CODE OF FEDERAL REGULATIONS

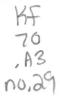

Title 29
Labor

Part 1910 (§ 1910.1000 to end of part 1910)

Revised as of July 1, 2019

Containing a codification of documents
of general applicability and future effect

As of July 1, 2019

Published by the Office of the Federal Register
National Archives and Records Administration
as a Special Edition of the Federal Register

U.S. GOVERNMENT OFFICIAL EDITION NOTICE

Legal Status and Use of Seals and Logos

The seal of the National Archives and Records Administration (NARA) authenticates the Code of Federal Regulations (CFR) as the official codification of Federal regulations established under the Federal Register Act. Under the provisions of 44 U.S.C. 1507, the contents of the CFR, a special edition of the Federal Register, shall be judicially noticed. The CFR is prima facie evidence of the original documents published in the Federal Register (44 U.S.C. 1510).

It is prohibited to use NARA's official seal and the stylized Code of Federal Regulations logo on any republication of this material without the express, written permission of the Archivist of the United States or the Archivist's designee. Any person using NARA's official seals and logos in a manner inconsistent with the provisions of 36 CFR part 1200 is subject to the penalties specified in 18 U.S.C. 506, 701, and 1017.

Use of ISBN Prefix

This is the Official U.S. Government edition of this publication and is herein identified to certify its authenticity. Use of the 0–16 ISBN prefix is for U.S. Government Publishing Office Official Editions only. The Superintendent of Documents of the U.S. Government Publishing Office requests that any reprinted edition clearly be labeled as a copy of the authentic work with a new ISBN.

 U.S. GOVERNMENT PUBLISHING OFFICE

U.S. Superintendent of Documents • Washington, DC 20402–0001

http://bookstore.gpo.gov

Phone: toll-free (866) 512-1800; DC area (202) 512-1800

Table of Contents

Cite this Code: **CFR**

To cite the regulations in this volume use title, part and section number. Thus, 29 CFR 1910.1000 *refers to title 29, part 1910, section 1000.*

Explanation

The Code of Federal Regulations is a codification of the general and permanent rules published in the Federal Register by the Executive departments and agencies of the Federal Government. The Code is divided into 50 titles which represent broad areas subject to Federal regulation. Each title is divided into chapters which usually bear the name of the issuing agency. Each chapter is further subdivided into parts covering specific regulatory areas.

Each volume of the Code is revised at least once each calendar year and issued on a quarterly basis approximately as follows:

Title 1 through Title 16...as of January 1
Title 17 through Title 27...as of April 1
Title 28 through Title 41...as of July 1
Title 42 through Title 50...as of October 1

The appropriate revision date is printed on the cover of each volume.

LEGAL STATUS

The contents of the Federal Register are required to be judicially noticed (44 U.S.C. 1507). The Code of Federal Regulations is prima facie evidence of the text of the original documents (44 U.S.C. 1510).

HOW TO USE THE CODE OF FEDERAL REGULATIONS

The Code of Federal Regulations is kept up to date by the individual issues of the Federal Register. These two publications must be used together to determine the latest version of any given rule.

To determine whether a Code volume has been amended since its revision date (in this case, July 1, 2019), consult the "List of CFR Sections Affected (LSA)," which is issued monthly, and the "Cumulative List of Parts Affected," which appears in the Reader Aids section of the daily Federal Register. These two lists will identify the Federal Register page number of the latest amendment of any given rule.

EFFECTIVE AND EXPIRATION DATES

Each volume of the Code contains amendments published in the Federal Register since the last revision of that volume of the Code. Source citations for the regulations are referred to by volume number and page number of the Federal Register and date of publication. Publication dates and effective dates are usually not the same and care must be exercised by the user in determining the actual effective date. In instances where the effective date is beyond the cutoff date for the Code a note has been inserted to reflect the future effective date. In those instances where a regulation published in the Federal Register states a date certain for expiration, an appropriate note will be inserted following the text.

OMB CONTROL NUMBERS

The Paperwork Reduction Act of 1980 (Pub. L. 96–511) requires Federal agencies to display an OMB control number with their information collection request.

Many agencies have begun publishing numerous OMB control numbers as amendments to existing regulations in the CFR. These OMB numbers are placed as close as possible to the applicable recordkeeping or reporting requirements.

PAST PROVISIONS OF THE CODE

Provisions of the Code that are no longer in force and effect as of the revision date stated on the cover of each volume are not carried. Code users may find the text of provisions in effect on any given date in the past by using the appropriate List of CFR Sections Affected (LSA). For the convenience of the reader, a "List of CFR Sections Affected" is published at the end of each CFR volume. For changes to the Code prior to the LSA listings at the end of the volume, consult previous annual editions of the LSA. For changes to the Code prior to 2001, consult the List of CFR Sections Affected compilations, published for 1949-1963, 1964-1972, 1973-1985, and 1986-2000.

"[RESERVED]" TERMINOLOGY

The term "[Reserved]" is used as a place holder within the Code of Federal Regulations. An agency may add regulatory information at a "[Reserved]" location at any time. Occasionally "[Reserved]" is used editorially to indicate that a portion of the CFR was left vacant and not accidentally dropped due to a printing or computer error.

INCORPORATION BY REFERENCE

What is incorporation by reference? Incorporation by reference was established by statute and allows Federal agencies to meet the requirement to publish regulations in the Federal Register by referring to materials already published elsewhere. For an incorporation to be valid, the Director of the Federal Register must approve it. The legal effect of incorporation by reference is that the material is treated as if it were published in full in the Federal Register (5 U.S.C. 552(a)). This material, like any other properly issued regulation, has the force of law.

What is a proper incorporation by reference? The Director of the Federal Register will approve an incorporation by reference only when the requirements of 1 CFR part 51 are met. Some of the elements on which approval is based are:

(a) The incorporation will substantially reduce the volume of material published in the Federal Register.

(b) The matter incorporated is in fact available to the extent necessary to afford fairness and uniformity in the administrative process.

(c) The incorporating document is drafted and submitted for publication in accordance with 1 CFR part 51.

What if the material incorporated by reference cannot be found? If you have any problem locating or obtaining a copy of material listed as an approved incorporation by reference, please contact the agency that issued the regulation containing that incorporation. If, after contacting the agency, you find the material is not available, please notify the Director of the Federal Register, National Archives and Records Administration, 8601 Adelphi Road, College Park, MD 20740-6001, or call 202-741-6010.

CFR INDEXES AND TABULAR GUIDES

A subject index to the Code of Federal Regulations is contained in a separate volume, revised annually as of January 1, entitled CFR INDEX AND FINDING AIDS. This volume contains the Parallel Table of Authorities and Rules. A list of CFR titles, chapters, subchapters, and parts and an alphabetical list of agencies publishing in the CFR are also included in this volume.

An index to the text of "Title 3—The President" is carried within that volume. The Federal Register Index is issued monthly in cumulative form. This index is based on a consolidation of the "Contents" entries in the daily Federal Register.

A List of CFR Sections Affected (LSA) is published monthly, keyed to the revision dates of the 50 CFR titles.

REPUBLICATION OF MATERIAL

There are no restrictions on the republication of material appearing in the Code of Federal Regulations.

INQUIRIES

For a legal interpretation or explanation of any regulation in this volume, contact the issuing agency. The issuing agency's name appears at the top of odd-numbered pages.

For inquiries concerning CFR reference assistance, call 202–741–6000 or write to the Director, Office of the Federal Register, National Archives and Records Administration, 8601 Adelphi Road, College Park, MD 20740-6001 or e-mail *fedreg.info@nara.gov.*

SALES

The Government Publishing Office (GPO) processes all sales and distribution of the CFR. For payment by credit card, call toll-free, 866-512-1800, or DC area, 202-512-1800, M-F 8 a.m. to 4 p.m. e.s.t. or fax your order to 202-512-2104, 24 hours a day. For payment by check, write to: US Government Publishing Office – New Orders, P.O. Box 979050, St. Louis, MO 63197-9000.

ELECTRONIC SERVICES

The full text of the Code of Federal Regulations, the LSA (List of CFR Sections Affected), The United States Government Manual, the Federal Register, Public Laws, Public Papers of the Presidents of the United States, Compilation of Presidential Documents and the Privacy Act Compilation are available in electronic format via *www.govinfo.gov.* For more information, contact the GPO Customer Contact Center, U.S. Government Publishing Office. Phone 202-512-1800, or 866-512-1800 (toll-free). E-mail, *ContactCenter@gpo.gov.*

The Office of the Federal Register also offers a free service on the National Archives and Records Administration's (NARA) World Wide Web site for public law numbers, Federal Register finding aids, and related information. Connect to NARA's web site at *www.archives.gov/federal-register.*

The e-CFR is a regularly updated, unofficial editorial compilation of CFR material and Federal Register amendments, produced by the Office of the Federal Register and the Government Publishing Office. It is available at *www.ecfr.gov.*

OLIVER A. POTTS,
Director,
Office of the Federal Register
July 1, 2019

THIS TITLE

Title 29—LABOR is composed of nine volumes. The parts in these volumes are arranged in the following order: Parts 0–99, parts 100–499, parts 500–899, parts 900–1899, part 1900–§1910.999, part 1910.1000–end of part 1910, parts 1911–1925, part 1926, and part 1927 to end. The contents of these volumes represent all current regulations codified under this title as of July 1, 2019.

The OMB control numbers for title 29 CFR part 1910 appear in §1910.8. For the convenience of the user, §1910.8 appears in the Finding Aids section of the volume containing §1910.1000 to the end.

For this volume, Cheryl E. Sirofchuck was Chief Editor. The Code of Federal Regulations publication program is under the direction of John Hyrum Martinez, assisted by Stephen J. Frattini.

Title 29—Labor

(This book contains part 1910, § 1910.1000 to end of part 1910)

SUBTITLE B—REGULATIONS RELATING TO LABOR (CONTINUED)

1

Subtitle B—Regulations Relating to Labor (Continued)

CHAPTER XVII—OCCUPATIONAL SAFETY AND HEALTH ADMINISTRATION, DEPARTMENT OF LABOR (CONTINUED)

PART 1910—OCCUPATIONAL SAFETY AND HEALTH STANDARDS (CONTINUED)

Subpart Z—Toxic and Hazardous Substances

Subpart Z—Toxic and Hazardous Substances

AUTHORITY: 29 U.S.C. 653, 655, 657; Secretary of Labor's Order No. 12–71 (36 FR 8754), 8–76 (41 FR 25059), 9–83 (48 FR 35736), 1–90 (55 FR 9033), 6–96 (62 FR 111), 3–2000 (65 FR 50017), 5–2002 (67 FR 65008), 5–2007 (72 FR 31160), 4–2010 (75 FR 55355), or 1–2012 (77 FR 3912); 29 CFR part 1911; and 5 U.S.C. 553, as applicable. Section 1910.1030 also issued under Public Law 106–430, 114 Stat. 1901. Section 1910.1201 also issued under 40 U.S.C. 5101 et seq.

EFFECTIVE DATE NOTE: At 84 FR 21458, May 14, 2019, the authority citation for part 1910, subpart Z was revised, effective July 15, 2019. For the convenience of the user, the revised text is set forth as follows:
AUTHORITY: 29 U.S.C. 653, 655, 657; Secretary of Labor's Order No. 12–71 (36 FR 8754), 8–76 (41 FR 25059), 9–83 (48 FR 35736), 1–90 (55 FR 9033), 6–96 (62 FR 111), 3–2000 (65 FR 50017), or 5–2007 (72 FR 31159), 4–2010 (75 FR 55355) or 1–2012 (77 FR 3912), as applicable; and 29 CFR part 1911.
All of subpart Z issued under 29 U.S.C. 655(b), except those substances that have exposure limits listed in Tables Z–1, Z–2, and Z–3 of § 1910.1000. The latter were issued under 29 U.S.C. 655(a).
Section 1910.1000, Tables Z–1, Z–2 and Z–3 also issued under 5 U.S.C. 553, but not under 29 CFR part 1911 except for the arsenic (organic compounds), benzene, cotton dust, and chromium (VI) listings.
Section 1910.1001 also issued under 40 U.S.C. 3704 and 5 U.S.C. 553.
Section 1910.1002 also issued under 5 U.S.C. 553, but not under 29 U.S.C. 655 or 29 CFR part 1911.
Sections 1910.1018, 1910.1029, and 1910.1200 also issued under 29 U.S.C. 653.
Section 1910.1030 also issued under Public Law 106–430, 114 Stat. 1901.
Section 1910.1201 also issued under 49 U.S.C. 1801–1819 and 5 U.S.C. 553.

SOURCE: 39 FR 23502, June 27, 1974, unless otherwise noted. Redesignated at 40 FR 23072, May 28, 1975.

EFFECTIVE DATE NOTE: At 84 FR 21597, May 14, 2019, part 1910 was amended by removing the phrases "and social security number", "social security number" and "social security numbers" from several sections, effective July 15, 2019.

§ 1910.1000 Air contaminants.

An employee's exposure to any substance listed in Tables Z–1, Z–2, or Z–3 of this section shall be limited in accordance with the requirements of the following paragraphs of this section.

(a) *Table Z–1*—(1) *Substances with limits preceded by* "*C*"—*Ceiling Values.* An employee's exposure to any substance in Table Z–1, the exposure limit of which is preceded by a "C", shall at no time exceed the exposure limit given for that substance. If instantaneous monitoring is not feasible, then the ceiling shall be assessed as a 15-minute time weighted average exposure which shall not be exceeded at any time during the working day.

(2) *Other substances—8-hour Time Weighted Averages.* An employee's exposure to any substance in Table Z–1, the exposure limit of which is not preceded by a "C", shall not exceed the 8-hour Time Weighted Average given for that substance in any 8-hour work shift of a 40-hour work week.

(b) *Table Z–2.* An employee's exposure to any substance listed in Table Z–2 shall not exceed the exposure limits specified as follows:

(1) *8-hour time weighted averages.* An employee's exposure to any substance listed in Table Z–2, in any 8-hour work shift of a 40-hour work week, shall not exceed the 8-hour time weighted average limit given for that substance in Table Z–2.

(2) *Acceptable ceiling concentrations.* An employee's exposure to a substance listed in Table Z–2 shall not exceed at any time during an 8-hour shift the acceptable ceiling concentration limit given for the substance in the table, except for a time period, and up to a concentration not exceeding the maximum duration and concentration allowed in the column under "acceptable maximum peak above the acceptable ceiling concentration for an 8-hour shift."

(3) *Example.* During an 8-hour work shift, an employee may be exposed to a concentration of Substance A (with a 10 ppm TWA, 25 ppm ceiling and 50 ppm peak) above 25 ppm (but never above 50 ppm) only for a maximum period of 10 minutes. Such exposure must be compensated by exposures to concentrations less than 10 ppm so that the cumulative exposure for the entire 8-hour work shift does not exceed a weighted average of 10 ppm.

(c) *Table Z–3.* An employee's exposure to any substance listed in Table Z–3, in any 8-hour work shift of a 40-hour work week, shall not exceed the 8-hour time weighted average limit given for that substance in the table.

(d) *Computation formulae.* The computation formula which shall apply to employee exposure to more than one substance for which 8-hour time weighted averages are listed in subpart Z of 29 CFR part 1910 in order to determine whether an employee is exposed over the regulatory limit is as follows:

(1)(i) The cumulative exposure for an 8-hour work shift shall be computed as follows:

$$E = (C_a\, T_a + C_b\, T_b + \ldots C_n\, T_n) \div 8$$

Where:

E is the equivalent exposure for the working shift.

C is the concentration during any period of time T where the concentration remains constant.

T is the duration in hours of the exposure at the concentration C.

The value of E shall not exceed the 8-hour time weighted average specified in subpart Z of 29 CFR part 1910 for the substance involved.

(ii) To illustrate the formula prescribed in paragraph (d)(1)(i) of this section, assume that Substance A has an 8-hour time weighted average limit of 100 ppm noted in Table Z–1. Assume that an employee is subject to the following exposure:

Two hours exposure at 150 ppm
Two hours exposure at 75 ppm
Four hours exposure at 50 ppm

Substituting this information in the formula, we have

$$(2 \times 150 + 2 \times 75 + 4 \times 50) \div 8 = 81.25 \text{ ppm}$$

Since 81.25 ppm is less than 100 ppm, the 8-hour time weighted average limit, the exposure is acceptable.

(2)(i) In case of a mixture of air contaminants an employer shall compute the equivalent exposure as follows:

$$E_m = (C_1 \div L_1 + C_2 \div L_2) + \ldots (C_n \div L_n)$$

Where:

E_m is the equivalent exposure for the mixture.

C is the concentration of a particular contaminant.

L is the exposure limit for that substance specified in subpart Z of 29 CFR part 1910.

The value of E_m shall not exceed unity (1).

(ii) To illustrate the formula prescribed in paragraph (d)(2)(i) of this section, consider the following exposures:

Substance	Actual concentration of 8-hour exposure (ppm)	8-hour TWA PEL (ppm)
B	500	1,000
C	45	200

Substance	Actual concentration of 8-hour exposure (ppm)	8-hour TWA PEL (ppm)
D	40	200

Substituting in the formula, we have:

$E_m = 500 \div 1,000 + 45 \div 200 + 40 \div 200$

$E_m = 0.500 + 0.225 + 0.200$

$E_m = 0.925$

Since E_m is less than unity (1), the exposure combination is within acceptable limits.

(e) To achieve compliance with paragraphs (a) through (d) of this section, administrative or engineering controls must first be determined and implemented whenever feasible. When such controls are not feasible to achieve full compliance, protective equipment or any other protective measures shall be used to keep the exposure of employees to air contaminants within the limits prescribed in this section. Any equipment and/or technical measures used for this purpose must be approved for each particular use by a competent industrial hygienist or other technically qualified person. Whenever respirators are used, their use shall comply with 1910.134.

TABLE Z–1—LIMITS FOR AIR CONTAMINANTS

Substance	CAS No. (c)	ppm (a)[1]	mg/m³ (b)[1]	Skin designation
Acetaldehyde	75–07–0	200	360	
Acetic acid	64–19–7	10	25	
Acetic anhydride	108–24–7	5	20	
Acetone	67–64–1	1000	2400	
Acetonitrile	75–05–8	40	70	
2-Acetylaminofluorine; see 1910.1014	53–96–3			
Acetylene dichloride; see 1,2-Dichloroethylene.				
Acetylene tetrabromide	79–27–6	1	14	
Acrolein	107–02–8	0.1	0.25	
Acrylamide	79–06–1	....	0.3	X
Acrylonitrile; see 1910.1045	107–13–1			
Aldrin	309–00–2	....	0.25	X
Allyl alcohol	107–18–6	2	5	X
Allyl chloride	107–05–1	1	3	
Allyl glycidyl ether (AGE)	106–92–3	(C)10	(C)45	
Allyl propyl disulfide	2179–59–1	2	12	
alpha-Alumina	1344–28–1			
Total dust		....	15	
Respirable fraction		....	5	
Aluminum, metal (as Al)	7429–90–5			
Total dust		....	15	
Respirable fraction		....	5	
4-Aminodiphenyl; see 1910.1011	92–67–1			
2-Aminoethanol; see Ethanolamine.				
2-Aminopyridine	504–29–0	0.5	2	
Ammonia	7664–41–7	50	35	
Ammonium sulfamate	7773–06–0			
Total dust		....	15	
Respirable fraction		....	5	
n-Amyl acetate	628–63–7	100	525	
sec-Amyl acetate	626–38–0	125	650	
Aniline and homologs	62–53–3	5	19	X
Anisidine (o-, p-isomers)	29191–52–4	....	0.5	X
Antimony and compounds (as Sb)	7440–36–0	....	0.5	
ANTU (alpha Naphthylthiourea)	86–88–4	....	0.3	
Arsenic, inorganic compounds (as As); see 1910.1018	7440–38–2			
Arsenic, organic compounds (as As)	7440–38–2	....	0.5	
Arsine	7784–42–1	0.05	0.2	
Asbestos; see 1910.1001	(4)			
Azinphos-methyl	86–50–0	....	0.2	X
Barium, soluble compounds (as Ba)	7440–39–3	....	0.5	
Barium sulfate	7727–43–7			
Total dust		....	15	
Respirable fraction		....	5	
Benomyl	17804–35–2			
Total dust		....	15	
Respirable fraction		....	5	
Benzene; see 1910.1028	71–43–2			
See Table Z–2 for the limits applicable in the operations or sectors excluded in 1910.1028[d]				
Benzidine; see 1910.1010	92–87–5			

9

TABLE Z–1—LIMITS FOR AIR CONTAMINANTS—Continued

Substance	CAS No. (c)	ppm (a) [1]	mg/m³ (b) [1]	Skin designation
p-Benzoquinone; see Quinone.			*	
Benzo(a)pyrene; see Coal tar pitch volatiles..				
Benzoyl peroxide	94–36–0		5	
Benzyl chloride	100–44–7	1	5	
Beryllium and beryllium compounds (as Be); see 1926.1124 [8].	7440–41–7			
Biphenyl; see Diphenyl.				
Bismuth telluride, Undoped	1304–82–1			
Total dust			15	
Respirable fraction			5	
Boron oxide	1303–86–2			
Total dust			15	
Boron trifluoride	7637–07–2	(C)1	(C)3	
Bromine	7726–95–6	0.1	0.7	
Bromoform	75–25–2	0.5	5	X
Butadiene (1,3-Butadiene); See 29 CFR 1910.1051; 29 CFR 1910.19(l).	106–99–0	1 ppm/5 ppm STEL		
Butanethiol; see Butyl mercaptan.				
2-Butanone (Methyl ethyl ketone)	78–93–3	200	590	
2-Butoxyethanol	111–76–2	50	240	X
n-Butyl-acetate	123–86–4	150	710	
sec-Butyl acetate	105–46–4	200	950	
tert-Butyl acetate	540–88–5	200	950	
n-Butyl alcohol	71–36–3	100	300	
sec-Butyl alcohol	78–92–2	150	450	
tert-Butyl alcohol	75–65–0	100	300	
Butylamine	109–73–9	(C)5	(C)15	X
tert-Butyl chromate (as CrO₃); see 1910.1026 [6]	1189–85–1			
n-Butyl glycidyl ether (BGE)	2426–08–6	50	270	
Butyl mercaptan	109–79–5	10	35	
p-tert-Butyltoluene	98–51–1	10	60	
Cadmium (as Cd); see 1910.1027	7440–43–9			
Calcium carbonate	1317–65–3			
Total dust			15	
Respirable fraction			5	
Calcium hydroxide	1305–62–0			
Total dust			15	
Respirable fraction			5	
Calcium oxide	1305–78–8		5	
Calcium silicate	1344–95–2			
Total dust			15	
Respirable fraction			5	
Calcium sulfate	7778–18–9			
Total dust			15	
Respirable fraction			5	
Camphor, synthetic	76–22–2		2	
Carbaryl (Sevin)	63–25–2		5	
Carbon black	1333–86–4		3.5	
Carbon dioxide	124–38–9	5000	9000	
Carbon disulfide	75–15–0		(²)	
Carbon monoxide	630–08–0	50	55	
Carbon tetrachloride	56–23–5		(²)	
Cellulose	9004–34–6			
Total dust			15	
Respirable fraction			5	
Chlordane	57–74–9		0.5	X
Chlorinated camphene	8001–35–2		0.5	X
Chlorinated diphenyl oxide	55720–99–5		0.5	
Chlorine	7782–50–5	(C)1	(C)3	
Chlorine dioxide	10049–04–4	0.1	0.3	
Chlorine trifluoride	7790–91–2	(C)0.1	(C)0.4	
Chloroacetaldehyde	107–20–0	(C)1	(C)3	
a-Chloroacetophenone (Phenacyl chloride)	532–27–4	0.05	0.3	
Chlorobenzene	108–90–7	75	350	
o-Chlorobenzylidene malononitrile	2698–41–1	0.05	0.4	
Chlorobromomethane	74–97–5	200	1050	
2-Chloro-1,3-butadiene; see beta-Chloroprene.				
Chlorodiphenyl (42% Chlorine) (PCB)	53469–21–9		1	X
Chlorodiphenyl (54% Chlorine) (PCB)	11097–69–1		0.5	X
1-Chloro-2,3-epoxypropane; see Epichlorohydrin.				
2-Chloroethanol; see Ethylene chlorohydrin.				
Chloroethylene; see Vinyl chloride.				

TABLE Z–1—LIMITS FOR AIR CONTAMINANTS—Continued

Substance	CAS No. (c)	ppm (a)[1]	mg/m³ (b)[1]	Skin designation
Chloroform (Trichloromethane)	67–66–3	(C)50	(C)240	
bis(Chloromethyl) ether; see 1910.1008	542–88–1			
Chloromethyl methyl ether; see 1910.1006	107–30–2			
1-Chloro-1-nitropropane	600–25–9	20	100	
Chloropicrin	76–06–2	0.1	0.7	
beta-Chloroprene	126–99–8	25	90	X
2-Chloro-6-(trichloromethyl) pyridine	1929–82–4			
Total dust			15	
Respirable fraction			5	
Chromium (II) compounds.				
(as Cr)	7440–47–3		0.5	
Chromium (III) compounds.				
(as Cr)	7440–47–3		0.5	
Chromium (VI) compounds; See 1910.1026[5]				
Chromium metal and insol. salts (as Cr)	7440–47–3		1	
Chrysene; see Coal tar pitch volatiles.				
Clopidol	2971–90–6			
Total dust			15	
Respirable fraction			5	
Coal dust (less than 5% SiO₂), respirable fraction			(³)	
Coal dust (greater than or equal to 5% SiO₂), respirable fraction.			(³)	
Coal tar pitch volatiles (benzene soluble fraction), anthracene, BaP, phenanthrene, acridine, chrysene, pyrene.	65966–93–2		0.2	
Cobalt metal, dust, and fume (as Co)	7440–48–4		0.1	
Coke oven emissions; see 1910.1029.				
Copper	7440–50–8			
Fume (as Cu)			0.1	
Dusts and mists (as Cu)			1	
Cotton dust[e]; see 1910.1043			1	
Crag herbicide (Sesone)	136–78–7			
Total dust			15	
Respirable fraction			5	
Cresol, all isomers	1319–77–3	5	22	X
Crotonaldehyde	123–73–9; 4170–30–3	2	6	
Cumene	98–82–8	50	245	X
Cyanides (as CN)	(⁴)		5	X
Cyclohexane	110–82–7	300	1050	
Cyclohexanol	108–93–0	50	200	
Cyclohexanone	108–94–1	50	200	
Cyclohexene	110–83–8	300	1015	
Cyclopentadiene	542–92–7	75	200	
2,4-D (Dichlorophenoxyacetic acid)	94–75–7		10	
Decaborane	17702–41–9	0.05	0.3	X
Demeton (Systox)	8065–48–3		0.1	X
Diacetone alcohol (4-Hydroxy-4-methyl-2-pentanone)	123–42–2	50	240	
1,2-Diaminoethane; see Ethylenediamine.				
Diazomethane	334–88–3	0.2	0.4	
Diborane	19287–45–7	0.1	0.1	
1,2-Dibromo-3-chloropropane (DBCP); see 1910.1044	96–12–8			
1,2-Dibromoethane; see Ethylene dibromide.				
Dibutyl phosphate	107–66–4	1	5	
Dibutyl phthalate	84–74–2		5	
o-Dichlorobenzene	95–50–1	(C)50	(C)300	
p-Dichlorobenzene	106–46–7	75	450	
3,′-Dichlorobenzidine; see 1910.1007	91–94–1			
Dichlorodifluoromethane	75–71–8	1000	4950	
1,3-Dichloro-5,5-dimethyl hydantoin	118–52–5		0.2	
Dichlorodiphenyltrichloroethane (DDT)	50–29–3		1	X
1,1-Dichloroethane	75–34–3	100	400	
1,2-Dichloroethane; see Ethylene dichloride.				
1,2-Dichloroethylene	540–59–0	200	790	
Dichloroethyl ether	111–44–4	(C)15	(C)90	X
Dichloromethane; see Methylene chloride.				
Dichloromonofluoromethane	75–43–4	1000	4200	
1,1-Dichloro-1-nitroethane	594–72–9	(C)10	(C)60	
1,2-Dichloropropane; see Propylene dichloride.				
Dichlorotetrafluoroethane	76–14–2	1000	7000	
Dichlorvos (DDVP)	62–73–7		1	X
Dicyclopentadienyl iron	102–54–5			
Total dust			15	

11

TABLE Z-1—LIMITS FOR AIR CONTAMINANTS—Continued

Substance	CAS No. (c)	ppm (a)[1]	mg/m³ (b)[1]	Skin designation
Respirable fraction			5	
Dieldrin	60-57-1		0.25	X
Diethylamine	109-89-7	25	75	
2-Diethylaminoethanol	100-37-8	10	50	X
Diethyl ether; see Ethyl ether.				
Difluorodibromomethane	75-61-6	100	860	
Diglycidyl ether (DGE)	2238-07-5	(C)0.5	(C)2.8	
Dihydroxybenzene; see Hydroquinone.				
Diisobutyl ketone	108-83-8	50	290	
Diisopropylamine	108-18-9	5	20	X
4-Dimethylaminoazobenzene; see 1910.1015	60-11-7			
Dimethoxymethane; see Methylal.				
Dimethyl acetamide	127-19-5	10	35	X
Dimethylamine	124-40-3	10	18	
Dimethylaminobenzene; see Xylidine.				
Dimethylaniline (N,N-Dimethylaniline)	121-69-7	5	25	X
Dimethylbenzene; see Xylene.				
Dimethyl-1,2-dibromo-2,2-dichloroethyl phosphate	300-76-5		3	
Dimethylformamide	68-12-2	10	30	X
2,6-Dimethyl-4-heptanone; see Diisobutyl ketone.				
1,1-Dimethylhydrazine	57-14-7	0.5	1	X
Dimethylphthalate	131-11-3		5	
Dimethyl sulfate	77-78-1	1	5	X
Dinitrobenzene (all isomers)			1	X
(ortho)	528-29-0			
(meta)	99-65-0			
(para)	100-25-4			
Dinitro-o-cresol	534-52-1		0.2	X
Dinitrotoluene	25321-14-6		1.5	X
Dioxane (Diethylene dioxide)	123-91-1	100	360	X
Diphenyl (Biphenyl)	92-52-4	0.2	1	
Diphenylmethane diisocyanate; see Methylene bisphenyl isocyanate.				
Dipropylene glycol methyl ether	34590-94-8	100	600	X
Di-sec octyl phthalate (Di-(2-ethylhexyl) phthalate)	117-81-7		5	
Emery	12415-34-8			
Total dust			15	
Respirable fraction			5	
Endrin	72-20-8		0.1	X
Epichlorohydrin	106-89-8	5	19	X
EPN	2104-64-5		0.5	X
1,2-Epoxypropane; see Propylene oxide.				
2,3-Epoxy-1-propanol; see Glycidol.				
Ethanethiol; see Ethyl mercaptan.				
Ethanolamine	141-43-5	3	6	
2-Ethoxyethanol (Cellosolve)	110-80-5	200	740	X
2-Ethoxyethyl acetate (Cellosolve acetate)	111-15-9	100	540	X
Ethyl acetate	141-78-6	400	1400	
Ethyl acrylate	140-88-5	25	100	X
Ethyl alcohol (Ethanol)	64-17-5	1000	1900	
Ethylamine	75-04-7	10	18	
Ethyl amyl ketone (5-Methyl-3-heptanone)	541-85-5	25	130	
Ethyl benzene	100-41-4	100	435	
Ethyl bromide	74-96-4	200	890	
Ethyl butyl ketone (3-Heptanone)	106-35-4	50	230	
Ethyl chloride	75-00-3	1000	2600	
Ethyl ether	60-29-7	400	1200	
Ethyl formate	109-94-4	100	300	
Ethyl mercaptan	75-08-1	(C)10	(C)25	
Ethyl silicate	78-10-4	100	850	
Ethylene chlorohydrin	107-07-3	5	16	X
Ethylenediamine	107-15-3	10	25	
Ethylene dibromide	106-93-4		(2)	
Ethylene dichloride (1,2-Dichloroethane)	107-06-2		(2)	
Ethylene glycol dinitrate	628-96-6	(C)0.2	(C)1	X
Ethylene glycol methyl acetate; see Methyl cellosolve acetate.				
Ethyleneimine; see 1910.1012	151-56-4			
Ethylene oxide; see 1910.1047	75-21-8			
Ethylidene chloride; see 1,1-Dichloroethane.				
N-Ethylmorpholine	100-74-3	20	94	X
Ferbam	14484-64-1			

TABLE Z–1—LIMITS FOR AIR CONTAMINANTS—Continued

Substance	CAS No. (c)	ppm (a)[1]	mg/m³ (b)[1]	Skin designation
Total dust			15	
Ferrovanadium dust	12604–58–9		1	
Fluorides (as F)	(⁴)		2.5	
Fluorine	7782–41–4	0.1	0.2	
Fluorotrichloromethane (Trichlorofluoromethane)	75–69–4	1000	5600	
Formaldehyde; see 1910.1048	50–00–0			
Formic acid	64–18–6	5	9	
Furfural	98–01–1	5	20	X
Furfuryl alcohol	98–00–0	50	200	
Grain dust (oat, wheat, barley)			10	
Glycerin (mist)	56–81–5			
Total dust			15	
Respirable fraction			5	
Glycidol	556–52–5	50	150	
Glycol monoethyl ether; see 2-Ethoxyethanol.				
Graphite, natural, respirable dust	7782–42–5		(³)	
Graphite, synthetic.				
Total dust			15	
Respirable fraction			5	
Guthion; see Azinphos methyl.				
Gypsum	13397–24–5			
Total dust			15	
Respirable fraction			5	
Hafnium	7440–58–6		0.5	
Heptachlor	76–44–8		0.5	X
Heptane (n-Heptane)	142–82–5	500	2000	
Hexachloroethane	67–72–1	1	10	X
Hexachloronaphthalene	1335–87–1		0.2	X
n-Hexane	110–54–3	500	1800	
2-Hexanone (Methyl n-butyl ketone)	591–78–6	100	410	
Hexone (Methyl isobutyl ketone)	108–10–1	100	410	
sec-Hexyl acetate	108–84–9	50	300	
Hydrazine	302–01–2	1	1.3	X
Hydrogen bromide	10035–10–6	3	10	
Hydrogen chloride	7647–01–0	(C)5	(C)7	
Hydrogen cyanide	74–90–8	10	11	X
Hydrogen fluoride (as F)	7664–39–3		(²)	
Hydrogen peroxide	7722–84–1	1	1.4	
Hydrogen selenide (as Se)	7783–07–5	0.05	0.2	
Hydrogen sulfide	7783–06–4		(²)	
Hydroquinone	123–31–9		2	
Iodine	7553–56–2	(C)0.1	(C)1	
Iron oxide fume	1309–37–1		10	
Isoamyl acetate	123–92–2	100	525	
Isoamyl alcohol (primary and secondary)	123–51–3	100	360	
Isobutyl acetate	110–19–0	150	700	
Isobutyl alcohol	78–83–1	100	300	
Isophorone	78–59–1	25	140	
Isopropyl acetate	108–21–4	250	950	
Isopropyl alcohol	67–63–0	400	980	
Isopropylamine	75–31–0	5	12	
Isopropyl ether	108–20–3	500	2100	
Isopropyl glycidyl ether (IGE)	4016–14–2	50	240	
Kaolin	1332–58–7			
Total dust			15	
Respirable fraction			5	
Ketene	463–51–4	0.5	0.9	
Lead, inorganic (as Pb); see 1910.1025	7439–92–1			
Limestone	1317–65–3			
Total dust			15	
Respirable fraction			5	
Lindane	58–89–9		0.5	X
Lithium hydride	7580–67–8		0.025	
L.P.G. (Liquefied petroleum gas)	68476–85–7	1000	1800	
Magnesite	546–93–0			
Total dust			15	
Respirable fraction			5	
Magnesium oxide fume	1309–48–4			
Total particulate			15	
Malathion	121–75–5			X
Total dust			15	
Maleic anhydride	108–31–6	0.25	1	

13

TABLE Z-1—LIMITS FOR AIR CONTAMINANTS—Continued

Substance	CAS No. (c)	ppm (a) [1]	mg/m³ (b) [1]	Skin designation
Manganese compounds (as Mn)	7439–96–5		(C)5	
Manganese fume (as Mn)	7439–96–5		(C)5	
Marble	1317–65–3			
Total dust			15	
Respirable fraction			5	
Mercury (aryl and inorganic) (as Hg)	7439–97–6		([2])	
Mercury (organo) alkyl compounds (as Hg)	7439–97–6		([2])	
Mercury (vapor) (as Hg)	7439–97–6		([2])	
Mesityl oxide	141–79–7	25	100	
Methanethiol; see Methyl mercaptan.				
Methoxychlor	72–43–5			
Total dust			15	
2-Methoxyethanol (Methyl cellosolve)	109–86–4	25	80	X
2-Methoxyethyl acetate (Methyl cellosolve acetate)	110–49–6	25	120	X
Methyl acetate	79–20–9	200	610	
Methyl acetylene (Propyne)	74–99–7	1000	1650	
Methyl acetylene-propadiene mixture (MAPP)		1000	1800	
Methyl acrylate	96–33–3	10	35	X
Methylal (Dimethoxy-methane)	109–87–5	1000	3100	
Methyl alcohol	67–56–1	200	260	
Methylamine	74–89–5	10	12	
Methyl amyl alcohol; see Methyl isobutyl carbinol.				
Methyl n-amyl ketone	110–43–0	100	465	
Methyl bromide	74–83–9	(C)20	(C)80	X
Methyl butyl ketone; see 2-Hexanone.				
Methyl cellosolve; see 2-Methoxyethanol.				
Methyl cellosolve acetate; see 2-Methoxyethyl acetate.				
Methyl chloride	74–87–3		([2])	
Methyl chloroform (1,1,1-Trichloroethane)	71–55–6	350	1900	
Methylcyclohexane	108–87–2	500	2000	
Methylcyclohexanol	25639–42–3	100	470	
o-Methylcyclohexanone	583–60–8	100	460	X
Methylene chloride	75–09–2		([2])	
Methyl ethyl ketone (MEK); see 2-Butanone.				
Methyl formate	107–31–3	100	250	
Methyl hydrazine (Monomethyl hydrazine)	60–34–4	(C)0.2	(C)0.35	X
Methyl iodide	74–88–4	5	28	X
Methyl isoamyl ketone	110–12–3	100	475	
Methyl isobutyl carbinol	108–11–2	25	100	X
Methyl isobutyl ketone; see Hexone.				
Methyl isocyanate	624–83–9	0.02	0.05	X
Methyl mercaptan	74–93–1	(C)10	(C)20	
Methyl methacrylate	80–62–6	100	410	
Methyl propyl ketone; see 2-Pentanone.				
alpha-Methyl styrene	98–83–9	(C)100	(C)480	
Methylene bisphenyl isocyanate (MDI)	101–68–8	(C)0.02	(C)0.2	
Mica; see Silicates.				
Molybdenum (as Mo)	7439–98–7			
Soluble compounds			5	
Insoluble compounds.				
Total dust			15	
Monomethyl aniline	100–61–8	2	9	X
Monomethyl hydrazine; see Methyl hydrazine.				
Morpholine	110–91–8	20	70	X
Naphtha (Coal tar)	8030–30–6	100	400	
Naphthalene	91–20–3	10	50	
alpha-Naphthylamine; see 1910.1004	134–32–7			
beta-Naphthylamine; see 1910.1009	91–59–8			
Nickel carbonyl (as Ni)	13463–39–3	0.001	0.007	
Nickel, metal and insoluble compounds (as Ni)	7440–02–0		1	
Nickel, soluble compounds (as Ni)	7440–02–0		1	
Nicotine	54–11–5		0.5	X
Nitric acid	7697–37–2	2	5	
Nitric oxide	10102–43–9	25	30	
p-Nitroaniline	100–01–6	1	6	X
Nitrobenzene	98–95–3	1	5	X
p-Nitrochlorobenzene	100–00–5		1	X
4-Nitrodiphenyl; see 1910.1003	92–93–3			
Nitroethane	79–24–3	100	310	
Nitrogen dioxide	10102–44–0	(C)5	(C)9	
Nitrogen trifluoride	7783–54–2	10	29	
Nitroglycerin	55–63–0	(C)0.2	(C)2	X

TABLE Z-1—LIMITS FOR AIR CONTAMINANTS—Continued

Substance	CAS No. (c)	ppm (a)[1]	mg/m³ (b)[1]	Skin designation
Nitromethane	75–52–5	100	250	
1-Nitropropane	108–03–2	25	90	
2-Nitropropane	79–46–9	25	90	
N-Nitrosodimethylamine; see 1910.1016.				
Nitrotoluene (all isomers)		5	30	X
o-isomer	88–72–2			
m-isomer	99–08–1			
p-isomer	99–99–0			
Nitrotrichloromethane; see Chloropicrin.				
Octachloronaphthalene	2234–13–1		0.1	X
Octane	111–65–9	500	2350	
Oil mist, mineral	8012–95–1		5	
Osmium tetroxide (as Os)	20816–12–0		0.002	
Oxalic acid	144–62–7		1	
Oxygen difluoride	7783–41–7	0.05	0.1	
Ozone	10028–15–6	0.1	0.2	
Paraquat, respirable dust	4685–14–7;		0.5	X
	1910–42–5;			
	2074–50–2			
Parathion	56–38–2		0.1	X
Particulates not otherwise regulated (PNOR)[f].				
Total dust			15	
Respirable fraction			5	
PCB; see Chlorodiphenyl (42% and 54% chlorine).				
Pentaborane	19624–22–7	0.005	0.01	
Pentachloronaphthalene	1321–64–8		0.5	X
Pentachlorophenol	87–86–5		0.5	X
Pentaerythritol	115–77–5			
Total dust			15	
Respirable fraction			5	
Pentane	109–66–0	1000	2950	
2-Pentanone (Methyl propyl ketone)	107–87–9	200	700	
Perchloroethylene (Tetrachloroethylene)	127–18–4		(2)	
Perchloromethyl mercaptan	594–42–3	0.1	0.8	
Perchloryl fluoride	7616–94–6	3	13.5	
Petroleum distillates (Naphtha) (Rubber Solvent)		500	2000	
Phenol	108–95–2	5	19	X
p-Phenylene diamine	106–50–3		0.1	X
Phenyl ether, vapor	101–84–8	1	7	
Phenyl ether-biphenyl mixture, vapor		1	7	
Phenylethylene; see Styrene.				
Phenyl glycidyl ether (PGE)	122–60–1	10	60	
Phenylhydrazine	100–63–0	5	22	X
Phosdrin (Mevinphos)	7786–34–7		0.1	X
Phosgene (Carbonyl chloride)	75–44–5	0.1	0.4	
Phosphine	7803–51–2	0.3	0.4	
Phosphoric acid	7664–38–2		1	
Phosphorus (yellow)	7723–14–0		0.1	
Phosphorus pentachloride	10026–13–8		1	
Phosphorus pentasulfide	1314–80–3		1	
Phosphorus trichloride	7719–12–2	0.5	3	
Phthalic anhydride	85–44–9	2	12	
Picloram	1918–02–1			
Total dust			15	
Respirable fraction			5	
Picric acid	88–89–1		0.1	X
Pindone (2-Pivalyl-1,3-indandione)	83–26–1		0.1	
Plaster of Paris	26499–65–0			
Total dust			15	
Respirable fraction			5	
Platinum (as Pt)	7440–06–4			
Metal.				
Soluble salts			0.002	
Portland cement	65997–15–1			
Total dust			15	
Respirable fraction			5	
Propane	74–98–6	1000	1800	
beta-Propriolactone; see 1910.1013	57–57–8			
n-Propyl acetate	109–60–4	200	840	
n-Propyl alcohol	71–23–8	200	500	
n-Propyl nitrate	627–13–4	25	110	
Propylene dichloride	78–87–5	75	350	

TABLE Z-1—LIMITS FOR AIR CONTAMINANTS—Continued

Substance	CAS No. (c)	ppm (a)[1]	mg/m³ (b)[1]	Skin designation
Propylene imine	75-55-8	2	5	X
Propylene oxide	75-56-9	100	240	
Propyne; see Methyl acetylene.				
Pyrethrum	8003-34-7		5	
Pyridine	110-86-1	5	15	
Quinone	106-51-4	0.1	0.4	
RDX; see Cyclonite.				
Rhodium (as Rh), metal fume and insoluble compounds	7440-16-6		0.1	
Rhodium (as Rh), soluble compounds	7440-16-6		0.001	
Ronnel	299-84-3		15	
Rotenone	83-79-4		5	
Rouge.				
Total dust			15	
Respirable fraction			5	
Selenium compounds (as Se)	7782-49-2		0.2	
Selenium hexafluoride (as Se)	7783-79-1	0.05	0.4	
Silica, amorphous, precipitated and gel	112926-00-8		(3)	
Silica, amorphous, diatomaceous earth, containing less than 1% crystalline silica.	61790-53-2		(3)	
Silica, crystalline, respirable dust				
Cristobalite; see 1910.1053 [7]	14464-46-1			
Quartz; see 1910.1053 [7]	14808-60-7			
Tripoli (as quartz); see 1910.1053 [7]	1317-95-9			
Tridymite; see 1910.1053 [7]	15468-32-3			
Silica, fused, respirable dust	60676-86-0		(3)	
Silicates (less than 1% crystalline silica).				
Mica (respirable dust)	12001-26-2		(3)	
Soapstone, total dust			(3)	
Soapstone, respirable dust			(3)	
Talc (containing asbestos); use asbestos limit; see 29 CFR 1910.1001.			(3)	
Talc (containing no asbestos), respirable dust	14807-96-6		(3)	
Tremolite, asbestiform; see 1910.1001.				
Silicon	7440-21-3			
Total dust			15	
Respirable fraction			5	
Silicon carbide	409-21-2			
Total dust			15	
Respirable fraction			5	
Silver, metal and soluble compounds (as Ag)	7440-22-4		0.01	
Soapstone; see Silicates.				
Sodium fluoroacetate	62-74-8		0.05	X
Sodium hydroxide	1310-73-2		2	
Starch	9005-25-8			
Total dust			15	
Respirable fraction			5	
Stibine	7803-52-3	0.1	0.5	
Stoddard solvent	8052-41-3	500	2900	
Strychnine	57-24-9		0.15	
Styrene	100-42-5		(2)	
Sucrose	57-50-1			
Total dust			15	
Respirable fraction			5	
Sulfur dioxide	7446-09-5	5	13	
Sulfur hexafluoride	2551-62-4	1000	6000	
Sulfuric acid	7664-93-9		1	
Sulfur monochloride	10025-67-9	1	6	
Sulfur pentafluoride	5714-22-7	0.025	0.25	
Sulfuryl fluoride	2699-79-8	5	20	
Systox; see Demeton.				
2,4,5-T (2,4,5-trichlorophenoxyacetic acid)	93-76-5		10	
Talc; see Silicates.				
Tantalum, metal and oxide dust	7440-25-7		5	
TEDP (Sulfotep)	3689-24-5		0.2	X
Tellurium and compounds (as Te)	13494-80-9		0.1	
Tellurium hexafluoride (as Te)	7783-80-4	0.02	0.2	
Temephos	3383-96-8			
Total dust			15	
Respirable fraction			5	
TEPP (Tetraethyl pyrophosphate)	107-49-3		0.05	X
Terphenyls	26140-60-3	(C)1	(C)9	
1,1,1,2-Tetrachloro-2,2-difluoroethane	76-11-9	500	4170	

TABLE Z–1—LIMITS FOR AIR CONTAMINANTS—Continued

Substance	CAS No. (c)	ppm (a)[1]	mg/m³ (b)[1]	Skin designation
1,1,2,2-Tetrachloro-1,2-difluoroethane	76–12–0	500	4170	
1,1,2,2-Tetrachloroethane	79–34–5	5	35	X
Tetrachloroethylene; see Perchloroethylene.				
Tetrachloromethane; see Carbon tetrachloride.				
Tetrachloronaphthalene	1335–88–2		2	X
Tetraethyl lead (as Pb)	78–00–2		0.075	X
Tetrahydrofuran	109–99–9	200	590	
Tetramethyl lead (as Pb)	75–74–1		0.075	X
Tetramethyl succinonitrile	3333–52–6	0.5	3	X
Tetranitromethane	509–14–8	1	8	
Tetryl (2,4,6-Trinitrophenylmethylnitramine)	479–45–8		1.5	X
Thallium, soluble compounds (as Tl)	7440–28–0		0.1	X
4,4′-Thiobis (6-tert, Butyl-m-cresol)	96–69–5			
Total dust			15	
Respirable fraction			5	
Thiram	137–26–8		5	
Tin, inorganic compounds (except oxides) (as Sn)	7440–31–5		2	
Tin, organic compounds (as Sn)	7440–31–5		0.1	
Titanium dioxide	13463–67–7			
Total dust			15	
Toluene	108–88–3		(2)	
Toluene-2,4-diisocyanate (TDI)	584–84–9	(C)0.02	(C)0.14	
o-Toluidine	95–53–4	5	22	X
Toxaphene; see Chlorinated camphene.				
Tremolite; see Silicates.				
Tributyl phosphate	126–73–8		5	
1,1,1-Trichloroethane; see Methyl chloroform.				
1,1,2-Trichloroethane	79–00–5	10	45	X
Trichloroethylene	79–01–6		(2)	
Trichloromethane; see Chloroform.				
Trichloronaphthalene	1321–65–9		5	X
1,2,3-Trichloropropane	96–18–4	50	300	
1,1,2-Trichloro-1,2,2-trifluoroethane	76–13–1	1000	7600	
Triethylamine	121–44–8	25	100	
Trifluorobromomethane	75–63–8	1000	6100	
2,4,6-Trinitrophenol; see Picric acid.				
2,4,6-Trinitrophenylmethylnitramine; see Tetryl.				
2,4,6-Trinitrotoluene (TNT)	118–96–7		1.5	X
Triorthocresyl phosphate	78–30–8		0.1	
Triphenyl phosphate	115–86–6		3	
Turpentine	8006–64–2	100	560	
Uranium (as U)	7440–61–1			
Soluble compounds			0.05	
Insoluble compounds			0.25	
Vanadium	1314–62–1			
Respirable dust (as V₂O₅)			(C)0.5	
Fume (as V₂O₅)			(C)0.1	
Vegetable oil mist.				
Total dust			15	
Respirable fraction			5	
Vinyl benzene; see Styrene.				
Vinyl chloride; see 1910.1017	75–01–4			
Vinyl cyanide; see Acrylonitrile.				
Vinyl toluene	25013–15–4	100	480	
Warfarin	81–81–2		0.1	
Xylenes (o-, m-, p-isomers)	1330–20–7	100	435	
Xylidine	1300–73–8	5	25	X
Yttrium	7440–65–5		1	
Zinc chloride fume	7646–85–7		1	
Zinc oxide fume	1314–13–2		5	
Zinc oxide	1314–13–2			
Total dust			15	
Respirable fraction			5	
Zinc stearate	557–05–1			
Total dust			15	
Respirable fraction			5	
Zirconium compounds (as Zr)	7440–67–7		5	

[1] The PELs are 8-hour TWAs unless otherwise noted; a (C) designation denotes a ceiling limit. They are to be determined from breathing-zone air samples.

(a) Parts of vapor or gas per million parts of contaminated air by volume at 25 °C and 760 torr.

(b) Milligrams of substance per cubic meter of air. When entry is in this column only, the value is exact; when listed with a ppm entry, it is approximate.

17

(c) The CAS number is for information only. Enforcement is based on the substance name. For an entry covering more than one metal compound, measured as the metal, the CAS number for the metal is given—not CAS numbers for the individual compounds.

(d) The final benzene standard in 1910.1028 applies to all occupational exposures to benzene except in some circumstances the distribution and sale of fuels, sealed containers and pipelines, coke production, oil and gas drilling and production, natural gas processing, and the percentage exclusion for liquid mixtures; for the excepted subsegments, the benzene limits in Table Z-2 apply. See 1910.1028 for specific circumstances.

(e) This 8-hour TWA applies to respirable dust as measured by a vertical elutriator cotton dust sampler or equivalent instrument. The time-weighted average applies to the cottom waste processing operations of waste recycling (sorting, blending, cleaning and willowing) and garnetting. See also 1910.1043 for cotton dust limits applicable to other sectors.

(f) All inert or nuisance dusts, whether mineral, inorganic, or organic, not listed specifically by substance name are covered by the Particulates Not Otherwise Regulated (PNOR) limit which is the same as the inert or nuisance dust limit of Table Z-3.

[2] See Table Z-2.

[3] See Table Z-3.

[4] Varies with compound.

[5] See Table Z-2 for the exposure limit for any operations or sectors where the exposure limit in § 1910.1026 is stayed or is otherwise not in effect.

[6] If the exposure limit in § 1910.1026 is stayed or is otherwise not in effect, the exposure limit is a ceiling of 0.1 mg/m3.

[7] See Table Z-3 for the exposure limit for any operations or sectors where the exposure limit in § 1910.1053 is stayed or is otherwise not in effect.

[8] *See* Table Z-2 for the exposure limits for any operations or sectors where the exposure limits in § 1910.1024 are stayed or otherwise not in effect.

TABLE Z-2

Substance	8-hour time weighted average	Acceptable ceiling concentration	Acceptable maximum peak above the acceptable ceiling concentration for an 8-hr shift	
			Concentration	Maximum duration
Benzene [a] (Z37.40-1969)	10 ppm	25 ppm	50 ppm	10 minutes.
Beryllium and beryllium compounds (Z37.29-1970) [d]	2 µg/m3	5 µg/m3	25 µg/m3	30 minutes.
Cadmium fume [b] (Z37.5-1970)	0.1 mg/m3	0.3 mg/m3.		
Cadmium dust [b] (Z37.5-1970)	0.2 mg/m3	0.6 mg/m3.		
Carbon disulfide (Z37.3-1968)	20 ppm	30 ppm	100 ppm	30 minutes.
Carbon tetrachloride (Z37.17-1967)	10 ppm	25 ppm	200 ppm	5 min. in any 4 hrs.
Chromic acid and chromates (Z37.7-1971) (as CrO₃) [c]		1 mg/10m3.		
Ethylene dibromide (Z37.31-1970)	20 ppm	30 ppm	50 ppm	5 minutes.
Ethylene dichloride (Z37.21-1969)	50 ppm	100 ppm	200 ppm	5 min. in any 3 hrs.
Fluoride as dust (Z37.28-1969)	2.5 mg/m3.			
Formaldehyde; see 1910.1048.				
Hydrogen fluoride (Z37.28-1969)	3 ppm.			
Hydrogen sulfide (Z37.2-1966)		20 ppm	50 ppm	10 mins. once, only if no other meas. exp. occurs.
Mercury (Z37.8-1971)		1 mg/10m3.		
Methyl chloride (Z37.18-1969)	100 ppm	200 ppm	300 ppm	5 mins. in any 3 hrs.
Methylene Chloride: See § 1919.52..				
Organo (alkyl) mercury (Z37.30-1969)	0.01 mg/m3	0.04 mg/m3.		
Styrene (Z37.15-1969)	100 ppm	200 ppm	600 ppm	5 mins. in any 3 hrs.
Tetrachloroethylene (Z37.22-1967)	100 ppm	200 ppm	300 ppm	5 mins. in any 3 hrs.
Toluene (Z37.12-1967)	200 ppm	300 ppm	500 ppm	10 minutes.
Trichloroethylene (Z37.19-1967)	100 ppm	200 ppm	300 ppm	5 mins. in any 2 hrs.

[a] This standard applies to the industry segments exempt from the 1 ppm 8-hour TWA and 5 ppm STEL of the benzene standard at 1910.1028.

[b] This standard applies to any operations or sectors for which the Cadmium standard, 1910.1027, is stayed or otherwise not in effect.

[c] This standard applies to any operations or sectors for which the exposure limit in the Chromium (VI) standard, § 1910.1026, is stayed or is otherwise not in effect.

[d] This standard applies to any operations or sectors for which the exposure limits in the beryllium standard, § 1910.1024, are stayed or is otherwise not in effect.

TABLE Z-3—MINERAL DUSTS

Substance	mppcf [a]	mg/m3
Silica:		
Crystalline		
Quartz (Respirable) [f]	250 [b]	10 mg/m3 [e]
	% SiO₂ + 5	% SiO₂ + 2

TABLE Z–3—MINERAL DUSTS—Continued

Substance	mppcf[a]	mg/m³
Cristobalite: Use ½ the value calculated from the count or mass formulae for quartz[f]. Tridymite: Use ½ the value calculated from the formulae for quartz[f].		
Amorphous, including natural diatomaceous earth	20	80 mg/m³
		%SiO₂
Silicates (less than 1% crystalline silica):		
Mica	20	
Soapstone	20	
Talc (not containing asbestos)	20[c]	
Talc (containing asbestos) Use asbestos limit.		
Tremolite, asbestiform (see 29 CFR 1910.1001).		
Portland cement	50	
Graphite (Natural)	15	
Coal Dust:		
Respirable fraction less than 5% SiO₂		2.4 mg/m³ [e]
		10 mg/m³ [e]
Respirable fraction greater than 5% SiO₂		%SiO₂ + 2
Inert or Nuisance Dust:[d]		
Respirable fraction	15	5 mg/m³
Total dust	50	15 mg/m³

Note—Conversion factors - mppcf × 35.3 = million particles per cubic meter = particles per c.c.

[a] Millions of particles per cubic foot of air, based on impinger samples counted by light-field techniques.

[b] The percentage of crystalline silica in the formula is the amount determined from airborne samples, except in those instances in which other methods have been shown to be applicable.

[c] Containing less than 1% quartz; if 1% quartz or more, use quartz limit.

[d] All inert or nuisance dusts, whether mineral, inorganic, or organic, not listed specifically by substance name are covered by this limit, which is the same as the Particulates Not Otherwise Regulated (PNOR) limit in Table Z–1.

[e] Both concentration and percent quartz for the application of this limit are to be determined from the fraction passing a size-selector with the following characteristics:

Aerodynamic diameter (unit density sphere)	Percent passing selector
2	90
2.5	75
3.5	50
5.0	25
10	0

The measurements under this note refer to the use of an AEC (now NRC) instrument. The respirable fraction of coal dust is determined with an MRE; the figure corresponding to that of 2.4 mg/m³ in the table for coal dust is 4.5 mg/m³ᴷ.

[f] This standard applies to any operations or sectors for which the respirable crystalline silica standard, 1910.1053, is stayed or is otherwise not in effect.

[58 FR 35340, June 30, 1993; 58 FR 40191, July 27, 1993, as amended at 61 FR 56831, Nov. 4, 1996; 62 FR 1600, Jan. 10, 1997; 62 FR 42018, Aug. 4, 1997; 71 FR 10373, Feb. 28, 2006; 71 FR 16673, Apr. 3, 2006; 71 FR 36008, June 23, 2006; 81 FR 16861, Mar. 25, 2016; 81 FR 31167, May 18, 2016; 81 FR 60272, Sept. 1, 2016; 82 FR 2735, Jan. 9, 2017]

§1910.1001 Asbestos.

(a) *Scope and application.* (1) This section applies to all occupational exposures to asbestos in all industries covered by the Occupational Safety and Health Act, except as provided in paragraph (a)(2) and (3) of this section.

(2) This section does not apply to construction work as defined in 29 CFR 1910.12(b). (Exposure to asbestos in construction work is covered by 29 CFR 1926.1101).

(3) This section does not apply to ship repairing, shipbuilding and shipbreaking employments and related employments as defined in 29 CFR 1915.4. (Exposure to asbestos in these employments is covered by 29 CFR 1915.1001).

(b) *Definitions.* Asbestos includes chrysotile, amosite, crocidolite, tremolite asbestos, anthophyllite asbestos, actinolite asbestos, and any of these minerals that have been chemically treated and/or altered.

Asbestos-containing material (ACM) means any material containing more than 1% asbestos.

Assistant Secretary means the Assistant Secretary of Labor for Occupational Safety and Health, U.S. Department of Labor, or designee.

Authorized person means any person authorized by the employer and required by work duties to be present in regulated areas.

Building/facility owner is the legal entity, including a lessee, which exercises control over management and record keeping functions relating to a building and/or facility in which activities covered by this standard take place.

Certified industrial hygienist (CIH) means one certified in the practice of industrial hygiene by the American Board of Industrial Hygiene.

Director means the Director of the National Institute for Occupational Safety and Health, U.S. Department of Health and Human Services, or designee.

Employee exposure means that exposure to airborne asbestos that would occur if the employee were not using respiratory protective equipment.

Fiber means a particulate form of asbestos 5 micrometers or longer, with a length-to-diameter ratio of at least 3 to 1.

High-efficiency particulate air (HEPA) filter means a filter capable of trapping and retaining at least 99.97 percent of 0.3 micrometer diameter mono-disperse particles.

Homogeneous area means an area of surfacing material or thermal system insulation that is uniform in color and texture.

Industrial hygienist means a professional qualified by education, training, and experience to anticipate, recognize, evaluate and develop controls for occupational health hazards.

PACM means "presumed asbestos containing material."

Presumed asbestos containing material means thermal system insulation and surfacing material found in buildings constructed no later than 1980. The designation of a material as "PACM" may be rebutted pursuant to paragraph (j)(8) of this section.

Regulated area means an area established by the employer to demarcate areas where airborne concentrations of asbestos exceed, or there is a reasonable possibility they may exceed, the permissible exposure limits.

Surfacing ACM means surfacing material which contains more than 1% asbestos.

Surfacing material means material that is sprayed, troweled-on or otherwise applied to surfaces (such as acoustical plaster on ceilings and fireproofing materials on structural members, or other materials on surfaces for acoustical, fireproofing, and other purposes).

Thermal System Insulation (TSI) means ACM applied to pipes, fittings, boilers, breeching, tanks, ducts or other structural components to prevent heat loss or gain.

Thermal System Insulation ACM means thermal system insulation which contains more than 1% asbestos.

(c) *Permissible exposure limit (PELS)*—(1) *Time-weighted average limit (TWA)*. The employer shall ensure that no employee is exposed to an airborne concentration of asbestos in excess of 0.1 fiber per cubic centimeter of air as an eight (8)-hour time-weighted average (TWA) as determined by the method prescribed in appendix A to this section, or by an equivalent method.

(2) *Excursion limit*. The employer shall ensure that no employee is exposed to an airborne concentration of asbestos in excess of 1.0 fiber per cubic centimeter of air (1 f/cc) as averaged over a sampling period of thirty (30) minutes as determined by the method prescribed in appendix A to this section, or by an equivalent method.

(d) *Exposure monitoring*—(1) *General*. (i) Determinations of employee exposure shall be made from breathing zone air samples that are representative of the 8-hour TWA and 30-minute short-term exposures of each employee.

(ii) Representative 8-hour TWA employee exposures shall be determined on the basis of one or more samples representing full-shift exposures for each shift for each employee in each job classification in each work area. Representative 30-minute short-term employee exposures shall be determined on the basis of one or more samples representing 30 minute exposures associated with operations that are most likely to produce exposures above the excursion limit for each shift for each job classification in each work area.

(2) *Initial monitoring.* (i) Each employer who has a workplace or work operation covered by this standard, except as provided for in paragraphs (d)(2)(ii) and (d)(2)(iii) of this section, shall perform initial monitoring of employees who are, or may reasonably be expected to be exposed to airborne concentrations at or above the TWA permissible exposure limit and/or excursion limit.

(ii) Where the employer has monitored after March 31, 1992, for the TWA permissible exposure limit and/or the excursion limit, and the monitoring satisfies all other requirements of this section, the employer may rely on such earlier monitoring results to satisfy the requirements of paragraph (d)(2)(i) of this section.

(iii) Where the employer has relied upon objective data that demonstrate that asbestos is not capable of being released in airborne concentrations at or above the TWA permissible exposure limit and/or excursion limit under the expected conditions of processing, use, or handling, then no initial monitoring is required.

(3) *Monitoring frequency (periodic monitoring) and patterns.* After the initial determinations required by paragraph (d)(2)(i) of this section, samples shall be of such frequency and pattern as to represent with reasonable accuracy the levels of exposure of the employees. In no case shall sampling be at intervals greater than six months for employees whose exposures may reasonably be foreseen to exceed the TWA permissible exposure limit and/or excursion limit.

(4) *Changes in monitoring frequency.* If either the initial or the periodic monitoring required by paragraphs (d)(2) and (d)(3) of this section statistically indicates that employee exposures are below the TWA permissible exposure limit and/or excursion limit, the employer may discontinue the monitoring

for those employees whose exposures are represented by such monitoring.

(5) *Additional monitoring.* Notwithstanding the provisions of paragraphs (d)(2)(ii) and (d)(4) of this section, the employer shall institute the exposure monitoring required under paragraphs (d)(2)(i) and (d)(3) of this section whenever there has been a change in the production, process, control equipment, personnel or work practices that may result in new or additional exposures above the TWA permissible exposure limit and/or excursion limit or when the employer has any reason to suspect that a change may result in new or additional exposures above the PEL and/or excursion limit.

(6) *Method of monitoring.* (i) All samples taken to satisfy the monitoring requirements of paragraph (d) of this section shall be personal samples collected following the procedures specified in appendix A.

(ii) All samples taken to satisfy the monitoring requirements of paragraph (d) of this section shall be evaluated using the OSHA Reference Method (ORM) specified in appendix A of this section, or an equivalent counting method.

(iii) If an equivalent method to the ORM is used, the employer shall ensure that the method meets the following criteria:

(A) Replicate exposure data used to establish equivalency are collected in side-by-side field and laboratory comparisons; and

(B) The comparison indicates that 90% of the samples collected in the range 0.5 to 2.0 times the permissible limit have an accuracy range of plus or minus 25 percent of the ORM results at a 95% confidence level as demonstrated by a statistically valid protocol; and

(C) The equivalent method is documented and the results of the comparison testing are maintained.

(iv) To satisfy the monitoring requirements of paragraph (d) of this section, employers must use the results of monitoring analysis performed by laboratories which have instituted quality assurance programs that include the elements as prescribed in appendix A of this section.

(7) *Employee notification of monitoring results.* (i) The employer must, within

21

15 working days after the receipt of the results of any monitoring performed under this sections, notify each affected employee of these results either individually in writing or by posting the results in an appropriate location that is accessible to affected employees.

(ii) The written notification required by paragraph (d)(7)(i) of this section shall contain the corrective action being taken by the employer to reduce employee exposure to or below the TWA and/or excursion limit, wherever monitoring results indicated that the TWA and/or excursion limit had been exceeded.

(e) *Regulated Areas*—(1) *Establishment.* The employer shall establish regulated areas wherever airborne concentrations of asbestos and/or PACM are in excess of the TWA and/or excursion limit prescribed in paragraph (c) of this section.

(2) *Demarcation.* Regulated areas shall be demarcated from the rest of the workplace in any manner that minimizes the number of persons who will be exposed to asbestos.

(3) *Access.* Access to regulated areas shall be limited to authorized persons or to persons authorized by the Act or regulations issued pursuant thereto.

(4) *Provision of respirators.* Each person entering a regulated area shall be supplied with and required to use a respirator, selected in accordance with paragraph (g)(2) of this section.

(5) *Prohibited activities.* The employer shall ensure that employees do not eat, drink, smoke, chew tobacco or gum, or apply cosmetics in the regulated areas.

(f) *Methods of compliance*—(1) *Engineering controls and work practices.* (i) The employer shall institute engineering controls and work practices to reduce and maintain employee exposure to or below the TWA and/or excursion limit prescribed in paragraph (c) of this section, except to the extent that such controls are not feasible.

(ii) Wherever the feasible engineering controls and work practices that can be instituted are not sufficient to reduce employee exposure to or below the TWA and/or excursion limit prescribed in paragraph (c) of this section, the employer shall use them to reduce employee exposure to the lowest levels achievable by these controls and shall

supplement them by the use of respiratory protection that complies with the requirements of paragraph (g) of this section.

(iii) For the following operations, wherever feasible engineering controls and work practices that can be instituted are not sufficient to reduce employee exposure to or below the TWA and/or excursion limit prescribed in paragraph (c) of this section, the employer shall use them to reduce employee exposure to or below 0.5 fiber per cubic centimeter of air (as an eight-hour time-weighted average) or 2.5 fibers/cc for 30 minutes (short-term exposure) and shall supplement them by the use of any combination of respiratory protection that complies with the requirements of paragraph (g) of this section, work practices and feasible engineering controls that will reduce employee exposure to or below the TWA and to or below the excursion limit permissible prescribed in paragraph (c) of this section: Coupling cutoff in primary asbestos cement pipe manufacturing; sanding in primary and secondary asbestos cement sheet manufacturing; grinding in primary and secondary friction product manufacturing; carding and spinning in dry textile processes; and grinding and sanding in primary plastics manufacturing.

(iv) *Local exhaust ventilation.* Local exhaust ventilation and dust collection systems shall be designed, constructed, installed, and maintained in accordance with good practices such as those found in the American National Standard Fundamentals Governing the Design and Operation of Local Exhaust Systems, ANSI Z9.2–1979.

(v) *Particular tools.* All hand-operated and power-operated tools which would produce or release fibers of asbestos, such as, but not limited to, saws, scorers, abrasive wheels, and drills, shall be provided with local exhaust ventilation systems which comply with paragraph (f)(1)(iv) of this section.

(vi) *Wet methods.* Insofar as practicable, asbestos shall be handled, mixed, applied, removed, cut, scored, or otherwise worked in a wet state sufficient to prevent the emission of airborne fibers so as to expose employees to levels in excess of the TWA and/or excursion limit, prescribed in paragraph (c) of this section, unless the usefulness of the product would be diminished thereby.

(vii) [Reserved]

(viii) *Particular products and operations.* No asbestos cement, mortar, coating, grout, plaster, or similar material containing asbestos, shall be removed from bags, cartons, or other containers in which they are shipped, without being either wetted, or enclosed, or ventilated so as to prevent effectively the release of airborne fibers.

(ix) *Compressed air.* Compressed air shall not be used to remove asbestos or materials containing asbestos unless the compressed air is used in conjunction with a ventilation system which effectively captures the dust cloud created by the compressed air.

(x) *Flooring.* Sanding of asbestos-containing flooring material is prohibited.

(2) *Compliance program.* (i) Where the TWA and/or excursion limit is exceeded, the employer shall establish and implement a written program to reduce employee exposure to or below the TWA and to or below the excursion limit by means of engineering and work practice controls as required by paragraph (f)(1) of this section, and by the use of respiratory protection where required or permitted under this section.

(ii) Such programs shall be reviewed and updated as necessary to reflect significant changes in the status of the employer's compliance program.

(iii) Written programs shall be submitted upon request for examination and copying to the Assistant Secretary, the Director, affected employees and designated employee representatives.

(iv) The employer shall not use employee rotation as a means of compliance with the TWA and/or excursion limit.

(3) Specific compliance methods for brake and clutch repair:

(i) Engineering controls and work practices for brake and clutch repair and service. During automotive brake and clutch inspection, disassembly, repair and assembly operations, the employer shall institute engineering controls and work practices to reduce employee exposure to materials containing asbestos using a negative pressure enclosure/HEPA vacuum system method or low pressure/wet cleaning method, which meets the detailed requirements set out in appendix F to this section. The employer may also comply using an equivalent method which follows written procedures which the employer demonstrates can achieve results equivalent to Method A in appendix F to this section. For facilities in which no more than 5 pair of brakes or 5 clutches are inspected, disassembled, repaired, or assembled per week, the method set forth in paragraph [D] of appendix F to this section may be used.

(ii) The employer may also comply by using an equivalent method which follows written procedures, which the employer demonstrates can achieve equivalent exposure reductions as do the two "preferred methods." Such demonstration must include monitoring data conducted under workplace conditions closely resembling the process, type of asbestos containing materials, control method, work practices and environmental conditions which the equivalent method will be used, or objective data, which document that under all reasonably foreseeable conditions of brake and clutch repair applications, the method results in exposures which are equivalent to the methods set out in appendix F to this section.

(g) *Respiratory protection*—(1) *General.* For employees who use respirators required by this section, the employer must provide each employee an appropriate respirator that complies with the requirements of this paragraph. Respirators must be used during:

(i) Periods necessary to install or implement feasible engineering and work-practice controls.

(ii) Work operations, such as maintenance and repair activities, for which engineering and work-practice controls are not feasible.

(iii) Work operations for which feasible engineering and work-practice controls are not yet sufficient to reduce employee exposure to or below the TWA and/or excursion limit.

(iv) Emergencies.

23

(2) *Respirator program.* (i) The employer must implement a respiratory protection program in accordance with 29 CFR 134 (b) through (d) (except (d)(1)(iii)), and (f) through (m), which covers each employee required by this section to use a respirator.

(ii) Employers must provide an employee with a tight-fitting, powered air-purifying respirator (PAPR) instead of a negative pressure respirator selected according to paragraph (g)(3) of this standard when the employee chooses to use a PAPR and it provides adequate protection to the employee.

(iii) No employee must be assigned to tasks requiring the use of respirators if, based on their most recent medical examination, the examining physician determines that the employee will be unable to function normally using a respirator, or that the safety or health of the employee or other employees will be impaired by the use of a respirator. Such employees must be assigned to another job or given the opportunity to transfer to a different position, the duties of which they can perform. If such a transfer position is available, the position must be with the same employer, in the same geographical area, and with the same seniority, status, and rate of pay the employee had just prior to such transfer.

(3) *Respirator selection.* Employers must:

(i) Select, and provide to employees, the appropriate respirators specified in paragraph (d)(3)(i)(A) of 29 CFR 1910.134; however, employers must not select or use filtering facepiece respirators for protection against asbestos fibers.

(ii) Provide HEPA filters for powered and non-powered air-purifying respirators.

(h) *Protective work clothing and equipment*—(1) *Provision and use.* If an employee is exposed to asbestos above the TWA and/or excursion limit, or where the possibility of eye irritation exists, the employer shall provide at no cost to the employee and ensure that the employee uses appropriate protective work clothing and equipment such as, but not limited to:

(i) Coveralls or similar full-body work clothing;

(ii) Gloves, head coverings, and foot coverings; and

(iii) Face shields, vented goggles, or other appropriate protective equipment which complies with 1910.133 of this part.

(2) *Removal and storage.* (i) The employer shall ensure that employees remove work clothing contaminated with asbestos only in change rooms provided in accordance with paragraph (i)(1) of this section.

(ii) The employer shall ensure that no employee takes contaminated work clothing out of the change room, except those employees authorized to do so for the purpose of laundering, maintenance, or disposal.

(iii) Contaminated work clothing shall be placed and stored in closed containers which prevent dispersion of the asbestos outside the container.

(iv) The employer shall ensure that containers of contaminated protective devices or work clothing, which are to be taken out of change rooms or the workplace for cleaning, maintenance or disposal, bear labels in accordance with paragraph (j) of this section.

(3) *Cleaning and replacement.* (i) The employer shall clean, launder, repair, or replace protective clothing and equipment required by this paragraph to maintain their effectiveness. The employer shall provide clean protective clothing and equipment at least weekly to each affected employee.

(ii) The employer shall prohibit the removal of asbestos from protective clothing and equipment by blowing or shaking. (iii) Laundering of contaminated clothing shall be done so as to prevent the release of airborne fibers of asbestos in excess of the permissible exposure limits prescribed in paragraph (c) of this section.

(iv) Any employer who gives contaminated clothing to another person for laundering shall inform such person of the requirement in paragraph (h)(3)(iii) of this section to effectively prevent the release of airborne fibers of asbestos in excess of the permissible exposure limits.

(v) The employer shall inform any person who launders or cleans protective clothing or equipment contaminated with asbestos of the potentially harmful effects of exposure to asbestos.

(vi) The employer shall ensure that contaminated clothing is transported in sealed impermeable bags, or other closed, impermeable containers, and labeled in accordance with paragraph (j) of this section.

(i) *Hygiene facilities and practices*—(1) *Change rooms.* (i) The employer shall provide clean change rooms for employees who work in areas where their airborne exposure to asbestos is above the TWA and/or excursion limit.

(ii) The employer shall ensure that change rooms are in accordance with 1910.141(e) of this part, and are equipped with two separate lockers or storage facilities, so separated as to prevent contamination of the employee's street clothes from his protective work clothing and equipment.

(2) *Showers.* (i) The employer shall ensure that employees who work in areas where their airborne exposure is above the TWA and/or excursion limit, shower at the end of the work shift.

(ii) The employer shall provide shower facilities which comply with 1910.141(d)(3) of this part.

(iii) The employer shall ensure that employees who are required to shower pursuant to paragraph (i)(2)(i) of this section do not leave the workplace wearing any clothing or equipment worn during the work shift.

(3) *Lunchrooms.* (i) The employer shall provide lunchroom facilities for employees who work in areas where their airborne exposure is above the TWA and/or excursion limit.

(ii) The employer shall ensure that lunchroom facilities have a positive pressure, filtered air supply, and are readily accessible to employees.

(iii) The employer shall ensure that employees who work in areas where their airborne exposure is above the PEL and/or excursion limit wash their hands and faces prior to eating, drinking or smoking.

(iv) The employer shall ensure that employees do not enter lunchroom facilities with protective work clothing or equipment unless surface asbestos fibers have been removed from the clothing or equipment by vacuuming or other method that removes dust without causing the asbestos to become airborne.

(4) *Smoking in work areas.* The employer shall ensure that employees do not smoke in work areas where they are occupationally exposed to asbestos because of activities in that work area.

(j) *Communication of hazards to employees—Introduction.* This section applies to the communication of information concerning asbestos hazards in general industry to facilitate compliance with this standard. Asbestos exposure in general industry occurs in a wide variety of industrial and commercial settings. Employees who manufacture asbestos-containing products may be exposed to asbestos fibers. Employees who repair and replace automotive brakes and clutches may be exposed to asbestos fibers. In addition, employees engaged in housekeeping activities in industrial facilities with asbestos product manufacturing operations, and in public and commercial buildings with installed asbestos containing materials may be exposed to asbestos fibers. Most of these workers are covered by this general industry standard, with the exception of state or local governmental employees in non-state plan states. It should be noted that employees who perform housekeeping activities during and after construction activities are covered by the asbestos construction standard, 29 CFR 1926.1101, formerly 1926.58. However, housekeeping employees, regardless of industry designation, should know whether building components they maintain may expose them to asbestos. The same hazard communication provisions will protect employees who perform housekeeping operations in all three asbestos standards; general industry, construction, and shipyard employment. As noted in the construction standard, building owners are often the only and/or best source of information concerning the presence of previously installed asbestos containing building materials. Therefore they, along with employers of potentially exposed employees, are assigned specific information conveying and retention duties under this section.

(1) *Hazard communication—general.* (i) Chemical manufacturers, importers, distributors and employers shall comply with all requirements of the Hazard

25

Communication Standard (HCS) (§ 1910.1200) for asbestos.

(ii) In classifying the hazards of asbestos at least the following hazards are to be addressed: Cancer and lung effects.

(iii) Employers shall include asbestos in the hazard communication program established to comply with the HCS (§ 1910.1200). Employers shall ensure that each employee has access to labels on containers of asbestos and to safety data sheets, and is trained in accordance with the requirements of HCS and paragraph (j)(7) of this section.

(2) *Installed Asbestos Containing Material.* Employers and building owners are required to treat installed TSI and sprayed on and troweled-on surfacing materials as ACM in buildings constructed no later than 1980 for purposes of this standard. These materials are designated "presumed ACM or PACM", and are defined in paragraph (b) of this section. Asphalt and vinyl flooring material installed no later than 1980 also must be treated as asbestos-containing. The employer or building owner may demonstrate that PACM and flooring material do not contain asbestos by complying with paragraph (j)(8)(iii) of this section.

(3) *Duties of employers and building and facility owners.* (i) Building and facility owners shall determine the presence, location, and quantity of ACM and/or PACM at the work site. Employers and building and facility owners shall exercise due diligence in complying with these requirements to inform employers and employees about the presence and location of ACM and PACM.

(ii) Building and facility owners shall maintain records of all information required to be provided pursuant to this section and/or otherwise known to the building owner concerning the presence, location and quantity of ACM and PACM in the building/facility. Such records shall be kept for the duration of ownership and shall be transferred to successive owners.

(iii) Building and facility owners shall inform employers of employees, and employers shall inform employees who will perform housekeeping activities in areas which contain ACM and/or PACM of the presence and location of ACM and/or PACM in such areas which may be contacted during such activities.

(4) *Warning signs—*(i) *Posting.* Warning signs shall be provided and displayed at each regulated area. In addition, warning signs shall be posted at all approaches to regulated areas so that an employee may read the signs and take necessary protective steps before entering the area.

(ii) *Sign specifications:*

(A) The warning signs required by paragraph (j)(4)(i) of this section shall bear the following legend:

DANGER
ASBESTOS
MAY CAUSE CANCER
CAUSES DAMAGE TO LUNGS
AUTHORIZED PERSONNEL ONLY

(B) In addition, where the use of respirators and protective clothing is required in the regulated area under this section, the warning signs shall include the following:

WEAR RESPIRATORY PROTECTION AND
  PROTECTIVE CLOTHING IN THIS AREA

(C) Prior to June 1, 2016, employers may use the following legend in lieu of that specified in paragraph (j)(4)(ii)(A) of this section:

DANGER
ASBESTOS
CANCER AND LUNG DISEASE
HAZARD
AUTHORIZED PERSONNEL ONLY

(D) Prior to June 1, 2016, employers may use the following legend in lieu of that specified in paragraph (j)(4)(ii)(B) of this section:

RESPIRATORS AND PROTECTIVE CLOTH-
  ING ARE REQUIRED IN THIS AREA

(iii) The employer shall ensure that employees working in and contiguous to regulated areas comprehend the warning signs required to be posted by paragraph (j)(4)(i) of this section. Means to ensure employee comprehension may include the use of foreign languages, pictographs and graphics.

(iv) At the entrance to mechanical rooms/areas in which employees reasonably can be expected to enter and which contain ACM and/or PACM, the building owner shall post signs which identify the material which is present, its location, and appropriate work

26

practices which, if followed, will ensure that ACM and/or PACM will not be disturbed. The employer shall ensure, to the extent feasible, that employees who come in contact with these signs can comprehend them. Means to ensure employee comprehension may include the use of foreign languages, pictographs, graphics, and awareness training.

(5) *Warning labels*—(i) *Labeling.* Labels shall be affixed to all raw materials, mixtures, scrap, waste, debris, and other products containing asbestos fibers, or to their containers. When a building owner or employer identifies previously installed ACM and/or PACM, labels or signs shall be affixed or posted so that employees will be notified of what materials contain ACM and/or PACM. The employer shall attach such labels in areas where they will clearly be noticed by employees who are likely to be exposed, such as at the entrance to mechanical room/areas. Signs required by paragraph (j) of this section may be posted in lieu of labels so long as they contain the information required for labeling.

(ii) *Label specifications.* In addition to the requirements of paragraph (j)(1), the employer shall ensure that labels of bags or containers of protective clothing and equipment, scrap, waste, and debris containing asbestos fibers include the following information:

DANGER
CONTAINS ASBESTOS FIBERS
MAY CAUSE CANCER
CAUSES DAMAGE TO LUNGS
DO NOT BREATHE DUST
AVOID CREATING DUST

(iii) Prior to June 1, 2015, employers may include the following information on raw materials, mixtures or labels of bags or containers of protective clothing and equipment, scrap, waste, and debris containing asbestos fibers in lieu of the labeling requirements in paragraphs (j)(1)(i) and (j)(5)(ii) of this section:

DANGER
CONTAINS ASBESTOS FIBERS
AVOID CREATING DUST
CANCER AND LUNG DISEASE HAZARD

(6) The provisions for labels and for safety data sheets required by para-

graph (j) of this section do not apply where:

(i) Asbestos fibers have been modified by a bonding agent, coating, binder, or other material provided that the manufacturer can demonstrate that during any reasonably foreseeable use, handling, storage, disposal, processing, or transportation, no airborne concentrations of fibers of asbestos in excess of the TWA permissible exposure level and/or excursion limit will be released or

(ii) Asbestos is present in a product in concentrations less than 1.0%.

(7) *Employee information and training.* (i) The employer shall train each employee who is exposed to airborne concentrations of asbestos at or above the PEL and/or excursion limit in accordance with the requirements of this section. The employer shall institute a training program and ensure employee participation in the program.

(ii) Training shall be provided prior to or at the time of initial assignment and at least annually thereafter.

(iii) The training program shall be conducted in a manner which the employee is able to understand. The employer shall ensure that each employee is informed of the following:

(A) The health effects associated with asbestos exposure;

(B) The relationship between smoking and exposure to asbestos producing lung cancer;

(C) The quantity, location, manner of use, release, and storage of asbestos, and the specific nature of operations which could result in exposure to asbestos;

(D) The engineering controls and work practices associated with the employee's job assignment;

(E) The specific procedures implemented to protect employees from exposure to asbestos, such as appropriate work practices, emergency and clean-up procedures, and personal protective equipment to be used;

(F) The purpose, proper use, and limitations of respirators and protective clothing, if appropriate;

(G) The purpose and a description of the medical surveillance program required by paragraph (l) of this section;

(H) The content of this standard, including appendices.

27

(I) The names, addresses and phone numbers of public health organizations which provide information, materials, and/or conduct programs concerning smoking cessation. The employer may distribute the list of such organizations contained in appendix I to this section, to comply with this requirement.

(J) The requirements for posting signs and affixing labels and the meaning of the required legends for such signs and labels.

(iv) The employer shall also provide, at no cost to employees who perform housekeeping operations in an area which contains ACM or PACM, an asbestos awareness training course, which shall at a minimum contain the following elements: health effects of asbestos, locations of ACM and PACM in the building/facility, recognition of ACM and PACM damage and deterioration, requirements in this standard relating to housekeeping, and proper response to fiber release episodes, to all employees who perform housekeeping work in areas where ACM and/or PACM is present. Each such employee shall be so trained at least once a year.

(v) Access to information and training materials.

(A) The employer shall make a copy of this standard and its appendices readily available without cost to all affected employees.

(B) The employer shall provide, upon request, all materials relating to the employee information and training program to the Assistant Secretary and the training program to the Assistant Secretary and the Director.

(C) The employer shall inform all employees concerning the availability of self-help smoking cessation program material. Upon employee request, the employer shall distribute such material, consisting of NIH Publication No. 89–1647, or equivalent self-help material, which is approved or published by a public health organization listed in appendix I to this section.

(8) *Criteria to rebut the designation of installed material as PACM.* (i) At any time, an employer and/or building owner may demonstrate, for purposes of this standard, that PACM does not contain asbestos. Building owners and/or employers are not required to communicate information about the presence of building material for which such a demonstration pursuant to the requirements of paragraph (j)(8)(ii) of this section has been made. However, in all such cases, the information, data and analysis supporting the determination that PACM does not contain asbestos, shall be retained pursuant to paragraph (m) of this section.

(ii) An employer or owner may demonstrate that PACM does not contain asbestos by the following:

(A) Having a completed inspection conducted pursuant to the requirements of AHERA (40 CFR 763, subpart E) which demonstrates that no ACM is present in the material; or

(B) Performing tests of the material containing PACM which demonstrate that no ACM is present in the material. Such tests shall include analysis of bulk samples collected in the manner described in 40 CFR 763.86. The tests, evaluation and sample collection shall be conducted by an accredited inspector or by a CIH. Analysis of samples shall be performed by persons or laboratories with proficiency demonstrated by current successful participation in a nationally recognized testing program such as the National Voluntary Laboratory Accreditation Program (NVLAP) or the National Institute for Standards and Technology (NIST) or the Round Robin for bulk samples administered by the American Industrial Hygiene Association (AIHA) or an equivalent nationally-recognized round robin testing program.

(iii) The employer and/or building owner may demonstrate that flooring material including associated mastic and backing does not contain asbestos, by a determination of an industrial hygienist based upon recognized analytical techniques showing that the material is not ACM.

(k) *Housekeeping.* (1) All surfaces shall be maintained as free as practicable of ACM waste and debris and accompanying dust.

(2) All spills and sudden releases of material containing asbestos shall be cleaned up as soon as possible.

(3) Surfaces contaminated with asbestos may not be cleaned by the use of compressed air.

(4) *Vacuuming.* HEPA-filtered vacuuming equipment shall be used for vacuuming asbestos containing waste and debris. The equipment shall be used and emptied in a manner which minimizes the reentry of asbestos into the workplace.

(5) Shoveling, dry sweeping and dry clean-up of asbestos may be used only where vacuuming and/or wet cleaning are not feasible.

(6) *Waste disposal.* Waste, scrap, debris, bags, containers, equipment, and clothing contaminated with asbestos consigned for disposal, shall be collected, recycled and disposed of in sealed impermeable bags, or other closed, impermeable containers.

(7) Care of asbestos-containing flooring material.

(i) Sanding of asbestos-containing floor material is prohibited.

(ii) Stripping of finishes shall be conducted using low abrasion pads at speeds lower than 300 rpm and wet methods.

(iii) Burnishing or dry buffing may be performed only on asbestos-containing flooring which has sufficient finish so that the pad cannot contact the asbestos-containing material.

(8) Waste and debris and accompanying dust in an area containing accessible ACM and/or PACM or visibly deteriorated ACM, shall not be dusted or swept dry, or vacuumed without using a HEPA filter.

(1) *Medical surveillance*—(1) *General*—(i) *Employees covered.* The employer shall institute a medical surveillance program for all employees who are or will be exposed to airborne concentrations of fibers of asbestos at or above the TWA or excursion limit.

(ii) *Examination by a physician.* (A) The employer shall ensure that all medical examinations and procedures are performed by or under the supervision of a licensed physician, and shall be provided without cost to the employee and at a reasonable time and place.

(B) Persons other than licensed physicians, who administer the pulmonary function testing required by this section, shall complete a training course in spirometry sponsored by an appropriate academic or professional institution.

(2) *Pre-placement examinations.* (i) Before an employee is assigned to an occupation exposed to airborne concentrations of asbestos fibers at or above the TWA and/or excursion limit, a pre-placement medical examination shall be provided or made available by the employer.

(ii) Such examination shall include, as a minimum, a medical and work history; a complete physical examination of all systems with emphasis on the respiratory system, the cardiovascular system and digestive tract; completion of the respiratory disease standardized questionnaire in appendix D to this section, part 1; a chest roentgenogram (posterior-anterior 14 × 17 inches); pulmonary function tests to include forced vital capacity (FVC) and forced expiratory volume at 1 second (FEV(1.0)); and any additional tests deemed appropriate by the examining physician. Interpretation and classification of chest roentgenogram shall be conducted in accordance with appendix E to this section.

(3) *Periodic examinations.* (i) Periodic medical examinations shall be made available annually.

(ii) The scope of the medical examination shall be in conformance with the protocol established in paragraph (l)(2)(ii) of this section, except that the frequency of chest roentgenogram shall be conducted in accordance with Table 1, and the abbreviated standardized questionnaire contained in, part 2 of appendix D to this section shall be administered to the employee.

TABLE 1—FREQUENCY OF CHEST ROENTGENOGRAM

Years since first exposure	Age of employee		
	15 to 35	35 + to 45	45 +
0 to 10	Every 5 years	Every 5 years	Every 5 years.
10 + ...	Every 5 years	Every 2 years	Every 1 year.

29

(4) *Termination of employment examinations.* (i) The employer shall provide, or make available, a termination of employment medical examination for any employee who has been exposed to airborne concentrations of fibers of asbestos at or above the TWA and/or excursion limit.

(ii) The medical examination shall be in accordance with the requirements of the periodic examinations stipulated in paragraph (l)(3) of this section, and shall be given within 30 calendar days before or after the date of termination of employment.

(5) *Recent examinations.* No medical examination is required of any employee, if adequate records show that the employee has been examined in accordance with any of paragraphs ((l)(2) through (l)(4)) of this section within the past 1 year period. A pre-employment medical examination which was required as a condition of employment by the employer, may not be used by that employer to meet the requirements of this paragraph, unless the cost of such examination is borne by the employer.

(6) *Information provided to the physician.* The employer shall provide the following information to the examining physician:

(i) A copy of this standard and Appendices D and E.

(ii) A description of the affected employee's duties as they relate to the employee's exposure.

(iii) The employee's representative exposure level or anticipated exposure level.

(iv) A description of any personal protective and respiratory equipment used or to be used.

(v) Information from previous medical examinations of the affected employee that is not otherwise available to the examining physician.

(7) *Physician's written opinion.* (i) The employer shall obtain a written opinion from the examining physician. This written opinion shall contain the results of the medical examination and shall include:

(A) The physician's opinion as to whether the employee has any detected medical conditions that would place the employee at an increased risk of material health impairment from exposure to asbestos;

(B) Any recommended limitations on the employee or upon the use of personal protective equipment such as clothing or respirators;

(C) A statement that the employee has been informed by the physician of the results of the medical examination and of any medical conditions resulting from asbestos exposure that require further explanation or treatment; and

(D) A statement that the employee has been informed by the physician of the increased risk of lung cancer attributable to the combined effect of smoking and asbestos exposure.

(ii) The employer shall instruct the physician not to reveal in the written opinion given to the employer specific findings or diagnoses unrelated to occupational exposure to asbestos.

(iii) The employer shall provide a copy of the physician's written opinion to the affected employee within 30 days from its receipt.

(m) *Recordkeeping—*(1) *Exposure measurements.*

NOTE: The employer may utilize the services of competent organizations such as industry trade associations and employee associations to maintain the records required by this section.

(i) The employer shall keep an accurate record of all measurements taken to monitor employee exposure to asbestos as prescribed in paragraph (d) of this section.

(ii) This record shall include at least the following information:

(A) The date of measurement;

(B) The operation involving exposure to asbestos which is being monitored;

(C) Sampling and analytical methods used and evidence of their accuracy;

(D) Number, duration, and results of samples taken;

(E) Type of respiratory protective devices worn, if any; and

(F) Name, social security number and exposure of the employees whose exposure are represented.

(iii) The employer shall maintain this record for at least thirty (30) years, in accordance with 29 CFR 1910.20.

(2) *Objective data for exempted operations.* (i) Where the processing, use, or

handling of products made from or containing asbestos is exempted from other requirements of this section under paragraph (d)(2)(iii) of this section, the employer shall establish and maintain an accurate record of objective data reasonably relied upon in support of the exemption.

(ii) The record shall include at least the following:

(A) The product qualifying for exemption;

(B) The source of the objective data;

(C) The testing protocol, results of testing, and/or analysis of the material for the release of asbestos;

(D) A description of the operation exempted and how the data support the exemption; and

(E) Other data relevant to the operations, materials, processing, or employee exposures covered by the exemption.

(iii) The employer shall maintain this record for the duration of the employer's reliance upon such objective data.

(3) *Medical surveillance.* (i) The employer shall establish and maintain an accurate record for each employee subject to medical surveillance by paragraph (l)(1)(i) of this section, in accordance with 29 CFR 1910.1020.

(ii) The record shall include at least the following information:

(A) The name and social security number of the employee;

(B) Physician's written opinions;

(C) Any employee medical complaints related to exposure to asbestos; and

(D) A copy of the information provided to the physician as required by paragraph (l)(6) of this section.

(iii) The employer shall ensure that this record is maintained for the duration of employment plus thirty (30) years, in accordance with 29 CFR 1910.1020.

(4) *Training.* The employer shall maintain all employee training records for one (1) year beyond the last date of employment of that employee.

(5) *Availability.* (i) The employer, upon written request, shall make all records required to be maintained by this section available to the Assistant Secretary and the Director for examination and copying.

(ii) The employer, upon request shall make any exposure records required by paragraph (m)(1) of this section available for examination and copying to affected employees, former employees, designated representatives and the Assistant Secretary, in accordance with 29 CFR 1910.1020 (a) through (e) and (g) through (i).

(iii) The employer, upon request, shall make employee medical records required by paragraph (m)(3) of this section available for examination and copying to the subject employee, to anyone having the specific written consent of the subject employee, and the Assistant Secretary, in accordance with 29 CFR 1910.1020.

(6) *Transfer of records.* The employer shall comply with the requirements concerning transfer of records set forth in 29 CFR 1910.1020(h).

(n) *Observation of monitoring*—(1) *Employee observation.* The employer shall provide affected employees or their designated representatives an opportunity to observe any monitoring of employee exposure to asbestos conducted in accordance with paragraph (d) of this section.

(2) *Observation procedures.* When observation of the monitoring of employee exposure to asbestos requires entry into an area where the use of protective clothing or equipment is required, the observer shall be provided with and be required to use such clothing and equipment and shall comply with all other applicable safety and health procedures.

(o) *Appendices.* (1) Appendices A, C, D, E, and F to this section are incorporated as part of this section and the contents of these Appendices are mandatory.

(2) Appendices B, G, H, I, and J to this section are informational and are not intended to create any additional obligations not otherwise imposed or to detract from any existing obligations.

APPENDIX A TO §1910.1001—OSHA REFERENCE METHOD—MANDATORY

This mandatory appendix specifies the procedure for analyzing air samples for asbestos and specifies quality control procedures that must be implemented by laboratories performing the analysis. The sampling and analytical methods described below represent

31

the elements of the available monitoring methods (such as appendix B of their regulation, the most current version of the OSHA method ID–160, or the most current version of the NIOSH Method 7400). All employers who are required to conduct air monitoring under paragraph (d) of the standard are required to utilize analytical laboratories that use this procedure, or an equivalent method, for collecting and analyzing samples.

Sampling and Analytical Procedure

1. The sampling medium for air samples shall be mixed cellulose ester filter membranes. These shall be designated by the manufacturer as suitable for asbestos counting. See below for rejection of blanks.

2. The preferred collection device shall be the 25-mm diameter cassette with an open-faced 50-mm electrically conductive extension cowl. The 37-mm cassette may be used if necessary but only if written justification for the need to use the 37-mm filter cassette accompanies the sample results in the employee's exposure monitoring record. Do not reuse or reload cassettes for asbestos sample collection.

3. An air flow rate between 0.5 liter/min and 2.5 liters/min shall be selected for the 25-mm cassette. If the 37-mm cassette is used, an air flow rate between 1 liter/min and 2.5 liters/min shall be selected.

4. Where possible, a sufficient air volume for each air sample shall be collected to yield between 100 and 1,300 fibers per square millimeter on the membrane filter. If a filter darkens in appearance or if loose dust is seen on the filter, a second sample shall be started.

5. Ship the samples in a rigid container with sufficient packing material to prevent dislodging the collected fibers. Packing material that has a high electrostatic charge on its surface (e.g., expanded polystyrene) cannot be used because such material can cause loss of fibers to the sides of the cassette.

6. Calibrate each personal sampling pump before and after use with a representative filter cassette installed between the pump and the calibration devices.

7. Personal samples shall be taken in the "breathing zone" of the employee (*i.e.*, attached to or near the collar or lapel near the worker's face).

8. Fiber counts shall be made by positive phase contrast using a microscope with an 8 to 10× eyepiece and a 40 to 45× objective for a total magnification of approximately 400× and a numerical aperture of 0.65 to 0.75. The microscope shall also be fitted with a green or blue filter.

9. The microscope shall be fitted with a Walton-Beckett eyepiece graticule calibrated for a field diameter of 100 micrometers (±2 micrometers).

10. The phase-shift detection limit of the microscope shall be about 3 degrees measured using the HSE phase shift test slide as outlined below.

a. Place the test slide on the microscope stage and center it under the phase objective.

b. Bring the blocks of grooved lines into focus.

NOTE: The slide consists of seven sets of grooved lines (ca. 20 grooves to each block) in descending order of visibility from sets 1 to 7, seven being the least visible. The requirements for asbestos counting are that the microscope optics must resolve the grooved lines in set 3 completely, although they may appear somewhat faint, and that the grooved lines in sets 6 and 7 must be invisible. Sets 4 and 5 must be at least partially visible but may vary slightly in visibility between microscopes. A microscope that fails to meet these requirements has either too low or too high a resolution to be used for asbestos counting.

c. If the image deteriorates, clean and adjust the microscope optics. If the problem persists, consult the microscope manufacturer.

11. Each set of samples taken will include 10% field blanks or a minimum of 2 field blanks. These blanks must come from the same lot as the filters used for sample collection. The field blank results shall be averaged and subtracted from the analytical results before reporting. A set consists of any sample or group of samples for which an evaluation for this standard must be made. Any samples represented by a field blank having a fiber count in excess of the detection limit of the method being used shall be rejected.

12. The samples shall be mounted by the acetone/triacetin method or a method with an equivalent index of refraction and similar clarity.

13. Observe the following counting rules.

a. Count only fibers equal to or longer than 5 micrometers. Measure the length of curved fibers along the curve.

b. In the absence of other information, count all particles as asbesto that have a length-to-width ratio (aspect ratio) of 3:1 or greater.

c. Fibers lying entirely within the boundary of the Walton-Beckett graticule field shall receive a count of 1. Fibers crossing the boundary once, having one end within the circle, shall receive the count of one half (½). Do not count any fiber that crosses the graticule boundary more than once. Reject and do not count any other fibers even though they may be visible outside the graticule area.

d. Count bundles of fibers as one fiber unless individual fibers can be identified by observing both ends of an individual fiber.

e. Count enough graticule fields to yield 100 fibers. Count a minimum of 20 fields; stop counting at 100 fields regardless of fiber count.

14. Blind recounts shall be conducted at the rate of 10 percent.

Quality Control Procedures

1. Intralaboratory program. Each laboratory and/or each company with more than one microscopist counting slides shall establish a statistically designed quality assurance program involving blind recounts and comparisons between microscopists to monitor the variability of counting by each microscopist and between microscopists. In a company with more than one laboratory, the program shall include all laboratories and shall also evaluate the laboratory-to-laboratory variability.

2.a. Interlaboratory program. Each laboratory analyzing asbestos samples for compliance determination shall implement an interlaboratory quality assurance program that as a minimum includes participation of at least two other independent laboratories. Each laboratory shall participate in round robin testing at least once every 6 months with at least all the other laboratories in its interlaboratory quality assurance group. Each laboratory shall submit slides typical of its own work load for use in this program. The round robin shall be designed and results analyzed using appropriate statistical methodology.

2.b. All laboratories should also participate in a national sample testing scheme such as the Proficiency Analytical Testing Program (PAT), or the Asbestos Registry sponsored by the American Industrial Hygiene Association (AIHA).

3. All individuals performing asbestos analysis must have taken the NIOSH course for sampling and evaluating airborne asbestos dust or an equalivalent course.

4. When the use of different microscopes contributes to differences between counters and laboratories, the effect of the different microscope shall be evaluated and the microscope shall be replaced, as necessary.

5. Current results of these quality assurance programs shall be posted in each laboratory to keep the microscopists informed.

APPENDIX B TO §1910.1001—DETAILED PROCEDURES FOR ASBESTOS SAMPLING AND ANALYSIS—NON-MANDATORY

Matrix Air:
OSHA Permissible Exposure Limits:
Time Weighted Average ...... 0.1 fiber/cc
Excursion Level (30 minutes). 1.0 fiber/cc

Collection Procedure:

A known volume of air is drawn through a 25-mm diameter cassette containing a mixed-cellulose ester filter. The cassette must be equipped with an electrically conductive 50-mm extension cowl. The sampling time and rate are chosen to give a fiber density of between 100 to 1,300 fibers/mm² on the filter.

Recommended Sampling Rate .... 0.5 to 5.0 liters/minute (L/min)

Recommended Air Volumes:
Minimum .... 25 L
Maximum .... 2,400 L

Analytical Procedure: A portion of the sample filter is cleared and prepared for asbestos fiber counting by Phase Contrast Microscopy (PCM) at 400X.

Commercial manufacturers and products mentioned in this method are for descriptive use only and do not constitute endorsements by USDOL-OSHA. Similar products from other sources can be substituted.

1. Introduction

This method describes the collection of airborne asbestos fibers using calibrated sampling pumps with mixed-cellulose ester (MCE) filters and analysis by phase contrast microscopy (PCM). Some terms used are unique to this method and are defined below:

Asbestos: A term for naturally occurring fibrous minerals. Asbestos includes chrysotile, crocidolite, amosite (cummingtonite-grunerite asbestos), tremolite asbestos, actinolite asbestos, anthophyllite asbestos, and any of these minerals that have been chemically treated and/or altered. The precise chemical formulation of each species will vary with the location from which it was mined. Nominal compositions are listed:

Chrysotile .... $Mg_3 Si_2 O_5(OH)_4$

Crocidolite .... $Na_2 Fe_32 + Fe_23 + Si_8 O_{22} (OH)^2$

Amosite .... $(Mg,Fe)_7 Si_8 O_{22} (OH)_2$

Tremolite-actinolite $Ca_2(Mg,Fe)_5 Si_8 O_{22} (OH)_2$

Anthophyllite .... $(Mg,Fe)_7 Si_8 O_{22} (OH)_2$

Asbestos Fiber: A fiber of asbestos which meets the criteria specified below for a fiber.

Aspect Ratio: The ratio of the length of a fiber to it's diameter (e.g. 3:1, 5:1 aspect ratios).

Cleavage Fragments: Mineral particles formed by comminution of minerals, especially those characterized by parallel sides and a moderate aspect ratio (usually less than 20:1).

Detection Limit: The number of fibers necessary to be 95% certain that the result is greater than zero.

Differential Counting: The term applied to the practice of excluding certain kinds of fibers from the fiber count because they do not appear to be asbestos.

Fiber: A particle that is 5 μm or longer, with a length-to-width ratio of 3 to 1 or longer.

33

Field: The area within the graticule circle that is superimposed on the microscope image.

Set: The samples which are taken, submitted to the laboratory, analyzed, and for which, interim or final result reports are generated.

Tremolite, Anthophyllite, and Actinolite: The non-asbestos form of these minerals which meet the definition of a fiber. It includes any of these minerals that have been chemically treated and/or altered.

Walton-Beckett Graticule: An eyepiece graticule specifically designed for asbestos fiber counting. It consists of a circle with a projected diameter of 100 2 µm (area of about 0.00785 mm²) with a crosshair having tic-marks at 3-µm intervals in one direction and 5-µm in the orthogonal direction. There are marks around the periphery of the circle to demonstrate the proper sizes and shapes of fibers. This design is reproduced in Figure 1. The disk is placed in one of the microscope eyepieces so that the design is superimposed on the field of view.

1.1. History

Early surveys to determine asbestos exposures were conducted using impinger counts of total dust with the counts expressed as million particles per cubic foot. The British Asbestos Research Council recommended filter membrane counting in 1969. In July 1969, the Bureau of Occupational Safety and Health published a filter membrane method for counting asbestos fibers in the United States. This method was refined by NIOSH and published as P CAM 239. On May 29, 1971, OSHA specified filter membrane sampling with phase contrast counting for evaluation of asbestos exposures at work sites in the United States. The use of this technique was again required by OSHA in 1986. Phase contrast microscopy has continued to be the method of choice for the measurement of occupational exposure to asbestos.

1.2. Principle

Air is drawn through a MCE filter to capture airborne asbestos fibers. A wedge shaped portion of the filter is removed, placed on a glass microscope slide and made transparent. A measured area (field) is viewed by PCM. All the fibers meeting defined criteria for asbestos are counted and considered a measure of the airborne asbestos concentration.

1.3. Advantages and Disadvantages

There are four main advantages of PCM over other methods:

(1) The technique is specific for fibers. Phase contrast is a fiber counting technique which excludes non-fibrous particles from the analysis.

(2) The technique is inexpensive and does not require specialized knowledge to carry out the analysis for total fiber counts.

(3) The analysis is quick and can be performed on-site for rapid determination of air concentrations of asbestos fibers.

(4) The technique has continuity with historical epidemiological studies so that estimates of expected disease can be inferred from long-term determinations of asbestos exposures.

The main disadvantage of PCM is that it does not positively identify asbestos fibers. Other fibers which are not asbestos may be included in the count unless differential counting is performed. This requires a great deal of experience to adequately differentiate asbestos from non-asbestos fibers. Positive identification of asbestos must be performed by polarized light or electron microscopy techniques. A further disadvantage of PCM is that the smallest visible fibers are about 0.2 µm in diameter while the finest asbestos fibers may be as small as 0.02 µm in diameter. For some exposures, substantially more fibers may be present than are actually counted.

1.4. Workplace Exposure

Asbestos is used by the construction industry in such products as shingles, floor tiles, asbestos cement, roofing felts, insulation and acoustical products. Non-construction uses include brakes, clutch facings, paper, paints, plastics, and fabrics. One of the most significant exposures in the workplace is the removal and encapsulation of asbestos in schools, public buildings, and homes. Many workers have the potential to be exposed to asbestos during these operations.

About 95% of the asbestos in commercial use in the United States is chrysotile. Crocidolite and amosite make up most of the remainder. Anthophyllite and tremolite or actinolite are likely to be encountered as contaminants in various industrial products.

1.5. Physical Properties

Asbestos fiber possesses a high tensile strength along its axis, is chemically inert, non-combustible, and heat resistant. It has a high electrical resistance and good sound absorbing properties. It can be weaved into cables, fabrics or other textiles, and also matted into asbestos papers, felts, or mats.

2. Range and Detection Limit

2.1. The ideal counting range on the filter is 100 to 1,300 fibers/mm². With a Walton-Beckett graticule this range is equivalent to 0.8 to 10 fibers/field. Using NIOSH counting statistics, a count of 0.8 fibers/field would give an approximate coefficient of variation (CV) of 0.13.

2.2. The detection limit for this method is 4.0 fibers per 100 fields or 5.5 fibers/mm². This was determined using an equation to estimate the maximum CV possible at a specific concentration (95% confidence) and a Lower Control Limit of zero. The CV value was then used to determine a corresponding concentration from historical CV vs fiber relationships. As an example:

Lower Control Limit (95% Confidence) = AC − 1.645(CV)(AC)

Where:

AC = Estimate of the airborne fiber concentration (fibers/cc) Setting the Lower Control Limit = 0 and solving for CV:

0 = AC − 1.645(CV)(AC)
CV = 0.61

This value was compared with CV vs. count curves. The count at which CV = 0.61 for Leidel-Busch counting statistics or for an OSHA Salt Lake Technical Center (OSHA-SLTC) CV curve (see appendix A for further information) was 4.4 fibers or 3.9 fibers per 100 fields, respectively. Although a lower detection limit of 4 fibers per 100 fields is supported by the OSHA-SLTC data, both data sets support the 4.5 fibers per 100 fields value.

3. Method Performance—Precision and Accuracy

Precision is dependent upon the total number of fibers counted and the uniformity of the fiber distribution on the filter. A general rule is to count at least 20 and not more than 100 fields. The count is discontinued when 100 fibers are counted, provided that 20 fields have already been counted. Counting more than 100 fibers results in only a small gain in precision. As the total count drops below 10 fibers, an accelerated loss of precision is noted.

At this time, there is no known method to determine the absolute accuracy of the asbestos analysis. Results of samples prepared through the Proficiency Analytical Testing (PAT) Program and analyzed by the OSHA-SLTC showed no significant bias when compared to PAT reference values. The PAT samples were analyzed from 1987 to 1989 (N = 36) and the concentration range was from 120 to 1,300 fibers/mm^2.

4. Interferences

Fibrous substances, if present, may interfere with asbestos analysis.

Some common fibers are:
fiberglass
anhydrite
plant fibers
perlite veins
gypsum
some synthetic fibers
membrane structures
sponge spicules
diatoms
microorganisms
wollastonite

The use of electron microscopy or optical tests such as polarized light, and dispersion staining may be used to differentiate these materials from asbestos when necessary.

5. Sampling

5.1. Equipment

5.1.1. Sample assembly (The assembly is shown in Figure 3). Conductive filter holder consisting of a 25-mm diameter, 3-piece cassette having a 50-mm long electrically conductive extension cowl. Backup pad, 25-mm, cellulose. Membrane filter, mixed-cellulose ester (MCE), 25-mm, plain, white, 0.4 to 1.2-µm pore size.

NOTES: (a) Do not re-use cassettes.

(b) Fully conductive cassettes are required to reduce fiber loss to the sides of the cassette due to electrostatic attraction.

(c) Purchase filters which have been selected by the manufacturer for asbestos counting or analyze representative filters for fiber background before use. Discard the filter lot if more than 4 fibers/100 fields are found.

(d) To decrease the possibility of contamination, the sampling system (filter-backup pad-cassette) for asbestos is usually preassembled by the manufacturer.

(e) Other cassettes, such as the Bellmouth, may be used within the limits of their validation.

5.1.2. Gel bands for sealing cassettes.

5.1.3. Sampling pump.

Each pump must be a battery operated, self-contained unit small enough to be placed on the monitored employee and not interfere with the work being performed. The pump must be capable of sampling at the collection rate for the required sampling time.

5.1.4. Flexible tubing, 6-mm bore.

5.1.5. Pump calibration.

Stopwatch and bubble tube/burette or electronic meter.

5.2. Sampling Procedure

5.2.1. Seal the point where the base and cowl of each cassette meet with a gel band or tape.

5.2.2. Charge the pumps completely before beginning.

5.2.3. Connect each pump to a calibration cassette with an appropriate length of 6-mm bore plastic tubing. Do not use luer connectors—the type of cassette specified above has built-in adapters.

5.2.4. Select an appropriate flow rate for the situation being monitored. The sampling flow rate must be between 0.5 and 5.0 L/min for personal sampling and is commonly set between 1 and 2 L/min. Always choose a flow rate that will not produce overloaded filters.

5.2.5. Calibrate each sampling pump before and after sampling with a calibration cassette in-line (Note: This calibration cassette should be from the same lot of cassettes used

35

for sampling). Use a primary standard (e.g. bubble burette) to calibrate each pump. If possible, calibrate at the sampling site.

NOTE: If sampling site calibration is not possible, environmental influences may affect the flow rate. The extent is dependent on the type of pump used. Consult with the pump manufacturer to determine dependence on environmental influences. If the pump is affected by temperature and pressure changes, correct the flow rate using the formula shown in the section "Sampling Pump Flow Rate Corrections" at the end of this appendix.

5.2.6. Connect each pump to the base of each sampling cassette with flexible tubing. Remove the end cap of each cassette and take each air sample open face. Assure that each sample cassette is held open side down in the employee's breathing zone during sampling. The distance from the nose/mouth of the employee to the cassette should be about 10 cm. Secure the cassette on the collar or lapel of the employee using spring clips or other similar devices.

5.2.7. A suggested minimum air volume when sampling to determine TWA compliance is 25 L. For Excursion Limit (30 min sampling time) evaluations, a minimum air volume of 48 L is recommended.

5.2.8. The most significant problem when sampling for asbestos is overloading the filter with non-asbestos dust. Suggested maximum air sample volumes for specific environments are:

Environment	Air vol. (L)
Asbestos removal operations (visible dust)	100
Asbestos removal operations (little dust)	240
Office environments	400 to 2,400

Caution: Do not overload the filter with dust. High levels of non-fibrous dust particles may obscure fibers on the filter and lower the count or make counting impossible. If more than about 25 to 30% of the field area is obscured with dust, the result may be biased low. Smaller air volumes may be necessary when there is excessive non-asbestos dust in the air.

While sampling, observe the filter with a small flashlight. If there is a visible layer of dust on the filter, stop sampling, remove and seal the cassette, and replace with a new sampling assembly. The total dust loading should not exceed 1 mg.

5.2.9. Blank samples are used to determine if any contamination has occurred during sample handling. Prepare two blanks for the first 1 to 20 samples. For sets containing greater than 20 samples, prepare blanks as 10% of the samples. Handle blank samples in the same manner as air samples with one exception: Do not draw any air through the

blank samples. Open the blank cassette in the place where the sample cassettes are mounted on the employee. Hold it open for about 30 seconds. Close and seal the cassette appropriately. Store blanks for shipment with the sample cassettes.

5.2.10. Immediately after sampling, close and seal each cassette with the base and plastic plugs. Do not touch or puncture the filter membrane as this will invalidate the analysis.

5.2.11 Attach and secure a sample seal around each sample cassette in such a way as to assure that the end cap and base plugs cannot be removed without destroying the seal. Tape the ends of the seal together since the seal is not long enough to be wrapped end-to-end. Also wrap tape around the cassette at each joint to keep the seal secure.

5.3. Sample Shipment

5.3.1. Send the samples to the laboratory with paperwork requesting asbestos analysis. List any known fibrous interferences present during sampling on the paperwork. Also, note the workplace operation(s) sampled.

5.3.2. Secure and handle the samples in such that they will not rattle during shipment nor be exposed to static electricity. Do not ship samples in expanded polystyrene peanuts, vermiculite, paper shreds, or excelsior. Tape sample cassettes to sheet bubbles and place in a container that will cushion the samples in such a manner that they will not rattle.

5.3.3. To avoid the possibility of sample contamination, always ship bulk samples in separate mailing containers.

6. *Analysis*

6.1. Safety Precautions

6.1.1. Acetone is extremely flammable and precautions must be taken not to ignite it. Avoid using large containers or quantities of acetone. Transfer the solvent in a ventilated laboratory hood. Do not use acetone near any open flame. For generation of acetone vapor, use a spark free heat source.

6.1.2. Any asbestos spills should be cleaned up immediately to prevent dispersal of fibers. Prudence should be exercised to avoid contamination of laboratory facilities or exposure of personnel to asbestos. Asbestos spills should be cleaned up with wet methods and/or a High Efficiency Particulate-Air (HEPA) filtered vacuum.

Caution: Do not use a vacuum without a HEPA filter—It will disperse fine asbestos fibers in the air.

6.2. Equipment

6.2.1. Phase contrast microscope with binocular or trinocular head.

6.2.2. Widefield or Huygenian 10X eyepieces (NOTE: The eyepiece containing the graticule must be a focusing eyepiece. Use a 40X phase objective with a numerical aperture of 0.65 to 0.75).

6.2.3. Kohler illumination (if possible) with green or blue filter.

6.2.4. Walton-Beckett Graticule, type G–22 with 100 ±2 μm projected diameter.

6.2.5. Mechanical stage.
A rotating mechanical stage is convenient for use with polarized light.

6.2.6. Phase telescope.

6.2.7. Stage micrometer with 0.01–mm subdivisions.

6.2.8. Phase-shift test slide, mark II (Available from PTR optics Ltd., and also McCrone).

6.2.9. Precleaned glass slides, 25 mm × 75 mm. One end can be frosted for convenience in writing sample numbers, etc., or paste-on labels can be used.

6.2.10. Cover glass #1 ½.

6.2.11. Scalpel (#10, curved blade).

6.2.12. Fine tipped forceps.

6.2.13. Aluminum block for clearing filter (see appendix D and Figure 4).

6.2.14. Automatic adjustable pipette, 100- to 500-μL.

6.2.15. Micropipette, 5 μL.

6.3. Reagents

6.3.1. Acetone (HPLC grade).

6.3.2. Triacetin (glycerol triacetate).

6.3.3. Lacquer or nail polish.

6.4. Standard Preparation

A way to prepare standard asbestos samples of known concentration has not been developed. It is possible to prepare replicate samples of nearly equal concentration. This has been performed through the PAT program. These asbestos samples are distributed by the AIHA to participating laboratories.

Since only about one-fourth of a 25–mm sample membrane is required for an asbestos count, any PAT sample can serve as a "standard" for replicate counting.

6.5. Sample Mounting

NOTE: See Safety Precautions in Section 6.1. before proceeding. The objective is to produce samples with a smooth (non-grainy) background in a medium with a refractive index of approximately 1.46. The technique below collapses the filter for easier focusing and produces permanent mounts which are useful for quality control and interlaboratory comparison.

An aluminum block or similar device is required for sample preparation.

6.5.1. Heat the aluminum block to about 70 °C. The hot block should not be used on any surface that can be damaged by either the heat or from exposure to acetone.

6.5.2. Ensure that the glass slides and cover glasses are free of dust and fibers.

6.5.3. Remove the top plug to prevent a vacuum when the cassette is opened. Clean the outside of the cassette if necessary. Cut the seal and/or tape on the cassette with a razor blade. Very carefully separate the base from the extension cowl, leaving the filter and backup pad in the base.

6.5.4. With a rocking motion cut a triangular wedge from the filter using the scalpel. This wedge should be one-sixth to one-fourth of the filter. Grasp the filter wedge with the forceps on the perimeter of the filter which was clamped between the cassette pieces. DO NOT TOUCH the filter with your finger. Place the filter on the glass slide sample side up. Static electricity will usually keep the filter on the slide until it is cleared.

6.5.5. Place the tip of the micropipette containing about 200 μL acetone into the aluminum block. Insert the glass slide into the receiving slot in the aluminum block. Inject the acetone into the block with slow, steady pressure on the plunger while holding the pipette firmly in place. Wait 3 to 5 seconds for the filter to clear, then remove the pipette and slide from the aluminum block.

6.5.6. Immediately (less than 30 seconds) place 2.5 to 3.5 μL of triacetin on the filter (Note: Waiting longer than 30 seconds will result in increased index of refraction and decreased contrast between the fibers and the preparation. This may also lead to separation of the cover slip from the slide).

6.5.7. Lower a cover slip gently onto the filter at a slight angle to reduce the possibility of forming air bubbles. If more than 30 seconds have elapsed between acetone exposure and triacetin application, glue the edges of the cover slip to the slide with lacquer or nail polish.

6.5.8. If clearing is slow, warm the slide for 15 min on a hot plate having a surface temperature of about 50 °C to hasten clearing. The top of the hot block can be used if the slide is not heated too long.

6.5.9. Counting may proceed immediately after clearing and mounting are completed.

6.6. Sample Analysis

Completely align the microscope according to the manufacturer's instructions. Then, align the microscope using the following general alignment routine at the beginning of every counting session and more often if necessary.

6.6.1. Alignment
(1) Clean all optical surfaces. Even a small amount of dirt can significantly degrade the image.
(2) Rough focus the objective on a sample.
(3) Close down the field iris so that it is visible in the field of view. Focus the image of the iris with the condenser focus. Center the image of the iris in the field of view.
(4) Install the phase telescope and focus on the phase rings. Critically center the rings.

Misalignment of the rings results in astigmatism which will degrade the image.

(5) Place the phase-shift test slide on the microscope stage and focus on the lines. The analyst must see line set 3 and should see at least parts of 4 and 5 but, not see line set 6 or 6. A microscope/microscopist combination which does not pass this test may not be used.

6.6.2. Counting Fibers

(1) Place the prepared sample slide on the mechanical stage of the microscope. Position the center of the wedge under the objective lens and focus upon the sample.

(2) Start counting from one end of the wedge and progress along a radial line to the other end (count in either direction from perimeter to wedge tip). Select fields randomly, without looking into the eyepieces, by slightly advancing the slide in one direction with the mechanical stage control.

(3) Continually scan over a range of focal planes (generally the upper 10 to 15 µm of the filter surface) with the fine focus control during each field count. Spend at least 5 to 15 seconds per field.

(4) Most samples will contain asbestos fibers with fiber diameters less than 1 µm. Look carefully for faint fiber images. The small diameter fibers will be very hard to see. However, they are an important contribution to the total count.

(5) Count only fibers equal to or longer than 5 µm. Measure the length of curved fibers along the curve.

(6) Count fibers which have a length to width ratio of 3:1 or greater.

(7) Count all the fibers in at least 20 fields. Continue counting until either 100 fibers are counted or 100 fields have been viewed; whichever occurs first. Count all the fibers in the final field.

(8) Fibers lying entirely within the boundary of the Walton-Beckett graticule field shall receive a count of 1. Fibers crossing the boundary once, having one end within the circle shall receive a count of ½. Do not count any fiber that crosses the graticule boundary more than once. Reject and do not count any other fibers even though they may be visible outside the graticule area. If a fiber touches the circle, it is considered to cross the line.

(9) Count bundles of fibers as one fiber unless individual fibers can be clearly identified and each individual fiber is clearly not connected to another counted fiber. See Figure 1 for counting conventions.

(10) Record the number of fibers in each field in a consistent way such that filter non-uniformity can be assessed.

(11) Regularly check phase ring alignment.

(12) When an agglomerate (mass of material) covers more than 25% of the field of view, reject the field and select another. Do not include it in the number of fields counted.

(13) Perform a "blind recount" of 1 in every 10 filter wedges (slides). Re-label the slides using a person other than the original counter.

6.7. Fiber Identification

As previously mentioned in Section 1.3., PCM does not provide positive confirmation of asbestos fibers. Alternate differential counting techniques should be used if discrimination is desirable. Differential counting may include primary discrimination based on morphology, polarized light analysis of fibers, or modification of PCM data by Scanning Electron or Transmission Electron Microscopy.

A great deal of experience is required to routinely and correctly perform differential counting. It is discouraged unless it is legally necessary. Then, only if a fiber is obviously not asbestos should it be excluded from the count. Further discussion of this technique can be found in reference 8.10.

If there is a question whether a fiber is asbestos or not, follow the rule:

"WHEN IN DOUBT, COUNT."

6.8. Analytical Recommendations—Quality Control System

6.8.1. All individuals performing asbestos analysis must have taken the NIOSH course for sampling and evaluating airborne asbestos or an equivalent course.

6.8.2. Each laboratory engaged in asbestos counting shall set up a slide trading arrangement with at least two other laboratories in order to compare performance and eliminate inbreeding of error. The slide exchange occurs at least semiannually. The round robin results shall be posted where all analysts can view individual analyst's results.

6.8.3. Each laboratory engaged in asbestos counting shall participate in the Proficiency Analytical Testing Program, the Asbestos Analyst Registry or equivalent.

6.8.4. Each analyst shall select and count prepared slides from a "slide bank". These are quality assurance counts. The slide bank shall be prepared using uniformly distributed samples taken from the workload. Fiber densities should cover the entire range routinely analyzed by the laboratory. These slides are counted blind by all counters to establish an original standard deviation. This historical distribution is compared with the quality assurance counts. A counter must have 95% of all quality control samples counted within three standard deviations of the historical mean. This count is then integrated into a new historical mean and standard deviation for the slide.

The analyses done by the counters to establish the slide bank may be used for an interim quality control program if the data are treated in a proper statistical fashion.

7. Calculations

7.1. Calculate the estimated airborne asbestos fiber concentration on the filter sample using the following formula:
where:

AC = Airborne fiber concentration

$$AC = \frac{\left[\left(\dfrac{FB}{FL}\right) - \left(\dfrac{BFB}{BFL}\right)\right] \times ECA}{1000 \times FR \times T \times MFA}$$

FB = Total number of fibers greater than 5 μm counted
FL = Total number of fields counted on the filter
BFB = Total number of fibers greater than 5 μm counted in the blank
BFL = Total number of fields counted on the blank
ECA = Effective collecting area of filter (385 mm² nominal for a 25-mm filter.)
FR = Pump flow rate (L/min)
MFA = Microscope count field area (mm²). This is 0.00785 mm² for a Walton-Beckett Graticule.
T = Sample collection time (min)
1,000 = Conversion of L to cc

NOTE: The collection area of a filter is seldom equal to 385 mm². It is appropriate for laboratories to routinely monitor the exact diameter using an inside micrometer. The collection area is calculated according to the formula:
Area = π(d/2)²

7.2. Short-cut Calculation

Since a given analyst always has the same interpupillary distance, the number of fields per filter for a particular analyst will remain constant for a given size filter. The field size for that analyst is constant (*i.e.*, the analyst is using an assigned microscope and is not changing the reticle).

For example, if the exposed area of the filter is always 385 mm² and the size of the field is always 0.00785 mm², the number of fields per filter will always be 49,000. In addition it is necessary to convert liters of air to cc. These three constants can then be combined such that ECA/(1,000 × MFA) = 49. The previous equation simplifies to:

$$AC = \frac{\left(\dfrac{FB}{FL}\right) - \left(\dfrac{BFB}{BFL}\right) \times 49}{FR \times T}$$

7.3. Recount Calculations

As mentioned in step 13 of Section 6.6.2., a "blind recount" of 10% of the slides is performed. In all cases, differences will be observed between the first and second counts of the same filter wedge. Most of these differences will be due to chance alone, that is, due to the random variability (precision) of the count method. Statistical recount criteria enables one to decide whether observed differences can be explained due to chance alone or are probably due to systematic differences between analysts, microscopes, or other biasing factors.

The following recount criterion is for a pair of counts that estimate AC in fibers/cc. The criterion is given at the type-I error level. That is, there is 5% maximum risk that we will reject a pair of counts for the reason that one might be biased, when the large observed difference is really due to chance.

Reject a pair of counts if:

$$\left|\sqrt{AC_2} - \sqrt{AC_1}\right| > 2.78$$

$$\times \left(\sqrt{AC_{AVG}}\right) \times CV_{FB}$$

Where:
AC1 = lower estimated airborne fiber concentration
AC2 = higher estimated airborne fiber concentration
ACavg = average of the two concentration estimates
CV_{FB} = CV for the average of the two concentration estimates

If a pair of counts are rejected by this criterion then, recount the rest of the filters in the submitted set. Apply the test and reject any other pairs failing the test. Rejection shall include a memo to the industrial hygienist stating that the sample failed a statistical test for homogeneity and the true air concentration may be significantly different than the reported value.

7.4. Reporting Results

Report results to the industrial hygienist as fibers/cc. Use two significant figures. If multiple analyses are performed on a sample, an average of the results is to be reported unless any of the results can be rejected for cause.

8. References

8.1. Dreesen, W.C., et al, *U.S. Public Health Service: A Study of Asbestosis in the Asbestos Textile Industry*, (Public Health Bulletin No. 241), US Treasury Dept., Washington, DC, 1938.

8.2. *Asbestos Research Council: The Measurement of Airborne Asbestos Dust by the Membrane Filter Method* (Technical Note), Asbestos Research Council, Rockdale, Lancashire, Great Britain, 1969.

8.3. Bayer, S.G., Zumwalde, R.D., Brown, T.A., *Equipment and Procedure for Mounting Millipore Filters and Counting Asbestos Fibers* by *Phase Contrast Microscopy*, Bureau of Occupational Health, U.S. Dept. of Health, Education and Welfare, Cincinnati, OH, 1969.

8.4. *NIOSH Manual of Analytical Methods*, 2nd ed., Vol. 1 (DHEW/NIOSH Pub. No. 77-157-A). National Institute for Occupational Safety and Health, Cincinnati, OH, 1977. pp. 239-1-239-21.

8.5. *Asbestos*, Code of Federal Regulations 29 CFR 1910.1001. 1971.

8.6. *Occupational Exposure to Asbestos, Tremolite, Anthophyllite, and Actinolite. Final Rule*, FEDERAL REGISTER 51:119 (20 June 1986). pp.22612-22790.

8.7. *Asbestos, Tremolite, Anthophyllite, and Actinolite*, Code of Federal Regulations 1910.1001. 1988. pp 711-752.

8.8. *Criteria for a Recommended Standard— Occupational Exposure to Asbestos* (DHEW/ NIOSH Pub. No. HSM 72-10267), National Institute for Occupational Safety and Health NIOSH, Cincinnati,OH, 1972. pp. III-1-III-24.

8.9. Leidel, N.A., Bayer,S.G., Zumwalde, R.D.,Busch, K.A., *USPHS/NIOSH Membrane Filter Method for Evaluating Airborne Asbestos Fibers* (DHEW/NIOSH Pub. No. 79-127). National Institute for Occupational Safety and Health, Cincinnati, OH, 1979.

8.10. Dixon, W.C., *Applications of Optical Microscopy in Analysis of Asbestos and Quartz*, Analytical Techniques in Occupational Health Chemistry, edited by D.D. Dollberg and A.W. Verstuyft. Wash. DC: American Chemical Society, (ACS Symposium Series 120) 1980. pp. 13-41.

Quality Control

The OSHA asbestos regulations require each laboratory to establish a quality control program. The following is presented as an example of how the OSHA-SLTC constructed its internal CV curve as part of meeting this requirement. Data is from 395 samples collected during OSHA compliance inspections and analyzed from October 1980 through April 1986.

Each sample was counted by 2 to 5 different counters independently of one another. The standard deviation and the CV statistic was calculated for each sample. This data was then plotted on a graph of CV vs. fibers/mm^2. A least squares regression was performed using the following equation:

CV = antilog1$_{10}$[A(log$_{10}$(x))^2 + B(log$_{10}$(x)) + C]

where:

x = the number of fibers/mm^2

Application of least squares gave:

A = 0.182205
B = − 0.973343
C = 0.327499

Using these values, the equation becomes:

CV　　=　　antilog$_{10}$　　[0.182205(log$_{10}$ (x))^2 − 0.973343(log$_{10}$ (x)) + 0.327499]

Sampling Pump Flow Rate Corrections

This correction is used if a difference greater than 5% in ambient temperature and/ or pressure is noted between calibration and sampling sites and the pump does not compensate for the differences.

$$Q_{act} = Q_{cal} \times \sqrt{\left(\frac{P_{cal}}{P_{act}}\right) \times \left(\frac{T_{act}}{T_{cal}}\right)}$$

Where:

Q_{act} = actual flow rate
Q_{cal} = calibrated flow rate (if a rotameter was used, the rotameter value)
P_{cal} = uncorrected air pressure at calibration
P_{act} = uncorrected air pressure at sampling site
T_{act} = temperature at sampling site (K)
T_{cal} = temperature at calibration (K)

Walton-Beckett Graticule

When ordering the Graticule for asbestos counting, specify the exact disc diameter needed to fit the ocular of the microscope and the diameter (mm) of the circular counting area. Instructions for measuring the dimensions necessary are listed:

(1) Insert any available graticule into the focusing eyepiece and focus so that the graticule lines are sharp and clear.

(2) Align the microscope.

(3) Place a stage micrometer on the microscope object stage and focus the microscope on the graduated lines.

(4) Measure the magnified grid length, PL (μm), using the stage micrometer.

(5) Remove the graticule from the microscope and measure its actual grid length, AL (mm). This can be accomplished by using a mechanical stage fitted with verniers, or a jeweler's loupe with a direct reading scale.

(6) Let D = 100 μm. Calculate the circle diameter, d_c (mm), for the Walton-Beckett graticule and specify the diameter when making a purchase:

$$d_c = \frac{AL \times D}{PL}$$

Example: If PL = 108 μm, AL = 2.93 mm and D = 100 μm, then,

$$d_c = \frac{2.93 \times 100}{108} = 2.71 mm$$

(7) Each eyepiece-objective-reticle combination on the microscope must be calibrated. Should any of the three be changed (by zoom adjustment, disassembly, replacement, etc.), the combination must be recalibrated. Calibration may change if interpupillary distance is changed. Measure the field diameter, D (acceptable range: 100±2 μm)

with a stage micrometer upon receipt of the graticule from the manufacturer. Determine the field area (mm²).

Field Area = Δ(D/2)²
If D = 100 μm = 0.1 mm, then
Field Area = Δ(0.1 mm/2)² = 0.00785 mm²

The Graticule is available from: Graticules Ltd., Morley Road, Tonbridge TN9 IRN, Kent, England (Telephone 011–44–732–359061). Also available from PTR Optics Ltd., 145 Newton Street, Waltham, MA 02154 [telephone (617) 891–6000] or McCrone Accessories and Components, 2506 S. Michigan Ave., Chicago, IL 60616 [phone (312)-842-7100]. The graticule is custom made for each microscope.

COUNTS FOR THE FIBERS IN THE FIGURE

Structure No.	Count	Explanation
1 to 6	1	Single fibers all contained within the circle.
7	½	Fiber crosses circle once.
8	0	Fiber too short.
9	2	Two crossing fibers.
10	0	Fiber outside graticule.
11	0	Fiber crosses graticule twice.
12	½	Although split, fiber only crosses once.

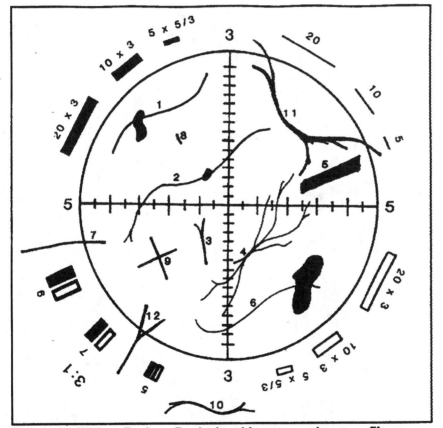

Figure 1: Walton-Beckett Graticule with some explanatory fibers.

APPENDIX C TO § 1910.1001 [RESERVED]

APPENDIX D TO § 1910.1001—MEDICAL
QUESTIONNAIRES; MANDATORY

This mandatory appendix contains the medical questionnaires that must be administered to all employees who are exposed to asbestos above the permissible exposure limit, and who will therefore be included in their employer's medical surveillance program. Part 1 of the appendix contains the Initial Medical Questionnaire, which must be obtained for all new hires who will be covered by the medical surveillance requirements. Part 2 includes the abbreviated Periodical Medical Questionnaire, which must be administered to all employees who are provided periodic medical examinations under the medical surveillance provisions of the standard.

Part 1
INITIAL MEDICAL QUESTIONNAIRE

1. NAME _____

2. SOCIAL SECURITY # ___ ___ ___ ___ ___ ___ ___ ___ ___
                     1   2   3   4   5   6   7   8   9

3. CLOCK NUMBER
                 ___ ___ ___ ___ ___ ___
                 10 11 12 13 14 15

4. PRESENT OCCUPATION _____

5. PLANT _____

6. ADDRESS _____

7. _____
                        (Zip Code)

8. TELEPHONE NUMBER _____

9. INTERVIEWER _____

10. DATE _____ ___ ___ ___ ___ ___ ___
                         16 17 18 19 20 21

11. Date of Birth _____ ___ ___ ___ ___ ___ ___
              Month Day Year 22 23 24 25 26 27

12. Place of Birth _____

13. Sex   1. Male   ___
                      2. Female ___

14. What is your marital status?   1. Single ___   4. Separated/
                             2. Married ___   Divorced ___
                             3. Widowed ___

15. Race   1. White ___ 4. Hispanic ___
                     2. Black ___ 5. Indian ___
                     3. Asian ___ 6. Other   ___

16. What is the highest grade completed in school? _____
    (For example 12 years is completion of high school)

OCCUPATIONAL HISTORY

17A. Have you ever worked full time (30 hours   1. Yes ___ 2. No __
     per week or more) for 6 months or more?

    IF YES TO 17A:

  B. Have you ever worked for a year or more in   1. Yes ___ 2. No __
     any dusty job?   3. Does Not Apply __

Specify job/industry _____   Total Years Worked ____

Was dust exposure: 1. Mild ___   2. Moderate ___   3. Severe ___

C. Have you even been exposed to gas or   1. Yes ___ 2. No ___
   chemical fumes in your work?
   Specify job/industry _____   Total Years Worked ___

   Was exposure: 1. Mild ___   2. Moderate ___   3. Severe ___

D. What has been your usual occupation or job--the one you have
   worked at the longest?

   1. Job occupation _____

   2. Number of years employed in this occupation _____

   3. Position/job title _____

   4. Business, field or
industry _____

(Record on lines the years in which you have worked in any of these
industries, e.g. 1960-1969)

Have you ever worked:

		YES	NO
E.	In a mine?.................................	[__]	[__]
F.	In a quarry?..............................	[__]	[__]
G.	In a foundry?.............................	[__]	[__]
H.	In a pottery?.............................	[__]	[__]
I.	In a cotton, flax or hemp mill?...........	[__]	[__]
J.	With asbestos?............................	[__]	[__]

18. PAST MEDICAL HISTORY

	YES	NO
A. Do you consider yourself to be in good health?	[__]	[__]

        If "NO" state reason _____

| B. Have you any defect of vision?............... | [__] | [__] |

        If "YES" state nature of defect _____

| C. Have you any hearing defect?................. | [__] | [__] |

        If "YES" state nature of defect _____

44

D. Are you suffering from or have you ever suffered from:

   a. Epilepsy (or fits, seizures, convulsions)?   [__]   [__]

   b. Rheumatic fever?   [__]   [__]

   c. Kidney disease?   [__]   [__]

   d. Bladder disease?   [__]   [__]

   e. Diabetes?   [__]   [__]

   f. Jaundice?   [__]   [__]

19. <u>CHEST COLDS AND CHEST ILLNESSES</u>

19A. If you get a cold, does it <u>usually</u> go to your   1. Yes __   2. No __
chest? (Usually means more than 1/2 the time)   3. Don't get colds __

20A. During the past 3 years, have you had any chest   1. Yes __   2. No __
illnesses that have kept you off work, indoors at
home, or in bed?

      IF YES TO 20A:
B. Did you produce phlegm with any of these chest   1. Yes __   2. No __
illnesses?   3. Does Not Apply __

C. In the last 3 years, how many such illnesses   Number of illnesses __
with (increased) phlegm did you have which   No such illnesses __
lasted a week or more?

21. Did you have any lung trouble before the age of   1. Yes __   2. No __
16?

22. Have you ever had any of the following?

   1A. Attacks of bronchitis?   1. Yes __   2. No __

      IF YES TO 1A:
   B. Was it confirmed by a doctor?   1. Yes __   2. No __
                              3. Does Not Apply __

   C. At what age was your first attack?   Age in Years __
                                      Does Not Apply __

   2A. Pneumonia (include bronchopneumonia)?   1. Yes __   2. No __

      IF YES TO 2A:
   B. Was it confirmed by a doctor?   1. Yes __   2. No __
                              3. Does Not Apply __

   C. At what age did you first have it?   Age in Years __
                                      Does Not Apply __

3A. Hay Fever?   1. Yes __   2. No __

    IF YES TO 3A:
  B. Was it confirmed by a doctor?   1. Yes __   2. No __
                                       3. Does Not Apply __

  C. At what age did it start?   Age in Years   __
                                        Does Not Apply __

23A. Have you ever had chronic bronchitis?   1. Yes __   2. No __

    IF YES TO 23A:
  B. Do you still have it?   1. Yes __   2. No __
                                        3. Does Not Apply __

  C. Was it confirmed by a doctor?   1. Yes __   2. No __
                                        3. Does Not Apply __

  D. At what age did it start?   Age in Years   __
                                        Does Not Apply __

24A. Have you ever had emphysema?   1. Yes __   2. No __

    IF YES TO 24A:
  B. Do you still have it?   1. Yes __   2. No __
                                        3. Does Not Apply __

  C. Was it confirmed by a doctor?   1. Yes __   2. No __
                                        3. Does Not Apply __

  D. At what age did it start?   Age in Years   __
                                        Does Not Apply __

25A. Have you ever had asthma?   1. Yes __   2. No __

    IF YES TO 25A:
  B. Do you still have it?   1. Yes __   2. No __
                                        3. Does Not Apply __

  C. Was it confirmed by a doctor?   1. Yes __   2. No __
                                        3. Does Not Apply __

  D. At what age did it start?   Age in Years   __
                                        Does Not Apply __

  E. If you no longer have it, at what age did it   Age stopped   __
    stop?   Does Not Apply __

26. Have you ever had:

  A. Any other chest illness?   1. Yes __   2. No __

    If yes, please specify _____

B. Any chest operations?   1. Yes __   2. No __

    If yes, please specify _____

C. Any chest injuries?   1. Yes __   2. No __

    If yes, please specify _____

27A. Has a doctor ever told you that you had heart   1. Yes __   2. No __
    trouble?

    IF YES TO 27A:
B. Have you ever had treatment for heart trouble   1. Yes __   2. No __
   in the past 10 years?   3. Does Not Apply __

28A. Has a doctor ever told you that you had high   1. Yes __   2. No __
    blood pressure?

    IF YES TO 28A:
B. Have you had any treatment for high blood   1. Yes __   2. No __
   pressure (hypertension) in the past 10 years?   3. Does Not Apply __

29. When did you last have your chest X-rayed?   (Year) ___ ___ ___ ___
                                                       25   26   27   28

30. Where did you last have your chest X-rayed (if known)? _____

    What was the outcome? _____

FAMILY HISTORY

31. Were either of your natural parents ever told by a doctor that they had a
    chronic lung condition such as:

	FATHER				MOTHER		
	1. Yes	2. No	3. Don't Know		1. Yes	2. No	3. Don't Know
A. Chronic Bronchitis?	___	___	___		___	___	___
B. Emphysema?	___	___	___		___	___	___
C. Asthma?	___	___	___		___	___	___
D. Lung cancer?	___	___	___		___	___	___
E. Other chest conditions	___	___	___		___	___	___
F. Is parent currently alive?	___	___	___		___	___	___

G. Please Specify   ___ Age if Living   ___ Age if Living
                      ___ Age at Death   ___ Age at Death
                      ___ Don't Know   ___ Don't Know

H. Please specify cause of death
_____   _____

COUGH

32A. Do you usually have a cough? (Count   1. Yes __   2. No __
     a cough with first smoke or on first
     going out of doors. Exclude clearing
     of throat.) [If no, skip to question
     32C.]

   B. Do you usually cough as much as 4 to   1. Yes __   2. No __
      6 times a day 4 or more days out of
      the week?

   C. Do you usually cough at all on getting   1. Yes __   2. No __
      up or first thing in the morning?

   D. Do you usually cough at all during the   1. Yes __   2. No __
      rest of the day or at night?

IF YES TO ANY OF ABOVE (32A, B, C, or D), ANSWER THE FOLLOWING.   IF NO
TO ALL, CHECK DOES NOT APPLY AND SKIP TO NEXT PAGE

   E. Do you usually cough like this on most   1. Yes __   2. No __
      days for 3 consecutive months or more   3. Does not apply __
      during the year?

   F. For how many years have you had the cough? Number of years __
                                                  Does not apply __

33A. Do you usually bring up phlegm from your   1. Yes __   2. No __
     chest?
     (Count phlegm with the first smoke or
     on first going out of doors. Exclude
     phlegm from the nose. Count swallowed
     phlegm.) (If no, skip to 33C)

   B. Do you usually bring up phlegm like this   1. Yes __   2. No __
      as much as twice a day 4 or more days
      out of the week?

   C. Do you usually bring up phlegm at all on   1. Yes __   2. No __
      getting up or first thing in the morning?

   D. Do you usually bring up phlegm at all   1. Yes __   2. No __
      during the rest of the day or at night?

IF YES TO ANY OF THE ABOVE (33A, B, C, or D), ANSWER THE FOLLOWING:
IF NO TO ALL, CHECK DOES NOT APPLY AND SKIP TO 34A.

   E. Do you bring up phlegm like this on most   1. Yes __   2. No __
      days for 3 consecutive months or more   3. Does not apply __
      during the year?

48

F. For how many years have you had trouble   Number of years __
   with phlegm?   Does not apply __

EPISODES OF COUGH AND PHLEGM

34A. Have you had periods or episodes of (in-   1. Yes __   2. No __
     creased*) cough and phlegm lasting for 3
     weeks or more each year?
     *(For persons who usually have cough and/or
     phlegm)

     If YES TO 34A
  B. For how long have you had at least 1 such   Number of years __
     episode per year?   Does not apply __

WHEEZING

35A. Does your chest ever sound wheezy or
     whistling
              1. When you have a cold?   1. Yes __   2. No __
              2. Occasionally apart from colds? 1. Yes __   2. No __
              3. Most days or nights?   1. Yes __   2. No __

     IF YES TO 1, 2, or 3 in 35A
  B. For how many years has this been present?   Number of years __
                                                        Does not apply __

36A. Have you ever had an attack of wheezing   1. Yes __   2. No __
     that has made you feel short of breath?

     IF YES TO 36A
  B. How old were you when you had your first   Age in years   __
     such attack?   Does not apply   __

  C. Have you had 2 or more such episodes?   1. Yes __   2. No __
                                                 3. Does not apply __

  D. Have you ever required medicine or   1. Yes __   2. No __
     treatment for the(se) attack(s·)?   3. Does not apply __

BREATHLESSNESS

37. If disabled from walking by any condition
     other than heart or lung disease, please
     describe and proceed to question 39A.
     Nature of condition(s)_____

38A. Are you troubled by shortness of breath when   1. Yes __   2. No __
     hurrying on the level or walking up a
     slight hill?

IF YES TO 38A

B. Do you have to walk slower than people of your age on the level because of breathlessness?

1. Yes __   2. No __
3. Does not apply __

C. Do you ever have to stop for breath when walking at your own pace on the level?

1. Yes __   2. No __
3. Does not apply __

D. Do you ever have to stop for breath after walking about 100 yards (or after a few minutes) on the level?

1. Yes __   2. No __
3. Does not apply __

E. Are you too breathless to leave the house or breathless on dressing or climbing one flight of stairs?

1. Yes __   2. No __
3. Does not apply __

TOBACCO SMOKING

39A. Have you ever smoked cigarettes? (No means less than 20 packs of cigarettes or 12 oz. of tobacco in a lifetime or less than 1 cigarette a day for 1 year.)

1. Yes __   2. No __

IF YES TO 39A

B. Do you now smoke cigarettes (as of one month ago)

1. Yes __   2. No __
3. Does not apply __

C. How old were you when you first started regular cigarette smoking?

Age in years __
Does not apply __

D. If you have stopped smoking cigarettes completely, how old were you when you stopped?

Age stopped __
Check if still smoking __
Does not apply __

E. How many cigarettes do you smoke per day now?

Cigarettes per day __
Does not apply __

F. On the average of the entire time you smoked, how many cigarettes did you smoke per day?

Cigarettes per day __
Does not apply __

G. Do or did you inhale the cigarette smoke?

1. Does not apply __
2. Not at all __
3. Slightly __
4. Moderately __
5. Deeply __

40A. Have you ever smoked a pipe regularly? (Yes means more than 12 oz. of tobacco in a lifetime.)

1. Yes __   2. No __

IF YES TO 40A:
FOR PERSONS WHO HAVE EVER SMOKED A PIPE

B. 1. How old were you when you started to
smoke a pipe regularly?   Age __

   2. If you have stopped smoking a pipe   Age stopped   __
      completely, how old were you when you   Check if still
      stopped?   smoking pipe   __
                                               Does not apply   __

C. On the average over the entire time you   __ oz. per week (a standard
   smoked a pipe, how much pipe tobacco did   pouch of tobacco contains
   you smoke per week?   1 1/2 oz.)
                                               __ Does not apply

D. How much pipe tobacco are you smoking now? oz. per week   __
                                               Not currently
                                               smoking a pipe   __

E. Do you or did you inhale the pipe smoke?   1. Never smoked   __
                                               2. Not at all   __
                                               3. Slightly   __
                                               4. Moderately   __
                                               5. Deeply   __

41A. Have you ever smoked cigars regularly?   1. Yes __   2. No __
     (Yes means more than 1 cigar a week for a
     year)

IF YES TO 41A
FOR PERSONS WHO HAVE EVER SMOKED CIGARS

B. 1. How old were you when you started   Age __
      smoking cigars regularly?

   2. If you have stopped smoking cigars   Age stopped   __
      completely, how old were you when   Check if still
      you stopped.   smoking cigars   __
                                               Does not apply   __

C. On the average over the entire time you   Cigars per week   __
   smoked cigars, how many cigars did you   Does not apply   __
   smoke per week?

D. How many cigars are you smoking per week   Cigars per week   __
   now?   Check if not
                                               smoking cigars
                                               currently   __

E. Do or did you inhale the cigar smoke?   1. Never smoked   __
                                               2. Not at all   __
                                               3. Slightly   __
                                               4. Moderately   __
                                               5. Deeply   __

Signature _____   Date _____

51

Part 2
PERIODIC MEDICAL QUESTIONNAIRE

1. NAME _____

2. SOCIAL SECURITY # __ __ __ __ __ __ __ __ __ __
                        1   2   3   4   5   6 7 8   9

3. CLOCK NUMBER   __ __   __ __ __ __   __
                                    10 11   12 13 14 15

4. PRESENT OCCUPATION _____

5. PLANT _____

6. ADDRESS _____

7. _____
                              (Zip Code)

8. TELEPHONE NUMBER _____

9. INTERVIEWER _____

10. DATE _____ __ __   __ __ __ __   __
                                          16 17   18 19 20 21

11. What is your marital status?   1. Single ___   4. Separated/
                                       2. Married ___   Divorced ___
                                       3. Widowed ___

12. OCCUPATIONAL HISTORY

12A. In the past year, did you work   1. Yes ___   2. No ___
     full time (30 hours per week
     or more) for 6 months or more?

     IF YES TO 12A:

12B. In the past year, did you work   1. Yes ___   2. No ___
     in a dusty job?   3. Does Not Apply ___

12C. Was dust exposure: 1. Mild ___   2. Moderate ___   3. Severe ___

12D. In the past year, were you   1. Yes ___   2. No ___
     exposed to gas or chemical
     fumes in your work?

12E. Was exposure: 1. Mild ___   2. Moderate ___   3. Severe ___

12F. In the past year,
     what was your: 1. Job/occupation? _____
                             2. Position/job title? _____

52

13. RECENT MEDICAL HISTORY

13A. Do you consider yourself to
be in good health?   Yes ___   No ___

If NO, state reason _____

13B. In the past year, have you
developed: Yes   No
                              Epilepsy?   ___   ___
                              Rheumatic fever?   ___   ___
                              Kidney disease?   ___   ___
                              Bladder disease?   ___   ___
                              Diabetes?   ___   ___
                              Jaundice?   ___   ___
                              Cancer?   ___   ___

14. CHEST COLDS AND CHEST ILLNESSES

14A. If you get a cold, does it usually go to your chest?
(Usually means more than 1/2 the time)
                                          1. Yes ___   2. No ___
                                          3. Don't get colds ___

15A. During the past year, have you had
any chest illnesses that have kept you   1. Yes ___   2. No ___
off work, indoors at home, or in bed?   3. Does Not Apply ___

IF YES TO 15A:

15B. Did you produce phlegm with any   1. Yes ___   2. No ___
of these chest illnesses?   3. Does Not Apply ___

15C. In the past year, how many such   Number of illnesses ___
illnesses with (increased) phlegm   No such illnesses ___
did you have which lasted a week
or more?

16. RESPIRATORY SYSTEM

In the past year have you had:

                              Yes or No   Further Comment on Positive
                                                         Answers
Asthma   _____

Bronchitis   _____

Hay Fever   _____

Other Allergies   _____

	Yes or No	Further Comment on Positive Answers
Pneumonia	_____	
Tuberculosis	_____	
Chest Surgery	_____	
Other Lung Problems	_____	
Heart Disease	_____	

Do you have:

	Yes or No	Further Comment on Positive Answers
Frequent colds	_____	
Chronic cough	_____	
Shortness of breath when walking or climbing one flight or stairs	_____	

Do you:

	Yes or No	
Wheeze	_____	
Cough up phlegm	_____	
Smoke cigarettes	_____	Packs per day ____ How many years ____

Date _____   Signature _____

APPENDIX E TO § 1910.1001—INTERPRETATION AND CLASSIFICATION OF CHEST ROENTGENOGRAMS—MANDATORY

(a) Chest roentgenograms shall be interpreted and classified in accordance with a professionally accepted Classification system and recorded on an interpretation form following the format of the CDC/NIOSH (M) 2.8 form. As a minimum, the content within the bold lines of this form (items 1 though 4) shall be included. This form is not to be submitted to NIOSH.

(b) Roentgenograms shall be interpreted and classified only by a B-reader, a board eligible/certified radiologist, or an experienced physician with known expertise in pneumoconioses.

(c) All interpreters, whenever interpreting chest roentgenograms made under this section, shall have immediately available for reference a complete set of the ILO-U/C International Classification of Radiographs for Pneumoconioses, 1980.

APPENDIX F TO § 1910.1001—WORK PRACTICES AND ENGINEERING CONTROLS FOR AUTOMOTIVE BRAKE AND CLUTCH INSPECTION, DISASSEMBLY, REPAIR AND ASSEMBLY—MANDATORY

This mandatory appendix specifies engineering controls and work practices that must be implemented by the employer during automotive brake and clutch inspection, disassembly, repair, and assembly operations. Proper use of these engineering controls and work practices by trained employees will reduce employees' asbestos exposure below the permissible exposure level during clutch and brake inspection, disassembly, repair, and assembly operations. The employer shall institute engineering controls and work practices using either the method set forth in paragraph [A] or paragraph [B] of this appendix, or any other method which the employer can demonstrate to be equivalent in terms of reducing employee exposure to asbestos as defined and which meets the requirements described in paragraph [C] of this appendix, for those facilities in which no more than 5 pairs of brakes or 5 clutches are inspected, disassembled, reassembled and/or repaired per week, the method set forth in paragraph [D] of this appendix may be used:

[A] Negative Pressure Enclosure/HEPA Vacuum System Method

(1) The brake and clutch inspection, disassembly, repair, and assembly operations shall be enclosed to cover and contain the clutch or brake assembly and to prevent the release of asbestos fibers into the worker's breathing zone.

(2) The enclosure shall be sealed tightly and thoroughly inspected for leaks before work begins on brake and clutch inspection, disassembly, repair, and assembly.

(3) The enclosure shall be such that the worker can clearly see the operation and shall provide impermeable sleeves through which the worker can handle the brake and clutch inspection, disassembly, repair and assembly. The integrity of the sleeves and ports shall be examined before work begins.

(4) A HEPA-filtered vacuum shall be employed to maintain the enclosure under negative pressure throughout the operation. Compressed-air may be used to remove asbestos fibers or particles from the enclosure.

(5) The HEPA vacuum shall be used first to loosen the asbestos containing residue from the brake and clutch parts and then to evacuate the loosened asbestos containing material from the enclosure and capture the material in the vacuum filter.

(6) The vacuum's filter, when full, shall be first wetted with a fine mist of water, then removed and placed immediately in an impermeable container, labeled according to paragraph (j)(5) of this section and disposed of according to paragraph (k) of this section.

(7) Any spills or releases of asbestos containing waste material from inside of the enclosure or vacuum hose or vacuum filter shall be immediately cleaned up and disposed of according to paragraph (k) of this section.

[B] Low Pressure/Wet Cleaning Method

(1) A catch basin shall be placed under the brake assembly, positioned to avoid splashes and spills.

(2) The reservoir shall contain water containing an organic solvent or wetting agent. The flow of liquid shall be controlled such that the brake assembly is gently flooded to prevent the asbestos-containing brake dust from becoming airborne.

(3) The aqueous solution shall be allowed to flow between the brake drum and brake support before the drum is removed.

(4) After removing the brake drum, the wheel hub and back of the brake assembly shall be thoroughly wetted to suppress dust.

(5) The brake support plate, brake shoes and brake components used to attach the brake shoes shall be thoroughly washed before removing the old shoes.

(6) In systems using filters, the filters, when full, shall be first wetted with a fine mist of water, then removed and placed immediately in an impermeable container, labeled according to paragraph (j)(4) of this section and disposed of according to paragraph (k) of this section.

(7) Any spills of asbestos-containing aqueous solution or any asbestos-containing waste material shall be cleaned up immediately and disposed of according to paragraph (k) of this section.

(8) The use of dry brushing during low pressure/wet cleaning operations is prohibited.

[C] Equivalent Methods

An equivalent method is one which has sufficient written detail so that it can be reproduced and has been demonstrated that the exposures resulting from the equivalent method are equal to or less than the exposures which would result from the use of the method described in paragraph [A] of this appendix. For purposes of making this comparison, the employer shall assume that exposures resulting from the use of the method described in paragraph [A] of this appendix shall not exceed 0.016 f/cc, as measured by the OSHA reference method and as averaged over at least 18 personal samples.

[D] Wet Method.

(1) A spray bottle, hose nozzle, or other implement capable of delivering a fine mist of water or amended water or other delivery system capable of delivering water at low pressure, shall be used to first thoroughly wet the brake and clutch parts. Brake and clutch components shall then be wiped clean with a cloth.

(2) The cloth shall be placed in an impermeable container, labelled according to paragraph (j)(4) of this section and then disposed of according to paragraph (k) of this section, or the cloth shall be laundered in a way to prevent the release of asbestos fibers in excess of 0.1 fiber per cubic centimeter of air.

(3) Any spills of solvent or any asbestos containing waste material shall be cleaned up immediately according to paragraph (k) of this section.

(4) The use of dry brushing during the wet method operations is prohibited.

APPENDIX G TO §1910.1001—SUBSTANCE TECHNICAL INFORMATION FOR ASBESTOS—NONMANDATORY

I. Substance Identification

A. Substance: "Asbestos" is the name of a class of magnesium-silicate minerals that occur in fibrous form. Minerals that are included in this group are chrysotile, crocidolite, amosite, tremolite asbestos, anthophyllite asbestos, and actinolite asbestos.

B. Asbestos is used in the manufacture of heat-resistant clothing, automative brake and clutch linings, and a variety of building materials including floor tiles, roofing felts, ceiling tiles, asbestos-cement pipe and sheet, and fire-resistant drywall. Asbestos is also present in pipe and boiler insulation materials, and in sprayed-on materials located on beams, in crawlspaces, and between walls.

C. The potential for a product containing asbestos to release breatheable fibers depends on its degree of friability. Friable means that the material can be crumbled with hand pressure and is therefore likely to emit fibers. The fibrous or fluffy sprayed-on materials used for fireproofing, insulation, or sound proofing are considered to be friable, and they readily release airborne fibers if disturbed. Materials such as vinyl-asbestos floor tile or roofing felts are considered nonfriable and generally do not emit airborne fibers unless subjected to sanding or sawing operations. Asbestos-cement pipe or sheet can emit airborne fibers if the materials are cut or sawed, or if they are broken during demolition operations.

D. Permissible exposure: Exposure to airborne asbestos fibers may not exceed 0.2 fibers per cubic centimeter of air (0.1 f/cc) averaged over the 8-hour workday.

II. Health Hazard Data

A. Asbestos can cause disabling respiratory disease and various types of cancers if the fibers are inhaled. Inhaling or ingesting fibers from contaminated clothing or skin can also result in these diseases. The symptoms of these diseases generally do not appear for 20 or more years after initial exposure.

B. Exposure to asbestos has been shown to cause lung cancer, mesothelioma, and cancer of the stomach and colon. Mesothelioma is a rare cancer of the thin membrane lining of the chest and abdomen. Symptoms of mesothelioma include shortness of breath, pain in the walls of the chest, and/or abdominal pain.

III. Respirators and Protective Clothing

A. Respirators: You are required to wear a respirator when performing tasks that result in asbestos exposure that exceeds the permissible exposure limit (PEL) of 0.1 f/cc. These conditions can occur while your employer is in the process of installing engineering controls to reduce asbestos exposure, or where engineering controls are not feasible to reduce asbestos exposure. Air-purifying respirators equipped with a high-efficiency particulate air (HEPA) filter can be used where airborne asbestos fiber concentrations do not exceed 2 f/cc; otherwise, air-supplied, positive-pressure, full facepiece respirators must be used. Disposable respirators or dust masks are not permitted to be used for asbestos work. For effective protection, respirators must fit your face and head snugly. Your employer is required to conduct fit tests when you are first assigned a respirator and every 6 months thereafter. Respirators should not be loosened or removed in work situations where their use is required.

B. Protective clothing: You are required to wear protective clothing in work areas where asbestos fiber concentrations exceed the permissible exposure limit.

IV. Disposal Procedures and Cleanup

A. Wastes that are generated by processes where asbestos is present include:
1. Empty asbestos shipping containers.
2. Process wastes such as cuttings, trimmings, or reject material.
3. Housekeeping waste from sweeping or vacuuming.
4. Asbestos fireproofing or insulating material that is removed from buildings.
5. Building products that contain asbestos removed during building renovation or demolition.
6. Contaminated disposable protective clothing.

B. Empty shipping bags can be flattened under exhaust hoods and packed into airtight containers for disposal. Empty shipping drums are difficult to clean and should be sealed.

C. Vacuum bags or disposable paper filters should not be cleaned, but should be sprayed with a fine water mist and placed into a labeled waste container.

D. Process waste and housekeeping waste should be wetted with water or a mixture of water and surfactant prior to packaging in disposable containers.

E. Material containing asbestos that is removed from buildings must be disposed of in leak-tight 6-mil thick plastic bags, plastic-lined cardboard containers, or plastic-lined metal containers. These wastes, which are removed while wet, should be sealed in containers before they dry out to minimize the release of asbestos fibers during handling.

V. Access to Information

A. Each year, your employer is required to inform you of the information contained in this standard and appendices for asbestos. In addition, your employer must instruct you in the proper work practices for handling materials containing asbestos, and the correct use of protective equipment.

B. Your employer is required to determine whether you are being exposed to asbestos. You or your representative has the right to observe employee measurements and to record the results obtained. Your employer is required to inform you of your exposure, and, if you are exposed above the permissible limit, he or she is required to inform you of the actions that are being taken to reduce your exposure to within the permissible limit.

C. Your employer is required to keep records of your exposures and medical examinations. These exposure records must be kept for at least thirty (30) years. Medical records must be kept for the period of your employment plus thirty (30) years.

D. Your employer is required to release your exposure and medical records to your physician or designated representative upon your written request.

APPENDIX H TO § 1910.1001—MEDICAL SURVEILLANCE GUIDELINES FOR ASBESTOS NON-MANDATORY

I. Route of Entry Inhalation, Ingestion

II. Toxicology

Clinical evidence of the adverse effects associated with exposure to asbestos is present in the form of several well-conducted epidemiological studies of occupationally exposed workers, family contacts of workers, and persons living near asbestos mines. These studies have shown a definite association between exposure to asbestos and an increased incidence of lung cancer, pleural and peritoneal mesothelioma, gastrointestinal cancer, and asbestosis. The latter is a disabling fibrotic lung disease that is caused only by exposure to asbestos. Exposure to asbestos has also been associated with an increased incidence of esophageal, kidney, laryngeal, pharyngeal, and buccal cavity cancers. As with other known chronic occupational diseases, disease associated with asbestos generally appears about 20 years following the first occurrence of exposure: There are no known acute effects associated with exposure to asbestos.

Epidemiological studies indicate that the risk of lung cancer among exposed workers who smoke cigarettes is greatly increased over the risk of lung cancer among non-exposed smokers or exposed nonsmokers. These studies suggest that cessation of smoking will reduce the risk of lung cancer for a person exposed to asbestos but will not reduce it to the same level of risk as that existing for an exposed worker who has never smoked.

III. Signs and Symptoms of Exposure-Related Disease

The signs and symptoms of lung cancer or gastrointestinal cancer induced by exposure to asbestos are not unique, except that a chest X-ray of an exposed patient with lung cancer may show pleural plaques, pleural calcification, or pleural fibrosis. Symptoms characteristic of mesothelioma include shortness of breath, pain in the walls of the chest, or abdominal pain. Mesothelioma has a much longer latency period compared with lung cancer (40 years versus 15–20 years), and mesothelioma is therefore more likely to be found among workers who were first exposed to asbestos at an early age. Mesothelioma is always fatal.

Asbestosis is pulmonary fibrosis caused by the accumulation of asbestos fibers in the lungs. Symptoms include shortness of breath, coughing, fatigue, and vague feelings of sickness. When the fibrosis worsens, shortness of breath occurs even at rest. The diagnosis of asbestosis is based on a history of exposure to asbestos, the presence of characteristic radiologic changes, end-inspiratory crackles (rales), and other clinical features of fibrosing lung disease. Pleural plaques and thickening are observed on X-rays taken during the early stages of the disease. Asbestosis is often a progressive disease even in the absence of continued exposure, although this appears to be a highly individualized characteristic. In severe cases, death may be caused by respiratory or cardiac failure.

IV. Surveillance and Preventive Considerations

As noted above, exposure to asbestos has been linked to an increased risk of lung cancer, mesothelioma, gastrointestinal cancer, and asbestosis among occupationally exposed workers. Adequate screening tests to determine an employee's potential for developing serious chronic diseases, such as cancer, from exposure to asbestos do not presently exist. However, some tests, particularly chest X-rays and pulmonary function tests, may indicate that an employee has been overexposed to asbestos increasing his or her risk of developing exposure-related chronic diseases. It is important for the physician to become familiar with the operating conditions in which occupational exposure to asbestos is likely to occur. This is particularly important in evaluating medical and work histories and in conducting physical examinations. When an active employee has been identified as having been overexposed to asbestos, measures taken by the employer to eliminate or mitigate further exposure should also lower the risk of serious long-term consequences.

The employer is required to institute a medical surveillance program for all employees who are or will be exposed to asbestos at or above the permissible exposure limit (0.1 fiber per cubic centimeter of air). All examinations and procedures must be performed by or under the supervision of a licensed physician, at a reasonable time and place, and at no cost to the employee.

Although broad latitude is given to the physician in prescribing specific tests to be included in the medical surveillance program, OSHA requires inclusion of the following elements in the routine examination:

(i) Medical and work histories with special emphasis directed to symptoms of the respiratory system, cardiovascular system, and digestive tract.

(ii) Completion of the respiratory disease questionnaire contained in appendix D.

(iii) A physical examination including a chest roentgenogram and pulmonary function test that includes measurement of the employee's forced vital capacity (FVC) and forced expiratory volume at one second (FEV$_1$).

(iv) Any laboratory or other test that the examining physician deems by sound medical practice to be necessary.

The employer is required to make the prescribed tests available at least annually to those employees covered; more often than specified if recommended by the examining physician; and upon termination of employment.

The employer is required to provide the physician with the following information: A copy of this standard and appendices; a description of the mployee's duties as they relate to asbestos exposure; the employee's representative level of exposure to asbestos; a description of any personal protective and respiratory equipment used; and information from previous medical examinations of the affected employee that is not otherwise available to the physician. Making this information available to the physician will aid in the evaluation of the employee's health in relation to assigned duties and fitness to wear personal protective equipment, if required.

The employer is required to obtain a written opinion from the examining physician containing the results of the medical examination; the physician's opinion as to whether the employee has any detected medical conditions that would place the employee at an increased risk of exposure-related disease; any recommended limitations on the employee or on the use of personal protective equipment; and a statement that the employee has been informed by the physician of the results of the medical examination and of any medical conditions related to asbestos exposure that require further explanation or treatment. This written opinion must not reveal specific findings or diagnoses unrelated to exposure to asbestos, and a copy of the opinion must be provided to the affected employee.

APPENDIX I TO § 1910.1001—SMOKING CESSATION PROGRAM INFORMATION FOR ASBESTOS—NON-MANDATORY

The following organizations provide smoking cessation information and program material.

1. The National Cancer Institute operates a toll-free Cancer Information Service (CIS) with trained personnel to help you. Call 1-800-4-CANCER* to reach the CIS office serving your area, or write: Office of Cancer Communications, National Cancer Institute, National Institutes of Health, Building 31, Room 10A24, Bethesda, Maryland 20892.

2. American Cancer Society, 3340 Peachtree Road, NE., Atlanta, Georgia 30062, (404) 320-3333.

The American Cancer Society (ACS) is a voluntary organization composed of 58 divisions and 3,100 local units. Through "The Great American Smokeout" in November, the annual Cancer Crusade in April, and numerous educational materials, ACS helps people learn about the health hazards of smoking and become successful ex-smokers.

3. American Heart Association, 7320 Greenville Avenue, Dallas, Texas 75231, (214) 750-5300.

The American Heart Association (AHA) is a voluntary organization with 130,000 members (physicians, scientists, and laypersons) in 55 state and regional groups. AHA produces a variety of publications and audiovisual materials about the effects of smoking on the heart. AHA also has developed a guidebook for incorporating a weight-control component into smoking cessation programs.

4. American Lung Association, 1740 Broadway, New York, New York 10019, (212) 245-8000.

A voluntary organization of 7,500 members (physicians, nurses, and laypersons), the American Lung Association (ALA) conducts numerous public information programs about the health effect of smoking. ALA has 59 state and 85 local units. The organization actively supports legislation and information campaigns for non-smokers' rights and provides help for smokers who want to quit, for example, through "Freedom From Smoking," a self-help smoking cessation program.

5. Office on Smoking and Health, U.S. Department of Health and, Human Services, 5600 Fishers Lane, Park Building, Room 110, Rockville, Maryland 20857.

The Office on Smoking and Health (OSH) is the Department of Health and Human Services' lead agency in smoking control. OSH has sponsored distribution of publications on smoking-realted topics, such as free flyers on relapse after initial quitting, helping a friend or family member quit smoking, the health hazards of smoking, and the effects of parental smoking on teenagers.

*In Hawaii, on Oahu call 524-1234 (call collect from neighboring islands),

Spanish-speaking staff members are available during daytime hours to callers from the following areas: California, Florida, Georgia, Illinois, New Jersey (area code 210), New York, and Texas. Consult your local telephone directory for listings of local chapters.

APPENDIX J TO § 1910.1001—POLARIZED LIGHT MICROSCOPY OF ASBESTOS—NON-MANDATORY

Method number: ID–191
Matrix: Bulk

Collection Procedure

Collect approximately 1 to 2 grams of each type of material and place into separate 20 mL scintillation vials.

Analytical Procedure

A portion of each separate phase is analyzed by gross examination, phase-polar examination, and central stop dispersion microscopy.

Commercial manufacturers and products mentioned in this method are for descriptive use only and do not constitute endorsements by USDOL-OSHA. Similar products from other sources may be substituted.

1. Introduction

This method describes the collection and analysis of asbestos bulk materials by light microscopy techniques including phase-polar illumination and central-stop dispersion microscopy. Some terms unique to asbestos analysis are defined below:

Amphibole: A family of minerals whose crystals are formed by long, thin units which have two thin ribbons of double chain silicate with a brucite ribbon in between. The shape of each unit is similar to an "I beam". Minerals important in asbestos analysis include cummingtonite-grunerite, crocidolite, tremolite-actinolite and anthophyllite.

Asbestos: A term for naturally occurring fibrous minerals. Asbestos includes chrysotile, cummingtonite-grunerite asbestos (amosite), anthophyllite asbestos, tremolite asbestos, crocidolite, actinolite asbestos and any of these minerals which have been chemically treated or altered. The precise chemical formulation of each species varies with the location from which it was mined. Nominal compositions are listed:

Chrysotile .... $Mg_3 Si_2 O_5(OH)_4$
Crocidolite
(Riebeckite as-
bestos) .... $Na_2 Fe_3^{2+} + Fe_2^{3+} + Si_8 O_{22}(OH)_2$
Cummingtonite-
Grunerite as-
bestos
(Amosite) .... $(Mg,Fe)_7 Si_8 O_{22}(OH)_2$
Tremolite-Actin-
olite asbestos .. $Ca_2(Mg,Fe)_5 Si_8 O_{22}(OH)_2$
Anthophyllite as-
bestos .... $(Mg,Fe)_7 Si_8 O_{22}(OH)_2$

Asbestos Fiber: A fiber of asbestos meeting the criteria for a fiber. (See section 3.5.)

Aspect Ratio: The ratio of the length of a fiber to its diameter usually defined as "length : width", e.g. 3:1.

Brucite: A sheet mineral with the composition $Mg(OH)_2$.

Central Stop Dispersion Staining (microscope): This is a dark field microscope technique that images particles using only light refracted by the particle, excluding light that travels through the particle unrefracted. This is usually accomplished with a McCrone objective or other arrangement which places a circular stop with apparent aperture equal to the objective aperture in the back focal plane of the microscope.

Cleavage Fragments: Mineral particles formed by the comminution of minerals, especially those characterized by relatively parallel sides and moderate aspect ratio.

Differential Counting: The term applied to the practice of excluding certain kinds of fibers from a phase contrast asbestos count because they are not asbestos.

Fiber: A particle longer than or equal to 5 µm with a length to width ratio greater than or equal to 3:1. This may include cleavage fragments. (see section 3.5 of this appendix).

Phase Contrast: Contrast obtained in the microscope by causing light scattered by small particles to destructively interfere with unscattered light, thereby enhancing the visibility of very small particles and particles with very low intrinsic contrast.

Phase Contrast Microscope: A microscope configured with a phase mask pair to create phase contrast. The technique which uses this is called Phase Contrast Microscopy (PCM).

Phase-Polar Analysis: This is the use of polarized light in a phase contrast microscope. It is used to see the same size fibers that are visible in air filter analysis. Although fibers finer than 1 µm are visible, analysis of these is inferred from analysis of larger bundles that are usually present.

Phase-Polar Microscope: The phase-polar microscope is a phase contrast microscope which has an analyzer, a polarizer, a first order red plate and a rotating phase condenser all in place so that the polarized light image is enhanced by phase contrast.

Sealing Encapsulant: This is a product which can be applied, preferably by spraying, onto an asbestos surface which will seal the surface so that fibers cannot be released.

Serpentine: A mineral family consisting of minerals with the general composition $Mg_3(Si2O_5(OH)_4$ having the magnesium in brucite layer over a silicate layer. Minerals important in asbestos analysis included in this family are chrysotile, lizardite, antigorite.

1.1. History

Light microscopy has been used for well over 100 years for the determination of mineral species. This analysis is carried out using specialized polarizing microscopes as well as bright field microscopes. The identification of minerals is an on-going process with many new minerals described each year. The first recorded use of asbestos was in Finland about 2500 B.C. where the material was used in the mud wattle for the wooden huts the people lived in as well as strengthening for pottery. Adverse health aspects of the mineral were noted nearly 2000 years ago when Pliny the Younger wrote about the poor health of slaves in the asbestos mines. Although known to be injurious for centuries, the first modern references to its toxicity were by the British Labor Inspectorate when it banned asbestos dust from the workplace in 1898. Asbestosis cases were described in the literature after the turn of the century. Cancer was first suspected in the mid 1930's and a causal link to mesothelioma was made in 1965. Because of the public concern for worker and public safety with the use of this material, several different types of analysis were applied to the determination of asbestos content. Light microscopy requires a great deal of experience and craft. Attempts were made to apply less subjective methods to the analysis. X-ray diffraction was partially successful in determining the mineral types but was unable to separate out the fibrous portions from the non-fibrous portions. Also, the minimum detection limit for asbestos analysis by X-ray diffraction (XRD) is about 1%. Differential Thermal Analysis (DTA) was no more successful. These provide useful corroborating information when the presence of asbestos has been shown by microscopy; however, neither can determine the difference between fibrous and non-fibrous minerals when both habits are present. The same is true of Infrared Absorption (IR).

When electron microscopy was applied to asbestos analysis, hundreds of fibers were discovered present too small to be visible in any light microscope. There are two different types of electron microscope used for asbestos analysis: Scanning Electron Microscope (SEM) and Transmission Electron Microscope (TEM). Scanning Electron Microscopy is useful in identifying minerals. The SEM can provide two of the three pieces of information required to identify fibers by electron microscopy: morphology and chemistry. The third is structure as determined by Selected Area Electron Diffraction—SAED which is performed in the TEM. Although the resolution of the SEM is sufficient for very fine fibers to be seen, accuracy of chemical analysis that can be performed on the fibers varies with fiber diameter in fibers of less than 0.2 μm diameter. The TEM is a powerful tool to identify fibers too small to be resolved by light microscopy and should be used in conjunction with this method when necessary. The TEM can provide all three pieces of information required

for fiber identification. Most fibers thicker than 1 μm can adequately be defined in the light microscope. The light microscope remains as the best instrument for the determination of mineral type. This is because the minerals under investigation were first described analytically with the light microscope. It is inexpensive and gives positive identification for most samples analyzed. Further, when optical techniques are inadequate, there is ample indication that alternative techniques should be used for complete identification of the sample.

1.2. Principle

Minerals consist of atoms that may be arranged in random order or in a regular arrangement. Amorphous materials have atoms in random order while crystalline materials have long range order. Many materials are transparent to light, at least for small particles or for thin sections. The properties of these materials can be investigated by the effect that the material has on light passing through it. The six asbestos minerals are all crystalline with particular properties that have been identified and cataloged. These six minerals are anisotropic. They have a regular array of atoms, but the arrangement is not the same in all directions. Each major direction of the crystal presents a different regularity. Light photons travelling in each of these main directions will encounter different electrical neighborhoods, affecting the path and time of travel. The techniques outlined in this method use the fact that light traveling through fibers or crystals in different directions will behave differently, but predictably. The behavior of the light as it travels through a crystal can be measured and compared with known or determined values to identify the mineral species. Usually, Polarized Light Microscopy (PLM) is performed with strain-free objectives on a bright-field microscope platform. This would limit the resolution of the microscope to about 0.4 μm. Because OSHA requires the counting and identification of fibers visible in phase contrast, the phase contrast platform is used to visualize the fibers with the polarizing elements added into the light path. Polarized light methods cannot identify fibers finer than about 1 μm in diameter even though they are visible. The finest fibers are usually identified by inference from the presence of larger, identifiable fiber bundles. When fibers are present, but not identifiable by light microscopy, use either SEM or TEM to determine the fiber identity.

1.3. Advantages and Disadvantages

The advantages of light micropy are:
(a) Basic identification of the materials was first performed by light microscopy and gross analysis. This provides a large base of

published information against which to check analysis and analytical technique.

(b) The analysis is specific to fibers. The minerals present can exist in asbestiform, fibrous, prismatic, or massive varieties all at the same time. Therefore, bulk methods of analysis such as X-ray diffraction, IR analysis, DTA, etc. are inappropriate where the material is not known to be fibrous.

(c) The analysis is quick, requires little preparation time, and can be performed on-site if a suitably equipped microscope is available.

The disadvantages are:

(a) Even using phase-polar illumination, not all the fibers present may be seen. This is a problem for very low asbestos concentrations where agglomerations or large bundles of fibers may not be present to allow identification by inference.

(b) The method requires a great degree of sophistication on the part of the microscopist. An analyst is only as useful as his mental catalog of images. Therefore, a microscopist's accuracy is enhanced by experience. The mineralogical training of the analyst is very important. It is the basis on which subjective decisions are made.

(c) The method uses only a tiny amount of material for analysis. This may lead to sampling bias and false results (high or low). This is especially true if the sample is severely inhomogeneous.

(d) Fibers may be bound in a matrix and not distinguishable as fibers so identification cannot be made.

1.4. Method Performance

1.4.1. This method can be used for determination of asbestos content from 0 to 100% asbestos. The detection limit has not been adequately determined, although for selected samples, the limit is very low, depending on the number of particles examined. For mostly homogeneous, finely divided samples, with no difficult fibrous interferences, the detection limit is below 1%. For inhomogeneous samples (most samples), the detection limit remains undefined. NIST has conducted proficiency testing of laboratories on a national scale. Although each round is reported statistically with an average, control limits, etc., the results indicate a difficulty in establishing precision especially in the low concentration range. It is suspected that there is significant bias in the low range especially near 1%. EPA tried to remedy this by requiring a mandatory point counting scheme for samples less than 10%. The point counting procedure is tedious, and may introduce significant biases of its own. It has not been incorporated into this method.

1.4.2. The precision and accuracy of the quantitation tests performed in this method are unknown. Concentrations are easier to determine in commercial products where asbestos was deliberately added because the

amount is usually more than a few percent. An analyst's results can be "calibrated" against the known amounts added by the manufacturer. For geological samples, the degree of homogeneity affects the precision.

1.4.3. The performance of the method is analyst dependent. The analyst must choose carefully and not necessarily randomly the portions for analysis to assure that detection of asbestos occurs when it is present. For this reason, the analyst must have adequate training in sample preparation, and experience in the location and identification of asbestos in samples. This is usually accomplished through substantial on-the-job training as well as formal education in mineralogy and microscopy.

1.5. Interferences

Any material which is long, thin, and small enough to be viewed under the microscope can be considered an interference for asbestos. There are literally hundreds of interferences in workplaces. The techniques described in this method are normally sufficient to eliminate the interferences. An analyst's success in eliminating the interferences depends on proper training.

Asbestos minerals belong to two mineral families: the serpentines and the amphiboles. In the serpentine family, the only common fibrous mineral is chrysotile. Occasionally, the mineral antigorite occurs in a fibril habit with morphology similar to the amphiboles. The amphibole minerals consist of a score of different minerals of which only five are regulated by federal standard: amosite, crocidolite, anthophyllite asbestos, tremolite asbestos and actinolite asbestos. These are the only amphibole minerals that have been commercially exploited for their fibrous properties; however, the rest can and do occur occasionally in asbestiform habit.

In addition to the related mineral interferences, other minerals common in building material may present a problem for some microscopists: gypsum, anhydrite, brucite, quartz fibers, talc fibers or ribbons, wollastonite, perlite, attapulgite, etc. Other fibrous materials commonly present in workplaces are: fiberglass, mineral wool, ceramic wool, refractory ceramic fibers, kevlar, nomex, synthetic fibers, graphite or carbon fibers, cellulose (paper or wood) fibers, metal fibers, etc.

Matrix embedding material can sometimes be a negative interference. The analyst may not be able to easily extract the fibers from the matrix in order to use the method. Where possible, remove the matrix before the analysis, taking careful note of the loss of weight. Some common matrix materials are: vinyl, rubber, tar, paint, plant fiber, cement, and epoxy. A further negative interference is that the asbestos fibers themselves may be either too small to be seen in Phase contrast Microscopy (PCM) or of a very low fibrous quality, having the appearance of plant fibers. The analyst's ability to deal with these materials increases with experience.

1.6. Uses and Occupational Exposure

Asbestos is ubiquitous in the environment. More than 40% of the land area of the United States is composed of minerals which may contain asbestos. Fortunately, the actual formation of great amounts of asbestos is relatively rare. Nonetheless, there are locations in which environmental exposure can be severe such as in the Serpentine Hills of California.

There are thousands of uses for asbestos in industry and the home. Asbestos abatement workers are the most current segment of the population to have occupational exposure to great amounts of asbestos. If the material is undisturbed, there is no exposure. Exposure occurs when the asbestos-containing material is abraded or otherwise disturbed during maintenance operations or some other activity. Approximately 95% of the asbestos in place in the United States is chrysotile.

Amosite and crocidolite make up nearly all the difference. Tremolite and anthophyllite make up a very small percentage. Tremolite is found in extremely small amounts in certain chrysotile deposits. Actinolite exposure is probably greatest from environmental sources, but has been identified in vermiculite containing, sprayed-on insulating materials which may have been certified as asbestos-free.

1.7. Physical and Chemical Properties

The nominal chemical compositions for the asbestos minerals were given in Section 1. Compared to cleavage fragments of the same minerals, asbestiform fibers possess a high tensile strength along the fiber axis. They are chemically inert, non- combustible, and heat resistant. Except for chrysotile, they are insoluble in Hydrochloric acid (HCl). Chrysotile is slightly soluble in HCl. Asbestos has high electrical resistance and good sound absorbing characteristics. It can be woven into cables, fabrics or other textiles, or matted into papers, felts, and mats.

1.8. Toxicology (This section is for Information Only and Should Not Be Taken as OSHA Policy)

Possible physiologic results of respiratory exposure to asbestos are mesothelioma of the pleura or peritoneum, interstitial fibrosis, asbestosis, pneumoconiosis, or respiratory cancer. The possible consequences of asbestos exposure are detailed in the NIOSH Criteria Document or in the OSHA Asbestos Standards 29 CFR 1910.1001 and 29 CFR 1926.1101 and 29 CFR 1915.1001.

2. Sampling Procedure

2.1. Equipment for Sampling

(a) Tube or cork borer sampling device
(b) Knife
(c) 20 mL scintillation vial or similar vial
(d) Sealing encapsulant

2.2. Safety Precautions

Asbestos is a known carcinogen. Take care when sampling. While in an asbestos-containing atmosphere, a properly selected and fit-tested respirator should be worn. Take samples in a manner to cause the least amount of dust. Follow these general guidelines:

(a) Do not make unnecessary dust.
(b) Take only a small amount (1 to 2 g).
(c) Tightly close the sample container.
(d) Use encapsulant to seal the spot where the sample was taken, if necessary.

2.3. Sampling Procedure

Samples of any suspect material should be taken from an inconspicuous place. Where the material is to remain, seal the sampling wound with an encapsulant to eliminate the potential for exposure from the sample site. Microscopy requires only a few milligrams of material. The amount that will fill a 20 mL scintillation vial is more than adequate. Be sure to collect samples from all layers and phases of material. If possible, make separate samples of each different phase of the material. This will aid in determining the actual hazard. *DO NOT USE ENVELOPES, PLASTIC OR PAPER BAGS OF ANY KIND TO COLLECT SAMPLES.* The use of plastic bags presents a contamination hazard to laboratory personnel and to other samples. When these containers are opened, a bellows effect blows fibers out of the container onto everything, including the person opening the container.

If a cork-borer type sampler is available, push the tube through the material all the way, so that all layers of material are sampled. Some samplers are intended to be disposable. These should be capped and sent to the laboratory. If a non-disposable cork borer is used, empty the contents into a scintillation vial and send to the laboratory. Vigorously and completely clean the cork borer between samples.

2.4 Shipment

Samples packed in glass vials must not touch or they might break in shipment.

(a) Seal the samples with a sample seal over the end to guard against tampering and to identify the sample.
(b) Package the bulk samples in separate packages from the air samples. They may cross-contaminate each other and will invalidate the results of the air samples.

(c) Include identifying paperwork *with* the samples, but not in contact with the suspected asbestos.

(d) To maintain sample accountability, ship the samples by certified mail, overnight express, or hand carry them to the laboratory.

3. Analysis

The analysis of asbestos samples can be divided into two major parts: sample preparation and microscopy. Because of the different asbestos uses that may be encountered by the analyst, each sample may need different preparation steps. The choices are outlined below. There are several different tests that are performed to identify the asbestos species and determine the percentage. They will be explained below.

3.1. Safety

(a) Do not create unnecessary dust. Handle the samples in HEPA-filter equipped hoods. If samples are received in bags, envelopes or other inappropriate container, open them only in a hood having a face velocity at or greater than 100 fpm. Transfer a small amount to a scintillation vial and only handle the smaller amount.

(b) Open samples in a hood, never in the open lab area.

(c) Index of refraction oils can be toxic. Take care not to get this material on the skin. Wash immediately with soap and water if this happens.

(d) Samples that have been heated in the muffle furnace or the drying oven may be hot. Handle them with tongs until they are cool enough to handle.

(e) Some of the solvents used, such as THF (tetrahydrofuran), are toxic and should only be handled in an appropriate fume hood and according to instructions given in the Safety data sheet (SDS).

3.2. Equipment

(a) Phase contrast microscope with 10x, 16x and 40x objectives, 10x wide-field eyepieces, G–22 Walton-Beckett graticule, Whipple disk, polarizer, analyzer and first order red or gypsum plate, 100 Watt illuminator, rotating position condenser with oversize phase rings, central stop dispersion objective, Kohler illumination and a rotating mechanical stage.

(b) Stereo microscope with reflected light illumination, transmitted light illumination, polarizer, analyzer and first order red or gypsum plate, and rotating stage.

(c) Negative pressure hood for the stereo microscope

(d) Muffle furnace capable of 600 °C

(e) Drying oven capable of 50–150 °C

(f) Aluminum specimen pans

(g) Tongs for handling samples in the furnace

(h) High dispersion index of refraction oils (Special for dispersion staining.)

n = 1.550
n = 1.585
n = 1.590
n = 1.605
n = 1.620
n = 1.670
n = 1.680
n = 1.690

(i) A set of index of refraction oils from about n = 1.350 to n = 2.000 in n = 0.005 increments. (Standard for Becke line analysis.)

(j) Glass slides with painted or frosted ends 1 × 3 inches 1mm thick, precleaned.

(k) Cover Slips 22 × 22 mm, #1½

(l) Paper clips or dissection needles

(m) Hand grinder

(n) Scalpel with both #10 and #11 blades

(o) 0.1 molar HCl

(p) Decalcifying solution (Baxter Scientific Products) Ethylenediaminetetraacetic Acid, Tetrasodium ....0.7 g/l
Sodium Potassium Tartrate ....8.0 mg/liter
Hydrochloric Acid ....99.2 g/liter
Sodium Tartrate...........................0.14 g/liter

(q) Tetrahydrofuran (THF)

(r) Hotplate capable of 60 °C

(s) Balance

(t) Hacksaw blade

(u) Ruby mortar and pestle

3.3. Sample Pre-Preparation

Sample preparation begins with pre-preparation which may include chemical reduction of the matrix, heating the sample to dryness or heating in the muffle furnace. The end result is a sample which has been reduced to a powder that is sufficiently fine to fit under the cover slip. Analyze different phases of samples separately, e.g., tile and the tile mastic should be analyzed separately as the mastic may contain asbestos while the tile may not.

(a) *Wet samples*

Samples with a high water content will not give the proper dispersion colors and must be dried prior to sample mounting. Remove the lid of the scintillation vial, place the bottle in the drying oven and heat at 100 °C to dryness (usually about 2 h). Samples which are not submitted to the lab in glass must be removed and placed in glass vials or aluminum weighing pans before placing them in the drying oven.

(b) *Samples With Organic Interference—Muffle Furnace*

These may include samples with tar as a matrix, vinyl asbestos tile, or any other organic that can be reduced by heating. Remove the sample from the vial and weigh in a balance to determine the weight of the submitted portion. Place the sample in a muffle

63

furnace at 500 °C for 1 to 2 h or until all obvious organic material has been removed. Retrieve, cool and weigh again to determine the weight loss on ignition. This is necessary to determine the asbestos content of the submitted sample, because the analyst will be looking at a reduced sample.

NOTE: Heating above 600 °C will cause the sample to undergo a structural change which, given sufficient time, will convert the chrysotile to forsterite. Heating even at lower temperatures for 1 to 2 h may have a measurable effect on the optical properties of the minerals. If the analyst is unsure of what to expect, a sample of standard asbestos should be heated to the same temperature for the same length of time so that it can be examined for the proper interpretation.

(c) *Samples With Organic Interference—THF*

Vinyl asbestos tile is the most common material treated with this solvent, although, substances containing tar will sometimes yield to this treatment. Select a portion of the material and then grind it up if possible. Weigh the sample and place it in a test tube. Add sufficient THF to dissolve the organic matrix. This is usually about 4 to 5 mL. *Remember, THF is highly flammable.* Filter the remaining material through a tared silver membrane, dry and weigh to determine how much is left after the solvent extraction. Further process the sample to remove carbonate or mount directly.

(d) *Samples With Carbonate Interference*

Carbonate material is often found on fibers and sometimes must be removed in order to perform dispersion microscopy. Weigh out a portion of the material and place it in a test tube. Add a sufficient amount of 0.1 M HCl or decalcifying solution in the tube to react all the carbonate as evidenced by gas formation; i.e., when the gas bubbles stop, add a little more solution. If no more gas forms, the reaction is complete. Filter the material out through a tared silver membrane, dry and weigh to determine the weight lost.

3.4. Sample Preparation

Samples must be prepared so that accurate determination can be made of the asbestos type and amount present. The following steps are carried out in the low-flow hood (a low-flow hood has less than 50 fpm flow):

(1) If the sample has large lumps, is hard, or cannot be made to lie under a cover slip, the grain size must be reduced. Place a small amount between two slides and grind the material between them or grind a small amount in a clean mortar and pestle. The choice of whether to use an alumina, ruby, or diamond mortar depends on the hardness of the material. Impact damage can alter the asbestos mineral if too much mechanical

shock occurs. (Freezer mills can completely destroy the observable crystallinity of asbestos and should not be used). For some samples, a portion of material can be shaved off with a scalpel, ground off with a hand grinder or hack saw blade.

The preparation tools should either be disposable or cleaned thoroughly. Use vigorous scrubbing to loosen the fibers during the washing. Rinse the implements with copious amounts of water and air-dry in a dust-free environment.

(2) If the sample is powder or has been reduced as in (1) above, it is ready to mount. Place a glass slide on a piece of optical tissue and write the identification on the painted or frosted end. Place two drops of index of refraction medium n = 1.550 on the slide. (The medium n = 1.550 is chosen because it is the matching index for chrysotile. Dip the end of a clean paper-clip or dissecting needle into the droplet of refraction medium on *the slide* to moisten it. Then dip the probe into the powder sample. Transfer what sticks on the probe to the slide. The material on the end of the probe should have a diameter of about 3 mm for a good mount. If the material is very fine, less sample may be appropriate. For non-powder samples such as fiber mats, forceps should be used to transfer a small amount of material to the slide. Stir the material in the medium on the slide, spreading it out and making the preparation as uniform as possible. Place a cover-slip on the preparation by gently lowering onto the slide and allowing it to fall "trapdoor" fashion on the preparation to push out any bubbles. Press gently on the cover slip to even out the distribution of particulate on the slide. If there is insufficient mounting oil on the preparation, one or two drops may be placed near the edge of the coverslip on the slide. Capillary action will draw the necessary amount of liquid into the preparation. Remove excess oil with the point of a laboratory wiper.

Treat at least two different areas of each phase in this fashion. Choose representative areas of the sample. It may be useful to select particular areas or fibers for analysis. This is useful to identify asbestos in severely inhomogeneous samples.

When it is determined that amphiboles may be present, repeat the above process using the appropriate high-dispersion oils until an identification is made or all six asbestos minerals have been ruled out. Note that percent determination must be done in the index medium 1.550 because amphiboles tend to disappear in their matching mediums.

3.5. Analytical Procedure

NOTE: This method presumes some knowledge of mineralogy and optical petrography.

The analysis consists of three parts: The determination of whether there is asbestos present, what type is present and the determination of how much is present. The general flow of the analysis is:

(1) Gross examination.

(2) Examination under polarized light on the stereo microscope.

(3) Examination by phase-polar illumination on the compound phase microscope.

(4) Determination of species by dispersion stain. Examination by Becke line analysis may also be used; however, this is usually more cumbersome for asbestos determination.

(5) Difficult samples may need to be analyzed by SEM or TEM, or the results from those techniques combined with light microscopy for a definitive identification. Identification of a particle as asbestos requires that it be asbestiform. Description of particles should follow the suggestion of Campbell. (Figure 1)

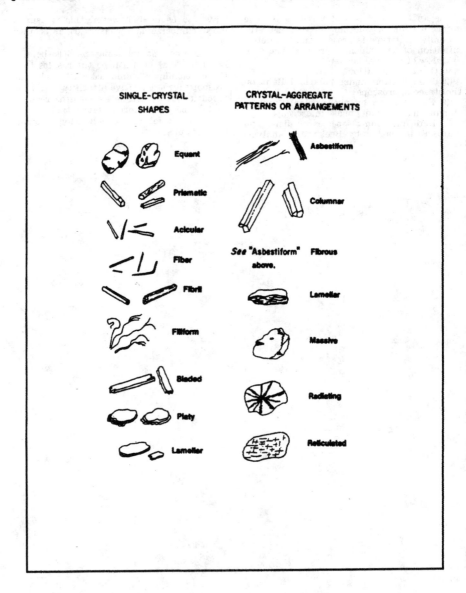

Figure 1. Particle definitions showing mineral growth habits.
From the U.S. Bureau of Mines

For the purpose of regulation, the mineral must be one of the six minerals covered and must be in the asbestos growth habit. Large specimen samples of asbestos generally have the gross appearance of wood. Fibers are easily parted from it. Asbestos fibers are very long compared with their widths. The fibers have a very high tensile strength as demonstrated by bending without breaking. Asbestos fibers exist in bundles that are easily parted, show longitudinal fine structure and may be tufted at the ends showing "bundle of sticks" morphology. In the microscope

66

some of these properties may not be observable. Amphiboles do not always show striations along their length even when they are asbestos. Neither will they always show tufting. They generally do not show a curved nature except for very long fibers. Asbestos and asbestiform minerals are usually characterized in groups by extremely high aspect ratios (greater than 100:1). While aspect ratio analysis is useful for characterizing populations of fibers, it cannot be used to identify individual fibers of intermediate to short aspect ratio. Observation of many fibers is often necessary to determine whether a sample consists of "cleavage fragments" or of asbestos fibers.

Most cleavage fragments of the asbestos minerals are easily distinguishable from true asbestos fibers. This is because true cleavage fragments usually have larger diameters than 1 µm. Internal structure of particles larger than this usually shows them to have no internal fibrillar structure. In addition, cleavage fragments of the monoclinic amphiboles show inclined extinction under crossed polars with no compensator. Asbestos fibers usually show extinction at zero degrees or ambiguous extinction if any at all. Morphologically, the larger cleavage fragments are obvious by their blunt or stepped ends showing prismatic habit. Also, they tend to be acicular rather than filiform.

Where the particles are less than 1 µm in diameter and have an aspect ratio greater than or equal to 3:1, it is recommended that the sample be analyzed by SEM or TEM if there is any question whether the fibers are cleavage fragments or asbestiform particles.

Care must be taken when analyzing by electron microscopy because the interferences are different from those in light microscopy and may structurally be very similar to asbestos. The classic interference is between anthophyllite and biopyribole or intermediate fiber. Use the same morphological clues for electron microscopy as are used for light microscopy, e.g. fibril splitting, internal longitudinal striation, fraying, curvature, etc.

(1) Gross examination:

Examine the sample, preferably in the glass vial. Determine the presence of any obvious fibrous component. Estimate a percentage based on previous experience and current observation. Determine whether any pre- preparation is necessary. Determine the number of phases present. This step may be carried out or augmented by observation at 6 to 40 × under a stereo microscope.

(2) After performing any necessary pre-preparation, prepare slides of each phase as described above. Two preparations of the same phase in the same index medium can be made side-by-side on the same glass for convenience. Examine with the polarizing stereo microscope. Estimate the percentage of as-

bestos based on the amount of birefringent fiber present.

(3) Examine the slides on the phase-polar microscopes at magnifications of 160 and 400 × . Note the morphology of the fibers. Long, thin, very straight fibers with little curvature are indicative of fibers from the amphibole family. Curved, wavy fibers are usually indicative of chrysotile. Estimate the percentage of asbestos on the phase-polar microscope under conditions of crossed polars and a gypsum plate. Fibers smaller than 1.0 µm in thickness must be identified by inference to the presence of larger, identifiable fibers and morphology. If no larger fibers are visible, electron microscopy should be performed. At this point, only a tentative identification can be made. Full identification must be made with dispersion microscopy. Details of the tests are included in the appendices.

(4) Once fibers have been determined to be present, they must be identified. Adjust the microscope for dispersion mode and observe the fibers. The microscope has a rotating stage, one polarizing element, and a system for generating dark-field dispersion microscopy (see Section 4.6. of this appendix). Align a fiber with its length parallel to the polarizer and note the color of the Becke lines. Rotate the stage to bring the fiber length perpendicular to the polarizer and note the color. Repeat this process for every fiber or fiber bundle examined. The colors must be consistent with the colors generated by standard asbestos reference materials for a positive identification. In n = 1.550, amphiboles will generally show a yellow to straw-yellow color indicating that the fiber indices of refraction are higher than the liquid. If long, thin fibers are noted and the colors are yellow, prepare further slides as above in the suggested matching liquids listed below:

Type of asbestos	Index of refraction
Chrysotile	n = 1.550.
Amosite	n = 1.670 or 1.680.
Crocidolite	n = 1.690.
Anthophyllite	n = 1.605 and 1.620.
Tremolite	n = 1.605 and 1.620.
Actinolite	n = 1.620.

Where more than one liquid is suggested, the first is preferred; however, in some cases this liquid will not give good dispersion color. Take care to avoid interferences in the other liquid; e.g., wollastonite in n = 1.620 will give the same colors as tremolite. In n = 1.605 wollastonite will appear yellow in all directions. Wollastonite may be determined under crossed polars as it will change from blue to yellow as it is rotated along its fiber axis by tapping on the cover slip. Asbestos minerals will not change in this way.

Determination of the angle of extinction may, when present, aid in the determination of anthophyllite from tremolite. True asbestos fibers usually have 0° extinction or ambiguous extinction, while cleavage fragments have more definite extinction.

Continue analysis until both preparations have been examined and all present species of asbestos are identified. If there are no fibers present, or there is less than 0.1% present, end the analysis with the minimum number of slides (2).

(5) Some fibers have a coating on them which makes dispersion microscopy very difficult or impossible. Becke line analysis or electron microscopy may be performed in those cases. Determine the percentage by light microscopy. TEM analysis tends to overestimate the actual percentage present.

(6) Percentage determination is an estimate of occluded area, tempered by gross observation. Gross observation information is used to make sure that the high magnification microscopy does not greatly over- or under- estimate the amount of fiber present. This part of the analysis requires a great deal of experience. Satisfactory models for asbestos content analysis have not yet been developed, although some models based on metallurgical grain-size determination have found some utility. Estimation is more easily handled in situations where the grain sizes visible at about 160 × are about the same and the sample is relatively homogeneous.

View all of the area under the cover slip to make the percentage determination. View the fields while moving the stage, paying attention to the clumps of material. These are not usually the best areas to perform dispersion microscopy because of the interference from other materials. But, they are the areas most likely to represent the accurate percentage in the sample. Small amounts of asbestos require slower scanning and more frequent analysis of individual fields.

Report the area occluded by asbestos as the concentration. This estimate does not generally take into consideration the difference in density of the different species present in the sample. For most samples this is adequate. Simulation studies with similar materials must be carried out to apply microvisual estimation for that purpose and is beyond the scope of this procedure.

(7) Where successive concentrations have been made by chemical or physical means, the amount reported is the percentage of the material in the "as submitted" or original state. The percentage determined by microscopy is multiplied by the fractions remaining after pre-preparation steps to give the percentage in the original sample. For example:

Step 1. 60% remains after heating at 550 °C for 1 h.

Step 2. 30% of the residue of step 1 remains after dissolution of carbonate in 0.1 m HCl.

Step 3. Microvisual estimation determines that 5% of the sample is chrysotile asbestos.

The reported result is:

R = (Microvisual result in percent) × (Fraction remaining after step 2) × (Fraction remaining of original sample after step 1)

R = (5) × (.30) × (.60) = 0.9%

(8) Report the percent and type of asbestos present. For samples where asbestos was identified, but is less than 1.0%, report "Asbestos present, less than 1.0%." There must have been at least two observed fibers or fiber bundles in the two preparations to be reported as present. For samples where asbestos was not seen, report as "None Detected."

4. Auxiliary Information

Because of the subjective nature of asbestos analysis, certain concepts and procedures need to be discussed in more depth. This information will help the analyst understand why some of the procedures are carried out the way they are.

4.1. Light

Light is electromagnetic energy. It travels from its source in packets called quanta. It is instructive to consider light as a plane wave. The light has a direction of travel. Perpendicular to this and mutually perpendicular to each other, are two vector components. One is the magnetic vector and the other is the electric vector. We shall only be concerned with the electric vector. In this description, the interaction of the vector and the mineral will describe all the observable phenomena. From a light source such a microscope illuminator, light travels in all different direction from the filament.

In any given direction away from the filament, the electric vector is perpendicular to the direction of travel of a light ray. While perpendicular, its orientation is random about the travel axis. If the electric vectors from all the light rays were lined up by passing the light through a filter that would only let light rays with electric vectors oriented in one direction pass, the light would then be *POLARIZED*.

Polarized light interacts with matter in the direction of the electric vector. This is the polarization direction. Using this property it is possible to use polarized light to probe different materials and identify them by how they interact with light.

The speed of light in a vacuum is a constant at about 2.99×10^8 m/s. When light travels in different materials such as air, water, minerals or oil, it does not travel at this speed. It travels slower. This slowing is a function of both the material through which the light is traveling and the wavelength or frequency of the light. In general, the more dense the material, the slower the light travels. Also, generally, the higher the frequency, the slower the light will travel. The ratio of the speed of light in a vacuum to that in a material is called the index of refraction (n). It is usually measured at 589 nm (the sodium D line). If white light (light containing all the visible wavelengths) travels through a material, rays of longer wavelengths will travel faster than those of shorter wavelengths, this separation is called dispersion. Dispersion is used as an identifier of materials as described in Section 4.6.

4.2. Material Properties

Materials are either amorphous or crystalline. The difference between these two descriptions depends on the positions of the atoms in them. The atoms in amorphous materials are randomly arranged with no long range order. An example of an amorphous material is glass. The atoms in crystalline materials, on the other hand, are in regular arrays and have long range order. Most of the atoms can be found in highly predictable locations. Examples of crystalline material are salt, gold, and the asbestos minerals. It is beyond the scope of this method to describe the different types of crystalline materials that can be found, or the full description of the classes into which they can fall. However, some general crystallography is provided below to give a foundation to the procedures described.

With the exception of anthophyllite, all the asbestos minerals belong to the monoclinic crystal type. The unit cell is the basic repeating unit of the crystal and for monoclinic crystals can be described as having three unequal sides, two 90° angles and one angle not equal to 90°. The orthorhombic group, of which anthophyllite is a member has three unequal sides and three 90° angles. The unequal sides are a consequence of the complexity of fitting the different atoms into the unit cell. Although the atoms are in a regular array, that array is not symmetrical in all directions. There is long range order in the three major directions of the crystal. However, the order is different in each of the three directions. This has the effect that the index of refraction is different in each of the three directions. Using polarized light, we can investigate the index of refraction in each of the directions and identify the mineral or material under investigation. The indices α, β, and γ are used to identify the lowest, middle, and highest index of refraction respectively. The x direction, associated with α is called the fast axis. Conversely, the z direction is associated with γ and is the slow direction. Crocidolite has α along the fiber length making it "length-fast". The remainder of the asbestos minerals have the γ axis along the fiber length. They are called "length-slow". This orientation to fiber length is used to aid in the identification of asbestos.

4.3. Polarized Light Technique

Polarized light microscopy as described in this section uses the phase-polar microscope described in Section 3.2. A phase contrast microscope is fitted with two polarizing elements, one below and one above the sample. The polarizers have their polarization directions at right angles to each other. Depending on the tests performed, there may be a compensator between these two polarizing elements. Light emerging from a polarizing element has its electric vector pointing in the polarization direction of the element. The light will not be subsequently transmitted through a second element set at a right angle to the first element. Unless the light is altered as it passes from one element to the other, there is no transmission of light.

4.4. Angle of Extinction

Crystals which have different crystal regularity in two or three main directions are said to be anisotropic. They have a different index of refraction in each of the main directions. When such a crystal is inserted between the crossed polars, the field of view is no longer dark but shows the crystal in color. The color depends on the properties of the crystal. The light acts as if it travels through the crystal along the optical axes. If a crystal optical axis were lined up along one of the polarizing directions (either the polarizer or the analyzer) the light would appear to travel only in that direction, and it would blink out or go dark. The difference in degrees between the fiber direction and the angle at which it blinks out is called the angle of extinction. When this angle can be measured, it is useful in identifying the mineral. The procedure for measuring the angle of extinction is to first identify the polarization direction in the microscope. A commercial alignment slide can be used to establish the polarization directions or use anthophyllite or another suitable mineral. This mineral has a zero degree angle of extinction and will go dark to extinction as it aligns with the polarization directions. When a fiber of anthophyllite has gone to extinction, align the eyepiece reticle or graticule with the fiber so that there is a visual cue as to the direction of polarization in the field of view. Tape or otherwise secure the eyepiece in this position so it will not shift.

After the polarization direction has been identified in the field of view, move the particle of interest to the center of the field of view and align it with the polarization direction. For fibers, align the fiber along this direction. Note the angular reading of the rotating stage. Looking at the particle, rotate the stage until the fiber goes dark or "blinks

69

out". Again note the reading of the stage. The difference in the first reading and the second is an angle of extinction.

The angle measured may vary as the orientation of the fiber changes about its long axis. Tables of mineralogical data usually report the maximum angle of extinction. Asbestos forming minerals, when they exhibit an angle of extinction, usually do show an angle of extinction close to the reported maximum, or as appropriate depending on the substitution chemistry.

4.5. Crossed Polars with Compensator

When the optical axes of a crystal are not lined up along one of the polarizing directions (either the polarizer or the analyzer) part of the light travels along one axis and part travels along the other visible axis. This is characteristic of birefringent materials.

The color depends on the difference of the two visible indices of refraction and the thickness of the crystal. The maximum difference available is the difference between the α and the γ axes. This maximum difference is usually tabulated as the birefringence of the crystal.

For this test, align the fiber at 45° to the polarization directions in order to maximize the contribution to each of the optical axes. The colors seen are called retardation colors. They arise from the recombination of light which has traveled through the two separate directions of the crystal. One of the rays is retarded behind the other since the light in that direction travels slower. On recombination, some of the colors which make up white light are enhanced by constructive interference and some are suppressed by destructive interference. The result is a color dependent on the difference between the indices and the thickness of the crystal. The proper colors, thicknesses, and retardations are shown on a Michel-Levy chart. The three items, retardation, thickness and birefringence are related by the following relationship:

$R = t(n_\gamma - n_\alpha)$
R = retardation, t = crystal thickness in µm, and
$n_{\alpha,\gamma}$ = indices of refraction.

Examination of the equation for asbestos minerals reveals that the visible colors for almost all common asbestos minerals and fiber sizes are shades of gray and black. The eye is relatively poor at discriminating different shades of gray. It is very good at discriminating different colors. In order to compensate for the low retardation, a compensator is added to the light train between the polarization elements. The compensator used for this test is a gypsum plate of known thickness and birefringence. Such a compensator when oriented at 45° to the polarizer direction, provides a retardation of 530 nm of the 530 nm wavelength color. This enhances the red color and gives the background a characteristic red to red-magenta color. If this "full-wave" compensator is in place when the asbestos preparation is inserted into the light train, the colors seen on the fibers are quite different. Gypsum, like asbestos has a fast axis and a slow axis. When a fiber is aligned with its fast axis in the same direction as the fast axis of the gypsum plate, the ray vibrating in the slow direction is retarded by both the asbestos and the gypsum. This results in a higher retardation than would be present for either of the two minerals. The color seen is a second order blue. When the fiber is rotated 90° using the rotating stage, the slow direction of the fiber is now aligned with the fast direction of the gypsum and the fast direction of the fiber is aligned with the slow direction of the gypsum. Thus, one ray vibrates faster in the fast direction of the gypsum, and slower in the slow direction of the fiber; the other ray will vibrate slower in the slow direction of the gypsum and faster in the fast direction of the fiber. In this case, the effect is subtractive and the color seen is a first order yellow. As long as the fiber thickness does not add appreciably to the color, the same basic colors will be seen for all asbestos types except crocidolite. In crocidolite the colors will be weaker, may be in the opposite directions, and will be altered by the blue absorption color natural to crocidolite. Hundreds of other materials will give the same colors as asbestos, and therefore, this test is not definitive for asbestos. The test is useful in discriminating against fiberglass or other amorphous fibers such as some synthetic fibers. Certain synthetic fibers will show retardation colors different than asbestos; however, there are some forms of polyethylene and aramid which will show morphology and retardation colors similar to asbestos minerals. This test must be supplemented with a positive identification test when birefringent fibers are present which can not be excluded by morphology. This test is relatively ineffective for use on fibers less than 1 µm in diameter. For positive confirmation TEM or SEM should be used if no larger bundles or fibers are visible.

4.6. Dispersion Staining

Dispersion microscopy or dispersion staining is the method of choice for the identification of asbestos in bulk materials. Becke line analysis is used by some laboratories and yields the same results as does dispersion staining for asbestos and can be used in lieu of dispersion staining. Dispersion staining is performed on the same platform as the phase-polar analysis with the analyzer and compensator removed. One polarizing element remains to define the direction of the light so that the different indices of refraction of the fibers may be separately determined. Dispersion microscopy is a dark-field technique when used for asbestos. Particles are imaged with scattered light. Light which is unscattered is blocked from reaching the eye either by the back field image mask in a McCrone objective or a back field image mask in the phase condenser. The most convenient method is to use the rotating phase condenser to move an oversized phase ring into place. The ideal size for this ring is for the central disk to be just larger than the objective entry aperture as viewed in the back focal plane. The larger the disk, the less scattered light reaches the eye. This will have the effect of diminishing the intensity of dispersion color and will shift the actual color seen. The colors seen vary even on microscopes from the same manufacturer. This is due to the different bands of wavelength exclusion by different mask sizes. The mask may either reside in the condenser or in the objective back focal plane. It is imperative that the analyst determine by experimentation with asbestos standards what the appropriate colors should be for each asbestos type. The colors depend also on the temperature of the preparation and the exact chemistry of the asbestos. Therefore, some slight differences from the standards should be allowed. This is not a serious problem for commercial asbestos uses. This technique is used for identification of the indices of refraction for fibers by recognition of color. There is no direct numerical readout of the index of refraction. Correlation of color to actual index of refraction is possible by referral to published conversion tables. This is not necessary for the analysis of asbestos. Recognition of appropriate colors along with the proper morphology are deemed sufficient to identify the commercial asbestos minerals. Other techniques including SEM, TEM, and XRD may be required to provide additional information in order to identify other types of asbestos.

Make a preparation in the suspected matching high dispersion oil, e.g., n = 1.550 for chrysotile. Perform the preliminary tests to determine whether the fibers are birefringent or not. Take note of the morphological character. Wavy fibers are indicative of chrysotile while long, straight, thin, frayed fibers are indicative of amphibole asbestos. This can aid in the selection of the appropriate matching oil. The microscope is set up and the polarization direction is noted as in Section 4.4. Align a fiber with the polarization direction. Note the color. This is the color parallel to the polarizer. Then rotate the fiber rotating the stage 90° so that the polarization direction is across the fiber. This is the perpendicular position. Again note the color. Both colors must be consistent with standard asbestos minerals in the correct direction for a positive identi-

fication of asbestos. If only one of the colors is correct while the other is not, the identification is not positive. If the colors in both directions are bluish-white, the analyst has chosen a matching index oil which is higher than the correct matching oil, e.g. the analyst has used n = 1.620 where chrysotile is present. The next lower oil (Section 3.5.) should be used to prepare another specimen. If the color in both directions is yellow-white to straw-yellow-white, this indicates that the index of the oil is lower than the index of the fiber, e.g. the preparation is in n = 1.550 while anthophyllite is present. Select the next higher oil (Section 3.5.) and prepare another slide. Continue in this fashion until a positive identification of all asbestos species present has been made or all possible asbestos species have been ruled out by negative results in this test. Certain plant fibers can have similar dispersion colors as asbestos. Take care to note and evaluate the morphology of the fibers or remove the plant fibers in pre- preparation. Coating material on the fibers such as carbonate or vinyl may destroy the dispersion color. Usually, there will be some outcropping of fiber which will show the colors sufficient for identification. When this is not the case, treat the sample as described in Section 3.3. and then perform dispersion staining. Some samples will yield to Becke line analysis if they are coated or electron microscopy can be used for identification.

5. References

5.1. Crane, D.T., *Asbestos in Air*, OSHA method ID160, Revised November 1992.

5.2. Ford, W.E., *Dana's Textbook of Mineralogy;* Fourth Ed.; John Wiley and Son, New York, 1950, p. vii.

5.3. Selikoff,.I.J., Lee, D.H.K., *Asbestos and Disease,* Academic Press, New York, 1978, pp. 3,20.

5.4. *Women Inspectors of Factories.* Annual Report for 1898, H.M. Statistical Office, London, p. 170 (1898).

5.5. Selikoff, I.J., Lee, D.H.K., *Asbestos and Disease,* Academic Press, New York, 1978, pp. 26,30.

5.6. Campbell, W.J., et al, *Selected Silicate Minerals and Their Asbestiform Varieties,* United States Department of the Interior, Bureau of Mines, Information Circular 8751, 1977.

5.7. *Asbestos,* Code of Federal Regulations, 29 CFR 1910.1001 and 29 CFR 1926.58.

5.8. *National Emission Standards for Hazardous Air Pollutants; Asbestos NESHAP Revision,* FEDERAL REGISTER, Vol. 55, No. 224, 20 November 1990, p. 48410.

5.9. Ross, M. *The Asbestos Minerals: Definitions, Description, Modes of Formation, Physical and Chemical Properties and Health Risk to the Mining Community,* Nation Bureau of Standards Special Publication, Washington, DC, 1977.

5.10. Lilis, R., Fibrous Zeolites and Endemic Mesothelioma in Cappadocia, Turkey, *J. Occ Medicine*, 1981, 23,(8),548–550.

5.11. *Occupational Exposure to Asbestos—1972*, U.S. Department of Health, Education and Welfare, Public Health Service, Center for Disease Control, National Institute for Occupational Safety and Health, HSM–72–10267.

5.12. Campbell, W.J., et al, Relationship of Mineral Habit to Size *Characteristics for Tremolite Fragments and Fibers*, United States Department of the Interior, Bureau of Mines, Information Circular 8367, 1979.

5.13. Mefford, D., DCM Laboratory, Denver, private communication, July 1987.

5.14. Deer, W.A., Howie, R.A., Zussman, J., *Rock Forming Minerals*, Longman, Thetford, UK, 1974.

5.15. Kerr, P.F., *Optical Mineralogy;* Third Ed. McGraw-Hill, New York, 1959.

5.16. Veblen, D.R. (Ed.), *Amphiboles and Other Hydrous Pyriboles—Mineralogy, Reviews in Mineralogy*, Vol 9A, Michigan, 1982, pp 1–102.

5.17. Dixon, W.C., *Applications of Optical Microscopy in the Analysis of Asbestos* and Quartz, ACS Symposium Series, No. 120, Analytical Techniques in Occupational Health Chemistry, 1979.

5.18. Polarized Light Microscopy, McCrone Research Institute, Chicago, 1976.

5.19. Asbestos Identification, McCrone Research Institute, G & G printers, Chicago, 1987.

5.20. McCrone, W.C., Calculation of Refractive Indices from Dispersion Staining Data, The Microscope, No 37, Chicago, 1989.

5.21. Levadie, B. (Ed.), *Asbestos and Other Health Related Silicates*, ASTM Technical Publication 834, ASTM, Philadelphia 1982.

5.22. Steel, E. and Wylie, A., Riordan, P.H. (Ed.), Mineralogical Characteristics of Asbestos, *Geology of Asbestos Deposits*, pp. 93–101, SME-AIME, 1981.

5.23. Zussman, J., The Mineralogy of Asbestos, *Asbestos: Properties, Applications and Hazards*, pp. 45–67 Wiley, 1979.

[51 FR 22733, June 20, 1986]

EDITORIAL NOTE: For FEDERAL REGISTER citations affecting § 1910.1001, see the List of CFR Sections Affected, which appears in the Finding Aids section of the printed volume and at *www.govinfo.gov*.

EFFECTIVE DATE NOTE: At 84 FR 21458, May 14, 2019, § 1910.1001 was amended by revising paragraphs (l)(2)(ii) and (l)(3)(ii), the heading to Table 1, and appendices D, E, and H, sections III and IV, effective July 15, 2019. For the convenience of the user, the revised text is set forth as follows:

§ 1910.1001   Asbestos.

*   *   *   *   *

(1) * * *

(2) * * *

(ii) Such examination shall include, as a minimum, a medical and work history; a complete physical examination of all systems with emphasis on the respiratory system, the cardiovascular system and digestive tract; completion of the respiratory disease standardized questionnaire in appendix D to this section, part 1; a 14- by 17-inch or other reasonably-sized standard film or digital posterior-anterior chest X-ray; pulmonary function tests to include forced vital capacity (FVC) and forced expiratory volume at 1 second (FEV$_1$); and any additional tests deemed appropriate by the examining physician. Classification of all chest X-rays shall be conducted in accordance with appendix E to this section.

(3) * * *

(ii) The scope of the medical examination shall be in conformance with the protocol established in paragraph (l)(2)(ii) of this section, except that the frequency of chest X-rays shall be conducted in accordance with Table 1 to this section, and the abbreviated standardized questionnaire contained in part 2 of appendix D to this section shall be administered to the employee.

Table 1 to § 1910.1001—Frequency of Chest X-ray

*   *   *   *   *

APPENDIX D TO § 1910.1001—MEDICAL QUESTIONNAIRES; MANDATORY

This mandatory appendix contains the medical questionnaires that must be administered to all employees who are exposed to asbestos above the permissible exposure limit, and who will therefore be included in their employer's medical surveillance program. Part 1 of this appendix contains the Initial Medical Questionnaire, which must be obtained for all new hires who will be covered by the medical surveillance requirements. Part 2 includes the abbreviated Periodical Medical Questionnaire, which must be administered to all employees who are provided periodic medical examinations under the medical surveillance provisions of the standard in this section.

Part 1
INITIAL MEDICAL QUESTIONNAIRE

1. NAME_____

2. CLOCK NUMBER_____

3. PRESENT OCCUPATION_____

4. PLANT _____

5. ADDRESS_____

6. _____
    (Zip Code)

7. TELEPHONE NUMBER_____

8. INTERVIEWER_____

9. DATE _____

10. Date of Birth _____
           Month   Day   Year

11. Place of Birth _____

12. Sex   1. Male ___
                                 2. Female ___

13. What is your marital status?   1. Single ___   4. Separated/
                                     2. Married ___   Divorced ___
                                     3. Widowed ___

14. Race (Check all that apply)
                    1. White ___   4. Hispanic or Latino ___
                    2. Black or African American ___   5. American Indian or
                                                           Alaska Native ___
                    3. Asian ___   6. Native Hawaiian or
                                                        Other Pacific Islander ___

15. What is the highest grade completed in school? _____
    (For example 12 years is completion of high school)

OCCUPATIONAL HISTORY

16A. Have you ever worked full time (30 hours per   1. Yes ___   2. No ___
     week or more) for 6 months or more?

     IF YES TO 16A:

B. Have you ever worked for a year or more in any   1. Yes ___   2. No ___
dusty job?   3. Does Not Apply ___

Specify job/industry _____   Total Years Worked ___

Was dust exposure: 1. Mild ___   2. Moderate ___   3. Severe ___

C. Have you ever been exposed to gas or   1. Yes ___   2. No ___
chemical fumes in your work?

Specify job/industry _____   Total Years Worked ___

Was exposure: 1. Mild ___   2. Moderate ___   3. Severe ___

D. What has been your usual occupation or job—the one you have worked at the
   longest?

1. Job occupation _____

2. Number of years employed in this occupation _____

3. Position/job title _____

4. Business, field or industry _____

(Record on lines the years in which you have worked in any of these industries, e.g. 1960-1969)

Have you ever worked:	YES	NO
E. In a mine?	_____	_____
F. In a quarry?	_____	_____
G. In a foundry?	_____	_____
H. In a pottery?	_____	_____
I. In a cotton, flax or hemp mill?....	_____	_____
J. With asbestos?	_____	_____

17. <u>PAST MEDICAL HISTORY</u>	YES	NO
A. Do you consider yourself to be in good health?	_____	_____

If "NO" state reason _____

| B. Have you any defect of vision? | _____ | _____ |

If "YES" state nature of defect _____

| C. Have you any hearing defect? | _____ | _____ |

If "YES" state nature of defect _____

	YES	NO
D. Are you suffering from or have you ever suffered from:		
a. Epilepsy (or fits, seizures, convulsions)?	____	____
b. Rheumatic fever?	____	____
c. Kidney disease?	____	____
d. Bladder disease?	____	____
e. Diabetes?	____	____
f. Jaundice?	____	____

18. CHEST COLDS AND CHEST ILLNESSES

18A. If you get a cold, does it "usually" go to your chest? (Usually means more than 1/2 the time)

1. Yes ___   2. No ___
3. Don't get colds ___

19A. During the past 3 years, have you had any chest illnesses that have kept you off work, indoors at home, or in bed?

1. Yes ___   2. No ___

IF YES TO 19A:

B. Did you produce phlegm with any of these chest illnesses?

1. Yes ___   2. No ___
3. Does Not Apply ___

C. In the last 3 years, how many such illnesses with (increased) phlegm did you have which lasted a week or more?

Number of illnesses ___
No such illnesses ___

20. Did you have any lung trouble before the age of 16?

1. Yes ___   2. No ___

21. Have you ever had any of the following?

1A. Attacks of bronchitis?

1. Yes ___   2. No ___

IF YES TO 1A:

B. Was it confirmed by a doctor?   1. Yes ___   2. No ___
                                                3. Does Not Apply   ___

C. At what age was your first attack?   Age in Years   ___
                                                Does Not Apply   ___

2A. Pneumonia (include   1. Yes ___   2. No ___
    bronchopneumonia)?

IF YES TO 2A:

B. Was it confirmed by a doctor?   1. Yes ___   2. No ___
                                                3. Does Not Apply   ___

C. At what age did you first have it?   Age in Years   ___
                                                Does Not Apply   ___

3A. Hay Fever?   1. Yes ___   2. No ___

IF YES TO 3A:

B. Was it confirmed by a doctor?   1. Yes ___   2. No ___
                                                3. Does Not Apply   ___

C. At what age did it start?   Age in Years   ___
                                                Does Not Apply   ___

22A. Have you ever had chronic bronchitis?   1. Yes ___   2. No ___

IF YES TO 22A:

B. Do you still have it?   1. Yes ___   2. No ___
                                                3. Does Not Apply   ___

C. Was it confirmed by a doctor?   1. Yes ___   2. No ___
                                                3. Does Not Apply   ___

D. At what age did it start?   Age in Years   ___
                                                Does Not Apply   ___

23A. Have you ever had emphysema?   1. Yes ___   2. No ___

IF YES TO 23A:

B. Do you still have it?   1. Yes ___   2. No ___
                                            3. Does Not Apply   ___

C. Was it confirmed by a doctor?   1. Yes ___   2. No ___
                                            3. Does Not Apply   ___

D. At what age did it start?   Age in Years   ___
                                            Does Not Apply   ___

24A. Have you ever had asthma?   1. Yes ___   2. No ___

IF YES TO 24A:

B. Do you still have it?   1. Yes ___   2. No ___
                                            3. Does Not Apply   ___

C. Was it confirmed by a doctor?   1. Yes ___   2. No ___
                                            3. Does Not Apply   ___

D. At what age did it start?   Age in Years   ___
                                            Does Not Apply   ___

E. If you no longer have it, at what age did   Age stopped   ___
   it stop?   Does Not Apply   ___

25. Have you ever had:

A. Any other chest illness?   1. Yes ___   2. No ___

If yes, please specify _____

B. Any chest operations?   1. Yes ___   2. No ___

If yes, please specify _____

C. Any chest injuries?   1. Yes ___   2. No ___

If yes, please specify _____

26A. Has a doctor ever told   1. Yes ___   2. No ___
   you that you had heart
   trouble?

IF YES TO 26A:

B. Have you ever had
treatment for heart
trouble in the past 10
years?

1. Yes ___   2. No ___
3. Does Not Apply ___

27A. Has a doctor told you
that you had high blood
pressure?

1. Yes ___   2. No ___

IF YES TO 27A:

B. Have you had any
treatment for high
blood pressure
(hypertension) in the
past 10 years?

1. Yes ___   2. No ___
3. Does Not Apply ___

28. When did you last have your chest X-rayed?   (Year) ___ ___ ___ ___

29. Where did you last have
your chest X-rayed (if
known)?

_____

What was the outcome?

_____

FAMILY HISTORY

30. Were either of your natural parents ever told by a doctor that they had a chronic lung condition such as:

	FATHER			MOTHER		
	1. Yes	2. No	3. Don't know	1. Yes	2. No	3. Don't know
A. Chronic Bronchitis?	___	___	___	___	___	___
B. Emphysema?	___	___	___	___	___	___
C. Asthma?	___	___	___	___	___	___
D. Lung cancer?	___	___	___	___	___	___
E. Other chest conditions?	___	___	___	___	___	___
F. Is parent currently alive?	___	___	___	___	___	___

G. Please Specify
___ Age if Living   ___ Age if Living
___ Age at Death   ___ Age at Death
___ Don't Know   ___ Don't Know

H. Please specify cause of   _____   _____
   death

COUGH

31A. Do you usually have a cough? (Count a cough with first smoke or on first going out of doors. Exclude clearing of throat.) (If no, skip to question 31C.)   1. Yes ___   2. No ___

B. Do you usually cough as much as 4 to 6 times a day 4 or more days out of the week?   1. Yes ___   2. No ___

C. Do you usually cough at all on getting up or first thing in the morning?   1. Yes ___   2. No ___

D. Do you usually cough at all during the   1. Yes ___   2. No ___
rest of the day or at night?

IF YES TO ANY OF ABOVE (31A, B, C, OR D), ANSWER THE FOLLOWING. IF
NO TO ALL, CHECK "DOES NOT APPLY" AND SKIP TO NEXT PAGE

E. Do you usually cough like this on most   1. Yes ___   2. No ___
days for 3 consecutive months or more   3. Does not apply   ___
during the year?

F. For how many years have you had the   Number of years ___
cough?   Does not apply   ___

32A. Do you usually bring up phlegm from   1. Yes ___   2. No ___
your chest?
Count phlegm with the first smoke or on
first going out of doors. Exclude phlegm
from the nose. Count swallowed phlegm.)
(If no, skip to 32C)

B. Do you usually bring up phlegm like this   1. Yes ___   2. No ___
as much as twice a day 4 or more days out
of the week?

C. Do you usually bring up phlegm at all on   1. Yes ___   2. No ___
getting up or first thing in the morning?

D. Do you usually bring up phlegm at all on   1. Yes ___   2. No ___
during the rest of the day or at night?

IF YES TO ANY OF THE ABOVE (32A, B, C, OR D), ANSWER THE FOLLOWING:

IF NO TO ALL, CHECK "DOES NOT APPLY" AND SKIP TO 33A

E. Do you bring up phlegm like   1. Yes ___   2. No ___
this on most days for 3   3. Does not apply   ___
consecutive months or more
during the year?

F. For how many years have you   Number of years ___
had trouble with phlegm?   Does not apply   ___

EPISODES OF COUGH AND PHLEGM

33A. Have you had periods or   1. Yes ___   2. No ___
episodes of (increased*) cough
and phlegm lasting for 3 weeks
or more each year?
*(For persons who usually have
cough and/or phlegm)

IF YES TO 33A

B. For how long have you had at   Number of years ___
least 1 such episode per year?   Does not apply ___

WHEEZING

34A. Does your chest ever sound
wheezy or whistling

   1. When you have a cold?   1. Yes ___   2. No ___

   2. Occasionally apart from colds?   1. Yes ___   2. No ___

   3. Most days or nights?   1. Yes ___   2. No ___

   B. For how many years has this   Number of years ___
been present?   Does not apply ___

35A. Have you ever had an attack of   1. Yes ___   2. No ___
wheezing that has made you
feel short of breath?

IF YES TO 35A

B. How old were you when you   Age in years ___
had your first such attack?   Does not apply ___

C. Have you had 2 or more such   1. Yes ___   2. No ___
episodes?   3. Does not apply ___

D. Have you ever required   1. Yes ___   2. No ___
medicine or treatment for   3. Does not apply ___
the(se) attack(s)?

BREATHLESSNESS

36. If disabled from walking by any
    condition other than heart or
    lung disease, please describe
    and proceed to question 38A.

Nature of condition(s)

_____

_____

37A. Are you troubled by shortness   1. Yes ___   2. No ___
     of breath when hurrying on the
     level or walking up a slight hill?

IF YES TO 37A

B. Do you have to walk slower   1. Yes ___   2. No ___
   than people of your age on the   3. Does not apply   ___
   level because of
   breathlessness?

C. Do you ever have to stop for   1. Yes ___   2. No ___
   breath when walking at your   3. Does not apply   ___
   own pace on the level?

D. Do you ever have to stop for   1. Yes ___   2. No ___
   breath after walking about 100   3. Does not apply   ___
   yards (or after a few minutes)
   on the level?

E. Are you too breathless to leave   1. Yes ___   2. No ___
   the house or breathless on   3. Does not apply   ___
   dressing or climbing one flight
   of stairs?

TOBACCO SMOKING

38A. Have you ever smoked   1. Yes ___   2. No ___
     cigarettes?
     (No means less than 20 packs
     of cigarettes or 12 oz. of
     tobacco in a lifetime or less
     than 1 cigarette a day for 1
     year.)

IF YES TO 38A

B. Do you now smoke cigarettes   1. Yes ___   2. No ___
   (as of one month ago)   3. Does not apply   ___

C. How old were you when you   Age in years   ___
first started regular cigarette   Does not apply   ___
smoking?

D. If you have stopped smoking   Age stopped   ___
cigarettes completely, how old   Check if still
were you when you stopped?   smoking   ___
                                    Does not apply   ___

E. How many cigarettes do you   Cigarettes
smoke per day now?   per day   ___
                                    Does not apply   ___

F. On the average of the entire   Cigarettes
time you smoked, how many   per day   ___
cigarettes did you smoke per   Does not apply   ___
day?

G. Do or did you inhale the   1. Does not apply   ___
cigarette smoke?   2. Not at all   ___
                                    3. Slightly   ___
                                    4. Moderately   ___
                                    5. Deeply   ___

39A. Have you ever smoked a pipe   1. Yes ___   2. No ___
regularly?
(Yes means more than 12 oz. of
tobacco in a lifetime.)

IF YES TO 39A:
FOR PERSONS WHO HAVE EVER SMOKED A PIPE

B. 1. How old were you when   Age ___
you started to smoke a pipe
regularly?

2. If you have stopped   Age stopped   ___
smoking a pipe completely,   Check if still smoking pipe ___
how old were you when   Does not apply   ___
you stopped?

C. On the average over the entire time you smoked a pipe, how much pipe tobacco did you smoke per week?

___ oz. per week (a standard pouch of tobacco contains 1 1/2 oz.)

___ Does not apply

D. How much pipe tobacco are you smoking now?

oz. per week ___
Not currently smoking a pipe ___

E. Do you or did you inhale the pipe smoke?

1. Never smoked ___
2. Not at all ___
3. Slightly ___
4. Moderately ___
5. Deeply ___

40A. Have you ever smoked cigars regularly?

1. Yes ___ 2. No ___

(Yes means more than 1 cigar a week for a year)

IF YES TO 40A

FOR PERSONS WHO HAVE EVER SMOKED A CIGAR

B. 1. How old were you when you started smoking cigars regularly?

Age ___

2. If you have stopped smoking cigars completely, how old were you when you stopped smoking cigars?

Age stopped ___
Check if still ___
Does not apply ___

C. On the average over the entire time you smoked cigars, how many cigars did you smoke per week?

Cigars per week ___
Does not apply ___

D. How many cigars are you smoking per week now?

Cigars per week ___
Check if not smoking cigars currently ___

E. Do or did you inhale the cigar smoke?

1. Never smoked ___
2. Not at all ___
3. Slightly ___
4. Moderately ___
5. Deeply ___

Signature _____   Date _____

Part 2

PERIODIC MEDICAL QUESTIONNAIRE

1. NAME _____

2. CLOCK NUMBER __ __ __ __ __ __ __

3. PRESENT OCCUPATION _____

4. PLANT _____

5. ADDRESS _____

6. _____
   (Zip Code)

7. TELEPHONE NUMBER _____

8. INTERVIEWER _____

9. DATE _____

10. What is your marital status?   1. Single   ___   4. Separated/
                                   2. Married   ___   Divorced ___
                                   3. Widowed ___

11. OCCUPATIONAL HISTORY

11A. In the past year, did you work   1. Yes ___   2. No ___
     full time (30 hours per week
     or more) for 6 months or more?

     IF YES TO 11A:

11B. In the past year, did you work   1. Yes ___   2. No ___
     in a dusty job?   3. Does not Apply ___

11C. Was dust exposure: 1. Mild ___   2. Moderate ___   3. Severe ___

11D. In the past year, were you   1. Yes ___   2. No ___
     exposed to gas or chemical
     fumes in your work?

11E. Was exposure: 1. Mild ___   2. Moderate ___   3. Severe ___

11F. In the past year,
    what was your: 1. Job/occupation? _____
                                 2. Position/job title? _____

12. RECENT MEDICAL HISTORY

12A. Do you consider yourself to
    be in good health?   Yes ___   No ___

If NO, state reason _____

12B. In the past year, have you developed:

	Yes	No
Epilepsy?	___	___
Rheumatic fever?	___	___
Kidney disease?	___	___
Bladder disease?	___	___
Diabetes?	___	___
Jaundice?	___	___
Cancer?	___	___

13. CHEST COLDS AND CHEST ILLNESSES

13A. If you get a cold, does it "usually" go to your chest? (usually means more than 1/2
    the time)
                             1. Yes ___ 2. No ___
                             3. Don't get colds ___

14A. During the past year, have you had
    any chest illnesses that have kept you   1. Yes ___ 2. No ___
    off work, indoors at home, or in bed?   3. Does Not Apply ___

    IF YES TO 14A:

14B. Did you produce phlegm with any   1. Yes ___ 2. No ___
    of these chest illnesses?   3. Does Not Apply ___

14C. In the past year, how many such   Number of illnesses ___
    illnesses with (increased) phlegm   No such illnesses   ___
    did you have which lasted a week
    or more?

15. RESPIRATORY SYSTEM

In the past year have you had:

	Yes or No	Further Comment on Positive Answers
Asthma	_____	
Bronchitis	_____	
Hay Fever	_____	
Other Allergies	_____	

	Yes or No	Further Comment on Positive Answers
Pneumonia	_____	
Tuberculosis	_____	
Chest Surgery	_____	
Other Lung Problems	_____	
Heart Disease	_____	

Do you have:

	Yes or No	Further Comment on Positive Answers
Frequent colds	_____	
Chronic cough	_____	
Shortness of breath when walking or climbing one flight or stairs	_____	

Do you:

Wheeze	_____	
Cough up phlegm	_____	
Smoke cigarettes	_____ Packs per day ____ How many years ___	

Date _____ Signature _____

APPENDIX E TO § 1910.1001—CLASSIFICATION OF CHEST X-RAYS—MANDATORY

(a) Chest X-rays shall be classified in accordance with the Guidelines for the use of the ILO International Classification of Radiographs of Pneumoconioses (revised edition 2011) (incorporated by reference, see §1910.6), and recorded on a classification form following the format of the CDC/NIOSH (M) 2.8 form. As a minimum, the content within the bold lines of this form (items 1 through 4) shall be included. This form is not to be submitted to NIOSH.

(b) All X-rays shall be classified only by a B-Reader, a board eligible/certified radiologist, or an experienced physician with known expertise in pneumoconioses.

(c) Whenever classifying chest X-ray film, the physician shall have immediately available for reference a complete set of the ILO standard format radiographs provided for use with the Guidelines for the use of the ILO International Classification of Radiographs of Pneumoconioses (revised edition 2011).

(d) Whenever classifying digitally-acquired chest X-rays, the physician shall have immediately available for reference a complete set of ILO standard digital chest radiographic images provided for use with the Guidelines for the Use of the ILO International Classification of Radiographs of Pneumoconioses (revised edition 2011). Classification of digitally-acquired chest X-rays shall be based on the viewing of images displayed as electronic copies and shall not be based on the viewing of hard copy printed transparencies of images.

*   *   *   *   *

APPENDIX H TO § 1910.1001—MEDICAL SURVEILLANCE GUIDELINES FOR ASBESTOS NON-MANDATORY

*   *   *   *   *

III. SIGNS AND SYMPTOMS OF EXPOSURE-RELATED DISEASE

The signs and symptoms of lung cancer or gastrointestinal cancer induced by exposure to asbestos are not unique, except that a chest X-ray of an exposed patient with lung cancer may show pleural plaques, pleural calcification, or pleural fibrosis, and may also show asbestosis (i.e., small irregular parenchymal opacities). Symptoms characteristic of mesothelioma include shortness of breath, pain in the chest or abdominal pain. Mesothelioma has a much longer average latency period compared with lung cancer (40 years versus 15–20 years), and mesothelioma is therefore more likely to be found among workers who were first exposed to asbestos at an early age. Mesothelioma is a fatal disease.

Asbestosis is pulmonary fibrosis caused by the accumulation of asbestos fibers in the lungs. Symptoms include shortness of breath, coughing, fatigue, and vague feelings of sickness. When the fibrosis worsens, shortness of breath occurs even at rest. The diagnosis of asbestosis is most commonly based on a history of exposure to asbestos, the presence of characteristic radiologic abnormalities, end-inspiratory crackles (rales), and other clinical features of fibrosing lung disease. Pleural plaques and thickening may be observed on chest X-rays. Asbestosis is often a progressive disease even in the absence of continued exposure, although this appears to be a highly individualized characteristic. In severe cases, death may be caused by respiratory or cardiac failure.

IV. SURVEILLANCE AND PREVENTIVE CONSIDERATIONS

As noted in section III of this appendix, exposure to asbestos has been linked to an increased risk of lung cancer, mesothelioma, gastrointestinal cancer, and asbestosis among occupationally exposed workers. Adequate screening tests to determine an employee's potential for developing serious chronic diseases, such as cancer, from exposure to asbestos do not presently exist. However, some tests, particularly chest X-rays and pulmonary function tests, may indicate that an employee has been overexposed to asbestos increasing his or her risk of developing exposure-related chronic diseases. It is important for the physician to become familiar with the operating conditions in which occupational exposure to asbestos is likely to occur. This is particularly important in evaluating medical and work histories and in conducting physical examinations. When an active employee has been identified as having been overexposed to asbestos, measures taken by the employer to eliminate or mitigate further exposure should also lower the risk of serious long-term consequences.

The employer is required to institute a medical surveillance program for all employees who are or will be exposed to asbestos at or above the permissible exposure limit (0.1 fiber per cubic centimeter of air). All examinations and procedures must be performed by or under the supervision of a licensed physician, at a reasonable time and place, and at no cost to the employee.

Although broad latitude is given to the physician in prescribing specific tests to be included in the medical surveillance program, OSHA requires inclusion of the following elements in the routine examination:

(i) Medical and work histories with special emphasis directed to symptoms of the respiratory system, cardiovascular system, and digestive tract.

(ii) Completion of the respiratory disease questionnaire contained in appendix D of this section.

(iii) A physical examination including a chest X-ray and pulmonary function test that includes measurement of the employee's forced vital capacity (FVC) and forced expiratory volume at one second (FEV$_1$).

(iv) Any laboratory or other test that the examining physician deems by sound medical practice to be necessary.

The employer is required to make the prescribed tests available at least annually to those employees covered; more often than specified if recommended by the examining physician; and upon termination of employment.

The employer is required to provide the physician with the following information: A copy of the standard in this section (including all appendices to this section); a description of the employee's duties as they relate to asbestos exposure; the employee's representative level of exposure to asbestos; a description of any personal protective and respiratory equipment used; and information from previous medical examinations of the affected employee that is not otherwise available to the physician. Making this information available to the physician will aid in the evaluation of the employee's health in relation to assigned duties and fitness to wear personal protective equipment, if required.

The employer is required to obtain a written opinion from the examining physician containing the results of the medical examination; the physician's opinion as to whether the employee has any detected medical conditions that would place the employee at an increased risk of exposure-related disease; any recommended limitations on the employee or on the use of personal protective equipment; and a statement that the employee has been informed by the physician of the results of the medical examination and of any medical conditions related to asbestos exposure that require further explanation or treatment. This written opinion must not reveal specific findings or diagnoses unrelated to exposure to asbestos, and a copy of the opinion must be provided to the affected employee.

* * * * *

§ 1910.1002 Coal tar pitch volatiles; interpretation of term.

As used in § 1910.1000 (Table Z-1), coal tar pitch volatiles include the fused polycyclic hydrocarbons which volatilize from the distillation residues of coal, petroleum (excluding asphalt), wood, and other organic matter. Asphalt (CAS 8052-42-4, and CAS 64742-93-4) is not covered under the "coal tar pitch volatiles" standard.

[48 FR 2768, Jan. 21, 1983]

§ 1910.1003 13 Carcinogens (4-Nitrobiphenyl, etc.).

(a) *Scope and application.* (1) This section applies to any area in which the 13 carcinogens addressed by this section are manufactured, processed, repackaged, released, handled, or stored, but shall not apply to transshipment in sealed containers, except for the labeling requirements under paragraphs (e)(2), (3) and (4) of this section. The 13 carcinogens are the following:

4-Nitrobiphenyl, Chemical Abstracts Service Register Number (CAS No.) 92933;
alpha-Naphthylamine, CAS No. 134327;
methyl chloromethyl ether, CAS No. 107302;
3,'-Dichlorobenzidine (and its salts) CAS No. 91941;
bis-Chloromethyl ether, CAS No. 542881;
beta-Naphthylamine, CAS No. 91598;
Benzidine, CAS No. 92875;
4-Aminodiphenyl, CAS No. 92671;
Ethyleneimine, CAS No. 151564;
beta-Propiolactone, CAS No. 57578;
2-Acetylaminofluorene, CAS No. 53963;
4-Dimethylaminoazo-benzene, CAS No. 60117; and
N-Nitrosodimethylamine, CAS No. 62759.

(2) This section shall not apply to the following:

(i) Solid or liquid mixtures containing less than 0.1 percent by weight or volume of 4–Nitrobiphenyl; methyl chloromethyl ether; bis-chloromethyl ether; beta-Naphthylamine; benzidine or 4–Aminodiphenyl; and

(ii) Solid or liquid mixtures containing less than 1.0 percent by weight or volume of alpha-Naphthylamine; 3,'-Dichlorobenzidine (and its salts); Ethyleneimine; beta-Propiolactone; 2-Acetylaminofluorene; 4-Dimethylaminoazobenzene, or N-Nitrosodimethylamine.

(b) *Definitions.* For the purposes of this section:

Absolute filter is one capable of retaining 99.97 percent of a mono disperse aerosol of 0.3 µm particles.

Authorized employee means an employee whose duties require him to be in the regulated area and who has been specifically assigned by the employer.

Clean change room means a room where employees put on clean clothing and/or protective equipment in an environment free of the 13 carcinogens addressed by this section. The clean change room shall be contiguous to and have an entry from a shower room, when the shower room facilities are otherwise required in this section.

Closed system means an operation involving a carcinogen addressed by this section where containment prevents the release of the material into regulated areas, non-regulated areas, or the external environment.

Decontamination means the inactivation of a carcinogen addressed by this section or its safe disposal.

Director means the Director, National Institute for Occupational Safety and Health, or any person directed by him or the Secretary of Health and Human Services to act for the Director.

Disposal means the safe removal of the carcinogens addressed by this section from the work environment.

Emergency means an unforeseen circumstance or set of circumstances resulting in the release of a carcinogen addressed by this section that may result in exposure to or contact with the material.

External environment means any environment external to regulated and nonregulated areas.

Isolated system means a fully enclosed structure other than the vessel of containment of a carcinogen addressed by this section that is impervious to the passage of the material and would prevent the entry of the carcinogen addressed by this section into regulated areas, nonregulated areas, or the external environment, should leakage or spillage from the vessel of containment occur.

Laboratory-type hood is a device enclosed on the three sides and the top and bottom, designed and maintained so as to draw air inward at an average linear face velocity of 150 feet per minute with a minimum of 125 feet per minute; designed, constructed, and maintained in such a way that an operation involving a carcinogen addressed by this section within the hood does not require the insertion of any portion of any employee's body other than his hands and arms.

Nonregulated area means any area under the control of the employer where entry and exit is neither restricted nor controlled.

Open-vessel system means an operation involving a carcinogen addressed by this section in an open vessel that is not in an isolated system, a laboratory-type hood, nor in any other system affording equivalent protection against the entry of the material into regulated areas, non-regulated areas, or the external environment.

Protective clothing means clothing designed to protect an employee against contact with or exposure to a carcinogen addressed by this section.

Regulated area means an area where entry and exit is restricted and controlled.

(c) *Requirements for areas containing a carcinogen addressed by this section.* A regulated area shall be established by an employer where a carcinogen addressed by this section is manufactured, processed, used, repackaged, released, handled or stored. All such areas shall be controlled in accordance with the requirements for the following category or categories describing the operation involved:

(1) *Isolated systems.* Employees working with a carcinogen addressed by this section within an isolated system such as a "glove box" shall wash their hands and arms upon completion of the assigned task and before engaging in other activities not associated with the isolated system.

(2) *Closed system operation.* (i) Within regulated areas where the carcinogens addressed by this section are stored in sealed containers, or contained in a closed system, including piping systems, with any sample ports or openings closed while the carcinogens addressed by this section are contained within, access shall be restricted to authorized employees only.

(ii) Employees exposed to 4-Nitrobiphenyl; alpha-Naphthylamine; 3,'-Dichlorobenzidine (and its salts); beta-Naphthylamine; benzidine; 4-Aminodiphenyl; 2-Acetylaminofluorene; 4-Dimethylaminoazo-benzene; and N-Nitrosodimethylamine shall be required to wash hands, forearms, face, and neck upon each exit from the regulated areas, close to the point of exit, and before engaging in other activities.

(3) *Open-vessel system operations.* Open-vessel system operations as defined in paragraph (b)(13) of this section are prohibited.

(4) *Transfer from a closed system, charging or discharging point operations, or otherwise opening a closed system.* In operations involving "laboratory-type hoods," or in locations where the carcinogens addressed by this section are contained in an otherwise "closed system," but is transferred, charged, or discharged into other normally closed containers, the provisions of this paragraph shall apply.

(i) Access shall be restricted to authorized employees only.

(ii) Each operation shall be provided with continuous local exhaust ventilation so that air movement is always from ordinary work areas to the operation. Exhaust air shall not be discharged to regulated areas, nonregulated areas or the external environment unless decontaminated. Clean makeup air shall be introduced in sufficient volume to maintain the correct operation of the local exhaust system.

(iii) Employees shall be provided with, and required to wear, clean, full body protective clothing (smocks, coveralls, or long-sleeved shirt and pants), shoe covers and gloves prior to entering the regulated area.

(iv) Employers must provide each employee engaged in handling operations involving the carcinogens 4-Nitrobiphenyl, alpha-Naphthylamine, 3,3'-Dichlorobenzidine (and its salts), beta-Naphthylamine, Benzidine, 4-Aminodiphenyl, 2-Acetylaminofluorene, 4-Dimethylaminoazo-benzene, and N-Nitrosodimethylamine, addressed by this section, with, and ensure that each of these employees wears and uses, a NIOSH-certified air-purifying, half-mask respirator with particulate filters. Employers also must provide each employee engaged in handling operations involving the carcinogens methyl chloromethyl ether, bis-Chloromethyl ether, Ethyleneimine, and beta-Propiolactone, addressed by this section, with, and ensure that each of these employees wears and uses any self-contained breathing apparatus that has a full facepiece and is operated in a pressure-demand or other positive-pressure mode, or any supplied-air respirator that has a full facepiece and is operated in a pressure-demand or other positive-pressure mode in combination with an auxiliary self-contained positive-pressure breathing apparatus. Employers may substitute a respirator affording employees higher levels of protection than these respirators.

(v) Prior to each exit from a regulated area, employees shall be required to remove and leave protective clothing and equipment at the point of exit and at the last exit of the day, to place used clothing and equipment in impervious containers at the point of exit for purposes of decontamination or disposal. The contents of such impervious containers shall be identified, as required under paragraph (e) of this section.

(vi) Drinking fountains are prohibited in the regulated area.

(vii) Employees shall be required to wash hands, forearms, face, and neck on each exit from the regulated area, close to the point of exit, and before engaging in other activities and employees exposed to 4-Nitrobiphenyl; alpha-Naphthylamine; 3,'-Dichlorobenzidine (and its salts); beta-Naphthylamine; Benzidine; 4-Aminodiphenyl; 2-Acetylaminofluorene; 4-Dimethylaminoazo-benzene; and N-Nitrosodimethylamine shall be required to shower after the last exit of the day.

(5) *Maintenance and decontamination activities.* In cleanup of leaks of spills, maintenance, or repair operations on contaminated systems or equipment, or any operations involving work in an area where direct contact with a carcinogen addressed by this section could result, each authorized employee entering that area shall:

(i) Be provided with and required to wear clean, impervious garments, including gloves, boots, and continuous-air supplied hood in accordance with §1910.134;

(ii) Be decontaminated before removing the protective garments and hood;

(iii) Be required to shower upon removing the protective garments and hood.

(d) *General regulated area requirements*—(1) *Respiratory program.* The employer must implement a respiratory protection program in accordance with §1910.134 (b), (c), (d) (except (d)(1)(iii) and (iv), and (d)(3)), and (e) through (m), which covers each employee required by this section to use a respirator.

(2) *Emergencies.* In an emergency, immediate measures including, but not limited to, the requirements of paragraphs (d)(2) (i) through (v) of this section shall be implemented.

(i) The potentially affected area shall be evacuated as soon as the emergency has been determined.

(ii) Hazardous conditions created by the emergency shall be eliminated and the potentially affected area shall be

93

decontaminated prior to the resumption of normal operations.

(iii) Special medical surveillance by a physician shall be instituted within 24 hours for employees present in the potentially affected area at the time of the emergency.

(iv) Where an employee has a known contact with a carcinogen addressed by this section, such employee shall be required to shower as soon as possible, unless contraindicated by physical injuries.

(v) Emergency deluge showers and eyewash fountains supplied with running potable water shall be located near, within sight of, and on the same level with locations where a direct exposure to Ethyleneimine or beta-Propiolactone only would be most likely as a result of equipment failure or improper work practice.

(3) *Hygiene facilities and practices.* (i) Storage or consumption of food, storage or use of containers of beverages, storage or application of cosmetics, smoking, storage of smoking materials, tobacco products or other products for chewing, or the chewing of such products are prohibited in regulated areas.

(ii) Where employees are required by this section to wash, washing facilities shall be provided in accordance with § 1910.141(d) (1) and (2) (ii) through (vii).

(iii) Where employees are required by this section to shower, shower facilities shall be provided in accordance with § 1910.141(d)(3).

(iv) Where employees wear protective clothing and equipment, clean change rooms shall be provided for the number of such employees required to change clothes, in accordance with § 1910.141(e).

(v) Where toilets are in regulated areas, such toilets shall be in a separate room.

(4) *Contamination control.* (i) Except for outdoor systems, regulated areas shall be maintained under pressure negative with respect to nonregulated areas. Local exhaust ventilation may be used to satisfy this requirement. Clean makeup air in equal volume shall replace air removed.

(ii) Any equipment, material, or other item taken into or removed from a regulated area shall be done so in a manner that does not cause contamination in nonregulated areas or the external environment.

(iii) Decontamination procedures shall be established and implemented to remove carcinogens addressed by this section from the surfaces of materials, equipment, and the decontamination facility.

(iv) Dry sweeping and dry mopping are prohibited for 4-Nitrobiphenyl; alpha-Naphthylamine; 3,'-Dichlorobenzidine (and its salts); beta-Naphthylamine; Benzidine; 4-Aminodiphenyl; 2-Acetylaminofluorene; 4-Dimethylaminoazo-benzene and N-Nitrosodimethylamine.

(e) *Communication of hazards—(1) Hazard communication.* (i) Chemical manufacturers, importers, distributors and employers shall comply with all requirements of the Hazard Communication Standard (HCS) (§ 1910.1200) for each carcinogen listed in paragraph (e)(1)(iv) of this section.

(ii) In classifying the hazards of carcinogens listed in paragraph (e)(1)(iv) of this section, at least the hazards listed in paragraph (e)(1)(iv) are to be addressed.

(iii) Employers shall include the carcinogens listed in paragraph (e)(1)(iv) of this section in the hazard communication program established to comply with the HCS (§ 1910.1200). Employers shall ensure that each employee has access to labels on containers of the carcinogens listed in paragraph (e)(1)(iv) and to safety data sheets, and is trained in accordance with the requirements of HCS and paragraph (e)(4) of this section.

(iv) List of Carcinogens:

(A) 4-Nitrobiphenyl: Cancer.

(B) alpha-Naphthylamine: Cancer; skin irritation; and acute toxicity effects.

(C) Methyl chloromethyl ether: Cancer; skin, eye and respiratory effects; acute toxicity effects; and flammability.

(D) 3,3'-Dichlorobenzidine (and its salts): Cancer and skin sensitization.

(E) bis-Chloromethyl ether: Cancer; skin, eye, and respiratory tract effects; acute toxicity effects; and flammability.

(F) beta-Naphthylamine: Cancer and acute toxicity effects.

(G) Benzidine: Cancer and acute toxicity effects.

(H) 4-Aminodiphenyl: Cancer.

(I) Ethyleneimine: Cancer; mutagenicity; skin and eye effects; liver effects; kidney effects; acute toxicity effects; and flammability.

(J) beta-Propiolactone: Cancer; skin irritation; eye effects; and acute toxicity effects.

(K) 2-Acetylaminofluorene: Cancer.

(L) 4-Dimethylaminoazo-benzene: Cancer; skin effects; and respiratory tract irritation.

(M) N-Nitrosodimethylamine: Cancer; liver effects; and acute toxicity effects.

(2) *Signs.* (i) The employer shall post entrances to regulated areas with signs bearing the legend:

DANGER
(CHEMICAL IDENTIFICATION)
MAY CAUSE CANCER
AUTHORIZED PERSONNEL ONLY

(ii) The employer shall post signs at entrances to regulated areas containing operations covered in paragraph (c)(5) of this section. The signs shall bear the legend:

DANGER
(CHEMICAL IDENTIFICATION)
MAY CAUSE CANCER
WEAR AIR-SUPPLIED HOODS, IMPERVIOUS SUITS, AND PROTECTIVE EQUIPMENT IN THIS AREA
AUTHORIZED PERSONNEL ONLY

(iii) Prior to June 1, 2016, employers may use the following legend in lieu of that specified in paragraph (e)(2)(i) of this section:

CANCER-SUSPECT AGENT
AUTHORIZED PERSONNEL ONLY

(iv) Prior to June 1, 2016, employers may use the following legend in lieu of that specified in paragraph (e)(2)(ii) of this section:

CANCER-SUSPECT AGENT EXPOSED IN THIS AREA
IMPERVIOUS SUIT INCLUDING GLOVES, BOOTS, AND AIR-SUPPLIED HOOD REQUIRED AT ALL TIMES
AUTHORIZED PERSONNEL ONLY

(v) Appropriate signs and instructions shall be posted at the entrance to, and exit from, regulated areas, informing employees of the procedures that must be followed in entering and leaving a regulated area.

(3) *Prohibited statements.* No statement shall appear on or near any required sign, label, or instruction that contradicts or detracts from the effect of any required warning, information, or instruction.

(4) *Training and indoctrination.* (i) Each employee prior to being authorized to enter a regulated area, shall receive a training and indoctrination program including, but not necessarily limited to:

(A) The nature of the carcinogenic hazards of a carcinogen addressed by this section, including local and systemic toxicity;

(B) The specific nature of the operation involving a carcinogen addressed by this section that could result in exposure;

(C) The purpose for and application of the medical surveillance program, including, as appropriate, methods of self-examination;

(D) The purpose for and application of decontamination practices and purposes;

(E) The purpose for and significance of emergency practices and procedures;

(F) The employee's specific role in emergency procedures;

(G) Specific information to aid the employee in recognition and evaluation of conditions and situations which may result in the release of a carcinogen addressed by this section;

(H) The purpose for and application of specific first aid procedures and practices;

(I) A review of this section at the employee's first training and indoctrination program and annually thereafter.

(ii) Specific emergency procedures shall be prescribed, and posted, and employees shall be familiarized with their terms, and rehearsed in their application.

(iii) All materials relating to the program shall be provided upon request to authorized representatives of the Assistant Secretary and the Director.

(f) [Reserved]

(g) *Medical surveillance.* At no cost to the employee, a program of medical surveillance shall be established and implemented for employees considered for assignment to enter regulated areas, and for authorized employees.

(1) *Examinations.* (i) Before an employee is assigned to enter a regulated area, a preassignment physical examination by a physician shall be provided. The examination shall include the personal history of the employee, family and occupational background, including genetic and environmental factors.

(ii) Authorized employees shall be provided periodic physical examinations, not less often than annually, following the preassignment examination.

(iii) In all physical examinations, the examining physician shall consider whether there exist conditions of increased risk, including reduced immunological competence, those undergoing treatment with steroids or cytotoxic agents, pregnancy, and cigarette smoking.

(2) *Records.* (i) Employers of employees examined pursuant to this paragraph shall cause to be maintained complete and accurate records of all such medical examinations. Records shall be maintained for the duration of the employee's employment.

(ii) Records required by this paragraph shall be provided upon request to employees, designated representatives, and the Assistant Secretary in accordance with 29 CFR 1910.1020 (a) through (e) and (g) through (i). These records shall also be provided upon request to the Director.

(iii) Any physician who conducts a medical examination required by this paragraph shall furnish to the employer a statement of the employee's suitability for employment in the specific exposure.

[61 FR 9242, Mar. 7, 1996, as amended at 63 FR 1286, Jan. 8, 1998; 63 FR 20099, Apr. 23, 1998; 70 FR 1141, Jan. 5, 2005; 71 FR 16672, Apr. 3, 2006; 73 FR 75584, Dec. 2, 2008; 76 FR 33608, June 8, 2011; 76 FR 80740, Dec. 27, 2011; 77 FR 17779, Mar. 26, 2012]

§1910.1004   alpha-Naphthylamine.

See §1910.1003, *13 carcinogens.*

[61 FR 9245, Mar. 7, 1996]

§1910.1005   [Reserved]

§1910.1006   Methyl chloromethyl ether.

See §1910.1003, *13 carcinogens.*

[61 FR 9245, Mar. 7, 1996]

§1910.1007   3,′-Dichlorobenzidine (and its salts).

See §1910.1003, *13 carcinogens.*

[61 FR 9245, Mar. 7, 1996]

§1910.1008   bis-Chloromethyl ether.

See §1910.1003, *13 carcinogens.*

[61 FR 9245, Mar. 7, 1996]

§1910.1009   beta-Naphthylamine.

See §1910.1003, *13 carcinogens.*

[61 FR 9245, Mar. 7, 1996]

§1910.1010   Benzidine.

See §1910.1003, *13 carcinogens.*

[61 FR 9245, Mar. 7, 1996]

§1910.1011   4-Aminodiphenyl.

See §1910.1003, *13 carcinogens.*

[61 FR 9245, Mar. 7, 1996]

§1910.1012   Ethyleneimine.

See §1910.1003, *13 carcinogens.*

[61 FR 9245, Mar. 7, 1996]

§1910.1013   beta-Propiolactone.

See §1910.1003, *13 carcinogens.*

[61 FR 9245, Mar. 7, 1996]

§1910.1014   2-Acetylaminofluorene.

See §1910.1003, *13 carcinogens.*

[61 FR 9245, Mar. 7, 1996]

§1910.1015   4-Dimethylaminoazobenzene.

See §1910.1003, *13 carcinogens.*

[61 FR 9245, Mar. 7, 1996]

§1910.1016   N-Nitrosodimethylamine.

See §1910.1003, *13 carcinogens.*

[61 FR 9245, Mar. 7, 1996]

§1910.1017   Vinyl chloride.

(a) *Scope and application.* (1) This section includes requirements for the control of employee exposure to vinyl chloride (chloroethene), Chemical Abstracts Service Registry No. 75014.

(2) This section applies to the manufacture, reaction, packaging, repackaging, storage, handling or use of vinyl chloride or polyvinyl chloride, but does

not apply to the handling or use of fabricated products made of polyvinyl chloride.

(3) This section applies to the transportation of vinyl chloride or polyvinyl chloride except to the extent that the Department of Transportation may regulate the hazards covered by this section.

(b) *Definitions*—(1) *Action level* means a concentration of vinyl chloride of 0.5 ppm averaged over an 8-hour work day.

(2) *Assistant Secretary* means the Assistant Secretary of Labor for Occupational Safety and Health, U.S. Department of Labor, or his designee.

(3) *Authorized person* means any person specifically authorized by the employer whose duties require him to enter a regulated area or any person entering such an area as a designated representative of employees for the purpose of exercising an opportunity to observe monitoring and measuring procedures.

(4) *Director* means the Director, National Institute for Occupational Safety and Health, U.S. Department of Health and Human Services, or his designee.

(5) *Emergency* means any occurrence such as, but not limited to, equipment failure, or operation of a relief device which is likely to, or does, result in massive release of vinyl chloride.

(6) *Fabricated product* means a product made wholly or partly from polyvinyl chloride, and which does not require further processing at temperatures, and for times, sufficient to cause mass melting of the polyvinyl chloride resulting in the release of vinyl chloride.

(7) *Hazardous operation* means any operation, procedure, or activity where a release of either vinyl chloride liquid or gas might be expected as a consequence of the operation or because of an accident in the operation, which would result in an employee exposure in excess of the permissible exposure limit.

(8) *OSHA Area Director* means the Director for the Occupational Safety and Health Administration Area Office having jurisdiction over the geographic area in which the employer's establishment is located.

(9) *Polyvinyl chloride* means polyvinyl chloride homopolymer or copolymer before such is converted to a fabricated product.

(10) *Vinyl chloride* means vinyl chloride monomer.

(c) *Permissible exposure limit.* (1) No employee may be exposed to vinyl chloride at concentrations greater than 1 ppm averaged over any 8-hour period, and

(2) No employee may be exposed to vinyl chloride at concentrations greater than 5 ppm averaged over any period not exceeding 15 minutes.

(3) No employee may be exposed to vinyl chloride by direct contact with liquid vinyl chloride.

(d) *Monitoring.* (1) A program of initial monitoring and measurement shall be undertaken in each establishment to determine if there is any employee exposed, without regard to the use of respirators, in excess of the action level.

(2) Where a determination conducted under paragraph (d)(1) of this section shows any employee exposures, without regard to the use of respirators, in excess of the action level, a program for determining exposures for each such employee shall be established. Such a program:

(i) Must be repeated at least quarterly for any employee exposed, without regard to the use of respirators, in excess of the permissible exposure limit.

(ii) Must be repeated not less than every 6 months for any employee exposed without regard to the use of respirators, at or above the action level.

(iii) May be discontinued for any employee only when at least two consecutive monitoring determinations, made not less than 5 working days apart, show exposures for that employee at or below the action level.

(3) Whenever there has been a production, process or control change which may result in an increase in the release of vinyl chloride, or the employer has any other reason to suspect that any employee may be exposed in excess of the action level, a determination of employee exposure under paragraph (d)(1) of this section shall be performed.

(4) The method of monitoring and measurement shall have an accuracy

97

(with a confidence level of 95 percent) of not less than plus or minus 50 percent from 0.25 through 0.5 ppm, plus or minus 35 percent from over 0.5 ppm through 1.0 ppm, and plus or minus 25 percent over 1.0 ppm. (Methods meeting these accuracy requirements are available in the "NIOSH Manual of Analytical Methods").

(5) Employees or their designated representatives shall be afforded reasonable opportunity to observe the monitoring and measuring required by this paragraph.

(e) *Regulated area.* (1) A regulated area shall be established where:

(i) Vinyl chloride or polyvinyl chloride is manufactured, reacted, repackaged, stored, handled or used; and

(ii) Vinyl chloride concentrations are in excess of the permissible exposure limit.

(2) Access to regulated areas shall be limited to authorized persons.

(f) *Methods of compliance.* Employee exposures to vinyl chloride shall be controlled to at or below the permissible exposure limit provided in paragraph (c) of this section by engineering, work practice, and personal protective controls as follows:

(1) Feasible engineering and work practice controls shall immediately be used to reduce exposures to at or below the permissible exposure limit.

(2) Wherever feasible engineering and work practice controls which can be instituted immediately are not sufficient to reduce exposures to at or below the permissible exposure limit, they shall nonetheless be used to reduce exposures to the lowest practicable level, and shall be supplemented by respiratory protection in accordance with paragraph (g) of this section. A program shall be established and implemented to reduce exposures to at or below the permissible exposure limit, or to the greatest extent feasible, solely by means of engineering and work practice controls, as soon as feasible.

(3) Written plans for such a program shall be developed and furnished upon request for examination and copying to authorized representatives of the Assistant Secretary and the Director. Such plans must be updated at least annually.

(g) *Respiratory protection*—(1) *General.* For employees who use respirators required by this section, the employer must provide each employee an appropriate respirator that complies with the requirements of this paragraph.

(2) *Respirator program.* The employer must implement a respiratory protection program in accordance § 1910.134 (b) through (d) (except (d)(1)(iii), and (d)(3)(iii)(B)(1) and (2)), and (f) through (m) which covers each employee required by this section to use a respirator.

(3) *Respirator selection.* (i) Employers must:

(A) Select, and provide to employees, the appropriate respirators specified in paragraph (d)(3)(i)(A) of 29 CFR 1910.134.

(B) Provide an organic vapor cartridge that has a service life of at least one hour when using a chemical cartridge respirator at vinyl chloride concentrations up to 10 ppm.

(C) Select a canister that has a service life of at least four hours when using a powered air-purifying respirator having a hood, helmet, or full or half facepiece, or a gas mask with a front-or back-mounted canister, at vinyl chloride concentrations up to 25 ppm.

(ii) When air-purifying respirators are used:

(A) Air-purifying canisters or cartridges must be replaced prior to the expiration of their service life or the end of the shift in which they are first used, whichever occurs first.

(B) A continuous-monitoring and alarm system must be provided when concentrations of vinyl chloride could reasonably exceed the allowable concentrations for the devices in use. Such a system must be used to alert employees when vinyl chloride concentrations exceed the allowable concentrations for the devices in use.

(h) *Hazardous operations.* (1) Employees engaged in hazardous operations, including entry of vessels to clean polyvinyl chloride residue from vessel walls, shall be provided and required to wear and use;

(i) Respiratory protection in accordance with paragraphs (c) and (g) of this section; and

(ii) Protective garments to prevent skin contact with liquid vinyl chloride or with polyvinyl chloride residue from vessel walls. The protective garments shall be selected for the operation and its possible exposure conditions.

(2) Protective garments shall be provided clean and dry for each use.

(i) *Emergency situations.* A written operational plan for emergency situations shall be developed for each facility storing, handling, or otherwise using vinyl chloride as a liquid or compressed gas. Appropriate portions of the plan shall be implemented in the event of an emergency. The plan shall specifically provide that:

(1) Employees engaged in hazardous operations or correcting situations of existing hazardous releases shall be equipped as required in paragraph (h) of this section;

(2) Other employees not so equipped shall evacuate the area and not return until conditions are controlled by the methods required in paragraph (f) of this section and the emergency is abated.

(j) *Training.* Each employee engaged in vinyl chloride or polyvinyl chloride operations shall be provided training in a program relating to the hazards of vinyl chloride and precautions for its safe use.

(1) The program shall include:

(i) The nature of the health hazard from chronic exposure to vinyl chloride including specifically the carcinogenic hazard;

(ii) The specific nature of operations which could result in exposure to vinyl chloride in excess of the permissible limit and necessary protective steps;

(iii) The purpose for, proper use, and limitations of respiratory protective devices;

(iv) The fire hazard and acute toxicity of vinyl chloride, and the necessary protective steps;

(v) The purpose for and a description of the monitoring program;

(vi) The purpose for, and a description of, the medical surveillance program;

(vii) Emergency procedures;

(viii) Specific information to aid the employee in recognition of conditions which may result in the release of vinyl chloride; and

(ix) A review of this standard at the employee's first training and indoctrination program, and annually thereafter.

(2) All materials relating to the program shall be provided upon request to the Assistant Secretary and the Director.

(k) *Medical surveillance.* A program of medical surveillance shall be instituted for each employee exposed, without regard to the use of respirators, to vinyl chloride in excess of the action level. The program shall provide each such employee with an opportunity for examinations and tests in accordance with this paragraph. All medical examinations and procedures shall be performed by or under the supervision of a licensed physician, and shall be provided without cost to the employee.

(1) At the time of initial assignment, or upon institution of medical surveillance;

(i) A general physical examination shall be performed, with specific attention to detecting enlargement of liver, spleen or kidneys, or dysfunction in these organs, and for abnormalities in skin, connective tissues and the pulmonary system (See appendix A).

(ii) A medical history shall be taken, including the following topics:

(A) Alcohol intake;

(B) Past history of hepatitis;

(C) Work history and past exposure to potential hepatotoxic agents, including drugs and chemicals;

(D) Past history of blood transfusions; and

(E) Past history of hospitalizations.

(iii) A serum specimen shall be obtained and determinations made of:

(A) Total bilirubin;

(B) Alkaline phosphatase;

(C) Serum glutamic oxalacetic transaminase (SGOT);

(D) Serum glutamic pyruvic transaminase (SGPT); and

(E) Gamma glustamyl transpeptidase.

(2) Examinations must be provided in accordance with this paragraph at least annually.

(3) Each employee exposed to an emergency shall be afforded appropriate medical surveillance.

(4) A statement of each employee's suitability for continued exposure to

vinyl chloride including use of protective equipment and respirators, shall be obtained from the examining physician promptly after any examination. A copy of the physician's statement shall be provided each employee.

(5) If any employee's health would be materially impaired by continued exposure, such employee shall be withdrawn from possible contact with vinyl chloride.

(6) Laboratory analyses for all biological specimens included in medical examination shall be performed by accredited laboratories.

(7) If the examining physician determines that alternative medical examinations to those required by paragraph (k)(1) of this section will provide at least equal assurance of detecting medical conditions pertinent to the exposure to vinyl chloride, the employer may accept such alternative examinations as meeting the requirements of paragraph (k)(1) of this section, if the employer obtains a statement from the examining physician setting forth the alternative examinations and the rationale for substitution. This statement shall be available upon request for examination and copying to authorized representatives of the Assistant Secretary and the Director.

(l) *Communication of hazards*—(1) *Hazard communication*—*general.* (i) Chemical manufacturers, importers, distributors and employers shall comply with all requirements of the Hazard Communication Standard (HCS) (§ 1910.1200) for vinyl chloride and polyvinyl chloride.

(ii) In classifying the hazards of vinyl chloride at least the following hazards are to be addressed: Cancer; central nervous system effects; liver effects; blood effects; and flammability.

(iii) Employers shall include vinyl chloride in the hazard communication program established to comply with the HCS (§ 1910.1200). Employers shall ensure that each employee has access to labels on containers of vinyl chloride and to safety data sheets, and is trained in accordance with the requirements of HCS and paragraph (j) of this section.

(2) *Signs.* (i) The employer shall post entrances to regulated areas with legible signs bearing the legend:

DANGER
VINYL CHLORIDE
MAY CAUSE CANCER
AUTHORIZED PERSONNEL ONLY

(ii) The employer shall post signs at areas containing hazardous operations or where emergencies currently exist. The signs shall be legible and bear the legend:

DANGER
VINYL CHLORIDE
MAY CAUSE CANCER
WEAR RESPIRATORY PROTECTION AND
  PROTECTIVE CLOTHING IN THIS AREA
AUTHORIZED PERSONNEL ONLY

(iii) Prior to June 1, 2016, employers may use the following legend in lieu of that specified in paragraph (l)(2)(i) of this section:

CANCER-SUSPECT AGENT AREA
AUTHORIZED PERSONNEL ONLY

(iv) Prior to June 1, 2016, employers may use the following legend in lieu of that specified in paragraph (l)(2)(ii) of this section:

CANCER-SUSPECT AGENT IN THIS AREA
PROTECTIVE EQUIPMENT REQUIRED
AUTHORIZED PERSONNEL ONLY

(3) *Labels.* (i) In addition to the other requirements in this paragraph (l), the employer shall ensure that labels for containers of polyvinyl chloride resin waste from reactors or other waste contaminated with vinyl chloride are legible and include the following information:

CONTAMINATED WITH VINYL CHLORIDE
MAY CAUSE CANCER

(ii) Prior to June 1, 2015, employers may include the following information on labels of containers of polyvinyl chloride resin waste from reactors or other waste contaminated with vinyl chloride in lieu of the labeling requirements in paragraphs (l)(3)(i) of this section:

CONTAMINATED WITH VINYL CHLORIDE
CANCER-SUSPECT AGENT

(4) Prior to June 1, 2015, employers may include the following information for containers of polyvinyl chloride in lieu of the labeling requirements in paragraphs (l)(1)(i) of this section:

POLYVINYL   CHLORIDE   (OR   TRADE
  NAME)
Contains

VINYL CHLORIDE
VINYL CHLORIDE IS A CANCER-SUSPECT
AGENT

(5)(i) Prior to June 1, 2015, employers may include either the following information in either paragraph (l)(5)(i) or (l)(5)(ii) of this section on containers of vinyl chloride in lieu of the labeling requirements in paragraph (l)(1)(i) of this section:

VINYL CHLORIDE
EXTREMELY FLAMMABLE GAS UNDER
PRESSURE
CANCER-SUSPECT AGENT

(ii) In accordance with 49 CFR Parts 170–189, with the additional legend applied near the label or placard:

CANCER-SUSPECT AGENT

(6) No statement shall appear on or near any required sign, label, or instruction which contradicts or detracts from the effect of any required warning, information, or instruction.

(m) *Records.* (1) All records maintained in accordance with this section shall include the name and social security number of each employee where relevant.

(2) Records of required monitoring and measuring and medical records shall be provided upon request to employees, designated representatives, and the Assistant Secretary in accordance with 29 CFR 1910.1020 (a) through (e) and (g) through (i). These records shall be provided upon request to the Director. Authorized personnel rosters shall also be provided upon request to the Assistant Secretary and the Director.

(i) Monitoring and measuring records shall:

(A) State the date of such monitoring and measuring and the concentrations determined and identify the instruments and methods used;

(B) Include any additional information necessary to determine individual employee exposures where such exposures are determined by means other than individual monitoring of employees; and

(C) Be maintained for not less than 30 years.

(ii) [Reserved]

(iii) Medical records shall be maintained for the duration of the employment of each employee plus 20 years, or 30 years, whichever is longer.

(n) The employer must, within 15 working days after the receipt of the results of any monitoring performed under this section, notify each affected employee of these results and the steps being taken to reduce exposures within the permissible exposure limit either individually in writing or by posting the results in an appropriate location that is accessible to affected employees.

APPENDIX A TO § 1910.1017—SUPPLEMENTARY
MEDICAL INFORMATION

When required tests under paragraph (k)(1) of this section show abnormalities, the tests should be repeated as soon as practicable, preferably within 3 to 4 weeks. If tests remain abnormal, consideration should be given to withdrawal of the employee from contact with vinyl chloride, while a more comprehensive examination is made.

Additional tests which may be useful:

A. For kidney dysfunction: urine examination for albumin, red blood cells, and exfoliative abnormal cells.

B. Pulmonary system: Forced vital capacity, Forced expiratory volume at 1 second, and chest roentgenogram (posterior-anterior, 14 × 17 inches).

C. Additional serum tests: Lactic acid dehydrogenase, lactic acid dehydrogenase isoenzyme, protein determination, and protein electrophoresis.

D. For a more comprehensive examination on repeated abnormal serum tests: Hepatitis B antigen, and liver scanning.

[39 FR 35896, Oct. 4, 1974. Redesignated at 40 FR 23072, May 28, 1975]

EDITORIAL NOTE: For FEDERAL REGISTER citations affecting § 1910.1017, see the List of CFR Sections Affected, which appears in the Finding Aids section of the printed volume and at www.govinfo.gov.

§ 1910.1018 Inorganic arsenic.

(a) *Scope and application.* This section applies to all occupational exposures to inorganic arsenic except that this section does not apply to employee exposures in agriculture or resulting from pesticide application, the treatment of wood with preservatives or the utilization of arsenically preserved wood.

(b) *Definitions. Action level* means a concentration of inorganic arsenic of 5 micrograms per cubic meter of air (5 $\mu g/m^3$) averaged over any eight (8) hour period.

Assistant Secretary means the Assistant Secretary of Labor for Occupational Safety and Health, U.S. Department of Labor, or designee.

Authorized person means any person specifically authorized by the employer whose duties require the person to enter a regulated area, or any person entering such an area as a designated representative of employees for the purpose of exercising the right to observe monitoring and measuring procedures under paragraph (e) of this section.

Director means the Director, National Institute for Occupational Safety and Health, U.S. Department of Health and Human Services, or designee.

Inorganic arsenic means copper acetoarsenite and all inorganic compounds containing arsenic except arsine, measured as arsenic (As).

(c) *Permissible exposure limit.* The employer shall assure that no employee is exposed to inorganic arsenic at concentrations greater than 10 micrograms per cubic meter of air (10 μg/m³), averaged over any 8-hour period.

(d) [Reserved]

(e) *Exposure monitoring*—(1) *General.* (i) Determinations of airborne exposure levels shall be made from air samples that are representative of each employee's exposure to inorganic arsenic over an eight (8) hour period.

(ii) For the purposes of this section, employee exposure is that exposure which would occur if the employee were not using a respirator.

(iii) The employer shall collect full shift (for at least 7 continuous hours) personal samples including at least one sample for each shift for each job classification in each work area.

(2) *Initial monitoring.* Each employer who has a workplace or work operation covered by this standard shall monitor each such workplace and work operation to accurately determine the airborne concentration of inorganic arsenic to which employees may be exposed.

(3) *Frequency.* (i) If the initial monitoring reveals employee exposure to be below the action level the measurements need not be repeated except as otherwise provided in paragraph (e)(4) of this section.

(ii) If the initial monitoring, required by this section, or subsequent monitoring reveals employee exposure to be above the permissible exposure limit, the employer shall repeat monitoring at least quarterly.

(iii) If the initial monitoring, required by this section, or subsequent monitoring reveals employee exposure to be above the action level and below the permissible exposure limit the employer shall repeat monitoring at least every six months.

(iv) The employer shall continue monitoring at the required frequency until at least two consecutive measurements, taken at least seven (7) days apart, are below the action level at which time the employer may discontinue monitoring for that employee until such time as any of the events in paragraph (e)(4) of this section occur.

(4) *Additional monitoring.* Whenever there has been a production, process, control or personal change which may result in new or additional exposure to inorganic arsenic, or whenever the employer has any other reason to suspect a change which may result in new or additional exposures to inorganic arsenic, additional monitoring which complies with paragraph (e) of this section shall be conducted.

(5) *Employee notification.* (i) The employer must, within 15 working days after the receipt of the results of any monitoring performed under this section, notify each affected employee of these results either individually in writing or by posting the results in an appropriate location that is accessible to affected employees.

(ii) Whenever the results indicate that the representative employee exposure exceeds the permissible exposure limit, the employer shall include in the written notice a statement that the permissible exposure limit was exceeded and a description of the corrective action taken to reduce exposure to or below the permissible exposure limit.

(6) *Accuracy of measurement.* (i) The employer shall use a method of monitoring and measurement which has an accuracy (with a confidence level of 95 percent) of not less than plus or minus 25 percent for concentrations of inorganic arsenic greater than or equal to 10 μg/m³.

(ii) The employer shall use a method of monitoring and measurement which has an accuracy (with confidence level of 95 percent) of not less than plus or minus 35 percent for concentrations of inorganic arsenic greater than 5 μg/m³ but less than 10 μg/m³.

(f) *Regulated area*—(1) *Establishment.* The employer shall establish regulated areas where worker exposures to inorganic arsenic, without regard to the use of respirators, are in excess of the permissible limit.

(2) *Demarcation.* Regulated areas shall be demarcated and segregated from the rest of the workplace in any manner that minimizes the number of persons who will be exposed to inorganic arsenic.

(3) *Access.* Access to regulated areas shall be limited to authorized persons or to persons otherwise authorized by the Act or regulations issued pursuant thereto to enter such areas.

(4) *Provision of respirators.* All persons entering a regulated area shall be supplied with a respirator, selected in accordance with paragraph (h)(2) of this section.

(5) *Prohibited activities.* The employer shall assure that in regulated areas, food or beverages are not consumed, smoking products, chewing tobacco and gum are not used and cosmetics are not applied, except that these activities may be conducted in the lunchrooms, change rooms and showers required under paragraph (m) of this section. Drinking water may be consumed in the regulated area.

(g) *Methods of compliance*—(1) *Controls.* (i) The employer shall institute at the earliest possible time but not later than December 31, 1979, engineering and work practice controls to reduce exposures to or below the permissible exposure limit, except to the extent that the employer can establish that such controls are not feasible.

(ii) Where engineering and work practice controls are not sufficient to reduce exposures to or below the permissible exposure limit, they shall nonetheless be used to reduce exposures to the lowest levels achievable by these controls and shall be supplemented by the use of respirators in accordance with paragraph (h) of this section and other necessary personal protective equipment. Employee rotation is not required as a control strategy before respiratory protection is instituted.

(2) *Compliance Program.* (i) The employer shall establish and implement a written program to reduce exposures to or below the permissible exposure limit by means of engineering and work practice controls.

(ii) Written plans for these compliance programs shall include at least the following:

(A) A description of each operation in which inorganic arsenic is emitted; e.g. machinery used, material processed, controls in place, crew size, operating procedures and maintenance practices;

(B) Engineering plans and studies used to determine methods selected for controlling exposure to inorganic arsenic;

(C) A report of the technology considered in meeting the permissible exposure limit;

(D) Monitoring data;

(E) A detailed schedule for implementation of the engineering controls and work practices that cannot be implemented immediately and for the adaption and implementation of any additional engineering and work practices necessary to meet the permissible exposure limit;

(F) Whenever the employer will not achieve the permissible exposure limit with engineering controls and work practices by December 31, 1979, the employer shall include in the compliance plan an analysis of the effectiveness of the various controls, shall install engineering controls and institute work practices on the quickest schedule feasible, and shall include in the compliance plan and implement a program to minimize the discomfort and maximize the effectiveness of respirator use; and

(G) Other relevant information.

(iii) Written plans for such a program shall be submitted upon request to the Assistant Secretary and the Director, and shall be available at the worksite for examination and copying by the Assistant Secretary, Director, any affected employee or authorized employee representatives.

(iv) The plans required by this paragraph must be revised and updated at

103

least annually to reflect the current status of the program.

(h) *Respiratory protection*—(1) *General.* For employees who use respirators required by this section, the employer must provide each employee an appropriate respirator that complies with the requirements of this paragraph. Respirators must be used during:

(i) Periods necessary to install or implement feasible engineering or work-practice controls.

(ii) Work operations, such as maintenance and repair activities, for which the employer establishes that engineering and work-practice controls are not feasible.

(iii) Work operations for which engineering and work-practice controls are not yet sufficient to reduce employee exposures to or below the permissible exposure limit.

(iv) Emergencies.

(2) *Respirator program.* (i) The employer must implement a respiratory protection program in accordance with § 1910.134(b) through (d) (except (d)(1)(iii)), and (f) through (m), which covers each employee required by this section to use a respirator.

(ii) If an employee exhibits breathing difficulty during fit testing or respirator use, they must be examined by a physician trained in pulmonary medicine to determine whether they can use a respirator while performing the required duty.

(3) *Respirator selection.* (i) Employers must:

(A) Select, and provide to employees, the appropriate respirators specified in paragraph (d)(3)(i)(A) of 29 CFR 1910.134.

(B) Ensure that employees do not use half mask respirators for protection against arsenic trichloride because it is absorbed rapidly through the skin.

(C) Provide HEPA filters for powered and non-powered air-purifying respirators.

(D) Select for employee use:

(*1*) Air-purifying respirators that have a combination HEPA filter with an appropriate gas-sorbent cartridge or canister when the employee's exposure exceeds the permissible exposure level for inorganic arsenic and the relevant limit for other gases.

(*2*) Front-or back-mounted gas masks equipped with HEPA filters and acid gas canisters or any full facepiece supplied-air respirators when the inorganic arsenic concentration is at or below 500 mg/m³; and half mask air-purifying respirators equipped with HEPA filters and acid gas cartridges when the inorganic arsenic concentration is at or below 100 µg/m³.

(ii) Employees required to use respirators may choose, and the employer must provide, a powered air-purifying respirator if it will provide proper protection. In addition, the employer must provide a combination dust and acid-gas respirator to employees who are exposed to gases over the relevant exposure limits.

(i) [Reserved]

(j) *Protective work clothing and equipment*—(1) *Provision and use.* Where the possibility of skin or eye irritation from inorganic arsenic exists, and for all workers working in regulated areas, the employer shall provide at no cost to the employee and assure that employees use appropriate and clean protective work clothing and equipment such as, but not limited to:

(i) Coveralls or similar full-body work clothing;

(ii) Gloves, and shoes or coverlets;

(iii) Face shields or vented goggles when necessary to prevent eye irritation, which comply with the requirements of § 1910.133(a) (2)–(6); and

(iv) Impervious clothing for employees subject to exposure to arsenic trichloride.

(2) *Cleaning and replacement.* (i) The employer shall provide the protective clothing required in paragraph (j) (1) of this section in a freshly laundered and dry condition at least weekly, and daily if the employee works in areas where exposures are over 100 µg/m³ of inorganic arsenic or in areas where more frequent washing is needed to prevent skin irritation.

(ii) The employer shall clean, launder, or dispose of protective clothing required by paragraph (j) (1) of this section.

(iii) The employer shall repair or replace the protective clothing and equipment as needed to maintain their effectiveness.

(iv) The employer shall assure that all protective clothing is removed at the completion of a work shift only in change rooms prescribed in paragraph (m) (1) of this section.

(v) The employer shall assure that contaminated protective clothing which is to be cleaned, laundered, or disposed of, is placed in a closed container in the change-room which prevents dispersion of inorganic arsenic outside the container.

(vi) The employer shall inform in writing any person who cleans or launders clothing required by this section, of the potentially harmful effects including the carcinogenic effects of exposure to inorganic arsenic.

(vii) Labels on contaminated protective clothing and equipment.

(A) The employer shall ensure that the containers of contaminated protective clothing and equipment in the workplace or which are to be removed from the workplace are labeled and that the labels include the following information:

DANGER: CONTAMINATED WITH INORGANIC ARSENIC. MAY CAUSE CANCER. DO NOT REMOVE DUST BY BLOWING OR SHAKING. DISPOSE OF INORGANIC ARSENIC CONTAMINATED WASH WATER IN ACCORDANCE WITH APPLICABLE LOCAL, STATE OR FEDERAL REGULATIONS.

(B) Prior to June 1, 2015, employers may include the following information on containers of protective clothing and equipment in lieu of the labeling requirements in paragraphs (j)(2)(vii) of this section:

CAUTION: Clothing contaminated with inorganic arsenic; do not remove dust by blowing or shaking. Dispose of inorganic arsenic contaminated wash water in accordance with applicable local, State or Federal regulations.

(viii) The employer shall prohibit the removal of inorganic arsenic from protective clothing or equipment by blowing or shaking.

(k) *Housekeeping*—(1) *Surfaces.* All surfaces shall be maintained as free as practicable of accumulations of inorganic arsenic.

(2) *Cleaning floors.* Floors and other accessible surfaces contaminated with inorganic arsenic may not be cleaned by the use of compressed air, and shoveling and brushing may be used only where vacuuming or other relevant methods have been tried and found not to be effective.

(3) *Vacuuming.* Where vacuuming methods are selected, the vacuums shall be used and emptied in a manner to minimize the reentry of inorganic arsenic into the workplace.

(4) *Housekeeping plan.* A written housekeeping and maintenance plan shall be kept which shall list appropriate frequencies for carrying out housekeeping operations, and for cleaning and maintaining dust collection equipment. The plan shall be available for inspection by the Assistant Secretary.

(5) *Maintenance of equipment.* Periodic cleaning of dust collection and ventilation equipment and checks of their effectiveness shall be carried out to maintain the effectiveness of the system and a notation kept of the last check of effectiveness and cleaning or maintenance.

(l) [Reserved]

(m) *Hygiene facilities and practices*—(1) *Change rooms.* The employer shall provide for employees working in regulated areas or subject to the possibility of skin or eye irritation from inorganic arsenic, clean change rooms equipped with storage facilities for street clothes and separate storage facilities for protective clothing and equipment in accordance with 29 CFR 1910.141(e).

(2) *Showers.* (i) The employer shall assure that employees working in regulated areas or subject to the possibility of skin or eye irritation from inorganic arsenic shower at the end of the work shift.

(ii) The employer shall provide shower facilities in accordance with §1910.141(d)(3).

(3) *Lunchrooms.* (i) The employer shall provide for employees working in regulated areas, lunchroom facilities which have a temperature controlled, positive pressure, filtered air supply, and which are readily accessible to employees working in regulated areas.

(ii) The employer shall assure that employees working in the regulated area or subject to the possibility of skin or eye irritation from exposure to inorganic arsenic wash their hands and face prior to eating.

(4) *Lavatories*. The employer shall provide lavatory facilities which comply with § 1910.141(d) (1) and (2).

(5) *Vacuuming clothes*. The employer shall provide facilities for employees working in areas where exposure, without regard to the use of respirators, exceeds 100 μg/m³ to vacuum their protective clothing and clean or change shoes worn in such areas before entering change rooms, lunchrooms or shower rooms required by paragraph (j) of this section and shall assure that such employees use such facilities.

(6) *Avoidance of skin irritation*. The employer shall assure that no employee is exposed to skin or eye contact with arsenic trichloride, or to skin or eye contact with liquid or particulate inorganic arsenic which is likely to cause skin or eye irritation.

(n) *Medical surveillance—(1) General—(i) Employees covered*. The employer shall institute a medical surveillance program for the following employees:

(A) All employees who are or will be exposed above the action level, without regard to the use of respirators, at least 30 days per year; and

(B) All employees who have been exposed above the action level, without regard to respirator use, for 30 days or more per year for a total of 10 years or more of combined employment with the employer or predecessor employers prior to or after the effective date of this standard. The determination of exposures prior to the effective date of this standard shall be based upon prior exposure records, comparison with the first measurements taken after the effective date of this standard, or comparison with records of exposures in areas with similar processes, extent of engineering controls utilized and materials used by that employer.

(ii) *Examination by physician*. The employer shall assure that all medical examinations and procedures are performed by or under the supervision of a licensed physician, and shall be provided without cost to the employee, without loss of pay and at a reasonable time and place.

(2) *Initial examinations*. By December 1, 1978, for employees initially covered by the medical provisions of this section, or thereafter at the time of initial assignment to an area where the employee is likely to be exposed over the action level at least 30 days per year, the employer shall provide each affected employee an opportunity for a medical examination, including at least the following elements:

(i) A work history and a medical history which shall include a smoking history and the presence and degree of respiratory symptoms such as breathlessness, cough, sputum production and wheezing.

(ii) A medical examination which shall include at least the following:

(A) A standard posterior-anterior chest x-ray;

(B) A nasal and skin examination; and

(C) Other examinations which the physician believes appropriate because of the employees exposure to inorganic arsenic or because of required respirator use.

(3) *Periodic examinations*. (i) Examinations must be provided in accordance with this paragraph at least annually.

(ii) Whenever a covered employee has not taken the examinations specified in paragraphs (n)(2)(i) and (n)(2)(ii) of this section within six (6) months preceding the termination of employment, the employer shall provide such examinations to the employee upon termination of employment.

(4) *Additional examinations*. If the employee for any reason develops signs or symptoms commonly associated with exposure to inorganic arsenic the employer shall provide an appropriate examination and emergency medical treatment.

(5) *Information provided to the physician*. The employer shall provide the following information to the examining physician:

(i) A copy of this standard and its appendices;

(ii) A description of the affected employee's duties as they relate to the employee's exposure;

(iii) The employee's representative exposure level or anticipated exposure level;

(iv) A description of any personal protective equipment used or to be used; and

(v) Information from previous medical examinations of the affected employee which is not readily available to the examining physician.

(6) *Physician's written opinion.* (i) The employer shall obtain a written opinion from the examining physician which shall include:

(A) The results of the medical examination and tests performed;

(B) The physician's opinion as to whether the employee has any detected medical conditions which would place the employee at increased risk of material impairment of the employee's health from exposure to inorganic arsenic;

(C) Any recommended limitations upon the employee's exposure to inorganic arsenic or upon the use of protective clothing or equipment such as respirators; and

(D) A statement that the employee has been informed by the physician of the results of the medical examination and any medical conditions which require further explanation or treatment.

(ii) The employer shall instruct the physician not to reveal in the written opinion specific findings or diagnoses unrelated to occupational exposure.

(iii) The employer shall provide a copy of the written opinion to the affected employee.

(o) *Employee information and training*—(1) *Training program.* (i) The employer shall train each employee who is subject to exposure to inorganic arsenic above the action level without regard to respirator use, or for whom there is the possibility of skin or eye irritation from inorganic arsenic, in accordance with the requirements of this section. The employer shall institute a training program and ensure employee participation in the program.

(ii) The training program shall be provided by October 1, 1978, for employees covered by this provision, at the time of initial assignment for those subsequently covered by this provision, and at least annually for other covered employees thereafter; and the employer shall assure that each employee is informed of the following:

(A) The information contained in appendix A;

(B) The quantity, location, manner of use, storage, sources of exposure, and the specific nature of operations which could result in exposure to inorganic arsenic as well as any necessary protective steps;

(C) The purpose, proper use, and limitation of respirators;

(D) The purpose and a description of the medical surveillance program as required by paragraph (n) of this section;

(E) The engineering controls and work practices associated with the employee's job assignment; and

(F) A review of this standard.

(2) *Access to training materials.* (i) The employer shall make readily available to all affected employees a copy of this standard and its appendices.

(ii) The employer shall provide; upon request, all materials relating to the employee information and training program to the Assistant Secretary and the Director.

(p) *Communication of hazards*—(1) *Hazard communication—General.* (i) Chemical manufacturers, importers, distributors and employers shall comply with all requirements of the Hazard Communication Standard (HCS) (§1910.1200) for inorganic arsenic.

(ii) In classifying the hazards of inorganic arsenic at least the following hazards are to be addressed: Cancer; liver effects; skin effects; respiratory irritation; nervous system effects; and acute toxicity effects.

(iii) Employers shall include inorganic arsenic in the hazard communication program established to comply with the HCS (§1910.1200). Employers shall ensure that each employee has access to labels on containers of inorganic arsenic and to safety data sheets, and is trained in accordance with the requirements of HCS and paragraph (o) of this section.

(iv) The employer shall ensure that no statement appears on or near any sign or label required by this paragraph (p) which contradicts or detracts from the meaning of the required sign or label.

(2) *Signs.* (i) The employer shall post signs demarcating regulated areas bearing the legend:

DANGER
INORGANIC ARSENIC
MAY CAUSE CANCER
DO NOT EAT, DRINK OR SMOKE

WEAR RESPIRATORY PROTECTION IN THIS AREA
AUTHORIZED PERSONNEL ONLY

(ii) Prior to June 1, 2016, employers may use the following legend in lieu of that specified in paragraph (p)(2)(i) of this section:

DANGER
INORGANIC ARSENIC
CANCER HAZARD
AUTHORIZED PERSONNEL ONLY
NO SMOKING OR EATING
RESPIRATOR REQUIRED

(iii) The employer shall ensure that signs required by this paragraph (p) are illuminated and cleaned as necessary so that the legend is readily visible.

(3)(i) Prior to June 1, 2015, in lieu of the labeling requirements in paragraphs (p)(1)(i) of this section, employers may apply precautionary labels to all shipping and storage containers of inorganic arsenic, and to all products containing inorganic arsenic, bearing the following legend:

DANGER
CONTAINS INORGANIC ARSENIC
CANCER HAZARD
HARMFUL IF INHALED OR SWALLOWED
USE ONLY WITH ADEQUATE VENTILA-
TION OR RESPIRATORY PROTECTION

(ii) Labels are not required when the inorganic arsenic in the product is bound in such a manner so as to make unlikely the possibility of airborne exposure to inorganic arsenic. (Possible examples of products not requiring labels are semiconductors, light emitting diodes and glass.)

(q) *Recordkeeping*—(1) *Exposure monitoring.* (i) The employer shall establish and maintain an accurate record of all monitoring required by paragraph (e) of this section.

(ii) This record shall include:

(A) The date(s), number, duration location, and results of each of the samples taken, including a description of the sampling procedure used to determine representative employee exposure where applicable;

(B) A description of the sampling and analytical methods used and evidence of their accuracy;

(C) The type of respiratory protective devices worn, if any;

(D) Name, social security number, and job classification of the employees monitored and of all other employees whose exposure the measurement is intended to represent; and

(E) The environmental variables that could affect the measurement of the employee's exposure.

(iii) The employer shall maintain these monitoring records for at least 40 years or for the duration of employment plus 20 years, whichever, is longer.

(2) *Medical surveillance.* (i) The employer shall establish and maintain an accurate record for each employee subject to medical surveillance as required by paragraph (n) of this section.

(ii) This record shall include:

(A) The name, social security number, and description of duties of the employee;

(B) A copy of the physician's written opinions;

(C) Results of any exposure monitoring done for that employee and the representative exposure levels supplied to the physician; and

(D) Any employee medical complaints related to exposure to inorganic arsenic.

(iii) The employer shall in addition keep, or assure that the examining physician keeps, the following medical records;

(A) A copy of the medical examination results including medical and work history required under paragraph (n) of this section;

(B) A description of the laboratory procedures and a copy of any standards or guidelines used to interpret the test results or references to that information;

(C) The initial X-ray;

(D) The X-rays for the most recent 5 years; and

(E) Any X-rays with a demonstrated abnormality and all subsequent X-rays;

(iv) The employer shall maintain or assure that the physician maintains those medical records for at least 40 years, or for the duration of employment plus 20 years whichever is longer.

(3) *Availability.* (i) The employer shall make available upon request all records required to be maintained by paragraph (q) of this section to the Assistant Secretary and the Director for examination and copying.

(ii) Records required by this paragraph shall be provided upon request to employees, designated representatives, and the Assistant Secretary in accordance with 29 CFR 1910.1020 (a) through (e) and (g) through (i).

(4) *Transfer of records.* (i) Whenever the employer ceases to do business, the successor employer shall receive and retain all records required to be maintained by this section.

(ii) The employer shall also comply with any additional requirements involving the transfer of records set in 29 CFR 1910.1020(h).

(r) *Observation of monitoring*—(1) *Employee observation.* The employer shall provide affected employees or their designated representatives an opportunity to observe any monitoring of employee exposure to inorganic arsenic conducted pursuant to paragraph (e) of this section.

(2) *Observation procedures.* (i) Whenever observation of the monitoring of employee exposure to inorganic arsenic requires entry into an area where the use of respirators, protective clothing, or equipment is required, the employer shall provide the observer with and assure the use of such respirators, clothing, and such equipment, and shall require the observer to comply with all other applicable safety and health procedures.

(ii) Without interfering with the monitoring, observers shall be entitled to;

(A) Receive an explanation of the measurement procedures;

(B) Observe all steps related to the monitoring of inorganic arsenic performed at the place of exposure; and

(C) Record the results obtained or receive copies of the results when returned by the laboratory.

(s) *Appendices.* The information contained in the appendices to this section is not intended by itself, to create any additional obligations not otherwise imposed by this standard nor detract from any existing obligation.

APPENDIX A TO § 1910.1018—INORGANIC ARSENIC SUBSTANCE INFORMATION SHEET

I. SUBSTANCE IDENTIFICATION

A. *Substance.* Inorganic Arsenic.

B. *Definition.* Copper acetoarsenite, arsenic and all inorganic compounds containing arsenic except arsine, measured as arsenic (As).

C. *Permissible Exposure Limit.* 10 micrograms per cubic meter of air as determined as an average over an 8-hour period. No employee may be exposed to any skin or eye contact with arsenic trichloride or to skin or eye contact likely to cause skin or eye irritation.

D. *Regulated Areas.* Only employees authorized by your employer should enter a regulated area.

II. HEALTH HAZARD DATA

A. *Comments.* The health hazard of inorganic arsenic is high.

B. *Ways in which the chemical affects your body.* Exposure to airborne concentrations of inorganic arsenic may cause lung cancer, and can be a skin irritant. Inorganic arsenic may also affect your body if swallowed. One compound in particular, arsenic trichloride, is especially dangerous because it can be absorbed readily through the skin. Because inorganic arsenic is a poison, you should wash your hands thoroughly prior to eating or smoking.

III. PROTECTIVE CLOTHING AND EQUIPMENT

A. *Respirators.* Respirators will be provided by your employer at no cost to you for routine use if your employer is in the process of implementing engineering and work practice controls or where engineering and work practice controls are not feasible or insufficient. You must wear respirators for nonroutine activities or in emergency situations where you are likely to be exposed to levels of inorganic arsenic in excess of the permissible exposure limit. Since how well your respirator fits your face is very important, your employer is required to conduct fit tests to make sure the respirator seals properly when you wear it. These tests are simple and rapid and will be explained to you during training sessions.

B. *Protective clothing.* If you work in a regulated area, your employer is required to provide at no cost to you, and you must wear, appropriate, clean, protective clothing and equipment. The purpose of this equipment is to prevent you from bringing to your home arsenic-contaminated dust and to protect your body from repeated skin contact with inorganic arsenic likely to cause skin irritation. This clothing should include such items as coveralls or similar full-body clothing, gloves, shoes or coverlets, and aprons. Protective equipment should include face shields or vented goggles, where eye irritation may occur. y

IV. HYGIENE FACILITIES AND PRACTICES

You must not eat, drink, smoke, chew gum or tobacco, or apply cosmetics in the regulated area, except that drinking water is permitted. If you work in a regulated area your employer is required to provide lunchrooms and other areas for these purposes.

If you work in a regulated area, your employer is required to provide showers, washing facilities, and change rooms. You must wash your face, and hands before eating and must shower at the end of the work shift. Do not take used protective clothing out of change rooms without your employer's permission. Your employer is required to provide for laundering or cleaning of your protective clothing.

V. SIGNS AND LABELS

Your employer is required to post warning signs and labels for your protection. Signs must be posted in regulated areas. The signs must warn that a cancer hazard is present, that only authorized employees may enter the area, and that no smoking or eating is allowed, and that respirators must be worn.

VI. MEDICAL EXAMINATIONS

If your exposure to arsenic is over the Action Level (5 μg/m³)—(including all persons working in regulated areas) at least 30 days per year, or you have been exposed to arsenic for more than 10 years over the Action Level, your employer is required to provide you with a medical examination. The examination shall be every 6 months for employees over 45 years old or with more than 10 years exposure over the Action Level and annually for other covered employees. The medical examination must include a medical history; a chest x-ray; a skin examination and a nasal examination. The examining physician will provide a written opinion to your employer containing the results of your medical exams. You should also receive a copy of this opinion. The physician must not tell your employer any conditions he detects unrelated to occupational exposure to arsenic but must tell you those conditions.

VII. OBSERVATION OF MONITORING

Your employer is required to monitor your exposure to arsenic and you or your representatives are entitled to observe the monitoring procedure. You are entitled to receive an explanation of the measurement procedure, and to record the results obtained. When the monitoring procedure is taking place in an area where respirators or personal protective clothing and equipment are required to be worn, you must also be provided with and must wear the protective clothing and equipment.

VIII. ACCESS TO RECORDS

You or your representative are entitled to records of your exposure to inorganic arsenic and your medical examination records if you request your employer to provide them.

IX. TRAINING AND NOTIFICATION

Additional information on all of these items plus training as to hazards of exposure to inorganic arsenic and the engineering and work practice controls associated with your job will also be provided by your employer. If you are exposed over the permissible exposure limit, your employer must inform you of that fact and the actions he is taking to reduce your exposures.

APPENDIX B TO § 1910.1018—SUBSTANCE TECHNICAL GUIDELINES

ARSENIC, ARSENIC TRIOXIDE, ARSENIC TRICHLORIDE (THREE EXAMPLES)

I. Physical and chemical properties

A. Arsenic (metal).
1. Formula: As.
2. Appearance: Gray metal.
3. Melting point: Sublimes without melting at 613C.
4. Specific Gravity: (H20 = 1):5.73.
5. Solubility in water: Insoluble.
B. Arsenic Trioxide.
1. Formula: As203, (As406).
2. Appearance: White powder.
3. Melting point: 315C.
4. Specific Gravity (H20 = 1):3.74.
5. Solubility in water: 3.7 grams in 100cc of water at 20c.
C. Arsenic Trichloride (liquid).
1. Formula: AsCl3.
2. Appearance: Colorless or pale yellow liquid.
3. Melting point: −8.5C.
4. Boiling point: 130.2C.
5. Specific Gravity (H20 = 1):2.16 at 20C.
6. Vapor Pressure: 10mm Hg at 23.5C.
7. Solubility in Water: Decomposes in water.

II. Fire, explosion and reactivity data.

A. Fire: Arsenic, arsenic Trioxide and Arsenic Trichloride are nonflammable.
B. Reactivity:
1. Conditions Contributing to instability: Heat.
2. Incompatibility: Hydrogen gas can react with inorganic arsenic to form the highly toxic gas arsine.

III. Monitoring and Measurement Procedures

Samples collected should be full shift (at least 7-hour) samples. Sampling should be done using a personal sampling pump at a flow rate of 2 liters per minute. Samples should be collected on 0.8 micrometer pore size membrane filter (37mm diameter). Volatile arsenicals such as arsenic trichloride can be most easily collected in a midget bubbler filled with 15 ml. of 0.1 N NaOH.

The method of sampling and analysis should have an accuracy of not less than ±25 percent (with a confidence limit of 95 percent) for 10 micrograms per cubic meter of air (10 µg/m³) and ±35 percent (with a confidence limit of 95 percent) for concentrations of inorganic arsenic between 5 and 10 µg/m³.

APPENDIX C TO § 1910.1018—MEDICAL
SURVEILLANCE GUIDELINES

I. GENERAL

Medical examinations are to be provided for all employees exposed to levels of inorganic arsenic above the action level (5 µg/m³) for at least 30 days per year (which would include among others, all employees who work in regulated areas). Examinations are also to be provided to all employees who have had 10 years or more exposure above the action level for more than 30 days per year while working for the present or predecessor employer though they may no longer be exposed above the level.

An initial medical examination is to be provided to all such employees by December 1, 1978. In addition, an initial medical examination is to be provided to all employees who are first assigned to areas in which worker exposure will probably exceed 5 µg/m³ (after the effective date of this standard) at the time of initial assignment. In addition to its immediate diagnostic usefulness, the initial examination will provide a baseline for comparing future test results. The initial examination must include as a minimum the following elements:

(1) A work and medical history, including a smoking history, and presence and degree of respiratory symptoms such as breathlessness, cough, sputum production, and wheezing;

(2) A 14″ by 17″ posterior-anterior chest X-ray;

(3) A nasal and skin examination; and

(4) Other examinations which the physician believes appropriate because of the employee's exposure to inorganic arsenic or because of required respirator use.

Periodic examinations are also to be provided to the employees listed above. The periodic examinations shall be given annually for those covered employees 45 years of age or less with fewer than 10 years employment in areas where employee exposure exceeds the action level (5 µg/m³). Periodic examinations need not include sputum cytology and only an updated medical history is required.

Periodic examinations for other covered employees, shall be provided every six (6) months. These examinations shall include all tests required in the initial examination, except that the medical history need only be updated.

The examination contents are minimum requirements. Additional tests such as lateral and oblique X-rays or pulmonary function tests may be useful. For workers exposed to three arsenicals which are associated with lymphatic cancer, copper acetoarsenite, potassium arsenite, or sodium arsenite the examination should also include palpation of superficial lymph nodes and complete blood count.

II. NONCARCINOGENIC EFFECTS

The OSHA standard is based on minimizing risk of exposed workers dying of lung cancer from exposure to inorganic arsenic. It will also minimize skin cancer from such exposures.

The following three sections quoted from "Occupational Diseases: A Guide to Their Recognition", Revised Edition, June 1977, National Institute for Occupational Safety and Health is included to provide information on the nonneoplastic effects of exposure to inorganic arsenic. Such effects should not occur if the OSHA standards are followed.

A. *Local*—Trivalent arsenic compounds are corrosive to the skin. Brief contact has no effect but prolonged contact results in a local hyperemia and later vesicular or pustular eruption. The moist mucous membranes are most sensitive to the irritant action. Conjunctiva, moist and macerated areas of skin, the eyelids, the angles of the ears, nose, mouth, and respiratory mucosa are also vulnerable to the irritant effects. The wrists are common sites of dermatitis, as are the genitalia if personal hygiene is poor. Perforations of the nasal septum may occur. Arsenic trioxide and pentoxide are capable of producing skin sensitization and contact dermatitis. Arsenic is also capable of producing keratoses, especially of the palms and soles.

B. *Systemic*—The acute toxic effects of arsenic are generally seen following ingestion of inorganic arsenical compounds. This rarely occurs in an industrial setting. Symptoms develop within ½ to 4 hours following ingestion and are usually characterized by constriction of the throat followed by dysphagia, epigastric pain, vomiting, and watery diarrhea. Blood may appear in vomitus and stools. If the amount ingested is sufficiently high, shock may develop due to severe fluid loss, and death may ensue in 24 hours. If the acute effects are survived, exfoliative dermatitis and peripheral neuritis may develop.

Cases of acute arsenical poisoning due to inhalation are exceedingly rare in industry. When it does occur, respiratory tract symptoms—cough, chest pain, dyspnea—giddiness, headache, and extreme general weakness precede gastrointestinal symptoms. The acute toxic symptoms of trivalent arsenical poisoning are due to severe inflammation of the mucous membranes and greatly increased permeability of the blood capillaries.

Chronic arsenical poisoning due to ingestion is rare and generally confined to patients taking prescribed medications. However, it can be a concomitant of inhaled inorganic arsenic from swallowed sputum and improper eating habits. Symptoms are weight loss, nausea and diarrhea alternating with constipation, pigmentation and eruption of the skin, loss of hair, and peripheral neuritis. Chronic hepatitis and cirrhosis have been described. Polyneuritis may be the salient feature, but more frequently there are numbness and parasthenias of "glove and stocking" distribution. The skin lesions are usually melanotic and keratotic and may occasionally take the form of an intradermal cancer of the squamous cell type, but without infiltrative properties. Horizontal white lines (striations) on the fingernails and toenails are commonly seen in chronic arsenical poisoning and are considered to be a diagnostic accompaniment of arsenical polyneuritis.

Inhalation of inorganic arsenic compounds is the most common cause of chronic poisoning in the industrial situation. This condition is divided into three phases based on signs and symptoms.

First Phase: The worker complains of weakness, loss of appetite, some nausea, occasional vomiting, a sense of heaviness in the stomach, and some diarrhea.

Second Phase: The worker complains of conjunctivitis, a catarrhal state of the mucous membranes of the nose, larynx, and respiratory passage. Coryza, hoarseness, and mild tracheobronchitis may occur. Perforation of the nasal septum is common, and is probably the most typical lesion of the upper respiratory tract in occupational exposure to arsenical dust. Skin lesions, eczematoid and allergic in type, are common.

Third Phase: The worker complains of symptoms of peripheral neuritis, initially of hands and feet, which is essentially sensory. In more severe cases, motor paralyses occur; the first muscles affected are usually the toe extensors and the peronei. In only the most severe cases will paralysis of flexor muscles of the feet or of the extensor muscles of hands occur.

Liver damage from chronic arsenical poisoning is still debated, and as yet the question is unanswered. In cases of chronic and acute arsenical poisoning, toxic effects to the myocardium have been reported based on EKG changes. These findings, however, are now largely discounted and the EKG changes are ascribed to electrolyte disturbances concomitant with arsenicalism. Inhalation of arsenic trioxide and other inorganic arsenical dusts does not give rise to radiological evidence or pneumoconiosis. Arsenic does have a depressant effect upon the bone marrow, with disturbances of both erythropoiesis and myelopoiesis.

BIBLIOGRAPHY

Dinman, B. D. 1960. Arsenic; chronic human intoxication. J. Occup. Med. 2:137.

Elkins, H. B. 1959. The Chemistry of Industrial Toxicology, 2nd ed. John Wiley and Sons, New York.

Holmquist, L. 1951. Occupational arsenical dermatitis; a study among employees at a copper-ore smelting works including investigations of skin reactions to contact with arsenic compounds. Acta. Derm. Venereol. (Supp. 26) 31:1.

Pinto, S. S., and C. M. McGill. 1953. Arsenic trioxide exposure in industry. Ind. Med. Surg. 22:281.

Pinto, S. S., and K. W. Nelson. 1976. Arsenic toxicology and industrial exposure. Annu. Rev. Pharmacol. Toxicol. 16:95.

Vallee, B. L., D. D. Ulmer, and W. E. C. Wacker. 1960. Arsenic toxicology and biochemistry. AMA Arch. Indust. Health 21:132.

[39 FR 23502, June 27, 1974, as amended at 43 FR 19624, May 5, 1978; 43 FR 28472, June 30, 1978; 45 FR 35282, May 23, 1980; 54 FR 24334, June 7, 1989; 58 FR 35310, June 30, 1993; 61 FR 5508, Feb. 13, 1996; 61 FR 9245, Mar. 7, 1996; 63 FR 1286, Jan. 8, 1998; 63 FR 33468, June 18, 1998; 70 FR 1141, Jan. 5, 2005; 71 FR 16672, 16673, Apr. 3, 2006; 71 FR 50189, Aug. 24, 2006; 73 FR 75585, Dec. 12, 2008; 76 FR 33608, June 8, 2011; 77 FR 17780, Mar. 26, 2012]

EFFECTIVE DATE NOTE: At 84 FR 21476, May 14, 2019, § 1910.1018 was amended by revising paragraphs (n)(2)(ii)(A) and (n)(3)(i) and (ii), appendix A, section VI, and appendix C, section I, effective July 15, 2019. For the convenience of the user, the revised text is set forth as follows:

§ 1910.1018 Inorganic arsenic.

*   *   *   *   *

(n) * * *
(2) * * *
(ii) * * *
(A) A standard film or digital posterior-anterior chest X-ray;

*   *   *   *   *

(3) * * *
(i) Examinations must be provided in accordance with paragraphs (n)(2)(i) and (n)(2)(ii)(B) and (C) of this section at least annually.
(ii) Whenever a covered employee has not taken the examinations specified in paragraphs (n)(2)(i) and (n)(2)(ii)(B) and (C) of this section within six (6) months preceding the termination of employment, the employer shall provide such examinations to

the employee upon termination of employment.

*   *   *   *   *

APPENDIX A TO § 1910.1018—INORGANIC
ARSENIC SUBSTANCE INFORMATION SHEET

*   *   *   *   *

VI. MEDICAL EXAMINATIONS

If your exposure to arsenic is over the Action Level (5 µg/m3)—(including all persons working in regulated areas) at least 30 days per year, or you have been exposed to arsenic for more than 10 years over the Action Level, your employer is required to provide you with a medical examination. The examination shall be every 6 months for employees over 45 years old or with more than 10 years exposure over the Action Level and annually for other covered employees. The medical examination must include a medical history; a chest X-ray (during initial examination only); skin examination and a nasal examination. The examining physician will provide a written opinion to your employer containing the results of the medical exams. You should also receive a copy of this opinion. The physician must not tell your employer any conditions he detects unrelated to occupational exposure to arsenic but must tell you those conditions.

*   *   *   *   *

APPENDIX C TO § 1910.1018—MEDICAL
SURVEILLANCE GUIDELINES

I. GENERAL

Medical examinations are to be provided for all employees exposed to levels of inorganic arsenic above the action level (5 µg/m3) for at least 30 days per year (which would include among others, all employees, who work in regulated areas). Examinations are also to be provided to all employees who have had 10 years or more exposure above the action level for more than 30 days per year while working for the present or predecessor employer though they may no longer be exposed above the level.

An initial medical examination is to be provided to all such employees by December 1, 1978. In addition, an initial medical examination is to be provided to all employees who are first assigned to areas in which worker exposure will probably exceed 5 µg/m3 (after August 1, 1978) at the time of initial assignment. In addition to its immediate diagnostic usefulness, the initial examination will provide a baseline for comparing future test results. The initial examination must include as a minimum the following elements:

(1) A work and medical history, including a smoking history, and presence and degree of respiratory symptoms such as breathlessness, cough, sputum production, and wheezing;

(2) A 14″ by 17″ or other reasonably-sized standard film or digital posterior-anterior chest X-ray;

(3) A nasal and skin examination; and

(4) Other examinations which the physician believes appropriate because of the employee's exposure to inorganic arsenic or because of required respirator use.

Periodic examinations are also to be provided to the employees listed in the first paragraph of this section. The periodic examinations shall be given annually for those covered employees 45 years of age or less with fewer than 10 years employment in areas where employee exposure exceeds the action level (5 µg/m3). Periodic examinations need not include sputum cytology or chest X-ray and only an updated medical history is required.

Periodic examinations for other covered employees shall be provided every six (6) months. These examinations shall include all tests required in the initial examination, except the chest X-ray, and the medical history need only be updated.

The examination contents are minimum requirements. Additional tests such as lateral and oblique X-rays or pulmonary function tests may be useful. For workers exposed to three arsenicals which are associated with lymphatic cancer, copper acetoarsenite, potassium arsenite, or sodium arsenite the examination should also include palpation of superficial lymph nodes and complete blood count.

*   *   *   *   *

§ 1910.1020 Access to employee exposure and medical records.

(a) *Purpose.* The purpose of this section is to provide employees and their designated representatives a right of access to relevant exposure and medical records; and to provide representatives of the Assistant Secretary a right of access to these records in order to fulfill responsibilities under the Occupational Safety and Health Act. Access by employees, their representatives, and the Assistant Secretary is necessary to yield both direct and indirect improvements in the detection, treatment, and prevention of occupational disease. Each employer is responsible for assuring compliance with this section, but the activities involved in complying with the access to medical records provisions can be carried out, on behalf of the employer, by the physician or other health care personnel in charge of employee medical records. Except as expressly provided, nothing in this section is intended to affect existing legal and ethical obligations concerning the maintenance and confidentiality of employee medical information, the duty to disclose information to a patient/employee or any other aspect of the medical-care relationship, or affect existing legal obligations concerning the protection of trade secret information.

(b) *Scope and application.* (1) This section applies to each general industry, maritime, and construction employer who makes, maintains, contracts for, or has access to employee exposure or medical records, or analyses thereof, pertaining to employees exposed to toxic substances or harmful physical agents.

(2) This section applies to all employee exposure and medical records, and analyses thereof, of such employees, whether or not the records are mandated by specific occupational safety and health standards.

(3) This section applies to all employee exposure and medical records, and analyses thereof, made or maintained in any manner, including on an in-house of contractual (e.g., fee-for-service) basis. Each employer shall assure that the preservation and access requirements of this section are complied with regardless of the manner in which the records are made or maintained.

(c) *Definitions*—(1) *Access* means the right and opportunity to examine and copy.

(2) *Analysis using exposure or medical records* means any compilation of data or any statistical study based at least in part on information collected from individual employee exposure or medical records or information collected from health insurance claims records, provided that either the analysis has been reported to the employer or no further work is currently being done by the person responsible for preparing the analysis.

(3) *Designated representative* means any individual or organization to whom an employee gives written authorization to exercise a right of access. For the purposes of access to employee exposure records and analyses using exposure or medical records, a recognized or certified collective bargaining agent shall be treated automatically as a designated representative without regard to written employee authorization.

(4) *Employee* means a current employee, a former employee, or an employee being assigned or transferred to work where there will be exposure to toxic substances or harmful physical agents. In the case of a deceased or legally incapacitated employee, the employee's legal representative may directly exercise all the employee's rights under this section.

(5) *Employee exposure record* means a record containing any of the following kinds of information:

(i) Environmental (workplace) monitoring or measuring of a toxic substance or harmful physical agent, including personal, area, grab, wipe, or other form of sampling, as well as related collection and analytical methodologies, calculations, and other background data relevant to interpretation of the results obtained;

(ii) Biological monitoring results which directly assess the absorption of a toxic substance or harmful physical agent by body systems (e.g., the level of a chemical in the blood, urine, breath, hair, fingernails, etc) but not including results which assess the biological effect of a substance or agent or which assess an employee's use of alcohol or drugs;

(iii) Material safety data sheets indicating that the material may pose a hazard to human health; or

(iv) In the absence of the above, a chemcial inventory or any other record which reveals where and when used and the identity (e.g., chemical, common, or trade name) of a toxic substance or harmful physical agent.

(6)(i) *Employee medical record* means a record concerning the health status of an employee which is made or maintained by a physician, nurse, or other health care personnel or technician, including:

(A) Medical and employment questionnaires or histories (including job description and occupational exposures),

114

(B) The results of medical examinations (pre-employment, pre-assignment, periodic, or episodic) and laboratory tests (including chest and other X-ray examinations taken for the purposes of establishing a base-line or detecting occupational illness, and all biological monitoring not defined as an "employee exposure record"),

(C) Medical opinions, diagnoses, progress notes, and recommendations,

(D) First aid records,

(E) Descriptions of treatments and prescriptions, and

(F) Employee medical complaints.

(ii) "Employee medical record" does not include medical information in the form of:

(A) Physical specimens (e.g., blood or urine samples) which are routinely discarded as a part of normal medical practice; or

(B) Records concerning health insurance claims if maintained separately from the employer's medical program and its records, and not accessible to the employer by employee name or other direct personal identifier (e.g., social security number, payroll number, etc.); or

(C) Records created solely in preparation for litigation which are privileged from discovery under the applicable rules of procedure or evidence; or

(D) Records concerning voluntary employee assistance programs (alcohol, drug abuse, or personal counseling programs) if maintained separately from the employer's medical program and its records.

(7) *Employer* means a current employer, a former employer, or a successor employer.

(8) *Exposure* or *exposed* means that an employee is subjected to a toxic substance or harmful physical agent in the course of employment through any route of entry (inhalation, ingestion, skin contact or absorption, etc.), and includes past exposure and potential (e.g., accidental or possible) exposure, but does not include situations where the employer can demonstrate that the toxic substance or harmful physical agent is not used, handled, stored, generated, or present in the workplace in any manner different from typical nonoccupational situations.

(9) *Health Professional* means a physician, occupational health nurse, industrial hygienist, toxicologist, or epidemiologist, providing medical or other occupational health services to exposed employees.

(10) *Record* means any item, collection, or grouping of information regardless of the form or process by which it is maintained (e.g., paper document, microfiche, microfilm, X-ray film, or automated data processing).

(11) *Specific chemical identity* means the chemical name, Chemical Abstracts Service (CAS) Registry Number, or any other information that reveals the precise chemical designation of the substance.

(12)(i) *Specific written consent* means a written authorization containing the following:

(A) The name and signature of the employee authorizing the release of medical information,

(B) The date of the written authorization,

(C) The name of the individual or organization that is authorized to release the medical information,

(D) The name of the designated representative (individual or organization) that is authorized to receive the released information,

(E) A general description of the medical information that is authorized to be released,

(F) A general description of the purpose for the release of the medical information, and

(G) A date or condition upon which the written authorization will expire (if less than one year).

(ii) A written authorization does not operate to authorize the release of medical information not in existence on the date of written authorization, unless the release of future information is expressly authorized, and does not operate for more than one year from the date of written authorization.

(iii) A written authorization may be revoked in writing prospectively at any time.

(13) *Toxic substance or harmful physical agent* means any chemical substance, biological agent (bacteria, virus, fungus, etc.), or physical stress (noise, heat, cold, vibration, repetitive

115

motion, ionizing and non-ionizing radiation, hypo-or hyperbaric pressure, etc.) which:

(i) Is listed in the latest printed edition of the National Institute for Occupational Safety and Health (NIOSH) Registry of Toxic Effects of Chemical Substances (RTECS), which is incorporated by reference as specified in § 1910.6; or

(ii) Has yielded positive evidence of an acute or chronic health hazard in testing conducted by, or known to, the employer; or

(iii) Is the subject of a material safety data sheet kept by or known to the employer indicating that the material may pose a hazard to human health.

(14) *Trade secret* means any confidential formula, pattern, process, device, or information or compilation of information that is used in an employer's business and that gives the employer an opportunity to obtain an advantage over competitors who do not know or use it.

(d) *Preservation of records.* (1) Unless a specific occupational safety and health standard provides a different period of time, each employer shall assure the preservation and retention of records as follows:

(i) *Employee medical records.* The medical record for each employee shall be preserved and maintained for at least the duration of employment plus thirty (30) years, except that the following types of records need not be retained for any specified period:

(A) Health insurance claims records maintained separately from the employer's medical program and its records,

(B) First aid records (not including medical histories) of one-time treatment and subsequent observation of minor scratches, cuts, burns, splinters, and the like which do not involve medical treatment, loss of consciousness, restriction of work or motion, or transfer to another job, if made on-site by a non-physician and if maintained separately from the employer's medical program and its records, and

(C) The medical records of employees who have worked for less than (1) year for the employer need not be retained beyond the term of employment if they are provided to the employee upon the termination of employment.

(ii) *Employee exposure records.* Each employee exposure record shall be preserved and maintained for at least thirty (30) years, except that:

(A) Background data to environmental (workplace) monitoring or measuring, such as laboratory reports and worksheets, need only be retained for one (1) year as long as the sampling results, the collection methodology (sampling plan), a description of the analytical and mathematical methods used, and a summary of other background data relevant to interpretation of the results obtained, are retained for at least thirty (30) years; and

(B) Material safety data sheets and paragraph (c)(5)(iv) records concerning the identity of a substance or agent need not be retained for any specified period as long as some record of the identity (chemical name if known) of the substance or agent, where it was used, and when it was used is retained for at least thirty (30) years;[1] and

(C) Biological monitoring results designated as exposure records by specific occupational safety and health standards shall be preserved and maintained as required by the specific standard.

(iii) *Analyses using exposure or medical records.* Each analysis using exposure or medial records shall be preserved and maintained for at least thirty (30) years.

(2) Nothing in this section is intended to mandate the form, manner, or process by which an employer preserves a record as long as the information contained in the record is preserved and retrievable, except that chest X-ray films shall be preserved in their original state.

(e) *Access to records—*(1) *General.* (i) Whenever an employee or designated representative requests access to a record, the employer shall assure that access is provided in a reasonable time, place, and manner. If the employer cannot reasonably provide access to the record within fifteen (15) working

---

[1] Material safety data sheets must be kept for those chemicals currently in use that are effected by the Hazard Communication Standard in accordance with 29 CFR 1910.1200(g).

days, the employer shall within the fifteen (15) working days apprise the employee or designated representative requesting the record of the reason for the delay and the earliest date when the record can be made available.

(ii) The employer may require of the requester only such information as should be readily known to the requester and which may be necessary to locate or identify the records being requested (e.g. dates and locations where the employee worked during the time period in question).

(iii) Whenever an employee or designated representative requests a copy of a record, the employer shall assure that either:

(A) A copy of the record is provided without cost to the employee or representative,

(B) The necessary mechanical copying facilities (e.g., photocopying) are made available without cost to the employee or representative for copying the record, or

(C) The record is loaned to the employee or representative for a reasonable time to enable a copy to be made.

(iv) In the case of an original X-ray, the employer may restrict access to on-site examination or make other suitable arrangements for the temporary loan of the X-ray.

(v) Whenever a record has been previously provided without cost to an employee or designated representative, the employer may charge reasonable, non-discriminatory administrative costs (i.e., search and copying expenses but not including overhead expenses) for a request by the employee or designated representative for additional copies of the record, except that

(A) An employer shall not charge for an initial request for a copy of new information that has been added to a record which was previously provided; and

(B) An employer shall not charge for an initial request by a recognized or certified collective bargaining agent for a copy of an employee exposure record or an analysis using exposure or medical records.

(vi) Nothing in this section is intended to preclude employees and collective bargaining agents from collectively bargaining to obtain access to information in addition to that available under this section.

(2) *Employee and designated representative access*—(i) *Employee exposure records.* (A) Except as limited by paragraph (f) of this section, each employer shall, upon request, assure the access to each employee and designated representative to employee exposure records relevant to the employee. For the purpose of this section, an exposure record relevant to the employee consists of:

(1) A record which measures or monitors the amount of a toxic substance or harmful physical agent to which the employee is or has been exposed;

(2) In the absence of such directly relevant records, such records of other employees with past or present job duties or working conditions related to or similar to those of the employee to the extent necessary to reasonably indicate the amount and nature of the toxic substances or harmful physical agents to which the employee is or has been subjected, and

(3) Exposure records to the extent necessary to reasonably indicate the amount and nature of the toxic substances or harmful physical agents at workplaces or under working conditions to which the employee is being assigned or transferred.

(B) Requests by designated representatives for unconsented access to employee exposure records shall be in writing and shall specify with reasonable particularity:

(1) The records requested to be disclosed; and

(2) The occupational health need for gaining access to these records.

(ii) *Employee medical records.* (A) Each employer shall, upon request, assure the access of each employee to employee medical records of which the employee is the subject, except as provided in paragraph (e)(2)(ii)(D) of this section.

(B) Each employer shall, upon request, assure the access of each designated representative to the employee medical records of any employee who has given the designated representative specific written consent. appendix A to this section contains a sample form which may be used to establish specific written consent for access to employee medical records.

(C) Whenever access to employee medical records is requested, a physician representing the employer may recommend that the employee or designated representative:

(*1*) Consult with the physician for the purposes of reviewing and discussing the records requested,

(*2*) Accept a summary of material facts and opinions in lieu of the records requested, or

(*3*) Accept release of the requested records only to a physician or other designated representative.

(D) Whenever an employee requests access to his or her employee medical records, and a physician representing the employer believes that direct employee access to information contained in the records regarding a specific diagnosis of a terminal illness or a psychiatric condition could be detrimental to the employee's health, the employer may inform the employee that access will only be provided to a designated representative of the employee having specific written consent, and deny the employee's request for direct access to this information only. Where a designated representative with specific written consent requests access to information so withheld, the employer shall assure the access of the designated representative to this information, even when it is known that the designated representative will give the information to the employee.

(E) A physician, nurse, or other responsible health care personnel maintaining medical records may delete from requested medical records the identity of a family member, personal friend, or fellow employee who has provided confidential information concerning an employee's health status.

(iii) *Analyses using exposure or medical records.* (A) Each employee shall, upon request, assure the access of each employee and designated representative to each analysis using exposure or medical records concerning the employee's working conditions or workplace.

(B) Whenever access is requested to an analysis which reports the contents of employee medical records by either direct identifier (name, address, social security number, payroll number, etc.) or by information which could reasonably be used under the circumstances indirectly to identify specific employees (exact age, height, weight, race, sex, date of initial employment, job title, etc.), the employer shall assure that personal identifiers are removed before access is provided. If the employer can demonstrate that removal of personal identifiers from an analysis is not feasible, access to the personally identifiable portions of the analysis need not be provided.

(3) *OSHA access.* (i) Each employer shall, upon request, and without derogation of any rights under the Constitution or the Occupational Safety and Health Act of 1970, 29 U.S.C. 651 *et seq.*, that the employer chooses to exercise, assure the prompt access of representatives of the Assistant Secretary of Labor for Occupational Safety and Health to employee exposure and medical records and to analyses using exposure or medical records. Rules of agency practice and procedure governing OSHA access to employee medical records are contained in 29 CFR 1913.10.

(ii) Whenever OSHA seeks access to personally identifiable employee medical information by presenting to the employer a written access order pursuant to 29 CFR 1913.10(d), the employer shall prominently post a copy of the written access order and its accompanying cover letter for at least fifteen (15) working days.

(f) *Trade secrets.* (1) Except as provided in paragraph (f)(2) of this section, nothing in this section precludes an employer from deleting from records requested by a health professional, employee, or designated representative any trade secret data which discloses manufacturing processes, or discloses the percentage of a chemical substance in mixture, as long as the health professional, employee, or designated representative is notified that information has been deleted. Whenever deletion of trade secret information substantially impairs evaluation of the place where or the time when exposure to a toxic substance or harmful physical agent occurred, the employer shall provide alternative information which is sufficient to permit the requesting party to identify where and when exposure occurred.

(2) The employer may withhold the specific chemical identity, including the chemical name and other specific identification of a toxic substance from a disclosable record provided that:

(i) The claim that the information withheld is a trade secret can be supported;

(ii) All other available information on the properties and effects of the toxic substance is disclosed;

(iii) The employer informs the requesting party that the specific chemical identity is being withheld as a trade secret; and

(iv) The specific chemical identity is made available to health professionals, employees and designated representatives in accordance with the specific applicable provisions of this paragraph.

(3) Where a treating physician or nurse determines that a medical emergency exists and the specific chemical identity of a toxic substance is necessary for emergency or first-aid treatment, the employer shall immediately disclose the specific chemical identity of a trade secret chemical to the treating physician or nurse, regardless of the existence of a written statement of need or a confidentiality agreement. The employer may require a written statement of need and confidentiality agreement, in accordance with the provisions of paragraphs (f)(4) and (f)(5), as soon as circumstances permit.

(4) In non-emergency situations, an employer shall, upon request, disclose a specific chemical identity, otherwise permitted to be withheld under paragraph (f)(2) of this section, to a health professional, employee, or designated representative if:

(i) The request is in writing;

(ii) The request describes with reasonable detail one or more of the following occupational health needs for the information:

(A) To assess the hazards of the chemicals to which employees will be exposed;

(B) To conduct or assess sampling of the workplace atmosphere to determine employee exposure levels;

(C) To conduct pre-assignment or periodic medical surveillance of exposed employees;

(D) To provide medical treatment to exposed employees;

(E) To select or assess appropriate personal protective equipment for exposed employees;

(F) To design or assess engineering controls or other protective measures for exposed employees; and

(G) To conduct studies to determine the health effects of exposure.

(iii) The request explains in detail why the disclosure of the specific chemical identity is essential and that, in lieu thereof, the disclosure of the following information would not enable the health professional, employee or designated representative to provide the occupational health services described in paragraph (f)(4)(ii) of this section:

(A) The properties and effects of the chemical;

(B) Measures for controlling workers' exposure to the chemical;

(C) Methods of monitoring and analyzing worker exposure to the chemical; and,

(D) Methods of diagnosing and treating harmful exposures to the chemical;

(iv) The request includes a description of the procedures to be used to maintain the confidentiality of the disclosed information; and,

(v) The health professional, employee, or designated representative and the employer or contractor of the services of the health professional or designated representative agree in a written confidentiality agreement that the health professional, employee or designated representative will not use the trade secret information for any purpose other than the health need(s) asserted and agree not to release the information under any circumstances other than to OSHA, as provided in paragraph (f)(7) of this section, except as authorized by the terms of the agreement or by the employer.

(5) The confidentiality agreement authorized by paragraph (f)(4)(iv) of this section:

(i) May restrict the use of the information to the health purposes indicated in the written statement of need;

(ii) May provide for appropriate legal remedies in the event of a breach of the agreement, including stipulation of a

119

reasonable pre-estimate of likely damages; and,

(iii) May not include requirements for the posting of a penalty bond.

(6) Nothing in this section is meant to preclude the parties from pursuing non-contractual remedies to the extent permitted by law.

(7) If the health professional, employee or designated representative receiving the trade secret information decides that there is a need to disclose it to OSHA, the employer who provided the information shall be informed by the health professional prior to, or at the same time as, such disclosure.

(8) If the employer denies a written request for disclosure of a specific chemical identity, the denial must:

(i) Be provided to the health professional, employee or designated representative within thirty days of the request;

(ii) Be in writing;

(iii) Include evidence to support the claim that the specific chemical identity is a trade secret;

(iv) State the specific reasons why the request is being denied; and,

(v) Explain in detail how alternative information may satisfy the specific medical or occupational health need without revealing the specific chemical identity.

(9) The health professional, employee, or designated representative whose request for information is denied under paragraph (f)(4) of this section may refer the request and the written denial of the request to OSHA for consideration.

(10) When a heath professional employee, or designated representative refers a denial to OSHA under paragraph (f)(9) of this section, OSHA shall consider the evidence to determine if:

(i) The employer has supported the claim that the specific chemical identity is a trade secret;

(ii) The health professional employee, or designated representative has supported the claim that there is a medical or occupational health need for the information; and

(iii) The health professional, employee or designated representative has demonstrated adequate means to protect the confidentiality.

(11)(i) If OSHA determines that the specific chemical identity requested under paragraph (f)(4) of this section is not a *bona fide* trade secret, or that it is a trade secret but the requesting health professional, employee or designated representatives has a legitimate medical or occupational health need for the information, has executed a written confidentiality agreement, and has shown adequate means for complying with the terms of such agreement, the employer will be subject to citation by OSHA.

(ii) If an employer demonstrates to OSHA that the execution of a confidentiality agreement would not provide sufficient protection against the potential harm from the unauthorized disclosure of a trade secret specific chemical identity, the Assistant Secretary may issue such orders or impose such additional limitations or conditions upon the disclosure of the requested chemical information as may be appropriate to assure that the occupational health needs are met without an undue risk of harm to the employer.

(12) Notwithstanding the existence of a trade secret claim, an employer shall, upon request, disclose to the Assistant Secretary any information which this section requires the employer to make available. Where there is a trade secret claim, such claim shall be made no later than at the time the information is provided to the Assistant Secretary so that suitable determinations of trade secret status can be made and the necessary protections can be implemented.

(13) Nothing in this paragraph shall be construed as requiring the disclosure under any circumstances of process or percentage of mixture information which is trade secret.

(g) *Employee information.* (1) Upon an employee's first entering into employment, and at least annually thereafter, each employer shall inform current employees covered by this section of the following:

(i) The existence, location, and availability of any records covered by this section;

(ii) The person responsible for maintaining and providing access to records; and

(iii) Each employee's rights of access to these records.

(2) Each employer shall keep a copy of this section and its appendices, and make copies readily available, upon request, to employees. The employer shall also distribute to current employees any informational materials concerning this section which are made available to the employer by the Assistant Secretary of Labor for Occupational Safety and Health.

(h) *Transfer of records.* (1) Whenever an employer is ceasing to do business, the employer shall transfer all records subject to this section to the successor employer. The successor employer shall receive and maintain these records.

(2) Whenever an employer is ceasing to do business and there is no successor employer to receive and maintain the records subject to this standard, the employer shall notify affected current employees of their rights of access to records at least three (3) months prior to the cessation of the employer's business.

(i) *Appendices.* The information contained in appendices A and B to this section is not intended, by itself, to create any additional obligations not otherwise imposed by this section nor detract from any existing obligation.

APPENDIX A TO §1910.1020—SAMPLE AUTHORIZATION LETTER FOR THE RELEASE OF EMPLOYEE MEDICAL RECORD INFORMATION TO A DESIGNATED REPRESENTATIVE (NON-MANDATORY)

I, _____ (full name of worker/patient), hereby authorize _____ (individual or organization holding the medical records) to release to _____ (individual or organization authorized to receive the medical information), the following medical information from my personal medical records:

_____

(Describe generally the information desired to be released)
I give my permission for this medical information to be used for the following purpose:

_____

but I do not give permission for any other use or re-disclosure of this information.

NOTE: Several extra lines are provided below so that you can place additional restrictions on this authorization letter if you want to. You may, however, leave these lines

blank. On the other hand, you may want to (1) specify a particular expiration date for this letter (if less than one year); (2) describe medical information to be created in the future that you intend to be covered by this authorization letter; or (3) describe portions of the medical information in your records which you do not intend to be released as a result of this letter.)

_____

_____

_____

Full name of Employee or Legal Representative

Signature of Employee or Legal Representative

Date of Signature

APPENDIX B TO §1910.1020—AVAILABILITY OF NIOSH REGISTRY OF TOXIC EFFECTS OF CHEMICAL SUBSTANCES (RTECS) (NON-MANDATORY)

The final regulation, 29 CFR 1910.20, applies to all employee exposure and medical records, and analyses thereof, of employees exposed to toxic substances or harmful physical agents (paragraph (b)(2)). The term *toxic substance or harmful physical agent* is defined by paragraph (c)(13) to encompass chemical substances, biological agents, and physical stresses for which there is evidence of harmful health effects. The regulation uses the latest printed edition of the National Institute for Occupational Safety and Health (NIOSH) Registry of Toxic Effects of Chemical Substances (RTECS) as one of the chief sources of information as to whether evidence of harmful health effects exists. If a substance is listed in the latest printed RTECS, the regulation applies to exposure and medical records (and analyses of these records) relevant to employees exposed to the substance.

It is appropriate to note that the final regulation does not require that employers purchase a copy of RTECS, and many employers need not consult RTECS to ascertain whether their employee exposure or medical records are subject to the rule. Employers who do not currently have the latest printed edition of the NIOSH RTECS, however, may desire to obtain a copy. The RTECS is issued in an annual printed edition as mandated by section 20(a)(6) of the Occupational Safety and Health Act (29 U.S.C. 669(a)(6)).

The Introduction to the 1980 printed edition describes the RTECS as follows:

"The 1980 edition of the Registry of Toxic Effects of Chemical Substances, formerly known as the Toxic Substances list, is the ninth revision prepared in compliance with the requirements of Section 20(a)(6) of the Occupational Safety and Health Act of 1970 (Public Law 91–596). The original list was completed on June 28, 1971, and has been updated annually in book format. Beginning in October 1977, quarterly revisions have been provided in microfiche. This edition of the Registry contains 168,096 listings of chemical substances: 45,156 are names of different chemicals with their associated toxicity data and 122,940 are synonyms. This edition includes approximately 5,900 new chemical compounds that did not appear in the 1979 Registry. (p. xi)

"The Registry's purposes are many, and it serves a variety of users. It is a single source document for basic toxicity information and for other data, such as chemical identifiers ad information necessary for the preparation of safety directives and hazard evaluations for chemical substances. The various types of toxic effects linked to literature citations provide researchers and occupational health scientists with an introduction to the toxicological literature, making their own review of the toxic hazards of a given substance easier. By presenting data on the lowest reported doses that produce effects by several routes of entry in various species, the Registry furnishes valuable information to those responsible for preparing safety data sheets for chemical substances in the workplace. Chemical and production engineers can use the Registry to identify the hazards which may be associated with chemical intermediates in the development of final products, and thus can more readily select substitutes or alternative processes which may be less hazardous. Some organizations, including health agencies and chemical companies, have included the NIOSH Registry accession numbers with the listing of chemicals in their files to reference toxicity information associated with those chemicals. By including foreign language chemical names, a start has been made toward providing rapid identification of substances produced in other countries. (p. xi)

"In this edition of the Registry, the editors intend to identify "all known toxic substances" which may exist in the environment and to provide pertinent data on the toxic effects from known doses entering an organism by any route described. (p xi)

"It must be reemphasized that the entry of a substance in the Registry does not automatically mean that it must be avoided. A listing does mean, however, that the substance has the documented potential of being harmful if misused, and care must be exercised to prevent tragic consequences. Thus, the Registry lists many substances that are common in everyday life and are in nearly every household in the United States. One can name a variety of such dangerous substances: prescription and non-prescription drugs; food additives; pesticide concentrates,

sprays, and dusts; fungicides; herbicides; paints; glazes, dyes; bleaches and other household cleaning agents; alkalies; and various solvents and diluents. The list is extensive because chemicals have become an integral part of our existence."

The RTECS printed edition may be purchased from the Superintendent of Documents, U.S. Government Printing Office (GPO), Washington, DC 20402 (202–783–3238).

Some employers may desire to subscribe to the quarterly update to the RTECS which is published in a microfiche edition. An annual subscription to the quarterly microfiche may be purchased from the GPO (Order the "Microfiche Edition, Registry of Toxic Effects of Chemical Substances"). Both the printed edition and the microfiche edition of RTECS are available for review at many university and public libraries throughout the country. The latest RTECS editions may also be examined at the OSHA Technical Data Center, Room N2439—Rear, United States Department of Labor, 200 Constitution Avenue, NW., Washington, DC 20210 (202–523–9700), or at any OSHA Regional or Area Office (*See,* major city telephone directories under United States Government-Labor Department).

[53 FR 38163, Sept. 29, 1988; 53 FR 49981, Dec. 13, 1988, as amended at 54 FR 24333, June 7, 1989; 55 FR 26431, June 28, 1990; 61 FR 9235, Mar. 7, 1996. Redesignated at 61 FR 31430, June 20, 1996, as amended at 71 FR 16673, Apr. 3, 2006; 76 FR 33608, June 8, 2011]

§ 1910.1024   Beryllium.

(a) *Scope and application.* (1) This standard applies to occupational exposure to beryllium in all forms, compounds, and mixtures in general industry, except those articles and materials exempted by paragraphs (a)(2) and (a)(3) of this standard.

(2) This standard does not apply to articles, as defined in the Hazard Communication standard (HCS) (§ 1910.1200(c)), that contain beryllium and that the employer does not process.

(3) This standard does not apply to materials containing less than 0.1% beryllium by weight where the employer has objective data demonstrating that employee exposure to beryllium will remain below the action level as an 8-hour TWA under any foreseeable conditions.

(b) *Definitions.* As used in this standard:

Action level means a concentration of airborne beryllium of 0.1 micrograms per cubic meter of air (µg/m³) calculated as an 8-hour time-weighted average (TWA).

Airborne exposure and *airborne exposure to beryllium* mean the exposure to airborne beryllium that would occur if the employee were not using a respirator.

Assistant Secretary means the Assistant Secretary of Labor for Occupational Safety and Health, United States Department of Labor, or designee.

Beryllium lymphocyte proliferation test (BeLPT) means the measurement of blood lymphocyte proliferation in a laboratory test when lymphocytes are challenged with a soluble beryllium salt.

Beryllium work area means any work area:

(i) Containing a process or operation that can release beryllium and that involves material that contains at least 0.1 percent beryllium by weight; and

(ii) Where employees are, or can reasonably be expected to be, exposed to airborne beryllium at any level or where there is the potential for dermal contact with beryllium.

CBD diagnostic center means a medical diagnostic center that has an on-site pulmonary specialist and on-site facilities to perform a clinical evaluation for the presence of chronic beryllium disease (CBD). This evaluation must include pulmonary function testing (as outlined by the American Thoracic Society criteria), bronchoalveolar lavage (BAL), and transbronchial biopsy. The CBD diagnostic center must also have the capacity to transfer BAL samples to a laboratory for appropriate diagnostic testing within 24 hours. The on-site pulmonary specialist must be able to interpret the biopsy pathology and the BAL diagnostic test results.

Chronic beryllium disease (CBD) means a chronic lung disease associated with airborne exposure to beryllium.

Confirmed positive means the person tested has beryllium sensitization, as indicated by two abnormal BeLPT test results, an abnormal and a borderline test result, or three borderline test results. It also means the result of a more reliable and accurate test indicating a person has been identified as having beryllium sensitization.

Contaminated with beryllium and *beryllium-contaminated* mean contaminated with dust, fumes, mists, or solutions containing beryllium in concentrations greater than or equal to 0.1 percent by weight.

Dermal contact with beryllium means skin exposure to:

(i) Soluble beryllium compounds containing beryllium in concentrations greater than or equal to 0.1 percent by weight;

(ii) Solutions containing beryllium in concentrations greater than or equal to 0.1 percent by weight; or

(iii) Dust, fumes, or mists containing beryllium in concentrations greater than or equal to 0.1 percent by weight.

Director means the Director of the National Institute for Occupational Safety and Health (NIOSH), U.S. Department of Health and Human Services, or designee.

Emergency means any occurrence such as, but not limited to, equipment failure, rupture of containers, or failure of control equipment, which may or does result in an uncontrolled and unintended release of airborne beryllium that presents a significant hazard.

High-efficiency particulate air (HEPA) filter means a filter that is at least 99.97 percent efficient in removing particles 0.3 micrometers in diameter.

Objective data means information, such as air monitoring data from industry-wide surveys or calculations based on the composition of a substance, demonstrating airborne exposure to beryllium associated with a particular product or material or a specific process, task, or activity. The data must reflect workplace conditions closely resembling or with a higher airborne exposure potential than the processes, types of material, control methods, work practices, and environmental conditions in the employer's current operations.

Physician or other licensed health care professional (PLHCP) means an individual whose legally permitted scope of practice (i.e., license, registration, or certification) allows the individual to independently provide or be delegated the responsibility to provide some or all of the health care services required by paragraph (k) of this standard.

123

Regulated area means an area, including temporary work areas where maintenance or non-routine tasks are performed, where an employee's airborne exposure exceeds, or can reasonably be expected to exceed, either the time-weighted average (TWA) permissible exposure limit (PEL) or short term exposure limit (STEL).

This standard means this beryllium standard, 29 CFR 1910.1024.

(c) *Permissible Exposure Limits (PELs)*—(1) *Time-weighted average (TWA) PEL.* The employer must ensure that no employee is exposed to an airborne concentration of beryllium in excess of 0.2 µg/m³ calculated as an 8-hour TWA.

(2) *Short-term exposure limit (STEL).* The employer must ensure that no employee is exposed to an airborne concentration of beryllium in excess of 2.0 µg/m³ as determined over a sampling period of 15 minutes.

(d) *Exposure assessment*—(1) *General.* The employer must assess the airborne exposure of each employee who is or may reasonably be expected to be exposed to airborne beryllium in accordance with either the performance option in paragraph (d)(2) or the scheduled monitoring option in paragraph (d)(3) of this standard.

(2) *Performance option.* The employer must assess the 8-hour TWA exposure and the 15-minute short-term exposure for each employee on the basis of any combination of air monitoring data and objective data sufficient to accurately characterize airborne exposure to beryllium.

(3) *Scheduled monitoring option.* (i) The employer must perform initial monitoring to assess the 8-hour TWA exposure for each employee on the basis of one or more personal breathing zone air samples that reflect the airborne exposure of employees on each shift, for each job classification, and in each work area.

(ii) The employer must perform initial monitoring to assess the short-term exposure from 15-minute personal breathing zone air samples measured in operations that are likely to produce airborne exposure above the STEL for each work shift, for each job classification, and in each work area.

(iii) Where several employees perform the same tasks on the same shift and in the same work area, the employer may sample a representative fraction of these employees in order to meet the requirements of this paragraph (d)(3). In representative sampling, the employer must sample the employee(s) expected to have the highest airborne exposure to beryllium.

(iv) If initial monitoring indicates that airborne exposure is below the action level and at or below the STEL, the employer may discontinue monitoring for those employees whose airborne exposure is represented by such monitoring.

(v) Where the most recent exposure monitoring indicates that airborne exposure is at or above the action level but at or below the TWA PEL, the employer must repeat such monitoring within six months of the most recent monitoring.

(vi) Where the most recent exposure monitoring indicates that airborne exposure is above the TWA PEL, the employer must repeat such monitoring within three months of the most recent 8-hour TWA exposure monitoring.

(vii) Where the most recent (non-initial) exposure monitoring indicates that airborne exposure is below the action level, the employer must repeat such monitoring within six months of the most recent monitoring until two consecutive measurements, taken 7 or more days apart, are below the action level, at which time the employer may discontinue 8-hour TWA exposure monitoring for those employees whose exposure is represented by such monitoring, except as otherwise provided in paragraph (d)(4) of this standard.

(viii) Where the most recent exposure monitoring indicates that airborne exposure is above the STEL, the employer must repeat such monitoring within three months of the most recent short-term exposure monitoring until two consecutive measurements, taken 7 or more days apart, are below the STEL, at which time the employer may discontinue short-term exposure monitoring for those employees whose exposure is represented by such monitoring, except as otherwise provided in paragraph (d)(4) of this standard.

(4) *Reassessment of exposure.* The employer must reassess airborne exposure whenever a change in the production, process, control equipment, personnel, or work practices may reasonably be expected to result in new or additional airborne exposure at or above the action level or STEL, or when the employer has any reason to believe that new or additional airborne exposure at or above the action level or STEL has occurred.

(5) *Methods of sample analysis.* The employer must ensure that all air monitoring samples used to satisfy the monitoring requirements of paragraph (d) of this standard are evaluated by a laboratory that can measure beryllium to an accuracy of plus or minus 25 percent within a statistical confidence level of 95 percent for airborne concentrations at or above the action level.

(6) *Employee notification of assessment results.* (i) Within 15 working days after completing an exposure assessment in accordance with paragraph (d) of this standard, the employer must notify each employee whose airborne exposure is represented by the assessment of the results of that assessment individually in writing or post the results in an appropriate location that is accessible to each of these employees.

(ii) Whenever an exposure assessment indicates that airborne exposure is above the TWA PEL or STEL, the employer must describe in the written notification the corrective action being taken to reduce airborne exposure to or below the exposure limit(s) exceeded where feasible corrective action exists but had not been implemented when the monitoring was conducted.

(7) *Observation of monitoring.* (i) The employer must provide an opportunity to observe any exposure monitoring required by this standard to each employee whose airborne exposure is measured or represented by the monitoring and each employee's representative(s).

(ii) When observation of monitoring requires entry into an area where the use of personal protective clothing or equipment (which may include respirators) is required, the employer must provide each observer with appropriate personal protective clothing and equipment at no cost to the observer and must ensure that each observer uses such clothing and equipment.

(iii) The employer must ensure that each observer follows all other applicable safety and health procedures.

(e) *Beryllium work areas and regulated areas*—(1) *Establishment.* (i) The employer must establish and maintain a beryllium work area wherever the criteria for a "beryllium work area" set forth in paragraph (b) of this standard are met.

(ii) The employer must establish and maintain a regulated area wherever employees are, or can reasonably be expected to be, exposed to airborne beryllium at levels above the TWA PEL or STEL.

(2) *Demarcation.* (i) The employer must identify each beryllium work area through signs or any other methods that adequately establish and inform each employee of the boundaries of each beryllium work area.

(ii) The employer must identify each regulated area in accordance with paragraph (m)(2) of this standard.

(3) *Access.* The employer must limit access to regulated areas to:

(i) Persons the employer authorizes or requires to be in a regulated area to perform work duties;

(ii) Persons entering a regulated area as designated representatives of employees for the purpose of exercising the right to observe exposure monitoring procedures under paragraph (d)(7) of this standard; and

(iii) Persons authorized by law to be in a regulated area.

(4) *Provision of personal protective clothing and equipment, including respirators.* The employer must provide and ensure that each employee entering a regulated area uses:

(i) Respiratory protection in accordance with paragraph (g) of this standard; and

(ii) Personal protective clothing and equipment in accordance with paragraph (h) of this standard.

(f) *Methods of compliance*—(1) *Written exposure control plan.* (i) The employer must establish, implement, and maintain a written exposure control plan, which must contain:

(A) A list of operations and job titles reasonably expected to involve airborne exposure to or dermal contact with beryllium;

(B) A list of operations and job titles reasonably expected to involve airborne exposure at or above the action level;

(C) A list of operations and job titles reasonably expected to involve airborne exposure above the TWA PEL or STEL;

(D) Procedures for minimizing cross-contamination, including preventing the transfer of beryllium between surfaces, equipment, clothing, materials, and articles within beryllium work areas;

(E) Procedures for keeping surfaces as free as practicable of beryllium;

(F) Procedures for minimizing the migration of beryllium from beryllium work areas to other locations within or outside the workplace;

(G) A list of engineering controls, work practices, and respiratory protection required by paragraph (f)(2) of this standard;

(H) A list of personal protective clothing and equipment required by paragraph (h) of this standard; and

(I) Procedures for removing, laundering, storing, cleaning, repairing, and disposing of beryllium-contaminated personal protective clothing and equipment, including respirators.

(ii) The employer must review and evaluate the effectiveness of each written exposure control plan at least annually and update it, as necessary, when:

(A) Any change in production processes, materials, equipment, personnel, work practices, or control methods results, or can reasonably be expected to result, in new or additional airborne exposure to beryllium;

(B) The employer is notified that an employee is eligible for medical removal in accordance with paragraph (l)(1) of this standard, referred for evaluation at a CBD diagnostic center, or shows signs or symptoms associated with airborne exposure to or dermal contact with beryllium; or

(C) The employer has any reason to believe that new or additional airborne exposure is occurring or will occur.

(iii) The employer must make a copy of the written exposure control plan accessible to each employee who is, or can reasonably be expected to be, exposed to airborne beryllium in accordance with OSHA's Access to Employee Exposure and Medical Records (Records Access) standard (§ 1910.1020(e)).

(2) *Engineering and work practice controls.* (i) The employer must use engineering and work practice controls to reduce and maintain employee airborne exposure to beryllium to or below the PEL and STEL, unless the employer can demonstrate that such controls are not feasible. Wherever the employer demonstrates that it is not feasible to reduce airborne exposure to or below the PELs with engineering and work practice controls, the employer must implement and maintain engineering and work practice controls to reduce airborne exposure to the lowest levels feasible and supplement these controls using respiratory protection in accordance with paragraph (g) of this standard.

(ii) For each operation in a beryllium work area that releases airborne beryllium, the employer must ensure that at least one of the following is in place to reduce airborne exposure:

(A) Material and/or process substitution;

(B) Isolation, such as ventilated partial or full enclosures;

(C) Local exhaust ventilation, such as at the points of operation, material handling, and transfer; or

(D) Process control, such as wet methods and automation.

(iii) An employer is exempt from using the controls listed in paragraph (f)(2)(ii) of this standard to the extent that:

(A) The employer can establish that such controls are not feasible; or

(B) The employer can demonstrate that airborne exposure is below the action level, using no fewer than two representative personal breathing zone samples taken at least 7 days apart, for each affected operation.

(3) *Prohibition of rotation.* The employer must not rotate employees to different jobs to achieve compliance with the PELs.

(g) *Respiratory protection—*(1) *General.* The employer must provide respiratory protection at no cost to the employee and ensure that each employee uses respiratory protection:

(i) During periods necessary to install or implement feasible engineering and work practice controls where airborne exposure exceeds, or can reasonably be expected to exceed, the TWA PEL or STEL;

(ii) During operations, including maintenance and repair activities and non-routine tasks, when engineering and work practice controls are not feasible and airborne exposure exceeds, or can reasonably be expected to exceed, the TWA PEL or STEL;

(iii) During operations for which an employer has implemented all feasible engineering and work practice controls when such controls are not sufficient to reduce airborne exposure to or below the TWA PEL or STEL;

(iv) During emergencies; and

(v) When an employee who is eligible for medical removal under paragraph (l)(1) chooses to remain in a job with airborne exposure at or above the action level, as permitted by paragraph (l)(2)(ii) of this standard.

(2) *Respiratory protection program.* Where this standard requires an employer to provide respiratory protection, the selection and use of such respiratory protection must be in accordance with the Respiratory Protection standard (§1910.134).

(3) The employer must provide at no cost to the employee a powered air-purifying respirator (PAPR) instead of a negative pressure respirator when

(i) Respiratory protection is required by this standard;

(ii) An employee entitled to such respiratory protection requests a PAPR; and

(iii) The PAPR provides adequate protection to the employee in accordance with paragraph (g)(2) of this standard.

(h) *Personal protective clothing and equipment*—(1) *Provision and use.* The employer must provide at no cost, and ensure that each employee uses, appropriate personal protective clothing and equipment in accordance with the written exposure control plan required under paragraph (f)(1) of this standard and OSHA's Personal Protective Equipment standards (subpart I of this part):

(i) Where airborne exposure exceeds, or can reasonably be expected to exceed, the TWA PEL or STEL; or

(ii) Where there is a reasonable expectation of dermal contact with beryllium.

(2) *Removal and storage.* (i) The employer must ensure that each employee removes all beryllium-contaminated personal protective clothing and equipment at the end of the work shift, at the completion of tasks involving beryllium, or when personal protective clothing or equipment becomes visibly contaminated with beryllium, whichever comes first.

(ii) The employer must ensure that each employee removes beryllium-contaminated personal protective clothing and equipment as specified in the written exposure control plan required by paragraph (f)(1) of this standard.

(iii) The employer must ensure that each employee stores and keeps beryllium-contaminated personal protective clothing and equipment separate from street clothing and that storage facilities prevent cross-contamination as specified in the written exposure control plan required by paragraph (f)(1) of this standard.

(iv) The employer must ensure that no employee removes beryllium-contaminated personal protective clothing or equipment from the workplace, except for employees authorized to do so for the purposes of laundering, cleaning, maintaining or disposing of beryllium-contaminated personal protective clothing and equipment at an appropriate location or facility away from the workplace.

(v) When personal protective clothing or equipment required by this standard is removed from the workplace for laundering, cleaning, maintenance or disposal, the employer must ensure that personal protective clothing and equipment are stored and transported in sealed bags or other closed containers that are impermeable and are labeled in accordance with paragraph (m)(3) of this standard and the HCS (§1910.1200).

(3) *Cleaning and replacement.* (i) The employer must ensure that all reusable personal protective clothing and equipment required by this standard is

cleaned, laundered, repaired, and replaced as needed to maintain its effectiveness.

(ii) The employer must ensure that beryllium is not removed from beryllium-contaminated personal protective clothing and equipment by blowing, shaking, or any other means that disperses beryllium into the air.

(iii) The employer must inform in writing the persons or the business entities who launder, clean or repair the personal protective clothing or equipment required by this standard of the potentially harmful effects of airborne exposure to and dermal contact with beryllium and that the personal protective clothing and equipment must be handled in accordance with this standard.

(i) *Hygiene areas and practices*—(1) *General.* For each employee working in a beryllium work area, the employer must:

(i) Provide readily accessible washing facilities in accordance with this standard and the Sanitation standard (§ 1910.141) to remove beryllium from the hands, face, and neck; and

(ii) Ensure that employees who have dermal contact with beryllium wash any exposed skin at the end of the activity, process, or work shift and prior to eating, drinking, smoking, chewing tobacco or gum, applying cosmetics, or using the toilet.

(2) *Change rooms.* In addition to the requirements of paragraph (i)(1)(i) of this standard, the employer must provide employees who work in a beryllium work area with a designated change room in accordance with this standard and the Sanitation standard (§ 1910.141) where employees are required to remove their personal clothing.

(3) *Showers.* (i) The employer must provide showers in accordance with the Sanitation standard (§ 1910.141) where:

(A) Airborne exposure exceeds, or can reasonably be expected to exceed, the TWA PEL or STEL; and

(B) Employee's hair or body parts other than hands, face, and neck can reasonably be expected to become contaminated with beryllium.

(ii) Employers required to provide showers under paragraph (i)(3)(i) of this standard must ensure that each employee showers at the end of the work shift or work activity if:

(A) The employee reasonably could have had airborne exposure above the TWA PEL or STEL; and

(B) The employee's hair or body parts other than hands, face, and neck could reasonably have become contaminated with beryllium.

(4) *Eating and drinking areas.* Wherever the employer allows employees to consume food or beverages at a worksite where beryllium is present, the employer must ensure that:

(i) Beryllium-contaminated surfaces in eating and drinking areas are as free as practicable of beryllium;

(ii) No employees enter any eating or drinking area with beryllium-contaminated personal protective clothing or equipment unless, prior to entry, surface beryllium has been removed from the clothing or equipment by methods that do not disperse beryllium into the air or onto an employee's body; and

(iii) Eating and drinking facilities provided by the employer are in accordance with the Sanitation standard (§ 1910.141).

(5) *Prohibited activities.* The employer must ensure that no employees eat, drink, smoke, chew tobacco or gum, or apply cosmetics in regulated areas.

(j) *Housekeeping*—(1) *General.* (i) The employer must maintain all surfaces in beryllium work areas and regulated areas as free as practicable of beryllium and in accordance with the written exposure control plan required under paragraph (f)(1) and the cleaning methods required under paragraph (j)(2) of this standard; and

(ii) The employer must ensure that all spills and emergency releases of beryllium are cleaned up promptly and in accordance with the written exposure control plan required under paragraph (f)(1) and the cleaning methods required under paragraph (j)(2) of this standard.

(2) *Cleaning methods.*

(i) The employer must ensure that surfaces in beryllium work areas and regulated areas are cleaned by HEPA-filtered vacuuming or other methods that minimize the likelihood and level of airborne exposure.

(ii) The employer must not allow dry sweeping or brushing for cleaning surfaces in beryllium work areas or regulated areas unless HEPA-filtered vacuuming or other methods that minimize the likelihood and level of airborne exposure are not safe or effective.

(iii) The employer must not allow the use of compressed air for cleaning beryllium-contaminated surfaces unless the compressed air is used in conjunction with a ventilation system designed to capture the particulates made airborne by the use of compressed air.

(iv) Where employees use dry sweeping, brushing, or compressed air to clean beryllium-contaminated surfaces, the employer must provide, and ensure that each employee uses, respiratory protection and personal protective clothing and equipment in accordance with paragraphs (g) and (h) of this standard.

(v) The employer must ensure that cleaning equipment is handled and maintained in a manner that minimizes the likelihood and level of airborne exposure and the re-entrainment of airborne beryllium in the workplace.

(3) *Disposal and recycling.* For materials that contain beryllium in concentrations of 0.1 percent by weight or more or are contaminated with beryllium, the employer must ensure that:

(i) Materials designated for disposal are disposed of in sealed, impermeable enclosures, such as bags or containers, that are labeled in accordance with paragraph (m)(3) of this standard; and

(ii) Materials designated for recycling are cleaned to be as free as practicable of surface beryllium contamination and labeled in accordance with paragraph (m)(3) of this standard, or place in sealed, impermeable enclosures, such as bags or containers, that are labeled in accordance with paragraph (m)(3) of this standard.

(k) *Medical surveillance*—(1) *General.* (i) The employer must make medical surveillance required by this paragraph available at no cost to the employee, and at a reasonable time and place, to each employee:

(A) Who is or is reasonably expected to be exposed at or above the action level for more than 30 days per year;

(B) Who shows signs or symptoms of CBD or other beryllium-related health effects;

(C) Who is exposed to beryllium during an emergency; or

(D) Whose most recent written medical opinion required by paragraph (k)(6) or (k)(7) of this standard recommends periodic medical surveillance.

(ii) The employer must ensure that all medical examinations and procedures required by this standard are performed by, or under the direction of, a licensed physician.

(2) *Frequency.* The employer must provide a medical examination:

(i) Within 30 days after determining that:

(A) An employee meets the criteria of paragraph (k)(1)(i)(A), unless the employee has received a medical examination, provided in accordance with this standard, within the last two years; or

(B) An employee meets the criteria of paragraph (k)(1)(i)(B) or (C).

(ii) At least every two years thereafter for each employee who continues to meet the criteria of paragraph (k)(1)(i)(A), (B), or (D) of this standard.

(iii) At the termination of employment for each employee who meets any of the criteria of paragraph (k)(1)(i) of this standard at the time the employee's employment terminates, unless an examination has been provided in accordance with this standard during the six months prior to the date of termination.

(3) *Contents of examination.* (i) The employer must ensure that the PLHCP conducting the examination advises the employee of the risks and benefits of participating in the medical surveillance program and the employee's right to opt out of any or all parts of the medical examination.

(ii) The employer must ensure that the employee is offered a medical examination that includes:

(A) A medical and work history, with emphasis on past and present airborne exposure to or dermal contact with beryllium, smoking history, and any history of respiratory system dysfunction;

(B) A physical examination with emphasis on the respiratory system;

(C) A physical examination for skin rashes;

(D) Pulmonary function tests, performed in accordance with the guidelines established by the American Thoracic Society including forced vital capacity (FVC) and forced expiratory volume in one second (FEV_1);

(E) A standardized BeLPT or equivalent test, upon the first examination and at least every two years thereafter, unless the employee is confirmed positive. If the results of the BeLPT are other than normal, a follow-up BeLPT must be offered within 30 days, unless the employee has been confirmed positive. Samples must be analyzed in a laboratory certified under the College of American Pathologists/Clinical Laboratory Improvement Amendments (CLIA) guidelines to perform the BeLPT.

(F) A low dose computed tomography (LDCT) scan, when recommended by the PLHCP after considering the employee's history of exposure to beryllium along with other risk factors, such as smoking history, family medical history, sex, age, and presence of existing lung disease; and

(G) Any other test deemed appropriate by the PLHCP.

(4) *Information provided to the PLHCP.* The employer must ensure that the examining PLHCP (and the agreed-upon CBD diagnostic center, if an evaluation is required under paragraph (k)(7) of this standard) has a copy of this standard and must provide the following information, if known:

(i) A description of the employee's former and current duties that relate to the employee's airborne exposure to and dermal contact with beryllium;

(ii) The employee's former and current levels of airborne exposure;

(iii) A description of any personal protective clothing and equipment, including respirators, used by the employee, including when and for how long the employee has used that personal protective clothing and equipment; and

(iv) Information from records of employment-related medical examinations previously provided to the employee, currently within the control of the employer, after obtaining written consent from the employee.

(5) *Licensed physician's written medical report for the employee.* The employer

must ensure that the employee receives a written medical report from the licensed physician within 45 days of the examination (including any follow-up BeLPT required under paragraph (k)(3)(ii)(E) of this standard) and that the PLHCP explains the results of the examination to the employee. The written medical report must contain:

(i) A statement indicating the results of the medical examination, including the licensed physician's opinion as to whether the employee has

(A) Any detected medical condition, such as CBD or beryllium sensitization (*i.e.*, the employee is confirmed positive, as defined in paragraph (b) of this standard), that may place the employee at increased risk from further airborne exposure, and

(B) Any medical conditions related to airborne exposure that require further evaluation or treatment.

(ii) Any recommendations on:

(A) The employee's use of respirators, protective clothing, or equipment; or

(B) Limitations on the employee's airborne exposure to beryllium.

(iii) If the employee is confirmed positive or diagnosed with CBD or if the licensed physician otherwise deems it appropriate, the written report must also contain a referral for an evaluation at a CBD diagnostic center.

(iv) If the employee is confirmed positive or diagnosed with CBD the written report must also contain a recommendation for continued periodic medical surveillance.

(v) If the employee is confirmed positive or diagnosed with CBD the written report must also contain a recommendation for medical removal from airborne exposure to beryllium, as described in paragraph (l) of this standard.

(6) *Licensed physician's written medical opinion for the employer.* (i) The employer must obtain a written medical opinion from the licensed physician within 45 days of the medical examination (including any follow-up BeLPT required under paragraph (k)(3)(ii)(E) of this standard). The written medical opinion must contain only the following:

(A) The date of the examination;

(B) A statement that the examination has met the requirements of this standard;

(C) Any recommended limitations on the employee's use of respirators, protective clothing, or equipment; and

(D) A statement that the PLHCP has explained the results of the medical examination to the employee, including any tests conducted, any medical conditions related to airborne exposure that require further evaluation or treatment, and any special provisions for use of personal protective clothing or equipment;

(ii) If the employee provides written authorization, the written opinion must also contain any recommended limitations on the employee's airborne exposure to beryllium.

(iii) If the employee is confirmed positive or diagnosed with CBD or if the licensed physician otherwise deems it appropriate, and the employee provides written authorization, the written opinion must also contain a referral for an evaluation at a CBD diagnostic center.

(iv) If the employee is confirmed positive or diagnosed with CBD and the employee provides written authorization, the written opinion must also contain a recommendation for continued periodic medical surveillance.

(v) If the employee is confirmed positive or diagnosed with CBD and the employee provides written authorization, the written opinion must also contain a recommendation for medical removal from airborne exposure to beryllium, as described in paragraph (l) of this standard.

(vi) The employer must ensure that each employee receives a copy of the written medical opinion described in paragraph (k)(6) of this standard within 45 days of any medical examination (including any follow-up BeLPT required under paragraph (k)(3)(ii)(E) of this standard) performed for that employee.

(7) *CBD diagnostic center.* (i) The employer must provide an evaluation at no cost to the employee at a CBD diagnostic center that is mutually agreed upon by the employer and the employee. The examination must be provided within 30 days of:

(A) The employer's receipt of a physician's written medical opinion to the employer that recommends referral to a CBD diagnostic center; or

(B) The employee presenting to the employer a physician's written medical report indicating that the employee has been confirmed positive or diagnosed with CBD, or recommending referral to a CBD diagnostic center.

(ii) The employer must ensure that the employee receives a written medical report from the CBD diagnostic center that contains all the information required in paragraph (k)(5)(i), (ii), (iv), and (v) of this standard and that the PLHCP explains the results of the examination to the employee within 30 days of the examination.

(iii) The employer must obtain a written medical opinion from the CBD diagnostic center within 30 days of the medical examination. The written medical opinion must contain only the information in paragraph (k)(6)(i), as applicable, unless the employee provides written authorization to release additional information. If the employee provides written authorization, the written opinion must also contain the information from paragraphs (k)(6)(ii), (iv), and (v), if applicable.

(iv) The employer must ensure that each employee receives a copy of the written medical opinion from the CBD diagnostic center described in paragraph (k)(7) of this standard within 30 days of any medical examination performed for that employee.

(v) After an employee has received the initial clinical evaluation at a CBD diagnostic center described in paragraph (k)(7)(i) of this standard, the employee may choose to have any subsequent medical examinations for which the employee is eligible under paragraph (k) of this standard performed at a CBD diagnostic center mutually agreed upon by the employer and the employee, and the employer must provide such examinations at no cost to the employee.

(l) *Medical removal.* (1) An employee is eligible for medical removal, if the employee works in a job with airborne exposure at or above the action level and either:

(i) The employee provides the employer with:

131

(A) A written medical report indicating a confirmed positive finding or CBD diagnosis; or

(B) A written medical report recommending removal from airborne exposure to beryllium in accordance with paragraph (k)(5)(v) or (k)(7)(ii) of this standard; or

(ii) The employer receives a written medical opinion recommending removal from airborne exposure to beryllium in accordance with paragraph (k)(6)(v) or (k)(7)(iii) of this standard.

(2) If an employee is eligible for medical removal, the employer must provide the employee with the employee's choice of:

(i) Removal as described in paragraph (l)(3) of this standard; or

(ii) Remaining in a job with airborne exposure at or above the action level, provided that the employer provides, and ensures that the employee uses, respiratory protection that complies with paragraph (g) of this standard whenever airborne exposures are at or above the action level.

(3) If the employee chooses removal:

(i) If a comparable job is available where airborne exposures to beryllium are below the action level, and the employee is qualified for that job or can be trained within one month, the employer must remove the employee to that job. The employer must maintain for six months from the time of removal the employee's base earnings, seniority, and other rights and benefits that existed at the time of removal.

(ii) If comparable work is not available, the employer must maintain the employee's base earnings, seniority, and other rights and benefits that existed at the time of removal for six months or until such time that comparable work described in paragraph (l)(3)(i) becomes available, whichever comes first.

(4) The employer's obligation to provide medical removal protection benefits to a removed employee shall be reduced to the extent that the employee receives compensation for earnings lost during the period of removal from a publicly or employer-funded compensation program, or receives income from another employer made possible by virtue of the employee's removal.

(m) *Communication of hazards*—(1) *General.* (i) Chemical manufacturers, importers, distributors, and employers must comply with all requirements of the HCS (§ 1910.1200) for beryllium.

(ii) In classifying the hazards of beryllium, at least the following hazards must be addressed: Cancer; lung effects (CBD and acute beryllium disease); beryllium sensitization; skin sensitization; and skin, eye, and respiratory tract irritation.

(iii) Employers must include beryllium in the hazard communication program established to comply with the HCS. Employers must ensure that each employee has access to labels on containers of beryllium and to safety data sheets, and is trained in accordance with the requirements of the HCS (§ 1910.1200) and paragraph (m)(4) of this standard.

(2) *Warning signs.* (i) *Posting.* The employer must provide and display warning signs at each approach to a regulated area so that each employee is able to read and understand the signs and take necessary protective steps before entering the area.

(ii) *Sign specification.* (A) The employer must ensure that the warning signs required by paragraph (m)(2)(i) of this standard are legible and readily visible.

(B) The employer must ensure each warning sign required by paragraph (m)(2)(i) of this standard bears the following legend:

DANGER
REGULATED AREA
BERYLLIUM
MAY CAUSE CANCER
CAUSES DAMAGE TO LUNGS
AUTHORIZED PERSONNEL ONLY
WEAR RESPIRATORY PROTECTION AND
  PERSONAL PROTECTIVE CLOTHING
  AND EQUIPMENT IN THIS AREA

(3) *Warning labels.* Consistent with the HCS (§ 1910.1200), the employer must label each bag and container of clothing, equipment, and materials contaminated with beryllium, and must, at a minimum, include the following on the label:

DANGER
CONTAINS BERYLLIUM
MAY CAUSE CANCER
CAUSES DAMAGE TO LUNGS
AVOID CREATING DUST

DO NOT GET ON SKIN

(4) *Employee information and training.*
(i) For each employee who has, or can reasonably be expected to have, airborne exposure to or dermal contact with beryllium:

(A) The employer must provide information and training in accordance with the HCS (§1910.1200(h));

(B) The employer must provide initial training to each employee by the time of initial assignment; and

(C) The employer must repeat the training required under this standard annually for each employee.

(ii) The employer must ensure that each employee who is, or can reasonably be expected to be, exposed to airborne beryllium can demonstrate knowledge and understanding of the following:

(A) The health hazards associated with airborne exposure to and contact with beryllium, including the signs and symptoms of CBD;

(B) The written exposure control plan, with emphasis on the location(s) of beryllium work areas, including any regulated areas, and the specific nature of operations that could result in airborne exposure, especially airborne exposure above the TWA PEL or STEL;

(C) The purpose, proper selection, fitting, proper use, and limitations of personal protective clothing and equipment, including respirators;

(D) Applicable emergency procedures;

(E) Measures employees can take to protect themselves from airborne exposure to and contact with beryllium, including personal hygiene practices;

(F) The purpose and a description of the medical surveillance program required by paragraph (k) of this standard including risks and benefits of each test to be offered;

(G) The purpose and a description of the medical removal protection provided under paragraph (l) of this standard;

(H) The contents of the standard; and

(I) The employee's right of access to records under the Records Access standard (§1910.1020).

(iii) When a workplace change (such as modification of equipment, tasks, or procedures) results in new or increased airborne exposure that exceeds, or can reasonably be expected to exceed, either the TWA PEL or the STEL, the employer must provide additional training to those employees affected by the change in airborne exposure.

(iv) *Employee information.* The employer must make a copy of this standard and its appendices readily available at no cost to each employee and designated employee representative(s).

(n) *Recordkeeping*—(1) *Air monitoring data.* (i) The employer must make and maintain a record of all exposure measurements taken to assess airborne exposure as prescribed in paragraph (d) of this standard.

(ii) This record must include at least the following information:

(A) The date of measurement for each sample taken;

(B) The task that is being monitored;

(C) The sampling and analytical methods used and evidence of their accuracy;

(D) The number, duration, and results of samples taken;

(E) The type of personal protective clothing and equipment, including respirators, worn by monitored employees at the time of monitoring; and

(F) The name, social security number, and job classification of each employee represented by the monitoring, indicating which employees were actually monitored.

(iii) The employer must ensure that exposure records are maintained and made available in accordance with the Records Access standard (§1910.1020).

(2) *Objective data.* (i) Where an employer uses objective data to satisfy the exposure assessment requirements under paragraph (d)(2) of this standard, the employer must make and maintain a record of the objective data relied upon.

(ii) This record must include at least the following information:

(A) The data relied upon;

(B) The beryllium-containing material in question;

(C) The source of the objective data;

(D) A description of the process, task, or activity on which the objective data were based; and

(E) Other data relevant to the process, task, activity, material, or airborne exposure on which the objective data were based.

(iii) The employer must ensure that objective data are maintained and made available in accordance with the Records Access standard (§ 1910.1020).

(3) *Medical surveillance.* (i) The employer must make and maintain a record for each employee covered by medical surveillance under paragraph (k) of this standard.

(ii) The record must include the following information about each employee:

(A) Name, social security number, and job classification;

(B) A copy of all licensed physicians' written medical opinions for each employee; and

(C) A copy of the information provided to the PLHCP as required by paragraph (k)(4) of this standard.

(iii) The employer must ensure that medical records are maintained and made available in accordance with the Records Access standard (§ 1910.1020).

(4) *Training.* (i) At the completion of any training required by this standard, the employer must prepare a record that indicates the name, social security number, and job classification of each employee trained, the date the training was completed, and the topic of the training.

(ii) This record must be maintained for three years after the completion of training.

(5) *Access to records.* Upon request, the employer must make all records maintained as a requirement of this standard available for examination and copying to the Assistant Secretary, the Director, each employee, and each employee's designated representative(s) in accordance the Records Access standard (§ 1910.1020).

(6) *Transfer of records.* The employer must comply with the requirements involving transfer of records set forth in the Records Access standard (§ 1910.1020).

(o) *Dates*—(1) *Effective date.* This standard shall become effective March 10, 2017.

(2) *Compliance dates.* (i) Obligations contained in paragraphs (c), (d), (g), (k), and (l) of this standard: March 12, 2018;

(ii) Change rooms and showers required by paragraph (i) of this standard: March 11, 2019;

(iii) Engineering controls required by paragraph (f) of this standard: March 10, 2020; and

(iv) All other obligations of this standard: December 12, 2018.

(p) *Appendix.* Appendix A—Control Strategies to Minimize Beryllium Exposure of this standard is non-mandatory.

APPENDIX A TO § 1910.1024—CONTROL STRATEGIES TO MINIMIZE BERYLLIUM EXPOSURE (NON-MANDATORY)

Paragraph (f)(2)(i) of this standard requires employers to use one or more of the control methods listed in paragraph (f)(2)(i) to minimize worker exposure in each operation in a beryllium work area, unless the operation is exempt under paragraph (f)(2)(ii). This appendix sets forth a non-exhaustive list of control options that employers could use to comply with paragraph (f)(2)(i) for a number of specific beryllium operations.

TABLE A.1—EXPOSURE CONTROL RECOMMENDATIONS

Operation	Minimal control strategy *	Application group
Beryllium Oxide Forming (e.g., pressing, extruding).	For pressing operations: .... (1) Install local exhaust ventilation (LEV) on oxide press tables, oxide feed drum breaks, press tumblers, powder rollers, and die set disassembly stations; (2) Enclose the oxide presses; and (3) Install mechanical ventilation (make-up air) in processing areas For extruding operations: (1) Install LEV on extruder powder loading hoods, oxide supply bottles, rod breaking operations, centerless grinders, rod laydown tables, dicing operations, surface grinders, discharge end of extrusion presses; (2) Enclose the centerless grinders; and (3) Install mechanical ventilation (make-up air) in processing areas.	Primary Beryllium Production; Beryllium Oxide Ceramics and Composites.

TABLE A.1—EXPOSURE CONTROL RECOMMENDATIONS—Continued

Operation	Minimal control strategy *	Application group
Chemical Processing Operations (e.g., leaching, pickling, degreasing, etching, plating).	For medium and high gassing operations: .... (1) Perform operation with a hood having a maximum of one open side; and (2) Design process so as to minimize spills; if accidental spills occur, perform immediate cleanup.	Primary Beryllium Production; Beryllium Oxide Ceramics and Composites; Copper Rolling, Drawing and Extruding.
Finishing (e.g., grinding, sanding, polishing, deburring).	(1) Perform portable finishing operations in a ventilated hood. The hood should include both downdraft and backdraft ventilation, and have at least two sides and a top. (2) Perform stationary finishing operations using a ventilated and enclosed hood at the point of operation. The grinding wheel of the stationary unit should be enclosed and ventilated.	Secondary Smelting; Fabrication of Beryllium Alloy Products; Dental Labs.
Furnace Operations (e.g., Melting and Casting).	(1) Use LEV on furnaces, pelletizer; arc furnace ingot machine discharge; pellet sampling; arc furnace bins and conveyors; beryllium hydroxide drum dumper and dryer; furnace rebuilding; furnace tool holders; arc furnace tundish and tundish skimming, tundish preheat hood, and tundish cleaning hoods; dross handling equipment and drums; dross recycling; and tool repair station, charge make-up station, oxide screener, product sampling locations, drum changing stations, and drum cleaning stations (2) Use mechanical ventilation (make-up air) in furnace building	Primary Beryllium Production; Beryllium Oxide Ceramics and Composites; Nonferrous Foundries; Secondary Smelting.
Machining	Use (1) LEV consistent with ACGIH® ventilation guidelines on deburring hoods, wet surface grinder enclosures, belt sanding hoods, and electrical discharge machines (for operations such as polishing, lapping, and buffing); (2) high velocity low volume hoods or ventilated enclosures on lathes, vertical mills, CNC mills, and tool grinding operations; (3) for beryllium oxide ceramics, LEV on lapping, dicing, and laser cutting; and (4) wet methods (e.g., coolants).	Primary Beryllium Production; Beryllium Oxide Ceramics and Composites; Copper Rolling, Drawing, and Extruding; Precision Turned Products.
Mechanical Processing (e.g., material handling (including scrap), sorting, crushing, screening, pulverizing, shredding, pouring, mixing, blending).	(1) Enclose and ventilate sources of emission; (2) Prohibit open handling of materials; and (3) Use mechanical ventilation (make-up air) in processing areas	Primary Beryllium Production; Beryllium Oxide Ceramics and Composites; Aluminum and Copper Foundries; Secondary Smelting.
Metal Forming (e.g., rolling, drawing, straightening, annealing, extruding).	(1) For rolling operations, install LEV on mill stands and reels such that a hood extends the length of the mill; (2) For point and chamfer operations, install LEV hoods at both ends of the rod; (3) For annealing operations, provide an inert atmosphere for annealing furnaces, and LEV hoods at entry and exit points; (4) For swaging operations, install LEV on the cutting head; (5) For drawing, straightening, and extruding operations, install LEV at entry and exit points; and (6) For all metal forming operations, install mechanical ventilation (make-up air) for processing areas.	Primary Beryllium Production; Copper Rolling, Drawing, and Extruding; Fabrication of Beryllium Alloy Products.
Welding	For fixed welding operations: .... (1) Enclose work locations around the source of fume generation and use local exhaust ventilation; and (2) Install close capture hood enclosure designed so as to minimize fume emission from the enclosure welding operation. For manual operations: (1) Use portable local exhaust and general ventilation	Primary Beryllium Production; Fabrication of Beryllium Alloy Products; Welding.

* All LEV specifications should be in accordance with the ACGIH® Publication No. 2094, "Industrial Ventilation—A Manual of Recommended Practice" wherever applicable.

[82 FR 2736, Jan. 9, 2017, as amended at 83 FR 19948, May 7, 2018; 83 FR 39360, Aug. 9, 2018]

§ 1910.1025 Lead.

(a) *Scope and application.* (1) This section applies to all occupational exposure to lead, except as provided in paragraph (a)(2).

(2) This section does not apply to the construction industry or to agricultural operations covered by 29 CFR part 1928.

(b) *Definitions. Action level* means employee exposure, without regard to the use of respirators, to an airborne concentration of lead of 30 micrograms per cubic meter of air (30 μg/m³) averaged over an 8-hour period.

Assistant Secretary means the Assistant Secretary of Labor for Occupational Safety and Health, U.S. Department of Labor, or designee.

Director means the Director, National Institute for Occupational Safety and Health (NIOSH), U.S. Department of Health, Education, and Welfare, or designee.

Lead means metallic lead, all inorganic lead compounds, and organic lead soaps. Excluded from this definition are all other organic lead compounds.

(c) *Permissible exposure limit (PEL).* (1) The employer shall assure that no employee is exposed to lead at concentrations greater than fifty micrograms per cubic meter of air (50 μg/m³) averaged over an 8-hour period.

(2) If an employee is exposed to lead for more than 8 hours in any work day, the permissible exposure limit, as a time weighted average (TWA) for that day, shall be reduced according to the following formula:

Maximum permissible limit (in μg/m³) = 400 ÷ hours worked in the day.

(3) When respirators are used to supplement engineering and work practice controls to comply with the PEL and all the requirements of paragraph (f) have been met, employee exposure, for the purpose of determining whether the employer has complied with the PEL, may be considered to be at the level provided by the protection factor of the respirator for those periods the respirator is worn. Those periods may be averaged with exposure levels during periods when respirators are not worn to determine the employee's daily TWA exposure.

(d) *Exposure monitoring—*(1) *General.* (i) For the purposes of paragraph (d), employee exposure is that exposure which would occur if the employee were not using a respirator.

(ii) With the exception of monitoring under paragraph (d)(3), the employer shall collect full shift (for at least 7 continuous hours) personal samples including at least one sample for each shift for each job classification in each work area.

(iii) Full shift personal samples shall be representative of the monitored employee's regular, daily exposure to lead.

(2) *Initial determination.* Each employer who has a workplace or work operation covered by this standard shall determine if any employee may be exposed to lead at or above the action level.

(3) *Basis of initial determination.* (i) The employer shall monitor employee exposures and shall base initial determinations on the employee exposure monitoring results and any of the following, relevant considerations:

(A) Any information, observations, or calculations which would indicate employee exposure to lead;

(B) Any previous measurements of airborne lead; and

(C) Any employee complaints of symptoms which may be attributable to exposure to lead.

(ii) Monitoring for the initial determination may be limited to a representative sample of the exposed employees who the employer reasonably believes are exposed to the greatest airborne concentrations of lead in the workplace.

(iii) Measurements of airborne lead made in the preceding 12 months may be used to satisfy the requirement to monitor under paragraph (d)(3)(i) if the sampling and analytical methods used meet the accuracy and confidence levels of paragraph (d)(9) of this section.

(4) *Positive initial determination and initial monitoring.* (i) Where a determination conducted under paragraphs (d) (2) and (3) of this section shows the possibility of any employee exposure at or above the action level, the employer shall conduct monitoring which is representative of the exposure for each employee in the workplace who is exposed to lead.

(ii) Measurements of airborne lead made in the preceding 12 months may be used to satisfy this requirement if the sampling and analytical methods used meet the accuracy and confidence levels of paragraph (d)(9) of this section.

(5) *Negative initial determination.* Where a determination, conducted under paragraphs (d) (2) and (3) of this section is made that no employee is exposed to airborne concentrations of lead at or above the action level, the

employer shall make a written record of such determination. The record shall include at least the information specified in paragraph (d)(3) of this section and shall also include the date of determination, location within the worksite, and the name and social security number of each employee monitored.

(6) *Frequency.* (i) If the initial monitoring reveals employee exposure to be below the action level the measurements need not be repeated except as otherwise provided in paragraph (d)(7) of this section.

(ii) If the initial determination or subsequent monitoring reveals employee exposure to be at or above the action level but below the permissible exposure limit the employer shall repeat monitoring in accordance with this paragraph at least every 6 months. The employer shall continue monitoring at the required frequency until at least two consecutive measurements, taken at least 7 days apart, are below the action level at which time the employer may discontinue monitoring for that employee except as otherwise provided in paragraph (d)(7) of this section.

(iii) If the initial monitoring reveals that employee exposure is above the permissible exposure limit the employer shall repeat monitoring quarterly. The employer shall continue monitoring at the required frequency until at least two consecutive measurements, taken at least 7 days apart, are below the PEL but at or above the action level at which time the employer shall repeat monitoring for that employee at the frequency specified in paragraph (d)(6)(ii), except as otherwise provided in paragraph (d)(7) of this section.

(7) *Additional monitoring.* Whenever there has been a production, process, control or personnel change which may result in new or additional exposure to lead, or whenever the employer has any other reason to suspect a change which may result in new or additional exposures to lead, additional monitoring in accordance with this paragraph shall be conducted.

(8) *Employee notification.* (i) The employer must, within 15 working days after the receipt of the results of any monitoring performed under this sec-

tion, notify each affected employee of these results either individually in writing or by posting the results in an appropriate location that is accessible to affected employees.

(ii) Whenever the results indicate that the representative employee exposure, without regard to respirators, exceeds the permissible exposure limit, the employer shall incude in the written notice a statement that the permissible exposure limit was exceeded and a description of the corrective action taken or to be taken to reduce exposure to or below the permissible exposure limit.

(9) *Accuracy of measurement.* The employer shall use a method of monitoring and analysis which has an accuracy (to a confidence level of 95%) of not less than plus or minus 20 percent for airborne concentrations of lead equal to or greater than 30 µg/m³.

(e) *Methods of compliance*—(1) *Engineering and work practice controls.* (i) Where any employee is exposed to lead above the permissible exposure limit for more than 30 days per year, the employer shall implement engineering and work practice controls (including administrative controls) to reduce and maintain employee exposure to lead in accordance with the implementation schedule in Table I below, except to the extent that the employer can demonstrate that such controls are not feasible. Wherever the engineering and work practice controls which can be instituted are not sufficient to reduce employee exposure to or below the permissible exposure limit, the employer shall nonetheless use them to reduce exposures to the lowest feasible level and shall supplement them by the use of respiratory protection which complies with the requirements of paragraph (f) of this section.

(ii) Where any employee is·exposed to lead above the permissible exposure limit, but for 30 days or less per year, the employer shall implement engineering controls to reduce exposures to 200 µg/m³, but thereafter may implement any combination of engineering, work practice (including administrative controls), and respiratory controls to reduce and maintain employee exposure to lead to or below 50 µg/m³.

TABLE I

Industry	Compliance dates:[1] (50 µg/m³)
Lead chemicals, secondary copper smelting.	July 19, 1996.
Nonferrous foundries	July 19, 1996.[2]
Brass and bronze ingot manufacture	6 years.[3]

[1] Calculated by counting from the date the stay on implementation of paragraph (e)(1) was lifted by the U.S. Court of Appeals for the District of Columbia, the number of years specified in the 1978 lead standard and subsequent amendments for compliance with the PEL of 50 µg/m³ for exposure to airborne concentrations of lead levels for the particular industry.

[2] Large nonferrous foundries (20 or more employees) are required to achieve the PEL of 50 µg/m³ by means of engineering and work practice controls. Small nonferrous foundries (fewer than 20 employees) are required to achieve an 8-hour TWA of 75 µg/m³ by such controls.

[3] Expressed as the number of years from the date on which the Court lifts the stay on the implementation of paragraph (e)(1) for this industry for employers to achieve a lead in air concentration of 75 µg/m³. Compliance with paragraph (e) in this industry is determined by a compliance directive that incorporates elements from the settlement agreement between OSHA and representatives of the industry.

(2) *Respiratory protection.* Where engineering and work practice controls do not reduce employee exposure to or below the 50 µg/m³ permissible exposure limit, the employer shall supplement these controls with respirators in accordance with paragraph (f).

(3) *Compliance program.* (i) Each employer shall establish and implement a written compliance program to reduce exposures to or below the permissible exposure limit, and interim levels if applicable, solely by means of engineering and work practice controls in accordance with the implementation schedule in paragraph (e)(1).

(ii) Written plans for these compliance programs shall include at least the following:

(A) A description of each operation in which lead is emitted; e.g. machinery used, material processed, controls in place, crew size, employee job responsibilities, operating procedures and maintenance practices;

(B) A description of the specific means that will be employed to achieve compliance, including engineering plans and studies used to determine methods selected for controlling exposure to lead;

(C) A report of the technology considered in meeting the permissible exposure limit;

(D) Air monitoring data which documents the source of lead emissions;

(E) A detailed schedule for implementation of the program, including documentation such as copies of purchase orders for equipment, construction contracts, etc.;

(F) A work practice program which includes items required under paragraphs (g), (h) and (i) of this regulation;

(G) An administrative control schedule required by paragraph (e)(6), if applicable;

(H) Other relevant information.

(iii) Written programs shall be submitted upon request to the Assistant Secretary and the Director, and shall be available at the worksite for examination and copying by the Assistant Secretary, Director, any affected employee or authorized employee representatives.

(iv) Written programs must be revised and updated at least annually to reflect the current status of the program.

(4) *Mechanical ventilation.* (i) When ventilation is used to control exposure, measurements which demonstrate the effectiveness of the system in controlling exposure, such as capture velocity, duct velocity, or static pressure shall be made at least every 3 months. Measurements of the system's effectiveness in controlling exposure shall be made within 5 days of any change in production, process, or control which might result in a change in employee exposure to lead.

(ii) *Recirculation of air.* If air from exhaust ventilation is recirculated into the workplace, the employer shall assure that (A) the system has a high efficiency filter with reliable back-up filter; and (B) controls to monitor the concentration of lead in the return air and to bypass the recirculation system automatically if it fails are installed, operating, and maintained.

(5) *Administrative controls.* If administrative controls are used as a means of reducing employees TWA exposure to lead, the employer shall establish and implement a job rotation schedule which includes:

(i) Name or identification number of each affected employee;

(ii) Duration and exposure levels at each job or work station where each affected employee is located; and

(iii) Any other information which may be useful in assessing the reliability of administrative controls to reduce exposure to lead.

(f) *Respiratory protection*—(1) *General.* For employees who use respirators required by this section, the employer must provide each employee an appropriate respirator that complies with the requirements of this paragraph. Respirators must be used during:

(i) Periods necessary to install or implement engineering or work-practice controls.

(ii) Work operations for which engineering and work-practice controls are not sufficient to reduce employee exposures to or below the permissible exposure limit.

(iii) Periods when an employee requests a respirator.

(2) *Respirator program.* (i) The employer must implement a respiratory protection program in accordance with § 1910.134(b) through (d) (except (d)(1)(iii)), and (f) through (m), which covers each employee required by this section to use a respirator.

(ii) If an employee has breathing difficulty during fit testing or respirator use, the employer must provide the employee with a medical examination in accordance with paragraph (j)(3)(i)(C) of this section to determine whether or not the employee can use a respirator while performing the required duty.

(3) *Respirator selection.* (i) Employers must:

(A) Select, and provide to employees, the appropriate respirators specified in paragraph (d)(3)(i)(A) of 29 CFR 1910.134.

(B) Provide employees with full facepiece respirators instead of half mask respirators for protection against lead aerosols that cause eye or skin irritation at the use concentrations.

(C) Provide HEPA filters for powered and non-powered air-purifying respirators.

(ii) Employers must provide employees with a powered air-purifying respirator (PAPR) instead of a negative pressure respirator selected according to paragraph (f)(3)(i) of this standard when an employee chooses to use a PAPR and it provides adequate protection to the employee as specified by paragraph (f)(3)(i) of this standard.

(g) *Protective work clothing and equipment*—(1) *Provision and use.* If an employee is exposed to lead above the PEL, without regard to the use of respirators or where the possibility of skin or eye irritation exists, the employer shall provide at no cost to the employee and assure that the employee uses appropriate protective work clothing and equipment such as, but not limited to:

(i) Coveralls or similar full-body work clothing;

(ii) Gloves, hats, and shoes or disposable shoe coverlets; and

(iii) Face shields, vented goggles, or other appropriate protective equipment which complies with § 1910.133 of this Part.

(2) *Cleaning and replacement.* (i) The employer shall provide the protective clothing required in paragraph (g)(1) of this section in a clean and dry condition at least weekly, and daily to employees whose exposure levels without regard to a respirator are over 200 µg/m³ of lead as an 8-hour TWA.

(ii) The employer shall provide for the cleaning, laundering, or disposal of protective clothing and equipment required by paragraph (g)(1) of this section.

(iii) The employer shall repair or replace required protective clothing and equipment as needed to maintain their effectiveness.

(iv) The employer shall assure that all protective clothing is removed at the completion of a work shift only in change rooms provided for that purpose as prescribed in paragraph (i)(2) of this section.

(v) The employer shall assure that contaminated protective clothing which is to be cleaned, laundered, or disposed of, is placed in a closed container in the change-room which prevents dispersion of lead outside the container.

(vi) The employer shall inform in writing any person who cleans or launders protective clothing or equipment of the potentially harmful effects of exposure to lead.

(vii) Labeling of contaminated protective clothing and equipment.

(A) The employer shall ensure that labels of bags or containers of contaminated protective clothing and equipment include the following information:

DANGER: CLOTHING AND EQUIPMENT CONTAMINATED WITH LEAD. MAY DAMAGE FERTILITY OR THE UNBORN CHILD. CAUSES DAMAGE TO THE CENTRAL NERVOUS SYSTEM. DO NOT EAT, DRINK OR SMOKE WHEN HANDLING. DO NOT REMOVE DUST BY BLOWING OR SHAKING. DISPOSE OF LEAD CONTAMINATED WASH WATER IN ACCORDANCE WITH APPLICABLE LOCAL, STATE, OR FEDERAL REGULATIONS.

(B) Prior to June 1, 2015, employers may include the following information on bags or containers of contaminated protective clothing and equipment in lieu of the labeling requirements in paragraphs (g)(2)(vii)(A) of this section:

CAUTION: CLOTHING CONTAMINATED WITH LEAD. DO NOT REMOVE DUST BY BLOWING OR SHAKING. DISPOSE OF LEAD CONTAMINATED WASH WATER IN ACCORDANCE WITH APPLICABLE LOCAL, STATE, OR FEDERAL REGULATIONS.

(viii) The employer shall prohibit the removal of lead from protective clothing or equipment by blowing, shaking, or any other means which disperses lead into the air.

(h) *Housekeeping*—(1) *Surfaces.* All surfaces shall be maintained as free as practicable of accumulations of lead.

(2) *Cleaning floors.* (i) Floors and other surfaces where lead accumulates may not be cleaned by the use of compressed air.

(ii) Shoveling, dry or wet sweeping, and brushing may be used only where vacuuming or other equally effective methods have been tried and found not to be effective.

(3) *Vacuuming.* Where vacuuming methods are selected, the vacuums shall be used and emptied in a manner which minimizes the reentry of lead into the workplace.

(i) *Hygiene facilities and practices.* (1) The employer shall assure that in areas where employees are exposed to lead above the PEL, without regard to the use of respirators, food or beverage is not present or consumed, tobacco products are not present or used, and cosmetics are not applied, except in

change rooms, lunchrooms, and showers required under paragraphs (i)(2) through (i)(4) of this section.

(2) *Change rooms.* (i) The employer shall provide clean change rooms for employees who work in areas where their airborne exposure to lead is above the PEL, without regard to the use of respirators.

(ii) The employer shall assure that change rooms are equipped with separate storage facilities for protective work clothing and equipment and for street clothes which prevent cross-contamination.

(3) *Showers.* (i) The employer shall assure that employees who work in areas where their airborne exposure to lead is above the PEL, without regard to the use of respirators, shower at the end of the work shift.

(ii) The employer shall provide shower facilities in accordance with § 1910.141 (d)(3) of this part.

(iii) The employer shall assure that employees who are required to shower pursuant to paragraph (i)(3)(i) do not leave the workplace wearing any clothing or equipment worn during the work shift.

(4) *Lunchrooms.* (i) The employer shall provide lunchroom facilities for employees who work in areas where their airborne exposure to lead is above the PEL, without regard to the use of respirators.

(ii) The employer shall assure that lunchroom facilities have a temperature controlled, positive pressure, filtered air supply, and are readily accessible to employees.

(iii) The employer shall assure that employees who work in areas where their airborne exposure to lead is above the PEL without regard to the use of a respirator wash their hands and face prior to eating, drinking, smoking or applying cosmetics.

(iv) The employer shall assure that employees do not enter lunchroom facilities with protective work clothing or equipment unless surface lead dust has been removed by vacuuming, downdraft booth, or other cleaning method.

(5) *Lavatories.* The employer shall provide an adequate number of lavatory facilities which comply with § 1910.141(d) (1) and (2) of this part.

(j) *Medical surveillance*—(1) *General.* (i) The employer shall institute a medical surveillance program for all employees who are or may be exposed at or above the action level for more than 30 days per year.

(ii) The employer shall assure that all medical examinations and procedures are performed by or under the supervision of a licensed physician.

(iii) The employer shall provide the required medical surveillance including multiple physician review under paragraph (j)(3)(iii) without cost to employees and at a reasonable time and place.

(2) *Biological monitoring*—(i) *Blood lead and ZPP level sampling and analysis.* The employer shall make available biological monitoring in the form of blood sampling and analysis for lead and zinc protoporphyrin levels to each employee covered under paragraph (j)(1)(i) of this section on the following schedule:

(A) At least every 6 months to each employee covered under paragraph (j)(1)(i) of this section;

(B) At least every two months for each employee whose last blood sampling and analysis indicated a blood lead level at or above 40 µg/100 g of whole blood. This frequency shall continue until two consecutive blood samples and analyses indicate a blood lead level below 40 µg/100 g of whole blood; and

(C) At least monthly during the removal period of each employee removed from exposure to lead due to an elevated blood lead level.

(ii) *Follow-up blood sampling tests.* Whenever the results of a blood lead level test indicate that an employee's blood lead level is at or above the numerical criterion for medical removal under paragraph (k)(1)(i)(A) of this section, the employer shall provide a second (follow-up) blood sampling test within two weeks after the employer receives the results of the first blood sampling test.

(iii) *Accuracy of blood lead level sampling and analysis.* Blood lead level sampling and analysis provided pursuant to this section shall have an accuracy (to a confidence level of 95 percent) within plus or minus 15 percent or 6 µg/100ml, whichever is greater, and shall be conducted by a laboratory licensed by the Center for Disease Con-

trol, United States Department of Health, Education and Welfare (CDC) or which has received a satisfactory grade in blood lead proficiency testing from CDC in the prior twelve months.

(iv) *Employee notification.* Within five working days after the receipt of biological monitoring results, the employer shall notify in writing each employee whose blood lead level is at or above 40 µg/100 g:

(A) Of that employee's blood lead level; and

(B) That the standard requires temporary medical removal with Medical Removal Protection benefits when an employee's blood lead level is at or above the numerical criterion for medical removal under paragraph (k)(1)(i) of this section.

(3) *Medical examinations and consultations*—(i) *Frequency.* The employer shall make available medical examinations and consultations to each employee covered under paragraph (j)(1)(i) of this section on the following schedule:

(A) At least annually for each employee for whom a blood sampling test conducted at any time during the preceding 12 months indicated a blood lead level at or above 40 µg/100 g;

(B) Prior to assignment for each employee being assigned for the first time to an area in which airborne concentrations of lead are at or above the action level;

(C) As soon as possible, upon notification by an employee either that the employee has developed signs or symptoms commonly associated with lead intoxication, that the employee desires medical advice concerning the effects of current or past exposure to lead on the employee's ability to procreate a healthy child, or that the employee has demonstrated difficulty in breathing during a respirator fitting test or during use; and

(D) As medically appropriate for each employee either removed from exposure to lead due to a risk of sustaining material impairment to health, or otherwise limited pursuant to a final medical determination.

(ii) *Content.* Medical examinations made available pursuant to paragraph (j)(3)(i) (A) through (B) of this section shall include the following elements:

(A) A detailed work history and a medical history, with particular attention to past lead exposure (occupational and non-occupational), personal habits (smoking, hygiene), and past gastrointestinal, hematologic, renal, cardiovascular, reproductive and neurological problems;

(B) A thorough physical examination, with particular attention to teeth, gums, hematologic, gastrointestinal, renal, cardiovascular, and neurological systems. Pulmonary status should be evaluated if respiratory protection will be used;

(C) A blood pressure measurement;

(D) A blood sample and analysis which determines:

(1) Blood lead level;

(2) Hemoglobin and hematocrit determinations, red cell indices, and examination of peripheral smear morphology;

(3) Zinc protoporphyrin;

(4) Blood urea nitrogen; and,

(5) Serum creatinine;

(E) A routine urinalysis with microscopic examination; and

(F) Any laboratory or other test which the examining physician deems necessary by sound medical practice.

The content of medical examinations made available pursuant to paragraph (j)(3)(i) (C) through (D) of this section shall be determined by an examining physician and, if requested by an employee, shall include pregnancy testing or laboratory evaluation of male fertility.

(iii) *Multiple physician review mechanism.* (A) If the employer selects the initial physician who conducts any medical examination or consultation provided to an employee under this section, the employee may designate a second physician:

(1) To review any findings, determinations or recommendations of the initial physician; and

(2) To conduct such examinations, consultations, and laboratory tests as the second physician deems necessary to facilitate this review.

(B) The employer shall promptly notify an employee of the right to seek a second medical opinion after each occasion that an initial physician conducts a medical examination or consultation pursuant to this section. The

employer may condition its participation in, and payment for, the multiple physician review mechanism upon the employee doing the following within fifteen (15) days after receipt of the foregoing notification, or receipt of the initial physician's written opinion, whichever is later:

(1) The employee informing the employer that he or she intends to seek a second medical opinion, and

(2) The employee initiating steps to make an appointment with a second physician.

(C) If the findings, determinations or recommendations of the second physician differ from those of the initial physician, then the employer and the employee shall assure that efforts are made for the two physicians to resolve any disagreement.

(D) If the two physicians have been unable to quickly resolve their disagreement, then the employer and the employee through their respective physicians shall designate a third physician:

(1) To review any findings, determinations or recommendations of the prior physicians; and

(2) To conduct such examinations, consultations, laboratory tests and discussions with the prior physicians as the third physician deems necessary to resolve the disagreement of the prior physicians.

(E) The employer shall act consistent with the findings, determinations and recommendations of the third physician, unless the employer and the employee reach an agreement which is otherwise consistent with the recommendations of at least one of the three physicians.

(iv) *Information provided to examining and consulting physicians.* (A) The employer shall provide an initial physician conducting a medical examination or consultation under this section with the following information:

(1) A copy of this regulation for lead including all Appendices;

(2) A description of the affected employee's duties as they relate to the employee's exposure;

(3) The employee's exposure level or anticipated exposure level to lead and to any other toxic substance (if applicable);

(4) A description of any personal protective equipment used or to be used;

(5) Prior blood lead determinations; and

(6) All prior written medical opinions concerning the employee in the employer's possession or control.

(B) The employer shall provide the foregoing information to a second or third physician conducting a medical examination or consultation under this section upon request either by the second or third physician, or by the employee.

(v) *Written medical opinions.* (A) The employer shall obtain and furnish the employee with a copy of a written medical opinion from each examining or consulting physician which contains the following information:

(1) The physician's opinion as to whether the employee has any detected medical condition which would place the employee at increased risk of material impairment of the employee's health from exposure to lead;

(2) Any recommended special protective measures to be provided to the employee, or limitations to be placed upon the employee's exposure to lead;

(3) Any recommended limitation upon the employee's use of respirators, including a determination of whether the employee can wear a powered air purifying respirator if a physician determines that the employee cannot wear a negative pressure respirator; and

(4) The results of the blood lead determinations.

(B) The employer shall instruct each examining and consulting physician to:

(1) Not reveal either in the written opinion, or in any other means of communication with the employer, findings, including laboratory results, or diagnoses unrelated to an employee's occupational exposure to lead; and

(2) Advise the employee of any medical condition, occupational or non-occupational, which dictates further medical examination or treatment.

(vi) *Alternate Physician Determination Mechanisms.* The employer and an employee or authorized employee representative may agree upon the use of any expeditious alternate physician determination mechanism in lieu of the multiple physician review mechanism provided by this paragraph so long as the alternate mechanism otherwise satisfies the requirements contained in this paragraph.

(4) *Chelation.* (i) The employer shall assure that any person whom he retains, employs, supervises or controls does not engage in prophylactic chelation of any employee at any time.

(ii) If therapeutic or diagnostic chelation is to be performed by any person in paragraph (j)(4)(i), the employer shall assure that it be done under the supervision of a licensed physician in a clinical setting with thorough and appropriate medical monitoring and that the employee is notified in writing prior to its occurrence.

(k) *Medical Removal Protection*—(1) *Temporary medical removal and return of an employee*—(i) *Temporary removal due to elevated blood lead levels.* (A) The employer shall remove an employee from work having an exposure to lead at or above the action level on each occasion that a periodic and a follow-up blood sampling test conducted pursuant to this section indicate that the employee's blood lead level is at or above 60 μg/100 g of whole blood; and

(B) The employer shall remove an employee from work having an exposure to lead at or above the action level on each occasion that the average of the last three blood sampling tests conducted pursuant to this section (or the average of all blood sampling tests conducted over the previous six (6) months, whichever is longer) indicates that the employee's blood lead level is at or above 50 μg/100 g of whole blood; provided, however, that an employee need not be removed if the last blood sampling test indicates a blood lead level below 40 μg/100 g of whole blood.

(ii) *Temporary removal due to a final medical determination.* (A) The employer shall remove an employee from work having an exposure to lead at or above the action level on each occasion that a final medical determination results in a medical finding, determination, or opinion that the employee has a detected medical condition which places the employee at increased risk of material impairment to health from exposure to lead.

(B) For the purposes of this section, the phrase "final medical determination" shall mean the outcome of the multiple physician review mechanism or alternate medical determination mechanism used pursuant to the medical surveillance provisions of this section.

(C) Where a final medical determination results in any recommended special protective measures for an employee, or limitations on an employee's exposure to lead, the employer shall implement and act consistent with the recommendation.

(iii) *Return of the employee to former job status.* (A) The employer shall return an employee to his or her former job status:

(*1*) For an employee removed due to a blood lead level at or above 60 µg/100 g, or due to an average blood lead level at or above 50 µg/100 g, when two consecutive blood sampling tests indicate that the employee's blood lead level is below 40 µg/100 g of whole blood;

(*2*) For an employee removed due to a final medical determination, when a subsequent final medical determination results in a medical finding, determination, or opinion that the employee no longer has a detected medical condition which places the employee at increased risk of material impairment to health from exposure to lead.

(B) For the purposes of this section, the requirement that an employer return an employee to his or her former job status is not intended to expand upon or restrict any rights an employee has or would have had, absent temporary medical removal, to a specific job classification or position under the terms of a collective bargaining agreement.

(iv) *Removal of other employee special protective measure or limitations.* The employer shall remove any limitations placed on an employee or end any special protective measures provided to an employee pursuant to a final medical determination when a subsequent final medical determination indicates that the limitations or special protective measures are no longer necessary.

(v) *Employer options pending a final medical determination.* Where the multiple physician review mechanism, or alternate medical determination mechanism used pursuant to the medical surveillance provisions of this section, has not yet resulted in a final medical determination with respect to an employee, the employer shall act as follows:

(A) *Removal.* The employer may remove the employee from exposure to lead, provide special protective measures to the employee, or place limitations upon the employee, consistent with the medical findings, determinations, or recommendations of any of the physicians who have reviewed the employee's health status.

(B) *Return.* The employer may return the employee to his or her former job status, end any special protective measures provided to the employee, and remove any limitations placed upon the employee, consistent with the medical findings, determinations, or recommendations of any of the physicians who have reviewed the employee's health status, with two exceptions. If

(*1*) the initial removal, special protection, or limitation of the employee resulted from a final medical determination which differed from the findings, determinations, or recommendations of the initial physician or

(*2*) The employee has been on removal status for the preceding eighteen months due to an elevated blood lead level, then the employer shall await a final medical determination.

(2) *Medical removal protection benefits*—(i) *Provision of medical removal protection benefits.* The employer shall provide to an employee up to eighteen (18) months of medical removal protection benefits on each occasion that an employee is removed from exposure to lead or otherwise limited pursuant to this section.

(ii) *Definition of medical removal protection benefits.* For the purposes of this section, the requirement that an employer provide medical removal protection benefits means that the employer shall maintain the earnings, seniority and other employment rights and benefits of an employee as though the employee had not been removed from normal exposure to lead or otherwise limited.

(iii) *Follow-up medical surveillance during the period of employee removal or limitation.* During the period of time that an employee is removed from normal exposure to lead or otherwise limited, the employer may condition the provision of medical removal protection benefits upon the employee's participation in follow-up medical surveillance made available pursuant to this section.

(iv) *Workers' compensation claims.* If a removed employee files a claim for workers' compensation payments for a lead-related disability, then the employer shall continue to provide medical removal protection benefits pending disposition of the claim. To the extent that an award is made to the employee for earnings lost during the period of removal, the employer's medical removal protection obligation shall be reduced by such amount. The employer shall receive no credit for workers' compensation payments received by the employee for treatment related expenses.

(v) *Other credits.* The employer's obligation to provide medical removal protection benefits to a removed employee shall be reduced to the extent that the employee receives compensation for earnings lost during the period of removal either from a publicly or employer-funded compensation program, or receives income from employment with another employer made possible by virtue of the employee's removal.

(vi) *Employees whose blood lead levels do not adequately decline within 18 months of removal.* The employer shall take the following measures with respect to any employee removed from exposure to lead due to an elevated blood lead level whose blood lead level has not declined within the past eighteen (18) months of removal so that the employee has been returned to his or her former job status:

(A) The employer shall make available to the employee a medical examination pursuant to this section to obtain a final medical determination with respect to the employee;

(B) The employer shall assure that the final medical determination obtained indicates whether or not the employee may be returned to his or her former job status, and if not, what steps should be taken to protect the employee's health;

(C) Where the final medical determination has not yet been obtained, or once obtained indicates that the employee may not yet be returned to his or her former job status, the employer shall continue to provide medical removal protection benefits to the employee until either the employee is returned to former job status, or a final medical determination is made that the employee is incapable of ever safely returning to his or her former job status.

(D) Where the employer acts pursuant to a final medical determination which permits the return of the employee to his or her former job status despite what would otherwise be an unacceptable blood lead level, later questions concerning removing the employee again shall be decided by a final medical determination. The employer need not automatically remove such an employee pursuant to the blood lead level removal criteria provided by this section.

(vii) *Voluntary Removal or Restriction of An Employee.* Where an employer, although not required by this section to do so, removes an employee from exposure to lead or otherwise places limitations on an employee due to the effects of lead exposure on the employee's medical condition, the employer shall provide medical removal protection benefits to the employee equal to that required by paragraph (k)(2)(i) of this section.

(1) *Employee information and training—*(1) *Training program.* (i) Each employer who has a workplace in which there is a potential exposure to airborne lead at any level shall inform employees of the content of Appendices A and B of this regulation.

(ii) The employer shall train each employee who is subject to exposure to lead at or above the action level, or for whom the possibility of skin or eye irritation exists, in accordance with the requirements of this section. The employer shall institute a training program and ensure employee participation in the program.

(iii) The employer shall provide initial training by 180 days from the effective date for those employees covered by paragraph (l)(1) (ii) on the standard's effective date and prior to the time of initial job assignment for those employees subsequently covered by this paragraph.

(iv) The training program shall be repeated at least annually for each employee.

(v) The employer shall assure that each employee is informed of the following:

(A) The content of this standard and its appendices;

(B) The specific nature of the operations which could result in exposure to lead above the action level;

(C) The purpose, proper selection, fitting, use, and limitations of respirators;

(D) The purpose and a description of the medical surveillance program, and the medical removal protection program including information concerning the adverse health effects associated with excessive exposure to lead (with particular attention to the adverse reproductive effects on both males and females);

(E) The engineering controls and work practices associated with the employee's job assignment;

(F) The contents of any compliance plan in effect; and

(G) Instructions to employees that chelating agents should not routinely be used to remove lead from their bodies and should not be used at all except under the direction of a licensed physician;

(2) *Access to information and training materials.* (i) The employer shall make readily available to all affected employees a copy of this standard and its appendices.

(ii) The employer shall provide, upon request, all materials relating to the employee information and training program to the Assistant Secretary and the Director.

(iii) In addition to the information required by paragraph (l)(1)(v), the employer shall include as part of the training program, and shall distribute to employees, any materials pertaining to the Occupational Safety and Health Act, the regulations issued pursuant to that Act, and this lead standard, which are made available to the employer by the Assistant Secretary.

(m) *Communication of hazards—*(1) *Hazard communication—general.* (i)

Chemical manufacturers, importers, distributors and employers shall comply with all requirements of the Hazard Communication Standard (HCS) (§ 1910.1200) for lead.

(ii) In classifying the hazards of lead at least the following hazards are to be addressed: Reproductive/developmental toxicity; central nervous system effects; kidney effects; blood effects; and acute toxicity effects.

(iii) Employers shall include lead in the hazard communication program established to comply with the HCS (§ 1910.1200). Employers shall ensure that each employee has access to labels on containers of lead and to safety data sheets, and is trained in accordance with the requirements of HCS and paragraph (l) of this section.

(2) *Signs.* (i) The employer shall post the following warning signs in each work area where the PEL is exceeded:

DANGER
LEAD
MAY DAMAGE FERTILITY OR THE UN-
BORN CHILD
CAUSES DAMAGE TO THE CENTRAL
NERVOUS SYSTEM
DO NOT EAT, DRINK OR SMOKE IN THIS
AREA

(ii) The employer shall ensure that no statement appears on or near any sign required by this paragraph (m)(2) which contradicts or detracts from the meaning of the required sign.

(iii) The employer shall ensure that signs required by this paragraph (m)(2) are illuminated and cleaned as necessary so that the legend is readily visible.

(iv) The employer may use signs required by other statutes, regulations, or ordinances in addition to, or in combination with, signs required by this paragraph (m)(2).

(v) Prior to June 1, 2016, employers may use the following legend in lieu of that specified in paragraph (m)(2)(ii) of this section:

WARNING
LEAD WORK AREA
POISON
NO SMOKING OR EATING

(n) *Recordkeeping—*(1) *Exposure monitoring.* (i) The employer shall establish and maintain an accurate record of all monitoring required in paragraph (d) of this section.

(ii) This record shall include:

(A) The date(s), number, duration, location and results of each of the samples taken, including a description of the sampling procedure used to determine representative employee exposure where applicable;

(B) A description of the sampling and analytical methods used and evidence of their accuracy;

(C) The type of respiratory protective devices worn, if any;

(D) Name, social security number, and job classification of the employee monitored and of all other employees whose exposure the measurement is intended to represent; and

(E) The environmental variables that could affect the measurement of employee exposure.

(iii) The employer shall maintain these monitoring records for at least 40 years or for the duration of employment plus 20 years, whichever is longer.

(2) *Medical surveillance.* (i) The employer shall establish and maintain an accurate record for each employee subject to medical surveillance as required by paragraph (j) of this section.

(ii) This record shall include:

(A) The name, social security number, and description of the duties of the employee;

(B) A copy of the physician's written opinions;

(C) Results of any airborne exposure monitoring done for that employee and the representative exposure levels supplied to the physician; and

(D) Any employee medical complaints related to exposure to lead.

(iii) The employer shall keep, or assure that the examining physician keeps, the following medical records:

(A) A copy of the medical examination results including medical and work history required under paragraph (j) of this section;

(B) A description of the laboratory procedures and a copy of any standards or guidelines used to interpret the test results or references to that information;

(C) A copy of the results of biological monitoring.

(iv) The employer shall maintain or assure that the physician maintains those medical records for at least 40 years, or for the duration of employment plus 20 years, whichever is longer.

(3) *Medical removals.* (i) The employer shall establish and maintain an accurate record for each employee removed from current exposure to lead pursuant to paragraph (k) of this section.

(ii) Each record shall include:

(A) The name and social security number of the employee;

(B) The date on each occasion that the employee was removed from current exposure to lead as well as the corresponding date on which the employee was returned to his or her former job status;

(C) A brief explanation of how each removal was or is being accomplished; and

(D) A statement with respect to each removal indicating whether or not the reason for the removal was an elevated blood lead level.

(iii) The employer shall maintain each medical removal record for at least the duration of an employee's employment.

(4) *Availability.* (i) The employer shall make available upon request all records required to be maintained by paragraph (n) of this section to the Assistant Secretary and the Director for examination and copying.

(ii) Environmental monitoring, medical removal, and medical records required by this paragraph shall be provided upon request to employees, designated representatives, and the Assistant Secretary in accordance with 29 CFR 1910.1020 (a)–(e) and (2)–(i). Medical removal records shall be provided in the same manner as environmental monitoring records.

(5) *Transfer of records.* (i) Whenever the employer ceases to do business, the successor employer shall receive and retain all records required to be maintained by paragraph (n) of this section.

(ii) The employer shall also comply with any additional requirements involving transfer of records set forth in 29 CFR 1910.1020(h).

(o) *Observation of monitoring*—(1) *Employee observation.* The employer shall provide affected employees or their designated representatives an opportunity to observe any monitoring of employee exposure to lead conducted pursuant to paragraph (d) of this section.

(2) *Observation procedures.* (i) Whenever observation of the monitoring of employee exposure to lead requires entry into an area where the use of respirators, protective clothing or equipment is required, the employer shall provide the observer with and assure the use of such respirators, clothing and such equipment, and shall require the observer to comply with all other applicable safety and health procedures.

(ii) Without interfering with the monitoring, observers shall be entitled to:

(A) Receive an explanation of the measurement procedures;

(B) Observe all steps related to the monitoring of lead performed at the place of exposure; and

(C) Record the results obtained or receive copies of the results when returned by the laboratory.

(p) *Appendices.* The information contained in the appendices to this section is not intended by itself, to create any additional obligations not otherwise imposed by this standard nor detract from any existing obligation.

APPENDIX A TO § 1910.1025—SUBSTANCE DATA SHEET FOR OCCUPATIONAL EXPOSURE TO LEAD

I. SUBSTANCE IDENTIFICATION

A. *Substance:* Pure lead (Pb) is a heavy metal at room temperature and pressure and is a basic chemical element. It can combine with various other substances to form numerous lead compounds.

B. *Compounds Covered by the Standard:* The word "lead" when used in this standard means elemental lead, all inorganic lead compounds and a class of organic lead compounds called lead soaps. This standard does not apply to other organic lead compounds.

C. *Uses:* Exposure to lead occurs in at least 120 different occupations, including primary and secondary lead smelting, lead storage battery manufacturing, lead pigment manufacturing and use, solder manufacturing and use, shipbuilding and ship repairing, auto manufacturing, and printing.

D. *Permissible Exposure:* The Permissible Exposure Limit (PEL) set by the standard is 50 micrograms of lead per cubic meter of air (50 µg/m³), averaged over an 8-hour workday.

E. *Action Level:* The standard establishes an action level of 30 micrograms per cubic meter of air (30 µg/m³), time weighted average, based on an 8-hour work-day. The action level initiates several requirements of the standard, such as exposure monitoring, medical surveillance, and training and education.

II. HEALTH HAZARD DATA

A. *Ways in which lead enters your body.* When absorbed into your body in certain doses lead is a toxic substance. The object of the lead standard is to prevent absorption of harmful quantities of lead. The standard is intended to protect you not only from the immediate toxic effects of lead, but also from the serious toxic effects that may not become apparent until years of exposure have passed.

Lead can be absorbed into your body by inhalation (breathing) and ingestion (eating). Lead (except for certain organic lead compounds not covered by the standard, such as tetraethyl lead) is not absorbed through your skin. When lead is scattered in the air as a dust, fume or mist it can be inhaled and absorbed through you lungs and upper respiratory tract. Inhalation of airborne lead is generally the most important source of occupational lead absorption. You can also absorb lead through your digestive system if lead gets into your mouth and is swallowed. If you handle food, cigarettes, chewing tobacco, or make-up which have lead on them or handle them with hands contaminated with lead, this will contribute to ingestion.

A significant portion of the lead that you inhale or ingest gets into your blood stream. Once in your blood stream, lead is circulated throughout your body and stored in various organs and body tissues. Some of this lead is quickly filtered out of your body and excreted, but some remains in the blood and other tissues. As exposure to lead continues, the amount stored in your body will increase if you are absorbing more lead than your body is excreting. Even though you may not be aware of any immediate symptoms of disease, this lead stored in your tissues can be slowly causing irreversible damage, first to individual cells, then to your organs and whole body systems.

B. *Effects of overexposure to lead*—(1) *Short term (acute) overexposure.* Lead is a potent, systemic poison that serves no known useful function once absorbed by your body. Taken in large enough doses, lead can kill you in a matter of days. A condition affecting the brain called acute encephalopathy may arise which develops quickly to seizures, coma, and death from cardiorespiratory arrest. A short term dose of lead can lead to acute encephalopathy. Short term occupational exposures of this magnitude are highly unusual, but not impossible. Similar forms of encephalopathy may, however, arise from extended, chronic exposure to lower doses of lead. There is no sharp dividing line between rapidly developing acute effects of lead, and chronic effects which take longer to acquire.

Lead adversely affects numerous body systems, and causes forms of health impairment and disease which arise after periods of exposure as short as days or as long as several years.

(2) *Long-term (chronic) overexposure.* Chronic overexposure to lead may result in severe damage to your blood-forming, nervous, urinary and reproductive systems. Some common symptoms of chronic overexposure include loss of appetite, metallic taste in the mouth, anxiety, constipation, nausea, pallor, excessive tiredness, weakness, insomnia, headache, nervous irritability, muscle and joint pain or soreness, fine tremors, numbness, dizziness, hyperactivity and colic. In lead colic there may be severe abdominal pain.

Damage to the central nervous system in general and the brain (encephalopathy) in particular is one of the most severe forms of lead poisoning. The most severe, often fatal, form of encephalopathy may be preceded by vomiting, a feeling of dullness progressing to drowsiness and stupor, poor memory, restlessness, irritability, tremor, and convulsions. It may arise suddenly with the onset of seizures, followed by coma, and death. There is a tendency for muscular weakness to develop at the same time. This weakness may progress to paralysis often observed as a characteristic "wrist drop" or "foot drop" and is a manifestation of a disease to the nervous system called peripheral neuropathy.

Chronic overexposure to lead also results in kidney disease with few, if any, symptoms appearing until extensive and most likely permanent kidney damage has occurred. Routine laboratory tests reveal the presence of this kidney disease only after about two-thirds of kidney function is lost. When overt symptoms of urinary dysfunction arise, it is often too late to correct or prevent worsening conditions, and progression to kidney dialysis or death is possible.

Chronic overexposure to lead impairs the reproductive systems of both men and women. Overexposure to lead may result in decreased sex drive, impotence and sterility in men. Lead can alter the structure of sperm cells raising the risk of birth defects. There is evidence of miscarriage and stillbirth in women whose husbands were exposed to lead or who were exposed to lead themselves. Lead exposure also may result in decreased fertility, and abnormal menstrual cycles in women. The course of pregnancy may be adversely affected by exposure to lead since lead crosses the placental barrier and poses risks to developing fetuses. Children born of parents either one of whom were exposed to excess lead levels are more likely to have birth defects, mental retardation, behavioral disorders or die during the first year of childhood.

Overexposure to lead also disrupts the blood-forming system resulting in decreased hemoglobin (the substance in the blood that carries oxygen to the cells) and ultimately anemia. Anemia is characterized by weakness, pallor and fatigability as a result of decreased oxygen carrying capacity in the blood.

(3) *Health protection goals of the standard.* Prevention of adverse health effects for most workers from exposure to lead throughout a working lifetime requires that worker blood lead (PbB) levels be maintained at or below forty micrograms per one hundred grams of whole blood (40 µg/100g). The blood lead levels of workers (both male and female workers) who intend to have children should be maintained below 30 µg/100g to minimize adverse reproductive health effects to the parents and to the developing fetus.

The measurement of your blood lead level is the most useful indicator of the amount of lead being absorbed by your body. Blood lead levels (PbB) are most often reported in units of milligrams (mg) or micrograms (µg) of lead (1 mg = 1000 µg) per 100 grams (100g), 100 milliliters (100 ml) or deciliter (dl) of blood. These three units are essentially the same. Sometime PbB's are expressed in the form of mg% or µg%. This is a shorthand notation for 100g, 100 ml, or dl.

PbB measurements show the amount of lead circulating in your blood stream, but do not give any information about the amount of lead stored in your various tissues. PbB measurements merely show current absorption of lead, not the effect that lead is having on your body or the effects that past lead exposure may have already caused. Past research into lead-related diseases, however, has focused heavily on associations between PbBs and various diseases. As a result, your PbB is an important indicator of the likelihood that you will gradually acquire a lead-related health impairment or disease.

Once your blood lead level climbs above 40 µg/100g, your risk of disease increases. There is a wide variability of individual response to lead, thus it is difficult to say that a particular PbB in a given person will cause a particular effect. Studies have associated fatal encephalopathy with PbBs as low as 150 µg/100g. Other studies have shown other forms of diseases in some workers with PbBs well below 80 µg/100g. Your PbB is a crucial indicator of the risks to your health, but one other factor is also extremely important. This factor is the length of time you have had elevated PbBs. The longer you have an elevated PbB, the greater the risk that large quantities of lead are being gradually stored in your organs and tissues (body burden). The greater your overall body burden, the greater the chances of substantial permanent damage.

The best way to prevent all forms of lead-related impairments and diseases—both

149

short term and long term- is to maintain your PbB below 40 µg/100g. The provisions of the standard are designed with this end in mind. Your employer has prime responsibility to assure that the provisions of the standard are complied with both by the company and by individual workers. You as a worker, however, also have a responsibility to assist your employer in complying with the standard. You can play a key role in protecting your own health by learning about the lead hazards and their control, learning what the standard requires, following the standard where it governs your own actions, and seeing that your employer complies with provisions governing his actions.

(4) *Reporting signs and symptoms of health problems.* You should immediately notify your employer if you develop signs or symptoms associated with lead poisoning or if you desire medical advice concerning the effects of current or past exposure to lead on your ability to have a healthy child. You should also notify your employer if you have difficulty breathing during a respirator fit test or while wearing a respirator. In each of these cases your employer must make available to you appropriate medical examinations or consultations. These must be provided at no cost to you and at a reasonable time and place.

The standard contains a procedure whereby you can obtain a second opinion by a physician of your choice if the employer selected the initial physician.

APPENDIX B TO § 1910.1025—EMPLOYEE STANDARD SUMMARY

This appendix summarizes key provisions of the standard that you as a worker should become familiar with.

I. PERMISSIBLE EXPOSURE LIMIT (PEL)— PARAGRAPH (c)

The standards sets a permissible exposure limit (PEL) of fifty micrograms of lead per cubic meter of air (50 µg/m³), averaged over an 8-hour work-day. This is the highest level of lead in air to which you may be permissibly exposed over an 8-hour workday. Since it is an 8-hour average it permits short exposures above the PEL so long as for each 8-hour work day your average exposure does not exceed the PEL.

This standard recognizes that your daily exposure to lead can extend beyond a typical 8-hour workday as the result of overtime or other alterations in your work schedule. To deal with this, the standard contains a formula which reduces your permissible exposure when you are exposed more than 8 hours. For example, if you are exposed to lead for 10 hours a day, the maximum permitted average exposure would be 40 µg/m³.

II. EXPOSURE MONITORING—PARAGRAPH (d)

If lead is present in the workplace where you work in any quantity, your employer is required to make an initial determination of whether the action level is exceeded for any employee. This initial determination must include instrument monitoring of the air for the presence of lead and must cover the exposure of a representative number of employees who are reasonably believed to have the highest exposure levels. If your employer has conducted appropriate air sampling for lead in the past year he may use these results. If there have been any employee complaints of symptoms which may be attributable to exposure to lead or if there is any other information or observations which would indicate employee exposure to lead, this must also be considered as part of the initial determination. This initial determination must have been completed by March 31, 1979. If this initial determination shows that a reasonable possibility exists that *any* employee may be exposed, without regard to respirators, over the action level (30 µg/m³) your employer must set up an air monitoring program to determine the exposure level of every employee exposed to lead at your workplace.

In carrying out this air monitoring program, your employer is not required to monitor the exposure of every employee, but he must monitor a representative number of employees and job types. Enough sampling must be done to enable each employee's exposure level to be reasonably least one full shift (at least 7 hours) air sample. In addition, these air samples must be taken under conditions which represent each employee's *regular*, daily exposure to lead. All initial exposure monitoring must have been completed by May 30, 1979.

If you are exposed to lead and air sampling is performed, your employer is required to quickly notify you in writing of air monitoring results which represent your exposure. If the results indicate your exposure exceeds the PEL (without regard to your use of respirators), then your employer must also notify you of this in writing, and provide you with a description of the corrective action that will be taken to reduce your exposure.

Your exposure must be rechecked by monitoring every six months if your exposure is over the action level but below the PEL. Air monitoring must be repeated every 3 months if you are exposed over the PEL. Your employer may discontinue monitoring for you if 2 consecutive measurements, taken at least two weeks apart, are below the action level. However, whenever there is a production, process, control, or personnel change at your workplace which may result in new or additional exposure to lead, or whenever there is any other reason to suspect a change which may result in new or additional exposure to lead, your employer must perform additional monitoring.

III. METHODS OF COMPLIANCE—PARAGRAPH (e)

Your employer is required to assure that no employee is exposed to lead in excess of the PEL. The standard establishes a priority of methods to be used to meet the PEL.

IV. RESPIRATORY PROTECTION—PARAGRAPH (f)

Your employer is required to provide and assure your use of respirators when your exposure to lead is not controlled below the PEL by other means. The employer must pay the cost of the respirator. Whenever you request one, your employer is also required to provide you a respirator even if your air exposure level does not exceed the PEL. You might desire a respirator when, for example, you have received medical advice that your lead absorption should be decreased. Or, you may intend to have children in the near future, and want to reduce the level of lead in your body to minimize adverse reproductive effects. While respirators are the least satisfactory means of controlling your exposure, they are capable of providing significant protection if properly chosen, fitted, worn, cleaned, maintained, and replaced when they stop providing adequate protection.

Your employer is required to select respirators from the seven types listed in Table II of the Respiratory Protection section of the standard (§1910.1025(f)). Any respirator chosen must be approved by the National Institute for Occupational Safety and Health (NIOSH) under the provisions of 42 CFR part 84. This respirator selection table will enable your employer to choose a type of respirator that will give you a proper amount of protection based on your airborne lead exposure. Your employer may select a type of respirator that provides greater protection than that required by the standard; that is, one recommended for a higher concentration of lead than is present in your workplace. For example, a powered air-purifying respirator (PAPR) is much more protective than a typical negative pressure respirator, and many also be more comfortable to wear. A PAPR has a filter, cartridge, or canister to clean the air, and a power source that continuously blows filtered air into your breathing zone. Your employer might make a PAPR available to you to ease the burden of having to wear a respirator for long periods of time. The standard provides that you can obtain a PAPR upon request.

Your employer must also start a Respiratory Protection Program. This program must include written procedures for the proper selection, use, cleaning, storage, and maintenance of respirators.

Your employer must ensure that your respirator facepiece fits properly. Proper fit of a respirator facepiece is critical to your protection from airborne lead. Obtaining a proper fit on each employee may require your employer to make available several different types of respirator masks. To ensure that your respirator fits properly and that facepiece leakage is minimal, your employer must give you either a qualitative or quantitative fit test as specified in appendix A of the Respiratory Protection standard located at 29 CFR 1910.134.

You must also receive from your employer proper training in the use of respirators. Your employer is required to teach you how to wear a respirator, to know why it is needed, and to understand its limitations.

The standard provides that if your respirator uses filter elements, you must be given an opportunity to change the filter elements whenever an increase in breathing resistance is detected. You also must be permitted to periodically leave your work area to wash your face and respirator facepiece whenever necessary to prevent skin irritation. If you ever have difficulty in breathing during a fit test or while using a respirator, your employer must make a medical examination available to you to determine whether you can safely wear a respirator. The result of this examination may be to give you a positive pressure respirator (which reduces breathing resistance) or to provide alternative means of protection.

V. PROTECTIVE WORK CLOTHING AND
EQUIPMENT—PARAGRAPH (g)

If you are exposed to lead above the PEL, or if you are exposed to lead compounds such as lead arsenate or lead azide which can cause skin and eye irritation, your employer must provide you with protective work clothing and equipment appropriate for the hazard. If work clothing is provided, it must be provided in a clean and dry condition at least weekly, and daily if your airborne exposure to lead is greater than 200 µg/m³. Appropriate protective work clothing and equipment can include coveralls or similar full-body work clothing, gloves, hats, shoes or disposable shoe coverlets, and face shields or vented goggles. Your employer is required to provide all such equipment at no cost to you. He is responsible for providing repairs and replacement as necessary, and also is responsible for the cleaning, laundering or disposal of protective clothing and equipment. Contaminated work clothing or equipment must be removed in change rooms and not worn home or you will extend your exposure and expose your family since lead from your clothing can accumulate in your house, car, etc. Contaminated clothing which is to be cleaned, laundered or disposed of must be placed in closed containers in the change room. At no time may lead be removed from protective clothing or equipment by any means which disperses lead into the work-room air.

VI. HOUSEKEEPING—PARAGRAPH (h)

Your employer must establish a house-keeping program sufficient to maintain all surfaces as free as practicable of accumulations of lead dust. Vacuuming is the preferred method of meeting this requirement, and the use of compressed air to clean floors and other surfaces is absolutely prohibited. Dry or wet sweeping, shoveling, or brushing may not be used except where vaccuming or other equally effective methods have been tried and do not work. Vacuums must be used and emptied in a manner which minimizes the reentry of lead into the workplace.

VII. HYGIENE FACILITIES AND PRACTICES— PARAGRAPH (i)

The standard requires that change rooms, showers, and filtered air lunchrooms be constructed and made available to workers exposed to lead above the PEL. When the PEL is exceeded the employer must assure that food and beverage is not present or consumed, tobacco products are not present or used, and cosmetics are not applied, except in these facilities. Change rooms, showers, and lunchrooms, must be used by workers exposed in excess of the PEL. After showering, *no* clothing or equipment worn during the shift may be worn home, and this includes shoes and underwear. Your own clothing worn during the shift should be carried home and cleaned carefully so that it does not contaminate your home. Lunchrooms may not be entered with protective clothing or equipment unless surface dust has been removed by vacuuming, downdraft booth, or other cleaning method. Finally, workers exposed above the PEL must wash both their hands and faces prior to eating, drinking, smoking or applying cosmetics.

All of the facilities and hygiene practices just discussed are essential to minimize additional sources of lead absorption from inhalation or ingestion of lead that may accumulate on you, your clothes, or your possessions. Strict compliance with these provisions can virtually eliminate several sources of lead exposure which significantly contribute to excessive lead absorption.

VIII. MEDICAL SURVEILLANCE—PARAGRAPH (j)

The medical surveillance program is part of the standard's comprehensive approach to the prevention of lead-related disease. Its purpose is to supplement the main thrust of the standard which is aimed at minimizing airborne concentrations of lead and sources of ingestion. Only medical surveillance can determine if the other provisions of the standard have affectively protected you as an individual. Compliance with the standard's provision will protect most workers from the adverse effects of lead exposure, but may not be satisfactory to protect individual workers (1) who have high body burdens of lead acquired over past years, (2) who have additional uncontrolled sources of non-occupational lead exposure, (3) who exhibit unusual variations in lead absorption rates, or (4) who have specific non-work related medical conditions which could be aggravated by lead exposure (e.g., renal disease, anemia). In addition, control systems may fail, or hygiene and respirator programs may be inadequate. Periodic medical surveillance of individual workers will help detect those failures. Medical surveillance will also be important to protect your reproductive ability—regardless of whether you are a man or woman.

All medical surveillance required by the standard must be performed by or under the supervision of a licensed physician. The employer must provide required medical surveillance without cost to employees and at a reasonable time and place. The standard's medical surveillance program has two parts—periodic biological monitoring and medical examinations.

Your employer's obligation to offer you medical surveillance is triggered by the results of the air monitoring program. Medical surveillance must be made available to all employees who are exposed in excess of the action level for more than 30 days a year. The initial phase of the medical surveillance program, which includes blood lead level tests and medical examinations, must be completed for all covered employees no later than August 28, 1979. Priority within this first round of medical surveillance must be given to employees whom the employer believes to be at greatest risk from continued exposure (for example, those with the longest prior exposure to lead, or those with the highest current exposure). Thereafter, the employer must periodically make medical surveillance—both biological monitoring and medical examinations—available to all covered employees.

Biological monitoring under the standard consists of blood lead level (PbB) and zinc protoporphyrin tests at least every 6 months after the initial PbB test. A zinc protoporphyrin (ZPP) test is a very useful blood test which measures an effect of lead on your body. Thus biological monitoring under the standard is currently limited to PbB testing. If a worker's PbB exceeds 40 μg/100g the monitoring frequency must be increased from every 6 months to at least every 2 months and not reduced until two consecutive PbBs indicate a blood lead level below 40 μg/100g. Each time your PbB is determined to be over 40 μg/100g, your employer must notify you of this in writing within five working days of his receipt of the test results. The employer must also inform you that the standard requires temporary medical removal with economic protection when your PbB exceeds certain criteria. (See Discussion of Medical Removal Protection—Paragraph (k).) During the first year of the standard, this removal criterion is 80 µg/100g. Anytime your PbB exceeds 80 µg/100g your employer must make available to you a prompt follow-up PbB test to ascertain your PbB. If the two tests both exceed 80 µg/100g and you are temporarily removed, then your employer must make successive PbB tests available to you on a monthly basis during the period of your removal.

Medical examinations beyond the initial one must be made available on an annual basis if your blood lead level exceeds 40 µg/100g at any time during the preceding year. The initial examination will provide information to establish a baseline to which subsequent data can be compared. An initial medical examination must also be made available (prior to assignment) for each employee being assigned for the first time to an area where the airborne concentration of lead equals or exceeds the action level. In addition, a medical examination or consultation must be made available as soon as possible if you notify your employer that you are experiencing signs or symptoms commonly associated with lead poisoning or that you have difficulty breathing while wearing a respirator or during a respirator fit test. You must also be provided a medical examination or consultation if you notify your employer that you desire medical advice concerning the effects of current or past exposure to lead on your ability to procreate a healthy child.

Finally, appropriate follow-up medical examinations or consultations may also be provided for employees who have been temporarily removed from exposure under the medical removal protection provisions of the standard. (See part IX, below.)

The standard specifies the minimum content of pre-assignment and annual medical examinations. The content of other types of medical examinations and consultations is left up to the sound discretion of the examining physician. Pre-assignment and annual medical examinations must include (1) a detailed work history and medical history, (2) a thorough physical examination, and (3) a series of laboratory tests designed to check your blood chemistry and your kidney function. In addition, at any time upon your request, a laboratory evaluation of male fertility will be made (microscopic examination of a sperm sample), or a pregnancy test will be given.

The standard does not require that you participate in any of the medical procedures, tests, etc. which your employer is required to make available to you. Medical surveillance can, however, play a very important role in protecting your health. You are strongly encouraged, therefore, to participate in a meaningful fashion. The standard contains a multiple physician review mechanism which would give you a chance to have a physician of your choice directly participate in the medical surveillance program. If you were dissatisfied with an examination by a physician chosen by your employer, you could select a second physician to conduct an independent analysis. The two doctors would attempt to resolve any differences of opinion, and select a third physician to resolve any firm dispute. Generally your employer will choose the physician who conducts medical surveillance under the lead standard—unless you and your employer can agree on the choice of a physician or physicians. Some companies and unions have agreed in advance, for example, to use certain independent medical laboratories or panels of physicians. Any of these arrangements are acceptable so long as required medical surveillance is made available to workers.

The standard requires your employer to provide certain information to a physician to aid in his or her examination of you. This information includes (1) the standard and its appendices, (2) a description of your duties as they relate to lead exposure, (3) your exposure level, (4) a description of personal protective equipment you wear, (5) prior blood lead level results, and (6) prior written medical opinions concerning you that the employer has. After a medical examination or consultation the physician must prepare a written report which must contain (1) the physician's opinion as to whether you have any medical condition which places you at increased risk of material impairment to health from exposure to lead, (2) any recommended special protective measures to be provided to you, (3) any blood lead level determinations, and (4) any recommended limitation on your use of respirators. This last element must include a determination of whether you can wear a powered air purifying respirator (PAPR) if you are found unable to wear a negative pressure respirator.

The medical surveillance program of the lead standard may at some point in time serve to notify certain workers that they have acquired a disease or other adverse medical condition as a result of occupational lead exposure. If this is true, these workers might have legal rights to compensation from public agencies, their employers, firms that supply hazardous products to their employers, or other persons. Some states have laws, including worker compensation laws, that disallow a worker who learns of a job-related health impairment to sue, unless the worker sues within a short period of time after learning of the impairment. (This period of time may be a matter of months or years.) An attorney can be consulted about these possibilities. It should be stressed that

153

OSHA is in no way trying to either encourage or discourage claims or lawsuits. However, since results of the standard's medical surveillance program can significantly affect the legal remedies of a worker who has acquired a job-related disease or impairment, it is proper for OSHA to make you aware of this.

The medical surveillance section of the standard also contains provisions dealing with chelation. Chelation is the use of certain drugs (administered in pill form or injected into the body) to reduce the amount of lead absorbed in body tissues. Experience accumulated by the medical and scientific communities has largely confirmed the effectiveness of this type of therapy for the treatment of very severe lead poisoning. On the other hand, it has also been established that there can be a long list of extremely harmful side effects associated with the use of chelating agents. The medical community has balanced the advantages and disadvantages resulting from the use of chelating agents in various circumstances and has established when the use of these agents is acceptable. The standard includes these accepted limitations due to a history of abuse of chelation therapy by some lead companies. The most widely used chelating agents are calcium disodium EDTA, (Ca Na$_2$ EDTA), Calcium Disodium Versenate (Versenate), and d-penicillamine (pencillamine or Cupramine).

The standard prohibits "prophylactic chelation" of any employee by any person the employer retains, supervises or controls. "Prophylactic chelation" is the routine use of chelating or similarly acting drugs to *prevent* elevated blood levels in workers who are occupationally exposed to lead, or the use of these drugs to *routinely* lower blood lead levels to predesignated concentrations believed to be 'safe'. It should be emphasized that where an employer takes a worker who has no symptoms of lead poisoning and has chelation carried out by a physician (either inside or outside of a hospital) solely to reduce the worker's blood lead level, that will generally be considered prophylactic chelation. The use of a hospital and a physician does not mean that prophylactic chelation is not being performed. Routine chelation to prevent increased or reduce current blood lead levels is unacceptable whatever the setting.

The standard allows the use of "therapeutic" or "diagnostic" chelation if administered under the supervision of a licensed physician in a clinical setting with thorough and appropriate medical monitoring. Therapeutic chelation responds to severe lead poisoning where there are marked symptoms. Diagnostic chelation involved giving a patient a dose of the drug then collecting all urine excreted for some period of time as an aid to the diagnosis of lead poisoning.

In cases where the examining physician determines that chelation is appropriate, you must be notified in writing of this fact before such treatment. This will inform you of a potentially harmful treatment, and allow you to obtain a second opinion.

IX. MEDICAL REMOVAL PROTECTION—
PARAGRAPH (k)

Excessive lead absorption subjects you to increased risk of disease. Medical removal protection (MRP) is a means of protecting you when, for whatever reasons, other methods, such as engineering controls, work practices, and respirators, have failed to provide the protection you need. MRP involves the temproary removal of a worker from his or her regular job to a place of significantly lower exposure without any loss of earnings, seniority, or other employment rights or benefits. The purpose of this program is to cease further lead absorption and allow your body to naturally excrete lead which has previously been absorbed. Temporary medical removal can result from an elevated blood lead level, or a medical opinion. Up to 18 months of protection is provided as a result of either form of removal. The vast majority of removed workers, however, will return to their former jobs long before their eighteen month period expires. The standard contains special provisions to deal with the extraordinary but possible case where a longterm worker's blood lead level does not adequately decline during eighteen months of removal.

During the first year of the standard, if your blood lead level is 80 µg/100g or above you must be removed from any exposure where your air lead level without a respirator would be 100 µg/m³ or above. If you are removed from your normal job you may not be returned until your blood lead level declines to at least 60 µg/100g. These criteria for removal and return will change according to the following schedule:

	Removal blood lead (µg/100 g)	Air lead (µg/m³)	Return blood lead (µg/100 g)
After Mar. 1, 1980	70 and above	50 and above	At or below 50.
After Mar. 1, 1981	60 and above	30 and above	At or below 40.
After Mar. 1, 1983	50 and above averaged over six months.	30 and above	Do.

You may also be removed from exposure even if your blood lead levels are below these criteria if a final medical determination indicates that you temporarily need reduced lead exposure for medical reasons. If the physician who is implementing your employers medical program makes a final written opinion recommending your removal or other special protective measures, your employer must implement the physician's recommendation. If you are removed in this manner, you may only be returned when the doctor indicates that it is safe for you to do so.

The standard does not give specific instructions dealing with what an employer must do with a removed worker. Your job assignment upon removal is a matter for you, your employer and your union (if any) to work out consistent with existing procedures for job assignments. Each removal must be accomplished in a manner consistent with existing collective bargaining relationships. Your employer is given broad discretion to implement temporary removals so long as no attempt is made to override existing agreements. Similarly, a removed worker is provided no right to veto an employer's choice which satisfies the standard.

In most cases, employers will likely transfer removed employees to other jobs with sufficiently low lead exposure. Alternatively, a worker's hours may be reduced so that the time weighted average exposure is reduced, or he or she may be temporarily laid off if no other alternative is feasible.

In all of these situation, MRP benefits must be provided during the period of removal—i.e., you continue to receive the same earnings, seniority, and other rights and benefits you would have had if you had not been removed. Earnings includes more than just your base wage; it includes overtime, shift differentials, incentives, and other compensation you would have earned if you had not been removed. During the period of removal you must also be provided with appropriate follow-up medical surveillance. If you were removed because your blood lead level was too high, you must be provided with a monthly blood test. If a medical opinion caused your removal, you must be provided medical tests or examinations that the doctor believes to be appropriate. If you do not participate in this follow up medical surveillance, you may lose your eligibility for MRP benefits.

When you are medically eligible to return to your former job, your employer must return you to your "former job status." This means that you are entitled to the position, wages, benefits, etc., you would have had if you had not been removed. If you would still be in your old job if no removal had occurred that is where you go back. If not, you are returned consistent with whatever job assignment discretion your employer would have

had if no removal had occurred. MRP only seeks to maintain your rights, not expand them or diminish them.

If you are removed under MRP and you are also eligible for worker compensation or other compensation for lost wages, your employer's MRP benefits obligation is reduced by the amount that you *actually* receive from these other sources. This is also true if you obtain other employment during the time you are laid off with MRP benefits.

The standard also covers situations where an employer *voluntarily* removes a worker from exposure to lead due to the effects of lead on the employee's medical condition, even though the standard does not require removal. In these situations MRP benefits must still be provided as though the standard required removal. Finally, it is important to note that in all cases where removal is required, respirators cannot be used as a substitute. Respirators may be used before removal becomes necessary, but not as an alternative to a transfer to a low exposure job, or to a lay-off with MRP benefits.

X. EMPLOYEE INFORMATION AND TRAINING—
PARAGRAPH (l)

Your employer is required to provide an information and training program for all employees exposed to lead above the action level or who may suffer skin or eye irritation from lead. This program must inform these employees of the specific hazards associated with their work environment, protective measures which can be taken, the danger of lead to their bodies (including their reproductive systems), and their rights under the standard. In addition your employer must make readily available to all employees, including those exposed below the action level, a copy of the standard and its appendices and must distribute to all employees any materials provided to the employer by the Occupational Safety and Health Administration (OSHA).

Your employer is required to complete this training program for all employees by August 28, 1979. After this date, all new employees must be trained prior to initial assignment to areas where there is a possibility of exposure over the action level.

This training program must also be provided at least annually thereafter.

xi. SIGNS—PARAGRAPH (m)

The standard requires that the following warning sign be posted in the work areas when the exposure to lead exceeds the PEL:

DANGER
LEAD
MAY DAMAGE FERTILITY OR THE UN-
    BORN CHILD
CAUSES DAMAGE TO THE CENTRAL
    NERVOUS SYSTEM

DO NOT EAT, DRINK OR SMOKE IN THIS AREA

However, prior to June 1, 2016, employers may use the following legend in lieu of that specified above:

WARNING
LEAD WORK AREA
POISON
NO SMOKING OR EATING

XII. RECORDKEEPING—PARAGRAPH (n)

Your employer is required to keep all records of exposure monitoring for airborne lead. These records must include the name and job classification of employees measured, details of the sampling and analytic techniques, the results of this sampling, and the type of respiratory protection being worn by the person sampled. Your employer is also required to keep all records of biological monitoring and medical examination results. These must include the names of the employees, the physician's written opinion, and a copy of the results of the examination. All of the above kinds of records must be kept for 40 years, or for at least 20 years after your termination of employment, whichever is longer.

Recordkeeping is also required if you are temporarily removed from your job under the medical removal protection program. This record must include your name and social security number, the date of your removal and return, how the removal was or is being accomplished, and whether or not the reason for the removal was an elevated blood lead level. Your employer is required to keep each medical removal record only for as long as the duration of an employee's employment.

The standard requires that if you request to see or copy environmental monitoring, blood lead level monitoring, or medical removal records, they must be made available to you or to a representative that you authorize. Your union also has access to these records. Medical records other than PbB's must also be provided upon request to you, to your physician or to any other person whom you may specifically designate. Your union does not have access to your personal medical records unless you authorize their access.

XIII. OBSERVATIONS OF MONITORING—PARAGRAPH (o)

When air monitoring for lead is performed at your workplace as required by this standard, your employer must allow you or someone you designate to act as an observer of the monitoring. Observers are entitled to an explanation of the measurement procedure, and to record the results obtained. Since results will not normally be available at the time of the monitoring, observers are entitled to record or receive the results of the monitoring when returned by the laboratory. Your employer is required to provide the observer with any personal protective devices required to be worn by employees working in the area that is being monitored. The employer must require the observer to wear all such equipment and to comply with all other applicable safety and health procedures.

XIV. FOR ADDITIONAL INFORMATION

A. Copies of the Standard and explanatory material may be obtained by writing or calling the OSHA Docket Office, U.S. Department of Labor, room N2634, 200 Constitution Avenue, N.W., Washington, DC 20210. Telephone: (202) 219-7894.

1. The standard and summary of the statement of reasons (preamble), FEDERAL REGISTER, Volume 43, pp. 52952–53014, November 14, 1978.

2. The full statement of reasons (preamble) FEDERAL REGISTER, vol. 43, pp. 54354–54509, November 21, 1978.

3. Partial Administrative Stay and Corrections to the standard, (44 FR 5446–5448) January 26, 1979.

4. Notice of the Partial Judicial Stay (44 FR 14554–14555) March 13, 1979.

5. Corrections to the preamble, FEDERAL REGISTER, vol. 44, pp. 20680–20681, April 6, 1979.

6. Additional correction to the preamble concerning the construction industry, FEDERAL REGISTER, vol. 44, p. 50338, August 28, 1979.

7. Appendices to the standard (Appendices A, B, C), FEDERAL REGISTER, Vol. 44, pp. 60980–60995, October 23, 1979.

8. Corrections to appendices, FEDERAL REGISTER, Vol. 44, 68828, November 30, 1979.

9. Revision to the standard and an additional appendix (Appendix D), FEDERAL REGISTER, Vol. 47, pp. 51117–51119, November 12, 1982.

10. Notice of reopening of lead rulemaking for nine remand industry sectors, FEDERAL REGISTER, vol. 53, pp. 11511–11513, April 7, 1988.

11. Statement of reasons, FEDERAL REGISTER, vol. 54, pp. 29142–29275, July 11, 1989.

12. Statement of reasons, FEDERAL REGISTER, vol. 55, pp. 3146–3167, January 30, 1990.

13. Correction to appendix B, FEDERAL REGISTER, vol. 55, pp. 4998–4999, February 13, 1991.

14. Correction to appendices, FEDERAL REGISTER, vol. 56, p. 24686, May 31, 1991.

B. Additional information about the standard, its enforcement, and your employer's compliance can be obtained from the nearest OSHA Area Office listed in your telephone directory under United States Government/Department of Labor.

APPENDIX C TO §1910.1025—MEDICAL
SURVEILLANCE GUIDELINES

INTRODUCTION

The primary purpose of the Occupational Safety and Health Act of 1970 is to assure, so far as possible, safe and healthful working conditions for every working man and woman. The occupational health standard for inorganic lead[1] was promulgated to protect workers exposed to inorganic lead including metallic lead, all inorganic lead compounds and organic lead soaps.

Under this final standard in effect as of March 1, 1979, occupational exposure to inorganic lead is to be limited to 50 µg/m³ (micrograms per cubic meter) based on an 8 hour time-weighted average (TWA). This level of exposure eventually must be achieved through a combination of engineering, work practice and other administrative controls. Periods of time ranging from 1 to 10 years are provided for different industries to implement these controls. The schedule which is based on individual industry considerations is given in Table 1. Until these controls are in place, respirators must be used to meet the 50 µg/m³ exposure limit.

The standard also provides for a program of biological monitoring and medical surveillance for all employees exposed to levels of inorganic lead above the action level of 30 µg/m³ (TWA) for more than 30 days per year. The purpose of this document is to outline the medical surveillance provisions of the standard for inorganic lead, and to provide

further information to the physician regarding the examination and evaluation of workers exposed to inorganic lead.

Section 1 provides a detailed description of the monitoring procedure including the required frequency of blood testing for exposed workers, provisions for medical removal protection (MRP), the recommended right of the employee to a second medical opinion, and notification and recordkeeping requirements of the employer. A discussion of the requirements for respirator use and respirator monitoring and OSHA's position on prophylactic chelation therapy are also included in this section.

Section 2 discusses the toxic effects and clinical manifestations of lead poisoning and effects of lead intoxication on enzymatic pathways in heme synthesis. The adverse effects on both male and female reproductive capacity and on the fetus are also discussed.

Section 3 outlines the recommended medical evaluation of the worker exposed to inorganic lead including details of the medical history, physical examination, and recommended laboratory tests, which are based on the toxic effects of lead as discussed in Section 2.

Section 4 provides detailed information concerning the laboratory tests available for the monitoring of exposed workers. Included also is a discussion of the relative value of each test and the limitations and precautions which are necessary in the interpretation of the laboratory results.

TABLE 1

Permissible airborne lead levels by industry (µg/m³)[1]	Effective date					
	Mar. 1, 1979	Mar. 1, 1980	Mar. 1, 1981	Mar. 1, 1982	Mar. 1, 1984	Mar. 1, 1989 (final)
1. Primary lead production	200	200	200	100	100	50
2. Secondary lead production	200	200	200	100	50	50
3. Lead-acid battery manufacturing	200	200	100	100	50	50
4. Nonferrous foundries	200	100	100	100	50	50
5. Lead pigment manufacturing	200	200	200	100	50	50
6. All other industries	200	50	50	50	50	50

[1] Airborne levels to be achieved without reliance or respirator protection through a combination of engineering, work practice and other administrative controls. While these controls are being implemented respirators must be used to meet the 50 µg/m³ exposure limit.

I. MEDICAL SURVEILLANCE AND MONITORING REQUIREMENTS FOR WORKERS EXPOSED TO INORGANIC LEAD

Under the occupational health standard for inorganic lead, a program of biological monitoring and medical surveillance is to be made available to all employees exposed to lead above the action level of 30 µg/m³ TWA for more than 30 days each year. This pro-

gram consists of periodic blood sampling and medical evaluation to be performed on a schedule which is defined by previous laboratory results, worker complaints or concerns, and the clinical assessment of the examining physician.

Under this program, the blood lead level of all employees who are exposed to lead above

[1]The term inorganic lead used throughout the medical surveillance appendices is meant

to be synonymous with the definition of lead set forth in the standard.

the action level of 30 µg/m³ is to be determined at least every six months. The frequency is increased to every two months for employees whose last blood lead level was between 40 µg/100 g whole blood and the level requiring employee medical removal to be discussed below. For employees who are removed from exposure to lead due to an elevated blood lead, a new blood lead level must be measured monthly. A zinc protoporphyrin (ZPP) is required on each occasion that a blood lead level measurement is made.

An annual medical examination and consultation performed under the guidelines discussed in Section 3 is to be made available to each employee for whom a blood test conducted at any time during the preceding 12 months indicated a blood lead level at or above 40 µg/100 g. Also, an examination is to be given to all employees prior to their assignment to an area in which airborne lead concentrations reach or exceed the action level. In addition, a medical examination must be provided as soon as possible after notification by an employee that the employee has developed signs or symptoms commonly associated with lead intoxication,

that the employee desires medical advice regarding lead exposure and the ability to procreate a healthy child, or that the employee has demonstrated difficulty in breathing during a respirator fitting test or during respirator use. An examination is also to be made available to each employee removed from exposure to lead due to a risk of sustaining material impairment to health, or otherwise limited or specially protected pursuant to medical recommendations.

Results of biological monitoring or the recommendations of an examining physician may necessitate removal of an employee from further lead exposure pursuant to the standard's medical removal protection (MRP) program. The object of the MRP program is to provide temporary medical removal to workers either with substantially elevated blood lead levels or otherwise at risk of sustaining material health impairment from continued substantial exposure to lead. The following guidelines which are summarized in Table 2 were created under the standard for the temporary removal of an exposed employee and his or her subsequent return to work in an exposure area.

TABLE 2

	Effective date				
	Mar. 1, 1979	Mar. 1, 1980	Mar. 1, 1981	Mar. 1, 1982	Mar. 1, 1983 (final)
A. Blood lead level requiring employee medical removal. (Level must be confirmed with second follow-up blood lead level within two weeks of first report.).	≥80 µg/100 g	≥70µg/100 g	≥60 µg/100 g	≥60 µg/100 g	≥60µg/100 g or average of last three blood samples or all blood samples over previous 6 months (whichever is over a longer time period) is 50 µg/100 g or greater unless last blood sample is 40 µg/100 g or less.
B. Frequency which employees exposed to action level of lead (30 µg/m³ TWA) must have blood lead level checked (ZPP is also required in each occasion that a blood lead is obtained.):					
1. Last blood lead level less than 40 µg/100 g.	Every 6 months	Every 6 months	Every 6 months	Every 6 months	Every 6 months.
2. Last blood lead level between 40 µg/100 g and level requiring medical removal (see A above).	Every 2 months	Every 2 months	Every 2 months	Every 2 months	Every 2 months.
3. Employees removed from exposure to lead because of an elevated blood lead level.	Every 1 month	Every 1 month	Every 1 month	Every 1 month	Every 1 month.
C. Permissible airborne exposure limit for workers removed from work due to an elevated blood lead level (without regard to respirator protection).	100 µg/m³ 8 hr TWA	50 µg/m³ 8 hr TWA	30 µg/m³ 8 hr TWA	30 µg/m³ 8 hr TWA	30 µg/m³ 8 hr TWA.

TABLE 2—Continued

	Effective date				
	Mar. 1, 1979	Mar. 1, 1980	Mar. 1, 1981	Mar. 1, 1982	Mar. 1, 1983 (final)
D. Blood lead level confirmed with a second blood analysis, at which employee may return to work. Permissible exposure without regard to respirator protection is listed by industry in Table I.	·60 μg/100 g	·50 μg/100 g	·40 μg/100 g	·40 μg/100 g	·40 μg/100 g.

NOTE: When medical opinion indicates that an employee is at risk of material impairment from exposure to lead, the physician can remove an employee from exposures exceeding the action level (or less) or recommend special protective measures as deemed appropriate and necessary. Medical monitoring during the medical removal period can be more stringent than noted in the table above if the physician so specifies. Return to work or removal of limitations and special protections is permitted when the physician indicates that the worker is no longer at risk of material impairment.

Under the standard's ultimate worker removal criteria, a worker is to be removed from any work having any eight hour TWA exposure to lead of 30 μg/m³ or more whenever either of the following circumstances apply: (1) a blood lead level of 60 μg/100 g or greater is obtained and confirmed by a second follow-up blood lead level performed within two weeks after the employer receives the results of the first blood sampling test, or (2) the average of the previous three blood lead determinations or the average of all blood lead determinations conducted during the previous six months, whichever encompasses the longest time period, equals or exceeds 50 μg/100 g, unless the last blood sample indicates a blood lead level at or below 40 μg/100 g in which case the employee need not be removed. Medical removal is to continue until two consecutive blood lead levels are 40 μg/100 g or less.

During the first two years that the ultimate removal criteria are being phased in, the return criteria have been set to assure that a worker's blood lead level has substantially declined during the period of removal. From March 1, 1979 to March 1, 1980, the blood lead level requiring employee medical removal is 80 μg/100 g. Workers found to have a confirmed blood lead at this level or greater need only be removed from work having a daily 8 hour TWA exposure to lead at or above 100 μg/m³. Workers so removed are to be returned to work when their blood lead levels are at or below 60 μg/100 g of whole blood. From March 1, 1980 to March 1, 1981, the blood lead level requiring medical removal is 70 μg/100 g. During this period workers need only be removed from jobs having a daily 8 hour TWA exposure to lead at or above 50 μg/m³ and are to be returned to work when a level of 50 μg/100 g is achieved. Beginning March 1, 1981, return depends on a worker's blood lead level declining to 40 μg/100 g of whole blood.

As part of the standard, the employer is required to notify in writing each employee whose blood lead level exceeds 40 μg/100 g. In addition each such employee is to be in-

formed that the standard requires medical removal with MRP benefits, discussed below, when an employee's blood lead level exceeds the above defined limits.

In addition to the above blood lead level criteria, temporary worker removal may also take place as a result of medical determinations and recommendations. Written medical opinions must be prepared after each examination pursuant to the standard. If the examining physician includes a medical finding, determination or opinion that the employee has a medical condition which places the employee at increased risk of material health impairment from exposure to lead, then the employee must be removed from exposure to lead at or above the action level. Alternatively, if the examining physician recommends special protective measures for an employee (e.g., use of a powered air purifying respirator) or recommends limitations on an employee's exposure to lead, then the employer must implement these recommendations. Recommendations may be more stringent than the specific provisions of the standard. The examining physician, therefore, is given broad flexibility to tailor special protective procedures to the needs of individual employees. This flexibility extends to the evaluation and management of pregnant workers and male and female workers who are planning to raise children. Based on the history, physical examination, and laboratory studies, the physician might recommend special protective measures or medical removal for an employee who is pregnant or who is planning to conceive a child when, in the physician's judgment, continued exposure to lead at the current job would pose a significant risk. The return of the employee to his or her former job status, or the removal of special protections or limitations, depends upon the examining physician determining that the employee is no longer at increased risk of material impairment or that special measures are no longer needed.

During the period of any form of special protection or removal, the employer must maintain the worker's earnings, seniority,

159

and other employment rights and benefits (as though the worker had not been removed) for a period of up to 18 months. This economic protection will maximize meaningful worker participation in the medical surveillance program, and is appropriate as part of the employer's overall obligation to provide a safe and healthful workplace. The provisions of MRP benefits during the employee's removal period may, however, be conditioned upon participation in medical surveillance.

On rare occasions, an employee's blood lead level may not acceptably decline within 18 months of removal. This situation will arise only in unusual circumstances, thus the standard relies on an individual medical examination to determine how to protect such an employee. This medical determination is to be based on both laboratory values, including lead levels, zinc protoporphyrin levels, blood counts, and other tests felt to be warranted, as well as the physician's judgment that any symptoms or findings on physical examination are a result of lead toxicity. The medical determination may be that the employee is incapable of ever safely returning to his or her former job status. The medical determination may provide additional removal time past 18 months for some employees or specify special protective measures to be implemented.

The lead standard provides for a multiple physician review in cases where the employee wishes a second opinion concerning potential lead poisoning or toxicity. If an employee wishes a second opinion, he or she can make an appointment with a physician of his or her choice. This second physician will review the findings, recommendations or determinations of the first physician and conduct any examinations, consultations or tests deemed necessary in an attempt to make a final medical determination. If the first and second physicians do not agree in their assessment they must try to resolve their differences. If they cannot reach an agreement then they must designate a third physician to resolve the dispute.

The employer must provide examining and consulting physicians with the following specific information: a copy of the lead regulations and all appendices, a description of the employee's duties as related to exposure, the exposure level to lead and any other toxic substances (if applicable), a description of personal protective equipment used, blood lead levels, and all prior written medical opinions regarding the employee in the employer's possession or control. The employer must also obtain from the physician and provide the employee with a written medical opinion containing blood lead levels, the physicians's opinion as to whether the employee is at risk of material impairment to health, any recommended protective measures for the employee if further exposure is permitted, as well as any recommended limi-

tations upon an employee's use of respirators.

Employers must instruct each physician not to reveal to the employer in writing or in any other way his or her findings, laboratory results, or diagnoses which are felt to be unrelated to occupational lead exposure. They must also instruct each physician to advise the employee of any occupationally or non-occupationally related medical condition requiring further treatment or evaluation.

The standard provides for the use of respirators where engineering and other primary controls have not been fully implemented. However, the use of respirator protection shall not be used in lieu of temporary medical removal due to elevated blood lead levels or findings that an employee is at risk of material health impairment. This is based on the numerous inadequacies of respirators including skin rash where the facepiece makes contact with the skin, unacceptable stress to breathing in some workers with underlying cardiopulmonary impairment, difficulty in providing adequate fit, the tendency for respirators to create additional hazards by interfering with vision, hearing, and mobility, and the difficulties of assuring the maximum effectiveness of a complicated work practice program involving respirators. Respirators do, however, serve a useful function where engineering and work practice controls are inadequate by providing supplementary, interim, or short-term protection, provided they are properly selected for the environment in which the employee will be working, properly fitted to the employee, maintained and cleaned periodically, and worn by the employee when required.

In its final standard on occupational exposure to inorganic lead, OSHA has prohibited prophylactic chelation. Diagnostic and therapeutic chelation are permitted only under the supervision of a licensed physician with appropriate medical monitoring in an acceptable clinical setting. The decision to initiate chelation therapy must be made on an individual basis and take into account the severity of symptoms felt to be a result of lead toxicity along with blood lead levels, ZPP levels, and other laboratory tests as appropriate. EDTA and penicillamine which are the primary chelating agents used in the therapy of occupational lead poisoning have significant potential side effects and their use must be justified on the basis of expected benefits to the worker. Unless frank and severe symptoms are present, therapeutic chelation is not recommended given the opportunity to remove a worker from exposure and allow the body to naturally excrete accumulated lead. As a diagnostic aid, the chelation mobilization test using CA-EDTA has limited applicability. According to some investigators, the test can differentiate between lead-induced and other nephropathies.

The test may also provide an estimation of the mobile fraction of the total body lead burden.

Employers are required to assure that accurate records are maintained on exposure monitoring, medical surveillance, and medical removal for each employee. Exposure monitoring and medical surveillance records must be kept for 40 years or the duration of employment plus 20 years, whichever is longer, while medical removal records must be maintained for the duration of employment. All records required under the standard must be made available upon request to the Assistant Secretary of Labor for Occupational Safety and Health and the Director of the National Institute for Occupational Safety and Health. Employers must also make environmental and biological monitoring and medical removal records available to affected employees and to former employees or their authorized employee representatives. Employees or their specifically designated representatives have access to their entire medical surveillance records.

In addition, the standard requires that the employer inform all workers exposed to lead at or above the action level of the provisions of the standard and all its appendices, the purpose and description of medical surveillance and provisions for medical removal protection if temporary removal is required. An understanding of the potential health effects of lead exposure by all exposed employees along with full understanding of their rights under the lead standard is essential for an effective monitoring program.

II. ADVERSE HEALTH EFFECTS OF INORGANIC LEAD

Although the toxicity of lead has been known for 2,000 years, the knowledge of the complex relationship between lead exposure and human response is still being refined. Significant research into the toxic properties of lead continues throughout the world, and it should be anticipated that our understanding of thresholds of effects and margins of safety will be improved in future years. The provisions of the lead standard are founded on two prime medical judgments: first, the prevention of adverse health effects from exposure to lead throughout a working lifetime requires that worker blood lead levels be maintained at or below 40 μg/100 g and second, the blood lead levels of workers, male or female, who intend to parent in the near future should be maintained below 30 μg/100 g to minimize adverse reproductive health effects to the parents and developing fetus. The adverse effects of lead on reproduction are being actively researched and OSHA encourages the physician to remain abreast of recent developments in the area to best advise pregnant workers or workers planning to conceive children.

The spectrum of health effects caused by lead exposure can be subdivided into five developmental stages: normal, physiological changes of uncertain significance, pathophysiological changes, overt symptoms (morbidity), and mortality. Within this process there are no sharp distinctions, but rather a continuum of effects. Boundaries between categories overlap due to the wide variation of individual responses and exposures in the working population. OSHA's development of the lead standard focused on pathophysiological changes as well as later stages of disease.

1. *Heme Synthesis Inhibition.* The earliest demonstrated effect of lead involves its ability to inhibit at least two enzymes of the heme synthesis pathway at very low blood levels. Inhibition of delta aminolevulinic acid dehydrase (ALA-D) which catalyzes conversion of delta-aminolevulinic acid (ALA) to protoporphyrin is observed at a blood lead level below 20 μg/100 g whole blood. At a blood lead level of 40 ug/100 g, more than 20% of the population would have 70% inhibition of ALA-D. There is an exponential increase in ALA excretion at blood lead levels greater than 40 μg/100 g.

Another enzyme, ferrochelatase, is also inhibited at low blood lead levels. Inhibition of ferrochelatase leads to increased free erythrocyte protoporphyrin (FEP) in the blood which can then bind to zinc to yield zinc protoporphyrin. At a blood lead level of 50 μg/100 g or greater, nearly 100% of the population will have an increase in FEP. There is also an exponential relationship between blood lead levels greater than 40 μg/100 g and the associated ZPP level, which has led to the development of the ZPP screening test for lead exposure.

While the significance of these effects is subject to debate, it is OSHA's position that these enzyme disturbances are early stages of a disease process which may eventually result in the clinical symptoms of lead poisoning. Whether or not the effects do progress to the later stages of clinical disease, disruption of these enzyme processes over a working lifetime is considered to be a material impairment of health.

One of the eventual results of lead-induced inhibition of enzymes in the heme synthesis pathway is anemia which can be asymptomatic if mild but associated with a wide array of symptoms including dizziness, fatigue, and tachycardia when more severe. Studies have indicated that lead levels as low as 50 μg/100 g can be associated with a definite decreased hemoglobin, although most cases of lead-induced anemia, as well as shortened red-cell survival times, occur at lead levels exceeding 80 μg/100 g. Inhibited hemoglobin synthesis is more common in chronic cases whereas shortened erythrocyte life span is more common in acute cases.

In lead-induced anemias, there is usually a reticulocytosis along with the presence of basophilic stippling, and ringed sideroblasts, although none of the above are pathognomonic for lead-induced anemia.

2. *Neurological Effects.* Inorganic lead has been found to have toxic effects on both the central and peripheral nervous systems. The earliest stages of lead-induced central nervous system effects first manifest themselves in the form of behavioral disturbances and central nervous system symptoms including irritability, restlessness, insomnia and other sleep disturbances, fatigue, vertigo, headache, poor memory, tremor, depression, and apathy. With more severe exposure, symptoms can progress to drowsiness, stupor, hallucinations, delerium, convulsions and coma.

The most severe and acute form of lead poisoning which usually follows ingestion or inhalation of large amounts of lead is acute encephalopathy which may arise precipitously with the onset of intractable seizures, coma, cardiorespiratory arrest, and death within 48 hours.

While there is disagreement about what exposure levels are needed to produce the earliest symptoms, most experts agree that symptoms definitely can occur at blood lead levels of 60 µg/100 g whole blood and therefore recommend a 40 µg/100 g maximum. The central nervous system effects frequently are not reversible following discontinued exposure or chelation therapy and when improvement does occur, it is almost always only partial.

The peripheral neuropathy resulting from lead exposure characteristically involves only motor function with minimal sensory damage and has a marked predilection for the extensor muscles of the most active extremity. The peripheral neuropathy can occur with varying degrees of severity. The earliest and mildest form which can be detected in workers with blood lead levels as low as 50 µg/100 g is manifested by slowing of motor nerve conduction velocity often without clinical symptoms. With progression of the neuropathy there is development of painless extensor muscle weakness usually involving the extensor muscles of the fingers and hand in the most active upper extremity, followed in severe cases by wrist drop or, much less commonly, foot drop.

In addition to slowing of nerve conduction, electromyographical studies in patients with blood lead levels greater than 50 µg/100 g have demonstrated a decrease in the number of acting motor unit potentials, an increase in the duration of motor unit potentials, and spontaneous pathological activity including fibrillations and fasciculations. Whether these effects occur at levels of 40 µg/100 g is undetermined.

While the peripheral neuropathies can occasionally be reversed with therapy, again such recovery is not assured particularly in the more severe neuropathies and often improvement is only partial. The lack of reversibility is felt to be due in part to segmental demyelination.

3. *Gastrointestinal.* Lead may also affect the gastrointestinal system producing abdominal colic or diffuse abdominal pain, constipation, obstipation, diarrhea, anorexia, nausea and vomiting. Lead colic rarely develops at blood lead levels below 80 µg/100 g.

4. *Renal.* Renal toxicity represents one of the most serious health effects of lead poisoning. In the early stages of disease nuclear inclusion bodies can frequently be identified in proximal renal tubular cells. Renal function remains normal and the changes in this stage are probably reversible. With more advanced disease there is progressive interstitial fibrosis and impaired renal function. Eventually extensive interstitial fibrosis ensues with sclerotic glomeruli and dilated and atrophied proximal tubules; all represent end stage kidney disease. Azotemia can be progressive, eventually resulting in frank uremia necessitating dialysis. There is occasionally associated hypertension and hyperuricemia with or without gout.

Early kidney disease is difficult to detect. The urinalysis is normal in early lead nephropathy and the blood urea nitrogen and serum creatinine increase only when two-thirds of kidney function is lost. Measurement of creatinine clearance can often detect earlier disease as can other methods of measurement of glomerular filtration rate. An abnormal Ca-EDTA mobilization test has been used to differentiate between lead-induced and other nephropathies, but this procedure is not widely accepted. A form of Fanconi syndrome with aminoaciduria, glycosuria, and hyperphosphaturia indicating severe injury to the proximal renal tubules is occasionally seen in children.

5. *Reproductive effects.* Exposure to lead can have serious effects on reproductive function in both males and females. In male workers exposed to lead there can be a decrease in sexual drive, impotence, decreased ability to produce healthy sperm, and sterility. Malformed sperm (teratospermia), decreased number of sperm (hypospermia), and sperm with decreased motility (asthenospermia) can all occur. Teratospermia has been noted at mean blood lead levels of 53 µg/100 g and hypospermia and asthenospermia at 41 µg/100 g. Furthermore, there appears to be a dose-response relationship for teratospermia in lead exposed workers.

Women exposed to lead may experience menstrual disturbances including dysmenorrhea, menorrhagia and amenorrhea. Following exposure to lead, women have a higher frequency of sterility, premature births, spontaneous miscarriages, and stillbirths.

Germ cells can be affected by lead and cause genetic damage in the egg or sperm cells before conception and result in failure to implant, miscarriage, stillbirth, or birth defects.

Infants of mothers with lead poisoning have a higher mortality during the first year and suffer from lowered birth weights, slower growth, and nervous system disorders.

Lead can pass through the placental barrier and lead levels in the mother's blood are comparable to concentrations of lead in the umbilical cord at birth. Transplacental passage becomes detectable at 12–14 weeks of gestation and increases until birth.

There is little direct data on damage to the fetus from exposure to lead but it is generally assumed that the fetus and newborn would be at least as susceptible to neurological damage as young children. Blood lead levels of 50–60 µg/100 g in children can cause significant neurobehavioral impairments and there is evidence of hyperactivity at blood levels as low as 25 µg/100 g. Given the overall body of literature concerning the adverse health effects of lead in children, OSHA feels that the blood lead level in children should be maintained below 30 µg/100 g with a population mean of 15 µg/100 g. Blood lead levels in the fetus and newborn likewise should not exceed 30 µg/100 g.

Because of lead's ability to pass through the placental barrier and also because of the demonstrated adverse effects of lead on reproductive function in both the male and female as well as the risk of genetic damage of lead on both the ovum and sperm, OSHA recommends a 30 µg/100 g maximum permissible blood lead level in both males and females who wish to bear children.

6. *Other toxic effects.* Debate and research continue on the effects of lead on the human body. Hypertension has frequently been noted in occupationally exposed individuals although it is difficult to assess whether this is due to lead's adverse effects on the kidney or if some other mechanism is involved. Vascular and electrocardiogarphic changes have been detected but have not been well characterized. Lead is thought to impair thyroid function and interfere with the pituitary-adrenal axis, but again these effects have not been well defined.

III. MEDICAL EVALUATION

The most important principle in evaluating a worker for any occupational disease including lead poisoning is a high index of suspicion on the part of the examining physician. As discussed in Section 2, lead can affect numerous organ systems and produce a wide array of signs and symptoms, most of which are non-specific and subtle in nature at least in the early stages of disease. Unless serious concern for lead toxicity is present, many of the early clues to diagnosis may easily be overlooked.

The crucial initial step in the medical evaluation is recognizing that a worker's employment can result in exposure to lead. The worker will frequently be able to define exposures to lead and lead containing materials but often will not volunteer this information unless specifically asked. In other situations the worker may not know of any exposures to lead but the suspicion might be raised on the part of the physician because of the industry or occupation of the worker. Potential occupational exposure to lead and its compounds occur in at least 120 occupations, including lead smelting, the manufacture of lead storage batteries, the manufacture of lead pigments and products containing pigments, solder manufacture, shipbuilding and ship repair, auto manufacturing, construction, and painting.

Once the possibility for lead exposure is raised, the focus can then be directed toward eliciting information from the medical history, physical exam, and finally from laboratory data to evaluate the worker for potential lead toxicity.

A complete and detailed work history is important in the initial evaluation. A listing of all previous employment with information on work processes, exposure to fumes or dust, known exposures to lead or other toxic substances, respiratory protection used, and previous medical surveillance should all be included in the worker's record. Where exposure to lead is suspected, information concerning on-the-job personal hygiene, smoking or eating habits in work areas, laundry procedures, and use of any protective clothing or respiratory protection equipment should be noted. A complete work history is essential in the medical evaluation of a worker with suspected lead toxicity, especially when long term effects such as neurotoxicity and nephrotoxicity are considered.

The medical history is also of fundamental importance and should include a listing of all past and current medical conditions, current medications including proprietary drug intake, previous surgeries and hospitalizations, allergies, smoking history, alcohol consumption, and also non-occupational lead exposures such as hobbies (hunting, riflery). Also known childhood exposures should be elicited. Any previous history of hematological, neurological, gastrointestinal, renal, psychological, gynecological, genetic, or reproductive problems should be specifically noted.

A careful and complete review must be performed to assess both recognized complaints and subtle or slowly acquired symptoms which the worker might not appreciate as being significant. The review of symptoms should include the following:

General—weight loss, fatigue, decreased appetite.

Head, Eyes, Ears, Nose, Throat (HEENT)—headaches, visual disturbances or decreased visual acuity, hearing deficits or tinnitus, pigmentation of the oral mucosa, or metallic taste in mouth.

Cardio-pulmonary—shortness of breath, cough, chest pains, palpitations, or orthopnea.

Gastrointestinal—nausea, vomiting, heartburn, abdominal pain, constipation or diarrhea.

Neurologic—irritability, insomnia, weakness (fatigue), dizziness, loss of memory, confusion, hallucinations, incoordination, ataxia, decreased strength in hands or feet, disturbances in gait, difficulty in climbing stairs, or seizures.

Hematologic—pallor, easy fatigability, abnormal blood loss, melena.

Reproductive (male and female and spouse where relevant)—history of infertility, impotence, loss of libido, abnormal menstrual periods, history of miscarriages, stillbirths, or children with birth defects.

Musculo-skeletal—muscle and joint pains.

The physical examination should emphasize the neurological, gastrointestinal, and cardiovascular systems. The worker's weight and blood pressure should be recorded and the oral mucosa checked for pigmentation characteristic of a possible Burtonian or lead line on the gingiva. It should be noted, however, that the lead line may not be present even in severe lead poisoning if good oral hygiene is practiced.

The presence of pallor on skin examination may indicate an anemia, which if severe might also be associated with a tachycardia. If an anemia is suspected, an active search for blood loss should be undertaken including potential blood loss through the gastrointestinal tract.

A complete neurological examination should include an adequate mental status evaluation including a search for behavioral and psychological disturbances, memory testing, evaluation for irritability, insomnia, hallucinations, and mental clouding. Gait and coordination should be examined along with close observation for tremor. A detailed evaluation of peripheral nerve function including careful sensory and motor function testing is warranted. Strength testing particularly of extensor muscle groups of all extremities is of fundamental importance.

Cranial nerve evaluation should also be included in the routine examination.

The abdominal examination should include auscultation for bowel sounds and abdominal bruits and palpation for organomegaly, masses, and diffuse abdominal tenderness.

Cardiovascular examination should evaluate possible early signs of congestive heart failure. Pulmonary status should be addressed particularly if respirator protection is contemplated.

As part of the medical evaluation, the lead standard requires the following laboratory studies:

1. Blood lead level

2. Hemoglobin and hematocrit determinations, red cell indices, and examination of the peripheral blood smear to evaluate red blood cell morphology

3. Blood urea nitrogen

4. Serum creatinine

5. Routine urinalysis with microscopic examination.

6. A zinc protoporphyrin level

In addition to the above, the physician is authorized to order any further laboratory or other tests which he or she deems necessary in accordance with sound medical practice. The evaluation must also include pregnancy testing or laboratory evaluation of male fertility if requested by the employee.

Additional tests which are probably not warranted on a routine basis but may be appropriate when blood lead and ZPP levels are equivocal include delta aminolevulinic acid and coproporphyrin concentrations in the urine, and dark-field illumination for detection of basophilic stippling in red blood cells.

If an anemia is detected further studies including a careful examination of the peripheral smear, reticulocyte count, stool for occult blood, serum iron, total iron binding capacity, bilirubin, and, if appropriate, vitamin B12 and folate may be of value in attempting to identify the cause of the anemia.

If a peripheral neuropathy is suspected, nerve conduction studies are warranted both for diagnosis and as a basis to monitor any therapy.

If renal disease is questioned, a 24 hour urine collection for creatinine clearance, protein, and electrolytes may be indicated. Elevated uric acid levels may result from lead-induced renal disease and a serum uric acid level might be performed.

An electrocardiogram and chest x-ray may be obtained as deemed appropriate.

Sophisticated and highly specialized testing should not be done routinely and where indicated should be under the direction of a specialist.

IV. LABORATORY EVALUATION

The blood lead level at present remains the single most important test to monitor lead exposure and is the test used in the medical surveillance program under the lead standard to guide employee medical removal. The ZPP has several advantages over the blood lead level. Because of its relatively recent development and the lack of extensive data concerning its interpretation, the ZPP currently remains an ancillary test.

This section will discuss the blood lead level and ZPP in detail and will outline their relative advantages and disadvantages. Other blood tests currently available to evaluate lead exposure will also be reviewed.

The blood lead level is a good index of current or recent lead absorption when there is no anemia present and when the worker has not taken any chelating agents. However, blood lead levels along with urinary lead levels do not necessarily indicate the total body burden of lead and are not adequate measures of past exposure. One reason for this is that lead has a high affinity for bone and up to 90% of the body's total lead is deposited there. A very important component of the total lead body burden is lead in soft tissue (liver, kidney, and brain). This fraction of the lead body burden, the biologically active lead, is not entirely reflected by blood lead levels since it is a function of the dynamics of lead absorption, distribution, deposition in bone and excretion. Following discontinuation of exposure to lead, the excess body burden is only slowly mobilized from bone and other relatively stable body stores and excreted. Consequently, a high blood lead level may only represent recent heavy exposure to lead without a significant total body excess and likewise a low blood lead level does not exclude an elevated total body burden of lead.

Also due to its correlation with recent exposures, the blood lead level may vary considerably over short time intervals.

To minimize laboratory error and erroneous results due to contamination, blood specimens must be carefully collected after thorough cleaning of the skin with appropriate methods using lead-free blood containers and analyzed by a reliable laboratory. Under the standard, samples must be analyzed in laboratories which are approved by the Center for Disease Control (CDC) or which have received satisfactory grades in proficiency testing by the CDC in the previous year. Analysis is to be made using atomic absorption spectrophotometry, anodic stripping voltammetry or any method which meets the accuracy requirements set forth by the standard.

The determination of lead in urine is generally considered a less reliable monitoring technique than analysis of whole blood primarily due to individual variability in urinary excretion capacity as well as the technical difficulty of obtaining accurate 24 hour urine collections. In addition, workers with renal insufficiency, whether due to lead or some other cause, may have decreased lead clearance and consequently urine lead levels may underestimate the true lead burden. Therefore, urine lead levels should not be used as a routine test.

The zinc protoporphyrin test, unlike the blood lead determination, measures an adverse metabolic effect of lead and as such is a better indicator of lead toxicity than the level of blood lead itself. The level of ZPP reflects lead absorption over the preceding 3 to 4 months, and therefore is a better indicator of lead body burden. The ZPP requires more time than the blood lead to read significantly elevated levels; the return to normal

after discontinuing lead exposure is also slower. Furthermore, the ZPP test is simpler, faster, and less expensive to perform and no contamination is possible. Many investigators believe it is the most reliable means of monitoring chronic lead absorption.

Zinc protoporphyrin results from the inhibition of the enzyme ferrochelatase which catalyzes the insertion of an iron molecule into the protoporphyrin molecule, which then becomes heme. If iron is not inserted into the molecule then zinc, having a greater affinity for protoporphyrin, takes the place of the iron, forming ZPP.

An elevation in the level of circulating ZPP may occur at blood lead levels as low as 20–30 µg/100 g in some workers. Once the blood lead level has reached 40 µg/100 g there is more marked rise in the ZPP value from its normal range of less than 100 µg/100 ml. Increases in blood lead levels beyond 40 µg/100 g are associated with exponential increases in ZPP.

Whereas blood lead levels fluctuate over short time spans, ZPP levels remain relatively stable. ZPP is measured directly in red blood cells and is present for the cell's entire 120 day life-span. Therefore, the ZPP level in blood reflects the average ZPP production over the previous 3–4 months and consequently the average lead exposure during that time interval.

It is recommended that a hematocrit be determined whenever a confirmed ZPP of 50 µg/100 ml whole blood is obtained to rule out a significant underlying anemia. If the ZPP is in excess of 100 µg/100 ml and not associated with abnormal elevations in blood lead levels, the laboratory should be checked to be sure that blood leads were determined using atomic absorption spectrophotometry anodic stripping voltammetry, or any method which meets the accuracy requirements set forth by the standard by a CDC approved laboratory which is experienced in lead level determinations. Repeat periodic blood lead studies should be obtained in all individuals with elevated ZPP levels to be certain that an associated elevated blood lead level has not been missed due to transient fluctuations in blood leads.

ZPP has a characteristic fluorescence spectrum with a peak at 594 nm which is detectable with a hematofluorimeter. The hematofluorimeter is accurate and portable and can provide on-site, instantaneous results for workers who can be frequently tested via a finger prick.

However, careful attention must be given to calibration and quality control procedures. Limited data on blood lead—ZPP correlations and the ZPP levels which are associated with the adverse health effects discussed in Section 2 are the major limitations of the test. Also it is difficult to correlate ZPP levels with environmental exposure and

165

there is some variation of response with age and sex. Nevertheless, the ZPP promises to be an important diagnostic test for the early detection of lead toxicity and its value will increase as more data is collected regarding its relationship to other manifestations of lead poisoning.

Levels of delta-aminolevulinic acid (ALA) in the urine are also used as a measure of lead exposure. Increasing concentrations of ALA are believed to result from the inhibition of the enzyme delta-aminolevulinic acid dehydrase (ALA-D). Although the test is relatively easy to perform, inexpensive, and rapid, the disadvantages include variability in results, the necessity to collect a complete 24 hour urine sample which has a specific gravity greater than 1.010, and also the fact that ALA decomposes in the presence of light.

The pattern of porphyrin excretion in the urine can also be helpful in identifying lead intoxication. With lead poisoning, the urine concentrations of coproporphyrins I and II, porphobilinogen and uroporphyrin I rise. The most important increase, however, is that of coproporphyrin III; levels may exceed 5,000 µg/1 in the urine in lead poisoned individuals, but its correlation with blood lead levels and ZPP are not as good as those of ALA. Increases in urinary porphyrins are not diagnostic of lead toxicity and may be seen in porphyria, some liver diseases, and in patients with high reticulocyte counts.

Summary. The Occupational Safety and Health Administration's standard for inorganic lead places significant emphasis on the medical surveillance of all workers exposed to levels of inorganic lead above the action level of 30 µg/m³ TWA. The physician has a fundamental role in this surveillance program, and in the operation of the medical removal protection program.

Even with adequate worker education on the adverse health effects of lead and appropriate training in work practices, personal hygiene and other control measures, the physician has a primary responsibility for evaluating potential lead toxicity in the worker. It is only through a careful and detailed medical and work history, a complete physical examination and appropriate laboratory testing that an accurate assessment can be made. Many of the adverse health effects of lead toxicity are either irreversible or only partially reversible and therefore early detection of disease is very important.

This document outlines the medical monitoring program as defined by the occupational safety and health standard for inorganic lead. It reviews the adverse health effects of lead poisoning and describes the important elements of the history and physical examinations as they relate to these adverse effects. Finally, the appropriate laboratory testing for evaluating lead exposure and toxicity is presented.

It is hoped that this review and discussion will give the physician a better understanding of the OSHA standard with the ultimate goal of protecting the health and wellbeing of the worker exposed to lead under his or her care.

[43 FR 53007, Nov. 14, 1978]

EDITORIAL NOTE: For FEDERAL REGISTER citations affecting § 1910.1025, see the List of CFR Sections Affected, which appears in the Finding Aids section of the printed volume and at *www.govinfo.gov.*

§ 1910.1026   Chromium (VI).

(a) *Scope.* (1) This standard applies to occupational exposures to chromium (VI) in all forms and compounds in general industry, except:

(2) Exposures that occur in the application of pesticides regulated by the Environmental Protection Agency or another Federal government agency (e.g., the treatment of wood with preservatives);

(3) Exposures to portland cement; or

(4) Where the employer has objective data demonstrating that a material containing chromium or a specific process, operation, or activity involving chromium cannot release dusts, fumes, or mists of chromium (VI) in concentrations at or above 0.5 µgm/m³ as an 8-hour time-weighted average (TWA) under any expected conditions of use.

(b) *Definitions.* For the purposes of this section the following definitions apply:

Action level means a concentration of airborne chromium (VI) of 2.5 micrograms per cubic meter of air (2.5 µgm/m³) calculated as an 8-hour time-weighted average (TWA).

Assistant Secretary means the Assistant Secretary of Labor for Occupational Safety and Health, U.S. Department of Labor, or designee.

Chromium (VI) [hexavalent chromium or Cr(VI)] means chromium with a valence of positive six, in any form and in any compound.

Director means the Director of the National Institute for Occupational Safety and Health (NIOSH), U.S. Department of Health and Human Services, or designee.

Emergency means any occurrence that results, or is likely to result, in an uncontrolled release of chromium (VI). If an incidental release of chromium

(VI) can be controlled at the time of release by employees in the immediate release area, or by maintenance personnel, it is not an emergency.

Employee exposure means the exposure to airborne chromium (VI) that would occur if the employee were not using a respirator.

High-efficiency particulate air [HEPA] filter means a filter that is at least 99.97 percent efficient in removing mono-dispersed particles of 0.3 micrometers in diameter or larger.

Historical monitoring data means data from chromium (VI) monitoring conducted prior to May 30, 2006, obtained during work operations conducted under workplace conditions closely resembling the processes, types of material, control methods, work practices, and environmental conditions in the employer's current operations.

Objective data means information such as air monitoring data from industry-wide surveys or calculations based on the composition or chemical and physical properties of a substance demonstrating the employee exposure to chromium (VI) associated with a particular product or material or a specific process, operation, or activity. The data must reflect workplace conditions closely resembling the processes, types of material, control methods, work practices, and environmental conditions in the employer's current operations.

Physician or other licensed health care professional [PLHCP] is an individual whose legally permitted scope of practice (*i.e.*, license, registration, or certification) allows him or her to independently provide or be delegated the responsibility to provide some or all of the particular health care services required by paragraph (k) of this section.

Regulated area means an area, demarcated by the employer, where an employee's exposure to airborne concentrations of chromium (VI) exceeds, or can reasonably be expected to exceed, the PEL.

This section means this §1910.1026 chromium (VI) standard.

(c) *Permissible exposure limit (PEL).* The employer shall ensure that no employee is exposed to an airborne concentration of chromium (VI) in excess of 5 micrograms per cubic meter of air

(5 µgm/m³), calculated as an 8-hour time-weighted average (TWA).

(d) *Exposure determination*—(1) *General.* Each employer who has a workplace or work operation covered by this section shall determine the 8-hour TWA exposure for each employee exposed to chromium (VI). This determination shall be made in accordance with either paragraph (d)(2) or paragraph (d)(3) of this section.

(2) *Scheduled monitoring option.* (i) The employer shall perform initial monitoring to determine the 8-hour TWA exposure for each employee on the basis of a sufficient number of personal breathing zone air samples to accurately characterize full shift exposure on each shift, for each job classification, in each work area. Where an employer does representative sampling instead of sampling all employees in order to meet this requirement, the employer shall sample the employee(s) expected to have the highest chromium (VI) exposures.

(ii) If initial monitoring indicates that employee exposures are below the action level, the employer may discontinue monitoring for those employees whose exposures are represented by such monitoring.

(iii) If monitoring reveals employee exposures to be at or above the action level, the employer shall perform periodic monitoring at least every six months.

(iv) If monitoring reveals employee exposures to be above the PEL, the employer shall perform periodic monitoring at least every three months.

(v) If periodic monitoring indicates that employee exposures are below the action level, and the result is confirmed by the result of another monitoring taken at least seven days later, the employer may discontinue the monitoring for those employees whose exposures are represented by such monitoring.

(vi) The employer shall perform additional monitoring when there has been any change in the production process, raw materials, equipment, personnel, work practices, or control methods that may result in new or additional exposures to chromium (VI), or when the employer has any reason to believe

167

that new or additional exposures have occurred.

(3) *Performance-oriented option.* The employer shall determine the 8-hour TWA exposure for each employee on the basis of any combination of air monitoring data, historical monitoring data, or objective data sufficient to accurately characterize employee exposure to chromium (VI).

(4) *Employee notification of determination results.* (i) Within 15 work days after making an exposure determination in accordance with paragraph (d)(2) or paragraph (d)(3) of this section, the employer shall individually notify each affected employee in writing of the results of that determination or post the results in an appropriate location accessible to all affected employees.

(ii) Whenever the exposure determination indicates that employee exposure is above the PEL, the employer shall describe in the written notification the corrective action being taken to reduce employee exposure to or below the PEL.

(5) *Accuracy of measurement.* Where air monitoring is performed to comply with the requirements of this section, the employer shall use a method of monitoring and analysis that can measure chromium (VI) to within an accuracy of plus or minus 25 percent (±25%) and can produce accurate measurements to within a statistical confidence level of 95 percent for airborne concentrations at or above the action level.

(6) *Observation of monitoring.* (i) Where air monitoring is performed to comply with the requirements of this section, the employer shall provide affected employees or their designated representatives an opportunity to observe any monitoring of employee exposure to chromium (VI).

(ii) When observation of monitoring requires entry into an area where the use of protective clothing or equipment is required, the employer shall provide the observer with clothing and equipment and shall assure that the observer uses such clothing and equipment and complies with all other applicable safety and health procedures.

(e) *Regulated areas—*(1) *Establishment.* The employer shall establish a regu-

lated area wherever an employee's exposure to airborne concentrations of chromium (VI) is, or can reasonably be expected to be, in excess of the PEL.

(2) *Demarcation.* The employer shall ensure that regulated areas are demarcated from the rest of the workplace in a manner that adequately establishes and alerts employees of the boundaries of the regulated area.

(3) *Access.* The employer shall limit access to regulated areas to:

(i) Persons authorized by the employer and required by work duties to be present in the regulated area;

(ii) Any person entering such an area as a designated representative of employees for the purpose of exercising the right to observe monitoring procedures under paragraph (d) of this section; or

(iii) Any person authorized by the Occupational Safety and Health Act or regulations issued under it to be in a regulated area.

(f) *Methods of compliance—*(1) *Engineering and work practice controls.* (i) Except as permitted in paragraph (f)(1)(ii) and paragraph (f)(1)(iii) of this section, the employer shall use engineering and work practice controls to reduce and maintain employee exposure to chromium (VI) to or below the PEL unless the employer can demonstrate that such controls are not feasible. Wherever feasible engineering and work practice controls are not sufficient to reduce employee exposure to or below the PEL, the employer shall use them to reduce employee exposure to the lowest levels achievable, and shall supplement them by the use of respiratory protection that complies with the requirements of paragraph (g) of this section.

(ii) Where painting of aircraft or large aircraft parts is performed in the aerospace industry, the employer shall use engineering and work practice controls to reduce and maintain employee exposure to chromium (VI) to or below 25 μgm/m^3 unless the employer can demonstrate that such controls are not feasible. The employer shall supplement such engineering and work practice controls with the use of respiratory protection that complies with the requirements of paragraph (g) of this section to achieve the PEL.

(iii) Where the employer can demonstrate that a process or task does not result in any employee exposure to chromium (VI) above the PEL for 30 or more days per year (12 consecutive months), the requirement to implement engineering and work practice controls to achieve the PEL does not apply to that process or task.

(2) *Prohibition of rotation.* The employer shall not rotate employees to different jobs to achieve compliance with the PEL.

(g) *Respiratory protection*—(1) *General.* Where respiratory protection is required by this section, the employer must provide each employee an appropriate respirator that complies with the requirements of this paragraph. Respiratory protection is required during:

(i) Periods necessary to install or implement feasible engineering and work practice controls;

(ii) Work operations, such as maintenance and repair activities, for which engineering and work practice controls are not feasible;

(iii) Work operations for which an employer has implemented all feasible engineering and work practice controls and such controls are not sufficient to reduce exposures to or below the PEL;

(iv) Work operations where employees are exposed above the PEL for fewer than 30 days per year, and the employer has elected not to implement engineering and work practice controls to achieve the PEL; or

(v) Emergencies.

(2) *Respiratory protection program.* Where respirator use is required by this section, the employer shall institute a respiratory protection program in accordance with §1910.134, which covers each employee required to use a respirator.

(h) *Protective work clothing and equipment*—(1) *Provision and use.* Where a hazard is present or is likely to be present from skin or eye contact with chromium (VI), the employer shall provide appropriate personal protective clothing and equipment at no cost to employees, and shall ensure that employees use such clothing and equipment.

(2) *Removal and storage.* (i) The employer shall ensure that employees re-move all protective clothing and equipment contaminated with chromium (VI) at the end of the work shift or at the completion of their tasks involving chromium (VI) exposure, whichever comes first.

(ii) The employer shall ensure that no employee removes chromium (VI)-contaminated protective clothing or equipment from the workplace, except for those employees whose job it is to launder, clean, maintain, or dispose of such clothing or equipment.

(iii) When contaminated protective clothing or equipment is removed for laundering, cleaning, maintenance, or disposal, the employer shall ensure that it is stored and transported in sealed, impermeable bags or other closed, impermeable containers.

(iv) The employer shall ensure that bags or containers of contaminated protective clothing or equipment that are removed from change rooms for laundering, cleaning, maintenance, or disposal are labeled in accordance with the requirements of the Hazard Communication Standard, §1910.1200.

(3) *Cleaning and replacement.* (i) The employer shall clean, launder, repair and replace all protective clothing and equipment required by this section as needed to maintain its effectiveness.

(ii) The employer shall prohibit the removal of chromium (VI) from protective clothing and equipment by blowing, shaking, or any other means that disperses chromium (VI) into the air or onto an employee's body.

(iii) The employer shall inform any person who launders or cleans protective clothing or equipment contaminated with chromium (VI) of the potentially harmful effects of exposure to chromium (VI) and that the clothing and equipment should be laundered or cleaned in a manner that minimizes skin or eye contact with chromium (VI) and effectively prevents the release of airborne chromium (VI) in excess of the PEL.

(i) *Hygiene areas and practices*—(1) *General.* Where protective clothing and equipment is required, the employer shall provide change rooms in conformance with 29 CFR 1910.141. Where skin contact with chromium (VI) occurs, the employer shall provide washing facilities in conformance with 29 CFR

169

1910.141. Eating and drinking areas provided by the employer shall also be in conformance with § 1910.141.

(2) *Change rooms.* The employer shall assure that change rooms are equipped with separate storage facilities for protective clothing and equipment and for street clothes, and that these facilities prevent cross-contamination.

(3) *Washing facilities.* (i) The employer shall provide readily accessible washing facilities capable of removing chromium (VI) from the skin, and shall ensure that affected employees use these facilities when necessary.

(ii) The employer shall ensure that employees who have skin contact with chromium (VI) wash their hands and faces at the end of the work shift and prior to eating, drinking, smoking, chewing tobacco or gum, applying cosmetics, or using the toilet.

(4) *Eating and drinking areas.* (i) Whenever the employer allows employees to consume food or beverages at a worksite where chromium (VI) is present, the employer shall ensure that eating and drinking areas and surfaces are maintained as free as practicable of chromium (VI).

(ii) The employer shall ensure that employees do not enter eating and drinking areas with protective work clothing or equipment unless surface chromium (VI) has been removed from the clothing and equipment by methods that do not disperse chromium (VI) into the air or onto an employee's body.

(5) *Prohibited activities.* The employer shall ensure that employees do not eat, drink, smoke, chew tobacco or gum, or apply cosmetics in regulated areas, or in areas where skin or eye contact with chromium (VI) occurs; or carry the products associated with these activities, or store such products in these areas.

(j) *Housekeeping*—(1) *General.* The employer shall ensure that:

(i) All surfaces are maintained as free as practicable of accumulations of chromium (VI).

(ii) All spills and releases of chromium (VI) containing material are cleaned up promptly.

(2) *Cleaning methods.* (i) The employer shall ensure that surfaces contaminated with chromium (VI) are cleaned by HEPA-filter vacuuming or other methods that minimize the likelihood of exposure to chromium (VI).

(ii) Dry shoveling, dry sweeping, and dry brushing may be used only where HEPA-filtered vacuuming or other methods that minimize the likelihood of exposure to chromium (VI) have been tried and found not to be effective.

(iii) The employer shall not allow compressed air to be used to remove chromium (VI) from any surface unless:

(A) The compressed air is used in conjunction with a ventilation system designed to capture the dust cloud created by the compressed air; or

(B) No alternative method is feasible.

(iv) The employer shall ensure that cleaning equipment is handled in a manner that minimizes the reentry of chromium (VI) into the workplace.

(3) *Disposal.* The employer shall ensure that:

(i) Waste, scrap, debris, and any other materials contaminated with chromium (VI) and consigned for disposal are collected and disposed of in sealed, impermeable bags or other closed, impermeable containers.

(ii) Bags or containers of waste, scrap, debris, and any other materials contaminated with chromium (VI) that are consigned for disposal are labeled in accordance with the requirements of the Hazard Communication Standard, 29 CFR 1910.1200.

(k) *Medical surveillance*—(1) *General.* (i) The employer shall make medical surveillance available at no cost to the employee, and at a reasonable time and place, for all employees:

(A) Who are or may be occupationally exposed to chromium (VI) at or above the action level for 30 or more days a year;

(B) Experiencing signs or symptoms of the adverse health effects associated with chromium (VI) exposure; or

(C) Exposed in an emergency.

(ii) The employer shall assure that all medical examinations and procedures required by this section are performed by or under the supervision of a PLHCP.

(2) *Frequency.* The employer shall provide a medical examination:

(i) Within 30 days after initial assignment, unless the employee has received a chromium (VI) related medical examination that meets the requirements of this paragraph within the last twelve months;

(ii) Annually;

(iii) Within 30 days after a PLHCP's written medical opinion recommends an additional examination;

(iv) Whenever an employee shows signs or symptoms of the adverse health effects associated with chromium (VI) exposure;

(v) Within 30 days after exposure during an emergency which results in an uncontrolled release of chromium (VI); or

(vi) At the termination of employment, unless the last examination that satisfied the requirements of paragraph (k) of this section was less than six months prior to the date of termination.

(3) *Contents of examination.* A medical examination consists of:

(i) A medical and work history, with emphasis on: Past, present, and anticipated future exposure to chromium (VI); any history of respiratory system dysfunction; any history of asthma, dermatitis, skin ulceration, or nasal septum perforation; and smoking status and history;

(ii) A physical examination of the skin and respiratory tract; and

(iii) Any additional tests deemed appropriate by the examining PLHCP.

(4) *Information provided to the PLHCP.* The employer shall ensure that the examining PLHCP has a copy of this standard, and shall provide the following information:

(i) A description of the affected employee's former, current, and anticipated duties as they relate to the employee's occupational exposure to chromium (VI);

(ii) The employee's former, current, and anticipated levels of occupational exposure to chromium (VI);

(iii) A description of any personal protective equipment used or to be used by the employee, including when and for how long the employee has used that equipment; and

(iv) Information from records of employment-related medical examinations previously provided to the affected employee, currently within the control of the employer.

(5) *PLHCP's written medical opinion.* (i) The employer shall obtain a written medical opinion from the PLHCP, within 30 days for each medical examination performed on each employee, which contains:

(A) The PLHCP's opinion as to whether the employee has any detected medical condition(s) that would place the employee at increased risk of material impairment to health from further exposure to chromium (VI);

(B) Any recommended limitations upon the employee's exposure to chromium (VI) or upon the use of personal protective equipment such as respirators;

(C) A statement that the PLHCP has explained to the employee the results of the medical examination, including any medical conditions related to chromium (VI) exposure that require further evaluation or treatment, and any special provisions for use of protective clothing or equipment.

(ii) The PLHCP shall not reveal to the employer specific findings or diagnoses unrelated to occupational exposure to chromium (VI).

(iii) The employer shall provide a copy of the PLHCP's written medical opinion to the examined employee within two weeks after receiving it.

(l) *Communication of chromium (VI) hazards to employees*—(1) *Hazard communication—general*—(i) Chemical manufacturers, importers, distributors and employers shall comply with all requirements of the Hazard Communication Standard (HCS) (§1910.1200) for chromium (VI).

(ii) In classifying the hazards of chromium (VI) at least the following hazards are to be addressed: Cancer, eye irritation, and skin sensitization.

(iii) Employers shall include chromium (VI) in the hazard communication program established to comply with the HCS (§1910.1200). Employers shall ensure that each employee has access to labels on containers of chromium (VI) and to safety data sheets, and is trained in accordance with the requirements of HCS and paragraph (l)(2) of this section.

(2) *Employee information and training.* (i) The employer shall ensure that each

171

employee can demonstrate knowledge of at least the following:

(A) The contents of this section; and

(B) The purpose and a description of the medical surveillance program required by paragraph (k) of this section.

(ii) The employer shall make a copy of this section readily available without cost to all affected employees.

(m) *Recordkeeping*—(1) *Air monitoring data.* (i) The employer shall maintain an accurate record of all air monitoring conducted to comply with the requirements of this section.

(ii) This record shall include at least the following information:

(A) The date of measurement for each sample taken;

(B) The operation involving exposure to chromium (VI) that is being monitored;

(C) Sampling and analytical methods used and evidence of their accuracy;

(D) Number, duration, and the results of samples taken;

(E) Type of personal protective equipment, such as respirators worn; and

(F) Name, social security number, and job classification of all employees represented by the monitoring, indicating which employees were actually monitored.

(iii) The employer shall ensure that exposure records are maintained and made available in accordance with 29 CFR 1910.1020.

(2) *Historical monitoring data.* (i) Where the employer has relied on historical monitoring data to determine exposure to chromium (VI), the employer shall establish and maintain an accurate record of the historical monitoring data relied upon.

(ii) The record shall include information that reflects the following conditions:

(A) The data were collected using methods that meet the accuracy requirements of paragraph (d)(5) of this section;

(B) The processes and work practices that were in use when the historical monitoring data were obtained are essentially the same as those to be used during the job for which exposure is being determined;

(C) The characteristics of the chromium (VI) containing material being handled when the historical monitoring data were obtained are the same as those on the job for which exposure is being determined;

(D) Environmental conditions prevailing when the historical monitoring data were obtained are the same as those on the job for which exposure is being determined; and

(E) Other data relevant to the operations, materials, processing, or employee exposures covered by the exception.

(iii) The employer shall ensure that historical exposure records are maintained and made available in accordance with 29 CFR 1910.1020.

(3) *Objective data.* (i) The employer shall maintain an accurate record of all objective data relied upon to comply with the requirements of this section.

(ii) This record shall include at least the following information:

(A) The chromium containing material in question;

(B) The source of the objective data;

(C) The testing protocol and results of testing, or analysis of the material for the release of chromium (VI);

(D) A description of the process, operation, or activity and how the data support the determination; and

(E) Other data relevant to the process, operation, activity, material, or employee exposures.

(iii) The employer shall ensure that objective data are maintained and made available in accordance with 29 CFR 1910.1020.

(4) *Medical surveillance.* (i) The employer shall establish and maintain an accurate record for each employee covered by medical surveillance under paragraph (k) of this section.

(ii) The record shall include the following information about the employee:

(A) Name and social security number;

(B) A copy of the PLHCP's written opinions;

(C) A copy of the information provided to the PLHCP as required by paragraph (k)(4) of this section.

(iii) The employer shall ensure that medical records are maintained and made available in accordance with 29 CFR 1910.1020.

172

(n) *Dates.* (1) For employers with 20 or more employees, all obligations of this section, except engineering controls required by paragraph (f) of this section, commence November 27, 2006.

(2) For employers with 19 or fewer employees, all obligations of this section, except engineering controls required by paragraph (f) of this section, commence May 30, 2007.

(3) Except as provided in (n)(4), for all employers, engineering controls required by paragraph (f) of this section shall be implemented no later than May 31, 2010.

(4) In facilities that become parties to the settlement agreement included in appendix A, engineering controls required by paragraph (f) of this section shall be implemented no later than December 31, 2008.

APPENDIX A TO § 1910.1026

IN THE UNITED STATES COURT OF APPEALS FOR THE THIRD CIRCUIT

Surface Finishing Industry Council et al., Petitioners, v. U.S. Occupational Safety and Health Administration, Respondent.

[Docket No. 06–2272 and consolidated cases]

Public Citizen Health Research Group et al., Petitioners, v. Occupational Safety and Health Administration, United States Department of Labor, Respondent.

[Docket No. 06–1818]

SETTLEMENT AGREEMENT

The parties to this Settlement Agreement ("Agreement") are the Occupational Safety and Health Administration, United States Department of Labor ("OSHA"), the Surface Finishing Industry Council or its successors ("SFIC"), surface-finishing and metal-finishing facilities which have opted into this Agreement pursuant to paragraph 7 ("Company" or "Companies"), Public Citizen Health Research Group ("HRG"), and the United Steel, Paper and Forestry, Rubber, Manufacturing, Energy, Allied Industrial and Service Workers International Union ("Steelworkers").

Whereas, On February 28, 2006, OSHA promulgated a revised hexavalent chromium standard for general industry ("the Standard") that includes a permissible exposure limit ("PEL") for hexavalent chromium of 5 micrograms per cubic meter ("µg/m³") measured as an 8-hour time-weighted average ("TWA"), and a deadline of May 31, 2010, for employers to come into compliance with this PEL through the implementation of engi-

neering controls. The deadline for compliance with the remaining provisions of the Standard, including those requiring the use of respiratory protection to comply with the PEL, is November 27, 2006, for employers with twenty (20) or more employees, and May 30, 2007, for employers with nineteen (19) or fewer employees. 29 CFR 1910.1026, 71 FR 10100 (Feb. 28, 2006);

Whereas, SFIC filed a Petition for Review of the Standard in the Eleventh Circuit that was consolidated with other Petitions in the Third Circuit (Case No. 06–2272);

Whereas, SFIC filed a Motion for Leave to Intervene in the matter of HRG's Petition for Review in the Third Circuit (Case No. 06–1818), which has been granted;

Now, therefore, the parties to this Agreement do hereby agree to the following terms:

1. *Term of this Agreement.* This Agreement will be effective upon execution and will expire on May 31, 2010.

2. *Accelerated implementation of engineering controls.* The Companies agree that in accordance with 29 CFR 1910.1026(f)(1) they will implement those feasible engineering controls necessary to reduce hexavalent chromium levels at their facilities by December 31, 2008, to or below the 5 µg/m³ PEL. In fulfilling this obligation, the Companies may select from the engineering and work practice controls listed in Exhibit A to this Agreement or adopt any other controls.

3. *Compliance plan and monitoring.* In accordance with 29 CFR 1910.1026(d)(4)(ii), each Company will prepare, and update as required, a written plan setting forth the specific control steps being taken to reduce employee exposure to or below the PEL by December 31, 2008. In addition, Companies will make an initial exposure determination as required by 29 CFR 1910.1026(d)(1) using either the procedures for personal breathing zone air samples described in 29 CFR 1910.1026(d)(2) or the performance-oriented option described at 29 CFR 1910.1026(d)(3). Thereafter, Companies will conduct periodic monitoring in accordance with the "Scheduled Monitoring Option" provisions at 29 CFR 1910.1026(d)(2) and related provisions at 29 CFR 1910.1026(d)(4)–(6). The Companies agree that upon request compliance plans prepared in accordance with this paragraph, as well as all monitoring results obtained in compliance with this paragraph, will be provided to OSHA, affected employees and employee representatives.

4. *Respirator use.* The respiratory protection provisions at 29 CFR 1910.1026(f) and (g) will apply to the Companies in accordance with the terms and dates set forth in the Standard, except that prior to December 31, 2008, for Companies that are in compliance with this Agreement, OSHA will enforce those respiratory protection provisions only with respect to employees who fall into one

173

of the following six (6) categories: (1) Employees who are exposed to hexavalent chromium in excess of the PEL while performing tasks described in Exhibit B to this Agreement; (2) through November 30, 2007, employees whose exposures to hexavalent chromium exceed a "respirator threshold" of 20 µg/m^3 (measured as an 8-hour TWA); (3) beginning December 1, 2007, employees whose exposures to hexavalent chromium exceed a "respirator threshold" of 12.5 µg/m^3 (measured as an 8-hour TWA); (4) employees who are exposed to hexavalent chromium and request a respirator; (5) any other employees who are required by the Companies to wear a respirator; and (6) employees with exposures for which respirators were required under the previous hexavalent chromium standard (1910.1000) and any other employees covered by respirator programs in effect on May 30, 2006.

5. *Employee information and training.* Company employees will be trained pursuant to the provisions of 29 CFR 1910.1026(l)(2). In addition, the Companies agree to train employees in the provisions of this Agreement within sixty (60) days of the Opt-In Date (defined in paragraph 7 of this Agreement). The training regarding this Agreement shall be provided in language the employees can understand.

6. *Enforcement.* Within thirty (30) days of the execution of this Agreement, OSHA will publish a notice in the FEDERAL REGISTER amending 29 CFR 1910.1026 as follows: (1) A copy of this Agreement will be attached to the Standard as appendix A; (2) a new paragraph, 1910.1026(n)(4), will be added to the Standard, and will read: "In facilities that become parties to the settlement agreement included in appendix A, engineering controls required by paragraph (f) of this section shall be implemented no later than December 31, 2008"; and (3) existing paragraph 1910.1026(n)(3) will be amended to read: "Except as provided in (n)(4), for all employers, engineering controls required by paragraph (f) of this section shall be implemented no later than May 31, 2010."

7. *Opt-In Date for Companies to become parties to this Agreement.* The FEDERAL REGISTER notice described in paragraph 6 of this Agreement will provide notice of the provisions of this Agreement, and of the revisions to the Standard described in paragraph 6, and will provide until November 30, 2006, for eligible facilities to become parties to this Agreement, and be subject to all of the duties, obligations, and rights herein. The last date for signing by facilities shall be referred to as the Opt-In Date. The opt in option will be available on a facility by facility basis and only to SFIC members and other surface-finishing and metal-finishing job shop facilities within the jurisdiction of Federal OSHA. (For purposes of this Agreement, a "job shop" is defined as a facility that sells plat-ing or anodizing services to other companies.) Moreover, the terms of this Agreement apply only with respect to the performance of surface-finishing and metal-finishing operations in those facilities. Although this Agreement applies only to facilities within the jurisdiction of Federal OSHA, OSHA will encourage States with OSHA-approved State occupational safety and health plans to either honor and implement the terms of this Agreement, including the amendments to the standard described in paragraph 6, or to take an alternative position, which may include entering into separate arrangements with surface- and metal-finishing job shop facilities (or their representatives) in their jurisdiction.

8. *Effect on third parties.* Nothing in this Agreement constitutes an admission by SFIC or the Companies that a significant risk of material health impairment exists for hexavalent chromium justifying a reduction of the PEL to 5 µg/m^3. Nor does anything in this Agreement constitute any other admission by SFIC or the Companies for purposes of this litigation or future litigation or standards-setting. This Agreement is not intended to give any rights to any third party except as expressly provided herein.

9. *OSHA inspections.* OSHA may do monitoring inspections to assess compliance with and progress under this Agreement and the Standard, and nothing in this Agreement limits OSHA's right to conduct inspections at Companies" facilities in accordance with the Occupational Safety and Health Act.

10. *Scope of Agreement.* The terms of this Agreement apply only in the circumstances and to the Companies specified herein. In entering into this Agreement, OSHA is not making any representations regarding its enforcement policy with respect to either (1) The hexavalent chromium standard as applied to employers who are not parties to this Agreement or (2) any other occupational safety or health standards.

11. *Effect of invalidation of the Standard.* If the Standard is invalidated, nothing in this Agreement shall prevent the application to SFIC or the Companies of any PEL that. is promulgated by OSHA on remand. This Agreement would not foreclose SFIC or the Companies from participating in rulemaking proceedings or otherwise challenging any new PEL promulgated by OSHA on remand.

12. *Withdrawal of Petitions and Interventions.* SFIC agrees to move to withdraw its Petition for Review in the above-captioned case, Case No. 06–2272, within five (5) working days of the execution of this Agreement. SFIC further will move to dismiss its motion to intervene in Case No. 06–1818 and all other challenges simultaneously with its motion to withdraw in Case No. 06–2272 as Petitioner.

13. *Attorneys' fees.* Each party agrees to bear its own attorneys' fees, costs, and other

expenses that have been incurred in connection with SFIC's Petition for Review, SFIC's intervention in HRG's Petition for Review, and the negotiation of this Agreement up to and including filing of the motions to dismiss.

14. *Support of Agreement.* In the event that all or any portion of this Agreement is challenged in any forum, the signatories below agree to move to intervene in support of this Agreement.

Agreed to this 25th day of October, 2006.

Baruch A. Fellner,

Counsel for SFIC, Gibson, Dunn & Crutcher LLP, 1050 Connecticut Avenue, NW., Washington, DC 20036, (202) 955-8500.

Lauren S. Goodman,

Counsel for OSHA, United States Department of Labor, Office of the Solicitor, 200 Constitution Avenue, NW., Washington, DC 20210, (202) 693-5445.

Scott L. Nelson,

Counsel for HRG and the Steelworkers, Public Citizen Litigation Group, 1600 20th Street, NW., Washington, DC 20009, (202) 588-7724.

EXHIBIT A

AVAILABLE ENGINEERING AND WORK PRACTICE CONTROLS

The Companies agree that work towards the implementation of these available engineering and work practice controls should not be delayed to accommodate their completion by December 31, 2008. The Companies are encouraged to implement from among these controls as soon as practicable.

1. Parts Transfer Practices

• *Minimize droplet formation.* Instruments akin to garden hoses are used to rinse off parts coming out of chemical baths. This causes many small droplets to form, which are easily atomized or vaporized and contribute to airborne chromium concentration. The industry is currently developing ways to minimize the formation of small droplets, dripping, or splashing, possibly by reducing hose pressure.

• *Minimize air current flow.* Strong air currents across these droplets may contribute to their vaporization, and therefore minimizing air current flow across the droplets may reduce airborne hexavalent chromium levels.

• *Slow part speeds as feasible.* The speed at which parts are pulled out of a chemical tank causes splashing, which adds to chromium vaporization. By slowing the speed at which parts are taken out of tanks, splashing and vaporization can be minimized. The feasibility of this control must be evaluated in light of the negative effect on productivity.

2. Plating Bath Surface Tension Management and Fume Suppression

• *Lower surface tension.* Lower surface tension in chemical baths leads to fewer drops forming. Chromium baths currently have a surface tension of 35 dynes per centimeter. As a comparison, water has a surface tension of 72 dynes per centimeter. Lowering surface tension further would lead to reduced airborne hexavalent chromium levels.

• *Fume suppressants.* Fume suppressants create a physical barrier between the chemical bath and the air, which prevents vaporization. Some suppressants, however, may cause pitting or other metal damage, and therefore their use is not always possible.

3. Facility Air Disturbance Monitoring

• *Improvement of local exhaust ventilation (LEV) capture efficiency.* The majority of electroplating facilities are not air-conditioned. As a result, doors are kept open to let in cool air, but this causes air currents that prevent the LEVs from performing efficiently. The use of fans has a similar effect. Industry is researching how to minimize these air currents so that LEVs can perform as designed. Such methods may include the use of partitions to degrade air current flow, or checklists that may include location and positioning of cross drafts, fans, doors, windows, partitions and process equipment that Companies can use to audit their workplaces in order to improve their capture efficiency.

4. Technology Enhancements In Lieu of LEV Retrofitting

• *Eductors.* Many chemical baths are currently mixed via air agitation: Air pipes bubble air into the tank to keep the chemicals mixed and to prevent them from settling. An adverse effect of this agitation is that air bubbles escape at the surface of the tank, resulting in some chromium vaporization. By using eductors (horn-shaped nozzles) in tanks, the chemicals flow from a pump to create solution movement below the surface without the use of air bubbles, and the amount of chromium vaporization can be significantly reduced.

5. Different Means of Chromium Additions

• *Liquid Chromium.* Dry hexavalent chromium flakes are occasionally added to tanks, which can generate airborne particulates of hexavalent chromium. Adding liquid chromium at or near the surface of a tank would lower airborne chromium levels and reduce splashing from tanks.

• *Hydration of flakes before addition.* To add liquid chromium to tanks, the dry flakes must be hydrated. Whether this process is performed by chemical suppliers that provide plating solutions to metal finishing companies or by metal finishing companies that have the necessary experience and equipment, appropriate work practices such as mixing techniques must be implemented to minimize the potential airborne levels of hexavalent chromium.

6. Dust Control

• *Better housekeeping.* Chrome dust that comes off products that are polished or grinded is actually elemental chromium, not hexavalent chromium, so polishing and grinding contribute little to airborne hexavalent chromium levels. However, Companies should use good housekeeping practices, including wet mopping, and wet wipedowns, to reduce the amount of dust present.

7. Improvement and Maintenance of Existing LEVs

• *Improvement and maintenance of existing LEVs.* Companies may repair and maintain their current LEVs. Because the final rule indicates that at least 75 percent of the industry is in compliance with the PEL with LEVs working at 40% of capacity, increasing LEV function can materially affect compliance.

8. Other Controls

• *Other methods.* Companies are constantly determining best work practices and technological controls through laboratory research and practical experience. Companies will implement other engineering and work practice controls as necessary and as practicable to reduce potential hexavalent chromium workplace exposures.

EXHIBIT B

WORKPLACE TASKS REQUIRING RESPIRATORS WHERE PEL IS EXCEEDED

Some well-known and relatively few, discrete tasks related to metal finishing activities result in potentially higher workplace exposures of hexavalent chromium. Where the applicable PEL for hexavalent chromium is exceeded, respirators shall be worn to conduct the following activities:

(1) Hexavalent chromium chemical additions. In order to have the metal deposited onto the part, hexavalent chromium must be added to the plating tank periodically. This is a discrete activity that involves the addition of either a dry flake of hexavalent chromium chemicals or a liquid solution of hexavalent chromium into the plating tank. Respirators shall be worn during the period it takes to add the hexavalent chromium chemical to the tank.

(2) Hexavalent chromium preparation and mixing. Different mixtures of hexavalent chromium chemicals are needed for different types of chromium plating processes. For example, hard chromium plating can require higher concentrations of hexavalent chro-

mium because a thicker coating and longer plating process may be needed for the critical product quality and performance. Similarly, different types of decorative chromium plating processes may need different levels of hexavalent chromium and other chemicals such as catalysts. These mixtures can be in the form of dry flakes or liquid solutions. All of these different hexavalent chromium chemical mixtures are generally prepared by metal finishing suppliers and distributors. Some metal finishing companies may also prepare hexavalent chromium solutions from the dry flakes prior to addition to the plating tanks. Respirators shall be worn during the period it takes to prepare these hexavalent chromium mixtures and solutions whether the activity is conducted at a chemical supplier or a metal finishing company.

(3) Hexavalent chromium tank cleaning. Occasionally, the tanks used for chromium plating may need to be emptied and cleaned. This process would involve the draining of the solution and then the removal of any residues in the tank. Workers cleaning out these tanks may have to enter the tank or reach into it to remove the residues. Respirators (as well as other appropriate PPE) shall be worn during the period it takes to clean the tanks and prepare them for use again.

(4) Hexavalent chromium painting operations. Some metal finishing operations apply paints with higher concentrations of hexavalent chromium to a line of parts, particularly for aerospace applications when a high degree of corrosion protection is needed for critical product performance. Paints are generally applied in such operations with some type of spray mechanism or similar dispersion practice. In some instances, it may be difficult to keep workplace exposures below the PEL for such paint spraying activities. Respirators shall be worn during such spray painting operations.

[71 FR 10374, Feb. 28, 2006, as amended at 71 FR 63242, Oct. 30, 2006; 73 FR 75585, Dec. 12, 2008; 75 FR 12686, Mar. 17, 2010; 77 FR 17781, Mar. 26, 2012]

§ 1910.1027 Cadmium.

(a) *Scope.* This standard applies to all occupational exposures to cadmium and cadmium compounds, in all forms, and in all industries covered by the Occupational Safety and Health Act, except the construction-related industries, which are covered under 29 CFR 1926.63.

(b) *Definitions. Action level* (AL) is defined as an airborne concentration of cadmium of 2.5 micrograms per cubic meter of air (2.5 µg/m³), calculated as an 8-hour time-weighted average (TWA).

Assistant Secretary means the Assistant Secretary of Labor for Occupational Safety and Health, U.S. Department of Labor, or designee.

Authorized person means any person authorized by the employer and required by work duties to be present in regulated areas or any person authorized by the OSH Act or regulations issued under it to be in regulated areas.

Director means the Director of the National Institute for Occupational Safety and Health (NIOSH), U.S. Department of Health and Human Services, or designee.

Employee exposure and similar language referring to the air cadmium level to which an employee is exposed means the exposure to airborne cadmium that would occur if the employee were not using respiratory protective equipment.

Final medical determination is the written medical opinion of the employee's health status by the examining physician under paragraphs (l)(3)-(12) of this section or, if multiple physician review under paragraph (l)(13) of this section or the alternative physician determination under paragraph (l)(14) of this section is invoked, it is the final, written medical finding, recommendation or determination that emerges from that process.

High-efficiency particulate air (HEPA) filter means a filter capable of trapping and retaining at least 99.97 percent of mono-dispersed particles of 0.3 micrometers in diameter.

Regulated area means an area demarcated by the employer where an employee's exposure to airborne concentrations of cadmium exceeds, or can reasonably be expected to exceed, the permissible exposure limit (PEL).

This section means this cadmium standard.

(c) *Permissible Exposure Limit (PEL).* The employer shall assure that no employee is exposed to an airborne concentration of cadmium in excess of five micrograms per cubic meter of air (5 µg/m³), calculated as an eight-hour time-weighted average exposure (TWA).

(d) *Exposure monitoring—*(1) *General.* (i) Each employer who has a workplace or work operation covered by this section shall determine if any employee may be exposed to cadmium at or above the action level.

(ii) Determinations of employee exposure shall be made from breathing zone air samples that reflect the monitored employee's regular, daily 8-hour TWA exposure to cadmium.

(iii) Eight-hour TWA exposures shall be determined for each employee on the basis of one or more personal breathing zone air samples reflecting full shift exposure on each shift, for each job classification, in each work area. Where several employees perform the same job tasks, in the same job classification, on the same shift, in the same work area, and the length, duration, and level of cadmium exposures are similar, an employer may sample a representative fraction of the employees instead of all employees in order to meet this requirement. In representative sampling, the employer shall sample the employee(s) expected to have the highest cadmium exposures.

(2) *Specific.* (i) Initial monitoring. Except as provided for in paragraphs (d)(2)(ii) and (d)(2)(iii) of this section, the employer shall monitor employee exposures and shall base initial determinations on the monitoring results.

(ii) Where the employer has monitored after September 14, 1991, under conditions that in all important aspects closely resemble those currently prevailing and where that monitoring satisfies all other requirements of this section, including the accuracy and confidence levels of paragraph (d)(6) of this section, the employer may rely on such earlier monitoring results to satisfy the requirements of paragraph (d)(2)(i) of this section.

(iii) Where the employer has objective data, as defined in paragraph (n)(2) of this section, demonstrating that employee exposure to cadmium will not exceed the action level under the expected conditions of processing, use, or handling, the employer may rely upon such data instead of implementing initial monitoring.

(3) *Monitoring Frequency (periodic monitoring).* (i) If the initial monitoring or periodic monitoring reveals employee exposures to be at or above the

177

action level, the employer shall monitor at a frequency and pattern needed to represent the levels of exposure of employees and where exposures are above the PEL to assure the adequacy of respiratory selection and the effectiveness of engineering and work practice controls. However, such exposure monitoring shall be performed at least every six months. The employer, at a minimum, shall continue these semi-annual measurements unless and until the conditions set out in paragraph (d)(3)(ii) of this section are met.

(ii) If the initial monitoring or the periodic monitoring indicates that employee exposures are below the action level and that result is confirmed by the results of another monitoring taken at least seven days later, the employer may discontinue the monitoring for those employees whose exposures are represented by such monitoring.

(4) *Additional Monitoring.* The employer also shall institute the exposure monitoring required under paragraphs (d)(2)(i) and (d)(3) of this section whenever there has been a change in the raw materials, equipment, personnel, work practices, or finished products that may result in additional employees being exposed to cadmium at or above the action level or in employees already exposed to cadmium at or above the action level being exposed above the PEL, or whenever the employer has any reason to suspect that any other change might result in such further exposure.

(5) *Employee Notification of Monitoring Results.* (i) The employer must, within 15 working days after the receipt of the results of any monitoring performed under this section, notify each affected employee of these results either individually in writing or by posting the results in an appropriate location that is accessible to employees.

(ii) Wherever monitoring results indicate that employee exposure exceeds the PEL, the employer shall include in the written notice a statement that the PEL has been exceeded and a description of the corrective action being taken by the employer to reduce employee exposure to or below the PEL.

(6) *Accuracy of measurement.* The employer shall use a method of monitoring and analysis that has an accuracy of not less than plus or minus 25 percent (±25%), with a confidence level of 95 percent, for airborne concentrations of cadmium at or above the action level, the permissible exposure limit (PEL), and the separate engineering control air limit (SECAL).

(e) *Regulated areas*—(1) *Establishment.* The employer shall establish a regulated area wherever an employee's exposure to airborne concentrations of cadmium is, or can reasonably be expected to be in excess of the permissible exposure limit (PEL).

(2) *Demarcation.* Regulated areas shall be demarcated from the rest of the workplace in any manner that adequately establishes and alerts employees of the boundaries of the regulated area.

(3) *Access.* Access to regulated areas shall be limited to authorized persons.

(4) *Provision of respirators.* Each person entering a regulated area shall be supplied with and required to use a respirator, selected in accordance with paragraph (g)(2) of this section.

(5) *Prohibited activities.* The employer shall assure that employees do not eat, drink, smoke, chew tobacco or gum, or apply cosmetics in regulated areas, carry the products associated with these activities into regulated areas, or store such products in those areas.

(f) *Methods of compliance*—(1) *Compliance hierarchy.* (i) Except as specified in paragraphs (f)(1) (ii), (iii) and (iv) of this section the employer shall implement engineering and work practice controls to reduce and maintain employee exposure to cadmium at or below the PEL, except to the extent that the employer can demonstrate that such controls are not feasible.

(ii) Except as specified in paragraphs (f)(1) (iii) and (iv) of this section, in industries where a separate engineering control air limit (SECAL) has been specified for particular processes (See Table 1 in this paragraph (f)(1)(ii)), the employer shall implement engineering and work practice controls to reduce and maintain employee exposure at or below the SECAL, except to the extent that the employer can demonstrate that such controls are not feasible.

TABLE I—SEPARATE ENGINEERING CONTROL AIRBORNE LIMITS (SECALS) FOR PROCESSES IN SELECTED INDUSTRIES

Industry	Process	SECAL ($\mu g/m^3$)
Nickel cadmium battery	Plate making, plate preparation	50
	All other processes	15
Zinc/Cadmium refining*	Cadmium refining, casting, melting, oxide production, sinter plant	50
Pigment manufacture	Calcine, crushing, milling, blending	50
	All other processes	15
Stabilizers*	Cadmium oxide charging, crushing, drying, blending	50
Lead smelting*	Sinter plant, blast furnace, baghouse, yard area	50
Plating*	Mechanical plating	15

*Processes in these industries that are not specified in this table must achieve the PEL using engineering controls and work practices as required in f(1)(i).

(iii) The requirement to implement engineering and work practice controls to achieve the PEL or, where applicable, the SECAL does not apply where the employer demonstrates the following:

(A) The employee is only intermittently exposed; and

(B) The employee is not exposed above the PEL on 30 or more days per year (12 consecutive months).

(iv) Wherever engineering and work practice controls are required and are not sufficient to reduce employee exposure to or below the PEL or, where applicable, the SECAL, the employer nonetheless shall implement such controls to reduce exposures to the lowest levels achievable. The employer shall supplement such controls with respiratory protection that complies with the requirements of paragraph (g) of this section and the PEL.

(v) The employer shall not use employee rotation as a method of compliance.

(2) *Compliance program.* (i) Where the PEL is exceeded, the employer shall establish and implement a written compliance program to reduce employee exposure to or below the PEL by means of engineering and work practice controls, as required by paragraph (f)(1) of this section. To the extent that engineering and work practice controls cannot reduce exposures to or below the PEL, the employer shall include in the written compliance program the use of appropriate respiratory protection to achieve compliance with the PEL.

(ii) Written compliance programs shall include at least the following:

(A) A description of each operation in which cadmium is emitted; e.g., machinery used, material processed, controls in place, crew size, employee job responsibilities, operating procedures, and maintenance practices;

(B) A description of the specific means that will be employed to achieve compliance, including engineering plans and studies used to determine methods selected for controlling exposure to cadmium, as well as, where necessary, the use of appropriate respiratory protection to achieve the PEL;

(C) A report of the technology considered in meeting the PEL;

(D) Air monitoring data that document the sources of cadmium emissions;

(E) A detailed schedule for implementation of the program, including documentation such as copies of purchase orders for equipment, construction contracts, etc.;

(F) A work practice program that includes items required under paragraphs (h), (i), and (j) of this section;

(G) A written plan for emergency situations, as specified in paragraph (h) of this section; and

(H) Other relevant information.

(iii) The written compliance programs shall be reviewed and updated at least annually, or more often if necessary, to reflect significant changes in the employer's compliance status.

(iv) Written compliance programs shall be provided upon request for examination and copying to affected employees, designated employee representatives as well as to the Assistant Secretary, and the Director.

(3) *Mechanical ventilation.* (i) When ventilation is used to control exposure, measurements that demonstrate the effectiveness of the system in controlling exposure, such as capture velocity, duct velocity, or static pressure shall be made as necessary to maintain its effectiveness.

(ii) Measurements of the system's effectiveness in controlling exposure shall be made as necessary within five working days of any change in production, process, or control that might result in a significant increase in employee exposure to cadmium.

(iii) *Recirculation of air.* If air from exhaust ventilation is recirculated into the workplace, the system shall have a high efficiency filter and be monitored to assure effectiveness.

(iv) Procedures shall be developed and implemented to minimize employee exposure to cadmium when maintenance of ventilation systems and changing of filters is being conducted.

(g) *Respiratory protection*—(1) *General.* For employees who use respirators required by this section, the employer must provide each employee an appropriate respirator that complies with the requirements of this paragraph. Respirators must be used during:

(i) Periods necessary to install or implement feasible engineering and work-practice controls when employee exposure levels exceed the PEL.

(ii) Maintenance and repair activities, and brief or intermittent operations, for which employee exposures exceed the PEL and engineering and work-practice controls are not feasible or are not required.

(iii) Activities in regulated areas specified in paragraph (e) of this section.

(iv) Work operations for which the employer has implemented all feasible engineering and work-practice controls and such controls are not sufficient to reduce employee exposures to or below the PEL.

(v) Work operations for which an employee is exposed to cadmium at or above the action level, and the employee requests a respirator.

(vi) Work operations for which an employee is exposed to cadmium above the PEL and engineering controls are not required by paragraph (f)(1)(ii) of this section.

(vii) Emergencies.

(2) *Respirator program.* (i) The employer must implement a respiratory protection program in accordance with § 1910.134(b) through (d) (except (d)(1)(iii)), and (f) through (m), which covers each employee required by this section to use a respirator.

(ii) No employees must use a respirator if, based on their most recent medical examination, the examining physician determines that they will be unable to continue to function normally while using a respirator. If the physician determines that the employee must be limited in, or removed from, their current job because of their inability to use a respirator, the limitation or removal must be in accordance with paragraphs (l) (11) and (12) of this section.

(iii) If an employee has breathing difficulty during fit testing or respirator use, the employer must provide the employee with a medical examination in accordance with paragraph (l)(6)(ii) of this section to determine if the employee can use a respirator while performing the required duties.

(3) *Respirator selection.* (i) Employers must:

(A) Select, and provide to employees, the appropriate respirators specified in paragraph (d)(3)(i)(A) of 29 CFR 1910.134.

(B) Provide employees with full facepiece respirators when they experience eye irritation.

(C) Provide HEPA filters for powered and non-powered air-purifying respirators.

(ii) The employer must provide an employee with a powered air-purifying respirator instead of a negative-pressure respirator when an employee who is entitled to a respirator chooses to use this type of respirator and such a respirator provides adequate protection to the employee.

(h) *Emergency situations.* The employer shall develop and implement a written plan for dealing with emergency situations involving substantial releases of airborne cadmium. The plan shall include provisions for the use of appropriate respirators and personal protective equipment. In addition, employees not essential to correcting the emergency situation shall be restricted from the area and normal operations halted in that area until the emergency is abated.

(i) *Protective work clothing and equipment*—(1) *Provision and use.* If an employee is exposed to airborne cadmium above the PEL or where skin or eye irritation is associated with cadmium exposure at any level, the employer shall provide at no cost to the employee, and assure that the employee uses, appropriate protective work clothing and equipment that prevents contamination of the employee and the employee's garments. Protective work clothing and equipment includes, but is not limited to:

(i) Coveralls or similar full-body work clothing;

(ii) Gloves, head coverings, and boots or foot coverings; and

(iii) Face shields, vented goggles, or other appropriate protective equipment that complies with 29 CFR 1910.133.

(2) *Removal and storage.* (i) The employer shall assure that employees remove all protective clothing and equipment contaminated with cadmium at the completion of the work shift and do so only in change rooms provided in accordance with paragraph (j)(1) of this section.

(ii) The employer shall assure that no employee takes cadmium-contaminated protective clothing or equipment from the workplace, except for employees authorized to do so for purposes of laundering, cleaning, maintaining, or disposing of cadmium contaminated protective clothing and equipment at an appropriate location or facility away from the workplace.

(iii) The employer shall assure that contaminated protective clothing and equipment, when removed for laundering, cleaning, maintenance, or disposal, is placed and stored in sealed, impermeable bags or other closed, impermeable containers that are designed to prevent dispersion of cadmium dust.

(iv) The employer shall assure that bags or containers of contaminated protective clothing and equipment that are to be taken out of the change rooms or the workplace for laundering, cleaning, maintenance or disposal shall bear labels in accordance with paragraph (m)(3) of this section.

(3) *Cleaning, replacement, and disposal.* (i) The employer shall provide the protective clothing and equipment required by paragraph (i)(1) of this section in a clean and dry condition as often as necessary to maintain its effectiveness, but in any event at least weekly. The employer is responsible for cleaning and laundering the protective clothing and equipment required by this paragraph to maintain its effectiveness and is also responsible for disposing of such clothing and equipment.

(ii) The employer also is responsible for repairing or replacing required protective clothing and equipment as needed to maintain its effectiveness. When rips or tears are detected while an employee is working they shall be immediately mended, or the worksuit shall be immediately replaced.

(iii) The employer shall prohibit the removal of cadmium from protective clothing and equipment by blowing, shaking, or any other means that disperses cadmium into the air.

(iv) The employer shall assure that any laundering of contaminated clothing or cleaning of contaminated equipment in the workplace is done in a manner that prevents the release of airborne cadmium in excess of the permissible exposure limit prescribed in paragraph (c) of this section.

(v) The employer shall inform any person who launders or cleans protective clothing or equipment contaminated with cadmium of the potentially harmful effects of exposure to cadmium and that the clothing and equipment should be laundered or cleaned in a manner to effectively prevent the release of airborne cadmium in excess of the PEL.

(j) *Hygiene areas and practices*—(1) *General.* For employees whose airborne exposure to cadmium is above the PEL, the employer shall provide clean change rooms, handwashing facilities, showers, and lunchroom facilities that comply with 29 CFR 1910.141.

(2) *Change rooms.* The employer shall assure that change rooms are equipped with separate storage facilities for street clothes and for protective clothing and equipment, which are designed

181

to prevent dispersion of cadmium and contamination of the employee's street clothes.

(3) *Showers and handwashing facilities.* (i) The employer shall assure that employees who are exposed to cadmium above the PEL shower during the end of the work shift.

(ii) The employer shall assure that employees whose airborne exposure to cadmium is above the PEL wash their hands and faces prior to eating, drinking, smoking, chewing tobacco or gum, or applying cosmetics.

(4) *Lunchroom facilities.* (i) The employer shall assure that the lunchroom facilities are readily accessible to employees, that tables for eating are maintained free of cadmium, and that no employee in a lunchroom facility is exposed at any time to cadmium at or above a concentration of 2.5 µg/m^3.

(ii) The employer shall assure that employees do not enter lunchroom facilities with protective work clothing or equipment unless surface cadmium has been removed from the clothing and equipment by HEPA vacuuming or some other method that removes cadmium dust without dispersing it.

(k) *Housekeeping.* (1) All surfaces shall be maintained as free as practicable of accumulations of cadmium.

(2) All spills and sudden releases of material containing cadmium shall be cleaned up as soon as possible.

(3) Surfaces contaminated with cadmium shall, wherever possible, be cleaned by vacuuming or other methods that minimize the likelihood of cadmium becoming airborne.

(4) HEPA-filtered vacuuming equipment or equally effective filtration methods shall be used for vacuuming. The equipment shall be used and emptied in a manner that minimizes the reentry of cadmium into the workplace.

(5) Shoveling, dry or wet sweeping, and brushing may be used only where vacuuming or other methods that minimize the likelihood of cadmium becoming airborne have been tried and found not to be effective.

(6) Compressed air shall not be used to remove cadmium from any surface unless the compressed air is used in conjunction with a ventilation system designed to capture the dust cloud created by the compressed air.

(7) Waste, scrap, debris, bags, containers, personal protective equipment, and clothing contaminated with cadmium and consigned for disposal shall be collected and disposed of in sealed impermeable bags or other closed, impermeable containers. These bags and containers shall be labeled in accordance with paragraph (m) of this section.

(l) *Medical surveillance*—(1) *General*—(i) *Scope.* (A) Currently exposed—The employer shall institute a medical surveillance program for all employees who are or may be exposed to cadmium at or above the action level unless the employer demonstrates that the employee is not, and will not be, exposed at or above the action level on 30 or more days per year (twelve consecutive months); and,

(B) Previously exposed—The employer shall also institute a medical surveillance program for all employees who prior to the effective date of this section might previously have been exposed to cadmium at or above the action level by the employer, unless the employer demonstrates that the employee did not prior to the effective date of this section work for the employer in jobs with exposure to cadmium for an aggregated total of more than 60 months.

(ii) To determine an employee's fitness for using a respirator, the employer shall provide the limited medical examination specified in paragraph (l)(6) of this section.

(iii) The employer shall assure that all medical examinations and procedures required by this standard are performed by or under the supervision of a licensed physician, who has read and is familiar with the health effects section of appendix A to this section, the regulatory text of this section, the protocol for sample handling and laboratory selection in appendix F to this section, and the questionnaire of appendix D to this section. These examinations and procedures shall be provided without cost to the employee and at a time and place that is reasonable and convenient to employees.

(iv) The employer shall assure that the collecting and handling of biological samples of cadmium in urine (CdU), cadmium in blood (CdB), and beta-2 microglobulin in urine (β_2-M) taken from employees under this section is done in a manner that assures their reliability and that analysis of biological samples of cadmium in urine (CdU), cadmium in blood (CdB), and beta-2 microglobulin in urine (β_2-M) taken from employees under this section is performed in laboratories with demonstrated proficiency for that particular analyte. (See appendix F to this section.)

(2) *Initial examination.* (i) The employer shall provide an initial (preplacement) examination to all employees covered by the medical surveillance program required in paragraph (l)(1)(i) of this section. The examination shall be provided to those employees within 30 days after initial assignment to a job with exposure to cadmium or no later than 90 days after the effective date of this section, whichever date is later.

(ii) The initial (preplacement) medical examination shall include:

(A) A detailed medical and work history, with emphasis on: Past, present, and anticipated future exposure to cadmium; any history of renal, cardiovascular, respiratory, hematopoietic, reproductive, and/or musculo-skeletal system dysfunction; current usage of medication with potential nephrotoxic side-effects; and smoking history and current status; and

(B) Biological monitoring that includes the following tests:

(1) Cadmium in urine (CdU), standardized to grams of creatinine (g/Cr);

(2) Beta-2 microglobulin in urine (β_2-M), standardized to grams of creatinine (g/Cr), with pH specified, as described in appendix F to this section; and

(3) Cadmium in blood (CdB), standardized to liters of whole blood (lwb).

(iii) Recent Examination: An initial examination is not required to be provided if adequate records show that the employee has been examined in accordance with the requirements of paragraph (l)(2)(ii) of this section within the past 12 months. In that case, such records shall be maintained as part of the employee's medical record and the

prior exam shall be treated as if it were an initial examination for the purposes of paragraphs (l)(3) and (4) of this section.

(3) *Actions triggered by initial biological monitoring:* (i) If the results of the initial biological monitoring tests show the employee's CdU level to be at or below 3 μg/g Cr, β_2-M level to be at or below 300 μg/g Cr and CdB level to be at or below 5 μg/lwb, then:

(A) For currently exposed employees, who are subject to medical surveillance under paragraph (l)(1)(i)(A) of this section, the employer shall provide the minimum level of periodic medical surveillance in accordance with the requirements in paragraph (l)(4)(i) of this section; and

(B) For previously exposed employees, who are subject to medical surveillance under paragraph (l)(1)(i)(B) of this section, the employer shall provide biological monitoring for CdU, β_2-M, and CdB one year after the initial biological monitoring and then the employer shall comply with the requirements of paragraph (l)(4)(v) of this section.

(ii) For all employees who are subject to medical surveillance under paragraph (l)(1)(i) of this section, if the results of the initial biological monitoring tests show the level of CdU to exceed 3 μg/g Cr, the level of β_2-M to exceed 300 μg/g Cr, or the level of CdB to exceed 5 μg/lwb, the employer shall:

(A) Within two weeks after receipt of biological monitoring results, reassess the employee's occupational exposure to cadmium as follows:

(1) Reassess the employee's work practices and personal hygiene;

(2) Reevaluate the employee's respirator use, if any, and the respirator program;

(3) Review the hygiene facilities;

(4) Reevaluate the maintenance and effectiveness of the relevant engineering controls;

(5) Assess the employee's smoking history and status;

(B) Within 30 days after the exposure reassessment, specified in paragraph (l)(3)(ii)(A) of this section, take reasonable steps to correct any deficiencies found in the reassessment that may be responsible for the employee's excess exposure to cadmium; and,

(C) Within 90 days after receipt of biological monitoring results, provide a full medical examination to the employee in accordance with the requirements of paragraph (l)(4)(ii) of this section. After completing the medical examination, the examining physician shall determine in a written medical opinion whether to medically remove the employee. If the physician determines that medical removal is not necessary, then until the employee's CdU level falls to or below 3 $\mu g/g$ Cr, β_2-M level falls to or below 300 $\mu g/g$ Cr and CdB level falls to or below 5 $\mu g/lwb$, the employer shall:

(1) Provide biological monitoring in accordance with paragraph (l)(2)(ii)(B) of this section on a semiannual basis; and

(2) Provide annual medical examinations in accordance with paragraph (l)(4)(ii) of this section.

(iii) For all employees who are subject to medical surveillance under paragraph (l)(1)(i) of this section, if the results of the initial biological monitoring tests show the level of CdU to be in excess of 15 $\mu g/g$ Cr, or the level of CdB to be in excess of 15 $\mu g/lwb$, or the level of β_2-M to be in excess of 1,500 $\mu g/g$ Cr, the employer shall comply with the requirements of paragraphs (l)(3)(ii)(A)–(B) of this section. Within 90 days after receipt of biological monitoring results, the employer shall provide a full medical examination to the employee in accordance with the requirements of paragraph (l)(4)(ii) of this section. After completing the medical examination, the examining physician shall determine in a written medical opinion whether to medically remove the employee. However, if the initial biological monitoring results and the biological monitoring results obtained during the medical examination both show that: CdU exceeds 15 $\mu g/g$ Cr; or CdB exceeds 15 $\mu g/lwb$; or β_2-M exceeds 1500 $\mu g/g$ Cr, and in addition CdU exceeds 3 $\mu g/g$ Cr or CdB exceeds 5 $\mu g/liter$ of whole blood, then the physician shall medically remove the employee from exposure to cadmium at or above the action level. If the second set of biological monitoring results obtained during the medical examination does not show that a mandatory removal trigger level has been exceeded,

then the employee is not required to be removed by the mandatory provisions of this paragraph. If the employee is not required to be removed by the mandatory provisions of this paragraph or by the physician's determination, then until the employee's CdU level falls to or below 3 $\mu g/g$ Cr, β_2-M level falls to or below 300 $\mu g/g$ Cr and CdB level falls to or below 5 $\mu g/lwb$, the employer shall:

(A) Periodically reassess the employee's occupational exposure to cadmium;

(B) Provide biological monitoring in accordance with paragraph (l)(2)(ii)(B) of this section on a quarterly basis; and

(C) Provide semiannual medical examinations in accordance with paragraph (l)(4)(ii) of this section.

(iv) For all employees to whom medical surveillance is provided, beginning on January 1, 1999, and in lieu of paragraphs (l)(3)(i)–(iii) of this section:

(A) If the results of the initial biological monitoring tests show the employee's CdU level to be at or below 3 $\mu g/g$ Cr, β_2-M level to be at or below 300 $\mu g/g$ Cr and CdB level to be at or below 5 $\mu g/lwb$, then for currently exposed employees, the employer shall comply with the requirements of paragraph (l)(3)(i)(A) of this section, and for previously exposed employees, the employer shall comply with the requirements of paragraph (l)(3)(i)(B) of this section;

(B) If the results of the initial biological monitoring tests show the level of CdU to exceed 3 $\mu g/g$ Cr, the level of β_2-M to exceed 300 $\mu g/g$ Cr, or the level of CdB to exceed 5 $\mu g/lwb$, the employer shall comply with the requirements of paragraphs (l)(3)(ii)(A)–(C) of this section; and,

(C) If the results of the initial biological monitoring tests show the level of CdU to be in excess of 7 $\mu g/g$ Cr, or the level of CdB to be in excess of 10 $\mu g/lwb$, or the level of β_2-M to be in excess of 750 $\mu g/g$ Cr, the employer shall: Comply with the requirements of paragraphs (l)(3)(ii)(A)–(B) of this section; and, within 90 days after receipt of biological monitoring results, provide a full medical examination to the employee in accordance with the requirements of paragraph (l)(4)(ii) of this section. After completing the medical examination, the examining physician shall determine in a written medical opinion whether to medically remove the employee. However, if the initial biological monitoring results and the biological monitoring results obtained during the medical examination both show that: CdU exceeds 7 µg/g Cr; or CdB exceeds 10 µg/lwb; or β_2-M exceeds 750 µg/g Cr, and in addition CdU exceeds 3 µg/g Cr or CdB exceeds 5 µg/liter of whole blood, then the physician shall medically remove the employee from exposure to cadmium at or above the action level. If the second set of biological monitoring results obtained during the medical examination does not show that a mandatory removal trigger level has been exceeded, then the employee is not required to be removed by the mandatory provisions of this paragraph. If the employee is not required to be removed by the mandatory provisions of this paragraph or by the physician's determination, then until the employee's CdU level falls to or below 3 µg/g Cr, β_2-M level falls to or below 300 µg/g Cr and CdB level falls to or below 5 µg/lwb, the employer shall: periodically reassess the employee's occupational exposure to cadmium; provide biological monitoring in accordance with paragraph (l)(2)(ii)(B) of this section on a quarterly basis; and provide semiannual medical examinations in accordance with paragraph (l)(4)(ii) of this section.

(4) *Periodic medical surveillance.* (i) For each employee who is covered under paragraph (l)(1)(i)(A) of this section, the employer shall provide at least the minimum level of periodic medical surveillance, which consists of periodic medical examinations and periodic biological monitoring. A periodic medical examination shall be provided within one year after the initial examination required by paragraph (l)(2) of this section and thereafter at least biennially. Biological sampling shall be provided at least annually, either as part of a periodic medical examination or separately as periodic biological monitoring.

(ii) The periodic medical examination shall include:

(A) A detailed medical and work history, or update thereof, with emphasis on: Past, present and anticipated future exposure to cadmium; smoking history and current status; reproductive history; current use of medications with potential nephrotoxic side-effects; any history of renal, cardiovascular, respiratory, hematopoietic, and/or musculo-skeletal system dysfunction; and as part of the medical and work history, for employees who wear respirators, questions 3–11 and 25–32 in appendix D to this section;

(B) A complete physical examination with emphasis on: Blood pressure, the respiratory system, and the urinary system;

(C) A 14 inch by 17 inch, or a reasonably standard sized posterior-anterior chest X-ray (after the initial X-ray, the frequency of chest X-rays is to be determined by the examining physician);

(D) Pulmonary function tests, including forced vital capacity (FVC) and forced expiratory volume at 1 second (FEV1);

(E) Biological monitoring, as required in paragraph (l)(2)(ii)(B) of this section;

(F) Blood analysis, in addition to the analysis required under paragraph (l)(2)(ii)(B) of this section, including blood urea nitrogen, complete blood count, and serum creatinine;

(G) Urinalysis, in addition to the analysis required under paragraph (l)(2)(ii)(B) of this section, including the determination of albumin, glucose, and total and low molecular weight proteins;

(H) For males over 40 years old, prostate palpation, or other at least as effective diagnostic test(s); and

(I) Any additional tests deemed appropriate by the examining physician.

(iii) Periodic biological monitoring shall be provided in accordance with paragraph (l)(2)(ii)(B) of this section.

(iv) If the results of periodic biological monitoring or the results of biological monitoring performed as part of the periodic medical examination show the level of the employee's CdU, β_2-M, or CdB to be in excess of the levels specified in paragraphs (l)(3)(ii) or (iii); or, beginning on January 1, 1999, in excess of the levels specified in paragraphs (l)(3)(ii) or (iv) of this section, the employer shall take the appropriate actions specified in paragraphs (l)(3)(ii)–(iv) of this section.

(v) For previously exposed employees under paragraph (l)(1)(i)(B) of this section:

(A) If the employee's levels of CdU did not exceed 3 µg/g Cr, CdB did not exceed 5 µg/lwb, and β₂-M did not exceed 300 µg/g Cr in the initial biological monitoring tests, and if the results of the followup biological monitoring required by paragraph (l)(3)(i)(B) of this section one year after the initial examination confirm the previous results, the employer may discontinue all periodic medical surveillance for that employee.

(B) If the initial biological monitoring results for CdU, CdB, or β₂-M were in excess of the levels specified in paragraph (l)(3)(i) of this section, but subsequent biological monitoring results required by paragraph (l)(3)(ii)–(iv) of this section show that the employee's CdU levels no longer exceed 3 µg/g Cr, CdB levels no longer exceed 5 µg/lwb, and β₂-M levels no longer exceed 300 µg/g Cr, the employer shall provide biological monitoring for CdU, CdB, and β₂-M one year after these most recent biological monitoring results. If the results of the followup biological monitoring, specified in this paragraph, confirm the previous results, the employer may discontinue all periodic medical surveillance for that employee.

(C) However, if the results of the follow-up tests specified in paragraph (l)(4)(v)(A) or (B) of this section indicate that the level of the employee's CdU, β₂-M, or CdB exceeds these same levels, the employer is required to provide annual medical examinations in accordance with the provisions of paragraph (l)(4)(ii) of this section until the results of biological monitoring are consistently below these levels or the examining physician determines in a written medical opinion that further medical surveillance is not required to protect the employee's health.

(vi) A routine, biennial medical examination is not required to be provided in accordance with paragraphs (l)(3)(i) and (l)(4) of this section if adequate medical records show that the employee has been examined in accordance with the requirements of paragraph (l)(4)(ii) of this section within the past 12 months. In that case, such records shall be maintained by the employer as part of the employee's medical record, and the next routine, periodic medical examination shall be made available to the employee within two years of the previous examination.

(5) *Actions triggered by medical examinations.* (i) If the results of a medical examination carried out in accordance with this section indicate any laboratory or clinical finding consistent with cadmium toxicity that does not require employer action under paragraph (l)(2), (3) or (4) of this section, the employer, within 30 days, shall reassess the employee's occupational exposure to cadmium and take the following corrective action until the physician determines they are no longer necessary:

(A) Periodically reassess: The employee's work practices and personal hygiene; the employee's respirator use, if any; the employee's smoking history and status; the respiratory protection program; the hygiene facilities; and the maintenance and effectiveness of the relevant engineering controls;

(B) Within 30 days after the reassessment, take all reasonable steps to correct the deficiencies found in the reassessment that may be responsible for the employee's excess exposure to cadmium;

(C) Provide semiannual medical reexaminations to evaluate the abnormal clinical sign(s) of cadmium toxicity until the results are normal or the employee is medically removed; and

(D) Where the results of tests for total proteins in urine are abnormal, provide a more detailed medical evaluation of the toxic effects of cadmium on the employee's renal system.

(6) *Examination for respirator use.* (i) To determine an employee's fitness for respirator use, the employer shall provide a medical examination that includes the elements specified in paragraph (l)(6)(i)(A)–(D) of this section. This examination shall be provided prior to the employee's being assigned to a job that requires the use of a respirator or no later than 90 days after this section goes into effect, whichever date is later, to any employee without a medical examination within the preceding 12 months that satisfies the requirements of this paragraph.

(A) A detailed medical and work history, or update thereof, with emphasis on: Past exposure to cadmium; smoking history and current status; any history of renal, cardiovascular, respiratory, hematopoietic, and/or musculoskeletal system dysfunction; a description of the job for which the respirator is required; and questions 3–11 and 25–32 in appendix D to this section;

(B) A blood pressure test;

(C) Biological monitoring of the employee's levels of CdU, CdB and β_2-M in accordance with the requirements of paragraph (l)(2)(ii)(B) of this section, unless such results already have been obtained within the previous 12 months; and

(D) Any other test or procedure that the examining physician deems appropriate.

(ii) After reviewing all the information obtained from the medical examination required in paragraph (l)(6)(i) of this section, the physician shall determine whether the employee is fit to wear a respirator.

(iii) Whenever an employee has exhibited difficulty in breathing during a respirator fit test or during use of a respirator, the employer, as soon as possible, shall provide the employee with a periodic medical examination in accordance with paragraph (l)(4)(ii) of this section to determine the employee's fitness to wear a respirator.

(iv) Where the results of the examination required under paragraph (l)(6)(i), (ii), or (iii) of this section are abnormal, medical limitation or prohibition of respirator use shall be considered. If the employee is allowed to wear a respirator, the employee's ability to continue to do so shall be periodically evaluated by a physician.

(7) *Emergency examinations.* (i) In addition to the medical surveillance required in paragraphs (l)(2)–(6) of this section, the employer shall provide a medical examination as soon as possible to any employee who may have been acutely exposed to cadmium because of an emergency.

(ii) The examination shall include the requirements of paragraph (l)(4)(ii) of this section, with emphasis on the respiratory system, other organ systems considered appropriate by the examining physician, and symptoms of acute overexposure, as identified in paragraphs II (B)(1)–(2) and IV of appendix A to this section.

(8) *Termination of employment examination.* (i) At termination of employment, the employer shall provide a medical examination in accordance with paragraph (l)(4)(ii) of this section, including a chest X-ray, to any employee to whom at any prior time the employer was required to provide medical surveillance under paragraphs (l)(1)(i) or (l)(7) of this section. However, if the last examination satisfied the requirements of paragraph (l)(4)(ii) of this section and was less than six months prior to the date of termination, no further examination is required unless otherwise specified in paragraphs (l)(3) or (l)(5) of this section;

(ii) However, for employees covered by paragraph (l)(1)(i)(B) of this section, if the employer has discontinued all periodic medical surveillance under paragraph (l)(4)(v) of this section, no termination of employment medical examination is required.

(9) *Information provided to the physician.* The employer shall provide the following information to the examining physician:

(i) A copy of this standard and appendices;

(ii) A description of the affected employee's former, current, and anticipated duties as they relate to the employee's occupational exposure to cadmium;

(iii) The employee's former, current, and anticipated future levels of occupational exposure to cadmium;

(iv) A description of any personal protective equipment, including respirators, used or to be used by the employee, including when and for how long the employee has used that equipment; and

(v) relevant results of previous biological monitoring and medical examinations.

(10) *Physician's written medical opinion.* (i) The employer shall promptly obtain a written, medical opinion from the examining physician for each medical examination performed on each employee. This written opinion shall contain:

187

(A) The physician's diagnosis for the employee;

(B) The physician's opinion as to whether the employee has any detected medical condition(s) that would place the employee at increased risk of material impairment to health from further exposure to cadmium, including any indications of potential cadmium toxicity;

(C) The results of any biological or other testing or related evaluations that directly assess the employee's absorption of cadmium;

(D) Any recommended removal from, or limitation on the activities or duties of the employee or on the employee's use of personal protective equipment, such as respirators;

(E) A statement that the physician has clearly and carefully explained to the employee the results of the medical examination, including all biological monitoring results and any medical conditions related to cadmium exposure that require further evaluation or treatment, and any limitation on the employee's diet or use of medications.

(ii) The employer promptly shall obtain a copy of the results of any biological monitoring provided by an employer to an employee independently of a medical examination under paragraphs (l)(2) and (l)(4) of this section, and, in lieu of a written medical opinion, an explanation sheet explaining those results.

(iii) The employer shall instruct the physician not to reveal orally or in the written medical opinion given to the employer specific findings or diagnoses unrelated to occupational exposure to cadmium.

(11) *Medical Removal Protection (MRP)*—(i) *General.* (A) The employer shall temporarily remove an employee from work where there is excess exposure to cadmium on each occasion that medical removal is required under paragraph (l)(3), (l)(4), or (l)(6) of this section and on each occasion that a physician determines in a written medical opinion that the employee should be removed from such exposure. The physician's determination may be based on biological monitoring results, inability to wear a respirator, evidence of illness, other signs or symptoms of cadmium-related dysfunction or disease, or any other reason deemed medically sufficient by the physician.

(B) The employer shall medically remove an employee in accordance with paragraph (l)(11) of this section regardless of whether at the time of removal a job is available into which the removed employee may be transferred.

(C) Whenever an employee is medically removed under paragraph (l)(11) of this section, the employer shall transfer the removed employee to a job where the exposure to cadmium is within the permissible levels specified in that paragraph as soon as one becomes available.

(D) For any employee who is medically removed under the provisions of paragraph (l)(11)(i) of this section, the employer shall provide follow-up biological monitoring in accordance with (l)(2)(ii)(B) of this section at least every three months and follow-up medical examinations semi-annually at least every six months until in a written medical opinion the examining physician determines that either the employee may be returned to his/her former job status as specified under paragraph (l)(11)(iv)–(v) of this section or the employee must be permanently removed from excess cadmium exposure.

(E) The employer may not return an employee who has been medically removed for any reason to his/her former job status until a physician determines in a written medical opinion that continued medical removal is no longer necessary to protect the employee's health.

(ii) Where an employee is found unfit to wear a respirator under paragraph (l)(6)(ii) of this section, the employer shall remove the employee from work where exposure to cadmium is above the PEL.

(iii) Where removal is based on any reason other than the employee's inability to wear a respirator, the employer shall remove the employee from work where exposure to cadmium is at or above the action level.

(iv) Except as specified in paragraph (l)(11)(v) of this section, no employee who was removed because his/her level of CdU, CdB and/or β_2-M exceeded the medical removal trigger levels in paragraph (l)(3) or (l)(4) of this section may be returned to work with exposure to cadmium at or above the action level until the employee's levels of CdU fall to or below 3 µg/g Cr, CdB falls to or below 5 µg/lwb, and β2-M falls to or below 300 µg/g Cr.

(v) However, when in the examining physician's opinion continued exposure to cadmium will not pose an increased risk to the employee's health and there are special circumstances that make continued medical removal an inappropriate remedy, the physician shall fully discuss these matters with the employee, and then in a written determination may return a worker to his/her former job status despite what would otherwise be unacceptably high biological monitoring results. Thereafter, the returned employee shall continue to be provided with medical surveillance as if he/she were still on medical removal until the employee's levels of CdU fall to or below 3 µg/g Cr, CdB falls to or below 5 µg/lwb, and β2-M falls to or below 300 µg/g Cr.

(vi) Where an employer, although not required by paragraph (l)(11)(i)–(iii) of this section to do so, removes an employee from exposure to cadmium or otherwise places limitations on an employee due to the effects of cadmium exposure on the employee's medical condition, the employer shall provide the same medical removal protection benefits to that employee under paragraph (l)(12) of this section as would have been provided had the removal been required under paragraph (l)(11)(i)–(iii) of this section.

(12) *Medical Removal Protection Benefits (MRPB)*. (i) The employer shall provide MRPB for up to a maximum of 18 months to an employee each time and while the employee is temporarily medically removed under paragraph (l)(11) of this section.

(ii) For purposes of this section, the requirement that the employer provide MRPB means that the employer shall maintain the total normal earnings, seniority, and all other employee rights and benefits of the removed employee, including the employee's right to his/her former job status, as if the employee had not been removed from the employee's job or otherwise medically limited.

(iii) Where, after 18 months on medical removal because of elevated biological monitoring results, the employee's monitoring results have not declined to a low enough level to permit the employee to be returned to his/her former job status:

(A) The employer shall make available to the employee a medical examination pursuant to this section in order to obtain a final medical determination as to whether the employee may be returned to his/her former job status or must be permanently removed from excess cadmium exposure; and

(B) The employer shall assure that the final medical determination indicates whether the employee may be returned to his/her former job status and what steps, if any, should be taken to protect the employee's health.

(iv) The employer may condition the provision of MRPB upon the employee's participation in medical surveillance provided in accordance with this section.

(13) *Multiple physician review.* (i) If the employer selects the initial physician to conduct any medical examination or consultation provided to an employee under this section, the employee may designate a second physician to:

(A) Review any findings, determinations, or recommendations of the initial physician; and

(B) Conduct such examinations, consultations, and laboratory tests as the second physician deems necessary to facilitate this review.

(ii) The employer shall promptly notify an employee of the right to seek a second medical opinion after each occasion that an initial physician provided by the employer conducts a medical examination or consultation pursuant to this section. The employer may condition its participation in, and payment for, multiple physician review upon the employee doing the following within fifteen (15) days after receipt of this notice, or receipt of the initial physician's written opinion, whichever is later:

(A) Informing the employer that he or she intends to seek a medical opinion; and

(B) Initiating steps to make an appointment with a second physician.

(iii) If the findings, determinations, or recommendations of the second physician differ from those of the initial physician, then the employer and the employee shall assure that efforts are made for the two physicians to resolve any disagreement.

(iv) If the two physicians have been unable to quickly resolve their disagreement, then the employer and the employee, through their respective physicians, shall designate a third physician to:

(A) Review any findings, determinations, or recommendations of the other two physicians; and

(B) Conduct such examinations, consultations, laboratory tests, and discussions with the other two physicians as the third physician deems necessary to resolve the disagreement among them.

(v) The employer shall act consistently with the findings, determinations, and recommendations of the third physician, unless the employer and the employee reach an agreement that is consistent with the recommendations of at least one of the other two physicians.

(14) *Alternate physician determination.* The employer and an employee or designated employee representative may agree upon the use of any alternate form of physician determination in lieu of the multiple physician review provided by paragraph (l)(13) of this section, so long as the alternative is expeditious and at least as protective of the employee.

(15) *Information the employer must provide the employee.* (i) The employer shall provide a copy of the physician's written medical opinion to the examined employee within two weeks after receipt thereof.

(ii) The employer shall provide the employee with a copy of the employee's biological monitoring results and an explanation sheet explaining the results within two weeks after receipt thereof.

(iii) Within 30 days after a request by an employee, the employer shall provide the employee with the information the employer is required to provide the examining physician under paragraph (l)(9) of this section.

(16) *Reporting.* In addition to other medical events that are required to be reported on the OSHA Form No. 200, the employer shall report any abnormal condition or disorder caused by occupational exposure to cadmium associated with employment as specified in Chapter (V)(E) of the Reporting Guidelines for Occupational Injuries and Illnesses.

(m) *Communication of cadmium hazards to employees*—(1) *Hazard communication.—general.* (i) Chemical manufacturers, importers, distributors and employers shall comply with all requirements of the Hazard Communication Standard (HCS) (§1910.1200) for cadmium.

(ii) In classifying the hazards of cadmium at least the following hazards are to be addressed: Cancer; lung effects; kidney effects; and acute toxicity effects.

(iii) Employers shall include cadmium in the hazard communication program established to comply with the HCS (§1910.1200). Employers shall ensure that each employee has access to labels on containers of cadmium and to safety data sheets, and is trained in accordance with the requirements of HCS and paragraph (m)(4) of this section.

(2) *Warning signs.* (i) Warning signs shall be provided and displayed in regulated areas. In addition, warning signs shall be posted at all approaches to regulated areas so that an employee may read the signs and take necessary protective steps before entering the area.

(ii) Warning signs required by paragraph (m)(2)(i) of this section shall bear the following legend:

DANGER
CADMIUM
MAY CAUSE CANCER
CAUSES DAMAGE TO LUNGS AND KIDNEYS
WEAR RESPIRATORY PROTECTION IN THIS AREA
AUTHORIZED PERSONNEL ONLY

(iii) The employer shall ensure that signs required by this paragraph (m)(2) are illuminated, cleaned, and maintained as necessary so that the legend is readily visible.

(iv) Prior to June 1, 2016, employers may use the following legend in lieu of that specified in paragraph (m)(2)(ii) of this section:

DANGER
CADMIUM
CANCER HAZARD
CAN CAUSE LUNG AND KIDNEY DISEASE
AUTHORIZED PERSONNEL ONLY
RESPIRATORS REQUIRED IN THIS AREA

(3) *Warning labels.* (i) Shipping and storage containers containing cadmium or cadmium compounds shall bear appropriate warning labels, as specified in paragraph (m)(1) of this section.

(ii) The warning labels for containers of contaminated protective clothing, equipment, waste, scrap, or debris shall include at least the following information:

DANGER
CONTAINS CADMIUM
MAY CAUSE CANCER
CAUSES DAMAGE TO LUNGS AND KIDNEYS
AVOID CREATING DUST

(iii) Prior to June 1, 2015, employers may include the following information on shipping and storage containers containing cadmium, cadmium compounds, or cadmium contaminated clothing, equipment, waste, scrap, or debris in lieu of the labeling requirements specified in paragraphs (m)(1)(i) and (m)(3)(ii) of this section:

DANGER
CONTAINS CADMIUM
CANCER HAZARD
AVOID CREATING DUST
CAN CAUSE LUNG AND KIDNEY DISEASE

(iv) Where feasible, installed cadmium products shall have a visible label or other indication that cadmium is present.

(4) *Employee information and training.* (i) The employer shall train each employee who is potentially exposed to cadmium in accordance with the requirements of this section. The employer shall institute a training program, ensure employee participation in the program, and maintain a record of the contents of such program.

(ii) Training shall be provided prior to or at the time of initial assignment to a job involving potential exposure to cadmium and at least annually thereafter.

(iii) The employer shall make the training program understandable to the employee and shall assure that each employee is informed of the following:

(A) The health hazards associated with cadmium exposure, with special attention to the information incorporated in appendix A to this section;

(B) The quantity, location, manner of use, release, and storage of cadmium in the workplace and the specific nature of operations that could result in exposure to cadmium, especially exposures above the PEL;

(C) The engineering controls and work practices associated with the employee's job assignment;

(D) The measures employees can take to protect themselves from exposure to cadmium, including modification of such habits as smoking and personal hygiene, and specific procedures the employer has implemented to protect employees from exposure to cadmium such as appropriate work practices, emergency procedures, and the provision of personal protective equipment;

(E) The purpose, proper selection, fitting, proper use, and limitations of respirators and protective clothing;

(F) The purpose and a description of the medical surveillance program required by paragraph (l) of this section;

(G) The contents of this section and its appendices; and

(H) The employee's rights of access to records under §1910.1020(e) and (g).

(iv) Additional access to information and training program and materials.

(A) The employer shall make a copy of this section and its appendices readily available without cost to all affected employees and shall provide a copy if requested.

(B) The employer shall provide to the Assistant Secretary or the Director, upon request, all materials relating to the employee information and the training program.

(n) *Recordkeeping*—(1) *Exposure monitoring.* (i) The employer shall establish and keep an accurate record of all air monitoring for cadmium in the workplace.

(ii) This record shall include at least the following information:

191

(A) The monitoring date, duration, and results in terms of an 8-hour TWA of each sample taken;

(B) The name, social security number, and job classification of the employees monitored and of all other employees whose exposures the monitoring is intended to represent;

(C) A description of the sampling and analytical methods used and evidence of their accuracy;

(D) The type of respiratory protective device, if any, worn by the monitored employee;

(E) A notation of any other conditions that might have affected the monitoring results.

(iii) The employer shall maintain this record for at least thirty (30) years, in accordance with 29 CFR 1910.1020.

(2) *Objective data for exemption from requirement for initial monitoring.* (i) For purposes of this section, objective data are information demonstrating that a particular product or material containing cadmium or a specific process, operation, or activity involving cadmium cannot release dust or fumes in concentrations at or above the action level even under the worst-case release conditions. Objective data can be obtained from an industry-wide study or from laboratory product test results from manufacturers of cadmium-containing products or materials. The data the employer uses from an industry-wide survey must be obtained under workplace conditions closely resembling the processes, types of material, control methods, work practices and environmental conditions in the employer's current operations.

(ii) The employer shall establish and maintain a record of the objective data for at least 30 years.

(3) *Medical surveillance.* (i) The employer shall establish and maintain an accurate record for each employee covered by medical surveillance under paragraph (l)(1)(i) of this section.

(ii) The record shall include at least the following information about the employee:

(A) Name, social security number, and description of the duties;

(B) A copy of the physician's written opinions and an explanation sheet for biological monitoring results;

(C) A copy of the medical history, and the results of any physical examination and all test results that are required to be provided by this section, including biological tests, X-rays, pulmonary function tests, etc., or that have been obtained to further evaluate any condition that might be related to cadmium exposure;

(D) The employee's medical symptoms that might be related to exposure to cadmium; and

(E) A copy of the information provided to the physician as required by paragraph (l)(9)(ii)–(v) of this section.

(iii) The employer shall assure that this record is maintained for the duration of employment plus thirty (30) years, in accordance with 29 CFR 1910.1020.

(4) *Availability.* (i) Except as otherwise provided for in this section, access to all records required to be maintained by paragraphs (n)(1) through (3) of this section shall be in accordance with the provisions of 29 CFR 1910.1020.

(ii) Within 15 days after a request, the employer shall make an employee's medical records required to be kept by paragraph (n)(3) of this section available for examination and copying to the subject employee, to designated representatives, to anyone having the specific written consent of the subject employee, and after the employee's death or incapacitation, to the employee's family members.

(6) *Transfer of records.* Whenever an employer ceases to do business and there is no successor employer to receive and retain records for the prescribed period or the employer intends to dispose of any records required to be preserved for at least 30 years, the employer shall comply with the requirements concerning transfer of records set forth in 29 CFR 1910.1020 (h).

(o) *Observation of monitoring*—(1) *Employee observation.* The employer shall provide affected employees or their designated representatives an opportunity to observe any monitoring of employee exposure to cadmium.

(2) *Observation procedures.* When observation of monitoring requires entry into an area where the use of protective clothing or equipment is required, the employer shall provide the observer with that clothing and equipment and

192

shall assure that the observer uses such clothing and equipment and complies with all other applicable safety and health procedures.

(p) *Dates*—(1) *Effective date.* This section shall become effective December 14, 1992.

(2) *Start-up dates.* All obligations of this section commence on the effective date except as follows:

(i) *Exposure monitoring.* Except for small businesses (nineteen (19) or fewer employees), initial monitoring required by paragraph (d)(2) of this section shall be completed as soon as possible and in any event no later than 60 days after the effective date of this standard. For small businesses, initial monitoring required by paragraph (d)(2) of this section shall be completed as soon as possible and in any event no later than 120 days after the effective date of this standard.

(ii) *Regulated areas.* Except for small business, defined under paragraph (p)(2)(i) of this section, regulated areas required to be established by paragraph (e) of this section shall be set up as soon as possible after the results of exposure monitoring are known and in any event no later than 90 days after the effective date of this section. For small businesses, regulated areas required to be established by paragraph (e) of this section shall be set up as soon as possible after the results of exposure monitoring are known and in any event no later than 150 days after the effective date of this section.

(iii) *Respiratory protection.* Except for small businesses, defined under paragraph (p)(2)(i) of this section, respiratory protection required by paragraph (g) of this section shall be provided as soon as possible and in any event no later than 90 days after the effective date of this section. For small businesses, respiratory protection required by paragraph (g) of this section shall be provided as soon as possible and in any event no later than 150 days after the effective date of this section.

(iv) *Compliance program.* Written compliance programs required by paragraph (f)(2) of this section shall be completed and available for inspection and copying as soon as possible and in any event no later than 1 year after the effective date of this section.

(v) *Methods of compliance.* The engineering controls required by paragraph (f)(1) of this section shall be implemented as soon as possible and in any event no later than two (2) years after the effective date of this section. Work practice controls shall be implemented as soon as possible. Work practice controls that are directly related to engineering controls to be implemented in accordance with the compliance plan shall be implemented as soon as possible after such engineering controls are implemented.

(vi) *Hygiene and lunchroom facilities.* (A) Handwashing facilities, permanent or temporary, shall be provided in accordance with 29 CFR 1910.141 (d)(1) and (2) as soon as possible and in any event no later than 60 days after the effective date of this section.

(B) Change rooms, showers, and lunchroom facilities shall be completed as soon as possible and in any event no later than 1 year after the effective date of this section.

(vii) *Employee information and training.* Except for small businesses, defined under paragraph (p)(2)(i) of this section, employee information and training required by paragraph (m)(4) of this section shall be provided as soon as possible and in any event no later than 90 days after the effective date of this standard. For small businesses, employee information and training required by paragraph (m)(4) of this standard shall be provided as soon as possible and in any event no later than 180 days after the effective date of this standard.

(viii) *Medical surveillance.* Except for small businesses, defined under paragraph (p)(2)(i) of this section, initial medical examinations required by paragraph (l) of this section shall be provided as soon as possible and in any event no later than 90 days after the effective date of this standard. For small businesses, initial medical examinations required by paragraph (l) of this section shall be provided as soon as possible and in any event no later than 180 days after the effective date of this standard.

(q) *Appendices.* Except where portions of appendices A, B, D, E, and F to this section are expressly incorporated in requirements of this section, these appendices are purely informational and are not intended to create any additional obligations not otherwise imposed or to detract from any existing obligations.

APPENDIX A TO § 1910.1027—SUBSTANCE
SAFETY DATA SHEET

CADMIUM

I. Substance Identification

A. Substance: Cadmium.
B. 8-Hour, Time-weighted-average, Permissible Exposure Limit (TWA PEL):
1. TWA PEL: Five micrograms of cadmium per cubic meter of air 5 µg/m^3, time-weighted average (TWA) for an 8-hour workday.
C. Appearance: Cadmium metal—soft, blue-white, malleable, lustrous metal or grayish-white powder. Some cadmium compounds may also appear as a brown, yellow, or red powdery substance.

II. Health Hazard Data

A. Routes of Exposure. Cadmium can cause local skin or eye irritation. Cadmium can affect your health if you inhale it or if you swallow it.
B. Effects of Overexposure.
1. Short-term (acute) exposure: Cadmium is much more dangerous by inhalation than by ingestion. High exposures to cadmium that may be immediately dangerous to life or health occur in jobs where workers handle large quantities of cadmium dust or fume; heat cadmium-containing compounds or cadmium-coated surfaces; weld with cadmium solders or cut cadmium-containing materials such as bolts.
2. Severe exposure may occur before symptoms appear. Early symptoms may include mild irritation of the upper respiratory tract, a sensation of constriction of the throat, a metallic taste and/or a cough. A period of 1-10 hours may precede the onset of rapidly progressing shortness of breath, chest pain, and flu-like symptoms with weakness, fever, headache, chills, sweating and muscular pain. Acute pulmonary edema usually develops within 24 hours and reaches a maximum by three days. If death from asphyxia does not occur, symptoms may resolve within a week.
3. Long-term (chronic) exposure. Repeated or long-term exposure to cadmium, even at relatively low concentrations, may result in kidney damage and an increased risk of cancer of the lung and of the prostate.
C. Emergency First Aid Procedures.
1. Eye exposure: Direct contact may cause redness or pain. Wash eyes immediately with large amounts of water, lifting the upper and lower eyelids. Get medical attention immediately.

2. Skin exposure: Direct contact may result in irritation. Remove contaminated clothing and shoes immediately. Wash affected area with soap or mild detergent and large amounts of water. Get medical attention immediately.
3. Ingestion: Ingestion may result in vomiting, abdominal pain, nausea, diarrhea, headache and sore throat. Treatment for symptoms must be administered by medical personnel. Under no circumstances should the employer allow any person whom he retains, employs, supervises or controls to engage in therapeutic chelation. Such treatment is likely to translocate cadmium from pulmonary or other tissue to renal tissue. Get medical attention immediately.
4. Inhalation: If large amounts of cadmium are inhaled, the exposed person must be moved to fresh air at once. If breathing has stopped, perform cardiopulmonary resuscitation. Administer oxygen if available. Keep the affected person warm and at rest. Get medical attention immediately.
5. Rescue: Move the affected person from the hazardous exposure. If the exposed person has been overcome, attempt rescue only after notifying at least one other person of the emergency and putting into effect established emergency procedures. Do not become a casualty yourself. Understand your emergency rescue procedures and know the location of the emergency equipment before the need arises.

III. Employee Information

A. Protective Clothing and Equipment.
1. Respirators: You may be required to wear a respirator for non-routine activities; in emergencies; while your employer is in the process of reducing cadmium exposures through engineering controls; and where engineering controls are not feasible. If respirators are worn in the future, they must have a joint Mine Safety and Health Administration (MSHA) and National Institute for Occupational Safety and Health (NIOSH) label of approval. Cadmium does not have a detectable odor except at levels well above the permissible exposure limits. If you can smell cadmium while wearing a respirator, proceed immediately to fresh air. If you experience difficulty breathing while wearing a respirator, tell your employer.
2. Protective Clothing: You may be required to wear impermeable clothing, gloves, foot gear, a face shield, or other appropriate protective clothing to prevent skin contact with cadmium. Where protective clothing is required, your employer must provide clean garments to you as necessary to assure that the clothing protects you adequately. The employer must replace or repair protective clothing that has become torn or otherwise damaged.

3. Eye Protection: You may be required to wear splash-proof or dust resistant goggles to prevent eye contact with cadmium.

B. Employer Requirements.

1. Medical: If you are exposed to cadmium at or above the action level, your employer is required to provide a medical examination, laboratory tests and a medical history according to the medical surveillance provisions under paragraph (1) of this standard. (See summary chart and tables in this appendix A.) These tests shall be provided without cost to you. In addition, if you are accidentally exposed to cadmium under conditions known or suspected to constitute toxic exposure to cadmium, your employer is required to make special tests available to you.

2. Access to Records: All medical records are kept strictly confidential. You or your representative are entitled to see the records of measurements of your exposure to cadmium. Your medical examination records can be furnished to your personal physician or designated representative upon request by you to your employer.

3. Observation of Monitoring: Your employer is required to perform measurements that are representative of your exposure to cadmium and you or your designated representative are entitled to observe the monitoring procedure. You are entitled to observe the steps taken in the measurement procedure, and to record the results obtained. When the monitoring procedure is taking place in an area where respirators or personal protective clothing and equipment are required to be worn, you or your representative must also be provided with, and must wear the protective clothing and equipment.

C. Employee Requirements—You will not be able to smoke, eat, drink, chew gum or tobacco, or apply cosmetics while working with cadmium in regulated areas. You will also not be able to carry or store tobacco products, gum, food, drinks or cosmetics in regulated areas because these products easily become contaminated with cadmium from the workplace and can therefore create another source of unnecessary cadmium exposure.

Some workers will have to change out of work clothes and shower at the end of the day, as part of their workday, in order to wash cadmium from skin and hair. Handwashing and cadmium-free eating facilities shall be provided by the employer and proper hygiene should always be performed before eating. It is also recommended that you do not smoke or use tobacco products, because among other things, they naturally contain cadmium. For further information, read the labeling on such products.

IV. Physician Information

A. Introduction. The medical surveillance provisions of paragraph (1) generally are aimed at accomplishing three main interrelated purposes: First, identifying employees at higher risk of adverse health effects from excess, chronic exposure to cadmium; second, preventing cadmium-induced disease; and third, detecting and minimizing existing cadmium-induced disease. The core of medical surveillance in this standard is the early and periodic monitoring of the employee's biological indicators of: (a) Recent exposure to cadmium; (b) cadmium body burden; and (c) potential and actual kidney damage associated with exposure to cadmium.

The main adverse health effects associated with cadmium overexposure are lung cancer and kidney dysfunction. It is not yet known how to adequately biologically monitor human beings to specifically prevent cadmium-induced lung cancer. By contrast, the kidney can be monitored to provide prevention and early detection of cadmium-induced kidney damage. Since, for non-carcinogenic effects, the kidney is considered the primary target organ of chronic exposure to cadmium, the medical surveillance provisions of this standard effectively focus on cadmium-induced kidney disease. Within that focus, the aim, where possible, is to prevent the onset of such disease and, where necessary, to minimize such disease as may already exist. The by-products of successful prevention of kidney disease are anticipated to be the reduction and prevention of other cadmium-induced diseases.

B. Health Effects. The major health effects associated with cadmium overexposure are described below.

1. Kidney: The most prevalent non-malignant disease observed among workers chronically exposed to cadmium is kidney dysfunction. Initially, such dysfunction is manifested as proteinuria. The proteinuria associated with cadmium exposure is most commonly characterized by excretion of low-molecular weight proteins (15,000 to 40,000 MW) accompanied by loss of electrolytes, uric acid, calcium, amino acids, and phosphate. The compounds commonly excreted include: beta-2-microglobulin (β_2-M), retinol binding protein (RBP), immunoglobulin light chains, and lysozyme. Excretion of low molecular weight proteins are characteristic of damage to the proximal tubules of the kidney (Iwao *et al.*, 1980).

It has also been observed that exposure to cadmium may lead to urinary excretion of high-molecular weight proteins such as albumin, immunoglobulin G, and glycoproteins (Ex. 29). Excretion of high-molecular weight proteins is typically indicative of damage to the glomeruli of the kidney. Bernard *et al.*, (1979) suggest that damage to the glomeruli and damage to the proximal tubules of the kidney may both be linked to cadmium exposure but they may occur independently of each other.

Several studies indicate that the onset of low-molecular weight proteinuria is a sign of irreversible kidney damage (Friberg *et al.*, 1974; Roels *et al.*, 1982; Piscator 1984; Elinder *et al.*, 1985; Smith *et al.*, 1986). Above specific levels of β_2-M associated with cadmium exposure it is unlikely that β_2-M levels return to normal even when cadmium exposure is eliminated by removal of the individual from the cadmium work environment (Friberg, Ex. 29, 1990).

Some studies indicate that such proteinuria may be progressive; levels of β_2-M observed in the urine increase with time even after cadmium exposure has ceased. See, for example, Elinder *et al.*, 1985. Such observations, however, are not universal, and it has been suggested that studies in which proteinuria has not been observed to progress may not have tracked patients for a sufficiently long time interval (Jarup, Ex. 8–661).

When cadmium exposure continues after the onset of proteinuria, chronic nephrotoxicity may occur (Friberg, Ex. 29). Uremia results from the inability of the glomerulus to adequately filter blood. This leads to severe disturbance of electrolyte concentrations and may lead to various clinical complications including kidney stones (L–140–50).

After prolonged exposure to cadmium, glomerular proteinuria, glucosuria, aminoaciduria, phosphaturia, and hypercalciuria may develop (Exs. 8–86, 4–28, 14–18). Phosphate, calcium, glucose, and amino acids are essential to life, and under normal conditions, their excretion should be regulated by the kidney. Once low molecular weight proteinuria has developed, these elements dissipate from the human body. Loss of glomerular function may also occur, manifested by decreased glomerular filtration rate and increased serum creatinine. Severe cadmium-induced renal damage may eventually develop into chronic renal failure and uremia (Ex. 55).

Studies in which animals are chronically exposed to cadmium confirm the renal effects observed in humans (Friberg *et al.*, 1986). Animal studies also confirm problems with calcium metabolism and related skeletal effects which have been observed among humans exposed to cadmium in addition to the renal effects. Other effects commonly reported in chronic animal studies include anemia, changes in liver morphology, immunosuppression and hypertension. Some of these effects may be associated with cofactors. Hypertension, for example, appears to be associated with diet as well as cadmium exposure. Animals injected with cadmium have also shown testicular necrosis (Ex. 8–86B).

2. Biological Markers

It is universally recognized that the best measures of cadmium exposures and its ef-

fects are measurements of cadmium in biological fluids, especially urine and blood. Of the two, CdU is conventionally used to determine body burden of cadmium in workers without kidney disease. CdB is conventionally used to monitor for recent exposure to cadmium. In addition, levels of CdU and CdB historically have been used to predict the percent of the population likely to develop kidney disease (Thun *et al.*, Ex. L–140–50; WHO, Ex. 8–674; ACGIH, Exs. 8–667, 140–50).

The third biological parameter upon which OSHA relies for medical surveillance is Beta-2-microglobulin in urine (β_2-M), a low molecular weight protein. Excess β_2-M has been widely accepted by physicians and scientists as a reliable indicator of functional damage to the proximal tubule of the kidney (Exs. 8–447, 144–3–C, 4–47, L–140–45, 19–43–A).

Excess β_2-M is found when the proximal tubules can no longer reabsorb this protein in a normal manner. This failure of the proximal tubules is an early stage of a kind of kidney disease that commonly occurs among workers with excessive cadmium exposure. Used in conjunction with biological test results indicating abnormal levels of CdU and CdB, the finding of excess β_2-M can establish for an examining physician that any existing kidney disease is probably cadmium-related (Trs. 6/6/90, pp. 82–86, 122, 134). The upper limits of normal levels for cadmium in urine and cadmium in blood are 3 µg Cd/gram creatinine in urine and 5 µgCd/liter whole blood, respectively. These levels were derived from broad-based population studies.

Three issues confront the physicians in the use of β_2-M as a marker of kidney dysfunction and material impairment. First, there are a few other causes of elevated levels of β_2-M not related to cadmium exposures, some of which may be rather common diseases and some of which are serious diseases (e.g., myeloma or transient flu, Exs. 29 and 8–086). These can be medically evaluated as alternative causes (Friberg, Ex. 29). Also, there are other factors that can cause β_2-M to degrade so that low levels would result in workers with tubular dysfunction. For example, regarding the degradation of β_2-M, workers with acidic urine (pH<6) might have β_2-M levels that are within the "normal" range when in fact kidney dysfunction has occurred (Ex. L–140–1) and the low molecular weight proteins are degraded in acid urine. Thus, it is very important that the pH of urine be measured, that urine samples be buffered as necessary (See appendix F.), and that urine samples be handled correctly, i.e., measure the pH of freshly voided urine samples, then if necessary, buffer to pH>6 (or above for shipping purposes), measure pH again and then, perhaps, freeze the sample for storage and shipping. (See also appendix F.) Second, there is debate over the pathological significance of proteinuria, however, most world experts believe that β_2-M levels greater than 300 μg/g Cr are abnormal (Elinder, Ex. 55, Friberg, Ex. 29). Such levels signify kidney dysfunction that constitutes material impairment of health. Finally, detection of β_2-M at low levels has often been considered difficult, however, many laboratories have the capability of detecting excess β_2-M using simple kits, such as the Phadebas Delphia test, that are accurate to levels of 100 μg β_2-M/g Cr U (Ex. L–140–1).

Specific recommendations for ways to measure β_2-M and proper handling of urine samples to prevent degradation of β_2-M have been addressed by OSHA in appendix F, in the section on laboratory standardization. All biological samples must be analyzed in a laboratory that is proficient in the analysis of that particular analyte, under paragraph (l)(1)(iv). (See appendix F). Specifically, under paragraph (l)(1)(iv), the employer to assure that the collecting and handling of biological samples of cadmium in urine (CdU), cadmium in blood (CdB), and beta-2 microglobulin in urine (β_2-M) taken from employees is collected in a manner that assures reliability. The employer must also assure that analysis of biological samples of cadmium in urine (CdU), cadmium in blood (CdB), and beta-2 microglobulin in urine (β_2-M) taken from employees is performed in laboratories with demonstrated proficiency for that particular analyte. (See appendix F.)

3. Lung and Prostate Cancer

The primary sites for cadmium-associated cancer appear to be the lung and the prostate (L–140–50). Evidence for an association between cancer and cadmium exposure derives from both epidemiological studies and animal experiments. Mortality from prostate cancer associated with cadmium is slightly elevated in several industrial cohorts, but the number of cases is small and there is not clear dose-response relationship. More substantive evidence exists for lung cancer.

The major epidemiological study of lung cancer was conducted by Thun et al., (Ex. 4–68). Adequate data on cadmium exposures were available to allow evaluation of dose-response relationships between cadmium exposure and lung cancer. A statistically significant excess of lung cancer attributed to cadmium exposure was observed in this study even when confounding variables such as co-exposure to arsenic and smoking habits were taken into consideration (Ex. L–140–50).

The primary evidence for quantifying a link between lung cancer and cadmium exposure from animal studies derives from two rat bioassay studies; one by Takenaka et al., (1983), which is a study of cadmium chloride and a second study by Oldiges and Glaser (1990) of four cadmium compounds.

Based on the above cited studies, the U.S. Environmental Protection Agency (EPA) classified cadmium as "B1", a probable human carcinogen, in 1985 (Ex. 4–4). The

International Agency for Research on Cancer (IARC) in 1987 also recommended that cadmium be listed as "2A", a probable human carcinogen (Ex. 4–15). The American Conference of Governmental Industrial Hygienists (ACGIH) has recently recommended that cadmium be labeled as a carcinogen. Since 1984, NIOSH has concluded that cadmium is possibly a human carcinogen and has recommended that exposures be controlled to the lowest level feasible.

4. Non-carcinogenic Effects

Acute pneumonitis occurs 10 to 24 hours after initial acute inhalation of high levels of cadmium fumes such as fever and chest pain (Exs. 30, 8–86B). In extreme exposure cases pulmonary edema may develop and cause death several days after exposure. Little actual exposure measurement data is available on the level of airborne cadmium exposure that causes such immediate adverse lung effects, nonetheless, it is reasonable to believe a cadmium concentration of approximately 1 mg/m^3 over an eight hour period is "immediately dangerous" (55 FR 4052, ANSI; Ex. 8–86B).

In addition to acute lung effects and chronic renal effects, long term exposure to cadmium may cause other severe effects on the respiratory system. Reduced pulmonary function and chronic lung disease indicative of emphysema have been observed in workers who have had prolonged exposure to cadmium dust or fumes (Exs. 4–29, 4–22, 4–42, 4–50, 4–63). In a study of workers conducted by Kazantzis et al., a statistically significant excess of worker deaths due to chronic bronchitis was found, which in his opinion was directly related to high cadmium exposures of 1 mg/m^3 or more (Tr. 6/8/90, pp. 156–157).

Cadmium need not be respirable to constitute a hazard. Inspirable cadmium particles that are too large to be respirable but small enough to enter the tracheobronchial region of the lung can lead to bronchoconstriction, chronic pulmonary disease, and cancer of that portion of the lung. All of these diseases have been associated with occupational exposure to cadmium (Ex. 8–86B). Particles that are constrained by their size to the extra-thoracic regions of the respiratory system such as the nose and maxillary sinuses can be swallowed through mucocillary clearance and be absorbed into the body (ACGIH, Ex. 8–692). The impaction of these particles in the upper airways can lead to anosmia, or loss of sense of smell, which is an early indication of overexposure among workers exposed to heavy metals. This condition is commonly reported among cadmium-exposed workers (Ex. 8–86–B).

C. Medical Surveillance

In general, the main provisions of the medical surveillance section of the standard,

197

under paragraphs (l)(1)–(17) of the regulatory text, are as follows:

1. Workers exposed above the action level are covered;

2. Workers with intermittent exposures are not covered;

3. Past workers who are covered receive biological monitoring for at least one year;

4. Initial examinations include a medical questionnaire and biological monitoring of cadmium in blood (CdB), cadmium in urine (CdU), and Beta-2-microglobulin in urine (β2-M);

5. Biological monitoring of these three analytes is performed at least annually; full medical examinations are performed biennially;

6. Until five years from the effective date of the standard, medical removal is required when CdU is greater than 15 µg/gram creatinine (g Cr), or CdB is greater than 15 µg/liter whole blood (lwb), or β2-M is greater than 1500 µg/g Cr, and CdB is greater than 5 µg/lwb or CdU is greater than 3 µg/g Cr;

7. Beginning five years after the standard is in effect, medical removal triggers will be reduced;

8. Medical removal protection benefits are to be provided for up to 18 months;

9. Limited initial medical examinations are required for respirator usage;

10. Major provisions are fully described under section (l) of the regulatory text; they are outlined here as follows:

A. Eligibility

B. Biological monitoring

C. Actions triggered by levels of CdU, CdB, and β2-M (See Summary Charts and Tables in Attachment-1.)

D. Periodic medical surveillance

E. Actions triggered by periodic medical surveillance (See appendix A Summary Chart and Tables in Attachment-1.)

F. Respirator usage

G. Emergency medical examinations

H. Termination examination

I. Information to physician

J. Physician's medical opinion

K. Medical removal protection

L. Medical removal protection benefits

M. Multiple physician review

N. Alternate physician review

O. Information employer gives to employee

P. Recordkeeping

Q. Reporting on OSHA form 200

11. The above mentioned summary of the medical surveillance provisions, the summary chart, and tables for the actions triggered at different levels of CdU, CdB and β2-M (in appendix A Attachment-1) are included only for the purpose of facilitating understanding of the provisions of paragraphs (l)(3) of the final cadmium standard. The summary of the provisions, the summary chart, and the tables do not add to or reduce the requirements in paragraph (l)(3).

D. Recommendations to Physicians

1. It is strongly recommended that patients with tubular proteinuria are counseled on: The hazards of smoking; avoidance of nephrotoxins and certain prescriptions and over-the-counter medications that may exacerbate kidney symptoms; how to control diabetes and/or blood pressure; proper hydration, diet, and exercise (Ex. 19–2). A list of prominent or common nephrotoxins is attached. (See appendix A Attachment-2.)

2. DO NOT CHELATE; KNOW WHICH DRUGS ARE NEPHROTOXINS OR ARE ASSOCIATED WITH NEPHRITIS.

3. The gravity of cadmium-induced renal damage is compounded by the fact there is no medical treatment to prevent or reduce the accumulation of cadmium in the kidney (Ex. 8–619). Dr. Friberg, a leading world expert on cadmium toxicity, indicated in 1992, that there is no form of chelating agent that could be used without substantial risk. He stated that tubular proteinuria has to be treated in the same way as other kidney disorders (Ex. 29).

4. After the results of a workers' biological monitoring or medical examination are received the employer is required to provide an information sheet to the patient, briefly explaining the significance of the results. (See Attachment 3 of this appendix A.)

5. For additional information the physician is referred to the following additional resources:

a. The physician can always obtain a copy of the preamble, with its full discussion of the health effects, from OSHA's Computerized Information System (OCIS).

b. The Docket Officer maintains a record of the rulemaking. The Cadmium Docket (H–057A), is located at 200 Constitution Ave. NW., room N–2625, Washington, DC 20210; telephone: 202–219–7894.

c. The following articles and exhibits in particular from that docket (H–057A):

Exhibit number	Author and paper title
8–447	Lauwerys *et. al.*, Guide for physicians, "Health Maintenance of Workers Exposed to Cadmium," published by the Cadmium Council.
4–67	Takenaka, S., H. Oldiges, H. Konig, D. Hochrainer, G. Oberdorster. "Carcinogenicity of Cadmium Chloride Aerosols in Wistar Rats". *JNCI* 70:367–373, 1983. (32)
4–68	Thun, M.J., T.M. Schnoor, A.B. Smith, W.E. Halperin, R.A. Lemen. "Mortality Among a Cohort of U.S. Cadmium Production Workers—An Update." *JNCI* 74(2):325–33, 1985. (8)
4–25	Elinder, C.G., Kjellstrom, T., Hogstedt, C., *et al.*, "Cancer Mortality of Cadmium Workers." *Brit. J. Ind. Med.* 42:651–655, 1985. (14)

Exhibit number	Author and paper title
4–26	Ellis, K.J. *et al.*, "Critical Concentrations of Cadmium in Human Renal Cortex: Dose Effect Studies to Cadmium Smelter Workers." *J. Toxicol. Environ. Health* 7:691–703, 1981. (76)
4–27	Ellis, K.J., S.H. Cohn and T.J. Smith. "Cadmium Inhalation Exposure Estimates: Their Significance with Respect to Kidney and Liver Cadmium Burden." *J. Toxicol. Environ. Health* 15:173–187, 1985.
4–28	Falck, F.Y., Jr., Fine, L.J., Smith, R.G., McClatchey, K.D., Annesley, T., England, B., and Schork, A.M. "Occupational Cadmium Exposure and Renal Status." *Am. J. Ind. Med.* 4:541, 1983. (64)
8–86A	Friberg, L., C.G. Elinder, *et al.*, "Cadmium and Health a Toxicological and Epidemiological Appraisal, Volume I, Exposure, Dose, and Metabolism." CRC Press, Inc., Boca Raton, FL, 1986. (Available from the OSHA Technical Data Center)
8–86B	Friberg, L., C.G. Elinder, *et al.*, "Cadmium and Health: A Toxicological and Epidemiological Appraisal, Volume II, Effects and Response." CRC Press, Inc., Boca Raton, FL, 1986. (Available from the OSHA Technical Data Center)
L–140–45	Elinder, C.G., "Cancer Mortality of Cadmium Workers", *Brit. J. Ind. Med.*, 42, 651–655, 1985.
L–140–50	Thun, M., Elinder, C.G., Friberg, L, "Scientific Basis for an Occupational Standard for Cadmium, *Am. J. Ind. Med.*, 20; 629–642, 1991.

V. Information Sheet

The information sheet (appendix A Attachment-3.) or an equally explanatory one should be provided to you after any biological monitoring results are reviewed by the physician, or where applicable, after any medical examination.

ATTACHMENT 1—APPENDIX A SUMMARY CHART AND TABLES A AND B OF ACTIONS TRIGGERED BY BIOLOGICAL MONITORING

APPENDIX A SUMMARY CHART: SECTION (1)(3) MEDICAL SURVEILLANCE

Categorizing Biological Monitoring Results

(A) Biological monitoring results categories are set forth in appendix A Table A for the periods ending December 31, 1998 and for the period beginning January 1, 1999.

(B) The results of the biological monitoring for the initial medical exam and the subsequent exams shall determine an employee's biological monitoring result category.

Actions Triggered by Biological Monitoring

(A)

(i) The actions triggered by biological monitoring for an employee are set forth in appendix A Table B.

(ii) The biological monitoring results for each employee under section (1)(3) shall determine the actions required for that employee. That is, for any employee in biological monitoring category C, the employer will perform all of the actions for which there is an X in column C of appendix A Table B.

(iii) An employee is assigned the alphabetical category ("A" being the lowest) depending upon the test results of the three biological markers.

(iv) An employee is assigned category A if monitoring results for all three biological markers fall at or below the levels indicated in the table listed for category A.

(v) An employee is assigned category B if any monitoring result for any of the three biological markers fall in the range of levels indicated in the table listed for category B, providing no result exceeds the levels listed for category B.

(vi) An employee is assigned category C if any monitoring result for any of the three biological markers are above the levels listed for category C.

(B) The user of appendix A Tables A and B should know that these tables are provided only to facilitate understanding of the relevant provisions of paragraph (1)(3) of this section. appendix A Tables A and B are not meant to add to or subtract from the requirements of those provisions.

APPENDIX A TABLE A—CATEGORIZATION OF BIOLOGICAL MONITORING RESULTS

APPLICABLE THROUGH 1998 ONLY

Biological marker	Monitoring result categories		
	A	B	C
Cadmium in urine (CdU) (μg/g creatinine)	≤3	>3 and ≤15	>15
β₂-microglobulin (β₂–M) (μg/g creatinine)	≤300	>300 and ≤1500	>1500*
Cadmium in blood (CdB) (μg/liter whole blood)	≤5	>5 and ≤15	>15

* If an employee's β_2–M levels are above 1,500 μg/g creatinine, in order for mandatory medical removal to be required (See appendix A Table B.), either the employee's CdU level must also be >3 μg/g creatinine or CdB level must also be >5 μg/liter whole blood.

199

APPLICABLE BEGINNING JANUARY 1, 1999

Biological marker	Monitoring result categories		
	A	B	C
Cadmium in urine (CdU) (µg/g creatinine)	≤3	>3 and ≤7	>7
β₂-microglobulin (β₂–M) (µg/g creatinine)	≤300	>300 and ≤750	>750*
Cadmium in blood (CdB) (µg/liter whole blood)	≤5	>5 and ≤10	>10

*If an employee's β₂–M levels are above 750 µg/g creatinine, in order for mandatory medical removal to be required (See appendix A Table B.), either the employee's CdU level must also be >3 µg/g creatinine or CdB level must also be >5 µg/liter whole blood.

APPENDIX A TABLE B—ACTIONS DETERMINED BY BIOLOGICAL MONITORING

This table presents the actions required based on the monitoring result in appendix A Table A. Each item is a separate require-ment in citing non-compliance. For example, a medical examination within 90 days for an employee in category B is separate from the requirement to administer a periodic medical examination for category B employees on an annual basis.

Required actions	Monitoring result category		
	A [1]	B [1]	C [1]
(1) Biological monitoring:			
(a) Annual.	X		
(b) Semiannual		X	
(c) Quarterly			X
(2) Medical examination:			
(a) Biennial	X		
(b) Annual.		X	
(c) Semiannual.			X
(d) Within 90 days		X	X
(3) Assess within two weeks:			
(a) Excess cadmium exposure		X	X
(b) Work practices		X	X
(c) Personal hygiene		X	X
(d) Respirator usage		X	X
(e) Smoking history		X	X
(f) Hygiene facilities		X	X
(g) Engineering controls		X	X
(h) Correct within 30 days		X	X
(i) Periodically assess exposures			X
(4) Discretionary medical removal		X	X
(5) Mandatory medical removal			X [2]

[1] For all employees covered by medical surveillance exclusively because of exposures prior to the effective date of this standard, if they are in Category A, the employer shall follow the requirements of paragraphs (l)(3)(i)(B) and (l)(4)(v)(A). If they are in Category B or C, the employer shall follow the requirements of paragraphs (l)(4)(v)(B)–(C).

[2] See footnote appendix A Table A.

APPENDIX A—ATTACHMENT 2—LIST OF MEDICATIONS

A list of the more common medications that a physician, and the employee, may wish to review is likely to include some of the following: (1) Anticonvulsants: Paramethadione, phenytoin, trimethadone; (2) antihypertensive drugs: Captopril, methyldopa; (3) antimicrobials: Aminoglycosides, amphotericin B, cephalosporins, ethambutol; (4) antineoplastic agents: Cisplatin, methotrexate, mitomycin-C, nitrosoureas, radiation; (4) sulfonamide diuretics: Acetazolamide, chlorthalidone, furosemide, thiazides; (5) halogenated alkanes, hydrocarbons, and solvents that may occur in some settings: Carbon tetrachloride, ethylene glycol, toluene; iodinated radiographic contrast media; nonsteroidal anti-inflammatory drugs; and, (7) other miscellaneous compounds: Acetominophen, allopurinol, amphetamines, azathioprine, cimetidine, cyclosporine, lithium, methoxyflurane, methysergide, D-penicillamine, phenacetin, phenendione. A list of drugs associated with acute interstitial nephritis includes: (1) Antimicrobial drugs: Cephalosporins, chloramphenicol, colistin, erythromycin, ethambutol, isoniazid, para-aminosalicylic acid, penicillins, polymyxin B, rifampin, sulfonamides, tetracyclines, and vancomycin; (2) other miscellaneous drugs: Allopurinol, antipyrene, azathioprine, captopril, cimetidine, clofibrate, methyldopa, phenindione, phenylpropanolamine, phenytoin, probenecid, sulfinpyrazone, sulfonamid diuretics, triamterene; and, (3) metals: Bismuth, gold.

This list have been derived from commonly available medical textbooks (e.g., Ex. 14–18). The list has been included merely to facilitate the physician's, employer's, and employee's understanding. The list does not represent an official OSHA opinion or policy regarding the use of these medications for particular employees. The use of such medications should be under physician discretion.

ATTACHMENT 3—BIOLOGICAL MONITORING AND MEDICAL EXAMINATION RESULTS

Employee _____
Testing Date _____
Cadmium in Urine _____ μg/g Cr—Normal Levels: ≤3 μg/g Cr.
Cadmium in Blood _____ μg/lwb—Normal Levels: ≤5 μg/lwb.
Beta-2-microglobulin in Urine _____ μg/g Cr—Normal Levels: ≤300 μg/g Cr.
Physical Examination Results: N/A _____ Satisfactory _____ Unsatisfactory _____ (see physician again).
Physician's Review of Pulmonary Function Test: N/A _____ Normal _____ Abnormal _____.

Next biological monitoring or medical examination scheduled for _____

The biological monitoring program has been designed for three main purposes: 1) to identify employees at risk of adverse health effects from excess, chronic exposure to cadmium; 2) to prevent cadmium-induced disease(s); and 3) to detect and minimize existing cadmium-induced disease(s).

The levels of cadmium in the urine and blood provide an estimate of the total amount of cadmium in the body. The amount of a specific protein in the urine (beta-2-microglobulin) indicates changes in kidney function. All three tests must be evaluated together. A single mildly elevated result may not be important if testing at a later time indicates that the results are normal and the workplace has been evaluated to decrease possible sources of cadmium exposure. The levels of cadmium or beta-2-microglobulin may change over a period of days to months and the time needed for those changes to occur is different for each worker.

If the results for biological monitoring are above specific "high levels" [cadmium urine greater than 10 micrograms per gram of creatinine (μg/g Cr), cadmium blood greater than 10 micrograms per liter of whole blood (μg/lwb), or beta-2-microglobulin greater than 1000 micrograms per gram of creatinine (μg/g Cr)], the worker has a much greater chance of developing other kidney diseases.

One way to measure for kidney function is by measuring beta-2-microglobulin in the urine. Beta-2-microglobulin is a protein which is normally found in the blood as it is being filtered in the kidney, and the kidney reabsorbs or returns almost all of the beta-2-

microglobulin to the blood. A very small amount (less than 300 μg/g Cr in the urine) of beta-2-microglobulin is not reabsorbed into the blood, but is released in the urine. If cadmium damages the kidney, the amount of beta-2-microglobulin in the urine increases because the kidney cells are unable to reabsorb the beta-2-microglobulin normally. An increase in the amount of beta-2-microglobulin in the urine is a very early sign of kidney dysfunction. A small increase in beta-2-microglobulin in the urine will serve as an early warning sign that the worker may be absorbing cadmium from the air, cigarettes contaminated in the workplace, or eating in areas that are cadmium contaminated.

Even if cadmium causes permanent changes in the kidney's ability to reabsorb beta-2-microglobulin, and the beta-2-microglobulin is above the "high levels", the loss of kidney function may not lead to any serious health problems. Also, renal function naturally declines as people age. The risk for changes in kidney function for workers who have biological monitoring results between the "normal values" and the "high levels" is not well known. Some people are more cadmium-tolerant, while others are more cadmium-susceptible.

For anyone with even a slight increase of beta-2-microglobulin, cadmium in the urine, or cadmium in the blood, it is very important to protect the kidney from further damage. Kidney damage can come from other sources than excess cadmium-exposure so it is also recommended that if a worker's levels are "high" he/she should receive counseling about drinking more water; avoiding cadmium-tainted tobacco and certain medications (nephrotoxins, acetaminophen); controlling diet, vitamin intake, blood pressure and diabetes; etc.

APPENDIX B TO §1910.1027—SUBSTANCE TECHNICAL GUIDELINES FOR CADMIUM

I. Cadmium Metal

A. *Physical and Chemical Data.*

1. *Substance Identification.*

Chemical name: Cadmium.

Formula: Cd.

Molecular Weight: 112.4.

Chemical Abstracts Service (CAS) Registry No.: 7740–43–9.

Other Identifiers: RETCS EU9800000; EPA D006; DOT 2570 53.

Synonyms: Colloidal Cadmium: Kadmium (German): CI 77180.

2. *Physical data.*

Boiling point: (760 mm Hg): 765 degrees C.

Melting point: 321 degrees C.

Specific Gravity: (H_2 O=@ 20 °C): 8.64.

Solubility: Insoluble in water; soluble in dilute nitric acid and in sulfuric acid.

Appearance: Soft, blue-white, malleable, lustrous metal or grayish-white powder.

B. *Fire, Explosion and Reactivity Data.*

1. *Fire.*

Fire and Explosion Hazards: The finely divided metal is pyrophoric, that is the dust is a severe fire hazard and moderate explosion hazard when exposed to heat or flame. Burning material reacts violently with extinguishing agents such as water, foam, carbon dioxide, and halons.

Flash point: Flammable (dust).

Extinguishing media: Dry sand, dry dolomite, dry graphite, or sodimum chloride.

2. *Reactivity.*

Conditions contributing to instability: Stable when kept in sealed containers under normal temperatures and pressure, but dust may ignite upon contact with air. Metal tarnishes in moist air.

Incompatibilities: Ammonium nitrate, fused: Reacts violently or explosively with cadmium dust below 20 °C. Hydrozoic acid: Violent explosion occurs after 30 minutes. Acids: Reacts violently, forms hydrogen gas. Oxidizing agents or metals: Strong reaction with cadmium dust. Nitryl fluoride at slightly elevated temperature: Glowing or white incandescence occurs. Selenium: Reacts exothermically. Ammonia: Corrosive reaction. Sulfur dioxide: Corrosive reaction. Fire extinguishing agents (water, foam, carbon dioxide, and halons): Reacts violently. Tellurium: Incandescent reaction in hydrogen atmosphere.

Hazardous decomposition products: The heated metal rapidly forms highly toxic, brownish fumes of oxides of cadmium.

C. *Spill, Leak and Disposal Procedures.*

1. *Steps to be taken if the materials is released or spilled.* Do not touch spilled material. Stop leak if you can do it without risk. Do not get water inside container. For large spills, dike spill for later disposal. Keep unnecessary people away. Isolate hazard area and deny entry. The Superfund Amendments and Reauthorization Act of 1986 Section 304 requires that a release equal to or greater than the reportable quantity for this substance (1 pound) must be immediately reported to the local emergency planning committee, the state emergency response commission, and the National Response Center (800) 424-8802; in Washington, DC metropolitan area (202) 426-2675.

II. Cadmium Oxide

A. *Physical and Chemical Date.*

1. *Substance identification.*

Chemical name: Cadmium Oxide.

Formula: CdO.

Molecular Weight: 128.4.

CAS No.: 1306-19-0.

Other Identifiers: RTECS EV1929500.

Synonyms: Kadmu tlenek (Polish).

2. *Physical data.*

Boiling point (760 mm Hg): 950 degrees C decomposes.

Melting point: 1500 °C.

Specific Gravity: (H_2 O = 1@20 °C): 7.0.

Solubility: Insoluble in water; soluble in acids and alkalines.

Appearance: Red or brown crystals.

B. *Fire, Explosion and Reactivity Data.*

1. *Fire.*

Fire and Explosion Hazards: Negligible fire hazard when exposed to heat or flame.

Flash point: Nonflammable.

Extinguishing media: Dry chemical, carbon dioxide, water spray or foam.

2. *Reactivity.*

Conditions contributing to instability: Stable under normal temperatures and pressures.

Incompatibilities: Magnesium may reduce CdO_2 explosively on heating.

Hazardous decomposition products: Toxic fumes of cadmium.

C. *Spill Leak and Disposal Procedures.*

1. *Steps to be taken if the material is released or spilled.* Do not touch spilled material. Stop leak if you can do it without risk. For small spills, take up with sand or other absorbent material and place into containers for later disposal. For small dry spills, use a clean shovel to place material into clean, dry container and then cover. Move containers from spill area. For larger spills, dike far ahead of spill for later disposal. Keep unnecessary people away. Isolate hazard area and deny entry. The Superfund Amendments and Reauthorization Act of 1986 Section 304 requires that a release equal to or greater than the reportable quantity for this substance (1 pound) must be immediately reported to the local emergency planning committee, the state emergency response commission, and the National Response Center (800) 424-8802; in Washington, DC metropolitan area (202) 426-2675.

III. Cadmium Sulfide.

A. *Physical and Chemical Data.*

1. *Substance Identification.*

Chemical name: Cadmium sulfide.

Formula: CdS.

Molecular weight: 144.5.

CAS No. 1306-23-6.

Other Identifiers: RTECS EV3150000.

Synonyms: Aurora yellow; Cadmium Golden 366; Cadmium Lemon Yellow 527; Cadmium Orange; Cadmium Primrose 819; Cadmium Sulphide; Cadmium Yellow; Cadmium Yellow 000; Cadmium Yellow Conc. Deep; Cadmium Yellow Conc. Golden; Cadmium Yellow Conc. Lemon; Cadmium Yellow Conc. Primrose; Cadmium Yellow Oz. Dark; Cadmium Yellow Primrose 47-1400; Cadmium Yellow 10G Conc.; Cadmium Yellow 892; Cadmopur Golden Yellow N; Cadmopur Yellow: Capsebon; C.I. 77199; C.I. Pigment Orange 20; CI Pigment Yellow 37; Ferro Lemon Yellow; Ferro Orange Yellow; Ferro Yellow; Greenockite; NCI-C02711.

2. *Physical data.*

Boiling point (760 mm. Hg): sublines in N_2 at 980 °C.

Melting point: 1750 degrees C (100 atm).

Specific Gravity: (H_2 O = 1@ 20 °C): 4.82.

Solubility: Slightly soluble in water; soluble in acid.

Appearance: Light yellow or yellow-orange crystals.

B. *Fire, Explosion and Reactivity Data.*

1. *Fire.*

Fire and Explosion Hazards: Neglible fire hazard when exposed to heat or flame.

Flash point: Nonflammable.

Extinguishing media: Dry chemical, carbon dioxide, water spray or foam.

2. *Reactivity.*

Conditions contributing to instability: Generally non-reactive under normal conditions. Reacts with acids to form toxic hydrogen sulfide gas.

Incompatibilities: Reacts vigorously with iodinemonochloride.

Hazardous decomposition products: Toxic fumes of cadmium and sulfur oxides.

C. *Spill Leak and Disposal Procedures.*

1. *Steps to be taken if the material is released or spilled.* Do not touch spilled material. Stop leak if you can do it without risk. For small, dry spills, with a clean shovel place material into clean, dry container and cover. Move containers from spill area. For larger spills, dike far ahead of spill for later disposal. Keep unnecessary people away. Isolate hazard and deny entry.

IV. *Cadmium Chloride.*

A. *Physical and Chemical Data.*

1. *Substance Identification.*

Chemcail name: Cadmium chloride.

Formula: $CdCl_2$.

Molecular weight: 183.3.

CAS No. 10108–64–2.

Other Identifiers: RTECS EY0175000.

Synonyms: Caddy; Cadmium dichloride; NA 2570 (DOT); UI-CAD; dichlorocadmium.

2. *Physical data.*

Boiling point (760 mm Hg): 960 degrees C.

Melting point: 568 degrees C.

Specific Gravity: (H_2 O = 1 @ 20 °C): 4.05.

Solubility: Soluble in water (140 g/100 cc); soluble in acetone.

Appearance: Small, white crystals.

B. *Fire, Explosion and Reactivity Data.*

1. *Fire.*

Fire and Explosion Hazards: Negligible fire and negligible explosion hazard in dust form when exposed to heat or flame.

Flash point: Nonflamable.

Extinguishing media: Dry chemical, carbon dioxide, water spray or foam.

2. *Reactivity.*

Conditions contributing to instability: Generally stable under normal temperatures and pressures.

Incompatibilities: Bromine trifluoride rapidly attacks cadmium chloride. A mixture of potassium and cadmium chloride may produce a strong explosion on impact.

Hazardous decomposition products: Thermal ecomposition may release toxic fumes of hydrogen chloride, chloride, chlorine or oxides of cadmium.

C. *Spill Leak and Disposal Procedures.*

1. *Steps to be taken if the materials is released or spilled.* Do not touch spilled material. Stop leak if you can do it without risk. For small, dry spills, with a clean shovel place material into clean, dry container and cover. Move containers from spill area. For larger spills, dike far ahead of spill for later disposal. Keep unnecessary people away. Isolate hazard and deny entry. The Superfund Amendments and Reauthorization Act of 1986 Section 304 requires that a release equal to or greater than the reportable quantity for this substance (100 pounds) must be immediately reported to the local emergency planning committee, the state emergency response commission, and the National Response Center (800) 424–8802; in Washington, DC Metropolitan area (202) 426–2675.

APPENDIX C TO § 1910.1027 [RESERVED]

APPENDIX D TO § 1910.1027—OCCUPATIONAL HEALTH HISTORY INTERVIEW WITH REFERENCE TO CADMIUM EXPOSURE

Directions

(To be read by employee and signed prior to the interview)

Please answer the questions you will be asked as completely and carefully as you can. These questions are asked of everyone who works with cadmium. You will also be asked to give blood and urine samples. The doctor will give your employer a written opinion on whether you are physically capable of working with cadmium. Legally, the doctor cannot share personal information you may tell him/her with your employer. The following information is considered strictly confidential. The results of the tests will go to you, your doctor and your employer. You will also receive an information sheet explaining the results of any biological monitoring or physical examinations performed.

If you are just being hired, the results of this interview and examination will be used to:

(1) Establish your health status and see if working with cadmium might be expected to cause unusual problems,

(2) Determine your health status today and see if there are changes over time,

(3) See if you can wear a respirator safely. If you are not a new hire:

OSHA says that everyone who works with cadmium can have periodic medical examinations performed by a doctor. The reasons for this are:

(a) If there are changes in your health, either because of cadmium or some other reason, to find them early,

(b) to prevent kidney damage.

Please sign below.

I have read these directions and understand them:

203

Employee signature

Date

Thank you for answering these questions. (Suggested Format)

Name _____

Age _____

Social Security # _____

Company _____

Job _____

Type of Preplacement Exam:

[ ] Periodic
[ ] Termination
[ ] Initial
[ ] Other

Blood Pressure _____

Pulse Rate _____

1. How long have you worked at the job listed above?

[ ] Not yet hired
[ ] Number of months
[ ] Number of years

2. Job Duties etc.

_____

3. Have you *ever* been told by a doctor that you had bronchitis?

[ ] Yes
[ ] No

If yes, how long ago?

[ ] Number of months
[ ] Number of years

4. Have you *ever* been told by a doctor that you had emphysema?

[ ] Yes
[ ] No

If yes, how long ago?

[ ] Number of years
[ ] Number of months

5. Have you ever been told by a doctor that you had other lung problems?

[ ] Yes
[ ] No

If yes, please describe type of lung problems and when you had these problems

_____

6. In the past year, have you had a cough?

[ ] Yes
[ ] No

If yes, did you cough up sputum?

[ ] Yes
[ ] No

If yes, how long did the cough with sputum production last?

[ ] Less than 3 months
[ ] 3 months or longer

If yes, for how many years have you had episodes of cough with sputum production lasting this long?

[ ] Less than one
[ ] 1
[ ] 2

[ ] Longer than 2

7. Have you ever smoked cigarettes?

[ ] Yes
[ ] No

8. Do you now smoke cigarettes?

[ ] Yes
[ ] No

9. If you smoke or have smoked cigarettes, for how many years have you smoked, or did you smoke?

[ ] Less than 1 year
[ ] Number of years

What is or was the greatest number of packs per day that you have smoked?

[ ] Number of packs

If you quit smoking cigarettes, how many years ago did you quit?

[ ] Less than 1 year
[ ] Number of years

How many packs a day do you now smoke?

[ ] Number of packs per day

10. Have you ever been told by a doctor that you had a kidney or urinary tract disease or disorder?

[ ] Yes
[ ] No

11. Have you ever had any of these disorders?

Kidney stones	[ ] Yes	[ ] No
Protein in urine	[ ] Yes	[ ] No
Blood in urine	[ ] Yes	[ ] No
Difficulty urinating	[ ] Yes	[ ] No
Other kidney/Urinary disorders.	[ ] Yes	[ ] No

Please describe problems, age, treatment, and follow up for any kidney or urinary problems you have had:

_____

12. Have you ever been told by a doctor or other health care provider who took your blood pressure that your blood pressure was high?

[ ] Yes
[ ] No

13. Have you ever been advised to take any blood pressure medication?

[ ] Yes
[ ] No

14. Are you presently taking any blood pressure medication?

[ ] Yes
[ ] No

15. Are you presently taking any other medication?

[ ] Yes
[ ] No

16. Please list any blood pressure or other medications and describe how long you have been taking each one:

Medicine:

_____

How Long Taken

_____

17. Have you ever been told by a doctor that you have diabetes? (sugar in your blood or urine)
[ ] Yes
[ ] No
If yes, do you presently see a doctor about your diabetes?
[ ] Yes
[ ] No
If yes, how do you control your blood sugar?
[ ] Diet alone
[ ] Diet plus oral medicine
[ ] Diet plus insulin (injection)
18. Have you ever been told by a doctor that you had:

Anemia .... [ ] Yes [ ] No
A low blood count? .... [ ] Yes [ ] No

19. Do you presently feel that you tire or run out of energy sooner than normal or sooner than other people your age?
[ ] Yes
[ ] No
If yes, for how long have you felt that you tire easily?
[ ] Less than 1 year
[ ] Number of years
20. Have you given blood within the last year?
[ ] Yes
[ ] No
If yes, how many times?
[ ] Number of times
How long ago was the last time you gave blood?
[ ] Less than 1 month
[ ] Number of months
21. Within the last year have you had any injuries with heavy bleeding?
[ ] Yes
[ ] No
If yes, how long ago?
[ ] Less than 1 month
[ ] Number of months
Describe: _____
_____
_____

22. Have you recently had any surgery?
[ ] Yes
[ ] No
If yes, please describe: _____
_____

23. Have you seen any blood lately in your stool or after a bowel movement?
[ ] Yes
[ ] No
24. Have you ever had a test for blood in your stool?
[ ] Yes
[ ] No
If yes, did the test show any blood in the stool?

[ ] Yes
[ ] No
What further evaluation and treatment were done? _____

_____

The following questions pertain to the ability to wear a respirator. Additional information for the physician can be found in The Respiratory Protective Devices Manual.
25. Have you ever been told by a doctor that you have asthma?
[ ] Yes
[ ] No
If yes, are you presently taking any medication for asthma? Mark all that apply.
[ ] Shots
[ ] Pills
[ ] Inhaler
26. Have you ever had a heart attack?
[ ] Yes
[ ] No
If yes, how long ago?
[ ] Number of years
[ ] Number of months
27. Have you ever had pains in your chest?
[ ] Yes
[ ] No
If yes, when did it usually happen?
[ ] While resting
[ ] While working
[ ] While exercising
[ ] Activity didn't matter
28. Have you ever had a thyroid problem?
[ ] Yes
[ ] No
29. Have you ever had a seizure or fits?
[ ] Yes
[ ] No
30. Have you ever had a stroke (cerebrovascular accident)?
[ ] Yes
[ ] No
31. Have you ever had a ruptured eardrum or a serious hearing problem?
[ ] Yes
[ ] No
32. Do you now have a claustrophobia, meaning fear of crowded or closed in spaces or any psychological problems that would make it hard for you to wear a respirator?
[ ] Yes
[ ] No
The following questions pertain to reproductive history.
33. Have you or your partner had a problem conceiving a child?
[ ] Yes
[ ] No
If yes, specify:
[ ] Self
[ ] Present mate
[ ] Previous mate
34. Have you or your partner consulted a physician for a fertility or other reproductive problem?

[ ] Yes
[ ] No
If yes, specify who consulted the physician:
[ ] Self
[ ] Spouse/partner
[ ] Self and partner
If yes, specify diagnosis made: _____

35. Have you or your partner ever conceived a child resulting in a miscarriage, still birth or deformed offspring?
[ ] Yes
[ ] No
If yes, specify:
[ ] Miscarriage
[ ] Still birth
[ ] Deformed offspring
If outcome was a deformed offspring, please specify type: _____

_____
_____

36. Was this outcome a result of a pregnancy of:
[ ] Yours with present partner
[ ] Yours with a previous partner
37. Did the timing of any abnormal pregnancy outcome coincide with present employment?
[ ] Yes
[ ] No
List dates of occurrences: _____

_____

38. What is the occupation of your spouse or partner?

_____
_____

For Women Only

39. Do you have menstrual periods?
[ ] Yes
[ ] No
Have you had menstrual irregularities?
[ ] Yes
[ ] No
If yes, specify type: _____

_____
_____

If yes, what was the approximated date this problem began? _____

_____

Approximate date problem stopped? _____

_____

For Men Only

40. Have you ever been diagnosed by a physician as having prostate gland problem(s)?
[ ] Yes
[ ] No
If yes, please describe type of problem(s) and what was done to evaluate and treat the problem(s):

_____
_____
_____

APPENDIX E TO § 1910.1027—CADMIUM IN WORKPLACE ATMOSPHERES

Method Number: ID–189
Matrix: Air
OSHA Permissible Exposure Limits: 5 µg/m³ (TWA), 2.5 µg/m³ (Action Level TWA)
Collection Procedure: A known volume of air is drawn through a 37-mm diameter filter cassette containing a 0.8-µm mixed cellulose ester membrane filter (MCEF).
Recommended Air Volume: 960 L
Recommended Sampling Rate: 2.0 L/min
Analytical Procedure: Air filter samples are digested with nitric acid. After digestion, a small amount of hydrochloric acid is added. The samples are then diluted to volume with deionized water and analyzed by either flame atomic absorption spectroscopy (AAS) or flameless atomic absorption spectroscopy using a heated graphite furnace atomizer (AAS-HGA).
Detection Limits:
Qualitative: 0.2 µg/m³ for a 200 L sample by Flame AAS, 0.007 µg/m³ for a 60 L sample by AAS-HGA
Quantitative: 0.70 µg/m³ for a 200 L sample by Flame AAS, 0.025 µg/m³ for a 60 L sample by AAS-HGA
Precision and Accuracy: (Flame AAS Analysis and AAS-HGA Analysis):
Validation Level: 2.5 to 10 µg/m³ for a 400 L air vol, 1.25 to 5.0 µg/m³ for a 60 L air vol
CV_1 (pooled): 0.010, 0.043
Analytical Bias: + 4.0%, − 5.8%
Overall Analytical Error:±6.0%, ±14.2%
Method Classification: Validated
Date: June, 1992
Inorganic Service Branch II, OSHA Salt Lake Technical Center, Salt Lake City, Utah
Commercial manufacturers and products mentioned in this method are for descriptive use only and do not constitute endorsements by USDOL-OSHA. Similar products from other sources can be substituted.

1. INTRODUCTION

1.1. Scope

This method describes the collection of airborne elemental cadmium and cadmium compounds on 0.8-µm mixed cellulose ester membrane filters and their subsequent analysis by either flame atomic absorption spectroscopy (AAS) or flameless atomic absorption spectroscopy using a heated graphite furnace atomizer (AAS-HGA). It is applicable for both TWA and Action Level TWA Permissible Exposure Level (PEL) measurements. The two atomic absorption analytical techniques included in the method do not differentiate between cadmium fume and cadmium dust samples. They also do not differentiate between elemental cadmium and its compounds.

1.2. Principle

Airborne elemental cadmium and cadmium compounds are collected on a 0.8-μm mixed cellulose ester membrane filter (MCEF). The air filter samples are digested with concentrated nitric acid to destroy the organic matrix and dissolve the cadmium analytes. After digestion, a small amount of concentrated hydrochloric acid is added to help dissolve other metals which may be present. The samples are diluted to volume with deionized water and then aspirated into the oxidizing air/acetylene flame of an atomic absorption spectrophotometer for analysis of elemental cadmium.

If the concentration of cadmium in a sample solution is too low for quantitation by this flame AAS analytical technique, and the sample is to be averaged with other samples for TWA calculations, aliquots of the sample and a matrix modifier are later injected onto a L'vov platform in a pyrolytically-coated graphite tube of a Zeeman atomic absorption spectrophotometer/graphite furnace assembly for analysis of elemental cadmium. The matrix modifier is added to stabilize the cadmium metal and minimize sodium chloride as an interference during the high temperature charring step of the analysis (5.1., 5.2.).

1.3. History

Previously, two OSHA sampling and analytical methods for cadmium were used concurrently (5.3., 5.4.). Both of these methods also required 0.8-μm mixed cellulose ester membrane filters for the collection of air samples. These cadmium air filter samples were analyzed by either flame atomic absorption spectroscopy (5.3.) or inductively coupled plasma/atomic emission spectroscopy (ICP-AES) (5.4.). Neither of these two analytical methods have adequate sensitivity for measuring workplace exposure to airborne cadmium at the new lower TWA and Action Level TWA PEL levels when consecutive samples are taken on one employee and the sample results need to be averaged with other samples to determine a single TWA.

The inclusion of two atomic absorption analytical techniques in the new sampling and analysis method for airborne cadmium permits quantitation of sample results over a broad range of exposure levels and sampling periods. The flame AAS analytical technique included in this method is similar to the previous procedure given in the General Metals Method ID–121 (5.3.) with some modifications. The sensitivity of the AAS-HGA analytical technique included in this method is adequate to measure exposure levels at ¹⁄₁₀ the Action Level TWA, or lower, when less than full-shift samples need to be averaged together.

1.4. Properties (5.5.)

Elemental cadmium is a silver-white, blue-tinged, lustrous metal which is easily cut with a knife. It is slowly oxidized by moist air to form cadmium oxide. It is insoluble in water, but reacts readily with dilute nitric acid. Some of the physical properties and other descriptive information of elemental cadmium are given below:

CAS No.....................................7440–43–9
Atomic Number 48
Atomic Symbol.......................................Cd
Atomic Weight 112.41
Melting Point ....321 °C
Boiling Point ....765 °C
Density ....8.65 g/mL (25 °C)

The properties of specific cadmium compounds are described in reference 5.5.

1.5. Method Performance

A synopsis of method performance is presented below. Further information can be found in Section 4.

1.5.1. The qualitative and quantitative detection limits for the flame AAS analytical technique are 0.04 μg (0.004 μg/mL) and 0.14 μg (0.014 μg/mL) cadmium, respectively, for a 10 mL solution volume. These correspond, respectively, to 0.2 μg/m³ and 0.70 μg/m³ for a 200 L air volume.

1.5.2. The qualitative and quantitative detection limits for the AAS-HGA analytical technique are 0.44 ng (0.044 ng/mL) and 1.5 ng (0.15 ng/mL) cadmium, respectively, for a 10 mL solution volume. These correspond, respectively, to 0.007 μg/m³ and 0.025 μg/m³ for a 60 L air volume.

1.5.3. The average recovery by the flame AAS analytical technique of 17 spiked MCEF samples containing cadmium in the range of 0.5 to 2.0 times the TWA target concentration of 5 μg/m³ (assuming a 400 L air volume) was 104.0% with a pooled coefficient of variation (CV₁) of 0.010. The flame analytical technique exhibited a positive bias of + 4.0% for the validated concentration range. The overall analytical error (OAE) for the flame AAS analytical technique was ±6.0%.

1.5.4. The average recovery by the AAS-HGA analytical technique of 18 spiked MCEF samples containing cadmium in the range of 0.5 to 2.0 times the Action Level TWA target concentration of 2.5 μg/m³ (assuming a 60 L air volume) was 94.2% with a pooled coefficient of variation (CV₁) of 0.043. The AAS-HGA analytical technique exhibited a negative bias of −5.8% for the validated concentration range. The overall analytical error (OAE) for the AAS-HGA analytical technique was ±14.2%.

1.5.5. Sensitivity in flame atomic absorption is defined as the characteristic concentration of an element required to produce a signal of 1% absorbance (0.0044 absorbance units). Sensitivity values are listed for each element by the atomic absorption spectrophotometer manufacturer and have proved to be a very valuable diagnostic tool to determine if instrumental parameters are optimized and if the instrument is performing up to specification. The sensitivity of the spectrophotometer used in the validation of the flame AAS analytical technique agreed with the manufacturer specifications (5.6.); the 2 µg/mL cadmium standard gave an absorbance reading of 0.350 abs. units.

1.5.6. Sensitivity in graphite furnace atomic absorption is defined in terms of the characteristic mass, the number of picograms required to give an integrated absorbance value of 0.0044 absorbance-second (5.7.). Data suggests that under Stabilized Temperature Platform Furnace (STPF) conditions (see Section 1.6.2.), characteristic mass values are transferable between properly functioning instruments to an accuracy of about 20% (5.2.). The characteristic mass for STPF analysis of cadmium with Zeeman background correction listed by the manufacturer of the instrument used in the validation of the AAS-HGA analytical technique was 0.35 pg. The experimental characteristic mass value observed during the determination of the working range and detection limits of the AAS-HGA analytical technique was 0.41 pg.

1.6. Interferences

1.6.1. High concentrations of silicate interfere in determining cadmium by flame AAS (5.6.). However, silicates are not significantly soluble in the acid matrix used to prepare the samples.

1.6.2. Interferences, such as background absorption, are reduced to a minimum in the AAS-HGA analytical technique by taking full advantage of the Stabilized Temperature Platform Furnace (STPF) concept. STPF includes all of the following parameters (5.2.):

a. Integrated Absorbance,
b. Fast Instrument Electronics and Sampling Frequency,
c. Background Correction,
d. Maximum Power Heating,
e. Atomization off the L'vov platform in a pyrolytically coated graphite tube,
f. Gas Stop during Atomization,
g. Use of Matrix Modifiers.

1.7. Toxicology (5.14.)

Information listed within this section is synopsis of current knowledge of the physiological effects of cadmium and is not intended to be used as the basis for OSHA policy. IARC classifies cadmium and certain of its compounds as Group 2A carcinogens (probably carcinogenic to humans). Cadmium fume is intensely irritating to the respiratory tract. Workplace exposure to cadmium can cause both chronic and acute effects. Acute effects include

tracheobronchitis, pneumonitis, and pulmonary edema. Chronic effects include anemia, rhinitis/anosmia, pulmonary emphysema, proteinuria and lung cancer. The primary target organs for chronic disease are the kidneys (non-carcinogenic) and the lungs (carcinogenic).

2. SAMPLING

2.1. Apparatus

2.1.1. Filter cassette unit for air sampling: A 37-mm diameter mixed cellulose ester membrane filter with a pore size of 0.8-µm contained in a 37-mm polystyrene two- or three-piece cassette filter holder (part no. MAWP 037 A0, Millipore Corp., Bedford, MA). The filter is supported with a cellulose backup pad. The cassette is sealed prior to use with a shrinkable gel band.

2.1.2. A calibrated personal sampling pump whose flow is determined to an accuracy of ±5% at the recommended flow rate with the filter cassette unit in line.

2.2. Procedure

2.2.1. Attach the prepared cassette to the calibrated sampling pump (the backup pad should face the pump) using flexible tubing. Place the sampling device on the employee such that air is sampled from the breathing zone.

2.2.2. Collect air samples at a flow rate of 2.0 L/min. If the filter does not become overloaded, a full-shift (at least seven hours) sample is strongly recommended for TWA and Action Level TWA measurements with a maximum air volume of 960 L. If overloading occurs, collect consecutive air samples for shorter sampling periods to cover the full workshift.

2.2.3. Replace the end plugs into the filter cassettes immediately after sampling. Record the sampling conditions.

2.2.4. Securely wrap each sample filter cassette end-to-end with an OSHA Form 21 sample seal.

2.2.5. Submit at least one blank sample with each set of air samples. The blank sample should be handled the same as the other samples except that no air is drawn through it.

2.2.6. Ship the samples to the laboratory for analysis as soon as possible in a suitable container designed to prevent damage in transit.

3. ANALYSIS

3.1. Safety Precautions

3.1.1. Wear safety glasses, protective clothing and gloves at all times.

3.1.2. Handle acid solutions with care. Handle all cadmium samples and solutions with extra care (see Sect. 1.7.). Avoid their direct contact with work area surfaces, eyes, skin and clothes. Flush acid solutions which contact the skin or eyes with copious amounts of water.

3.1.3. Perform all acid digestions and acid dilutions in an exhaust hood while wearing a face shield. To avoid exposure to acid vapors, do not remove beakers containing concentrated acid solutions from the exhaust hood until they have returned to room temperature and have been diluted or emptied.

3.1.4. Exercise care when using laboratory glassware. Do not use chipped pipets, volumetric flasks, beakers or any glassware with sharp edges exposed in order to avoid the possibility of cuts or abrasions.

3.1.5. Never pipet by mouth.

3.1.6. Refer to the instrument instruction manuals and SOPs (5.8., 5.9.) for proper and safe operation of the atomic absorption spectrophotometer, graphite furnace atomizer and associated equipment.

3.1.7. Because metallic elements and other toxic substances are vaporized during AAS flame or graphite furnace atomizer operation, it is imperative that an exhaust vent be used. Always ensure that the exhaust system is operating properly during instrument use.

3.2. Apparatus for Sample and Standard Preparation

3.2.1. Hot plate, capable of reaching 150 °C, installed in an exhaust hood.

3.2.2. Phillips beakers, 125 mL.

3.2.3. Bottles, narrow-mouth, polyethylene or glass with leakproof caps: used for storage of standards and matrix modifier.

3.2.4. Volumetric flasks, volumetric pipets, beakers and other associated general laboratory glassware.

3.2.5. Forceps and other associated general laboratory equipment.

3.3. Apparatus for Flame AAS Analysis

3.3.1. Atomic absorption spectrophotometer consisting of a(an):

Nebulizer and burner head
Pressure regulating devices capable of maintaining constant oxidant and fuel pressures
Optical system capable of isolating the desired wavelength of radiation (228.8 nm)
Adjustable slit
Light measuring and amplifying device
Display, strip chart, or computer interface for indicating the amount of absorbed radiation
Cadmium hollow cathode lamp or electrodeless discharge lamp (EDL) and power supply

3.3.2. Oxidant: compressed air, filtered to remove water, oil and other foreign substances.

3.3.3. Fuel: standard commercially available tanks of acetylene dissolved in acetone; tanks should be equipped with flash arresters.

CAUTION: Do not use grades of acetylene containing solvents other than acetone because they may damage the PVC tubing used in some instruments.

3.3.4. Pressure-reducing valves: two gauge, two-stage pressure regulators to maintain fuel and oxidant pressures somewhat higher than the controlled operating pressures of the instrument.

3.3.5. Exhaust vent installed directly above the spectrophotometer burner head.

3.4. Apparatus for AAS-HGA Analysis

3.4.1. Atomic absorption spectrophotometer consisting of a(an):

Heated graphite furnace atomizer (HGA) with argon purge system
Pressure-regulating devices capable of maintaining constant argon purge pressure
Optical system capable of isolating the desired wavelength of radiation (228.8 nm)
Adjustable slit
Light measuring and amplifying device
Display, strip chart, or computer interface for indicating the amount of absorbed radiation (as integrated absorbance, peak area)
Background corrector: Zeeman or deuterium arc. The Zeeman background corrector is recommended
Cadmium hollow cathode lamp or electrodeless discharge lamp (EDL) and power supply
Autosampler capable of accurately injecting 5 to 20 µL sample aliquots onto the L'vov Platform in a graphite tube

3.4.2. Pyrolytically coated graphite tubes containing solid, pyrolytic L'vov platforms.

3.4.3. Polyethylene sample cups, 2.0 to 2.5 mL, for use with the autosampler.

3.4.4. Inert purge gas for graphite furnace atomizer: compressed gas cylinder of purified argon.

3.4.5. Two gauge, two-stage pressure regulator for the argon gas cylinder.

3.4.6. Cooling water supply for graphite furnace atomizer.

3.4.7. Exhaust vent installed directly above the graphite furnace atomizer.

3.5. Reagents

All reagents should be ACS analytical reagent grade or better.

3.5.1. Deionized water with a specific conductance of less than 10 µS.

3.5.2. Concentrated nitric acid, HNO_3.

3.5.3. Concentrated hydrochloric acid, HCl.

3.5.4. Ammonium phosphate, monobasic, $NH_4 H_2 PO_4$.

3.5.5. Magnesium nitrate, $Mg(NO_3)_2 \cdot 6H_2 O$.

3.5.6. Diluting solution (4% HNO_3, 0.4% HCl): Add 40 mL HNO_3 and 4 mL HCl carefully to approximately 500 mL deionized water and dilute to 1 L with deionized water.

3.5.7. Cadmium standard stock solution, 1,000 µg/mL: Use a commercially available certified 1,000 µg/mL cadmium standard or, alternatively, dissolve 1.0000 g of cadmium metal in a minimum volume of 1:1 HCl and dilute to 1 L with 4% HNO_3. Observe expiration dates of commercial standards. Properly dispose of commercial standards with no expiration dates or prepared standards one year after their receipt or preparation date.

3.5.8. Matrix modifier for AAS-HGA analysis: Dissolve 1.0 g NH_4 H_2 PO_4 and 0.15 g $Mg(NO_3)_2$ · $6H_2$ O in approximately 200 mL deionized water. Add 1 mL HNO_3 and dilute to 500 mL with deionized water.

3.5.9 Nitric Acid, 1:1 HNO_3/DI H_2 O mixture: Carefully add a measured volume of concentrated HNO_3 to an equal volume of DI H_2 O.

3.5.10. Nitric acid, 10% v/v: Carefully add 100 mL of concentrated HNO_3 to 500 mL of DI H_2 O and dilute to 1 L.

3.6. Glassware Preparation

3.6.1. Clean Phillips beakers by refluxing with 1:1 nitric acid on a hot plate in a fume hood. Thoroughly rinse with deionized water and invert the beakers to allow them to drain dry.

3.6.2. Rinse volumetric flasks and all other glassware with 10% nitric acid and deionized water prior to use.

3.7. Standard Preparation for Flame AAS Analysis

3.7.1. Dilute stock solutions: Prepare 1, 5, 10 and 100 μg/mL cadmium standard stock solutions by making appropriate serial dilutions of 1,000 μg/mL cadmium standard stock solution with the diluting solution described in Section 3.5.6.

3.7.2. Working standards: Prepare cadmium working standards in the range of 0.02 to 2.0 μg/mL by making appropriate serial dilutions of the dilute stock solutions with the same diluting solution. A suggested method of preparation of the working standards is given below.

Working standard	Std solution	Aliquot	Final vol.
(μg/mL)	(μg/mL)	(mL)	(mL)
0.02	1	10	500
0.05	5	5	500
0.1	10	5	500
0.2	10	10	500
0.5	10	25	500
1	100	5	500
2	100	10	500

Store the working standards in 500-mL, narrow-mouth polyethylene or glass bottles with leak proof caps. Prepare every twelve months.

3.8. Standard Preparation for AAS-HGA Analysis

3.8.1. Dilute stock solutions: Prepare 10, 100 and 1,000 ng/mL cadmium standard stock so-

lutions by making appropriate ten-fold serial dilutions of the 1,000 μg/mL cadmium standard stock solution with the diluting solution described in Section 3.5.6.

3.8.2. Working standards: Prepare cadmium working standards in the range of 0.2 to 20 ng/mL by making appropriate serial dilutions of the dilute stock solutions with the same diluting solution. A suggested method of preparation of the working standards is given below.

Working standard	Std solution	Aliquot	Final vol.
(ng/mL)	(ng/mL)	(mL)	(mL)
0.2	10	2	100
0.5	10	5	100
1	10	10	100
2	100	2	100
5	100	5	100
10	100	10	100
20	1,000	2	100

Store the working standards in narrow-mouth polyethylene or glass bottles with leakproof caps. Prepare monthly.

3.9. Sample Preparation

3.9.1. Carefully transfer each sample filter with forceps from its filter cassette unit to a clean, separate 125-mL Phillips beaker along with any loose dust found in the cassette. Label each Phillips beaker with the appropriate sample number.

3.9.2. Digest the sample by adding 5 mL of concentrated nitric acid (HNO_3) to each Phillips beaker containing an air filter sample. Place the Phillips beakers on a hot plate in an exhaust hood and heat the samples until approximately 0.5 mL remains. The sample solution in each Phillips beaker should become clear. If it is not clear, digest the sample with another portion of concentrated nitric acid.

3.9.3. After completing the HNO_3 digestion and cooling the samples, add 40 μL (2 drops) of concentrated HCl to each air sample solution and then swirl the contents. Carefully add about 5 mL of deionized water by pouring it down the inside of each beaker.

3.9.4. Quantitatively transfer each cooled air sample solution from each Phillips beaker to a clean 10-mL volumetric flask. Dilute each flask to volume with deionized water and mix well.

3.10. Flame AAS Analysis

Analyze all of the air samples for their cadmium content by flame atomic absorption spectroscopy (AAS) according to the instructions given below.

3.10.1. Set up the atomic absorption spectrophotometer for the air/acetylene flame analysis of cadmium according to the SOP

(5.8.) or the manufacturer's operational instructions. For the source lamp, use the cadmium hollow cathode or electrodeless discharge lamp operated at the manufacturer's recommended rating for continuous operation. Allow the lamp to warm up 10 to 20 min or until the energy output stabilizes. Optimize conditions such as lamp position, burner head alignment, fuel and oxidant flow rates, etc. See the SOP or specific instrument manuals for details. Instrumental parameters for the Perkin-Elmer Model 603 used in the validation of this method are given in Attachment 1.

3.10.2. Aspirate and measure the absorbance of a standard solution of cadmium. The standard concentration should be within the linear range. For the instrumentation used in the validation of this method a 2 µg/mL cadmium standard gives a net absorbance reading of about 0.350 abs. units (see Section 1.5.5.) when the instrument and the source lamp are performing to manufacturer specifications.

3.10.3. To increase instrument response, scale expand the absorbance reading of the aspirated 2 µg/mL working standard approximately four times. Increase the integration time to at least 3 seconds to reduce signal noise.

3.10.4. Autozero the instrument while aspirating a deionized water blank. Monitor the variation in the baseline absorbance reading (baseline noise) for a few minutes to insure that the instrument, source lamp and associated equipment are in good operating condition.

3.10.5. Aspirate the working standards and samples directly into the flame and record their absorbance readings. Aspirate the deionized water blank immediately after every standard or sample to correct for and monitor any baseline drift and noise. Record the baseline absorbance reading of each deionized water blank. Label each standard and sample reading and its accompanying baseline reading.

3.10.6. It is recommended that the entire series of working standards be analyzed at the beginning and end of the analysis of a set of samples to establish a concentration-response curve, ensure that the standard readings agree with each other and are reproducible. Also, analyze a working standard after every five or six samples to monitor the performance of the spectrophotometer. Standard readings should agree within ±10 to 15% of the readings obtained at the beginning of the analysis.

3.10.7. Bracket the sample readings with standards during the analysis. If the absorbance reading of a sample is above the absorbance reading of the highest working standard, dilute the sample with diluting solution and reanalyze. Use the appropriate dilution factor in the calculations.

3.10.8. Repeat the analysis of approximately 10% of the samples for a check of precision.

3.10.9. If possible, analyze quality control samples from an independent source as a check on analytical recovery and precision.

3.10.10. Record the final instrument settings at the end of the analysis. Date and label the output.

3.11. AAS-HGA Analysis

Initially analyze all of the air samples for their cadmium content by flame atomic absorption spectroscopy (AAS) according to the instructions given in Section 3.10. If the concentration of cadmium in a sample solution is less than three times the quantitative detection limit [0.04 µg/mL (40 ng/mL) for the instrumentation used in the validation] and the sample results are to be averaged with other samples for TWA calculations, proceed with the AAS-HGA analysis of the sample as described below.

3.11.1. Set up the atomic absorption spectrophotometer and HGA for flameless atomic absorption analysis of cadmium according to the SOP (5.9.) or the manufacturer's operational instructions and allow the instrument to stabilize. The graphite furnace atomizer is equipped with a pyrolytically coated graphite tube containing a pyrolytic platform. For the source lamp, use a cadmium hollow cathode or electrodeless discharge lamp operated at the manufacturer's recommended setting for graphite furnace operation. The Zeeman background corrector and EDL are recommended for use with the L'vov platform. Instrumental parameters for the Perkin-Elmer Model 5100 spectrophotometer and Zeeman HGA-600 graphite furnace used in the validation of this method are given in Attachment 2.

3.11.2. Optimize the energy reading of the spectrophotometer at 228.8 nm by adjusting the lamp position and the wavelength according to the manufacturer's instructions.

3.11.3. Set up the autosampler to inject a 5-µL aliquot of the working standard, sample or reagent blank solution onto the L'vov platform along with a 10-µL overlay of the matrix modifier.

3.11.4. Analyze the reagent blank (diluting solution, Section 3.5.6.) and then autozero the instrument before starting the analysis of a set of samples. It is recommended that the reagent blank be analyzed several times during the analysis to assure the integrated absorbance (peak area) reading remains at or near zero.

3.11.5. Analyze a working standard approximately midway in the linear portion of the working standard range two or three times to check for reproducibility and sensitivity (see sections 1.5.5. and 1.5.6.) before starting the analysis of samples. Calculate the experimental characteristic mass value from the average integrated absorbance reading and injection volume of the analyzed working standard. Compare this value to the manufacturer's suggested value as a check of proper instrument operation.

3.11.6. Analyze the reagent blank, working standard, and sample solutions. Record and label the peak area (abs-sec) readings and the peak and background peak profiles on the printer/plotter.

3.11.7. It is recommended the entire series of working standards be analyzed at the beginning and end of the analysis of a set of samples. Establish a concentration-response curve and ensure standard readings agree with each other and are reproducible. Also, analyze a working standard after every five or six samples to monitor the performance of the system. Standard readings should agree within ±15% of the readings obtained at the beginning of the analysis.

3.11.8. Bracket the sample readings with standards during the analysis. If the peak area reading of a sample is above the peak area reading of the highest working standard, dilute the sample with the diluting solution and reanalyze. Use the appropriate dilution factor in the calculations.

3.11.9. Repeat the analysis of approximately 10% of the samples for a check of precision.

3.11.10. If possible, analyze quality control samples from an independent source as a check of analytical recovery and precision.

3.11.11. Record the final instrument settings at the end of the analysis. Date and label the output.

3.12. Calculations

NOTE: Standards used for HGA analysis are in ng/mL. Total amounts of cadmium from calculations will be in ng (not µg) unless a prior conversion is made.

3.12.1. Correct for baseline drift and noise in flame AAS analysis by subtracting each baseline absorbance reading from its corresponding working standard or sample absorbance reading to obtain the net absorbance reading for each standard and sample.

3.12.2. Use a least squares regression program to plot a concentration-response curve of net absorbance reading (or peak area for HGA analysis) versus concentration (µg/mL or ng/mL) of cadmium in each working standard.

3.12.3. Determine the concentration (µg/mL or ng/mL) of cadmium in each sample from the resulting concentration-response curve. If the concentration of cadmium in a sample solution is less than three times the quantitative detection limit [0.04 µg/mL (40 ng/mL) for the instrumentation used in the validation of the method] and if consecutive samples were taken on one employee and the sample results are to be averaged with other samples to determine a single TWA, reanalyze the sample by AAS-HGA as described in

Section 3.11. and report the AAS-HGA analytical results.

3.12.4. Calculate the total amount (µg or ng) of cadmium in each sample from the sample solution volume (mL):

W = (C)(sample vol, mL)(DF)

Where:

W = Total cadmium in sample
C = Calculated concentration of cadmium
DF = Dilution Factor (if applicable)

3.12.5. Make a blank correction for each air sample by subtracting the total amount of cadmium in the corresponding blank sample from the total amount of cadmium in the sample.

3.12.6. Calculate the concentration of cadmium in an air sample (mg/m^3 or $µg/m^3$) by using one of the following equations:

$$mg/m^3 = W_{bc}/(\text{Air vol sampled, L})$$

or

$$µg/m^3 = (W_{bc})(1{,}000 \text{ ng/µg})/(\text{Air vol sampled, L})$$

Where:

W_{bc} = blank corrected total µg cadmium in the sample. (1µg = 1,000 ng)

4. BACKUP DATA

4.1. Introduction

4.1.1. The purpose of this evaluation is to determine the analytical method recovery, working standard range, and qualitative and quantitative detection limits of the two atomic absorption analytical techniques included in this method. The evaluation consisted of the following experiments:

1. An analysis of 24 samples (six samples each at 0.1, 0.5, 1 and 2 times the TWA-PEL) for the analytical method recovery study of the flame AAS analytical technique.

2. An analysis of 18 samples (six samples each at 0.5, 1 and 2 times the Action Level TWA-PEL) for the analytical method recovery study of the AAS-HGA analytical technique.

3. Multiple analyses of the reagent blank and a series of standard solutions to determine the working standard range and the qualitative and quantitative detection limits for both atomic absorption analytical techniques.

4.1.2. The analytical method recovery results at all test levels were calculated from concentration-response curves and statistically examined for outliers at the 99% confidence level. Possible outliers were determined using the Treatment of Outliers test (5.10.). In addition, the sample results of the two analytical techniques, at 0.5, 1.0 and 2.0 times their target concentrations, were tested for homogeneity of variances also at the 99% confidence level. Homogeneity of the coefficients of variation was determined using the Bartlett's test (5.11.). The overall analytical error (OAE) at the 95% confidence level was calculated using the equation (5.12.):

OAE = ±[| Bias| + (1.96)(CV_1(pooled))(100%)]

4.1.3. A derivation of the International Union of Pure and Applied Chemistry (IUPAC) detection limit equation (5.13.) was used to determine the qualitative and quantitative detection limits for both atomic absorption analytical techniques:

C_{ld} = k(sd)/m   (Equation 1)

Where:

C_{ld} = the smallest reliable detectable concentration an analytical instrument can determine at a given confidence level.

k = 3 for the Qualitative Detection Limit at the 99.86% Confidence Level

= 10 for the Quantitative Detection Limit at the 99.99% Confidence Level.

sd = standard deviation of the reagent blank (Rbl) readings.

m = analytical sensitivity or slope as calculated by linear regression.

4.1.4. Collection efficiencies of metallic fume and dust atmospheres on 0.8-μm mixed cellulose ester membrane filters are well documented and have been shown to be excellent (5.11.). Since elemental cadmium and the cadmium component of cadmium compounds are nonvolatile, stability studies of cadmium spiked MCEF samples were not performed.

4.2. Equipment

4.2.1. A Perkin-Elmer (PE) Model 603 spectrophotometer equipped with a manual gas control system, a stainless steel nebulizer, a burner mixing chamber, a flow spoiler and a 10 cm. (one-slot) burner head was used in the experimental validation of the flame AAS analytical technique. A PE cadmium hollow cathode lamp, operated at the manufacturer's recommended current setting for continuous operation (4 mA), was used as the source lamp. Instrument parameters are listed in Attachment 1.

4.2.2. A PE Model 5100 spectrophotometer, Zeeman HGA–600 graphite furnace atomizer and AS–60 HGA autosampler were used in the experimental validation of the AAS-HGA analytical technique. The spectrophotometer was equipped with a PE Series 7700 professional computer and Model PR–310 printer. A PE System 2 cadmium electrodeless discharge lamp, operated at the manufacturer's recommended current setting for modulated operation (170 mA), was used as the source lamp. Instrument parameters are listed in Attachment 2.

4.3. Reagents

4.3.1. J.T. Baker Chem. Co. (Analyzed grade) concentrated nitric acid, 69.0–71.0%, and concentrated hydrochloric acid, 36.5–38.0%, were used to prepare the samples and standards.

4.3.2. Ammonium phosphate, monobasic, NH_4 H_2 PO_4 and magnesium nitrate, $Mg(NO_3)_2 6H_2$ O, both manufactured by the Mallinckrodt Chem. Co., were used to prepare the matrix modifier for AAS-HGA analysis.

4.4. Standard Preparation for Flame AAS Analysis

4.4.1. Dilute stock solutions: Prepared 0.01, 0.1, 1, 10 and 100 μg/mL cadmium standard stock solutions by making appropriate serial dilutions of a commercially available 1,000 μg/mL cadmium standard stock solution (RICCA Chemical Co., Lot# A102) with the diluting solution (4% HNO_3, 0.4% HCl).

4.4.2. Analyzed Standards: Prepared cadmium standards in the range of 0.001 to 2.0 μg/mL by pipetting 2 to 10 mL of the appropriate dilute cadmium stock solution into a 100-mL volumetric flask and diluting to volume with the diluting solution. (See Section 3.7.2.)

4.5. Standard Preparation for AAS-HGA Analysis

4.5.1. Dilute stock solutions: Prepared 1, 10, 100 and 1,000 ng/mL cadmium standard stock solutions by making appropriate serial dilutions of a commercially available 1,000 μg/mL cadmium standard stock solution (J.T. Baker Chemical Co., Instra-analyzed, Lot# D22642) with the diluting solution (4% HNO_3, 0.4% HCl).

4.5.2. Analyzed Standards: Prepared cadmium standards in the range of 0.1 to 40 ng/mL by pipetting 2 to 10 mL of the appropriate dilute cadmium stock solution into a 100-mL volumetric flask and diluting to volume with the diluting solution. (See Section 3.8.2.)

4.6. Detection Limits and Standard Working Range for Flame AAS Analysis

4.6.1. Analyzed the reagent blank solution and the entire series of cadmium standards in the range of 0.001 to 2.0 μg/mL three to six times according to the instructions given in Section 3.10. The diluting solution (4% HNO_3, 0.4% HCl) was used as the reagent blank. The integration time on the PE 603 spectrophotometer was set to 3.0 seconds and a fourfold expansion of the absorbance reading of the 2.0 μg/mL cadmium standard was made prior to analysis. The 2.0 μg/mL standard gave a net absorbance reading of 0.350 abs. units prior to expansion in agreement with the manufacturer's specifications (5.6.).

4.6.2. The net absorbance readings of the reagent blank and the low concentration Cd standards from 0.001 to 0.1 μg/mL and the statistical analysis of the results are shown in Table I. The standard deviation, sd, of the six net absorbance readings of the reagent blank is 1.05 abs. units. The slope, m, as calculated by a linear regression plot of the net absorbance readings (shown in Table II) of the 0.02 to 1.0 μg/mL cadmium standards versus their concentration is 772.7 abs. units/ (μg/mL).

4.6.3. If these values for sd and the slope, m, are used in Eqn. 1 (Sect. 4.1.3.), the qualitative and quantitative detection limits as determined by the IUPAC Method are:

C_{ld} = (3)(1.05 abs. units)/(772.7 abs. units/(μg/mL))

= 0.0041 μg/mL for the qualitative detection limit.

C_{ld} = (10)(1.05 abs. units)/(772.7 abs. units/μg/mL))

= 0.014 μg/mL for the quantitative detection limit.

The qualitative and quantitative detection limits for the flame AAS analytical technique are 0.041 μg and 0.14 μg cadmium, respectively, for a 10 mL solution volume. These correspond, respectively, to 0.2 μg/m^3 and 0.70 μg/m^3 for a 200 L air volume.

4.6.4. The recommended Cd standard working range for flame AAS analysis is 0.02 to 2.0 μg/mL. The net absorbance readings of the reagent blank and the recommended working range standards and the statistical analysis of the results are shown in Table II. The standard of lowest concentration in the working range, 0.02 μg/mL, is slightly greater than the calculated quantitative detection limit, 0.014 μg/mL. The standard of highest concentration in the working range, 2.0 μg/mL, is at the upper end of the linear working range suggested by the manufacturer (5.6.). Although the standard net absorbance readings are not strictly linear at concentrations above 0.5 μg/mL, the deviation from linearity is only about 10% at the upper end of the recommended standard working range. The deviation from linearity is probably caused by the four-fold expansion of the signal suggested in the method. As shown in Table II, the precision of the standard net absorbance readings are excellent throughout the recommended working range; the relative standard deviations of the readings range from 0.009 to 0.064.

4.7. Detection Limits and Standard Working Range for AAS-HGA Analysis

4.7.1. Analyzed the reagent blank solution and the entire series of cadmium standards in the range of 0.1 to 40 ng/mL according to the instructions given in Section 3.11. The diluting solution (4% HNO_3, 0.4% HCl) was used as the reagent blank. A fresh aliquot of the reagent blank and of each standard was used for every analysis. The experimental characteristic mass value was 0.41 pg, calculated from the average peak area (abs-sec) reading of the 5 ng/mL standard which is approximately midway in the linear portion of the working standard range. This agreed within 20% with the characteristic mass value, 0.35 pg, listed by the manufacturer of the instrument (5.2.).

4.7.2. The peak area (abs-sec) readings of the reagent blank and the low concentration Cd standards from 0.1 to 2.0 ng/mL and statistical analysis of the results are shown in Table III. Five of the reagent blank peak area readings were zero and the sixth reading was 1 and was an outlier. The near lack of a blank signal does not satisfy a strict interpretation of the IUPAC method for determining the detection limits. Therefore, the standard deviation of the six peak area readings of the 0.2 ng/mL cadmium standard, 0.75 abs-sec, was used to calculate the detection limits by the IUPAC method. The slope, m, as calculated by a linear regression plot of the peak area (abs-sec) readings (shown in Table IV) of the 0.2 to 10 ng/mL cadmium standards versus their concentration is 51.5 abs-sec/(ng/mL).

4.7.3. If 0.75 abs-sec (sd) and 51.5 abs-sec/(ng/ml) (m) are used in Eqn. 1 (Sect. 4.1.3.), the qualitative and quantitative detection limits as determined by the IUPAC method are:

C_{ld} = (3)(0.75 abs-sec)/(51.5 abs-sec/(ng/mL))

= 0.044 ng/mL for the qualitative detection limit.

C_{ld}= (10)(0.75 abs-sec)/(51.5 abs-sec/(ng/mL)) = 0.15 ng/mL for the quantitative detection limit.

The qualitative and quantitative detection limits for the AAS-HGA analytical technique are 0.44 ng and 1.5 ng cadmium, respectively, for a 10 mL solution volume. These correspond, respectively, to 0.007 μg/m^3 and 0.025 μg/m^3 for a 60 L air volume.

4.7.4. The peak area (abs-sec) readings of the Cd standards from 0.2 to 40 ng/mL and the statistical analysis of the results are given in Table IV. The recommended standard working range for AAS-HGA analysis is 0.2 to 20 ng/mL. The standard of lowest concentration in the recommended working range is slightly greater than the calculated quantitative detection limit, 0.15 ng/mL. The deviation from linearity of the peak area readings of the 20 ng/mL standard, the highest concentration standard in the recommended working range, is approximately 10%. The deviations from linearity of the peak area readings of the 30 and 40 ng/mL standards are significantly greater than 10%. As shown in Table IV, the precision of the peak area readings are satisfactory throughout the recommended working range; the relative standard deviations of the readings range from 0.025 to 0.083.

4.8. Analytical Method Recovery for Flame AAS Analysis

4.8.1. Four sets of spiked MCEF samples were prepared by injecting 20 μL of 10, 50, 100 and 200 μg/mL dilute cadmium stock solutions on 37 mm diameter filters (part no. AAWP 037 00, Millipore Corp., Bedford, MA) with a calibrated micropipet. The dilute stock solutions were prepared by making appropriate serial dilutions of a commercially available 1,000 µg/mL cadmium standard stock solution (RICCA Chemical Co., Lot# A102) with the diluting solution (4% HNO₃, 0.4% HCl). Each set contained six samples and a sample blank. The amount of cadmium in the prepared sets were equivalent to 0.1, 0.5, 1.0 and 2.0 times the TWA PEL target concentration of 5 µg/m³ for a 400 L air volume.

4.8.2. The air-dried spiked filters were digested and analyzed for their cadmium content by flame atomic absorption spectroscopy (AAS) following the procedure described in Section 3. The 0.02 to 2.0µg/mL cadmium standards (the suggested working range) were used in the analysis of the spiked filters.

4.8.3. The results of the analysis are given in Table V. One result at 0.5 times the TWA PEL target concentration was an outlier and was excluded from statistical analysis. Experimental justification for rejecting it is that the outlier value was probably due to a spiking error. The coefficients of variation for the three test levels at 0.5 to 2.0 times TWA PEL target concentration passed Bartlett's test and were pooled.

4.8.4. The average recovery of the six spiked filter samples at 0.1 times the TWA PEL target concentration was 118.2% with a coefficient of variation (CV₁) of 0.128. The average recovery of the spiked filter samples in the range of 0.5 to 2.0 times the TWA target concentration was 104.0% with a pooled coefficient of variation (CV₁) of 0.010. Consequently, the analytical bias found in these spiked sample results over the tested concentration range was + 4.0% and the OAE was ±6.0%.

4.9. Analytical Method Recovery for AAS-HGA Analysis

4.9.1. Three sets of spiked MCEF samples were prepared by injecting 15µL of 5, 10 and 20 µg/mL dilute cadmium stock solutions on 37 mm diameter filters (part no. AAWP 037 00, Millipore Corp., Bedford, MA) with a calibrated micropipet. The dilute stock solutions were prepared by making appropriate serial dilutions of a commercially available certified 1,000 µg/mL cadmium standard stock solution (Fisher Chemical Co., Lot# 913438–24) with the diluting solution (4% HNO₃, 0.4% HCl). Each set contained six samples and a sample blank. The amount of cadmium in the prepared sets were equivalent to 0.5, 1 and 2 times the Action Level TWA target concentration of 2.5 µg/m³ for a 60 L air volume.

4.9.2. The air-dried spiked filters were digested and analyzed for their cadmium content by flameless atomic absorption spectroscopy using a heated graphite furnace atomizer following the procedure described in Section 3. A five-fold dilution of the spiked

filter samples at 2 times the Action Level TWA was made prior to their analysis. The 0.05 to 20 ng/mL cadmium standards were used in the analysis of the spiked filters.

4.9.3. The results of the analysis are given in Table VI. There were no outliers. The coefficients of variation for the three test levels at 0.5 to 2.0 times the Action Level TWA PEL passed the Bartlett's test and were pooled. The average recovery of the spiked filter samples was 94.2% with a pooled coefficient of variation (CV₁) of 0.043. Consequently, the analytical bias was − 5.8% and the OAE was ±14.2%.

4.10. Conclusions

The experiments performed in this evaluation show the two atomic absorption analytical techniques included in this method to be precise and accurate and have sufficient sensitivity to measure airborne cadmium over a broad range of exposure levels and sampling periods.

5. REFERENCES

5.1. Slavin, W. Graphite Furnace AAS—A Source Book; Perkin-Elmer Corp., Spectroscopy Div.: Ridgefield, CT, 1984; p. 18 and pp. 83–90.

5.2. Grosser, Z., Ed.; Techniques in Graphite Furnace Atomic Absorption Spectrophotometry; Perkin-Elmer Corp., Spectroscopy Div.: Ridgefield, CT, 1985.

5.3. Occupational Safety and Health Administration Salt Lake Technical Center: Metal and Metalloid Particulate in Workplace Atmospheres (Atomic Absorption) (USDOL/OSHA Method No. ID–121). In OSHA Analytical Methods Manual 2nd ed. Cincinnati, OH: American Conference of Governmental Industrial Hygienists, 1991.

5.4. Occupational Safety and Health Administration Salt Lake Technical Center: Metal and Metalloid Particulate in Workplace Atmospheres (ICP) (USDOL/OSHA Method No. ID–125G). In OSHA Analytical Methods Manual 2nd ed. Cincinnati, OH: American Conference of Governmental Industrial Hygienists, 1991.

5.5. Windholz, M., Ed.; The Merck Index, 10th ed.; Merck & Co.: Rahway, NJ, 1983.

5.6. Analytical Methods for Atomic Absorption Spectrophotometry, The Perkin-Elmer Corporation: Norwalk, CT, 1982.

5.7. Slavin, W., D.C. Manning, G. Carnrick, and E. Pruszkowska: Properties of the Cadmium Determination with the Platform Furnace and Zeeman Background Correction. Spectrochim. Acta 38B:1157–1170 (1983).

5.8. Occupational Safety and Health Administration Salt Lake Technical Center: Standard Operating Procedure for Atomic Absorption. Salt Lake City, UT: USDOL/OSHA-SLTC, In progress.

5.9. Occupational Safety and Health Administration Salt Lake Technical Center:

AAS-HGA Standard Operating Procedure. Salt Lake City, UT: USDOL/OSHA-SLTC, In progress.

5.10. Mandel, J.: Accuracy and Precision, Evaluation and Interpretation of Analytical Results, The Treatment of Outliers. In Treatise On Analytical Chemistry, 2nd ed., Vol.1, edited by I. M. Kolthoff and P. J. Elving. New York: John Wiley and Sons, 1978. pp. 282–285.

5.11. National Institute for Occupational Safety and Health: Documentation of the NIOSH Validation Tests by D. Taylor, R. Kupel, and J. Bryant (DHEW/NIOSH Pub. No. 77–185). Cincinnati, OH: National Institute for Occupational Safety and Health, 1977.

5.12. Occupational Safety and Health Administration Analytical Laboratory: Precision and Accuracy Data Protocol for Laboratory Validations. In OSHA Analytical Methods Manual 1st ed. Cincinnati, OH: American Conference of Governmental Industrial Hygienists (Pub. No. ISBN: 0–936712–66–X), 1985.

5.13. Long, G.L. and J.D. Winefordner: Limit of Detection—A Closer Look at the IUPAC Definition. Anal.Chem. 55:712A–724A (1983).

5.14. American Conference of Governmental Industrial Hygienists: Documentation of Threshold Limit Values and Biological Exposure Indices. 5th ed. Cincinnati, OH: American Conference of Governmental Industrial Hygienists, 1986.

TABLE I—CD DETECTION LIMIT STUDY

[Flame AAS Analysis]

STD (µg/mL)	Absorbance reading at 228.8 nm		Statistical analysis
Reagent blank	5	2	n = 6.
	4	3	mean = 3.50.
	4	3	std dev = 1.05.
			CV = 0.30.
0.001	6	6	n = 6.
	2	4	mean = 5.00.
	6	6	std dev = 1.67.
			CV = 0.335.
0.002	5	7	n = 6.
	7	3	mean = 5.50.
	7	4	std dev = 1.76.
			CV = 0.320.
0.005	7	7	n = 6.
	8	8	mean = 7.33.
	8	6	std dev = 0.817.
			CV = 0.111.
0.010	10	9	n = 6.
	10	13	mean = 10.3.
	10	10	std dev = 1.37.
			CV = 0.133.
0.020	20	23	n = 6.
	20	22	mean = 20.8.
	20	20	std dev = 1.33.
			CV = 0.064.
0.050	42	42	n = 6.
	42	42	mean = 42.5.
	42	45	std dev = 1.22.
			CV = 0.029.

TABLE I—CD DETECTION LIMIT STUDY— Continued

[Flame AAS Analysis]

STD (µg/mL)	Absorbance reading at 228.8 nm	Statistical analysis
0.10	84	n = 3.
	80	mean = 82.3.
	83	std dev = 2.08.
		CV = 0.025.

TABLE II—CD STANDARD WORKING RANGE STUDY

[Flame AAS Analysis]

STD (µg/mL)	Absorbance reading at 228.8 nm		Statistical analysis
Reagent blank	5	2	n = 6.
	4	3	mean = 3.50.
	4	3	std dev = 1.05.
			CV = 0.30.
0.020	20	23	n = 6.
	20	22	mean = 20.8.
	20	20	std dev = 1.33.
			CV = 0.064.
0.050	42	42	n = 6.
	42	42	mean = 42.5.
	42	45	std dev = 1.22.
			CV = 0.029.
0.10	84		n = 3.
	80		mean = 82.3.
	83		std dev = 2.08.
			CV = 0.025.
0.20	161		n = 3.
	161		mean = 160.0.
	158		std dev = 1.73.
			CV = 0.011.
0.50	391		n = 3.
	389		mean = 391.0.
	393		std dev = 2.00.
			CV = 0.005.
1.00	760		n = 3.
	748		mean = 753.3.
	752		std dev = 6.11.
			CV = 0.008.
2.00	1416		n = 3.
	1426		mean = 1414.3.
	1401		std dev = 12.6.
			CV = 0.009.

TABLE III—CD DETECTION LIMIT STUDY

[AAS-HGA Analysis]

STD (ng/mL)	Peak area readings × 10^3 at 228.8 nm		Statistical analysis
Reagent blank	0	0	n = 6.
	0	1	mean = 0.167.
	0	0	std dev = 0.41.
			CV = 2.45.
0.1	8	6	n = 6.
	5	7	mean = 7.7.
	13	7	std dev = 2.8.
			CV = 0.366.
0.2	11	13	n = 6.
	11	12	mean = 11.8.
	12	12	std dev = 0.75.
			CV = 0.064.

216

TABLE III—CD DETECTION LIMIT STUDY— Continued
[AAS-HGA Analysis]

STD (ng/mL)	Peak area readings × 10^3 at 228.8 nm		Statistical analysis
0.5	28	33	n = 6.
	26	28	mean = 28.8.
	28	30	std dev = 2.4.
			CV = 0.083.
1.0	52	55	n = 6.
	56	58	mean = 54.8.
	54	54	std dev = 2.0.
			CV = 0.037.
2.0	101	112	n = 6.
	110	110	mean = 108.8.
	110	110	std dev = 3.9.
			CV = 0.036.

TABLE IV—CD STANDARD WORKING RANGE STUDY
[AAS-HGA Analysis]

STD (ng/mL)	Peak area readings × 10^3 at 228.8 nm		Statistical analysis
0.2	11	13	n = 6.
	11	12	mean = 11.8.
	12	12	std dev = 0.75.
			CV = 0.064.
0.5	28	33	n = 6.
	26	28	mean = 28.8.
	28	30	std dev = 2.4.
			CV = 0.083.

TABLE IV—CD STANDARD WORKING RANGE STUDY—Continued
[AAS-HGA Analysis]

STD (ng/mL)	Peak area readings × 10^3 at 228.8 nm		Statistical analysis
1.0	52	55	n = 6.
	56	58	mean = 54.8.
	54	54	std dev = 2.0.
			CV = 0.037.
2.0	101	112	n = 6.
	110	110	mean = 108.8.
	110	110	std dev = 3.9.
			CV = 0.036.
5.0	247	265	n = 6.
	268	275	mean = 265.5.
	259	279	std dev = 11.5.
			CV = 0.044.
10.0	495	520	n = 6.
	523	513	mean = 516.7.
	516	533	std dev = 12.7.
			CV = 0.025.
20.0	950	953	n = 6.
	951	958	mean = 941.8.
	949	890	std dev = 25.6.
			CV = 0.027.
30.0	1269	1291	n = 6.
	1303	1307	mean = 1293.
	1295	1290	std dev = 13.3.
			CV = 0.010.
40.0	1505	1567	n = 6.
	1535	1567	mean = 1552.
	1566	1572	std dev = 26.6.
			CV = 0.017.

TABLE V—ANALYTICAL METHOD RECOVERY
[Flame AAS Analysis]

Test level	0.5 ×	Percent rec.	µg taken	1.0 ×	Percent rec.	µg taken	2.0 ×	Percent rec.
µg taken	µg found			µg found			µg found	
1.00	1.0715	107.2	2.00	2.0688	103.4	4.00	4.1504	103.8
1.00	1.0842	108.4	2.00	2.0174	100.9	4.00	4.1108	102.8
1.00	1.0842	108.4	2.00	2.0431	102.2	4.00	4.0581	101.5
1.00	*1.0081	*100.8	2.00	2.0431	102.2	4.00	4.0844	102.1
1.00	1.0715	107.2	2.00	2.0174	100.9	4.00	4.1504	103.8
1.00	1.0842	108.4	2.00	2.0045	100.2	4.00	4.1899	104.7

n=	5	6	6
mean =	107.9	101.6	103.1
std dev =	0.657	1.174	1.199
CV_1=	0.006	0.011	0.012
	CV_1 (pooled) = 0.010		

*Rejected as an outlier—this value did not pass the outlier T-test at the 99% confidence level.

Test level	0.1 ×	Percent rec.
µg taken	µg found	
0.200	0.2509	125.5
0.200	0.2509	125.5
0.200	0.2761	138.1
0.200	0.2258	112.9
0.200	0.2258	112.9
0.200	0.1881	94.1

n=	6

mean = ... 118.2
std dev = ... 15.1
CV_1= 0.128

TABLE VI—ANALYTICAL METHOD RECOVERY

[AAS-HGA analysis]

| Test level | 0.5 × | | 1.0 × | | 2.0 × | |
ng taken	ng found	Percent rec.	ng taken	ng found	Percent rec.	ng taken	ng found	Percent rec.
75	71.23	95.0	150	138.00	92.0	300	258.43	86.1
75	71.47	95.3	150	138.29	92.2	300	258.46	86.2
75	70.02	93.4	150	136.30	90.9	300	280.55	93.5
75	77.34	103.1	150	146.62	97.7	300	288.34	96.1
75	78.32	104.4	150	145.17	96.8	300	261.74	87.2
75	71.96	95.9	150	144.88	96.6	300	277.22	92.4
n=	6			6			6	
mean =	97.9			94.4			90.3	
std dev =	4.66			2.98			4.30	
CV_1=	0.048			0.032			0.048	
	CV_1(pooled) = 0.043							

ATTACHMENT 1

Instrumental Parameters for Flame AAS Analysis

Atomic Absorption Spectrophotometer
(Perkin-Elmer Model 603)

Flame: Air/Acetylene—lean, blue
Oxidant Flow: 55
Fuel Flow: 32
Wavelength: 228.8 nm
Slit: 4 (0.7 nm)
Range: UV
Signal: Concentration (4 exp)
Integration Time: 3 sec

ATTACHMENT 2

Instrumental Parameters for HGA Analysis

Atomic Absorption Spectrophotometer
(Perkin-Elmer Model 5100)

Signal Type: Zeeman AA
Slitwidth: 0.7 nm
Wavelength: 228.8 nm
Measurement: Peak Area
Integration Time: 6.0 sec
BOC Time: 5 sec

BOC = Background Offset Correction.

ZEEMAN GRAPHITE FURNACE (PERKIN-ELMER MODEL HGA–600)

Step	Ramp time (sec)	Hold time (sec)	Temp. (°C)	Argon flow (mL/min)	Read (sec)
1) Predry	5	10	90	300	
2) Dry	30	10	140	300	
3) Char	10	20	900	300	
4) Cool Down	1	8	30	300	
5) Atomize	0	5	1600	0	−1
6) Burnout	1	8	2500	300	....

APPENDIX F TO § 1910.1027—NONMANDATORY PROTOCOL FOR BIOLOGICAL MONITORING

1.00 Introduction

Under the final OSHA cadmium rule (29 CFR part 1910), monitoring of biological specimens and several periodic medical examinations are required for eligible employees. These medical examinations are to be conducted regularly, and medical monitoring is to include the periodic analysis of cadmium in blood (CDB), cadmium in urine (CDU) and beta-2-microglobulin in urine

(B2MU). As CDU and B2MU are to be normalized to the concentration of creatinine in urine (CRTU), then CRTU must be analyzed in conjunction with CDU and B2MU analyses.

The purpose of this protocol is to provide procedures for establishing and maintaining the quality of the results obtained from the analyses of CDB, CDU and B2MU by commercial laboratories. Laboratories conforming to the provisions of this nonmandatory protocol shall be known as "participating laboratories." The biological monitoring data from these laboratories will be evaluated by physicians responsible for biological monitoring to determine the conditions under which employees may continue to work in locations exhibiting airborne-cadmium concentrations at or above defined actions levels (see paragraphs (l)(3) and (l)(4) of the final rule). These results also may be used to support a decision to remove workers from such locations.

Under the medical monitoring program for cadmium, blood and urine samples must be collected at defined intervals from workers by physicians responsible for medical monitoring; these samples are sent to commercial laboratories that perform the required analyses and report results of these analyses to the responsible physicians. To ensure the accuracy and reliability of these laboratory analyses, the laboratories to which samples are submitted should participate in an ongoing and efficacious proficiency testing program. Availability of proficiency testing programs may vary with the analyses performed.

To test proficiency in the analysis of CDB, CDU and B2MU, a laboratory should participate either in the interlaboratory comparison program operated by the Centre de Toxicologie du Quebec (CTQ) or an equivalent program. (Currently, no laboratory in the U.S. performs proficiency testing on CDB, CDU or B2MU.) Under this program, CTQ sends participating laboratories 18 samples of each analyte (CDB, CDU and/or B2MU) annually for analysis. Participating laboratories must return the results of these analyses to CTQ within four to five weeks after receiving the samples.

The CTQ program pools analytical results from many participating laboratories to derive consensus mean values for each of the samples distributed. Results reported by each laboratory then are compared against these consensus means for the analyzed samples to determine the relative performance of each laboratory. The proficiency of a participating laboratory is a function of the extent of agreement between results submitted by the participating laboratory and the consensus values for the set of samples analyzed.

Proficiency testing for CRTU analysis (which should be performed with CDU and B2MU analyses to evaluate the results properly) also is recommended. In the U.S., only the College of American Pathologists (CAP) currently conducts CRTU proficiency testing; participating laboratories should be accredited for CRTU analysis by the CAP.

Results of the proficiency evaluations will be forwarded to the participating laboratory by the proficiency-testing laboratory, as well as to physicians designated by the participating laboratory to receive this information. In addition, the participating laboratory should, on request, submit the results of

their internal Quality Assurance/Quality Control (QA/QC) program for each analytic procedure (*i.e.*, CDB, CDU and/or B2MU) to physicians designated to receive the proficiency results. For participating laboratories offering CDU and/or B2MU analyses, QA/QC documentation also should be provided for CRTU analysis. (Laboratories should provide QA/QC information regarding CRTU analysis directly to the requesting physician if they perform the analysis in-house; if CRTU analysis is performed by another laboratory under contract, this information should be provided to the physician by the contract laboratory.)

QA/QC information, along with the actual biological specimen measurements, should be provided to the responsible physician using standard formats. These physicians then may collate the QA/QC information with proficiency test results to compare the relative performance of laboratories, as well as to facilitate evaluation of the worker monitoring data. This information supports decisions made by the physician with regard to the biological monitoring program, and for mandating medical removal.

This protocol describes procedures that may be used by the responsible physicians to identify laboratories most likely to be proficient in the analysis of samples used in the biological monitoring of cadmium; also provided are procedures for record keeping and reporting by laboratories participating in proficiency testing programs, and recommendations to assist these physicians in interpreting analytical results determined by participating laboratories. As the collection and handling of samples affects the quality of the data, recommendations are made for these tasks. Specifications for analytical methods to be used in the medical monitoring program are included in this protocol as well.

In conclusion, this document is intended as a supplement to characterize and maintain the quality of medical monitoring data collected under the final cadmium rule promulgated by OSHA (29 CFR part 1910). OSHA has been granted authority under the Occupational Safety and Health Act of 1970 to protect workers from the effects of exposure to hazardous substances in the work place and to mandate adequate monitoring of workers to determine when adverse health effects may be occurring. This nonmandatory protocol is intended to provide guidelines and recommendations to improve the accuracy and reliability of the procedures used to analyze the biological samples collected as part of the medical monitoring program for cadmium.

2.0 Definitions

When the terms below appear in this protocol, use the following definitions.

Accuracy: A measure of the bias of a data set. Bias is a systematic error that is either inherent in a method or caused by some artifact or idiosyncracy of the measurement system. Bias is characterized by a consistent deviation (positive or negative) in the results from an accepted reference value.

Arithmetic Mean: The sum of measurements in a set divided by the number of measurements in a set.

Blind Samples: A quality control procedure in which the concentration of analyte in the samples should be unknown to the analyst at the time that the analysis is performed.

Coefficient of Variation: The ratio of the standard deviation of a set of measurements to the mean (arithmetic or geometric) of the measurements.

Compliance Samples: Samples from exposed workers sent to a participating laboratory for analysis.

Control Charts: Graphic representations of the results for quality control samples being analyzed by a participating laboratory.

Control Limits: Statistical limits which define when an analytic procedure exceeds acceptable parameters; control limits provide a method of assessing the accuracy of analysts, laboratories, and discrete analytic runs.

Control Samples: Quality control samples.

F/T: The measured amount of an analyte divided by the theoretical value (defined below) for that analyte in the sample analyzed; this ratio is a measure of the recovery for a quality control sample.

Geometric Mean: The natural antilog of the mean of a set of natural log-transformed data.

Geometric Standard Deviation: The antilog of the standard deviation of a set of natural log-transformed data.

Limit of Detection: Using a predefined level of confidence, this is the lowest measured value at which some of the measured material is likely to have come from the sample.

Mean: A central tendency of a set of data; in this protocol, this mean is defined as the *arithmetic mean* (see definition of *arithmetic mean* above) unless stated otherwise.

Performance: A measure of the overall quality of data reported by a laboratory.

Pools: Groups of quality-control samples to be established for each target value (defined below) of an analyte. For the protocol provided in attachment 3, for example, the theoretical value of the quality control samples of the pool must be within a range defined as plus or minus (±) 50% of the target value. Within each analyte pool, there must be quality control samples of at least 4 theoretical values.

Precision: The extent of agreement between repeated, independent measurements of the same quantity of an analyte.

Proficiency: The ability to satisfy a specified level of analyte performance.

Proficiency Samples: Specimens, the values of which are unknown to anyone at a participating laboratory, and which are submitted by a participating laboratory for proficiency testing.

Quality or Data Quality: A measure of the confidence in the measurement value.

Quality Control (QC) Samples: Specimens, the value of which is unknown to the analyst, but is known to the appropriate QA/QC personnel of a participating laboratory; when used as part of a laboratory QA/QC program, the theoretical values of these samples should not be known to the analyst until the analyses are complete. QC samples are to be run in sets consisting of one QC sample from each pool (see definition of "pools" above).

Sensitivity: For the purposes of this protocol, the limit of detection.

Standard Deviation: A measure of the distribution or spread of a data set about the mean; the standard deviation is equal to the positive square root of the variance, and is expressed in the same units as the original measurements in the data set.

Standards: Samples with values known by the analyst and used to calibrate equipment and to check calibration throughout an analytic run. In a laboratory QA/QC program, the values of the standards must exceed the values obtained for compliance samples such that the lowest standard value is near the limit of detection and the highest standard is higher than the highest compliance sample or QC sample. Standards of at least three different values are to be used for calibration, and should be constructed from at least 2 different sources.

Target Value: Those values of CDB, CDU or B2MU which trigger some action as prescribed in the medical surveillance section of the regulatory text of the final cadmium rule. For CDB, the target values are 5, 10 and 15 µg/l. For CDU, the target values are 3, 7, and 15 µg/g CRTU. For B_2 MU, the target values are 300, 750 and 1500 µg/g CRTU. (Note that target values may vary as a function of time.)

Theoretical Value (or Theoretical Amount): The reported concentration of a quality-control sample (or calibration standard) derived from prior characterizations of the sample.

Value or Measurement Value: The numerical result of a measurement.

Variance: A measure of the distribution or spread of a data set about the mean; the variance is the sum of the squares of the differences between the mean and each discrete measurement divided by one less than the number of measurements in the data set.

3.0 Protocol

This protocol provides procedures for characterizing and maintaining the quality of analytic results derived for the medical monitoring program mandated for workers under the final cadmium rule.

3.1 Overview

The goal of this protocol is to assure that medical monitoring data are of sufficient quality to facilitate proper interpretation. The data quality objectives (DQOs) defined for the medical monitoring program are summarized in Table 1. Based on available information, the DQOs presented in Table 1 should be achievable by the majority of laboratories offering the required analyses commercially; OSHA recommends that only laboratories meeting these DQOs be used for the analysis of biological samples collected for monitoring cadmium exposure.

TABLE 1—RECOMMENDED DATA QUALITY OBJECTIVES (DQOS) FOR THE CADMIUM MEDICAL MONITORING PROGRAM

Analyte/concentration pool	Limit of detection	Precision (CV) (%)	Accuracy
Cadmium in blood	0.5 µg/l	....	±1 µg/l or 15% of the mean.
≤2 µg/l	....	40	
>2µg/l	....	20	
Cadmium in urine	0.5 µg/g creatinine	....	±1 µg/l or 15% of the mean.
≤2 µg/l creatinine	....	40	
>2µg/l creatinine	....	20	
β-2-microglobulin in urine: 100 µg/g creatine.	100 µg/g creatinine	5	±15% of the mean.

To satisfy the DQOs presented in Table 1, OSHA provides the following guidelines:

1. Procedures for the collection and handling of blood and urine are specified (Section 3.4.1 of this protocol);

2. Preferred analytic methods for the analysis of CDB, CDU and B2MU are defined (and a method for the determination of CRTU also is specified since CDU and B2MU results are to be normalized to the level of CRTU).

3. Procedures are described for identifying laboratories likely to provide the required analyses in an accurate and reliable manner;

4. These guidelines (Sections 3.2.1 to 3.2.3, and Section 3.3) include recommendations regarding internal QA/QC programs for participating laboratories, as well as levels of proficiency through participation in an interlaboratory proficiency program;

5. Procedures for QA/QC record keeping (Section 3.3.2), and for reporting QC/QA results are described (Section 3.3.3); and,

6. Procedures for interpreting medical monitoring results are specified (Section 3.4.3).

Methods recommended for the biological monitoring of eligible workers are:

1. The method of Stoeppler and Brandt (1980) for CDB determinations (limit of detection: 0.5 µg/l);

2. The method of Pruszkowska et al. (1983) for CDU determinations (limit of detection: 0.5 µg/l of urine); and,

3. The Pharmacia Delphia test kit (Pharmacia 1990) for the determination of B2MU (limit of detection: 100 µg/l urine).

Because both CDU and B2MU should be reported in µg/g CRTU, an independent determination of CRTU is recommended. Thus, both the OSHA Salt Lake City Technical Center (OSLTC) method (OSHA, no date) and the Jaffe method (Du Pont, no date) for the determination of CRTU are specified under

this protocol (i.e., either of these 2 methods may be used). Note that although detection limits are not reported for either of these CRTU methods, the range of measurements expected for CRTU (0.9-1.7 µg/l) are well above the likely limit of detection for either of these methods (Harrison, 1987).

Laboratories using alternate methods should submit sufficient data to the responsible physicians demonstrating that the alternate method is capable of satisfying the defined data quality objectives of the program. Such laboratories also should submit a QA/QC plan that documents the performance of the alternate method in a manner entirely equivalent to the QA/QC plans proposed in Section 3.3.1.

3.2 Duties of the Responsible Physician

The responsible physician will evaluate biological monitoring results provided by participating laboratories to determine whether such laboratories are proficient and have satisfied the QA/QC recommendations. In determining which laboratories to employ for this purpose, these physicians should review proficiency and QA/QC data submitted to them by the participating laboratories.

Participating laboratories should demonstrate proficiency for each analyte (CDU, CDB and B2MU) sampled under the biological monitoring program. Participating laboratories involved in analyzing CDU and B2MU also should demonstrate proficiency for CRTU analysis, or provide evidence of a contract with a laboratory proficient in CRTU analysis.

3.2.1 Recommendations for Selecting Among Existing Laboratories

OSHA recommends that existing laboratories providing commercial analyses for

221

CDB, CDU and/or B2MU for the medical monitoring program satisfy the following criteria:

1. Should have performed commercial analyses for the appropriate analyte (CDB, CDU and/or B2MU) on a regular basis over the last 2 years;

2. Should provide the responsible physician with an internal QA/QC plan;

3. If performing CDU or B2MU analyses, the participating laboratory should be accredited by the CAP for CRTU analysis, and should be enrolled in the corresponding CAP survey (note that alternate credentials may be acceptable, but acceptability is to be determined by the responsible physician); and,

4. Should have enrolled in the CTQ interlaboratory comparison program for the appropriate analyte (CDB, CDU and/or B2MU).

Participating laboratories should submit appropriate documentation demonstrating compliance with the above criteria to the responsible physician. To demonstrate compliance with the first of the above criteria, participating laboratories should submit the following documentation for each analyte they plan to analyze (note that each document should cover a period of at least 8 consecutive quarters, and that the period designated by the term "regular analyses" is at least once a quarter):

1. Copies of laboratory reports providing results from regular analyses of the appropriate analyte (CDB, CDU and/or B2MU);

2. Copies of 1 or more signed and executed contracts for the provision of regular analyses of the appropriate analyte (CDB, CDU and/or B2MU); or,

3. Copies of invoices sent to 1 or more clients requesting payment for the provision of regular analyses of the appropriate analyte (CDB, CDU and/or B2MU). Whatever the form of documentation submitted, the specific analytic procedures conducted should be identified directly. The forms that are copied for submission to the responsible physician also should identify the laboratory which provided these analyses.

To demonstrate compliance with the second of the above criteria, a laboratory should submit to the responsible physician an internal QA/QC plan detailing the standard operating procedures to be adopted for satisfying the recommended QA/QC procedures for the analysis of each specific analyte (CDB, CDU and/or B2MU). Procedures for internal QA/QC programs are detailed in Section 3.3.1 below.

To satisfy the third of the above criteria, laboratories analyzing for CDU or B2MU also should submit a QA/QC plan for creatinine analysis (CRTU); the QA/QC plan and characterization analyses for CRTU must come from the laboratory performing the CRTU analysis, even if the CRTU analysis is being performed by a contract laboratory.

Laboratories enrolling in the CTQ program (to satisfy the last of the above criteria) must remit, with the enrollment application, an initial fee of approximately $100 per analyte. (Note that this fee is only an estimate, and is subject to revision without notice.) Laboratories should indicate on the application that they agree to have proficiency test results sent by the CTQ directly to the physicians designated by participating laboratories.

Once a laboratory's application is processed by the CTQ, the laboratory will be assigned a code number which will be provided to the laboratory on the initial confirmation form, along with identification of the specific analytes for which the laboratory is participating. Confirmation of participation will be sent by the CTQ to physicians designated by the applicant laboratory.

3.2.2 Recommended Review of Laboratories Selected To Perform Analyses

Six months after being selected initially to perform analyte determinations, the status of participating laboratories should be reviewed by the responsible physicians. Such reviews should then be repeated every 6 months or whenever additional proficiency or QA/QC documentation is received (whichever occurs first).

As soon as the responsible physician has received the CTQ results from the first 3 rounds of proficiency testing (i.e., 3 sets of 3 samples each for CDB, CDU and/or B2MU) for a participating laboratory, the status of the laboratory's continued participation should be reviewed. Over the same initial 6-month period, participating laboratories also should provide responsible physicians the results of their internal QA/QC monitoring program used to assess performance for each analyte (CDB, CDU and/or B2MU) for which the laboratory performs determinations. This information should be submitted using appropriate forms and documentation.

The status of each participating laboratory should be determined for each analyte (i.e., whether the laboratory satisfies minimum proficiency guidelines based on the proficiency samples sent by the CTQ and the results of the laboratory's internal QA/QC program). To maintain competency for analysis of CDB, CDU and/or B2MU during the first review, the laboratory should satisfy performance requirements for at least 2 of the 3 proficiency samples provided in each of the 3 rounds completed over the 6-month period. Proficiency should be maintained for the analyte(s) for which the laboratory conducts determinations.

To continue participation for CDU and/or B2MU analyse, laboratories also should either maintain accreditation for CRTU analysis in the CAP program and participate in the CAP surveys, or they should contract the CDU and B2MU analyses to a laboratory which satisfies these requirements (or which can provide documentation of accreditation/ participation in an equivalent program).

The performance requirement for CDB analysis is defined as an analytical result within ±1 μg/l blood or 15% of the consensus mean (whichever is greater). For samples exhibiting a consensus mean less than 1 μg/l, the performance requirement is defined as a concentration between the detection limit of the analysis and a maximum of 2 μg/l. The purpose for redefining the acceptable interval for low CDB values is to encourage proper reporting of the actual values obtained during measurement; laboratories, therefore, will not be penalized (in terms of a narrow range of acceptability) for reporting measured concentrations smaller than 1 μg/l.

The performance requirement for CDU analysis is defined as an analytical result within ±1 μg/l urine or 15% of the consensus mean (whichever is greater). For samples exhibiting a consensus mean less than 1 μg/l urine, the performance requirement is defined as a concentration between the detection limit of the analysis and a maximum of 2 μg/l urine. Laboratories also should demonstrate proficiency in creatinine analysis as defined by the CAP. Note that reporting CDU results, other than for the CTQ proficiency samples (*i.e.*, compliance samples), should be accompanied with results of analyses for CRTU, and these 2 sets of results should be combined to provide a measure of CDU in units of μg/g CRTU.

The performance requirement for B2MU is defined as analytical results within ±15% of the consensus mean. Note that reporting B2MU results, other than for CTQ proficiency samples (*i.e.*, compliance samples), should be accompanied with results of analyses for CRTU, and these 2 sets of results should be combined to provide a measure of B2MU in units of μg/g CRTU.

There are no recommended performance checks for CRTU analyses. As stated previously, laboratories performing CRTU analysis in support of CDU or B2MU analyses should be accredited by the CAP, and participating in the CAP's survey for CRTU.

Following the first review, the status of each participating laboratory should be re-evaluated at regular intervals (*i.e.*, corresponding to receipt of results from each succeeding round of proficiency testing and submission of reports from a participating laboratory's internal QA/QC program).

After a year of collecting proficiency test results, the following proficiency criterion should be added to the set of criteria used to determine the participating laboratory's status (for analyzing CDB, CDU and/or B2MU): A participating laboratory should not fail performance requirements for more than 4 samples from the 6 most recent consecutive rounds used to assess proficiency for CDB, CDU and/or B2MU separately (*i.e.*, a total of

18 discrete proficiency samples for each analyte). Note that this requirement does not replace, but supplements, the recommendation that a laboratory should satisfy the performance criteria for at least 2 of the 3 samples tested for each round of the program.

3.2.3 Recommendations for Selecting Among Newly-Formed Laboratories (or Laboratories That Previously Failed To Meet the Protocol Guidelines)

OSHA recommends that laboratories that have not previously provided commercial analyses of CDB, CDU and/or B2MU (or have done so for a period less than 2 years), or which have provided these analyses for 2 or more years but have not conformed previously with these protocol guidelines, should satisfy the following provisions for each analyte for which determinations are to be made prior to being selected to analyze biological samples under the medical monitoring program:

1. Submit to the responsible physician an internal QA/QC plan detailing the standard operating procedures to be adopted for satisfying the QA/QC guidelines (guidelines for internal QA/QC programs are detailed in Section 3.3.1);

2. Submit to the responsible physician the results of the initial characterization analyses for each analyte for which determinations are to be made;

3. Submit to the responsible physician the results, for the initial 6-month period, of the internal QA/QC program for each analyte for which determinations are to be made (if no commercial analyses have been conducted previously, a minimum of 2 mock standardization trials for each analyte should be completed per month for a 6-month period);

4. Enroll in the CTQ program for the appropriate analyte for which determinations are to be made, and arrange to have the CTQ program submit the initial confirmation of participation and proficiency test results directly to the designated physicians. Note that the designated physician should receive results from 3 completed rounds from the CTQ program before approving a laboratory for participation in the biological monitoring program;

5. Laboratories seeking participation for CDU and/or B2MU analyses should submit to the responsible physician documentation of accreditation by the CAP for CRTU analyses performed in conjunction with CDU and/or B2MU determinations (if CRTU analyses are conducted by a contract laboratory, this laboratory should submit proof of CAP accreditation to the responsible physician); and,

6. Documentation should be submitted on an appropriate form.

To participate in CDB, CDU and/or B2MU analyses, the laboratory should satisfy the above criteria for a minimum of 2 of the 3 proficiency samples provided in each of the 3 rounds of the CTQ program over a 6-month period; this procedure should be completed for each appropriate analyte. Proficiency should be maintained for each analyte to continue participation. Note that laboratories seeking participation for CDU or B2MU also should address the performance requirements for CRTU, which involves providing evidence of accreditation by the CAP and participation in the CAP surveys (or an equivalent program).

The performance requirement for CDB analysis is defined as an analytical result within ±1 µg/l or 15% of the consensus mean (whichever is greater). For samples exhibiting a consensus mean less than 1 µg/l, the performance requirement is defined as a concentration between the detection limit of the analysis and a maximum of 2 µg/l. The purpose of redefining the acceptable interval for low CDB values is to encourage proper reporting of the actual values obtained during measurement; laboratories, therefore, will not be penalized (in terms of a narrow range of acceptability) for reporting measured concentrations less than 1 µg/l.

The performance requirement for CDU analysis is defined as an analytical result within ±1 µg/l urine or 15% of the consensus mean (whichever is greater). For samples exhibiting a consensus mean less than 1 µg/l urine, the performance requirement is defined as a concentration that falls between the detection limit of the analysis and a maximum of 2 µg/l urine. Performance requirements for the companion CRTU analysis (defined by the CAP) also should be met. Note that reporting CDU results, other than for CTQ proficiency testing should be accompanied with results of CRTU analyses, and these 2 sets of results should be combined to provide a measure of CDU in units of µg/g CRTU.

The performance requirement for B2MU is defined as an analytical result within ±15% of the consensus mean. Note that reporting B2MU results, other than for CTQ proficiency testing should be accompanied with results of CRTU analysis, these 2 sets of results should be combined to provide a measure of B2MU in units of µg/g CRTU.

Once a new laboratory has been approved by the responsible physician for conducting analyte determinations, the status of this approval should be reviewed periodically by the responsible physician as per the criteria presented under Section 3.2.2.

Laboratories which have failed previously to gain approval of the responsible physician for conducting determinations of 1 or more analytes due to lack of compliance with the criteria defined above for existing laboratories (Section 3.2.1), may obtain approval by satisfying the criteria for newly-formed laboratories defined under this section; for these laboratories, the second of the above criteria may be satisfied by submitting a new set of characterization analyses for each analyte for which determinations are to be made.

Reevaluation of these laboratories is discretionary on the part of the responsible physician. Reevaluation, which normally takes about 6 months, may be expedited if the laboratory can achieve 100% compliance with the proficiency test criteria using the 6 samples of each analyte submitted to the CTQ program during the first 2 rounds of proficiency testing.

For laboratories seeking reevaluation for CDU or B2MU analysis, the guidelines for CRTU analyses also should be satisfied, including accreditation for CRTU analysis by the CAP, and participation in the CAP survey program (or accreditation/participation in an equivalent program).

3.2.4 Future Modifications to the Protocol Guidelines

As participating laboratories gain experience with analyses for CDB, CDU and B2MU, it is anticipated that the performance achievable by the majority of laboratories should improve until it approaches that reported by the research groups which developed each method. OSHA, therefore, may choose to recommend stricter performance guidelines in the future as the overall performance of participating laboratories improves.

3.3 Guidelines for Record Keeping and Reporting

To comply with these guidelines, participating laboratories should satisfy the above-stated performance and proficiency recommendations, as well as the following internal QA/QC, record keeping, and reporting provisions.

If a participating laboratory fails to meet the provisions of these guidelines, it is recommended that the responsible physician disapprove further analyses of biological samples by that laboratory until it demonstrates compliance with these guidelines. On disapproval, biological samples should be sent to a laboratory that can demonstrate compliance with these guidelines, at least until the former laboratory is reevaluated by the responsible physician and found to be in compliance.

The following record keeping and reporting procedures should be practiced by participating laboratories.

3.3.1 Internal Quality Assurance/Quality Control Procedures

Laboratories participating in the cadmium monitoring program should develop and maintain an internal quality assurance/quality control (QA/QC) program that incorporates procedures for establishing and maintaining control for each of the analytic procedures (determinations of CDB, CDU and/or B2MU) for which the laboratory is seeking participation. For laboratories analyzing CDU and/or B2MU, a QA/QC program for CRTU also should be established.

Written documentation of QA/QC procedures should be described in a formal QA/QC plan; this plan should contain the following information: Sample acceptance and handling procedures (*i.e.*, chain-of-custody); sample preparation procedures; instrument parameters; calibration procedures; and, calculations. Documentation of QA/QC procedures should be sufficient to identify analytical problems, define criteria under which analysis of compliance samples will be suspended, and describe procedures for corrective actions.

3.3.1.1 *QA/QC procedures for establishing control of CDB and CDU analyses*

The QA/QC program for CDB and CDU should address, at a minimum, procedures involved in calibration, establishment of control limits, internal QC analyses and maintaining control, and corrective-action protocols. Participating laboratory should develop and maintain procedures to assure that analyses of compliance samples are within control limits, and that these procedures are documented thoroughly in a QA/QC plan.

A nonmandatory QA/QC protocol is presented in Attachment 1. This attachment is illustrative of the procedures that should be addressed in a proper QA/QC program.

Calibration. Before any analytic runs are conducted, the analytic instrument should be calibrated. Calibration should be performed at the beginning of each day on which QC and/or compliance samples are run. Once calibration is established, QC or compliance samples may be run. Regardless of the type of samples run, about every fifth sample should serve as a standard to assure that calibration is being maintained.

Calibration is being maintained if the standard is within ±15% of its theoretical value. If a standard is more than ±15% of its theoretical value, the run has exceeded control limits due to calibration error; the entire set of samples then should be reanalyzed after recalibrating or the results should be recalculated based on a statistical curve derived from that set of standards.

It is essential that the value of the highest standard analyzed be higher than the highest sample analyzed; it may be necessary, therefore, to run a high standard at the end of the run, which has been selected based on results obtained over the course of the run (*i.e.*, higher than any standard analyzed to that point).

Standards should be kept fresh; as samples age, they should be compared with new standards and replaced if necessary.

Internal Quality Control Analyses. Internal QC samples should be determined interspersed with analyses of compliance samples. At a minimum, these samples should be run at a rate of 5% of the compliance samples or at least one set of QC samples per analysis of compliance samples, whichever is greater. If only 2 samples are run, they should contain different levels of cadmium.

Internal QC samples may be obtained as commercially-available reference materials and/or they may be internally prepared. Internally-prepared samples should be well characterized and traced, or compared to a reference material for which a consensus value is available.

Levels of cadmium contained in QC samples should not be known to the analyst prior to reporting the results of the analysis.

Internal QC results should be plotted or charted in a manner which describes sample recovery and laboratory control limits.

Internal Control Limits. The laboratory protocol for evaluating internal QC analyses per control limits should be clearly defined. Limits may be based on statistical methods (e.g., as $2\hat{\sigma}$ from the laboratory mean recovery), or on proficiency testing limits (e.g.,±1µg or 15% of the mean, whichever is greater). Statistical limits that exceed ±40% should be reevaluated to determine the source error in the analysis.

When laboratory limits are exceeded, analytic work should terminate until the source of error is determined and corrected; compliance samples affected by the error should be reanalyzed. In addition, the laboratory protocol should address any unusual trends that develop which may be biasing the results. Numerous, consecutive results above or below laboratory mean recoveries, or outside laboratory statistical limits, indicate that problems may have developed.

Corrective Actions. The QA/QC plan should document in detail specific actions taken if control limits are exceeded or unusual trends develop. Corrective actions should be noted on an appropriate form, accompanied by supporting documentation.

In addition to these actions, laboratories should include whatever additional actions are necessary to assure that accurate data are reported to the responsible physicians.

Reference Materials. The following reference materials may be available:

Cadmium in Blood (CDB)

1. Centre de Toxicologie du Quebec, Le Centre Hospitalier de l'Universite Laval, 2705 boul. Laurier, Quebec, Que., Canada G1V 4G2. (Prepared 6 times per year at 1–15 µg Cd/l.)

2. H. Marchandise, Community Bureau of Reference-BCR, Directorate General XII, Commission of the European Communities, 200, rue de la Loi, B–1049, Brussels, Belgium. (Prepared as Bl CBM–1 at 5.37 µg Cd/l, and Bl CBM–2 at 12.38 µg Cd/l.)

3. Kaulson Laboratories Inc., 691 Bloomfield Ave., Caldwell, NJ 07006; tel: (201) 226-9494, FAX (201) 226-3244. (Prepared as #0141 [As, Cd, Hg, Pb] at 2 levels.)

Cadmium in Urine (CDU)

1. Centre de Toxicologie du Quebec, Le Centre Hospitalier de l'Universite Laval, 2705 boul. Laurier, Quebec, Que., Canada G1V 4G2. (Prepared 6 times per year.)

2. National Institute of Standards and Technology (NIST), Dept. of Commerce, Gaithersburg, MD; tel: (301) 975-6776. (Prepared as SRM 2670 freeze-dried urine [metals]; set includes normal and elevated levels of metals; cadmium is certified for elevated level of 88.0 µg/l in reconstituted urine.)

3. Kaulson Laboratories Inc., 691 Bloomfield Ave., Caldwell, NJ 07006; tel: (201) 226-9494, FAX (201) 226-3244. (Prepared as #0140 [As, Cd, Hg, Pb] at 2 levels.)

3.3.1.2 *QA/QC procedures for establishing control of B2MU*

A written, detailed QA/QC plan for B2MU analysis should be developed. The QA/QC plan should contain a protocol similar to those protocols developed for the CDB/CDU analyses. Differences in analyses may warrant some differences in the QA/QC protocol, but procedures to ensure analytical integrity should be developed and followed.

Examples of performance summaries that can be provided include measurements of accuracy (*i.e.*, the means of measured values versus target values for the control samples) and precision (*i.e.*, based on duplicate analyses). It is recommended that the accuracy and precision measurements be compared to those reported as achievable by the Pharmacia Delphia kit (Pharmacia 1990) to determine if and when unsatisfactory analyses have arisen. If the measurement error of 1 or more of the control samples is more than 15%, the run exceeds control limits. Similarly, this decision is warranted when the average CV for duplicate samples is greater than 5%.

3.3.2 Procedures for Record Keeping

To satisfy reporting requirements for commercial analyses of CDB, CDU and/or B2MU performed for the medical monitoring program mandated under the cadmium rule, participating laboratories should maintain the following documentation for each analyte:

1. For each analytic instrument on which analyte determinations are made, records relating to the most recent calibration and QC sample analyses;

2. For these instruments, a tabulated record for each analyte of those determinations found to be within and outside of control limits over the past 2 years;

3. Results for the previous 2 years of the QC sample analyses conducted under the internal QA/QC program (this information should be: Provided for each analyte for which determinations are made and for each analytic instrument used for this purpose, sufficient to demonstrate that internal QA/QC programs are being executed properly, and consistent with data sent to responsible physicians.

4. Duplicate copies of monitoring results for each analyte sent to clients during the previous 5 years, as well as associated information; supporting material such as chain-of-custody forms also should be retained; and,

5. Proficiency test results and related materials received while participating in the CTQ interlaboratory program over the past 2 years; results also should be tabulated to provide a serial record of relative error (derived per Section 3.3.3 below).

3.3.3 Reporting Procedures

Participating laboratories should maintain these documents: QA/QC program plans; QA/QC status reports; CTQ proficiency program reports; and, analytical data reports. The information that should be included in these reports is summarized in Table 2; a copy of each report should be sent to the responsible physician.

TABLE 2—REPORTING PROCEDURES FOR LABORATORIES PARTICIPATING IN THE CADMIUM MEDICAL MONITORING PROGRAM

Report	Frequency (time frame)	Contents
1 QA/QC Program Plan	Once (initially)	A detailed description of the QA/QC protocol to be established by the laboratory to maintain control of analyte determinations.
2 QA/QC Status Report	Every 2 months	Results of the QC samples incorporated into regular runs for each instrument (over the period since the last report).
3 Proficiency Report	Attached to every data report	Results from the last full year of proficiency samples submitted to the CTQ program and Results of the 100 most recent QC samples incorporated into regular runs for each instrument.
4 Analytical Data Report	For all reports of data results ..	Date the sample was received; Date the sample was analyzed; Appropriate chain-of-custody information; Types of analyses performed; Results of the requested analyses and Copy of the most current proficiency report.

As noted in Section 3.3.1, a QA/QC program plan should be developed that documents internal QA/QC procedures (defined under Section 3.3.1) to be implemented by the participating laboratory for each analyte; this plan should provide a list identifying each instrument used in making analyte determinations.

A QA/QC status report should be written bimonthly for each analyte. In this report, the results of the QC program during the reporting period should be reported for each analyte in the following manner: The number (N) of QC samples analyzed during the period; a table of the target levels defined for each sample and the corresponding measured values; the mean of F/T value (as defined below) for the set of QC samples run during the period; and, use of $\bar{X} \pm 2\hat{\sigma}$ (as defined below) for the set of QC samples run during the period as a measure of precision.

As noted in Section 2, an F/T value for a QC sample is the ratio of the measured concentration of analyte to the established (i.e., reference) concentration of analyte for that QC sample. The equation below describes the derivation of the mean for F/T values, X, (with N being the total number of samples analyzed):

$$\bar{X} = \frac{\sum (F/T)}{N}$$

The standard deviation, $\hat{\sigma}$, for these measurements is derived using the following equation (note that $2\hat{\sigma}$ is twice this value):

$$\hat{\sigma} = \left[\frac{\sum (F/T - \bar{X})^2}{N-1} \right]^{\frac{1}{2}}$$

The nonmandatory QA/QC protocol (see Attachment 1) indicates that QC samples should be divided into several discrete pools, and a separate estimate of precision for each pools then should be derived. Several precision estimates should be provided for concentrations which differ in average value. These precision measures may be used to document improvements in performance with regard to the combined pool.

Participating laboratories should use the CTQ proficiency program for each analyte. Results of the this program will be sent by CTQ directly to physicians designated by the participating laboratories. Proficiency results from the CTQ program are used to establish the accuracy of results from each participating laboratory, and should be provided to responsible physicians for use in trend analysis. A proficiency report consisting of these proficiency results should accompany data reports as an attachment.

For each analyte, the proficiency report should include the results from the 6 previous proficiency rounds in the following format:

1. Number (N) of samples analyzed;
2. Mean of the target levels, $(1/N)\Sigma_i$, with T_i being a consensus mean for the sample;
3. Mean of the measurements, $(1/N)\Sigma_i$, with M_i being a sample measurement;
4. A measure of error defined by:

$$(1/N)\Sigma(T_i - M_i)^2$$

Analytical data reports should be submitted to responsible physicians directly. For each sample, report the following information: The date the sample was received; the date the sample was analyzed; appropriate chain-of-custody information; the type(s) of analyses performed; and, the results of the analyses. This information should be reported on a form similar to the form provided an appropriate form. The most recent proficiency program report should accompany the analytical data reports (as an attachment).

Confidence intervals for the analytical results should be reported as $X \pm 2\hat{\sigma}$, with X being the measured value and $2\hat{\sigma}$ the standard deviation calculated as described above.

For CDU or B2MU results, which are combined with CRTU measurements for proper reporting, the 95% confidence limits are derived from the limits for CDU or B2MU, (p), and the limits for CRTU, (q), as follows:

$$\frac{X}{Y} \pm \left(\frac{1}{Y^2} \right) \left(Y^2 \times p^2 + X^2 \times q^2 \right)^{\frac{1}{2}}$$

For these calculations, X ±p is the measurement and confidence limits for CDU or B2MU, and Y ±q is the measurement and confidence limit for CRTU.

Participating laboratories should notify responsible physicians as soon as they receive information indicating a change in their accreditation status with the CTQ or the CAP. These physicians should not be expected to wait until formal notice of a status change has been received from the CTQ or the CAP.

3.4 Instructions to Physicians

Physicians responsible for the medical monitoring of cadmium-exposed workers must collect the biological samples from workers; they then should select laboratories to perform the required analyses, and should interpret the analytic results.

3.4.1 Sample Collection and Holding Procedures

Blood Samples. The following procedures are recommended for the collection, shipment and storage of blood samples for CDB analysis to reduce analytical variablility;

these recommendations were obtained primarily through personal communications with J.P. Weber of the CTQ (1991), and from reports by the Centers for Disease Control (CDC, 1986) and Stoeppler and Brandt (1980). To the extent possible, blood samples should be collected from workers at the same time of day. Workers should shower or thoroughly wash their hands and arms before blood samples are drawn. The following materials are needed for blood sample collection: Alcohol wipes; sterile gauze sponges; band-aids; 20-gauge, 1.5-in. stainless steel needles (sterile); preprinted labels; tourniquets; vacutainer holders; 3-ml "metal free" vacutainer tubes (i.e., dark-blue caps), with EDTA as an anti-coagulant; and, styrofoam vacutainer shipping containers.

Whole blood samples are taken by venipuncture. Each blue-capped tube should be labeled or coded for the worker and company before the sample is drawn. (Blue-capped tubes are recommended instead of red-capped tubes because the latter may consist of red coloring pigment containing cadmium, which could contaminate the samples.) Immediately after sampling, the vacutainer tubes must be thoroughly mixed by inverting the tubes at least 10 times manually or mechanically using a Vortex device (for 15 sec). Samples should be refrigerated immediately or stored on ice until they can be packed for shipment to the participating laboratory for analysis.

The CDC recommends that blood samples be shipped with a "cool pak" to keep the samples cold during shipment. However, the CTQ routinely ships and receives blood samples for cadmium analysis that have not been kept cool during shipment. The CTQ has found no deterioration of cadmium in biological fluids that were shipped via parcel post without a cooling agent, even though these deliveries often take 2 weeks to reach their destination.

Urine Samples. The following are recommended procedures for the collection, shipment and storage of urine for CDU and B2MU analyses, and were obtained primarily through personal communications with J.P. Weber of the CTQ (1991), and from reports by the CDC (1986) and Stoeppler and Brandt (1980).

Single "spot" samples are recommended. As B2M can degrade in the bladder, workers should first empty their bladder and then drink a large glass of water at the start of the visit. Urine samples then should be collected within 1 hour. Separate samples should be collected for CDU and B2MU using the following materials: Sterile urine collection cups (250 ml); small sealable plastic bags; preprinted labels; 15-ml polypropylene or polyethylene screw-cap tubes; lab gloves ("metal free"); and, preservatives (as indicated).

The sealed collection cup should be kept in the plastic bag until collection time. The workers should wash their hands with soap and water before receiving the collection cup. The collection cup should not be opened until just before voiding and the cup should be sealed immediately after filling. It is important that the inside of the container and cap are not touched by, or come into contact with, the body, clothing or other surfaces.

For CDU analyzes, the cup is swirled gently to resuspend any solids, and the 15-ml tube is filled with 10-12 ml urine. The CDC recommends the addition of 100 μl concentrated HNO_3 as a preservative before sealing the tube and then freezing the sample. The CTQ recommends minimal handling and does not acidify their interlaboratory urine reference materials prior to shipment, nor do they freeze the sample for shipment. At the CTQ, if the urine sample has much sediment, the sample is acidified in the lab to free any cadmium in the precipitate.

For B2M, the urine sample should be collected directly into a polyethylene bottle previously washed with dilute nitric acid. The pH of the urine should be measured and adjusted to 8.0 with 0.1 N NaOH immediately following collection. Samples should be frozen and stored at -20 °C until testing is performed. The B2M in the samples should be stable for 2 days when stored at 2-8 °C, and for at least 2 months at -20 °C. Repeated freezing and thawing should be avoided to prevent denaturing the B2M (Pharmacia 1990).

3.4.2   Recommendations for Evaluating Laboratories

Using standard error data and the results of proficiency testing obtained from CTQ, responsible physicians can make an informed choice of which laboratory to select to analyze biological samples. In general, laboratories with small standard errors and little disparity between target and measured values tend to make precise and accurate sample determinations. Estimates of precision provided to the physicians with each set of monitoring results can be compared to previously-reported proficiency and precision estimates. The latest precision estimates should be at least as small as the standard error reported previously by the laboratory. Moreover, there should be no indication that precision is deteriorating (i.e., increasing values for the precision estimates). If precision is deteriorating, physicians may decide to use another laboratory for these analyses. QA/QC information provided by the participating laboratories to physicians can, therefore, assist physicians in evaluating laboratory performance.

3.4.3 Use and Interpretation of Results

When the responsible physician has received the CDB, CDU and/or B2MU results, these results must be compared to the action levels discussed in the final rule for cadmium. The comparison of the sample results to action levels is straightforward. The measured value reported from the laboratory can be compared directly to the action levels; if the reported value exceeds an action level, the required actions must be initiated.

4.0 Background

Cadmium is a naturally-occurring environmental contaminant to which humans are continually exposed in food, water, and air. The average daily intake of cadmium by the U.S. population is estimated to be 10–20 µg/day. Most of this intake is via ingestion, for which absorption is estimated at 4–7% (Kowal et al. 1979). An additional nonoccupational source of cadmium is smoking tobacco; smoking a pack of cigarettes a day adds an additional 2–4 µg cadmium to the daily intake, assuming absorption via inhalation of 25–35% (Nordberg and Nordberg 1988; Friberg and Elinder 1988; Travis and Haddock 1980).

Exposure to cadmium fumes and dusts in an occupational setting where air concentrations are 20–50 µg/m³ results in an additional daily intake of several hundred micrograms (Friberg and Elinder 1988, p. 563). In such a setting, occupational exposure to cadmium occurs primarily via inhalation, although additional exposure may occur through the ingestion of material via contaminated hands if workers eat or smoke without first washing. Some of the particles that are inhaled initially may be ingested when the material is deposited in the upper respiratory tract, where it may be cleared by mucociliary transport and subsequently swallowed.

Cadmium introduced into the body through inhalation or ingestion is transported by the albumin fraction of the blood plasma to the liver, where it accumulates and is stored principally as a bound form complexed with the protein metallothionein. Metallothionein-bound cadmium is the main form of cadmium subsequently transported to the kidney; it is these 2 organs, the liver and kidney, in which the majority of the cadmium body burden accumulates. As much as one half of the total body burden of cadmium may be found in the kidneys (Nordberg and Nordberg 1988).

Once cadmium has entered the body, elimination is slow; about 0.02% of the body burden is excreted per day via urinary/fecal elimination. The whole-body half-life of cadmium is 10–35 years, decreasing slightly with increasing age (Travis and Haddock 1980). The continual accumulation of cadmium is the basis for its chronic noncarcinogenic toxicity. This accumulation makes the kidney the target organ in which cadmium toxicity usually is first observed (Piscator 1964). Renal damage may occur when cadmium levels in the kidney cortex approach 200 µg/g wet tissue-weight (Travis and Haddock 1980).

The kinetics and internal distribution of cadmium in the body are complex, and depend on whether occupational exposure to cadmium is ongoing or has terminated. In general, cadmium in blood is related principally to recent cadmium exposure, while cadmium in urine reflects cumulative exposure (i.e., total body burden) (Lauwerys et al. 1976; Friberg and Elinder 1988).

4.1 Health Effects

Studies of workers in a variety of industries indicate that chronic exposure to cadmium may be linked to several adverse health effects including kidney dysfunction, reduced pulmonary function, chronic lung disease and cancer (FEDERAL REGISTER 1990). The primary sites for cadmium-associated cancer appear to be the lung and the prostate.

Cancer. Evidence for an association between cancer and cadmium exposure comes from both epidemiological studies and animal experiments. Pott (1965) found a statistically significant elevation in the incidence of prostate cancer among a cohort of cadmium workers. Other epidemiology studies also report an elevated incidence of prostate cancer; however, the increases observed in these other studies were not statistically significant (Meridian Research, Inc. 1989).

One study (Thun et al. 1985) contains sufficiently quantitative estimates of cadmium exposure to allow evaluation of dose-response relationships between cadmium exposure and lung cancer. A statistically significant excess of lung cancer attributed to cadmium exposure was found in this study, even after accounting for confounding variables such as coexposure to arsenic and smoking habits (Meridian Research, Inc. 1989).

Evidence for quantifying a link between lung cancer and cadmium exposure comes from a single study (Takenaka et al. 1983). In this study, dose-response relationships developed from animal data were extrapolated to humans using a variety of models. OSHA chose the multistage risk model for estimating the risk of cancer for humans using these animal data. Animal injection studies also suggest an association between cadmium exposure and cancer, particularly observations of an increased incidence of tumors at sites remote from the point of injection. The International Agency for Research on Cancer (IARC) (Supplement 7, 1987) indicates that this, and related, evidence is sufficient to classify cadmium as an animal carcinogen. However, the results of these injection studies cannot be used to quantify risks attendant to human occupational exposures due to differences in routes of exposure (Meridian Research, Inc. 1989).

Based on the above-cited studies, the U.S. Environmental Protection Agency (EPA) classifies cadmium as "B1," a probable human carcinogen (USEPA 1985). IARC in 1987 recommended that cadmium be listed as a probable human carcinogen.

Kidney Dysfunction. The most prevalent nonmalignant effect observed among workers chronically exposed to cadmium is kidney dysfunction. Initially, such dysfunction is manifested by proteinuria (Meridian Research, Inc. 1989; Roth Associates, Inc. 1989). Proteinuria associated with cadmium exposure is most commonly characterized by excretion of low-molecular weight proteins (15,000–40,000 MW), accompanied by loss of electrolytes, uric acid, calcium, amino acids, and phosphate. Proteins commonly excreted include β-2-microglobulin (B2M), retinol-binding protein (RBP), immunoglobulin light chains, and lysozyme. Excretion of low molecular weight proteins is characteristic of damage to the proximal tubules of the kidney (Iwao et al. 1980).

Exposure to cadmium also may lead to urinary excretion of high-molecular weight proteins such as albumin, immunoglobulin G, and glycoproteins (Meridian Research, Inc. 1989; Roth Associates, Inc. 1989). Excretion of high-molecular weight proteins is indicative of damage to the glomeruli of the kidney. Bernard et al. (1979) suggest that cadmium-associated damage to the glomeruli and damage to the proximal tubules of the kidney develop independently of each other, but may occur in the same individual.

Several studies indicate that the onset of low-molecular weight proteinuria is a sign of irreversible kidney damage (Friberg et al. 1974; Roels et al. 1982; Piscator 1984; Elinder et al. 1985; Smith et al. 1986). For many workers, once sufficiently elevated levels of B2M are observed in association with cadmium exposure, such levels do not appear to return to normal even when cadmium exposure is eliminated by removal of the worker from the cadmium-contaminated work environment (Friberg, exhibit 29, 1990).

Some studies indicate that cadmium-induced proteinuria may be progressive; levels of B2MU increase even after cadmium exposure has ceased (Elinder et al. 1985). Other researchers have reached similar conclusions (Frieburg testimony, OSHA docket exhibit 29, Elinder testimony, OSHA docket exhibit 55, and OSHA docket exhibits 8–86B). Such observations are not universal, however (Smith et al. 1986; Tsuchiya 1976). Studies in which proteinuria has not been observed, however, may have initiated the reassessment too early (Meridian Research, Inc.1989; Roth Associates, Inc. 1989; Roels 1989).

A quantitative assessment of the risks of developing kidney dysfunction as a result of cadmium exposure was performed using the data from Ellis et al. (1984) and Falck et al. (1983). Meridian Research, Inc. (1989) and Roth Associates, Inc. (1989) employed several mathematical models to evaluate the data from the 2 studies, and the results indicate that cumulative cadmium exposure levels between 5 and 100 μg-years/m³ correspond with a one-in-a-thousand probability of developing kidney dysfunction.

When cadmium exposure continues past the onset of early kidney damage (manifested as proteinuria), chronic nephrotoxicity may occur (Meridian Research, Inc. 1989; Roth Associates, Inc. 1989). Uremia, which is the loss of the glomerulus' ability to adequately filter blood, may result. This condition leads to severe disturbance of electrolyte concentrations, which may result in various clinical complications including atherosclerosis, hypertension, pericarditis, anemia, hemorrhagic tendencies, deficient cellular immunity, bone changes, and other problems. Progression of the disease may require dialysis or a kidney transplant.

Studies in which animals are chronically exposed to cadmium confirm the renal effects observed in humans (Friberg et al. 1986). Animal studies also confirm cadmium-related problems with calcium metabolism and associated skeletal effects, which also have been observed among humans. Other effects commonly reported in chronic animal studies include anemia, changes in liver morphology, immunosuppression and hypertension. Some of these effects may be associated with cofactors; hypertension, for example, appears to be associated with diet, as well as with cadmium exposure. Animals injected with cadmium also have shown testicular necrosis.

4.2 Objectives for Medical Monitoring

In keeping with the observation that renal disease tends to be the earliest clinical manifestation of cadmium toxicity, the final cadmium standard mandates that eligible workers must be medically monitored to prevent this condition (as well as cadmium-induced cancer). The objectives of medical-monitoring, therefore, are to: Identify workers at significant risk of adverse health effects from excess, chronic exposure to cadmium; prevent future cases of cadmium-induced disease; detect and minimize existing cadmium-induced disease; and, identify workers most in need of medical intervention.

The overall goal of the medical monitoring program is to protect workers who may be exposed continuously to cadmium over a 45-year occupational lifespan. Consistent with this goal, the medical monitoring program should assure that:

1. Current exposure levels remain sufficiently low to prevent the accumulation of cadmium body burdens sufficient to cause

disease in the future by monitoring CDB as an indicator of recent cadmium exposure;

2. Cumulative body burdens, especially among workers with undefined historical exposures, remain below levels potentially capable of leading to damage and disease by assessing CDU as an indicator of cumulative exposure to cadmium; and,

3. Health effects are not occurring among exposed workers by determining B2MU as an early indicator of the onset of cadmium-induced kidney disease.

4.3 Indicators of Cadmium Exposure and Disease

Cadmium is present in whole blood bound to albumin, in erythrocytes, and as a metallothionein-cadmium complex. The metallothionein-cadmium complex that represents the primary transport mechanism for cadmium delivery to the kidney. CDB concentrations in the general, nonexposed population average 1 µg Cd/l whole blood, with smokers exhibiting higher levels (see Section 5.1.6). Data presented in Section 5.1.6 shows that 95% of the general population not occupationally exposed to cadmium have CDB levels less than 5 µg Cd/l.

If total body burdens of cadmium remain low, CDB concentrations indicate recent exposure (i.e., daily intake). This conclusion is based on data showing that cigarette smokers exhibit CDB concentrations of 2–7 µg/l depending on the number of cigarettes smoked per day (Nordberg and Nordberg 1988), while CDB levels for those who quit smoking return to general population values (approximately 1 µg/l) within several weeks (Lauwerys et al. 1976). Based on these observations, Lauwerys et al. (1976) concluded that CDB has a biological half-life of a few weeks to less than 3 months. As indicated in Section 3.1.6, the upper 95th percentile for CDB levels observed among those who are not occupationally exposed to cadmium is 5 µg/l, which suggests that the absolute upper limit to the range reported for smokers by Nordberg and Nordberg may have been affected by an extreme value (i.e., beyond 2σ above the mean).

Among occupationally-exposed workers, the occupational history of exposure to cadmium must be evaluated to interpret CDB levels. New workers, or workers with low exposures to cadmium, exhibit CDB levels that are representative of recent exposures, similar to the general population. However, for workers with a history of chronic exposure to cadmium, who have accumulated significant stores of cadmium in the kidneys/liver, part of the CDB concentrations appear to indicate body burden. If such workers are removed from cadmium exposure, their CDB levels remain elevated, possibly for years, reflecting prior long-term accumulation of cadmium in body tissues. This condition tends to occur, however, only beyond some

threshold exposure value, and possibly indicates the capacity of body tissues to accumulate cadmium which cannot be excreted readily (Friberg and Elinder 1988; Nordberg and Nordberg 1988).

CDU is widely used as an indicator of cadmium body burdens (Nordberg and Nordberg 1988). CDU is the major route of elimination and, when CDU is measured, it is commonly expressed either as µg Cd/l urine (unadjusted), µg Cd/l urine (adjusted for specific gravity), or µg Cd/g CRTU (see Section 5.2.1). The metabolic model for CDU is less complicated than CDB, since CDU is dependentin large part on the body (i.e., kidney) burden of cadmium. However, a small proportion of CDU still be attributed to recent cadmium exposure, particularly if exposure to high airborne concentrations of cadmium occurred. Note that CDU is subject to larger interindividual and day-to-day variations than CDB, so repeated measurements are recommended for CDU evaluations.

CDU is bound principally to metallothionein, regardless of whether the cadmium originates from metallothionein in plasma or from the cadmium pool accumulated in the renal tubules. Therefore, measurement of metallothionein in urine may provide information similar to CDU, while avoiding the contamination problems that may occur during collection and handling urine for cadmium analysis (Nordberg and Nordberg 1988). However, a commercial method for the determination of metallothionein at the sensitivity levels required under the final cadmium rule is not currently available; therefore, analysis of CDU is recommended.

Among the general population not occupationally exposed to cadmium, CDU levels average less than 1 µg/l (see Section 5.2.7). Normalized for creatinine (CRTU), the average CDU concentration of the general population is less than 1 µg/g CRTU. As cadmium accumulates over the lifespan, CDU increases with age. Also, cigarette smokers may eventually accumulate twice the cadmium body burden of nonsmokers, CDU is slightly higher in smokers than in nonsmokers, even several years after smoking cessation (Nordberg and Nordberg 1988). Despite variations due to age and smoking habits, 95% of those not occupationally exposed to cadmium exhibit levels of CDU less than 3 µg/g CRTU (based on the data presented in Section 5.2.7).

About 0.02% of the cadmium body burden is excreted daily in urine. When the critical cadmium concentration (about 200 ppm) in the kidney is reached, or if there is sufficient cadmium-induced kidney dysfunction, dramatic increases in CDU are observed (Nordberg and Nordberg 1988). Above 200 ppm, therefore, CDU concentrations cease to be an indicator of cadmium body burden, and are instead an index of kidney failure.

231

Proteinuria is an index of kidney dysfunction, and is defined by OSHA to be a material impairment. Several small proteins may be monitored as markers for proteinuria. Below levels indicative of proteinuria, these small proteins may be early indicators of increased risk of cadmium-induced renal tubular disease. Analytes useful for monitoring cadmium-induced renal tubular damage include:

1. β-2-Microglobulin (B2M), currently the most widely used assay for detecting kidney dysfunction, is the best characterized analyte available (Iwao et al. 1980; Chia et al. 1989);

2. Retinol Binding Protein (RBP) is more stable than B2M in acidic urine (*i.e.*, B2M breakdown occurs if urinary pH is less than 5.5; such breakdown may result in false [i.e., low] B2M values [Bernard and Lauwerys, 1990]);

3. N-Acetyl-B-Glucosaminidase (NAG) is the analyte of an assay that is simple, inexpensive, reliable, and correlates with cadmium levels under 10 µg/g CRTU, but the assay is less sensitive than RBP or B2M (Kawada et al. 1989);

4. Metallothionein (MT) correlates with cadmium and B2M levels, and may be a better predictor of cadmium exposure than CDU and B2M (Kawada et al. 1989);

5. Tamm-Horsfall Glycoprotein (THG) increases slightly with elevated cadmium levels, but this elevation is small compared to increases in urinary albumin, RBP, or B2M (Bernard and Lauwerys 1990);

6. Albumin (ALB), determined by the biuret method, is not sufficiently sensitive to serve as an early indicator of the onset of renal disease (Piscator 1962);

7. Albumin (ALB), determined by the Amido Black method, is sensitive and reproducible, but involves a time-consuming procedure (Piscator 1962);

8. Glycosaminoglycan (GAG) increases among cadmium workers, but the significance of this effect is unknown because no relationship has been found between elevated GAG and other indices of tubular damage (Bernard and Lauwerys 1990);

9. Trehalase seems to increase earlier than B2M during cadmium exposure, but the procedure for analysis is complicated and unreliable (Iwata et al. 1988); and,

10. Kallikrein is observed at lower concentrations among cadmium-exposed workers than among normal controls (Roels et al. 1990).

Of the above analytes, B2M appears to be the most widely used and best characterized analyte to evaluate the presence/absence, as well as the extent of, cadmium-induced renal tubular damage (Kawada, Koyama, and Suzuki 1989; Shaikh and Smith 1984; Nogawa 1984). However, it is important that samples be collected and handled so as to minimize B2M degradation under acidic urine conditions.

The threshold value of B2MU commonly used to indicate the presence of kidney damage 300 µg/g CRTU (Kjellstrom et al. 1977a; Buchet et al. 1980; and Kowal and Zirkes 1983). This value represents the upper 95th or 97.5th percentile level of urinary excretion observed among those without tubular dysfunction (Elinder, exbt L–140–45, OSHA docket H057A). In agreement with these conclusions, the data presented in Section 5.3.7 of this protocol generally indicate that the level of 300 µg/g CRTU appears to define the boundary for kidney dysfunction. It is not clear, however, that this level represents the upper 95th percentile of values observed among those who fail to demonstrate proteinuria effects.

Although elevated B2MU levels appear to be a fairly specific indicator of disease associated with cadmium exposure, other conditions that may lead to elevated B2MU levels include high fevers from influenza, extensive physical exercise, renal disease unrelated to cadmium exposure, lymphomas, and AIDS (Iwao et al. 1980; Schardun and van Epps 1987). Elevated B2M levels observed in association with high fevers from influenza or from extensive physical exercise are transient, and will return to normal levels once the fever has abated or metabolic rates return to baseline values following exercise. The other conditions linked to elevated B2M levels can be diagnosed as part of a properly-designed medical examination. Consequently, monitoring B2M, when accompanied by regular medical examinations and CDB and CDU determinations (as indicators of present and past cadmium exposure), may serve as a specific, early indicator of cadmium-induced kidney damage.

4.4 Criteria for Medical Monitoring of Cadmium Workers

Medical monitoring mandated by the final cadmium rule includes a combination of regular medical examinations and periodic monitoring of 3 analytes: CDB, CDU and B2MU. As indicated above, CDB is monitored as an indicator of current cadmium exposure, while CDU serves as an indicator of the cadmium body burden; B2MU is assessed as an early marker of irreversible kidney damage and disease.

The final cadmium rule defines a series of action levels that have been developed for each of the 3 analytes to be monitored. These action levels serve to guide the responsible physician through a decision-making process. For each action level that is exceeded, a specific response is mandated. The sequence of action levels, and the attendant actions, are described in detail in the final cadmium rule.

Other criteria used in the medical decision-making process relate to tests performed during the medical examination (including a determination of the ability of a worker to wear a respirator). These criteria, however, are not affected by the results of the analyte determinations addressed in the above paragraphs and, consequently, will not be considered further in these guidelines.

4.5 Defining to Quality and Proficiency of the Analyte Determinations

As noted above in Sections 2 and 3, the quality of a measurement should be defined along with its value to properly interpret the results. Generally, it is necessary to know the accuracy and the precision of a measurement before it can be properly evaluated. The precision of the data from a specific laboratory indicates the extent to which the repeated measurements of the same sample vary within that laboratory. The accuracy of the data provides an indication of the extent to which these results deviate from average results determined from many laboratories performing the same measurement (*i.e.*, in the absence of an independent determination of the true value of a measurement). Note that terms are defined operationally relative to the manner in which they will be used in this protocol. Formal definitions for the terms in italics used in this section can be found in the list of definitions (Section 2).

Another data quality criterion required to properly evaluate measurement results is the limit of detection of that measurement. For measurements to be useful, the range of the measurement which is of interest for biological monitoring purposes must lie entirely above the limit of detection defined for that measurement.

The overall quality of a laboratory's results is termed the performance of that laboratory. The degree to which a laboratory satisfies a minimum performance level is referred to as the proficiency of the laboratory. A successful medical monitoring program, therefore, should include procedures developed for monitoring and recording laboratory performance; these procedures can be used to identify the most proficient laboratories.

5.0 Overview of Medical Monitoring Tests for CDB, CDU, B2MU and CRTU

To evaluate whether available methods for assessing CDB, CDU, B2MU and CRTU are adequate for determining the parameters defined by the proposed action levels, it is necessary to review procedures available for sample collection, preparation and analysis.

A variety of techniques for these purposes have been used historically for the determination of cadmium in biological matrices (including CDB and CDU), and for the determination of specific proteins in biological matrices (including B2MU). However, only the most recent techniques are capable of satisfying the required accuracy, precision and sensitivity (*i.e.*, limit of detection) for monitoring at the levels mandated in the final cadmium rule, while still facilitating automated analysis and rapid processing.

5.1 Measuring Cadmium in Blood (CDB)

Analysis of biological samples for cadmium requires strict analytical discipline regarding collection and handling of samples. In addition to occupational settings, where cadmium contamination would be apparent, cadmium is a ubiquitous environmental contaminant, and much care should be exercised to ensure that samples are not contaminated during collection, preparation or analysis. Many common chemical reagents are contaminated with cadmium at concentrations that will interfere with cadmium analysis; because of the widespread use of cadmium compounds as colored pigments in plastics and coatings, the analyst should continually monitor each manufacturer's chemical reagents and collection containers to prevent contamination of samples.

Guarding against cadmium contamination of biological samples is particularly important when analyzing blood samples because cadmium concentrations in blood samples from nonexposed populations are generally less than 2 µg/l (2 ng/ml), while occupationally-exposed workers can be at medical risk to cadmium toxicity if blood concentrations exceed 5 µg/l (ACGIH 1991 and 1992). This narrow margin between exposed and unexposed samples requires that exceptional care be used in performing analytic determinations for biological monitoring for occupational cadmium exposure.

Methods for quantifying cadmium in blood have improved over the last 40 years primarily because of improvements in analytical instrumentation. Also, due to improvements in analytical techniques, there is less need to perform extensive multi-step sample preparations prior to analysis. Complex sample preparation was previously required to enhance method sensitivity (for cadmium), and to reduce interference by other metals or components of the sample.

5.1.1 Analytical Techniques Used To Monitor Cadmium in Biological Matrices

233

TABLE 3—COMPARISON OF ANALYTICAL PROCEDURES/INSTRUMENTATION FOR DETERMINATION OF
CADMIUM IN BIOLOGICAL SAMPLES

Analytical procedure	Limit of detection [ng/(g or ml)]	Specified biological matrix	Reference	Comments
Flame Atomic Absorption Spectroscopy (FAAS).	≥1.0	Any matrix	Perkin-Elmer (1982).	Not sensitive enough for biomonitoring without extensive sample digestion, metal chelation and organic solvent extraction.
Graphite Furnace Atomic Absorption Spectroscopy (GFAAS).	0.04	Urine	Pruszkowska et al. (1983).	Methods of choice for routine cadmium analysis.
	≥0.20	Blood	Stoeppler and Brandt (1980).	
Inductively-Coupled Argon-Plasma Atomic Emission Spectroscopy (ICAP AES).	2.0	Any matrix	NIOSH (1984A) ...	Requires extensive sample preparation and concentration of metal with chelating resin. Advantage is simultaneous analyses for as many as 10 metals from 1 sample.
Neutron Activation Gamma Spectroscopy (NA).	1.5	In vivo (liver)	Ellis et al. (1983)	Only available *in vivo* method for direct determination of cadmium body tissue burdens; expensive; absolute determination of cadmium in reference materials.
Isotope Dilution Mass Spectroscopy (IDMS).	<1.0	Any matrix	Michiels and DeBievre (1986).	Suitable for absolute determination of cadmium in reference materials; expensive.
Differential Pulse Anodic Stripping Voltammetry (DPASV).	<1.0	Any matrix	Stoeppler and Brandt (1980).	Suitable for absolute determination of cadmium in reference materials; efficient method to check accuracy of analytical method.

A number of analytical techniques have been used for determining cadmium concentrations in biological materials. A summary of the characteristics of the most widely employed techniques is presented in Table 3. The technique most suitable for medical monitoring for cadmium is atomic absorption spectroscopy (AAS).

To obtain a measurement using AAS, a light source (*i.e.*, hollow cathode or lectrode-free discharge lamp) containing the element of interest as the cathode, is energized and the lamp emits a spectrum that is unique for that element. This light source is focused through a sample cell, and a selected wavelength is monitored by a monochrometer and photodetector cell. Any ground state atoms in the sample that match those of the lamp element and are in the path of the emitted light may absorb some of the light and decrease the amount of light that reaches the photodetector cell. The amount of light absorbed at each characteristic wavelength is proportional to the number of ground state atoms of the corresponding element that are in the pathway of the light between the source and detector.

To determine the amount of a specific metallic element in a sample using AAS, the sample is dissolved in a solvent and aspirated into a high-temperature flame as an aerosol. At high temperatures, the solvent is rapidly evaporated or decomposed and the solute is initially solidified; the majority of the sample elements then are transformed into an atomic vapor. Next, a light beam is focused above the flame and the amount of metal in the sample can be determined by measuring the degree of absorbance of the atoms of the target element released by the flame at a characteristic wavelength.

A more refined atomic absorption technique, flameless AAS, substitutes an electrothermal, graphite furnace for the flame. An aliquot (10–100 µl) of the sample is pipetted into the cold furnace, which is then heated rapidly to generate an atomic vapor of the element.

AAS is a sensitive and specific method for the elemental analysis of metals; its main drawback is nonspecific background absorbtion and scattering of the light beam by particles of the sample as it decomposes at high temperatures; nonspecific absorbance reduces the sensitivity of the analytical method. The problem of nonspecific absorbance and scattering can be reduced by extensive sample pretreatment, such as ashing and/or acid digestion of the sample to reduce its organic content.

Current AAS instruments employ background correction devices to adjust electronically for background absorbtion and scattering. A common method to correct for background effects is to use a deuterium arc lamp as a second light source. A continuum light source, such as the deuterium lamp, emits a broad spectrum of wavelengths instead of specific wavelengths characteristic of a particular element, as with the hollow cathode tube. With this system, light from the primary source and the continuum source are passed alternately through the sample cell. The target element effectively absorbs light only from the primary source (which is much brighter than the continuum source at the characteristic wavelengths), while the background matrix absorbs and scatters light from both sources equally. Therefore, when the ratio of the two beams is measured electronically, the effect of nonspecific background absorption and scattering is eliminated. A less common, but more sophisticated, backgrond correction system is based on the Zeeman effect, which uses a magnetically-activated light polarizer to compensate electronically for nonspecific absorbtion and scattering.

Atomic emission spectroscopy with inductively-coupled argon plasma (AES-ICAP) is widely used to analyze for metals. With this instrument, the sample is aspirated into an extremely hot argon plasma flame, which excites the metal atoms; emission spectra specific for the sample element then are generated. The quanta of emitted light passing through a monochrometer are amplified by photomultiplier tubes and measured by a photodetector to determine the amount of metal in the sample. An advantage of AES-ICAP over AAS is that multi-elemental analyses of a sample can be performed by simultaneously measuring specific elemental emission energies. However, AES-ICAP lacks the sensitivity of AAS, exhibiting a limit of detection which is higher than the limit of detection for graphite-furnace AAS (Table 3).

Neutron activation (NA) analysis and isotope dilution mass spectrometry (IDMS) are 2 additional, but highly specialized, methods that have been used for cadmium determinations. These methods are expensive because they require elaborate and sophisticated instrumentation.

NA analysis has the distinct advantage over other analytical methods of being able to determine cadmium body burdens in specific organs (e.g., liver, kidney) in vivo (Ellis et al. 1983). Neutron bombardment of the target transforms cadmium-113 to cadmium-114, which promptly decays ($<10^{-14}$ sec) to its ground state, emitting gamma rays that are measured using large gamma detectors; appropriate shielding and instrumentation are required when using this method.

IDMS analysis, a definitive but laborious method, is based on the change in the ratio of 2 isotopes of cadmium (cadmium 111 and 112) that occurs when a known amount of the element (with an artificially altered ratio of the same isotopes [i.e., a cadmium 111 "spike"] is added to a weighed aliquot of the sample (Michiels and De Bievre 1986).

5.1.2 Methods Developed for CDB Determinations

A variety of methods have been used for preparing and analyzing CDB samples; most of these methods rely on one of the analytical techniques described above. Among the earliest reports, Princi (1947) and Smith et al. (1955) employed a colorimetric procedure to analyze for CDB and CDU. Samples were dried and digested through several cycles with concentrated mineral acids (HNO_3 and H_2SO_4) and hydrogen peroxide (H_2O_2).'The digest was neutralized, and the cadmium was complexed with diphenylthiocarbazone and extracted with chloroform. The dithizonecadmium complex then was quantified using a spectrometer.

Colorimetric procedures for cadmium analyses were replaced by methods based on atomic absorption spectroscopy (AAS) in the early 1960s, but many of the complex sample preparation procedures were retained. Kjellstrom (1979) reports that in Japanese, American and Swedish laboratories during the early 1970s, blood samples were wet ashed with mineral acids or ashed at high temperature and wetted with nitric acid. The cadmium in the digest was complexed with metal chelators including diethyl dithiocarbamate (DDTC), ammonium pyrrolidine dithiocarbamate (APDC) or diphenylthiocarbazone (dithizone) in ammonia-citrate buffer and extracted with methyl isobutyl ketone (MIBK). The resulting solution then was analyzed by flame AAS or graphite-furnace AAS forcadmium determinations using deuterium-lamp background correction.

In the late 1970s, researchers began developing simpler preparation procedures. Roels et al. (1978) and Roberts and Clark (1986) developed simplified digestion procedures. Using the Roberts and Clark method, a 0.5 ml aliquot of blood is collected and transferred to a digestion tube containing 1 ml concentrated HNO_3. The blood is then digested at 110 °C for 4 hours. The sample is reduced in volume by continued heating, and 0.5 ml 30% H_2O_2 is added as the sample dries. The residue is dissolved in 5 ml dilute (1%) HNO_3, and 20 μl of sample is then analyzed by graphite-furnace AAS with deuterium-background correction.

The current trend in the preparation of blood samples is to dilute the sample and add matrix modifiers to reduce background interference, rather than digesting the sample to reduce organic content. The method of Stoeppler and Brandt (1980), and the abbreviated procedure published in the American Public Health Association's (APHA) *Methods for Biological Monitoring* (1988), are straightforward and are nearly identical. For the APHA method, a small aliquot (50–300 μl) of whole blood that has been stabilized with ethylenediaminetetraacetate (EDTA) is added to 1.0 ml 1MHNO₃, vigorously shaken and centrifuged. Aliquots (10–25 µl) of the supernatant then are then analyzed by graphite-furnace AAS with appropriate background correction.

Using the method of Stoeppler and Brandt (1980), aliquots (50–200 µl) of whole blood that have been stabilized with EDTA are pipetted into clean polystyrene tubes and mixed with 150-600 µl of 1 M HNO₃. After vigorous shaking, the solution is centrifuged and a 10–25 µl aliquot of the supernatant then is analyzed by graphite-furnace AAS with appropriate background correction.

Claeys-Thoreau (1982) and DeBenzo et al. (1990) diluted blood samples at a ratio of 1:10 with a matrix modifier (0.2% Triton X–100, a wetting agent) for direct determinations of CDB. DeBenzo et al. also demonstrated that aqueous standards of cadmium, instead of spiked, whole-blood samples, could be used to establish calibration curves if standards and samples are treated with additional small volumes of matrix modifiers (i.e., 1% HNO₃, 0.2% ammonium hydrogenphosphate and 1 mg/ml magnesium salts).

These direct dilution procedures for CDB analysis are simple and rapid. Laboratories can process more than 100 samples a day using a dedicated graphite-furnace AAS, an auto-sampler, and either a Zeeman- or a deuterium-background correction system. Several authors emphasize using optimum settings for graphite-furnace temperatures during the drying, charring, and atomization processes associated with the flameless AAS method, and the need to run frequent QC samples when performing automated analysis.

5.1.3 Sample Collection and Handling

Sample collection procedures are addressed primarily to identify ways to minimize the degree of variability that may be introduced by sample collection during medical monitoring. It is unclear at this point the extent to which collection procedures contribute to variability among CDB samples. Sources of variation that may result from sampling procedures include time-of-day effects and introduction of external contamination during the collection process. To minimize these sources, strict adherence to a sample collection protocol is recommended. Such a protocol must include provisions for thorough cleaning of the site from which blood will be extracted; also, every effort should be made to collect samples near the same time of day. It is also important to recognize that under the recent OSHA blood-borne pathogens standard (29 CFR 1910.1030), blood samples and certain body fluids must be handled and treated as if they are infectious.

5.1.4 Best Achievable Performance

The best achievable performance using a particular method for CDB determinations is assumed to be equivalent to the performance reported by research laboratories in which the method was developed.

For their method, Roberts and Clark (1986) demonstrated a limit of detection of 0.4 µg Cd/l in whole blood, with a linear response curve from 0.4 to 16.0 µg Cd/l. They report a coefficient of variation (CV) of 6.7% at 8.0 µg/l.

The APHA (1988) reports a range of 1.0–25 µg/l, with a CV of 7.3% (concentration not stated). Insufficient documentation was available to critique this method.

Stoeppler and Brandt (1980) achieved a detection limit of 0.2 µg Cd/l whole blood, with a linear range of 0.4–12.0 µg Cd/l, and a CV of 15–30%, for samples at <1.0 µg/l. Improved precision (CV of 3.8%) was reported for CDB concentrations at 9.3 µg/l.

5.1.5 General Method Performance

For any particular method, the performance expected from commercial laboratories may be somewhat lower than that reported by the research laboratory in which the method was developed. With participation in appropriate proficiency programs and use of a proper in-house QA/QC program incorporating provisions for regular corrective actions, the performance of commercial laboratories is expected to approach that reported by research laboratories. Also, the results reported for existing proficiency programs serve as a gauge of the likely level of performance that currently can be expected from commercial laboratories offering these analyses.

Weber (1988) reports on the results of the proficiency program run by the Centre de Toxicologie du Quebec (CTQ). As indicated previously, participants in that program receive 18 blood samples per year having cadmium concentrations ranging from 0.2–20 µg/l. Currently, 76 laboratories are participating in this program. The program is established for several analytes in addition to cadmium, and not all of these laboratories participate in the cadmium proficiency-testing program.

Under the CTQ program, cadmium results from individual laboratories are compared against the consensus mean derived for each sample. Results indicate that after receiving 60 samples (i.e., after participation for approximately three years), 60% of the laboratories in the program are able to report results that fall within ±1 µg/l or 15% of the mean, whichever is greater. (For this procedure, the 15% criterion was applied to concentrations exceeding 7 µg/l.) On any single sample of the last 20 samples, the percentage of laboratories falling within the specified range is between 55 and 80%.

The CTQ also evaluates the performance of participating laboratories against a less severe standard: ±2 µg/l or 15% of the mean, whichever is greater (Weber 1988); 90% of participating laboratories are able to satisfy this standard after approximately 3 years in the program. (The 15% criterion is used for concentrations in excess of 13 µg/l.) On any single sample of the last 15 samples, the percentage of samples falling within the specified range is between 80 and 95% (except for a single test for which only 60% of the laboratories achieved the desired performance).

Based on the data presented in Weber (1988), the CV for analysis of CDB is nearly constant at 20% for cadmium concentrations exceeding 5 µg/l, and increases for cadmium concentrations below 5 µg/l. At 2 µg/l, the reported CV rises to approximately 40%. At 1 µg/l, the reported CV is approximately 60%.

Participating laboratories also tend to overestimate concentrations for samples exhibiting concentrations less than 2 µg/l (see Figure 11 of Weber 1988). This problem is due in part to the proficiency evaluation criterion that allows reporting a minimum ±2.0 µg/l for evaluated CDB samples. There is currently little economic or regulatory incentive for laboratories participating in the CTQ program to achieve greater accuracy for CDB samples containing cadmium at concentrations less than 2.0 µg/l, even if the laboratory has the experience and competency to distinguish among lower concentrations in the samples obtained from the CTQ.

The collective experience of international agencies and investigators demonstrate the need for a vigorous QC program to ensure that CDB values reported by participating laboratories are indeed reasonably accurate. As Friberg (1988) stated:

"Information about the quality of published data has often been lacking. This is of concern as assessment of metals in trace concentrations in biological media are fraught with difficulties from the collection, handling, and storage of samples to the chemical analyses. This has been proven over and over again from the results of interlaboratory testing and quality control exercises. Large variations in results were reported even from 'experienced' laboratories."

The UNEP/WHO global study of cadmium biological monitoring set a limit for CDB accuracy using the maximum allowable deviation method at $Y = X \pm (0.1X + 1)$ for a targeted concentration of 10 µg Cd/l (Friberg and Vahter 1983). The performance of participating laboratories over a concentration range of 1.5–12 µg/l was reported by Lind et al. (1987). Of the 3 QC runs conducted during 1982 and 1983, 1 or 2 of the 6 laboratories failed each run. For the years 1983 and 1985, between zero and 2 laboratories failed each of the consecutive QC runs.

In another study (Vahter and Friberg 1988), QC samples consisting of both external (unknown) and internal (stated) concentrations were distributed to laboratories participating in the epidemiology research. In this study, the maximum acceptable deviation between the regression analysis of reported results and reference values was set at $Y = X \pm (0.05X + 0.2)$ for a concentration range of 0.3–5.0 µg Cd/l. It is reported that only 2 of 5 laboratories had acceptable data after the first QC set, and only 1 of 5 laboratories had acceptable data after the second QC set. By the fourth QC set, however, all 5 laboratories were judged proficient.

The need for high quality CDB monitoring is apparent when the toxicological and biological characteristics of this metal are considered; an increase in CDB from 2 to 4 µg/l could cause a doubling of the cadmium accumulation in the kidney, a critical target tissue for selective cadmium accumulation (Nordberg and Nordberg 1988).

Historically, the CDC's internal QC program for CDB cadmium monitoring program has found achievable accuracy to be ±10% of the true value at CDB concentrations ≥5.0 µg/l (Paschal 1990). Data on the performance of laboratories participating in this program currently are not available.

5.1.6 Observed CDB Concentrations

As stated in Section 4.3, CDB concentrations are representative of ongoing levels of exposure to cadmium. Among those who have been exposed chronically to cadmium for extended periods, however, CDB may contain a component attributable to the general cadmium body burden.

5.1.6.1 *CDB Concentrations Among Unexposed Samples*

Numerous studies have been conducted examining CDB concentrations in the general population, and in control groups used for comparison with cadmium-exposed workers. A number of reports have been published that present erroneously high values of CDB (Nordberg and Nordberg 1988). This problem was due to contamination of samples during sampling and analysis, and to errors in analysis. Early AAS methods were not sufficiently sensitive to accurately estimate CDB concentrations.

Table 4 presents results of recent studies reporting CDB levels for the general U.S. population not exposed occupationally to cadmium. Other surveys of tissue cadmium using U.S. samples and conducted as part of a cooperative effort among Japan, Sweden and the U.S., did not collect CDB data because standard analytical methodologies were unavailable, and because of analytic problems (Kjellstrom 1979; SWRI 1978).

237

TABLE 4—BLOOD CADMIUM CONCENTRATIONS OF U.S. POPULATION NOT OCCUPATIONALLY EXPOSED TO CADMIUM[A]

Study No.	No. in study (n)	Sex	Age	Smoking habits[b]	Arithmetic mean (±S.D.)[c]	Absolute range or (95% CI)[d]	Geometric mean (±GSD)[e]	Lower 95th percentile of distribution[f]	Upper 95th percentile of distribution[f]	Reference
1	80	M	4 to 69	NS,S	1.13	0.35–3.3	0.98±1.71	0.4	2.4	Kowal et al. (1979).
	88	F	4 to 69	NS,S	1.03	0.21–3.3	0.91±1.63	0.4	2.0	
	115	M/F	4 to 69	NS	0.95	0.21–3.3	0.85±1.59	0.4	1.8	
	31	M/F	4 to 69	S	1.54	0.4–3.3	1.37±1.65	0.6	3.2	
2	10	M	Adults	(?)	2.0±2.1	(0.5–5.0)		g(0)	g(5.8)	Ellis et al. (1983).
3	24	M	Adults	NS			0.6±1/87	0.2	1.8	Frieberg and Vahter (1983).
	20	M	Adults	S			1.2±2.13	0.3	4.4	
	64	F	Adults	NS			0.5±1.85	0.2	1.4	
	39	F	Adults	S			0.8±2.22	0.2	3.1	
4	32	M	Adults	S,NS			1.2±2.0	0.4	3.9	Thun et al. (1989).
5	35	M	Adults	(?)	2.1±2.1	(0.5–7.3)		g(0)	g(5.6)	Mueller et al. (1989).

[a] Concentrations reported in µg Cd/l blood unless otherwise stated.
[b] NS—never smoked; S—current cigarette smoker.
[c] S.D.—Arithmetic Standard Deviation.
[d] C.I.—Confidence interval.
[e] GSD—Geometric Standard Deviation.
[f] Based on an assumed lognormal distribution.
[g] Based on an assumed normal distribution.

Arithmetic and/or geometric means and standard deviations are provided in Table 4 for measurements among the populations defined in each study listed. The range of reported measurements and/or the 95% upper and lower confidence intervals for the means are presented when this information was reported in a study. For studies reporting either an arithmetic or geometric standard deviation along with a mean, the lower and upper 95th percentile for the distribution also were derived and reported in the table.

The data provided in table 4 from Kowal et al. (1979) are from studies conducted between 1974 and 1976 evaluating CDB levels for the general population in Chicago, and are considered to be representative of the U.S. population. These studies indicate that the average CDB concentration among those not occupationally exposed to cadmium is approximately 1 µg/l.

In several other studies presented in Table 4, measurements are reported separately for males and females, and for smokers and nonsmokers. The data in this table indicate that similar CDB levels are observed among males and females in the general population, but that smokers tend to exhibit higher CDB levels than nonsmokers. Based on the Kowal et al. (1979) study, smokers not occupationally exposed to cadmium exhibit an average CDB level of 1.4 µg/l.

In general, nonsmokers tend to exhibit levels ranging to 2 µg/l, while levels observed among smokers range to 5 µg/l. Based on the data presented in Table 4, 95% of those not occupationally exposed to cadmium exhibit CDB levels less than 5 µg/l.

5.1.6.2 *CDB concentrations among exposed workers*

Table 5 is a summary of results from studies reporting CDB levels among workers exposed to cadmium in the work place. As in Table 4, arithmetic and/or geometric means and standard deviations are provided if reported in the listed studies. The absolute range, or the 95% confidence interval around the mean, of the data in each study are provided when reported. In addition, the lower and upper 95th percentile of the distribution are presented for each study i which a mean and corresponding standard deviation were reported. Table 5 also provides estimates of the duration, and level, of exposure to cadmium in the work place if these data were reported in the listed studies. The data presented in table 5 suggest that CDB levels are dose related. Sukuri et al. (1983) show that higher CDB levels are observed among workers experiencing higher work place exposure. This trend appears to be true of the studies listed in the table.

CDB levels reported in table 5 are higher among those showing signs of cadmium-related kidney damage than those showing no such damage. Lauwerys et al. (1976) report CDB levels among workers with kidney lesions that generally are above the levels reported for workers without kidney lesions.

Ellis et al. (1983) report a similar observation comparing workers with and without renal dysfunction, although they found more overlap between the 2 groups than Lauwerys et al.

TABLE 5—BLOOD CADMIUM IN WORKERS EXPOSED TO CADMIUM IN THE WORKPLACE

Study number	Work environment (worker population monitored)	Number in study	Employment in years (mean)	Mean concentration of cadmium in air (µg/m³)	Concentrations of Cadmium in blood[a]					
					Arithmetic mean (±S.D.)[b]	Absolute range or (95% C.I.)[c]	Geometric mean (GSD)[d]	Lower 95th percentile of range[e] ( )[f]	Upper 95th percentile of range[e] ( )[f]	Reference
1	Ni-Cd battery plant and Cd production plant:	......	3–40 ...	≤90	....	....	....	......	......	Lauwerys et al. 1976.
	(Workers without kidney lesions).	96	....	....	21.4±1.9	....	....	(18)	(25).	
	(Workers with kidney lesions).	25	....	....	38.8±3.8	....	....	(32)	(45).	
2	Ni-Cd battery plant:	......	......	......	....	....	....	......	......	Adamsson et al. (1979).
	(Smokers)	7	(5)	10.1	22.7	7.3–67.2.				
	(Nonsmokers)	8	(9)	7.0	7.0	4.9–10.5.				
3	Cadmium alloy plant:	......	......	......	....	....	....	......	......	Sukuri et al. 1982.
	(High exposure group).	7	(10.6)	[1,000–5 yrs;.	20.8±7.1	....	....	(7.3) ...	(34).	
	(Low exposure group).	9	(7.3) ...	40–5 yrs].	7.1±1.1	....	....	(5.1) ...	(9.1).	
4	Retrospective study of workers with renal problems:	19	15–41	......	....	....	....	......	....	Roels et al. 1982.
	(Before removal).	....	(27.2)	....	39.9±3.7	11–179 ..	....	(34)	(46).	
	(After removal).	....	[g](4.2) ...	....	14.1±5.6	5.7–27.4	....	(4.4) ...	(24).	
5	Cadmium production plant:	......	......	......	....	....	....	......	......	Ellis et al. 1983.
	(Workers without renal dysfunction).	33	1–34 ...	....	15±5.7	7–31	....	(5.4) ...	(25).	
	(Workers with renal dysfunction).	18	10–34	....	24±8.5	10–34	....	(9.3) ...	(39).	
6	Cd-Cu alloy plant.	75	Up to 39.	....	....	....	8.8±1.1 ..	7.5	10	Mason et al. 1988.
7	Cadmium recovery operation—Current (19) and former (26) workers.	45	(19.0)	....	....	....	7.9±2.0 ..	2.5	25	Thun et al. 1989.
8	Cadmium recovery operation	40	....	....	10.2±5.3	2.2–18.8	....	(1.3) ...	(19)	Mueller et al. 1989.

[a] Concentrations reported in µg Cd/l blood unless otherwise stated.
[b] S.D.—Standard Deviation.
[c] C.I.—Confidence Interval.
[d] GSD—Geometric Standard Deviation.
[e] Based on an assumed lognormal distribution.
[f] Based on an assumed normal distribution.
[g] Years following removal.

The data in table 5 also indicate that CDB levels are higher among those experiencing current occupational exposure than those who have been removed from such exposure. Roels et al. (1982) indicate that CDB levels observed among workers experiencing ongoing exposure in the work place are almost entirely above levels observed among workers removed from such exposure. This finding suggests that CDB levels decrease once cadmium exposure has ceased.

A comparison of the data presented in tables 4 and 5 indicates that CDB levels observed among cadmium-exposed workers is significantly higher than levels observed among the unexposed groups. With the exception of 2 studies presented in table 5 (1 of which includes former workers in the sample group tested), the lower 95th percentile for CDB levels among exposed workers are greater than 5 µg/l, which is the value of the upper 95th percentile for CDB levels observed among those who are not occupationally exposed. Therefore, a CDB level of 5 µg/l represents a threshold above which significant work place exposure to cadmium may be occurring.

5.1.7 Conclusions and Recommendations for CDB

Based on the above evaluation, the following recommendations are made for a CDB proficiency program.

5.1.7.1 *Recommended method*

The method of Stoeppler and Brandt (1980) should be adopted for analyzing CDB. This method was selected over other methods for its straightforward sample-preparation procedures, and because limitations of the method were described adequately. It also is the method used by a plurality of laboratories currently participating in the CTQ proficiency program. In a recent CTQ interlaboratory comparison report (CTQ 1991), analysis of the methods used by laboratories to measure CDB indicates that 46% (11 of 24) of the participating laboratories used the Stoeppler and Brandt methodology (HNO$_3$ deproteinization of blood followed by analysis of the supernatant by GF-AAS). Other CDB methods employed by participating laboratories identified in the CTQ report include dilution of blood (29%), acid digestion (12%) and miscellaneous methods (12%).

Laboratories may adopt alternate methods, but it is the responsibility of the laboratory to demonstrate that the alternate methods meet the data quality objectives defined for the Stoeppler and Brandt method (see Section 5.1.7.2 below).

5.1.7.2 *Data quality objectives*

Based on the above evaluation, the following data quality objectives (DQOs) should facilitate interpretation of analytical results.

Limit of Detection. 0.5 µg/l should be achievable using the Stoeppler and Brandt method. Stoeppler and Brandt (1980) report a limit of detection equivalent to ≤0.2 µg/l in whole blood using 25 µl aliquots of deproteinized, diluted blood samples.

Accuracy. Initially, some of the laboratories performing CDB measurements may be expected to satisfy criteria similar to the less severe criteria specified by the CTQ program, i.e., measurements within 2 µg/l or 15% (whichever is greater) of the target value. About 60% of the laboratories enrolled in the CTQ program could meet this criterion on the first proficiency test (Weber 1988).

Currently, approximately 12 laboratories in the CTQ program are achieving an accuracy for CDB analysis within the more severe constraints of ±1 µg/l or 15% (whichever is greater). Later, as laboratories gain experience, they should achieve the level of accuracy exhibited by these 12 laboratories. The experience in the CTQ program has shown that, even without incentives, laboratories benefit from the feedback of the program; after they have analyzed 40–50 control samples from the program, performance improves to the point where about 60% of the laboratories can meet the stricter criterion of ±1 µg/l or 15% (Weber 1988). Thus, this stricter target accuracy is a reasonable DQO.

Precision. Although Stoeppler and Brandt (1980) suggest that a coefficient of variation (CV) near 1.3% (for a 10 µg/l concentration) is achievable for within-run reproducibility, it is recognized that other factors affecting within- and between-run comparability will increase the achievable CV. Stoeppler and Brandt (1980) observed CVs that were as high as 30% for low concentrations (0.4 µg/l), and CVs of less than 5% for higher concentrations.

For internal QC samples (see Section 3.3.1), laboratories should attain an overall precision near 25%. For CDB samples with concentrations less than 2 µg/l, a target precision of 40% is reasonable, while precisions of 20% should be achievable for concentrations greater than 2 µg/l. Although these values are more strict than values observed in the CTQ interlaboratory program reported by Webber (1988), they are within the achievable limits reported by Stoeppler and Brandt (1980).

5.1.7.3 *Quality assurance/quality control*

Commercial laboratories providing measurement of CDB should adopt an internal QA/QC program that incorporates the following components: Strict adherence to the selected method, including all calibration requirements; regular incorporation of QC samples during actual runs; a protocol for corrective actions, and documentation of these actions; and, participation in an inter-laboratory proficiency program. Note that the nonmandatory QA/QC program presented in Attachment 1 is based on the Stoeppler and Brandt method for CDB analysis. Should an alternate method be adopted, the laboratory should develop a QA/QC program satisfying the provisions of Section 3.3.1.

5.2 Measuring Cadmium in Urine (CDU)

As in the case of CDB measurement, proper determination of CDU requires strict analytical discipline regarding collection and handling of samples. Because cadmium is both ubiquitous in the environment and employed widely in coloring agents for industrial products that may be used during sample collection, preparation and analysis, care should be exercised to ensure that samples are not contaminated during the sampling procedure.

Methods for CDU determination share many of the same features as those employed for the determination of CDB. Thus, changes and improvements to methods for measuring CDU over the past 40 years parallel those used to monitor CDB. The direction of development has largely been toward the simplification of sample preparation techniques made possible because of improvements in analytic techniques.

5.2.1 Units of CDU Measurement

Procedures adopted for reporting CDU concentrations are not uniform. In fact, the situation for reporting CDU is more complicated than for CDB, where concentrations are normalized against a unit volume of whole blood.

Concentrations of solutes in urine vary with several biological factors (including the time since last voiding and the volume of liquid consumed over the last few hours); as a result, solute concentrations should be normalized against another characteristic of urine that represents changes in solute concentrations. The 2 most common techniques are either to standardize solute concentrations against the concentration of creatinine, or to standardize solute concentrations against the specific gravity of the urine. Thus, CDU concentrations have been reported in the literature as "uncorrected" concentrations of cadmium per volume of urine (i.e., µg Cd/l urine), "corrected" concentrations of cadmium per volume of urine at a standard specific gravity (i.e., µg Cd/l urine at a specific gravity of 1.020), or "corrected" mass concentration per unit mass of creatinine (i.e., µg Cd/g creatinine). (CDU concentrations [whether uncorrected or corrected for specific gravity, or normalized to creatinine] occasionally are reported in nanomoles [i.e., nmoles] of cadmium per unit mass or volume. In this protocol, these values are converted to µg of cadmium per unit

mass or volume using 89 nmoles of cadmium = 10 µg.)

While it is agreed generally that urine values of analytes should be normalized for reporting purposes, some debate exists over what correction method should be used. The medical community has long favored normalization based on creatinine concentration, a common urinary constituent. Creatinine is a normal product of tissue catabolism, is excreted at a uniform rate, and the total amount excreted per day is constant on a day-to-day basis (NIOSH 1984b). While this correction method is accepted widely in Europe, and within some occupational health circles, Kowals (1983) argues that the use of specific gravity (i.e., total solids per unit volume) is more straightforward and practical (than creatinine) in adjusting CDU values for populations that vary by age or gender.

Kowals (1983) found that urinary creatinine (CRTU) is lower in females than males, and also varies with age. Creatinine excretion is highest in younger males (20–30 years old), decreases at middle age (50–60 years), and may rise slightly in later years. Thus, cadmium concentrations may be underestimated for some workers with high CRTU levels.

Within a single void urine collection, urine concentration of any analyte will be affected by recent consumption of large volumes of liquids, and by heavy physical labor in hot environments. The absolute amount of analyte excreted may be identical, but concentrations will vary widely so that urine must be corrected for specific gravity (i.e., to normalize concentrations to the quantity of total solute) using a fixed value (e.g., 1.020 or 1.024). However, since heavy-metal exposure may increase urinary protein excretion, there is a tendency to underestimate cadmium concentrations in samples with high specific gravities when specific-gravity corrections are applied.

Despite some shortcomings, reporting solute concentrations as a function of creatinine concentration is accepted generally; OSHA therefore recommends that CDU levels be reported as the mass of cadmium per unit mass of creatinine (µg/g CTRU).

Reporting CDU as µg/g CRTU requires an additional analytical process beyond the analysis of cadmium: Samples must be analyzed independently for creatinine so that results may be reported as the ratio of cadmium to creatinine concentrations found in the urine sample. Consequently, the overall quality of the analysis depends on the combined performance by a laboratory on these 2 determinations. The analysis used for CDU determinations is addressed below in terms of µg Cd/l, with analysis of creatinine addressed separately. Techniques for assessing creatinine are discussed in Section 5.4.

Techniques for deriving cadmium as a ratio of CRTU, and the confidence limits for independent measurements of cadmium and CRTU, are provided in Section 3.3.3.

5.2.2 Analytical Techniques Used To Monitor CDU

Analytical techniques used for CDU determinations are similar to those employed for CDB determinations; these techniques are summarized in Table 3. As with CDB monitoring, the technique most suitable for CDU determinations is atomic absorption spectroscopy (AAS). AAS methods used for CDU determinations typically employ a graphite furnace, with background correction made using either the deuterium-lamp or Zeeman techniques; Section 5.1.1 provides a detailed description of AAS methods.

5.2.3 Methods Developed for CDU Determinations

Princi (1947), Smith et al. (1955), Smith and Kench (1957), and Tsuchiya (1967) used colorimetric procedures similar to those described in the CDB section above to estimate CDU concentrations. In these methods, urine (50 ml) is reduced to dryness by heating in a sand bath and digested (wet ashed) with mineral acids. Cadmium then is complexed with dithiazone, extracted with chloroform and quantified by spectrophotometry. These early studies typically report reagent blank values equivalent to 0.3 µg Cd/l, and CDU concentrations among nonexposed control groups at maximum levels of 10 µg Cd/l—erroneously high values when compared to more recent surveys of cadmium concentrations in the general population.

By the mid-1970s, most analytical procedures for CDU analysis used either wet ashing (mineral acid) or high temperatures (>400 °C) to digest the organic matrix of urine, followed by cadmium chelation with APDC or DDTC solutions and extraction with MIBK. The resulting aliquots were analyzed by flame or graphite-furnace AAS (Kjellstrom 1979).

Improvements in control over temperature parameters with electrothermal heating devices used in conjunction with flameless AAS techniques, and optimization of temperature programs for controlling the drying, charring, and atomization processes in sample analyses, led to improved analytical detection of diluted urine samples without the need for sample digestion or ashing. Roels et al. (1978) successfully used a simple sample preparation, dilution of 1.0 ml aliquots of urine with 0.1 N HNO₃, to achieve accurate low-level determinations of CDU.

In the method described by Pruszkowska et al. (1983), which has become the preferred method for CDU analysis, urine samples were diluted at a ratio of 1:5 with water; diammonium hydrogenphosphate in dilute HNO₃ was used as a matrix modifier. The matrix modifier allows for a higher charring

temperature without loss of cadmium through volatilization during preatomization. This procedure also employs a stabilized temperature platform in a graphite furnace, while nonspecific background absorbtion is corrected using the Zeeman technique. This method allows for an absolute detection limit of approximately 0.04 µg Cd/l urine.

5.2.4 Sample Collection and Handling

Sample collection procedures for CDU may contribute to variability observed among CDU measurements. Sources of variation attendant to sampling include time-of-day, the interval since ingestion of liquids, and the introduction of external contamination during the collection process. Therefore, to minimize contributions from these variables, strict adherence to a sample-collection protocol is recommended. This protocol should include provisions for normalizing the conditions under which urine is collected. Every effort also should be made to collect samples during the same time of day.

Collection of urine samples from an industrial work force for biological monitoring purposes usually is performed using "spot" (i.e., single-void) urine with the pH of the sample determined immediately. Logistic and sample-integrity problems arise when efforts are made to collect urine over long periods (e.g., 24 hrs). Unless single-void urines are used, there are numerous opportunities for measurement error because of poor control over sample collection, storage and environmental contamination.

To minimize the interval during which sample urine resides in the bladder, the following adaption to the "spot" collection procedure is recommended: The bladder should first be emptied, and then a large glass of water should be consumed; the sample may be collected within an hour after the water is consumed.

5.2.5 Best Achievable Performance

Performance using a particular method for CDU determinations is assumed to be equivalent to the performance reported by the research laboratories in which the method was developed. Pruszkowska et al. (1983) report a detection limit of 0.04 µg/l CDU, with a CV of <4% between 0–5 µg/l. The CDC reports a minimum CDU detection limit of 0.07 µg/l using a modified method based on Pruszkowska et al. (1983). No CV is stated in this protocol; the protocol contains only rejection criteria for internal QC parameters used during accuracy determinations with known standards (Attachment 8 of exhibit 106 of OSHA docket H057A). Stoeppler and Brandt (1980) report a CDU detection limit of 0.2 µ/l for their methodology.

5.2.6 General Method Performance

For any particular method, the expected initial performance from commercial laboratories may be somewhat lower than that reported by the research laboratory in which the method was developed. With participation in appropriate proficiency programs, and use of a proper in-house QA/QC program incorporating provisions for regular corrective actions, the performance of commercial laboratories may be expected to improve and approach that reported by a research laboratories. The results reported for existing proficiency programs serve to specify the initial level of performance that likely can be expected from commercial laboratories offering analysis using a particular method.

Weber (1988) reports on the results of the CTQ proficiency program, which includes CDU results for laboratories participating in the program. Results indicate that after receiving 60 samples (*i.e.*, after participating in the program for approximately 3 years), approximately 80% of the participating laboratories report CDU results ranging between ±2 µg/l or 15% of the consensus mean, whichever is greater. On any single sample of the last 15 samples, the proportion of laboratories falling within the specified range is between 75 and 95%, except for a single test for which only 60% of the laboratories reported acceptable results. For each of the last 15 samples, approximately 60% of the laboratories reported results within ±1 µg or 15% of the mean, whichever is greater. The range of concentrations included in this set of samples was not reported.

Another report from the CTQ (1991) summarizes preliminary CDU results from their 1991 interlaboratory program. According to the report, for 3 CDU samples with values of 9.0, 16.8, 31.5 µg/l, acceptable results (target of ±2 µg/l or 15 % of the consensus mean, whichever is greater) were achieved by only 44–52% of the 34 laboratories participating in the CDU program. The overall CVs for these 3 CDU samples among the 34 participating laboratories were 31%, 25%, and 49%, respectively. The reason for this poor performance has not been determined.

A more recent report from the CTQ (Weber, private communication) indicates that 36% of the laboratories in the program have been able to achieve the target of ±1 µg/l or 15% for more than 75% of the samples analyzed over the last 5 years, while 45% of participating laboratories achieved a target of ±2 µg/l or 15% for more than 75% of the samples analyzed over the same period.

Note that results reported in the interlaboratory programs are in terms of µg Cd/l of urine, unadjusted for creatinine. The performance indicated, therefore, is a measure of the performance of the cadmium portion of the analyses, and does not include variation that may be introduced during the analysis of CRTU.

5.2.7 Observed CDU Concentrations

Prior to the onset of renal dysfunction, CDU concentrations provide a general indication of the exposure history (*i.e.*, body burden) (see Section 4.3). Once renal dysfunction occurs, CDU levels appear to increase and are no longer indicative solely of cadmium body burden (Friberg and Elinder 1988).

5.2.7.1 *Range of CDU concentrations observed among unexposed samples*

Surveys of CDU concentrations in the general population were first reported from cooperative studies among industrial countries (*i.e.*, Japan, U.S. and Sweden) conducted in the mid-1970s. In summarizing these data, Kjellstrom (1979) reported that CDU concentrations among Dallas, Texas men (age range: <9–59 years; smokers and nonsmokers) varied from 0.11–1.12 µg/l (uncorrected for creatinine or specific gravity). These CDU concentrations are intermediate between population values found in Sweden (range: 0.11–0.80 µg/l) and Japan (range: 0.14–2.32 µg/l).

Kowal and Zirkes (1983) reported CDU concentrations for almost 1,000 samples collected during 1978–79 from the general U.S. adult population (*i.e.*, nine states; both genders; ages 20–74 years). They report that CDU concentrations are lognormally distributed; low levels predominated, but a small proportion of the population exhibited high levels. These investigators transformed the CDU concentrations values, and reported the same data 3 different ways: µg/l urine (unadjusted), µg/l (specific gravity adjusted to 1.020), and µg/g CRTU. These data are summarized in Tables 6 and 7.

Based on further statistical examination of these data, including the lifestyle characteristics of this group, Kowal (1988) suggested increased cadmium absorption (*i.e.*, body burden) was correlated with low dietary intakes of calcium and iron, as well as cigarette smoking.

CDU levels presented in Table 6 are adjusted for age and gender. Results suggest that CDU levels may be slightly different among men and women (*i.e.*, higher among men when values are unadjusted, but lower among men when the values are adjusted, for specific gravity or CRTU). Mean differences among men and women are small compared to the standard deviations, and therefore may not be significant. Levels of CDU also appear to increase with age. The data in Table 6 suggest as well that reporting CDU levels adjusted for specific gravity or as a function of CRTU results in reduced variability.

TABLE 6—URINE CADMIUM CONCENTRATIONS IN THE U.S. ADULT POPULATION: NORMAL AND
CONCENTRATION-ADJUSTED VALUES BY AGE AND SEX [1]

	Geometric means (and geometric standard deviations)		
	Unadjusted (µg/l)	SG-adjusted [2] µg/l at 1.020)	Creatine-adjusted (µg/g)
Sex:			
Male (n = 484)	0.55 (2.9)	0.73 (2.6)	0.55 (2.7)
Female (n = 498)	0.49 (3.0)	0.86 (2.7)	0.78 (2.7)
Age:			
20–29 (n = 222)	0.32 (3.0)	0.43 (2.7)	0.32 (2.7)
30–39 (n = 141)	0.46 (3.2)	0.70 (2.8)	0.54 (2.7)
40–49 (n = 142)	0.50 (3.0)	0.81 (2.6)	0.70 (2.7)
50–59 (n = 117)	0.61 (2.9)	0.99 (2.4)	0.90 (2.3)
60–69 (n = 272)	0.76 (2.6)	1.16 (2.3)	1.03 (2.3)

[1] From Kowal and Zirkes 1983.
[2] SC-adjusted is adjusted for specific gravity.

TABLE 7—URINE CADMIUM CONCENTRATIONS IN THE U.S. ADULT POPULATION: CUMULATIVE
FREQUENCY DISTRIBUTION OF URINARY CADMIUM (N = 982) [1]

Range of concentrations	Unadjusted (µg/l) percent	SG-adjusted (µg/l at 1.020) percent	Creatine-adjusted (µg/g) percent
<0.5	43.9	28.0	35.8
0.6–1.0	71.7	56.4	65.6
1.1–1.5	84.4	74.9	81.4
1.6–2.0	91.3	84.7	88.9
2.1–3.0	97.3	94.4	95.8
3.1–4.0	98.8	97.4	97.2
4.1–5.0	99.4	98.2	97.9
5.1–10.0	99.6	99.4	99.3
10.0–20.0	99.8	99.6	99.6

[1] Source: Kowal and Zirkes (1983).

The data in the Table 6 indicate the geometric mean of CDU levels observed among the general population is 0.52 µ/g Cd/l urine (unadjusted), with a geometric standard deviation of 3.0. Normalized for creatinine, the geometric mean for the population is 0.66 µ/g CRTU, with a geometric standard deviation of 2.7. Table 7 provides the distributions of CDU concentrations for the general population studied by Kowal and Zirkes. The data in this table indicate that 95% of the CDU levels observed among those not occupationally exposed to cadmium are below 3 µ/g CRTU.

5.2.7.2 *Range of CDU concentrations observed among exposed workers*

Table 8 is a summary of results from available studies of CDU concentrations observed among cadmium-exposed workers. In this table, arithmetic and/or geometric means and standard deviations are provided if reported in these studies. The absolute range for the data in each study, or the 95% confidence interval around the mean of each study, also are provided when reported. The lower and upper 95th percentile of the distribution are presented for each study in which a mean and corresponding standard deviation were reported. Table 8 also provides estimates of the years of exposure, and the levels of exposure, to cadmium in the work place if reported in these studies. Concentrations reported in this table are in µ/g CRTU, unless otherwise stated.

TABLE 8—URINE CADMIUM CONCENTRATIONS IN WORKERS EXPOSED TO CADMIUM IN THE WORKPLACE

Study number	Work environment (worker population monitored)	Number in Study (n)	Employment in years (mean)	Mean Concentration of cadmium in air (µg/m³)	Concentration of cadmium in Urine [a]					Reference
					Arithmetic mean (±S.D.) [b]	Absolute range or (95% C.I.) [c]	Geometric mean (GSD) [d]	Lower 95th percentile of range [e] ( ) [f]	Upper 95th percentile of range [e] ( ) [f]	
1	Ni-Cd battery plant and Cd production plant.		3–40	≤90						Lauwerys et al. 1976.
	(Workers without kidney lesions).	96			16.3±16.7			(0)	(44).	
	(Workers with kidney lesions).	25			48.2±42.6			(0)	(120).	
2	Ni-Cd battery plant									Adamsson et al. (1979).
	(Smokers)	7	(5)	10.1	5.5	1.0–14.7.				
	(Nonsmokers)	8	(9)	7.0	3.6	0.5–9.3.				
3	Cadmium salts production facility.	148	(15.4) [g]		15.8	2–150				Butchet et al. 1980.
4	Retrospective study of workers with renal problems.	19	15–41							Roels et al. 1982.
	(Before removal)		(27.2)		39.4±28.1	10.8–117		(0)	(88).	
	(After removal)		(4.2) [g]		16.4±9.0	80–42.3		(1.0)	(32).	
5	Cadmium production plant.									Ellis et al. 1983.
	(Workers without renal dysfunction).	33	1–34		9.4±6.9	2–27		(0)	(21).	
	(Workers with renal dysfunction).	18	10–34		22.8±12.7	8–55		(1)	(45).	
6	Cd-Cu alloy plant	75	Up to 39	Note h	6.9±9.4			(0)	(23).	Mason et al. 1988.
7	Cadmium recovery operation.	45	(19)	87	9.3±6.9			(0)	(21).	Thun et al. 1989.
8	Pigment manufacturing plant.	29	(12.8)	0.18–3.0		0.2–9.5	1.1			Mueller et al. 1989.
9	Pigment manufacturing plant.	26	(12.1)	≤3.0			1.25±2.45	0.3	6	Kawada et al. 1990.

a Concentrations reported in µg/g Cr.
b S.D.—Standard Deviation.
c C.I.—Confidence Interval.
d GSD—Geometric Standard Deviation.
e Based on an assumed lognormal distribution.
f Based on an assumed normal distribution.
g Years following removal.
h Equivalent to 50 for 20–22 yrs

Data in Table 8 from Lauwerys et al. (1976) and Ellis et al. (1983) indicate that CDU concentrations are higher among those exhibiting kidney lesions or dysfunction than among those lacking these symptoms. Data from the study by Roels et al. (1982) indicate that CDU levels decrease among workers removed from occupational exposure to cadmium in comparison to workers experiencing ongoing exposure. In both cases, however, the distinction between the 2 groups is not as clear as with CDB; there is more overlap in CDU levels observed among each of the paired populations than is true for corresponding CDB levels. As with CDB levels, the data in Table 8 suggest increased CDU concentrations among workers who experienced increased overall exposure.

Although a few occupationally-exposed workers in the studies presented in Table 8 exhibit CDU levels below 3 µg/g CRTU, most of those workers exposed to cadmium levels in excess of the PEL defined in the final cadmium rule exhibit CDU levels above 3 µg/g CRTU; this level represents the upper 95th percentile of the CDU distribution observed among those who are not occupationally exposed to cadmium (Table 7).

The mean CDU levels reported in Table 8 among occupationally-exposed groups studied (except 2) exceed 3 µg/g CRTU. Correspondingly, the level of exposure reported in these studies (with 1 exception) are significantly higher than what workers will experience under the final cadmium rule. The 2 exceptions are from the studies by Mueller et al. (1989) and Kawada et al. (1990); these studies indicate that workers exposed to cadmium during pigment manufacture do not exhibit CDU levels as high as those levels observed among workers exposed to cadmium in other occupations. Exposure levels, however, were lower in the pigment manufacturing plants studied. Significantly, workers removed from occupational cadmium exposure for an average of 4 years still exhibited CDU levels in excess of 3 µg/g CRTU (Roels et al. 1982). In the single-exception study with a reported level of cadmium exposure lower than levels proposed in the final rule (i.e., the study of a pigment manufacturing plant by Kawada et al. 1990), most of the workers exhibited CDU levels less than 3 µg/g CRTU (i.e., the mean value was only 1.3 µg/g CRTU). CDU levels among workers with such limited cadmium exposure are expected to be significantly lower than levels of other studies reported in Table 8.

Based on the above data, a CDU level of 3 µg/g CRTU appear to represent a threshold above which significant work place exposure to cadmium occurs over the work span of those being monitored. Note that this threshold is not as distinct as the corresponding threshold described for CDB. In general, the variability associated with CDU measurements among exposed workers appears to be higher than the variability associated with CDB measurements among similar workers.

5.2.8   Conclusions and Recommendations for CDU

The above evaluation supports the following recommendations for a CDU proficiency program. These recommendations address only sampling and analysis procedures for CDU determinations, which are to be reported as an unadjusted µg Cd/l urine. Normalizing this result to creatinine requires a second analysis for CRTU so that the ratio of the 2 measurements can be obtained. Creatinine analysis is addressed in Section 5.4. Formal procedures for combining the 2 measurements to derive a value and a confidence limit for CDU in µg/g CRTU are provided in Section 3.3.3.

5.2.8.1   *Recommended method*

The method of Pruszkowska et al. (1983) should be adopted for CDU analysis. This method is recommended because it is simple, straightforward and reliable (i.e., small variations in experimental conditions do not affect the analytical results).

A synopsis of the methods used by laboratories to determine CDU under the interlaboratory program administered by the CTQ (1991) indicates that more than 78% (24 of 31) of the participating laboratories use a dilution method to prepare urine samples for CDU analysis. Laboratories may adopt alternate methods, but it is the responsibility of the laboratory to demonstrate that the alternate methods provide results of comparable quality to the Pruszkowska method.

5.2.8.2   *Data quality objectives*

The following data quality objectives should facilitate interpretation of analytical results, and are achievable based on the above evaluation.

Limit of Detection. A level of 0.5 µg/l (i.e., corresponding to a detection limit of 0.5 µg/g CRTU, assuming 1 g CRT/l urine) should be achievable. Pruszkowska et al. (1983) achieved a limit of detection of 0.04 µg/l for CDU based on the slope of the curve for their working standards (0.35 pg Cd/0.0044, A signal = 1% absorbance using GF-AAS).

The CDC reports a minimum detection limit for CDU of 0.07 µg/l using a modified Pruszkowska method. This limit of detection was defined as 3 times the standard deviation calculated from 10 repeated measurements of a "low level" CDU test sample (Attachment 8 of exhibit 106 of OSHA docket H057A). Stoeppler and Brandt (1980) report a limit of detection for CDU of 0.2 µg/l using an aqueous dilution (1:2) of the urine samples.

Accuracy. A recent report from the CTQ (Weber, private communication) indicates that 36% of the laboratories in the program achieve the target of ±1 µg/l or 15% for more than 75% of the samples analyzed over the last 5 years, while 45% of participating laboratories achieve a target of ±2 µg/l or 15% for more than 75% of the samples analyzed over the same period. With time and a strong incentive for improvement, it is expected that the proportion of laboratories successfully achieving the stricter level of accuracy should increase. It should be noted, however, these indices of performance do not include variations resulting from the ancillary measurement of CRTU (which is recommended for the proper recording of results). The low cadmium levels expected to be measured indicate that the analysis of creatinine will contribute relatively little to the overall variability observed among creatinine-normalized CDU levels (see Section 5.4). The initial target value for reporting CDU under this program, therefore, is set at ±1 µg/g CRTU or 15% (whichever is greater).

Precision. For internal QC samples (which are recommended as part of an internal QA/QC program, Section 3.3.1), laboratories should attain an overall precision of 25%. For CDB samples with concentrations less than 2 µg/l, a target precision of 40% is acceptable, while precisions of 20% should be achievable for CDU concentrations greater than 2 µg/l. Although these values are more stringent than those observed in the CTQ interlaboratory program reported by Webber (1988), they are well within limits expected to be achievable for the method as reported by Stoeppler and Brandt (1980).

5.2.8.3 *Quality assurance/quality control*

Commercial laboratories providing CDU determinations should adopt an internal QA/QC program that incorporates the following components: Strict adherence to the selected method, including calibration requirements; regular incorporation of QC samples during actual runs; a protocol for corrective actions, and documentation of such actions; and, participation in an interlaboratory proficiency program. Note that the nonmandatory program presented in Attachment 1 as an example of an acceptable QA/QC program, is based on using the Pruszkowska method for CDU analysis. Should an alternate method be adopted by a laboratory, the laboratory should develop a QA/QC program equivalent to the nonmandatory program, and which satisfies the provisions of Section 3.3.1.

5.3 Monitoring β-2–Microglobulin in Urine (B2MU)

As indicated in Section 4.3, B2MU appears to be the best of several small proteins that may be monitored as early indicators of cadmium-induced renal damage. Several analytic techniques are available for measuring B2M.

5.3.1 Units of B2MU Measurement

Procedures adopted for reporting B2MU levels are not uniform. In these guidelines, OSHA recommends that B2MU levels be reported as µg/g CRTU, similar to reporting CDU concentrations. Reporting B2MU normalized to the concentration of CRTU requires an additional analytical process beyond the analysis of B2M: Independent analysis for creatinine so that results may be reported as a ratio of the B2M and creatinine concentrations found in the urine sample. Consequently, the overall quality of the analysis depends on the combined performance on these 2 analyses. The analysis used for B2MU determinations is described in terms of µg B2M/l urine, with analysis of creatinine addressed separately. Techniques used to measure creatinine are provided in Section 5.4. Note that Section 3.3.3 provides techniques for deriving the value of B2M as function of CRTU, and the confidence limits for independent measurements of B2M and CRTU.

5.3.2 Analytical Techniques Used To Monitor B2MU

One of the earliest tests used to measure B2MU was the radial immunodiffusion technique. This technique is a simple and specific method for identification and quantitation of a number of proteins found in human serum and other body fluids when the protein is not readily differentiated by standard electrophoretic procedures. A quantitative relationship exists between the concentration of a protein deposited in a well that is cut into a thin agarose layer containing corresponding monospecific antiserum, and the distance that the resultant complex diffuses. The wells are filled with an unknown serum and the standard (or control), and incubated in a moist environment at room temperature. After the optimal point of diffusion has been reached, the diameters of the resulting precipitation rings are measured. The diameter of a ring is related to the concentration of the constituent substance. For B2MU determinations required in the medical monitoring program, this method requires a process that may be insufficient to concentrate the protein to levels that are required for detection.

Radioimmunoassay (RIA) techniques are used widely in immunologic assays to measure the concentration of antigen or antibody in body-fluid samples. RIA procedures are based on competitive-binding techniques. If antigen concentration is being measured, the principle underlying the procedure is that radioactive-labeled antigen competes with the sample's unlabeled antigen for binding sites on a known amount of immobile antibody. When these 3 components are present in the system, an equilibrium exists. This equilibrium is followed by a separation of

247

the free and bound forms of the antigen. Either free or bound radioactive-labeled antigen can be assessed to determine the amount of antigen in the sample. The analysis is performed by measuring the level of radiation emitted either by the bound complex following removal of the solution containing the free antigen, or by the isolated solution containing the residual-free antigen. The main advantage of the RIA method is the extreme sensitivity of detection for emitted radiation and the corresponding ability to detect trace amounts of antigen. Additionally, large numbers of tests can be performed rapidly.

The enzyme-linked immunosorbent assay (ELISA) techniques are similar to RIA techniques except that nonradioactive labels are employed. This technique is safe, specific and rapid, and is nearly as sensitive as RIA techniques. An enzyme-labeled antigen is used in the immunologic assay; the labeled antigen detects the presence and quantity of unlabeled antigen in the sample. In a representative ELISA test, a plastic plate is coated with antibody (e.g., antibody to B2M). The antibody reacts with antigen (B2M) in the urine and forms an antigen-antibody complex on the plate. A second anti-B2M antibody (i.e., labeled with an enzyme) is added to the mixture and forms an antibody-antigen-antibody complex. Enzyme activity is measured spectrophotometrically after the addition of a specific chromogenic substrate which is activated by the bound enzyme. The results of a typical test are calculated by comparing the spectrophotometric reading of a serum sample to that of a control or reference serum. In general, these procedures are faster and require less laboratory work than other methods.

In a fluorescent ELISA technique (such as the one employed in the Pharmacia Delphia test for B2M), the labeled enzyme is bound to a strong fluorescent dye. In the Pharmacia Delphia test, an antigen bound to a fluorescent dye competes with unlabeled antigen in the sample for a predetermined amount of specific, immobile antibody. Once equilibrium is reached, the immobile phase is removed from the labeled antigen in the sample solution and washed; an enhancement solution then is added that liberates the fluorescent dye from the bound antigen-antibody complex. The enhancement solution also contains a chelate that complexes with the fluorescent dye in solution; this complex increases the fluorescent properties of the dye so that it is easier to detect.

To determine the quantity of B2M in a sample using the Pharmacia Delphia test, the intensity of the fluorescence of the enhancement solution is measured. This intensity is proportional to the concentration of labeled antigen that bound to the immobile antibody phase during the initial competi-

tion with unlabeled antigen from the sample. Consequently, the intensity of the fluorescence is an inverse function of the concentration of antigen (B2M) in the original sample. The relationship between the fluorescence level and the B2M concentration in the sample is determined using a series of graded standards, and extrapolating these standards to find the concentration of the unknown sample.

5.3.3 Methods Developed for B2MU Determinations

B2MU usually is measured by radioimmunoassay (RIA) or enzyme-linked immunosorbent assay (ELISA); however, other methods (including gel electrophoresis, radial immunodiffusion, and nephelometric assays) also have been described (Schardun and van Epps 1987). RIA and ELISA methods are preferred because they are sensitive at concentrations as low as micrograms per liter, require no concentration processes, are highly reliable and use only a small sample volume.

Based on a survey of the literature, the ELISA technique is recommended for monitoring B2MU. While RIAs provide greater sensitivity (typically about 1 μg/l, Evrin et al. 1971), they depend on the use of radioisotopes; use of radioisotopes requires adherence to rules and regulations established by the Atomic Energy Commission, and necessitates an expensive radioactivity counter for testing. Radioisotopes also have a relatively short half-life, which corresponds to a reduced shelf life, thereby increasing the cost and complexity of testing. In contrast, ELISA testing can be performed on routine laboratory spectrophotometers, do *not* necessitate adherence to additional rules and regulations governing the handling of radioactive substances, and the test kits have long shelf lives. Further, the range of sensitivity commonly achieved by the recommended ELISA test (i.e., the Pharmacia Delphia test) is approximately 100 μg/l (Pharmacia 1990), which is sufficient for monitoring B2MU levels resulting from cadmium exposure. Based on the studies listed in Table 9 (Section 5.3.7), the average range of B2M concentrations among the general, nonexposed population falls between 60 and 300 μg/g CRTU. The upper 95th percentile of distributions, derived from studies in Table 9 which reported standard deviations, range between 180 and 1,140 μg/g CRTU. Also, the Pharmacia Delphia test currently is the most widely used test for assessing B2MU.

5.3.4 Sample Collection and Handling

As with CDB or CDU, sample collection procedures are addressed primarily to identify ways to minimize the degree of variability introduced by sample collection during medical monitoring. It is unclear the extent to which sample collection contributes to B2MU variability. Sources of variation include time-of-day effects, the interval since consuming liquids and the quantity of liquids consumed, and the introduction of external contamination during the collection process. A special problem unique to B2M sampling is the sensitivity of this protein to degradation under acid conditions commonly found in the bladder. To minimize this problem, strict adherence to a sampling protocol is recommended. The protocol should include provisions for normalizing the conditions under which the urine is collected. Clearly, it is important to minimize the interval urine spends in the bladder. It also is recommended that every effort be made to collect samples during the same time of day.

Collection of urine samples for biological monitoring usually is performed using "spot" (*i.e.*, single-void) urine. Logistics and sample integrity become problems when efforts are made to collect urine over extended periods (e.g., 24 hrs). Unless single-void urines are used, numerous opportunities exist for measurement error because of poor control over sample collection, storage and environmental contamination.

To minimize the interval that sample urine resides in the bladder, the following adaption to the "spot" collection procedure is recommended: The bladder should be emptied and then a large glass of water should be consumed; the sample then should be collected within an hour after the water is consumed.

5.3.5 Best Achievable Performance

The best achievable performance is assumed to be equivalent to the performance reported by the manufacturers of the Pharmacia Delphia test kits (Pharmacia 1990). According to the insert that comes with these kits, QC results should be within ±2 SDs of the mean for each control sample tested; a CV of less than or equal to 5.2%

should be maintained. The total CV reported for test kits is less than or equal to 7.2%.

5.3.6 General Method Performance

Unlike analyses for CDB and CDU, the Pharmacia Delphia test is standardized in a commercial kit that controls for many sources of variation. In the absence of data to the contrary, it is assumed that the achievable performance reported by the manufacturer of this test will serve as an achievable performance objective. The CTQ proficiency testing program for B2MU analysis is expected to use the performance parameters defined by the test kit manufacturer as the basis of the B2MU proficiency testing program.

Note that results reported for the test kit are expressed in terms of µg B2M/l of urine, and have not been adjusted for creatinine. The indicated performance, therefore, is a measure of the performance of the B2M portion of the analyses only, and does not include variation that may have been introduced during the analysis of creatinine.

5.3.7 Observed B2MU Concentrations

As indicated in Section 4.3, the concentration of B2MU may serve as an early indicator of the onset of kidney damage associated with cadmium exposure.

5.3.7.1 *Range of B2MU concentrations among unexposed samples*

Most of the studies listed in Table 9 report B2MU levels for those who were not occupationally exposed to cadmium. Studies noted in the second column of this table (which contain the footnote "d") reported B2MU concentrations among cadmium-exposed workers who, nonetheless, showed *no* signs of proteinuria. These latter studies are included in this table because, as indicated in Section 4.3, monitoring B2MU is intended to provide advanced warning of the onset of kidney dysfunction associated with cadmium exposure, rather than to distinguish relative exposure. This table, therefore, indicates the range of B2MU levels observed among those who had no symptoms of renal dysfunction (including cadmium-exposed workers with none of these symptoms).

TABLE 9—B-2-MICROGLOBULIN CONCENTRATIONS OBSERVED IN URINE AMONG THOSE NOT OCCUPATIONALLY EXPOSED TO CADMIUM

Study No.	No. in study	Geo-metric mean	Geo-metric standard deviation	Lower 95th per-centile of distribu-tion [a]	Upper 95th per-centile of distribu-tion [a]	Reference
1	133 m [b]	115 µg/ g [c].	4.03	12	1,140 µg/ g [c].	Ishizaki et al. 1989.
2	161 f [b] ..	146 µg/ g [c].	3.11	23	940 µg/ g [c].	Ishizaki et al. 1989.

249

TABLE 9—B-2-MICROGLOBULIN CONCENTRATIONS OBSERVED IN URINE AMONG THOSE NOT
OCCUPATIONALLY EXPOSED TO CADMIUM—Continued

Study No.	No. in study	Geometric mean	Geometric standard deviation	Lower 95th percentile of distribution[a]	Upper 95th percentile of distribution[a]	Reference
3	10	84 µg/g	....	....	....	Ellis et al. 1983.
4	203	76 µg/l ..	....	....	....	Stewart and Hughes 1981.
5	9	103 µg/g	....	....	....	Chia et al. 1989.
6	47[d]	86 µg/L	1.9	30 µg/1 ..	250 µg/L	Kjellstrom et al. 1977.
7	1,000[e] ..	68.1 µg/ gr Cr[f].	3.1 m & f	<10 µg/gr Cr[h].	320 µg/gr Cr[h].	Kowal 1983.
8	87	71 µg/g[i]	....	7[h]	200[h]	Buchet et al. 1980.
9	10	0.073 mg/ 24h.	....	....	....	Evrin et al. 1971.
10	59	156 µg/g	1.1[j]	130	180	Mason et al. 1988.
11	8	118 µg/g	....	....	....	Iwao et al. 1980.
12	34	79 µg/g	....	....	....	Wibowo et al. 1982.
13	41 m	....	....	....	400 µg/gr Cr[k].	Falck et al. 1983.
14	35[n]	67	....	....	....	Roels et al. 1991.
15	31[d]	63	....	....	....	Roels et al. 1991.
16	36[d]	77[i]	....	....	....	Miksche et al. 1981.
17	18[n]	130	....	....	....	Kawada et al. 1989.
18	32[p]	122	....	....	....	Kawada et al. 1989.
19	18[d]	295	1.4	170	510	Thun et al. 1989.

a—Based on an assumed lognormal distribution.
b—m = males, f = females.
c—Aged general population from non-polluted area; 47.9% population aged 50–69; 52.1% ≥70 years of age; values reported in study.
d—Exposed workers without proteinuria.
e—492 females, 484 male.
f—Creatinine adjusted; males = 68.1 µg/g Cr, females = 64.3 µg/g Cr.
h—Reported in the study.
i—Arithmetic mean.
j—Geometric standard error.
k—Upper 95% tolerance limits: for Falck this is based on the 24 hour urine sample.
n—Controls.
p—Exposed synthetic resin and pigment workers without proteinuria; Cadmium in urine levels up to 10 µg/g Cr.

To the extent possible, the studies listed in Table 9 provide geometric means and geometric standard deviations for measurements among the groups defined in each study. For studies reporting a geometric standard deviation along with a mean, the lower and upper 95th percentile for these distributions were derived and reported in the table.

The data provided from 15 of the 19 studies listed in Table 9 indicate that the geometric mean concentration of B2M observed among those who were not occupationally exposed to cadmium is 70–170 µg/g CRTU. Data from the 4 remaining studies indicate that exposed workers who exhibit no signs of proteinuria show mean B2MU levels of 60–300 µg/g CRTU. B2MU values in the study by Thun et al. (1989), however, appear high in comparison to the other 3 studies. If this study is removed, B2MU levels for those who are not occupationally exposed to cadmium are similar to B2MU levels found among cadmium-exposed workers who exhibit no signs of kidney dysfunction. Although the mean is high in the study by Thun et al., the range of measurements reported in this study is within the ranges reported for the other studies.

Determining a reasonable upper limit from the range of B2M concentrations observed among those who do not exhibit signs of proteinuria is problematic. Elevated B2MU levels are among the signs used to define the onset of kidney dysfunction. Without access to the raw data from the studies listed in Table 9, it is necessary to rely on reported standard deviations to estimate an upper limit for normal B2MU concentrations (i.e., the upper 95th percentile for the distributions measured). For the 8 studies reporting a geometric standard deviation, the upper 95th percentiles for the distributions are 180–

1140 µg/g CRTU. These values are in general agreement with the upper 95th percentile for the distribution (*i.e.*, 631 µg/g CRTU) reported by Buchet et al. (1980). These upper limits also appear to be in general agreement with B2MU values (*i.e.*, 100–690 µg/g CRTU) reported as the normal upper limit by Iwao et al. (1980), Kawada et al. (1989), Wibowo et al. (1982), and Schardun and van Epps (1987). These values must be compared to levels reported among those exhibiting kidney dysfunction to define a threshold level for kidney dysfunction related to cadmium exposure.

5.3.7.2 *Range of B2MU concentrations among exposed workers*

Table 10 presents results from studies reporting B2MU determinations among those occupationally exposed to cadmium in the work place; in some of these studies, kidney dysfunction was observed among exposed workers, while other studies did not make an effort to distinguish among exposed workers based on kidney dysfunction. As with Table 9, this table provides geometric means and geometric standard deviations for the groups defined in each study if available. For studies reporting a geometric standard deviation along with a mean, the lower and upper 95th percentiles for the distributions are derived and reported in the table.

TABLE 10—B-2-MICROGLOBULIN CONCENTRATIONS OBSERVED IN URINE AMONG OCCUPATIONALLY-EXPOSED WORKERS

Study No.	N	Concentration of B-2-Microglobulin in urine				Reference
		Geometric mean (µg/g)[a]	Geom std dev	L 95% of range[b]	U 95% of range[b]	
1	1,424	160	6.19	8.1	3,300	Ishizaki et al., 1989.
2	1,754	260	6.50	12	5,600	Ishizaki et al., 1989.
3	33	210	....	....	....	Ellis et al., 1983.
4	65	210	....	....	....	Chia et al., 1989.
5	[c]44	5,700	6.49	[d]300	[d]98,000	Kjellstrom et al., 1977.
6	148	[e]180	....	[f]110	[f]280	Buchet et al., 1980.
7	37	160	3.90	17	1,500	Kenzaburo et al., 1979.
8	[c]45	3,300	8.7	[d]310	[d]89,000	Mason et al., 1988.
9	[c]10	6,100	5.99	[f]650	[f]57,000	Falck et al., 1983.
10	[c]11	3,900	2.96	[d]710	[d]15,000	Elinder et al., 1985.
11	[c]12	300	....	....	....	Roels et al., 1991.
12	[g]8	7,400	....	....	....	Roels et al., 1991.
13	[c]23	[h]1,800	....	....	....	Roels et al., 1991.
14	10	690	....	....	....	Iwao et al., 1980.
15	34	71	....	....	....	Wibowo et al., 1982.
16	[c]15	4,700	6.49	[d]590	[d]93,000	Thun et al., 1989.

[a] Unless otherwise stated.
[b] Based on an assumed lognormal distribution.
[c] Among workers diagnosed as having renal dysfunction; for Elinder this means β 2 levels greater than 300 micrograms per gram creatinine (µg/gr Cr); for Roels, 1991, range = 31 − 35, 170 µgβ2/gr Cr and geometric mean = 63 among healthy workers; for Mason β2 >300 µg/gr Cr.
[d] Based on a detailed review of the data by OSHA.
[e] Arithmetic mean.
[f] Reported in the study.
[g] Retired workers.
[h] 1,800 µgβ2/gr Cr for first survey; second survey = 1,600; third survey = 2,600; fourth survey = 2,600; fifth survey = 2,600.

The data provided in Table 10 indicate that the mean B2MU concentration observed among workers experiencing occupational exposure to cadmium (but with undefined levels of proteinuria) is 160–7400 µg/g CRTU. One of these studies reports geometric means lower than this range (*i.e.*, as low as 71 µg/g CRTU); an explanation for this wide spread in average concentrations is not available.

Seven of the studies listed in Table 10 report a range of B2MU levels among those diagnosed as having renal dysfunction. As indicated in this table, renal dysfunction (proteinuria) is defined in several of these studies by B2MU levels in excess of 300 µg/g CRTU (see footnote "c" of Table 10); therefore, the range of B2MU levels observed in these studies is a function of the operational definition used to identify those with renal dysfunction. Nevertheless, a B2MU level of 300 µg/g CRTU appears to be a meaningful threshold for identifying those having early signs of kidney damage. While levels much higher than 300 µg/g CRTU have been observed among those with renal dysfunction, the vast majority of those not occupationally exposed to cadmium exhibit much lower B2MU concentrations (see Table 9). Similarly, the vast majority of workers *not* exhibiting renal dysfunction are found to have levels below 300 µg/g CRTU (Table 9).

The 300 µg/g CRTU level for B2MU proposed in the above paragraph has support among researchers as the threshold level that distinguishes between cadmium-exposed workers with and without kidney dysfunction. For example, in the guide for physicians who must evaluate cadmium-exposed workers written for the Cadmium Council by Dr. Lauwerys, levels of B2M greater than 200–300 µg/g CRTU are considered to require additional medical evaluation for kidney dysfunction (exhibit 8–447, OSHA docket H057A). The most widely used test for measuring B2M (*i.e.*, the Pharmacia Delphia test) defines B2M levels above 300 µg/l as abnormal (exhibit L–140–1, OSHA docket H057A).

Dr. Elinder, chairman of the Department of Nephrology at the Karolinska Institute, testified at the hearings on the proposed cadmium rule. According to Dr. Elinder (exhibit L–140–45, OSHA docket H057A), the normal concentration of B2MU has been well documented (Evrin and Wibell 1972; Kjellstrom et al. 1977a; Elinder et al. 1978, 1983; Buchet et al. 1980; Jawaid et al. 1983; Kowal and Zirkes, 1983). Elinder stated that the upper 95 or 97.5 percentiles for B2MU among those without tubular dysfunction is below 300 µg/g CRTU (Kjellstrom et al. 1977a; Buchet et al. 1980; Kowal and Zirkes, 1983). Elinder defined levels of B2M above 300 µg/g CRTU as "slight" proteinuria.

5.3.8 Conclusions and Recommendations for B2MU

Based on the above evaluation, the following recommendations are made for a B2MU proficiency testing program. Note that the following discussion addresses only sampling and analysis for B2MU determinations (*i.e.*, to be reported as an unadjusted µg B2M/l urine). Normalizing this result to creatinine requires a second analysis for CRTU (see Section 5.4) so that the ratio of the 2 measurements can be obtained.

5.3.8.1 *Recommended method*

The Pharmacia Delphia method (Pharmacia 1990) should be adopted as the standard method for B2MU determinations.

Laboratories may adopt alternate methods, but it is the responsibility of the laboratory to demonstrate that alternate methods provide results of comparable quality to the Pharmacia Delphia method.

5.3.8.2 *Data quality objectives*

The following data quality objectives should facilitate interpretation of analytical results, and should be achievable based on the above evaluation.

Limit of Detection. A limit of 100 µg/l urine should be achievable, although the insert to the test kit (Pharmacia 1990) cites a detection limit of 150 µg/l; private conversations with representatives of Pharmacia, however, indicate that the lower limit of 100 µg/l should be achievable provided an additional standard of 100 µg/l B2M is run with the other standards to derive the calibration curve (Section 3.3.1.1). The lower detection limit is desirable due to the proximity of this detection limit to B2MU values defined for the cadmium medical monitoring program.

Accuracy. Because results from an interlaboratory proficiency testing program are not available currently, it is difficult to define an achievable level of accuracy. Given the general performance parameters defined by the insert to the test kits, however, an accuracy of ±15% of the target value appears achievable.

Due to the low levels of B2MU to be measured generally, it is anticipated that the analysis of creatinine will contribute relatively little to the overall variability observed among creatinine-normalized B2MU levels (see Section 5.4). The initial level of accuracy for reporting B2MU levels under this program should be set at ±15%.

Precision. Based on precision data reported by Pharmacia (1990), a precision value (*i.e.*, CV) of 5% should be achievable over the defined range of the analyte. For internal QC samples (*i.e.*, recommended as part of an internal QA/QC program, Section 3.3.1), laboratories should attain precision near 5% over the range of concentrations measured.

5.3.8.3 *Quality assurance/quality control*

Commercial laboratories providing measurement of B2MU should adopt an internal QA/QC program that incorporates the following components: Strict adherence to the Pharmacia Delphia method, including calibration requirements; regular use of QC samples during routine runs; a protocol for corrective actions, and documentation of these actions; and, participation in an interlaboratory proficiency program. Procedures that may be used to address internal QC requirements are presented in Attachment 1. Due to differences between analyses for B2MU and CDB/CDU, specific values presented in Attachment 1 may have to be modified. Other components of the program (including characterization runs), however, can be adapted to a program for B2MU.

5.4 Monitoring Creatinine in Urine (CRTU)

Because CDU and B2MU should be reported relative to concentrations of CRTU, these concentrations should be determined in addition CDU and B2MU determinations.

5.4.1 Units of CRTU Measurement

CDU should be reported as µg Cd/g CRTU, while B2MU should be reported as µg B2M/g CRTU. To derive the ratio of cadmium or B2M to creatinine, CRTU should be reported in units of g crtn/l of urine. Depending on the analytical method, it may be necessary to convert results of creatinine determinations accordingly.

5.4.2 Analytical Techniques Used To Monitor CRTU

Of the techniques available for CRTU determinations, an absorbance spectrophotometric technique and a high-performance liquid chromatography (HPLC) technique are identified as acceptable in this protocol.

5.4.3 Methods Developed for CRTU Determinations

CRTU analyse performed in support of either CDU or B2MU determinations should be performed using either of the following 2 methods:

1. The Du Pont method (*i.e.*, Jaffe method), in which creatinine in a sample reacts with picrate under alkaline conditions, and the resulting red chromophore is monitored (at 510 nm) for a fixed interval to determine the rate of the reaction; this reaction rate is proportional to the concentration of creatinine present in the sample (a copy of this method is provided in Attachment 2 of this protocol); or,

2. The OSHA SLC Technical Center (OSLTC) method, in which creatinine in an aliquot of sample is separated using an HPLC column equipped with a UV detector; the resulting peak is quantified using an electrical integrator (a copy of this method is provided in Attachment 3 of this protocol).

5.4.4 Sample Collection and Handling

CRTU samples should be segregated from samples collected for CDU or B2MU analysis. Sample-collection techniques have been described under Section 5.2.4. Samples should be preserved either to stabilize CDU (with HNO_3) or B2MU (with NaOH). Neither of these procedures should adversely affect CRTU analysis (see Attachment 3).

5.4.5 General Method Performance

Data from the OSLTC indicate that a CV of 5% should be achievable using the OSLTC method (Septon, L private communication). The achievable accuracy of this method has not been determined.

Results reported in surveys conducted by the CAP (CAP 1991a, 1991b and 1992) indicate that a CV of 5% is achievable. The accuracy achievable for CRTU determinations has not been reported.

Laboratories performing creatinine analysis under this protocol should be CAP accredited and should be active participants in the CAP surveys.

5.4.6 Observed CRTU Concentrations

Published data suggest the range of CRTU concentrations is 1.0–1.6 g in 24-hour urine samples (Harrison 1987). These values are equivalent to about 1 g/l urine.

5.4.7 Conclusions and Recommendations for CRTU

5.4.7.1 *Recommended method*

Use either the Jaffe method (Attachment 2) or the OSLTC method (Attachment 3). Alternate methods may be acceptable provided adequate performance is demonstrated in the CAP program.

5.4.7.2 *Data quality objectives*

Limit of Detection. This value has not been formally defined; however, a value of 0.1 g/l urine should be readily achievable.

Accuracy. This value has not been defined formally; accuracy should be sufficient to retain accreditation from the CAP.

Precision. A CV of 5% should be achievable using the recommended methods.

6.0 References

Adamsson E, Piscator M, and Nogawa K. (1979). Pulmonary and gastrointestinal exposure to cadmium oxide dust in a battery factory. *Environmental Health Perspectives, 28,* 219–222.

American Conference of Governmental Industrial Hygienists (ACGIH). (1986). *Documentation of the Threshold Limit Values and Biological Exposure Indices.* 5th edition. p. BEI–55.

Bernard A, Buchet J, Roels H, Masson P, and Lauwerys R. (1979). Renal excretion of proteins and enzymes in workers exposed to cadmium. *European Journal of Clinical Investigation, 9,* 11–22.

Bernard A and Lauwerys R. (1990). Early markers of cadmium nephrotoxicity: Biological significance and predictive value. *Toxocological and Environmental Chemistry, 27,* 65–72.

Braunwald E, Isselbacher K, Petersdorf R, Wilson J, Martin J, and Fauci A (Eds.).

(1987). *Harrison's Principles of Internal Medicine.* New York: McGraw-Hill Book Company.

Buchet J, Roels H, Bernard I, and Lauwerys R. (1980). Assessment of renal funcion of workers exposed to inorganic lead, cadmium, or mercury vapor. *Journal of Occupational Medicine,* 22, 741–750.

CAP. (1991). Urine Chemistry, Series 1: Survey (Set U-B). College of American Pathologists.

CAP. (1991). Urine Chemistry, Series 1: Survey (Set U-C). College of American Pathologists.

CAP. (1992). Urine Chemistry, Series 1: Survey (Set U-A). College of American Pathologists.

CDC. (1986). Centers for Disease Control, Division of Environmental Health Laboratory Sciences, Center for Environmental Health, Atlanta, Georgia. Docket No. 106A. Lake Couer d'Alene, Idaho cadmium and lead study: 86–0030, Specimen collection and shipping protocol.

CDC. (1990). Centers for Disease Control, Nutritional Biochemistry Branch. 4/27/90 Draft SOP for Method 0360A "Determination of cadmium in urine by graphite furnace atomic absorption spectrometry with Zeeman background correction.

Centre de Toxicologie du Quebec. (1991). Interlaboratory comparison program report for run #2. Shipping date 3/11/91. Addition BLR 9/19.

Chia K, Ong C, Ong H, and Endo G. (1989). Renal tubular function of workers exposed to low levels of cadmium. *British Journal of Industrial Medicine,* 46, 165–170.

Claeys-Thoreau F. (1982). Determination of low levels of cadmium and lead in biological fluids with simple dilution by atomic absorption spectrophotometry using Zeeman effect background absorption and the L'Vov platform. *Atomic Spectroscopy,* 3, 188–191.

DeBenzo Z, Fraile R, and Carrion N. (1990). Electrothermal atomization atomic absorption spectrometry with stabilized aqueous standards for the determination of cadmium in whole blood. *Analytica Chimica Acta,* 231, 283–288.

Elinder C, Edling C, Lindberg E, Kagedal B, and Vesterberg O. (1985). Assessment of renal function in workers previously exposed to cadmium. *British Journal of Internal Medicine,* 42, 754.

Ellis K, Cohn S, and Smith T. (1985). Cadmium inhalation exposure estimates: Their significance with respect to kidney and liver cadmium burden. *Journal of Toxicology and Environmental Health,* 15, 173–187.

Ellis K, Yasumura S, Vartsky D, and Cohn S. (1983). Evaluation of biological indicators of body burden of cadmium in humans. *Fundamentals and Applied Toxicology,* 3, 169–174.

Ellis K, Yeun K, Yasumura S, and Cohn S. (1984). Dose-response analysis of cadmium in man: Body burden vs kidney function. *Environmental Research,* 33, 216–226.

Evrin P, Peterson A, Wide I, and Berggard I. (1971). Radioimmunoassay of B-2-microglobulin in human biological fluids. *Scandanavian Journal of Clinical Laboratory Investigation,* 28, 439–443.

Falck F, Fine L, Smith R, Garvey J, Schork A, England B, McClatchey K, and Linton J. (1983). Metallothionein and occupational exposure to cadmium. *British Journal of Industrial Medicine,* 40, 305–313.

FEDERAL REGISTER. (1990). Occupational exposure to cadmium: Proposed rule. 55/22/4052–4147, February 6.

Friberg, Exhibit 29, (1990). Exhibit No. 29 of the OSHA Federal Docket H057A. Washington, DC.

Friberg L. (1988). Quality assurance. In T. Clarkson (Ed.), *Biological Monitoring of Toxic Metals* (pp. 103–105). New York: Plenum Press.

Friberg L, and Elinder C. (1988). Cadmium toxicity in humans. In *Essential and Trace Elements in Human Health and Disease* (pp. 559–587). Docket Number 8–660.

Friberg L, Elinder F, et al. (1986). *Cadmium and Health: A Toxicological and Epidemiological Appraisal. Volume II, Effects and Response.* Boca Raton, FL: CRC Press.

Friberg L, Piscator M, Nordberg G, and Kjellstrom T. (1974). *Cadmium in the Environment* (2nd ed.). Cleveland:CRC.

Friberg L and Vahter M. (1983). Assessment of exposure to lead and cadmium through biological monitoring: Results of a UNEP/WHO global study. *Environmental Research,* 30, 95–128.

Gunter E, and Miller D. (1986). Laboratory procedures used by the division of environmental health laboratory sciences center for environmental health, Centers for Disease Control for the hispanic health and nutrition examination survey (HHANES). Atlanta, GA: Centers for Disease Control.

Harrison. (1987). Harrison's Principles of Internal Medicine. Braunwald, E; Isselbacher, KJ; Petersdorf, RG; Wilson, JD; Martin, JB; and Fauci, AS Eds. Eleventh Ed. McGraw Hill Book Company. San Francisco.

Henry J. (1991). *Clinical Diagnosis and Management by Laboratory Methods* (18th edition). Philadelphia: WB Saunders Company.

IARC (1987). *IRAC Monographs on the Evaluation of Carcinogenic Risks to Humans. Overall Evaluation of Carcinogenicity: Update of Volume 1–42.* Supplemental 7, 1987.

Ishizaki M, Kido T, Honda R, Tsuritani I, Yamada Y, Nakagawa H, and Nogawa K. (1989). Dose-response relationship between urinary cadmium and B-2-microglobulin in a Japanese environmentally cadmium exposed population. *Toxicology,* 58, 121–131.

Iwao S, Tsuchiya K, and Sakurai H. (1980). Serum and urinary B-2-microglobulin among cadmium-exposed workers. *Journal of Occupational Medicine,* 22, 399–402.

Iwata K, Katoh T, Morikawa Y, Aoshima K, Nishijo M, Teranishi H, and Kasuya M.

(1988). Urinary trehalase activity as an indicator of kidney injury due to environmental cadmium exposure. *Archives of Toxicology, 62,* 435–439.

Kawada T, Koyama H, and Suzuki S. (1989). Cadmium, NAG activity, and B-2-microglobulin in the urine of cadmium pigment workers. *British Journal of Industrial Medicine, 46,* 52–55.

Kawada T, Tohyama C, and Suzuki S. (1990). Significance of the excretion of urinary indicator proteins for a low level of occupational exposure to cadmium. *International Archives of Occupational Environmental Health, 62,* 95–100.

Kjellstrom T. (1979). Exposure and accumulation of cadmium in populations from Japan, the United States, and Sweden. *Environmental Health Perspectives, 28,* 169–197.

Kjellstrom T, Evrin P, and Rahnster B. (1977). Dose-response analysis of cadmium-induced tubular proteinuria. *Environmental Research, 13,* 303–317.

Kjellstrom T, Shiroishi K, and Evrin P. (1977). Urinary B-2-microglobulin excretion among people exposed to cadmium in the general environment. *Environmental Research, 13,* 318–344.

Kneip T, & Crable J (Eds.). (1988). Method 107. Cadmium in blood. *Methods for biological monitoring* (pp.161–164). Washington, DC: American Public Health Association.

Kowal N. (1988). Urinary cadmium and B-2-microglobulin: Correlation with nutrition and smoking history. *Journal of Toxicology and Environmental Health, 25,* 179–183.

Kowal N, Johnson D, Kraemer D, and Pahren H. (1979). Normal levels of cadmium in diet, urine, blood, and tissues of inhabitants of the United States. *Journal of Toxicology and Environmental Health, 5,* 995–1014.

Kowal N and Zirkes M. (1983). Urinary cadmium and B-2-microglobulin: Normal values and concentration adjustment. *Journal of Toxicology and Environmental Health, 11,* 607–624.

Lauwerys R, Buchet J, and Roels H. (1976). The relationship between cadmium exposure or body burden and the concentration of cadmium in blood and urine in man. *International Archives of Occupational and Environmental Health, 36,* 275–285

Lauwerys R, Roels H, Regniers, Buchet J, and Bernard A. (1979). Significance of cadmium concentration in blood and in urine in workers exposed to cadmium. *Environmental Research, 20,* 375–391.

Lind B, Elinder C, Friberg L, Nilsson B, Svartengren M, and Vahter M. (1987). Quality control in the analysis of lead and cadmium in blood. *Fresenius' Zeitschrift fur Analytical Chemistry, 326,* 647–655.

Mason H, Davison A, Wright A, Guthrie C, Fayers P, Venables K, Smith N, Chettle D, Franklin D, Scott M, Holden H, Gompertz D, and Newman-Taylor A. (1988). Relations between liver cadmium, cumulative exposure, and renal function in cadmium alloy workers. *British Journal of Industrial Medicine, 45,* 793–802.

Meridian Research, Inc. (1989). *Quantitative Assessment of Cancer Risks Associated with Occupational Exposure to Cd.* Prepared by Meridian Research, Inc. and Roth Associates, Inc. for the Occupational Safety & Health Administration. June 12, 1989.

Meridian Research, Inc and Roth Associates, Inc. (1989). *Quantitative Assessment of the Risk of Kidney Dysfunction Associated with Occupational Exposure to Cd.* Prepared by Meridian Research, Inc. and Roth Associates, Inc. for the Occupational Safety & Health Administration. July 31 1989.

Micheils E and DeBievre P. (1986). Method 25–Determination of cadmium in whole blood by isotope dilution mass spectrometry. O'Neill I, Schuller P, and Fishbein L (Eds.), *Environmental Carcinogens Selected Methods of Analysis* (Vol. 8). Lyon, France: International Agency for Research on Cancer.

Mueller P, Smith S, Steinberg K, and Thun M. (1989). Chronic renal tubular effects in relation to urine cadmium levels. *Nephron, 52,* 45–54.

NIOSH. (1984a). Elements in blood or tissues. Method 8005 issued 5/15/85 and Metals in urine. Method 8310 issued 2/15/84 In P. Eller (Ed.), *NIOSH Manual of Analytical Methods* (Vol. 1, Ed. 3). Cincinnati, Ohio: US-DHHS.

NIOSH. (1984b). Lowry L. Section F: Special considerations for biological samples in *NIOSH Manual of Analytical Methods* (Vol. 1, 3rd ed.). P. Eller (Ed.). Cincinnati, Ohio: US-DHHS.

Nordberg G and Nordberg M. (1988). Biological monitoring of cadmium. In T. Clarkson, L. Friberg, G. Nordberg, and P. Sager (Eds.), *Biological Monitoring of Toxic Metals,* New York: Plenum Press.

Nogawa K. (1984). Biologic indicators of cadmium nephrotoxicity in persons with low-level cadmium exposure. *Environmental Health Perspectives, 54,* 163–169.

OSLTC (no date). Analysis of Creatinine for the Normalization of Cadmium and Beta-2-Microglobulin Concentrations in Urine. OSHA Salt Lake Technical Center. Salt Lake City, UT. Paschal. (1990). Attachment 8 of exhibit 106 of the OSHA docket H057A.

Perkin-Elmer Corporation. (1982). *Analytical Methods for Atomic Absorption Spectroscopy.*

Perkin-Elmer Corporation. (1977). *Analytical Methods Using the HGA Graphite Furnace.*

Pharmacia Diagnostics. (1990). Pharmacia DELFIA system B–2-microglobulin kit insert. Uppsala, Sweden: Pharmacia Diagnostics.

Piscator M. (1962). Proteinuria in chronic cadmium poisoning. *Archives of Environmental Health,5,* 55–62.

Potts, C.L. (1965). Cadmium Proteinuria—The Health Battery Workers Exposed to Cadmium Oxide dust. Ann Occup Hyg, 3:55–61, 1965.

Princi F. (1947). A study of industrial exposures to cadmium. *Journal of Industrial Hygiene and Toxicology*, *29*, 315–320.

Pruszkowska E, Carnick G, and Slavin W. (1983). Direct determination of cadmium in urine with use of a stabilized temperature platform furnace and Zeeman background correction. *Clinical Chemistry*, *29*, 477–480.

Roberts C and Clark J. (1986). Improved determination of cadmium in blood and plasma by flameless atomic absorption spectroscopy. *Bulletin of Environmental Contamination and Toxicology*, *36*, 496–499.

Roelandts I. (1989). Biological reference materials. *Soectrochimica Acta*, *44B*, 281–290.

Roels H, Buchet R, Lauwerys R, Bruaux P, Clays-Thoreau F, Laafontaine A, Overschelde J, and Verduyn J. (1978). Lead and cadmium absorption among children near a nonferrous metal plant. *Environmental Research*, *15*, 290–308.

Roels H, Djubgang J, Buchet J, Bernard A, and Lauwerys R. (1982). Evolution of cadmium-induced renal dysfunction in workers removed from exposure. *Scandanavian Journal of Work and Environmental Health*, *8*, 191–200.

Roels H, Lauwerys R, and Buchet J. (1989). Health significance of cadmium induced renal dysfunction: A five year follow-up. *British Journal of Industrial Medicine*, *46*, 755–764.

Roels J, Lauwerys R, Buchet J, Bernard A, Chettle D, Harvey T, and Al-Haddad I. (1981). In vivo measurements of liver and kidney cadmium in workers exposed to this metal: Its significance with respect to cadmium in blood and urine. *Environmental Research*, *26*, 217–240.

Roels H, Lauwerys R, Buchet J, Bernard A, Lijnen P, and Houte G. (1990). Urinary kallikrein activity in workers exposed to cadmium, lead, or mercury vapor. *British Journal of Industrial Medicine*, *47*, 331–337.

Sakurai H, Omae K, Toyama T, Higashi T, and Nakadate T. (1982). Cross-sectional study of pulmonary function in cadmium alloy workers. *Scandanavian Journal of Work and Environmental Health*, *8*, 122–130.

Schardun G and van Epps L. (1987). B–2-microglobulin: Its significance in the evaluation of renal function. *Kidney International*, *32*, 635–641.

Shaikh Z, and Smith L. (1984). Biological indicators of cadmium exposure and toxicity. *Experentia*, *40*, 36–43.

Smith J and Kench J. (1957). Observations on urinary cadmium and protein excretion in men exposed to cadmium oxide dust and fume. *British Journal of Industrial Medicine*, *14*, 240–245.

Smith J, Kench J, and Lane R. (1955). Determination of Cadmium in urine and obser- vations on urinary cadmium and protein excretion in men exposed to cadmium oxide dust. *British Journal of Industrial Medicine*, *12*, 698–701.

SWRI (Southwest Research Institute). (1978). The distribution of cadmium and other metals in human tissues. Health Effects Research Lab, Research Triangle Park, NC, Population Studies Division. NTIS No. PB–285–200.

Stewart M and Hughes E. (1981). Urinary B–2-microglobulin in the biological monitoring of cadmium workers. *British Journal of Industrial Medicine*, *38*, 170–174.

Stoeppler K and Brandt M. (1980). Contributions to automated trace analysis. part V. Determination of cadmium in whole blood and urine by electrothermal atomic absorption spectrophotometry. *Fresenius' Zeitschrift fur Analytical Chemistry*, *300*, 372–380.

Takenaka et al. (1983). *Carcinogencity of Cd Chloride Aerosols in White Rates*. INCI 70: 367–373, 1983.

Thun M, Osorio A, Schober S, Hannon W, Lewis B, and Halperin W. (1989). Nephropathy in cadmium workers: Assessment of risk from airborne occupational exposure to cadmium. *British Journal of Industrial Medicine*, *46*, 689–697.

Thun M, Schnorr T, Smith A, Halperin W, and Lemen R. (1985). Mortality among a cohort of US cadmium production workers—an update. *Journal of the National Cancer Institute*, *74*, 325–333.

Travis D and Haddock A. (1980). Interpretation of the observed age-dependency of cadmium body burdens in man. *Environmental Research*, *22*, 46–60.

Tsuchiya K. (1967). Proteinuria of workers exposed to cadmium fume. *Archives of Environmental Health*, *14*, 875–880.

Tsuchiya K. (1976). Proteinuria of cadmium workers. *Journal of Occupational Medicine*, *18*, 463–470.

Tsuchiya K, Iwao S, Sugita M, Sakurai H. (1979). Increased urinary B-2-microglobulin in cadmium exposure: Dose-effect relationship and biological significance of B-2-microglobulin. *Environmental Health Perspectives*, *28*, 147–153.

USEPA. (1985). Updated Mutagenicity and Carcinogenicity Assessments of Cd: Addendum to the Health Assessment Document for Cd (May 1981). Final Report. June 1985.

Vahter M and Friberg L. (1988). Quality control in integrated human exposure monitoring of lead and cadmium. *Fresenius' Zeitschrift fur Analytical Chemistry*, *332*, 726–731.

Weber J. (1988). An interlaboratory comparison programme for several toxic substances in blood and urine. *The Science of the Total Environment*, *71*, 111–123.

Weber J. (1991a). Accuracy and precision of trace metal determinations in biological fluids. In K. Subramanian, G. Iyengar, and K.

Okamot (Eds.), *Biological Trace Element Research*-Multidisciplinary Perspectives, ACS Symposium Series 445. Washington, DC: American Chemical Society.

Weber J. (1991b). Personal communication about interlaboratory program and shipping biological media samples for cadmium analyses.

Wibowo A, Herber R, van Deyck W, and Zielhuis R. (1982). Biological assessment of exposure in factories with second degree usage of cadmium compounds. *International Archives of Occupational Environmental Health, 49*, 265–273.

Attachment 1—Nonmandatory Protocol for an Internal Quality Assurance/Quality Control Program

The following is an example of the type of internal quality assurance/quality control program that assures adequate control to satisfy OSHA requirements under this protocol. However, other approaches may also be acceptable.

As indicated in Section 3.3.1 of the protocol, the QA/QC program for CDB and CDU should address, at a minimum, the following:
• calibration;
• establishment of control limits;
• internal QC analyses and maintaining control; and
• corrective action protocols.

This illustrative program includes both initial characterization runs to establish the performance of the method and ongoing analysis of quality control samples intermixed with compliance samples to maintain control.

Calibration

Before any analytical runs are conducted, the analytic instrument must be calibrated. This is to be done at the beginning of each day on which quality control samples and/or compliance samples are run. Once calibration is established, quality control samples or compliance samples may be run. Regardless of the type of samples run, every fifth sample must be a standard to assure that the calibration is holding.

Calibration is defined as holding if every standard is within plus or minus (±) 15% of its theoretical value. If a standard is more than plus or minus 15% of its theoretical value, then the run is out of control due to calibration error and the entire set of samples must either be reanalyzed after recalibrating or results should be recalculated based on a statistical curve derived from the measurement of all standards.

It is essential that the highest standard run is higher than the highest sample run. To assure that this is the case, it may be necessary to run a high standard at the end of the run, which is selected based on the results obtained over the course of the run.

All standards should be kept fresh, and as they get old, they should be compared with new standards and replaced if they exceed the new standards by ±15%.

Initial Characterization Runs and Establishing Control

A participating laboratory should establish four pools of quality control samples for each of the analytes for which determinations will be made. The concentrations of quality control samples within each pool are to be centered around each of the four target levels for the particular analyte identified in Section 4.4 of the protocol.

Within each pool, at least 4 quality control samples need to be established with varying concentrations ranging between plus or minus 50% of the target value of that pool. Thus for the medium-high cadmium in blood pool, the theoretical values of the quality control samples may range from 5 to 15 µg/l, (the target value is 10 µg/l). At least 4 unique theoretical values must be represented in this pool.

The range of theoretical values of plus or minus 50% of the target value of a pool means that there will be overlap of the pools. For example, the range of values for the medium-low pool for cadmium in blood is 3.5 to 10.5 µg/l while the range of values for the medium-high pool is 5 to 15 µg/l. Therefore, it is possible for a quality control sample from the medium-low pool to have a higher concentration than a quality control sample from the medium-high pool.

Quality control samples may be obtained as commercially available reference materials, internally prepared, or both. Internally prepared samples should be well characterized and traced or compared to a reference material for which a consensus value for concentration is available. Levels of analyte in the quality control samples must be concealed from the analyst prior to the reporting of analytical results. Potential sources of materials that may be used to construct quality control samples are listed in Section 3.3.1 of the protocol.

Before any compliance samples are analyzed, control limits must be established. Control limits should be calculated for every pool of each analyte for which determinations will be made and control charts should be kept for each pool of each analyte. A separate set of control charts and control limits should be established for each analytical instrument in a laboratory that will be used for analysis of compliance samples.

At the beginning of this QA/QC program, control limits should be based on the results of the analysis of 20 quality control samples from each pool of each analyte. For any given pool, the 20 quality control samples should be run on 20 different days. Although no more than one sample should be run from

257

any single pool on a particular day, a laboratory may run quality control samples from different pools on the same day. This constitutes a set of initial characterization runs.

For each quality control sample analyzed, the value F/T (defined in the glossary) should be calculated. To calculate the control limits for a pool of an analyte, it is first necessary to calculate the mean, $\bar{X}$, of the F/T values for each quality control sample in a pool and then to calculate its standard deviation σ. Thus, for the control limit for a pool, $\bar{X}$ is calculated as:

$$\frac{\left(\sum \dfrac{F}{T}\right)}{N}$$

and σ is calculated as

$$\left[\frac{\sum\left(\dfrac{F}{T}-\bar{X}\right)^2}{N-1}\right]^{\frac{1}{2}}$$

Where N is the number of quality control samples run for a pool.

The control limit for a particular pool is then given by the mean plus or minus 2 standard deviations (X ±3σ).

The control limits may be no greater than 40% of the mean F/T value. If three standard deviations are greater than 40% of the mean F/T value, then analysis of compliance samples may not begin.[1] Instead, an investigation into the causes of the large standard deviation should begin, and the inadequacies must be remedied. Then, control limits must be reestablished which will mean repeating the running 20 quality control samples from each pool over 20 days.

Internal Quality Control Analyses and Maintaining Control

Once control limits have been established for each pool of an analyte, analysis of compliance samples may begin. During any run of compliance samples, quality control samples are to be interspersed at a rate of no less than 5% of the compliance sample workload. When quality control samples are run, however, they should be run in sets consisting of one quality control sample from each pool. Therefore, it may be necessary, at times, to intersperse quality control samples at a rate greater than 5%.

There should be at least one set of quality control samples run with any analysis of compliance samples. At a minimum, for example, 4 quality control samples should be run even if only 1 compliance sample is run. Generally, the number of quality control samples that should be run are a multiple of four with the minimum equal to the smallest multiple of four that is greater than 5% of the total number of samples to be run. For example, if 300 compliance samples of an analyte are run, then at least 16 quality control samples should be run (16 is the smallest multiple of four that is greater than 15, which is 5% of 300).

Control charts for each pool of an analyte (and for each instrument in the laboratory to be used for analysis of compliance samples) should be established by plotting F/T versus date as the quality control sample results are reported. On the graph there should be lines representing the control limits for the pool, the mean F/T limits for the pool, and the theoretical F/T of 1.000. Lines representing plus or minus (±) $\hat{\sigma}$ should also be represented on the charts. A theoretical example of a control chart is presented in Figure 1.

FIGURE 1—THEORETICAL EXAMPLE OF A CONTROL CHART FOR A POOL OF AN ANALYTE

			X					1.162 (Upper Control Limit)
	X							1.096 (Upper 2$\hat{\sigma}$ Line)
X								1.000 (Theoretical Mean)
		X	X			X		0.964 (Mean)
				X	X			
	X							0.832 (Lower 2$\hat{\sigma}$ Line)
					X			0.766 (Lower Control Limit)
March	2	2	3	5	6	9	10	13	16	17

[1] Note that the value, "40%" may change over time as experience is gained with the program.

All quality control samples should be plotted on the chart, and the charts should be checked for visual trends. If a quality control sample falls above or below the control limits for its pool, then corrective steps must be taken (see the section on corrective actions below). Once a laboratory's program has been established, control limits should be updated every 2 months.

The updated control limits should be calculated from the results of the last 100 quality control samples run for each pool. If 100 quality control samples from a pool have not been run at the time of the update, then the limits should be based on as many as have been run provided at least 20 quality control samples from each pool have been run over 20 different days.

The trends that should be looked for on the control charts are:

1. 10 consecutive quality control samples falling above or below the mean;
2. 3 consecutive quality control samples falling more than 2σ from the mean (above or below the 2σ lines of the chart); or
3. the mean calculated to update the control limits falls more than 10% above or below the theoretical mean of 1.000.

If any of these trends is observed, then all analysis must be stopped, and an investigation into the causes of the errors must begin. Before the analysis of compliance samples may resume, the inadequacies must be remedied and the control limits must be reestablished for that pool of an analyte. Reestablishment of control limits will entail running 20 sets of quality control samples over 20 days.

Note that alternative procedures for defining internal quality control limits may also be acceptable. Limits may be based, for example, on proficiency testing, such as ±1 μg or 15% of the mean (whichever is greater). These should be clearly defined.

Corrective actions

Corrective action is the term used to describe the identification and remediation of errors occurring within an analysis. Corrective action is necessary whenever the result of the analysis of any quality control sample falls outside of the established control limits. The steps involved may include simple things like checking calculations of basic instrument maintenance, or it may involve more complicated actions like major instrument repair. Whatever the source of error, it must be identified and corrected (and a Corrective Action Report (CAR) must be completed. CARs should be kept on file by the laboratory.

Attachment 2—Creatinine in Urine (Jaffe Procedure)

Intended use: The CREA pack is used in the Du Pont ACA® discrete clinical analyzer to quantitatively measure creatinine in serum and urine.

Summary: The CREA method employs a modification of the kinetic Jaffe reaction reported by Larsen. This method has been reported to be less susceptible than conventional methods to interference from non-creatinine, Jaffe-positive compounds.[1]

A split sample comparison between the CREA method and a conventional Jaffe procedure on Autoanalyzer® showed a good correlation. (See Specific Performance Characteristics).

*Note: Numbered subscripts refer to the bibliography and lettered subscripts refer to footnotes.

Autoanalyzer®, is a registered trademark of Technicon Corp., Tarrytown, NY.

Principles of Procedure: In the presence of a strong base such as NaOH, picrate reacts with creatinine to form a red chromophore. The rate of increasing absorbance at 510 nm due to the formation of this chromophore during a 17.07-second measurement period is directly proportional to the creatinine concentration in the sample.

$$\text{Creatinine} + \text{Picrate} \xrightarrow{\text{NaOH}} \text{Red chromophore (absorbs at 510 nm)}$$

Reagents:

Compartment[a]	Form	Ingredient	Quantity[b]
No. 2, 3, & 4	Liquid	Picrate	0.11 mmol.
6	Liquid	NaOH (for pH adjustment)[c].	

a. Compartments are numbered 1–7, with compartment #7 located closest to pack fill position #2.
b. Nominal value at manufacture.
c. See Precautions.

Precautions: Compartment #6 contains 75μL of 10 N NaOH; avoid contact; skin irritant; rinse contacted area with water. Comply with OSHA'S Bloodborne Pathogens Standard while handling biological samples (29 CFR 1910.1039).

Used packs contain human body fluids; handle with appropriate care.

FOR IN VITRO DIAGNOSTIC USE

Mixing and Diluting:

Mixing and diluting are automatically performed by the ACA® discrete clinical analyzer. The sample cup must contain sufficient quantity to accommodate the sample volume plus the "dead volume"; precise cup filling is not required.

SAMPLE CUP VOLUMES (μL)

Analyzer	Standard		Microsystem	
	Dead	Total	Dead	Total
II, III	120	3000	10	500
IV, SX	120	3000	30	500
V	90	3000	10	500

Storage of Unprocessed Packs: Store at 2–8 °C. Do not freeze. Do not expose to temperatures above 35 °C or to direct sunlight.

Expiration: Refer to EXPIRATION DATE on the tray label.

Specimen Collection: Serum or urine can be collected and stored by normal procedures. [2]

Known Interfering Substances [3]

• Serum Protein Influence—Serum protein levels exert a direct influence on the CREA assay. The following should be taken into account when this method is used for urine samples and when it is calibrated:

Aqueous creatinine standards or urine specimens will give CREA results depressed by approximately 0.7 mg/dL [62 μmol/L] [d] and will be less precise than samples containing more than 3 g/dL [30 g/L] protein.

All urine specimens should be diluted with an albumin solution to give a final protein concentration of at least 3 g/dL [30 g/L]. Du Pont Enzyme Diluent (Cat. #790035–901) may be used for this purpose.

• High concentration of endogenous bilirubin (>20 mg/dL [>342 μmol/L]) will give depressed CREA results (average depression 0.8 mg/dL [71 μmol/L]). [4]

• Grossly hemolyzed (hemoglobin >100 mg/dL [>62 μmol/L]) or visibly lipemic specimens may cause falsely elevated CREA results. [5][6]

• The following cephalosporin antibiotics do not interfere with the CREA method when present at the concentrations indicated. Systematic inaccuracies (bias) due to these substances are less than or equal to 0.1 mg/dL [8.84 μmol/L] at CREA concentrations of approximately 1 mg/dL [88 μmol/L].

Antibiotic	Peak serum level [7][8][9]		Drug concentration	
	mg/dL	[mmol/L]	mg/dL	[mmol/L]
Cephaloridine	1.4	0.3	25	6.0
Cephalexin	0.6–2.0	0.2–0.6	25	7.2
Cephamandole	1.3–2.5	0.3–0.5	25	4.9
Cephapirin	2.0	D0.4	25	5.6
Cephradine	1.5–2.0	0.4–0.6	25	7.1
Cefazolin	2.5–5.0	0.55–1.1	50	11.0

• The following cephalosporin antibiotics have been shown to affect CREA results when present at the indicated concentrations. System inaccuracies (bias) due to these substances are greater that 0.1 mg/dL [8.84 μmol/L] at CREA concentrations of:

Antibiotic	Peak serum level [8][10]		Drug concentration		
	mg/dL	[mmol/L]	mg/dL	[mmol/L]	Effect
Cephalothin	1–6	0.2–1.5	100	25.2	↓20–25%
Cephoxitin	2.0	0.5	5.0	1.2	↑35–40%

• The single wavelength measurement used in this method eliminates interference from chromophores whose 510 nm absorbance is constant throughout the measurement period.

• Each laboratory should determine the acceptability of its own blood collection tubes and serum separation products. Variations in these products may exist between manufacturers and, at times, from lot to lot.

d. Systeme International d'unites (S.I. Units) are in brackets.

Procedure:

TEST MATERIALS

Item	II, III Du Pont Cat. No.	IV, SX Du Pont Cat. No.	V Du Pont Cat. No.
ACA ® CREA Analytical Test Pack	701976901	701976901	701976901
Sample System Kit or	710642901	710642901	713697901
Micro Sample System Kit and	702694901	710356901	NA
Micro Sample System Holders	702785000	NA	NA
DYLUX ® Photosensitive.			
Printer Paper	700036000	NA	NA
Thermal Printer Paper	NA	710639901	713645901
Du Pont Purified Water	704209901	710615901	710815901
Cell Wash Solution	701864901	710664901	710864901

Test Steps: The operator need only load the sample kit and appropriate test pack(s) into a properly prepared ACA® discrete clinical analyzer. It automatically advances the pack(s) through the test steps and prints a result(s). See the Instrument Manual of the ACA® analyzer for details of mechanical travel of the test pack(s).

Preset Creatinine (CREA)—Test Conditions

• Sample Volume: 200 µL
• Diluent: Purified Water
• Temperature: 37.0 ±0.1 °C
• Reaction Period: 29 seconds
• Type of Measurement: Rate
• Measurement Period: 17.07 seconds
• Wavelength: 510 nm
• Units: mg/dL [µmol/L]

CALIBRATION: The general calibration procedure is described in the Calibration/Verification chapter of the Manuals.

The following information should be considered when calibrating the CREA method.

• Assay Range: 0–20 mg/mL [0–1768 µmol/L][e].
• Reference Material: Protein containing primary standards[f] or secondary calibrators such as Du Pont Elevated Chemistry Control (Cat. #790035903) and Normal Chemistry Control (Cat. #790035905)[g].
• Suggested Calibration Levels: 1,5,20, mg/mL [88, 442, 1768 µmol/L].
• Calibration Scheme: 3 levels, 3 packs per level.
• Frequency: Each new pack lot. Every 3 months for any one pack lot.

e. For the results in S.I. units [µmol/L] the conversion factory is 88.4.

f. Refer to the Creatinine Standard Preparation and Calibration Procedure available on request from a Du Pont Representative.

g. If the Du Pont Chemistry Controls are being used, prepare them according to the instructions on the product insert sheets.

PRESET CREATININE (CREA) TEST CONDITIONS

Item	ACA ® II analyzer	ACA ® III, IV, SX, V analyzer
Count by	One (1) .... [Five (5)]	NA
Decimal Point	0.0 mg/dL .... [000.0 µmol/L]	000.0 mg/dL [000 µmol/L]
Location .... Assigned Starting	999.8	−1.000 E1
Point or Offset C_0	[9823.]	[−8.840 E2]
Scale Factor or Assigned	0.2000 .... mg/dL/count[h]	2.004 E-1[h]
Linear Term C_1 h	[0.3536 µmol/L/count]	[1.772E1]

h. The preset scale factor (linear term) was derived from the molar absorptivity of the indicator and is based on an absorbance to activity relationship (sensitivity) of 0.596 (mA/min)/(U/L). Due to small differences in filters and electronic components between instruments, the actual scale factor (linear term) may differ slightly from that given above.

Quality Control: Two types of quality control procedures are recommended:

• General Instrument Check. Refer to the Filter Balance Procedure and the Absorbance Test Method described in the ACA Analyzer Instrument Manual. Refer also to the ABS Test Methodology literature.

• Creatinine Method Check. At least once daily run a CREA test on a solution of known creatinine activity such as an assayed control or calibration standard other than that used to calibrate the CREA method. For further details review the Quality Assurance Section of the Chemistry Manual. The result obtained should fall within acceptable limits defined by the day-to-day variability of the system as measured in the user's laboratory. (See SPECIFIC PERFORMANCE CHARACTERISTICS for guidance.) If the result falls outside the laboratory's acceptable limits, follow the procedure outlined in the Chemistry Troubleshooting Section of the Chemistry Manual.

A possible system malfunction is indicated when analysis of a sample with five consecutive test packs gives the following results:

Level	SD
1 mg/dL	>0.15 mg/dL
[88 µmol/L]	[>13 µmol/L]
20 mg/dL	>0.68 mg/dL
[1768 µmol/L]	[>60 µmol/L]

Refer to the procedure outlined in the Trouble Shooting Section of the Manual.

Results: The ACA® analyzer automatically calculates and prints the CREA result in mg/dL [µmol/L].

Limitation of Procedure: Results >20 mg/dL [1768 µmol/L]:

• Dilute with suitable protein base diluent. Reassay. Correct for diluting before reporting.

The reporting system contains error messages to warn the operator of specific malfunctions. Any report slip containing a letter code or word immediately following the numerical value should not be reported. Refer to the Manual for the definition of error codes.

Reference Interval

Serum: [11] [i]

Males	0.8–1.3 md/dL
	[71–115 µmol/L]
Females	0.6–1.0 md/dL
	[53–88 µmol/L]

Urine: [12]

Males	0.6–2.5 g/24 hr
	[53–221 mmol/24 hr]
Females	0.6–1.5 g/24 hr
	[53–133 mmol/24 hr]

i. Reference interval data obtained from 200 apparently healthy individuals (71 males, 129 females) between the ages of 19 and 72.

Each laboratory should establish its own reference intervals for CREA as performed on the analyzer.

Specific Performance Characteristics [j]

REPRODUCIBILITY [k]

Material	Mean	Standard deviation (% CV)	
		Within-run	Between-day
Lyophilized Control	1.3 [115]	0.05 (3.7) [4.4]	0.05 (3.7) [4.4]
Lyophilized Control	20.6 [1821]	0.12 (0.6) [10.6]	0.37 (1.8) [32.7]

CORRELATION—REGRESSION STATISTICS [L]

Comparative method	Slope	Intercept	Correlation coefficient	n
Autoanalyzer®	1.03	0.03[2.7]	0.997	260

j. All specific performance characteristics tests were run after normal recommended equipment quality control checks were performed (see Instrument Manual).

k. Specimens at each level were analyzed in duplicate for twenty days. The within-run

and between-day standard deviations were calculated by the analysis of variance method.

l. Model equation for regression statistics is:

Result of ACA® Analyzer = Slope (Comparative method result) + intercept

Assay Range [m]

0.0–20.0 mg/dl
[0–1768 μmol]

m. See REPRODUCIBILITY for method performance within the assay range.

Analytical Specificity

See KNOWN INTERFERING SUBSTANCES section for details.

BIBLIOGRAPHY

[1] Larsen, K, Clin Chem Acta 41, 209 (1972).
[2] Tietz, NW, Fundamentals of Clinical Chemistry, W. B. Saunders Co., Philadelphia, PA, 1976, pp 47–52, 1211.
[3] Supplementary information pertaining to the effects of various drugs and patient conditions on in vivo or in vitro diagnostic levels can be found in "Drug Interferences with Clinical Laboratory Tests," Clin. Chem 21 (5) (1975), and "Effects of Disease on Clinical Laboratory Tests," Clin Chem, 26 (4) 1D–476D (1980).
[4] Watkins, R. Fieldkamp, SC, Thibert, RJ, and Zak, B, Clin Chem, 21, 1002 (1975).
[5] Kawas, EE, Richards, AH, and Bigger, R, An Evaluation of a Kinetic Creatinine Test for the Du Pont ACA, Du Pont Company, Wilmington, DE (February 1973). (Reprints available from DuPont Company, Diagnostic Systems)
[6] Westgard, JO, Effects of Hemolysis and Lipemia on ACA Creatinine Method, 0.200 μL, Sample Size, Du Pont Company, Wilmington, DE (October 1972).
[7] Physicians' Desk Reference, Medical Economics Company, 33 Edition, 1979.
[8] Henry, JB, Clinical Diagnosis and Management by Laboratory Methods, W.B. Saunders Co., Philadelphia, PA 1979, Vol. III.
[9] Krupp, MA, Tierney, LM Jr., Jawetz, E, Roe, RI, Camargo, CA, Physicians Handbook, Lange Medical Publications, Los Altos, CA, 1982 pp 635–636.
[10] Sarah, AJ, Koch, TR, Drusano, GL, Celoxitin Falsely Elevates Creatinine Levels, JAMA 247, 205–206 (1982).
[11] Gadsden, RH, and Phelps, CA, A Normal Range Study of Amylase in Urine and Serum on the Du Pont ACA, Du Pont Company, Wilmington, DE (March 1978). (Reprints available from DuPont Company, Diagnostic Systems)
[12] Dicht, JJ, Reference Intervals for Serum Amylase and Urinary Creatinine on the Du Pont ACA® Discrete Clinical Analyzer, Du Pont Company, Wilmington, DE (November 1984).

Attachment 3—Analysis of Creatinine for the Normalization of Cadmium and Beta-2-Microglobulin Concentrations in Urine (OSLTC Procedure).

Matrix: Urine.

Target concentration: 1.1 g/L (this amount is representative of creatinine concentrations found in urine).

Procedure: A 1.0 ml aliquot of urine is passed through a C18 SEP-PAK® (Waters Associates). Approximately 30 mL of HPLC (high performance liquid chromatography) grade water is then run through the SEP-PAK. The resulting solution is diluted to volume in a 100-mL volumetric flask and analyzed by HPLC using an ultraviolet (UV) detector.

Special requirements: After collection, samples should be appropriately stabilized for cadmium (Cd) analysis by using 10% high purity (with low Cd background levels) nitric acid (exactly 1.0 mL of 10% nitric acid per 10 mL of urine) or stabilized for Beta-2-Microglobulin (B2M) by taking to pH 7 with dilute NaOH (exactly 1.0 mL of 0.11 N NaOH per 10 mL of urine). If not immediately analyzed, the samples should be frozen and shipped by overnight mail in an insulated container.

Dated: January 1992.

David B. Armitage,

Duane Lee,

Chemists.

Organic Service Branch II, OSHA Technical Center, Salt Lake City, Utah

1. General Discussion

1.1 Background
1.1.1. History of procedure
Creatinine has been analyzed by several methods in the past. The earliest methods were of the wet chemical type. As an example, creatinine reacts with sodium picrate in basic solution to form a red complex, which is then analyzed colorimetrically (Refs. 5.1. and 5.2.).

Since industrial hygiene laboratories will be analyzing for Cd and B2M in urine, they will be normalizing those concentrations to the concentration of creatinine in urine. A literature search revealed several HPLC methods (Refs. 5.3., 5.4., 5.5. and 5.6.) for creatinine in urine and because many industrial hygiene laboratories have HPLC equipment, it was desirable to develop an industrial hygiene HPLC method for creatinine in urine. The method of Hausen, Fuchs, and Wachter was chosen as the starting point for method development. SEP-PAKs were used for sample clarification and cleanup

263

in this method to protect the analytical column. The urine aliquot which has been passed through the SEP-PAK is then analyzed by reverse-phase HPLC using ion-pair techniques.

This method is very similar to that of Ogata and Taguchi (Ref. 5.6.), except they used centrifugation for sample clean-up. It is also of note that they did a comparison of their HPLC results to those of the Jaffe method (a picric acid method commonly used in the health care industry) and found a linear relationship of close to 1:1. This indicates that either HPLC or colorimetric methods may be used to measure creatinine concentrations in urine.

1.1.2. Physical properties (Ref. 5.7.)

Molecular weight: 113.12

Molecular formula: $C_4–H_7–N_3–0$

Chemical name: 2-amino-1,5-dihydro-1-methyl-4H-imidazol-4-one

CAS No.: 60–27–5

Melting point: 300 °C (decomposes)

Appearance: white powder

Solubility: soluble in water; slightly soluble in alcohol; practically insoluble in acetone, ether, and chloroform

Synonyms: 1-methylglycocyamidine, 1-methylhydantoin-2-imide

Structure: see Figure #1

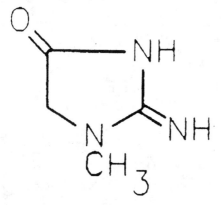

Figure #1

1.2. Advantages

1.2.1. This method offers a simple, straightforward, and specific alternative method to the Jaffe method.

1.2.2. HPLC instrumentation is commonly found in many industrial hygiene laboratories.

2. Sample stabilization procedure

2.1. Apparatus

Metal-free plastic container for urine sample.

2.2. Reagents

2.2.1. Stabilizing Solution—

(1) Nitric acid (10%, high purity with low Cd background levels) for stabilizing urine for Cd analysis or

(2) NaOH, 0.11 N, for stabilizing urine for B2M analysis.

2.2.2. HPLC grade water

2.3. Technique

2.3.1. Stabilizing solution is added to the urine sample (see section 2.2.1.). The stabilizing solution should be such that for each 10 mL of urine, add exactly 1.0 mL of stabilizer solution. (Never add water or urine to acid or base. Always add acid or base to water or urine.) Exactly 1.0 mL of 0.11 N NaOH added to 10 mL of urine should result in a pH of 7. Or add 1.0 mL of 10% nitric acid to 10 mL of urine.

2.3.2. After sample collection seal the plastic bottle securely and wrap it with an appropriate seal. Urine samples should be frozen and then shipped by overnight mail (if shipping is necessary) in an insulated container. (Do not fill plastic bottle too full. This will allow for expansion of contents during the freezing process.)

2.4. The Effect of Preparation and Stabilization Techniques on Creatinine Concentrations

Three urine samples were prepared by making one sample acidic, not treating a second sample, and adjusting a third sample to pH 7. The samples were analyzed in duplicate by two different procedures. For the first procedure a 1.0 mL aliquot of urine was put in a 100-mL volumetric flask, diluted to volume with HPLC grade water, and then analyzed directly on an HPLC. The other procedure used SEP-PAKs. The SEP-PAK was rinsed with approximately 5 mL of methanol followed by approximately 10 mL of HPLC grade water and both rinses were discarded. Then, 1.0 mL of the urine sample was put through the SEP-PAK, followed by 30 mL of HPLC grade water. The urine and water were transferred to a 100-mL volumetric flask, diluted to volume with HPLC grade water, and analyzed by HPLC. These three urine samples were analyzed on the day they were obtained and then frozen. The results show that whether the urine is acidic, untreated or adjusted to pH 7, the resulting answer for creatinine is essentially unchanged. The purpose of stabilizing the urine by making it acidic or neutral is for the analysis of Cd or B2M respectively.

COMPARISON OF PREPARATION & STABILIZATION TECHNIQUES

Sample	w/o SEP-PAK g/L creatinine	with SEP-PAK g/L creatinine
Acid	1.10	1.10
Acid	1.11	1.10
Untreated	1.12	1.11
Untreated	1.11	1.12
pH 7	1.08	1.02
pH 7	1.11	1.08

2.5. Storage

After 4 days and 54 days of storage in a freezer, the samples were thawed, brought to room temperature and analyzed using the same procedures as in section 2.4. The results of several days of storage show that the resulting answer of creatinine is essentially unchanged.

STORAGE DATA

| Sample | 4 days | | 54 days | |
	w/o SEP-PAK g/L creatinine	with SEP-PAK g/L creatinine	w/o SEP-PAK g/L creatinine	with SEP-PAK g/L creatinine
Acid	1.09	1.09	1.08	1.09
Acid	1.10	1.10	1.09	1.10
Acid			1.09	1.09
Untreated	1.13	1.14	1.09	1.11
Untreated	1.15	1.14	1.10	1.10
Untreated			1.09	1.10
pH 7	1.14	1.13	1.12	1.12
pH 7	1.14	1.13	1.12	1.12
pH 7			1.12	1.12

2.6. Interferences

None.

2.7. Safety precautions

2.7.1. Make sure samples are properly sealed and frozen before shipment to avoid leakage.

2.7.2. Follow the appropriate shipping procedures.

The following modified special safety precautions are based on those recommended by the Centers for Disease Control (CDC) (Ref. 5.8.). and OSHA's Bloodborne Pathogens standard (29 CFR 1910.1039).

2.7.3. Wear gloves, lab coat, and safety glasses while handling all human urine products. Disposable plastic, glass, and paper (pipet tips, gloves, etc.) that contact urine should be placed in a biohazard autoclave bag. These bags should be kept in appropriate containers until sealed and autoclaved. Wipe down all work surfaces with 10% sodium hypochlorite solution when work is finished.

2.7.4. Dispose of all biological samples and diluted specimens in a biohazard autoclave bag at the end of the analytical run.

2.7.5. Special care should be taken when handling and dispensing nitric acid. Always remember to add acid to water (or urine). Nitric acid is a corrosive chemical capable of severe eye and skin dam-age. Wear metal-free gloves, a lab coat, and safety glasses. If the nitric acid comes in contact with any part of the body, quickly wash with copious quantities of water for at least 15 minutes.

2.7.6. Special care should be taken when handling and dispensing NaOH. Always remember to add base to water (or urine). NaOH can cause severe eye and skin damage. Always wear the appropriate gloves, a lab coat, and safety glasses. If the NaOH comes in contact with any part of the body, quickly wash with copious quantities of water for at least 15 minutes.

3. Analytical procedure

3.1. Apparatus

3.1.1. A high performance liquid chromatograph equipped with pump, sample injector and UV detector.

3.1.2. A C18 HPLC column; 25 cm × 4.6 mm I.D.

3.1.3. An electronic integrator, or some other suitable means of determining analyte response.

3.1.4. Stripchart recorder.

3.1.5. C18 SEP-PAKs (Waters Associates) or equivalent.

3.1.6. Luer-lock syringe for sample preparation (5 mL or 10 mL).

3.1.7. Volumetric pipettes and flasks for standard and sample preparation.

3.1.8. Vacuum system to aid sample preparation (optional).

3.2. Reagents

3.2.1. Water, HPLC grade.

3.2.2. Methanol, HPLC grade.

3.2.3. PIC B–7® (Waters Associates) in small vials.

3.2.4. Creatinine, anhydrous, Sigma hemical Corp., purity not listed.

3.2.5. 1–Heptanesulfonic acid, sodium salt monohydrate.

3.2.6. Phosphoric acid.

3.2.7. Mobile phase. It can be prepared by mixing one vial of PIC B–7 into a 1 L solution of 50% methanol and 50% water. The mobile phase can also be made by preparing a solution that is 50% methanol and 50% water with 0.005M heptanesulfonic acid and adjusting the pH of the solution to 3.5 with phosphoric acid.

3.3. Standard preparation

3.3.1. Stock standards are prepared by weighing 10 to 15 mg of creatinine. This is transferred to a 25-mL volumetric flask and diluted to volume with HPLC grade water.

3.3.2. Dilutions to a working range of 3 to 35 µg/mL are made in either HPLC grade water or HPLC mobile phase (standards give the same detector response in either solution).

3.4. Sample preparation

3.4.1. The C18 SEP-PAK is connected to a Luer-lock syringe. It is rinsed with 5 mL HPLC grade methanol and then 10 mL of HPLC grade water. These rinses are discarded.

3.4.2. Exactly 1.0 mL of urine is pipetted into the syringe. The urine is put through the SEP-PAK into a suitable container using a vacuum system.

3.4.3. The walls of the syringe are rinsed in several stages with a total of approximately 30 mL of HPLC grade water. These rinses are put through the SEP-PAK into the same container. The resulting solution is transferred to a 100-mL volumetric flask and then brought to volume with HPLC grade water.

3.5. Analysis (conditions and hardware are those used in this evaluation.)

3.5.1. Instrument conditions

Column: Zorbax® ODS, 5–6 µm particle size; 25 cm × 4.6 mm I.D.

Mobile phase: See Section 3.2.7.

Detector: Dual wavelength UV; 229 nm (primary) 254 nm (secondary)

Flow rate: 0.7 mL/ minute

Retention time: 7.2 minutes

Sensitivity: 0.05 AUFS

Injection volume: 20µl

3.5.2. Chromatogram (see Figure #2)

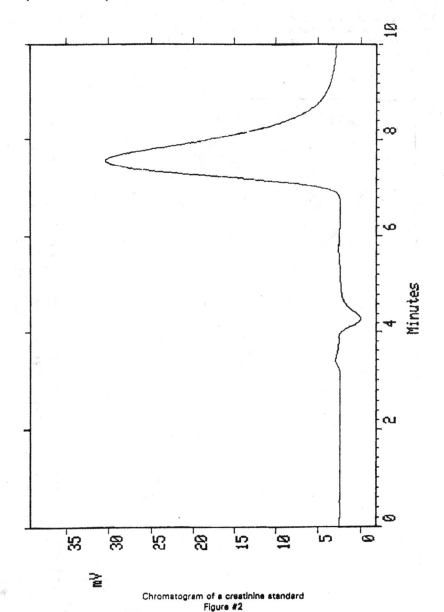

Chromatogram of a creatinine standard
Figure #2

3.6. Interferences

3.6.1. Any compound that has the same retention time as creatinine and absorbs at 229 nm is an interference.

3.6.2. HPLC conditions may be varied to circumvent interferences. In addition, analysis at another UV wavelength (*i.e.*, 254 nm) would allow a comparison of the ratio of response of a standard to that of a sample. Any deviations would indicate an interference.

3.7. Calculations

267

3.7.1. A calibration curve is constructed by plotting detector response versus standard concentration (See Figure #3).

3.7.2. The concentration of creatinine in a sample is determined by finding the concentration corresponding to its detector response. (See Figure #3).

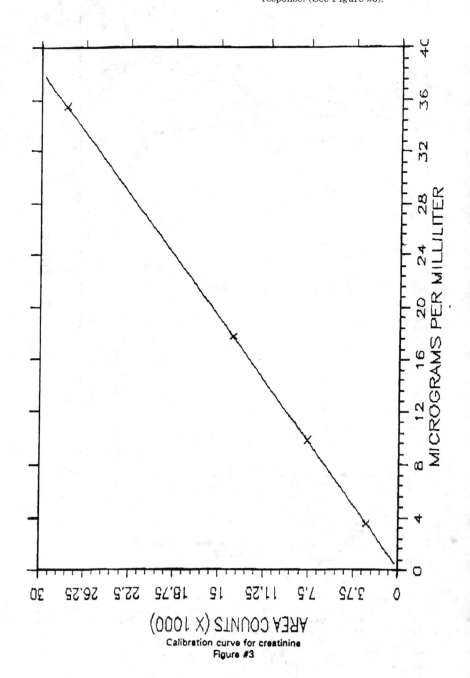

Calibration curve for creatinine
Figure #3

3.7.3. The µg/mL creatinine from section 3.7.2. is then multiplied by 100 (the dilution factor). This value is equivalent to the micrograms of creatinine in the 1.0 mL stabilized urine aliquot or the milligrams of creatinine per liter of urine. The desired units, g/L, is determined by the following relationship:

$$g/L = \frac{\mu g/mL}{1000} = \frac{mg/L}{1000}$$

3.7.4. The resulting value for creatinine is used to normalize the urinary concentration of the desired analyte (A) (Cd or B2M) by using the following formula.

$$\mu g\ A/g\ creatinine = \frac{\mu g\ A/L\ (experimental)}{g/L\ creatinine}$$

Where A is the desired analyte. The protocol of reporting such normalized results is µg A/g creatinine.

3.8. Safety precautions See section 2.7.

4. Conclusions

The determination of creatinine in urine by HPLC is a good alternative to the Jaffe method for industrial hygiene laboratories. Sample clarification with SEP-PAKs did not change the amount of creatinine found in urine samples. However, it does protect the analytical column. The results of this creatinine in urine procedure are unaffected by the pH of the urine sample under the conditions tested by this procedure. Therefore, no special measures are required for creatinine analysis whether the urine sample has been stabilized with 10% nitric acid for the Cd analysis or brought to a pH of 7 with 0.11 N NaOH for the B2M analysis.

5. References

5.1. Clark, L.C.; Thompson, H.L.; *Anal. Chem.* 1949, 21, 1218.

5.2. Peters, J.H.; *J. Biol. Chem.* 1942, 146, 176.

5.3. Hausen, V.A.; Fuchs, D.; Wachter, H.; *J. Clin. Chem. Clin. Biochem.* 1981, 19, 373–378.

5.4. Clark, P.M.S.; Kricka L.J.; Patel, A.; *J. Liq. Chrom.* 1980, 3(7), 1031–1046.

5.5. Ballerini, R.; Chinol, M.; Cambi, A.; *J. Chrom.* 1979, 179, 365–369.

5.6. Ogata, M.; Taguchi, T.; *Industrial Health* 1987, 25, 225–228.

5.7. "Merck Index", 11th ed.; Windholz, Martha Ed.; Merck: Rahway, N.J., 1989; p 403.

5.8. Kimberly, M.; *"Determination of Cadmium in Urine by Graphite Furnace Atomic Absorption Spectrometry with Zeeman Background Correction."*, Centers for Disease Control, Atlanta, Georgia, unpublished, update 1990.

[57 FR 42389, Sept. 14, 1992, as amended at 57 FR 49272, Oct. 30, 1992; 58 FR 21781, Apr. 23, 1993; 61 FR 5508, Feb. 13, 1996; 63 FR 1288, Jan. 8, 1998; 70 FR 1142, Jan. 5, 2005; 71 FR 16672, 16673, Apr. 3, 2006; 71 FR 50189, Aug. 24, 2006; 73 FR 75585, Dec. 12, 2008; 76 FR 33608, June 8, 2011; 77 FR 17781, Mar. 26, 2012]

EFFECTIVE DATE NOTE: At 84 FR21477, May 14, 2019, § 1910.1027 was amended by revising paragraph (l)(4)(ii)(C) and appendix D, effective July 15, 2019. For the convenience of the user, the revised text is set forth as follows:

§ 1910.1027 Cadmium.

*   *   *   *   *

(1) * * *
(4) * * *
(ii) * * *
(C) A 14 inch by 17 inch or other reasonably-sized standard film or digital posterior-anterior chest X-ray (after the initial X-ray, the frequency of chest X-rays is to be determined by the examining physician);

*   *   *   *   *

APPENDIX D TO § 1910.1027—OCCUPATIONAL HEALTH HISTORY INTERVIEW WITH

REFERENCE TO CADMIUM EXPOSURE

Directions

(To be read by employee and signed prior to the interview)

Please answer the questions you will be asked as completely and carefully as you can. These questions are asked of everyone who works with cadmium. You will also be asked to give blood and urine samples. The doctor will give your employer a written opinion on whether you are physically capable of working with cadmium. Legally, the doctor cannot share personal information you may tell him/her with your employer. The following information is considered strictly confidential. The results of the tests will go to you, your doctor and your employer. You will also receive an information sheet explaining the results of any biological monitoring or physical examinations performed. If you are just being hired, the results of this interview and examination will be used to:

(1) Establish your health status and see if working with cadmium might be expected to cause unusual problems,

(2) Determine your health status today and see if there are changes over time,

(3) See if you can wear a respirator safely.

If you are not a new hire:

OSHA says that everyone who works with cadmium can have periodic medical examinations performed by a doctor. The reasons for this are:

a) If there are changes in your health, either because of cadmium or some other reason, to find them early,

b) to prevent kidney damage.

Please sign below.

I have read these directions and understand them:

_____

Employee signature

_____

Date

Thank you for answering these questions. (Suggested Format)

Name_____

Age _____

Company_____

Job_____

Type of Preplacement Exam:

[ ] Periodic

[ ] Termination

[ ] Initial

[ ] Other

Blood Pressure_____

Pulse Rate_____

1. How long have you worked at the job listed above?
   [ ] Not yet hired

   [ ] Number of months

   [ ] Number of years

2. Job Duties etc.

_____

_____

_____

3. Have you ever been told by a doctor that you had bronchitis?

   [ ] Yes

   [ ] No

   If yes, how long ago?

   [ ] Number of months

   [ ] Number of years

4. Have you ever been told by a doctor that you had emphysema?

   [ ] Yes

   [ ] No

   If yes, how long ago?

   [ ] Number of years

   [ ] Number of months

5. Have you ever been told by a doctor that you had other lung problems?

   [ ] Yes

   [ ] No

   If yes, please describe type of lung problems and when you had these problems.

_____

_____

_____

6. In the past year, have you had a cough?

[ ] Yes

[ ] No

If yes, did you cough up sputum?

[ ] Yes

[ ] No

If yes, how long did the cough with sputum production last?

[ ] Less than 3 months

[ ] 3 months or longer

If yes, for how many years have you had episodes of cough with sputum production lasting this long?

[ ] Less than one

[ ] 1

[ ] 2

[ ] Longer than 2

7. Have you ever smoked cigarettes?

[ ] Yes

[ ] No

8. Do you now smoke cigarettes?

[ ] Yes

[ ] No

9. If you smoke or have smoked cigarettes, for how many years have you smoked, or did you smoke?

[ ] Less than 1 year

[ ] Number of years

What is or was the greatest number of packs per day that you have smoked?

[ ] Number of packs

If you quit smoking cigarettes, how many years ago did you quit?

[ ] Less than 1 year

[ ] Number of years

How many packs a day do you now smoke?

[ ] Number of packs per day

10. Have you ever been told by a doctor that you had a kidney or urinary tract disease or disorder?
    [ ] Yes

    [ ] No

11. Have you ever had any of these disorders?

Kidney stones...[ ] Yes   [ ] No

Protein in urine..[ ] Yes   [ ] No

Blood in urine ....[ ] Yes   [ ] No

Difficulty urinating...[ ] Yes   [ ] No

Other kidney/Urinary disorders..[ ] Yes   [ ] No

Please describe problems, age, treatment, and follow up for any kidney or urinary problems you have had:

_____

_____

_____

12. Have you ever been told by a doctor or other health care provider who took your blood pressure that your blood pressure was high?
    [ ] Yes

    [ ] No

274

13. Have you ever been advised to take any blood pressure medication?
    [ ] Yes

    [ ] No

14. Are you presently taking any blood pressure medication?
    [ ] Yes

    [ ] No

15. Are you presently taking any other medication?
    [ ] Yes

    [ ] No

16. Please list any blood pressure or other medications and describe how long you have been taking each one:

Medicine	How long Taken

17. Have you ever been told by a doctor that you have diabetes? (sugar in your blood or urine)
    [ ] Yes

    [ ] No

If yes, do you presently see a doctor about your diabetes?
    [ ] Yes

    [ ] No

If yes, how do you control your blood sugar?

[ ] Diet alone

[ ] Diet plus oral medicine

[ ] Diet plus insulin (injection)

18. Have you ever been told by a doctor that you had:

Anemia	[ ] Yes	[ ] No
A low blood count?	[ ] Yes	[ ] No

19. Do you presently feel that you tire or run out of energy sooner than normal or sooner than other people your age?

[ ] Yes

[ ] No

If yes, for how long have you felt that you tire easily?

[ ] Less than 1 year

[ ] Number of years

20. Have you given blood within the last year?

[ ] Yes

[ ] No

If yes, how many times?

[ ] Number of times

How long ago was the last time you gave blood?

[ ] Less than 1 month

[ ] Number of months

21. Within the last year have you had any injuries with heavy bleeding?
    [ ] Yes

    [ ] No

    If yes, how long ago?
    [ ] Less than 1 month

    [ ] Number of months

Describe: _____

_____

_____

22. Have you recently had any surgery?
    [ ] Yes

    [ ] No

If yes, please describe: _____

_____

_____

23. Have you seen any blood lately in your stool or after a bowel movement?
    [ ] Yes

    [ ] No

24. Have you ever had a test for blood in your stool?
    [ ] Yes

    [ ] No

    If yes, did the test show any blood in the stool?

    [ ] Yes

    [ ] No

What further evaluation and treatment were done? _____ .

_____

_____

_____

_____

The following questions pertain to the ability to wear a respirator.
Additional information for the physician can be found in The Respiratory Protective
Devices Manual.

25. Have you ever been told by a doctor that you have asthma?
   [ ] Yes

   [ ] No

   If yes, are you presently taking any medication for asthma? Mark all that apply.

   [ ] Shots

   [ ] Pills

   [ ] Inhaler

26. Have you ever had a heart attack?
   [ ] Yes

   [ ] No

   If yes, how long ago?

   [ ] Number of years

   [ ] Number of months

27. Have you ever had pains in your chest?
   [ ] Yes

   [ ] No

   If yes, when did it usually happen?

   [ ] While resting

   [ ] While working

   [ ] While exercising

   [ ] Activity didn't matter

28. Have you ever had a thyroid problem?
    [ ] Yes

    [ ] No

29. Have you ever had a seizure or fits?
    [ ] Yes

    [ ] No

30. Have you ever had a stroke (cerebrovascular accident)?
    [ ] Yes

    [ ] No

31. Have you ever had a ruptured eardrum or a serious hearing problem?
    [ ] Yes

    [ ] No

32. Do you now have a claustrophobia, meaning fear of crowded or closed in spaces or any psychological problems that would make it hard for you to wear a respirator?
    [ ] Yes

    [ ] No

The following questions pertain to reproductive history.

33. Have you or your partner had a problem conceiving a child?
    [ ] Yes

    [ ] No

    If yes, specify:

    [ ] Self

    [ ] Present mate

    [ ] Previous mate

34. Have you or your partner consulted a physician for a fertility or other reproductive problem?

[ ] Yes

[ ] No

If yes, specify who consulted the physician:

[ ] Self

[ ] Spouse/partner

[ ] Self and partner

If yes, specify diagnosis made: _____

_____

_____

_____

35. Have you or your partner ever conceived a child resulting in a miscarriage, still birth or a child with malformations or birth defects?

[ ] Yes

[ ] No

If yes, specify:

[ ] Miscarriage

[ ] Still birth

[ ] Malformations or birth defects

If outcome was a child with malformations or birth defects, please specify type:

_____

_____

36. Was this outcome a result of a pregnancy of:

[ ] Yours with present partner

[ ] Yours with a previous partner

37. Did the timing of any abnormal pregnancy outcome coincide with present employment?

[ ] Yes

[ ] No

List dates of occurrences: _____

_____

_____

38. What is the occupation of your spouse or partner?

_____

_____

For Women Only

39. Do you have menstrual periods?

[ ] Yes

[ ] No

Have you had menstrual irregularities?

[ ] Yes

[ ] No

If yes, specify type: _____

_____

_____

If yes, what was the approximated date this problem began? _____

_____

Approximate date problem stopped? _____

_____

For Men Only

40. Have you ever been diagnosed by a physician as having prostate gland problem(s)?
[ ] Yes

[ ] No

If yes, please describe type of problem(s) and what was done to evaluate and treat the problem(s): _____

_____

_____

*   *   *   *   *

§1910.1028 Benzene.

(a) *Scope and application.* (1) This section applies to all occupational exposures to benzene. Chemical Abstracts Service Registry No. 71–43–2, except as provided in paragraphs (a)(2) and (a)(3) of this section.

(2) This section does not apply to:

(i) The storage, transportation, distribution, dispensing, sale or use of gasoline, motor fuels, or other fuels containing benzene subsequent to its final discharge from bulk wholesale storage facilities, except that operations where gasoline or motor fuels are dispensed for more than 4 hours per day in an indoor location are covered by this section.

(ii) Loading and unloading operations at bulk wholesale storage facilities which use vapor control systems for all loading and unloading operations, except for the provisions of 29 CFR 1910.1200 as incorporated into this section and the emergency provisions of paragraphs (g) and (i)(4) of this section.

(iii) The storage, transportation, distribution or sale of benzene or liquid mixtures containing more than 0.1 percent benzene in intact containers or in transportation pipelines while sealed in such a manner as to contain benzene vapors or liquid, except for the provisions of 29 CFR 1910.1200 as incorporated into this section and the emergency provisions of paragraphs (g) and (i)(4) of this section.

(iv) Containers and pipelines carrying mixtures with less than 0.1 percent benzene and natural gas processing plants processing gas with less than 0.1 percent benzene.

(v) Work operations where the only exposure to benzene is from liquid mixtures containing 0.5 percent or less of benzene by volume, or the vapors released from such liquids until September 12, 1988; work operations where the only exposure to benzene is from liquid mixtures containing 0.3 percent or less of benzene by volume or the vapors released from such liquids from September 12, 1988, to September 12, 1989; and work operations where the only exposure to benzene is from liquid mixtures containing 0.1 percent or less of benzene by volume or the vapors released from such liquids after September 12, 1989; except that tire building machine operators using solvents with more than 0.1 percent benzene are covered by paragraph (i) of this section.

(vi) Oil and gas drilling, production and servicing operations.

(vii) Coke oven batteries.

(3) The cleaning and repair of barges and tankers which have contained benzene are excluded from paragraph (f) methods of compliance, paragraph (e)(1) exposure monitoring-general, and paragraph (e)(6) accuracy of monitoring. Engineering and work practice controls shall be used to keep exposures below 10 ppm unless it is proven to be not feasible.

(b) *Definitions. Action level* means an airborne concentration of benzene of 0.5 ppm calculated as an 8-hour time-weighted average.

Assistant Secretary means the Assistant Secretary of Labor for Occupational Safety and Health, U.S. Department of Labor, or designee.

Authorized person means any person specifically authorized by the employer whose duties require the person to enter a regulated area, or any person entering such an area as a designated representative of employees for the purpose of exercising the right to observe monitoring and measuring procedures under paragraph (l) of this section, or any other person authorized by the Act or regulations issued under the Act.

Benzene ($C_6 H_6$) (CAS Registry No. 71–43–2) means liquefied or gaseous benzene. It includes benzene contained in liquid mixtures and the benzene vapors released by these liquids. It does not include trace amounts of unreacted benzene contained in solid materials.

Bulk wholesale storage facility means a bulk terminal or bulk plant where fuel is stored prior to its delivery to wholesale customers.

Container means any barrel, bottle, can, cylinder, drum, reaction vessel, storage tank, or the like, but does not include piping systems.

Day means any part of a calendar day.

Director means the Director of the National Institute for Occupational Safety and Health, U.S. Department of Health and Human Services, or designee.

Emergency means any occurrence such as, but not limited to, equipment failure, rupture of containers, or failure of control equipment which may or does result in an unexpected significant release of benzene.

Employee exposure means exposure to airborne benzene which would occur if the employee were not using respiratory protective equipment.

Regulated area means any area where airborne concentrations of benzene exceed or can reasonably be expected to exceed, the permissible exposure limits, either the 8-hour time weighted average exposure of 1 ppm or the short-term exposure limit of 5 ppm for 15 minutes.

Vapor control system means any equipment used for containing the total vapors displaced during the loading of gasoline, motor fuel or other fuel tank trucks and the displacing of these vapors through a vapor processing system or balancing the vapor with the storage tank. This equipment also includes systems containing the vapors displaced from the storage tank during the unloading of the tank truck which balance the vapors back to the tank truck.

(c) *Permissible exposure limits (PELs)*— (1) *Time-weighted average limit (TWA)*. The employer shall assure that no employee is exposed to an airborne concentration of benzene in excess of one part of benzene per million parts of air (1 ppm) as an 8-hour time-weighted average.

(2) *Short-term exposure limit (STEL)*. The employer shall assure that no employee is exposed to an airborne concentration of benzene in excess of five (5) ppm as averaged over any 15 minute period.

(d) *Regulated areas*. (1) The employer shall establish a regulated area wherever the airborne concentration of benzene exceeds or can reasonably be expected to exceed the permissible exposure limits, either the 8-hour time weighted average exposure of 1 ppm or the short-term exposure limit of 5 ppm for 15 minutes.

(2) Access to regulated areas shall be limited to authorized persons.

(3) Regulated areas shall be determined from the rest of the workplace in any manner that minimizes the number of employees exposed to benzene within the regulated area.

(e) *Exposure monitoring*—(1) *General*. (i) Determinations of employee exposure shall be made from breathing zone air samples that are representative of each employee's average exposure to airborne benzene.

(ii) Representative 8-hour TWA employee exposures shall be determined on the basis of one sample or samples representing the full shift exposure for each job classification in each work area.

(iii) Determinations of compliance with the STEL shall be made from 15 minute employee breathing zone samples measured at operations where there is reason to believe exposures are high, such as where tanks are opened, filled, unloaded or gauged; where containers or process equipment are opened and where benzene is used for cleaning or as a solvent in an uncontrolled situation. The employer may use objective data, such as measurements from brief period measuring devices, to determine where STEL monitoring is needed.

(iv) Except for initial monitoring as required under paragraph (e)(2) of this section, where the employer can document that one shift will consistently have higher employee exposures for an operation, the employer shall only be required to determine representative employee exposure for that operation during the shift on which the highest exposure is expected.

(2) *Initial monitoring.* (i) Each employer who has a place of employment covered under paragraph (a)(1) of this section shall monitor each of these workplaces and work operations to determine accurately the airborne concentrations of benzene to which employees may be exposed.

(ii) The initial monitoring required under paragraph (e)(2)(i) of this section shall be completed by 60 days after the effective date of this standard or within 30 days of the introduction of benzene into the workplace. Where the employer has monitored within one year prior to the effective date of this standard and the monitoring satisfies all other requirements of this section, the employer may rely on such earlier monitoring results to satisfy the requirements of paragraph (e)(2)(i) of this section.

(3) *Periodic monitoring and monitoring frequency.* (i) If the monitoring required by paragraph (e)(2)(i) of this section reveals employee exposure at or above the action level but at or below the TWA, the employer shall repeat such monitoring for each such employee at least every year.

(ii) If the monitoring required by paragraph (e)(2)(i) of this section reveals employee exposure above the TWA, the employer shall repeat such monitoring for each such employee at least every six (6) months.

(iii) The employer may alter the monitoring schedule from every six months to annually for any employee for whom two consecutive measure-

ments taken at least 7 days apart indicate that the employee exposure has decreased to the TWA or below, but is at or above the action level.

(iv) Monitoring for the STEL shall be repeated as necessary to evaluate exposures of employees subject to short term exposures.

(4) *Termination of monitoring.* (i) If the initial monitoring required by paragraph (e)(2)(i) of this section reveals employee exposure to be below the action level the employer may discontinue the monitoring for that employee, except as otherwise required by paragraph (e)(5) of this section.

(ii) If the periodic monitoring required by paragraph (e)(3) of this section reveals that employee exposures, as indicated by at least two consecutive measurements taken at least 7 days apart, are below the action level the employer may discontinue the monitoring for that employee, except as otherwise required by paragraph (e)(5).

(5) *Additional monitoring.* (i) The employer shall institute the exposure monitoring required under paragraphs (e)(2) and (e)(3) of this section when there has been a change in the production, process, control equipment, personnel or work practices which may result in new or additional exposures to benzene, or when the employer has any reason to suspect a change which may result in new or additional exposures.

(ii) Whenever spills, leaks, ruptures or other breakdowns occur that may lead to employee exposure, the employer shall monitor (using area or personal sampling) after the cleanup of the spill or repair of the leak, rupture or other breakdown to ensure that exposures have returned to the level that existed prior to the incident.

(6) *Accuracy of monitoring.* Monitoring shall be accurate, to a confidence level of 95 percent, to within plus or minus 25 percent for airborne concentrations of benzene.

(7) *Employee notification of monitoring results.* (i) The employer must, within 15 working days after the receipt of the results of any monitoring performed under this section, notify each affected employee of these results either individually in writing or by posting the

results in an appropriate location that is accessible to employees.

(ii) Whenever the PELs are exceeded, the written notification required by paragraph (e)(7)(i) of this section shall contain the corrective action being taken by the employer to reduce the employee exposure to or below the PEL, or shall refer to a document available to the employee which states the corrective actions to be taken.

(f) *Methods of compliance*—(1) *Engineering controls and work practices.* (i) The employer shall institute engineering controls and work practices to reduce and maintain employee exposure to benzene at or below the permissible exposure limits, except to the extent that the employer can establish that these controls are not feasible or where the provisions of paragraph (f)(1)(iii) or (g)(1) of this section apply.

(ii) Wherever the feasible engineering controls and work practices which can be instituted are not sufficient to reduce employee exposure to or below the PELs, the employer shall use them to reduce employee exposure to the lowest levels achievable by these controls and shall supplement them by the use of respiratory protection which complies with the requirements of paragraph (g) of this section.

(iii) Where the employer can document that benzene is used in a workplace less than a total of 30 days per year, the employer shall use engineering controls, work practice controls or respiratory protection or any combination of these controls to reduce employee exposure to benzene to or below the PELs, except that employers shall use engineering and work practice controls, if feasible, to reduce exposure to or below 10 ppm as an 8-hour TWA.

(2) *Compliance program.* (i) When any exposures are over the PEL, the employer shall establish and implement a written program to reduce employee exposure to or below the PEL primarily by means of engineering and work practice controls, as required by paragraph (f)(1) of this section.

(ii) The written program shall include a schedule for development and implementation of the engineering and work practice controls. These plans shall be reviewed and revised as appropriate based on the most recent exposure monitoring data, to reflect the current status of the program.

(iii) Written compliance programs shall be furnished upon request for examination and copying to the Assistant Secretary, the Director, affected employees and designated employee representatives.

(g) *Respiratory protection*—(1) *General.* For employees who use respirators required by this section, the employer must provide each employee an appropriate respirator that complies with the requirements of this paragraph. Respirators must be used during:

(i) Periods necessary to install or implement feasible engineering and work-practice controls.

(ii) Work operations for which the employer establishes that compliance with either the TWA or STEL through the use of engineering and work-practice controls is not feasible; for example, some maintenance and repair activities, vessel cleaning, or other operations for which engineering and work-practice controls are infeasible because exposures are intermittent and limited in duration.

(iii) Work operations for which feasible engineering and work-practice controls are not yet sufficient, or are not required under paragraph (f)(1)(iii) of this section, to reduce employee exposure to or below the PELs.

(iv) Emergencies.

(2) *Respirator program.* (i) The employer must implement a respiratory protection program in accordance with §1910.134(b) through (d) (except (d)(1)(iii), (d)(3)(iii)(b)(1) and (2)), and (f) through (m), which covers each employee required by this section to use a respirator.

(ii) For air-purifying respirators, the employer must replace the air-purifying element at the expiration of its service life or at the beginning of each shift in which such elements are used, whichever comes first.

(iii) If NIOSH approves an air-purifying element with an end-of-service-life indicator for benzene, such an element may be used until the indicator shows no further useful life.

(3) *Respirator selection.* (i) Employers must:

(A) Select, and provide to employees, the appropriate respirators specified in paragraph (d)(3)(i)(A) of 29 CFR 1910.134.

(B) Provide employees with any organic vapor gas mask or any self-contained breathing apparatus with a full facepiece to use for escape.

(C) Use an organic vapor cartridge or canister with powered and non-powered air-purifying respirators, and a chin-style canister with full facepiece gas masks.

(D) Ensure that canisters used with non-powered air-purifying respirators have a minimum service life of four hours when tested at 150 ppm benzene at a flow rate of 64 liters per minute (LPM), a temperature of 25 °C, and a relative humidity of 85%; for canisters used with tight-fitting or loose-fitting powered air-purifying respirators, the flow rates for testing must be 115 LPM and 170 LPM, respectively.

(ii) Any employee who cannot use a negative-pressure respirator must be allowed to use a respirator with less breathing resistance, such as a powered air-purifying respirator or supplied-air respirator.

(h) *Protective clothing and equipment.* Personal protective clothing and equipment shall be worn where appropriate to prevent eye contact and limit dermal exposure to liquid benzene. Protective clothing and equipment shall be provided by the employer at no cost to the employee and the employer shall assure its use where appropriate. Eye and face protection shall meet the requirements of 29 CFR 1910.133.

(i) *Medical surveillance*—(1) *General.* (i) The employer shall make available a medical surveillance program for employees who are or may be exposed to benzene at or above the action level 30 or more days per year; for employees who are or may be exposed to benzene at or above the PELs 10 or more days per year; for employees who have been exposed to more than 10 ppm of benzene for 30 or more days in a year prior to the effective date of the standard when employed by their current employer; and for employees involved in the tire building operations called tire building machine operators, who use solvents containing greater than 0.1 percent benzene.

(ii) The employer shall assure that all medical examinations and proce-dures are performed by or under the supervision of a licensed physician and that all laboratory tests are conducted by an accredited laboratory.

(iii) The employer shall assure that persons other than licensed physicians who administer the pulmonary function testing required by this section shall complete a training course in spirometry sponsored by an appropriate governmental, academic or professional institution.

(iv) The employer shall assure that all examinations and procedures are provided without cost to the employee and at a reasonable time and place.

(2) *Initial examination.* (i) Within 60 days of the effective date of this standard, or before the time of initial assignment, the employer shall provide each employee covered by paragraph (i)(1)(i) of this section with a medical examination including the following elements:

(A) A detailed occupational history which includes:

(*1*) Past work exposure to benzene or any other hematological toxins,

(*2*) A family history of blood dyscrasias including hematological neoplasms;

(*3*) A history of blood dyscrasias including genetic hemoglobin abnormalities, bleeding abnormalities, abnormal function of formed blood elements;

(*4*) A history of renal or liver dysfunction;

(*5*) A history of medicinal drugs routinely taken;

(*6*) A history of previous exposure to ionizing radiation and

(*7*) Exposure to marrow toxins outside of the current work situation.

(B) A complete physical examination.

(C) *Laboratory tests.* A complete blood count including a leukocyte count with differential, a quantitative thrombocyte count, hematocrit, hemoglobin, erythrocyte count and erythrocyte indices (MCV, MCH, MCHC). The results of these tests shall be reviewed by the examining physician.

(D) Additional tests as necessary in the opinion of the examining physician, based on alterations to the components of the blood or other signs which may be related to benzene exposure; and

(E) For all workers required to wear respirators for at least 30 days a year, the physical examination shall pay special attention to the cardiopulmonary system and shall include a pulmonary function test.

(ii) No initial medical examination is required to satisfy the requirements of paragraph (i)(2)(i) of this section if adequate records show that the employee has been examined in accordance with the procedures of paragraph (i)(2)(i) of this section within the twelve months prior to the effective date of this standard.

(3) *Periodic examinations.* (i) The employer shall provide each employee covered under paragraph (i)(1)(i) of this section with a medical examination annually following the previous examination. These periodic examinations shall incude at least the following elements:

(A) A brief history regarding any new exposure to potential marrow toxins, changes in medicinal drug use, and the appearance of physical signs relating to blood disorders:

(B) A complete blood count including a leukocyte count with differential, quantitative thrombocyte count, hemoglobin, hematocrit, erythrocyte count and erythrocyte indices (MCV, MCH, MCHC); and

(C) Appropriate additional tests as necessary, in the opinion of the examining physician, in consequence of alterations in the components of the blood or other signs which may be related to benzene exposure.

(ii) Where the employee develops signs and symptoms commonly associated with toxic exposure to benzene, the employer shall provide the employee with an additional medical examination which shall include those elements considered appropriate by the examining physician.

(iii) For persons required to use respirators for at least 30 days a year, a pulmonary function test shall be performed every three (3) years. A specific evaluation of the cardiopulmonary system shall be made at the time of the pulmonary function test.

(4) *Emergency examinations.* (i) In addition to the surveillance required by (i)(1)(i), if an employee is exposed to benzene in an emergency situation, the employer shall have the employee provide a urine sample at the end of the employee's shift and have a urinary

phenol test performed on the sample within 72 hours. The urine specific gravity shall be corrected to 1.024.

(ii) If the result of the urinary phenol test is below 75 mg phenol/L of urine, no further testing is required.

(iii) If the result of the urinary phenol test is equal to or greater than 75 mg phenol/L of urine, the employer shall provide the employee with a complete blood count including an erythrocyte count, leukocyte count with differential and thrombocyte count at monthly intervals for a duration of three (3) months following the emergency exposure.

(iv) If any of the conditions specified in paragraph (i)(5)(i) of this section exists, then the further requirements of paragraph (i)(5) of this section shall be met and the employer shall, in addition, provide the employees with periodic examinations if directed by the physician.

(5) *Additional examinations and referrals.* (i) Where the results of the complete blood count required for the initial and periodic examinations indicate any of the following abnormal conditions exist, then the blood count shall be repeated within 2 weeks.

(A) The hemoglobin level or the hematocrit falls below the normal limit [outside the 95% confidence interval (C.I.)] as determined by the laboratory for the particular geographic area and/or these indices show a persistent downward trend from the individual's pre-exposure norms; provided these findings cannot be explained by other medical reasons.

(B) The thrombocyte (platelet) count varies more than 20 percent below the employee's most recent values or falls outside the normal limit (95% C.I.) as determined by the laboratory.

(C) The leukocyte count is below 4,000 per mm^3 or there is an abnormal differential count.

(ii) If the abnormality persists, the examining physician shall refer the employee to a hematologist or an internist for further evaluation unless the physician has good reason to believe such referral is unnecessary. (See appendix C for examples of conditions where a referral may be unnecessary.)

(iii) The employer shall provide the hematologist or internist with the information required to be provided to the physician under paragraph (i)(6) of this section and the medical record required to be maintained by paragraph (k)(2)(ii) of this section.

(iv) The hematologist's or internist's evaluation shall include a determination as to the need for additional tests, and the employer shall assure that these tests are provided.

(6) *Information provided to the physician.* The employer shall provide the following information to the examining physician:

(i) A copy of this regulation and its appendices;

(ii) A description of the affected employee's duties as they relate to the employee's exposure;

(iii) The employee's actual or representative exposure level:

(iv) A description of any personal protective equipment used or to be used; and

(v) Information from previous employment-related medical examinations of the affected employee which is not otherwise available to the examining physician.

(7) *Physician's written opinions.* (i) For each examination under this section, the employer shall obtain and provide the employee with a copy of the examining physician's written opinion within 15 days of the examination. The written opinion shall be limited to the following information:

(A) The occupationally pertinent results of the medical examination and tests;

(B) The physician's opinion concerning whether the employee has any detected medical conditions which would place the employee's health at greater than normal risk of material impairment from exposure to benzene;

(C) The physician's recommended limitations upon the employee's exposure to benzene or upon the employee's use of protective clothing or equipment and respirators.

(D) A statement that the employee has been informed by the physician of the results of the medical examination and any medical conditions resulting from benzene exposure which require further explanation or treatment.

(ii) The written opinion obtained by the employer shall not reveal specific records, findings and diagnoses that have no bearing on the employee's ability to work in a benzene-exposed workplace.

(8) *Medical removal plan.* (i) When a physician makes a referral to a hematologist/internist as required under paragraph (i)(5)(ii) of this section, the employee shall be removed from areas where exposures may exceed the action level until such time as the physician makes a determination under paragraph (i)(8)(ii) of this section.

(ii) Following the examination and evaluation by the hematologist/internist, a decision to remove an employee from areas where benzene exposure is above the action level or to allow the employee to return to areas where benzene exposure is above the action level shall be made by the physician in consultation with the hematologist/internist. This decision shall be communicated in writing to the employer and employee. In the case of removal, the physician shall state the required probable duration of removal from occupational exposure to benzene above the action level and the requirements for future medical examinations to review the decision.

(iii) For any employee who is removed pursuant to paragraph (i)(8)(ii) of this section, the employer shall provide a follow-up examination. The physician, in consultation with the hematologist/internist, shall make a decision within 6 months of the date the employee was removed as to whether the employee shall be returned to the usual job or whether the employee should be removed permanently.

(iv) Whenever an employee is temporarily removed from benzene exposure pursuant to paragraph (i)(8)(i) or (i)(8)(ii) of this section, the employer shall transfer the employee to a comparable job for which the employee is qualified (or can be trained for in a short period) and where benzene exposures are as low as possible, but in no event higher than the action level. The employer shall maintain the employee's current wage rate, seniority and other benefits. If there is no such job available, the employer shall provide medical removal protection benefits until such a job becomes available or for 6 months, whichever comes first.

(v) Whenever an employee is removed permanently from benzene exposure based on a physician's recommendation pursuant to paragraph (i)(8)(iii) of this section, the employee shall be given the opportunity to transfer to another position which is available or later becomes available for which the employee is qualified (or can be trained for in a short period) and where benzene exposures are as low as possible but in no event higher than the action level. The employer shall assure that such employee suffers no reduction in current wage rate, seniority or other benefits as a result of the transfer.

(9) *Medical removal protection benefits.* (i) The employer shall provide to an employee 6 months of medical removal protection benefits immediately following each occasion an employee is removed from exposure to benzene because of hematological findings pursuant to paragraphs (i)(8) (i) and (ii) of this section, unless the employee has been transferred to a comparable job where benzene exposures are below the action level.

(ii) For the purposes of this section, the requirement that an employer provide medical removal protection benefits means that the employer shall maintain the current wage rate, seniority and other benefits of an employee as though the employee had not been removed.

(iii) The employer's obligation to provide medical removal protection benefits to a removed employee shall be reduced to the extent that the employee receives compensation for earnings lost during the period of removal either from a publicly or employer-funded compensation program, or from employment with another employer made possible by virtue of the employee's removal.

(j) *Communication of hazards—*(1) *Hazard communication—general.* Chemical manufacturers, importers, distributors and employers shall comply with all requirements of the Hazard Communication Standard (HCS) (§ 1910.1200) for benzene.

(ii) In classifying the hazards of benzene at least the following hazards are to be addressed: Cancer; central nerv-

ous system effects; blood effects; aspiration; skin, eye, and respiratory tract irritation; and flammability.

(iii) Employers shall include benzene in the hazard communication program established to comply with the HCS (§ 1910.1200). Employers shall ensure that each employee has access to labels on containers of benzene and to safety data sheets, and is trained in accordance with the requirements of HCS and paragraph (j)(3) of this section.

(2) *Warning signs and labels.* (i)The employer shall post signs at entrances to regulated areas. The signs shall bear the following legend:

DANGER
BENZENE
MAY CAUSE CANCER
HIGHLY   FLAMMABLE   LIQUID   AND
 VAPOR
DO NOT SMOKE
WEAR RESPIRATORY PROTECTION IN
 THIS AREA
AUTHORIZED PERSONNEL ONLY

(ii) Prior to June 1, 2016, employers may use the following legend in lieu of that specified in paragraph (j)(2)(i) of this section:

DANGER
BENZENE
CANCER HAZARD
FLAMMABLE—NO SMOKING
AUTHORIZED PERSONNEL ONLY
RESPIRATOR REQUIRED

(iii) The employer shall ensure that labels or other appropriate forms of warning are provided for containers of benzene within the workplace. There is no requirement to label pipes. The labels shall comply with the requirements of paragraph (j)(1) of this section and § 1910.1200(f).

(iv) Prior to June 1, 2015, employers shall include the following legend or similar language on the labels or other appropriate forms of warning:

DANGER
CONTAINS BENZENE
CANCER HAZARD

(3) *Information and training.* (i) The employer shall provide employees with information and training at the time of their initial assignment to a work area where benzene is present. If exposures are above the action level, employees shall be provided with information and training at least annually thereafter.

(ii) The training program shall be in accordance with the requirements of 29 CFR 1910.1200(h) (1) and (2), and shall include specific information on benzene for each category of information included in that section.

(iii) In addition to the information required under 29 CFR 1910.1200, the employer shall:

(A) Provide employees with an explanation of the contents of this section, including Appendices A and B, and indicate to them where the standard is available; and

(B) Describe the medical surveillance program required under paragraph (i) of this section, and explain the information contained in appendix C.

(k) *Recordkeeping*—(1) *Exposure measurements.* (i) The employer shall establish and maintain an accurate record of all measurements required by paragraph (e) of this section, in accordance with 29 CFR 1910.20.

(ii) This record shall include:

(A) The dates, number, duration, and results of each of the samples taken, including a description of the procedure used to determine representative employee exposures;

(B) A description of the sampling and analytical methods used;

(C) A description of the type of respiratory protective devices worn, if any; and

(D) The name, social security number, job classification and exposure levels of the employee monitored and all other employees whose exposure the measurement is intended to represent.

(iii) The employer shall maintain this record for at least 30 years, in accordance with 29 CFR 1910.20.

(2) *Medical surveillance.* (i) The employer shall establish and maintain an accurate record for each employee subject to medical surveillance required by paragraph (i) of this section, in accordance with 29 CFR 1910.20.

(ii) This record shall include:

(A) The name and social security number of the employee;

(B) The employer's copy of the physician's written opinion on the initial, periodic and special examinations, including results of medical examinations and all tests, opinions and recommendations;

(C) Any employee medical complaints related to exposure to benzene;

(D) A copy of the information provided to the physician as required by paragraphs (i)(6) (ii) through (v) of this section; and

(E) A copy of the employee's medical and work history related to exposure to benzene or any other hematologic toxins.

(iii) The employer shall maintain this record for at least the duration of employment plus 30 years, in accordance with 29 CFR 1910.20.

(3) *Availability.* (i) The employer shall assure that all records required to be maintained by this section shall be made available upon request to the Assistant Secretary and the Director for examination and copying.

(ii) Employee exposure monitoring records required by this paragraph shall be provided upon request for examination and copying to employees, employee representatives, and the Assistant Secretary in accordance with 29 CFR 1910.20 (a) through (e) and (g) through (i).

(iii) Employee medical records required by this paragraph shall be provided upon request for examination and copying, to the subject employee, to anyone having the specific written consent of the subject employee, and to the Assistant Secretary in accordance with 29 CFR 1910.20.

(4) *Transfer of records.* The employer shall comply with the requirements involving transfer of records as set forth in 29 CFR 1910.1020(h).

(l) *Observation of monitoring*—(1) *Employee observation.* The employer shall provide affected employees, or their designated representatives, an opportunity to observe the measuring or monitoring of employee exposure to benzene conducted pursuant to paragraph (e) of this section.

(2) *Observation procedures.* When observation of the measuring or monitoring of employee exposure to benzene requires entry into areas where the use of protective clothing and equipment or respirators is required, the employer shall provide the observer with personal protective clothing and equipment or respirators required to be worn

by employees working in the area, assure the use of such clothing and equipment or respirators, and require the observer to comply with all other applicable safety and health procedures.

(m) [Reserved]

(n) *Appendices.* The information contained in Appendices A, B, C, and D is not intended, by itself, to create any additional obligations not otherwise imposed or to detract from any existing obligations.

APPENDIX A TO § 1910.1028—SUBSTANCE SAFETY DATA SHEET, BENZENE

I. SUBSTANCE IDENTIFICATION

A. Substance: Benzene.

B. Permissible Exposure: Except as to the use of gasoline, motor fuels and other fuels subsequent to discharge from bulk terminals and other exemptions specified in § 1910.1028(a)(2):

1. Airborne: The maximum time-weighted average (TWA) exposure limit is 1 part of benzene vapor per million parts of air (1 ppm) for an 8-hour workday and the maximum short-term exposure limit (STEL) is 5 ppm for any 15-minute period.

2. Dermal: Eye contact shall be prevented and skin contact with liquid benzene shall be limited.

C. Appearance and odor: Benzene is a clear, colorless liquid with a pleasant, sweet odor. The odor of benzene does not provide adequate warning of its hazard.

II. HEALTH HAZARD DATA

A. *Ways in which benzene affects your health.* Benzene can affect your health if you inhale it, or if it comes in contact with your skin or eyes. Benzene is also harmful if you happen to swallow it.

B. *Effects of overexposure.* 1. Short-term (acute) overexposure: If you are overexposed to high concentrations of benzene, well above the levels where its odor is first recognizable, you may feel breathless, irritable, euphoric, or giddy; you may experience irritation in eyes, nose, and respiratory tract. You may develop a headache, feel dizzy, nauseated, or intoxicated. Severe exposures may lead to convulsions and loss of consciousness.

2. Long-term (chronic) exposure. Repeated or prolonged exposure to benzene, even at relatively low concentrations, may result in various blood disorders, ranging from anemia to leukemia, an irreversible, fatal disease. Many blood disorders associated with benzene exposure may occur without symptoms.

III. PROTECTIVE CLOTHING AND EQUIPMENT

A. *Respirators.* Respirators are required for those operations in which engineering controls or work practice controls are not feasible to reduce exposure to the permissible level. However, where employers can document that benzene is present in the workplace less than 30 days a year, respirators may be used in lieu of engineering controls. If respirators are worn, they must have joint Mine Safety and Health Administration and the National Institute for Occupational Safety and Health (NIOSH) seal of approval, and cartridge or canisters must be replaced before the end of their service life, or the end of the shift, whichever occurs first. If you experience difficulty breathing while wearing a respirator, you may request a positive pressure respirator from your employer. You must be thoroughly trained to use the assigned respirator, and the training will be provided by your employer.

B. *Protective Clothing.* You must wear appropriate protective clothing (such as boots, gloves, sleeves, aprons, etc.) over any parts of your body that could be exposed to liquid benzene.

C. *Eye and Face Protection.* You must wear splash-proof safety goggles if it is possible that benzene may get into your eyes. In addition, you must wear a face shield if your face could be splashed with benzene liquid.

IV. EMERGENCY AND FIRST AID PROCEDURES

A. *Eye and face exposure.* If benzene is splashed in your eyes, wash it out immediately with large amounts of water. If irritation persists or vision appears to be affected see a doctor as soon as possible.

B. *Skin exposure.* If benzene is spilled on your clothing or skin, remove the contaminated clothing and wash the exposed skin with large amounts of water and soap immediately. Wash contaminated clothing before you wear it again.

C. *Breathing.* If you or any other person breathes in large amounts of benzene, get the exposed person to fresh air at once. Apply artificial respiration if breathing has stopped. Call for medical assistance or a doctor as soon as possible. Never enter any vessel or confined space where the benzene concentration might be high without proper safety equipment and at least one other person present who will stay outside. A life line should be used.

D. *Swallowing.* If benzene has been swallowed and the patient is conscious, do not induce vomiting. Call for medical assistance or a doctor immediately.

V. MEDICAL REQUIREMENTS

If you are exposed to benzene at a concentration at or above 0.5 ppm as an 8-hour time-weighted average, or have been exposed at or above 10 ppm in the past while employed by your current employer, your employer is required to provide a medical examination and history and laboratory tests within 60 days of the effective date of this standard and annually thereafter. These tests shall be provided without cost to you. In addition, if you are accidentally exposed to benzene (either by ingestion, inhalation, or skin/eye contact) under emergency conditions known or suspected to constitute toxic exposure to benzene, your employer is required to make special laboratory tests available to you.

VI. OBSERVATION OF MONITORING

Your employer is required to perform measurements that are representative of your exposure to benzene and you or your designated representative are entitled to observe the monitoring procedure. You are entitled to observe the steps taken in the measurement procedure, and to record the results obtained. When the monitoring procedure is taking place in an area where respirators or personal protective clothing and equipment are required to be worn, you or your representative must also be provided with, and must wear the protective clothing and equipment.

VII. ACCESS TO RECORDS

You or your representative are entitled to see the records of measurements of your exposure to benzene upon written request to your employer. Your medical examination records can be furnished to yourself, your physician or designated representative upon request by you to your employer.

VIII. PRECAUTIONS FOR SAFE USE, HANDLING AND STORAGE

Benzene liquid is highly flammable. It should be stored in tightly closed containers in a cool, well ventilated area. Benzene vapor may form explosive mixtures in air. All sources of ignition must be controlled. Use nonsparking tools when opening or closing benzene containers. Fire extinguishers, where provided, must be readily available. Know where they are located and how to operate them. Smoking is prohibited in areas where benzene is used or stored. Ask your supervisor where benzene is used in your area and for additional plant safety rules.

APPENDIX B TO § 1910.1028—SUBSTANCE TECHNICAL GUIDELINES, BENZENE

I. PHYSICAL AND CHEMICAL DATA

A. Substance identification.

1. *Synonyms:* Benzol, benzole, coal naphtha, cyclohexatriene, phene, phenyl hydride, pyrobenzol. (Benzin, petroleum benzin and Benzine do not contain benzene).

2. *Formula:* $C_6 H_6$ (CAS Registry Number: 71–43–2)

B. Physical data.

1. Boiling Point (760 mm Hg); 80.1 °C (176 °F)

2. Specific Gravity (water = 1): 0.879

3. Vapor Density (air = 1): 2.7

4. Melting Point: 5.5 °C (42 °F)

5. Vapor Pressure at 20 °C (68 °F): 75 mm Hg

6. Solubility in Water: .06%

7. Evaporation Rate (ether = 1): 2.8

8. Appearance and Odor: Clear, colorless liquid with a distinctive sweet odor.

II. FIRE, EXPLOSION, AND REACTIVITY HAZARD DATA

A. Fire.

1. Flash Point (closed cup): −11 °C (12 °F)

2. Autoignition Temperature: 580 °C (1076 °F)

3. Flammable limits in Air. % by Volume: Lower: 1.3%, Upper: 7.5%

4. Extinguishing Media: Carbon dioxide, dry chemical, or foam.

5. Special Fire-Fighting procedures: Do not use solid stream of water, since stream will scatter and spread fire. Fine water spray can be used to keep fire-exposed containers cool.

6. Unusual fire and explosion hazards: Benzene is a flammable liquid. Its vapors can form explosive mixtures. All ignition sources must be controlled when benzene is used, handled, or stored. Where liquid or vapor may be released, such areas shall be considered as hazardous locations. Benzene vapors are heavier than air; thus the vapors may travel along the ground and be ignited by open flames or sparks at locations remote from the site at which benzene is handled.

7. Benzene is classified as a 1 B flammable liquid for the purpose of conforming to the requirements of 29 CFR 1910.106. A concentration exceeding 3,250 ppm is considered a potential fire explosion hazard. Locations where benzene may be present in quantities sufficient to produce explosive or ignitable mixtures are considered Class I Group D for the purposes of conforming to the requirements of 29 CFR 1910.309.

B. Reactivity.

1. Conditions contributing to instability: Heat.

2. Incompatibility: Heat and oxidizing materials.

3. Hazardous decomposition products: Toxic gases and vapors (such as carbon monoxide).

III. SPILL AND LEAK PROCEDURES

A. Steps to be taken if the material is released or spilled. As much benzene as possible should be absorbed with suitable materials, such as dry sand or earth. That remaining must be flushed with large amounts of water. Do not flush benzene into a confined space, such as a sewer, because of explosion danger. Remove all ignition sources. Ventilate enclosed places.

B. Waste disposal method. Disposal methods must conform to other jurisdictional regulations. If allowed, benzene may be disposed of: (a) By absorbing it in dry sand or earth and disposing in a sanitary landfill; (b) if small quantities, by removing it to a safe location from buildings or other combustible sources, pouring it in dry sand or earth and cautiously igniting it; and (c) if large quantities, by atomizing it in a suitable combustion chamber.

IV. MISCELLANEOUS PRECAUTIONS

A. High exposure to benzene can occur when transferring the liquid from one container to another. Such operations should be well ventilated and good work practices must be established to avoid spills.

B. Use non-sparking tools to open benzene containers which are effectively grounded and bonded prior to opening and pouring.

C. Employers must advise employees of all plant areas and operations where exposure to benzene could occur. Common operations in which high exposures to benzene may be encountered are: the primary production and utilization of benzene, and transfer of benzene.

APPENDIX C TO §1910.1028—MEDICAL SURVEILLANCE GUIDELINES FOR BENZENE

I. ROUTE OF ENTRY

Inhalation; skin absorption.

II. TOXICOLOGY

Benzene is primarily an inhalation hazard. Systemic absorption may cause depression of the hematopoietic system, pancytopenia, aplastic anemia, and leukemia. Inhalation of high concentrations can affect central nervous system function. Aspiration of small amounts of liquid benzene immediately causes pulmonary edema and hemorrhage of pulmonary tissue. There is some absorption through the skin. Absorption may be more rapid in the case of abraded skin, and benzene may be more readily absorbed if it is present in a mixture or as a contaminant in solvents which are readily absorbed. The defatting action of benzene may produce primary irritation due to repeated or prolonged contact with the skin. High concentration are irritating to the eyes and the mucuous membranes of the nose, and respiratory tract.

III. SIGNS AND SYMPTOMS

Direct skin contact with benzene may cause erythema. Repeated or prolonged contact may result in drying, scaling dermatitis, or development of secondary skin infections. In addition, there is benzene absorption through the skin. Local effects of benzene vapor or liquid on the eye are slight. Only at very high concentrations is there any smarting sensation in the eye. Inhalation of high concentrations of benzene may have an initial stimulatory effect on the central nervous system characterized by exhilaration, nervous excitation, and/or giddiness, followed by a period of depression, drowsiness, or fatigue. A sensation of tightness in the chest accompanied by breathlessness may occur and ultimately the victim may lose consciousness. Tremors, convulsions and death may follow from respiratory paralysis or circulatory collapse in a few minutes to several hours following severe exposures.

The detrimental effect on the blood-forming system of prolonged exposure to small quantities of benzene vapor is of extreme importance. The hematopoietic system is the chief target for benzene's toxic effects which are manifested by alterations in the levels of formed elements in the peripheral blood. These effects have occurred at concentrations of benzene which may not cause irritation of mucous membranes, or any unpleasant sensory effects. Early signs and symptoms of benzene morbidity are varied, often not readily noticed and non-specific. Subjective complaints of headache, dizziness, and loss of appetite may precede or follow clinical signs. Rapid pulse and low blood pressure, in addition to a physical appearance of anemia, may accompany a subjective complaint of shortness of breath and excessive tiredness. Bleeding from the nose, gums, or mucous membranes, and the development of purpuric spots (small bruises) may occur as the condition progresses. Clinical evidence of leukopenia, anemia, and thrombocytopenia, singly or in combination, has been frequently reported among the first signs. Bone marrow may appear normal, aplastic, or hyperplastic, and may not, in all situations, correlate with peripheral blood forming tissues. Because of variations in the susceptibility to benzene morbidity, there is no "typical" blood picture. The onset of effects of prolonged benzene exposure may be delayed for many months or years after the actual exposure has ceased and identification or correlation with benzene exposure must be sought out in the occupational history.

IV. TREATMENT OF ACUTE TOXIC EFFECTS

Remove from exposure immediately. Make sure you are adequately protected and do not risk being overcome by fumes. Give oxygen or artificial resuscitation if indicated. Flush eyes, wash skin if contaminated and remove all contaminated clothing. Symptoms of intoxication may persist following severe exposures. Recovery from mild exposures is usually rapid and complete.

V. SURVEILLANCE AND PREVENTIVE CONSIDERATIONS

A. General

The principal effects of benzene exposure which form the basis for this regulation are pathological changes in the hematopoietic system, reflected by changes in the peripheral blood and manifesting clinically as pancytopenia, aplastic anemia, and leukemia. Consequently, the medical surveillance program is designed to observe, on a regular basis, blood indices for early signs of these effects, and although early signs of leukemia are not usually available, emerging diagnostic technology and innovative regimes make consistent surveillance for leukemia, as well as other hematopoietic effects, essential.

Initial examinations are to be provided within 60 days of the effective date of this standard, or at the time of initial assignment, and periodic examinations annually thereafter. There are special provisions for medical tests in the event of hematologic abnormalities or for emergency situations.

The blood values which require referral to a hematologist or internist are noted in the standard in paragraph (i)(5). The standard specifies that blood abnormalities that persist must be referred "unless the physician has good reason to believe such referral is unnecessary" (paragraph (i)(5)). Examples of conditions that could make a referral unnecessary despite abnormal blood limits are iron or folate deficiency, menorrhagia, or blood loss due to some unrelated medical abnormality.

Symptoms and signs of benzene toxicity can be non-specific. Only a detailed history and appropriate investigative procedures will enable a physician to rule out or confirm conditions that place the employee at increased risk. To assist the examining physician with regard to which laboratory tests are necessary and when to refer an employee to the specialist, OSHA has established the following guidelines.

B. Hematology Guidelines

A minimum battery of tests is to be performed by strictly standardized methods.

1. Red cell, white cell, platelet counts, white blood cell differential, hematacrit and red cell indices must be performed by an accredited laboratory. The normal ranges for the red cell and white cell counts are influenced by altitude, race, and sex, and therefore should be determined by the accredited laboratory in the specific area where the tests are performed.

Either a decline from an absolute normal or an individual's base line to a subnormal value or a rise to a supra-normal value, are indicative of potential toxicity, particularly if all blood parameters decline. The normal total white blood count is approximately 7,200/mm³ plus or minus 3,000. For cigarette smokers the white count may be higher and the upper range may be 2,000 cells higher than normal for the laboratory. In addition, infection, allergies and some drugs may raise the white cell count. The normal platelet count is approximately 250,000 with a range

of 140,000 to 400,000. Counts outside this range should be regarded as possible evidence of benzene toxicity.

Certain abnormalities found through routine screening are of greater significance in the benzene-exposed worker and require prompt consultation with a specialist, namely:

a. Thrombocytopenia.

b. A trend of decreasing white cell, red cell, or platelet indices in an individual over time is more worrisome than an isolated abnormal finding at one test time. The importance of trend highlights the need to compare an individual's test results to baseline and/or previous periodic tests.

c. A constellation or pattern of abnormalities in the different blood indices is of more significance than a single abnormality. A low white count not associated with any abnormalities in other cell indices may be a normal statistical variation, whereas if the low white count is accompanied by decreases in the platelet and/or red cell indices, such a pattern is more likely to be associated with benzene toxicity and merits thorough investigation.

Anemia, leukopenia, macrocytosis or an abnormal differential white blood cell count should alert the physician to further investigate and/or refer the patient if repeat tests confirm the abnormalities. If routine screening detects an abnormality, follow-up tests which may be helpful in establishing the etiology of the abnormality are the peripheral blood smear and the reticulocyte count.

The extreme range of normal for reticulocytes is 0.4 to 2.5 percent of the red cells, the usual range being 0.5 to 1.2 percent of the red cells, but the typical value is in the range of 0.8 to 1.0 percent. A decline in reticulocytes to levels of less than 0.4 percent is to be regarded as possible evidence (unless another specific cause is found) of benzene toxicity requiring accelerated surveillance. An increase in reticulocyte levels to about 2.5 percent may also be consistent with (but is not as characteristic of) benzene toxicity.

2. An important diagnostic test is a careful examination of the peripheral blood smear. As with reticulocyte count the smear should be with fresh uncoagulated blood obtained from a needle tip following venipuncture or from a drop of earlobe blood (capillary blood). If necessary, the smear may, under certain limited conditions, be made from a blood sample anticoagulated with EDTA (but never with oxalate or heparin). When the smear is to be prepared from a specimen of venous blood which has been collected by a commercial Vacutainer® type tube containing neutral EDTA, the smear should be made as soon as possible after the venesection. A delay of up to 12 hours is permissible between the drawing of the blood specimen into EDTA and the preparation of

the smear if the blood is stored at refrigerator (not freezing) temperature.

3. The minimum mandatory observations to be made from the smear are:

a. The differential white blood cell count.

b. Description of abnormalities in the appearance of red cells.

c. Description of any abnormalities in the platelets.

d. A careful search must be made throughout of every blood smear for immature white cells such as band forms (in more than normal proportion, i.e., over 10 percent of the total differential count), any number of metamyelocytes, myelocytes or myeloblasts. Any nucleate or multinucleated red blood cells should be reported. Large "giant" platelets or fragments of megakaryocytes must be recognized.

An increase in the proportion of band forms among the neutrophilic granulocytes is an abnormality deserving special mention, for it may represent a change which should be considered as an early warning of benzene toxicity in the absence of other causative factors (most commonly infection). Likewise, the appearance of metamyelocytes, in the absence of another probable cause, must be considered a possible indication of benzene-induced toxicity.

An upward trend in the number of basophils, which normally do not exceed about 2.0 percent of the total white cells, is to be regarded as possible evidence of benzene toxicity. A rise in the eosinophil count is less specific but also may be suspicious of toxicity if the rises above 6.0 percent of the total white count.

The normal range of monocytes is from 2.0 to 8.0 percent of the total white count with an average of about 5.0 percent. About 20 percent of individuals reported to have mild but persisting abnormalities caused by exposure to benzene show a persistent monocytosis. The findings of a monocyte count which persists at more than 10 to 12 percent of the normal white cell count (when the total count is normal) or persistence of an absolute monocyte count in excess of 800/mm³ should be regarded as a possible sign of benzene-induced toxicity.

A less frequent but more serious indication of benzene toxicity is the finding in the peripheral blood of the so-called "pseudo" (or acquired) Pelger-Huet anomaly. In this anomaly many, or sometimes the majority, of the neutrophilic granulocytes possess two round nuclear segments—less often one or three round segments—rather than three normally elongated segments. When this anomaly is not hereditary, it is often but not invariably predictive of subsequent leukemia. However, only about two percent of patients who ultimately develop acute myelogenous leukemia show the acquired Pelger-Huet anomaly. Other tests that can be administered to investigate blood abnormalities are discussed below; however, such procedures should be undertaken by the hematologist.

An uncommon sign, which cannot be detected from the smear, but can be elicited by a "sucrose water test" of peripheral blood, is transient paroxysmal nocturnal hemoglobinuria (PNH), which may first occur insidiously during a period of established aplastic anemia, and may be followed within one to a few years by the appearance of rapidly fatal acute myelogenous leukemia. Clinical detection of PNH, which occurs in only one or two percent of those destined to have acute myelogenous leukemia, may be difficult; if the "sucrose water test" is positive, the somewhat more definitive Ham test, also known as the acid-serum hemolysis test, may provide confirmation.

e. Individuals documented to have developed acute myelogenous leukemia years after initial exposure to benzene may have progressed through a preliminary phase of hematologic abnormality. In some instances pancytopenia (i.e., a lowering in the counts of all circulating blood cells of bone marrow origin, but not to the extent implied by the term "aplastic anemia") preceded leukemia for many years. Depression of a single blood cell type or platelets may represent a harbinger of aplasia or leukemia. The finding of two or more cytopenias, or pancytopenia in a benzene-exposed individual, must be regarded as highly suspicious of more advanced although still reversible, toxicity. "Pancytopenia" coupled with the appearance of immature cells (myelocytes, myeloblasts, erythroblasts, etc.), with abnormal cells (pseudo Pelger-Huet anomaly, atypical nuclear heterochromatin, etc.), or unexplained elevations of white blood cells must be regarded as evidence of benzene overexposure unless proved otherwise. Many severely aplastic patients manifested the ominous finding of 5–10 percent myeloblasts in the marrow, occasional myeloblasts and myelocytes in the blood and 20–30% monocytes. It is evident that isolated cytopenias, pancytopenias, and even aplastic anemias induced by benzene may be reversible and complete recovery has been reported on cessation of exposure. However, since any of these abnormalities is serious, the employee must immediately be removed from any possible exposure to benzene vapor. Certain tests may substantiate the employee's prospects for progression or regression. One such test would be an examination of the bone marrow, but the decision to perform a bone marrow aspiration or needle biopsy is made by the hematologist.

The findings of basophilic stippling in circulating red blood cells (usually found in 1 to 5% of red cells following marrow injury), and detection in the bone marrow of what are termed "ringed sideroblasts" must be taken seriously, as they have been noted in recent years to be premonitory signs of subsequent leukemia.

Recently peroxidase-staining of circulating or marrow neutrophil granulocytes, employing benzidine dihydrochloride, have revealed the disappearance of, or diminution in, peroxidase in a sizable proportion of the granulocytes, and this has been reported as an early sign of leukemia. However, relatively few patients have been studied to date. Granulocyte granules are normally strongly peroxidase positive. A steady decline in leukocyte alkaline phosphatase has also been reported as suggestive of early acute leukemia. Exposure to benzene may cause an early rise in serum iron, often but not always associated with a fall in the reticulocyte count. Thus, serial measurements of serum iron levels may provide a means of determining whether or not there is a trend representing sustained suppression of erythropoiesis.

Measurement of serum iron, determination of peroxidase and of alkaline phosphatase activity in peripheral granulocytes can be performed in most pathology laboratories. Peroxidase and alkaline phosphatase staining are usually undertaken when the index of suspecion for leukemia is high.

APPENDIX D TO § 1910.1028—SAMPLING AND ANALYTICAL METHODS FOR BENZENE MONITORING AND MEASUREMENT PROCEDURES

Measurements taken for the purpose of determining employee exposure to benzene are best taken so that the representative average 8-hour exposure may be determined from a single 8-hour sample or two (2) 4-hour samples. Short-time interval samples (or grab samples) may also be used to determine average exposure level if a minimum of five measurements are taken in a random manner over the 8-hour work shift. Random sampling means that any portion of the work shift has the same change of being sampled as any other. The arithmetic average of all such random samples taken on one work shift is an estimate of an employee's average level of exposure for that work shift. Air samples should be taken in the employee's breathing zone (air that would most nearly represent that inhaled by the employee). Sampling and analysis must be performed with procedures meeting the requirements of the standard.

There are a number of methods available for monitoring employee exposures to benzene. The sampling and analysis may be performed by collection of the benzene vaptor or charcoal absorption tubes, with subsequent chemical analysis by gas chromatography. Sampling and analysis may also be performed by portable direct reading instruments, real-time continuous monitoring systems, passive dosimeters or other suitable methods. The employer has the obligation of selecting a monitoring method which meets

the accuracy and precision requirements of the standard under his unique field conditions. The standard requires that the method of monitoring must have an accuracy, to a 95 percent confidence level, of not less than plus or minus 25 percent for concentrations of benzene greater than or equal to 0.5 ppm.

The OSHA Laboratory modified NIOSH Method S311 and evaluated it at a benzene air concentration of 1 ppm. A procedure for determining the benzene concentration in bulk material samples was also evalauted. This work, reported in OSHA Laboratory Method No. 12, includes the following two analytical procedures:

I. OSHA METHOD 12 FOR AIR SAMPLES

Analyte: Benzene
Matrix: Air
Procedure: Adsorption on charcoal, desorption with carbon disulfide, analysis by GC.

Detection limit: 0.04 ppm
Recommended air volume and sampling rate: 10L to 0.2 L/min.

1. Principle of the Method.

1.1 A known volume of air is drawn through a charcoal tube to trap the organic vapors present.

1.2. The charcoal in the tube is transferred to a small, stoppered vial, and the anlyte is desorbed with carbon disulfide.

1.3. An aliquot of the desorbed sample is injected into a gas chromatograph.

1.4 The area of the resulting peak is determined and compared with areas obtained from standards.

2. Advantages and disadvantages of the method.

2.1 The sampling device is small, portable, and involved no liquids. Interferences are minimal, and most of those which do occur can be eliminated by altering chromatographic conditions. The samples are analyzed by means of a quick, instrumental method.

2.2 The amount of sample which can be taken is limited by the number of milligrams that the tube will hold before overloading. When the sample value obtained for the backup section of the charcoal tube exceeds 25 percent of that found on the front section, the possibility of sample loss exists.

3. Apparatus.

3.1 A calibrated personal sampling pump whose flow can be determined within ±5 percent at the recommended flow rate.

3.2. Charcoal tubes: Glass with both ends flame sealed, 7 cm long with a 6-mm O.D. and a 4-mm I.D., containing 2 sections of 20/40 mesh activated charcoal separated by a 2-mm portion of urethane foam. The activated charcoal is prepared from coconut shells and is fired at 600 °C prior to packing. The adsorbing section contains 100 mg of charcoal, the back-up section 50 mg. A 3-mm portion of urethane foam is placed between the outlet end of the tube and the back-up section. A plug of silanized glass wool is placed in front of the adsorbing section. The pressure drop across the tube must be less than one inch of mercury at a flow rate of 1 liter per minute.

3.3. Gas chromatograph equipped with a flame ionization detector.

3.4. Column (10-ft × ⅛-in stainless steel) packed with 80/100 Supelcoport coated with 20 percent SP 2100, 0.1 percent CW 1500.

3.5. An electronic integrator or some other suitable method for measuring peak area.

3.6. Two-milliliter sample vials with Teflon-lined caps.

3.7. Microliter syringes: 10-microliter (10-μL syringe, and other convenient sizes for making standards, 1-μL syringe for sample injections.

3.8. Pipets: 1.0 mL delivery pipets

3.9. Volumetric flasks: convenient sizes for making standard solutions.

4. Reagents.

4.1. Chromatographic quality carbon disulfide (CS_2). Most commercially available carbon disulfide contains a trace of benzene which must be removed. It can be removed with the following procedure:

Heat under reflux for 2 to 3 hours, 500 mL of carbon disulfide, 10 mL concentrated sulfuric acid, and 5 drops of concentrated nitric acid. The benzene is converted to nitrobenzene. The carbon disulfide layer is removed, dried with anhydrous sodium sulfate, and distilled. The recovered carbon disulfide should be benzene free. (It has recently been determined that benzene can also be removed by passing the carbon disulfide through 13x molecular sieve).

4.2. Benzene, reagent grade.

4.3. p-Cymene, reagent grade, (internal standard).

4.4. Desorbing reagent. The desorbing reagent is prepared by adding 0.05 mL of p-cymene per milliliter of carbon disulfide. The internal standard offers a convenient means correcting analytical response for slight inconsistencies in the size of sample injec-tions. If the external standard technique is preferred, the internal standard can be eliminated).

4.5. Purified GC grade helium, hydrogen and air.

5. Procedure.

5.1. Cleaning of equipment. All glassware used for the laboratory analysis should be properly cleaned and free of organics which could interfere in the analysis.

5.2. Calibration of personal pumps. Each pump must be calibrated with a representative charcoal tube in the line.

5.3. Collection and shipping of samples.

5.3.1. Immediately before sampling, break the ends of the tube to provide an opening at least one-half the internal diameter of the tube (2 mm).

5.3.2. The smaller section of the charcoal is used as the backup and should be placed nearest the sampling pump.

5.3.3. The charcoal tube should be placed in a vertical position during sampling to minimize channeling through the charcoal.

5.3.4 Air being sampled should not be passed through any hose or tubing before entering the charcoal tube.

5.3.5. A sample size of 10 liters is recommended. Sample at a flow rate of approximately 0.2 liters per minute. The flow rate should be known with an accuracy of at least ±5 percent.

5.3.6. The charcoal tubes should be capped with the supplied plastic caps immediately after sampling.

5.3.7. Submit at least one blank tube (a charcoal tube subjected to the same handling procedures, without having any air drawn through it) with each set of samples.

5.3.8. Take necessary shipping and packing precautions to minimize breakage of samples.

5.4. Analysis of samples.

5.4.1. Preparation of samples. In preparation for analysis, each charcoal tube is scored with a file in front of the first section of charcoal and broken open. The glass wool is removed and discarded. The charcoal in the first (larger) section is transferred to a 2-ml vial. The separating section of foam is removed and discarded; the second section is transferred to another capped vial. These two sections are analyzed separately.

5.4.2. Desorption of samples. Prior to analysis, 1.0 mL of desorbing solution is pipetted into each sample container. The desorbing solution consists of 0.05 μL internal standard per mL of carbon disulfide. The sample vials are capped as soon as the solvent is added. Desorption should be done for 30 minutes with occasional shaking.

5.4.3. GC conditions. Typical operating conditions for the gas chromatograph are:

1.30 mL/min (60 psig) helium carrier gas flow.

2.30 mL/min (40 psig) hydrogen gas flow to detector.

3.240 mL/min (40 psig) air flow to detector.

4.150 °C injector temperature.

5.250 °C detector temperature.

6.100 °C column temperature.

5.4.4. Injection size. 1 μL.

5.4.5. Measurement of area. The peak areas are measured by an electronic integrator or some other suitable form of area measurement.

5.4.6. An internal standard procedure is used. The integrator is calibrated to report results in ppm for a 10 liter air sample after correction for desorption efficiency.

5.5. Determination of desorption efficiency.

5.5.1. Importance of determination. The desorption efficiency of a particular compound can vary from one laboratory to another and from one lot of chemical to another. Thus, it is necessary to determine, at least once, the percentage of the specific compound that is removed in the desorption process, provided the same batch of charcoal is used.

5.5.2. Procedure for determining desorption efficiency. The reference portion of the charcoal tube is removed. To the remaining portion, amounts representing 0.5X, 1X, and 2X and (X represents target concentration) based on a 10 L air sample are injected into several tubes at each level. Dilutions of benzene with carbon disulfide are made to allow injection of measurable quantities. These tubes are then allowed to equilibrate at least overnight. Following equilibration they are analyzed following the same procedure as the samples. Desorption efficiency is determined by dividing the amount of benzene found by amount spiked on the tube.

6. Calibration and standards. A series of standards varying in concentration over the range of interest is prepared and analyzed under the same GC conditions that will be used on the samples. A calibration curve is prepared by plotting concentration (µg/mL) versus peak area.

7. Calculations. Benzene air concentration can be calculated from the following equation:

$$mg/m^3 = (A)(B)/(C)(D)$$

Where:

A = µg/mL benzene, obtained from the calibration curve

B = desorption volume (1 mL)

C = Liters of air sampled

D = desorption efficiency

The concentration in mg/m^3 can be converted to ppm (at 25° and 760 mm) with following equation:

$$ppm = (mg/m^3)(24.46)/(78.11)$$

Where:

24.46 = molar volume of an ideal gas 25 °C and 760 mm

78.11 = molecular weight of benzene

8. Backup Data.

8.1 Detection limit—Air Samples. The detection limit for the analytical procedure is 1.28 ng with a coefficient of variation of 0.023 at this level. This would be equivalent to an air concentration of 0.04 ppm for a 10 L air sample. This amount provided a chromatographic peak that could be identifiable in the presence of possible interferences. The detection limit data were obtained by making 1 µL injections of a 1.283 µg/mL standard.

Injection	Area Count
1	655.4

Injection	Area Count	
2	617.5	X̄ = 640.2
3	662.0	SD = 14.9
4	641.1	CV = 0.023
5	636.4	
6	629.2	

8.2. Pooled coefficient of variation—Air Samples. The pooled coefficient of variation for the analytical procedure was determined by 1 µL replicate injections of analytical standards. The standards were 16.04, 32.08, and 64.16 µg/mL, which are equivalent to 0.5, 1.0, and 2.0 ppm for a 10 L air sample respectively.

Injection	Area Counts		
	0.5 ppm	1.0 ppm	2.0 ppm
1	3996.5	8130.2	16481
2	4059.4	8235.6	16493
3	4052.0	8307.9	16535
4	4027.2	8263.2	16609
5	4046.8	8291.1	16552
6	4137.9	8288.8	16618
X̄=	4053.3	8254.0	16548.3
SD=	47.2	62.5	57.1
CV =	0.0116	0.0076	0.0034
C̄V = 0.008			

8.3. Storage data—Air Samples

Samples were generated at 1.03 ppm benzene at 80% relative humidity, 22 °C, and 643 mm. All samples were taken for 50 minutes at 0.2 L/min. Six samples were analyzed immediately and the rest of the samples were divided into two groups by fifteen samples each. One group was stored at refrigerated temperature of −25 °C, and the other group was stored at ambient temperature (approximately 23 °C). These samples were analyzed over a period of fifteen days. The results are tabulated below.

PERCENT RECOVERY

Day analyzed	Refrigerated			Ambient		
0	97.4	98.7	98.9	97.4	98.7	98.9
0	97.1	100.6	100.9	97.1	100.6	100.9
2	95.8	96.4	95.4	95.4	96.6	96.9
5	93.9	94.3	92.4	92.4	94.3	94.1
9	93.6	95.5	94.6	95.2	95.6	96.6
13	94.3	95.3	93.7	91.0	95.0	94.6
15	96.8	95.8	94.2	92.9	96.3	95.9

8.4. Desorption data.

Samples were prepared by injecting liquid benzene onto the A section of charcoal tubes. Samples were prepared that would be equivalent to 0.5, 1.0, and 2.0 ppm for a 10 L air sample.

PERCENT RECOVERY

Sample	0.5 ppm	1.0 ppm	2.0 ppm
1	99.4	98.8	99.5
2	99.5	98.7	99.7

PERCENT RECOVERY—Continued

Sample	0.5 ppm	1.0 ppm	2.0 ppm
3	99.2	98.6	99.8
4	99.4	99.1	100.0
5	99.2	99.0	99.7
6	99.8	99.1	99.9
X̄=	99.4	98.9	99.8
SD=	0.22	0.21	0.18
CV =	0.0022	0.0021	0.0018
X̄ = 99.4			

8.5. Carbon disulfide.

Carbon disulfide from a number of sources was analyzed for benzene contamination. The results are given in the following table. The benzene contamiant can be removed with the procedures given in section 4.1.

Sample	µg Ben-zene/mL	ppm equiva-lent (for 10 L air sample)
Aldrich Lot 83017	4.20	0.13
Baker Lot 720364	1.01	0.03
Baker Lot 822351	1.01	0.03
Malinkrodt Lot WEMP	1.74	0.05
Malinkrodt Lot WDSJ	5.65	0.18
Malinkrodt Lot WHGA	2.90	0.09
Treated CS$_2$		

II. OSHA LABORATORY METHOD NO. 12 FOR BULK SAMPLES

Analyte: Benzene.

Matrix: Bulk Samples.

Procedure: Bulk Samples are analyzed directly by high performance liquid chromatography (HPLC).

Detection limits: 0.01% by volume.

1. Principle of the method.

1.1. An aliquot of the bulk sample to be analyzed is injected into a liquid chromatograph.

1.2. The peak area for benzene is determined and compared to areas obtained from standards.

2. Advantages and disadvantages of the method.

2.1. The analytical procedure is quick, sensitive, and reproducible.

2.2. Reanalysis of samples is possible.

2.3. Interferences can be circumvented by proper selection of HPLC parameters.

2.4. Samples must be free of any particulates that may clog the capillary tubing in the liquid chromatograph. This may require distilling the sample or clarifying with a clarification kit.

3. Apparatus.

3.1. Liquid chromatograph equipped with a UV detector.

3.2. HPLC Column that will separate benzene from other components in the bulk sample being analyzed. The column used for validation studies was a Waters uBondapack C18, 30 cm × 3.9 mm.

3.3. A clarification kit to remove any particulates in the bulk if necessary.

3.4. A micro-distillation apparatus to distill any samples if necessary.

3.5. An electronic integrator or some other suitable method of measuring peak areas.

3.6. Microliter syringes—10 µL syringe and other convenient sizes for making standards. 10 µL syringe for sample injections.

3.7. Volumetric flasks, 5 mL and other convenient sizes for preparing standards and making dilutions.

4. Reagents.

4.1. Benzene, reagent grade.

4.2. HPLC grade water, methyl alcohol, and isopropyl alcohol.

5. Collection and shipment of samples.

5.1. Samples should be transported in glass containers with Teflon-lined caps.

5.2. Samples should not be put in the same container used for air samples.

6. Analysis of samples.

6.1. Sample preparation.

If necessary, the samples are distilled or clarified. Samples are analyzed undiluted. If the benzene concentration is out of the working range, suitable dilutions are made with isopropyl alcohol.

6.2. HPLC conditions.

The typical operating conditions for the high performance liquid chromatograph are:

1. Mobile phase—Methyl alcohol/water, 50/50

1. Analytical wavelength—254 nm

3. Injection size—10 µL

6.3. Measurement of peak area and calibration.

Peak areas are measured by an integrator or other suitable means. The integrator is calibrated to report results % in benzene by volume.

7. Calculations.

Since the integrator is programmed to report results in % benzene by volume in an undiluted sample, the following equation is used:

% Benzene by Volume = A × B

Where:

A = % by volume on report

B = Dilution Factor

(B = 1 for undiluted sample)

8. Backup Data.

8.1. Detection limit—Bulk Samples.

The detection limit for the analytical procedure for bulk samples is 0.88 µg, with a coefficient of variation of 0.019 at this level. This amount provided a chromatographic peak that could be identifiable in the presence of possible interferences. The detection limit date were obtained by making 10 µL injections of a 0.10% by volume standard.

Injection	Area Count
1	45386
2	44214
3	43822

X̄ = 44040.1

Injection	Area Count	
4	44062	SD = 852.5
6	42724	CV = 0.019

8.2. Pooled coefficient of variation—Bulk Samples.

The pooled coefficient of variation for analytical procedure was determined by 50 µL replicate injections of analytical standards. The standards were 0.01, 0.02, 0.04, 0.10, 1.0, and 2.0% benzene by volume.

AREA COUNT (PERCENT)

Injection No.	0.01	0.02	0.04	0.10	1.0	2.0
1	45386	84737	166097	448497	4395380	9339150
2	44241	84300	170832	441299	4590800	9484900
3	43822	83835	164160	443719	4593200	9557580
4	44062	84381	164445	444842	4642350	9677060
5	44006	83012	168398	442564	4646430	9766240
6	42724	81957	173002	443975	4646260	
X̄ =	44040.1	83703.6	167872	444149	4585767	9564986
SD =	852.5	1042.2	3589.8	2459.1	96839.3	166233
CV =	0.0194	0.0125	0.0213	0.0055	0.0211	0.0174
C̄V =	0.017					

[52 FR 34562, Sept. 11, 1987, as amended at 54 FR 24334, June 7, 1989; 61 FR 5508, Feb. 13, 1996; 63 FR 1289, Jan. 8, 1998; 63 FR 20099, Apr. 23, 1998; 70 FR 1142, Jan. 5, 2005; 71 FR 16673, Apr. 3, 2006; 71 FR 50189, Aug. 24, 2006; 73 FR 75585, Dec. 12, 2008; 76 FR 33608, June 8, 2011; 77 FR 17781, Mar. 26, 2012]

§ 1910.1029 Coke oven emissions.

(a) *Scope and application.* This section applies to the control of employee exposure to coke oven emissions, except that this section shall not apply to working conditions with regard to which other Federal agencies exercise statutory authority to prescribe or enforce standards affecting occupational safety and health.

(b) *Definitions.* For the purpose of this section:

Authorized person means any person specifically authorized by the employer whose duties require the person to enter a regulated area, or any person entering such an area as a designated representative of employees for the purpose of exercising the opportunity to observe monitoring and measuring procedures under paragraph (n) of this section.

Beehive oven means a coke oven in which the products of carbonization other than coke are not recovered, but are released into the ambient air.

Coke oven means a retort in which coke is produced by the destructive distillation or carbonization of coal.

Coke oven battery means a structure containing a number of slot-type coke ovens.

Coke oven emissions means the benzene-soluble fraction of total particulate matter present during the destructive distillation or carbonization of coal for the production of coke.

Director means the Director, National Institute for Occupational Safety and Health, U.S. Department of Health, Education, and Welfare, or his or her designee.

Emergency means any occurance such as, but not limited to, equipment failure which is likely to, or does, result in any massive release of coke oven emissions.

Existing coke oven battery means a battery in operation or under construction on January 20, 1977, and which is not a rehabilitated coke oven battery.

Rehabilitated coke oven battery means a battery which is rebuilt, overhauled, renovated, or restored such as from the pad up, after January 20, 1977.

Secretary means the Secretary of Labor, U.S. Department of Labor, or his or her designee.

Stage charging means a procedure by which a predetermined volume of coal in each larry car hopper is introduced into an oven such that no more than two hoppers are discharging simultaneously.

Sequential charging means a procedure, usually automatically timed, by which a predetermined volume of coal in each larry car hopper is introduced into an oven such that no more than two hoppers commence or finish discharging simultaneously although, at

300

some point, all hoppers are discharging simultaneously.

Pipeline charging means any apparatus used to introduce coal into an oven which uses a pipe or duct permanently mounted onto an oven and through which coal is charged.

Green plush means coke which when removed from the oven results in emissions due to the presence of unvolatilized coal.

(c) *Permissible exposure limit.* The employer shall assure that no employee in the regulated area is exposed to coke oven emissions at concentrations greater than 150 micrograms per cubic meter of air (150 $\mu g/m^3$), averaged over any 8-hour period.

(d) *Regulated areas.* (1) The employer shall establish regulated areas and shall limit access to them to authorized persons.

(2) The employer shall establish the following as regulated areas:

(i) The coke oven battery including topside and its machinery, pushside and its machinery, coke side and its machinery, and the battery ends; the wharf; and the screening station;

(ii) The beehive oven and its machinery.

(e) *Exposure monitoring and measurement*—(1) *Monitoring program.* (i) Each employer who has a place of employment where coke oven emissions are present shall monitor employees employed in the regulated area to measure their exposure to coke oven emissions.

(ii) The employer shall obtain measurements which are representative of each employee's exposure to coke oven emissions over an eight-hour period. All measurements shall determine exposure without regard to the use of respiratory protection.

(iii) The employer shall collect fullshift (for at least seven continuous hours) personal samples, including at least one sample during each shift for each battery and each job classification within the regulated areas including at least the following job classifications:

(a) Lidman;

(b) Tar chaser;

(c) Larry car operator;

(d) Luterman;

(e) Machine operator, coke side;

(f) Benchman, coke side;

(g) Benchman, pusher side;

(h) Heater;

(i) Quenching car operator;

(j) Pusher machine operator;

(k) Screening station operator;

(l) Wharfman;

(m) Oven patcher;

(n) Oven repairman;

(o) Spellman; and

(p) Maintenance personnel.

(iv) The employer shall repeat the monitoring and measurements required by this paragraph (e)(1) at least every three months.

(2) *Redetermination.* Whenever there has been a production, process, or control change which may result in new or additional exposure to coke oven emissions, or whenever the employer has any other reason to suspect an increase in employee exposure, the employer shall repeat the monitoring and measurements required by paragraph (e)(1) of this section for those employees affected by such change or increase.

(3) *Employee notification.* (i) The employer must, within 15 working days after the receipt of the results of any monitoring performed under this section, notify each affected employee of these results either individually in writing or by posting the results in an appropriate location that is accessible to employees.

(ii) Whenever such results indicate that the representative employee exposure exceeds the permissible exposure limit, the employer shall, in such notification, inform each employee of that fact and of the corrective action being taken to reduce exposure to or below the permissible exposure limit.

(4) *Accuracy of measurement.* The employer shall use a method of monitoring and measurement which has an accuracy (with a confidence level of 95%) of not less than plus or minus 35% for concentrations of coke oven emissions greater than or equal to 150 $\mu g/m^3$.

(f) *Methods of compliance.* The employer shall control employee exposure to coke oven emissions by the use of engineering controls, work practices and respiratory protection as follows:

(1) *Priority of compliance methods*—(i) *Existing coke oven batteries.* (a) The employer shall institute the engineering

and work practice controls listed in paragraphs (f)(2), (f)(3) and (f)(4) of this section in existing coke oven batteries at the earliest possible time, but not later than January 20, 1980, except to the extent that the employer can establish that such controls are not feasible. In determining the earliest possible time for institution of engineering and work practice controls, the requirement, effective August 27, 1971, to implement feasible administrative or engineering controls to reduce exposures to coal tar pitch volatiles, shall be considered. Wherever the engineering and work practice controls which can be instituted are not sufficient to reduce employee exposures to or below the permissible exposure limit, the employer shall nonetheless use them to reduce exposures to the lowest level achievable by these controls and shall supplement them by the use of respiratory protection which complies with the requirements of paragraph (g) of this section.

(b) The engineering and work practice controls required under paragraphs (f)(2), (f)(3) and (f)(4) of this section are minimum requirements generally applicable to all existing coke oven batteries. If, after implementing all controls required by paragraphs (f)(2), (f)(3) and (f)(4) of this section, or after January 20, 1980, whichever is sooner, employee exposures still exceed the permissible exposure limit, employers shall implement any other engineering and work practice controls necessary to reduce exposure to or below the permissible exposure limit except to the extent that the employer can establish that such controls are not feasible. Whenever the engineering and work practice controls which can be instituted are not sufficient to reduce employee exposures to or below the permissible exposure limit, the employer shall nonetheless use them to reduce exposures to the lowest level achievable by these controls and shall supplement them by the use of respiratory protection which complies with the requirements of paragraph (g) of this section.

(ii) *New or rehabilitated coke oven batteries.* (a) The employer shall institute the best available engineering and work practice controls on all new or re-

habilitated coke oven batteries to reduce and maintain employee exposures at or below the permissible exposure limit, except to the extent that the employer can establish that such controls are not feasible. Wherever the engineering and work practice controls which can be instituted are not sufficient to reduce employee exposures to or below the permissible exposure limit, the employer shall nonetheless use them to reduce exposures to the lowest level achievable by these controls and shall supplement them by the use of respiratory protection which complies with the requirements of paragraph (g) of this section.

(b) If, after implementing all the engineering and work practice controls required by paragraph (f)(1)(ii)(a) of this section, employee exposures still exceed the permissible exposure limit, the employer shall implement any other engineering and work practice controls necessary to reduce exposure to or below the permissible exposure limit except to the extent that the employer can establish that such controls are not feasible. Wherever the engineering and work practice controls which can be instituted are not sufficient to reduce employee exposures to or below the permissible exposure limit, the employer shall nonetheless use them to reduce exposures to the lowest level achievable by these controls and shall supplement them by the use of respiratory protection which complies with the requirements of paragraph (g) of this section.

(iii) *Beehive ovens.* (a) The employer shall institute engineering and work practice controls on all beehive ovens at the earliest possible time to reduce and maintain employee exposures at or below the permissible exposure limit, except to the extent that the employer can establish that such controls are not feasible. In determining the earliest possible time for institution of engineering and work practice controls, the requirement, effective August 27, 1971, to implement feasible administrative or engineering controls to reduce exposures to coal tar pitch volatiles, shall be considered. Wherever the engineering and work practice controls which can be instituted are not sufficient to reduce employee exposures to or below the permissible exposure limit, the employer shall nonetheless use them to reduce exposures to the lowest level achievable by these controls and shall supplement them by the use of respiratory protection which complies with the requirements of paragraph (g) of this section.

(b) If, after implementing all engineering and work practice controls required by paragraph (f)(1)(iii)(a) of this section, employee exposures still exceed the permissible exposure limit, the employer shall implement any other engineering and work practice controls necessary to reduce exposures to or below the permissible exposure limit except to the extent that the employer can establish that such controls are not feasible. Whenever the engineering and work practice controls which can be instituted are not sufficient to reduce employee exposures to or below the permissible exposure limit, the employer shall nonetheless use them to reduce exposures to the lowest level achievable by these controls and shall supplement them by the use of respiratory protection which complies with the requirements of paragraph (g) of this section.

(2) *Engineering controls*—(i) *Charging.* The employer shall equip and operate existing coke oven batteries with all of the following engineering controls to control coke oven emissions during charging operations:

(a) One of the following methods of charging:

(1) Stage charging as described in paragraph (f)(3)(i)(b) of this section; or

(2) Sequential charging as described in paragraph (f)(3)(i)(b) of this section except that paragraph (f)(3)(i)(b)(3)(iv) of this section does not apply to sequential charging; or

(3) Pipeline charging or other forms of enclosed charging in accordance with paragraph (f)(2)(i) of this section, except that paragraphs (f)(2)(i)(b), (d), (e), (f) and (h) of this section do not apply;

(b) Drafting from two or more points in the oven being charged, through the use of double collector mains, or a fixed or moveable jumper pipe system to another oven, to effectively remove the gases from the oven to the collector mains;

(c) Aspiration systems designed and operated to provide sufficient negative pressure and flow volume to effectively move the gases evolved during charging into the collector mains, including sufficient steam pressure, and steam jets of sufficient diameter;

(d) Mechanical volumetric controls on each larry car hopper to provide the proper amount of coal to be charged through each charging hole so that the tunnel head will be sufficient to permit the gases to move from the oven into the collector mains;

(e) Devices to facilitate the rapid and continuous flow of coal into the oven being charged, such as stainless steel liners, coal vibrators or pneumatic shells;

(f) Individually operated larry car drop sleeves and slide gates designed and maintained so that the gases are effectively removed from the oven into the collector mains;

(g) Mechanized gooseneck and standpipe cleaners;

(h) Air seals on the pusher machine leveler bars to control air infiltration during charging; and

(i) Roof carbon cutters or a compressed air system or both on the pusher machine rams to remove roof carbon.

(ii) *Coking.* The employer shall equip and operate existing coke oven batteries with all of the following engineering controls to control coke emissions during coking operations;

(a) A pressure control system on each battery to obtain uniform collector main pressure;

(b) Ready access to door repair facilities capable of prompt and efficient repair of doors, door sealing edges and all door parts;

(c) An adequate number of spare doors available for replacement purposes;

(d) Chuck door gaskets to control chuck door emissions until such door is repaired, or replaced; and

(e) Heat shields on door machines.

(3) *Work practice controls*—(i) *Charging.* The employer shall operate existing coke oven batteries with all of the following work practices to control coke oven emissions during the charging operation:

(a) Establishment and implementation of a detailed, written inspection and cleaning procedure for each battery consisting of at least the following elements:

(1) Prompt and effective repair or replacement of all engineering controls;

(2) Inspection and cleaning of goosenecks and standpipes prior to each charge to a specified minimum diameter sufficient to effectively move the evolved gases from the oven to the collector mains;

(3) Inspection for roof carbon build-up prior to each charge and removal of roof carbon as necessary to provide an adequate gas channel so that the gases are effectively moved from the oven into the collector mains;

(4) Inspection of the steam aspiration system prior to each charge so that sufficient pressure and volume is maintained to effectively move the gases from the oven to the collector mains;

(5) Inspection of steam nozzles and liquor sprays prior to each charge and cleaning as necessary so that the steam nozzles and liquor sprays are clean;

(6) Inspection of standpipe caps prior to each charge and cleaning and luting or both as necessary so that the gases are effectively moved from the oven to the collector mains; and

(7) Inspection of charging holes and lids for cracks, warpage and other defects prior to each charge and removal of carbon to prevent emissions, and application of luting material to standpipe and charging hole lids where necessary to obtain a proper seal.

(b) Establishment and implementation of a detailed written charging procedure, designed and operated to eliminate emissions during charging for each battery, consisting of at least the following elements:

(1) Larry car hoppers filled with coal to a predetermined level in accordance with the mechanical volumetric controls required under paragraph (f)(2)(i)(d) of this section so as to maintain a sufficient gas passage in the oven to be charged;

(2) The larry car aligned over the oven to be charged, so that the drop sleeves fit tightly over the charging holes; and

(3) The oven charged in accordance with the following sequence of requirements:

(i) The aspiration system turned on;

(ii) Coal charged through the outermost hoppers, either individually or together depending on the capacity of the aspiration system to collect the gases involved;

(iii) The charging holes used under paragraph (f)(3)(i)(b)(3)(ii) of this section relidded or otherwise sealed off to prevent leakage of coke oven emissions;

(iv) If four hoppers are used, the third hopper discharged and relidded or otherwise sealed off to prevent leakage of coke oven emissions;

(v) The final hopper discharged until the gas channel at the top of the oven is blocked and then the chuck door opened and the coal leveled;

(vi) When the coal from the final hopper is discharged and the leveling operation complete, the charging hole relidded or otherwise sealed off to prevent leakage of coke oven emissions; and

(vii) The aspiration system turned off only after the charging holes have been closed.

(c) Establishment and implementation of a detailed written charging procedure, designed and operated to eliminate emissions during charging of each pipeline or enclosed charged battery.

(ii) *Coking.* The employer shall operate existing coke oven batteries pursuant to a detailed written procedure established and implemented for the control of coke oven emissions during coking, consisting of at least the following elements:

(a) Checking oven back pressure controls to maintain uniform pressure conditions in the collecting main;

(b) Repair, replacement and adjustment of oven doors and chuck doors and replacement of door jambs so as to provide a continuous metal-to-metal fit;

(c) Cleaning of oven doors, chuck doors and door jambs each coking cycle so as to provide an effective seal;

(d) An inspection system and corrective action program to control door emissions to the maximum extent possible; and

(e) Luting of doors that are sealed by luting each coking cycle and reluting, replacing or adjusting as necessary to control leakage.

(iii) *Pushing.* The employer shall operate existing coke oven batteries with the following work practices to control coke oven emissions during pushing operations:

(a) Coke and coal spillage quenched as soon as practicable and not shoveled into a heated oven; and

(b) A detailed written procedure for each battery established and implemented for the control of emissions during pushing consisting of the following elements:

(1) Dampering off the ovens and removal of charging hole lids to effectively control coke oven emissions during the push;

(2) Heating of the coal charge uniformly for a sufficient period so as to obtain proper coking including preventing green pushes;

(3) Prevention of green pushes to the maximum extent possible;

(4) Inspection, adjustment and correction of heating flue temperatures and defective flues at least weekly and after any green push, so as to prevent green pushes;

(5) Cleaning of heating flues and related equipment to prevent green pushes, at least weekly and after any green push.

(iv) *Maintenance and repair.* The employer shall operate existing coke oven batteries pursuant to a detailed written procedure of maintenance and repair established and implemented for the effective control of coke oven emissions consisting of the following elements:

(a) Regular inspection of all controls, including goosenecks, standpipes, standpipe caps, charging hold lids and castings, jumper pipes and air seals for cracks, misalignment or other defects and prompt implementation of the necessary repairs as soon as possible;

(b) Maintaining the regulated area in a neat, orderly condition free of coal and coke spillage and debris;

(c) Regular inspection of the damper system, aspiration system and collector main for cracks or leakage, and prompt implementation of the necessary repairs;

(d) Regular inspection of the heating system and prompt implementation of the necessary repairs;

(e) Prevention of miscellaneous fugitive topside emissions;

(f) Regular inspection and patching of oven brickwork;

(g) Maintenance of battery equipment and controls in good working order;

(h) Maintenance and repair of coke oven doors, chuck doors, door jambs and seals; and

(i) Repairs instituted and completed as soon as possible, including temporary repair measures instituted and completed where necessary, including but not limited to:

(1) Prevention of miscellaneous fugitive topside emissions; and

(2) Chuck door gaskets, which shall be installed prior to the start of the next coking cycle.

(4) *Filtered air.* (i) The employer shall provided positive-pressure, temperature controlled filtered air for larry car, pusher machine, door machine, and quench car cabs.

(ii) The employer shall provide standby pulpits on the battery topside, at the wharf, and at ther screening station, equipped with positive-pressure, temperature controlled filtered air.

(5) *Emergencies.* Whenever an emergency occurs, the next coking cycle may not begin until the cause of the emergency is determined and corrected, unless the employer can establish that it is necessary to initiate the next coking cycle in order to determine the cause of the emergency.

(6) *Compliance program.* (i) Each employer shall establish and implement a written program to reduce exposures solely by means of the engineering and work practice controls required in paragraph (f) of this section.

(ii) The written program shall include at least the following:

(a) A description of each coke oven operation by battery, including work force and operating crew, coking time, operating procedures and maintenance practices;

(b) Engineering plans and other studies used to determine the controls for the coke battery;

305

(c) A report of the technology considered in meeting the permissible exposure limit;

(d) Monitoring data obtained in accordance with paragraph (e) of this section;

(e) A detailed schedule for the implementation of the engineering and work practice controls required in paragraph (f) of this section; and

(f) Other relevant information.

(iii) If, after implementing all controls required by paragraph (f)(2)–(f)(4) of this section, or after January 20, 1980, whichever is sooner, or after completion of a new or rehabilitated battery the permissible exposure limit is still exceeded, the employer shall develop a detailed written program and schedule for the implementation of any additional engineering controls and work practices necessary to reduce exposure to or below the permissible exposure limit.

(iv) Written plans for such programs shall be submitted, upon request, to the Secretary and the Director, and shall be available at the worksite for examination and copying by the Secretary, the Director, and the authorized employee representative. The plans required under paragraph (f)(6) of this section shall be revised and updated at least annually to reflect the current status of the program.

(7) *Training in compliance procedures.* The employer shall incorporate all written procedures and schedules required under this paragraph (f) in the information and training program required under paragraph (k) of this section and, where appropriate, post in the regulated area.

(g) *Respiratory protection*—(1) *General.* For employees who use respirators required by this section, the employer must provide each employee an appropriate respirator that complies with the requirements of this paragraph. Respirators must be used during:

(i) Periods necessary to install or implement feasible engineering and work-practice controls.

(ii) Work operations, such as maintenance and repair activity, for which engineering and work-practice controls are technologically not feasible.

(iii) Work operations for which feasible engineering and work-practice controls are not yet sufficient to reduce employee exposure to or below the permissible exposure limit.

(iv) Emergencies.

(2) *Respirator program.* The employer must implement a respiratory protection program in accordance with § 1910.134(b) through (d) (except (d)(1)(iii)), and (f) through (m), which covers each employee required by this section to use a respirator.

(3) *Respirator selection.* Employers must select, and provide to employees, the appropriate respirators specified in paragraph (d)(3)(i)(A) of 29 CFR 1910.134; however, employers may use a filtering facepiece respirator only when it functions as a filter respirator for coke oven emissions particulates.

(h) *Protective clothing and equipment*—(1) *Provision and use.* The employer shall provide and assure the use of appropriate protective clothing and equipment, such as but not limited to:

(i) Flame resistant jacket and pants;

(ii) Flame resistant gloves;

(iii) Face shields or vented goggles which comply with § 1910.133(a)(2) of this part;

(iv) Footwear providing insulation from hot surfaces for footwear;

(v) Safety shoes which comply with § 1910.136 of this part; and

(vi) Protective helmets which comply with § 1910.135 of this part.

(2) *Cleaning and replacement.* (i) The employer shall provide the protective clothing required by paragraphs (h)(1) (i) and (ii) of this section in a clean and dry condition at least weekly.

(ii) The employer shall clean, launder, or dispose of protective clothing required by paragraphs (h)(1) (i) and (ii) of this section.

(iii) The employer shall repair or replace the protective clothing and equipment as needed to maintain their effectiveness.

(iv) The employer shall assure that all protective clothing is removed at the completion of a work shift only in change rooms prescribed in paragraph (i)(1) of this section.

(v) The employer shall assure that contaminated protective clothing which is to be cleaned, laundered, or disposed of, is placed in a closable container in the change room.

(vi) The employer shall inform any person who cleans or launders protective clothing required by this section, of the potentially harmful effects of exposure to coke oven emissions.

(i) *Hygiene facilities and practices*—(1) *Change rooms.* The employer shall provide clean change rooms equipped with storage facilities for street clothes and separate storage facilities for protective clothing and equipment whenever employees are required to wear protective clothing and equipment in accordance with paragraph (h)(1) of this section.

(2) *Showers.* (i) The employer shall assure that employees working in the regulated area shower at the end of the work shift.

(ii) The employer shall provide shower facilities in accordance with §1910.141(d)(3) of this part.

(3) *Lunchrooms.* The employer shall provide lunchroom facilities which have a temperature controlled, positive pressure, filtered air supply, and which are readily accessible to employees working in the regulated area.

(4) *Lavatories.* (i) The employer shall assure that employees working in the regulated area wash their hands and face prior to eating.

(ii) The employer shall provide lavatory facilities in accordance with §1910.141(d) (1) and (2) of this part.

(5) *Prohibition of activities in the regulated area.* (i) The employer shall assure that in the regulated area, food or beverages are not present or consumed, smoking products are not present or used, and cosmetics are not applied, except that these activities may be conducted in the lunchrooms, change rooms and showers required under paragraphs (i)(1)–(i)(3) of this section.

(ii) Drinking water may be consumed in the regulated area.

(j) *Medical surveillance*—(1) *General requirements.* (i) Each employer shall institute a medical surveillance program for all employees who are employed in a regulated area at least 30 days per year.

(ii) This program shall provide each employee covered under paragraph (j)(1)(i) of this section with an opportunity for medical examinations in accordance with this paragraph (j).

(iii) The employer shall inform any employee who refuses any required medical examination of the possible health consequences of such refusal and shall obtain a signed statement from the employee indicating that the employee understands the risk involved in the refusal to be examined.

(iv) The employer shall assure that all medical examinations and procedures are performed by or under the supervision of a licensed physician, and are provided without cost to the employee.

(2) *Initial examinations.* At the time of initial assignment to a regulated area or upon the institution of the medical surveillance program, the employer shall provide a medical examination for employees covered under paragraph (j)(1)(i) of this section including at least the following elements:

(i) A work history and medical history which shall include smoking history and the presence and degree of respiratory symptoms, such as breathlessness, cough, sputum production, and wheezing;

(ii) A standard posterior-anterior chest x-ray;

(iii) Pulmonary function tests including forced vital capacity (FVC) and forced expiratory volume at one second (FEV 1.0) with recording of type of equipment used;

(iv) Weight;

(v) A skin examination;

(vi) Urinalysis for sugar, albumin, and hematuria; and

(vii) A urinary cytology examination.

(3) *Periodic examinations.* (i) The employer shall provide the examinations specified in paragraphs (j)(2) (i)–(vi) of this section at least annually for employees covered under paragraph (j)(1)(i) of this section.

(ii) The employer must provide the examinations specified in paragraphs (j)(2)(i) through (j)(2)(vii) of this section at least annually for employees 45 years of age or older or with five (5) or more years employment in the regulated area.

(iii) Whenever an employee who is 45 years of age or older or with five (5) or more years employment in a regulated area transfers or is transferred from employment in a regulated area, the employer must continue to provide the

307

examinations specified in paragraphs (j)(2)(i) through (j)(2)(vii) of this section at least annually as long as that employee is employed by the same employer or a successor employer.

(iv) Whenever an employee has not taken the examinations specified in paragraphs (j)(3) (i)–(iii) of this section with the six (6) months preceding the termination of employment the employer shall provide such examinations to the employee upon termination of employment.

(4) *Information provided to the physician.* The employer shall provide the following information to the examining physician:

(i) A copy of this regulation and its Appendixes;

(ii) A description of the affected employee's duties as they relate to the employee's exposure;

(iii) The employee's exposure level or estimated exposure level;

(iv) A description of any personal protective equipment used or to be used; and

(v) Information from previous medical examinations of the affected employee which is not readily available to the examining physician.

(5) *Physician's written opinion.* (i) The employer shall obtain a written opinion from the examining physician which shall include:

(a) The results of the medical examinations;

(b) The physician's opinion as to whether the employee has any detected medical conditions which would place the employee at increased risk of material impairment of the employee's health from exposure to coke oven emissions;

(c) Any recommended limitations upon the employee's exposure to coke oven emissions or upon the use of protective clothing or equipment such as respirators; and

(d) A statement that the employee has been informed by the physician of the results of the medical examination and any medical conditions which require further explanation or treatment.

(ii) The employer shall instruct the physician not to reveal in the written opinion specific findings or diagnoses unrelated to occupational exposure.

(iii) The employer shall provide a copy of the written opinion to the affected employee.

(k) *Employee information and training*—(1) *Training program.* (i) The employer shall train each employee who is employed in a regulated area in accordance with the requirements of this section. The employer shall institute a training program and ensure employee participation in the program.

(ii) The training program shall be provided as of January 27, 1977 for employees who are employed in the regulated area at that time or at the time of initial assignment to a regulated area.

(iii) The training program shall be provided at least annually for all employees who are employed in the regulated area, except that training regarding the occupational safety and health hazards associated with exposure to coke oven emissions and the purpose, proper use, and limitations of respiratory protective devices shall be provided at least quarterly until January 20, 1978.

(iv) The training program shall include informing each employee of:

(a) The information contained in the substance information sheet for coke oven emissions (Appendix A);

(b) The purpose, proper use, and limitations of respiratory protective devices required in accordance with paragraph (g) of this section;

(c) The purpose for and a description of the medical surveillance program required by paragraph (j) of this section including information on the occupational safety and health hazards associated with exposure to coke oven emissions;

(d) A review of all written procedures and schedules required under paragraph (f) of this section; and

(e) A review of this standard.

(2) *Access to training materials.* (i) The employer shall make a copy of this standard and its appendixes readily available to all employees who are employed in the regulated area.

(ii) The employer shall provide upon request all materials relating to the employee information and training program to the Secretary and the Director.

(1) *Communication of hazards*—(1) *Hazard communication—general.* The employer shall include coke oven emissions in the program established to comply with the Hazard Communication Standard (HCS) (§1910.1200). The employer shall ensure that each employee has access to labels on containers of chemicals and substances associated with coke oven processes and to safety data sheets, and is trained in accordance with the provisions of HCS and paragraph (k) of this section. The employer shall ensure that at least the following hazard is addressed: Cancer.

(2) *Signs.* (i) The employer shall post signs in the regulated area bearing the legend:

DANGER
COKE OVEN EMISSIONS
MAY CAUSE CANCER
DO NOT EAT, DRINK OR SMOKE
WEAR RESPIRATORY PROTECTION IN THIS AREA
AUTHORIZED PERSONNEL ONLY

(ii) In addition, the employer shall post signs in the areas where the permissible exposure limit is exceeded bearing the legend:

WEAR RESPIRATORY PROTECTION IN THIS AREA

(iii) The employer shall ensure that no statement appears on or near any sign required by this paragraph (l) which contradicts or detracts from the effects of the required sign.

(iv) The employer shall ensure that signs required by this paragraph (l)(2) are illuminated and cleaned as necessary so that the legend is readily visible.

(v) Prior to June 1, 2016, employers may use the following legend in lieu of that specified in paragraph (l)(2)(i) of this section:

DANGER
CANCER HAZARD
AUTHORIZED PERSONNEL ONLY
NO SMOKING OR EATING

(vi) Prior to June 1, 2016, employers may use the following legend in lieu of that specified in paragraph (l)(2)(ii) of this section:

DANGER
RESPIRATOR REQUIRED

(3) *Labels.* (i) The employer shall ensure that labels of containers of contaminated protective clothing and equipment include the following information:

CONTAMINATED WITH COKE EMISSIONS
MAY CAUSE CANCER
DO NOT REMOVE DUST BY BLOWING OR SHAKING

(ii) Prior to June 1, 2015, employers may include the following information on contaminated protective clothing and equipment in lieu of the labeling requirements in paragraph (l)(3)(i) of this section:

CAUTION
CLOTHING CONTAMINATED WITH COKE EMISSIONS
DO NOT REMOVE DUST BY BLOWING OR SHAKING

(m) *Recordkeeping*—(1) *Exposure measurements.* The employer shall establish and maintain an accurate record of all measurements taken to monitor employee exposure to coke oven emissions required in paragraph (e) of this section.

(i) This record shall include:

(*a*) Name, social security number, and job classification of the employees monitored;

(*b*) The date(s), number, duration and results of each of the samples taken, including a description of the sampling procedure used to determine representative employee exposure where applicable;

(*c*) The type of respiratory protective devices worn, if any;

(*d*) A description of the sampling and analytical methods used and evidence of their accuracy; and

(*e*) The environmental variables that could affect the measurement of employee exposure.

(ii) The employer shall maintain this record for at lest 40 years or for the duration of employment plus 20 years, whichever is longer.

(2) *Medical surveillance.* The employer shall establish and maintain an accurate record for each employee subject to medical surveillance as required by paragraph (j) of this section.

(i) The record shall include:

(*a*) The name, social security number, and description of duties of the employee;

(*b*) A copy of the physician's written opinion;

309

(c) The signed statement of any refusal to take a medical examination under paragraph (j)(1)(ii) of this section; and

(d) Any employee medical complaints related to exposure to coke oven emissions.

(ii) The employer shall keep, or assure that the examining physician keeps, the following medical records:

(a) A copy of the medical examination results including medical and work history required under paragraph (j)(2) of this section;

(b) A description of the laboratory procedures used and a copy of any standards or guidelines used to interpret the test results;

(c) The initial x-ray;

(d) The x-rays for the most recent five (5) years;

(e) Any x-ray with a demonstrated abnormality and all subsequent x-rays;

(f) The initial cytologic examination slide and written description;

(g) The cytologic examination slide and written description for the most recent 10 years; and

(h) Any cytologic examination slides with demonstrated atypia, if such atypia persists for 3 years, and all subsequent slides and written descriptions.

(iii) The employer shall maintain medical records required under paragraph (m)(2) of this section for at least 40 years, or for the duration of employment plus 20 years, whichever is longer.

(3) *Availability.* (i) The employer shall make available upon request all records required to be maintained by paragraph (m) of this section to the Secretary and the Director for examination and copying.

(ii) Employee exposure measurement records and employee medical records required by this paragraph shall be provided upon request to employees, designated representatives, and the Assistant Secretary in accordance with 29 CFR 1910.1020(a)–(e) and (g)–(i).

(4) *Transfer of records.* (i) Whenever the employer ceases to do business, the successor employer shall receive and retain all records required to be maintained by paragraph (m) of this section.

(ii) The employer shall also comply with any additional requirements involving transfer of records set forth in 29 CFR 1910.1020(h).

(n) *Observation of monitoring*—(1) *Employee observation.* The employer shall provide affected employees or their representatives an opportunity to observe any measuring or monitoring of employee exposure to coke oven emissions conducted pursuant to paragraph (e) of this section.

(2) *Observation procedures.* (i) Whenever observation of the measuring or monitoring of employee exposure to coke oven emissions requires entry into an area where the ues of protective clothing or equipment is required, the employer shall provide the observer with and assure the use of such equipment and shall require the observer to comply with all other applicable safety and health procedures.

(ii) Without interfering with the measurement, observers shall be entitled to:

(a) An Explanation of the measurement procedures;

(b) Observe all steps related to the measurement of coke oven emissions performed at the place of exposure; and

(c) Record the results obtained.

(o) [Reserved]

(p) *Appendices.* The information contained in the appendixes to this section is not intended, by itself, to create any additional obligations not otherwise imposed or to detract from any existing obligation.

APPENDIX A TO § 1910.1029—COKE OVEN EMISSIONS SUBSTANCE INFORMATION SHEET

I. SUBSTANCE IDENTIFICATION

A. *Substance:* Coke Oven Emissions

B. *Definition:* The benzene-soluble fraction of total particulate matter present during the destructive distillation or carbonization of coal for the production of coke.

C. *Permissible Exposure Limit:* 150 micrograms per cubic meter of air determined as an average over an 8-hour period.

D. *Regulated areas:* Only employees authorized by your employer should enter a regulated area. The employer is required to designate the following areas as regulated areas: the coke oven battery, including topside and its machinery, pushside and its machinery, cokeside and its machinery, and the battery ends; the screening station; and the wharf; and the beehive ovens and their machinery.

II. HEALTH HAZARD DATA

Exposure to coke oven emissions is a cause of lung cancer, and kidney cancer, in humans. Although there have not been an excess number of skin cancer cases in humans, repeated skin contact with coke oven emissions should be avoided.

III. PROTECTIVE CLOTHING AND EQUIPMENT

A. *Respirators:* Respirators will be provided by your employer for routine use if your employer is in the process of implementing engineering and work practice controls or where engineering and work practice controls are not feasible or insufficient to reduce exposure to or below the PEL. You must wear respirators for non-routine activities or in emergency situations where you are likely to be exposed to levels of coke oven emissions in excess of the permissible exposure limit. Until January 20, 1978, the routine wearing of respirators is voluntary. Until that date, if you choose not to wear a respirator you do not have to do so. You must still have your respirator with you and you must still wear it if you are near visible emissions. Since how well your respirator fits your face is very important, your employer is required to conduct fit tests to make sure the respirator seals properly when you wear it. These tests are simple and rapid and will be explained to you during your training sessions.

B. *Protective clothing:* Your employer is required to provide, and you must wear, appropriate, clean, protective clothing and equipment to protect your body from repeated skin contact with coke oven emissions and from the heat generated during the coking process. This clothing should include such items as jacket and pants and flame resistant gloves. Protective equipment should include face shield or vented goggles, protective helmets and safety shoes, insulated from hot surfaces where appropriate.

IV. HYGIENE FACILITIES AND PRACTICES

You must not eat, drink, smoke, chew gum or tobacco, or apply cosmetics in the regulated area, except that drinking water is permitted. Your employer is required to provide lunchrooms and other areas for these purposes.

Your employer is required to provide showers, washing facilities, and change rooms. If you work in a regulated area, you must wash your face, and hands before eating. You must shower at the end of the work shift. Do not take used protective clothing out of the change rooms without your employer's permission. Your employer is required to provide for laundering or cleaning of your protective clothing.

V. SIGNS AND LABELS

Your employer is required to post warning signs and labels for your protection. Signs must be posted in regulated areas. The signs must warn that a cancer hazard is present, that only authorized employees may enter the area, and that no smoking or eating is allowed. In regulated areas where coke oven emissions are above the permissible exposure limit, the signs should also warn that respirators must be worn.

VI. MEDICAL EXAMINATIONS

If you work in a regulated area at least 30 days per year, your employer is required to provide you with a medical examination every year. The medical examination must include a medical history, a chest x-ray, pulmonary function test, weight comparison, skin examination, a urinalysis, and a urine cytology exam for early detection of urinary cancer. The urine cytology exam is only included in the initial exam until you are either 45 years or older, or have 5 or more years employment in the regulated areas when the medical exams including this test, but excepting the x-ray exam, are to be given every six months; under these conditions, you are to be given an x-ray exam at least once a year. The examining physician will provide a written opinion to your employer containing the results of the medical exams. You should also receive a copy of this opinion.

VII. OBSERVATION OF MONITORING

Your employer is required to monitor your exposure to coke oven emissions and you are entitled to observe the monitoring procedure. You are entitled to receive an explanation of the measurement procedure, observe the steps taken in the measurement procedure, and to record the results obtained. When the monitoring procedure is taking place in an area where respirators or personal protective clothing and equipment are required to be worn, you must also be provided with and must wear the protective clothing and equipment.

VIII. ACCESS TO RECORDS

You or your representative are entitled to records of your exposure to coke oven emissions upon request to your employer. Your medical examination records can be furnished to your physician upon request to your employer.

IX. TRAINING AND EDUCATION

Additional information on all of these items plus training as to hazards of coke oven emissions and the engineering and work practice controls associated with your job will also be provided by your employer.

APPENDIX B TO § 1910.1029—INDUSTRIAL HY-
GIENE AND MEDICAL SURVEILLANCE GUIDE-
LINES

I. INDUSTRIAL HYGIENE GUIDELINES

A. *Sampling* (Benzene-Soluble Fraction
Total Particulate Matter).

Samples collected should be full shift (at
least 7-hour) samples. Sampling should be
done using a personal sampling pump with
pulsation damper at a flow rate of 2 liters
per minute. Samples should be collected on
0.8 micrometer pore size silver membrane filters (37 mm diameter) preceded by Gelman
glass fiber type A-E filters encased in three-
piece plastic (polystyrene) field monitor cassettes. The cassette face cap should be on
and the plug removed. The rotameter should
be checked every hour to ensure that proper
flow rates are maintained.

A minimum of three full-shift samples
should be collected for each job classification on each battery, at least one from each
shift. If disparate results are obtained for
particular job classification, sampling
should be repeated. It is advisable to sample
each shift on more than one day to account
for environmental variables (wind, precipitation, etc.) which may affect sampling. Differences in exposures among different work
shifts may indicate a need to improve work
practices on a particular shift. Sampling results from different shifts for each job classification should not be averaged. Multiple
samples from same shift on each battery
may be used to calculate an average exposure for a particular job classification.

B. *Analysis.*

1. All extraction glassware is cleaned with
dichromic acid cleaning solution, rinsed with
tap water, then dionized water, acetone, and
allowed to dry completely. The glassware is
rinsed with nanograde benzene before use.
The Teflon cups are cleaned with benzene
then with acetone.

2. Pre-weigh the 2 ml Teflon cups to one
hundredth of a milligram (0.01 mg) on an
autobalance AD 2 Tare weight of the cups is
about 50 mg.

3. Place the silver membrane filter and
glass fiber filter into a 15 ml test tube.

4. Extract with 5 ml of benzene for five
minutes in an ultrasonic cleaner.

5. Filter the extract in 15 ml medium glass
fritted funnels.

6. Rinse test tube and filters with two 1.5
ml aliquots of benzene and filter through the
fritted glass funnel.

7. Collect the extract and two rinses in a 10
ml Kontes graduated evaporative concen-
trator.

8. Evaporate down to 1 ml while rinsing the
sides with benzene.

9. Pipet 0.5 ml into the Teflon cup and
evaporate to dryness in a vacuum oven at 40
°C for 3 hours.

10. Weigh the Teflon cup and the weight
gain is due to the benzene soluble residue in
half the Sample.

II. MEDICAL SURVEILLANCE GUIDELINES

A. *General.* The minimum requirements for
the medical examination for coke oven
workers are given in paragraph (j) of the
standard. The initial examination is to be
provided to all coke oven workers who work
at least 30 days in the regulated area. The
examination includes a 14″ × 17″ posterior-anterior chest x-ray reading, pulmonary function tests (FVC and FEV 1.0), weight, urinalysis, skin examination, and a urinary
cytologic examination. These tests are needed to serve as the baseline for comparing the
employee's future test results. Periodic
exams include all the elements of the initial
exam, except that the urine cytologic test is
to be performed only on those employees
who are 45 years or older or who have worked
for 5 or more years in the regulated area;
periodic exams, with the exception of x-rays,
are to be performed semiannually for this
group instead of annually; for this group, x-
rays will continue to be given at least annually. The examination contents are minimum requirements; additional tests such as
lateral and oblique x-rays or additional pulmonary function tests may be performed if
deemed necessary.

B. *Pulmonary function tests.*

Pulmonary function tests should be performed in a manner which minimizes subject
and operator bias. There has been shown to
be learning effects with regard to the results
obtained from certain tests, such as FEV 1.0.
Best results can be obtained by multiple
trials for each subject. The best of three
trials or the average of the last three of five
trials may be used in obtaining reliable results. The type of equipment used (manufacturer, model, etc.) should be recorded with
the results as reliability and accuracy varies
and such information may be important in
the evaluation of test results. Care should be
exercised to obtain the best possible testing
equipment.

[39 FR 23502, June 27, 1974, 41 FR 46784, Oct.
22, 1976, as amended at 42 FR 3304, Jan. 18,
1977; 45 FR 35283, May 23, 1980; 50 FR 37353,
37354, Sept. 13, 1985; 54 FR 24334, June 7, 1989;
61 FR 5508, Feb. 13, 1996; 63 FR 1290, Jan. 8,
1998; 63 FR 33468, June 18, 1998; 70 FR 1142,
Jan. 5, 2005; 71 FR 16672, 16673, Apr. 3, 2006; 71
FR 50189, Aug. 24, 2006; 73 FR 75585, Dec. 12,
2008; 76 FR 33608, June 8, 2011; 77 FR 17782,
Mar. 26, 2012]

EFFECTIVE DATE NOTE: At 84 FR 21490, May
14, 2019, § 1910.1029 was amended by revising
paragraphs (j)(2)(ii) and (j)(3), appendix A,
section VI, and appendix B, section II(A), effective July 15, 2019. For the convenience of
the user, the revised text is set forth as follows:

§ 1910.1029 Coke oven emissions.

*   *   *   *   *

(j) * * *

(2) * * *

(ii) A 14- by 17-inch or other reasonably-sized standard film or digital posterior-anterior chest X-ray;

*   *   *   *   *

(3) *Periodic examinations.* (i) The employer shall provide the examinations specified in paragraphs (j)(2)(i) and (iii) through (vi) of this section at least annually for employees covered under paragraph (j)(1)(i) of this section.

(ii) The employer must provide the examinations specified in paragraphs (j)(2)(i) and (iii) through (vii) of this section at least annually for employees 45 years of age or older or with five (5) or more years employment in the regulated area.

(iii) Whenever an employee who is 45 years of age or older or with five (5) or more years employment in a regulated area transfers or is transferred from employment in a regulated area, the employer must continue to provide the examinations specified in paragraphs (j)(2)(i) and (iii) through (vii) of this section at least annually as long as that employee is employed by the same employer or a successor employer.

*   *   *   *   *

APPENDIX A TO § 1910.1029—COKE OVEN
EMISSIONS SUBSTANCE INFORMATION SHEET

*   *   *   *   *

VI. MEDICAL EXAMINATIONS

If you work in a regulated area at least 30 days per year, your employer is required to provide you with a medical examination every year. The initial medical examination must include a medical history, a chest X-ray, pulmonary function test, weight comparison, skin examination, a urinalysis, and a urine cytology exam for early detection of urinary cancer. Periodic examinations shall include all tests required in the initial examination, except that (1) the x-ray is to be performed during initial examination only and (2) the urine cytologic test is to be performed only on those employees who are 45 years or older or who have worked for 5 or more years in the regulated area. The examining physician will provide a written opinion to your employer containing the results of the medical exams. You should also receive a copy of this opinion.

*   *   *   *   *

APPENDIX B TO § 1910.1029—INDUSTRIAL HYGIENE AND MEDICAL SURVEILLANCE GUIDELINES

*   *   *   *   *

II. MEDICAL SURVEILLANCE GUIDELINES

A. *General.* The minimum requirements for the medical examination for coke oven workers are given in the standard in paragraph (j) of this section. The initial examination is to be provided to all coke oven workers who work at least 30 days in the regulated area. The examination includes a 14″ by 17″ or other reasonably-sized standard film or digital posterior-anterior chest X-ray reading, pulmonary function tests (FVC and FEV$_1$), weight, urinalysis, skin examination, and a urinary cytological examination. These tests are needed to serve as the baseline for comparing the employee's future test results. Periodic exams include all the elements of the initial exams, except that (1) the x-ray is to be performed during initial examination only and (2) the urine cytologic test is to be performed only on those employees who are 45 years or older or who have worked for 5 or more years in the regulated area. The examination contents are minimum requirements; additional tests such as lateral and oblique X-rays or additional pulmonary function tests may be performed if deemed necessary.

*   *   *   *   *

§ 1910.1030 Bloodborne pathogens.

(a) *Scope and Application.* This section applies to all occupational exposure to blood or other potentially infectious materials as defined by paragraph (b) of this section.

(b) *Definitions.* For purposes of this section, the following shall apply:

Assistant Secretary means the Assistant Secretary of Labor for Occupational Safety and Health, or designated representative.

Blood means human blood, human blood components, and products made from human blood.

Bloodborne Pathogens means pathogenic microorganisms that are present in human blood and can cause disease in humans. These pathogens include, but are not limited to, hepatitis B virus (HBV) and human immunodeficiency virus (HIV).

Clinical Laboratory means a workplace where diagnostic or other screening procedures are performed on blood or other potentially infectious materials.

Contaminated means the presence or the reasonably anticipated presence of blood or other potentially infectious materials on an item or surface.

Contaminated Laundry means laundry which has been soiled with blood or other potentially infectious materials or may contain sharps.

Contaminated Sharps means any contaminated object that can penetrate the skin including, but not limited to, needles, scalpels, broken glass, broken capillary tubes, and exposed ends of dental wires.

Decontamination means the use of physical or chemical means to remove, inactivate, or destroy bloodborne pathogens on a surface or item to the point where they are no longer capable of transmitting infectious particles and the surface or item is rendered safe for handling, use, or disposal.

Director means the Director of the National Institute for Occupational Safety and Health, U.S. Department of Health and Human Services, or designated representative.

Engineering controls means controls (e.g., sharps disposal containers, self-sheathing needles, safer medical devices, such as sharps with engineered sharps injury protections and needleless systems) that isolate or remove the bloodborne pathogens hazard from the workplace.

Exposure Incident means a specific eye, mouth, other mucous membrane, non-intact skin, or parenteral contact with blood or other potentially infectious materials that results from the performance of an employee's duties.

Handwashing facilities means a facility providing an adequate supply of running potable water, soap, and single-use towels or air-drying machines.

Licensed Healthcare Professional is a person whose legally permitted scope of practice allows him or her to independently perform the activities required by paragraph (f) Hepatitis B Vaccination and Post-exposure Evaluation and Follow-up.

HBV means hepatitis B virus.

HIV means human immunodeficiency virus.

Needleless systems means a device that does not use needles for:

(1) The collection of bodily fluids or withdrawal of body fluids after initial venous or arterial access is established;

(2) The administration of medication or fluids; or

(3) Any other procedure involving the potential for occupational exposure to bloodborne pathogens due to percutaneous injuries from contaminated sharps.

Occupational Exposure means reasonably anticipated skin, eye, mucous membrane, or parenteral contact with blood or other potentially infectious materials that may result from the performance of an employee's duties.

Other Potentially Infectious Materials means

(1) The following human body fluids: semen, vaginal secretions, cerebrospinal fluid, synovial fluid, pleural fluid, pericardial fluid, peritoneal fluid, amniotic fluid, saliva in dental procedures, any body fluid that is visibly contaminated with blood, and all body fluids in situations where it is difficult or impossible to differentiate between body fluids;

(2) Any unfixed tissue or organ (other than intact skin) from a human (living or dead); and

(3) HIV-containing cell or tissue cultures, organ cultures, and HIV- or HBV-containing culture medium or other solutions; and blood, organs, or other tissues from experimental animals infected with HIV or HBV.

Parenteral means piercing mucous membranes or the skin barrier through such events as needlesticks, human bites, cuts, and abrasions.

Personal Protective Equipment is specialized clothing or equipment worn by an employee for protection against a hazard. General work clothes (e.g., uniforms, pants, shirts or blouses) not intended to function as protection against a hazard are not considered to be personal protective equipment.

Production Facility means a facility engaged in industrial-scale, large-volume or high concentration production of HIV or HBV.

Regulated Waste means liquid or semi-liquid blood or other potentially infectious materials; contaminated items that would release blood or other potentially infectious materials in a liquid or semi-liquid state if compressed; items that are caked with dried blood or other potentially infectious materials and are capable of releasing these materials during handling; contaminated sharps; and pathological and microbiological wastes containing blood or other potentially infectious materials.

Research Laboratory means a laboratory producing or using research-laboratory-scale amounts of HIV or HBV. Research laboratories may produce high concentrations of HIV or HBV but not in the volume found in production facilities.

Sharps with engineered sharps injury protections means a nonneedle sharp or a needle device used for withdrawing body fluids, accessing a vein or artery, or administering medications or other fluids, with a built-in safety feature or mechanism that effectively reduces the risk of an exposure incident.

Source Individual means any individual, living or dead, whose blood or other potentially infectious materials may be a source of occupational exposure to the employee. Examples include, but are not limited to, hospital and clinic patients; clients in institutions for the developmentally disabled; trauma victims; clients of drug and alcohol treatment facilities; residents of hospices and nursing homes; human remains; and individuals who donate or sell blood or blood components.

Sterilize means the use of a physical or chemical procedure to destroy all microbial life including highly resistant bacterial endospores.

Universal Precautions is an approach to infection control. According to the concept of Universal Precautions, all human blood and certain human body fluids are treated as if known to be infectious for HIV, HBV, and other bloodborne pathogens.

Work Practice Controls means controls that reduce the likelihood of exposure by altering the manner in which a task is performed (e.g., prohibiting recapping of needles by a two-handed technique).

(c) *Exposure control*—(1) *Exposure Control Plan.* (i) Each employer having an employee(s) with occupational exposure as defined by paragraph (b) of this section shall establish a written Exposure Control Plan designed to eliminate or minimize employee exposure.

(ii) The Exposure Control Plan shall contain at least the following elements:

(A) The exposure determination required by paragraph (c)(2),

(B) The schedule and method of implementation for paragraphs (d) Methods of Compliance, (e) HIV and HBV Research Laboratories and Production Facilities, (f) Hepatitis B Vaccination and Post-Exposure Evaluation and Follow-up, (g) Communication of Hazards to Employees, and (h) Recordkeeping, of this standard, and

(C) The procedure for the evaluation of circumstances surrounding exposure incidents as required by paragraph (f)(3)(i) of this standard.

(iii) Each employer shall ensure that a copy of the Exposure Control Plan is accessible to employees in accordance with 29 CFR 1910.20(e).

(iv) The Exposure Control Plan shall be reviewed and updated at least annually and whenever necessary to reflect new or modified tasks and procedures which affect occupational exposure and to reflect new or revised employee positions with occupational exposure. The review and update of such plans shall also:

(A) Reflect changes in technology that eliminate or reduce exposure to bloodborne pathogens; and

(B) Document annually consideration and implementation of appropriate commercially available and effective safer medical devices designed to eliminate or minimize occupational exposure.

(v) An employer, who is required to establish an Exposure Control Plan shall solicit input from non-managerial employees responsible for direct patient care who are potentially exposed to injuries from contaminated sharps in the identification, evaluation, and selection of effective engineering and work practice controls and shall document the solicitation in the Exposure Control Plan.

(vi) The Exposure Control Plan shall be made available to the Assistant Secretary and the Director upon request for examination and copying.

(2) *Exposure determination.* (i) Each employer who has an employee(s) with

occupational exposure as defined by paragraph (b) of this section shall prepare an exposure determination. This exposure determination shall contain the following:

(A) A list of all job classifications in which all employees in those job classifications have occupational exposure;

(B) A list of job classifications in which some employees have occupational exposure, and

(C) A list of all tasks and procedures or groups of closely related task and procedures in which occupational exposure occurs and that are performed by employees in job classifications listed in accordance with the provisions of paragraph (c)(2)(i)(B) of this standard.

(ii) This exposure determination shall be made without regard to the use of personal protective equipment.

(d) *Methods of compliance*—(1) *General.* Universal precautions shall be observed to prevent contact with blood or other potentially infectious materials. Under circumstances in which differentiation between body fluid types is difficult or impossible, all body fluids shall be considered potentially infectious materials.

(2) *Engineering and work practice controls.* (i) Engineering and work practice controls shall be used to eliminate or minimize employee exposure. Where occupational exposure remains after institution of these controls, personal protective equipment shall also be used.

(ii) Engineering controls shall be examined and maintained or replaced on a regular schedule to ensure their effectiveness.

(iii) Employers shall provide handwashing facilities which are readily accessible to employees.

(iv) When provision of handwashing facilities is not feasible, the employer shall provide either an appropriate antiseptic hand cleanser in conjunction with clean cloth/paper towels or antiseptic towelettes. When antiseptic hand cleansers or towelettes are used, hands shall be washed with soap and running water as soon as feasible.

(v) Employers shall ensure that employees wash their hands immediately or as soon as feasible after removal of gloves or other personal protective equipment.

(vi) Employers shall ensure that employees wash hands and any other skin with soap and water, or flush mucous membranes with water immediately or as soon as feasible following contact of such body areas with blood or other potentially infectious materials.

(vii) Contaminated needles and other contaminated sharps shall not be bent, recapped, or removed except as noted in paragraphs (d)(2)(vii)(A) and (d)(2)(vii)(B) below. Shearing or breaking of contaminated needles is prohibited.

(A) Contaminated needles and other contaminated sharps shall not be bent, recapped or removed unless the employer can demonstrate that no alternative is feasible or that such action is required by a specific medical or dental procedure.

(B) Such bending, recapping or needle removal must be accomplished through the use of a mechanical device or a one-handed technique.

(viii) Immediately or as soon as possible after use, contaminated reusable sharps shall be placed in appropriate containers until properly reprocessed. These containers shall be:

(A) Puncture resistant;

(B) Labeled or color-coded in accordance with this standard;

(C) Leakproof on the sides and bottom; and

(D) In accordance with the requirements set forth in paragraph (d)(4)(ii)(E) for reusable sharps.

(ix) Eating, drinking, smoking, applying cosmetics or lip balm, and handling contact lenses are prohibited in work areas where there is a reasonable likelihood of occupational exposure.

(x) Food and drink shall not be kept in refrigerators, freezers, shelves, cabinets or on countertops or benchtops where blood or other potentially infectious materials are present.

(xi) All procedures involving blood or other potentially infectious materials shall be performed in such a manner as to minimize splashing, spraying, spattering, and generation of droplets of these substances.

(xii) Mouth pipetting/suctioning of blood or other potentially infectious materials is prohibited.

(xiii) Specimens of blood or other potentially infectious materials shall be placed in a container which prevents leakage during collection, handling, processing, storage, transport, or shipping.

(A) The container for storage, transport, or shipping shall be labeled or color-coded according to paragraph (g)(1)(i) and closed prior to being stored, transported, or shipped. When a facility utilizes Universal Precautions in the handling of all specimens, the labeling/color-coding of specimens is not necessary provided containers are recognizable as containing specimens. This exemption only applies while such specimens/containers remain within the facility. Labeling or color-coding in accordance with paragraph (g)(1)(i) is required when such specimens/containers leave the facility.

(B) If outside contamination of the primary container occurs, the primary container shall be placed within a second container which prevents leakage during handling, processing, storage, transport, or shipping and is labeled or color-coded according to the requirements of this standard.

(C) If the specimen could puncture the primary container, the primary container shall be placed within a secondary container which is puncture-resistant in addition to the above characteristics.

(xiv) Equipment which may become contaminated with blood or other potentially infectious materials shall be examined prior to servicing or shipping and shall be decontaminated as necessary, unless the employer can demonstrate that decontamination of such equipment or portions of such equipment is not feasible.

(A) A readily observable label in accordance with paragraph (g)(1)(i)(H) shall be attached to the equipment stating which portions remain contaminated.

(B) The employer shall ensure that this information is conveyed to all affected employees, the servicing representative, and/or the manufacturer, as appropriate, prior to handling, servicing, or shipping so that appropriate precautions will be taken.

(3) *Personal protective equipment*—(i) *Provision.* When there is occupational exposure, the employer shall provide, at no cost to the employee, appropriate personal protective equipment such as, but not limited to, gloves, gowns, laboratory coats, face shields or masks and eye protection, and mouthpieces, resuscitation bags, pocket masks, or other ventilation devices. Personal protective equipment will be considered "appropriate" only if it does not permit blood or other potentially infectious materials to pass through to or reach the employee's work clothes, street clothes, undergarments, skin, eyes, mouth, or other mucous membranes under normal conditions of use and for the duration of time which the protective equipment will be used.

(ii) *Use.* The employer shall ensure that the employee uses appropriate personal protective equipment unless the employer shows that the employee temporarily and briefly declined to use personal protective equipment when, under rare and extraordinary circumstances, it was the employee's professional judgment that in the specific instance its use would have prevented the delivery of health care or public safety services or would have posed an increased hazard to the safety of the worker or co-worker. When the employee makes this judgement, the circumstances shall be investigated and documented in order to determine whether changes can be instituted to prevent such occurances in the future.

(iii) *Accessibility.* The employer shall ensure that appropriate personal protective equipment in the appropriate sizes is readily accessible at the worksite or is issued to employees. Hypoallergenic gloves, glove liners, powderless gloves, or other similar alternatives shall be readily accessible to those employees who are allergic to the gloves normally provided.

(iv) *Cleaning, Laundering, and Disposal.* The employer shall clean, launder, and dispose of personal protective equipment required by paragraphs (d) and (e) of this standard, at no cost to the employee.

(v) *Repair and Replacement.* The employer shall repair or replace personal protective equipment as needed to maintain its effectiveness, at no cost to the employee.

(vi) If a garment(s) is penetrated by blood or other potentially infectious

317

materials, the garment(s) shall be removed immediately or as soon as feasible.

(vii) All personal protective equipment shall be removed prior to leaving the work area.

(viii) When personal protective equipment is removed it shall be placed in an appropriately designated area or container for storage, washing, decontamination or disposal.

(ix) *Gloves.* Gloves shall be worn when it can be reasonably anticipated that the employee may have hand contact with blood, other potentially infectious materials, mucous membranes, and non-intact skin; when performing vascular access procedures except as specified in paragraph (d)(3)(ix)(D); and when handling or touching contaminated items or surfaces.

(A) Disposable (single use) gloves such as surgical or examination gloves, shall be replaced as soon as practical when contaminated or as soon as feasible if they are torn, punctured, or when their ability to function as a barrier is compromised.

(B) Disposable (single use) gloves shall not be washed or decontaminated for re-use.

(C) Utility gloves may be decontaminated for re-use if the integrity of the glove is not compromised. However, they must be discarded if they are cracked, peeling, torn, punctured, or exhibit other signs of deterioration or when their ability to function as a barrier is compromised.

(D) If an employer in a volunteer blood donation center judges that routine gloving for all phlebotomies is not necessary then the employer shall:

(*1*) Periodically reevaluate this policy;

(*2*) Make gloves available to all employees who wish to use them for phlebotomy;

(*3*) Not discourage the use of gloves for phlebotomy; and

(*4*) Require that gloves be used for phlebotomy in the following circumstances:

(*i*) When the employee has cuts, scratches, or other breaks in his or her skin;

(*ii*) When the employee judges that hand contamination with blood may occur, for example, when performing phlebotomy on an uncooperative source individual; and

(*iii*) When the employee is receiving training in phlebotomy.

(x) *Masks, Eye Protection, and Face Shields.* Masks in combination with eye protection devices, such as goggles or glasses with solid side shields, or chin-length face shields, shall be worn whenever splashes, spray, spatter, or droplets of blood or other potentially infectious materials may be generated and eye, nose, or mouth contamination can be reasonably anticipated.

(xi) *Gowns, Aprons, and Other Protective Body Clothing.* Appropriate protective clothing such as, but not limited to, gowns, aprons, lab coats, clinic jackets, or similar outer garments shall be worn in occupational exposure situations. The type and characteristics will depend upon the task and degree of exposure anticipated.

(xii) Surgical caps or hoods and/or shoe covers or boots shall be worn in instances when gross contamination can reasonably be anticipated (e.g., autopsies, orthopaedic surgery).

(4) *Housekeeping*—(i) *General.* Employers shall ensure that the worksite is maintained in a clean and sanitary condition. The employer shall determine and implement an appropriate written schedule for cleaning and method of decontamination based upon the location within the facility, type of surface to be cleaned, type of soil present, and tasks or procedures being performed in the area.

(ii) All equipment and environmental and working surfaces shall be cleaned and decontaminated after contact with blood or other potentially infectious materials.

(A) Contaminated work surfaces shall be decontaminated with an appropriate disinfectant after completion of procedures; immediately or as soon as feasible when surfaces are overtly contaminated or after any spill of blood or other potentially infectious materials; and at the end of the work shift if the surface may have become contaminated since the last cleaning.

(B) Protective coverings, such as plastic wrap, aluminum foil, or imperviously-backed absorbent paper used to cover equipment and environmental surfaces, shall be removed and replaced as soon as feasible when they become overtly contaminated or at the end of the workshift if they may have become contaminated during the shift.

(C) All bins, pails, cans, and similar receptacles intended for reuse which have a reasonable likelihood for becoming contaminated with blood or other potentially infectious materials shall be inspected and decontaminated on a regularly scheduled basis and cleaned and decontaminated immediately or as soon as feasible upon visible contamination.

(D) Broken glassware which may be contaminated shall not be picked up directly with the hands. It shall be cleaned up using mechanical means, such as a brush and dust pan, tongs, or forceps.

(E) Reusable sharps that are contaminated with blood or other potentially infectious materials shall not be stored or processed in a manner that requires employees to reach by hand into the containers where these sharps have been placed.

(iii) *Regulated Waste*—(A) *Contaminated Sharps Discarding and Containment.* (1) Contaminated sharps shall be discarded immediately or as soon as feasible in containers that are:

(i) Closable;

(ii) Puncture resistant;

(iii) Leakproof on sides and bottom; and

(iv) Labeled or color-coded in accordance with paragraph (g)(1)(i) of this standard.

(2) During use, containers for contaminated sharps shall be:

(i) Easily accessible to personnel and located as close as is feasible to the immediate area where sharps are used or can be reasonably anticipated to be found (e.g., laundries);

(ii) Maintained upright throughout use; and

(iii) Replaced routinely and not be allowed to overfill.

(3) When moving containers of contaminated sharps from the area of use, the containers shall be:

(i) Closed immediately prior to removal or replacement to prevent spillage or protrusion of contents during handling, storage, transport, or shipping;

(ii) Placed in a secondary container if leakage is possible. The second container shall be:

(A) Closable;

(B) Constructed to contain all contents and prevent leakage during handling, storage, transport, or shipping; and

(C) Labeled or color-coded according to paragraph (g)(1)(i) of this standard.

(4) Reusable containers shall not be opened, emptied, or cleaned manually or in any other manner which would expose employees to the risk of percutaneous injury.

(B) *Other Regulated Waste Containment*—(1) Regulated waste shall be placed in containers which are:

(i) Closable;

(ii) Constructed to contain all contents and prevent leakage of fluids during handling, storage, transport or shipping;

(iii) Labeled or color-coded in accordance with paragraph (g)(1)(i) this standard; and

(iv) Closed prior to removal to prevent spillage or protrusion of contents during handling, storage, transport, or shipping.

(2) If outside contamination of the regulated waste container occurs, it shall be placed in a second container. The second container shall be:

(i) Closable;

(ii) Constructed to contain all contents and prevent leakage of fluids during handling, storage, transport or shipping;

(iii) Labeled or color-coded in accordance with paragraph (g)(1)(i) of this standard; and

(iv) Closed prior to removal to prevent spillage or protrusion of contents during handling, storage, transport, or shipping.

(C) Disposal of all regulated waste shall be in accordance with applicable regulations of the United States, States and Territories, and political subdivisions of States and Territories.

(iv) *Laundry.* (A) Contaminated laundry shall be handled as little as possible with a minimum of agitation. (1) Contaminated laundry shall be bagged or containerized at the location where it was used and shall not be sorted or rinsed in the location of use.

(2) Contaminated laundry shall be placed and transported in bags or containers labeled or color-coded in accordance with paragraph (g)(1)(i) of this standard. When a facility utilizes Universal Precautions in the handling of all soiled laundry, alternative labeling or color-coding is sufficient if it permits all employees to recognize the containers as requiring compliance with Universal Precautions.

(3) Whenever contaminated laundry is wet and presents a reasonable likelihood of soak-through of or leakage from the bag or container, the laundry shall be placed and transported in bags or containers which prevent soak-through and/or leakage of fluids to the exterior.

(B) The employer shall ensure that employees who have contact with contaminated laundry wear protective gloves and other appropriate personal protective equipment.

(C) When a facility ships contaminated laundry off-site to a second facility which does not utilize Universal Precautions in the handling of all laundry, the facility generating the contaminated laundry must place such laundry in bags or containers which are labeled or color-coded in accordance with paragraph (g)(1)(i).

(e) *HIV and HBV Research Laboratories and Production Facilities.* (1) This paragraph applies to research laboratories and production facilities engaged in the culture, production, concentration, experimentation, and manipulation of HIV and HBV. It does not apply to clinical or diagnostic laboratories engaged solely in the analysis of blood, tissues, or organs. These requirements apply in addition to the other requirements of the standard.

(2) Research laboratories and production facilities shall meet the following criteria:

(i) *Standard microbiological practices.* All regulated waste shall either be incinerated or decontaminated by a method such as autoclaving known to effectively destroy bloodborne pathogens.

(ii) *Special practices.* (A) Laboratory doors shall be kept closed when work involving HIV or HBV is in progress.

(B) Contaminated materials that are to be decontaminated at a site away from the work area shall be placed in a durable, leakproof, labeled or color-coded container that is closed before being removed from the work area.

(C) Access to the work area shall be limited to authorized persons. Written policies and procedures shall be established whereby only persons who have been advised of the potential biohazard, who meet any specific entry requirements, and who comply with all entry and exit procedures shall be allowed to enter the work areas and animal rooms.

(D) When other potentially infectious materials or infected animals are present in the work area or containment module, a hazard warning sign incorporating the universal biohazard symbol shall be posted on all access doors. The hazard warning sign shall comply with paragraph (g)(1)(ii) of this standard.

(E) All activities involving other potentially infectious materials shall be conducted in biological safety cabinets or other physical-containment devices within the containment module. No work with these other potentially infectious materials shall be conducted on the open bench.

(F) Laboratory coats, gowns, smocks, uniforms, or other appropriate protective clothing shall be used in the work area and animal rooms. Protective clothing shall not be worn outside of the work area and shall be decontaminated before being laundered.

(G) Special care shall be taken to avoid skin contact with other potentially infectious materials. Gloves shall be worn when handling infected animals and when making hand contact with other potentially infectious materials is unavoidable.

(H) Before disposal all waste from work areas and from animal rooms shall either be incinerated or decontaminated by a method such as autoclaving known to effectively destroy bloodborne pathogens.

(I) Vacuum lines shall be protected with liquid disinfectant traps and high-efficiency particulate air (HEPA) filters or filters of equivalent or superior efficiency and which are checked routinely and maintained or replaced as necessary.

(J) Hypodermic needles and syringes shall be used only for parenteral injection and aspiration of fluids from laboratory animals and diaphragm bottles. Only needle-locking syringes or disposable syringe-needle units (*i.e.*, the needle is integral to the syringe) shall be used for the injection or aspiration of other potentially infectious materials. Extreme caution shall be used when handling needles and syringes. A needle shall not be bent, sheared, replaced in the sheath or guard, or removed from the syringe following use. The needle and syringe shall be promptly placed in a puncture-resistant container and autoclaved or decontaminated before reuse or disposal.

(K) All spills shall be immediately contained and cleaned up by appropriate professional staff or others properly trained and equipped to work with potentially concentrated infectious materials.

(L) A spill or accident that results in an exposure incident shall be immediately reported to the laboratory director or other responsible person.

(M) A biosafety manual shall be prepared or adopted and periodically reviewed and updated at least annually or more often if necessary. Personnel shall be advised of potential hazards, shall be required to read instructions on practices and procedures, and shall be required to follow them.

(iii) *Containment equipment.* (A) Certified biological safety cabinets (Class I, II, or III) or other appropriate combinations of personal protection or physical containment devices, such as special protective clothing, respirators, centrifuge safety cups, sealed centrifuge rotors, and containment caging for animals, shall be used for all activities with other potentially infectious materials that pose a threat of exposure to droplets, splashes, spills, or aerosols.

(B) Biological safety cabinets shall be certified when installed, whenever they are moved and at least annually.

(3) HIV and HBV research laboratories shall meet the following criteria:

(i) Each laboratory shall contain a facility for hand washing and an eye wash facility which is readily available within the work area.

(ii) An autoclave for decontamination of regulated waste shall be available.

(4) HIV and HBV production facilities shall meet the following criteria:

(i) The work areas shall be separated from areas that are open to unrestricted traffic flow within the building. Passage through two sets of doors shall be the basic requirement for entry into the work area from access corridors or other contiguous areas. Physical separation of the high-containment work area from access corridors or other areas or activities may also be provided by a double-doored clothes-change room (showers may be included), airlock, or other access facility that requires passing through two sets of doors before entering the work area.

(ii) The surfaces of doors, walls, floors and ceilings in the work area shall be water resistant so that they can be easily cleaned. Penetrations in these surfaces shall be sealed or capable of being sealed to facilitate decontamination.

(iii) Each work area shall contain a sink for washing hands and a readily available eye wash facility. The sink shall be foot, elbow, or automatically operated and shall be located near the exit door of the work area.

(iv) Access doors to the work area or containment module shall be self-closing.

(v) An autoclave for decontamination of regulated waste shall be available within or as near as possible to the work area.

(vi) A ducted exhaust-air ventilation system shall be provided. This system shall create directional airflow that draws air into the work area through the entry area. The exhaust air shall not be recirculated to any other area of the building, shall be discharged to the outside, and shall be dispersed away from occupied areas and air intakes. The proper direction of the airflow shall be verified (*i.e.*, into the work area).

(5) *Training Requirements.* Additional training requirements for employees in HIV and HBV research laboratories and HIV and HBV production facilities are specified in paragraph (g)(2)(ix).

(f) *Hepatitis B vaccination and post-exposure evaluation and follow-up*—(1) *General.* (i) The employer shall make available the hepatitis B vaccine and vaccination series to all employees who have occupational exposure, and post-exposure evaluation and follow-up to all employees who have had an exposure incident.

(ii) The employer shall ensure that all medical evaluations and procedures including the hepatitis B vaccine and vaccination series and post-exposure evaluation and follow-up, including prophylaxis, are:

(A) Made available at no cost to the employee;

(B) Made available to the employee at a reasonable time and place;

(C) Performed by or under the supervision of a licensed physician or by or under the supervision of another licensed healthcare professional; and

(D) Provided according to recommendations of the U.S. Public Health Service current at the time these evaluations and procedures take place, except as specified by this paragraph (f).

(iii) The employer shall ensure that all laboratory tests are conducted by an accredited laboratory at no cost to the employee.

(2) *Hepatitis B Vaccination.* (i) Hepatitis B vaccination shall be made available after the employee has received the training required in paragraph (g)(2)(vii)(I) and within 10 working days of initial assignment to all employees who have occupational exposure unless the employee has previously received the complete hepatitis B vaccination series, antibody testing has revealed that the employee is immune, or the vaccine is contraindicated for medical reasons.

(ii) The employer shall not make participation in a prescreening program a prerequisite for receiving hepatitis B vaccination.

(iii) If the employee initially declines hepatitis B vaccination but at a later date while still covered under the standard decides to accept the vaccination, the employer shall make available hepatitis B vaccination at that time.

(iv) The employer shall assure that employees who decline to accept hepatitis B vaccination offered by the employer sign the statement in appendix A.

(v) If a routine booster dose(s) of hepatitis B vaccine is recommended by the U.S. Public Health Service at a future date, such booster dose(s) shall be made available in accordance with section (f)(1)(ii).

(3) *Post-exposure Evaluation and Follow-up.* Following a report of an exposure incident, the employer shall make immediately available to the exposed employee a confidential medical evaluation and follow-up, including at least the following elements:

(i) Documentation of the route(s) of exposure, and the circumstances under which the exposure incident occurred;

(ii) Identification and documentation of the source individual, unless the employer can establish that identification is infeasible or prohibited by state or local law;

(A) The source individual's blood shall be tested as soon as feasible and after consent is obtained in order to determine HBV and HIV infectivity. If consent is not obtained, the employer shall establish that legally required consent cannot be obtained. When the source individual's consent is not required by law, the source individual's blood, if available, shall be tested and the results documented.

(B) When the source individual is already known to be infected with HBV or HIV, testing for the source individual's known HBV or HIV status need not be repeated.

(C) Results of the source individual's testing shall be made available to the exposed employee, and the employee shall be informed of applicable laws and regulations concerning disclosure of the identity and infectious status of the source individual.

(iii) Collection and testing of blood for HBV and HIV serological status;

(A) The exposed employee's blood shall be collected as soon as feasible and tested after consent is obtained.

(B) If the employee consents to baseline blood collection, but does not give consent at that time for HIV serologic testing, the sample shall be preserved for at least 90 days. If, within 90 days of the exposure incident, the employee elects to have the baseline sample tested, such testing shall be done as soon as feasible.

(iv) Post-exposure prophylaxis, when medically indicated, as recommended by the U.S. Public Health Service;

(v) Counseling; and

(vi) Evaluation of reported illnesses.

(4) *Information Provided to the Healthcare Professional.* (i) The employer shall ensure that the healthcare professional responsible for the employee's Hepatitis B vaccination is provided a copy of this regulation.

(ii) The employer shall ensure that the healthcare professional evaluating an employee after an exposure incident is provided the following information:

(A) A copy of this regulation;

(B) A description of the exposed employee's duties as they relate to the exposure incident;

(C) Documentation of the route(s) of exposure and circumstances under which exposure occurred;

(D) Results of the source individual's blood testing, if available; and

(E) All medical records relevant to the appropriate treatment of the employee including vaccination status which are the employer's responsibility to maintain.

(5) *Healthcare Professional's Written Opinion.* The employer shall obtain and provide the employee with a copy of the evaluating healthcare professional's written opinion within 15 days of the completion of the evaluation.

(i) The healthcare professional's written opinion for Hepatitis B vaccination shall be limited to whether Hepatitis B vaccination is indicated for an employee, and if the employee has received such vaccination.

(ii) The healthcare professional's written opinion for post-exposure evaluation and follow-up shall be limited to the following information:

(A) That the employee has been informed of the results of the evaluation; and

(B) That the employee has been told about any medical conditions resulting from exposure to blood or other potentially infectious materials which require further evaluation or treatment.

(iii) All other findings or diagnoses shall remain confidential and shall not be included in the written report.

(6) *Medical recordkeeping.* Medical records required by this standard shall be maintained in accordance with paragraph (h)(1) of this section.

(g) *Communication of hazards to employees*—(1) *Labels and signs*—(i) *Labels.* (A) Warning labels shall be affixed to containers of regulated waste, refrigerators and freezers containing blood or other potentially infectious material; and other containers used to store, transport or ship blood or other potentially infectious materials, except as provided in paragraph (g)(1)(i)(E), (F) and (G).

(B) Labels required by this section shall include the following legend:

BIOHAZARD

(C) These labels shall be fluorescent orange or orange-red or predominantly so, with lettering and symbols in a contrasting color.

(D) Labels shall be affixed as close as feasible to the container by string, wire, adhesive, or other method that prevents their loss or unintentional removal.

(E) Red bags or red containers may be substituted for labels.

(F) Containers of blood, blood components, or blood products that are labeled as to their contents and have been released for transfusion or other clinical use are exempted from the labeling requirements of paragraph (g).

(G) Individual containers of blood or other potentially infectious materials that are placed in a labeled container during storage, transport, shipment or disposal are exempted from the labeling requirement.

(H) Labels required for contaminated equipment shall be in accordance with this paragraph and shall also state

323

which portions of the equipment remain contaminated.

(I) Regulated waste that has been decontaminated need not be labeled or color-coded.

(ii) *Signs.* (A) The employer shall post signs at the entrance to work areas specified in paragraph (e), HIV and HBV Research Laboratory and Production Facilities, which shall bear the following legend:

BIOHAZARD

(Name of the Infectious Agent)
(Special requirements for entering the area)
(Name, telephone number of the laboratory
director or other responsible person.)

(B) These signs shall be fluorescent orange-red or predominantly so, with lettering and symbols in a contrasting color.

(2) *Information and Training.* (i) The employer shall train each employee with occupational exposure in accordance with the requirements of this section. Such training must be provided at no cost to the employee and during working hours. The employer shall institute a training program and ensure employee participation in the program.

(ii) Training shall be provided as follows:

(A) At the time of initial assignment to tasks where occupational exposure may take place;

(B) At least annually thereafter.

(iii) [Reserved]

(iv) Annual training for all employees shall be provided within one year of their previous training.

(v) Employers shall provide additional training when changes such as modification of tasks or procedures or institution of new tasks or procedures affect the employee's occupational exposure. The additional training may be limited to addressing the new exposures created.

(vi) Material appropriate in content and vocabulary to educational level, literacy, and language of employees shall be used.

(vii) The training program shall contain at a minimum the following elements:

(A) An accessible copy of the regulatory text of this standard and an explanation of its contents;

(B) A general explanation of the epidemiology and symptoms of bloodborne diseases;

(C) An explanation of the modes of transmission of bloodborne pathogens;

(D) An explanation of the employer's exposure control plan and the means by which the employee can obtain a copy of the written plan;

(E) An explanation of the appropriate methods for recognizing tasks and other activities that may involve exposure to blood and other potentially infectious materials;

(F) An explanation of the use and limitations of methods that will prevent or reduce exposure including appropriate engineering controls, work practices, and personal protective equipment;

(G) Information on the types, proper use, location, removal, handling, decontamination and disposal of personal protective equipment;

(H) An explanation of the basis for selection of personal protective equipment;

(I) Information on the hepatitis B vaccine, including information on its efficacy, safety, method of administration, the benefits of being vaccinated, and that the vaccine and vaccination will be offered free of charge;

(J) Information on the appropriate actions to take and persons to contact in an emergency involving blood or other potentially infectious materials;

(K) An explanation of the procedure to follow if an exposure incident occurs, including the method of reporting the incident and the medical follow-up that will be made available;

(L) Information on the post-exposure evaluation and follow-up that the employer is required to provide for the employee following an exposure incident;

(M) An explanation of the signs and labels and/or color coding required by paragraph (g)(1); and

(N) An opportunity for interactive questions and answers with the person conducting the training session.

(viii) The person conducting the training shall be knowledgeable in the subject matter covered by the elements contained in the training program as it relates to the workplace that the training will address.

(ix) Additional Initial Training for Employees in HIV and HBV Laboratories and Production Facilities. Employees in HIV or HBV research laboratories and HIV or HBV production facilities shall receive the following initial training in addition to the above training requirements.

(A) The employer shall assure that employees demonstrate proficiency in standard microbiological practices and techniques and in the practices and operations specific to the facility before being allowed to work with HIV or HBV.

(B) The employer shall assure that employees have prior experience in the handling of human pathogens or tissue cultures before working with HIV or HBV.

(C) The employer shall provide a training program to employees who have no prior experience in handling human pathogens. Initial work activities shall not include the handling of infectious agents. A progression of work activities shall be assigned as techniques are learned and proficiency is developed. The employer shall assure that employees participate in work activities involving infectious agents only after proficiency has been demonstrated.

(h) *Recordkeeping*—(1) *Medical Records.* (i) The employer shall establish and maintain an accurate record for each employee with occupational exposure, in accordance with 29 CFR 1910.1020.

(ii) This record shall include:

(A) The name and social security number of the employee;

(B) A copy of the employee's hepatitis B vaccination status including the dates of all the hepatitis B vaccinations and any medical records relative to the employee's ability to receive vaccination as required by paragraph (f)(2);

(C) A copy of all results of examinations, medical testing, and follow-up procedures as required by paragraph (f)(3);

(D) The employer's copy of the healthcare professional's written opinion as required by paragraph (f)(5); and

(E) A copy of the information provided to the healthcare professional as required by paragraphs (f)(4)(ii)(B)(C) and (D).

(iii) Confidentiality. The employer shall ensure that employee medical records required by paragraph (h)(1) are:

(A) Kept confidential; and

(B) Not disclosed or reported without the employee's express written consent to any person within or outside the workplace except as required by this section or as may be required by law.

(iv) The employer shall maintain the records required by paragraph (h) for at least the duration of employment plus 30 years in accordance with 29 CFR 1910.1020.

(2) *Training Records.* (i) Training records shall include the following information:

(A) The dates of the training sessions;

(B) The contents or a summary of the training sessions;

(C) The names and qualifications of persons conducting the training; and

(D) The names and job titles of all persons attending the training sessions.

(ii) Training records shall be maintained for 3 years from the date on which the training occurred.

(3) *Availability.* (i) The employer shall ensure that all records required to be maintained by this section shall be made available upon request to the Assistant Secretary and the Director for examination and copying.

(ii) Employee training records required by this paragraph shall be provided upon request for examination and copying to employees, to employee representatives, to the Director, and to the Assistant Secretary.

(iii) Employee medical records required by this paragraph shall be provided upon request for examination and copying to the subject employee, to anyone having written consent of the subject employee, to the Director, and to the Assistant Secretary in accordance with 29 CFR 1910.1020.

(4) *Transfer of Records.* The employer shall comply with the requirements involving transfer of records set forth in 29 CFR 1910.1020(h).

(5) *Sharps injury log.* (i) The employer shall establish and maintain a sharps injury log for the recording of percutaneous injuries from contaminated sharps. The information in the sharps injury log shall be recorded and maintained in such manner as to protect the confidentiality of the injured employee. The sharps injury log shall contain, at a minimum:

(A) The type and brand of device involved in the incident,

(B) The department or work area where the exposure incident occurred, and

(C) An explanation of how the incident occurred.

(ii) The requirement to establish and maintain a sharps injury log shall apply to any employer who is required to maintain a log of occupational injuries and illnesses under 29 CFR part 1904.

(iii) The sharps injury log shall be maintained for the period required by 29 CFR 1904.33.

(i) *Dates*—(1) *Effective Date.* The standard shall become effective on March 6, 1992.

(2) The Exposure Control Plan required by paragraph (c) of this section shall be completed on or before May 5, 1992.

(3) Paragraphs (g)(2) Information and Training and (h) Recordkeeping of this section shall take effect on or before June 4, 1992.

(4) Paragraphs (d)(2) Engineering and Work Practice Controls, (d)(3) Personal Protective Equipment, (d)(4) Housekeeping, (e) HIV and HBV Research Laboratories and Production Facilities, (f) Hepatitis B Vaccination and Post-Exposure Evaluation and Follow-up, and (g)(1) Labels and Signs of this section, shall take effect July 6, 1992.

APPENDIX A TO SECTION 1910.1030—HEPATITIS B VACCINE DECLINATION (MANDATORY)

I understand that due to my occupational exposure to blood or other potentially infectious materials I may be at risk of acquiring hepatitis B virus (HBV) infection. I have been given the opportunity to be vaccinated with hepatitis B vaccine, at no charge to myself. However, I decline hepatitis B vaccination at this time. I understand that by declining this vaccine, I continue to be at risk of acquiring hepatitis B, a serious disease. If in the future I continue to have occupational exposure to blood or other potentially infectious materials and I want to be vaccinated with hepatitis B vaccine, I can receive the vaccination series at no charge to me.

[56 FR 64175, Dec. 6, 1991, as amended at 57 FR 12717, Apr. 13, 1992; 57 FR 29206, July 1, 1992; 61 FR 5508, Feb. 13, 1996; 66 FR 5325, Jan. 18, 2001; 71 FR 16672, 16673, Apr. 3, 2006; 73 FR 75586, Dec. 12, 2008; 76 FR 33608, June 8, 2011; 76 FR 80740, Dec. 27, 2011; 77 FR 19934, Apr. 3, 2012]

§ 1910.1043   Cotton dust.

(a) *Scope and application.* (1) This section, in its entirety, applies to the control of employee exposure to cotton dust in all workplaces where employees engage in yarn manufacturing, engage in slashing and weaving operations, or work in waste houses for textile operations.

(2) This section does not apply to the handling or processing of woven or knitted materials; to maritime operations covered by 29 CFR Parts 1915 and 1918; to harvesting or ginning of cotton; or to the construction industry.

(3) Only paragraphs (h) Medical surveillance, (k)(2) through (4) Recordkeeping—Medical Records, and appendices B, C and D of this section apply in all work places where employees exposed to cotton dust engage in cottonseed processing or waste processing operations.

(4) This section applies to yarn manufacturing and slashing and weaving operations exclusively using washed cotton (as defined by paragraph (n) of this section) only to the extent specified by paragraph (n) of this section.

(5) This section, in its entirety, applies to the control of all employees exposure to the cotton dust generated in the preparation of washed cotton from opening until the cotton is thoroughly wetted.

(6) This section does not apply to knitting, classing or warehousing operations except that employers with these operations, if requested by NIOSH, shall grant NIOSH access to

their employees and workplaces for exposure monitoring and medical examinations for purposes of a health study to be performed by NIOSH on a sampling basis.

(b) *Definitions.* For the purpose of this section:

Assistant Secretary means the Assistant Secretary of Labor for Occupational Safety and Health, U.S. Department of Labor, or designee;

Blow down means the general cleaning of a room or a part of a room by the use of compressed air.

Blow off means the use of compressed air for cleaning of short duration and usually for a specific machine or any portion of a machine.

Cotton dust means dust present in the air during the handling or processing of cotton, which may contain a mixture of many substances including ground up plant matter, fiber, bacteria, fungi, soil, pesticides, non-cotton plant matter and other contaminants which may have accumulated with the cotton during the growing, harvesting and subsequent processing or storage periods. Any dust present during the handling and processing of cotton through the weaving or knitting of fabrics, and dust present in other operations or manufacturing processes using raw or waste cotton fibers or cotton fiber byproducts from textile mills are considered cotton dust within this definition. Lubricating oil mist associated with weaving operations is not considered cotton dust.

Director means the Director of the National Institute for Occupational Safety and Health (NIOSH), U.S. Department of Health and Human Services, or designee.

Equivalent Instrument means a cotton dust sampling device that meets the vertical elutriator equivalency requirements as described in paragraph (d)(1)(iii) of this section.

Lint-free respirable cotton dust means particles of cotton dust of approximately 15 micrometers or less aerodynamic equivalent diameter;

Vertical elutriator cotton dust sampler or *vertical elutriator* means a dust sampler which has a particle size cut-off at approximately 15 micrometers aerodynamic equivalent diameter when op-

erating at the flow rate of 7.4 ±0.2 liters of air per minute;

Waste processing means waste recycling (sorting, blending, cleaning and willowing) and garnetting.

Yarn manufacturing means all textile mill operations from opening to, but not including, slashing and weaving.

(c) *Permissible exposure limits and action levels*—(1) *Permissible exposure limits (PEL).* (i) The employer shall assure that no employee who is exposed to cotton dust in yarn manufacturing and cotton washing operations is exposed to airborne concentrations of lint-free respirable cotton dust greater than 200 µg/m³ mean concentration, averaged over an eight-hour period, as measured be a vertical elutriator or an equivalent instrument.

(ii) The employer shall assure that no employee who is exposed to cotton dust in textile mill waste house operations or is exposed in yarn manufacturing to dust from "lower grade washed cotton" as defined in paragraph (n)(5) of this section is exposed to airborne concentrations of lint-free respirable cotton dust greater than 500 µg/m³ mean concentration, averaged over an eight-hour period, as measured by a vertical elutriator or an equivalent instrument.

(iii) The employer shall assure that no employee who is exposed to cotton dust in the textile processes known as slashing and weaving is exposed to airborne concentrations of lint-free respirable cotton dust greater than 750 µg/m³ mean concentration, averaged over an eight hour period, as measured by a vertical elutriator or an equivalent instrument.

(2) *Action levels.* (i) The action level for yarn manufacturing and cotton washing operations is an airborne concentration of lint-free respirable cotton dust of 100 µg/m³ mean concentration, averaged over an eight-hour period, as measured by a vertical elutriator or an equivalent instrument.

(ii) The action level for waste houses for textile operations is an airborne concentration of lint-free respirable cotton dust of 250 µg/m³ mean concentration, averaged over an eight-hour period, as measured by a vertical elutriator or an equivalent instrument.

(iii) The action level for the textile processes known as slashing and weaving is an airborne concentration of lint-free respirable cotton dust of 375 µg/m³ mean concentration, averaged over an eight-hour period, as measured by a vertical elutriator or an equivalent instrument.

(d) *Exposure monitoring and measurement*—(1) *General.* (i) For the purposes of this section, employee exposure is that exposure which would occur if the employee were not using a respirator.

(ii) The sampling device to be used shall be either the vertical elutriator cotton dust sampler or an equivalent instrument.

(iii) If an alternative to the vertical elutriator cotton dust sampler is used, the employer shall establish equivalency by reference to an OSHA opinion or by documenting, based on data developed by the employer or supplied by the manufacturer, that the alternative sampling devices meets the following criteria:

(A) It collects respirable particulates in the same range as the vertical elutriator (approximately 15 microns);

(B) Replicate exposure data used to establish equivalency are collected in side-by-side field and laboratory comparisons; and

(C) A minimum of 100 samples over the range of 0.5 to 2 times the permissible exposure limit are collected, and 90% of these samples have an accuracy range of plus or minus 25 per cent of the vertical elutriator reading with a 95% confidence level as demonstrated by a statistically valid protocol. (An acceptable protocol for demonstrating equivalency is described in appendix E of this section.)

(iv) OSHA will issue a written opinion stating that an instrument is equivalent to a vertical elutriator cotton dust sampler if

(A) A manufacturer or employer requests an opinion in writing and supplies the following information:

(1) Sufficient test data to demonstrate that the instrument meets the requirements specified in this paragraph and the protocol specified in appendix E of this section;

(2) Any other relevant information about the instrument and its testing requested by OSHA; and

(3) A certification by the manufacturer or employer that the information supplied is accurate, and

(B) if OSHA finds, based on information submitted about the instrument, that the instrument meets the requirements for equivalency specified by paragraph (d) of this section.

(2) *Initial monitoring.* Each employer who has a place of employment within the scope of paragraph (a)(1), (a)(4), or (a)(5) of this section shall conduct monitoring by obtaining measurements which are representative of the exposure of all employees to airborne concentrations of lint-free respirable cotton dust over an eight-hour period. The sampling program shall include at least one determination during each shift for each work area.

(3) *Periodic monitoring.* (i) If the initial monitoring required by paragraph (d)(2) of this section or any subsequent monitoring reveals employee exposure to be at or below the permissible exposure limit, the employer shall repeat the monitoring for those employees at least annually.

(ii) If the initial monitoring required by paragraph (d)(2) of this section or any subsequent monitoring reveals employee exposure to be above the PEL, the employer shall repeat the monitoring for those employees at least every six months.

(iii) Whenever there has been a production, process, or control change which may result in new or additional exposure to cotton dust, or whenever the employer has any other reason to suspect an increase in employee exposure, the employer shall repeat the monitoring and measurements for those employees affected by the change or increase.

(4) *Employee notification.* (i) The employer must, within 15 working days after the receipt of the results of any monitoring performed under this section, notify each affected employee of these results either individually in writing or by posting the results in an appropriate location that is accessible to employees.

(ii) Whenever the results indicate that the employee's exposure exceeds the applicable permissible exposure limit specified in paragraph (c) of this section, the employer shall include in the written notice a statement that the permissible exposure limit was exceeded and a description of the corrective action taken to reduce exposure below the permissible exposure limit.

(e) *Methods of compliance*—(1) *Engineering and work practice controls.* The employer shall institute engineering and work practice controls to reduce and maintain employee exposure to cotton dust at or below the permissible exposure limit specified in paragraph (c) of this section, except to the extent that the employer can establish that such controls are not feasible.

(2) Whenever feasible engineering and work practice controls are not sufficient to reduce employee exposure to or below the permissible exposure limit, the employer shall nonetheless institute these controls to reduce exposure to the lowest feasible level, and shall supplement these controls with the use of respirators which shall comply with the provisions of paragraph (f) of this section.

(3) *Compliance program.* (i) Where the most recent exposure monitoring data indicates that any employee is exposed to cotton dust levels greater than the permissible exposure limit, the employer shall establish and implement a written program sufficient to reduce exposures to or below the permissible exposure limit solely by means of engineering controls and work practices as required by paragraph (e)(1) of this section.

(ii) The written program shall include at least the following:

(A) A description of each operation or process resulting in employee exposure to cotton dust at levels greater than the PEL;

(B) Engineering plans and other studies used to determine the controls for each process;

(C) A report of the technology considered in meeting the permissible exposure limit;

(D) Monitoring data obtained in accordance with paragraph (d) of this section;

(E) A detailed schedule for development and implementation of engineering and work practice controls, including exposure levels projected to be achieved by such controls;

(F) Work practice program; and

(G) Other relevant information.

(iii) The employer's schedule as set forth in the compliance program, shall project completion of the implementation of the compliance program no later than March 27, 1984 or as soon as possible if monitoring after March 27, 1984 reveals exposures over the PEL, except as provided in paragraph (m)(2)(ii)(B) of this section.

(iv) The employer shall complete the steps set forth in his program by the dates in the schedule.

(v) Written programs shall be submitted, upon request, to the Assistant Secretary and the Director, and shall be available at the worksite for examination and copying by the Assistant Secretary, the Director, and any affected employee or their designated representatives.

(vi) The written program required under paragraph (e)(3) of this section shall be revised and updated when necessary to reflect the current status of the program and current exposure levels.

(4) *Mechanical ventilation.* When mechanical ventilation is used to control exposure, measurements which demonstrate the effectiveness of the system to control exposure, such as capture velocity, duct velocity, or static pressure shall be made at reasonable intervals.

(f) *Respiratory protection*—(1) *General.* For employees who are required to use respirators by this section, the employer must provide each employee an appropriate respirator that complies with the requirements of this paragraph. Respirators must be used during:

(i) Periods necessary to install or implement feasible engineering and work-practice controls.

(ii) Maintenance and repair activities for which engineering and work-practice controls are not feasible.

(iii) Work operations for which feasible engineering and work-practice controls are not yet sufficient to reduce employee exposure to or below the permissible exposure limits.

(iv) Work operations specified under paragraph (g)(1) of this section.

(v) Periods for which an employee requests a respirator.

(2) *Respirator program.* (i) The employer must implement a respiratory protection program in accordance with § 1910.134(b) through (d) (except (d)(1)(iii)), and (f) through (m), which covers each employee required by this section to use a respirator.

(ii) Whenever a physician determines that an employee who works in an area in which the cotton-dust concentration exceeds the PEL is unable to use a respirator, including a powered air-purifying respirator, the employee must be given the opportunity to transfer to an available position, or to a position that becomes available later, that has a cotton-dust concentration at or below the PEL. The employer must ensure that such employees retain their current wage rate or other benefits as a result of the transfer.

(3) *Respirator selection.* (i) Employers must:

(A) Select, and provide to employees, the appropriate respirators specified in paragraph (d)(3)(i)(A) of 29 CFR 1910.134; however, employers must not select or use filtering facepieces for protection against cotton dust concentrations greater than five times (5 ×) the PEL.

(B) Provide HEPA filters for powered and non-powered air-purifying respirators used at cotton dust concentrations greater than ten times (10 ×) the PEL.

(ii) Employers must provide an employee with a powered air-purifying respirator (PAPR) instead of a non-powered air-purifying respirator selected according to paragraph (f)(3)(i) of this standard when the employee chooses to use a PAPR and it provides adequate protection to the employee as specified by paragraph (f)(3)(i) of this standard.

(g) *Work practices.* Each employer shall, regardless of the level of employee exposure, immediately establish and implement a written program of work practices which shall minimize cotton dust exposure. The following shall be included were applicable:

(1) Compressed air "blow down" cleaning shall be prohibited where alternative means are feasible. Where compressed air is used for cleaning, the employees performing the "blow down" or "blow off" shall wear suitable respirators. Employees whose presence is not required to perform "blow down" or "blow of" shall be required to leave the area affected by the "blow down" or "blow off" during this cleaning operation.

(2) Cleaning of clothing or floors with compressed air shall be prohibited.

(3) Floor sweeping shall be performed with a vacuum or with methods designed to minimize dispersal of dust.

(4) In areas where employees are exposed to concentrations of cotton dust greater than the permissible exposure limit, cotton and cotton waste shall be stacked, sorted, baled, dumped, removed or otherwise handled by mechanical means, except where the employer can show that it is infeasible to do so. Where infeasible, the method used for handling cotton and cotton waste shall be the method which reduces exposure to the lowest level feasible.

(h) *Medical surveillance*—(1) *General.* (i) Each employer covered by the standard shall institute a program of medical surveillance for all employees exposed to cotton dust.

(ii) The employer shall assure that all medical examinations and procedures are performed by or under the supervision of a licensed physician and are provided without cost to the employee.

(iii) Persons other than licensed physicians, who administer the pulmonary function testing required by this section shall have completed a NIOSH-approved training course in spirometry.

(2) *Initial examinations.* The employer shall provide medical surveillance to each employee who is or may be exposed to cotton dust. For new employees, this examination shall be provided prior to initial assignment. The medical surveillance shall include at least the following:

(i) A medical history;

(ii) The standardized questionnaire contained in appendix B; and

(iii) A pulmonary function measurement, including a determination of forced vital capacity (FVC) and forced expiratory volume in one second (FEV_1), the FEV_1/FVC ratio, and the percentage that the measured values of FEV_1 and FVC differ from the predicted values, using the standard tables in appendix C. These determinations shall be made for each employee before the employee enters the workplace on the first day of the work week, preceded by at least 35 hours of no exposure to cotton dust. The tests shall be repeated during the shift, no less than 4 and no more than 10 hours after the beginning of the work shift; and, in any event, no more than one hour after cessation of exposure. Such exposure shall be typical of the employee's usual workplace exposure. The predicted FEV_1 and FVC for blacks shall be multiplied by 0.85 to adjust for ethnic differences.

(iv) Based upon the questionnaire results, each employee shall be graded according to Schilling's byssinosis classification system.

(3) *Periodic examinations.* (i) The employer shall provide at least annual medical surveillance for all employees exposed to cotton dust above the action level in yarn manufacturing, slashing and weaving, cotton washing and waste house operations. The employer shall provide medical surveillance at least every two years for all employees exposed to cotton dust at or below the action level, for all employees exposed to cotton dust from washed cotton (except from washed cotton defined in paragraph (n)(3) of this section), and for all employees exposed to cotton dust in cottonseed processing and waste processing operations. Periodic medical surveillance shall include at least an update of the medical history, standardized questionnaire (App. B–111), Schilling byssinosis grade, and the pulmonary function measurements in paragraph (h)(2)(iii) of this section.

(ii) Medical surveillance as required in paragraph (h)(3)(i) of this section shall be provided every six months for all employees in the following categories:

(A) An FEV_1 of greater than 80 percent of the predicted value, but with an FEV_1 decrement of 5 percent or 200 ml. on a first working day;

(B) An FEV_1 of less than 80 percent of the predicted value; or

(C) Where, in the opinion of the physician, any significant change in questionnaire findings, pulmonary function results, or other diagnostic tests have occurred.

(iii) An employee whose FEV_1 is less than 60 percent of the predicted value shall be referred to a physician for a detailed pulmonary examination.

(iv) A comparison shall be made between the current examination results and those of previous examinations and a determination made by the physician as to whether there has been a significant change.

(4) *Information provided to the physician.* The employer shall provide the following information to the examination physician:

(i) A copy of this regulation and its Appendices:

(ii) A description of the affected employee's duties as they relate to the employee's exposure;

(iii) The employee's exposure level or anticipated exposure level;

(iv) A description of any personal protective equipment used or to be used; and

(v) Information from previous medical examinations of the affected employee which is not readily available to the examining physician.

(5) *Physician's written opinion.* (i) The employer shall obtain and furnish the employee with a copy of a written opinion from the examining physician containing the following:

(A) The results of the medical examination and tests including the FEV_1, FVC, AND FEV_1/FVC ratio;

(B) The physician's opinion as to whether the employee has any detected medical conditions which would place the employee at increased risk of material impairment of the employee's health from exposure to cotton dust;

(C) The physician's recommended limitations upon the employee's exposure to cotton dust or upon the employee's use of respirators including a determination of whether an employee can wear a negative pressure respirator, and where the employee cannot, a determination of the employee's ability to wear a powered air purifying respirator; and,

(D) A statement that the employee has been informed by the physician of the results of the medical examination and any medical conditions which require further examination or treatment.

331

(ii) The written opinion obtained by the employer shall not reveal specific findings or diagnoses unrelated to occupational exposure.

(i) *Employee education and training—* (1) *Training program.* (i) The employer shall train each employee exposed to cotton dust in accordance with the requirements of this section. The employer shall institute a training program and ensure employee participation in the program.

(ii) The training program shall be provided prior to initial assignment and shall be repeated annually for each employee exposed to cotton dust, when job assignments or work processes change and when employee performance indicates a need for retraining.

(2) *Access to training materials.* (i) Each employer shall post a copy of this section with its appendices in a public location at the workplace, and shall, upon request, make copies available to employees.

(ii) The employer shall provide all materials relating to the employee training and information program to the Assistant Secretary and the Director upon request.

(j) *Signs.* (1) The employer shall post the following warning sign in each work area where the permissible exposure limit for cotton dust is exceeded:

DANGER
COTTON DUST
CAUSES DAMAGE TO LUNGS
(BYSSINOSIS)
WEAR RESPIRATORY PROTECTION IN THIS AREA

(2) Prior to June 1, 2016, employers may use the following legend in lieu of that specified in paragraph (j)(1) of this section:

WARNING
COTTON DUST WORK AREA
MAY CAUSE ACUTE OR DELAYED
LUNG INJURY
(BYSSINOSIS)
RESPIRATORS
REQUIRED IN THIS AREA

(k) *Recordkeeping*—(1) *Exposure measurements.* (i) The employer shall establish and maintain an accurate record of all measurements required by paragraph (d) of this section.

(ii) The record shall include:

(A) A log containing the items listed in paragraph IV (a) of appendix A, and

the dates, number, duration, and results of each of the samples taken, including a description of the procedure used to determine representative employee exposure;

(B) The type of protective devices worn, if any, and length of time worn; and

(C) The names, social security numbers, job classifications, and exposure levels of employees whose exposure the measurement is intended to represent.

(iii) The employer shall maintain this record for at least 20 years.

(2) *Medical surveillance.* (i) The employer shall establish and maintain an accurate medical record for each employee subject to medical surveillance required by paragraph (h) of this section.

(ii) The record shall include:

(A) The name and social security number and description of the duties of the employee;

(B) A copy of the medical examination results including the medical history, questionnaire response, results of all tests, and the physician's recommendation;

(C) A copy of the physician's written opinion;

(D) Any employee medical complaints related to exposure to cotton dust;

(E) A copy of this standard and its appendices, except that the employer may keep one copy of the standard and the appendices for all employees, provided that he references the standard and appendices in the medical surveillance record of each employee; and

(F) A copy of the information provided to the physician as required by paragraph (h)(4) of this section.

(iii) The employer shall maintain this record for at least 20 years.

(3) *Availability.* (i) The employer shall make all records required to be maintained by paragraph (k) of this section available to the Assistant Secretary and the Director for examination and copying.

(ii) Employee exposure measurement records and employee medical records required by this paragraph shall be provided upon request to employees, designated representatives, and the Assistant Secretary in accordance with 29

CFR 1910.1020 (a) through (e) and (g) through (i).

(4) *Transfer of records.* (i) Whenever the employer ceases to do business, the successor employer shall receive and retain all records required to be maintained by paragraph (k) of this section.

(ii) The employer shall also comply with any additional requirements involving transfer of records set forth in 29 CFR 1910.1020(h).

(l) *Observation of monitoring.* (1) The employer shall provide affected employees or their designated representatives an opportunity to observe any measuring or monitoring of employee exposure to cotton dust conducted pursuant to paragraph (d) of this section.

(2) Whenever observation of the measuring or monitoring of employee exposure to cotton dust requires entry into an area where the use of personal protective equipment is required, the employer shall provide the observer with and assure the use of such equipment and shall require the observer to comply with all other applicable safety and health procedures.

(3) Without interfering with the measurement, observers shall be entitled to:

(i) An explanation of the measurement procedures;

(ii) An opportunity to observe all steps related to the measurement of airborne concentrations of cotton dust performed at the place of exposure; and

(iii) An opportunity to record the results obtained.

(m) *Washed Cotton—*(1) *Exemptions.* Cotton, after it has been washed by the processes described in this paragraph, is exempt from all or parts of this section as specified if the requirements of this paragraph are met.

(2) *Initial requirements.* (i) In order for an employer to qualify as exempt or partially exempt from this standard for operations using washed cotton, the employer must demonstrate that the cotton was washed in a facility which is open to inspection by the Assistant Secretary and the employer must provide sufficient accurate documentary evidence to demonstrate that the washing methods utilized meet the requirements of this paragraph.

(ii) An employer who handles or processes cotton which has been washed in a facility not under the employer's control and claims an exemption or partial exemption under this paragraph, must obtain from the cotton washer and make available at the worksite, to the Assistant Secretary, to any affected employee, or to their designated representative the following:

(A) A certification by the washer of the cotton of the grade of cotton, the type of washing process, and that the batch meets the requirements of this paragraph;

(B) Sufficient accurate documentation by the washer of the cotton grades and washing process; and

(C) An authorization by the washer that the Assistant Secretary or the Director may inspect the washer's washing facilities and documentation of the process.

(3) *Medical and dyed cotton.* Medical grade (USP) cotton, cotton that has been scoured, bleached and dyed, and mercerized yarn shall be exempt from all provisions of this standard.

(4) *Higher grade washed cotton.* The handling or processing of cotton classed as "low middling light spotted or better" (color grade 52 or better and leaf grade code 5 or better according to the 1993 USDA classification system) shall be exempt from all provisions of the standard except the requirements of paragraphs (h) medical surveillance, (k)(2) through (4) recordkeeping—medical records, and Appendices B, C, and D of this section, if they have been washed on one of the following systems:

(i) On a continuous batt system or a rayon rinse system including the following conditions:

(A) With water;

(B) At a temperature of no less than 60 °C;

(C) With a water-to-fiber ratio of no less than 40:1; and

(D) With the bacterial levels in the wash water controlled to limit bacterial contamination of the cotton.

(ii) On a batch kier washing system including the following conditions:

(A) With water;

(B) With cotton fiber mechanically opened and thoroughly prewetted before forming the cake;

333

(C) For low-temperature processing, at a temperature of no less than 60 °C with a water-to-fiber ratio of no less than 40:1; or, for high-temperature processing, at a temperature of no less than 93 °C with a water-to-fiber ratio of no less than 15:1;

(D) With a minimum of one wash cycle followed by two rinse cycles for each batch, using fresh water in each cycle, and

(E) With bacterial levels in the wash water controlled to limit bacterial contamination of the cotton.

(5) *Lower grade washed cotton.* The handling and processing of cotton of grades lower than "low middling light spotted," that has been washed as specified in paragraph (n)(4) of this section and has also been bleached, shall be exempt from all provisions of the standard except the requirements of paragraphs (c)(1)(ii) Permissible Exposure Limit, (d) Exposure Monitoring, (h) Medical Surveillance, (k) Recordkeeping, and Appendices B, C and D of this section.

(6) *Mixed grades of washed cotton.* If more than one grade of washed cotton is being handled or processed together, the requirements of the grade with the most stringent exposure limit, medical and monitoring requirements shall be followed.

(n) *Appendices.* (1) Appendices B, C, and D of this section are incorporated as part of this section and the contents of these appendices are mandatory.

(2) Appendix A of this section contains information which is not intended to create any additional obligations not otherwise imposed or to detract from any existing obligations.

(3) Appendix E of this section is a protocol which may be followed in the validation of alternative measuring devices as equivalent to the vertical elutriator cotton dust sampler. Other protocols may be used if it is demonstrated that they are statistically valid, meet the requirements in paragraph (d)(1)(iii) of this section, and are appropriate for demonstrating equivalency.

APPENDIX A TO § 1910.1043—AIR SAMPLING AND ANALYTICAL PROCEDURES FOR DETERMINING CONCENTRATIONS OF COTTON DUST

I. SAMPLING LOCATIONS

The sampling procedures must be designed so that samples of the actual dust concentrations are collected accurately and consistently and reflect the concentrations of dust at the place and time of sampling. Sufficient number of 6-hour area samples in each distinct work area of the plant should be collected at locations which provide representative samples of air to which the worker is exposed. In order to avoid filter overloading, sampling time may be shortened when sampling in dusty areas. Samples in each work area should be gathered simultaneously or sequentially during a normal operating period. The daily time-weighted average (TWA) exposure of each worker can then be determined by using the following formula:

Summation of hours spent in each location and the dust concentration in that location.

Total hours exposed

A time-weighted average concentration should be computed for each worker and properly logged and maintained on file for review.

II. SAMPLING EQUIPMENT

(a) Sampler. The instrument selected for monitoring is the Lumsden-Lynch vertical elutriator. It should operate at a flow rate of 7.4±0.2 liters/minute.

The samplers should be cleaned prior to sampling. The pumps should be monitored during sampling.

(b) Filter Holder. A three-piece cassette constructed of polystyrene designed to hold a 37-mm diameter filter should be used. Care must be exercised to insure that an adequate seal exists between elements of the cassette.

(c) Filers and Support Pads. The membrane filters used should be polyvinyl chloride with a 5-um pore size and 37-mm diameter. A support pad, commonly called a backup pad, should be used under the filter membrane in the field monitor cassette.

(d) Balance. A balance sensitive to 10 micrograms should be used.

(e) Monitoring equipment for use in Class III hazardous locations must be approved for use in such locations, in accordance with the requirements of the OSHA electrical standards in subpart S of part 1910.

III. INSTRUMENT CALIBRATION PROCEDURE

Samplers shall be calibrated when first received from the factory, after repair, and after receiving any abuse. The samplers should be calibrated in the laboratory both before they are used in the field and after

334

they have been used to collect a large number of field samples. The primary standard, such as a spirometer or other standard calibrating instruments such as a wet test meter or a large bubble meter or dry gas meter, should be used. Instructions for calibration with the wet test meter follow. If another calibration device is selected, equivalent procedures should be used:

(a) Level wet test meter. Check the water level which should just touch the calibration point at the left side of the meter. If water level is low, add water 1–2 °F. warmer than room temperature of till point. Run the meter for 30 minutes before calibration;

(b) Place the polyvinyl chloride membrane filter in the filter cassette;

(c) Assemble the calibration sampling train;

(d) Connect the wet test meter to the train.

The pointer on the meter should run clockwise and a pressure drop of not more than 1.0 inch of water indicated. If the pressure drop is greater than 1.0, disconnect and check the system;

(e) Operate the system for ten minutes before starting the calibration;

(f) Check the vacuum gauge on the pump to insure that the pressure drop across the orifice exceeds 17 inches of mercury;

(g) Record the following on calibration data sheets:

(1) Wet test meter reading, start and finish;

(2) Elapsed time, start and finish (at least two minutes);

(3) Pressure drop at manometer;

(4) Air temperature;

(5) Barometric pressure; and

(6) Limiting orifice number;

(h) Calculate the flow rate and compare against the flow of 7.4±0.2 liters/minute. If flow is between these limits, perform calibration again, average results, and record orifice number and flow rate. If flow is not within these limits, discard or modify orifice and repeat procedure;

(i) Record the name of the person performing the calibration, the date, serial number of the wet test meter, and the number of the critical orifices being calibrated.

IV. SAMPLING PROCEDURE

(a) Sampling data sheets should include a log of:

(1) The date of the sample collection;

(2) The time of sampling;

(3) The location of the sampler;

(4) The sampler serial number;

(5) The cassette number;

(6) The time of starting and stopping the sampling and the duration of sampling;

(7) The weight of the filter before and after sampling;

(8) The weight of dust collected (corrected for controls);

(9) The dust concentration measured;

(10) Other pertinent information; and

(11) Name of person taking sample

(b) Assembly of filter cassette should be as follows:

(1) Loosely assemble 3-piece cassette;

(2) Number cassette;

(3) Place absorbant pad in cassette;

(4) Weigh filter to an accuracy of 10 µg;

(5) Place filter in cassette;

(6) Record weight of filter in log, using cassette number for identification;

(7) Fully assemble cassette, using pressure to force parts tightly together;

(8) Install plugs top and bottom;

(9) Put shrink band on cassette, covering joint between center and bottom parts of cassette; and

(10) Set cassette aside until shrink band dries thoroughly.

(c) Sampling collection should be performed as follows:

(1) Clean lint out of the motor and elutriator;

(2) Install vertical elutriator in sampling locations specified above with inlet 4½ to 5½ feet from floor (breathing zone height);

(3) Remove top section of cassette;

(4) Install cassette in ferrule of elutriator;

(5) Tape cassette to ferrule with masking tape or similar material for air-tight seal;

(6) Remove bottom plug of cassette and attach hose containing critical orifice;

(7) Start elutriator pump and check to see if gauge reads above 17 in. of Hg vacuum;

(8) Record starting time, cassette number, and sampler number;

(9) At end of sampling period stop pump and record time; and

(10) Controls with each batch of samples collected, two additional filter cassettes should be subjected to exactly the same handling as the samples, except that they are not opened. These control filters should be weighed in the same manner as the sample filters.

Any difference in weight in the control filters would indicate that the procedure for handling sample filters may not be adequate and should be evaluated to ascertain the cause of the difference, whether and what necessary corrections must be made, and whether additional samples must be collected.

(d) Shipping. The cassette with samples should be collected, along with the appropriate number of blanks, and shipped to the analytical laboratory in a suitable container to prevent damage in transit.

(e) Weighing of the sample should be achieved as follows:

(1) Remove shrink band;

(2) Remove top and middle sections of cassette and botton plug;

(3) Remove filter from cassette and weigh to an accuracy of 10 µg; and

(4) Record weight in log against original weight

(f) Calculation of volume of air sampled should be determined as follows:

(1) From starting and stopping times of sampling period, determine length of time in minutes of sampling period; and

(2) Multiply sampling time in minutes by flow rate of critical orifice in liters per minute and divide by 1000 to find air quantity in cubic meters.

(g) Calculation of Dust Concentrations should be made as follows:

(1) Substract weight of clean filter from dirty filter and apply control correction to find actual weight of sample. Record this weight (in µg) in log; and

(2) Divide mass of sample in µg by air volume in cubic meters to find dust concentration in µg/m. Record in log.

APPENDIX B-1
RESPIRATORY QUESTIONNAIRE

A. IDENTIFICATION DATA

PLANT_____ SOCIAL SECURITY NO. _____
DAY   MONTH   YEAR
(figures) (last 2 digits)

NAME_____ _____ DATE OF INTERVIEW_____
(Surname)

_____ DATE OF BIRTH_____
(First Names)   M   F

ADDRESS_____ AGE _____(8,9) SEX _____(10)

_____RACE | W | | N | | IND. | | OTHER | (11)

INTERVIEWER: 1   2   3   4   5   6   7   8   (12)

WORK SHIFT·   1st_____   2nd_____3rd_____(13)   STANDING HEIGHT_____(14,15)

PRESENT WORK AREA   WEIGHT_____ _____(16,18)

If working in more than one specified work area, X area where most of the work shift is spent. If "other," but spending 25% of the work shift in one of the specified work areas, classify in that work area. If carding department employee, check area within that department where most of the work shift is spent (if in doubt, check "throughout"). For work areas such as spinning and weaving where many work rooms may be involved, be sure to check the specific work room to which the employee is assigned — if he works in more than one work room within a department classify as 7 (all) for that department.

	Workroom Number	(19) Open	(20) Pick	Area	(21) Card #1	'22) #2	(23) Spin	(24) Wind	(25) Twist	(26) Spool	(27) Warp	(28) Slash	(29) Weave	(30) Other
AT RISK (cotton & cotton blend)	1			Cards										
	2			Draw										
	3			Comb										
	4			Rove										
	5			Thru Out										
	6													
	7 (all)													
Control (synthetic & wool)	8													
Ex-Worker (cotton)	9													

337

Use actual wording of each question. Put X in appropriate square after each question. When in doubt record 'No'. When no square, circle appropriate answer.

B. COUGH

(on getting up)†

Do you usually cough first thing in the morning?_____Yes____No_____(31)
(Count a cough with first smoke or on "first going out of doors." Exclude clearing throat or a single cough.)

Do you usually cough during the day or at night?_____Yes____No_____(32)
(Ignore an occasional cough.)

If 'Yes' to either question (31-32):

Do you cough like this on most days for as much as three months a year?_____Yes____No_____(33)

Do you cough on any particular day of the week?   Yes____No_____(34)

(1)   (2)   (3)   (4)   (5)   (6)   (7)

If 'Yes': Which day?   Mon.   Tues.   Wed   Thur.   Fri.   Sat   Sun.   (35)

C. PHLEGM or alternative word to suit local custom.

(on getting up)†

Do you usually bring up any phlegm from your chest first thing in the morning? (Count phlegm with the first smoke or on "first going out of doors." Exclude phlegm from the nose. Count swallowed phlegm.)_____Yes____No_____(36)

Do you usually bring up any phlegm from your chest during the day or at night? (Accept twice or more.)_____Yes____No_____(37)

If 'Yes' to either question (36) or (37):

Do you bring up phlegm like this on most days for as much as three months each year?_____Yes____No_____(38)

If 'Yes' to question (33) or (38):

(cough)

How long have you had this phlegm?   (1)   ☐ 2 years or less   (39)
(Write in number of years   (2)   ☐ More than 2 years-9 years

                                     (3)   ☐ 10-19 years

                                     (4)   ☐ 20+ years

†These words are for subjects who work at night

D. CHEST ILLNESSES

In the past three years, have you had a period   (1)   ☐ No   (40)
of (increased) †cough and phlegm lasting for
3 weeks or more?_____(2)   ☐ Yes, only one period

                                     (3)   ☐ Yes, two or more periods

†For subjects who usually have phlegm

During the past 3 years have you had any chest illness which has kept you off work, indoors at home or in bed? (For as long as one week, flu?)   Yes____No_____(41)

If 'Yes' to (41):   Did you bring up (more) phlegm than usual in any of these illnesses?   Yes____No_____(42)

If 'Yes' to (42):   During the past three years have you had:
Only one such illness with increased phlegm?   (1)   ☐   (43)

More than one such illness: (2)   ☐   (44)

                                 Br. Grade_____

E. TIGHTNESS

Does your chest ever feel tight or your breathing become difficult?_____Yes_____No_____(45)

Is your chest tight or your breathing difficult on any particular day
of the week? (after a week or 10 days away from the mill) _____Yes_____No_____(46)

	(3)	(4)	(5)	(6)	(7)	(8)
If 'Yes': Which day? Mon.	Tues.	Wed.	Thur.	Fri.	Sat.	Sun.	(47)

(1) (2)
Sometimes Always

If 'Yes' Monday At what time on Monday does your chest   1 ☐ Before entering the mill   (48)
feel tight or your breathing difficult?

2 ☐ After entering the mill

(Ask only if NO to Question (45)

In the past, has your chest ever been tight or your breathing
difficult on any particular day of the week?_____Yes_____No_____(49)

	(3)	(4)	(5)	(6)	(7)	(8)
If 'Yes': Which day? Mon.	Tues.	Wed.	Thur.	Fri.	Sat.	Sun.	(50)

(1) (2)
Sometimes Always

F. BREATHLESSNESS

If disabled from walking by any condition other than
heart or lung disease put "X" here and leave
questions (52-60) unasked.   ☐   (51)

Are you ever troubled by shortness of breath, when hurrying on the
level or walking up a slight hill?_____Yes_____No_____(52)

If 'No', grade is 1. If 'Yes', proceed to next question

Do you get short of breath walking with other people at an
ordinary pace on the level?_____Yes_____No_____(53)

If 'No', grade is 2. If 'Yes', proceed to next question

Do you have to stop for breath when walking at your own pace
on the level?_____Yes_____No_____(54)

If 'No', grade is 3. If 'Yes', proceed to next question

Are you short of breath on washing or dressing?_____Yes_____No_____(55)

If 'No', grade is 4. If 'Yes', grade is 5.

Dyspnea Grd._____(56)

ON MONDAYS

Are you ever troubled by shortness of breath, when hurrying on the
level or walking up a slight hill?_____Yes_____No_____(57)

If 'No', grade is 1. If 'Yes', proceed to next question

Do you get short of breath walking with other people at an ordinary
pace on the level?_____Yes_____No_____(58)

If 'No', grade is 2. If 'Yes', proceed to next question

Do you have to stop for breath when walking at your own
pace on the level? _____Yes_____No_____(59)

If 'No', grade is 3. If 'Yes', proceed to next question

Are you short of breath on washing or dressing?_____Yes_____No_____(60)

If 'No', grade is 4. If 'Yes', grade is 5

B. Grd._____(61)

G. **OTHER ILLNESSES AND ALLERGY HISTORY**

Do you have a heart condition for which you are under a doctor's care? _____ Yes _____ No ___ (62)

Have you ever had asthma?   Yes   No   (63)

If 'Yes', did it begin   (1) ☐ Before age 30

                          (2) ☐ After age 30

If 'Yes' before 30 did you have asthma before ever going to work in
a textile mill? _____Yes _____ No ____ (64)

Have you ever had hay fever or other allergies (other than above)? _____Yes _____ No ____ (65)

H. **TOBACCO SMOKING***

Do you smoke?

Record 'Yes' if regular smoker up to one month ago (Cigarettes, cigar
or pipe) _____Yes _____ No_____ (66)

If 'No' to (63)

Have you ever smoked? (Cigarettes, cigars, pipe. Record 'No' if subject _____Yes ___ ___ No_____ (67)
has never smoked as much as one cigarette a day, or 1 oz of tobacco
a month, for as long as one year.)

If 'Yes' to (63) or (64), what have you smoked and for how many years?
(Write in specific number of years in the appropriate square)

	(1) (<5)	(2) (5-9)	(3) (10-14)	(4) (15-19)	(5) (20-24)	(6) (25-29)	(7) (30-34)	(8) (35-39)	(9) (>40)	
Years										
Cigarettes										(68)
Pipe										(69)
Cigars										(70)

If cigarettes, how many packs per day?   (1) ☐ less than 1/2 pack   (71)
(Write in number of cigarettes)   (2) ☐ 1/2 pack, but less than 1 pack
                                                      (3) ☐ 1 pack, but less than 1 1/2 packs
                                                      (4) ☐ 1-1/2 packs or more

Number of pack years: _____ (72,73)

If an ex smoker (cigarettes, cigar or pipe), how long since you stopped? _____ (74)
(Write in number of years)

                                                      (1) ☐ 0-1 year
                                                      (2) ☐ 1-4 years
                                                      (3) ☐ 5-9 years
                                                      (4) ☐ 10+ years

*Have you changed your smoking habits since last interview? If yes, specify what changes.

I. **OCCUPATIONAL HISTORY****

Have you ever worked in: A foundry? (As long as one year) _____Yes_____No ___ (75)

                          Stone or mineral mining, quarrying or processing?
                          (As long as one year) ___ ._____Yes_____No ___.__(76)

                          Asbestos milling or processing? (Ever) _____Yes _____ No_____(77)

                          Other dusts, fumes or smoke? If yes, specify ___ ___Yes_____ .No_____ (78)

                          Type of exposure _____

                          Length of exposure _____

**Ask only on first interview.

At what age did you first go to work in a textile mill? (Write in specific age in appropriate
square)

	(1) <20	(2) 20-24	(3) 25-29	(4) 30-34	(5) 35-39	(6) 40+

When you first worked in a textile mill, did you work with (1) ☐ Cotton or cotton blend   (79)

                                                            (2) ☐ Synthetic or wool   (80)

APPENDIX B-II

Respiratory Questionnaire
for
Non-Textile Workers for the
Cotton Industry

Identification No.	Interviewer Code

Location	Date of Interview

A. IDENTIFICATION

1. NAME (Last) (First) (Middle Initial)	3. PHONE NUMBER AREA CODE ( ) NO.	4 SOCIAL SECURITY # (optional see below)
2. CURRENT ADDRESS (Number, Street, or Rural Route, City or Town, County, State, Zip Code)	5. BIRTHDATE (Mo., Day, Yr.)	6. AGE LAST BIRTHDAY
	7. SEX 1 ☐ Male 2 ☐ Female	
	8. ETHNIC GROUP OR ANCESTRY 1. ☐ White, not of Hispanic Origin 2. ☐ Black, not of Hispanic Origin 3. ☐ Hispanic 4. ☐ American Indian or Alaskan Native 5. ☐ Asian or Pacific Islander 6. ☐ Other: _____	
9. STANDING HEIGHT _____ (cm)	10. WEIGHT _____	11. WORK SHIFT 1st ☐ 2nd ☐ 3rd ☐

12. PRESENT WORK AREA
Please indicate primary assigned work area and percent of time spent at that site. If at other locations, please indicate and note percent of time for each.

PRIMARY WORK AREA	
SPECIFIC JOB	

13. APPROPRIATE INDUSTRY

1 ☐ Garnetting   3 ☐ Cotton Warehouse   5 ☐ Cotton Classification

2 ☐ Cottonseed Oil Mill   4 ☐ Utilization   6 ☐ Cotton Ginning

(Furnishing your Social Security number is voluntary. Your refusal to provide this number will not affect any right, benefit, or privilege to which you would be entitled if you did provide your Social Security number. Your Social Security number is being requested since it will permit use in future determinations in statistical research studies.)

B. OCCUPATIONAL HISTORY TABLE

Complete the following table showing the entire work history of the individual from present to initial employment. Sporadic, part-time periods of employment, each of no significant duration, should be grouped if possible.

INDUSTRY AND LOCATION	TENURE OF EMPLOYMENT		SPECIFIC OCCUPATION	AVERAGE NO. DAYS WORKED PER WEEK	HAZARDOUS HEALTH EXPOSURE ASSOCIATED WITH WORK		
	FROM 19___	TO 19___			YES	NO	IF YES, DESCRIBE

C. SYMPTOMS

Use actual wording of each question. Put X in appropriate square after each question. When in doubt record "No".

COUGH

1. Do you usually cough first thing in the morning?
   (on getting up)*
   (Count a cough with first smoke or on
   "first going out of doors". Exclude
   clearing throat or a single cough.)   1 ☐ Yes   2 ☐ No

2. Do you usually cough during the day or at night?   1 ☐ Yes   2 ☐ No
   (Ignore an occasional cough.)

If YES to either question 1 or 2:

3. Do you cough like this on most days for as much as
   three months a year?   1 ☐ Yes   2 ☐ No   9 ☐ NA

4. Do you cough on any particular day of the week?   1 ☐ Yes   2 ☐ No

If YES:

5. Which day? Mon.   Tue.   Wed.   Thur.   Fri.   Sat.   Sun.   _____

PHLEGM

6. Do you usually bring up any phlegm from your
   chest first thing in the morning? (on getting
   up)* (Count phlegm with the first smoke or on
   "first going out of doors." Exclude phlegm
   from the nose. Count swallowed phlegm.)   1 ☐ Yes   2 ☐ No

7. Do you usually bring up any phlegm from your
   chest during the day or at night?
   (Accept twice or more.)   1 ☐ Yes   2 ☐ No

If YES to either question 6 or 7:

8. Do you bring up phlegm like this on most days
   for as much as three months each year?   1 ☐ Yes   2 ☐ No

If YES to question 3 or 8:

9. How long have you had this phlegm? (cough)   (1) ☐ 2 years or less
   (Write in number of years)
   (2) ☐ More than 2 years - 9 years

   (3) ☐ 10-19 years

*These words are for subjects who work at night   (4) ☐ 20+ years

CHEST ILLNESS

10. In the past three years, have you had a   (1) ☐ No
    period of (increased) cough and phlegm
    lasting for 3 weeks or more?   (2) ☐ Yes, only one period

                                                   (3) ☐ Yes, two or more periods

For subjects who usually have phlegm:

11. During the past 3 years have you had any chest   1 ☐ Yes   2 ☐ No
    illness which has kept you off work, indoors
    at home or in bed? (For as long as one week, flu?)

If YES to 11:

12. Did you bring up (more) phelgm than usual in any   1 ☐ Yes   2 ☐ No
    of these illnesses?

If YES to 12: During the past three years have you had:

13. Only one such illness with increased phelgm?   1 ☐ Yes   2 ☐ No

14. More than one such illness: 1 ☐ Yes   2 ☐ No

                                               Br. Brade _____

TIGHTNESS

15. Does your chest ever feel tight or your   1 ☐ Yes   2 ☐ No
    breathing become difficult?

16. Is your chest tight or your breathing difficult   1 ☐ Yes   2 ☐ No
    on any particular day of the week? (after a
    week or 10 days away from the mill)
                              (3)   (4)   (5)   (6)   (7)   (8)
17. If YES, Which day? Mon. ╱Tues.   Wed.   Thur.   Fri.   Sat.   Sun.
                         (1) ╲   (2)
                         Sometimes Always

18. If YES Monday: At what time on Monday does your chest   ☐ Before entering mill
             feel tight or your breathing difficult?
                                                            ☐ After entering mill

(ASK ONLY IF NO TO QUESTION 15)

19. In the past, has your chest ever been tight or   1 ☐ Yes   2 ☐ No
    your breathing difficult on any particular day of
    the week?
                              (3)   (4)   (5)   (6)   (7)   (8)
20. If YES, Which day? Mon. ╱Tues.   Wed.   Thur.   Fri.   Sat.   Sun.
                         (1) ╱   ╲ (2)
                         Sometimes Always

BREATHLESSNESS

21. If disabled from walking by any condition other than heart or lung disease put "X" in the space and leave questions (22-30) unasked. ▱

22. Are you ever troubled by shortness of breath, when hurrying on the level or walking up a slight hill? 1 ▱ Yes 2 ▱ No

   If NO, grade is 1. If YES, proceed to next question

23. Do you get short of breath walking with other people at an ordinary pace on the level? 1 ▱ Yes 2 ▱ No

   If NO, grade is 2. If YES, proceed to next question

24. Do you have to stop for breath when walking at your own pace on the level? 1 ▱ Yes 2 ▱ No

   If NO, grade is 3. If YES, proceed to next question

25. Are you short of breath on washing or dressing? 1 ▱ Yes 2 ▱ No

   If NO, grade is 4. If YES, grade is 5.

26. Dyspnea Grd. _____

ON MONDAYS:

27. Are you ever troubled by shortness of breath, when hurrying on the level or walking up a slight hill? 1 ▱ Yes 2 ▱ No

   If NO, grade is 1. If YES, proceed to next question

28. Do you get short of breath walking with other people at an ordinary pace on the level? 1 ▱ Yes 2 ▱ No

   If NO, grade is 2. If YES, proceed to next question

29. Do you have to stop for breath when walking at your own pace on the level? 1 ▱ Yes 2 ▱ No

   If NO, grade is 3. If YES, proceed to next question

30. Are you short of breath on washing or dressing? 1 ▱ Yes 2 ▱ No

   If NO, grade is 4. If YES, grade is 5

31. B. Grd. _____

OTHER ILLNESSES AND ALLERGY HISTORY

32. Do you have a heart condition for which you are under a doctor's care? 1 ▱ Yes 2 ▱ No

345

OTHER ILLNESSES AND ALLERGY HISTORY CONTINUED:

33. **Have you ever had asthma?**   1 ☐ Yes   2 ☐ No

    If yes, did it begin: (1) Before age 30 ☐

                     (2) After age 30   ☐

34. **If yes before 30: did you have asthma before**
    ever going to work in a textile mill?   1 ☐ Yes   2 ☐ No

35. **Have you ever had hay fever or other allergies**
    (other than above)?   1 ☐ Yes   2 ☐ No

TOBACCO SMOKING

36. **Do you smoke?**   1 ☐ Yes   2 ☐ No
    Record Yes if regular smoker up to one
    month ago. (Cigarettes, cigar or pipe)

  If NO to (33).

37. **Have you ever smoked? (Cigarettes, cigars,**   1 ☐ Yes   2 ☐ No
    pipe. Record NO if subject has never smoked
    as much as one cigarette a day, or 1 oz. of
    tobacco a month, for as long as one year.)

  If Yes to (33) or (34); what have you smoked for how
many years? (Write in specific number of years in
the appropriate square)

		(1)	(2)	(3)	(4)	(5)	(6)	(7)	(8)	(9)
	Years	(<5)	(5-9)	(10-14)	(15-19)	(20-24)	(25-29)	(30-34)	(35-39)	(>40)
38.	Cigarettes									
39.	Pipe									
40.	Cigars									

41. **If cigarettes, how many packs per day?**   ☐ Less than 1/2 pack
    Write in number of cigarettes   ☐ 1/2 pack, but less than 1 pack
    ————————   ☐ 1 pack, but less than 1 1/2 packs
                          ☐ 1-1/2 packs or more

42. **Number of pack years:**   ————————

43. **If an ex-smoker (cigarettes, cigar or pipe), how**   ————————
    long since you stopped? (Write in number of years.)
                                ☐ 0-1 year
                                ☐ 1-4 years
                                ☐ 5-9 years
                                ☐ 10+ years

OCCUPATIONAL HISTORY

Have you ever worked in:

44. A foundry? (As long as one year) 1 ☐ Yes 2 ☐ No

45. Stone or mineral mining, quarrying or processing? (As long as one year) 1 ☐ Yes 2 ☐ No

46. Asbestos milling or processing? (Ever) 1 ☐ Yes 2 ☐ No

47. Cotton or cotton blend mill? (For controls only) 1 ☐ Yes 2 ☐ No

48. Other dusts, fumes or smoke? If yes, specify. 1 ☐ Yes 2 ☐ No

Type of exposure _____

Length of exposure _____

347

APPENDIX B-III

ABBREVIATED RESPIRATORY QUESTIONNAIRE

A. IDENTIFICATION DATA

PLANT_____ SOCIAL SECURITY NO. _____

                                                                DAY   MONTH   YEAR
                                                               (figures) (last 2 digits)

NAME _____ DATE OF INTERVIEW_____
     (Surname)

_____ DATE OF BIRTH_____
     (First Names)   M   F

ADDRESS _____ AGE_____ (8,9) SEX _____ (10)

_____ RACE | W | N | IND. | OTHER | (11)

INTERVIEWER: 1   2   3   4   5   6   7   8   (12)

WORK SHIFT: 1st_____ 2nd_____3rd_____(13)   STANDING HEIGHT_____(14,15)

PRESENT WORK AREA   WEIGHT_____(16,18)

If working in more than one specified work area, X area where most of the work shift is spent. If "other," but spending 25% of the work shift in one of the specified work areas, classify in that work area. If carding department employee, check area within that department where most of the work shift is spent (if in doubt, check "throughout"). For work areas such as spinning and weaving where many work rooms may be involved, be sure to check the specific work room to which the employee is assigned — if he works in more than one work room within a department classify as 7 (all) for ..... department.

	Workroom Number	(19) Open	(20) Pick	Area	(21) Card #1	(22) #2	(23) Spin	(24) Wind	(25) Twist	(26) Spool	(27) Warp	(28) Slash	(29) Weave	(30) Other
AT RISK (cotton & cotton blend)	1			Cards										
	2			Draw										
	3			Comb										
	4			Rove										
	5			Thru Out										
	6													
	7 (all)													
Control (synthetic & wool)	8													
Ex-Worker (cotton)	9													

Use actual wording of each question. Put X in appropriate square after each question. When in doubt record 'No'. When no square, circle appropriate answer.

B. COUGH

(on getting up)†
Do you usually cough first thing in the morning?_____Yes____ No____ ___(31)
(Count a cough with first smoke or on "first going out of doors."
Exclude clearing throat or a single cough.)

Do you usually cough during the day or at night?_____Yes____ No_____ (32)
(Ignore an occasional cough.)

If 'Yes' to either question (31-32):

Do you cough like this on most days for as much as three months a year?_____Yes____ No_____ (33)

Do you cough on any particular day of the week?   Yes____ No_____ (34)

          (1)   (2)   (3)   (4)   (5)   (6)   (7)

If 'Yes': Which day?   Mon.   Tues.   Wed.   Thur.   Fri.   Sat   Sun.   (35)

C. PHLEGM or alternative word to suit local custom.

                               (on getting up)†
Do you usually bring up any phlegm from your chest first thing in
the morning? (Count phlegm with the first smoke or on "first going
out of doors." Exclude phlegm from the nose. Count swallowed
phlegm.)_____Yes____ No_____(36)

Do you usually bring up any phlegm from your chest during the day or at
night? (Accept twice or more.)_____Yes____ No_____(37)

If 'Yes' to either question (36) or (37):

Do you bring up phlegm like this on most days for as much as three
months each year?_____Yes____ No____ ____(38)

If 'Yes' to question (33) or (38):

                 (cough)   (1)   ☐ 2 years or less
How long have you had this phlegm?
          (Write in number of years   (2)   ☐ More than 2 years-9 years

                                  (3)   ☐ 10-19 years

                                  (4)   ☐ 20+ years

†These words are for subjects who work at night

D. TIGHTNESS

Does your chest ever feel tight or your breathing become difficult?_____Yes_____ No____ (39)

Is your chest tight or your breathing difficult on any particular day
of the week? (after a week or 10 days away from the mill)_____Yes_____ No____ (40)

             (3)   (4)   (5)   (6)   (7)   (8)
If 'Yes': Which day? Mon   Tues   Wed   Thur.   Fri.   Sat.   Sun.
           (1)   (2)   (41)
     Sometimes   Always

If 'Yes' Monday: At what time on Monday does your chest   1 ☐ Before entering the mill   (42)
                    feel tight or your breathing difficult?
                                      2 ☐ After entering the mill

(Ask only if NO to Question (45))

In the past, has your chest ever been tight or your breathing
difficult on any particular day of the week?_____Yes_____ No____ (43)

             (3)   (4)   (5)   (6)   (7)   (8)
If 'Yes': Which day? Mon   Tues   Wed   Thur   Fri.   Sat.   Sun   (44)
           (1)   (2)
     Sometimes   Always

E. TOBACCO SMOKING

*Have you changed your smoking habits since last interview?
If yes, specify what changes.

APPENDIX C—Spirometry Prediction Tables for Normal Males and Females

TABLE 1. PREDICTED FVC FOR MALES (KNUDSON, ET AL.: AM. REV. RESPIR. DIS. 1976, 113, 587.)

AGE

HT	17	19	21	23	25	27	29	31	33	35	37	39	41	43	45	47	49	51	53	55	57	59	61	63	65
60.0	3.44	3.59	3.75	3.90	3.72	3.66	3.60	3.55	3.49	3.43	3.37	3.32	3.26	3.20	3.14	3.08	3.03	2.97	2.91	2.85	2.79	2.74	2.68	2.62	2.56
60.5	3.50	3.66	3.81	3.96	3.80	3.74	3.68	3.63	3.57	3.51	3.45	3.40	3.34	3.28	3.22	3.16	3.11	3.05	2.99	2.93	2.87	2.82	2.76	2.70	2.64
61.0	3.56	3.72	3.88	4.03	3.89	3.83	3.77	3.72	3.66	3.60	3.54	3.49	3.43	3.37	3.31	3.25	3.20	3.14	3.08	3.02	2.96	2.90	2.84	2.79	2.73
61.5	3.63	3.78	3.94	4.09	3.97	3.91	3.85	3.80	3.74	3.68	3.62	3.57	3.51	3.45	3.39	3.33	3.28	3.22	3.16	3.10	3.04	2.98	2.93	2.87	2.81
62.0	3.69	3.85	4.00	4.15	4.05	3.99	3.93	3.88	3.82	3.76	3.70	3.65	3.59	3.53	3.47	3.41	3.36	3.30	3.24	3.18	3.12	3.07	3.01	2.95	2.89
62.5	3.76	3.91	4.07	4.22	4.13	4.07	4.01	3.96	3.90	3.84	3.78	3.73	3.67	3.61	3.55	3.49	3.44	3.38	3.32	3.26	3.20	3.15	3.09	3.03	2.97
63.0	3.82	3.97	4.13	4.28	4.22	4.16	4.10	4.05	3.99	3.93	3.87	3.82	3.76	3.70	3.64	3.58	3.53	3.47	3.41	3.35	3.29	3.23	3.17	3.12	3.06
63.5	3.88	4.04	4.19	4.34	4.30	4.24	4.18	4.13	4.07	4.01	3.95	3.90	3.84	3.78	3.72	3.66	3.61	3.55	3.49	3.43	3.37	3.31	3.26	3.20	3.14
64.0	3.95	4.10	4.26	4.41	4.38	4.32	4.26	4.21	4.15	4.09	4.03	3.98	3.92	3.86	3.80	3.74	3.69	3.63	3.57	3.51	3.45	3.40	3.34	3.28	3.22
64.5	4.01	4.17	4.32	4.47	4.46	4.40	4.34	4.29	4.23	4.17	4.11	4.06	4.00	3.94	3.88	3.82	3.77	3.71	3.65	3.59	3.53	3.48	3.42	3.36	3.30
65.0	4.07	4.23	4.39	4.54	4.55	4.49	4.43	4.38	4.32	4.26	4.20	4.15	4.09	4.03	3.97	3.91	3.86	3.80	3.74	3.68	3.62	3.56	3.50	3.45	3.39
65.5	4.14	4.29	4.45	4.60	4.63	4.57	4.51	4.46	4.40	4.34	4.28	4.23	4.17	4.11	4.05	3.99	3.94	3.88	3.82	3.76	3.70	3.64	3.59	3.53	3.47
66.0	4.20	4.36	4.51	4.66	4.71	4.65	4.59	4.54	4.48	4.42	4.36	4.31	4.25	4.19	4.13	4.07	4.02	3.96	3.90	3.84	3.78	3.73	3.67	3.61	3.55
66.5	4.26	4.42	4.58	4.73	4.80	4.74	4.68	4.63	4.57	4.51	4.45	4.40	4.34	4.28	4.22	4.16	4.11	4.05	3.99	3.93	3.87	3.81	3.75	3.69	3.64
67.0	4.33	4.48	4.64	4.79	4.88	4.82	4.76	4.71	4.65	4.59	4.53	4.48	4.42	4.36	4.30	4.24	4.19	4.13	4.07	4.01	3.95	3.89	3.83	3.78	3.72
67.5	4.39	4.55	4.70	4.85	4.96	4.90	4.84	4.79	4.73	4.67	4.61	4.56	4.50	4.44	4.38	4.32	4.27	4.21	4.15	4.09	4.03	3.97	3.92	3.86	3.80
68.0	4.45	4.61	4.77	4.92	5.04	4.98	4.92	4.87	4.81	4.75	4.69	4.64	4.58	4.52	4.46	4.40	4.35	4.29	4.23	4.17	4.11	4.06	4.00	3.94	3.88
68.5	4.52	4.67	4.83	4.98	5.13	5.07	5.01	4.96	4.90	4.84	4.78	4.73	4.67	4.61	4.55	4.49	4.44	4.38	4.32	4.26	4.20	4.14	4.08	4.02	3.97
69.0	4.58	4.74	4.89	5.04	5.21	5.15	5.09	5.04	4.98	4.92	4.86	4.81	4.75	4.69	4.63	4.57	4.52	4.46	4.40	4.34	4.28	4.22	4.16	4.11	4.05
69.5	4.64	4.80	4.96	5.11	5.29	5.23	5.17	5.12	5.06	5.00	4.94	4.89	4.83	4.77	4.71	4.65	4.60	4.54	4.48	4.42	4.36	4.30	4.25	4.19	4.13
70.0	4.71	4.86	5.02	5.17	5.37	5.31	5.25	5.20	5.14	5.08	5.02	4.97	4.91	4.85	4.79	4.73	4.68	4.62	4.56	4.50	4.44	4.39	4.33	4.27	4.21
70.5	4.77	4.93	5.08	5.23	5.46	5.40	5.34	5.29	5.23	5.17	5.11	5.06	5.00	4.94	4.88	4.82	4.77	4.71	4.65	4.59	4.53	4.47	4.41	4.35	4.30
71.0	4.83	4.99	5.15	5.30	5.54	5.48	5.42	5.37	5.31	5.25	5.19	5.14	5.08	5.02	4.96	4.90	4.85	4.79	4.73	4.67	4.61	4.55	4.49	4.44	4.38
71.5	4.90	5.05	5.21	5.36	5.62	5.56	5.50	5.45	5.39	5.33	5.27	5.22	5.16	5.10	5.04	4.98	4.93	4.87	4.81	4.75	4.69	4.63	4.58	4.52	4.46
72.0	4.96	5.12	5.27	5.42	5.70	5.64	5.58	5.53	5.47	5.41	5.35	5.30	5.24	5.18	5.12	5.06	5.01	4.95	4.89	4.83	4.77	4.72	4.66	4.60	4.54
72.5	5.03	5.18	5.34	5.49	5.79	5.73	5.67	5.62	5.56	5.50	5.44	5.39	5.33	5.27	5.21	5.15	5.10	5.04	4.98	4.92	4.86	4.80	4.74	4.68	4.63
73.0	5.09	5.24	5.40	5.55	5.87	5.81	5.75	5.70	5.64	5.58	5.52	5.47	5.41	5.35	5.29	5.23	5.18	5.12	5.06	5.00	4.94	4.88	4.82	4.76	4.71
73.5	5.15	5.31	5.46	5.61	5.95	5.89	5.83	5.78	5.72	5.66	5.60	5.55	5.49	5.43	5.37	5.31	5.26	5.20	5.14	5.08	5.02	4.96	4.91	4.85	4.79
74.0	5.22	5.37	5.53	5.68	6.04	5.98	5.92	5.87	5.81	5.75	5.69	5.64	5.58	5.52	5.46	5.40	5.35	5.29	5.23	5.17	5.11	5.05	4.99	4.93	4.88
74.5	5.28	5.44	5.59	5.74	6.12	6.06	6.00	5.95	5.89	5.83	5.77	5.72	5.66	5.60	5.54	5.48	5.43	5.37	5.31	5.25	5.19	5.13	5.07	5.01	4.96
75.0	5.34	5.50	5.65	5.80	6.20	6.14	6.08	6.03	5.97	5.91	5.85	5.80	5.74	5.68	5.62	5.56	5.51	5.45	5.39	5.33	5.27	5.21	5.15	5.10	5.04
75.5	5.41	5.56	5.72	5.87	6.28	6.22	6.16	6.11	6.05	5.99	5.93	5.88	5.82	5.76	5.70	5.64	5.59	5.53	5.47	5.41	5.35	5.29	5.24	5.18	5.12
76.0	5.47	5.63	5.78	5.93	6.36	6.30	6.24	6.19	6.13	6.07	6.01	5.96	5.90	5.84	5.78	5.72	5.67	5.61	5.55	5.49	5.43	5.38	5.32	5.26	5.20
76.5	5.53	5.69	5.85	6.00	6.45	6.39	6.33	6.28	6.22	6.16	6.10	6.05	5.99	5.93	5.87	5.81	5.76	5.70	5.64	5.58	5.52	5.46	5.40	5.34	5.29
77.0	5.60	5.75	5.91	6.06	6.53	6.47	6.41	6.36	6.30	6.24	6.18	6.13	6.07	6.01	5.95	5.89	5.84	5.78	5.72	5.66	5.60	5.54	5.48	5.43	5.37
77.5	5.66	5.82	5.97	6.12	6.61	6.55	6.49	6.44	6.38	6.32	6.26	6.21	6.15	6.09	6.03	5.97	5.92	5.86	5.80	5.74	5.68	5.63	5.57	5.51	5.45
78.0	5.72	5.88	6.04	6.19	6.69	6.63	6.57	6.52	6.46	6.40	6.34	6.29	6.23	6.17	6.11	6.05	6.00	5.94	5.88	5.82	5.76	5.71	5.65	5.59	5.53
78.5	5.79	5.94	6.10	6.25	6.78	6.72	6.66	6.61	6.55	6.49	6.43	6.38	6.32	6.26	6.20	6.14	6.09	6.03	5.97	5.91	5.85	5.79	5.73	5.67	5.62
79.0	5.85	6.01	6.16	6.31	6.86	6.80	6.74	6.69	6.63	6.57	6.51	6.46	6.40	6.34	6.28	6.22	6.17	6.11	6.05	5.99	5.93	5.87	5.81	5.76	5.70
79.5	5.91	6.07	6.23	6.38	6.94	6.88	6.82	6.77	6.71	6.65	6.59	6.54	6.48	6.42	6.36	6.30	6.25	6.19	6.13	6.07	6.01	5.96	5.90	5.84	5.78
80.0	5.98	6.13	6.29	6.44	7.02	6.96	6.90	6.85	6.79	6.73	6.67	6.62	6.56	6.50	6.44	6.38	6.33	6.27	6.21	6.15	6.09	6.04	5.98	5.92	5.86
80.5	6.04	6.20	6.35	6.50	7.11	7.05	6.99	6.94	6.88	6.82	6.76	6.71	6.65	6.59	6.53	6.47	6.42	6.36	6.30	6.24	6.18	6.12	6.06	6.01	5.95
81.0	6.10	6.26	6.42	6.57	7.19	7.13	7.07	7.02	6.96	6.90	6.84	6.79	6.73	6.67	6.61	6.55	6.50	6.44	6.38	6.32	6.26	6.20	6.15	6.09	6.03
81.5	6.17	6.32	6.48	6.63	7.27	7.21	7.15	7.10	7.04	6.98	6.92	6.87	6.81	6.75	6.69	6.63	6.58	6.52	6.46	6.40	6.34	6.29	6.23	6.17	6.11
82.0	6.23	6.39	6.54	6.69	7.35	7.29	7.23	7.18	7.12	7.06	7.00	6.95	6.89	6.83	6.77	6.71	6.66	6.60	6.54	6.48	6.42	6.37	6.31	6.25	6.19
82.5	6.30	6.45	6.61	6.76	7.44	7.38	7.32	7.27	7.21	7.15	7.09	7.04	6.98	6.92	6.86	6.80	6.75	6.69	6.63	6.57	6.51	6.45	6.39	6.33	6.28
83.0	6.36	6.51	6.67	6.82	7.52	7.46	7.40	7.35	7.29	7.23	7.17	7.12	7.06	7.00	6.94	6.88	6.83	6.77	6.71	6.65	6.59	6.53	6.48	6.41	6.36
83.5	6.42	6.58	6.73	6.88	7.60	7.54	7.48	7.43	7.37	7.31	7.25	7.20	7.14	7.08	7.02	6.96	6.91	6.85	6.79	6.73	6.67	6.62	6.56	6.50	6.44
84.0	6.49	6.64	6.80	6.95	7.68	7.62	7.56	7.51	7.45	7.39	7.33	7.28	7.22	7.16	7.10	7.04	6.99	6.93	6.87	6.81	6.75	6.70	6.64	6.58	6.52
84.5	6.55	6.71	6.86	7.01	7.77	7.71	7.65	7.60	7.54	7.48	7.42	7.37	7.31	7.25	7.19	7.13	7.08	7.02	6.96	6.90	6.84	6.78	6.72	6.66	6.61
85.0	6.61	6.77	6.92	7.07	7.85	7.79	7.73	7.68	7.62	7.56	7.50	7.45	7.39	7.33	7.27	7.21	7.16	7.10	7.04	6.98	6.92	6.86	6.81	6.75	6.69

TABLE 2. PREDICTED FEV_1 FOR MALES (KNUDSON, ET AL: AM. REV. RESPIR. DIS. 1976, 113, 587.)

HT \ AGE	17	19	21	23	25	27	29	31	33	35	37	39	41	43	45	47	49	51	53	55	57	59	61	63	65
60.0	2.97	3.06	3.15	3.24	3.05	2.99	2.94	2.88	2.83	2.78	2.72	2.67	2.61	2.56	2.51	2.45	2.40	2.34	2.29	2.24	2.18	2.13	2.07	2.02	1.97
60.5	3.03	3.11	3.20	3.30	3.12	3.06	3.00	2.95	2.90	2.84	2.79	2.73	2.68	2.63	2.56	2.52	2.46	2.41	2.36	2.30	2.25	2.19	2.14	2.09	2.03
61.0	3.08	3.17	3.26	3.35	3.18	3.12	3.07	3.02	2.96	2.91	2.85	2.80	2.75	2.69	2.64	2.58	2.53	2.48	2.42	2.37	2.31	2.26	2.21	2.14	2.10
61.5	3.14	3.23	3.32	3.41	3.24	3.19	3.14	3.08	3.03	2.97	2.92	2.85	2.81	2.76	2.69	2.65	2.60	2.54	2.49	2.43	2.38	2.32	2.27	2.22	2.16
62.0	3.20	3.29	3.38	3.47	3.31	3.26	3.20	3.15	3.09	3.04	2.99	2.93	2.88	2.82	2.77	2.72	2.66	2.61	2.55	2.50	2.45	2.39	2.34	2.28	2.23
62.5	3.26	3.35	3.44	3.53	3.38	3.32	3.27	3.21	3.16	3.11	3.05	2.99	2.95	2.88	2.82	2.78	2.73	2.68	2.62	2.57	2.51	2.45	2.41	2.35	2.30
63.0	3.32	3.41	3.50	3.59	3.44	3.39	3.34	3.28	3.22	3.17	3.12	3.07	3.01	2.96	2.90	2.85	2.80	2.74	2.69	2.63	2.58	2.53	2.47	2.42	2.36
63.5	3.38	3.47	3.56	3.65	3.51	3.46	3.40	3.35	3.29	3.24	3.18	3.13	3.08	3.02	2.97	2.92	2.86	2.81	2.75	2.70	2.65	2.59	2.54	2.48	2.43
64.0	3.43	3.52	3.61	3.70	3.58	3.52	3.47	3.41	3.36	3.31	3.25	3.20	3.14	3.09	3.04	2.98	2.93	2.87	2.82	2.77	2.71	2.66	2.60	2.55	2.50
64.5	3.49	3.58	3.67	3.76	3.64	3.59	3.53	3.47	3.43	3.37	3.31	3.26	3.21	3.16	3.10	3.05	3.00	2.94	2.89	2.83	2.78	2.72	2.67	2.62	2.56
65.0	3.55	3.64	3.73	3.82	3.71	3.65	3.60	3.53	3.49	3.44	3.38	3.33	3.28	3.22	3.17	3.11	3.06	3.01	2.95	2.90	2.84	2.79	2.74	2.68	2.63
65.5	3.61	3.70	3.79	3.88	3.77	3.72	3.67	3.60	3.56	3.50	3.45	3.40	3.34	3.29	3.23	3.18	3.13	3.07	3.02	2.96	2.91	2.86	2.80	2.75	2.69
66.0	3.67	3.76	3.85	3.94	3.84	3.79	3.73	3.67	3.62	3.57	3.52	3.46	3.41	3.35	3.30	3.25	3.19	3.14	3.08	3.03	2.98	2.92	2.87	2.81	2.76
66.5	3.73	3.82	3.91	4.00	3.91	3.85	3.80	3.73	3.69	3.64	3.58	3.53	3.47	3.42	3.37	3.31	3.26	3.20	3.15	3.10	3.04	2.99	2.93	2.88	2.83
67.0	3.79	3.88	3.97	4.06	3.97	3.92	3.86	3.81	3.76	3.70	3.65	3.59	3.54	3.49	3.43	3.38	3.32	3.27	3.22	3.16	3.11	3.06	3.00	2.95	2.89
67.5	3.84	3.93	4.02	4.11	4.04	3.98	3.93	3.88	3.82	3.77	3.71	3.66	3.61	3.55	3.50	3.44	3.39	3.34	3.28	3.23	3.17	3.12	3.07	3.01	2.96
68.0	3.90	3.99	4.08	4.17	4.10	4.05	4.00	3.94	3.89	3.83	3.78	3.73	3.67	3.62	3.56	3.51	3.46	3.40	3.35	3.28	3.24	3.19	3.13	3.08	3.02
68.5	3.96	4.05	4.14	4.23	4.17	4.12	4.06	4.01	3.95	3.90	3.85	3.78	3.74	3.68	3.62	3.58	3.52	3.47	3.40	3.36	3.31	3.25	3.20	3.14	3.09
69.0	4.02	4.11	4.20	4.29	4.24	4.18	4.13	4.07	4.02	3.97	3.91	3.86	3.80	3.75	3.70	3.64	3.59	3.53	3.48	3.43	3.37	3.32	3.26	3.21	3.16
69.5	4.08	4.17	4.26	4.35	4.30	4.25	4.19	4.14	4.09	4.03	3.98	3.91	3.87	3.82	3.75	3.71	3.65	3.60	3.55	3.49	3.44	3.38	3.33	3.28	3.22
70.0	4.14	4.23	4.32	4.41	4.37	4.31	4.26	4.21	4.15	4.10	4.04	3.98	3.94	3.88	3.83	3.77	3.72	3.67	3.61	3.56	3.50	3.45	3.40	3.33	3.29
70.5	4.19	4.28	4.37	4.46	4.44	4.38	4.33	4.27	4.22	4.16	4.11	4.04	4.00	3.95	3.88	3.84	3.79	3.72	3.68	3.62	3.57	3.51	3.46	3.41	3.35
71.0	4.25	4.34	4.43	4.52	4.50	4.45	4.39	4.34	4.28	4.23	4.18	4.12	4.07	4.01	3.96	3.91	3.85	3.79	3.74	3.69	3.64	3.58	3.53	3.46	3.42
71.5	4.31	4.40	4.49	4.58	4.57	4.51	4.46	4.40	4.35	4.30	4.24	4.18	4.14	4.08	4.01	3.97	3.92	3.85	3.81	3.76	3.70	3.64	3.59	3.54	3.49
72.0	4.37	4.46	4.55	4.64	4.63	4.58	4.52	4.47	4.42	4.36	4.31	4.25	4.20	4.15	4.09	4.04	3.98	3.92	3.88	3.82	3.77	3.71	3.66	3.61	3.55
72.5	4.43	4.52	4.61	4.70	4.70	4.64	4.59	4.54	4.48	4.43	4.37	4.31	4.27	4.21	4.16	4.10	4.05	3.99	3.94	3.89	3.83	3.77	3.73	3.67	3.62
73.0	4.49	4.58	4.67	4.76	4.76	4.71	4.66	4.60	4.54	4.49	4.44	4.39	4.33	4.28	4.22	4.17	4.12	4.05	4.00	3.95	3.90	3.84	3.79	3.74	3.68
73.5	4.54	4.63	4.72	4.81	4.83	4.78	4.72	4.67	4.61	4.56	4.51	4.45	4.40	4.34	4.29	4.24	4.18	4.12	4.07	4.02	3.97	3.90	3.86	3.80	3.75
74.0	4.60	4.69	4.78	4.87	4.90	4.84	4.79	4.73	4.67	4.63	4.57	4.51	4.46	4.41	4.36	4.30	4.25	4.18	4.14	4.09	4.03	3.97	3.92	3.87	3.82
74.5	4.66	4.75	4.84	4.93	4.96	4.91	4.85	4.80	4.75	4.69	4.64	4.58	4.53	4.47	4.42	4.37	4.31	4.25	4.19	4.15	4.10	4.04	3.99	3.94	3.88
75.0	4.72	4.81	4.90	4.99	5.03	4.97	4.92	4.87	4.81	4.76	4.70	4.64	4.60	4.54	4.49	4.44	4.38	4.32	4.26	4.22	4.16	4.10	4.06	4.00	3.94
75.5	4.78	4.87	4.96	5.05	5.09	5.04	4.98	4.93	4.87	4.82	4.77	4.72	4.66	4.61	4.55	4.50	4.45	4.39	4.33	4.28	4.23	4.18	4.12	4.07	4.01
76.0	4.84	4.93	5.02	5.11	5.16	5.11	5.05	5.00	4.94	4.89	4.84	4.78	4.73	4.67	4.62	4.57	4.51	4.45	4.40	4.35	4.30	4.24	4.19	4.13	4.08
76.5	4.90	4.99	5.08	5.17	5.22	5.17	5.12	5.06	5.01	4.96	4.90	4.84	4.79	4.74	4.68	4.63	4.58	4.52	4.46	4.42	4.36	4.30	4.25	4.20	4.15
77.0	4.95	5.04	5.13	5.22	5.29	5.24	5.18	5.13	5.08	5.02	4.97	4.91	4.86	4.81	4.75	4.70	4.64	4.58	4.54	4.48	4.43	4.37	4.32	4.27	4.21
77.5	5.01	5.10	5.19	5.28	5.35	5.30	5.25	5.20	5.15	5.09	5.03	4.97	4.93	4.87	4.81	4.76	4.71	4.65	4.60	4.55	4.49	4.43	4.39	4.33	4.28
78.0	5.07	5.16	5.25	5.34	5.42	5.37	5.31	5.26	5.21	5.15	5.10	5.05	4.99	4.94	4.88	4.83	4.78	4.72	4.67	4.61	4.56	4.51	4.45	4.40	4.34
78.5	5.13	5.22	5.31	5.40	5.48	5.44	5.38	5.33	5.28	5.22	5.17	5.11	5.06	5.00	4.94	4.90	4.84	4.79	4.73	4.68	4.63	4.56	4.52	4.46	4.41
79.0	5.19	5.28	5.37	5.46	5.55	5.50	5.45	5.39	5.34	5.29	5.23	5.18	5.12	5.07	5.02	4.96	4.91	4.84	4.80	4.75	4.69	4.64	4.58	4.53	4.48
79.5	5.25	5.34	5.43	5.52	5.62	5.57	5.51	5.46	5.41	5.35	5.30	5.23	5.19	5.14	5.07	5.03	4.97	4.91	4.87	4.81	4.76	4.69	4.65	4.60	4.54
80.0	5.30	5.39	5.48	5.57	5.69	5.63	5.58	5.53	5.47	5.42	5.36	5.31	5.26	5.20	5.15	5.09	5.04	4.97	4.93	4.88	4.82	4.77	4.72	4.66	4.61
80.5	5.36	5.45	5.54	5.63	5.75	5.70	5.65	5.59	5.54	5.48	5.43	5.38	5.32	5.27	5.20	5.16	5.11	5.04	5.00	4.94	4.89	4.82	4.78	4.73	4.67
81.0	5.42	5.51	5.60	5.69	5.82	5.77	5.71	5.66	5.60	5.55	5.50	5.43	5.39	5.33	5.28	5.23	5.17	5.11	5.06	5.01	4.96	4.90	4.85	4.79	4.74
81.5	5.48	5.57	5.66	5.75	5.89	5.83	5.78	5.72	5.67	5.62	5.56	5.50	5.45	5.40	5.35	5.29	5.23	5.18	5.13	5.08	5.02	4.97	4.91	4.86	4.81
82.0	5.54	5.63	5.72	5.81	5.96	5.90	5.84	5.79	5.73	5.68	5.63	5.56	5.52	5.47	5.41	5.36	5.30	5.24	5.20	5.14	5.09	5.03	4.98	4.93	4.87
82.5	5.60	5.69	5.78	5.87	6.02	5.96	5.91	5.86	5.80	5.75	5.69	5.64	5.59	5.53	5.48	5.42	5.37	5.32	5.26	5.21	5.15	5.10	5.05	4.99	4.94
83.0	5.65	5.74	5.83	5.92	6.08	6.03	5.98	5.92	5.86	5.81	5.76	5.71	5.65	5.60	5.55	5.49	5.44	5.38	5.33	5.27	5.22	5.15	5.11	5.06	5.00
83.5	5.71	5.80	5.90	5.98	6.15	6.10	6.04	5.99	5.93	5.88	5.83	5.77	5.72	5.66	5.61	5.56	5.50	5.45	5.39	5.34	5.29	5.23	5.18	5.12	5.07
84.0	5.77	5.86	5.95	6.04	6.21	6.16	6.11	6.05	6.00	5.95	5.89	5.83	5.78	5.73	5.68	5.62	5.57	5.51	5.46	5.41	5.35	5.30	5.24	5.19	5.14
84.5	5.83	5.92	6.01	6.10	6.28	6.23	6.17	6.12	6.07	6.01	5.96	5.90	5.85	5.80	5.74	5.69	5.63	5.58	5.53	5.47	5.42	5.36	5.31	5.26	5.20
85.0	5.89	5.98	6.07	6.16	6.36	6.29	6.24	6.19	6.13	6.06	6.02	5.97	5.92	5.86	5.81	5.75	5.70	5.65	5.59	5.54	5.48	5.43	5.38	5.32	5.27

351

TABLE 3. PREDICTED FVC FOR FEMALES (KNUDSON, ET AL.: AM. REV. RESPIR. DIS. 1976, 113, 587.)

AGE

HT	17	19	21	23	25	27	29	31	33	35	37	39	41	43	45	47	49	51	53	55	57	59	61	63	65
52.0	2.45	2.64	2.65	2.61	2.56	2.52	2.47	2.43	2.39	2.34	2.30	2.25	2.21	2.16	2.12	2.08	2.03	1.99	1.95	1.90	1.86	1.81	1.77	1.73	1.68
52.5	2.50	2.68	2.70	2.65	2.61	2.57	2.52	2.48	2.43	2.39	2.35	2.30	2.26	2.21	2.17	2.13	2.08	2.04	2.00	1.95	1.91	1.86	1.82	1.77	1.73
53.0	2.54	2.72	2.74	2.70	2.66	2.61	2.57	2.52	2.48	2.44	2.39	2.35	2.30	2.26	2.21	2.17	2.13	2.08	2.04	2.00	1.95	1.91	1.86	1.82	1.78
53.5	2.58	2.76	2.79	2.75	2.70	2.66	2.62	2.57	2.53	2.48	2.44	2.39	2.35	2.31	2.26	2.22	2.18	2.13	2.09	2.04	2.00	1.95	1.91	1.87	1.82
54.0	2.62	2.81	2.84	2.79	2.75	2.71	2.66	2.62	2.57	2.53	2.49	2.44	2.40	2.35	2.31	2.27	2.22	2.18	2.14	2.09	2.05	2.00	1.96	1.91	1.87
54.5	2.66	2.85	2.89	2.84	2.80	2.75	2.71	2.67	2.62	2.58	2.53	2.49	2.45	2.40	2.36	2.31	2.27	2.23	2.18	2.14	2.09	2.05	2.01	1.96	1.92
55.0	2.71	2.89	2.93	2.89	2.84	2.80	2.76	2.71	2.67	2.62	2.58	2.54	2.49	2.45	2.40	2.36	2.32	2.27	2.23	2.18	2.14	2.10	2.05	2.01	1.96
55.5	2.75	2.93	2.98	2.94	2.89	2.84	2.80	2.76	2.72	2.67	2.63	2.58	2.54	2.50	2.45	2.41	2.36	2.32	2.28	2.23	2.19	2.14	2.10	2.06	2.01
56.0	2.79	2.97	3.03	2.98	2.94	2.89	2.85	2.81	2.76	2.72	2.67	2.63	2.59	2.54	2.50	2.45	2.41	2.37	2.32	2.28	2.23	2.19	2.15	2.10	2.06
56.5	2.83	3.01	3.07	3.03	2.99	2.94	2.90	2.85	2.81	2.77	2.72	2.68	2.63	2.59	2.55	2.50	2.46	2.41	2.37	2.33	2.28	2.23	2.19	2.15	2.11
57.0	2.87	3.06	3.12	3.08	3.03	2.99	2.94	2.90	2.86	2.81	2.77	2.72	2.68	2.64	2.59	2.55	2.50	2.46	2.42	2.37	2.33	2.28	2.24	2.20	2.15
57.5	2.91	3.10	3.17	3.12	3.08	3.03	2.99	2.95	2.90	2.86	2.82	2.77	2.72	2.68	2.64	2.60	2.55	2.51	2.47	2.42	2.38	2.33	2.29	2.24	2.20
58.0	2.96	3.14	3.21	3.17	3.13	3.08	3.04	2.99	2.95	2.91	2.86	2.82	2.77	2.73	2.69	2.64	2.60	2.55	2.51	2.47	2.42	2.38	2.33	2.29	2.25
58.5	3.00	3.18	3.26	3.22	3.17	3.13	3.09	3.04	3.00	2.95	2.91	2.87	2.82	2.78	2.73	2.69	2.65	2.60	2.56	2.51	2.47	2.43	2.38	2.34	2.29
59.0	3.04	3.22	3.31	3.26	3.22	3.17	3.13	3.09	3.05	3.00	2.96	2.91	2.87	2.82	2.78	2.74	2.69	2.65	2.61	2.56	2.52	2.47	2.43	2.38	2.34
59.5	3.08	3.27	3.36	3.31	3.27	3.22	3.18	3.14	3.09	3.05	3.00	2.96	2.92	2.87	2.83	2.78	2.74	2.70	2.65	2.61	2.56	2.52	2.48	2.43	2.39
60.0	3.12	3.31	3.40	3.36	3.31	3.27	3.23	3.18	3.14	3.09	3.05	3.01	2.96	2.92	2.87	2.83	2.79	2.74	2.70	2.65	2.61	2.57	2.52	2.48	2.43
60.5	3.17	3.35	3.45	3.41	3.36	3.32	3.27	3.23	3.19	3.14	3.10	3.05	3.01	2.97	2.92	2.88	2.83	2.79	2.75	2.70	2.66	2.61	2.57	2.53	2.48
61.0	3.21	3.39	3.50	3.45	3.41	3.36	3.32	3.28	3.23	3.19	3.14	3.10	3.06	3.01	2.97	2.92	2.88	2.84	2.80	2.75	2.70	2.66	2.62	2.57	2.53
61.5	3.25	3.43	3.54	3.50	3.46	3.41	3.37	3.32	3.28	3.24	3.19	3.15	3.10	3.06	3.02	2.97	2.93	2.88	2.84	2.80	2.75	2.71	2.66	2.62	2.58
62.0	3.29	3.48	3.59	3.55	3.50	3.46	3.41	3.37	3.33	3.28	3.24	3.19	3.15	3.11	3.06	3.02	2.97	2.93	2.89	2.84	2.80	2.75	2.71	2.67	2.62
62.5	3.33	3.52	3.64	3.59	3.55	3.51	3.46	3.42	3.37	3.33	3.28	3.24	3.20	3.15	3.11	3.07	3.02	2.98	2.94	2.89	2.85	2.80	2.76	2.71	2.67
63.0	3.38	3.56	3.68	3.64	3.60	3.55	3.51	3.46	3.42	3.38	3.33	3.29	3.24	3.20	3.16	3.11	3.07	3.02	2.98	2.94	2.89	2.85	2.80	2.76	2.72
63.5	3.42	3.60	3.73	3.69	3.64	3.60	3.56	3.51	3.47	3.42	3.38	3.34	3.29	3.25	3.20	3.16	3.12	3.07	3.03	2.98	2.94	2.89	2.85	2.81	2.76
64.0	3.46	3.64	3.78	3.73	3.69	3.65	3.60	3.56	3.51	3.47	3.43	3.38	3.34	3.29	3.25	3.21	3.16	3.12	3.08	3.03	2.99	2.94	2.90	2.85	2.81
64.5	3.50	3.69	3.83	3.78	3.74	3.69	3.65	3.61	3.56	3.52	3.47	3.43	3.39	3.34	3.30	3.25	3.21	3.16	3.12	3.08	3.03	2.99	2.95	2.90	2.86
65.0	3.54	3.73	3.87	3.83	3.78	3.74	3.70	3.65	3.61	3.56	3.52	3.48	3.43	3.39	3.34	3.30	3.26	3.21	3.17	3.12	3.08	3.04	2.99	2.95	2.90
65.5	3.59	3.77	3.92	3.88	3.83	3.79	3.74	3.70	3.65	3.61	3.57	3.52	3.48	3.44	3.39	3.35	3.30	3.26	3.22	3.17	3.13	3.08	3.04	3.00	2.95
66.0	3.63	3.81	3.97	3.92	3.88	3.83	3.79	3.75	3.70	3.66	3.61	3.57	3.53	3.48	3.44	3.39	3.35	3.30	3.26	3.22	3.17	3.13	3.09	3.04	3.00
66.5	3.67	3.85	4.01	3.97	3.93	3.88	3.84	3.79	3.75	3.70	3.66	3.62	3.57	3.53	3.48	3.44	3.40	3.35	3.31	3.27	3.22	3.18	3.13	3.09	3.05
67.0	3.71	3.89	4.06	4.02	3.97	3.93	3.88	3.84	3.80	3.75	3.71	3.66	3.62	3.58	3.53	3.49	3.44	3.40	3.36	3.31	3.27	3.22	3.18	3.14	3.09
67.5	3.75	3.94	4.11	4.06	4.02	3.98	3.93	3.89	3.84	3.80	3.76	3.71	3.67	3.62	3.58	3.54	3.49	3.45	3.40	3.36	3.32	3.27	3.23	3.18	3.14
68.0	3.79	3.98	4.15	4.11	4.07	4.02	3.98	3.93	3.89	3.85	3.80	3.76	3.71	3.67	3.62	3.58	3.54	3.49	3.45	3.41	3.36	3.32	3.27	3.23	3.19
68.5	3.84	4.02	4.20	4.16	4.11	4.07	4.03	3.98	3.94	3.89	3.85	3.81	3.76	3.72	3.67	3.63	3.58	3.54	3.50	3.45	3.41	3.37	3.32	3.28	3.23
69.0	3.88	4.06	4.25	4.20	4.16	4.12	4.07	4.03	3.98	3.94	3.90	3.85	3.81	3.76	3.72	3.68	3.63	3.59	3.55	3.50	3.46	3.41	3.37	3.32	3.28
69.5	3.92	4.10	4.30	4.25	4.21	4.16	4.12	4.08	4.03	3.99	3.94	3.90	3.86	3.81	3.77	3.72	3.68	3.63	3.59	3.55	3.50	3.46	3.42	3.37	3.33
70.0	3.96	4.15	4.34	4.30	4.25	4.21	4.17	4.12	4.08	4.03	3.99	3.95	3.90	3.86	3.81	3.77	3.73	3.68	3.64	3.59	3.55	3.51	3.46	3.42	3.37
70.5	4.00	4.19	4.39	4.35	4.30	4.26	4.21	4.17	4.13	4.08	4.04	3.99	3.95	3.91	3.86	3.82	3.77	3.73	3.69	3.64	3.60	3.55	3.51	3.47	3.42
71.0	4.05	4.23	4.44	4.39	4.35	4.30	4.26	4.22	4.17	4.13	4.08	4.04	4.00	3.95	3.91	3.86	3.82	3.77	3.73	3.69	3.64	3.60	3.56	3.51	3.47
71.5	4.09	4.27	4.48	4.44	4.40	4.35	4.31	4.26	4.22	4.18	4.13	4.09	4.04	4.00	3.95	3.91	3.87	3.82	3.78	3.74	3.69	3.65	3.60	3.56	3.52
72.0	4.13	4.31	4.53	4.49	4.44	4.40	4.35	4.31	4.27	4.22	4.18	4.13	4.09	4.05	4.00	3.96	3.91	3.87	3.83	3.78	3.74	3.69	3.65	3.61	3.56
72.5	4.17	4.36	4.58	4.53	4.49	4.44	4.40	4.36	4.31	4.27	4.23	4.18	4.14	4.09	4.05	4.01	3.96	3.91	3.88	3.83	3.79	3.74	3.70	3.65	3.61
73.0	4.21	4.40	4.62	4.58	4.54	4.49	4.45	4.40	4.36	4.32	4.27	4.23	4.18	4.14	4.10	4.05	4.01	3.96	3.92	3.88	3.83	3.79	3.74	3.70	3.66
73.5	4.26	4.44	4.67	4.63	4.58	4.54	4.50	4.45	4.41	4.36	4.32	4.27	4.23	4.19	4.14	4.10	4.06	4.01	3.97	3.92	3.88	3.83	3.79	3.75	3.70
74.0	4.30	4.48	4.72	4.67	4.63	4.59	4.54	4.50	4.45	4.41	4.37	4.32	4.28	4.23	4.19	4.15	4.10	4.06	4.02	3.97	3.93	3.88	3.84	3.79	3.75
74.5	4.34	4.52	4.77	4.72	4.68	4.63	4.59	4.55	4.50	4.46	4.41	4.37	4.33	4.28	4.24	4.19	4.15	4.10	4.06	4.02	3.97	3.93	3.89	3.84	3.80
75.0	4.38	4.57	4.81	4.77	4.72	4.68	4.64	4.59	4.55	4.50	4.46	4.42	4.37	4.33	4.28	4.24	4.20	4.15	4.11	4.06	4.02	3.98	3.93	3.89	3.84
75.5	4.42	4.61	4.86	4.82	4.77	4.73	4.68	4.64	4.59	4.55	4.51	4.46	4.42	4.38	4.33	4.29	4.24	4.20	4.16	4.11	4.07	4.02	3.98	3.94	3.89
76.0	4.47	4.65	4.91	4.86	4.82	4.77	4.73	4.69	4.64	4.60	4.55	4.51	4.47	4.42	4.38	4.33	4.29	4.24	4.20	4.16	4.11	4.07	4.03	3.98	3.94
76.5	4.51	4.69	4.95	4.91	4.87	4.82	4.78	4.73	4.69	4.65	4.60	4.56	4.51	4.47	4.43	4.38	4.34	4.29	4.25	4.21	4.16	4.12	4.07	4.03	3.99
77.0	4.55	4.73	5.00	4.96	4.91	4.87	4.82	4.78	4.74	4.69	4.65	4.60	4.56	4.52	4.47	4.43	4.38	4.34	4.30	4.25	4.21	4.16	4.12	4.08	4.03

TABLE 4. PREDICTED FEV$_1$ FOR FEMALES (KNUDSON, ET AL.: AM. REV. RESPIR. DIS. 1976, 113, 587.)

AGE

HT	17	19	21	23	25	27	29	31	33	35	37	39	41	43	45	47	49	51	53	55	57	59	61	63	65
52.0	2.31	2.48	2.33	2.29	2.25	2.21	2.16	2.12	2.08	2.04	2.00	1.95	1.91	1.87	1.83	1.79	1.74	1.70	1.66	1.62	1.58	1.53	1.49	1.45	1.41
52.5	2.34	2.51	2.37	2.32	2.28	2.24	2.20	2.16	2.11	2.07	2.03	1.99	1.95	1.90	1.86	1.82	1.78	1.74	1.69	1.65	1.61	1.57	1.53	1.48	1.44
53.0	2.38	2.55	2.40	2.36	2.32	2.27	2.23	2.19	2.15	2.11	2.06	2.02	1.98	1.94	1.90	1.85	1.81	1.77	1.73	1.69	1.64	1.60	1.56	1.52	1.48
53.5	2.41	2.58	2.43	2.39	2.35	2.31	2.27	2.22	2.18	2.14	2.10	2.06	2.01	1.97	1.93	1.89	1.85	1.80	1.76	1.72	1.68	1.64	1.59	1.55	1.51
54.0	2.45	2.62	2.47	2.43	2.39	2.34	2.30	2.26	2.22	2.17	2.13	2.09	2.05	2.00	1.96	1.92	1.88	1.84	1.80	1.75	1.72	1.67	1.63	1.59	1.54
54.5	2.48	2.65	2.50	2.46	2.42	2.38	2.33	2.29	2.25	2.21	2.17	2.12	2.08	2.04	2.00	1.96	1.91	1.87	1.83	1.79	1.75	1.70	1.66	1.62	1.58
55.0	2.51	2.68	2.54	2.49	2.46	2.41	2.37	2.33	2.28	2.24	2.20	2.16	2.12	2.07	2.03	1.99	1.95	1.91	1.86	1.82	1.78	1.74	1.70	1.65	1.61
55.5	2.55	2.72	2.57	2.53	2.49	2.45	2.40	2.36	2.32	2.28	2.24	2.19	2.15	2.11	2.07	2.03	1.98	1.94	1.90	1.86	1.82	1.77	1.73	1.69	1.65
56.0	2.58	2.75	2.61	2.56	2.52	2.48	2.44	2.40	2.35	2.31	2.27	2.23	2.19	2.14	2.10	2.06	2.02	1.98	1.93	1.89	1.86	1.81	1.77	1.72	1.68
56.5	2.62	2.79	2.64	2.60	2.56	2.51	2.47	2.43	2.39	2.35	2.30	2.26	2.22	2.18	2.14	2.09	2.05	2.01	1.97	1.93	1.88	1.84	1.80	1.76	1.72
57.0	2.65	2.82	2.67	2.63	2.59	2.55	2.51	2.46	2.42	2.38	2.34	2.30	2.25	2.21	2.17	2.13	2.09	2.04	2.00	1.96	1.92	1.88	1.83	1.79	1.75
57.5	2.69	2.86	2.71	2.67	2.62	2.58	2.54	2.50	2.46	2.41	2.37	2.33	2.29	2.25	2.20	2.16	2.12	2.08	2.04	1.99	1.95	1.91	1.87	1.83	1.78
58.0	2.72	2.89	2.74	2.70	2.66	2.62	2.57	2.53	2.49	2.45	2.41	2.36	2.32	2.28	2.24	2.20	2.15	2.11	2.07	2.03	1.98	1.94	1.90	1.86	1.82
58.5	2.75	2.92	2.78	2.73	2.69	2.65	2.61	2.57	2.52	2.48	2.44	2.40	2.36	2.31	2.27	2.23	2.19	2.15	2.10	2.06	2.02	1.98	1.94	1.89	1.85
59.0	2.79	2.96	2.81	2.77	2.73	2.69	2.64	2.60	2.56	2.52	2.48	2.43	2.39	2.35	2.31	2.27	2.22	2.18	2.14	2.10	2.06	2.01	1.97	1.93	1.89
59.5	2.82	2.99	2.85	2.80	2.76	2.72	2.68	2.63	2.59	2.55	2.51	2.47	2.43	2.38	2.34	2.30	2.26	2.22	2.17	2.13	2.09	2.05	2.01	1.96	1.92
60.0	2.86	3.03	2.88	2.84	2.80	2.75	2.71	2.67	2.63	2.59	2.54	2.50	2.46	2.42	2.38	2.33	2.29	2.25	2.21	2.17	2.12	2.08	2.04	2.00	1.96
60.5	2.89	3.06	2.91	2.87	2.83	2.79	2.75	2.70	2.66	2.62	2.58	2.54	2.49	2.45	2.41	2.37	2.33	2.28	2.24	2.20	2.16	2.12	2.07	2.03	1.99
61.0	2.93	3.10	2.95	2.91	2.86	2.82	2.78	2.74	2.70	2.65	2.61	2.57	2.53	2.49	2.44	2.40	2.36	2.32	2.28	2.23	2.19	2.15	2.11	2.07	2.02
61.5	2.96	3.13	2.98	2.94	2.90	2.86	2.81	2.77	2.73	2.69	2.65	2.60	2.56	2.52	2.48	2.44	2.39	2.35	2.31	2.27	2.23	2.18	2.14	2.10	2.06
62.0	2.99	3.16	3.02	2.97	2.93	2.89	2.85	2.81	2.76	2.72	2.68	2.64	2.60	2.55	2.51	2.47	2.43	2.39	2.34	2.30	2.26	2.22	2.18	2.13	2.09
62.5	3.03	3.20	3.05	3.01	2.97	2.92	2.88	2.84	2.80	2.76	2.72	2.67	2.63	2.59	2.55	2.51	2.46	2.42	2.38	2.34	2.30	2.25	2.21	2.17	2.13
63.0	3.06	3.23	3.09	3.04	3.00	2.96	2.92	2.88	2.83	2.79	2.75	2.71	2.67	2.62	2.58	2.54	2.50	2.46	2.41	2.37	2.33	2.29	2.25	2.20	2.16
63.5	3.10	3.27	3.12	3.08	3.04	2.99	2.95	2.91	2.87	2.83	2.78	2.74	2.70	2.66	2.62	2.57	2.53	2.49	2.45	2.41	2.36	2.32	2.28	2.24	2.20
64.0	3.13	3.30	3.15	3.11	3.07	3.03	2.99	2.94	2.90	2.86	2.82	2.78	2.73	2.69	2.65	2.61	2.57	2.52	2.48	2.44	2.40	2.36	2.31	2.27	2.23
64.5	3.17	3.34	3.19	3.15	3.10	3.06	3.02	2.98	2.94	2.90	2.85	2.81	2.77	2.73	2.68	2.64	2.60	2.56	2.52	2.48	2.43	2.39	2.35	2.31	2.26
65.0	3.20	3.37	3.22	3.18	3.14	3.10	3.05	3.01	2.97	2.93	2.89	2.85	2.80	2.76	2.72	2.68	2.63	2.59	2.55	2.51	2.47	2.42	2.38	2.34	2.30
65.5	3.23	3.40	3.26	3.21	3.17	3.13	3.09	3.05	3.00	2.96	2.92	2.88	2.84	2.79	2.75	2.71	2.67	2.63	2.58	2.54	2.50	2.46	2.42	2.37	2.33
66.0	3.27	3.44	3.29	3.25	3.21	3.16	3.12	3.08	3.04	3.00	2.96	2.91	2.87	2.83	2.79	2.75	2.70	2.66	2.62	2.58	2.54	2.49	2.45	2.41	2.37
66.5	3.30	3.47	3.33	3.28	3.24	3.20	3.16	3.12	3.07	3.03	2.99	2.95	2.91	2.86	2.82	2.78	2.74	2.70	2.65	2.61	2.57	2.53	2.49	2.44	2.40
67.0	3.34	3.51	3.36	3.32	3.28	3.23	3.19	3.15	3.11	3.07	3.02	2.98	2.94	2.90	2.86	2.81	2.77	2.73	2.69	2.65	2.61	2.56	2.52	2.48	2.44
67.5	3.37	3.54	3.39	3.35	3.31	3.27	3.23	3.18	3.14	3.10	3.06	3.02	2.97	2.93	2.89	2.85	2.81	2.76	2.72	2.68	2.64	2.60	2.55	2.51	2.47
68.0	3.41	3.58	3.43	3.39	3.34	3.30	3.26	3.22	3.18	3.13	3.09	3.05	3.01	2.97	2.92	2.88	2.84	2.80	2.76	2.72	2.67	2.63	2.59	2.55	2.50
68.5	3.44	3.61	3.46	3.42	3.38	3.34	3.29	3.25	3.21	3.17	3.13	3.08	3.04	3.00	2.96	2.92	2.87	2.83	2.79	2.75	2.71	2.66	2.62	2.58	2.54
69.0	3.47	3.64	3.50	3.46	3.41	3.37	3.33	3.29	3.25	3.20	3.16	3.12	3.08	3.04	2.99	2.95	2.91	2.87	2.83	2.79	2.74	2.70	2.66	2.62	2.57
69.5	3.51	3.68	3.53	3.49	3.45	3.41	3.36	3.32	3.28	3.24	3.20	3.15	3.11	3.07	3.03	2.99	2.94	2.90	2.86	2.82	2.78	2.73	2.69	2.65	2.61
70.0	3.54	3.71	3.57	3.52	3.48	3.44	3.40	3.36	3.31	3.27	3.23	3.19	3.15	3.10	3.06	3.02	2.98	2.94	2.89	2.86	2.81	2.77	2.73	2.68	2.64
70.5	3.58	3.75	3.60	3.56	3.52	3.47	3.43	3.39	3.35	3.31	3.27	3.22	3.18	3.14	3.10	3.05	3.01	2.97	2.93	2.89	2.85	2.80	2.76	2.72	2.68
71.0	3.61	3.78	3.63	3.59	3.55	3.51	3.47	3.42	3.38	3.34	3.30	3.26	3.21	3.17	3.13	3.09	3.05	3.00	2.96	2.93	2.88	2.84	2.79	2.75	2.71
71.5	3.65	3.82	3.67	3.63	3.58	3.54	3.50	3.46	3.42	3.37	3.33	3.29	3.25	3.21	3.16	3.12	3.08	3.04	3.00	2.96	2.92	2.87	2.83	2.79	2.74
72.0	3.68	3.85	3.70	3.66	3.62	3.58	3.53	3.49	3.45	3.41	3.37	3.32	3.28	3.24	3.20	3.16	3.12	3.07	3.03	2.99	2.95	2.90	2.86	2.82	2.78
72.5	3.71	3.88	3.74	3.70	3.65	3.61	3.57	3.53	3.49	3.44	3.40	3.36	3.32	3.28	3.23	3.19	3.15	3.11	3.07	3.03	2.98	2.94	2.90	2.86	2.81
73.0	3.75	3.92	3.77	3.73	3.69	3.65	3.60	3.56	3.52	3.48	3.44	3.39	3.35	3.31	3.27	3.23	3.18	3.14	3.10	3.06	3.02	2.97	2.93	2.89	2.85
73.5	3.78	3.95	3.81	3.76	3.72	3.68	3.64	3.60	3.55	3.51	3.47	3.43	3.39	3.34	3.30	3.26	3.22	3.18	3.13	3.10	3.05	3.01	2.97	2.92	2.88
74.0	3.82	3.99	3.84	3.80	3.76	3.71	3.67	3.63	3.59	3.55	3.50	3.46	3.42	3.38	3.34	3.29	3.25	3.21	3.17	3.13	3.09	3.04	3.00	2.96	2.92
74.5	3.85	4.02	3.87	3.83	3.79	3.75	3.71	3.66	3.62	3.58	3.54	3.50	3.45	3.41	3.37	3.33	3.29	3.24	3.20	3.16	3.12	3.08	3.03	2.99	2.95
75.0	3.89	4.06	3.91	3.87	3.83	3.78	3.74	3.70	3.66	3.61	3.57	3.53	3.49	3.45	3.41	3.36	3.32	3.28	3.24	3.20	3.16	3.11	3.07	3.03	2.98
75.5	3.92	4.09	3.94	3.90	3.86	3.82	3.77	3.73	3.69	3.65	3.61	3.56	3.52	3.48	3.44	3.40	3.36	3.31	3.27	3.24	3.19	3.14	3.10	3.06	3.02
76.0	3.95	4.12	3.98	3.94	3.89	3.85	3.81	3.77	3.73	3.68	3.64	3.60	3.56	3.52	3.47	3.43	3.39	3.35	3.31	3.27	3.23	3.18	3.14	3.10	3.05
76.5	3.99	4.16	4.01	3.97	3.93	3.89	3.84	3.80	3.76	3.72	3.68	3.63	3.59	3.55	3.51	3.47	3.42	3.38	3.34	3.31	3.26	3.21	3.17	3.13	3.09
77.0	4.02	4.19	4.05	4.00	3.96	3.92	3.88	3.84	3.79	3.75	3.71	3.67	3.63	3.58	3.54	3.50	3.46	3.42	3.37	3.34	3.29	3.25	3.21	3.16	3.12

APPENDIX D TO § 1910.1043—PULMONARY FUNC-
TION STANDARDS FOR COTTON DUST STAND-
ARD

The spirometric measurements of pulmonary function shall conform to the following minimum standards, and these standards are not intended to preclude additional
testing or alternate methods which can be
determined to be superior.

I. APPARATUS

a. The instrument shall be accurate to
within ±50 milliliters or within ±3 percent of
reading, whichever is greater.

b. The instrument should be capable of
measuring vital capacity from 0 to 7 liters
BTPS.

c. The instrument shall have a low inertia
and offer low resistance to airflow such that
the resistance to airflow at 12 liters per second must be less than 1.5 cm H_2 O/(liter/sec).

d. The zero time point for the purpose of
timing the FEV_1 shall be determined by extrapolating the steepest portion of the volume time curve back to the maximal inspiration volume (1, 2, 3, 4) or by an equivalent
method.

e. Instruments incorporating measurements of airflow to determine volume shall
conform to the same volume accuracy stated
in (a) of this section when presented with
flow rates from at least 0 to 12 liters per second.

f. The instrument or user of the instrument must have a means of correcting volumes to body temperature saturated with
water vapor (BTPS) under conditions of
varying ambient spirometer temperatures
and barometric pressures.

g. The instrument used shall provide a
tracing or display of either flow versus volume or volume versus time during the entire
forced expiration. A tracing or display is
necessary to determine whether the patient
has performed the test properly. The tracing
must be stored and available for recall and
must be of sufficient size that hand measurements may be made within requirement of
paragraph (a) of this section. If a paper
record is made it must have a paper speed of
at least 2 cm/sec and a volume sensitivity of
at least 10.0 mm of chart per liter of volume.

h. The instrument shall be capable of accumulating volume for a minimum of 10 seconds and shall not stop accumulating volume
before (1) the volume change for a 0.5 second
interval is less than 25 milliliters, or (2) the
flow is less than 50 milliliters per second for
a 0.5 second interval.

i. The forced vital capacity (FVC) and
forced expiratory volume in 1 second ($FEV_{1.0}$)
measurements shall comply with the accuracy requirements stated in paragraph (a) of
this section. That is, they should be accurately measured to within ±50 ml or within
±3 percent of reading, whichever is greater.

j. The instrument must be capable of being
calibrated in the field with respect to the
FEV_1 and FVC. This calibration of the FEV_1
and FVC may be either directly or indirectly
through volume and time base measurements. The volume calibration source should
provide a volume displacement of at least 2
liters and should be accurate to within ±30
milliliters.

II. TECHNIQUE FOR MEASUREMENT OF FORCED
VITAL CAPACITY MANEUVER

a. Use of a nose clip is recommended but
not required. The procedures shall be explained in simple terms to the patient who
shall be instructed to loosen any tight clothing and stand in front of the apparatus. The
subject may sit, but care should be taken on
repeat testing that the same position be used
and, if possible, the same spirometer. Particular attention shall be given to insure
that the chin is slightly elevated with the
neck slightly extended. The patient shall be
instructed to make a full inspiration from a
normal breathing pattern and then blow into
the apparatus, without interruption, as hard,
fast, and completely as possible. At least
three forced expirations shall be carried out.
During the maneuvers, the patient shall be
observed for compliance with instruction.
The expirations shall be checked visually for
reproducibility from flow-volume or volume-
time tracings or displays. The following efforts shall be judged unacceptable when the
patient:

1. Has not reached full inspiration preceding the forced expiration,

2. Has not used maximal effort during the
entire forced expiration,

3. Has not continued the expiration for at
least 5 seconds or until an obvious plateau in
the volume time curve has occurred,

4. Has coughed or closed his glottis,

5. Has an obstructed mouthpiece or a leak
around the mouthpiece (obstruction due to
tongue being placed in front of mouthpiece,
false teeth falling in front of mouthpiece,
etc.)

6. Has an unsatisfactory start of expiration, one characterized by excessive hesitation (or false starts), and therefore not allowing back extrapolation of time 0 (extrapolated volume on the volume time tracing
must be less than 10 percent of the FVC.)

7. Has an excessive variability between the
three acceptable curves. The variation between the two largest FVC's and FEV_1's of
the three satisfactory tracings should not
exceed 10 percent or ±100 milliliters, whichever is greater.

b. Periodic and routine recalibration of the
instrument or method for recording FVC and
$FEV_{1.0}$ should be performed using a syringe
or other volume source of at least 2 liters.

III. INTERPRETATION OF SPIROGRAM

a. The first step in evaluating a spirogram should be to determine whether or not the patient has performed the test properly or as described in II above. From the three satisfactory tracings, the forced vital capacity (FVC) and forced expiratory volume in 1 second ($FEV_{1.0}$) shall be measured and recorded. The largest observed FVC and largest observed FEV_1 shall be used in the analysis regardless of the curve(s) on which they occur.

b. The following guidelines are recommended by NIOSH for the evaluation and management of workers exposed to cotton dust. It is important to note that employees who show reductions in FEV_1/FVC ratio below .75 or drops in Monday FEV_1 of 5 percent or greater on their initial screening exam, should be re-evaluated within a month of the first exam. Those who show consistent decrease in lung function, as shown on the following table, should be managed as recommended.

IV. QUALIFICATIONS OF PERSONNEL ADMINISTERING THE TEST

Technicians who perform pulmonary function testing should have the basic knowledge required to produce meaningful results. Training consisting of approximately 16 hours of formal instruction should cover the following areas.

a. Basic physiology of the forced vital capacity maneuver and the determinants of airflow limitation with emphasis on the relation to reproducibility of results.

b. Instrumentation requirements including calibration procedures, sources of error and their correction.

c. Performance of the testing including subject coaching, recognition of improperly performed maneuvers and corrective actions.

d. Data quality with emphasis on reproducibility.

e. Actual use of the equipment under supervised conditions.

f. Measurement of tracings and calculations of results.

APPENDIX E TO §1910.1043—VERTICAL ELUTRIATOR EQUIVALENCY PROTOCOL

a. *Samples to be taken*—In order to ascertain equivalency, it is necessary to collect a total of 100 samples from at least 10 sites in a mill. That is, there should be 10 replicate readings at each of 10 sites. The sites should represent dust levels which vary over the allowable range of 0.5 to 2 times the permissible exposure limit. Each sample requires the use of two vertical elutriators (VE's) and at least one but not more than two alternative devices (AD's). Thus, the end result is 200 VE readings and either 100 or 200 AD readings. The 2 VE readings and the 1 or 2 AD readings at each time and site must be made simultaneously. That is, the two VE's and one or

two AD's must be arranged together in such a way that they are measuring essentially the same dust levels.

b. *Data averaging*—The two VE readings taken at each site are then averaged. These averages are to be used as the 100 VE readings. If two alternate devices were used, their test results are also averaged. Thus, after this step is accomplished, there will be 100 VE readings and 100 AD readings.

c. *Differences*—For each of the 100 sets of measurements (VE and AD) the difference is obtained as the average VE reading minus the AD reading. Call these differences D_i. Thus, we have.

$$D_i = VE_i - AD_i, \ i = 1, 2, \ldots, 100 \quad (1)$$

Next we compute the arithmetic mean and standard deviations of the differences, using equations (2) and (3), respectively.

$$\overline{X}_D = \frac{1}{N} \sum_{i=1}^{N} D_i \quad (2)$$

$$S_D = \sqrt{\frac{\sum D_i^2 - \frac{\left(\sum D_i\right)^2}{N}}{N-1}} \quad (3)$$

where N equals the number of differences (100 in this case), X_D is the arithmetic mean and S_D is the standard deviation.

We next calculate the critical value as $T = KS_D + |\overline{X}_D|$ where $K = 1.87$, based on 100 samples.

d. *Equivalency test*. The next step is to obtain the average of the 100 VE readings. This is obtained by equation (4)

$$\overline{X}_{VE} = \frac{1}{n}\left(\sum_{i=1}^{N} VE_i\right) \quad (4)$$

We next multiply 0.25 by $\overline{X}_{VE}$. If $T \leq 0.25$ $\overline{X}_{VE}$, we can say that the alternate device has passed the equivalency test.

[43 FR 27394, June 23, 1978; 43 FR 35035, Aug. 8, 1978, as amended at 45 FR 67340, Oct. 10, 1980; 50 FR 51173, Dec. 13, 1985; 51 FR 24325, July 3, 1986; 54 FR 24334, June 7, 1989; 61 FR 5508, Feb. 13, 1996; 63 FR 1290, Jan. 8, 1998; 65 FR 76567, Dec. 7, 2000; 70 FR 1142, Jan. 5, 2005; 71 FR 16672, 16673, Apr. 3, 2006; 71 FR 50189, Aug. 24, 2006; 73 FR 75586, Dec. 12, 2008; 76 FR 33609, June 8, 2011; 77 FR 17782, Mar. 26, 2012]

EFFECTIVE DATE NOTE: At 84 FR 21490, May 14, 2019, §1910.1043 was amended by revising paragraphs (h)(2)(iii), (h)(3)(ii), and (n)(1) and appendices B-I, B-II, and B-III; removing and reserving appendix C; and revising appendix D, effective July 15, 2019. For the convenience of the user, the revised text is set forth as follows:

§ 1910.1043   Cotton dust.

*   *   *   *   *

(h) * * *

(2) * * *

(iii) A pulmonary function measurement, including forced vital capacity (FVC) and forced expiratory volume in one second (FEV_1), and determination of the FEV_1/FVC ratio shall be made. FVC, FEV_1, and FEV_1/FVC ratio values shall be compared to appropriate race/ethnicity-specific Lower Limit of Normal (LLN) values and predicted values published in Spirometric Reference Values from a Sample of the General U.S. Population, American Journal of Respiratory and Critical Care Medicine, 159(1): 179–187, January 1999 (commonly known as the NHANES III reference data set) (incorporated by reference, see § 1910.6). To obtain reference values for Asian-Americans, Spirometric Reference Values FEV_1 and FVC predicted and LLN values for Caucasians shall be multiplied by 0.88 to adjust for ethnic differences. These determinations shall be made for each employee before the employee enters the workplace on the first day of the work week, preceded by at least 35 hours of no exposure to cotton dust. The tests shall be repeated during the shift, no less than 4 and no more than 10 hours after the beginning of the work shift; and, in any event, no more than one hour after cessation of exposure. Such exposure shall be typical of the employee's usual workplace exposure.

*   *   *   *   *

(3) * * *

(ii) Medical surveillance as required in paragraph (h)(3)(i) of this section shall be provided every six months for all employees in the following categories:

(A) An FEV_1 greater than the LLN, but with an FEV_1 decrement of 5 percent or 200 ml. on a first working day;

(B) An FEV_1 of less than the LLN; or

(C) Where, in the opinion of the physician, any significant change in questionnaire findings, pulmonary function results, or other diagnostic tests have occurred.

*   *   *   *   *

(n) * * *

(1) Appendices B and D of this section are incorporated as part of this section and the contents of these appendices are mandatory.

*   *   *   *   *

APPENDIX B-I -- RESPIRATORY QUESTIONNAIRE

RESPIRATORY QUESTIONNAIRE

A. IDENTIFICATION DATA

PLANT _____

DAY   MONTH   YEAR

(figures) (last 2 digits)

NAME _____ DATE OF INTERVIEW _____

(Surname)

_____ DATE OF BIRTH _____

(First Names)

M   F

ADDRESS _____ AGE ____ (8, 9) SEX _____(10)

RACE (11) (Check all that apply)

    1. White ___   4. Hispanic or Latino ___

    2. Black or African American ___   5. American Indian or Alaska Native ___

    3. Asian ___   6. Native Hawaiian or

                              Other Pacific Islander ___

INTERVIEWER: 1 2 3 4 5 6 7 8   (12)

WORK SHIFT: 1st _____ 2nd _____ 3rd _____   (13)

STANDING HEIGHT _____   (14, 15)

WEIGHT _____   (16, 18)

PRESENT WORK AREA

If working in more than one specified work area, X area where most of the work shift is spent. If "other," but spending 25% of the work shift in one of the specified work areas, classify in that work area. If carding department employee, check area within that department where most of the work shift is spent (if in doubt, check "throughout"). For work areas such as spinning and weaving where many work rooms may be involved, be sure to check to specific work room to which the employee is assigned - if he works in more than one work room within a department classify as 7 (all) for that department.

	Work-room Number	(19) Open	(20) Pick	Area	(21) Card #1	(22) #2	(23) Spin	(24) Wind	(25) Twist
AT	1			Cards					
RISK	2			Draw					
(cotton &	3			Comb					
cotton blend)	4			Thru Out					
	5								
	6								
	7 (all)								
Control (synthe-tic & wo ol)	8								
Ex-Worker (cotton)	9								

Continued –

Work-Room Number	(26) Spool	(27) Warp	(28) Slash	(29) Weave	(30) Other
AT RISK (cotton & cotton blend) 1					
2					
3					
4					
5					
6					
7 (all)					
Control (synthetic & wool) 8					
Ex-Worker (cotton) 9					

Use actual wording of each question. Put X in appropriate square after each question. When in doubt record "No". When no square, circle appropriate answer.

B. COUGH

(on getting up)
Do you usually cough first thing in the morning?   _____

Yes _____ No _____ (31)

(Count a cough with first smoke or on "first going out of doors." Exclude clearing throat or a single cough.)

359

Do you usually cough during the day or at night?   Yes _____ No _____ (32)

(Ignore an occasional cough.)

If `Yes' to either question (31-32):

Do you cough like this on most days for as much as
three months a year?   Yes _____ No _____ (33)

Do you cough on any particular day of the week?   Yes _____ No _____ (34)

               (1)   (2)   (3)   (4)   (5) (6) (7)

If 'Yes': Which day?   Mon   Tues   Wed   Thur   Fri   Sat   Sun   (35)

C. PHLEGM or alternative word to suit local custom.

            (on getting up)

Do you usually bring up any phlegm from your
chest first thing in the morning? (Count phlegm
with the first smoke or on "first going out of
doors." Exclude phlegm from the nose. Count
swallowed phlegm.)   Yes _____ No _____ (36)

Do you usually bring up any phlegm from your
chest during the day or at night?
(Accept twice or more.)   Yes _____ No _____ (37)

If `Yes' to question (36) or (37):

Do you bring up any phlegm like this on most   Yes _____ No _____ (38)
days for as much as three months each year?

360

If `Yes' to question (33) or (38):

(cough)

How long have you had this phlegm?   (1) ____ 2 years or less   (39)

(Write in number of years)   (2) ____ More than 2 year-9 years

                                        (3) ____ 10-19 years

                                        (4) ____ 20+ years

* These words are for subjects who work at night

D. CHEST ILLNESSES

In the past three years, have you had a period   (1) ____ No   (40)
of (increased) *cough and phlegm lasting for
3 weeks or more?   (2) ____ Yes, only one period

                                                   (3) ____ Yes, two or more periods

*For subjects who usually have phlegm

During the past 3 years have you had any chest
illness which has kept you off work, indoors at
home or in bed? (For as long as one week, flu?)   Yes _____ No _____ (41)

If `Yes' to (41):

Did you bring up (more) phlegm than usual in   Yes _____ No _____ (42)
any of these illnesses?

If `Yes' to (42):

During the past three years have you had: Only one such illness
                                              with increased
                                              phlegm?   (1) _____ (43)

                                              More than
                                              one such illness: (2) _____(44)

                                              Br. Grade _____

E. TIGHTNESS

Does your chest ever feel tight or your breathing
become difficult?

                                                    Yes _____ No _____ (45)

Is your chest tight or your breathing difficult on any
particular day of the week? (after a week or 10 days   Yes _____ No _____ (46)
from the mill)

If `Yes': Which day?   (3)   (4)   (5)   (6) (7) (8)

                          Mon. ^ Tues. Wed. Thur. Fri. Sat. Sun.   (47)

                          (1) / \ (2)

                          Sometimes Always

If `Yes' Monday: At what time on   (1) ___ Before entering the mill (48)
Monday does your chest feel tight or your
breathing difficult?   (2) ___ After entering the mill

(Ask only if NO to Question (45))

In the past, has your chest ever been tight or
your breathing difficult on any particular day
of the week?

                                          Yes _____ No _____   (49)

If `Yes': Which day?   (3)   (4)   (5)   (6) (7) (8)

                          Mon. ^ Tues. Wed. Thur. Fri. Sat. Sun.   (50)

                          (1) /   \ (2)

                          Sometimes Always

F. BREATHLESSNESS

If disabled from walking by any condition other than heart or lung disease put "X" here and leave questions (52-60) unasked.

_____(51)

Are you ever troubled by shortness of breath, when hurrying on the level or walking up a slight hill?

Yes _____ No _____ (52)

If `No', grade is 1.

If `Yes', proceed to next question.

Do you get short of breath walking with other people at an ordinary pace on the level?

Yes _____ No _____ (53)

If `No', grade is 2.

If `Yes', proceed to next question.

Do you have to stop for breath when walking at your own pace on the level?

Yes _____ No _____ (54)

If `No', grade is 3.

If `Yes', proceed to next question.

Are you short of breath on washing or dressing? Yes _____ No _____ (55)

If `No', grade is 4.

If `Yes' grade is 5.

Dyspnea Grd. _____ (56)

ON MONDAYS

Are you ever troubled by shortness of breath, when hurrying on the level or walking up a slight hill?

Yes _____ No _____ (57)

If `No', grade is 1.

If `Yes', proceed to next question.

Do you get short of breath walking with other people at ordinary pace on the level?

Yes _____ No _____ (58)

363

If 'No', grade is 2.

If 'Yes', proceed to next question.

Do you have to stop for breath when walking at
your own pace on level ground?

Yes _____ No _____ (59)

If 'No', grade is 3.

If 'Yes', proceed to next question.

Are you short of breath on washing or dressing?   Yes _____ No _____ (60)

If 'No', grade is 4.

If 'Yes', grade is 5.   B. Grd. _____ (61)

G. OTHER ILLNESSES AND ALLERGY HISTORY

Do you have a heart condition for which you are
under a doctor's care?

Yes _____ No _____ (62)

Have you ever had asthma?   Yes _____ No _____ (63)

If 'Yes', did it begin: (1) _____ Before age 30

                                                   (2) _____ After age 30

If 'Yes' before 30 did you have asthma before ever
going to work in a textile mill?

Yes _____ No _____ (64)

Have you ever had hay fever or other allergies
(other than above)?

Yes _____ No _____ (65)

H. TOBACCO SMOKING*

Do you smoke?

Record 'Yes', if regular smoker up
to one month ago (Cigarettes, cigar
or pipe)

Yes _____ No _____ (66)

If `No' to (63)

Have you ever smoked? (Cigarettes, cigars, pipe.
Record `No' if subject has never smoked as much
as one cigarette a day, or 1 oz of tobacco a
month, for as long as one year.)   Yes _____ No _____ (67)

If `Yes' to (63) or (64), what have you smoked and for how many years?
(Write in specific number of years in the appropriate square)

	(1)	(2)	(3)	(4)	(5)	(6)	(7)	(8)	(9)	
Years	<5	5-9	10-14	15-19	20-24	25-29	30-34	35-39	>40	
Cigarettes										(68)
Pipe										(69)
Cigars										(70)

If cigarettes, how many packs per day?   (1) _____ Less than 1/2 pack   (71)
(Write in number of cigarettes)

(2) _____ 1/2 pack, but less than 1 pack

(3) _____ 1 pack, but less than 1 ½ pack
s

(4) _____ 1 1/2 packs or more

Number of years   _____ (72, 73)

If an ex-smoker (cigarettes, cigar or pipe),
how long since you stopped?   _____ (74)
(Write in number of years)

(1) _____ 0-1 year

(2) _____ 1-4 years

(3) _____ 5-9 years

(4) _____ 10+ years

* Have you changed your smoking habits since last interview? If yes, specify what
changes.

I. OCCUPATIONAL HISTORY**

Have you ever worked in:

A foundry? (As long as one year)   Yes _____ No _____ (75)

Stone or mineral mining, quarry or processing?
(As long as one year)
                                                    Yes _____ No _____ (76)

Asbestos milling or processing?   Yes _____ No _____ (77)

Other dusts, fumes or smoke?   Yes _____ No _____ (78)

   If yes, specify.

Type of exposure   _____

Length of exposure   _____

** Ask only on first interview.

At what age did you first go to work in a textile mill?

(Write in specific age in appropriate square)

(1)	(2)	(3)	(4)	(5)	(6)
<20	20-24	25-29	30-34	35-39	40+

When you first worked in a textile mill,
did you work with:
                          (1) _____ Cotton or cotton blend (79)

                          (2) _____ Synthetic or wool   (80)

APPENDIX B-II -- RESPIRATORY QUESTIONNAIRE FOR NON-TEXTILE
WORKERS FOR THE COTTON INDUSTRY

Respiratory Questionnaire for Non-Textile Workers for the
Cotton Industry

Identification No.   Interviewer Code

Location   Date of Interview

A.   IDENTIFICATION

1. NAME   (Last)   (First)   (Middle Initial)

2. CURRENT ADDRESS (Number, Street, or Rural Route, City or Town,
   County, State, Zip Code)

3. PHONE NUMBER   AREA CODE   NO.

   (__ __ __) __ __ __ - __ __ __ __

4. BIRTHDATE   (Mo., Day, Yr.)

5. SEX

   1. _____   Male   2. _____ Female

6. ETHNIC GROUP OR ANCESTRY (Check all that apply)

   1. ____ White
   2. ____ Black or African American
   3. ____ Asian

4. ____ Hispanic or Latino
5. ____ American Indian or Alaska Native
6. ____ Native Hawaiian or Other Pacific Islander

7. STANDING HEIGHT

_____ (in)

8. WEIGHT (lbs)

_____

9. WORK SHIFT

1st _____   2nd _____   3rd _____

10. PRESENT WORK AREA
Please indicate primary assigned work area and percent of time spent at that site.
If at other locations, please indicate and note percent of time for each.

PRIMARY WORK AREA	
SPECIFIC JOB	

11. APPROPRIATE INDUSTRY
1. _____ Garnetting
2. _____ Cottonseed Oil Mill
3. _____ Cotton Warehouse
4. _____ Utilization
5. _____ Cotton Classification
6. _____ Cotton Ginning

B. OCCUPATIONAL HISTORY TABLE

Complete the following table showing the entire work history of the individual from present to initial employment. Sporadic, part-time periods of employment, each of no significant duration, should be grouped if possible.

INDUSTRY AND LOCATION	TENURE OF EMPLOYMENT		SPECIFIC OCCUPATION	AVER-AGE NO. DAYS WORK-	HAZARDOUS HEALTH EXPOSURE ASSOCIATED WITH WORK		
	FROM (year)	TO (year)		ED PER WEEK	YES	NO	IF YES, DESCR-IBE

C.   SYMPTOMS

Use actual wording of each question. Put X in appropriate square after each question. When in doubt record "No.".

COUGH

1. Do you usually cough first thing in the morning? (on getting up)* (Count a cough with first smoke or on "first going out of doors". Exclude clearing throat or a single cough.)   1.____Yes   2.____No

2. Do you usually cough during the day or at night? (Ignore an occasional cough.)   1.____ Yes   2.____ No

If YES to either 1 or 2:

3. Do you cough like this on days   1. ____ Yes   2. ____ No
    for as much as three months a   3. ____ NA
    year?

4. Do you cough on any particular   1. ____ Yes   2. _____ No
    day of the week?

   If YES:

5. Which day?   Mon. Tue. Wed. Thur. Fri. Sat. Sun. _____

PHLEGM

6. Do you usually bring up any   1. ____ Yes   2. ____ No
    phlegm from your chest first
    thing in the morning? (on
    getting up)* (Count phlegm
    with the first smoke or on "first
    going out of doors." Exclude
    phlegm from the nose. Count
    swallowed phlegm.

7. Do you usually bring up any   1. ____ Yes   2. ____ No
    phlegm from your chest during
    the day or at night?
    (Accept twice or more.)

If YES to either question 6 or 7:

8. Do you bring up phlegm like   1. ____ Yes   2. ____ No
    this on most days for as much
    as three months each year?

If YES to question 3 or 8:

9. How long have you had this phlegm?
   (cough)
   (Write in number of years)

(1) ____ 2 years or less
(2) ____ More than 2 years - 9 years
(3) ____ 10-19 years
(4) ____ 20+ years

* These words are for subjects who work at night.

<u>CHEST ILLNESS</u>

10. In the past three years, have you had a period of (increased) cough and phlegm lasting for 3 weeks or more?

(1) ____ No
(2) ____ Yes, only one period
(3) ____ Yes, two or more periods

For subjects who usually have phlegm:

11. During the past 3 years have you had any chest illness which has kept you off work, indoors at home or in bed? (For as long as one week, flu?)

1. ____ Yes   2. ____ No

If YES to 11:

12. Did you bring up (more) phlegm than usual in any of these illnesses?

1. ____ Yes   2. ____ No

13. Only one such illness with increased phlegm?

1. ____ Yes   2. ____ No

If YES to 12: During the past three years have you had:

14. More than one such illness:

1. ____ Yes   2. ____ No

Br. Grade _____

TIGHTNESS

15. Does your chest ever feel   1. ____ Yes   2. ____ No
    tight or your breathing
    become difficult?

16. Is your chest tight or your   1. ____ Yes   2. ____ No
    breathing difficult on any
    particular day of the week?
    (after a week or 10 days away
    from the mill)

17. If `Yes': Which day?   (3)   (4)   (5)   (6)   (7)   (8)
                                     Mon. ^   Tues. Wed. Thur. Fri. Sat. Sun.
                                     (1) / \ (2)
                                 Sometimes   Always

18. If YES Monday: _____ Before entering mill
    At what time on Monday
    does your chest feel tight or   _____ After entering mill
    your breathing difficult?

(Ask only if NO to Question (15))

19. In the past, has your chest ever
been tight or your breathing
difficult on any particular day of
the week?   1. ____ Yes   2. ____ No

20. If `Yes': Which day?   (3)   (4)   (5)   (6)   (7)   (8)
                                     Mon. ^   Tues. Wed. Thur. Fri. Sat. Sun.
                                     (1) / \ (2)
                                 Sometimes   Always

BREATHLESSNESS

21. If disabled from walking by any condition
    other than heart or lung disease put "X" in
    the space and leave questions (22-30)   _____
    unasked.

22. Are you ever troubled by shortness of
    breath, when hurrying on the level or

372

walking up a slight hill? 1. ____ Yes 2. ____ No

If NO, grade is 1. If YES, proceed to next question.

23. Do you get short of breath walking with other people at an ordinary pace on the level?   1. ____ Yes 2. ____ No

If NO, grade is 2. If YES, proceed to next question.

24. Do you have to stop for breath when walking at your own pace on the level?   1. ____ Yes 2. ____ No

If NO, grade is 3. If YES, proceed to next question.

25. Are you short of breath on washing or dressing?   1. ____ Yes 2. ____ No

If NO, grade is 4, If YES, grade is 5.

26.   Dyspnea Grd. _____

ON MONDAYS:

27. Are you ever troubled by shortness of breath, when hurrying on the level or walking up a slight hill?   1. ____ Yes 2. ____ No

If NO, grade is 1, If YES, proceed to next question.

28. Do you get short of breath walking with other people at an ordinary pace on the level?   1. ____ Yes 2. ____ No

If NO, grade is 2, If YES, proceed to next

question.

29. Do you have to stop for breath when   1. ____ Yes 2. ____ No
    walking at your own pace on the level?

If NO, grade is 3, If YES, proceed to next
question.

30. Are you short of breath on washing or   1. ____ Yes 2. ____ No
    dressing?

If NO, grade is 4, If YES, grade is 5.

                                                B. Grd. _____

OTHER ILLNESSES AND ALLERGY HISTORY

32. Do you have a heart condition for which   1. ____ Yes 2. ____ No
    you are under a doctor's care?

33. Have you ever had asthma?   1. ____ Yes 2. ____ No

If yes, did it begin:

                                                (1) Before age 30 _____

                                                (2) After age 30 _____

34. If yes before 30: did you have asthma   1. ____ Yes 2. ____ No
    before ever going to work in a textile
    mill?

35. Have you ever had hay fever or other   1. ____ Yes 2. ____ No
    allergies (other than above)?

TOBACCO SMOKING

36. Do you smoke?   1. ____ Yes 2. ____ No
    Record Yes if regular smoker up to one
    month ago. (Cigarettes, cigar or pipe)

If NO to (33).

37. Have you ever smoked? 1. _____ Yes 2. _____ No
(Cigarettes, cigars, pipe. Record NO if
subject has never smoked as much as one
cigarette a day, or 1 oz. of tobacco a
month, for as long as one year.)

If YES to (33) or (34); what have you smoked for how many years?
(Write in specific number of years in the appropriate square)

	(1)	(2)	(3)	(4)	(5)	(6)	(7)	(8)	(9)	
Years	<5	5-9	10-14	15-19	20-24	25-29	30-34	35-39	>40	
Cigarettes										(38)
Pipe										(39)
Cigars										(40)

41. If cigarettes, how many packs per
day?
Write in number of cigarettes   _____

_____ Less than 1/2 pack

_____ 1/2 pack, but less than 1 pack

_____ 1 pack, but less than 1 1/2 packs

_____ 1-1/2 packs or more

42. Number of pack years: _____

43. If an ex-smoker (Cigarettes, cigar or
pipe), how long since you stopped? (Write
in number of years.)   _____

_____ 0-1 year
_____ 1-4 years
_____ 5-9 years
_____ 10+ years

OCCUPATIONAL HISTORY

Have you ever worked in:

44. A foundry?   1. ____ Yes 2. ____ No
    (As long as one year)

45. Stone or mineral mining, quarrying   1. ____ Yes 2. ____ No
or
    processing?
    (As long as one year)

46. Asbestos milling or processing?   1. ____ Yes 2. ____ No
    (Ever)

47. Cotton or cotton blend mill?   1. ____ Yes 2. ____ No
    (For controls only)

48. Other dusts, fumes or smoke?   1. ____ Yes 2. ____ No
    If yes, specify.

Type of exposure _____

Length of exposure _____

APPENDIX B-III -- ABBREVIATED RESPIRATORY QUESTIONNAIRE

ABBREVIATED RESPIRATORY QUESTIONNAIRE

A. IDENTIFICATION DATA

PLANT _____

                                            DAY   MONTH   YEAR

                                            (figures) (last 2 digits)

NAME _____ DATE OF INTERVIEW _____

        (Surname)

_____ DATE OF BIRTH _____

        (First Names)

                                            M   F

ADDRESS _____ AGE ____ (8, 9) SEX _____(10)

RACE (11) (Check all that apply)

    1. White ___   4. Hispanic or Latino ___

    2. Black or African American ___   5. American Indian or Alaska Native ___

    3. Asian ___   6. Native Hawaiian or
                                       Other Pacific Islander ___

INTERVIEWER: 1 2 3 4 5 6 7 8   (12)

WORK SHIFT: 1st _____ 2nd _____ 3rd _____   (13)

STANDING HEIGHT _____   (14, 15)

WEIGHT _____   (16, 18)

PRESENT WORK AREA

  If working in more than one specified work area, X area where most of the work shift is spent. If "other," but spending 25% of the work shift in one of the specified work areas, classify in that work area. If carding department employee, check area within that department where most of the work shift is spent (if in doubt, check "throughout"). For work areas such as spinning and weaving where many work rooms may be involved, be sure to check to specific work room to which the employee is assigned - if he works in more than one work room within a department classify as 7 (all) for that department.

		(19)	(20)		(21)	(22)	(23)	(24)	(25)
	Work-room Number	Open	Pick	Area	Card #1	#2	Spin	Wind	Twist
AT	1			Cards					
RISK	2			Draw					
(cotton & Cotton blend)	3			Comb					
	4			Thru Out					
	5								
	6								
	7 (all)								
Control (synthetic & wool)	8								
Ex-Worker	9								

(cotton)									

Continued –

	Work-Room Number	(26) Spool	(27) Warp	(28) Slash	(29) Weave	(30) Other
AT	1					
RISK	2					
(cotton & cotton blend)	3					
	4					
	5					
	6					
	7 (all)					
Control (synthetic & wool)	8					
Ex-Worker (cotton)	9					

Use actual wording of each question. Put X in appropriate square after each question. When in doubt record `No'. When no square, circle appropriate answer.

B. COUGH

(on getting up)
Do you usually cough first thing in the morning? _____

Yes _____ No _____ (31)

379

(Count a cough with first smoke or on "first going out of doors." Exclude clearing throat or a single cough.)

Do you usually cough during the day or at night?   Yes _____ No _____ (32)

(Ignore an occasional cough.)

If `Yes' to either question (31-32):

Do you cough like this on most days for as much as three months a year?

Yes _____ No _____ (33)

Do you cough on any particular day of the week?   Yes _____ No _____ (34)

| | (1) | (2) | (3) | (4) | (5) | (6) | (7) | |
| If 'Yes': Which day? | Mon | Tues | Wed | Thur | Fri | Sat | Sun | (35) |

C. PHLEGM or alternative word to suit local custom.

(on getting up)

Do you usually bring up any phlegm from your chest first thing in the morning? (Count phlegm with the first smoke or on "first going out of doors." Exclude phlegm from the nose. Count swallowed phlegm.)

Yes _____ No _____ (36)

Do you usually bring up any phlegm from your chest during the day or at night?
(Accept twice or more.)

Yes _____ No _____ (37)

If `Yes' to question (36) or (37):

Do you bring up any phlegm like this on most   Yes _____ No _____ (38)
days for as much as three months each year?

If `Yes' to question (33) or (38):

(cough)

How long have you had this phlegm? (1) ____ 2 years or less

(Write in number of years) (2) ____ More than 2 years-9 years

(3) ____ 10-19 years

(4) ____ 20+ years

* These words are for subjects who work at night

D. TIGHTNESS

Does your chest ever feel tight or your breathing become difficult?

Yes _____ No _____ (39)

Is your chest tight or your breathing difficult on any particular day of the week? (after a week or 10 days from the mill)

Yes _____ No _____ (40)

If `Yes': Which day? (3) (4) (5) (6) (7) (8)

Mon. ^ Tues. Wed. Thur. Fri. Sat. Sun. (41)

(1) / \ (2)

Sometimes Always

If `Yes' Monday At what time on Monday does your chest feel tight or your breathing difficult?

(1) ____ Before entering the mill (42)

(2) ____ After entering the mill

(Ask only if NO to Question (45))

In the past, has your chest ever been tight or your breathing difficult on any particular day of the week?

Yes _____ No _____ (43)

If `Yes': Which day?

(3)   (4)   (5)   (6)   (7)   (8)

Mon. ^ Tues. Wed. Thur. Fri. Sat. Sun.   (44)

(1) /   \ (2)

Sometimes   Always

E. TOBACCO SMOKING

* Have you changed your smoking habits since last interview?

If yes, specify what changes.

APPENDIX C TO § 1910.1043 [RESERVED]

APPENDIX D TO § 1910.1043—PULMONARY FUNCTION STANDARDS FOR COTTON DUST STANDARD

The spirometric measurements of pulmonary function shall conform to the following minimum standards, and these standards are not intended to preclude additional testing or alternate methods which can be determined to be superior.

I. APPARATUS

a. The instrument shall be accurate to within ±50 milliliters or within ±3 percent of reading, whichever is greater.

b. 1. Instruments purchased on or before May 14, 2020 should be capable of measuring vital capacity from 0 to 7 liters BTPS

2. Instruments purchased after May 14, 2020 should be capable of measuring vital capacity from 0 to 8 liters BTPS.

c. The instrument shall have a low inertia and offer low resistance to airflow such that the resistance to airflow at 12 liters per second must be less than 1.5 cm $H_2 O$/(liter/sec).

d. The zero time point for the purpose of timing the FEV_1 shall be determined by extrapolating the steepest portion of the volume time curve back to the maximal inspiration volume (1, 2, 3, 4) or by an equivalent method.

e. 1. Instruments purchased on or before May 14, 2020 that incorporate measurements of airflow to determine volume shall conform to the same volume accuracy stated in paragraph (a) of this section I when presented with flow rates from at least 0 to 12 liters per second.

2. Instruments purchased after May 14, 2020 that incorporate measurements of airflow to determine volume shall conform to the same volume accuracy stated in paragraph (a) of this section I when presented with flow rates from at least 0 to 14 liters per second.

f. The instrument or user of the instrument must have a means of correcting volumes to body temperature saturated with water vapor (BTPS) under conditions of varying ambient spirometer temperatures and barometric pressures.

g. 1. Instruments purchased on or before May 14, 2020 shall provide a tracing or display of either flow versus volume or volume versus time during the entire forced expiration. A tracing or display is necessary to determine whether the patient has performed the test properly. The tracing must be stored and available for recall and must be of sufficient size that hand measurements may be made within the volume accuracy requirements of paragraph (a) of this section I. If a paper record is made it must have a paper speed of at least 2 cm/sec and a volume sensitivity of at least 10.0 mm of chart per liter of volume.

2. Instruments purchased after May 14, 2020 shall provide during testing a paper tracing or real-time display of flow versus volume and volume versus time for the entire forced expiration. Such a tracing or display is necessary to determine whether the worker has performed the test properly. Flow-volume and volume-time curves must be stored and available for recall. Real-time displays shall have a volume scale of at least 5 mm/L, a time scale of at least 10 mm/s, and a flow scale of at least 2.5 mm/L/s, when both flow-volume and volume-time displays are visible. If hand measurements will be made, paper tracings must be of sufficient size to allow those measurements to be made within the volume accuracy requirements of paragraph (a) of this section I. If a paper record is made it must have a paper speed of at least 2 cm/sec and a volume sensitivity of at least 10.0 mm of chart per liter of volume.

h. 1. Instruments purchased on or before May 14, 2020 shall be capable of accumulating volume for a minimum of 10 seconds and shall not stop accumulating volume before (i) the volume change for a 0.5-second interval is less than 25 milliliters, or (ii) the flow is less than 50 milliliters per second for a 0.5 second interval.

2. Instruments purchased after May 14, 2020 shall be capable of accumulating volume for a minimum of 15 seconds and shall not stop accumulating volume before the volume change for a 1-second interval is less than 25 milliliters.

i. The forced vital capacity (FVC) and forced expiratory volume in 1 second (FEV_1) measurements shall comply with the accuracy requirements stated in paragraph (a) of this section. That is, they should be accurately measured to within ±50 ml or within ±3 percent of reading, whichever is greater.

j. 1. Instruments purchased on or before May 14, 2020 must be capable of being calibrated in the field with respect to the FEV_1 and FVC. This calibration of the FEV_1 and FVC may be either directly or indirectly through volume and time base measurements. The volume calibration source should provide a volume displacement of at least 2 liters and should be accurate to within + or − 30 milliliters.

2. Instruments purchased after May 14, 2020 must be capable of having its calibration checked in the field and be recalibrated, if necessary, if the spirometer requires the technician to do so. The volume-calibration syringe shall provide a volume displacement of at least 3 liters and shall be accurate to within ± 0.5 percent of 3 liters (15 milliliters).

II. TECHNIQUE FOR MEASUREMENT OF FORCED VITAL CAPACITY MANEUVER

a. Use of a nose clip is recommended but not required. The procedures shall be explained in simple terms to the worker who shall be instructed to loosen any tight clothing and stand in front of the apparatus. The worker may sit, but care should be taken on repeat testing that the same position be used and, if possible, the same spirometer. Particular attention shall be given to ensure that the chin is slightly elevated with the neck slightly extended. The worker shall be instructed to make a full inspiration from a normal breathing pattern and then blow into the apparatus, without interruption, as hard, fast, and completely as possible. At least three and no more than eight forced expirations shall be carried out. During the maneuvers, the worker shall be observed for compliance with instruction. The expirations shall be checked visually for technical acceptability and repeatability from flow-volume or volume-time tracings or displays. The following efforts shall be judged technically unacceptable when the worker:

1. Has not reached full inspiration preceding the forced expiration,

2. Has not used maximal effort during the entire forced expiration,

3. Has not tried to exhale continuously for at least 6 seconds and the volume-time curve shows no change in volume (<0.025 L) for at least one second,

4. Has coughed in the first second or closed the glottis,

5. Has an obstructed mouthpiece or a leak around the mouthpiece (obstruction due to tongue being placed in front of mouthpiece, false teeth falling in front of mouthpiece, etc.),

6. Has an unsatisfactory start of expiration, one characterized by excessive hesitation (or false starts), and, therefore, not allowing back extrapolation of time 0 (extrapolated volume on the volume-time tracing must be less than 150 milliliters or 5 percent of the FVC, whichever is greater.), and

7. Has an excessive variability between the acceptable curves. The difference between the two largest FVCs from the satisfactory tracings shall not exceed 150 milliliters and the difference between the two largest FEV_1s of the satisfactory tracings shall not exceed 150 milliliters.

b. Calibration checks of the volume accuracy of the instrument for recording FVC and FEV_1 shall be performed daily or more frequently if specified by the spirometer manufacturer, using a 3-liter syringe. Calibration checks to ensure that the spirometer is recording 3 liters of injected air to within ±3.5 percent, or 2.90 to 3.10 liters, shall be conducted. Calibration checks of flow-type spirometers shall include injection of 3 liters air over a range of speeds, with injection times of 0.5 second, 3 seconds, and 6 or more seconds. Checks of volume-type spirometers shall include a single calibration check and a check to verify that the spirometer is not leaking more than 30 milliliters/minute air.

III. INTERPRETATION OF SPIROGRAM

a. The first step in evaluating a spirogram should be to determine whether or not the worker has performed the test properly or as described in section II of this appendix. From the three satisfactory tracings, the forced vital capacity (FVC) and forced expiratory volume in 1 second (FEV_1) shall be measured and recorded. The largest observed FVC and largest observed FEV_1 shall be used in the analysis regardless of the curve(s) on which they occur.

b. [Reserved]

IV. QUALIFICATIONS OF PERSONNEL ADMINISTERING THE TEST

Technicians who perform pulmonary function testing should have the basic knowledge required to produce meaningful results. Training consisting of approximately 16 hours of formal instruction should cover the following areas.

a. Basic physiology of the forced vital-capacity maneuver and the determinants of airflow limitation, with emphasis on the relation to repeatability of results.

b. Instrumentation requirements, including calibration check procedures, sources of error, and their correction.

c. Performance of the testing including worker coaching, recognition of improperly performed maneuvers and corrective actions.

d. Data quality with emphasis on repeatability.

e. Actual use of the equipment under supervised conditions.

f. Measurement of tracings and calculations of results.

§ 1910.1044 1,2-dibromo-3-chloropropane.

(a) *Scope and application.* (1) This section applies to occupational exposure to 1,2-dibromo-3-chloropropane (DBCP).

(2) This section does not apply to:

(i) Exposure to DBCP which results solely from the application and use of DBCP as a pesticide; or

(ii) The storage, transportation, distribution or sale of DBCP in intact containers sealed in such a manner as to prevent exposure to DBCP vapors or liquid, except for the requirements of paragraphs (i), (n) and (o) of this section.

(b) *Definitions. Authorized person* means any person required by his duties to be present in regulated areas and authorized to do so by his employer, by this section, or by the Act. *Authorized person* also includes any person entering such areas as a designated representative of employees exercising an opportunity to observe employee exposure monitoring.

DBCP means 1,2-dibromo-3-chloropropane, Chemical Abstracts Service Registry Number 96–12–8, and includes all forms of DBCP.

Director means the Director, National Institute for Occupational Safety and Health, U.S. Department of Health and Human Services, or designee.

Emergency means any occurrence such as, but not limited to equipment failure, rupture of containers, or failure of control equipment which may, or does, result in an unexpected release of DBCP.

OSHA Area Office means the Area Office of the Occupational Safety and Health Administration having jurisdiction over the geographic area where the affected workplace is located.

Assistant Secretary means the Assistant Secretary of Labor for Occupational Safety and Health, U.S. Department of Labor, or designee.

(c) *Permissible exposure limit*—(1) *Inhalation.* The employer shall assure that no employee is exposed to an airborne concentration of DBCP in excess of 1 part DBCP per billion parts of air (ppb) as an 8-hour time-weighted average.

(2) *Dermal and eye exposure.* The employer shall assure that no employee is exposed to eye or skin contact with DBCP.

(d) [Reserved]

(e) *Regulated areas.* (1) The employer shall establish, within each place of employment, regulated areas wherever DBCP concentrations are in excess of the permissible exposure limit.

(2) The employer shall limit access to regulated areas to authorized persons.

(f) *Exposure monitoring*—(1) *General.* (i) Determinations of airborne exposure levels shall be made from air samples that are representative of each employee's exposure to DBCP over an 8-hour period.

(ii) For the purposes of this paragraph, employee exposure is that exposure which would occur if the employee were not using a respirator.

(2) *Initial.* Each employer who has a place of employment in which DBCP is present, shall monitor each workplace and work operation to accurately determine the airborne concentrations of DBCP to which employees may be exposed.

(3) *Frequency.* (i) If the monitoring required by this section reveals employee exposures to be at or below the permissible exposure limit, the employer must repeat these measurements at least every 6 months.

(ii) If the monitoring required by this section reveals employee exposures to be in excess of the permissible exposure limit, the employer must repeat these measurements for each such employee at least quarterly. The employer must continue quarterly monitoring until at least two consecutive measurements, taken at least seven (7) days apart, are at or below the permissible exposure limit. Thereafter the employer must monitor at least every 6 months.

(4) *Additional.* Whenever there has been a production, process, control, or personnel change which may result in any new or additional exposure to DBCP, or whenever the employer has any reason to suspect new or additional exposures to DBCP, the employer shall monitor the employees potentially affected by such change for the purpose of redetermining their exposure.

(5) *Employee notification.* (i) The employer must, within 15 working days after the receipt of the results of any monitoring performed under this section, notify each employee of these results either individually in writing or by posting the results in an appropriate location that is accessible to employees.

(ii) Whenever the results indicate that employee exposure exceeds the permissible exposure limit, the employer shall include in the written notice a statement that the permissible exposure limit was exceeded and a description of the corrective action being taken to reduce exposure to or below the permissible exposure limit.

(6) *Accuracy of measurement.* The employer shall use a method of measurement which has an accuracy, to a confidence level of 95 percent, of not less than plus or minus 25 percent for concentrations of DBCP at or above the permissible exposure limit.

(g) *Methods of compliance—*(1) *Priority of compliance methods.* The employer shall institute engineering and work practice controls to reduce and maintain employee exposures to DBCP at or below the permissible exposure limit, except to the extent that the employer establishes that such controls are not feasible. Where feasible engineering and work practice controls are not sufficient to reduce employee exposures to within the permissible exposure limit, the employer shall nonetheless use them to reduce exposures to the lowest level achievable by these controls, and shall supplement them by use of respiratory protection.

(2) *Compliance program.* (i) The employer shall establish and implement a written program to reduce employee exposures to DBCP to or below the per-

missible exposure limit solely by means of engineering and work practice controls as required by paragraph (g)(1) of this section.

(ii) The written program shall include a detailed schedule for development and implementation of the engineering and work practice controls. These plans must be revised at least annually to reflect the current status of the program.

(iii) Written plans for these compliance programs shall be submitted upon request to the Assistant Secretary and the Director, and shall be available at the worksite for examination and copying by the Assistant Secretary, the Director, and any affected employee or designated representative of employees.

(iv) The employer shall institute and maintain at least the controls described in his most recent written compliance program.

(h) *Respiratory protection—*(1) *General.* For employees who are required to use respirators by this section, the employer must provide each employee an appropriate respirator that complies with the requirements of this paragraph. Respirators must be used during:

(i) Periods necessary to install or implement feasible engineering and work-practice controls.

(ii) Maintenance and repair activities for which engineering and work-practice controls are not feasible.

(iii) Work operations for which feasible engineering and work-practice controls are not yet sufficient to reduce employee exposure to or below the permissible exposure limit.

(iv) Emergencies.

(2) *Respirator program.* The employer must implement a respiratory protection program in accordance with § 1910.134(b) through (d) (except (d)(1)(iii)), and (f) through (m), which covers each employee required by this section to use a respirator.

(3) *Respirator selection.* Employers must:

(i) Select, and provide to employees, the appropriate atmosphere-supplying respirator specified in paragraph (d)(3)(i)(A) of 29 CFR 1910.134.

(ii) Provide employees with one of the following respirator options to use for entry into, or escape from, unknown DBCP concentrations:

(A) A combination respirator that includes a supplied-air respirator with a full facepiece operated in a pressure-demand or other positive-pressure or continuous-flow mode, as well as an auxiliary self-contained breathing apparatus (SCBA) operated in a pressure-demand or positive-pressure mode.

(B) An SCBA with a full facepiece operated in a pressure-demand or other positive-pressure mode.

(i) *Emergency situations*—(1) *Written plans.* (i) A written plan for emergency situations shall be developed for each workplace in which DBCP is present.

(ii) Appropriate portions of the plan shall be implemented in the event of an emergency.

(2) Employees engaged in correcting emergency conditions shall be equipped as required in paragraphs (h) and (j) of this section until the emergency is abated.

(3) *Evacuation.* Employees not engaged in correcting the emergency shall be removed and restricted from the area and normal operations in the affected area shall not be resumed until the emergency is abated.

(4) *Alerting employees.* Where there is a possibility of employee exposure to DBCP due to the occurrence of an emergency, a general alarm shall be installed and maintained to promptly alert employees of such occurrences.

(5) *Medical surveillance.* For any employee exposed to DBCP in an emergency situation, the employer shall provide medical surveillance in accordance with paragraph (m)(6) of this section.

(6) *Exposure monitoring.* (i) Following an emergency, the employer shall conduct monitoring which complies with paragraph (f) of this section.

(ii) In workplaces not normally subject to periodic monitoring, the employer may terminate monitoring when two consecutive measurements indicate exposures below the permissible exposure limit.

(j) *Protective clothing and equipments*—(1) *Provision and use.* Where there is any possibility of eye or dermal contact with liquid or solid DBCP, the employer shall provide, at no cost to the employee, and assure that the employee wears impermeable protective clothing and equipment to protect the area of the body which may come in contact with DBCP. Eye and face protection shall meet the requirements of § 1910.133 of this part.

(2) *Removal and storage.* (i) The employer shall assure that employees remove DBCP contaminated work clothing only in change rooms provided in accordance with paragraph (l) (1) of this section.

(ii) The employer shall assure that employees promptly remove any protective clothing and equipment which becomes contaminated with DBCP-containing liquids and solids. This clothing shall not be reworn until the DBCP has been removed from the clothing or equipment.

(iii) The employer shall assure that no employee takes DBCP contaminated protective devices and work clothing out of the change room, except those employees authorized to do so for the purpose of laundering, maintenance, of disposal.

(iv) DBCP-contaminated protective devices and work clothing shall be placed and stored in closed containers which prevent dispersion of the DBCP outside the container.

(v) Containers of DBCP-contaminated protective devices or work clothing which are to be taken out of change rooms or the workplace for cleaning, maintenance or disposal shall bear labels with the following information: CONTAMINATED WITH 1,2–Dibromo-3-chloropropane (DBCP), MAY CAUSE CANCER.

(3) *Cleaning and replacement.* (i) The employer shall clean, launder, repair, or replace protective clothing and equipment required by this paragraph to maintain their effectiveness. The employer shall provide clean protective clothing and equipment at least daily to each affected employee.

(ii) The employer shall inform any person who launders or clean DBCP-contaminated protective clothing or equipment of the potentially harmful effects of exposure to DBCP.

(iii) The employer shall prohibit the removal of DBCP from protective clothing and equipment by blowing or shaking.

(k) *Housekeeping*—(1) *Surfaces.* (i) All workplace surfaces shall be maintained free of visible accumulations of DBCP.

(ii) Dry sweeping and the use of compressed air for the cleaning of floors and other surfaces is prohibited where DBCP dusts or liquids are present.

(iii) Where vacuuming methods are selected to clean floors and other surfaces, either portable units or a permanent system may be used.

(*a*) If a portable unit is selected, the exhaust shall be attached to the general workplace exhaust ventilation system or collected within the vacuum unit, equipped with high efficiency filters or other appropriate means of contaminant removal, so that DBCP is not reintroduced into the workplace air; and

(*b*) Portable vacuum units used to collect DBCP may not be used for other cleaning purposes and shall be labeled as prescribed by paragraph (j)(2)(v) of this section.

(iv) Cleaning of floors and other surfaces contaminated with DBCP-containing dusts shall not be performed by washing down with a hose, unless a fine spray has first been laid down.

(2) *Liquids.* Where DBCP is present in a liquid form, or as a resultant vapor, all containers or vessels containing DBCP shall be enclosed to the maximum extent feasible and tightly covered when not in use.

(3) *Waste disposal.* DBCP waste scrap, debris, containers or equipment, shall be disposed of in sealed bags or other closed containers which prevent dispersion of DBCP outside the container.

(1) *Hygiene facilities and practices*—(1) *Change rooms.* The employer shall provide clean change rooms equipped with storage facilities for street clothes and separate storage facilities for protective clothing and equipment whenever employees are required to wear protective clothing and equipment in accordance with paragraphs (h) and (j) of this section.

(2) *Showers.* (i) The employer shall assure that employees working in the regulated area shower at the end of the work shift.

(ii) The employer shall assure that employees whose skin becomes contaminated with DBCP-containing liquids or solids immediately wash or shower to remove any DBCP from the skin.

(iii) The employer shall provide shower facilities in accordance with 29 CFR 1910.141(d)(3).

(3) *Lunchrooms.* The employer shall provide lunchroom facilities which have a temperature controlled, positive pressure, filtered air supply, and which are readily accessible to employees working in regulated areas.

(4) *Lavatories.* (i) The employer shall assure that employees working in the regulated area remove protective clothing and wash their hands and face prior to eating.

(ii) The employer shall provide a sufficient number of lavatory facilities which comply with 29 CFR 1910.141(d) (1) and (2).

(5) *Prohibition of activities in regulated areas.* The employer shall assure that, in regulated areas, food or beverages are not present or consumed, smoking products and implements are not present or used, and cosmetics are not present or applied.

(m) *Medical surveillance*—(1) *General.* (i) The employer shall make available a medical surveillance program for employees who work in regulated areas and employees who are subjected to DBCP exposures in an emergency situation.

(ii) All medical examinations and procedures shall be performed by or under the supervision of a licensed physician, and shall be provided without cost to the employee.

(2) *Frequency and content.* At the time of initial assignment, and annually thereafter, the employer shall provide a medical examination for employees who work in regulated areas, which includes at least the following:

(i) A medical and occupational history including reproductive history.

(ii) A physical examination, including examination of the genito-urinary tract, testicle size and body habitus, including a determination of sperm count.

(iii) A serum specimen shall be obtained and the following determinations made by radioimmunoassay techniques utilizing National Institutes of Health (NIH) specific antigen or one of equivalent sensitivity:

(a) Serum follicle stimulating hormone (FSH);

(b) Serum luteinizing hormone (LH); and

(c) Serum total estrogen (females).

(iv) Any other tests deemed appropriate by the examining physician.

(3) *Additional examinations.* If the employee for any reason develops signs or symptoms commonly associated with exposure to DBCP, the employer shall provide the employee with a medical examination which shall include those elements considered appropriate by the examining physician.

(4) *Information provided to the physician.* The employer shall provide the following information to the examining physician:

(i) A copy of this regulation and its appendices;

(ii) A description of the affected employee's duties as they relate to the employee's exposure;

(iii) The level of DBCP to which the employee is exposed; and

(iv) A description of any personal protective equipment used or to be used.

(5) *Physician's written opinion.* (i) For each examination under this section, the employer shall obtain and provide the employee with a written opinion from the examining physician which shall include:

(a) The results of the medical tests performed;

(b) The physician's opinion as to whether the employee has any detected medical condition which would place the employee at an increased risk of material impairment of health from exposure to DBCP; and

(c) Any recommended limitations upon the employee's exposure to DBCP or upon the use of protective clothing and equipment such as respirators.

(ii) The employer shall instruct the physician not to reveal in the written opinion specific findings or diagnoses unrelated to occupational exposure.

(6) *Emergency situations.* If the employee is exposed to DBCP in an emergency situation, the employer shall provide the employee with a sperm count test as soon as practicable, or, if the employee has been vasectionized or is unable to produce a semen specimen, the hormone tests contained in paragraph (m)(2)(iii) of this section. The employer shall provide these same tests three months later.

(n) *Employee information and training*—(1) *Training program.* (i) The employer shall train each employee who may be exposed to DBCP in accordance with the requirements of this section. The employer shall institute a training program and ensure employee participation in the program.

(ii) The employer shall assure that each employee is informed of the following:

(a) The information contained in appendix A;

(b) The quantity, location, manner of use, release or storage of DBCP and the specific nature of operations which could result in exposure to DBCP as well as any necessary protective steps;

(c) The purpose, proper use, and limitations of respirators;

(d) The purpose and description of the medical surveillance program required by paragraph (m) of this section; and

(e) A review of this standard, including appendices.

(2) *Access to training materials.* (i) The employer shall make a copy of this standard and its appendices readily available to all affected employees.

(ii) The employer shall provide, upon request, all materials relating to the employee information and training program to the Assistant Secretary and the Director.

(o) *Communication of hazards*—(1) *Hazard communication—general.* (i) Chemical manufacturers, importers, distributors and employers shall comply with all requirements of the Hazard Communication Standard (HCS) (§ 1910.1200) for DBCP.

(ii) In classifying the hazards of DBCP at least the following hazards are to be addressed: Cancer; reproductive effects; liver effects; kidney effects; central nervous system effects; skin, eye and respiratory tract irritation; and acute toxicity effects.

(iii) Employers shall include DBCP in the hazard communication program established to comply with the HCS (§ 1910.1200). Employers shall ensure that each employee has access to labels on containers of DBCP and to safety data sheets, and is trained in accordance with the requirements of HCS and paragraph (n) of this section.

(iv) The employer shall ensure that no statement appears on or near any sign or label required by this paragraph (o) which contradicts or detracts from the meaning of the required sign or label.

(2) *Signs.* (i) The employer shall post signs to clearly indicate all regulated areas. These signs shall bear the legend:

DANGER
1,2-Dibromo-3-chloropropane
MAY CAUSE CANCER
WEAR RESPIRATORY PROTECTION IN THIS AREA
AUTHORIZED PERSONNEL ONLY

(ii) Prior to June 1, 2016, employers may use the following legend in lieu of that specified in paragraph (o)(2) of this section:

DANGER
1,2-Dibromo-3-chloropropane
(Insert appropriate trade or common names)
CANCER HAZARD
AUTHORIZED PERSONNEL ONLY
RESPIRATOR REQUIRED

(3) *Labels.* (i) Where DBCP or products containing DBCP are sold, distributed or otherwise leave the employer's workplace bearing appropriate labels required by EPA under the regulations in 40 CFR Part 162, the labels required by this paragraph (o)(3) need not be affixed.

(ii) The employer shall ensure that the precautionary labels required by this paragraph (o)(3) are readily visible and legible.

(iii) Prior to June 1, 2015, employers may include the following information on containers of DBCP or products containing DBCP, DBCP-contaminated protective devices or work clothing or DBCP-contaminated portable vacuums in lieu of the labeling requirements in paragraphs (j)(2)(v), (k)(l)(iii)(b) and (o)(1)(i) of this section:

DANGER
1,2-Dibromo-3-chloropropane
CANCER HAZARD

(p) *Recordkeeping*—(1) *Exposure monitoring.* (i) The employer shall establish and maintain an accurate record of all monitoring required by paragraph (f) of this section.

(ii) This record shall include:

(*a*) The dates, number, duration and results of each of the samples taken, including a description of the sampling procedure used to determine representative employee exposure;

(*b*) A description of the sampling and analytical methods used;

(*c*) Type of respiratory protective devices worn, if any; and

(*d*) Name, social security number, and job classification of the employee monitored and of all other employees whose exposure the measurement is intended to represent.

(iii) The employer shall maintain this record for at least 40 years or the duration of employment plus 20 years, whichever is longer.

(2) *Medical surveillance.* (i) The employer shall establish and maintain an accurate record for each employee subject to medical surveillance required by paragraph (m) of this section.

(ii) This record shall include:

(*a*) The name and social security number of the employee;

(*b*) A copy of the physician's written opinion;

(*c*) Any employee medical complaints related to exposure to DBCP;

(*d*) A copy of the information provided the physician as required by paragraphs (m)(4)(ii) through (m)(4)(iv) of this section; and

(*e*) A copy of the employee's medical and work history.

(iii) The employer shall maintain this record for at least 40 years or the duration of employment plus 20 years, whichever is longer.

(3) *Availability.* (i) The employer shall assure that all records required to be maintained by this section be made available upon request to the Assistant Secretary and the Director for examination and copying.

(ii) Employee exposure monitoring records and employee medical records required by this paragraph shall be provided upon request to employees, designated representatives, and the Assistant Secretary in accordance with 29 CFR 1910.1020 (a) through (e) and (g) through (i).

(4) *Transfer of records.* (i) If the employer ceases to do business, the successor employer shall receive and retain all records required to be maintained by paragraph (p) of this section for the prescribed period.

(ii) The employer shall also comply with any additional requirements involving transfer of records set forth in 29 CFR 1910.1020(h).

(q) *Observation of monitoring*—(1) *Employee observation.* The employer shall provide affected employees, or their designated representatives, with an opportunity to observe any monitoring of employee exposure to DBCP required by this section.

(2) *Observation procedures.* (i) Whenever observation of the measuring or monitoring of employee exposure to DBCP requires entry into an area where the use of protective clothing or equipment is required, the employer shall provide the observer with personal protective clothing or equipment required to be worn by employees working in the area, assure the use of such clothing and equipment, and require the observer to comply with all other applicable safety and health procedures.

(ii) Without interfering with the monitoring or measurement, observers shall be entitled to:

(*a*) Receive an explanation of the measurement procedures;

(*b*) Observe all steps related to the measurement of airborne concentrations of DBCP performed at the place of exposure; and

(*c*) Record the results obtained.

(r) *Appendices.* The information contained in the appendices is not intended, by itself, to create any additional obligations not otherwise imposed or to detract from any existing obligation.

APPENDIX A TO § 1910.1044—SUBSTANCE
SAFETY DATA SHEET FOR DBCP

I. SUBSTANCE IDENTIFICATION

A. Synonyms and trades names: DBCP; Dibromochloropropane; Fumazone (Dow Chemical Company TM); Nemafume; Nemagon (Shell Chemical Co. TM); Nemaset; BBC 12; and OS 1879.

B. Permissible exposure:

1. *Airborne.* 1 part DBCP vapor per billion parts of air (1 ppb); time-weighted average (TWA) for an 8-hour workday.

2. *Dermal.* Eye contact and skin contact with DBCP are prohibited.

C. Appearance and odor: Technical grade DBCP is a dense yellow or amber liquid with a pungent odor. It may also appear in granular form, or blended in varying concentrations with other liquids.

D. Uses: DBCP is used to control nematodes, very small worm-like plant parasites, on crops including cotton, soybeans, fruits, nuts, vegetables and ornamentals.

II. HEALTH HAZARD DATA

A. Routes of entry: Employees may be exposed:

1. Through inhalation (breathing);

2. Through ingestion (swallowing);

3. Skin contact; and

4. Eye contact.

B. Effects of exposure:

1. *Acute exposure.* DBCP may cause drowsiness, irritation of the eyes, nose, throat and skin, nausea and vomiting. In addition, overexposure may cause damage to the lungs, liver or kidneys.

2. *Chronic exposure.* Prolonged or repeated exposure to DBCP has been shown to cause sterility in humans. It also has been shown to produce cancer and sterility in laboratory animals and has been determined to constitute an increased risk of cancer in man.

3. *Reporting Signs and Symptoms.* If you develop any of the above signs or symptoms that you think are caused by exposure to DBCP, you should inform your employer.

III. EMERGENCY FIRST AID PROCEDURES

A. *Eye exposure.* If DBCP liquid or dust containing DBCP gets into your eyes, wash your eyes immediately with large amounts of water, lifting the lower and upper lids occasionally. Get medical attention immediately. Contact lenses should not be worn when working with DBCP.

B. *Skin exposure.* If DBCP liquids or dusts containing DBCP get on your skin, immediately wash using soap or mild detergent and water. If DBCP liquids or dusts containing DBCP penetrate through your clothing, remove the clothing immediately and wash. If irritation is present after washing get medical attention.

C. *Breathing.* If you or any person breathe in large amounts of DBCP, move the exposed person to fresh air at once. If breathing has stopped, perform artificial respiration. Do not use mouth-to-mouth. Keep the affected person warm and at rest. Get medical attention as soon as possible.

D. *Swallowing.* When DBCP has been swallowed and the person is conscious, give the person large amounts of water immediately. After the water has been swallowed, try to get the person to vomit by having him touch the back of his throat with his finger. Do not make an unconscious person vomit. Get medical attention immediately.

E. *Rescue.* Notify someone. Put into effect the established emergency rescue procedures. Know the locations of the emergency rescue equipment before the need arises.

IV. RESPIRATORS AND PROTECTIVE CLOTHING

A. *Respirators.* You may be required to wear a respirator in emergencies and while your employer is in the process of reducing DBCP exposures through engineering controls. If respirators are worn, they must have a National Institute for Occupational Safety and Health (NIOSH) approval label (Older respirators may have a Bureau of Mines Approval label). For effective protection, a respirator must fit your face and head snugly. The respirator should not be loosened or removed in work situations where its use is required. DBCP does not have a detectable odor except at 1,000 times or more above the permissible exposure limit. If you can smell DBCP while wearing a respirator, the respirator is not working correctly; go immediately to fresh air. If you experience difficulty breathing while wearing a respirator, tell your employer.

B. *Protective clothing.* When working with DBCP you must wear for your protection impermeable work clothing provided by your employer. (Standard rubber and neoprene protective clothing do not offer adequate protection).

DBCP must never be allowed to remain on the skin. Clothing and shoes must not be allowed to become contaminated with DBCP, and if they do, they must be promptly removed and not worn again until completely free of DBCP. Turn in impermeable clothing that has developed leaks for repair or replacement.

C. *Eye protection.* You must wear splash-proof safety goggles where there is any possibility of DBCP liquid or dust contacting your eyes.

V. PRECAUTIONS FOR SAFE USE, HANDLING, AND STORAGE

A. DBCP must be stored in tightly closed containers in a cool, well-ventilated area.

B. If your work clothing may have become contaminated with DBCP, or liquids or dusts containing DBCP, you must change into uncontaminated clothing before leaving the work premises.

C. You must promptly remove any protective clothing that becomes contaminated with DBCP. This clothing must not be reworn until the DBCP is removed from the clothing.

D. If your skin becomes contaminated with DBCP, you must immediately and thoroughly wash or shower with soap or mild detergent and water to remove any DBCP from your skin.

E. You must not keep food, beverages, cosmetics, or smoking materials, nor eat or smoke, in regulated areas.

F. If you work in a regulated area, you must wash your hands thoroughly with soap or mild detergent and water, before eating, smoking or using toilet facilities.

G. If you work in a regulated area, you must remove any protective equipment or clothing before leaving the regulated area.

H. Ask your supervisor where DBCP is used in your work area and for any additional safety and health rules.

VI. ACCESS TO INFORMATION

A. Each year, your employer is required to inform you of the information contained in this Substance Safety Data Sheet for DBCP. In addition, your employer must instruct you in the safe use of DBCP, emergency procedures, and the correct use of protective equipment.

B. Your employer is required to determine whether you are being exposed to DBCP. You or your representative have the right to observe employee exposure measurements and to record the result obtained. Your employer is required to inform you of your exposure. If your employer determines that you are being overexposed, he is required to inform you of the actions which are being taken to reduce your exposure.

C. Your employer is required to keep records of your exposure and medical examinations. Your employer is required to keep exposure and medical data for at least 40 years or the duration of your employment plus 20 years, whichever is longer.

D. Your employer is required to release exposure and medical records to you, your physician, or other individual designated by you upon your written request.

APPENDIX B TO § 1910.1044—SUBSTANCE
TECHNICAL GUIDELINES FOR DBCP

I. PHYSICAL AND CHEMICAL DATA

A. Substance Identification

1. Synonyms: 1,2-dibromo-3-chloropropane; DBCP, Fumazone; Nemafume; Nemagon; Nemaset; BBC 12; OS 1879. DBCP is also included in agricultural pesticides and fumigants which include the phrase "Nema—" in their name.

2. Formula: C3H5Br2 Cl.

3. Molecular Weight: 236.

B. Physical Data:

1. Boiling point (760 mm HG): 195C (383F)

2. Specific gravity (water = 1): 2.093.

3. Vapor density (air = 1 at boiling point of DBCP): Data not available.

4. Melting point: 6C (43F).

5. Vapor pressure at 20C (68F): 0.8 mm Hg

6. Solubility in water: 1000 ppm.

7. Evaporation rate (Butyl Acetate = 1): very much less than 1.

8. Appearance and odor: Dense yellow or amber liquid with a pungent odor at high concentrations. Any detectable odor of DBCP indicates overexposure.

II. FIRE EXPLOSION AND REACTIVITY HAZARD DATA

A. Fire

1. Flash point: 170F (77C)

2. Autoignition temperature: Data not available.

3. Flammable limits in air, percent by volume: Data not available.

4. Extinguishing media: Carbon dioxide, dry chemical.

5. Special fire-fighting procedures: Do not use a solid stream of water since a stream will scatter and spread the fire. Use water spray to cool containers exposed to a fire.

6. Unusual fire and explosion hazards: None known.

7. For purposes of complying with the requirements of § 1910.106, liquid DBCP is classified as a Category 4 flammable liquid.

8. For the purpose of complying with § 1910.309, the classification of hazardous locations as described in article 500 of the National Electrical Code for DBCP shall be Class I, Group D.

9. For the purpose of compliance with § 1910.157, DBCP is classified as a Class B fire hazard.

10. For the purpose of compliance with § 1910.178, locations classified as hazardous locations due to the presence of DBCP shall be Class I, Group D.

11. Sources of ignition are prohibited where DBCP presents a fire or explosion hazard.

B. Reactivity

1. Conditions contributing to instability: None known.

2. Incompatibilities: Reacts with chemically active metals, such as aluminum, magnesium and tin alloys.

3. Hazardous decomposition products: Toxic gases and vapors (such as HBr, HCl and carbon monoxide) may be released in a fire involving DBCP.

4. Special precautions: DBCP will attack some rubber materials and coatings.

III. SPILL, LEAK AND DISPOSAL PROCEDURES

A. If DBCP is spilled or leaked, the following steps should be taken:

1. The area should be evacuated at once and re-entered only after thorough ventilation.

2. Ventilate area of spill or leak.

3. If in liquid form, collect for reclamation or absorb in paper, vermiculite, dry sand, earth or similar material.

4. If in solid form, collect spilled material in the most convenient and safe manner for reclamation or for disposal.

B. Persons not wearing protective equipment must be restricted from areas of spills or leaks until cleanup has been completed.

C. Waste Disposal Methods:

1. For small quantities of liquid DBCP, absorb on paper towels, remove to a safe place (such as a fume hood) and burn the paper. Large quantities can be reclaimed or collected and atomized in a suitable combustion chamber equipped with an appropriate effluent gas cleaning device. If liquid DBCP is absorbed in vermiculite, dry sand, earth or similar material and placed in sealed containers it may be disposed of in a State-approved sanitary landfill.

2. If in solid form, for small quantities, place on paper towels, remove to a safe place (such as a fume hood) and burn. Large quantities may be reclaimed. However, if this is not practical, dissolve in a flammable solvent (such as alcohol) and atomize in a suitable combustion chamber equipped with an appropriate effluent gas cleaning device. DBCP in solid form may also be disposed in a state-approved sanitary landfill.

IV. MONITORING AND MEASUREMENT PROCEDURES

A. Exposure above the permissible exposure limit.

1. *Eight Hour Exposure Evaluation:* Measurements taken for the purpose of determining employee exposure under this section are best taken so that the average 8-hour exposure may be determined from a single 8-hour sample or two (2) 4-hour samples. Air samples should be taken in the employee's breathing zone (air that would most nearly represent that inhaled by the employee).

2. *Monitoring Techniques:* The sampling and analysis under this section may be performed by collecting the DBCP vapor on petroleum based charcoal absorption tubes with subsequent chemical analyses. The method of measurement chosen should determine the concentration of airborne DBCP at the permissible exposure limit to an accuracy of plus or minus 25 percent. If charcoal tubes are used, a total volume of 10 liters should be collected at a flow rate of 50 cc. per minute for each tube. Analyze the resultant samples as you would samples of halogenated solvent.

B. Since many of the duties relating to employee protection are dependent on the results of monitoring and measuring procedures, employers should assure that the evaluation of employee exposures is performed by a competent industrial hygienist or other technically qualified person.

V. PROTECTIVE CLOTHING

Employees should be required to wear appropriate protective clothing to prevent any possibility of skin contact with DBCP. Because DBCP is absorbed through the skin, it is important to prevent skin contact with both liquid and solid forms of DBCP. Protective clothing should include impermeable coveralls or similar fullbody work clothing, gloves, headcoverings, and workshoes or shoe coverings. Standard rubber and neoprene gloves do not offer adequate protection and should not be relied upon to keep DBCP off the skin. DBCP should never be allowed to remain on the skin. Clothing and shoes should not be allowed to become contaminated with the material, and if they do, they should be promptly removed and not worn again until completely free of the material. Any protective clothing which has developed leaks or is otherwise found to be defective should be repaired or replaced. Employees should also be required to wear splash-proof safety goggles where there is any possibility of DBCP contacting the eyes.

VI. HOUSEKEEPING AND HYGIENE FACILITIES

1. The workplace must be kept clean, orderly and in a sanitary condition;

2. Dry sweeping and the use of compressed air is unsafe for the cleaning of floors and other surfaces where DBCP dust or liquids are found. To minimize the contamination of air with dust, vacuuming with either portable or permanent systems must be used. If a portable unit is selected, the exhaust must be attached to the general workplace exhaust ventilation system, or collected within the vacuum unit equipped with high efficiency filters or other appropriate means of contamination removal and not used for other purposes. Units used to collect DBCP must be labeled.

3. Adequate washing facilities with hot and cold water must be provided, and maintained in a sanitary condition. Suitable cleansing agents should also be provided to assure the effective removal of DBCP from the skin.

4. Change or dressing rooms with individual clothes storage facilities must be provided to prevent the contamination of street clothes with DBCP. Because of the hazardous nature of DBCP, contaminated protective clothing must be stored in closed containers for cleaning or disposal.

VII. MISCELLANEOUS PRECAUTIONS

A. Store DBCP in tightly closed containers in a cool, well ventilated area.

B. Use of supplied-air suits or other impervious clothing (such as acid suits) may be necessary to prevent skin contact with DBCP. Supplied-air suits should be selected, used, and maintained under the supervision of persons knowlegeable in the limitations and potential life-endangering characteristics of supplied-air suits.

C. The use of air-conditioned suits may be necessary in warmer climates.

D. Advise employees of all areas and operations where exposure to DBCP could occur.

VIII. COMMON OPERATIONS

Common operations in which exposure to DBCP is likely to occur are: during its production; and during its formulation into pesticides and fumigants.

APPENDIX C TO § 1910.1044—MEDICAL SURVEILLANCE GUIDELINES FOR DBCP

I. ROUTE OF ENTRY

Inhalation; skin absorption

II. TOXICOLOGY

Recent data collected on workers involved in the manufacture and formulation of DBCP has shown that DBCP can cause sterility at very low levels of exposure. This finding is supported by studies showing that DBCP causes sterility in animals. Chronic exposure to DBCP resulted in pronounced necrotic action on the parenchymatous organs (i.e., liver, kidney, spleen) and on the testicles of rats at concentrations as low as 5 ppm. Rats that were chronically exposed to DBCP also showed changes in the composition of the blood, showing low RBC, hemoglobin, and WBC, and high reticulocyte levels as well as functional hepatic disturbance, manifesting itself in a long prothrombin time. Reznik et al. noted a single dose of 100 mg produced profound depression of the nervous system of rats. Their condition gradually improved. Acute exposure also resulted in the destruction of the sex gland activity of male rats as well as causing changes in the estrous cycle in female rats. Animal studies have also associated DBCP with an increased incidence of carcinoma. Olson, et al. orally administered DBCP to rats and mice 5 times per week at experimentally predetermined maximally tolerated doses and at half those doses. As early as ten weeks after initiation of treatment, DBCP induced a high incidence of squamous cell carcinomas of the stomach with metastases in both species. DBCP also induced mammary adenocarcinomas in the female rats at both dose levels.

III. SIGNS AND SYMPTOMS

A. Inhalation: Nausea, eye irritation, conjunctivitis, respiratory irritation, pulmonary congestion or edema, CNS depression with apathy, sluggishness, and ataxia.

B. Dermal: Erythema or inflammation and dermatitis on repeated exposure.

IV. SPECIAL TESTS

A. *Semen analysis:* The following information excerpted from the document "Evaluation of Testicular Function", submitted by the Corporate Medical Department of the Shell Oil Company (exhibit 39–3), may be useful to physicians conducting the medical surveillance program;

In performing semen analyses certain minimal but specific criteria should be met:

393

1. It is recommended that a minimum of three valid semen analyses be obtained in order to make a determination of an individual's average sperm count.

2. A period of sexual abstinence is necessary prior to the collection of each masturbatory sample. It is recommended that intercourse or masturbation be performed 48 hours before the actual specimen collection. A period of 48 hours of abstinence would follow; then the masturbatory sample would be collected.

3. Each semen specimen should be collected in a clean, widemouthed, glass jar (not necessarily pre-sterilized) in a manner designated by the examining physician. Any part of the seminal fluid exam should be initialed *only after liquifaction* is complete, i.e., 30 to 45 minutes after collection.

4. Semen volume should be measured to the nearest ⅒ of a cubic centimeter.

5. Sperm density should be determined using routine techniques involving the use of a white cell pipette and a hemocytometer chamber. The immobilizing fluid most effective and most easily obtained for this process is distilled water.

6. Thin, dry smears of the semen should be made for a morphologic classification of the sperm forms and should be stained with either hematoxalin or the more difficult, yet more precise, Papanicolaou technique. Also of importance to record is obvious sperm agglutination, pyospermia, delayed liquifaction (greater than 30 minutes), and hyperviscosity. In addition, pH, using nitrazine paper, should be determined.

7. A total morphology evaluation should include percentages of the following:

  a. Normal (oval) forms,

  b. Tapered forms,

  c. Amorphous forms (include large and small sperm shapes),

  d. Duplicated (either heads or tails) forms, and

  e. Immature forms.

8. Each sample should be evaluated for sperm *viability* (percent viable sperm moving at the time of examination) as well as sperm *motility* (subjective characterization of "purposeful forward sperm progression" of the majority of those viable sperm analyzed) within two hours after collection, ideally by the same or equally qualified examiner.

B. *Serum determinations:* The following serum determinations should be performed by radioimmuno-assay techniques using National Institutes of Health (NIH) specific antigen or antigen preparations of equivalent sensitivity:

1. Serum follicle stimulating hormone (FSH);

2. Serum luteinizing hormone (LH); and

3. Serum total estrogen (females only).

V. TREATMENT

Remove from exposure immediately, give oxygen or artificial resuscitation if indicated. Contaminated clothing and shoes should be removed immediately. Flush eyes and wash contaminated skin. If swallowed and the person is conscious, induce vomiting. Recovery from mild exposures is usually rapid and complete.

VI. SURVEILLANCE AND PREVENTIVE CONSIDERATIONS

A. *Other considerations.* DBCP can cause both acute and chronic effects. It is important that the physician become familiar with the operating conditions in which exposure to DBCP occurs. Those with respiratory disorders may not tolerate the wearing of negative pressure respirators.

B. *Surveillance and screening.* Medical histories and laboratory examinations are required for each employee subject to exposure to DBCP. The employer should screen employees for history of certain medical conditions (listed below) which might place the employee at increased risk from exposure.

1. *Liver disease.* The primary site of biotransformation and detoxification of DBCP is the liver. Liver dysfunctions likely to inhibit the conjugation reactions will tend to promote the toxic actions of DBCP. These precautions should be considered before exposing persons with impaired liver function to DBCP.

2. *Renal disease.* Because DBCP has been associated with injury to the kidney it is important that special consideration be given to those with possible impairment of renal function.

3. *Skin desease.* DBCP can penetrate the skin and can cause erythema on prolonged exposure. Persons with pre-existing skin disorders may be more susceptible to the effects of DBCP.

4. *Blood dyscrasias.* DBCP has been shown to decrease the content of erythrocytes, hemoglobin, and leukocytes in the blood, as well as increase the prothrombin time. Persons with existing blood disorders may be more susceptible to the effects of DBCP.

5. *Reproductive disorders.* Animal studies have associated DBCP with various effects on the reproductive organs. Among these effects are atrophy of the testicles and changes in the estrous cycle. Persons with pre-existing reproductive disorders may be at increased risk to these effects of DBCP.

REFERENCES

1. Reznik, Ya. B. and Sprinchan, G. K.: Experimental Data on the Gonadotoxic effect of Nemagon, *Gig. Sanit.*, (6), 1975, pp. 101–102, (translated from Russian).

2. Faydysh, E. V., Rakhmatullaev, N. N. and Varshavskii, V. A.: The Cytotoxic Action of Nemagon in a Subacute Experiment,

Med. Zh. Uzbekistana, (No. 1), 1970, pp. 64–65, (translated from Russian).

3. Rakhmatullaev, N. N.: Hygienic Characteristics of the Nematocide Nemagon in Relation to Water Pollution Control, Hyg. Sanit., 36(3), 1971, pp. 344–348, (translated from Russian).

4. Olson, W. A. et al.: Induction of Stomach Cancer in Rats and Mice by Halogenated Aliphatic Fumigants, Journal of the National Cancer Institute, (51), 1973, pp. 1993–1995.

5. Torkelson, T. R. et al.: Toxicologic Investigations of 1,2-Dibromo-3-chloropropane, Toxicology and Applied Pharmacology, 3, 1961 pp. 545–559.

[43 FR 11527, Mar. 17, 1978, as amended at 45 FR 35283, May 23, 1980; 49 FR 18295, Apr. 30, 1984; 54 FR 24334, June 7, 1989; 58 FR 35310, June 30, 1993; 61 FR 5508, Feb. 13, 1996; 63 FR 1291, Jan. 8, 1998; 70 FR 1142, Jan. 5, 2005; 71 FR 16772, Apr. 3, 2006; 71 FR 50189, Aug. 24, 2006; 73 FR 75586, Dec. 12, 2008; 76 FR 33609, June 8, 2011; 77 FR 17782, Mar. 26, 2012; 78 FR 9313, Feb. 8, 2013]

§1910.1045 Acrylonitrile.

(a) Scope and application. (1) This section applies to all occupational exposures to acrylonitrile (AN), Chemical Abstracts Service Registry No. 000107131, except as provided in paragraphs (a)(2) and (a)(3) of this section.

(2) This section does not apply to exposures which result solely from the processing, use, and handling of the following materials:

(i) ABS resins, SAN resins, nitrile barrier resins, solid nitrile elastomers, and acrylic and modacrylic fibers, when these listed materials are in the form of finished polymers, and products fabricated from such finished polymers;

(ii) Materials made from and/or containing AN for which objective data is reasonably relied upon to demonstrate that the material is not capable of releasing AN in airborne concentrations in excess of 1 ppm as an eight (8)-hour time-weighted average, under the expected conditions of processing, use, and handling which will cause the greatest possible release; and

(iii) Solid materials made from and/or containing AN which will not be heated above 170 °F during handling, use, or processing.

(3) An employer relying upon exemption under paragraph (a)(2)(ii) shall maintain records of the objective data supporting that exemption, and of the basis of the employer's reliance on the data, as provided in paragraph (q) of this section.

(b) Definitions. Acrylonitrile or AN means acrylonitrile monomer, chemical formula $CH_2 = CHCN$.

Action level means a concentration of AN of 1 ppm as an eight (8)-hour time-weighted average.

Assistant Secretary means the Assistant Secretary of Labor for Occupational Safety and Health, U.S. Department of Labor, or designee.

Authorized person means any person specifically authorized by the employer whose duties require the person to enter a regulated area, or any person entering such an area as a designated representative of employees for the purpose of exercising the opportunity to observe monitoring procedures under paragraph (r) of this section.

Decontamination means treatment of materials and surfaces by water washdown, ventilation, or other means, to assure that the materials will not expose employees to airborne concentrations of AN above 1 means the Director, National Institute for Occupational Safety and Health, U.S. Department of Health and Human Services, or designee.

Emergency means any occurrence such as, but not limited to, equipment failure, rupture of containers, or failure of control equipment, which results in an unexpected massive release of AN.

Liquid AN means AN monomer in liquid form, and liquid or semiliquid polymer intermediates, including slurries, suspensions, emulsions, and solutions, produced during the polymerization of AN.

OSHA Area Office means the Area Office of the Occupational Safety and Health Administration having jurisdiction over the geographic area where the affected workplace is located.

(c) Permissible exposure limits—(1) Inhalation. (i) Time weighted average limit (TWA). The employer shall assure that no employee is exposed to an airborne concentration of acrylonitrile in excess of two (2) parts acrylonitrile per million parts of air (2 ppm) as an eight (8)-hour time-weighted average.

(ii) Ceiling limit. The employer shall assure that no employee is exposed to an airborne concentration of acrylonitrile in excess of ten (10) ppm as averaged over any fifteen (15)-minute period during the work day.

(2) *Dermal and eye exposure.* The employer shall assure that no employee is exposed to skin contact or eye contact with liquid AN.

(d) [Reserved]

(e) *Exposure monitoring*—(1) *General.* (i) Determinations of airborne exposure levels shall be made from air samples that are representative of each employee's exposure to AN over an eight (8)-hour period.

(ii) For the purposes of this section, employee exposure is that exposure which would occur if the employee were not using a respirator.

(2) *Initial monitoring.* Each employer who has a place of employment in which AN is present shall monitor each such workplace and work operation to accurately determine the airborne concentrations of AN to which employees may be exposed.

(3) *Frequency.* (i) If the monitoring required by this section reveals employee exposure to be below the action level, the employer may discontinue monitoring for that employee.

(ii) If the monitoring required by this section reveals employee exposure to be at or above the action level but at or below the permissible exposure limits, the employer must repeat such monitoring for each such employee at least every 6 months. The employer must continue these measurements every 6 months until at least two consecutive measurements taken at least seven (7) days a part, are below the action level, and thereafter the employer may discontinue monitoring for that employee.

(iii) If the monitoring required by this section reveals employee exposure to be in excess of the permissible exposure limits, the employer must repeat these determinations for each such employee at least quarterly. The employer must continue these quarterly measurements until at least two consecutive measurements, taken at least seven (7) days apart, are at or below the permissible exposure limits, and thereafter the employer must monitor at least every 6 months.

(4) *Additional monitoring.* Whenever there has been a production, process, control, or personnel change which may result in new or additional exposures to AN, or whenever the employer has any other reason to suspect a change which may result in new or additional exposures to AN, additional monitoring which complies with this paragraph shall be conducted.

(5) *Employee notification.* (i) The employer must, within 15 working days after the receipt of the results of any monitoring performed under this section, notify each affected employee of these results either individually in writing or by posting the results in an appropriate location that is accessible to employees.

(ii) Whenever the results indicate that the representative employee exposure exceeds the permissible exposure limits, the employer shall include in the written notice a statement that the permissible exposure limits were exceeded and a description of the corrective action being taken to reduce exposure to or below the permissible exposure limits.

(6) *Accuracy of measurement.* The method of measurement of employee exposures shall be accurate to a confidence level of 95 percent, to within plus or minus 35 percent for concentrations of AN at or above the permissible exposure limits, and plus or minus 50 percent for concentrations of AN below the permissible exposure limits.

(f) *Regulated areas.* (1) The employer shall establish regulated areas where AN concentrations are in excess of the permissible exposure limits.

(2) Regulated areas shall be demarcated and segregated from the rest of the workplace, in any manner that minimizes the number of persons who will be exposed to AN.

(3) Access to regulated areas shall be limited to authorized persons or to persons otherwise authorized by the act or regulations issued pursuant thereto.

(4) The employer shall assure that food or beverages are not present or consumed, tobacco products are not present or used, and cosmetics are not applied in the regulated area.

(g) *Methods of compliance*—(1) *Engineering and work practice controls.* (i) By November 2, 1980, the employer shall institute engineering and work practice controls to reduce and maintain employee exposures to AN, to or below the permissible exposure limits, except to the extent that the employer establishes that such controls are not feasible.

(ii) Wherever the engineering and work practice controls which can be instituted are not sufficient to reduce employee exposures to or below the permissible exposure limits, the employer shall nonetheless use them to reduce exposures to the lowest levels achievable by these controls, and shall supplement them by the use of respiratory protection which complies with the requirements of paragraph (h) of this section.

(2) *Compliance program.* (i) The employer shall establish and implement a written program to reduce employee exposures to or below the permissible exposure limits solely by means of engineering and work practice controls, as required by paragraph (g)(1) of this section.

(ii) Written plans for these compliance programs shall include at least the following:

(A) A description of each operation or process resulting in employee exposure to AN above the permissible exposure limits;

(B) An outline of the nature of the engineering controls and work practices to be applied to the operation or process in question;

(C) A report of the technology considered in meeting the permissible exposure limits;

(D) A schedule for implementation of engineering and work practice controls for the operation or process, which shall project completion no later than November 2, 1980; and

(E) Other relevant information.

(iii) The employer shall complete the steps set forth in the compliance program by the dates in the schedule.

(iv) Written plans shall be submitted upon request to the Assistant Secretary and the Director, and shall be available at the worksite for examination and copying by the Assistant Secretary, the Director, or any affected employee or representative.

(v) The plans required by this paragraph must be revised and updated at least annually to reflect the current status of the program.

(h) *Respiratory protection*—(1) *General.* For employees who use respirators required by this section, the employer must provide each employee an appropriate respirator that complies with the requirements of this paragraph. Respirators must be used during:

(i) Periods necessary to install or implement feasible engineering and work-practice controls.

(ii) Work operations, such as maintenance and repair activities or reactor cleaning, for which the employer establishes that engineering and work-practice controls are not feasible.

(iii) Work operations for which feasible engineering and work-practice controls are not yet sufficient to reduce employee exposure to or below the permissible exposure limits.

(iv) Emergencies.

(2) *Respirator program.* (i) The employer must implement a respiratory protection program in accordance with §1910.134(b) through (d) (except (d)(1)(iii), (d)(3)(iii)(b)(1), and (2)), and (f) through (m), which covers each employee required by this section to use a respirator.

(ii) If air-purifying respirators (chemical-cartridge or chemical-canister types) are used:

(A) The air-purifying canister or cartridge must be replaced prior to the expiration of its service life or at the completion of each shift, whichever occurs first.

(B) A label must be attached to the cartridge or canister to indicate the date and time at which it is first installed on the respirator.

(3) *Respirator selection.* Employers must:

(i) Select, and provide to employees, the appropriate respirators specified in paragraph (d)(3)(i)(A) of 29 CFR 1910.134.

(ii) For escape, provide employees with any organic vapor respirator or any self-contained breathing apparatus permitted for use under paragraph (h)(3)(i) of this standard.

(i) *Emergency situations*—(1) *Written plans.* (i) A written plan for emergency situations shall be developed for each workplace where liquid AN is present. Appropriate portions of the plan shall be implemented in the event of an emergency.

(ii) The plan shall specifically provide that employees engaged in correcting emergency conditions shall be equipped as required in paragraph (h) of this section until the emergency is abated.

(iii) Employees not engaged in correcting the emergency shall be evacuated from the area and shall not be permitted to return until the emergency is abated.

(2) *Alerting employees.* Where there is the possibility of employee exposure to AN in excess of the ceiling limit, a general alarm shall be installed and used to promptly alert employees of such occurrences.

(j) *Protective clothing and equipment—* (1) *Provision and use.* Where eye or skin contact with liquid AN may occur, the employer shall provide at no cost to the employee, and assure that employees wear, impermeable protective clothing or other equipment to protect any area of the body which may come in contact with liquid AN. The provision of §§ 1910.132 and 1910.133 shall be complied with.

(2) *Cleaning and replacement.* (i) The employer shall clean, launder, maintain, or replace protective clothing and equipment required by this section as needed to maintain their effectiveness.

(ii) The employer shall assure that impermeable protective clothing which contacts or is likely to have contacted liquid AN shall be decontaminated before being removed by the employee.

(iii) The employer shall assure that an employee whose nonimpermeable clothing becomes wetted with liquid AN shall immediately remove that clothing and proceed to shower. The clothing shall be decontaminated before it is removed from the regulated area.

(iv) The employer shall assure that no employee removes protective clothing or equipment from the change room, except for those employees authorized to do so for the purpose of laundering, maintenance, or disposal.

(v) The employer shall inform any person who launders or cleans protective clothing or equipment of the potentially harmful effects of exposure to AN.

(k) *Housekeeping.* (1) All surfaces shall be maintained free of visible accumulations of liquid AN.

(2) For operations involving liquid AN, the employer shall institute a program for detecting leaks and spills of liquid AN, including regular visual inspections.

(3) Where spills of liquid AN are detected, the employer shall assure that surfaces contacted by the liquid AN are decontaminated. Employees not engaged in decontamination activities shall leave the area of the spill, and shall not be permitted in the area until decontamination is completed.

(l) *Waste disposal.* AN waste, scrap, debris, bags, containers, or equipment shall be decontaminated before being incorporated in the general waste disposal system.

(m) *Hygiene facilities and practices.* (1) Where employees are exposed to airborne concentrations of AN above the permissible exposure limits, or where employees are required to wear protective clothing or equipment pursuant to paragraph (j) of this section, the facilities required by 29 CFR 1910.141, including clean change rooms and shower facilities, shall be provided by the employer for the use of those employees, and the employer shall assure that the employees use the facilities provided.

(2) The employer shall assure that employees wearing protective clothing or equipment for protection from skin contact with liquid AN shall shower at the end of the work shift.

(3) The employer shall assure that, in the event of skin or eye exposure to liquid AN, the affected employee shall shower immediately to minimize the danger of skin absorption.

(4) The employer shall assure that employees working in the regulated area wash their hands and faces prior to eating.

(n) *Medical surveillance*—(1) *General.* (i) The employer shall institute a program of medical surveillance for each employee who is or will be exposed to AN at or above the action level, without regard to the use of respirators. The employer shall provide each such employee with an opportunity for medical examinations and tests in accordance with this paragraph.

(ii) The employer shall assure that all medical examinations and procedures are performed by or under the supervision of a licensed physician, and that they shall be provided without cost to the employee.

(2) *Initial examinations.* At the time of initial assignment, or upon institution of the medical surveillance program, the employer shall provide each affected employee an opportunity for a medical examination, including at least the following elements:

(i) A work history and medical history with special attention to skin, respiratory, and gastrointestinal systems, and those nonspecific symptoms, such as headache, nausea, vomiting, dizziness, weakness, or other central nervous system dysfunctions that may be associated with acute or with chronic exposure to AN;

(ii) A complete physical examination giving particular attention to the peripheral and central nervous system, gastrointestinal system, respiratory system, skin, and thyroid;

(iii) A 14- by 17-inch posteroanterior chest X-ray; and

(iv) Further tests of the intestinal tract, including fecal occult blood screening, for all workers 40 years of age or older, and for any other affected employees for whom, in the opinion of the physician, such testing is appropriate.

(3) *Periodic examinations.* (i) The employer shall provide the examinations specified in paragraph (n)(2) of this section at least annually for all employees specified in paragraph (n)(1) of this section.

(ii) If an employee has not had the examination specified in paragraph (n)(2) of this section within 6 months preceding termination of employment, the employer shall make such examination available to the employee prior to such termination.

(4) *Additional examinations.* If the employee for any reason develops signs or symptoms which may be associated with exposure to AN, the employer shall provide an appropriate examination and emergency medical treatment.

(5) *Information provided to the physician.* The employer shall provide the following information to the examining physician:

(i) A copy of this standard and its appendixes;

(ii) A description of the affected employee's duties as they relate to the employee's exposure;

(iii) The employee's representative exposure level;

(iv) The employee's anticipated or estimated exposure level (for preplacement examinations or in cases of exposure due to an emergency);

(v) A description of any personal protective equipment used or to be used; and

(vi) Information from previous medical examinations of the affected employee, which is not otherwise available to the examining physician.

(6) *Physician's written opinion.* (i) The employer shall obtain a written opinion from the examining physician which shall include:

(A) The results of the medical examination and test performed;

(B) The physician's opinion as to whether the employee has any detected medical condition(s) which would place the employee at an increased risk of material impairment of the employee's health from exposure to AN;

(C) Any recommended limitations upon the employee's exposure to AN or upon the use of protective clothing and equipment such as respirators; and

(D) A statement that the employee has been informed by the physician of the results of the medical examination and any medical conditions which require further examination or treatment.

(ii) The employer shall instruct the physician not to reveal in the written opinion specific findings or diagnoses unrelated to occupational exposure to AN.

(iii) The employer shall provide a copy of the written opinion to the affected employee.

(o) *Employee information and training*—(1) *Training program.* (i) The employer shall train each employee exposed to AN above the action level, each employee whose exposures are maintained below the action level by engineering and work practice controls, and each employee subject to potential skin or eye contact with liquid

399

AN in accordance with the requirements of this section. The employer shall institute a training program and ensure employee participation in the program.

(ii) Training shall be provided at the time of initial assignment, or upon institution of the training program, and at least annually thereafter, and the employer shall assure that each employee is informed of the following:

(A) The information contained in appendixes A and B;

(B) The quantity, location, manner of use, release, or storage of AN, and the specific nature of operations which could result in exposure to AN, as well as any necessary protective steps;

(C) The purpose, proper use, and limitations of respirators and protective clothing;

(D) The purpose and a description of the medical surveillance program required by paragraph (n) of this section;

(E) The emergency procedures developed, as required by paragraph (i) of this section;

(F) Engineering and work practice controls, their function, and the employee's relationship to these controls; and

(G) A review of this standard.

(2) *Access to training materials.* (i) The employer shall make a copy of this standard and its appendixes readily available to all affected employees.

(ii) The employer shall provide, upon request, all materials relating to the employee information and training program to the Assistant Secretary and the Director.

(p) *Communication of hazards—*(1) *Hazard communication—general.* (i) Chemical manufacturers, importers, distributors and employers shall comply with all requirements of the Hazard Communication Standard (HCS) (§ 1910.1200) for AN and AN-based materials not exempted under paragraph (a)(2) of this section.

(ii) In classifying the hazards of AN and AN-based materials at least the following hazards are to be addressed: Cancer; central nervous system effects; liver effects; skin sensitization; skin, respiratory, and eye irritation; acute toxicity effects; and flammability.

(iii) Employers shall include AN and AN-based materials in the hazard communication program established to comply with the HCS (§ 1910.1200). Employers shall ensure that each employee has access to labels on containers of AN and AN-based materials and to safety data sheets, and is trained in accordance with the requirements of HCS and paragraph (o) of this section.

(iv) The employer shall ensure that no statement appears on or near any sign or label required by this paragraph (p) that contradicts or detracts from the required sign or label.

(2) *Signs.* (i) The employer shall post signs to clearly indicate all workplaces where AN concentrations exceed the permissible exposure limits. The signs shall bear the following legend:

DANGER
ACRYLONITRILE (AN)
MAY CAUSE CANCER
RESPIRATORY PROTECTION MAY BE REQUIRED IN THIS AREA
AUTHORIZED PERSONNEL ONLY

(ii) The employer shall ensure that signs required by this paragraph (p)(2) are illuminated and cleaned as necessary so that the legend is readily visible.

(iii) Prior to June 1, 2016, employers may use the following legend in lieu of that specified in paragraph (p)(2)(i) of this section:

DANGER
ACRYLONITRILE (AN)
CANCER HAZARD
AUTHORIZED PERSONNEL ONLY
RESPIRATORS MAY BE REQUIRED

(3) *Labels.* (i) The employer shall ensure that precautionary labels are in compliance with paragraph (p)(1)(i) of this section and are affixed to all containers of liquid AN and AN-based materials not exempted under paragraph (a)(2) of this section. The employer shall ensure that the labels remain affixed when the materials are sold, distributed, or otherwise leave the employer's workplace.

(ii) Prior to June 1, 2015, employers may include the following information on precautionary labels required by this paragraph (p)(3) in lieu of the labeling requirements in paragraph (p)(1) of this section:

DANGER
CONTAINS ACRYLONITRILE (AN)

CANCER HAZARD

(iii) The employer shall ensure that the precautionary labels required by this paragraph (p)(3) are readily visible and legible.

(q) *Recordkeeping*—(1) *Objective data for exempted operations.* (i) Where the processing, use, and handling of materials made from or containing AN are exempted pursuant to paragraph (a)(2)(ii) of this section, the employer shall establish and maintain an accurate record of objective data reasonably relied upon in support of the exemption.

(ii) This record shall include at least the following information:

(A) The material qualifying for exemption;

(B) The source of the objective data;

(C) The testing protocol, results of testing, and/or analysis of the material for the release of AN;

(D) A description of the operation exempted and how the data supports the exemption; and

(E) Other data relevant to the operations, materials, and processing covered by the exemption.

(iii) The employer shall maintain this record for the duration of the employer's reliance upon such objective data.

(2) *Exposure monitoring.* (i) The employer shall establish and maintain an accurate record of all monitoring required by paragraph (e) of this section.

(ii) This record shall include:

(A) The dates, number, duration, and results of each of the samples taken, including a description of the sampling procedure used to determine representative employee exposure;

(B) A description of the sampling and analytical methods used and the data relied upon to establish that the methods meet the accuracy and precision requirements of paragraph (e)(6) of this section;

(C) Type of respiratory protective devices worn, if any; and

(D) Name, social security number, and job classification of the employee monitored and of all other employees whose exposure the measurement is intended to represent.

(iii) The employer shall maintain this record for at least forty (40) years, or for the duration of employment plus twenty (20) years, whichever is longer.

(3) *Medical surveillance.* (i) The employer shall establish and maintain an accurate record for each employee subject to medical surveillance as required by paragraph (n) of this section.

(ii) This record shall include:

(A) A copy of the physician's written opinions;

(B) Any employee medical complaints related to exposure to AN;

(C) A copy of the information provided to the physician as required by paragraph (n)(5) of this section; and

(D) A copy of the employee's medical and work history.

(iii) The employer shall assure that this record be maintained for at least forty (40) years, or for the duration of employment plus twenty (20) years, whichever is longer.

(4) *Availability.* (i) The employer shall make all records required to be maintained by this section available, upon request, to the Assistant Secretary and the Director for examination and copying.

(ii) Records required by paragraphs (q)(1) through (q)(3) of this section shall be provided upon request to employees, designated representatives, and the Assistant Secretary in accordance with 29 CFR 1910.1020 (a) through (e) and (q) through (i). Records required by paragraph (q)(1) shall be provided in the same manner as exposure monitoring records.

(5) *Transfer of records.* (i) Whenever the employer ceases to do business, the successor employer shall receive and retain all records required to be maintained by this section for the prescribed period.

(ii) The employer shall also comply with any additional requirements involving transfer of records set forth in 29 CFR 1910.1020(h).

(r) *Observation of monitoring*—(1) *Employee observation.* The employer shall provide affected employees, or their designated representatives, an opportunity to observe any monitoring of employee exposure to AN conducted pursuant to paragraph (e) of this section.

(2) *Observation procedures.* (i) Whenever observation of the monitoring of employee exposure to AN requires

entry into an area where the use of protective clothing or equipment is required, the employer shall provide the observer with personal protective clothing and equipment required to be worn by employees working in the area, assure the use of such clothing and equipment, and require the observer to comply with all other applicable safety and health procedures.

(ii) Without interfering with the monitoring, observers shall be entitled:

(A) To receive an explanation of the measurement procedures;

(B) To observe all steps related to the measurement of airborne concentrations of AN performed at the place of exposure; and

(C) To record the results obtained.

(s) [Reserved]

(t) *Appendixes.* The information contained in the appendixes is not intended, by itself, to create any additional obligation not otherwise imposed, or to detract from any obligation.

APPENDIX A TO § 1910.1045—SUBSTANCE SAFETY DATA SHEET FOR ACRYLONITRILE

I. SUBSTANCE IDENTIFICATION

A. Substance: Acrylonitrile (CH₂ CHCN).

B. Synonyms: Propenenitrile; vinyl cyanide; cyanoethylene; AN; VCN; acylon; carbacryl; fumigrian; ventox.

C. Acrylonitrile can be found as a liquid or vapor, and can also be found in polymer resins, rubbers, plastics, polyols, and other polymers having acrylonitrile as a raw or intermediate material.

D. AN is used in the manufacture of acrylic and modiacrylic fibers, acrylic plastics and resins, speciality polymers, nitrile rubbers, and other organic chemicals. It has also been used as a fumigant.

E. Appearance and odor: Colorless to pale yellow liquid with a pungent odor which can only be detected at concentrations above the permissible exposure level, in a range of 13–19 parts AN per million parts of air (13–19 ppm).

F. Permissible exposure: Exposure may not exceed either:

1. Two parts AN per million parts of air (2 ppm) averaged over the 8-hour workday; or

2. Ten parts AN per million parts of air (10 ppm) averaged over any 15-minute period in the workday.

3. In addition, skin and eye contact with liquid AN is prohibited.

II. HEALTH HAZARD DATA

A. Acrylonitrile can affect your body if you inhale the vapor (breathing), if it comes in contact with your eyes or skin, or if you swallow it. It may enter your body through your skin.

B. Effects of overexposure: 1. Short-term exposure: Acrylonitrile can cause eye irritation, nausea, vomiting, headache, sneezing, weakness, and light-headedness. At high concentrations, the effects of exposure may go on to loss of consciousness and death. When acrylonitrile is held in contact with the skin after being absorbed into shoe leather or clothing, it may produce blisters following several hours of no apparent effect. Unless the shoes or clothing are removed immediately and the area washed, blistering will occur. Usually there is no pain or inflammation associated with blister formation.

2. Long-term exposure: Acrylonitrile has been shown to cause cancer in laboratory animals and has been associated with higher incidences of cancer in humans. Repeated or prolonged exposure of the skin to acrylonitrile may produce irritation and dermatitis.

3. Reporting signs and symptoms: You should inform your employer if you develop any signs or symptoms and suspect they are caused by exposure to acrylonitrile.

III. EMERGENCY FIRST AID PROCEDURES

A. Eye exposure: If acrylonitrile gets into your eyes, wash your eyes immediately with large amounts of water, lifting the lower and upper lids occasionally. Get medical attention immediately. Contact lenses should not be worn when working with this chemical.

B. Skin exposure: If acrylonitrile gets on your skin, immediately wash the contaminated skin with water. If acrylonitrile soaks through your clothing, especially your shoes, remove the clothing immediately and wash the skin with water. If symptoms occur after washing, get medical attention immediately. Thoroughly wash the clothing before reusing. Contaminated leather shoes or other leather articles should be discarded.

C. Inhalation: If you or any other person breathes in large amounts of acrylonitrile, move the exposed person to fresh air at once. If breathing has stopped, perform artificial respiration. Keep the affected person warm and at rest. Get medical attention as soon as possible.

D. Swallowing: When acrylonitrile has been swallowed, give the person large quantities of water immediately. After the water has been swallowed, try to get the person to vomit by having him touch the back of his throat with his finger. Do not make an unconscious person vomit. Get medical attention immediately.

E. Rescue: Move the affected person from the hazardous exposure. If the exposed person has been overcome, notify someone else and put into effect the established emergency procedures. Do not become a casualty yourself. Understand your emergency rescue procedures and know the location of the emergency equipment before the need arises.

F. Special first aid procedures: First aid kits containing an adequate supply (at least two dozen) of amyl nitrite pearls, each containing 0.3 ml, should be maintained at each site where acrylonitrile is used. When a person is suspected of receiving an overexposure to acrylonitrile, immediately remove that person from the contaminated area using established rescue procedures. Contaminated clothing must be removed and the acrylonitrile washed from the skin immediately. Artificial respiration should be started at once if breathing has stopped. If the person is unconscious, amyl nitrite may be used as an antidote by a properly trained individual in accordance with established emergency procedures. Medical aid should be obtained immediately.

IV. RESPIRATORS AND PROTECTIVE CLOTHING

A. Respirators. You may be required to wear a respirator for nonroutine activities, in emergencies, while your employer is in the process of reducing acrylonitrile exposures through engineering controls, and in areas where engineering controls are not feasible. If respirators are worn, they must have a label issued by the National Institute for Occupational Safety and Health under the provisions of 42 CFR part 84 stating that the respirators have been approved for use with organic vapors. For effective protection, respirators must fit your face and head snugly. Respirators must not be loosened or removed in work situations where their use is required.

Acrylonitrile does not have a detectable odor except at levels above the permissible exposure limits. Do not depend on odor to warn you when a respirator cartridge or canister is exhausted. Cartridges or canisters must be changed daily or before the end-of-service-life, whichever comes first. Reuse of these may allow acrylonitrile to gradually filter through the cartridge and cause exposures which you cannot detect by odor. If you can smell acrylonitrile while wearing a respirator, proceed immediately to fresh air. If you experience difficulty breathing while wearing a respirator, tell your employer.

B. Supplied-air suits: In some work situations, the wearing of supplied-air suits may be necessary. Your employer must instruct you in their proper use and operation.

C. Protective clothing: You must wear impervious clothing, gloves, face shield, or other appropriate protective clothing to prevent skin contact with liquid acrylonitrile. Where protective clothing is required, your employer is required to provide clean garments to you as necessary to assume that the clothing protects you adequately. Replace or repair impervious clothing that has developed leaks.

Acrylonitrile should never be allowed to remain on the skin. Clothing and shoes which are not impervious to acrylonitrile should not be allowed to become contaminated with acrylonitrile, and if they do the clothing and shoes should be promptly removed and decontaminated. The clothing should be laundered or discarded after the AN is removed. Once acrylonitrile penetrates shoes or other leather articles, they should not be worn again.

D. Eye protection: You must wear splashproof safety goggles in areas where liquid acrylonitrile may contact your eyes. In addition, contact lenses should not be worn in areas where eye contact with acrylonitrile can occur.

V. PRECAUTIONS FOR SAFE USE, HANDLING, AND STORAGE

A. Acrylonitrile is a flammable liquid, and its vapors can easily form explosive mixtures in air.

B. Acrylonitrile must be stored in tightly closed containers in a cool, well-ventilated area, away from heat, sparks, flames, strong oxidizers (especially bromine), strong bases, copper, copper alloys, ammonia, and amines.

C. Sources of ignition such as smoking and open flames are prohibited wherever acrylonitrile is handled, used, or stored in a manner that could create a potential fire or explosion hazard.

D. You should use non-sparking tools when opening or closing metal containers of acrylonitrile, and containers must be bonded and grounded when pouring or transferring liquid acrylonitrile.

E. You must immediately remove any non-impervious clothing that becomes wetted with acrylonitrile, and this clothing must not be reworn until the acrylonitrile is removed from the clothing.

F. Impervious clothing wet with liquid acrylonitrile can be easily ignited. This clothing must be washed down with water before you remove it.

G. If your skin becomes wet with liquid acrylonitrile, you must promptly and thoroughly wash or shower with soap or mild detergent to remove any acrylonitrile from your skin.

H. You must not keep food, beverages, or smoking materials, nor are you permitted to eat or smoke in regulated areas where acrylonitrile concentrations are above the permissible exposure limits.

I. If you contact liquid acrylonitrile, you must wash your hands thoroughly with soap or mild detergent and water before eating, smoking, or using toilet facilities.

J. Fire extinguishers and quick drenching facilities must be readily available, and you should know where they are and how to operate them.

K. Ask your supervisor where acrylonitrile is used in your work area and for any additional plant safety and health rules.

VI. ACCESS TO INFORMATION

A. Each year, your employer is required to inform you of the information contained in this Substance Safety Data Sheet for acrylonitrile. In addition, you employer must instruct you in the proper work practices for using acrylonitrile, emergency procedures, and the correct use of protective equipment.

B. Your employer is required to determine whether you are being exposed to acrylonitrile. You or your representative has the right to observe employee measurements and to record the results obtained. Your employer is required to inform you of your exposure. If your employer determines that you are being overexposed, he or she is required to inform you of the actions which are being taken to reduce your exposure to within permissible exposure limits.

C. Your employer is required to keep records of your exposures and medical examinations. These records must be kept by the employer for at least forty (40) years or for the period of your employment plus twenty (20) years, whichever is longer.

D. Your employer is required to release your exposure and medical records to you or your representative upon your request.

APPENDIX B TO § 1910.1045—SUBSTANCE
TECHNICAL GUIDELINES FOR ACRYLONITRILE

I. PHYSICAL AND CHEMICAL DATA

A. Substance identification: 1. Synonyms: AN; VCN; vinyl cyanide; propenenitrile; cyanoethylene; Acrylon; Carbacryl; Fumigrain; Ventox.

2. Formula: $CH_2 = CHCN$.

3. Molecular weight: 53.1.

B. Physical data: 1. Boiling point (760 mm Hg): 77.3 °C (171 °F);

2. Specific gravity (water = 1): 0.81 (at 20 °C or 68 °F);

3. Vapor density (air = 1 at boiling point of acrylonitrile): 1.83;

4. Melting point: −83 °C (−117 °F);

5. Vapor pressure (@20 °F): 83 mm Hg;

6. Solubility in water, percent by weight @20 °C (68 °F): 7.35;

7. Evaporation rate (Butyl Acetate = 1): 4.54; and

8. Appearance and odor: Colorless to pale yellow liquid with a pungent odor at concentrations above the permissible exposure level. Any detectable odor of acrylonitrile may indicate overexposure.

II. FIRE, EXPLOSION, AND REACTIVITY HAZARD DATA

A. Fire: 1. Flash point: −1 °C (30 °F) (closed cup).

2. Autoignition temperature: 481 °C (898 °F).

3. Flammable limits air, percent by volume: Lower: 3, Upper: 17.

4. Extinguishing media: Alcohol foam, carbon dioxide, and dry chemical.

5. Special fire-fighting procedures: Do not use a solid stream of water, since the stream will scatter and spread the fire. Use water to cool containers exposed to a fire.

6. Unusual fire and explosion hazards: Acrylonitrile is a flammable liquid. Its vapors can easily form explosive mixtures with air. All ignition sources must be controlled where acrylonitrile is handled, used, or stored in a manner that could create a potential fire or explosion hazard. Acrylonitrile vapors are heavier than air and may travel along the ground and be ignited by open flames or sparks at locations remote from the site at which acrylonitrile is being handled.

7. For purposes of compliance with the requirements of 29 CFR 1910.106, acrylonitrile is classified as a class IB flammable liquid. For example, 7,500 ppm, approximately one-fourth of the lower flammable limit, would be considered to pose a potential fire and explosion hazard.

8. For purposes of compliance with 29 CFR 1910.157, acrylonitrile is classified as a Class B fire hazard.

9. For purpose of compliance with 29 CFR 1919.309, locations classified as hazardous due to the presence of acrylonitrile shall be Class I, Group D.

B. Reactivity:

1. Conditions contributing to instability: Acrylonitrile will polymerize when hot, and the additional heat liberated by the polymerization may cause containers to explode. Pure AN may self-polymerize, with a rapid build-up of pressure, resulting in an explosion hazard. Inhibitors are added to the commercial product to prevent self-polymerization.

2. Incompatibilities: Contact with strong oxidizers (especially bromine) and strong bases may cause fires and explosions. Contact with copper, copper alloys, ammonia, and amines may start serious decomposition.

3. Hazardous decompostion products: Toxic gases and vapors (such as hydrogen cyanide, oxides of nitrogen, and carbon monoxide) may be released in a fire involving acrylonitrile and certain polymers made from acrylonitrile.

4. Special precautions: Liquid acrylonitrile will attack some forms of plastics, rubbers, and coatings.

404

III. SPILL, LEAK, AND DISPOSAL PROCEDURES

A. If acrylonitrile is spilled or leaked, the following steps should be taken:
1. Remove all ignition sources.
2. The area should be evacuated at once and re-entered only after the area has been thoroughly ventilated and washed down with water.
3. If liquid acrylonitrile or polymer intermediate, collect for reclamation or absorb in paper, vermiculite, dry sand, earth, or similar material, or wash down with water into process sewer system.

B. Persons not wearing protective equipment should be restricted from areas of spills or leaks until clean-up has been completed.

C. Waste disposal methods: Waste material shall be disposed of in a manner that is not hazardous to employees or to the general population. Spills of acrylonitrile and flushing of such spills shall be channeled for appropriate treatment or collection for disposal. They shall not be channeled directly into the sanitary sewer system. In selecting the method of waste disposal, applicable local, State, and Federal regulations should be consulted.

IV. MONITORING AND MEASUREMENT PROCEDURES

A. Exposure above the Permissible Exposure Limit:
1. Eight-hour exposure evaluation: Measurements taken for the purpose of determining employee exposure under this section are best taken so that the average 8-hour exposure may be determined from a single 8-hour sample or two (2) 4-hour samples. Air samples should be taken in the employee's breathing zone (air that would most nearly represent that inhaled by the employee.)
2. Ceiling evaluation: Measurements taken for the purpose of determining employee exposure under this section must be taken during periods of maximum expected airborne concentrations of acrylonitrile in the employee's breathing zone. A minimum of three (3) measurements should be taken on one work shift. The average of all measurements taken is an estimate of the employee's ceiling exposure.
3. Monitoring techniques: The sampling and analysis under this section may be performed by collecting the acrylonitrile vapor on charcoal adsorption tubes or other composition adsorption tubes, with subsequent chemical analysis. Sampling and analysis may also be performed by instruments such as real-time continuous monitoring systems, portable direct-reading instruments, or passive dosimeters. Analysis of resultant samples should be by gas chromatograph.

Appendix D lists methods of sampling and analysis which have been tested by NIOSH and OSHA for use with acrylonitrile. NIOSH and OSHA have validated modifications of NIOSH Method S–156 (See appendix D) under laboratory conditions for concentrations below 1 ppm. The employer has the obligation of selecting a monitoring method which meets the accuracy and precision requirements of the standard under his unique field conditions. The standard requires that methods of monitoring must be accurate, to a 95-percent confidence level, to ±35-percent for concentrations of AN at or above 2 ppm, and to ±50-percent for concentrations below 2 ppm. In addition to the methods described in appendix D, there are numerous other methods available for monitoring for AN in the workplace. Details on these other methods have been submitted by various companies to the rulemaking record, and are available at the OSHA Docket Office.

B. Since many of the duties relating to employee exposure are dependent on the results of monitoring and measuring procedures, employers shall assure that the evaluation of employee exposures is performed by a competent industrial hygienist or other technically qualified person.

V. PROTECTIVE CLOTHING

Employees shall be provided with and required to wear appropriate protective clothing to prevent any possibility of skin contact with liquid AN. Because acrylonitrile is absorbed through the skin, it is important to prevent skin contact with liquid AN. Protective clothing shall include impermeable coveralls or similar full-body work clothing, gloves, head-coverings, as appropriate to protect areas of the body which may come in contact with liquid AN.

Employers should ascertain that the protective garmets are impermeable to acrylonitrile. Non-impermeable clothing and shoes should not be allowed to become contaminated with liquid AN. If permeable clothing does become contaminated, it should be promptly removed, placed in a regulated area for removal of the AN, and not worn again until the AN is removed. If leather footwear or other leather garments become wet from acrylonitrile, they should be replaced and not worn again, due to the ability of leather to absorb acrylonitrile and hold it against the skin. Since there is no pain associated with the blistering which may result from skin contact with liquid AN, it is essential that the employee be informed of this hazard so that he or she can be protected.

Any protective clothing which has developed leaks or is otherwise found to be defective shall be repaired or replaced. Clean protective clothing shall be provided to the employee as necessary to assure its protectiveness. Whenever impervious clothing becomes wet with liquid AN, it shall be washed down with water before being removed by the employee. Employees are also required to wear splash-proof safety goggles where there is

405

any possibility of acrylonitrile contacting the eyes.

VI. HOUSEKEEPING AND HYGIENE FACILITIES

For purposes of complying with 29 CFR 1910.141, the following items should be emphasized:

A. The workplace should be kept clean, orderly, and in a sanitary condition. The employer is required to institute a leak and spill detection program for operations involving liquid AN in order to detect sources of fugitive AN emissions.

B. Dry sweeping and the use of compressed air is unsafe for the cleaning of floors and other surfaces where liquid AN may be found.

C. Adequate washing facilities with hot and cold water are to be provided, and maintained in a sanitary condition. Suitable cleansing agents are also to be provided to assure the effective removal of acrylonitrile from the skin.

D. Change or dressing rooms with individual clothes storage facilities must be provided to prevent the contamination of street clothes with acrylonitrile. Because of the hazardous nature of acrylonitrile, contaminated protective clothing should be placed in a regulated area designated by the employer for removal of the AN before the clothing is laundered or disposed of.

VII. MISCELLANEOUS PRECAUTIONS

A. Store acrylonitrile in tightly-closed containers in a cool, well-ventilated area and take necessary precautions to avoid any explosion hazard.

B. High exposures to acrylonitrile can occur when transferring the liquid from one container to another.

C. Non-sparking tools must be used to open and close metal acrylonitrile containers. These containers must be effectively grounded and bonded prior to pouring.

D. Never store uninhibited acrylonitrile.

E. Acrylonitrile vapors are not inhibited. They may form polymers and clog vents of storage tanks.

F. Use of supplied-air suits or other impervious coverings may be necessary to prevent skin contact with and provide respiratory protection from acrylonitrile where the concentration of acrylonitrile is unknown or is above the ceiling limit. Supplied-air suits should be selected, used, and maintained under the immediate supervision of persons knowledgeable in the limitations and potential life-endangering characteristics of supplied-air suits.

G. Employers shall advise employees of all areas and operations where exposure to acrylonitrile could occur.

VIII. COMMON OPERATIONS

Common operations in which exposure to acrylonitrile is likely to occur include the following: Manufacture of the acrylonitrile monomer; synthesis of acrylic fibers, ABS, SAN, and nitrile barrier plastics and resins, nitrile rubber, surface coatings, specialty chemicals, use as a chemical intermediate, use as a fumigant and in the cyanoethylation of cotton.

APPENDIX C TO § 1910.1045—MEDICAL SURVEILLANCE GUIDELINES FOR ACRYLONITRILE

I. ROUTE OF ENTRY

Inhalation; skin absorption; ingestion.

II. TOXICOLOGY

Acrylonitrile vapor is an asphyxiant due to inhibitory action on metabolic enzyme systems. Animals exposed to 75 or 100 ppm for 7 hours have shown signs of anoxia; in some animals which died at the higher level, cyanomethemoglobin was found in the blood. Two human fatalities from accidental poisioning have been reported; one was caused by inhalation of an unknown concentration of the vapor, and the other was thought to be caused by skin absorption or inhalation. Most cases of intoxication from industrial exposure have been mild, with rapid onset of eye irritation, headache, sneezing, and nausea. Weakness, lightheadedness, and vomiting may also occur. Exposure to high concentrations may produce profound weakness, asphyxia, and death. The vapor is a severe eye irritant. Prolonged skin contract with the liquid may result in absorption with systemic effects, and in the formation of large blisters after a latent period of several hours. Although there is usually little or no pain or inflammation, the affected skin resembles a second-degree thermal burn. Solutions spilled on exposed skin, or on areas covered only by a light layer of clothing, evaporate rapidly, leaving no irritation, or, at the most, mild transient redness. Repeated spills on exposed skin may result in dermatitis due to solvent effects.

Results after 1 year of a planned 2-year animal study on the effects of exposure to acrylonitrile have indicated that rats ingesting as little as 35 ppm in their drinking water develop tumors of the central nervous system. The interim results of this study have been supported by a similar study being conducted by the same laboratory, involving exposure of rats by inhalation of acrylonitrile vapor, which has shown similar types of tumors in animals exposed to 80 ppm.

In addition, the preliminary results of an epidemiological study being performed by duPont on a cohort of workers in their Camden, S.C. acrylic fiber plant indicate a statistically significant increase in the incidence of colon and lung cancers among employees exposed to acrylonitrile.

III. SIGNS AND SYMPTOMS OF ACUTE OVEREXPOSURE

Asphyxia and death can occur from exposure to high concentrations of acrylonitrile. Symptoms of overexposure include eye irritation, headache, sneezing, nausea and vomiting, weakness, and light-headedness. Prolonged skin contact can cause blisters on the skin with appearance of a second-degree burn, but with little or no pain. Repeated skin contact may produce scaling dermatits.

IV. TREATMENT OF ACUTE OVEREXPOSURE

Remove employee from exposure. Immediately flush eyes with water and wash skin with soap or mild detergent and water. If AN has been swallowed, and person is conscious, induce vomiting. Give artificial resuscitation if indicated. More severe cases, such as those associated with loss of consciousness, may be treated by the intravenous administration of sodium nitrite, followed by sodium thiosulfate, although this is not as effective for acrylonitrile poisoning as for inorganic cyanide poisoning.

V. SURVEILLANCE AND PREVENTIVE CONSIDERATIONS

A. As noted above, exposure to acrylonitrile has been linked to increased incidence of cancers of the colon and lung in employees of the duPont acrylic fiber plant in Camden, S.C. In addition, the animal testing of acrylonitrile has resulted in the development of cancers of the central nervous system in rats exposed by either inhalation or ingestion. The physician should be aware of the findings of these studies in evaluating the health of employees exposed to acrylonitrile.

Most reported acute effects of occupational exposure to acrylonitrile are due to its ability to cause tissue anoxia and asphyxia. The effects are similar to those caused by hydrogen cyanide. Liquid acrylonitrile can be absorbed through the skin upon prolonged contact. The liquid readily penetrates leather, and will produce burns of the feet if footwear contaminated with acrylonitrile is not removed.

It is important for the physician to become familiar with the operating conditions in which exposure to acrylonitrile may occur. Those employees with skin diseases may not tolerate the wearing of whatever protective clothing may be necessary to protect them from exposure. In addition, those with chronic respiratory disease may not tolerate the wearing of negative-pressure respirators.

B. Surveillance and screening. Medical histories and laboratory examinations are required for each employee subject to exposure to acrylonitrile above the action level. The employer must screen employees for history of certain medical conditions which might place the employee at increased risk from exposure.

1. *Central nervous system dysfunction.* Acute effects of exposure to acrylonitrile generally involve the central nervous system. Symptoms of acrylonitrile exposure include headache, nausea, dizziness, and general weakness. The animal studies cited above suggest possible carcinogenic effects of acrylonitrile on the central nervous system, since rats exposed by either inhalation or ingestion have developed similar CNS tumors.

2. *Respiratory disease.* The du Pont data indicate an increased risk of lung cancer among employees exposed to acrylonitrile.

3. *Gastrointestinal disease.* The du Pont data indicate an increased risk of cancer of the colon among employees exposed to acrylonitrile. In addition, the animal studies show possible tumor production in the stomachs of the rats in the ingestion study.

4. *Skin disease.* Acrylonitrile can cause skin burns when prolonged skin contact with the liquid occurs. In addition, repeated skin contact with the liquid can cause dermatitis.

5. *General.* The purpose of the medical procedures outlined in the standard is to establish a baseline for future health monitoring. Persons unusually susceptible to the effects of anoxia or those with anemia would be expected to be at increased risk. In addition to emphasis on the CNS, respiratory and gastro-intestinal systems, the cardiovascular system, liver, and kidney function should also be stressed.

APPENDIX D TO §1910.1045—SAMPLING AND ANALYTICAL METHODS FOR ACRYLONITRILE

There are many methods available for monitoring employee exposures to acrylonitrile. Most of these involve the use of charcoal tubes and sampling pumps, with analysis by gas chromatograph. The essential differences between the charcoal tube methods include, among others, the use of different desorbing solvents, the use of different lots of charcoal, and the use of different equipment for analysis of the samples.

Besides charcoal, considerable work has been performed on methods using porous polymer sampling tubes and passive dosimeters. In addition, there are several portable gas analyzers and monitoring units available on the open market.

This appendix contains details for the methods which have been tested at OSHA Analytical Laboratory in Salt Lake City, and NIOSH in Cincinnati. Each is a variation on NIOSH Method S–156, which is also included for reference. This does not indicate that these methods are the only ones which will be satisfactory. There also may be workplace situations in which these methods are

407

not adequate, due to such factors as high humidity. Copies of the other methods available to OSHA are available in the rulemaking record, and may be obtained from the OSHA Docket Office. These include, the Union Carbide, Monsanto, Dow Chemical and Dow Badische methods, as well as NISOH Method P & CAM 127.

Employers who note problems with sample breakthrough should try larger charcoal tubes. Tubes of larger capacity are available, and are often used for sampling vinyl chloride. In addition, lower flow rates and shorter sampling times should be beneficial in minimizing breakthrough problems.

Whatever method the employer chooses, he must assure himself of the method's accuracy and precision under the unique conditions present in his workplace.

NIOSH METHOD S-156 (UNMODIFIED)

Analyte: Acrylonitrile.

Matrix: Air.

Procedure: Absorption on charcoal, desorption with methanol, GC.

1. *Principle of the method* (Reference 11.1).

1.1 A known volume of air is drawn through a charcoal tube to trap the organic vapors present.

1.2 The charcoal in the tube is transferred to a small, stoppered sample container, and the analyte is desorbed with methanol.

1.3 An aliquot of the desorbed sample is injected into a gas chromatograph.

1.4 The area of the resulting peak is determined and compared with areas obtained for standards.

2. *Range and sensitivity*.

2.1 This method was validated over the range of 17.5-70.0 mg/cu m at an atmospheric temperature and pressure of 22 °C and 760 MM Hg, using a 20-liter sample. Under the conditions of sample size (20-liters) the probable useful range of this method is 4.5-135 mg-cu m. The method is capable of measuring much smaller amounts if the desorption efficiency is adequate. Desorption efficiency must be determined over the range used.

2.2 The upper limit of the range of the method is dependent on the adsorptive capacity of the charcoal tube. This capacity varies with the concentrations of acrylonitrile and other substances in the air. The first section of the charcoal tube was found to hold at least 3.97 mg of acrylonitrile when a test atmosphere containing 92.0 mg/cu m of acrylonitrile in air was sampled 0.18 liter per minute for 240 minutes; at that time the concentration of acrylonitrile in the effluent was less than 5 percent of that in the influent. (The charcoal tube consists of two sections of activated charcoal separated by a section of urethane foam. See section 6.2.) If a particular atmosphere is suspected of con-

taining a large amount of contaminant, a smaller sampling volume should be taken.

3. *Interference*.

3.1 When the amount of water in the air is so great that condensation actually occurs in the tube, organic vapors will not be trapped efficiently. Preliminary experiments using toluene indicate that high humidity severely decreases the breakthrough volume.

3.2 When interfering compounds are known or suspected to be present in the air, such information, including their suspected identities, should be transmitted with the sample.

3.3 It must be emphasized that any compound which has the same retention time as the analyte at the operating conditions described in this method is an interference. Retention time data on a single column cannot be considered proof of chemical identity.

3.4 If the possibility of interference exists, separation conditions (column packing, temperature, etc.) must be changed to circumvent the problem.

4. *Precision and accuracy*.

4.1 The Coefficient of Variation (CV_T) for the total analytical and sampling method in the range of 17.5-70.0 mg/cu m was 0.073. This value corresponds to a 3.3 mg/cu m standard deviation at the (previous) OSHA standard level (20 ppm). Statistical information and details of the validation and experimental test procedures can be found in Reference 11.2.

4.2 On the average the concentrations obtained at the 20 ppm level using the overall sampling and analytical method were 6.0 percent lower than the "true" concentrations for a limited number of laboratory experiments. Any difference between the "found" and "true" concentrations may not represent a bias in the sampling and analytical method, but rather a random variation from the experimentally determined "true" concentration. Therefore, no recovery correction should be applied to the final result in section 10.5.

5. *Advantages and disadvantages of the method*.

5.1 The sampling device is small, portable, and involves no liquids. Interferences are minimal, and most of those which do occur can be eliminated by altering chromatographic conditions. The tubes are analyzed by means of a quick, instrumental method.

The method can also be used for the simultaneous analysis of two or more substances suspected to be present in the same sample by simply changing gas chromatographic conditions.

5.2 One disadvantage of the method is that the amount of sample which can be taken is limited by the number of milligrams that the tube will hold before overloading. When the sample value obtained for the backup section of the charcoal tube exceeds 25 percent of that found on the front section, the possibility of sample loss exists.

5.3 Furthermore, the precision of the method is limited by the reproducibility of the pressure drop across the tubes. This drop will affect the flow rate and cause the volume to be imprecise, because the pump is usually calibrated for one tube only.

6. *Apparatus.*

6.1 A calibrated personal sampling pump whose flow can be determined within ±5 percent at the recommended flow rate. (Reference 11.3).

6.2 Charcoal tubes: Glass tubes with both ends flame sealed, 7 cm long with a 6-mm O.D. and a 4-mm I.D., containing 2 sections of 20/40 mesh activated charcoal separated by a 2-mm portion of urethane foam. The activated charcoals prepared from coconut shells and is fired at 600 °C prior to packing. The adsorbing section contains 100 mg of charcoal, the backup section 50 mg. A 3-mm portion of urethane foam is placed between the outlet end of the tube and the backup section. A plug of silicated glass wool is placed in front of the adsorbing section. The pressure drop across the tube must be less than 1 inch of mercury at a flow rate of 1 liter per minute.

6.3 Gas chromatograph equipped with a flame ionization detector.

6.4 Column (4-ft × ¼-in stainless steel) packed with 50/80 mesh Poropak, type Q.

6.5 An electronic integrator or some other suitable method for measuring peak areas.

6.6 Two-milliliter sample containers with glass stoppers or Teflon-lined caps. If an automatic sample injector is used, the associated vials may be used.

6.7 Microliter syringes: 10-microliter and other convenient sizes for making standards.

6.8 Pipets: 1.0-ml delivery pipets.

6.9 Volumetric flask: 10-ml or convenient sizes for making standard solutions.

7. *Reagents.*

7.1 Chromatographic quality methanol.

7.2 Acrylonitrile, reagent grade.

7.3 Hexane, reagent grade.

7.4 Purified nitrogen.

7.5 Prepurified hydrogen.

7.6 Filtered compressed air.

8. *Procedure.*

8.1 Cleaning of equipment. All glassware used for the laboratory analysis should be detergent washed and thoroughly rinsed with tap water and distilled water.

8.2 Calibration of personal pumps. Each personal pump must be calibrated with a representative charcoal tube in the line. This will minimize errors associated with uncertainties in the sample volume collected.

8.3 Collection and shipping of samples.

8.3.1 Immediately before sampling, break the ends of the tube to provide an opening at least one-half the internal diameter of the tube (2 mm).

8.3.2 The smaller section of charcoal is used as a backup and should be positioned nearest the sampling pump.

8.3.3 The charcoal tube should be placed in a vertical direction during sampling to minimize channeling through the charcoal.

8.3.4 Air being sampled should not be passed through any hose or tubing before entering the charcoal tube.

8.3.5 A maximum sample size of 20 liters is recommended. Sample at a flow of 0.20 liter per minute or less. The flow rate should be known with an accuracy of at least ±5 percent.

8.3.6 The temperature and pressure of the atmosphere being sampled should be recorded. If pressure reading is not available, record the elevation.

8.3.7 The charcoal tubes should be capped with the supplied plastic caps immediately after sampling. Under no circumstances should rubber caps be used.

8.3.8 With each batch of 10 samples submit one tube from the same lot of tubes which was used for sample collection and which is subjected to exactly the same handling as the samples except that no air is drawn through it. Label this as a blank.

8.3.9 Capped tubes should be packed tightly and padded before they are shipped to minimize tube breakage during shipping.

8.3.10 A sample of the bulk material should be submitted to the laboratory in a glass container with a Teflon-lined cap. This sample should not be transported in the same container as the charcoal tubes.

8.4 *Analysis of samples.*

8.4.1 Preparation of samples. In preparation for analysis, each charcoal tube is scored with a file in front of the first section of charcoal and broken open. The glass wool is removed and discarded. The charcoal in the first (larger) section is transferred to a 2-ml stoppered sample container. The separating section of foam is removed and discarded; the second section is transferred to another stoppered container. These two sections are analyzed separately.

8.4.2 Desorption of samples. Prior to analysis, 1.0 ml of methanol is pipetted into each sample container. Desorption should be done for 30 minutes. Tests indicate that this is adequate if the sample is agitated occasionally during this period. If an automatic sample injector is used, the sample vials should be capped as soon as the solvent is added to minimize volatilization.

8.4.3 GC conditions. The typical operating conditions for the gas chromatograph are:

1. 50 ml/min (60 psig) nitrogen carrier gas flow.

2. 65 ml/min (24 psig) hydrogen gas flow to detector.

3. 500 ml/min (50 psig) air flow to detector.

4. 235 °C injector temperature.

5. 255 °C manifold temperature (detector).

6. 155 °C column temperature.

8.4.4 Injection. The first step in the analysis is the injection of the sample into the gas chromatograph. To eliminate difficulties arising from blowback or distillation within the syringe needle, one should employ the solvent flush injection technique. The 10-microliter syringe is first flushed with solvent several times to wet the barrel and plunger. Three microliters of solvent are drawn into the syringe to increase the accuracy and reproducibility of the injected sample volume. The needle is removed from the solvent, and the plunger is pulled back about 0.2 microliter to separate the solvent flush from the sample with a pocket of air to be used as a marker. The needle is then immersed in the sample, and a 5-microliter aliquot is withdrawn, taking into consideration the volume of the needle, since the sample in the needle will be completely injected. After the needle is removed from the sample and prior to injection, the plunger is pulled back 1.2 microliters to minimize evaporation of the sample from the tip of the needle. Observe that the sample occupies 4.9–5.0 microliters in the barrel of the syringe. Duplicate injections of each sample and standard should be made. No more than a 3 percent difference in area is to be expected. An automatic sample injector can be used if it is shown to give reproducibility at least as good as the solvent flush method.

8.4.5 Measurement of area. The area of the sample peak is measured by an electronic integrator or some other suitable form of area measurement, and preliminary results are read from a standard curve prepared as discussed below.

8.5 Determination of desorption efficiency.

8.5.1 Importance of determination. The desorption efficiency of a particular compound can vary from one laboratory to another and also from one batch of charcoal to another. Thus, it is necessary to determine at least once the percentage of the specific compound that is removed in the desorption process, provided the same batch of charcoal is used.

8.5.2 Procedure for determining desorption efficiency. Activated charcoal equivalent to the amount in the first section of the sampling tube (100 mg) is measured into a 2.5 in, 4-mm I.D. glass tube, flame sealed at one end. This charcoal must be from the same batch as that used in obtaining the samples and can be obtained from unused charcoal tubes. The open end is capped with Parafilm. A known amount of hexane solution of acrylonitrile containing 0.239 g/ml is injected directly into the activated charcoal with a microliter syringe, and tube is capped with more Parafilm. When using an automatic sample injector, the sample injector vials, capped with Teflon-faced septa, may be used in place of the glass tube.

The amount injected is equivalent to that present in a 20-liter air sample at the selected level.

Six tubes at each of three levels (0.5X, 1X, and 2X of the standard) are prepared in this manner and allowed to stand for at least overnight to assure complete adsorption of the analyte onto the charcoal. These tubes are referred to as the sample. A parallel blank tube should be treated in the same manner except that no sample is added to it. The sample and blank tubes are desorbed and analyzed in exactly the same manner as the sampling tube described in section 8.4.

Two or three standards are prepared by injecting the same volume of compound into 1.0 ml of methanol with the same syringe used in the preparation of the samples. These are analyzed with the samples.

The desorption efficiency (D.E.) equals the average weight in mg recovered from the tube divided by the weight in mg added to the tube, or

$$D.E. = \frac{\text{Average weight recovered (mg)}}{\text{weight added (mg)}}$$

The desorption efficiency is dependent on the amount of analyte collected on the charcoal. Plot the desorption efficiency versus weight of analyte found. This curve is used in section 10.4 to correct for adsorption losses.

9. Calibration and standards.

It is convenient to express concentration of standards in terms of mg/1.0 ml methanol, because samples are desorbed in this amount of methanol. The density of the analyte is used to convert mg into microliters for easy measurement with a microliter syringe. A series of standards, varying in concentration over the range of interest, is prepared and analyzed under the same GC conditions and during the same time period as the unknown samples. Curves are established by plotting concentration in mg/1.0 ml versus peak area.

NOTE: Since no internal standard is used in the method, standard solutions must be analyzed at the same time that the sample analysis is done. This will minimize the effect of known day-to-day variations and variations during the same day of the FID response.

10. Calculations.

10.1 Read the weight, in mg, corresponding to each peak area from the standard curve. No volume corrections are needed, because the standard curve is based on mg/1.0 ml methanol and the volume of sample injected is identical to the volume of the standards injected.

10.2 Corrections for the bank must be made for each sample.

mg = mg sample − mg blank

Where:

mg sample = mg found in front section of sample tube.

mg sample = mg found in front section of blank tube.

A similar procedure is followed for the backup sections.

10.3 Add the weights found in the front and backup sections to get the total weight in the sample.

10.4 Read the desorption efficiency from the curve (see sec. 8.5.2) for the amount found in the front section. Divide the total weight by this desorption efficiency to obtain the corrected mg/sample.

$$\text{Corrected mg/sample} = \frac{\text{Total weight}}{\text{D.E.}}$$

10.5 The concentration of the analyte in the air sampled can be expressed in mg/cu m.

$$\text{mg/cu m} = \text{Corrected mg (section 10.4)} \times \frac{1,000 \text{ (liter/cu m)}}{\text{air volume sampled (liter)}}$$

10.6 Another method of expressing concentration is ppm.

ppm = m mg/cu × 24.45/M.W. × 760/P × T. + 273/298

Where:

P = Pressure (mm Hg) of air sampled.

T = Temperature (°C) of air sampled.

24.45 = Molar volume (liter/mole) at 25 °C and 760 mm Hg.

M.W. = Molecular weight (g/mole) of analyte.

760 = Standard pressure (mm Hg).

298 = Standard temperature (°K).

11. *References.*

11.1 White, L. D. et al., "A Convenient Optimized Method for the Analysis of Selected Solvent Vapors in the Industrial Atmosphere," *Amer. Ind. Hyg. Assoc. J., 31*:225 (1970).

11.2 Documentation of NIOSH Validation Tests, NIOSH Contract No. CDC–99–74–45.

11.3 Final Report, NIOSH Contract HSM–99–71–31, "Personal Sampler Pump for Charcoal Tubes," September 15, 1972.

NIOSH Modification of NIOSH Method S–156

The NIOSH recommended method for low levels for acrylonitrile is a modification of method S–156. It differs in the following respects:

(1) Samples are desorbed using 1 ml of 1 percent acetone in CS_2 rather than methanol.

(2) The analytical column and conditions are:

Column: 20 percent SP–1000 on 80/100 Supelcoport 10 feet × ⅛ inch S.S.

Conditions:

Injector temperature: 200 °C.

Detector temperature: 100 °C.

Column temperature: 85 °C.

Helium flow: 25 ml/min.

Air flow: 450 ml/min.

Hydrogen flow: 55 ml/min.

(3) A 2 µl injection of the desorbed analyte is used.

(4) A sampling rate of 100 ml/min is recommended.

OSHA Laboratory Modification of NIOSH Method S–156

Analyte: Acrylonitrile.

Matrix: Air.

Procedure: Adsorption on charcoal, desorption with methanol, GC.

1. *Principle of the Method* (Reference 1).

1.1 A known volume of air is drawn through a charcoal tube to trap the organic vapors present.

1.2 The charcoal in the tube is transferred to a small, stoppered sample vial, and the analyte is desorbed with methanol.

1.3 An aliquot of the desorbed sample is injected into a gas chromatograph.

1.4 The area of the resulting peak is determined and compared with areas obtained for standards.

2. *Advantages and disadvantages of the method.*

2.1 The sampling device is small, portable, and involves no liquids. Interferences are minimal, and most of those which do occur can be eliminated by altering chromatographic conditions. The tubes are analyzed by means of a quick, instrumental method.

2.2 This method may not be adequate for the simultaneous analysis of two or more substances.

2.3 The amount of sample which can be taken is limited by the number of milligrams that the tube will hold before overloading. When the sample value obtained for the backup section of the charcoal tube exceeds 25 percent of that found on the front section, the possibility of sample loss exists.

2.4 The precision of the method is limited by the reproducibility of the pressure drop across the tubes. This drop will affect the flow rate and cause the volume to be imprecise, because the pump is usually calibrated for one tube only.

3. *Apparatus.*

3.1 A calibrated personal sampling pump whose flow can be determined within ±5 percent at the recommended flow rate.

411

3.2 Charcoal tubes: Glass tube with both ends flame sealed, 7 cm long with a 6-mm O.D. and a 4-mm I.D., containing 2 sections of 20/40 mesh activated charcoal separated by a 2-mm portion of urethane foam. The activated charcoal is prepared from coconut shells and is fired at 600 °C prior to packing. The adsorbing section contains 100 mg of charcoal, the back-up section 50 mg. A 3-mm portion of urethane foam is placed between the outlet end of the tube and the back-up section. A plug of sililated glass wool is placed in front of the adsorbing section. The pressure drop across the tube must be less than one inch of mercury at a flow rate of 1 liter per minute.

3.3 Gas chromatograph equipped with a nitrogen phosphorus detector.

3.4 Column (10-ft × 1/8″-in stainless steel) packed with 100/120 Supelcoport coated with 10 percent SP 1000.

3.5 An electronic integrator or some other suitable method for measuring peak area.

3.6 Two-milliliter sample vials with Teflon-lined caps

3.7 Microliter syringes: 10-microliter, and other convenient sizes for making standards.

3.8 Pipets: 1.0-ml delivery pipets.

3.9 Volumetric flasks: convenient sizes for making standard solutions.

4. *Reagents.*

4.1 Chromatographic quality methanol.

4.2 Acrylonitrile, reagent grade.

4.3 Filtered compressed air.

4.4 Purified hydrogen.

4.5 Purified helium.

5. *Procedure.*

5.1 Cleaning of equipment. All glassware used for the laboratory analysis should be properly cleaned and free of organics which could interfere in the analysis.

5.2 Calibration of personal pumps. Each pump must be calibrated with a representative charcoal tube in the line.

5.3 Collection and shipping of samples.

5.3.1 Immediately before sampling, break the ends of the tube to provide an opening at least one-half the internal diameter of the tube (2 mm).

5.3.2 The smaller section of the charcoal is used as the backup and should be placed nearest the sampling pump.

5.3.3 The charcoal should be placed in a vertical position during sampling to minimize channeling through the charcoal.

5.3.4 Air being sampled should not be passed through any hose or tubing before entering the charcoal tube.

5.3.5 A sample size of 20 liters is recommended. Sample at a flow rate of approximately 0.2 liters per minute. The flow rate should be known with an accuracy of at least ±5 percent.

5.3.6 The temperature and pressure of the atmosphere being sampled should be recorded.

5.3.7 The charcoal tubes should be capped with the supplied plastic caps immediately after sampling. Rubber caps should not be used.

5.3.8 Submit at least one blank tube (a charcoal tube subjected to the same handling procedures, without having any air drawn through it) with each set of samples.

5.3.9. Take necessary shipping and packing precautions to minimize breakage of samples.

5.4 Analysis of samples.

5.4.1 Preparation of samples. In preparation for analysis, each charcoal tube is scored with a file in front of the first section of charcoal and broken open. The glass wool is removed and discarded. The charcoal in the first (larger) section is transferred to a 2-ml vial. The separating section of foam is removed and discarded; the section is transferred to another capped vial. These two sections are analyzed separately.

5.4.2 Desorption of samples. Prior to analysis, 1.0 ml of methanol is pipetted into each sample container. Desorption should be done for 30 minutes in an ultrasonic bath. The sample vials are recapped as soon as the solvent is added.

5.4.3 GC conditions. The typical operating conditions for the gas chromatograph are:

1. 30 ml/min (60 psig) helium carrier gas flow.

2. 3.0 ml/min (30 psig) hydrogen gas flow to detector.

3. 50 ml/min (60 psig) air flow to detector.

4. 200 °C injector temperature.

5. 200 °C dejector temperature.

6. 100 °C column temperature.

5.4.4 Injection. Solvent flush technique or equivalent.

5.4.5 Measurement of area. The area of the sample peak is measured by an electronic integator or some other suitable form of area measurement, and preliminary results are read from a standard curve prepared as discussed below.

5.5 Determination of desorption efficiency.

5.5.1 Importance of determination. The desorption efficiency of a particular compound can vary from one laboratory to another and also from one batch of charcoal to another. Thus, it is necessary to determine, at least once, the percentage of the specific compound that is removed in the desorption process, provided the same batch of charcoal is used.

5.5.2 Procedure for determining desorption efficiency. The reference portion of the charcoal tube is removed. To the remaining portion, amounts representing 0.5X, 1X, and 2X (X represents TLV) based on a 20 l air sample are injected onto several tubes at each level. Dilutions of acrylonitrile with methanol are made to allow injection of measurable quantities. These tubes are then allowed to equilibrate at least overnight. Following equilibration they are analyzed following the

same procedure as the samples A curve of
the desorption efficiency amt recovered/amt
added is plotted versus amount of analyte
found. This curve is used to correct for adsorption losses.

6. *Calibration and standards.*
A series of standards, varying in concentration over the range of interest, is prepared and analyzed under the same GC conditions and during the same time period as the
unknown samples. Curves are prepared by
plotting concentration versus peak area.

NOTE: Since no internal standard is used in
the method, standard solutions must be analyzed at the same time that the sample analysis is done. This will minimize the effect of
known day-to-day variations and variations
during the same day of the NPD response.
Multiple injections are necessary.

7. *Calculations.*
Read the weight, corresponding to each
peak area from the standard curve, correct
for the blank, correct for the desorption efficiency, and make necessary air volume corrections.

8. *Reference.* NIOSH Method S–156.

[43 FR 45809, Oct. 3, 1978, as amended at 45 FR
35283, May 23, 1980; 54 FR 24334, June 7, 1989;
58 FR 35310, June 30, 1993; 61 FR 5508, Feb. 13,
1996; 63 FR 1291, Jan. 8, 1998; 63 FR 20099, Apr.
23, 1998; 70 FR 1142, Jan. 5, 2005; 71 FR 16672,
16673, Apr. 3, 2006; 71 FR 50190, Aug. 24, 2006;
73 FR 75586, Dec. 12, 2008; 76 FR 33609, June 8,
2011; 77 FR 17783, Mar. 26, 2012]

EFFECTIVE DATE NOTE: At 84 FR 21518, May
14, 2019, § 1910.1045 was amended by revising
paragraphs (n)(2)(iii) and (n)(3)(i) and (ii) of
§ 1910.1045, effective July 15, 2019. For the
convenience of the user, the revised text is
set forth as follows:

§ 1910.1045 Acrylonitrile.

*   *   *   *   *

(n) * * *
(2) * * *
(iii) A 14- by 17-inch or other reasonably-
sized standard film or digital posterior-anterior chest X-ray; and

*   *   *   *   *

(3) * * *
(i) The employer shall provide the examinations specified in paragraphs (n)(2)(i), (ii),
and (iv) of this section at least annually for
all employees specified in paragraph (n)(1) of
this section.
(ii) If an employee has not had the examination specified in paragraphs (n)(2)(i), (ii),
and (iv) of this section within 6 months preceding termination of employment, the employer shall make such examination avail-

able to the employee prior to such termination.

*   *   *   *   *

§ 1910.1047 Ethylene oxide.

(a) *Scope and application.* (1) This section applies to all occupational exposures to ethylene oxide (EtO), Chemical Abstracts Service Registry No. 75–
21–8, except as provided in paragraph
(a)(2) of this section.

(2) This section does not apply to the
processing, use, or handling of products
containing EtO where objective data
are reasonably relied upon that demonstrate that the product is not capable of releasing EtO in airborne concentrations at or above the action
level, and may not reasonably be foreseen to release EtO in excess of the excursion limit, under the expected conditions of processing, use, or handling
that will cause the greatest possible release.

(3) Where products containing EtO
are exempted under paragraph (a)(2) of
this section, the employer shall maintain records of the objective data supporting that exemption and the basis
for the employer's reliance on the data,
as provided in paragraph (k)(1) of this
section.

(b) *Definitions:* For the purpose of this
section, the following definitions shall
apply:

Action level means a concentration of
airborne EtO of 0.5 ppm calculated as
an eight (8)-hour time-weighted average.

Assistant Secretary means the Assistant Secretary of Labor for Occupational Safety and Health, U.S. Department of Labor, or designee.

Authorized person means any person
specifically authorized by the employer
whose duties require the person to
enter a regulated area, or any person
entering such an area as a designated
representative of employees for the
purpose of exercising the right to observe monitoring and measuring procedures under paragraph (l) of this section, or any other person authorized by
the Act or regulations issued under the
Act.

Director means the Director of the
National Institute for Occupational
Safety and Health, U.S. Department of

Health and Human Services, or designee.

Emergency means any occurrence such as, but not limited to, equipment failure, rupture of containers, or failure of control equipment that is likely to or does result in an unexpected significant release of EtO.

Employee exposure means exposure to airborne EtO which would occur if the employee were not using respiratory protective equipment.

Ethylene oxide or *EtO* means the three-membered ring organic compound with chemical formula $C_2 H_4 O$.

(c) *Permissible exposure limits*—(1) *8-hour time weighted average (TWA)*. The employer shall ensure that no employee is exposed to an airborne concentration of EtO in excess of one (1) part EtO per million parts of air (1 ppm) as an 8-hour time-weighted average (8-hour TWA).

(2) *Excursion limit.* The employer shall ensure that no employee is exposed to an airborne concentration of EtO in excess of 5 parts of EtO per million parts of air (5 ppm) as averaged over a sampling period of fifteen (15) minutes.

(d) *Exposure monitoring*—(1) *General.* (i) Determinations of employee exposure shall be made from breathing zone air samples that are representative of the 8-hour TWA and 15-minute short-term exposures of each employee.

(ii) Representative 8-hour TWA employee exposure shall be determined on the basis of one or more samples representing full-shift exposure for each shift for each job classification in each work area. Representative 15-minute short-term employee exposures shall be determined on the basis of one or more samples representing 15-minute exposures associated with operations that are most likely to produce exposures above the excursion limit for each shift for each job classification in each work area.

(iii) Where the employer can document that exposure levels are equivalent for similar operations in different work shifts, the employer need only determine representative employee exposure for that operation during one shift.

(2) *Initial monitoring.* (i) Each employer who has a workplace or work operation covered by this standard, except as provided for in paragraph (a)(2) or (d)(2)(ii) of this section, shall perform initial monitoring to determine accurately the airborne concentrations of EtO to which employees may be exposed.

(ii) Where the employer has monitored after June 15, 1983 and the monitoring satisfies all other requirements of this section, the employer may rely on such earlier monitoring results to satisfy the requirements of paragraph (d)(2)(i) of this section.

(iii) Where the employer has previously monitored for the excursion limit and the monitoring satisfies all other requirements of this sections, the employer may rely on such earlier monitoring results to satisfy the requirements of paragraph (d)(2)(i) of this section.

(3) *Monitoring frequency (periodic monitoring).* (i) If the monitoring required by paragraph (d)(2) of this section reveals employee exposure at or above the action level but at or below the 8-hour TWA, the employer shall repeat such monitoring for each such employee at least every 6 months.

(ii) If the monitoring required by paragraph (d)(2)(i) of this section reveals employee exposure above the 8-hour TWA, the employer shall repeat such monitoring for each such employee at least every 3 months.

(iii) The employer may alter the monitoring schedule from quarterly to semiannually for any employee for whom two consecutive measurements taken at least 7 days apart indicate that the employee's exposure has decreased to or below the 8-hour TWA.

(iv) If the monitoring required by paragraph (d)(2)(i) of this section reveals employee exposure above the 15 minute excursion limit, the employer shall repeat such monitoring for each such employee at least every 3 months, and more often as necessary to evaluate exposure the employee's short-term exposures.

(4) *Termination of monitoring.* (i) If the initial monitoring required by paragraph (d)(2)(i) of this section reveals employee exposure to be below the action level, the employer may discontinue TWA monitoring for those employees whose exposures are represented by the initial monitoring.

(ii) If the periodic monitoring required by paragraph (d)(3) of this section reveals that employee exposures, as indicated by at least two consecutive measurements taken at least 7 days apart, are below the action level, the employer may discontinue TWA monitoring for those employees whose exposures are represented by such monitoring.

(iii) If the initial monitoring required by paragraph (d)(2)(1) of this section reveals employee exposure to be at or below the excursion limit, the employer may discontinue excursion limit monitoring for those employees whose exposures are represented by the initial monitoring.

(iv) If the periodic monitoring required by paragraph (d)(3) of this section reveals that employee exposures, as indicated by at least two consecutive measurements taken at least 7 days apart, are at or below the excursion limit, the employer may discontinue excursion limit monitoring for those employees whose exposures are represented by such monitoring.

(5) *Additional monitoring.* Notwithstanding the provisions of paragraph (d)(4) of this section, the employer shall institute the exposure monitoring required under paragraphs (d)(2)(i) and (d)(3) of this section whenever there has been a change in the production, process, control equipment, personnel or work practices that may result in new or additional exposures to EtO or when the employer has any reason to suspect that a change may result in new or additional exposures.

(6) *Accuracy of monitoring.* (i) Monitoring shall be accurate, to a confidence level of 95 percent, to within plus or minus 25 percent for airborne concentrations of EtO at the 1 ppm TWA and to within plus or minus 35 percent for airborne concentrations of EtO at the action level of 0.5 ppm.

(ii) Monitoring shall be accurate, to a confidence level of 95 percent, to within plus or minus 35 percent for airborne concentrations of EtO at the excursion limit.

(7) *Employee notification of monitoring results.* (i) The employer must, within 15 working days after the receipt of the results of any monitoring performed under this section, notify each affected employee of these results either individually in writing or by posting the results in an appropriate location that is accessible to employees.

(ii) The written notification required by paragraph (d)(7)(i) of this section shall contain the corrective action being taken by the employer to reduce employee exposure to or below the TWA and/or excursion limit, wherever monitoring results indicated that the TWA and/or excursion limit has been exceeded.

(e) *Regulated areas.* (1) The employer shall establish a regulated area wherever occupational exposure to airborne concentrations of EtO may exceed the TWA or wherever the EtO concentration exceeds or can reasonably be expected to exceed the excursion limit.

(2) Access to regulated areas shall be limited to authorized persons.

(3) Regulated areas shall be demarcated in any manner that minimizes the number of employees within the regulated area.

(f) *Methods of compliance*—(1) *Engineering controls and work practices.* (i) The employer shall institute engineering controls and work practices to reduce and maintain employee exposure to or below the TWA and to or below the excursion limit, except to the extent that such controls are not feasible.

(ii) Wherever the feasible engineering controls and work practices that can be instituted are not sufficient to reduce employee exposure to or below the TWA and to or below the excursion limit, the employer shall use them to reduce employee exposure to the lowest levels achievable by these controls and shall supplement them by the use of respiratory protection that complies with the requirements of paragraph (g) of this section.

(iii) Engineering controls are generally infeasible for the following operations: collection of quality assurance sampling from sterilized materials removal of sterilized materials: loading and unloading of tank cars; changing of ethylene oxide tanks on sterilizers; and vessel cleaning. For these operations, engineering controls are required only

415

where the Assistant Secretary demonstrates that such controls are feasible.

(2) *Compliance program.* (i) Where the TWA or excursion limit is exceeded, the employer shall establish and implement a written program to reduce exposure to or below the TWA and to or below the excursion limit by means of engineering and work practice controls, as required by paragraph (f)(1) of this section, and by the use of respiratory protection where required or permitted under this section.

(ii) The compliance program shall include a schedule for periodic leak detection surveys and a written plan for emergency situations, as specified in paragraph (h)(i) of this section.

(iii) Written plans for a program required in paragraph (f)(2) shall be developed and furnished upon request for examination and copying to the Assistant Secretary, the Director, affected employees and designated employee representatives. Such plans shall be reviewed at least every 12 months, and shall be updated as necessary to reflect significant changes in the status of the employer's compliance program.

(iv) The employer shall not implement a schedule of employee rotation as a means of compliance with the TWA or excursion limit.

(g) *Respiratory protection and personal protective equipment*—(1) *General.* For employees who use respirators required by this section, the employer must provide each employee an appropriate respirator that complies with the requirements of this paragraph. Respirators must be used during:

(i) Periods necessary to install or implement feasible engineering and work-practice controls.

(ii) Work operations, such as maintenance and repair activities and vessel cleaning, for which engineering and work-practice controls are not feasible.

(iii) Work operations for which feasible engineering and work-practice controls are not yet sufficient to reduce employee exposure to or below the TWA.

(iv) Emergencies.

(2) *Respirator program.* The employer must implement a respiratory protection program in accordance with § 1910.134(b) through (d) (except

(d)(i)(iii)), and (f) through (m), which covers each employee required by this section to use a respirator.

(3) *Respirator selection.* Employers must:

(i) Select, and provide to employees, the appropriate respirators specified in paragraph (d)(3)(i)(A) of 29 CFR 1910.134; however, employers must not select or use half masks of any type because EtO may cause eye irritation or injury.

(ii) Equip each air-purifying, full facepiece respirator with a front-or back-mounted canister approved for protection against ethylene oxide.

(iii) For escape, provide employees with any respirator permitted for use under paragraphs (g)(3)(i) and (ii) of this standard.

(4) *Protective clothing and equipment.* When employees could have eye or skin contact with EtO or EtO solutions, the employer must select and provide, at no cost to the employee, appropriate protective clothing or other equipment in accordance with 29 CFR 1910.132 and 1910.133 to protect any area of the employee's body that may come in contact with the EtO or EtO solution, and must ensure that the employee wears the protective clothing and equipment provided.

(h) *Emergency situations*—(1) *Written plan.* (i) A written plan for emergency situations shall be developed for each workplace where there is a possibility of an emergency. Appropriate portions of the plan shall be implemented in the event of an emergency.

(ii) The plan shall specifically provide that employees engaged in correcting emergency conditions shall be equipped with respiratory protection as required by paragraph (g) of this section until the emergency is abated.

(iii) The plan shall include the elements prescribed in 29 CFR 1910.38 and 29 CFR 1910.39, "Emergency action plans" and "Fire prevention plans," respectively.

(2) *Alerting employees.* Where there is the possibility of employee exposure to EtO due to an emergency, means shall be developed to alert potentially affected employees of such occurrences promptly. Affected employees shall be immediately evacuated from the area in the event that an emergency occurs.

416

(i) *Medical Surveillance*—(1) *General*— (i) *Employees covered.* (A) The employer shall institute a medical surveillance program for all employees who are or may be exposed to EtO at or above the action level, without regard to the use of respirators, for at least 30 days a year.

(B) The employer shall make available medical examinations and consultations to all employees who have been exposed to EtO in an emergency situation.

(ii) *Examination by a physician.* The employer shall ensure that all medical examinations and procedures are performed by or under the supervision of a licensed physician, and are provided without cost to the employee, without loss of pay, and at a reasonable time and place.

(2) *Medical examinations and consultations*—(i) *Frequency.* The employer shall make available medical examinations and consultations to each employee covered under paragraph (i)(1)(i) of this section on the following schedules:

(A) Prior to assignment of the employee to an area where exposure may be at or above the action level for at least 30 days a year.

(B) At least annually each employee exposed at or above the action level for at least 30 days in the past year.

(C) At termination of employment or reassignment to an area where exposure to EtO is not at or above the action level for at least 30 days a year.

(D) As medically appropriate for any employee exposed during an emergency.

(E) As soon as possible, upon notification by an employee either (1) that the employee has developed signs or symptoms indicating possible overexposure to EtO, or (2) that the employee desires medical advice concerning the effects of current or past exposure to EtO on the employee's ability to produce a healthy child.

(F) If the examining physician determines that any of the examinations should be provided more frequently than specified, the employer shall provide such examinations to affected employees at the frequencies recommended by the physician.

(ii) *Content.* (A) Medical examinations made available pursuant to paragraphs (i)(2)(i)(A)–(D) of this section shall include:

(1) A medical and work history with special emphasis directed to symptoms related to the pulmonary, hematologic, neurologic, and reproductive systems and to the eyes and skin.

(2) A physical examination with particular emphasis given to the pulmonary, hematologic, neurologic, and reproductive systems and to the eyes and skin.

(3) A complete blood count to include at least a white cell count (including differential cell count), red cell count, hematocrit, and hemoglobin.

(4) Any laboratory or other test which the examining physician deems necessary by sound medical practice.

(B) The content of medical examinations or consultation made available pursuant to paragraph (i)(2)(i)(E) of this section shall be determined by the examining physician, and shall include pregnancy testing or laboratory evaluation of fertility, if requested by the employee and deemed appropriate by the physician.

(3) *Information provided to the physician.* The employer shall provide the following information to the examining physician:

(i) A copy of this standard and Appendices A, B, and C.

(ii) A description of the affected employee's duties as they relate to the employee's exposure.

(iii) The employee's representative exposure level or anticipated exposure level.

(iv) A description of any personal protective and respiratory equipment used or to be used.

(v) Information from previous medical examinations of the affected employee that is not otherwise available to the examining physician.

(4) *Physician's written opinion.* (i) The employer shall obtain a written opinion from the examining physician. This written opinion shall contain the results of the medical examination and shall include:

(A) The physician's opinion as to whether the employee has any detected medical conditions that would place the employee at an increased risk of material health impairment from exposure to EtO;

417

(B) Any recommended limitations on the employee or upon the use of personal protective equipment such as clothing or respirators; and

(C) A statement that the employee has been informed by the physician of the results of the medical examination and of any medical conditions resulting from EtO exposure that require further explanation or treatment.

(ii) The employer shall instruct the physician not to reveal in the written opinion given to the employer specific findings or diagnoses unrelated to occupational exposure to EtO.

(iii) The employer shall provide a copy of the physician's written opinion to the affected employee within 15 days from its receipt.

(j) *Communication of hazards*—(1) *Hazard communication*—*general.* (i) Chemical manufacturers, importers, distributors and employers shall comply with all requirements of the Hazard Communication Standard (HCS) (§ 1910.1200) for EtO.

(ii) In classifying the hazards of EtO at least the following hazards are to be addressed: Cancer; reproductive effects; mutagenicity; central nervous system; skin sensitization; skin, eye and respiratory tract irritation; acute toxicity effects; and flammability.

(iii) Employers shall include EtO in the hazard communication program established to comply with the HCS (§ 1910.1200). Employers shall ensure that each employee has access to labels on containers of EtO and to safety data sheets, and is trained in accordance with the requirements of HCS and paragraph (j)(3) of this section.

(2) *Signs and labels*—(i) *Signs.* (A) The employer shall post and maintain legible signs demarcating regulated areas and entrances or access ways to regulated areas that bear the following legend:

DANGER
ETHYLENE OXIDE
MAY CAUSE CANCER
MAY DAMAGE FERTILITY OR THE UN-
   BORN CHILD
RESPIRATORY PROTECTION AND PRO-
   TECTIVE CLOTHING MAY BE REQUIRED
   IN THIS AREA
AUTHORIZED PERSONNEL ONLY

(B) Prior to June 1, 2016, employers may use the following legend in lieu of

that specified in paragraph (j)(2)(i)(A) of this section:

DANGER
ETHYLENE OXIDE
CANCER HAZARD AND REPRODUCTIVE
   HAZARD
AUTHORIZED PERSONNEL ONLY
RESPIRATORS AND PROTECTIVE CLOTH-
   ING MAY BE REQUIRED TO BE WORN IN
   THIS AREA

(ii) *Labels.* (A) The employer shall ensure that labels are affixed to all containers of EtO whose contents are capable of causing employee exposure at or above the action level or whose contents may reasonably be foreseen to cause employee exposure above the excursion limit, and that the labels remain affixed when the containers of EtO leave the workplace. For the purposes of this paragraph (j)(2)(ii), reaction vessels, storage tanks, and pipes or piping systems are not considered to be containers.

(B) Prior to June 1, 2015, employers may include the following information on containers of EtO in lieu of the labeling requirements in paragraph (j)(1)(i) of this section:

(*1*) DANGER
CONTAINS ETHYLENE OXIDE
CANCER HAZARD AND REPRODUCTIVE
   HAZARD;
(*2*) A warning statement against breathing airborne concentrations of EtO.

(C) The labeling requirements under this section do not apply where EtO is used as a pesticide, as such term is defined in the Federal Insecticide, Fungicide, and Rodenticide Act (7 U.S.C. 136 *et seq.*), when it is labeled pursuant to that Act and regulations issued under that Act by the Environmental Protection Agency.

(3) *Information and training.* (i) The employer shall provide employees who are potentially exposed to EtO at or above the action level or above the excursion limit with information and training on EtO at the time of initial assignment and at least annually thereafter.

(ii) Employees shall be informed of the following:

(A) The requirements of this section with an explanation of its contents, including Appendices A and B;

(B) Any operations in their work area where EtO is present;

(C) The location and availability of the written EtO final rule; and

(D) The medical surveillance program required by paragraph (i) of this section with an explanation of the information in appendix C.

(iii) Employee training shall include at least:

(A) Methods and observations that may be used to detect the presence or release of EtO in the work area (such as monitoring conducted by the employer, continuous monitoring devices, etc.);

(B) The physical and health hazards of EtO;

(C) The measures employees can take to protect themselves from hazards associated with EtO exposure, including specific procedures the employer has implemented to protect employees from exposure to EtO, such as work practices, emergency procedures, and personal protective equipment to be used; and

(D) The details of the hazard communication program developed by the employer, including an explanation of the labeling system and how employees can obtain and use the appropriate hazard information.

(k) *Recordkeeping*—(1) *Objective data for exempted operations.* (i) Where the processing, use, or handling of products made from or containing EtO are exempted from other requirements of this section under paragraph (a)(2) of this section, or where objective data have been relied on in lieu of initial monitoring under paragraph (d)(2)(ii) of this section, the employer shall establish and maintain an accurate record of objective data reasonably relied upon in support of the exemption.

(ii) This record shall include at least the following information:

(A) The product qualifying for exemption;

(B) The source of the objective data;

(C) The testing protocol, results of testing, and/or analysis of the material for the release of EtO;

(D) A description of the operation exempted and how the data support the exemption; and

(E) Other data relevant to the operations, materials, processing, or employee exposures covered by the exemption.

(iii) The employer shall maintain this record for the duration of the employer's reliance upon such objective data.

(2) *Exposure measurements.* (i) The employer shall keep an accurate record of all measurements taken to monitor employee exposure to EtO as prescribed in paragraph (d) of this section.

(ii) This record shall include at least the following information:

(A) The date of measurement;

(B) The operation involving exposure to EtO which is being monitored;

(C) Sampling and analytical methods used and evidence of their accuracy;

(D) Number, duration, and results of samples taken;

(E) Type of protective devices worn, if any; and

(F) Name, social security number and exposure of the employees whose exposures are represented.

(iii) The employer shall maintain this record for at least thirty (30) years, in accordance with 29 CFR 1910.1020.

(3) *Medical surveillance.* (i) The employer shall establish and maintain an accurate record for each employee subject to medical surveillance by paragraph (i)(1)(i) of this section, in accordance with 29 CFR 1910.1020.

(ii) The record shall include at least the following information:

(A) The name and social security number of the employee;

(B) Physicians' written opinions;

(C) Any employee medical complaints related to exposure to EtO; and

(D) A copy of the information provided to the physician as required by paragraph (i)(3) of this section.

(iii) The employer shall ensure that this record is maintained for the duration of employment plus thirty (30) years, in accordance with 29 CFR 1910.1020.

(4) *Availability.* (i) The employer, upon written request, shall make all records required to be maintained by this section available to the Assistant Secretary and the Director for examination and copying.

(ii) The employer, upon request, shall make any exemption and exposure records required by paragraphs (k) (1)

419

and (2) of this section available for examination and copying to affected employees, former employees, designated representatives and the Assistant Secretary, in accordance with 29 CFR 1910.1020 (a) through (e) and (g) through (i).

(iii) The employer, upon request, shall make employee medical records required by paragraph (k)(3) of this section available for examination and copying to the subject employee, anyone having the specific written consent of the subject employee, and the Assistant Secretary, in accordance with 29 CFR 1910.1020.

(5) *Transfer of records.* The employer shall comply with the requirements concerning transfer of records set forth in 29 CFR 1910.1020(h).

(1) *Observation of monitoring*—(1) *Employee observation.* The employer shall provide affected employees or their designated representatives an opportunity to observe any monitoring of employee exposure to EtO conducted in accordance with paragraph (d) of this section.

(2) *Observation procedures.* When observation of the monitoring of employee exposure to EtO requires entry into an area where the use of protective clothing or equipment is required, the observer shall be provided with and be required to use such clothing and equipment and shall comply with all other applicable safety and health procedures.

(m) [Reserved]

(n) *Appendices.* The information contained in the appendices is not intended by itself to create any additional obligations not otherwise imposed or to detract from any existing obligation.

APPENDIX A TO § 1910.1047—SUBSTANCE SAFETY DATA SHEET FOR ETHYLENE OXIDE (NON-MANDATORY)

I. SUBSTANCE IDENTIFICATION

A. Substance: Ethylene oxide ($C_2 H_4 O$).

B. Synonyms: dihydrooxirene, dimethylene oxide, EO, 1,2-epoxyethane, EtO, ETO, oxacyclopropane, oxane, oxidoethane, alpha/beta-oxidoethane, oxiran, oxirane.

C. Ethylene oxide can be found as a liquid or vapor.

D. EtO is used in the manufacture of ethylene glycol, surfactants, ethanolamines, glycol ethers, and other organic chemicals. EtO is also used as a sterilant and fumigant.

E. Appearance and odor: Colorless liquid below 10.7 °C (51.3 °F) or colorless gas with ether-like odor detected at approximately 700 parts EtO per million parts of air (700 ppm).

F. Permissible Exposure: Exposure may not exceed 1 part EtO per million parts of air averaged over the 8-hour workday.

II. HEALTH HAZARD DATA

A. Ethylene oxide can cause bodily harm if you inhale the vapor, if it comes into contact with your eyes or skin, or if you swallow it.

B. Effects of overexposure:

1. Ethylene oxide in liquid form can cause eye irritation and injury to the cornea, frostbite, and severe irritation and blistering of the skin upon prolonged or confined contact. Ingestion of EtO can cause gastric irritation and liver injury. Acute effects from inhalation of EtO vapors include respiratory irritation and lung injury, headache, nausea, vomiting, diarrhea, shortness of breath, and cyaonosis (blue or purple coloring of skin). Exposure has also been associated with the occurrence of cancer, reproductive effects, mutagenic changes, neurotoxicity, and sensitization.

1. EtO has been shown to cause cancer in laboratory animals and has been associated with higher incidences of cancer in humans. Adverse reproductive effects and chromosome damage may also occur from EtO exposure.

a. Reporting signs and symptoms: You should inform your employer if you develop any signs or symptoms and suspect that they are caused by exposure to EtO.

III. EMERGENCY FIRST AID PROCEDURES

A. Eye exposure: If EtO gets into your eyes, wash your eyes immediately with large amounts of water, lifting the lower and upper eyelids. Get medical attention immediately. Contact lenses should not be worn when working with this chemical.

B. Skin exposure: If EtO gets on your skin, immediately wash the contaminated skin with water. If EtO soaks through your clothing, especially your shoes, remove the clothing immediately and wash the skin with water using an emergency deluge shower. Get medical attention immediately. Thoroughly wash contaminated clothing before reusing. Contaminated leather shoes or other leather articles should not be reused and should be discarded.

C. Inhalation: If large amounts of EtO are inhaled, the exposed person must be moved to fresh air at once. If breathing has stopped, perform cardiopulmonary resuscitation. Keep the affected person warm and at rest. Get medical attention immediately.

D. Swallowing: When EtO has been swallowed, give the person large quantities of water immediately. After the water has been swallowed, try to get the person to vomit by having him or her touch the back of the throat with his or her finger. Do not make an unconscious person vomit. Get medical attention immediately.

E. Rescue: Move the affected person from the hazardous exposure. If the exposed person has been overcome, attempt rescue only after notifying at least one other person of the emergency and putting into effect established emergency procedures. Do not become a casualty yourself. Understand your emergency rescue procedures and know the location of the emergency equipment before the need arises.

IV. RESPIRATORS AND PROTECTIVE CLOTHING

A. Respirators. You may be required to wear a respirator for nonroutine activities, in emergencies, while your employer is in the process of reducing EtO exposures through engineering controls, and in areas where engineering controls are not feasible. As of the effective date of this standard, only air-supplied, positive-pressure, full-facepiece respirators are approved for protection against EtO. If air-purifying respirators are worn in the future, they must have a label issued by the National Institute for Occupational Safety and Health under the provisions of 42 CFR part 84 stating that the respirators have been approved for use with ethylene oxide. For effective protection, respirators must fit your face and head snugly. Respirators must not be loosened or removed in work situations where their use is required.

EtO does not have a detectable odor except at levels well above the permissible exposure limits. If you can smell EtO while wearing a respirator, proceed immediately to fresh air. If you experience difficulty breathing while wearing a respirator, tell your employer.

B. Protective clothing: You may be required to wear impermeable clothing, gloves, a face shield, or other appropriate protective clothing to prevent skin contact with liquid EtO or EtO-containing solutions. Where protective clothing is required, your employer must provide clean garments to you as necessary to assure that the clothing protects you adequately.

Replace or repair protective clothing that has become torn or otherwise damaged.

EtO must never be allowed to remain on the skin. Clothing and shoes which are not impermeable to EtO should not be allowed to become contaminated with EtO, and if they do, the clothing should be promptly removed and decontaminated. Contaminated leather shoes should be discarded. Once EtO penetrates shoes or other leather articles, they should not be worn again.

C. Eye protection: You must wear splashproof safety goggles in areas where liquid EtO or EtO-containing solutions may contact your eyes. In addition, contact lenses should not be worn in areas where eye contact with EtO can occur.

V. PRECAUTIONS FOR SAFE USE, HANDLING, AND STORAGE

A. EtO is a flammable liquid, and its vapors can easily form explosive mixtures in air.

B. EtO must be stored in tighly closed containers in a cool, well-ventilated area, away from heat, sparks, flames, strong oxidizers, alkalines, and acids, strong bases, acetylide-forming metals such as cooper, silver, mercury and their alloys.

C. Sources of ignition such as smoking material, open flames and some electrical devices are prohibited wherever EtO is handled, used, or stored in a manner that could create a potential fire or explosion hazard.

D. You should use non-sparking tools when opening or closing metal containers of EtO, and containers must be bonded and grounded in the rare instances in which liquid EtO is poured or transferred.

E. Impermeable clothing wet with liquid EtO or EtO-containing solutions may be easily ignited. If your are wearing impermeable clothing and are splashed with liquid EtO or EtO-containing solution, you should immediately remove the clothing while under an emergency deluge shower.

F. If your skin comes into contact with liquid EtO or EtO-containing solutions, you should immediately remove the EtO using an emergency deluge shower.

G. You should not keep food, beverages, or smoking materials in regulated areas where employee exposures are above the permissible exposure limits.

H. Fire extinguishers and emergency deluge showers for quick drenching should be readily available, and you should know where they are and how to operate them.

I. Ask your supervisor where EtO is used in your work area and for any additional plant safety and health rules.

VI. ACCESS TO INFORMATION

A. Each year, your employer is required to inform you of the information contained in this standard and appendices for EtO. In addition, your employer must instruct you in the proper work practices for using EtO emergency procedures, and the correct use of protective equipment.

B. Your employer is required to determine whether you are being exposed to EtO. You or your representative has the right to observe employee measurements and to record the results obtained. Your employer is required to inform you of your exposure. If your employer determine that you are being overexposed, he or she is required to inform you of the actions which are being taken to reduce your exposure to within permissible exposure limits.

C. Your employer is required to keep records of your exposures and medical examinations. These exposure records must be kept by the employer for at least thirty (30) years. Medical records must be kept for the period of your employment plus thirty (30) years.

D. Your employer is required to release your exposure and medical records to your physician or designated representative upon your written request.

VII. STERILANT USE OF ETO IN HOSPITALS AND HEALTH CARE FACILITIES

This section of appendix A, for informational purposes, sets forth EPA's recommendations for modifications in workplace design and practice in hospitals and health care facilities for which the Environmental Protection Agency has registered EtO for uses as a sterilant or fumigant under the Federal Insecticide, Funigicide, and Rodenticide Act, 7 U.S.C. 136 et seq. These new recommendations, published in the FEDERAL REGISTER by EPA at 49 FR 15268, as modified in today's REGISTER, are intended to help reduce the exposure of hospital and health care workers to EtO to 1 ppm. EPA's recommended workplace design and workplace practice are as follows:

1. Workplace Design

a. *Installation of gas line hand valves.* Hand valves must be installed on the gas supply line at the connection to the supply cylinders to minimize leakage during cylinder change.

b. *Installation of capture boxes.* Sterilizer operations result in a gas/water discharge at the completion of the process. This discharge is routinely piped to a floor drain which is generally located in an equipment or an adjacent room. When the floor drain is not in the same room as the sterilizer and workers are not normally present, all that is necessary is that the room be well ventilated.

The installation of a "capture box" will be required for those work place layouts where the floor drain is located in the same room as the sterilizer or in a room where workers are normally present. A "capture box" is a piece of equipment that totally encloses the floor drain where the discharge from sterilizer is pumped. The "capture box" is to be vented directly to a non-recirculating or dedicated ventilation system. Sufficient air intake should be allowed at the bottom of the box to handle the volume of air that is ventilated from the top of the box. The "capture box" can be made of metal, plastic, wood or other equivalent material. The box is intended to reduce levels of EtO dis-charged into the work room atmosphere. The use of a "capture box" is not required if: (1) The vacuum pump discharge floor drain is located in a well ventilated equipment or other room where workers are not normally present or (2) the water sealed vacuum pump discharges directly to a closed sealed sewer line (check local plumbing codes).

If it is impractical to install a vented "capture box" and a well ventilated equipment or other room is not feasible, a box that can be sealed over the floor drain may be used if: (1) The floor drain is located in a room where workers are not normally present and EtO cannot leak into an occupied area, and (2) the sterilizer in use is less than 12 cubic feet in capacity (check local plumbing codes).

c. *Ventilation of aeration units* i. *Existing aeration units.* Existing units must be vented to a non-recirculating or dedicated system or vented to an equipment or other room where workers are not normally present and which is well ventilated. Aerator units must be positioned as close as possible to the sterilizer to minimize the exposure from the off-gassing of sterilized items.

ii. *Installation of new aerator units (where none exist).* New aerator units must be vented as described above for existing aerators. Aerators must be in place by July 1, 1986.

d. *Ventilation during cylinder change.* Workers may be exposed to short but relatively high levels of EtO during the change of gas cylinders. To reduce exposure from this route, users must select one of three alternatives designed to draw off gas that may be released when the line from the sterilizer to the cylinder is disconnected:

i. Location of cylinders in a well ventilated equipment room or other room where workers are not normally present.

ii. Installation of a flexible hose (at least 4″ in diameter) to a non-recirculating or dedicated ventilation system and located in the area of cylinder change in such a way that the hose can be positioned at the point where the sterilizer gas line is disconnected from the cylinder.

iii. Installation of a hood that is part of a non-recirculating or dedicated system and positioned no more than one foot above the point where the change of cylinders takes place.

e. *Ventilation of sterilizer door area.* One of the major sources of exposure to EtO occurs when the sterilizer door is opened following the completion of the sterilization process. In order to reduce this avenue of exposure, a hood or metal canopy closed on each end must be installed over the sterilizer door. The hood or metal canopy must be connected to a non-recirculating or dedicated ventilation system or one that exhausts gases to a well ventilated equipment or other room where workers are not normally present. A hood or canopy over the sterilizer door is required for use even with those sterilizers that have a purge cycle and must be in place by July 1, 1986.

f. *Ventilation of sterilizer relief valve.* Sterilizers are typically equipped with a safety relief device to release gas in case of increased pressure in the sterilizer. Generally, such relief devices are used on pressure vessels. Although these pressure relief devices are rarely opened for hospital and health care sterilizers, it is suggested that they be designed to exhaust vapor from the sterilizer by one of the following methods:

i. Through a pipe connected to the outlet of the relief valve ventilated directly outdoors at a point high enough to be away from passers by, and not near any windows that open, or near any air conditioning or ventilation air intakes.

ii. Through a connection to an existing or new non-recirculating or dedicated ventilation system.

iii. Through a connection to a well ventilated equipment or other room where workers are not normally present.

g. *Ventilation systems.* Each hospital and health care facility affected by this notice that uses EtO for the sterilization of equipment and supplies must have a ventilation system which enables compliance with the requirements of section (b) through (f) in the manner described in these sections and within the timeframes allowed. Thus, each affected hospital and health care facility must have or install a non-recirculating or dedicated ventilation equipment or other room where workers are not normally present in which to vent EtO.

h. *Installation of alarm systems.* An audible and visual indicator alarm system must be installed to alert personnel of ventilation system failures, i.e., when the ventilation fan motor is not working.

2. Workplace Practices

All the workplace practices discussed in this unit must be permanently posted near the door of each sterilizer prior to use by any operator.

a. *Changing of supply line filters.* Filters in the sterilizer liquid line must be changed when necessary, by the following procedure:

i. Close the cylinder valve and the hose valve.

ii. Disconnect the cylinder hose (piping) from the cylinder.

iii. Open the hose valve and bleed slowly into a proper ventilating system at or near the in-use supply cylinders.

iv. Vacate the area until the line is empty.

v. Change the filter.

vi. Reconnect the lines and reverse the value position.

vii. Check hoses, filters, and valves for leaks with a fluorocarbon leak detector (for those sterilizers using the 88 percent chlorofluorocarbon, 12 percent ethylene oxide mixture (12/88)).

b. *Restricted access area.* i. Areas involving use of EtO must be designated as restricted access areas. They must be identified with signs or floor marks near the sterilizer door, aerator, vacuum pump floor drain discharge, and in-use cylinder storage.

ii. All personnel must be excluded from the restricted area when certain operations are in progress, such as discharging a vacuum pump, emptying a sterilizer liquid line, or venting a non-purge sterilizer with the door ajar or other operations where EtO might be released directly into the face of workers.

c. *Door opening procedures.* i. *Sterilizers with purge cycles.* A load treated in a sterilizer equipped with a purge cycle should be removed immediately upon completion of the cycle (provided no time is lost opening the door after cycle is completed). If this is not done, the purge cycle should be repeated before opening door.

ii. *Sterilizers without purge cycles.* For a load treated in a sterilizer not equipped with a purge cycle, the sterilizer door must be ajar 6″ for 15 minutes, and then fully opened for at least another 15 minutes before removing the treated load. The length of time of the second period should be established by peak monitoring for one hour after the two 15-minute periods suggested. If the level is above 10 ppm time-weighted average for 8 hours, more time should be added to the second waiting period (door wide open). However, in no case may the second period be shortened to less than 15 minutes.

d. *Chamber unloading procedures.* i. Procedures for unloading the chamber must include the use of baskets or rolling carts, or baskets and rolling tables to transfer treated loads quickly, thus avoiding excessive contact with treated articles, and reducing the duration of exposures.

ii. If rolling carts are used, they should be pulled not pushed by the sterilizer operators to avoid offgassing exposure.

e. *Maintenance.* A written log should be instituted and maintained documenting the date of each leak detection and any maintenance procedures undertaken. This is a suggested use practice and is not required.

i. *Leak detection.* Sterilizer door gaskets, cylinder and vacuum piping, hoses, filters, and valves must be checked for leaks under full pressure with a Fluorocarbon leak detector (for 12/88 systems only) every two weeks by maintenance personnel. Also, the cylinder piping connections must be checked after changing cylinders. Particular attention in leak detection should be given to the automatic solenoid valves that control the flow of EtO to the sterilizer. Specifically, a check should be made at the EtO gasline entrance port to the sterilizer, while the sterilizer door is open and the solenoid valves are in a closed position.

ii. *Maintenance procedures.* Sterilizer/ areator door gaskets, valves, and fittings must be replaced when necessary as determined by maintenance personnel in their biweekly checks; in addition, visual inspection of the door gaskets for cracks, debris, and other foreign substances should be conducted daily by the operator.

APPENDIX B TO § 1910.1047—SUBSTANCE TECHNICAL GUIDELINES FOR ETHYLENE OXIDE (NON-MANDATORY)

I. PHYSICAL AND CHEMICAL DATA

A. Substance identification:

1. Synonyms: dihydrooxirene, dimethylene oxide, EO, 1,2-epoxyethane, EtO ETO oxacyclopropane, oxane, oxidoethane, alpha/beta-oxidoethane, oxiran, oxirane.

2. Formula: ($C_2 H_4 O$).

3. Molecular weight: 44.06

B. Physical data:

1. Boiling point (760 mm Hg): 10.70 °C (51.3 °F);

2. Specific gravity (water = 1): 0.87 (at 20 °C or 68 °F)

3. Vapor density (air = 1): 1.49;

4. Vapor pressure (at 20 °C); 1,095 mm Hg;

5. Solubility in water: complete;

6. Appearance and odor: colorless liquid; gas at temperature above 10.7 °F or 51.3 °C with ether-like odor above 700 ppm.

II. FIRE, EXPLOSION, AND REACTIVITY HAZARD DATA

A. Fire:

1. Flash point: less than O °F (open cup);

2. Stability: decomposes violently at temperatures above 800 °F;

3. Flammable limits in air, percent by volume: Lower: 3, Upper: 100;

4. Extinguishing media: Carbon dioxide for small fires, polymer or alcohol foams for large fires;

5. Special fire fighting procedures: Dilution of ethylene oxide with 23 volumes of water renders it non-flammable;

6. Unusual fire and explosion hazards: Vapors of EtO will burn without the presence of air or other oxidizers. EtO vapors are heavier than air and may travel along the ground and be ignited by open flames or sparks at locations remote from the site at which EtO is being used.

7. For purposes of compliance with the requirements of 29 CFR 1910.106, EtO is classified as a flammable gas. For example, 7,500 ppm, approximately one-fourth of the lower flammable limit, would be considered to pose a potential fire and explosion hazard.

8. For purposes of compliance with 29 CFR 1910.155, EtO is classified as a Class B fire hazard.

9. For purpose of compliance with 29 CFR 1919.307, locations classified as hazardous due to the presence of EtO shall be Class I.

B. Reactivity:

1. Conditions contributing to instability: EtO will polymerize violently if contaminated with aqueous alkalies, amines, mineral acids, metal chlorides, or metal oxides. Violent decomposition will also occur at temperatures above 800 °F;

2. Incompatabilities: Alkalines and acids;

3. Hazardous decomposition products: Carbon monoxide and carbon dioxide.

III. SPILL, LEAK, AND DISPOSAL PROCEDURES

A. If EtO is spilled or leaked, the following steps should be taken:

1. Remove all ignition sources.

2. The area should be evacuated at once and re-entered only after the area has been thoroughly ventilated and washed down with water.

B. Persons not wearing appropriate protective equipment should be restricted from areas of spills or leaks until cleanup has been completed.

C. Waste disposal methods: Waste material should be disposed of in a manner that is not hazardous to employees or to the general population. In selecting the method of waste disposal, applicable local, State, and Federal regulations should be consulted.

IV. MONITORING AND MEASUREMENT PROCEDURES

A. Exposure above the Permissible Exposure Limit:

1. Eight-hour exposure evaluation: Measurements taken for the purpose of determining employee exposure under this section are best taken with consecutive samples covering the full shift. Air samples should be taken in the employee's breathing zone (air that would most nearly represent that inhaled by the employee.)

2. Monitoring techniques: The sampling and analysis under this section may be performed by collection of the EtO vapor on charcoal adsorption tubes or other composition adsorption tubes, with subsequent chemical analysis. Sampling and analysis may also be performed by instruments such as real-time continuous monitoring systems, portable direct reading instruments, or passive dosimeters as long as measurements taken using these methods accurately evaluate the concentration of EtO in employees' breathing zones.

Appendix D describes the validated method of sampling and analysis which has been tested by OSHA for use with EtO. Other available methods are also described in appendix D. The employer has the obligation of selecting a monitoring method which meets the accuracy and precision requirements of the standard under his unique field conditions. The standard requires that the method of monitoring should be accurate, to a 95 percent confidence level, to plus or minus 25 percent for concentrations of EtO at 1 ppm, and to plus or minus 35 percent for concentrations at 0.5 ppm. In addition to the method described in appendix D, there are numerous other methods available for monitoring for EtO in the workplace. Details on these other methods have been submitted by various companies to the rulemaking record, and are available at the OSHA Docket Office.

B. Since many of the duties relating to employee exposure are dependent on the results of measurement procedures, employers should assure that the evaluation of employee exposures is performed by a technically qualified person.

V. PROTECTIVE CLOTHING AND EQUIPMENT

Employees should be provided with and be required to wear appropriate protective clothing wherever there is significant potential for skin contact with liquid EtO or EtO-containing solutions. Protective clothing shall include impermeable coveralls or similar full-body work clothing, gloves, and head coverings, as appropriate to protect areas of the body which may come in contact with liquid EtO or EtO-containing solutions.

Employers should ascertain that the protective garments are impermeable to EtO. Permeable clothing, including items made of rubber, and leather shoes should not be allowed to become contaminated with liquid EtO. If permeable clothing does become contaminated, it should be immediately removed, while the employer is under an emergency deluge shower. If leather footwear or other leather garments become wet from EtO they should be discarded and not be worn again, because leather absorbs EtO and holds it against the skin.

Any protective clothing that has been damaged or is otherwise found to be defective should be repaired or replaced. Clean protective clothing should be provided to the employee as necessary to assure employee protection. Whenever impermeable clothing becomes wet with liquid EtO, it should be washed down with water before being removed by the employee. Employees are also required to wear splash-proof safety goggles where there is any possibility of EtO contacting the eyes.

VI. MISCELLANEOUS PRECAUTIONS

A. Store EtO in tightly closed containers in a cool, well-ventilated area and take all necessary precautions to avoid any explosion hazard.

B. Non-sparking tools must be used to open and close metal containers. These containers must be effectively grounded and bonded.

C. Do not incinerate EtO cartridges, tanks or other containers.

D. Employers should advise employees of all areas and operations where exposure to EtO occur.

VII. COMMON OPERATIONS

Common operations in which exposure to EtO is likely to occur include the following: Manufacture of EtO, surfactants, ethanolamines, glycol ethers, and specialty chemicals, and use as a sterilant in the hospital, health product and spice industries.

APPENDIX C TO § 1910.1047—MEDICAL SURVEILLANCE GUIDELINES FOR ETHYLENE OXIDE (NON-MANDATORY)

I. ROUTE OF ENTRY

Inhalation.

II. TOXICOLOGY

Clinical evidence of adverse effects associated with the exposure to EtO is present in the form of increased incidence of cancer in laboratory animals (leukemia, stomach, brain), mutation in offspring in animals, and resorptions and spontaneous abortions in animals and human populations respectively. Findings in humans and experimental animals exposed to airborne concentrations of EtO also indicate damage to the genetic material (DNA). These include hemoglobin alkylation, unscheduled DNA synthesis, sister chromatid exchange chromosomal aberration, and functional sperm abnormalities.

Ethylene oxide in liquid form can cause eye irritation and injury to the cornea, frostbite, severe irritation, and blistering of the skin upon prolonged or confined contact. Ingestion of EtO can cause gastric irritation and liver injury. Other effects from inhalation of EtO vapors include respiratory irritation and lung injury, headache, nausea, vomiting, diarrhea, dyspnea and cyanosis.

III. SIGNS AND SYMPTOMS OF ACUTE OVEREXPOSURE

The early effects of acute overexposure to EtO are nausea and vomiting, headache, and irritation of the eyes and respiratory passages. The patient may notice a "peculiar taste" in the mouth. Delayed effects can include pulmonary edema, drowsiness, weakness, and incoordination. Studies suggest that blood cell changes, an increase in chromosomal aberrations, and spontaneous abortion may also be causally related to acute overexposure to EtO.

Skin contact with liquid or gaseous EtO causes characteristic burns and possibly even an allergic-type sensitization. The edema and erythema occurring from skin contact with EtO progress to vesiculation with a tendency to coalesce into blebs with desquamation. Healing occurs within three weeks, but there may be a residual brown pigmentation. A 40–80% solution is extremely dangerous, causing extensive blistering after only brief contact. Pure liquid

EtO causes frostbite because of rapid evapo-ration. In contrast, the eye is relatively in-sensitive to EtO, but there may be some irri-tation of the cornea.

Most reported acute effects of occupational exposure to EtO are due to contact with EtO in liquid phase. The liquid readily penetrates rubber and leather, and will produce blis-tering if clothing or footwear contaminated with EtO are not removed.

IV. SURVEILLANCE AND PREVENTIVE CONSIDERATIONS

As noted above, exposure to EtO has been linked to an increased risk of cancer and re-productive effects including decreased male fertility, fetotoxicity, and spontaneous abor-tion. EtO workers are more likely to have chromosomal damage than similar groups not exposed to EtO. At the present, limited studies of chronic effects in humans result-ing from exposure to EtO suggest a causal association with leukemia. Animal studies indicate leukemia and cancers at other sites (brain, stomach) as well. The physician should be aware of the findings of these stud-ies in evaluating the health of employees ex-posed to EtO.

Adequate screening tests to determine an employee's potential for developing serious chronic diseases, such as cancer, from expo-sure to EtO do not presently exist. Labora-tory tests may, however, give evidence to suggest that an employee is potentially over-exposed to EtO. It is important for the physi-cian to become familiar with the operating conditions in which exposure to EtO is likely to occur. The physician also must become fa-miliar with the signs and symptoms that in-dicate a worker is receiving otherwise unrec-ognized and unacceptable exposure to EtO. These elements are especially important in evaluating the medical and work histories and in conducting the physical exam. When an unacceptable exposure in an active em-ployee is identified by the physician, meas-ures taken by the employer to lower expo-sure should also lower the risk of serious long-term consequences.

The employer is required to institute a medical surveillance program for all employ-ees who are or will be exposed to EtO at or above the action level (0.5 ppm) for at least 30 days per year, without regard to res-pirator use. All examinations and procedures must be performed by or under the super-vision of a licensed physician at a reasonable time and place for the employee and at no cost to the employee.

Although broad latitude in prescribing spe-cific tests to be included in the medical sur-veillance program is extended to the exam-ining physician, OSHA requires inclusion of the following elements in the routine exam-ination:

(i) Medical and work histories with special emphasis directed to symptoms related to the pulmonary, hematologic, neurologic, and reproductive systems and to the eyes and skin.

(ii) Physical examination with particular emphasis given to the pulmonary, hemato-logic, neurologic, and reproductive systems and to the eyes and skin.

(iii) Complete blood count to include at least a white cell count (including differen-tial cell count), red cell count, hematocrit, and hemoglobin.

(iv) Any laboratory or other test which the examining physician deems necessary by sound medical practice.

If requested by the employee, the medical examinations shall include pregnancy test-ing or laboratory evaluation of fertility as deemed appropriate by the physician.

In certain cases, to provide sound medical advice to the employer and the employee, the physician must evaluate situations not directly related to EtO. For example, em-ployees with skin diseases may be unable to tolerate wearing protective clothing. In ad-dition those with chronic respiratory dis-eases may not tolerate the wearing of nega-tive pressure (air purifying) respirators. Ad-ditional tests and procedures that will help the physician determine which employees are medically unable to wear such res-pirators should include: An evaluation of cardiovascular function, a baseline chest x-ray to be repeated at five year intervals, and a pulmonary function test to be repeated every three years. The pulmonary function test should include measurement of the em-ployee's forced vital capacity (FVC), forced expiratory volume at one second (FEV1), as well as calculation of the ratios of FEV1 to FVC, and measured FVC and measured FEV1 to expected values corrected for variation due to age, sex, race, and height.

The employer is required to make the pre-scribed tests available at least annually to employees who are or will be exposed at or above the action level, for 30 or more days per year; more often than specified if rec-ommended by the examining physician; and upon the employee's termination of employ-ment or reassignment to another work area. While little is known about the long term consequences of high short-term exposures, it appears prudent to monitor such affected employees closely in light of existing health data. The employer shall provide physician recommended examinations to any employee exposed to EtO in emergency conditions. Likewise, the employer shall make available medical consultations including physician recommended exams to employees who be-lieve they are suffering signs or symptoms of exposure to EtO.

The employer is required to provide the physician with the following informatin: a copy of this standard and its appendices; a description of the affected employee's duties as they relate to the employee exposure level; and information from the employee's previous medical examinations which is not readily available to the examining physician. Making this information available to the physician will aid in the evaluation of the employee's health in relation to assigned duties and fitness to wear personal protective equipment, when required.

The employer is required to obtain a written opinion from the examining physician containing the results of the medical examinations; the physician's opinion as to whether the employee has any detected medical conditions which would place the employee at increased risk of material impairment of his or her health from exposure to EtO; any recommended restrictions upon the employee's exposure to EtO, or upon the use of protective clothing or equipment such as respirators; and a statement that the employee has been informed by the physician of the results of the medical examination and of any medical conditions which require further explanation or treatment. This written opinion must not reveal specific findings or diagnoses unrelated to occupational exposure to EtO, and a copy of the opinion must be provided to the affected employee.

The purpose in requiring the examining physician to supply the employer with a written opinion is to provide the employer with a medical basis to aid in the determination of initial placement of employees and to assess the employee's ability to use protective clothing and equipment.

APPENDIX D TO § 1910.1047—SAMPLING AND ANALYTICAL METHODS FOR ETHYLENE OXIDE (NON-MANDATORY)

A number of methods are available for monitoring employee exposures to EtO. Most of these involve the use of charcoal tubes and sampling pumps, followed by analysis of the samples by gas chromatograph. The essential differences between the charcoal tube methods include, among others, the use of different desorbing solvents, the use of different lots of charcoal, and the use of different equipment for analysis of the samples.

Besides charcoal, methods using passive dosimeters, gas sampling bags, impingers, and detector tubes have been utilized for determination of EtO exposure. In addition, there are several commercially available portable gas analyzers and monitoring units.

This appendix contains details for the method which has been tested at the OSHA Analytical Laboratory in Salt Lake City. Inclusion of this method in the appendix does not mean that this method is the only one which will be satisfactory. Copies of descriptions of other methods available are available in the rulemaking record, and may be obtained from the OSHA Docket Office. These include the Union Carbide, Dow Chemical, 3M, and DuPont methods, as well as

NIOSH Method S–286. These methods are briefly described at the end of this appendix.

Employers who note problems with sample breakthrough using the OSHA or other charcoal methods should try larger charcoal tubes. Tubes of larger capacity are available. In addition, lower flow rates and shorter sampling times should be beneficial in minimizing breakthrough problems. Whatever method the employer chooses, he must assure himself of the method's accuracy and precision under the unique conditions present in his workplace.

ETHYLENE OXIDE

Method No.: 30.

Matrix: Air.

Target Concentration: 1.0 ppm (1.8 mg/m³).

Procedure: Samples are collected on two charcoal tubes in series and desorbed with 1% CS_2 in benzene. The samples are derivatized with HBr and treated with sodium carbonate. Analysis is done by gas chromatography with an electron capture detector.

Recommended Air Volume and Sampling Rate: 1 liter and 0.05 Lpm.

Detection Limit of the Overall Procedure: 13.3 ppb (0.024 mg/m³) (Based on 1.0 liter air sample).

Reliable Quantitation Limit: 52.2 ppb (0.094 mg/m³) (Based on 1.0 liter air sample).

Standard Error of Estimate: 6.59% (See Backup Section 4.6).

Special Requirements: Samples must be analyzed within 15 days of sampling date.

Status of Method: The sampling and analytical method has been subjected to the established evaluation procedures of the Organic Method Evaluations Branch.

Date: August 1981.

Chemist: Wayne D. Potter.

ORGANIC SOLVENTS BRANCH, OSHA ANALYTICAL LABORATORY, SALT LAKE CITY, UTAH

1. General Discussion.

1.1 Background.

1.1.1 History of Procedure.

Ethylene oxide samples analyzed at the OSHA Laboratory have normally been collected on activated charcoal and desorbed with carbon disulfide. The analysis is performed with a gas chromatograph equipped with a FID (Flame ionization detector) as described in NIOSH Method S286 (Ref. 5.1). This method is based on a PEL of 50 ppm and has a detection limit of about 1 ppm.

Recent studies have prompted the need for a method to analyze and detect ethylene oxide at very low concentrations.

Several attempts were made to form an ultraviolet (UV) sensitive derivative with ethylene oxide for analysis with HPLC. Among those tested that gave no detectable product were: p-anisidine, methylimidazole, aniline, and 2,3,6-trichlorobenzoic acid. Each

427

was tested with catalysts such as triethylamine, aluminum chloride, methylene chloride and sulfuric acid but no detectable derivative was produced.

The next derivatization attempt was to react ethylene oxide with HBr to form 2-bromoethanol. This reaction was successful. An ECD (electron capture detector) gave a very good response for 2-bromoethanol due to the presence of bromine. The use of carbon disulfide as the desorbing solvent gave too large a response and masked the 2-bromoethanol. Several other solvents were tested for both their response on the ECD and their ability to desorb ethylene oxide from the charcoal. Among those tested were toluene, xylene, ethyl benzene, hexane, cyclohexane and benzene. Benzene was the only solvent tested that gave a suitable response on the ECD and a high desorption. It was found that the desorption efficiency was improved by using 1% CS_2 with the benzene. The carbon disulfide did not significantly improve the recovery with the other solvents. SKC Lot 120 was used in all tests done with activated charcoal.

1.1.2 Physical Properties (Ref. 5.2–5.4).

Synonyms: Oxirane; dimethylene oxide, 1,2-epoxy-ethane; oxane; $C_2 H_4 O$; ETO;

Molecular Weight: 44.06

Boiling Point: 10.7 °C (51.3°)

Melting Point: −111 °C

Description: Colorless, flammable gas

Vapor Pressure: 1095 mm. at 20 °C

Odor: Ether-like odor

Lower Explosive Limits: 3.0% (by volume)

Flash Point (TOC): Below 0 °F

Molecular Structure: CH_2—CH_2

1.2 Limit Defining Parameters.

1.2.1 Detection Limit of the Analytical Procedure.

The detection limit of the analytical procedure is 12.0 picograms of ethylene oxide per injection. This is the amount of analyte which will give a peak whose height is five times the height of the baseline noise. (See Backup Data Section 4.1).

1.2.2 Detection Limit of the Overall Procedure.

The detection limit of the overall procedure is 24.0 ng of ethylene oxide per sample. This is the amount of analyte spiked on the sampling device which allows recovery of an amount of analyte equivalent to the detection limit of the analytical procedure. (See Backup Data Section 4.2).

1.2.3 Reliable Quantitation Limit.

The reliable quantitation limit is 94.0 nanograms of ethylene oxide per sample. This is the smallest amount of analyte which can be quantitated within the requirements of 75% recovery and 95% confidence limits. (See Backup Data Section 4.2).

It must be recognized that the reliable quantitation limit and detection limits reported in the method are based upon optimization of the instrument for the smallest possible amount of analyte. When the target concentration of an analyte is exceptionally higher than these limits, they may not be attainable at the routine operating parameters. In this case, the limits reported on analysis reports will be based on the operating parameters used during the analysis of the samples.

1.2.4 Sensitivity.

The sensitivity of the analytical procedure over a concentration range representing 0.5 to 2 times the target concentration based on the recommended air volume is 34105 area units per μg/mL. The sensitivity is determined by the slope of the calibration curve (See Backup Data Section 4.3).

The sensitivity will vary somewhat with the particular instrument used in the analysis.

1.2.5 Recovery.

The recovery of analyte from the collection medium must be 75% or greater. The average recovery from spiked samples over the range of 0.5 to 2 times the target concentration is 88.0% (See Backup Section 4.4). At lower concentrations the recovery appears to be non-linear.

1.2.6 Precision (Analytical Method Only).

The pooled coefficient of variation obtained from replicate determination of analytical standards at 0.5X, 1X and 2X the target concentration is 0.036 (See Backup Data Section 4.5).

1.2.7 Precision (Overall Procedure).

The overall procedure must provide results at the target concentration that are 25% of better at the 95% confidence level. The precision at the 95% confidence level for the 15 day storage test is plus or minus 12.9% (See Backup Data Section 4.6).

This includes an additional plus or minus 5% for sampling error.

1.3 Advantages.

1.3.1 The sampling procedure is convenient.

1.3.2 The analytical procedure is very sensitive and reproducible.

1.3.3 Reanalysis of samples is possible.

1.3.4 Samples are stable for at least 15 days at room temperature.

1.3.5 Interferences are reduced by the longer GC retention time of the new derivative.

1.4 Disadvantages.

1.4.1 Two tubes in series must be used because of possible breakthrough and migration.

1.4.2 The precision of the sampling rate may be limited by the reproducibility of the pressure drop across the tubes. The pumps are usually calibrated for one tube only.

1.4.3 The use of benzene as the desorption solvent increases the hazards of analysis because of the potential carcinogenic effects of benzene.

1.4.4 After repeated injections there can be a buildup of residue formed on the electron capture detector which decreases sensitivity.

1.4.5 Recovery from the charcoal tubes appears to be nonlinear at low concentrations.

2. Sampling Procedure.

2.1 Apparatus.

2.1.1 A calibrated personal sampling pump whose flow can be determined within plus or minus 5% of the recommended flow.

2.1.2 SKC Lot 120 Charcoal tubes: glass tube with both ends flame sealed, 7 cm long with a 6 mm O.D. and a 4-mm I.D., containing 2 sections of coconut shell charcoal separated by a 2-mm portion of urethane foam. The adsorbing section contains 100 mg of charcoal, the backup section 50 mg. A 3-mm portion of urethane foam is placed between the outlet end of the tube and the backup section. A plug of silylated glass wool is placed in front of the adsorbing section.

2.2 Reagents.

2.2.1 None required.

2.3 Sampling Technique.

2.3.1 Immediately before sampling, break the ends of the charcoal tubes. All tubes must be from the same lot.

2.3.2 Connect two tubes in series to the sampling pump with a short section of flexible tubing. A minimum amount of tubing is used to connect the two sampling tubes together. The tube closer to the pump is used as a backup. This tube should be identified as the backup tube.

2.3.3 The tubes should be placed in a vertical position during sampling to minimize channeling.

2.3.4 Air being sampled should not pass through any hose or tubing before entering the charcoal tubes.

2.3.5 Seal the charcoal tubes with plastic caps immediately after sampling. Also, seal each sample with OSHA seals lengthwise.

2.3.6 With each batch of samples, submit at least one blank tube from the same lot used for samples. This tube should be subjected to exactly the same handling as the samples (break, seal, transport) except that no air is drawn through it.

2.3.7 Transport the samples (and corresponding paperwork) to the lab for analysis.

2.3.8 If bulk samples are submitted for analysis, they shoud be transported in glass containers with Teflon-lined caps. These samples must be mailed separately from the container used for the charcoal tubes.

2.4 Breakthrough.

2.4.1 The breakthrough (5% breakthrough) volume for a 3.0 mg/m ethylene oxide sample stream at approximately 85% relative humidity, 22 °C and 633 mm is 2.6 liters sampled at 0.05 liters per minute. This is equivalent to 7.8 µg of ethylene oxide. Upon saturation of the tube it appeared that the water may be displacing ethylene oxide during sampling.

2.5 Desorption Efficiency.

2.5.1 The desorption efficiency, from liquid injection onto charcoal tubes, averaged 88.0% from 0.5 to 2.0 × the target concentration for a 1.0 liter air sample. At lower ranges it appears that the desorption efficiency is non-linear (See Backup Data Section 4.2).

2.5.2 The desorption efficiency may vary from one laboratory to another and also from one lot of charcoal to another. Thus, it is necessary to determine the desorption efficiency for a particular lot of charcoal.

2.6 Recommended Air Volume and Sampling Rate.

2.6.1 The recommended air volume is 1.0 liter.

2.6.2 The recommended maximum sampling rate is 0.05 Lpm.

2.7 Interferences.

2.7.1 Ethylene glycol and Freon 12 at target concentration levels did not interfere with the collection of ethylene oxide.

2.7.2 Suspected interferences should be listed on the sample data sheets.

2.7.3 The relative humidity may affect the sampling procedure.

2.8 Safety Precautions.

2.8.1 Attach the sampling equipment to the employee so that it does not interfere with work performance.

2.8.2 Wear safety glasses when breaking the ends of the sampling tubes.

2.8.3 If possible, place the sampling tubes in a holder so the sharp end is not exposed while sampling.

3. Analytical Method.

3.1 Apparatus.

3.1.1 Gas chromatograph equipped with a linearized electron capture detector.

3.1.2 GC column capable of separating the derivative of ethylene oxide (2-bromoethanol) from any interferences and the 1% CS_2 in benzene solvent. The column used for validation studies was: 10 ft × ⅛ inch stainless steel 20% SP–2100, .1% Carbowax 1500 on 100/120 Supelcoport.

3.1.3 An electronic integrator or some other suitable method of measuring peak areas.

3.1.4 Two milliliter vials with Teflon-lined caps.

3.1.5 Gas tight syringe—500 µL or other convenient sizes for preparing standards.

3.1.6 Microliter syringes—10 µL or other convenient sizes for diluting standards and 1 µL for sample injections.

3.1.7 Pipets for dispensing the 1% CS_2 in benzene solvent. The Glenco 1 mL dispenser is adequate and convenient.

3.1.8 Volumetric flasks—5 mL and other convenient sizes for preparing standards.

3.1.9 Disposable Pasteur pipets.

3.2 Reagents.

3.2.1 Benzene, reagent grade.

429

3.2.2 Carbon Disulfide, reagent grade.

3.2.3 Ethylene oxide, 99.7% pure.

3.2.4 Hydrobromic Acid, 48% reagent grade.

3.2.5 Sodium Carbonate, anhydrous, reagent grade.

3.2.6 Desorbing reagent, 99% Benzene/1% CS_2.

3.3 Sample Preparation.

3.3.1 The front and back sections of each sample are transferred to separate 2-mL vials.

3.3.2 Each sample is desorbed with 1.0 mL of desorbing reagent.

3.3.3 The vials are sealed immediately and allowed to desorb for one hour with occasional shaking.

3.3.4 Desorbing reagent is drawn off the charcoal with a disposable pipet and put into clean 2-mL vials.

3.3.5 One drop of HBr is added to each vial. Vials are resealed and HBr is mixed well with the desorbing reagent.

3.3.6 About 0.15 gram of sodium carbonate is carefully added to each vial. Vials are again resealed and mixed well.

3.4 Standard Preparation.

3.4.1 Standards are prepared by injecting the pure ethylene oxide gas into the desorbing reagent.

3.4.2 A range of standards are prepared to make a calibration curve. A concentration of 1.0 µL of ethylene oxide gas per 1 mL desorbing reagent is equivalent to 1.0 ppm air concentration (all gas volumes at 25 °C and 760 mm) for the recommended 1 liter air sample. This amount is uncorrected for desorption efficiency (See Backup Data Section 4.2. for desorption efficiency corrections).

3.4.3 One drop of HBr per mL of standard is added and mixed well.

3.4.4 About 0.15 grams of sodium carbonate is carefully added for each drop of HBr (A small reaction will occur).

3.5 Analysis.

3.5.1 GC Conditions.

Nitrogen flow rate—10mL/min.

Injector Temperature—250 °C

Detector Temperature—300 °C

Column Temperature—100 °C

Injection size—0.8 µL

Elution time—3.9 minutes

3.5.2 Peak areas are measured by an integrator or other suitable means.

3.5.3 The integrator results are in area units and a calibration curve is set up with concentration vs. area units.

3.6 Interferences.

3.6.1 Any compound having the same retention time of 2-bromoethanol is a potential interference. Possible interferences should be listed on the sample data sheets.

3.6.2 GC parameters may be changed to circumvent interferences.

3.6.3 There are usually trace contaminants in benzene. These contaminants, however, posed no problem of interference.

3.6.4 Retention time data on a single column is not considered proof of chemical identity. Samples over the 1.0 ppm target level should be confirmed by GC/Mass Spec or other suitable means.

3.7 Calculations

3.7.1 The concentration in µg/mL for a sample is determined by comparing the area of a particular sample to the calibration curve, which has been prepared from analytical standards.

3.7.2 The amount of analyte in each sample is corrected for desorption efficiency by use of a desorption curve.

3.7.3 Analytical results (A) from the two tubes that compose a particular air sample are added together.

3.7.4 The concentration for a sample is calculated by the following equation:

$$ETO, \ mg/m^3 = \frac{AXB}{C}$$

where:

A = µg/mL

B = desorption volume in milliliters

C = air volume in liters.

3.7.5 To convert mg/m³ to parts per million (ppm) the following relationship is used:

$$ETO, \ ppm = \frac{mg/m^3 \times 24.45}{44.05}$$

where:

mg/m³ = results from 3.7.4

24.45 = molar volume at 25 °C and 760mm Hg

44.05 = molecular weight of ETO.

3.8 Safety Precautions

3.8.1 Ethylene oxide and benzene are potential carcinogens and care must be exercised when working with these compounds.

3.8.2 All work done with the solvents (preparation of standards, desorption of samples, etc.) should be done in a hood.

3.8.3 Avoid any skin contact with all of the solvents.

3.8.4 Wear safety glasses at all times.

3.8.5 Avoid skin contact with HBr because it is highly toxic and a strong irritant to eyes and skin.

4. Backup Data.

4.1 Detection Limit Data.

The detection limit was determined by injecting 0.8 µL of a 0.015 µg/mL standard of ethylene oxide into 1% CS_2 in benzene. The detection limit of the analytical procedure is taken to be 1.20×10^{-5} µg per injection. This is equivalent to 8.3 ppb (0.015 mg/m³) for the recommended air volume.

4.2 Desorption Efficiency.

Ethylene oxide was spiked onto charcoal tubes and the following recovery data was obtained.

Amount spiked (μg)	Amount recovered (μg)	Percent recovery
4.5	4.32	96.0
3.0	2.61	87.0
2.25	2.025	90.0
1.5	1.365	91.0
1.5	1.38	92.0
.75	.6525	87.0
.375	.315	84.0
.375	.312	83.2
.1875	.151	80.5
.094	.070	74.5

At lower amounts the recovery appears to be non-linear.

4.3 Sensitivity Data.

The following data was used to determine the calibration curve.

Injection	0.5 × .75 μg/ mL	1 × 1.5 μg/mL	2 × 3.0 μg/mL
1	30904	59567	111778
2	30987	62914	106016
3	32555	58578	106122
4	32242	57173	109716
X	31672	59558	108408

Slope = 34.105.

4.4 Recovery.

The recovery was determined by spiking ethylene oxide onto lot 120 charcoal tubes and desorbing with 1% CS₂ in Benzene. Recoveries were done at 0.5, 1.0, and 2.0× the target concentration (1 ppm) for the recommended air volume.

PERCENT RECOVERY

Sample	0.5x	1.0x	2.0x
1	88.7	95.0	91.7
2	83.8	95.0	87.3
3	84.2	91.0	86.0
4	88.0	91.0	83.0
5	88.0	86.0	85.0
X	86.5	90.5	87.0

Weighted Average = 88.2.

4.5 Precision of the Analytical Procedure.

The following data was used to determine the precision of the analytical method:

Concentration	0.5 × .75 μg/ mL	1 × 1.5 μg/mL	2 × 3.0 μg/mL
Injection	.7421	1.4899	3.1184
	.7441	1.5826	3.0447
	.7831	1.4628	2.9149
	.7753	1.4244	2.9185
Average	.7612	1.4899	2.9991
Standard Deviation	.0211	.0674	.0998
CV	.0277	.0452	.0333

$$CV = \frac{3(.0277)^2 + 3(.0452)^2 + 3(.0333)^2}{3+3+3}$$

CV + 0.036

4.6 Storage Data.

Samples were generated at 1.5 mg/m³ ethylene oxide at 85% relative humidity, 22 °C and 633 mm. All samples were taken for 20 minutes at 0.05 Lpm. Six samples were analyzed as soon as possible and fifteen samples were stored at refrigerated temperature (5 °C) and fifteen samples were stored at ambient temperature (23 °C). These stored samples were analyzed over a period of nineteen days.

PERCENT RECOVERY

Day analyzed	Refrigerated	Ambient
1	87.0	87.0
1	93.0	93.0
1	94.0	94.0
1	92.0	92.0
4	92.0	91.0
4	93.0	88.0
4	91.0	89.0
6	92.0	
6	92.0	
8		92.0
8		86.0
10	91.7	
10	95.5	
10	95.7	
11		90.0
11		82.0
13	78.0	
13	81.4	
13	82.4	
14		78.5
14		72.1
18	66.0	
18	68.0	
19		64.0
19		77.0

4.7 Breakthrough Data.

Breakthrough studies were done at 2 ppm (3.6 mg/m³) at approximately 85% relative humidity at 22 °C (ambient temperature). Two charcoal tubes were used in series. The backup tube was changed every 10 minutes and analyzed for breakthrough. The flow rate was 0.050 Lpm.

Tube No.	Time (minutes)	Percent break-through
1	10	(¹)
2	20	(¹)
3	30	(¹)
4	40	1.23
5	50	3.46
6	60	18.71
7	70	39.2
8	80	53.3
9	90	72.0
10	100	96.0
11	110	113.0
12	120	133.9

¹ None.

The 5% breakthrough volume was reached when 2.6 liters of test atmosphere were drawn through the charcoal tubes.

5. References.

431

5.1 "NIOSH Manual of Analytical Methods," 2nd ed. NIOSH: Cincinnati, 1977; Method S286.

5.2 "IARC Monographs on the Evaluation of Carcinogenic Risk of Chemicals to Man," International Agency for Research on Cancer: Lyon, 1976; Vol. II, p. 157.

5.3 Sax., N.I. "Dangerous Properties of Industrial Materials," 4th ed.; Van Nostrand Reinhold Company. New York, 1975; p. 741.

5.4 "The Condensed Chemical Dictionary", 9th ed.; Hawley, G.G., ed.; Van Nostrand Reinhold Company, New York, 1977; p. 361.

Summary of Other Sampling Procedures

OSHA believes that served other types of monitoring equipment and techniques exist for monitoring time-weighted averages. Considerable research and method development is currently being performed, which will lead to improvements and a wider variety of monitoring techniques. A combination of monitoring procedures can be used. There probably is no one best method for monitoring personal exposure to ethylene oxide in all cases. There are advantages, disadvantages, and limitations to each method. The method of choice will depend on the need and requirements. Some commonly used methods include the use of charcoal tubes, passive dosimeters, Tedler gas sampling bags, detector tubes, photoionization detection units, infrared detection units and gas chromatographs. A number of these methods are described below.

A. Charcoal Tube Sampling Procedures

Qazi-Ketcham method (Ex. 11-133)—This method consists of collecting EtO on Columbia JXC activated carbon, desorbing the EtO with carbon disulfide and analyzing by gas chromatography with flame ionization detection. Union Carbide has recently updated and revalidated this monitoring procedures. This method is capable of determining both eight-hour time-weighted average exposures and short-term exposures. The method was validated to 0.5 ppm. Like other charcoal collecting procedures, the method requires considerable analytical expertise.

ASTM-proposed method—The Ethylene Oxide Industry Council (EOIC) has contracted with Clayton Environmental Consultants, Inc. to conduct a collaborative study for the proposed method. The ASTM-Proposed method is similar to the method published by Qazi and Ketcham is the November 1977 American Industrial Hygiene Association Journal, and to the method of Pilney and Coyne, presented at the 1979 American Industrial Hygiene Conference. After the air to be sampled is drawn through an activated charcoal tube, the ethylene oxide is desorbed from the tube using carbon disulfide and is quantitated by gas chroma-

tography utilizing a flame ionization detector. The ASTM-proposed method specifies a large two-section charcoal tube, shipment in dry ice, storage at less than -5 °C, and analysis within three weeks to prevent migration and sample loss. Two types of charcoal tubes are being tested— Pittsburgh Coconut-Based (PCB) and Columbia JXC charcoal. This collaborative study will give an indication of the inter- and intralaboratory precision and accuracy of the ASTM-proposed method. Several laboratories have considerable expertise using the Qazi-Ketcham and Dow methods.

B. Passive Monitors—Ethylene oxide diffuses into the monitor and is collected in the sampling media. The DuPont Pro-Tek badge collects EtO in an absorbing solution, which is analyzed colorimetrically to determine the amount of EtO present. The 3M 350 badge collects the EtO on chemically treated charcoal. Other passive monitors are currently being developed and tested. Both 3M and DuPont have submitted data indicating their dosimeters meet the precision and accuracy requirements of the proposed ethylene oxide standard. Both presented laboratory validation data to 0.2 ppm (Exs. 11-65, 4-20, 108, 109, 130).

C. Tedlar Gas Sampling Bags-Samples are collected by drawing a known volume of air into a Tedlar gas sampling bag. The ethylene oxide concentration is often determined on-site using a portable gas chromatograph or portable infrared spectometer.

D. Detector tubes—A known volume of air is drawn through a detector tube using a small hand pump. The concentration of EtO is related to the length of stain developed in the tube. Detector tubes are economical, easy to use, and give an immediate readout. Unfortunately, partly because they are nonspecific, their accuracy is often questionable. Since the sample is taken over a short period of time, they may be useful for determining the source of leaks.

E. Direct Reading Instruments—There are numerous types of direct reading instruments, each having its own strengths and weaknesses (Exs. 135B, 135C, 107, 11-78, 11-153). Many are relatively new, offering greater sensitivity and specificity. Popular ethylene oxide direct reading instruments include infrared detection units, photoionization detection units, and gas chromatographs.

Portable infrared analyzers provide an immediate, continuous indication of a concentration value; making them particularly useful for locating high concentration pockets, in leak detection and in ambient air monitoring. In infrared detection units, the amount of infrared light absorbed by the gas being analyzed at selected infrared wavelengths is related to the concentration of a particular component. Various models have either fixed or variable infrared filters, differing cell pathlengths, and microcomputer controls for greater sensitivity, automation, and interference elimination.

A fairly recent detection system is photoionization detection. The molecules are ionized by high energy ultraviolet light. The resulting current is measured. Since different substances have different ionization potentials, other organic compounds may be ionized. The lower the lamp energy, the better the selectivity. As a continuous monitor, photoionization detection can be useful for locating high concentration pockets, in leak detection, and continuous ambient air monitoring. Both portable and stationary gas chromatographs are available with various types of detectors, including photoionization detectors. A gas chromatograph with a photoionization detector retains the photoionization sensitivity, but minimizes or eliminates interferences. For several GC/PID units, the sensitivity is in the 0.1–0.2 ppm EtO range. The GC/PID with microprocessors can sample up to 20 sample points sequentially, calculate and record data, and activate alarms or ventilation systems. Many are quite flexible and can be configured to meet the specific analysis needs for the workplace.

DuPont presented their laboratory validation data of the accuracy of the Qazi-Ketcham charcoal tube, the PCB charcoal tube, Miran 103 IR analyzer, 3M #3550 monitor and the Du Pont C–70 badge. Quoting Elbert V. Kring:

We also believe that OSHA's proposed accuracy in this standard is appropriate. At plus or minus 25 percent at one part per million, and plus or minus 35 percent below that. And, our data indicates there's only one monitoring method, right now, that we've tested thoroughly, that meets that accuracy requirements. That is the Du Pont Pro-Tek badge* * *. We also believe that this kind of data should be confirmed by another independent laboratory, using the same type dynamic chamber testing (Tr. 1470)

Additional data by an independent laboratory following their exact protocol was not submitted. However, information was submitted on comparisons and precision and accuracy of those monitoring procedures which indicate far better precision and accuracy of those monitoring procedures than that obtained by Du Pont (Ex. 4–20, 130, 11–68, 11–133, 130, 135A).

The accuracy of any method depends to a large degree upon the skills and experience of those who not only collect the samples but also those who analyze the samples. Even for methods that are collaboratively tested, some laboratories are closer to the true values than others. Some laboratories may meet the precision and accuracy requirements of the method; others may consistently far exceed them for the same method.

[49 FR 25796, June 22, 1984, as amended at 50 FR 9801, Mar. 12, 1985; 50 FR 41494, Oct. 11, 1985; 51 FR 25053, July 10, 1986; 53 FR 11436, 11437, Apr. 6, 1988; 53 FR 27960, July 26, 1988; 54 FR 24334, June 7, 1989; 61 FR 5508, Feb. 13, 1996; 63 FR 1292, Jan. 8, 1998; 67 FR 67965, Nov. 7, 2002; 70 FR 1143, Jan. 5, 2005; 71 FR 16672, 16673, Apr. 3, 2006; 71 FR 50190, Aug. 24, 2006; 73 FR 75586, Dec. 12, 2008; 76 FR 33609, June 8, 2011; 77 FR 17783, Mar. 26, 2012]

§1910.1048 Formaldehyde.

(a) *Scope and application.* This standard applies to all occupational exposures to formaldehyde, i.e. from formaldehyde gas, its solutions, and materials that release formaldehyde.

(b) *Definitions.* For purposes of this standard, the following definitions shall apply:

Action level means a concentration of 0.5 part formaldehyde per million parts of air (0.5 ppm) calculated as an eight (8)-hour time-weighted average (TWA) concentration.

Assistant Secretary means the Assistant Secretary of Labor for the Occupational Safety and Health Administration, U.S. Department of Labor, or designee.

Authorized person means any person required by work duties to be present in regulated areas, or authorized to do so by the employer, by this section, or by the OSH Act of 1970.

Director means the Director of the National Institute for Occupational Safety and Health, U.S. Department of Health and Human Services, or designee.

Emergency is any occurrence, such as but not limited to equipment failure, rupture of containers, or failure of control equipment that results in an uncontrolled release of a significant amount of formaldehyde.

Employee exposure means the exposure to airborne formaldehyde which would occur without corrections for protection provided by any respirator that is in use.

Formaldehyde means the chemical substance, HCHO, Chemical Abstracts Service Registry No. 50–00–0.

(c) *Permissible Exposure Limit (PEL)*— (1) *TWA:* The employer shall assure that no employee is exposed to an airborne concentration of formaldehyde which exceeds 0.75 parts formaldehyde per million parts of air (0.75 ppm) as an 8-hour TWA.

(2) *Short Term Exposure Limit (STEL):* The employer shall assure that no employee is exposed to an airborne concentration of formaldehyde which exceeds two parts formaldehyde per million parts of air (2 ppm) as a 15-minute STEL.

(d) *Exposure monitoring*—(1) *General.* (i) Each employer who has a workplace covered by this standard shall monitor employees to determine their exposure to formaldehyde.

(ii) *Exception.* Where the employer documents, using objective data, that the presence of formaldehyde or formaldehyde-releasing products in the workplace cannot result in airborne concentrations of formaldehyde that would cause any employee to be exposed at or above the action level or the STEL under foreseeable conditions of use, the employer will not be required to measure employee exposure to formaldehyde.

(iii) When an employee's exposure is determined from representative sampling, the measurements used shall be representative of the employee's full shift or short-term exposure to formaldehyde, as appropriate.

(iv) Representative samples for each job classification in each work area shall be taken for each shift unless the employer can document with objective data that exposure levels for a given job classification are equivalent for different work shifts.

(2) *Initial monitoring.* The employer shall identify all employees who may be exposed at or above the action level or at or above the STEL and accurately determine the exposure of each employee so identified.

(i) Unless the employer chooses to measure the exposure of each employee potentially exposed to formaldehyde, the employer shall develop a representative sampling strategy and measure sufficient exposures within each job classification for each workshift to correctly characterize and not underestimate the exposure of any employee within each exposure group.

(ii) The initial monitoring process shall be repeated each time there is a change in production, equipment, process, personnel, or control measures which may result in new or additional exposure to formaldehyde.

(iii) If the employer receives reports of signs or symptoms of respiratory or dermal conditions associated with formaldehyde exposure, the employer shall promptly monitor the affected employee's exposure.

(3) *Periodic monitoring.* (i) The employer shall periodically measure and accurately determine exposure to formaldehyde for employees shown by the initial monitoring to be exposed at or above the action level or at or above the STEL.

(ii) If the last monitoring results reveal employee exposure at or above the action level, the employer shall repeat monitoring of the employees at least every 6 months.

(iii) If the last monitoring results reveal employee exposure at or above the STEL, the employer shall repeat monitoring of the employees at least once a year under worst conditions.

(4) *Termination of monitoring.* The employer may discontinue periodic monitoring for employees if results from two consecutive sampling periods taken at least 7 days apart show that employee exposure is below the action level and the STEL. The results must be statistically representative and consistent with the employer's knowledge of the job and work operation.

(5) *Accuracy of monitoring.* Monitoring shall be accurate, at the 95 percent confidence level, to within plus or minus 25 percent for airborne concentrations of formaldehyde at the TWA and the STEL and to within plus or minus 35 percent for airborne concentrations of formaldehyde at the action level.

(6) *Employee notification of monitoring results.* The employer must, within 15 working days after the receipt of the results of any monitoring performed under this section, notify each affected employee of these results either individually in writing or by posting the results in an appropriate location that is accessible to employees. If employee exposure is above the PEL, affected employees shall be provided with a description of the corrective actions being taken by the employer to decrease exposure.

(7) *Observation of monitoring.* (i) The employer shall provide affected employees or their designated representatives an opportunity to observe any monitoring of employee exposure to formaldehyde required by this standard.

(ii) When observation of the monitoring of employee exposure to formaldehyde requires entry into an area where the use of protective clothing or equipment is required, the employer shall provide the clothing and equipment to the observer, require the observer to use such clothing and equipment, and assure that the observer complies with all other applicable safety and health procedures.

(e) *Regulated areas*—(1) *Signs.* (i) The employer shall establish regulated areas where the concentration of airborne formaldehyde exceeds either the TWA or the STEL and post all entrances and access ways with signs bearing the following legend:

DANGER
FORMALDEHYDE
MAY CAUSE CANCER
CAUSES SKIN, EYE, AND RESPIRATORY IRRITATION
AUTHORIZED PERSONNEL ONLY

(ii) Prior to June 1, 2016, employers may use the following legend in lieu of that specified in paragraph (e)(1)(i) of this section:

DANGER
FORMALDEHYDE
IRRITANT AND POTENTIAL CANCER HAZARD
AUTHORIZED PERSONNEL ONLY

(2) The employer shall limit access to regulated areas to authorized persons who have been trained to recognize the hazards of formaldehyde.

(3) An employer at a multiemployer worksite who establishes a regulated area shall communicate the access restrictions and locations of these areas to other employers with work operations at that worksite.

(f) *Methods of compliance*—(1) *Engineering controls and work practices.* The employer shall institute engineering and work practice controls to reduce and maintain employee exposures to formaldehyde at or below the TWA and the STEL.

(2) *Exception.* Whenever the employer has established that feasible engineer-

ing and work practice controls cannot reduce employee exposure to or below either of the PELs, the employer shall apply these controls to reduce employee exposures to the extent feasible and shall supplement them with respirators which satisfy this standard.

(g) *Respiratory protection*—(1) *General.* For employees who use respirators required by this section, the employer must provide each employee an appropriate respirator that complies with the requirements of this paragraph. Respirators must be used during:

(i) Periods necessary to install or implement feasible engineering and work-practice controls.

(ii) Work operations, such as maintenance and repair activities or vessel cleaning, for which the employer establishes that engineering and work-practice controls are not feasible.

(iii) Work operations for which feasible engineering and work-practice controls are not yet sufficient to reduce employee exposure to or below the PELs.

(iv) Emergencies.

(2) *Respirator program.* (i) The employer must implement a respiratory protection program in accordance with §1910.134(b) through (d) (except (d)(1)(iii), (d)(3)(iii)(b)(1), and (2)), and (f) through (m), which covers each employee required by this section to use a respirator.

(ii) When employees use air-purifying respirators with chemical cartridges or canisters that do not contain end-of-service-life indicators approved by the National Institute for Occupational Safety and Health, employers must replace these cartridges or canisters as specified by paragraphs (d)(3)(iii)(B)(1) and (B)(2) of 29 CFR 1910.134, or at the end of the workshift, whichever condition occurs first.

(3) *Respirator selection.* (i) Employers must:

(A) Select, and provide to employees, the appropriate respirators specified in paragraph (d)(3)(i)(A) of 29 CFR 1910.134.

(B) Equip each air-purifying, full facepiece respirator with a canister or cartridge approved for protection against formaldehyde.

(C) For escape, provide employees with one of the following respirator options: A self-contained breathing apparatus operated in the demand or pressure-demand mode; or a full facepiece respirator having a chin-style, or a front-or back-mounted industrial-size, canister or cartridge approved for protection against formaldehyde.

(ii) Employers may substitute an air-purifying, half mask respirator for an air-purifying, full facepiece respirator when they equip the half mask respirator with a cartridge approved for protection against formaldehyde and provide the affected employee with effective gas-proof goggles.

(iii) Employers must provide employees who have difficulty using negative pressure respirators with powered air-purifying respirators permitted for use under paragraph (g)(3)(i)(A) of this standard and that affords adequate protection against formaldehyde exposures.

(h) *Protective equipment and clothing.* Employers shall comply with the provisions of 29 CFR 1910.132 and 29 CFR 1910.133. When protective equipment or clothing is provided under these provisions, the employer shall provide these protective devices at no cost to the employee and assure that the employee wears them.

(1) *Selection.* The employer shall select protective clothing and equipment based upon the form of formaldehyde to be encountered, the conditions of use, and the hazard to be prevented.

(i) All contact of the eyes and skin with liquids containing 1 percent or more formaldehyde shall be prevented by the use of chemical protective clothing made of material impervious to formaldehyde and the use of other personal protective equipment, such as goggles and face shields, as appropriate to the operation.

(ii) Contact with irritating or sensitizing materials shall be prevented to the extent necessary to eliminate the hazard.

(iii) Where a face shield is worn, chemical safety goggles are also required if there is a danger of formaldehyde reaching the area of the eye.

(iv) Full body protection shall be worn for entry into areas where concentrations exceed 100 ppm and for emergency reentry into areas of unknown concentration.

(2) *Maintenance of protective equipment and clothing.* (i) The employer shall assure that protective equipment and clothing that has become contaminated with formaldehyde is cleaned or laundered before its reuse.

(ii) When formaldehyde-contaminated clothing and equipment is ventilated, the employer shall establish storage areas so that employee exposure is minimized.

(A) *Signs.* Storage areas for contaminated clothing and equipment shall have signs bearing the following legend:

DANGER
FORMALDEHYDE-CONTAMINATED
[CLOTHING] EQUIPMENT
MAY CAUSE CANCER
CAUSES SKIN, EYE AND RESPIRATORY
IRRITATION
DO NOT BREATHE VAPOR
DO NOT GET ON SKIN

(B) *Labels.* The employer shall ensure containers for contaminated clothing and equipment are labeled consistent with the Hazard Communication Standard, § 1910.1200, and shall, as a minimum, include the following:

DANGER
FORMALDEHYDE-CONTAMINATED
[CLOTHING] EQUIPMENT
MAY CAUSE CANCER
CAUSES SKIN, EYE, AND RESPIRATORY
IRRITATION
DO NOT BREATHE VAPOR
DO NOT GET ON SKIN

(C) Prior to June 1, 2016, employers may use the following legend in lieu of that specified in paragraph (h)(2)(ii)(A) of this section:

DANGER
FORMALDEHYDE-CONTAMINATED
[CLOTHING] EQUIPMENT
AVOID INHALATION AND SKIN CONTACT

(D) Prior to June 1, 2015, employers may include the following information on containers of protective clothing and equipment in lieu of the labeling requirements in paragraphs (h)(2)(ii)(B) of this section:

DANGER
FORMALDEHYDE-CONTAMINATED
[CLOTHING] EQUIPMENT
AVOID INHALATION AND SKIN CONTACT

(iii) The employer shall assure that only persons trained to recognize the hazards of formaldehyde remove the contaminated material from the storage area for purposes of cleaning, laundering, or disposal.

(iv) The employer shall assure that no employee takes home equipment or clothing that is contaminated with formaldehyde.

(v) The employer shall repair or replace all required protective clothing and equipment for each affected employee as necessary to assure its effectiveness.

(vi) The employer shall inform any person who launders, cleans, or repairs such clothing or equipment of formaldehyde's potentially harmful effects and of procedures to safely handle the clothing and equipment.

(i) *Hygiene protection.* (1) The employer shall provide change rooms, as described in 29 CFR 1910.141 for employees who are required to change from work clothing into protective clothing to prevent skin contact with formaldehyde.

(2) If employees' skin may become spashed with solutions containing 1 percent or greater formaldehyde, for example, because of equipment failure or improper work practices, the employer shall provide conveniently located quick drench showers and assure that affected employees use these facilities immediately.

(3) If there is any possibility that an employee's eyes may be splashed with solutions containing 0.1 percent or greater formaldehyde, the employer shall provide acceptable eyewash facilities within the immediate work area for emergency use.

(j) *Housekeeping.* For operations involving formaldehyde liquids or gas, the employer shall conduct a program to detect leaks and spills, including regular visual inspections.

(1) Preventative maintenance of equipment, including surveys for leaks, shall be undertaken at regular intervals.

(2) In work areas where spillage may occur, the employer shall make provisions to contain the spill, to decontaminate the work area, and to dispose of the waste.

(3) The employer shall assure that all leaks are repaired and spills are cleaned promptly by employees wearing suitable protective equipment and trained in proper methods for cleanup and decontamination.

(4) Formaldehyde-contaminated waste and debris resulting from leaks or spills shall be placed for disposal in sealed containers bearing a label warning of formaldehyde's presence and of the hazards associated with formaldehyde. The employer shall ensure that the labels are in accordance with paragraph (m) of this section.

(k) *Emergencies.* For each workplace where there is the possibility of an emergency involving formaldehyde, the employer shall assure appropriate procedures are adopted to minimize injury and loss of life. Appropriate procedures shall be implemented in the event of an emergency.

(1) *Medical surveillance*—(1) *Employees covered.* (i) The employer shall institute medical surveillance programs for all employees exposed to formaldehyde at concentrations at or exceeding the action level or exceeding the STEL.

(ii) The employer shall make medical surveillance available for employees who develop signs and symptoms of overexposure to formaldehyde and for all employees exposed to formaldehyde in emergencies. When determining whether an employee may be experiencing signs and symptoms of possible overexposure to formaldehyde, the employer may rely on the evidence that signs and symptoms associated with formaldehyde exposure will occur only in exceptional circumstances when airborne exposure is less than 0.1 ppm and when formaldehyde is present in material in concentrations less than 0.1 percent.

(2) *Examination by a physician.* All medical procedures, including administration of medical disease questionnaires, shall be performed by or under the supervision of a licensed physician and shall be provided without cost to the employee, without loss of pay, and at a reasonable time and place.

(3) *Medical disease questionnaire.* The employer shall make the following medical surveillance available to employees prior to assignment to a job where formaldehyde exposure is at or

above the action level or above the STEL and annually thereafter. The employer shall also make the following medical surveillance available promptly upon determining that an employee is experiencing signs and symptoms indicative of possible overexposure to formaldehyde.

(i) Administration of a medical disease questionnaire, such as in appendix D, which is designed to elicit information on work history, smoking history, any evidence of eye, nose, or throat irritation; chronic airway problems or hyperreactive airway disease: allergic skin conditions or dermatitis; and upper or lower respiratory problems.

(ii) A determination by the physician, based on evaluation of the medical disease questionnaire, of whether a medical examination is necessary for employees not required to wear respirators to reduce exposure to formaldehyde.

(4) *Medical examinations.* Medical examinations shall be given to any employee who the physician feels, based on information in the medical disease questionnaire, may be at increased risk from exposure to formaldehyde and at the time of initial assignment and at least annually thereafter to all employees required to wear a respirator to reduce exposure to formaldehyde. The medical examination shall include:

(i) A physical examination with emphasis on evidence of irritation or sensitization of the skin and respiratory system, shortness of breath, or irritation of the eyes.

(ii) Laboratory examinations for respirator wearers consisting of baseline and annual pulmonary function tests. As a minimum, these tests shall consist of forced vital capacity (FVC), forced expiratory volume in one second (FEV$_1$), and forced expiratory flow (FEF).

(iii) Any other test which the examining physician deems necessary to complete the written opinion.

(iv) Counseling of employees having medical conditions that would be directly or indirectly aggravated by exposure to formaldehyde on the increased risk of impairment of their health.

(5) *Examinations for employees exposed in an emergency.* The employer shall

make medical examinations available as soon as possible to all employees who have been exposed to formaldehyde in an emergency.

(i) The examination shall include a medical and work history with emphasis on any evidence of upper or lower respiratory problems, allergic conditions, skin reaction or hypersensitivity, and any evidence of eye, nose, or throat irritation.

(ii) Other examinations shall consist of those elements considered appropriate by the examining physician.

(6) *Information provided to the physician.* The employer shall provide the following information to the examining physician:

(i) A copy of this standard and appendix A, C, D, and E;

(ii) A description of the affected employee's job duties as they relate to the employee's exposure to formaldehyde;

(iii) The representative exposure level for the employee's job assignment;

(iv) Information concerning any personal protective equipment and respiratory protection used or to be used by the employee; and

(v) Information from previous medical examinations of the affected employee within the control of the employer.

(vi) In the event of a nonroutine examination because of an emergency, the employer shall provide to the physician as soon as possible: A description of how the emergency occurred and the exposure the victim may have received.

(7) *Physician's written opinion.* (i) For each examination required under this standard, the employer shall obtain a written opinion from the examining physician. This written opinion shall contain the results of the medical examination except that it shall not reveal specific findings or diagnoses unrelated to occupational exposure to formaldehyde. The written opinion shall include:

(A) The physician's opinion as to whether the employee has any medical condition that would place the employee at an increased risk of material impairment of health from exposure to formaldehyde;

(B) Any recommended limitations on the employee's exposure or changes in the use of personal protective equipment, including respirators;

(C) A statement that the employee has been informed by the physician of any medical conditions which would be aggravated by exposure to formaldehyde, whether these conditions may have resulted from past formaldehyde exposure or from exposure in an emergency, and whether there is a need for further examination or treatment.

(ii) The employer shall provide for retention of the results of the medical examination and tests conducted by the physician.

(iii) The employer shall provide a copy of the physician's written opinion to the affected employee within 15 days of its receipt.

(8) *Medical removal.* (i) The provisions of paragraph (1)(8) apply when an employee reports significant irritation of the mucosa of the eyes or the upper airways, respiratory sensitization, dermal irritation, or dermal sensitization attributed to workplace formaldehyde exposure. Medical removal provisions do not apply in the case of dermal irritation or dermal sensitization when the product suspected of causing the dermal condition contains less than 0.05% formaldehyde.

(ii) An employee's report of signs or symptoms of possible overexposure to formaldehyde shall be evaluated by a physician selected by the employer pursuant to paragraph (1)(3). If the physician determines that a medical examination is not necessary under paragraph (1)(3)(ii), there shall be a two-week evaluation and remediation period to permit the employer to ascertain whether the signs or symptoms subside untreated or with the use of creams, gloves, first aid treatment or personal protective equipment. Industrial hygiene measures that limit the employee's exposure to formaldehyde may also be implemented during this period. The employee shall be referred immediately to a physician prior to expiration of the two-week period if the signs or symptoms worsen. Earnings, seniority and benefits may not be altered during the two-week period by virtue of the report.

(iii) If the signs or symptoms have not subsided or been remedied by the end of the two-week period, or earlier if signs or symptoms warrant, the employee shall be examined by a physician selected by the employer. The physician shall presume, absent contrary evidence, that observed dermal irritation or dermal sensitization are not attributable to formaldehyde when products to which the affected employee is exposed contain less than 0.1% formaldehyde.

(iv) Medical examinations shall be conducted in compliance with the requirements of paragraph (1)(5) (i) and (ii). Additional guidelines for conducting medical exams are contained in appendix C.

(v) If the physician finds that significant irritation of the mucosa of the eyes or of the upper airways, respiratory sensitization, dermal irritation, or dermal sensitization result from workplace formaldehyde exposure and recommends restrictions or removal, the employer shall promptly comply with the restrictions or recommendation of removal. In the event of a recommendation of removal, the employer shall remove the effected employee from the current formaldehyde exposure and if possible, transfer the employee to work having no or significantly less exposure to formaldehyde.

(vi) When an employee is removed pursuant to paragraph (1)(8)(v), the employer shall transfer the employee to comparable work for which the employee is qualified or can be trained in a short period (up to 6 months), where the formaldehyde exposures are as low as possible, but not higher than the action level. The employeer shall maintain the employee's current earnings, seniority, and other benefits. If there is no such work available, the employer shall maintain the employee's current earnings, seniority and other benefits until such work becomes available, until the employee is determined to be unable to return to workplace formaldehyde exposure, until the employee is determined to be able to return to the original job status, or for six months, whichever comes first.

(vii) The employer shall arrange for a follow-up medical examination to take place within six months after the employee is removed pursuant to this paragraph. This examination shall determine if the employee can return to the original job status, or if the removal is to be permanent. The physician shall make a decision within six months of the date the employee was removed as to whether the employee can be returned to the original job status, or if the removal is to be permanent.

(viii) An employer's obligation to provide earnings, seniority and other benefits to a removed employee may be reduced to the extent that the employee receives compensation for earnings lost during the period of removal either from a publicly or employer-funded compensation program or from employment with another employer made possible by virtue of the employee's removal.

(ix) In making determinations of the formaldehyde content of materials under this paragraph the employer may rely on objective data.

(9) *Multiple physician review.* (i) After the employer selects the initial physician who conducts any medical examination or consultation to determine whether medical removal or restriction is appropriate, the employee may designate a second physician to review any findings, determinations or recommendations of the initial physician and to conduct such examinations, consultations, and laboratory tests as the second physician deems necessary and appropriate to evaluate the effects of formaldehyde exposure and to facilitate this review.

(ii) The employer shall promptly notify an employee of the right to seek a second medical opinion after each occasion that an initial physician conducts a medical examination or consultation for the purpose of medical removal or restriction.

(iii) The employer may condition its participation in, and payment for, the multiple physician review mechanism upon the employee doing the following within fifteen (15) days after receipt of the notification of the right to seek a second medical opinion, or receipt of the initial physician's written opinion, whichever is later;

(A) The employee informs the employer of the intention to seek a second medical opinion, and

(B) The employee initiates steps to make an appointment with a second physician.

(iv) If the findings, determinations or recommendations of the second physician differ from those of the initial physician, then the employer and the employee shall assure that efforts are made for the two physicians to resolve the disagreement. If the two physicians are unable to quickly resolve their disagreement, then the employer and the employee through their respective physicians shall designate a third physician who shall be a specialist in the field at issue:

(A) To review the findings, determinations or recommendations of the prior physicians; and

(B) To conduct such examinations, consultations, laboratory tests and discussions with the prior physicians as the third physician deems necessary to resolve the disagreement of the prior physicians.

(v) In the alternative, the employer and the employee or authorized employee representative may jointly designate such third physician.

(vi) The employer shall act consistent with the findings, determinations and recommendations of the third physician, unless the employer and the employee reach an agreement which is otherwise consistent with the recommendations of at least one of the three physicians.

(m) *Communication of hazards—*(1) *Hazard communication—General.* (i) Chemical manufacturers, importers, distributors and employers shall comply with all requirements of the Hazard Communication Standard (HCS) (§ 1910.1200) for formaldehyde.

(ii) In classifying the hazards of formaldehyde at least the following hazards are to be addressed: Cancer; skin and respiratory sensitization; eye, skin and respiratory tract irritation; acute toxicity effects; and flammability.

(iii) Employers shall include formaldehyde in the hazard communication program established to comply with the HCS (§ 1910.1200). Employers shall ensure that each employee has access to labels on containers of formaldehyde and to safety data sheets, and is trained in accordance with the requirements of HCS and paragraph (n) of this section.

(iv) Paragraphs (m)(1)(i), (m)(1)(ii), and (m)(1)(iii) of this section apply to chemicals associated with formaldehyde gas, all mixtures or solutions composed of greater than 0.1 percent formaldehyde, and materials capable of releasing formaldehyde into the air at concentrations reaching or exceeding 0.1 ppm.

(v) In making the determinations of anticipated levels of formaldehyde release, the employer may rely on objective data indicating the extent of potential formaldehyde release under reasonably foreseeable conditions of use.

(2)(i) In addition to the requirements in paragraphs (m)(1) through (m)(1)(iv) of this section, for materials listed in paragraph (m)(1)(iv) capable of releasing formaldehyde at levels above 0.5 ppm, labels shall appropriately address all hazards as defined in paragraph (d) of § 1910.1200 and Appendices A and B to § 1910.1200, including cancer and respiratory sensitization, and shall contain the hazard statement "May Cause Cancer."

(ii) As a minimum, for all materials listed in paragraph (m)(1)(i) and (iv) of this section capable of releasing formaldehyde at levels of 0.1 ppm to 0.5 ppm, labels shall identify that the product contains formaldehyde; list the name and address of the responsible party; and state that physical and health hazard information is readily available from the employer and from safety data sheets.

(iii) Prior to June 1, 2015, employers may include the phrase "Potential Cancer Hazard" in lieu of "May Cause Cancer" as specified in paragraph (m)(2)(i) of this section.

(n) *Employee information and training*—(1) *Participation.* The employer shall assure that all employees who are assigned to workplaces where there is exposure to formaldehyde participate in a training program, except that where the employer can show, using objective data, that employees are not exposed to formaldehyde at or above 0.1 ppm, the employer is not required to provide training.

(2) *Frequency.* Employers shall provide such information and training to employees at the time of initial assignment, and whenever a new exposure to formaldehyde is introduced into the work area. The training shall be repeated at least annually.

(3) *Training program.* The training program shall be conducted in a manner which the employee is able to understand and shall include:

(i) A discussion of the contents of this regulation and the contents of the Material Safety Data Sheet.

(ii) The purpose for and a description of the medical surveillance program required by this standard, including:

(A) A description of the potential health hazards associated with exposure to formaldehyde and a description of the signs and symptoms of exposure to formaldehyde.

(B) Instructions to immediately report to the employer the development of any adverse signs or symptoms that the employee suspects is attributable to formaldehyde exposure.

(iii) Description of operations in the work area where formaldehyde is present and an explanation of the safe work practices appropriate for limiting exposure to formaldehyde in each job;

(iv) The purpose for, proper use of, and limitations of personal protective clothing and equipment;

(v) Instructions for the handling of spills, emergencies, and clean-up procedures;

(vi) An explanation of the importance of engineering and work practice controls for employee protection and any necessary instruction in the use of these controls; and

(vii) A review of emergency procedures including the specific duties or assignments of each employee in the event of an emergency.

(4) *Access to training materials.* (i) The employer shall inform all affected employees of the location of written training materials and shall make these materials readily available, without cost, to the affected employees.

(ii) The employer shall provide, upon request, all training materials relating to the employee training program to the Assistant Secretary and the Director.

(o) *Recordkeeping*—(1) *Exposure measurements.* The employer shall establish and maintain an accurate record of all measurements taken to monitor employee exposure to formaldehyde. This record shall include:

(i) The date of measurement;

(ii) The operation being monitored;

(iii) The methods of sampling and analysis and evidence of their accuracy and precision;

(iv) The number, durations, time, and results of samples taken;

(v) The types of protective devices worn; and

(vi) The names, job classifications, social security numbers, and exposure estimates of the employees whose exposures are represented by the actual monitoring results.

(2) *Exposure determinations.* Where the employer has determined that no monitoring is required under this standard, the employer shall maintain a record of the objective data relied upon to support the determination that no employee is exposed to formaldehyde at or above the action level.

(3) *Medical surveillance.* The employer shall establish and maintain an accurate record for each employee subject to medical surveillance under this standard. This record shall include:

(i) The name and social security number of the employee;

(ii) The physician's written opinion;

(iii) A list of any employee health complaints that may be related to exposure to formaldehyde; and

(iv) A copy of the medical examination results, including medical disease questionnaires and results of any medical tests required by the standard or mandated by the examining physician.

(4) *Respirator fit testing.* (i) The employer shall establish and maintain accurate records for employees subject to negative pressure respirator fit testing required by this standard.

(ii) This record shall include:

(A) A copy of the protocol selected for respirator fit testing.

(B) A copy of the results of any fit testing performed.

(C) The size and manufacturer of the types of respirators available for selection.

(D) The date of the most recent fit testing, the name and social security

number of each tested employee, and the respirator type and facepiece selected.

(5) *Record retention.* The employer shall retain records required by this standard for at least the following periods:

(i) Exposure records and determinations shall be kept for at least 30 years.

(ii) Medical records shall be kept for the duration of employment plus 30 years.

(iii) Respirator fit testing records shall be kept until replaced by a more recent record.

(6) *Availability of records.* (i) Upon request, the employer shall make all records maintained as a requirement of this standard available for examination and copying to the Assistant Secretary and the Director.

(ii) The employer shall make employee exposure records, including estimates made from representative monitoring and available upon request for examination, and copying to the subject employee, or former employee, and employee representatives in accordance with 29 CFR 1910.1020 (a)–(e) and (g)–(i).

(iii) Employee medical records required by this standard shall be provided upon request for examination and coying, to the subject employee or former employee or to anyone having the specific written consent of the subject employee or former employee in accordance with 29 CFR 1910.1020 (a)–(e) and (g)–(i).

APPENDIX A TO § 1910.1048—SUBSTANCE TECHNICAL GUIDELINES FOR FORMALIN

The following Substance Technical Guideline for Formalin provides information on uninhibited formalin solution (37% formaldehyde, no methanol stabilizer). It is designed to inform employees at the production level of their rights and duties under the formaldehyde standard whether their job title defines them as workers or supervisors. Much of the information provided is general; however, some information is specific for formalin. When employee exposure to formaldehyde is from resins capable of releasing formaldehyde, the resin itself and other impurities or decomposition products may also be toxic, and employers should include this information as well when informing employees of the hazards associated with the materials they handle. The precise hazards associated with exposure to formaldehyde depend both on the form (solid, liquid, or gas) of the material and the concentration of formaldehyde present. For example, 37–50 percent solutions of formaldehyde present a much greater hazard to the skin and eyes from spills or splashes than solutions containing less than 1 percent formaldehyde. Individual Substance Technical Guidelines used by the employer for training employees should be modified to properly give information on the material actually being used.

Substance Identification

Chemical Name: Formaldehyde
Chemical Family: Aldehyde
Chemical Formula: HCHO
Molecular Weight: 30.03
Chemical Abstracts Service Number (CAS Number): 50–00–0

Synonyms: Formalin; Formic Aldehyde; Paraform; Formol; Formalin (Methanolfree); Fyde; Formalith; Methanal; Methyl Aldehyde; Methylene Glycol; Methylene Oxide; Tetraoxymethalene; Oxomethane; Oxymethylene

Components and Contaminants

Percent: 37.0 Formaldehyde
Percent: 63.0 Water
(Note—Inhibited solutions contain methanol.)

Other Contaminants: Formic acid (alcohol free)
Exposure Limits:
OSHA TWA—0.75 ppm
OSHA STEL—2 ppm

Physical Data

Description: Colorless liquid, pungent odor
Boiling point: 214 °F (101 °C)
Specific Gravity: 1.08 (H_2 O = 1 @ 20 °C)
pH: 2.8–4.0
Solubility in Water: Miscible
Solvent Solubility: Soluble in alcohol and acetone
Vapor Density: 1.04 (Air = 1 @ 20 °C)
Odor Threshold: 0.8–1 ppm

Fire and Explosion Hazard

Moderate fire and explosion hazard when exposed to heat or flame.

The flash point of 37% formaldehyde solutions is above normal room temperature, but the explosion range is very wide, from 7 to 73% by volume in air.

Reaction of formaldehyde with nitrogen dioxide, nitromethane, perchloric acid and aniline, or peroxyformic acid yields explosive compounds.

Flash Point: 185 °F (85 °C) closed cup
Lower Explosion Limit: 7%
Upper Explosion Limit: 73%
Autoignition Temperature: 806 °F (430 °C)
Flammability (OSHA): Category 4 flammable liquid

Extinguishing Media: Use dry chemical, "alcohol foam", carbon dioxide, or water in flooding amounts as fog. Solid streams may not be effective. Cool fire-exposed containers with water from side until well after fire is out.

Use of water spray to flush spills can also dilute the spill to produce nonflammable mixtures. Water runoff, however, should be contained for treatment.

National Fire Protection Association Section 325M Designation:

Health: 2—Materials hazardous to health, but areas may be entered with full-faced mask self-contained breathing apparatus which provides eye protection.

Flammability: 2—Materials which must be moderately heated before ignition will occur. Water spray may be used to extinguish the fire because the material can be cooled below its flash point.

Reactivity: D—Materials which (in themselves) are normally stable even under fire exposure conditions and which are not reactive with water. Normal fire fighting procedures may be used.

Reactivity

Stability: Formaldehyde solutions may self-polymerize to form paraformaldehyde which precipitates.

Incompatibility (Materials to Avoid): Strong oxidizing agents, caustics, strong alkalies, isocyanates, anhydrides, oxides, and inorganic acids. Formaldehyde reacts with hydrochloric acid to form the potent carcinogen, bis-chloromethyl ether. Formaldehyde reacts with nitrogen dioxide, nitromethane, perchloric acid and aniline, or peroxyformic acid to yield explosive compounds. A violent reaction occurs when formaldehyde is mixed with strong oxidizers.

Hazardous Combustion or Decomposition Products: Oxygen from the air can oxidize formaldehyde to formic acid, especially when heated. Formic acid is corrosive.

Health Hazard Data

Acute Effects of Exposure

Ingestion (Swallowing): Liquids containing 10 to 40% formaldehyde cause severe irritation and inflammation of the mouth, throat, and stomach. Severe stomach pains will follow ingestion with possible loss of consciousness and death. Ingestion of dilute formaldehyde solutions (0.03–0.04%) may cause discomfort in the stomach and pharynx.

Inhalation (Breathing): Formaldehyde is highly irritating to the upper respiratory tract and eyes. Concentrations of 0.5 to 2.0 ppm may irritate the eyes, nose, and throat of some individuals. Concentrations of 3 to 5 ppm also cause tearing of the eyes and are intolerable to some persons. Concentrations of 10 to 20 ppm cause difficulty in breathing, burning of the nose and throat, cough, and heavy tearing of the eyes, and 25 to 30 ppm causes severe respiratory tract injury leading to pulmonary edema and pneumonitis. A concentration of 100 ppm is immediately dangerous to life and health. Deaths from accidental exposure to high concentrations of formaldehyde have been reported.

Skin (Dermal): Formalin is a severe skin irritant and a sensitizer. Contact with formalin causes white discoloration, smarting, drying, cracking, and scaling. Prolonged and repeated contact can cause numbness and a hardening or tanning of the skin. Previously exposed persons may react to future exposure with an allergic eczematous dermatitis or hives.

Eye Contact: Formaldehyde solutions splashed in the eye can cause injuries ranging from transient discomfort to severe, permanent corneal clouding and loss of vision. The severity of the effect depends on the concentration of formaldehyde in the solution and whether or not the eyes are flushed with water immediately after the accident.

NOTE. The perception of formaldehyde by odor and eye irritation becomes less sensitive with time as one adapts to formaldehyde. This can lead to overexposure if a worker is relying on formaldehyde's warning properties to alert him or her to the potential for exposure.

Acute Animal Toxicity:
Oral, rats: LD50 = 800 mg/kg
Oral, mouse: LD50 = 42 mg/kg
Inhalation, rats: LCLo = 250 mg/kg
Inhalation, mouse: LCLo = 900 mg/kg
Inhalation, rats: LC50 = 590 mg/kg

Chronic Effects of Exposure

Carcinogenicity: Formaldehyde has the potential to cause cancer in humans. Repeated and prolonged exposure increases the risk. Various animal experiments have conclusively shown formaldehyde to be a carcinogen in rats. In humans, formaldehyde exposure has been associated with cancers of the lung, nasopharynx and oropharynx, and nasal passages.

Mutagenicity: Formaldehyde is genotoxic in several *in vitro* test systems showing properties of both an initiator and a promoter.

Toxicity: Prolonged or repeated exposure to formaldehyde may result in respiratory impairment. Rats exposed to formaldehyde at 2 ppm developed benign nasal tumors and changes of the cell structure in the nose as well as inflamed mucous membranes of the nose. Structural changes in the epithelial cells in the human nose have also been observed. Some persons have developed asthma or bronchitis following exposure to formaldehyde, most often as the result of an accidental spill involving a single exposure to a high concentration of formaldehyde.

Emergency and First Aid Procedures

Ingestion (Swallowing): If the victim is conscious, dilute, inactivate, or absorb the ingested formaldehyde by giving milk, activated charcoal, or water. Any organic material will inactivate formaldehyde. Keep affected person warm and at rest. Get medical attention immediately. If vomiting occurs, keep head lower than hips.

Inhalation (Breathing): Remove the victim from the exposure area to fresh air immediately. Where the formaldehyde concentration may be very high, each rescuer must put on a self-contained breathing apparatus before attempting to remove the victim, and medical personnel should be informed of the formaldehyde exposure immediately. If breathing has stopped, give artificial respiration. Keep the affected person warm and at rest. Qualified first-aid or medical personnel should administer oxygen, if available, and maintain the patient's airways and blood pressure until the victim can be transported to a medical facility. If exposure results in a highly irritated upper respiratory tract and coughing continues for more than 10 minutes, the worker should be hospitalized for observation and treatment.

Skin Contact: Remove contaminated clothing (including shoes) immediately. Wash the affected area of your body with soap or mild detergent and large amounts of water until no evidence of the chemical remains (at least 15 to 20 minutes). If there are chemical burns, get first aid to cover the area with sterile, dry dressing, and bandages. Get medical attention if you experience appreciable eye or respiratory irritation.

Eye Contact: Wash the eyes immediately with large amounts of water occasionally lifting lower and upper lids, until no evidence of chemical remains (at least 15 to 20 minutes). In case of burns, apply sterile bandages loosely without medication. Get medical attention immediately. If you have experienced appreciable eye irritation from a splash or excessive exposure, you should be referred promptly to an opthamologist for evaluation.

Emergency Procedures

Emergencies: If you work in an area where a large amount of formaldehyde could be released in an accident or from equipment failure, your employer must develop procedures to be followed in event of an emergency. You should be trained in your specific duties in the event of an emergency, and it is important that you clearly understand these duties. Emergency equipment must be accessible and you should be trained to use any equipment that you might need. Formaldehyde contaminated equipment must be cleaned before reuse.

If a spill of appreciable quantity occurs, leave the area quickly unless you have specific emergency duties. Do not touch spilled material. Designated persons may stop the leak and shut off ignition sources if these procedures can be done without risk. Designated persons should isolate the hazard area and deny entry except for necessary people protected by suitable protective clothing and respirators adequate for the exposure. Use water spray to reduce vapors. Do not smoke, and prohibit all flames or flares in the hazard area.

Special Firefighting Procedures: Learn procedures and responsibilities in the event of a fire in your workplace. Become familiar with the appropriate equipment and supplies and their location. In firefighting, withdraw immediately in case of rising sound from venting safety device or any discoloration of storage tank due to fire.

Spill, Leak, and Disposal Procedures

Occupational Spill: For small containers, place the leaking container in a well ventilated area. Take up small spills with absorbent material and place the waste into properly labeled containers for later disposal. For larger spills, dike the spill to minimize contamination and facilitate salvage or disposal. You may be able to neutralize the spill with sodium hydroxide or sodium sulfite. Your employer must comply with EPA rules regarding the clean-up of toxic waste and notify state and local authorities, if required. If the spill is greater than 1,000 lb/day, it is reportable under EPA's Superfund legislation.

Waste Disposal: Your employer must dispose of waste containing formaldehyde in accordance with applicable local, state, and Federal law and in a manner that minimizes exposure of employees at the site and of the clean-up crew.

Monitoring and Measurement Procedures

Monitoring Requirements: If your exposure to formaldehyde exceeds the 0.5 ppm action level or the 2 ppm STEL, your employer must monitor your exposure. Your employer need not measure every exposure if a "high exposure" employee can be identified. This person usually spends the greatest amount of time nearest the process equipment. If you are a "representative employee", you will be asked to wear a sampling device to collect formaldehyde. This device may be a passive badge, a sorbent tube attached to a pump, or an impinger containing liquid. You should perform your work as usual, but inform the person who is conducting the monitoring of any difficulties you are having wearing the device.

Evaluation of 8-hour Exposure: Measurements taken for the purpose of determining time-weighted average (TWA) exposures are best taken with samples covering the full shift. Samples collected must be taken from the employee's breathing zone air.

Short-term Exposure Evaluation: If there are tasks that involve brief but intense exposure to formaldehyde, employee exposure must be measured to assure compliance with the STEL. Sample collections are for brief periods, only 15 minutes, but several samples may be needed to identify the peak exposure.

Monitoring Techniques: OSHA's only requirement for selecting a method for sampling and analysis is that the methods used accurately evaluate the concentration of formaldehyde in employees' breathing zones. Sampling and analysis may be performed by collection of formaldehyde on liquid or solid sorbents with subsequent chemical analysis. Sampling and analysis may also be performed by passive diffusion monitors and short-term exposure may be measured by instruments such as real-time continuous monitoring systems and portable direct reading instruments.

Notification of Results: Your employer must inform you of the results of exposure monitoring representative of your job. You may be informed in writing, but posting the results where you have ready access to them constitutes compliance with the standard.

Protective Equipment and Clothing

[Material impervious to formaldehyde is needed if the employee handles formaldehyde solutions of 1% or more. Other employees may also require protective clothing or equipment to prevent dermatitis.]

Respiratory Protection: Use NIOSH-approved full facepiece negative pressure respirators equipped with approved cartridges or canisters within the use limitations of these devices. (Present restrictions on cartridges and canisters do not permit them to be used for a full workshift.) In all other situations, use positive pressure respirators such as the positive-pressure air purifying respirator or the self-contained breathing apparatus (SCBA). If you use a negative pressure respirator, your employer must provide you with fit testing of the respirator at least once a year.

Protective Gloves: Wear protective (impervious) gloves provided by your employer, at no cost, to prevent contact with formalin. Your employer should select these gloves based on the results of permeation testing and in accordance with the ACGIH Guidelines for Selection of Chemical Protective Clothing.

Eye Protection: If you might be splashed in the eyes with formalin, it is essential that you wear goggles or some other type of complete protection for the eye. You may also need a face shield if your face is likely to be splashed with formalin, but you must not substitute face shields for eye protection.

445

(This section pertains to formaldehyde solutions of 1% or more.)

Other Protective Equipment: You must wear protective (impervious) clothing and equipment provided by your employer at no cost to prevent repeated or prolonged contact with formaldehyde liquids. If you are required to change into whole-body chemical protective clothing, your employer must provide a change room for your privacy and for storage of your normal clothing.

If you are splashed with formaldehyde, use the emergency showers and eyewash fountains provided by your employer immediately to prevent serious injury. Report the incident to your supervisor and obtain necessary medical support.

ENTRY INTO AN IDLH ATMOSPHERE

Enter areas where the formaldehyde concentration might be 100 ppm or more only with complete body protection including a self-contained breathing apparatus with a full facepiece operated in a positive pressure mode or a supplied air respirator with full facepiece and operated in a positive pressure mode. This equipment is essential to protect your life and health under such extreme conditions.

Engineering Controls

Ventilation is the most widely applied engineering control method for reducing the concentration of airborne substances in the breathing zones of workers. There are two distinct types of ventilation.

Local Exhaust: Local exhaust ventilation is designed to capture airborne contaminants as near to the point of generation as possible. To protect you, the direction of contaminant flow must always be toward the local exhaust system inlet and away from you.

General (Mechanical): General dilution ventilation involves continuous introduction of fresh air into the workroom to mix with the contaminated air and lower your breathing zone concentration of formaldehyde. Effectiveness depends on the number of air changes per hour. Where devices emitting formaldehyde are spread out over a large area, general dilution ventilation may be the only practical method of control.

Work Practices: Work practices and administrative procedures are an important part of a control system. If you are asked to perform a task in a certain manner to limit your exposure to formaldehyde, it is extremely important that you follow these procedures.

Medical Surveillance

Medical surveillance helps to protect employees' health. You are encouraged strongly to participate in the medical surveillance program.

Your employer must make a medical surveillance program available at no expense to you and at a reasonable time and place if you are exposed to formaldehyde at concentrations above 0.5 ppm as an 8-hour average or 2 ppm over any 15-minute period. You will be offered medical surveillance at the time of your initial assignment and once a year afterward as long as your exposure is at least 0.5 ppm (TWA) or 2 ppm (STEL). Even if your exposure is below these levels, you should inform your employer if you have signs and symptoms that you suspect, through your training, are related to your formaldehyde exposure because you may need medical surveillance to determine if your health is being impaired by your exposure.

The surveillance plan includes:

(a) A medical disease questionnaire.

(b) A physical examination if the physician determines this is necessary.

If you are required to wear a respirator, your employer must offer you a physical examination and a pulmonary function test every year.

The physician must collect all information needed to determine if you are at increased risk from your exposure to formaldehyde. At the physician's discretion, the medical examination may include other tests, such as a chest x-ray, to make this determination.

After a medical examination the physician will provide your employer with a written opinion which includes any special protective measures recommended and any restrictions on your exposure. The physician must inform you of any medical conditions you have which would be aggravated by exposure to formaldehyde.

All records from your medical examinations, including disease surveys, must be retained at your employer's expense.

EMERGENCIES

If you are exposed to formaldehyde in an emergency and develop signs or symptoms associated with acute toxicity from formaldehyde exposure, your employer must provide you with a medical examination as soon as possible. This medical examination will include all steps necessary to stabilize your health. You may be kept in the hospital for observation if your symptoms are severe to ensure that any delayed effects are recognized and treated.

APPENDIX B TO § 1910.1048—SAMPLING STRATEGY AND ANALYTICAL METHODS FOR FORMALDEHYDE

To protect the health of employees, exposure measurements must be unbiased and representative of employee exposure. The proper measurement of employee exposure requires more than a token commitment on the part of the employer. OSHA's mandatory requirements establish a baseline; under the best of circumstances all questions regarding employee exposure will be answered. Many employers, however, will wish to conduct more extensive monitoring before undertaking expensive commitments, such as engineering controls, to assure that the modifications are truly necessary. The following sampling strategy, which was developed at NIOSH by Nelson A. Leidel, Kenneth A. Busch, and Jeremiah R. Lynch and described in NIOSH publication No. 77–173 (Occupational Exposure Sampling Strategy Manual) will assist the employer in developing a strategy for determining the exposure of his or her employees.

There is no one correct way to determine employee exposure. Obviously, measuring the exposure of every employee exposed to formaldehyde will provide the most information on any given day. Where few employees are exposed, this may be a practical solution. For most employers, however, use of the following strategy will give just as much information at less cost.

Exposure data collected on a single day will not automatically guarantee the employer that his or her workplace is always in compliance with the formaldehyde standard. This does not imply, however, that it is impossible for an employer to be sure that his or her worksite is in compliance with the standard. Indeed, a properly designed sampling strategy showing that all employees are exposed below the PELs, at least with a 95 percent certainty, is compelling evidence that the exposure limits are being achieved provided that measurements are conducted using valid sampling strategy and approved analytical methods.

There are two PELs, the TWA concentration and the STEL. Most employers will find that one of these two limits is more critical in the control of their operations, and OSHA expects that the employer will concentrate monitoring efforts on the critical component. If the more difficult exposure is controlled, this information, along with calculations to support the assumptions, should be adequate to show that the other exposure limit is also being achieved.

Sampling Strategy

Determination of the Need for Exposure Measurements

The employer must determine whether employees may be exposed to concentrations in excess of the action level. This determination becomes the first step in an employee exposure monitoring program that minimizes employer sampling burdens while providing adequate employee protection. If employees may be exposed above the action level, the employer must measure exposure. Otherwise, an objective determination that employee exposure is low provides adequate

evidence that exposure potential has been examined.

The employer should examine all available relevant information, *eg.* insurance company and trade association data and information from suppliers or exposure data collected from similar operations. The employer may also use previously-conducted sampling including area monitoring. The employer must make a determination relevant to each operation although this need not be on a separate piece of paper. If the employer can demonstrate conclusively that no employee is exposed above the action level or the STEL through the use of objective data, the employer need proceed no further on employee exposure monitoring until such time that conditions have changed and the determination is no longer valid.

If the employer cannot determine that employee exposure is less than the action level and the STEL, employee exposure monitoring will have to be conducted.

Workplace Material Survey

The primary purpose of a survey of raw material is to determine if formaldehyde is being used in the work environment and if so, the conditions under which formaldehyde is being used.

The first step is to tabulate all situations where formaldehyde is used in a manner such that it may be released into the workplace atmosphere or contaminate the skin. This information should be available through analysis of company records and information on the MSDSs available through provisions of this standard and the Hazard Communication standard.

If there is an indication from materials handling records and accompanying MSDSs that formaldehyde is being used in the following types of processes or work operations, there may be a potential for releasing formaldehyde into the workplace atmosphere:

(1) Any operation that involves grinding, sanding, sawing, cutting, crushing, screening, sieving, or any other manipulation of material that generates formaldehyde-bearing dust

(2) Any processes where there have been employee complaints or symptoms indicative of exposure to formaldehyde

(3) Any liquid or spray process involving formaldehyde

(4) Any process that uses formaldehyde in preserved tissue

(5) Any process that involves the heating of a formaldehyde-bearing resin.

Processes and work operations that use formaldehyde in these manners will probably require further investigation at the worksite to determine the extent of employee monitoring that should be conducted.

Workplace Observations

To this point, the only intention has been to provide an indication as to the existence of potentially exposed employees. With this information, a visit to the workplace is needed to observe work operations, to identify potential health hazards, and to determine whether any employees may be exposed to hazardous concentrations of formaldehyde.

In many circumstances, sources of formaldehyde can be identified through the sense of smell. However, this method of detection should be used with caution because of olfactory fatigue.

Employee location in relation to source of formaldehyde is important in determining if an employee may be significantly exposed to formaldehyde. In most instances, the closer a worker is to the source, the higher the probability that a significant exposure will occur.

Other characteristics should be considered. Certain high temperature operations give rise to higher evaporation rates. Locations of open doors and windows provide natural ventilation that tend to dilute formaldehyde emissions. General room ventilation also provides a measure of control.

Calculation of Potential Exposure Concentrations

By knowing the ventilation rate in a workplace and the quantity of formaldehyde generated, the employer may be able to determine by calculation if the PELs might be exceeded. To account for poor mixing of formaldehyde into the entire room, locations of fans and proximity of employees to the work operation, the employer must include a safety factor. If an employee is relatively close to a source, particularly if he or she is located downwind, a safety factor of 100 may be necessary. For other situations, a factor of 10 may be acceptable. If the employer can demonstrate through such calculations that employee exposure does not exceed the action level or the STEL, the employer may use this information as objective data to demonstrate compliance with the standard.

Sampling Strategy

Once the employer determines that there is a possibility of substantial employee exposure to formaldehyde, the employer is obligated to measure employee exposure.

The next step is selection of a maximum risk employee. When there are different processes where employees may be exposed to formaldehyde, a maximum risk employee should be selected for each work operation.

Selection of the maximum risk employee requires professional judgment. The best procedure for selecting the maximum risk employee is to observe employees and select the person closest to the source of formaldehyde. Employee mobility may affect this selection; eg. if the closest employee is mobile in his tasks, he may not be the maximum risk employee. Air movement patterns and differences in work habits will also affect selection of the maximum risk employee.

When many employees perform essentially the same task, a maximum risk employee cannot be selected. In this circumstance, it is necessary to resort to random sampling of the group of workers. The objective is to select a subgroup of adequate size so that there is a high probability that the random sample will contain at least one worker with high exposure if one exists. The number of persons in the group influences the number that need to be sampled to ensure that at least one individual from the highest 10 percent exposure group is contained in the sample. For example, to have 90 percent confidence in the results, if the group size is 10, nine should be sampled; for 50, only 18 need to be sampled.

If measurement shows exposure to formaldehyde at or above the action level or the STEL, the employer needs to identify all other employees who may be exposed at or above the action level or STEL and measure or otherwise accurately characterize the exposure of these employees.

Whether representative monitoring or random sampling are conducted, the purpose remains the same—to determine if the exposure of any employee is above the action level. If the exposure of the most exposed employee is less than the action level and the STEL, regardless of how the employee is identified, then it is reasonable to assume that measurements of exposure of the other employees in that operation would be below the action level and the STEL.

Exposure Measurements

There is no "best" measurement strategy for all situations. Some elements to consider in developing a strategy are:

(1) Availability and cost of sampling equipment

(2) Availability and cost of analytic facilities

(3) Availability and cost of personnel to take samples

(4) Location of employees and work operations

(5) Intraday and interday variations in the process

(6) Precision and accuracy of sampling and analytic methods, and

(7) Number of samples needed.

Samples taken for determining compliance with the STEL differ from those that measure the TWA concentration in important ways. STEL samples are best taken in a nonrandom fashion using all available knowledge relating to the area, the individual, and the process to obtain samples during periods of maximum expected concentrations. At least three measurements on a shift are generally needed to spot gross errors or mistakes; however, only the highest value represents the STEL.

If an operation remains constant throughout the workshift, a much greater number of samples would need to be taken over the 32 discrete nonoverlapping periods in an 8-hour workshift to verify compliance with a STEL. If employee exposure is truly uniform throughout the workshift, however, an employer in compliance with the 1 ppm TWA would be in compliance with the 2 ppm STEL, and this determination can probably be made using objective data.

Need To Repeat the Monitoring Strategy

Interday and intraday fluctuations in employee exposure are mostly influenced by the physical processes that generate formaldehyde and the work habits of the employee. Hence, in-plant process variations influence the employer's determination of whether or not additional controls need to be imposed. Measurements that employee exposure is low on a day that is not representative of worst conditions may not provide sufficient information to determine whether or not additional engineering controls should be installed to achieve the PELs.

The person responsible for conducting sampling must be aware of systematic changes which will negate the validity of the sampling results. Systematic changes in formaldehyde exposure concentration for an employee can occur due to:

(1) The employee changing patterns of movement in the workplace

(2) Closing of plant doors and windows

(3) Changes in ventilation from season to season

(4) Decreases in ventilation efficiency or abrupt failure of engineering control equipment

(5) Changes in the production process or work habits of the employee.

Any of these changes, if they may result in additional exposure that reaches the next level of action (i.e. 0.5 or 1.0 ppm as an 8-hr average or 2 ppm over 15 minutes) require the employer to perform additional monitoring to reassess employee exposure.

A number of methods are suitable for measuring employee exposure to formaldehyde or for characterizing emissions within the worksite. The preamble to this standard describes some methods that have been widely used or subjected to validation testing. A detailed analytical procedure derived from the OSHA Method 52 for acrolein and formaldehyde is presented below for informational purposes. Inclusion of OSHA's method in this appendix in no way implies that it is the only acceptable way to measure employee exposure to formaldehyde. Other methods that are free from significant interferences and that can determine formaldehyde at the permissible exposure limits within ±25 percent of the "true" value at the 95 percent confidence level are also acceptable. Where applicable, the method should also be capable of measuring formaldehyde at the action level to ±35 percent of the "true" value with a 95 percent confidence level. OSHA encourages employers to choose methods that will be best for their individual needs. The employer must exercise caution, however, in choosing an appropriate method since some techniques suffer from interferences that are likely to be present in workplaces of certain industry sectors where formaldehyde is used.

OSHA's Analytical Laboratory Method

Method No: 52
Matrix: Air
Target Concentration: 1 ppm (1.2 mg/m³)
Procedures: Air samples are collected by drawing known volumes of air through sampling tubes containing XAD-2 adsorbent which have been coated with 2-(hydroxymethyl) piperidine. The samples are desorbed with toluene and then analyzed by gas chromatography using a nitrogen selective detector.
Recommended Sampling Rate and Air Volumes: 0.1 L/min and 24 L
Reliable Quantitation Limit: 16 ppb (20 μg/m³)
Standard Error of Estimate at the Target Concentration: 7.3%
Status of the Method: A sampling and analytical method that has been subjected to the established evaluation procedures of the Organic Methods Evaluation Branch.
Date: March 1985

1. General Discussion

1.1 *Background:* The current OSHA method for collecting acrolein vapor recommends the use of activated 13X molecular sieves. The samples must be stored in an ice bath during and after sampling and also they must be analyzed within 48 hours of collection. The current OSHA method for collecting formaldehyde vapor recommends the use of bubblers containing 10% methanol in water as the trapping solution.

This work was undertaken to resolve the sample stability problems associated with acrolein and also to eliminate the need to use bubblers to sample formaldehyde. A goal of this work was to develop and/or to evaluate a common sampling and analytical procedure for acrolein and formaldehyde. NIOSH has developed independent methodologies for acrolein and formaldehyde which recommend the use of reagent-coated adsorbent tubes to collect the aldehydes as stable derivatives. The formaldehyde sampling tubes contain Chromosorb 102 adsorbent coated with N-benzylethanolamine (BEA) which reacts with formaldehyde vapor to form a stable oxazolidine compound. The acrolein sampling tubes contain XAD-2 adsorbent coated with 2-(hydroxymethyl)piperidine (2-HMP) which reacts with acrolein vapor to form a different, stable oxazolidine derivative. Acrolein does not appear to react with BEA to give a suitable reaction product. Therefore, the formaldehyde procedure cannot provide a common method for both aldehydes. However, formaldehyde does react with 2-HMP to form a very suitable reaction product. It is the quantitative reaction of acrolein and formaldehyde with 2-HMP that provides the basis for this evaluation.

This sampling and analytical procedure is very similar to the method recommended by NIOSH for acrolein. Some changes in the NIOSH methodology were necessary to permit the simultaneous determination of both aldehydes and also to accommodate OSHA laboratory equipment and analytical techniques.

1.2 *Limit-defining parameters:* The analyte air concentrations reported in this method are based on the recommended air volume for each analyte collected separately and a desorption volume of 1 mL. The amounts are presented as acrolein and/or formaldehyde, even though the derivatives are the actual species analyzed.

1.2.1 *Detection limits of the analytical procedure:* The detection limit of the analytical procedure was 386 pg per injection for formaldehyde. This was the amount of analyte which gave a peak whose height was about five times the height of the peak given by the residual formaldehyde derivative in a typical blank front section of the recommended sampling tube.

1.2.2 *Detection limits of the overall procedure:* The detection limits of the overall procedure were 482 ng per sample (16 ppb or 20 $\mu g/m^3$ for formaldehyde). This was the amount of analyte spiked on the sampling device which allowed recoveries approximately equal to the detection limit of the analytical procedure.

1.2.3 *Reliable quantitation limits:* The reliable quantitation limit was 482 ng per sample (16 ppb or 20 $\mu g/m^3$) for formaldehyde. These were the smallest amounts of analyte which could be quantitated within the limits of a recovery of at least 75% and a precision (±1.96 SD) of ±25% or better.

The reliable quantitation limit and detection limits reported in the method are based upon optimization of the instrument for the smallest possible amount of analyte. When the target concentration of an analyte is exceptionally higher than these limits, they may not be attainable at the routine operating parameters.

1.2.4 *Sensitivity:* The sensitivity of the analytical procedure over concentration ranges representing 0.4 to 2 times the target concentration, based on the recommended air volumes, was 7,589 area units per $\mu g/mL$ for formaldehyde. This value was determined from the slope of the calibration curve. The sensitivity may vary with the particular instrument used in the analysis.

1.2.5 *Recovery:* The recovery of formaldehyde from samples used in an 18-day storage test remained above 92% when the samples were stored at ambient temperature. These values were determined from regression lines which were calculated from the storage data. The recovery of the analyte from the collection device must be at least 75% following storage.

1.2.6 *Precision (analytical method only):* The pooled coefficient of variation obtained from replicate determinations of analytical standards over the range of 0.4 to 2 times the target concentration was 0.0052 for formaldehyde (Section 4.3).

1.2.7 *Precision (overall procedure):* The precision at the 95% confidence level for the ambient temperature storage tests was ±14.3% for formaldehyde. These values each include an additional ±5% for sampling error. The overall procedure must provide results at the target concentrations that are ±25% at the 95% confidence level.

1.2.8 *Reproducibility:* Samples collected from controlled test atmospheres and a draft copy of this procedure were given to a chemist unassociated with this evaluation. The formaldehyde samples were analyzed following 15 days storage. The average recovery was 96.3% and the standard deviation was 1.7%.

1.3 *Advantages:*

1.3.1 The sampling and analytical procedures permit the simultaneous determination of acrolein and formaldehyde.

1.3.2 Samples are stable following storage at ambient temperature for at least 18 days.

1.4 *Disadvantages:* None.

2. Sampling Procedure

2.1 *Apparatus:*

2.1.1 Samples are collected by use of a personal sampling pump that can be calibrated to within ±5% of the recommended 0.1 L/min sampling rate with the sampling tube in line.

2.1.2 Samples are collected with laboratory prepared sampling tubes. The sampling tube is constructed of silane treated glass and is about 8-cm long. The ID is 4 mm and the OD is 6 mm. One end of the tube is tapered so that a glass wool end plug will hold the contents of the tube in place during sampling. The other end of the sampling tube is open to its full 4-mm ID to facilitate packing of the tube. Both ends of the tube are fire-polished for safety. The tube is packed with a 75-mg backup section, located nearest the tapered end and a 150-mg sampling section of pretreated XAD-2 adsorbent which has been coated with 2–HMP. The two sections of coated adsorbent are separated and retained with small plugs of silanized glass wool. Following packing, the sampling tubes are sealed with two 7/32 inch OD plastic end caps. Instructions for the pretreatment and the coating of XAD–2 adsorbent are presented in Section 4 of this method.

2.1.3 Sampling tubes, similar to those recommended in this method, are marketed by Supelco, Inc. These tubes were not available when this work was initiated; therefore, they were not evaluated.

2.2 *Reagents:* None required.

2.3 *Technique:*

2.3.1 Properly label the sampling tube before sampling and then remove the plastic end caps.

2.3.2 Attach the sampling tube to the pump using a section of flexible plastic tubing such that the large, front section of the sampling tube is exposed directly to the atmosphere. Do not place any tubing ahead of the sampling tube. The sampling tube should be attached in the worker's breathing zone in a vertical manner such that it does not impede work performance.

2.3.3 After sampling for the appropriate time, remove the sampling tube from the pump and then seal the tube with plastic end caps.

2.3.4 Include at least one blank for each sampling set. The blank should be handled in the same manner as the samples with the exception that air is not drawn through it.

2.3.5 List any potential interferences on the sample data sheet.

2.4 *Breakthrough:*

2.4.1 Breakthrough was defined as the relative amount of analyte found on a backup sample in relation to the total amount of analyte collected on the sampling train.

2.4.2 For formaldehyde collected from test atmospheres containing 6 times the PEL, the average 5% breakthrough air volume was 41 L. The sampling rate was 0.1 L/min and the average mass of formaldehyde collected was 250 µg.

2.5 *Desorption Efficiency:* No desorption efficiency corrections are necessary to compute air sample results because analytical standards are prepared using coated adsorbent. Desorption efficiencies were determined, however, to investigate the recoveries of the analytes from the sampling device. The average recovery over the range of 0.4 to 2 times the target concentration, based on the recommended air volumes, was 96.2% for formaldehyde. Desorption efficiencies were essentially constant over the ranges studied.

2.6 *Recommended Air Volume and Sampling Rate:*

2.6.1 The recommended air volume for formaldehyde is 24 L.

2.6.2 The recommended sampling rate is 0.1 L/min.

2.7 *Interferences:*

2.7.1 Any collected substance that is capable of reacting 2-HMP and thereby depleting the derivatizing agent is a potential interference. Chemicals which contain a carbonyl group, such as acetone, may be capable or reacting with 2-HMP.

2.7.2 There are no other known interferences to the sampling method.

2.8 *Safety Precautions:*

2.8.1 Attach the sampling equipment to the worker in such a manner that it well not interfere with work performance or safety.

2.8.2 Follow all safety practices that apply to the work area being sampled.

3. Analytical Procedure

3.1 *Apparatus:*

3.1.1 A gas chromatograph (GC), equipped with a nitrogen selective detector. A Hewlett-Packard Model 5840A GC fitted with a nitrogen-phosphorus flame ionization detector (NPD) was used for this evaluation. Injections were performed using a Hewlett-Packard Model 7671A automatic sampler.

3.1.2 A GC column capable of resolving the analytes from any interference. A 6 ft × ¼ in OD (2mm ID) glass GC column containing 10% UCON 50–HB–5100 + 2% KOH on 80/100 mesh Chromosorb W-AW was used for the evaluation. Injections were performed on-column.

3.1.3 Vials, glass 2-mL with Teflon-lined caps.

3.1.4 Volumetric flasks, pipets, and syringes for preparing standards, making dilutions, and performing injections.

3.2 *Reagents:*

3.2.1 Toluene and dimethylformamide. Burdick and Jackson solvents were used in this evaluation.

3.2.2 Helium, hydrogen, and air, GC grade.

3.2.3 Formaldehyde, 37%, by weight, in water. Aldrich Chemical, ACS Reagent Grade formaldehyde was used in this evaluation.

3.2.4 Amberlite XAD–2 adsorbent coated with 2-(hydroxymethyl—piperidine (2-HMP), 10% by weight (Section 4).

3.2.5 Desorbing solution with internal standard. This solution was prepared by adding 20 µL of dimethylformamide to 100 mL of toluene.

3.3 *Standard preparation:*

3.3.1 *Formaldehyde:* Prepare stock standards by diluting known volumes of 37% formaldehyde solution with methanol. A procedure to determine the formaldehyde content of these standards is presented in Section 4. A standard containing 7.7 mg/mL formaldehyde was prepared by diluting 1 mL of the 37% reagent to 50 mL with methanol.

3.3.2 It is recommended that analytical standards be prepared about 16 hours before the air samples are to be analyzed in order to ensure the complete reaction of the analytes with 2-HMP. However, rate studies have shown the reaction to be greater than 95% complete after 4 hours. Therefore, one or two standards can be analyzed after this reduced time if sample results are outside the concentration range of the prepared standards.

3.3.3 Place 150-mg portions of coated XAD–2 adsorbent, from the same lot number as used to collect the air samples, into each of several glass 2-mL vials. Seal each vial with a Teflon-lined cap.

3.3.4 Prepare fresh analytical standards each day by injecting appropriate amounts of the diluted analyte directly onto 150-mg portions of coated adsorbent. It is permissible to inject both acrolein and formaldehyde on the same adsorbent portion. Allow the standards to stand at room temperature. A standard, approximately the target levels, was prepared by injecting 11 µL of the acrolein and 12 µL of the formaldehyde stock standards onto a single coated XAD–2 adsorbent portion.

3.3.5 Prepare a sufficient number of standards to generate the calibration curves. Analytical standard concentrations should bracket sample concentrations. Thus, if samples are not in the concentration range of the prepared standards, additional standards must be prepared to determine detector response.

3.3.7 Desorb the standards in the same manner as the samples following the 16-hour reaction time.

3.4 *Sample preparation:*

3.4.1 Transfer the 150-mg section of the sampling tube to a 2-mL vial. Place the 75-mg section in a separate vial. If the glass wool plugs contain a significant number of adsorbent beads, place them with the appropriate sampling tube section. Discard the glass wool plugs if they do not contain a significant number of adsorbent beads.

3.4.2 Add 1 mL of desorbing solution to each vial.

3.4.3 Seal the vials with Teflon-lined caps and then allow them to desorb for one hour. Shake the vials by hand with vigorous force several times during the desorption time.

3.4.4 Save the used sampling tubes to be cleaned and recycled.

3.5 *Analysis:*

3.5.1 GC *Conditions*

Column Temperature:

Bi-level temperature program—First level: 100 to 140 °C at 4 °C/min following completion of the first level.

Second level: 140 to 180 °C at 20 °C/min following completion of the first level.

Isothermal period: Hold column at 180 °C until the recorder pen returns to baseline (usually about 25 min after injection).

Injector temperature: 180 °C

Helium flow rate: 30 mL/min (detector response will be reduced if nitrogen is substituted for helium carrier gas).

Injection volume: 0.8 µL

GC column: Six-ft × ¼-in OD (2 mm ID) glass GC column containing 10% UCON 50–HB–5100 + 2% KOH on 80/100 Chromosorb W-AW.

NPD conditions:

Hydrogen flow rate: 3 mL/min

Air flow rate: 50 mL/min

Detector temperature: 275 °C

3.5.2 *Chromatogram:* For an example of a typical chromatogram, see Figure 4.11 in OSHA Method 52.

3.5.3 Use a suitable method, such as electronic integration, to measure detector response.

3.5.4 Use an internal standard method to prepare the calibration curve with several standard solutions of different concentrations. Prepare the calibration curve daily. Program the integrator to report results in µg/mL.

3.5.5 Bracket sample concentrations with standards.

3.6 *Interferences (Analytical)*

3.6.1 Any compound with the same general retention time as the analytes and which also gives a detector response is a potential interference. Possible interferences should be reported to the laboratory with submitted samples by the industrial hygienist.

3.6.2 GC parameters (temperature, column, etc.) may be changed to circumvent interferences.

3.6.3 A useful means of structure designation is GC/MS. It is recommended this procedure be used to confirm samples whenever possible.

3.6.4 The coated adsorbent usually contains a very small amount of residual formaldehyde derivative (Section 4.8).

3.7 *Calculations:*

3.7.1 Results are obtained by use of calibration curves. Calibration curves are prepared by plotting detector response against concentration for each standard. The best line through the data points is determined by curve fitting.

3.7.2 The concentration, in µg/mL, for a particular sample is determined by comparing its detector response to the calibration curve. If either of the analytes is found on the backup section, it is added to the amount found on the front section. Blank corrections should be performed before adding the results together.

3.7.3 The acrolein and/or formaldehyde air concentration can be expressed using the following equation:

$$mg/m^3 = (A)(B)/C$$

where A = µg/mL from 3.7.2, B = desorption volume, and C = L of air sampled.

No desorption efficiency corrections are required.

3.7.4 The following equation can be used to convert results in mg/m³ to ppm.

$$ppm = (mg/m^3)(24.45)/MW$$

where mg/m^3 = result from 3.7.3, 24.45 = molar volume of an ideal gas at 760 mm Hg and 25 °C, MW = molecular weight (30.0).

4. Backup Data

4.1 Backup data on detection limits, reliable quantitation limits, sensitivity and precision of the analytical method, breakthrough, desorption efficiency, storage, reproducibility, and generation of test atmospheres are available in OSHA Method 52, developed by the Organics Methods Evaluation Branch, OSHA Analytical Laboratory, Salt Lake City, Utah.

4.2 *Procedure to Coat XAD–2 Adsorbent with 2–HMP:*

4.2.1 *Apparatus:* Soxhlet extraction apparatus, rotary evaporation apparatus, vacuum dessicator, 1–L vacuum flask, 1–L round-bottomed evaporative flask, 1–L Erlenmeyer flask, 250-mL Buchner funnel with a coarse fritted disc, etc.

4.2.2 *Reagents:*

4.2.2.1 Methanol, isooctane, and toluene.

4.2.2.2 2-(Hydroxymethyl)piperidine.

4.2.2.3 Amberlite XAD–2 non-ionic polymeric adsorbent, 20 to 60 mesh, Aldrich Chemical XAD–2 was used in this evaluation.

4.2.3 *Procedure:* Weigh 125 g of crude XAD–2 adsorbent into a 1–L Erlenmeyer flask. Add about 200 mL of water to the flask and then swirl the mixture to wash the adsorbent. Discard any adsorbent that floats to the top of the water and then filter the mixture using a fritted Buchner funnel. Air dry the adsorbent for 2 minutes. Transfer the adsorbent back to the Erlenmeyer flask and then add about 200 mL of methanol to the flask. Swirl and then filter the mixture as before. Transfer the washed adsorbent back to the Erlenmeyer flask and then add about 200 mL of methanol to the flask. Swirl and then filter the mixture as before. Transfer the washed adsorbent to a 1–L round-bottomed evaporative flask, add 13 g of 2–HMP and then 200 mL of methanol, swirl the mixture and then allow it to stand for one hour. Remove the methanol at about 40 °C and reduced pressure using a rotary evaporation apparatus. Transfer the coated adsorbent to a suitable container and store it in a vacuum desiccator at room temperature overnight. Transfer the coated adsorbent to a Soxhlet extractor and then extract the material with toluene for about 24 hours. Discard the con-

taminated toluene, add methanol in its place and then continue the Soxhlet extraction for an additional 4 hours. Transfer the adsorbent to a weighted 1–L round-bottom evaporative flask and remove the methanol using the rotary evaporation apparatus. Determine the weight of the adsorbent and then add an amount of 2-HMP, which is 10% by weight of the adsorbent. Add 200 mL of methanol and then swirl the mixture. Allow the mixture to stand for one hour. Remove the methanol by rotary evaporation. Transfer the coated adsorbent to a suitable container and store it in a vacuum desiccator until all traces of solvents are gone. Typically, this will take 2–3 days. The coated adsorbent should be protected from contamination. XAD–2 adsorbent treated in this manner will probably not contain residual acrolein derivative. However, this adsorbent will often contain residual formaldehyde derivative levels of about 0.1 µg per 150 mg of adsorbent. If the blank values for a batch of coated adsorbent are too high, then the batch should be returned to the Soxhlet extractor, extracted with toluene again and then recoated. This process can be repeated until the desired blank levels are attained.

The coated adsorbent is now ready to be packed into sampling tubes. The sampling tubes should be stored in a sealed container to prevent contamination. Sampling tubes should be stored in the dark at room temperature. The sampling tubes should be segregated by coated adsorbent lot number. A sufficient amount of each lot number of coated adsorbent should be retained to prepare analytical standards for use with air samples from that lot number.

4.3 *A Procedure to Determine Formaldehyde by Acid Titration:* Standardize the 0.1 N HCl solution using sodium carbonate and methyl orange indicator.

Place 50 mL of 0.1 M sodium sulfite and three drops of thymophthalein indicator into a 250-mL Erlenmeyer flask. Titrate the contents of the flask to a colorless endpoint with 0.1 N HCl (usually one or two drops is sufficient). Transfer 10 mL of the formaldehyde/methanol solution (prepared in 3.3.1) into the same flask and titrate the mixture with 0.1 N HCl, again, to a colorless endpoint. The formaldehyde concentration of the standard may be calculated by the following equation:

$$\text{Formaldehyde, mg/mL} = \frac{\text{acid titer} \times \text{acid normality} \times 30.0}{\text{mL of sample}}$$

This method is based on the quantitative liberation of sodium hydroxide when form-

aldehyde reacts with sodium sulfite to form the formaldehyde-bisulfite addition product.

The volume of sample may be varied depending on the formaldehyde content but the solution to be titrated must contain excess sodium sulfite. Formaldehyde solutions containing substantial amounts of acid or base must be neutralized before analysis.

APPENDIX C TO § 1910.1048—MEDICAL
SURVEILLANCE—FORMALDEHYDE

I. Health Hazards

The occupational health hazards of formaldehyde are primarily due to its toxic effects after inhalation, after direct contact with the skin or eyes by formaldehyde in liquid or vapor form, and after ingestion.

II. Toxicology

A. Acute Effects of Exposure

1. *Inhalation (breathing):* Formaldehyde is highly irritating to the upper airways. The concentration of formaldehyde that is immediately dangerous to life and health is 100 ppm. Concentrations above 50 ppm can cause severe pulmonary reactions within minutes. These include pulmonary edema, pneumonia, and bronchial irritation which can result in death. Concentrations above 5 ppm readily cause lower airway irritation characterized by cough, chest tightness and wheezing. There is some controversy regarding whether formaldehyde gas is a pulmonary sensitizer which can cause occupational asthma in a previously normal individual. Formaldehyde can produce symptoms of bronchial asthma in humans. The mechanism may be either sensitization of the individual by exposure to formaldehyde or direct irritation by formaldehyde in persons with pre-existing asthma. Upper airway irritation is the most common respiratory effect reported by workers and can occur over a wide range of concentrations, most frequently above 1 ppm. However, airway irritation has occurred in some workers with exposures to formaldehyde as low as 0.1 ppm. Symptoms of upper airway irritation include dry or sore throat, itching and burning sensations of the nose, and nasal congestion. Tolerance to this level of exposure may develop within 1–2 hours. This tolerance can permit workers remaining in an environment of gradually increasing formaldehyde concentrations to be unaware of their increasingly hazardous exposure.

2. *Eye contact:* Concentrations of formaldehyde between 0.05 ppm and 0.5 ppm produce a sensation of irritation in the eyes with burning, itching, redness, and tearing. Increased rate of blinking and eye closure generally protects the eye from damage at these low levels, but these protective mechanisms may interfere with some workers' work abilities. Tolerance can occur in workers continuously exposed to concentrations of formaldehyde in this range. Accidental splash injuries of human eyes to aqueous solutions of formaldehyde (formalin) have resulted in a wide range of ocular injuries including corneal opacities and blindness. The severity of the reactions have been directly dependent on the concentration of formaldehyde in solution and the amount of time lapsed before emergency and medical intervention.

3. *Skin contact:* Exposure to formaldehyde solutions can cause irritation of the skin and allergic contact dermatitis. These skin diseases and disorders can occur at levels well below those encountered by many formaldehyde workers. Symptoms include erythema, edema, and vesiculation or hives. Exposure to liquid formalin or formaldehyde vapor can provoke skin reactions in sensitized individuals even when airborne concentrations of formaldehyde are well below 1 ppm.

4. *Ingestion:* Ingestion of as little as 30 ml of a 37 percent solution of formaldehyde (formalin) can result in death. Gastrointestinal toxicity after ingestion is most severe in the stomach and results in symptoms which can include nausea, vomiting, and servere abdominal pain. Diverse damage to other organ systems including the liver, kidney, spleen, pancreas, brain, and central nervous systems can occur from the acute response to ingestion of formaldehyde.

B. Chronic Effects of Exposure

Long term exposure to formaldehyde has been shown to be associated with an increased risk of cancer of the nose and accessory sinuses, nasopharyngeal and oropharyngeal cancer, and lung cancer in humans. Animal experiments provide conclusive evidence of a causal relationship between nasal cancer in rats and formaldehyde exposure. Concordant evidence of carcinogenicity includes DNA binding, genotoxicity in short-term tests, and cytotoxic changes in the cells of the target organ suggesting both preneoplastic changes and a dose-rate effect. Formaldehyde is a complete carcinogen and appears to exert an effect on at least two stages of the carcinogenic process.

III. Surveillance considerations

A. History

1. *Medical and occupational history:* Along with its acute irritative effects, formaldehyde can cause allergic sensitization and cancer. One of the goals of the work history should be to elicit information on any prior or additional exposure to formaldehyde in either the occupational or the non-occupational setting.

2. *Respiratory history:* As noted above, formaldehyde has recognized properties as an airway irritant and has been reported by some authors as a cause of occupational asthma. In addition, formaldehyde has been associated with cancer of the entire respiratory system of humans. For these reasons, it is

appropriate to include a comprehensive review of the respiratory system in the medical history. Components of this history might include questions regarding dyspnea on exertion, shortness of breath, chronic airway complaints, hyperreactive airway disease, rhinitis, bronchitis, bronchiolitis, asthma, emphysema, respiratory allergic reaction, or other preexisting pulmonary disease.

In addition, generalized airway hypersensitivity can result from exposures to a single sensitizing agent. The examiner should, therefore, elicit any prior history of exposure to pulmonary irritants, and any short- or long-term effects of that exposure.

Smoking is known to decrease mucociliary clearance of materials deposited during respiration in the nose and upper airways. This may increase a worker's exposure to inhaled materials such as formaldehyde vapor. In addition, smoking is a potential confounding factor in the investigation of any chronic respiratory disease, including cancer. For these reasons, a complete smoking history should be obtained.

3. *Skin Disorders:* Because of the dermal irritant and sensitizing effects of formaldehyde, a history of skin disorders should be obtained. Such a history might include the existence of skin irritation, previously documented skin sensitivity, and other dermatologic disorders. Previous exposure to formaldehyde and other dermal sensitizers should be recorded.

4. *History of atopic or allergic diseases:* Since formaldehyde can cause allergic sensitization of the skin and airways, it might be useful to identify individuals with prior allergen sensitization. A history of atopic disease and allergies to formaldehyde or any other substances should also be obtained. It is not definitely known at this time whether atopic diseases and allergies to formaldehyde or any other substances should also be obtained. Also it is not definitely known at this time whether atopic individuals have a greater propensity to develop formaldehyde sensitivity than the general population, but identification of these individuals may be useful for ongoing surveillance.

5. *Use of disease questionnaires:* Comparison of the results from previous years with present results provides the best method for detecting a general deterioration in health when toxic signs and symptoms are measured subjectively. In this way recall bias does not affect the results of the analysis. Consequently, OSHA has determined that the findings of the medical and work histories should be kept in a standardized form for comparison of the year-to-year results.

B. Physical Examination

1. *Mucosa of eyes and airways:* Because of the irritant effects of formaldehyde, the examining physician should be alert to evidence of this irritation. A speculum exam-

ination of the nasal mucosa may be helpful in assessing possible irritation and cytotoxic changes, as may be indirect inspection of the posterior pharynx by mirror.

2. *Pulmonary system:* A conventional respiratory examination, including inspection of the thorax and auscultation and percussion of the lung fields should be performed as part of the periodic medical examination. Although routine pulmonary function testing is only required by the standard once every year for persons who are exposed over the TWA concentration limit, these tests have an obvious value in investigating possible respiratory dysfunction and should be used wherever deemed appropriate by the physician. In cases of alleged formaldehyde-induced airway disease, other possible causes of pulmonary disfunction (including exposures to other substances) should be ruled out. A chest radiograph may be useful in these circumstances. In cases of suspected airway hypersensitivity or allergy, it may be appropriate to use bronchial challenge testing with formaldehyde or methacholine to determine the nature of the disorder. Such testing should be performed by or under the supervision of a physician experienced in the procedures involved.

3. *Skin:* The physician should be alert to evidence of dermal irritation of sensitization, including reddening and inflammation, urticaria, blistering, scaling, formation of skin fissures, or other symptoms. Since the integrity of the skin barrier is compromised by other dermal diseases, the presence of such disease should be noted. Skin sensitivity testing carries with it some risk of inducing sensitivity, and therefore, skin testing for formaldehyde sensitivity should not be used as a routine screening test. Sensitivity testing may be indicated in the investigation of a suspected existing sensitivity. Guidelines for such testing have been prepared by the North American Contact Dermatitis Group.

C. Additional Examinations or Tests

The physician may deem it necessary to perform other medical examinations or tests as indicated. The standard provides a mechanism whereby these additional investigations are covered under the standard for occupational exposure to formaldehyde.

D. Emergencies

The examination of workers exposed in an emergency should be directed at the organ systems most likely to be affected. Much of the content of the examination will be similar to the periodic examination unless the patient has received a severe acute exposure requiring immediate attention to prevent serious consequences. If a severe overexposure requiring medical intervention or hospitalization has occurred, the physician must be alert to the possibility of delayed symptoms. Followup nonroutine examinations may be necessary to assure the patient's well-being.

E. Employer Obligations

The employer is required to provide the physician with the following information: A copy of this standard and appendices A, C, D, and E; a description of the affected employee's duties as they relate to his or her exposure concentration; an estimate of the employee's exposure including duration (e.g., 15 hr/wk, three 8-hour shifts, full-time); a description of any personal protective equipment, including respirators, used by the employee; and the results of any previous medical determinations for the affected employee related to formaldehyde exposure to the extent that this information is within the employer's control.

F. Physician's Obligations

The standard requires the employer to obtain a written statement from the physician. This statement must contain the physician's opinion as to whether the employee has any medical condition which would place him or her at increased risk of impaired health from exposure to formaldehyde or use of respirators, as appropriate. The physician must also state his opinion regarding any restrictions that should be placed on the employee's exposure to formaldehyde or upon the use of protective clothing or equipment such as respirators. If the employee wears a respirator as a result of his or her exposure to formaldehyde, the physician's opinion must also contain a statement regarding the suitability of the employee to wear the type of respirator assigned. Finally, the physician must inform the employer that the employee has been told the results of the medical examination and of any medical conditions which require further explanation or treatment. This written opinion is not to contain any information on specific findings or diagnoses unrelated to occupational exposure to formaldehyde.

The purpose in requiring the examining physician to supply the employer with a written opinion is to provide the employer with a medical basis to assist the employer in placing employees initially, in assuring that their health is not being impaired by formaldehyde, and to assess the employee's ability to use any required protective equipment.

APPENDIX D TO § 1910.1048—NONMANDATORY MEDICAL DISEASE QUESTIONNAIRE

A. Identification

Plant Name _____

Date _____

Employee Name _____

S.S. # _____

Job Title _____

Birthdate: _____

Age: _____

Sex: _____

Height: _____

Weight: _____

B. Medical History

1. Have you ever been in the hospital as a patient?
Yes ☐ No ☐
If yes, what kind of problem were you having? _____

2. Have you ever had any kind of operation?
Yes ☐ No ☐
If yes, what kind? _____

3. Do you take any kind of medicine regularly?
Yes ☐ No ☐
If yes, what kind? _____

4. Are you allergic to any drugs, foods, or chemicals?
Yes ☐ No ☐
If yes, what kind of allergy is it? _____
What causes the allergy? _____

5. Have you ever been told that you have asthma, hayfever, or sinusitis?
Yes ☐ No ☐

6. Have you ever been told that you have emphysema, bronchitis, or any other respiratory problems?
Yes ☐ No ☐

7. Have you ever been told you had hepatitis?
Yes ☐ No ☐

8. Have you ever been told that you had cirrhosis?
Yes ☐ No ☐

9. Have you ever been told that you had cancer?
Yes ☐ No ☐

10. Have you ever had arthritis or joint pain?
Yes ☐ No ☐

11. Have you ever been told that you had high blood pressure?
Yes ☐ No ☐

12. Have you ever had a heart attack or heart trouble?
Yes ☐ No ☐

B-1. Medical History Update

1. Have you been in the hospital as a patient any time within the past year?
Yes ☐ No ☐
If so, for what condition? _____

2. Have you been under the care of a physician during the past year?
Yes ☐ No ☐

If so, for what condition? _____

3. Is there any change in your breathing since last year?
Yes ☐ No ☐
Better? _____
Worse? _____
No change? _____
If change, do you know why? _____

4. Is your general health different this year from last year?
Yes ☐ No ☐
If different, in what way? _____

5. Have you in the past year or are you now taking any medication on a regular basis?
Yes ☐ No ☐
Name Rx _____
Condition being treated _____

C. Occupational History

1. How long have you worked for your present employer?

_____

2. What jobs have you held with this employer? Include job title and length of time in each job.

_____
_____
_____

3. In each of these jobs, how many hours a day were you exposed to chemicals?

4. What chemicals have you worked with most of the time?

5. Have you ever noticed any type of skin rash you feel was related to your work?
Yes ☐ No ☐
6. Have you ever noticed that any kind of chemical makes you cough?
Yes ☐ No ☐
Wheeze?
Yes ☐ No ☐
Become short of breath or cause your chest to become tight?
Yes ☐ No ☐
7. Are you exposed to any dust or chemicals at home?
Yes ☐ No ☐
If yes, explain: _____

8. In other jobs, have you ever had exposure to:
Wood dust?
Yes ☐ No ☐
Nickel or chromium?
Yes ☐ No ☐
Silica (foundry, sand blasting)?
Yes ☐ No ☐
Arsenic or asbestos?
Yes ☐ No ☐
Organic solvents?
Yes ☐ No ☐

Urethane foams?
Yes ☐ No ☐

C-1. Occupational History Update

1. Are you working on the same job this year as you were last year?
Yes ☐ No ☐
If not, how has your job changed? _____

2. What chemicals are you exposed to on your job?

_____

3. How many hours a day are you exposed to chemicals?

_____

4. Have you noticed any skin rash within the past year you feel was related to your work?
Yes ☐ No ☐
If so, explain circumstances: _____

_____

5. Have you noticed that any chemical makes you cough, be short of breath, or wheeze?
Yes ☐ No ☐
If so, can you identify it? _____

_____

D. Miscellaneous

1. Do you smoke?
Yes ☐ No ☐
If so, how much and for how long? _____

Pipe _____
Cigars _____
Cigarettes _____
2. Do you drink alcohol in any form?
Yes ☐ No ☐
If so, how much, how long, and how often?

_____

3. Do you wear glasses or contact lenses?
Yes ☐ No ☐
4. Do you get any physical exercise other than that required to do your job?
Yes ☐ No ☐
If so, explain: _____

5. Do you have any hobbies or "side jobs" that require you to use chemicals, such as furniture stripping, sand blasting, insulation or manufacture of urethane foam, furniture, etc?
Yes ☐ No ☐
If so, please describe, giving type of business or hobby, chemicals used and length of exposures.

_____

E. Symptoms Questionnaire

1. Do you ever have any shortness of breath?
Yes ☐ No ☐
If yes, do you have to rest after climbing several flights of stairs?
Yes ☐ No ☐

If yes, if you walk on the level with people your own age, do you walk slower than they do?
Yes ☐ No ☐
If yes, if you walk slower than a normal pace, do you have to limit the distance that you walk?
Yes ☐ No ☐
If yes, do you have to stop and rest while bathing or dressing?
Yes ☐ No ☐
2. Do you cough as much as three months out of the year?
Yes ☐ No ☐
If yes, have you had this cough for more than two years?
Yes ☐ No ☐
If yes, do you ever cough anything up from chest?
Yes ☐ No ☐
3. Do you ever have a feeling of smothering, unable to take a deep breath, or tightness in your chest?
Yes ☐ No ☐
If yes, do you notice that this on any particular day of the week?
Yes ☐ No ☐
If yes, what day or the week?
Yes ☐ No ☐
If yes, do you notice that this occurs at any particular place?
Yes ☐ No ☐
If yes, do you notice that this is worse after you have returned to work after being off for several days?
Yes ☐ No ☐
4. Have you ever noticed any wheezing in your chest?
Yes ☐ No ☐
If yes, is this only with colds or other infections?
Yes ☐ No ☐
Is this caused by exposure to any kind of dust or other material?
Yes ☐ No ☐
If yes, what kind? _____
5. Have you noticed any burning, tearing, or redness of your eyes when you are at work?
Yes ☐ No ☐
If so, explain circumstances: _____

6. Have you noticed any sore or burning throat or itchy or burning nose when you are at work?
Yes ☐ No ☐
If so, explain circumstances: _____

7. Have you noticed any stuffiness or dryness of your nose?
Yes ☐ No ☐
8. Do you ever have swelling of the eyelids or face?
Yes ☐ No ☐
9. Have you ever been jaundiced?
Yes ☐ No ☐
If yes, was this accompanied by any pain?

Yes ☐ No ☐
10. Have you ever had a tendency to bruise easily or bleed excessively?
Yes ☐ No ☐
11. Do you have frequent headaches that are not relieved by aspirin or tylenol?
Yes ☐ No ☐
If yes, do they occur at any particular time of the day or week?
Yes ☐ No ☐
If yes, when do they occur? _____

12. Do you have frequent episodes of nervousness or irritability?
Yes ☐ No ☐
13. Do you tend to have trouble concentrating or remembering?
Yes ☐ No ☐
14. Do you ever feel dizzy, light-headed, excessively drowsy or like you have been drugged?
Yes ☐ No ☐
15. Does your vision ever become blurred?
Yes ☐ No ☐
16. Do you have numbness or tingling of the hands or feet or other parts of your body?
Yes ☐ No ☐
17. Have you ever had chronic weakness or fatigue?
Yes ☐ No ☐
18. Have you ever had any swelling of your feet or ankles to the point where you could not wear your shoes?
Yes ☐ No ☐
19. Are you bothered by heartburn or indigestion?
Yes ☐ No ☐
20. Do you ever have itching, dryness, or peeling and scaling of the hands?
Yes ☐ No ☐
21. Do you ever have a burning sensation in the hands, or reddening of the skin?
Yes ☐ No ☐
22. Do you ever have cracking or bleeding of the skin on your hands?
Yes ☐ No ☐
23. Are you under a physician's care?
Yes ☐ No ☐
If yes, for what are you being treated? _____

24. Do you have any physical complaints today?
Yes ☐ No ☐
If yes, explain? _____

25. Do you have other health conditions not covered by these questions?
Yes ☐ No ☐
If yes, explain: _____

[57 FR 22310, May 27, 1992; 57 FR 27161, June 18, 1992; 61 FR 5508, Feb. 13, 1996; 63 FR 1292, Jan. 8, 1998; 63 FR 20099, Apr. 23, 1998; 71 FR 1143, Jan. 5, 2005; 71 FR 16672, 16673, Apr. 3, 2006; 71 FR 50190, Aug. 24, 2006; 73 FR 75586, Dec. 12, 2008; 77 FR 17784, Mar. 26, 2012]

EFFECTIVE DATE NOTE: At 84 FR 21518, May 14, 2019, § 1910.1048 was amended by revising appendix D, effective July 15, 2019. For the convenience of the user, the revised text is set forth as follows:

§ 1910.1048   Formaldehyde.

*   *   *   *   *

APPENDIX D TO § 1910.1048—NONMANDATORY MEDICAL DISEASE QUESTIONNAIRE

A. Identification

Plant Name: _____

Date: _____

Employee Name: _____

Job Title: _____

Birthdate: _____

Age: _____

Sex: _____

Height: _____

Weight: _____

B. Medical History

1. Have you ever been in the hospital as a patient?

    Yes__ No__

    If yes, what kind of problem were you having? _____

    _____

2. Have you ever had any kind of operation?

    Yes__ No__

    If yes, what kind? _____

    _____

3. Do you take any kind of medicine regularly?

    Yes__ No__

    If yes, what kind? _____

    _____

4. Are you allergic to any drugs, foods, or chemicals?

    Yes__ No__

    If yes, what kind of allergy is it? _____

    _____

    What causes the allergy? _____

    _____

5. Have you ever been told that you have asthma, hayfever, or sinusitis?
   Yes___ No___

6. Have you ever been told that you have emphysema, bronchitis, or any other respiratory problems?
   Yes___ No___

7. Have you ever been told you had hepatitis?
   Yes___ No___

8. Have you ever been told that you had cirrhosis?
   Yes___ No___

9. Have you ever been told that you had cancer?
   Yes___ No___

10. Have you ever had arthritis or joint pain?
    Yes___ No___

11. Have you ever been told that you had high blood pressure?
    Yes___ No___

12. Have you ever had a heart attack or heart trouble?
    Yes___ No___

B-1. Medical History Update

1. Have you been in the hospital as a patient any time within the past year?
   Yes___ No___

   If so, for what condition? _____

   _____

2. Have you been under the care of a physician during the past year?
   Yes___ No___

   If so, for what condition?_____

   _____

3. Is there any change in your breathing since last year?

    Yes__ No__

    Better? _____

    Worse? _____

    No change?_____

    If change, do you know why?_____

    _____

4. Is your general health different this year from last year?

    Yes__ No__

    If different, in what way?_____

    _____

5. Have you in the past year or are you now taking any medication on a regular basis?

    Yes__ No__

    Name Rx_____

    Condition being treated _____

C. Occupational History

1. How long have you worked for your present employer?

    _____

2. What jobs have you held with this employer? Include job title and length of time
   in each job _____

    _____

    _____

    _____

3. In each of these jobs, how many hours a day were you exposed to chemicals?

    _____

4. What chemicals have you worked with most of the time?

    _____

5. Have you ever noticed any type of skin rash you feel was related to your work?

    Yes__ No__

6. Have you ever noticed that any kind of chemical makes you cough?
   Yes__ No__

   Wheeze?

   Yes__ No__

   Become short of breath or cause your chest to become tight?

   Yes__ No__

7. Are you exposed to any dust or chemicals at home?
   Yes__ No__

   If yes, explain: _____

   _____

8. In other jobs, have you ever had exposure to:
   Wood dust?

   Yes__ No__

   Nickel or chromium?

   Yes__ No__

   Silica (foundry, sand blasting)?

   Yes__ No__

   Arsenic or asbestos?

   Yes__ No__

   Organic solvents?

   Yes__ No__

   Urethane foams?

   Yes__ No__

C-1. Occupational History Update

1. Are you working on the same job this year as you were last year?
   Yes__ No__

   If not, how has your job changed? _____

   _____

2. What chemicals are you exposed to on your job?

_____

3. How many hours a day are you exposed to chemicals?

_____

4. Have you noticed any skin rash within the past year you feel was related to your work?

Yes___ No___

If so, explain circumstances: _____

_____

5. Have you noticed that any chemical makes you cough, be short of breath, or wheeze?

Yes___ No___

If so, can you identify it? _____

_____

D. Miscellaneous

1. Do you smoke?

Yes___ No___

If so, how much and for how long? _____

_____

Pipe_____

Cigars_____

Cigarettes_____

2. Do you drink alcohol in any form?

Yes___ No___

If so, how much, how long, and how often? _____

_____

3. Do you wear glasses or contact lenses?

Yes___ No___

4. Do you get any physical exercise other than that required to do your job?

Yes___ No___

If so, explain: _____

_____

5. Do you have any hobbies or "side jobs" that require you to use chemicals, such as furniture stripping, sand blasting, insulation or manufacture of urethane foam, furniture, etc.?

Yes__ No__

If so, please describe, giving type of business or hobby, chemicals used and length of exposures.

_____

E. Symptoms Questionnaire

1. Do you ever have any shortness of breath?

Yes__ No__

If yes, do you have to rest after climbing several flights of stairs?

Yes__ No__

If yes, if you walk on the level with people your own age, do you walk slower than they do?

Yes__ No__

If yes, if you walk slower than a normal pace, do you have to limit the distance that you walk?

Yes__ No__

If yes, do you have to stop and rest while bathing or dressing?

Yes__ No__

2. Do you cough as much as three months out of the year?

Yes__ No__

If yes, have you had this cough for more than two years?

Yes__ No__

If yes, do you ever cough anything up from chest?

Yes__ No__

3. Do you ever have a feeling of smothering, unable to take a deep breath, or tightness in your chest?

Yes__ No__

If yes, do you notice that this on any particular day of the week?

Yes__ No__

If yes, what day or the week?

Yes__ No__

If yes, do you notice that this occurs at any particular place?

Yes__ No__

If yes, do you notice that this is worse after you have returned to work after being off for several days?

Yes__ No__

4. Have you ever noticed any wheezing in your chest?

Yes__ No__

If yes, is this only with colds or other infections?

Yes__ No__

Is this caused by exposure to any kind of dust or other material?

Yes__ No__

If yes, what kind? _____

5. Have you noticed any burning, tearing, or redness of your eyes when you are at work?

Yes__ No__

If so, explain circumstances: _____

_____

6. Have you noticed any sore or burning throat or itchy or burning nose when you are at work?

Yes__ No__

If so, explain circumstances: _____

_____

7. Have you noticed any stuffiness or dryness of your nose?

Yes__ No__

8. Do you ever have swelling of the eyelids or face?

   Yes__ No__

9. Have you ever been jaundiced?

   Yes__ No__

   If yes, was this accompanied by any pain?

   Yes__ No__

10. Have you ever had a tendency to bruise easily or bleed excessively?

    Yes__ No__

11. Do you have frequent headaches that are not relieved by aspirin or Tylenol?

    Yes__ No__

    If yes, do they occur at any particular time of the day or week?

    Yes__ No__

    If yes, when do they occur? _____

    _____

12. Do you have frequent episodes of nervousness or irritability?

    Yes__ No__

13. Do you tend to have trouble concentrating or remembering?

    Yes__ No__

14. Do you ever feel dizzy, light-headed, excessively drowsy or like you have been drugged?

    Yes__ No__

15. Does your vision ever become blurred?

    Yes__ No__

16. Do you have numbness or tingling of the hands or feet or other parts of your body?

    Yes__ No__

17. Have you ever had chronic weakness or fatigue?

    Yes__ No__

18. Have you ever had any swelling of your feet or ankles to the point where you could not wear your shoes?

    Yes__ No__

19. Are you bothered by heartburn or indigestion?

Yes__ No__

20. Do you ever have itching, dryness, or peeling and scaling of the hands?

Yes__ No__

21. Do you ever have a burning sensation in the hands, or reddening of the skin?

Yes__ No__

22. Do you ever have cracking or bleeding of the skin on your hands?

Yes__ No__

23. Are you under a physician's care?

Yes__ No__

If yes, for what are you being treated? _____

_____

24. Do you have any physical complaints today?

Yes__ No__

If yes, explain? _____

_____

25. Do you have other health conditions not covered by these questions?

Yes__ No__

If yes, explain: _____

_____

§ 1910.1050 Methylenedianiline.

(a) *Scope and application.* (1) This section applies to all occupational exposures to MDA, Chemical Abstracts Service Registry No. 101–77–9, except as provided in paragraphs (a)(2) through (a)(7) of this section.

(2) Except as provided in paragraphs (a)(8) and (e)(5) of this section, this section does not apply to the processing, use, and handling of products containing MDA where initial monitoring indicates that the product is not capable of releasing MDA in excess of the action level under the expected conditions of processing, use, and handling which will cause the greatest possible release; and where no "dermal exposure to MDA" can occur.

(3) Except as provided in paragraph (a)(8) of this section, this section does not apply to the processing, use, and handling of products containing MDA where objective data are reasonably relied upon which demonstrate the product is not capable of releasing MDA under the expected conditions of processing, use, and handling which will cause the greatest possible release; and where no "dermal exposure to MDA" can occur.

(4) This section does not apply to the storage, transportation, distribution or sale of MDA in intact containers sealed in such a manner as to contain the MDA dusts, vapors, or liquids, except for the provisions of 29 CFR 1910.1200 and paragraph (d) of this section.

(5) This section does not apply to the construction industry as defined in 29 CFR 1910.12(b). (Exposure to MDA in

the construction industry is covered by 29 CFR 1926.60).

(6) Except as provided in paragraph (a)(8) of this secton, this section does not apply to materials in any form which contain less than 0.1% MDA by weight or volume.

(7) Except as provided in paragraph (a)(8) of this section, this section does not apply to "finished articles containing MDA."

(8) Where products containing MDA are exempted under paragraphs (a)(2) through (a)(7) of this section, the employer shall maintain records of the initial monitoring results or objective data supporting that exemption and the basis for the employer's reliance on the data, as provided in the recordkeeping provision of paragraph (n) of this section.

(b) *Definitions.* For the purpose of this section, the following definitions shall apply:

Action level means a concentration of airborne MDA of 5 ppb as an eight (8)-hour time-weighted average.

Assistant Secretary means the Assistant Secretary of Labor for Occupational Safety and Health, U.S. Department of Labor, or designee.

Authorized person means any person specifically authorized by the employer whose duties require the person to enter a regulated area, or any person entering such an area as a designated representative of employees, for the purpose of exercising the right to observe monitoring and measuring procedures under paragraph (o) of this section, or any other person authorized by the Act or regulations issued under the Act.

Container means any barrel, bottle, can, cylinder, drum, reaction vessel, storage tank, commercial packaging or the like, but does not include piping systems.

Dermal exposure to MDA occurs where employees are engaged in the handling, application or use of mixtures or materials containing MDA, with any of the following non-airborne forms of MDA:

(i) Liquid, powdered, granular, or flaked mixtures containing MDA in concentrations greater than 0.1% by weight or volume; and

(ii) Materials other than "finished articles" containing MDA in concentra- tions greater than 0.1% by weight or volume.

Director means the Director of the National Institute for Occupational Safety and Health, U.S. Department of Health and Human Services, or designee.

Emergency means any occurrence such as, but not limited to, equipment failure, rupture of containers, or failure of control equipment which results in an unexpected and potentially hazardous release of MDA.

Employee exposure means exposure to MDA which would occur if the employee were not using respirators or protective work clothing and equipment.

Finished article containing MDA is defined as a manufactured item:

(i) Which is formed to a specific shape or design during manufacture;

(ii) Which has end use function(s) dependent in whole or part upon its shape or design during end use; and

(iii) Where applicable, is an item which is fully cured by virtue of having been subjected to the conditions (temperature, time) necessary to complete the desired chemical reaction.

4,4′ Methylenedianiline or MDA means the chemical, 4,4′-diaminodiphenylmethane, Chemical Abstract Service Registry number 101–77–9, in the form of a vapor, liquid, or solid. The definition also includes the salts of MDA.

Regulated areas means areas where airborne concentrations of MDA exceed or can reasonably be expected to exceed, the permissible exposure limits, or where dermal exposure to MDA can occur.

STEL means short term exposure limit as determined by any 15 minute sample period.

(c) *Permissible exposure limits (PEL).* The employer shall assure that no employee is exposed to an airborne concentration of MDA in excess of ten parts per billion (10 ppb) as an 8-hour time-weighted average or a STEL of 100 ppb.

(d) *Emergency situations*—(1) *Written plan.* (i) A written plan for emergency situations shall be developed for each workplace where there is a possibility of an emergency. Appropriate portions of the plan shall be implemented in the event of an emergency.

(ii) The plan shall specifically provide that employees engaged in correcting emergency conditions shall be equipped with the appropriate personal protective equipment and clothing as required in paragraphs (h) and (i) of this section until the emergency is abated.

(iii) The plan shall specifically include provisions for alerting and evacuating affected employees as well as the elements prescribed in 29 CFR 1910.38 and 29 CFR 1910.39, "Emergency action plans" and "Fire prevention plans," respectively.

(2) *Alerting employees.* Where there is the possibility of employee exposure to MDA due to an emergency, means shall be developed to alert promptly those employees who have the potential to be directly exposed. Affected employees not engaged in correcting emergency conditions shall be evacuated immediately in the event that an emergency occurs. Means shall also be developed and implemented for alerting other employees who may be exposed as a result of the emergency.

(e) *Exposure monitoring*—(1) *General.* (i) Determinations of employee exposure shall be made from breathing zone air samples that are representative of each employee's exposure to airborne MDA over an eight (8) hour period. Determination of employee exposure to the STEL shall be made from breathing zone air samples collected over a 15 minute sampling period.

(ii) Representative employee exposure shall be determined on the basis of one or more samples representing full shift exposure for each shift for each job classification in each work area where exposure to MDA may occur.

(iii) Where the employer can document that exposure levels are equivalent for similar operations in different work shifts, the employer shall only be required to determine representative employee exposure for that operation during one shift.

(2) *Initial monitoring.* Each employer who has a workplace or work operation covered by this standard shall perform initial monitoring to determine accurately the airborne concentrations of MDA to which employees may be exposed.

(3) *Periodic monitoring and monitoring frequency.* (i) If the monitoring required by paragraph (e)(2) of this section reveals employee exposure at or above the action level, but at or below the PELs, the employer shall repeat such representative monitoring for each such employee at least every six (6) months.

(ii) If the monitoring required by paragraph (e)(2) of this section reveals employee exposure above the PELs, the employer shall repeat such monitoring for each such employee at least every three (3) months.

(iii) The employer may alter the monitoring schedule from every three months to every six months for any employee for whom two consecutive measurements taken at least 7 days apart indicate that the employee exposure has decreased to below the TWA but above the action level.

(4) *Termination of monitoring.* (i) If the initial monitoring required by paragraph (e)(2) of this section reveals employee exposure to be below the action level, the employer may discontinue the monitoring for that employee, except as otherwise required by paragraph (e)(5) of this section.

(ii) If the periodic monitoring required by paragraph (e)(3) of this section reveals that employee exposures, as indicated by at least two consecutive measurements taken at least 7 days apart, are below the action level the employer may discontinue the monitoring for that employee, except as otherwise required by paragraph (e)(5) of this section.

(5) *Additional monitoring.* The employer shall institute the exposure monitoring required under paragraphs (e)(2) and (e)(3) of this section when there has been a change in production process, chemicals present, control equipment, personnel, or work practices which may result in new or additional exposures to MDA, or when the employer has any reason to suspect a change which may result in new or additional exposures.

(6) *Accuracy of monitoring.* Monitoring shall be accurate, to a confidence level of 95 percent, to within plus or minus

25 percent for airborne concentrations of MDA.

(7) *Employee notification of monitoring results.* (i) The employer shall, within 15 working days after the receipt of the results of any monitoring performed under this standard, notify each employee of these results, in writing, either individually or by posting of results in an appropriate location that is accessible to affected employees.

(ii) The written notification required by paragraph (e)(7)(i) of this section shall contain the corrective action being taken by the employer to reduce the employee exposure to or below the PELs, wherever the PELs are exceeded.

(8) *Visual monitoring.* The employer shall make routine inspections of employee hands, face and forearms potentially exposed to MDA. Other potential dermal exposures reported by the employee must be referred to the appropriate medical personnel for observation. If the employer determines that the employee has been exposed to MDA the employer shall:

(i) Determine the source of exposure;

(ii) Implement protective measures to correct the hazard; and

(iii) Maintain records of the corrective actions in accordance with paragraph (n) of this section.

(f) *Regulated areas—*(1) *Establishment—*(i) *Airborne exposures.* The employer shall establish regulated areas where airborne concentrations of MDA exceed or can reasonably be expected to exceed, the permissible exposure limits.

(ii) *Dermal exposures.* Where employees are subject to dermal exposure to MDA the employer shall establish those work areas as regulated areas.

(2) *Demarcation.* Regulated areas shall be demarcated from the rest of the workplace in a manner that minimizes the number of persons potentially exposed.

(3) *Access.* Access to regulated areas shall be limited to authorized persons.

(4) *Personal protective equipment and clothing.* Each person entering a regulated area shall be supplied with, and required to use, the appropriate personal protective clothing and equipment in accordance with paragraphs (h) and (i) of this section.

(5) *Prohibited activities.* The employer shall ensure that employees do not eat, drink, smoke, chew tobacco or gum, or apply cosmetics in regulated areas.

(g) *Methods of compliance—*(1) *Engineering controls and work practices.* (i) The employer shall institute engineering controls and work practices to reduce and maintain employee exposure to MDA at or below the PELs except to the extent that the employer can establish that these controls are not feasible or where the provisions of paragraph (g)(1)(ii) or (h)(1) (i) through (iv) of this section apply.

(ii) Wherever the feasible engineering controls and work practices which can be instituted are not sufficient to reduce employee exposure to or below the PELs, the employer shall use them to reduce employee exposure to the lowest levels achievable by these controls and shall supplement them by the use of respiratory protective devices which comply with the requirements of paragraph (h) of this section.

(2) *Compliance program.* (i) The employer shall establish and implement a written program to reduce employee exposure to or below the PELs by means of engineering and work practice controls, as required by paragraph (g)(1) of this section, and by use of respiratory protection where permitted under this section. The program shall include a schedule for periodic maintenance (e.g., leak detection) and shall include the written plan for emergency situations as specified in paragraph (d) of this section.

(ii) Upon request this written program shall be furnished for examination and copying to the Assistant Secretary, the Director, affected employees, and designated employee representatives. The employer shall review and, as necessary, update such plans at least once every 12 months to make certain they reflect the current status of the program.

(3) *Employee rotation.* Employee rotation shall not be permitted as a means of reducing exposure.

(h) *Respiratory protection—*(1) *General.* For employees who use respirators required by this section, the employer must provide each employee an appropriate respirator that complies with the requirements of this paragraph. Respirators must be used during:

(i) Periods necessary to install or implement feasible engineering and work-practice controls.

(ii) Work operations for which the employer establishes that engineering and work-practice controls are not feasible.

(iii) Work operations for which feasible engineering and work-practice controls are not yet sufficient to reduce employee exposure to or below the PEL.

(iv) Emergencies.

(2) *Respirator program.* The employer must implement a respiratory protection program in accordance with § 1910.134 (b) through (d) (except (d)(1)(iii)), and (f) through (m), which covers each employee required by this section to use a respirator.

(3) *Respirator selection.* (i) Employers must:

(A) Select, and provide to employees, the appropriate respirators specified in paragraph (d)(3)(i)(A) of 29 CFR 1910.134.

(B) Provide HEPA filters for powered and non-powered air-purifying respirators.

(C) For escape, provide employees with one of the following respirator options: Any self-contained breathing apparatus with a full facepiece or hood operated in the positive-pressure or continuous-flow mode; or a full facepiece air-purifying respirator.

(D) Provide a combination HEPA filter and organic vapor canister or cartridge with powered or non-powered air-purifying respirators when MDA is in liquid form or used as part of a process requiring heat.

(ii) Any employee who cannot use a negative-pressure respirator must be given the option of using a positive-pressure respirator, or a supplied-air respirator operated in the continuous-flow or pressure-demand mode.

(i) *Protective work clothing and equipment*—(1) *Provision and use.* Where employees are subject to dermal exposure to MDA, where liquids containing MDA can be splashed into the eyes, or where airborne concentrations of MDA are in excess of the PEL, the employer shall provide, at no cost to the employee, and ensure that the employee uses, appropriate protective work clothing and equipment which prevent contact with MDA such as, but not limited to:

(i) Aprons, coveralls or other full-body work clothing;

(ii) Gloves, head coverings, and foot coverings; and

(iii) Face shields, chemical goggles; or

(iv) Other appropriate protective equipment which comply with § 1910.133.

(2) *Removal and storage.* (i) The employer shall ensure that, at the end of their work shift, employees remove MDA-contaminated protective work clothing and equipment that is not routinely removed throughout the day in change rooms provided in accordance with the provisions established for change rooms.

(ii) The employer shall ensure that, during their work shift, employees remove all other MDA-contaminated protective work clothing or equipment before leaving a regulated area.

(iii) The employer shall ensure that no employee takes MDA-contaminated work clothing or equipment out of the change room, except those employees authorized to do so for the purpose of laundering, maintenance, or disposal.

(iv) MDA-contaminated work clothing or equipment shall be placed and stored in closed containers which prevent dispersion of the MDA outside the container.

(v) Containers of MDA-contaminated protective work clothing or equipment which are to be taken out of change rooms or the workplace for cleaning, maintenance, or disposal, shall bear labels warning of the hazards of MDA.

(3) *Cleaning and replacement.* (i) The employer shall provide the employee with clean protective clothing and equipment. The employer shall ensure that protective work clothing or equipment required by this paragraph is cleaned, laundered, repaired, or replaced at intervals appropriate to maintain its effectiveness.

(ii) The employer shall prohibit the removal of MDA from protective work clothing or equipment by blowing, shaking, or any methods which allow MDA to re-enter the workplace.

(iii) The employer shall ensure that laundering of MDA-contaminated clothing shall be done so as to prevent the release of MDA in the workplace.

(iv) Any employer who gives MDA-contaminated clothing to another person for laundering shall inform such person of the requirement to prevent the release of MDA.

(v) The employer shall inform any person who launders or cleans protective clothing or equipment contaminated with MDA of the potentially harmful effects of exposure.

(vi) MDA-contaminated clothing shall be transported in properly labeled, sealed, impermeable bags or containers.

(j) *Hygiene facilities and practices*—(1) *Change rooms.* (i) The employer shall provide clean change rooms for employees, who must wear protective clothing, or who must use protective equipment because of their exposure to MDA.

(ii) Change rooms must be equipped with separate storage for protective clothing and equipment and for street clothes which prevents MDA contamination of street clothes.

(2) *Showers.* (i) The employer shall ensure that employees, who work in areas where there is the potential for exposure resulting from airborne MDA (e.g., particulates or vapors) above the action level, shower at the end of the work shift.

(A) Shower facilities required by this paragraph shall comply with §1910.141(d)(3).

(B) The employer shall ensure that employees who are required to shower pursuant to the provisions contained herein do not leave the workplace wearing any protective clothing or equipment worn during the work shift.

(ii) Where dermal exposure to MDA occurs, the employer shall ensure that materials spilled or deposited on the skin are removed as soon as possible by methods which do not facilitate the dermal absorption of MDA.

(3) *Lunch facilities*—(i) *Availability and construction.* (A) Whenever food or beverages are consumed at the worksite and employees are exposed to MDA at or above the PEL or are subject to dermal exposure to MDA the employer shall provide readily accessible lunch areas.

(B) Lunch areas located within the workplace and in areas where there is the potential for airborne exposure to MDA at or above the PEL shall have a positive pressure, temperature controlled, filtered air supply.

(C) Lunch areas may not be located in areas within the workplace where the potential for dermal exposure to MDA exists.

(ii) The employer shall ensure that employees who have been subjected to dermal exposure to MDA or who have been exposed to MDA above the PEL wash their hands and faces with soap and water prior to eating, drinking, smoking, or applying cosmetics.

(iii) The employer shall ensure that employees exposed to MDA do not enter lunch facilities with MDA-contaminated protective work clothing or equipment.

(k) *Communication of hazards*—(1) *Hazard communication—general.*

(i) Chemical manufacturers, importers, distributors and employers shall comply with all requirements of the Hazard Communication Standard (HCS) (§1910.1200) for MDA.

(ii) In classifying the hazards of MDA at least the following hazards are to be addressed: Cancer; liver effects; and skin sensitization.

(iii) Employers shall include MDA in the hazard communication program established to comply with the HCS (§1910.1200). Employers shall ensure that each employee has access to labels on containers of MDA and to safety data sheets, and is trained in accordance with the requirements of HCS and paragraph (k)(4) of this section.

(2) *Signs and labels*—(i) *Signs.* (A) The employer shall post and maintain legible signs demarcating regulated areas and entrances or access ways to regulated areas that bear the following legend:

DANGER

MDA

MAY CAUSE CANCER

CAUSES DAMAGE TO THE LIVER

RESPIRATORY PROTECTION AND PROTECTIVE CLOTHING MAY BE REQUIRED IN THIS AREA

AUTHORIZED PERSONNEL ONLY

(B) Prior to June 1, 2016, employers may use the following legend in lieu of that specified in paragraph (k)(2)(i)(A) of this section:

DANGER
MDA
MAY CAUSE CANCER
LIVER TOXIN
AUTHORIZED PERSONNEL ONLY
RESPIRATORS AND PROTECTIVE CLOTH-
ING MAY BE REQUIRED TO BE WORN IN
THIS AREA

(ii) *Labels.* Prior to June 1, 2015, employers may include the following information workplace labels in lieu of the labeling requirements in paragraph (k)(1) of this section:

(A) For pure MDA:
DANGER
CONTAINS MDA
MAY CAUSE CANCER
LIVER TOXIN

(B) For mixtures containing MDA:
DANGER
CONTAINS MDA
CONTAINS MATERIALS WHICH MAY
CAUSE CANCER
LIVER TOXIN

(3) *Safety data sheets (SDS).* In meeting the obligation to provide safety data sheets, employers shall make appropriate use of the information found in Appendices A and B to § 1910.1050.

(4) *Information and training.* (i) The employer shall provide employees with information and training on MDA, in accordance with 29 CFR 1910.1200(h), at the time of initial assignment and at least annually thereafter.

(ii) In addition to the information required under 29 CFR 1910.1200, the employer shall:

(A) Provide an explanation of the contents of this section, including appendices A and B, and indicate to employees where a copy of the standard is available;

(B) Describe the medical surveillance program required under paragraph (m) of this section, and explain the information contained in appendix C; and

(C) Describe the medical removal provision required under paragraph (m) of this section.

(5) *Access to training materials.* (i) The employer shall make readily available to all affected employees, without cost, all written materials relating to the employee training program, including a copy of this regulation.

(ii) The employer shall provide to the Assistant Secretary and the Director, upon request, all information and training materials relating to the employee information and training program.

(l) *Housekeeping.* (1) All surfaces shall be maintained as free as practicable of visible accumulations of MDA.

(2) The employer shall institute a program for detecting MDA leaks, spills, and discharges, including regular visual inspections of operations involving liquid or solid MDA.

(3) All leaks shall be repaired and liquid or dust spills cleaned up promptly.

(4) Surfaces contaminated with MDA may not be cleaned by the use of compressed air.

(5) Shoveling, dry sweeping, and other methods of dry clean-up of MDA may be used where HEPA-filtered vacuuming and/or wet cleaning are not feasible or practical.

(6) Waste, scrap, debris, bags, containers, equipment, and clothing contaminated with MDA shall be collected and disposed of in a manner to prevent the re-entry of MDA into the workplace.

(m) *Medical surveillance*—(1) *General.* (i) The employer shall make available a medical surveillance program for employees exposed to MDA:

(A) Employees exposed at or above the action level for 30 or more days per year;

(B) Employees who are subject to dermal exposure to MDA for 15 or more days per year;

(C) Employees who have been exposed in an emergency situation;

(D) Employees whom the employer, based on results from compliance with paragraph (e)(8) of this section, has reason to believe are being dermally exposed; and

(E) Employees who show signs or symptoms of MDA exposure.

(ii) The employer shall ensure that all medical examinations and procedures are performed by, or under the supervision of, a licensed physician, at a reasonable time and place, and provided without cost to the employee.

(2) *Initial examinations.* (i) Within 150 days of the effective date of this standard, or before the time of initial assignment, the employer shall provide each

employee covered by paragraph (m)(1)(i) of this section with a medical examination including the following elements:

(A) A detailed history which includes:

(1) Past work exposure to MDA or any other toxic substances;

(2) A history of drugs, alcohol, tobacco, and medication routinely taken (duration and quantity); and

(3) A history of dermatitis, chemical skin sensitization, or previous hepatic disease.

(B) A physical examination which includes all routine physical examination parameters, skin examination, and signs of liver disease.

(C) Laboratory tests including:

(1) Liver function tests and

(2) Urinalysis.

(D) Additional tests as necessary in the opinion of the physician.

(ii) No initial medical examination is required if adequate records show that the employee has been examined in accordance with the requirements of this section within the previous six months prior to the effective date of this standard or prior to the date of initial assignment.

(3) *Periodic examinations.* (i) The employer shall provide each employee covered by this section with a medical examination at least annually following the initial examination. These periodic examinations shall include at least the following elements:

(A) A brief history regarding any new exposure to potential liver toxins, changes in drug, tobacco, and alcohol intake, and the appearance of physical signs relating to the liver, and the skin;

(B) The appropriate tests and examinations including liver function tests and skin examinations; and

(C) Appropriate additional tests or examinations as deemed necessary by the physician.

(ii) If in the physicians' opinion the results of liver function tests indicate an abnormality, the employee shall be removed from further MDA exposure in accordance with paragraph (m)(9) of this section. Repeat liver function tests shall be conducted on advice of the physician.

(4) *Emergency examinations.* If the employer determines that the employee has been exposed to a potentially hazardous amount of MDA in an emergency situation as addressed in paragraph (d) of this section, the employer shall provide medical examinations in accordance with paragraphs (m)(3)(i) and (ii) of this section. If the results of liver function testing indicate an abnormality, the employee shall be removed in accordance with paragraph (m)(9) of this section. Repeat liver function tests shall be conducted on the advice of the physician. If the results of the tests are normal, tests must be repeated two to three weeks from the initial testing. If the results of the second set of tests are normal and, on the advice of the physician, no additional testing is required.

(5) *Additional examinations.* Where the employee develops signs and symptoms associated with exposure to MDA, the employer shall provide the employee with an additional medical examination including a liver function test. Repeat liver function tests shall be conducted on the advice of the physician. If the results of the tests are normal, tests must be repeated two to three weeks from the initial testing. If the results of the second set of tests are normal and, on the advice of the physician, no additional testing is required.

(6) *Multiple physician review mechanism.* (i) If the employer selects the initial physician who conducts any medical examination or consultation provided to an employee under this section, and the employee has signs of symptoms of occupational exposure to MDA (which could include an abnormal liver function test), and the employee disagrees with the opinion of the examining physician, and this opinion could affect the employee's job status, the employee may designate an appropriate, mutually acceptable second physician:

(A) To review any findings, determinations, or recommendations of the initial physician; and

(B) To conduct such examinations, consultations, and laboratory tests as the second physician deems necessary to facilitate this review.

(ii) The employer shall promptly notify an employee of the right to seek a second medical opinion after each occasion that an initial physician conducts a medical examination or consultation pursuant to this section. The employer may condition its participation in, and payment for, the multiple physician review mechanism upon the employee doing the following within fifteen (15) days after receipt of the foregoing notification, or receipt of the initial physician's written opinion, whichever is later:

(A) The employee informing the employer that he or she intends to seek a second medical opinion, and

(B) The employee initiating steps to make an appointment with a second physician.

(iii) If the findings, determinations, or recommendations of the second physician differ from those of the initial physician, then the employer and the employee shall assure that efforts are made for the two physicians to resolve any disagreement.

(iv) If the two physicians have been unable to resolve quickly their disagreement, then the employer and the employee through their respective physicians shall designate a third physician;

(A) To review any findings, determinations, or recommendations of the prior physicians; and

(B) To conduct such examinations, consultations, laboratory tests, and discussions with the prior physicians as the third physician deems necessary to resolve the disagreement of the prior physicians.

(v) The employer shall act consistent with the findings, determinations, and recommendations of the third physician, unless the employer and the employee reach an agreement which is otherwise consistent with the recommendations of at least one of the three physicians.

(7) *Information provided to the examining and consulting physicians.* (i) The employer shall provide the following information to the examining physician:

(A) A copy of this regulation and its appendices;

(B) A description of the affected employee's duties as they relate to the employee's potential exposure to MDA;

(C) The employee's current actual or representative MDA exposure level;

(D) A description of any personal protective equipment used or to be used; and

(E) Information from previous employment-related medical examinations of the affected employee.

(ii) The employer shall provide the foregoing information to a second physician under this section upon request either by the second physician, or by the employee.

(8) *Physician's written opinion.* (i) For each examination under this section, the employer shall obtain, and provide the employee with a copy of, the examining physician's written opinion within 15 days of its receipt. The written opinion shall include the following:

(A) The occupationally-pertinent results of the medical examination and tests;

(B) The physician's opinion concerning whether the employee has any detected medical conditions which would place the employee at increased risk of material impairment of health from exposure to MDA;

(C) The physician's recommended limitations upon the employee's exposure to MDA or upon the employee's use of protective clothing or equipment and respirators; and

(D) A statement that the employee has been informed by the physician of the results of the medical examination and any medical conditions resulting from MDA exposure which require further explanation or treatment.

(ii) The written opinion obtained by the employer shall not reveal specific findings or diagnoses unrelated to occupational exposures.

(9) *Medical removal*—(i) *Temporary medical removal of an employee*—(A) *Temporary removal resulting from occupational exposure.* The employee shall be removed from work environments in which exposure to MDA is at or above the action level or where dermal exposure to MDA may occur, following an initial examination (paragraph (m)(2) of this section), periodic examinations (paragraph (m)(3) of this section), an emergency situation paragraph (m)(4) of this section, or an additional examination (paragraph (m)(5) of this section) in the following circumstances:

(1) When the employee exhibits signs and/or symptoms indicative of acute exposure to MDA; or

(2) When the examining physician determines that an employee's abnormal liver function tests are not associated with MDA exposure but that the abnormalities may be exacerbated as a result of occupational exposure to MDA.

(B) *Temporary removal due to a final medical determination.* (1) The employer shall remove an employee from work environments in which exposure to MDA is at or above the action level or where dermal exposure to MDA may occur, on each occasion that there is a final medical determination or opinion that the employee has a detected medical condition which places the employee at increased risk of material impairment to health from exposure to MDA.

(2) For the purposes of this section, the phrase "final medical determination" shall mean the outcome of the physician review mechanism used pursuant to the medical surveillance provisions of this section.

(3) Where a final medical determination results in any recommended special protective measures for an employee, or limitations on an employee's exposure to MDA, the employer shall implement and act consistent with the recommendation.

(ii) *Return of the employee to former job status.* (A) The employer shall return an employee to his or her former job status:

(1) When the employee no longer shows signs or symptoms of exposure to MDA, or upon the advice of the physician.

(2) When a subsequent final medical determination results in a medical finding, determination, or opinion that the employee no longer has a detected medical condition which places the employee at increased risk of material impairment to health from exposure to MDA.

(B) For the purposes of this section, the requirement that an employer return an employee to his or her former job status is not intended to expand upon or restrict any rights an employee has or would have had, absent temporary medical removal, to a specific job classification or position

under the terms of a collective bargaining agreement.

(iii) *Removal of other employee special protective measure or limitations.* The employer shall remove any limitations placed on an employee, or end any special protective measures provided to an employee, pursuant to a final medical determination, when a subsequent final medical determination indicates that the limitations or special protective measures are no longer necessary.

(iv) *Employer options pending a final medical determination.* Where the physician review mechanism used pursuant to the medical surveillance provisions of this section, has not yet resulted in a final medical determination with respect to an employee, the employer shall act as follows:

(A) *Removal.* The employer may remove the employee from exposure to MDA, provide special protective measures to the employee, or place limitations upon the employee, consistent with the medical findings, determinations, or recommendations of any of the physicians who have reviewed the employee's health status.

(B) *Return.* The employer may return the employee to his or her former job status, and end any special protective measures provided to the employee, consistent with the medical findings, determinations, or recommendations of any of the physicians who have reviewed the employee's health status, with two exceptions.

(1) If the initial removal, special protection, or limitation of the employee resulted from a final medical determination which differed from the findings, determinations, or recommendations of the initial physician; or

(2) If the employee has been on removal status for the preceding six months as a result of exposure to MDA, then the employer shall await a final medical determination.

(v) *Medical removal protection benefits—*(A) *Provisions of medical removal protection benefits.* The employer shall provide to an employee up to six (6) months of medical removal protection benefits on each occasion that an employee is removed from exposure to MDA or otherwise limited pursuant to this section.

477

(B) *Definition of medical removal protection benefits.* For the purposes of this section, the requirement that an employer provide medical removal protection benefits means that the employer shall maintain the earnings, seniority, and other employment rights and benefits of an employee as though the employee had not been removed from normal exposure to MDA or otherwise limited.

(C) *Follow-up medical surveillance during the period of employee removal or limitations.* During the period of time that an employee is removed from normal exposure to MDA or otherwise limited, the employer may condition the provision of medical removal protection benefits upon the employee's participation in follow-up medical surveillance made available pursuant to this section.

(D) *Workers' compensation claims.* If a removed employee files a claim for workers' compensation payments for a MDA-related disability, then the employer shall continue to provide medical removal protection benefits pending disposition of the claim. To the extent that an award is made to the employee for earnings lost during the period of removal, the employer's medical removal protection obligation shall be reduced by such amount. The employer shall receive no credit for workers' compensation payments received by the employee for treatment-related expenses.

(E) *Other credits.* The employer's obligation to provide medical removal protection benefits to a removed employee shall be reduced to the extent that the employee receives compensation for earnings lost during the period of removal either from a publicly or employer-funded compensation program, or receives income from non-MDA-related employment with any employer made possible by virtue of the employee's removal.

(F) *Employees who do not recover within the 6 months of removal.* The employer shall take the following measures with respect to any employee removed from exposure to MDA:

(1) The employer shall make available to the employee a medical examination pursuant to this section to obtain a final medical determination with respect to the employee;

(2) The employer shall assure that the final medical determination obtained indicates whether or not the employee may be returned to his or her former job status, and, if not, what steps should be taken to protect the employee's health;

(3) Where the final medical determination has not yet been obtained, or, once obtained indicates that the employee may not yet be returned to his or her former job status, the employer shall continue to provide medical removal protection benefits to the employee until either the employee is returned to former job status, or a final medical determination is made that the employee is incapable of ever safely returning to his or her former job status; and

(4) Where the employer acts pursuant to a final medical determination which permits the return of the employee to his or her former job status, despite what would otherwise be an abnormal liver function test, later questions concerning removing the employee again shall be decided by a final medical determination. The employer need not automatically remove such an employee pursuant to the MDA removal criteria provided by this section.

(vi) *Voluntary removal or restriction of an employee.* Where an employer, although not required by this section to do so, removes an employee from exposure to MDA or otherwise places limitations on an employee due to the effects of MDA exposure on the employee's medical condition, the employer shall provide medical removal protection benefits to the employee equal to that required by paragraph (m)(9)(v) of this section.

(n) *Recordkeeping—*(1) *Monitoring data for exempted employers.* (i) Where as a result of the initial monitoring the processing, use, or handling of products made from or containing MDA are exempted from other requirements of this section under paragraph (a)(2) of this section, the employer shall establish and maintain an accurate record of monitoring relied on in support of the exemption.

(ii) This record shall include at least the following information:

(A) The product qualifying for exemption;

(B) The source of the monitoring data (e.g., was monitoring performed by the employer or a private contractor);

(C) The testing protocol, results of testing, and/or analysis of the material for the release of MDA;

(D) A description of the operation exempted and how the data support the exemption (e.g., are the monitoring data representative of the conditions at the affected facility); and

(E) Other data relevant to the operations, materials, processing, or employee exposures covered by the exemption.

(iii) The employer shall maintain this record for the duration of the employer's reliance upon such objective data.

(2) *Objective data for exempted employers.* (i) Where the processing, use, or handling of products made from or containing MDA are exempted from other requirements of this section under paragraph (a) of this section, the employer shall establish and maintain an accurate record of objective data relied upon in support of the exemption.

(ii) This record shall include at least the following information:

(A) The product qualifying for exemption;

(B) The source of the objective data;

(C) The testing protocol, results of testing, and/or analysis of the material for the release of MDA;

(D) A description of the operation exempted and how the data support the exemption; and

(E) Other data relevant to the operations, materials, processing, or employee exposures covered by the exemption.

(iii) The employer shall maintain this record for the duration of the employer's reliance upon such objective data.

(3) *Exposure measurements.* (i) The employer shall establish and maintain an accurate record of all measurements required by paragraph (e) of this section, in accordance with 29 CFR 1910.1020.

(ii) This record shall include:

(A) The dates, number, duration, and results of each of the samples taken, including a description of the procedure used to determine representative employee exposures;

(B) Identification of the sampling and analytical methods used;

(C) A description of the type of respiratory protective devices worn, if any; and

(D) The name, social security number, job classification and exposure levels of the employee monitored and all other employees whose exposure the measurement is intended to represent.

(iii) The employer shall maintain this record for at least 30 years, in accordance with 29 CFR 1910.1020.

(4) *Medical surveillance.* (i) The employer shall establish and maintain an accurate record for each employee subject to medical surveillance required by paragraph (m) of this section, in accordance with 29 CFR 1910.1020.

(ii) This record shall include:

(A) The name, social security number and description of the duties of the employee;

(B) The employer's copy of the physician's written opinion on the initial, periodic, and any special examinations, including results of medical examination and all tests, opinions, and recommendations;

(C) Results of any airborne exposure monitoring done for that employee and the representative exposure levels supplied to the physician; and

(D) Any employee medical complaints related to exposure to MDA;

(iii) The employer shall keep, or assure that the examining physician keeps, the following medical records:

(A) A copy of this standard and its appendices, except that the employer may keep one copy of the standard and its appendices for all employees provided the employer references the standard and its appendices in the medical surveillance record of each employee;

(B) A copy of the information provided to the physician as required by any paragraphs in the regulatory text;

(C) A description of the laboratory procedures and a copy of any standards or guidelines used to interpret the test results or references to the information;

479

(D) A copy of the employee's medical and work history related to exposure to MDA; and

(iv) The employer shall maintain this record for at least the duration of employment plus 30 years, in accordance with 29 CFR 1910.1020.

(5) *Medical removals.* (i) The employer shall establish and maintain an accurate record for each employee removed from current exposure to MDA pursuant to paragraph (m) of this section.

(ii) Each record shall include:

(A) The name and social security number of the employee;

(B) The date of each occasion that the employee was removed from current exposure to MDA as well as the corresponding date on which the employee was returned to his or her former job status;

(C) A brief explanation of how each removal was or is being accomplished; and

(D) A statement with respect to each removal indicating the reason for the removal.

(iii) The employer shall maintain each medical removal record for at least the duration of an employee's employment plus 30 years.

(6) *Availability.* (i) The employer shall assure that records required to be maintained by this section shall be made available, upon request, to the Assistant Secretary and the Director for examination and copying.

(ii) Employee exposure monitoring records required by this section shall be provided upon request for examination and copying to employees, employee representatives, and the Assistant Secretary in accordance with 29 CFR 1910.1020 (a)–(e) and (g)–(i).

(iii) Employee medical records required by this section shall be provided upon request for examination and copying, to the subject employee, and to anyone having the specific written consent of the subject employee, and to the Assistant Secretary in accordance with 29 CFR 1910.1020.

(7) *Transfer of records.* The employer shall comply with the requirements involving transfer of records set forth in 29 CFR 1910.1020(h).

(o) *Observation of monitoring*—(1) *Employee observation.* The employer shall provide affected employees, or their designated representatives, an opportunity to observe the measuring or monitoring of employee exposure to MDA conducted pursuant to paragraph (e) of this section.

(2) *Observation procedures.* When observation of the measuring or monitoring of employee exposure to MDA requires entry into areas where the use of protective clothing and equipment or respirators is required, the employer shall provide the observer with personal protective clothing and equipment or respirators required to be worn by employees working in the area, assure the use of such clothing and equipment or respirators, and require the observer to comply with all other applicable safety and health procedures.

(p) [Reserved]

(q) *Appendices.* The information contained in Appendices A, B, C, and D of this section is not intended, by itself, to create any additional obligations not otherwise imposed by this standard nor detract from any existing obligation.

APPENDIX A TO § 1910.1050—SUBSTANCE DATA SHEET, FOR 4,4′-METHYLENEDIANILINE

I. Substance Identification

A. Substance: Methylenedianiline (MDA)

B. Permissible Exposure:

1. Airborne: Ten parts per billion parts of air (10 ppb), time-weighted average (TWA) for an 8-hour workday and an action level of five parts per billion parts of air (5 ppb).

2. Dermal: Eye contact and skin contact with MDA are not permitted.

C. Appearance and odor: White to tan solid; amine odor

II. Health Hazard Data

A. *Ways in which MDA affects your health.* MDA can affect your health if you inhale it, or if it comes in contact with your skin or eyes. MDA is also harmful if you happen to swallow it. Do not get MDA in eyes, on skin, or on clothing.

B. *Effects of overexposure.* 1. Short-term (acute) overexposure: Overexposure to MDA may produce fever, chills, loss of appetite, vomiting, jaundice. Contact may irritate skin, eyes and mucous membranes. Sensitization may occur.

2. *Long-term (chronic) exposure.* Repeated or prolonged exposure to MDA, even at relatively low concentrations, may cause cancer. In addition, damage to the liver, kidneys, blood, and spleen may occur with long term exposure.

3. *Reporting signs and symptoms.* You should inform your employer if you develop any signs or symptoms which you suspect are caused by exposure to MDA including yellow staining of the skin.

III. Protective Clothing and Equipment

A. Respirators. Respirators are required for those operations in which engineering controls or work-practice controls are not adequate or feasible to reduce exposure to the permissible limit. If respirators are worn, they must have a label issued by the National Institute for Occupational Safety and Health under the provisions of 42 CFR part 84 stating that the respirators have been approved for this purpose, and cartridges and canisters must be replaced in accordance with the requirements of 29 CFR 1910.134. If you experience difficulty breathing while wearing a respirator, you can request a positive-pressure respirator from your employer. You must be thoroughly trained to use the assigned respirator, and the training must be provided by your employer.

MDA does not have a detectable odor except at levels well above the permissible exposure limits. Do not depend on odor to warn you when a respirator canister is exhausted. If you can smell MDA while wearing a respirator, proceed immediately to fresh air. If you experience difficulty breathing while wearing a respirator, tell your employer.

B. *Protective Clothing.* You may be required to wear coveralls, aprons, gloves, face shields, or other appropriate protective clothing to prevent skin contact with MDA. Where protective clothing is required, your employer is required to provide clean garments to you, as necessary, to assure that the clothing protects you adequately. Replace or repair impervious clothing that has developed leaks.

MDA should never be allowed to remain on the skin. Clothing and shoes which are not impervious to MDA should not be allowed to become contaminated with MDA, and if they do, the clothing and shoes should be promptly removed and decontaminated. The clothing should be laundered to remove MDA or discarded. Once MDA penetrates shoes or other leather articles, they should not be worn again.

C. *Eye protection.* You must wear splashproof safety goggles in areas where liquid MDA may contact your eyes. Contact lenses should not be worn in areas where eye contact with MDA can occur. In addition, you must wear a face shield if your face could be splashed with MDA liquid.

IV. Emergency and First Aid Procedures

A. *Eye and face exposure.* If MDA is splashed into the eyes, wash the eyes for at least 15 minutes. See a doctor as soon as possible.

B. *Skin exposure.* If MDA is spilled on your clothing or skin, remove the contaminated clothing and wash the exposed skin with large amounts of soap and water immediately. Wash contaminated clothing before you wear it again.

C. *Breathing.* If you or any other person breathes in large amounts of MDA, get the exposed person to fresh air at once. Apply artificial respiration if breathing has stopped. Call for medical assistance or a doctor as soon as possible. Never enter any vessel or confined space where the MDA concentration might be high without proper safety equipment and at least one other person present who will stay outside. A life line should be used.

D. *Swallowing.* If MDA has been swallowed and the patient is conscious, do not induce vomiting. Call for medical assistance or a doctor immediately.

V. Medical Requirements

If you are exposed to MDA at a concentration at or above the action level for more than 30 days per year, or exposed to liquid mixtures more than 15 days per year, your employer is required to provide a medical examination, including a medical history and laboratory tests, within 60 days of the effective date of this standard and annually thereafter. These tests shall be provided without cost to you. In addition, if you are accidentally exposed to MDA (either by ingestion, inhalation, or skin/eye contact) under conditions known or suspected to constitute toxic exposure to MDA, your employer is required to make special examinations and tests available to you.

VI. Observation of Monitoring

Your employer is required to perform measurements that are representative of your exposure to MDA and you or your designated representative are entitled to observe the monitoring procedure. You are entitled to observe the steps taken in the measurement procedure and to record the results obtained. When the monitoring procedure is taking place in an area where respirators or personal protective clothing and equipment are required to be worn, you and your representative must also be provided with, and must wear, the protective clothing and equipment.

VII. Access to Records

You or your representative are entitled to see the records of measurements of your exposure to MDA upon written request to your employer. Your medical examination records can be furnished to your physician or designated representative upon request by you to your employer.

481

VIII. Precautions for Safe Use, Handling and Storage

A. *Material is combustible.* Avoid strong acids and their anhydrides. Avoid strong oxidants. Consult supervisor for disposal requirements.

B. *Emergency clean-up.* Wear self-contained breathing apparatus and fully clothe the body in the appropriate personal protective clothing and equipment.

APPENDIX B TO § 1910.1050—SUBSTANCE TECHNICAL GUIDELINES, MDA

I. Identification

A. Substance identification.
1. Synonyms: CAS No. 101–77–9. 4,4'-methylenedianiline; 4,4'-methylenebisaniline; methylenedianiline; dianilinomethane.
2. Formula: $C_{13} H_{14} N_2$

II. Physical Data

1. Appearance and Odor: White to tan solid; amine odor
2. Molecular Weight: 198.26
3. Boiling Point: 398–399 degrees C at 760 mm Hg
4. Melting Point: 88–93 degrees C (190–100 degrees F)
5. Vapor Pressure: 9 mmHg at 232 degrees C
6. Evaporation Rate (n-butyl acetate = 1): Negligible
7. Vapor Density (Air = 1): Not Applicable
8. Volatile Fraction by Weight: Negligible
9. Specific Gravity (Water = 1): Slight
10. Heat of Combustion: −8.40 kcal/g
11. Solubility in Water: Slightly soluble in cold water, very soluble in alcohol, benzene, ether, and many organic solvents.

III. Fire, Explosion, and Reactivity Hazard Data

1. Flash Point: 190 degrees C (374 degrees F) Setaflash closed cup
2. Flash Point: 226 degrees C (439 degrees F) Cleveland open cup
3. Extinguishing Media: Water spray; Dry Chemical; Carbon dioxide.
4. Special Fire Fighting Procedures: Wear self-contained breathing apparatus and protective clothing to prevent contact with skin and eyes.
5. Unusual Fire and Explosion Hazards: Fire or excessive heat may cause production of hazardous decomposition products.

IV. Reactivity Data

1. Stability: Stable
2. Incompatibility: Strong oxidizers
3. Hazardous Decomposition Products: As with any other organic material, combustion may produce carbon monoxide. Oxides of nitrogen may also be present.
4. Hazardous Polymerization: Will not occur.

V. Spill and Leak Procedures

1. Sweep material onto paper and place in fiber carton.
2. Package appropriately for safe feed to an incinerator or dissolve in compatible waste solvents prior to incineration.
3. Dispose of in an approved incinerator equipped with afterburner and scrubber or contract with licensed chemical waste disposal service.
4. Discharge treatment or disposal may be subject to federal, state, or local laws.
5. Wear appropriate personal protective equipment.

VI. Special Storage and Handling Precautions

A. High exposure to MDA can occur when transferring the substance from one container to another. Such operations should be well ventilated and good work practices must be established to avoid spills.
B. Pure MDA is a solid with a low vapor pressure. Grinding or heating operations increase the potential for exposure.
C. Store away from oxidizing materials.
D. Employers shall advise employees of all areas and operations where exposure to MDA could occur.

VII. Housekeeping and Hygiene Facilities

A. The workplace should be kept clean, orderly, and in a sanitary condition.
The employer should institute a leak and spill detection program for operations involving MDA in order to detect sources of fugitive MDA emissions.
B. Adequate washing facilities with hot and cold water are to be provided and maintained in a sanitary condition. Suitable cleansing agents should also be provided to assure the effective removal of MDA from the skin.

VIII. Common Operations

Common operations in which exposure to MDA is likely to occur include the following: Manufacture of MDA; Manufacture of Methylene diisocyanate; Curing agent for epoxy resin structures; Wire coating operations; and filament winding.

APPENDIX C TO § 1910.1050—MEDICAL SURVEILLANCE GUIDELINES FOR MDA

I. Route of Entry

Inhalation; skin absorption; ingestion. MDA can be inhaled, absorbed through the skin, or ingested.

II. Toxicology

MDA is a suspect carcinogen in humans. There are several reports of liver disease in humans and animals resulting from acute exposure to MDA. A well documented case of an acute cardiomyopathy secondary to exposure to MDA is on record. Numerous human cases of hepatitis secondary to MDA are known. Upon direct contact MDA may also cause damage to the eyes. Dermatitis and skin sensitization have been observed. Almost all forms of acute environmental hepatic injury in humans involve the hepatic parenchyma and produce hepatocellular jaundice. This agent produces intrahepatic cholestasis. The clinical picture consists of cholestatic jaundice, preceded or accompanied by abdominal pain, fever, and chills. Onset in about 60% of all observed cases is abrupt with severe abdominal pain. In about 30% of observed cases, the illness presented and evolved more slowly and less dramatically, with only slight abdominal pain. In about 10% of the cases only jaundice was evident. The cholestatic nature of the jaundice is evident in the prominence of itching, the histologic predominance of bile stasis, and portal inflammatory infiltration, accompanied by only slight parenchymal injury in most cases, and by the moderately elevated transaminase values. Acute, high doses, however, have been known to cause hepatocellular damage resulting in elevated SGPT, SGOT, alkaline phosphatase and bilirubin.

Absorption through the skin is rapid. MDA is metabolized and excreted over a 48-hour period. Direct contact may be irritating to the skin, causing dermatitis. Also MDA which is deposited on the skin is not thoroughly removed through washing.

MDA may cause bladder cancer in humans. Animal data supporting this assumption is not available nor is conclusive human data. However, human data collected on workers at a helicopter manufacturing facility where MDA is used suggests a higher incidence of bladder cancer among exposed workers.

III. Signs and Symptoms

Skin may become yellow from contact with MDA.

Repeated or prolonged contact with MDA may result in recurring dermatitis (red-itchy, cracked skin) and eye irritation. Inhalation, ingestion or absorption through the skin at high concentrations may result in hepatitis, causing symptoms such as fever and chills, nausea and vomiting, dark urine, anorexia, rash, right upper quadrant pain and jaundice. Corneal burns may occur when MDA is splashed in the eyes.

IV. Treatment of Acute Toxic Effects/Emergency Situation

If MDA gets into the eyes, immediately wash eyes with large amounts of water. If MDA is splashed on the skin, immediately wash contaminated skin with mild soap or detergent. Employee should be removed from exposure and given proper medical treatment. Medical tests required under the emergency section of the medical surveillance section (M)(4) must be conducted.

If the chemical is swallowed do not induce vomiting but remove by gastric lavage.

APPENDIX D TO §1910.1050—SAMPLING AND ANALYTICAL METHODS FOR MDA MONITORING AND MEASUREMENT PROCEDURES

Measurements taken for the purpose of determining employee exposure to MDA are best taken so that the representative average 8-hour exposure may be determined from a single 8-hour sample or two (2) 4-hour samples. Short-time interval samples (or grab samples) may also be used to determine average exposure level if a minimum of five measurements are taken in a random manner over the 8-hour work shift. Random sampling means that any portion of the work shift has the same chance of being sampled as any other. The arithmetic average of all such random samples taken on one work shift is an estimate of an employee's average level of exposure for that work shift. Air samples should be taken in the employee's breathing zone (air that would most nearly represent that inhaled by the employee).

There are a number of methods available for monitoring employee exposures to MDA. The method OSHA currently uses is included below.

The employer, however, has the obligation of selecting any monitoring method which meets the accuracy and precision requirements of the standard under his unique field conditions. The standard requires that the method of monitoring must have an accuracy, to a 95 percent confidence level, of not less than plus or minus 25 percent for the select PEL.

OSHA Methodology

Sampling Procedure

Apparatus

Samples are collected by use of a personal sampling pump that can be calibrated within ±5% of the recommended flow rate with the sampling filter in line.

Samples are collected on 37 mm Gelman type A/E glass fiber filters treated with sulfuric acid. The filters are prepared by soaking each filter with 0.5 mL of 0.26N H_2 SO_4. (0.26 N H_2 SO_4 can be prepared by diluting 1.5 mL of 36N H_2 SO_4 to 200 mL with deionized water.) The filters are dried in an oven at 100 degrees C for one hour and then assembled into two-piece 37 mm polystyrene cassettes with backup pads. The cassettes are sealed with shrink bands and the ends are plugged with plastic plugs.

After sampling, the filters are carefully removed from the cassettes and individually transferred to small vials containing approximately 2 mL deionized water. The vials must be tightly sealed. The water can be added before or after the filters are transferred. The vials must be sealable and capable of holding at least 7 mL of liquid. Small glass scintillation vials with caps containing Teflon liners are recommended.

Reagents

Deionized water is needed for addition to the vials.

Sampling Technique

Immediately before sampling, remove the plastic plugs from the filter cassettes.

Attach the cassette to the sampling pump with flexible tubing and place the cassette in the employee's breathing zone.

After sampling, seal the cassettes with plastic plugs until the filters are transferred to the vials containing deionized water.

At some convenient time within 10 hours of sampling, transfer the sample filters to vials.

Seal the small vials lengthwise.

Submit at least one blank filter with each sample set. Blanks should be handled in the same manner as samples, but no air is drawn through them.

Record sample volumes (in L of air) for each sample, along with any potential interferences.

Retention Efficiency

A retention efficiency study was performed by drawing 100 L of air (80% relative humidity) at 1 L/min through sample filters that had been spiked with 0.814 µg MDA. Instead of using backup pads, blank acid-treated filters were used as backups in each cassette. Upon analysis, the top filters were found to have an average of 91.8% of the spiked amount. There was no MDA found on the bottom filters, so the amount lost was probably due to the slight instability of the MDA salt.

Extraction Efficiency

The average extraction efficiency for six filters spiked at the target concentration is 99.6%.

The stability of extracted and derivatized samples was verified by reanalyzing the above six samples the next day using fresh standards. The average extraction efficiency for the reanalyzed samples is 98.7%.

Recommended Air Volume and Sampling Rate

The recommended air volume is 100 L.

The recommended sampling rate is 1 L/min.

Interferences (Sampling)

MDI appears to be a positive interference. It was found that when MDI was spiked onto an acid-treated filter, the MDI converted to MDA after air was drawn through it.

Suspected interferences should be reported to the laboratory with submitted samples.

Safety Precautions (Sampling)

Attach the sampling equipment to the employees so that it will not interfere with work performance or safety.

Follow all safety procedures that apply to the work area being sampled.

Analytical Procedure

Apparatus: The following are required for analysis.

A GC equipped with an electron capture detector. For this evaluation a Tracor 222 Gas Chromatograph equipped with a Nickel 63 High Temperature Electron Capture Detector and a Linearizer was used.

A GC column capable of separating the MDA derivative from the solvent and interferences. A 6 ft × 2 mm ID glass column packed with 3% OV–101 coated on 100/120 Gas Chrom Q was used in this evaluation.

A electronic integrator or some other suitable means of measuring peak areas or heights.

Small resealable vials with Teflon-lined caps capable of holding 4 mL.

A dispenser or pipet for toluene capable of delivering 2.0 mL.

Pipets (or repipets with plastic or Teflon tips) capable of delivering 1 mL for the sodium hydroxide and buffer solutions.

A repipet capable of delivering 25 µL HFAA.

Syringes for preparation of standards and injection of standards and samples into a GC.

Volumetric flasks and pipets to dilute the pure MDA in preparation of standards.

Disposable pipets to transfer the toluene layers after the samples are extracted.

Reagents

0.5 NaOH prepared from reagent grade NaOH.

Toluene, pesticide grade. Burdick and Jackson distilled in glass toluene was used.

Heptafluorobutyric acid anhydride (HFAA). HFAA from Pierce Chemical Company was used.

pH 7.0 phosphate buffer, prepared from 136 g potassium dihydrogen phosphate and 1 L deionized water. The pH is adjusted to 7.0 with saturated sodium hydroxide solution.

4,4′ -Methylenedianiline (MDA), reagent grade.

Standard Preparation

Concentrated stock standards are prepared by diluting pure MDA with toluene. Analytical standards are prepared by injecting uL amounts of diluted stock standards into vials that contain 2.0 mL toluene.

25 uL HFAA are added to each vial and the vials are capped and shaken for 10 seconds. After 10 min, 1 mL of buffer is added to each vial.

The vials are recapped and shaken for 10 seconds.

After allowing the layers to separate, aliquots of the toluene (upper) layers are removed with a syringe and analyzed by GC.

Analytical standard concentrations should bracket sample concentrations. Thus, if samples fall out of the range of prepared standards, additional standards must be prepared to ascertain detector response.

Sample Preparation

The sample filters are received in vials containing deionized water.

1 mL of 0.5N NaOH and 2.0 mL toluene are added to each vial.

The vials are recapped and shaken for 10 min.

After allowing the layers to separate, approximately 1 mL aliquots of the toluene (upper) layers are transferred to separate vials with clean disposable pipets.

The toluene layers are treated and analyzed.

Analysis

GC conditions

Zone temperatures:
Column—220 degrees C
Injector—235 degrees C
Detector—335 degrees C
Gas flows, Ar/CH$_4$ Column—28 mL/min
(95/5)   Purge—40 mL/min
Injection volume: 5.0 uL
Column: 6 ft × ⅛ in ID glass, 3% OV–101 on 100/120 Gas Chrom Q
Retention time of MDA derivative: 3.5 min

Chromatogram

Peak areas or heights are measured by an integrator or other suitable means.

A calibration curve is constructed by plotting response (peak areas or heights) of standard injections versus ug of MDA per sample. Sample concentrations must be bracketed by standards.

Interferences (Analytical)

Any compound that gives an electron capture detector response and has the same general retention time as the HFAA derivative of MDA is a potential interference. Suspected interferences reported to the laboratory with submitted samples by the industrial hygienist must be considered before samples are derivatized.

GC parameters may be changed to possibly circumvent interferences.

Retention time on a single column is not considered proof of chemical identity.

Analyte identity should be confirmed by GC/MS if possible.

Calculations

The analyte concentration for samples is obtained from the calibration curve in terms of ug MDA per sample. The extraction efficiency is 100%. If any MDA is found on the blank, that amount is subtracted from the sample amounts. The air concentrations are calculated using the following formulae.

$\mu g/m^3$ = (µg MDA per sample) (1000)/(L of air sampled)

ppb = ($\mu g/m^3$) (24.46) / (198.3) = ($\mu g/m^3$) (0.1233) where 24.46 is the molar volume at 25 degrees C and 760 mm Hg

Safety Precautions (Analytical)

Avoid skin contact and inhalation of all chemicals.

Restrict the use of all chemicals to a fume hood if possible.

Wear safety glasses and a lab coat at all times while in the lab area.

[57 FR 35666, Aug. 10, 1992, as amended at 57 FR 49649, Nov. 3, 1992; 61 FR 5508, Feb. 13, 1996; 63 FR 1293, Jan. 8, 1998; 67 FR 67965, Nov. 7, 2002; 71 FR 16672, 16673, Apr. 3, 2006; 71 FR 50190, Aug. 24, 2006; 73 FR 75586, Dec. 12, 2008; 76 FR 33609, June 8, 2011; 77 FR 17785, Mar. 26, 2012]

§1910.1051 1,3-Butadiene.

(a) *Scope and application.* (1) This section applies to all occupational exposures to 1,3-Butadiene (BD), Chemical Abstracts Service Registry No. 106–99–0, except as provided in paragraph (a)(2) of this section.

(2)(i) Except for the recordkeeping provisions in paragraph (m)(1) of this section, this section does not apply to the processing, use, or handling of products containing BD or to other work operations and streams in which BD is present where objective data are reasonably relied upon that demonstrate the work operation or the product or the group of products or operations to which it belongs may not reasonably be foreseen to release BD in airborne concentrations at or above the action level or in excess of the STEL under the expected conditions of processing, use, or handling that will cause the greatest possible release or in any plausible accident.

(ii) This section also does not apply to work operations, products or streams where the only exposure to BD is from liquid mixtures containing 0.1% or less of BD by volume or the vapors

485

released from such liquids, unless objective data become available that show that airborne concentrations generated by such mixtures can exceed the action level or STEL under reasonably predictable conditions of processing, use or handling that will cause the greatest possible release.

(iii) Except for labeling requirements and requirements for emergency response, this section does not apply to the storage, transportation, distribution or sale of BD or liquid mixtures in intact containers or in transportation pipelines sealed in such a manner as to fully contain BD vapors or liquid.

(3) Where products or processes containing BD are exempted under paragraph (a)(2) of this section, the employer shall maintain records of the objective data supporting that exemption and the basis for the employer's reliance on the data, as provided in paragraph (m)(1) of this section.

(b) *Definitions:* For the purpose of this section, the following definitions shall apply:

Action level means a concentration of airborne BD of 0.5 ppm calculated as an eight (8)-hour time-weighted average.

Assistant Secretary means the Assistant Secretary of Labor for Occupational Safety and Health, U.S. Department of Labor, or designee.

Authorized person means any person specifically designated by the employer, whose duties require entrance into a regulated area, or a person entering such an area as a designated representative of employees to exercise the right to observe monitoring and measuring procedures under paragraph (d)(8) of this section, or a person designated under the Act or regulations issued under the Act to enter a regulated area.

1,3–Butadiene means an organic compound with chemical formula $CH_2 = CH\text{-}CH = CH_2$ that has a molecular weight of approximately 54.15 gm/mole.

Business day means any Monday through Friday, except those days designated as federal, state, local or company specific holidays.

Complete Blood Count (CBC) means laboratory tests performed on whole blood specimens and includes the following: White blood cell count (WBC), hematocrit (Hct), red blood cell count (RBC), hemoglobin (Hgb), differential count of white blood cells, red blood cell morphology, red blood cell indices, and platelet count.

Day means any part of a calendar day.

Director means the Director of the National Institute for Occupational Safety and Health (NIOSH), U.S. Department of Health and Human Services, or designee.

Emergency situation means any occurrence such as, but not limited to, equipment failure, rupture of containers, or failure of control equipment that may or does result in an uncontrolled significant release of BD.

Employee exposure means exposure of a worker to airborne concentrations of BD which would occur if the employee were not using respiratory protective equipment.

Objective data means monitoring data, or mathematical modelling or calculations based on composition, chemical and physical properties of a material, stream or product.

Permissible Exposure Limits, PELs means either the 8 hour Time Weighted Average (8-hr TWA) exposure or the Short-Term Exposure Limit (STEL).

Physician or other licensed health care professional is an individual whose legally permitted scope of practice (*i.e.,* license, registration, or certification) allows him or her to independently provide or be delegated the responsibility to provide one or more of the specific health care services required by paragraph (k) of this section.

Regulated area means any area where airborne concentrations of BD exceed or can reasonably be expected to exceed the 8-hour time weighted average (8-hr TWA) exposure of 1 ppm or the short-term exposure limit (STEL) of 5 ppm for 15 minutes.

This section means this 1,3-butadiene standard.

(c) *Permissible exposure limits (PELs)—* (1) *Time-weighted average (TWA) limit.* The employer shall ensure that no employee is exposed to an airborne concentration of BD in excess of one (1) part BD per million parts of air (ppm) measured as an eight (8)-hour time-weighted average.

(2) *Short-term exposure limit (STEL).* The employer shall ensure that no employee is exposed to an airborne concentration of BD in excess of five parts of BD per million parts of air (5 ppm) as determined over a sampling period of fifteen (15) minutes.

(d) *Exposure monitoring—*(1) *General.* (i) Determinations of employee exposure shall be made from breathing zone air samples that are representative of the 8-hour TWA and 15-minute short-term exposures of each employee.

(ii) Representative 8-hour TWA employee exposure shall be determined on the basis of one or more samples representing full-shift exposure for each shift and for each job classification in each work area.

(iii) Representative 15-minute short-term employee exposures shall be determined on the basis of one or more samples representing 15-minute exposures associated with operations that are most likely to produce exposures above the STEL for each shift and for each job classification in each work area.

(iv) Except for the initial monitoring required under paragraph (d)(2) of this section, where the employer can document that exposure levels are equivalent for similar operations on different work shifts, the employer need only determine representative employee exposure for that operation from the shift during which the highest exposure is expected.

(2) *Initial monitoring.* (i) Each employer who has a workplace or work operation covered by this section, shall perform initial monitoring to determine accurately the airborne concentrations of BD to which employees may be exposed, or shall rely on objective data pursuant to paragraph (a)(2)(i) of this section to fulfill this requirement. The initial monitoring required under this paragraph shall be completed within 60 days of the introduction of BD into the workplace.

(ii) Where the employer has monitored within two years prior to the effective date of this section and the monitoring satisfies all other requirements of this section, the employer may rely on such earlier monitoring results to satisfy the requirements of paragraph (d)(2)(i) of this section, pro-

vided that the conditions under which the initial monitoring was conducted have not changed in a manner that may result in new or additional exposures.

(3) *Periodic monitoring and its frequency.* (i) If the initial monitoring required by paragraph (d)(2) of this section reveals employee exposure to be at or above the action level but at or below both the 8-hour TWA limit and the STEL, the employer shall repeat the representative monitoring required by paragraph (d)(1) of this section every twelve months.

(ii) If the initial monitoring required by paragraph (d)(2) of this section reveals employee exposure to be above the 8-hour TWA limit, the employer shall repeat the representative monitoring required by paragraph (d)(1)(ii) of this section at least every three months until the employer has collected two samples per quarter (each at least 7 days apart) within a two-year period, after which such monitoring must occur at least every six months.

(iii) If the initial monitoring required by paragraph (d)(2) of this section reveals employee exposure to be above the STEL, the employer shall repeat the representative monitoring required by paragraph (d)(1)(iii) of this section at least every three months until the employer has collected two samples per quarter (each at least 7 days apart) within a two-year period, after which such monitoring must occur at least every six months.

(iv) The employer may alter the monitoring schedule from every six months to annually for any required representative monitoring for which two consecutive measurements taken at least 7 days apart indicate that employee exposure has decreased to or below the 8-hour TWA, but is at or above the action level.

(4) *Termination of monitoring.* (i) If the initial monitoring required by paragraph (d)(2) of this section reveals employee exposure to be below the action level and at or below the STEL, the employer may discontinue the monitoring for employees whose exposures are represented by the initial monitoring.

487

(ii) If the periodic monitoring required by paragraph (d)(3) of this section reveals that employee exposures, as indicated by at least two consecutive measurements taken at least 7 days apart, are below the action level and at or below the STEL, the employer may discontinue the monitoring for those employees who are represented by such monitoring.

(5) *Additional monitoring.* (i) The employer shall institute the exposure monitoring required under paragraph (d) of this section whenever there has been a change in the production, process, control equipment, personnel or work practices that may result in new or additional exposures to BD or when the employer has any reason to suspect that a change may result in new or additional exposures.

(ii) Whenever spills, leaks, ruptures or other breakdowns occur that may lead to employee exposure above the 8-hr TWA limit or above the STEL, the employer shall monitor [using leak source, such as direct reading instruments, area or personal monitoring], after the cleanup of the spill or repair of the leak, rupture or other breakdown, to ensure that exposures have returned to the level that existed prior to the incident.

(6) *Accuracy of monitoring.* Monitoring shall be accurate, at a confidence level of 95 percent, to within plus or minus 25 percent for airborne concentrations of BD at or above the 1 ppm TWA limit and to within plus or minus 35 percent for airborne concentrations of BD at or above the action level of 0.5 ppm and below the 1 ppm TWA limit.

(7) *Employee notification of monitoring results.* (i) The employer must, within 15 working days after the receipt of the results of any monitoring performed under this section, notify each affected employee of these results either individually in writing or by posting the results in an appropriate location that is accessible to employees.

(ii) The employer shall, within 15 business days after receipt of any monitoring performed under this section indicating the 8-hour TWA or STEL has been exceeded, provide the affected employees, in writing, with information on the corrective action being taken by the employer to reduce employee exposure to or below the 8-hour TWA or STEL and the schedule for completion of this action.

(8) *Observation of monitoring*—(i) *Employee observation.* The employer shall provide affected employees or their designated representatives an opportunity to observe any monitoring of employee exposure to BD conducted in accordance with paragraph (d) of this section.

(ii) *Observation procedures.* When observation of the monitoring of employee exposure to BD requires entry into an area where the use of protective clothing or equipment is required, the employer shall provide the observer at no cost with protective clothing and equipment, and shall ensure that the observer uses this equipment and complies with all other applicable safety and health procedures.

(e) *Regulated areas.* (1) The employer shall establish a regulated area wherever occupational exposures to airborne concentrations of BD exceed or can reasonably be expected to exceed the permissible exposure limits, either the 8-hr TWA or the STEL.

(2) Access to regulated areas shall be limited to authorized persons.

(3) Regulated areas shall be demarcated from the rest of the workplace in any manner that minimizes the number of employees exposed to BD within the regulated area.

(4) An employer at a multi-employer worksite who establishes a regulated area shall communicate the access restrictions and locations of these areas to other employers with work operations at that worksite whose employees may have access to these areas.

(f) *Methods of compliance*—(1) *Engineering controls and work practices.* (i) The employer shall institute engineering controls and work practices to reduce and maintain employee exposure to or below the PELs, except to the extent that the employer can establish that these controls are not feasible or where paragraph (h)(1)(i) of this section applies.

(ii) Wherever the feasible engineering controls and work practices which can be instituted are not sufficient to reduce employee exposure to or below the 8-hour TWA or STEL, the employer shall use them to reduce employee exposure to the lowest levels achievable by these controls and shall supplement them by the use of respiratory protection that complies with the requirements of paragraph (h) of this section.

(2) *Compliance plan.* (i) Where any exposures are over the PELs, the employer shall establish and implement a written plan to reduce employee exposure to or below the PELs primarily by means of engineering and work practice controls, as required by paragraph (f)(1) of this section, and by the use of respiratory protection where required or permitted under this section. No compliance plan is required if all exposures are under the PELs.

(ii) The written compliance plan shall include a schedule for the development and implementation of the engineering controls and work practice controls including periodic leak detection surveys.

(iii) Copies of the compliance plan required in paragraph (f)(2) of this section shall be furnished upon request for examination and copying to the Assistant Secretary, the Director, affected employees and designated employee representatives. Such plans shall be reviewed at least every 12 months, and shall be updated as necessary to reflect significant changes in the status of the employer's compliance program.

(iv) The employer shall not implement a schedule of employee rotation as a means of compliance with the PELs.

(g) *Exposure Goal Program.* (1) For those operations and job classifications where employee exposures are greater than the action level, in addition to compliance with the PELs, the employer shall have an exposure goal program that is intended to limit employee exposures to below the action level during normal operations.

(2) Written plans for the exposure goal program shall be furnished upon request for examination and copying to the Assistant Secretary, the Director, affected employees and designated employee representatives.

(3) Such plans shall be updated as necessary to reflect significant changes in the status of the exposure goal program.

(4) Respirator use is not required in the exposure goal program.

(5) The exposure goal program shall include the following items unless the employer can demonstrate that the item is not feasible, will have no significant effect in reducing employee exposures, or is not necessary to achieve exposures below the action level:

(i) A leak prevention, detection, and repair program.

(ii) A program for maintaining the effectiveness of local exhaust ventilation systems.

(iii) The use of pump exposure control technology such as, but not limited to, mechanical double-sealed or seal-less pumps.

(iv) Gauging devices designed to limit employee exposure, such as magnetic gauges on rail cars.

(v) Unloading devices designed to limit employee exposure, such as a vapor return system.

(vi) A program to maintain BD concentration below the action level in control rooms by use of engineering controls.

(h) *Respiratory protection*—(1) *General.* For employees who use respirators required by this section, the employer must provide each employee an appropriate respirator that complies with the requirements of this paragraph. Respirators must be used during:

(i) Periods necessary to install or implement feasible engineering and work-practice controls.

(ii) Non-routine work operations that are performed infrequently and for which employee exposures are limited in duration.

(iii) Work operations for which feasible engineering and work-practice controls are not yet sufficient to reduce employee exposures to or below the PELs.

(iv) Emergencies.

(2) *Respirator program.* (i) The employer must implement a respiratory protection program in accordance with §1910.134(b) through (d) (except (d)(1)(iii), (d)(3)(iii)(B)(1), and (2)), and (f) through (m), which covers each employee required by this section to use a respirator.

(ii) If air-purifying respirators are used, the employer must replace the air-purifying filter elements according to the replacement schedule set for the class of respirators listed in Table 1 of this section, and at the beginning of each work shift.

(iii) Instead of using the replacement schedule listed in Table 1 of this section, the employer may replace cartridges or canisters at 90% of their expiration service life, provided the employer:

(A) Demonstrates that employees will be adequately protected by this procedure.

(B) Uses BD breakthrough data for this purpose that have been derived from tests conducted under worst-case conditions of humidity, temperature, and air-flow rate through the filter element, and the employer also describes the data supporting the cartridge-or canister-change schedule, as well as the basis for using the data in the employer's respirator program.

(iv) A label must be attached to each filter element to indicate the date and time it is first installed on the respirator.

(v) If NIOSH approves an end-of-service-life indicator (ESLI) for an air-purifying filter element, the element may be used until the ESLI shows no further useful service life or until the element is replaced at the beginning of the next work shift, whichever occurs first.

(vi) Regardless of the air-purifying element used, if an employee detects the odor of BD, the employer must replace the air-purifying element immediately.

(3) *Respirator selection.* (i) The employer must select appropriate respirators from Table 1 of this section.

TABLE 1—MINIMUM REQUIREMENTS FOR RESPIRATORY PROTECTION FOR AIRBORNE BD

Concentration of airborne BD (ppm) or condition of use	Minimum required respirator
Less than or equal to 5 ppm (5 times PEL)	(a) Air-purifying half mask or full facepiece respirator equipped with approved BD or organic vapor cartridges or canisters. Cartridges or canisters shall be replaced every 4 hours.
Less than or equal to 10 ppm (10 times PEL).	(a) Air-purifying half mask or full facepiece respirator equipped with approved BD or organic vapor cartridges or canisters. Cartridges or canisters shall be replaced every 3 hours.
Less than or equal to 25 ppm (25 times PEL).	(a) Air-purifying full facepiece respirator equipped with approved BD or organic vapor cartridges or canisters. Cartridges or canisters shall be replaced every 2 hours.
	(b) Any powered air-purifying respirator equipped with approved BD or organic vapor cartridges. PAPR cartridges shall be replaced every 2 hours.
	(c) Continuous flow supplied air respirator equipped with a hood or helmet.
Less than or equal to 50 ppm (50 times PEL).	(a) Air-purifying full facepiece respirator equipped with approved BD or organic vapor cartridges or canisters. Cartridges or canisters shall be replaced every (1) hour.
	(b) Powered air-purifying respirator equipped with a tight-fitting facepiece and an approved BD or organic vapor cartridges. PAPR cartridges shall be replaced every (1) hour.
Less than or equal to 1,000 ppm (1,000 times PEL).	(a) Supplied air respirator equipped with a half mask of full facepiece and operated in a pressure demand or other positive pressure mode.
Greater than 1000 ppm unknown concentration, or firefighting.	(a) Self-contained breathing apparatus equipped with a full facepiece and operated in a pressure demand or other positive pressure mode.
	(b) Any supplied air respirator equipped with a full facepiece and operated in a pressure demand or other positive pressure mode in combination with an auxiliary self-contained breathing apparatus operated in a pressure demand or other positive pressure mode.
Escape from IDLH conditions	(a) Any positive pressure self-contained breathing apparatus with an appropriate service life.
	(b) A air-purifying full facepiece respirator equipped with a front or back mounted BD or organic vapor canister.

NOTES: Respirators approved for use in higher concentrations are permitted to be used in lower concentrations. Full facepiece is required when eye irritation is anticipated.

(ii) Air-purifying respirators must have filter elements approved by NIOSH for organic vapors or BD.

(iii) When an employee whose job requires the use of a respirator cannot use a negative-pressure respirator, the employer must provide the employee with a respirator that has less breathing resistance than the negative-pressure respirator, such as a powered air-purifying respirator or supplied-air respirator, when the employee is able to use it and if it provides the employee adequate protection.

(i) *Protective clothing and equipment.* Where appropriate to prevent eye contact and limit dermal exposure to BD, the employer shall provide protective clothing and equipment at no cost to the employee and shall ensure its use. Eye and face protection shall meet the requirements of 29 CFR 1910.133.

(j) *Emergency situations. Written plan.* A written plan for emergency situations shall be developed, or an existing plan shall be modified, to contain the applicable elements specified in 29 CFR 1910.38 and 29 CFR 1910.39, "Emergency action plans" and "Fire prevention plans," respectively, and in 29 CFR 1910.120, "Hazardous Waste Operations and Emergency Response," for each workplace where there is the possibility of an emergency.

(k) *Medical screening and surveillance*—(1) *Employees covered.* The employer shall institute a medical screening and surveillance program as specified in this paragraph for:

(i) Each employee with exposure to BD at concentrations at or above the action level on 30 or more days or for employees who have or may have exposure to BD at or above the PELs on 10 or more days a year;

(ii) Employers (including successor owners) shall continue to provide medical screening and surveillance for employees, even after transfer to a non-BD exposed job and regardless of when the employee is transferred, whose work histories suggest exposure to BD:

(A) At or above the PELs on 30 or more days a year for 10 or more years;

(B) At or above the action level on 60 or more days a year for 10 or more years; or

(C) Above 10 ppm on 30 or more days in any past year; and

(iii) Each employee exposed to BD following an emergency situation.

(2) *Program administration.* (i) The employer shall ensure that the health questionnaire, physical examination and medical procedures are provided without cost to the employee, without loss of pay, and at a reasonable time and place.

(ii) Physical examinations, health questionnaires, and medical procedures shall be performed or administered by a physician or other licensed health care professional.

(iii) Laboratory tests shall be conducted by an accredited laboratory.

(3) *Frequency of medical screening activities.* The employer shall make medical screening available on the following schedule:

(i) For each employee covered under paragraphs (j)(1) (i)–(ii) of this section, a health questionnaire and complete blood count with differential and platelet count (CBC) every year, and a physical examination as specified below:

(A) An initial physical examination that meets the requirements of this rule, if twelve months or more have elapsed since the last physical examination conducted as part of a medical screening program for BD exposure;

(B) Before assumption of duties by the employee in a job with BD exposure;

(C) Every 3 years after the initial physical examination;

(D) At the discretion of the physician or other licensed health care professional reviewing the annual health questionnaire and CBC;

(E) At the time of employee reassignment to an area where exposure to BD is below the action level, if the employee's past exposure history does not meet the criteria of paragraph (j)(1)(ii) of this section for continued coverage in the screening and surveillance program, and if twelve months or more have elapsed since the last physical examination; and

(F) At termination of employment if twelve months or more have elapsed since the last physical examination.

(ii) Following an emergency situation, medical screening shall be conducted as quickly as possible, but not later than 48 hours after the exposure.

(iii) For each employee who must wear a respirator, physical ability to perform the work and use the respirator must be determined as required by 29 CFR 1910.134.

(4) *Content of medical screening.* (i) Medical screening for employees covered by paragraphs (j)(1) (i)–(ii) of this section shall include:

491

(A) A baseline health questionnaire that includes a comprehensive occupational and health history and is updated annually. Particular emphasis shall be placed on the hematopoietic and reticuloendothelial systems, including exposure to chemicals, in addition to BD, that may have an adverse effect on these systems, the presence of signs and symptoms that might be related to disorders of these systems, and any other information determined by the examining physician or other licensed health care professional to be necessary to evaluate whether the employee is at increased risk of material impairment of health from BD exposure. Health questionnaires shall consist of the sample forms in appendix C to this section, or be equivalent to those samples;

(B) A complete physical examination, with special emphasis on the liver, spleen, lymph nodes, and skin;

(C) A CBC; and

(D) Any other test which the examining physician or other licensed health care professional deems necessary to evaluate whether the employee may be at increased risk from exposure to BD.

(ii) Medical screening for employees exposed to BD in an emergency situation shall focus on the acute effects of BD exposure and at a minimum include: A CBC within 48 hours of the exposure and then monthly for three months; and a physical examination if the employee reports irritation of the eyes, nose throat, lungs, or skin, blurred vision, coughing, drowsiness, nausea, or headache. Continued employee participation in the medical screening and surveillance program, beyond these minimum requirements, shall be at the discretion of the physician or other licensed health care professional.

(5) *Additional medical evaluations and referrals.* (i) Where the results of medical screening indicate abnormalities of the hematopoietic or reticuloendothelial systems, for which a non-occupational cause is not readily apparent, the examining physician or other licensed health care professional shall refer the employee to an appropriate specialist for further evaluation and shall make available to the specialist the results of the medical screening.

(ii) The specialist to whom the employee is referred under this paragraph shall determine the appropriate content for the medical evaluation, e.g., examinations, diagnostic tests and procedures, etc.

(6) *Information provided to the physician or other licensed health care professional.* The employer shall provide the following information to the examining physician or other licensed health care professional involved in the evaluation:

(i) A copy of this section including its appendices;

(ii) A description of the affected employee's duties as they relate to the employee's BD exposure;

(iii) The employee's actual or representative BD exposure level during employment tenure, including exposure incurred in an emergency situation;

(iv) A description of pertinent personal protective equipment used or to be used; and

(v) Information, when available, from previous employment-related medical evaluations of the affected employee which is not otherwise available to the physician or other licensed health care professional or the specialist.

(7) *The written medical opinion.* (i) For each medical evaluation required by this section, the employer shall ensure that the physician or other licensed health care professional produces a written opinion and provides a copy to the employer and the employee within 15 business days of the evaluation. The written opinion shall be limited to the following information:

(A) The occupationally pertinent results of the medical evaluation;

(B) A medical opinion concerning whether the employee has any detected medical conditions which would place the employee's health at increased risk of material impairment from exposure to BD;

(C) Any recommended limitations upon the employee's exposure to BD; and

(D) A statement that the employee has been informed of the results of the medical evaluation and any medical conditions resulting from BD exposure that require further explanation or treatment.

(ii) The written medical opinion provided to the employer shall not reveal specific records, findings, and diagnoses that have no bearing on the employee's ability to work with BD.

NOTE: However, this provision does not negate the ethical obligation of the physician or other licensed health care professional to transmit any other adverse findings directly to the employee.

(8) *Medical surveillance.* (i) The employer shall ensure that information obtained from the medical screening program activities is aggregated (with all personal identifiers removed) and periodically reviewed, to ascertain whether the health of the employee population of that employer is adversely affected by exposure to BD.

(ii) Information learned from medical surveillance activities must be disseminated to covered employees, as defined in paragraph (k)(1) of this section, in a manner that ensures the confidentiality of individual medical information.

(1) *Communication of BD hazards to employees*—(1) *Hazard communication— general.* (i) Chemical manufacturers, importers, distributors and employers shall comply with all requirements of the Hazard Communication Standard (HCS) (§1910.1200) for BD.

(ii) In classifying the hazards of BD at least the following hazards are to be addressed: Cancer; eye and respiratory tract irritation; central nervous system effects; and flammability.

(iii) Employers shall include BD in the hazard communication program established to comply with the HCS (§1910.1200). Employers shall ensure that each employee has access to labels on containers of BD and to safety data sheets, and is trained in accordance with the requirements of HCS and paragraph (l)(2) of this section.

(2) *Employee information and training.* (i) The employer shall provide all employees exposed to BD with information and training in accordance with the requirements of the Hazard Communication Standard, 29 CFR 1910.1200, 29 CFR 1915.1200, and 29 CFR 1926.59.

(ii) The employer shall train each employee who is potentially exposed to BD at or above the action level or the STEL in accordance with the requirements of this section. The employer shall institute a training program, ensure employee participation in the program, and maintain a record of the contents of such program.

(iii) Training shall be provided prior to or at the time of initial assignment to a job potentially involving exposure to BD at or above the action level or STEL and at least annually thereafter.

(iv) The training program shall be conducted in a manner that the employee is able to understand. The employer shall ensure that each employee exposed to BD over the action level or STEL is informed of the following:

(A) The health hazards associated with BD exposure, and the purpose and a description of the medical screening and surveillance program required by this section;

(B) The quantity, location, manner of use, release, and storage of BD and the specific operations that could result in exposure to BD, especially exposures above the PEL or STEL;

(C) The engineering controls and work practices associated with the employee's job assignment, and emergency procedures and personal protective equipment;

(D) The measures employees can take to protect themselves from exposure to BD.

(E) The contents of this standard and its appendices, and

(F) The right of each employee exposed to BD at or above the action level or STEL to obtain:

(*1*) medical examinations as required by paragraph (j) of this section at no cost to the employee;

(*2*) the employee's medical records required to be maintained by paragraph (m)(4) of this section; and

(*3*) all air monitoring results representing the employee's exposure to BD and required to be kept by paragraph (m)(2) of this section.

(3) *Access to information and training materials.* (i) The employer shall make a copy of this standard and its appendices readily available without cost to all affected employees and their designated representatives and shall provide a copy if requested.

(ii) The employer shall provide to the Assistant Secretary or the Director, or the designated employee representatives, upon request, all materials relating to the employee information and the training program.

(m) *Recordkeeping*—(1) *Objective data for exemption from initial monitoring.* (i) Where the processing, use, or handling of products or streams made from or containing BD are exempted from other requirements of this section under paragraph (a)(2) of this section, or where objective data have been relied on in lieu of initial monitoring under paragraph (d)(2)(ii) of this section, the employer shall establish and maintain a record of the objective data reasonably relied upon in support of the exemption.

(ii) This record shall include at least the following information:

(A) The product or activity qualifying for exemption;

(B) The source of the objective data;

(C) The testing protocol, results of testing, and analysis of the material for the release of BD;

(D) A description of the operation exempted and how the data support the exemption; and

(E) Other data relevant to the operations, materials, processing, or employee exposures covered by the exemption.

(iii) The employer shall maintain this record for the duration of the employer's reliance upon such objective data.

(2) *Exposure measurements.* (i) The employer shall establish and maintain an accurate record of all measurements taken to monitor employee exposure to BD as prescribed in paragraph (d) of this section.

(ii) The record shall include at least the following information:

(A) The date of measurement;

(B) The operation involving exposure to BD which is being monitored;

(C) Sampling and analytical methods used and evidence of their accuracy;

(D) Number, duration, and results of samples taken;

(E) Type of protective devices worn, if any; and

(F) Name, social security number and exposure of the employees whose exposures are represented.

(G) The written corrective action and the schedule for completion of this ac-

tion required by paragraph (d)(7)(ii) of this section.

(iii) The employer shall maintain this record for at least 30 years in accordance with 29 CFR 1910.1020.

(3) [Reserved]

(4) *Medical screening and surveillance.* (i) The employer shall establish and maintain an accurate record for each employee subject to medical screening and surveillance under this section.

(ii) The record shall include at least the following information:

(A) The name and social security number of the employee;

(B) Physician's or other licensed health care professional's written opinions as described in paragraph (k)(7) of this section;

(C) A copy of the information provided to the physician or other licensed health care professional as required by paragraphs (k)(7)(ii)–(iv) of this section.

(iii) Medical screening and surveillance records shall be maintained for each employee for the duration of employment plus 30 years, in accordance with 29 CFR 1910.1020.

(5) *Availability.* (i) The employer, upon written request, shall make all records required to be maintained by this section available for examination and copying to the Assistant Secretary and the Director.

(ii) Access to records required to be maintained by paragraphs (l)(1)–(3) of this section shall be granted in accordance with 29 CFR 1910.1020(e).

(6) *Transfer of records.* The employer shall transfer medical and exposure records as set forth in 29 CFR 1910.1020(h).

(ii) The employer shall transfer medical and exposure records as set forth in 29 CFR 1910.1020(h).

(n) [Reserved]

(o) *Appendices.* (1) appendix E to this section is mandatory.

(2) Appendices A, B, C, D, and F to this section are informational and are not intended to create any additional obligations not otherwise imposed or to detract from any existing obligations.

APPENDIX A TO § 1910.1051—SUBSTANCE SAFETY DATA SHEET FOR 1,3-BUTADIENE (NON-MANDATORY)

I. SUBSTANCE IDENTIFICATION

A. Substance: 1,3-Butadiene (CH_2 = CH-CH = CH_2).

B. Synonyms: 1,3-Butadiene (BD); butadiene; biethylene; bi-vinyl; divinyl; butadiene-1,3; buta-1,3-diene; erythrene; NCI-C50602; CAS–106–99–0.

C. BD can be found as a gas or liquid.

D. BD is used in production of styrene-butadiene rubber and polybutadiene rubber for the tire industry. Other uses include copolymer latexes for carpet backing and paper coating, as well as resins and polymers for pipes and automobile and appliance parts. It is also used as an intermediate in the production of such chemicals as fungicides.

E. Appearance and odor: BD is a colorless, non-corrosive, flammable gas with a mild aromatic odor at standard ambient temperature and pressure.

F. Permissible exposure: Exposure may not exceed 1 part BD per million parts of air averaged over the 8-hour workday, nor may short-term exposure exceed 5 parts of BD per million parts of air averaged over any 15-minute period in the 8-hour workday.

II. HEALTH HAZARD DATA

A. BD can affect the body if the gas is inhaled or if the liquid form, which is very cold (cryogenic), comes in contact with the eyes or skin.

B. Effects of overexposure: Breathing very high levels of BD for a short time can cause central nervous system effects, blurred vision, nausea, fatigue, headache, decreased blood pressure and pulse rate, and unconsciousness. There are no recorded cases of accidental exposures at high levels that have caused death in humans, but this could occur. Breathing lower levels of BD may cause irritation of the eyes, nose, and throat. Skin contact with liquefied BD can cause irritation and frostbite.

C. Long-term (chronic) exposure: BD has been found to be a potent carcinogen in rodents, inducing neoplastic lesions at multiple target sites in mice and rats. A recent study of BD-exposed workers showed that exposed workers have an increased risk of developing leukemia. The risk of leukemia increases with increased exposure to BD. OSHA has concluded that there is strong evidence that workplace exposure to BD poses an increased risk of death from cancers of the lymphohematopoietic system.

D. Reporting signs and symptoms: You should inform your supervisor if you develop any of these signs or symptoms and suspect that they are caused by exposure to BD.

III. EMERGENCY FIRST AID PROCEDURES

In the event of an emergency, follow the emergency plan and procedures designated for your work area. If you have been trained in first aid procedures, provide the necessary first aid measures. If necessary, call for additional assistance from co-workers and emergency medical personnel.

A. Eye and Skin Exposures: If there is a potential that liquefied BD can come in contact with eye or skin, face shields and skin protective equipment must be provided and used. If liquefied BD comes in contact with the eye, immediately flush the eyes with large amounts of water, occasionally lifting the lower and the upper lids. Flush repeatedly. Get medical attention immediately. Contact lenses should not be worn when working with this chemical. In the event of skin contact, which can cause frostbite, remove any contaminated clothing and flush the affected area repeatedly with large amounts of tepid water.

B. Breathing: If a person breathes in large amounts of BD, move the exposed person to fresh air at once. If breathing has stopped, begin cardiopulmonary resuscitation (CPR) if you have been trained in this procedure. Keep the affected person warm and at rest. Get medical attention immediately.

C. Rescue: Move the affected person from the hazardous exposure. If the exposed person has been overcome, call for help and begin emergency rescue procedures. Use extreme caution so that you do not become a casualty. Understand the plant's emergency rescue procedures and know the locations of rescue equipment before the need arises.

IV. RESPIRATORS AND PROTECTIVE CLOTHING

A. Respirators: Good industrial hygiene practices recommend that engineering and work practice controls be used to reduce environmental concentrations to the permissible exposure level. However, there are some exceptions where respirators may be used to control exposure. Respirators may be used when engineering and work practice controls are not technically feasible, when such controls are in the process of being installed, or when these controls fail and need to be supplemented or during brief, non-routine, intermittent exposure. Respirators may also be used in situations involving non-routine work operations which are performed infrequently and in which exposures are limited in duration, and in emergency situations. In some instances cartridge respirator use is allowed, but only with strict time constraints. For example, at exposure below 5 ppm BD, a cartridge (or canister) respirator, either full or half face, may be used, but the cartridge or canister must be replaced at least every 4 hours, and it must be replaced every 3 hours when the exposure is between 5 and 10 ppm. If the use of respirators is necessary, the only respirators permitted are those that have been approved by the National Institute for Occupational Safety and Health (NIOSH). In addition to respirator selection, a complete respiratory protection program must be instituted which includes regular training, maintenance, fit testing, inspection, cleaning, and evaluation of respirators. If you can smell BD while wearing a respirator, proceed immediately to fresh air, and change cartridge (or canister) before re-entering an area where there is BD exposure. If you experience difficulty in breathing while wearing a respirator, tell your supervisor.

B. Protective Clothing: Employees should be provided with and required to use impervious clothing, gloves, face shields (eight-inch minimum), and other appropriate protective clothing necessary to prevent the skin from becoming frozen by contact with liquefied BD (or a vessel containing liquid BD).

Employees should be provided with and required to use splash-proof safety goggles where liquefied BD may contact the eyes.

V. Precautions for Safe Use, Handling, and Storage

A. Fire and Explosion Hazards: BD is a flammable gas and can easily form explosive mixtures in air. It has a lower explosive limit of 2%, and an upper explosive limit of 11.5%. It has an autoignition temperature of 420 °C (788 °F). Its vapor is heavier than air (vapor density, 1.9) and may travel a considerable distance to a source of ignition and flash back. Usually it contains inhibitors to prevent self-polymerization (which is accompanied by evolution of heat) and to prevent formation of explosive peroxides. At elevated temperatures, such as in fire conditions, polymerization may take place. If the polymerization takes place in a container, there is a possibility of violent rupture of the container.

B. Hazard: Slightly toxic. Slight respiratory irritant. Direct contact of liquefied BD on skin may cause freeze burns and frostbite.

C. Storage: Protect against physical damage to BD containers. Outside or detached storage of BD containers is preferred. Inside storage should be in a cool, dry, well-ventilated, noncombustible location, away from all possible sources of ignition. Store cylinders vertically and do not stack. Do not store with oxidizing material.

D. Usual Shipping Containers: Liquefied BD is contained in steel pressure apparatus.

E. Electrical Equipment: Electrical installations in Class I hazardous locations, as defined in Article 500 of the National Electrical Code, should be in accordance with Article 501 of the Code. If explosion-proof electrical equipment is necessary, it shall be suitable for use in Group B. Group D equipment may be used if such equipment is isolated in accordance with Section 501–5(a) by sealing all conduit ½- inch size or larger. See Venting of Deflagrations (NFPA No. 68, 1994), National Electrical Code (NFPA No. 70, 1996), Static Electricity (NFPA No. 77, 1993), Lightning Protection Systems (NFPA No. 780, 1995), and Fire Hazard Properties of Flammable Liquids, Gases and Volatile Solids (NFPA No. 325, 1994).

F. Fire Fighting: Stop flow of gas. Use water to keep fire-exposed containers cool. Fire extinguishers and quick drenching facilities must be readily available, and you should know where they are and how to operate them.

G. Spill and Leak: Persons not wearing protective equipment and clothing should be restricted from areas of spills or leaks until clean-up has been completed. If BD is spilled or leaked, the following steps should be taken:

1. Eliminate all ignition sources.

2. Ventilate area of spill or leak.

3. If in liquid form, for small quantities, allow to evaporate in a safe manner.

4. Stop or control the leak if this can be done without risk. If source of leak is a cylinder and the leak cannot be stopped in place, remove the leaking cylinder to a safe place and repair the leak or allow the cylinder to empty.

H. Disposal: This substance, when discarded or disposed of, is a hazardous waste according to Federal regulations (40 CFR part 261). It is listed as hazardous waste number D001 due to its ignitability. The transportation, storage, treatment, and disposal of this waste material must be conducted in compliance with 40 CFR parts 262, 263, 264, 268 and 270. Disposal can occur only in properly permitted facilities. Check state and local regulation of any additional requirements as these may be more restrictive than federal laws and regulation.

I. You should not keep food, beverages, or smoking materials in areas where there is BD exposure, nor should you eat or drink in such areas.

J. Ask your supervisor where BD is used in your work area and ask for any additional plant safety and health rules.

VI. Medical Requirements

Your employer is required to offer you the opportunity to participate in a medical screening and surveillance program if you are exposed to BD at concentrations exceeding the action level (0.5 ppm BD as an 8-hour TWA) on 30 days or more a year, or at or above the 8 hr TWA (1 ppm) or STEL (5 ppm for 15 minutes) on 10 days or more a year. Exposure for any part of a day counts. If you have had exposure to BD in the past, but have been transferred to another job, you may still be eligible to participate in the medical screening and surveillance program.

The OSHA rule specifies the past exposures that would qualify you for participation in the program. These past exposure are work histories that suggest the following: (1) That you have been exposed at or above the PELs on 30 days a year for 10 or more years; (2) that you have been exposed at or above the action level on 60 days a year for 10 or more years; or (3) that you have been exposed above 10 ppm on 30 days in any past year. Additionally, if you are exposed to BD in an emergency situation, you are eligible for a medical examination within 48 hours. The basic medical screening program includes a health questionnaire, physical examination, and blood test. These medical evaluations must be offered to you at a reasonable time and place, and without cost or loss of pay.

VII. Observation of Monitoring

Your employer is required to perform measurements that are representative of your exposure to BD and you or your designated representative are entitled to observe the monitoring procedure. You are entitled to observe the steps taken in the measurement procedure, and to record the results obtained. When the monitoring procedure is taking place in an area where respirators or personal protective clothing and equipment are required to be worn, you or your representative must also be provided with, and must wear, the protective clothing and equipment.

VIII. Access to Information

A. Each year, your employer is required to inform you of the information contained in this appendix. In addition, your employer must instruct you in the proper work practices for using BD, emergency procedures, and the correct use of protective equipment.

B. Your employer is required to determine whether you are being exposed to BD. You or your representative has the right to observe employee measurements and to record the results obtained. Your employer is required to inform you of your exposure. If your employer determines that you are being overexposed, he or she is required to inform you of the actions which are being taken to reduce your exposure to within permissible exposure limits and of the schedule to implement these actions.

C. Your employer is required to keep records of your exposures and medical examinations. These records must be kept by the employer for at least thirty (30) years.

D. Your employer is required to release your exposure and medical records to you or your representative upon your request.

APPENDIX B TO §1910.1051—SUBSTANCE TECHNICAL GUIDELINES FOR 1,3-BUTADIENE (NONMANDATORY)

I. Physical and Chemical Data

A. Substance identification:

1. Synonyms: 1,3-Butadiene (BD); butadiene; biethylene; bivinyl; divinyl; butadiene-1,3; buta-1,3-diene; erythrene; NCI-C50620; CAS–106–99–0.

2. Formula: $CH_2 = CH$-$CH = CH_2$.

3. Molecular weight: 54.1.

B. Physical data:

1. Boiling point (760 mm Hg): -4.7 °C (23.5 °F).

2. Specific gravity (water = 1): 0.62 at 20 °C (68 °F).

3. Vapor density (air = 1 at boiling point of BD): 1.87.

4. Vapor pressure at 20 °C (68 °F): 910 mm Hg.

5. Solubility in water, g/100 g water at 20 °C (68 °F): 0.05.

6. Appearance and odor: Colorless, flammable gas with a mildly aromatic odor. Liquefied BD is a colorless liquid with a mildly aromatic odor.

II. Fire, Explosion, and Reactivity Hazard Data

A. Fire:

1. Flash point: -76 °C (-105 °F) for take out; liquefied BD; Not applicable to BD gas.

2. Stability: A stabilizer is added to the monomer to inhibit formation of polymer during storage. Forms explosive peroxides in air in absence of inhibitor.

3. Flammable limits in air, percent by volume: Lower: 2.0; Upper: 11.5.

4. Extinguishing media: Carbon dioxide for small fires, polymer or alcohol foams for large fires.

5. Special fire fighting procedures: Fight fire from protected location or maximum possible distance. Stop flow of gas before extinguishing fire. Use water spray to keep fire-exposed cylinders cool.

6. Unusual fire and explosion hazards: BD vapors are heavier than air and may travel to a source of ignition and flash back. Closed containers may rupture violently when heated.

7. For purposes of compliance with the requirements of 29 CFR 1910.106, BD is classified as a flammable gas. For example, 7,500 ppm, approximately one-fourth of the lower flammable limit, would be considered to pose a potential fire and explosion hazard.

8. For purposes of compliance with 29 CFR 1910.155, BD is classified as a Class B fire hazard.

9. For purposes of compliance with 29 CFR 1910.307, locations classified as hazardous due to the presence of BD shall be Class I.

B. Reactivity:

1. Conditions contributing to instability: Heat. Peroxides are formed when inhibitor

497

concentration is not maintained at proper level. At elevated temperatures, such as in fire conditions, polymerization may take place.

2. Incompatibilities: Contact with strong oxidizing agents may cause fires and explosions. The contacting of crude BD (not BD monomer) with copper and copper alloys may cause formations of explosive copper compounds.

3. Hazardous decomposition products: Toxic gases (such as carbon monoxide) may be released in a fire involving BD.

4. Special precautions: BD will attack some forms of plastics, rubber, and coatings. BD in storage should be checked for proper inhibitor content, for self-polymerization, and for formation of peroxides when in contact with air and iron. Piping carrying BD may become plugged by formation of rubbery polymer.

C. Warning Properties:

1. Odor Threshold: An odor threshold of 0.45 ppm has been reported in The American Industrial Hygiene Association (AIHA) Report, *Odor Thresholds for Chemicals with Established Occupational Health Standards.* (Ex. 32–28C)

2. Eye Irritation Level: Workers exposed to vapors of BD (concentration or purity unspecified) have complained of irritation of eyes, nasal passages, throat, and lungs. Dogs and rabbits exposed experimentally to as much as 6700 ppm for 7½ hours a day for 8 months have developed no histologically demonstrable abnormality of the eyes.

3. Evaluation of Warning Properties: Since the mean odor threshold is about half of the 1 ppm PEL, and more than 10-fold below the 5 ppm STEL, most wearers of air purifying respirators should still be able to detect breakthrough before a significant overexposure to BD occurs.

III. Spill, Leak, and Disposal Procedures

A. Persons not wearing protective equipment and clothing should be restricted from areas of spills or leaks until cleanup has been completed. If BD is spilled or leaked, the following steps should be taken:

1. Eliminate all ignition sources.

2. Ventilate areas of spill or leak.

3. If in liquid form, for small quantities, allow to evaporate in a safe manner.

4. Stop or control the leak if this can be done without risk. If source of leak is a cylinder and the leak cannot be stopped in place, remove the leaking cylinder to a safe place and repair the leak or allow the cylinder to empty.

B. Disposal: This substance, when discarded or disposed of, is a hazardous waste according to Federal regulations (40 CFR part 261). It is listed by the EPA as hazardous waste number D001 due to its ignitability. The transportation, storage, treatment, and disposal of this waste material must be conducted in compliance with 40

CFR parts 262, 263, 264, 268 and 270. Disposal can occur only in properly permitted facilities. Check state and local regulations for any additional requirements because these may be more restrictive than federal laws and regulations.

IV. Monitoring and Measurement Procedures

A. Exposure above the Permissible Exposure Limit (8-hr TWA) or Short-Term Exposure Limit (STEL):

1. 8-hr TWA exposure evaluation: Measurements taken for the purpose of determining employee exposure under this standard are best taken with consecutive samples covering the full shift. Air samples must be taken in the employee's breathing zone (air that would most nearly represent that inhaled by the employee).

2. STEL exposure evaluation: Measurements must represent 15 minute exposures associated with operations most likely to exceed the STEL in each job and on each shift.

3. Monitoring frequencies: Table 1 gives various exposure scenarios and their required monitoring frequencies, as required by the final standard for occupational exposure to butadiene.

TABLE 1—FIVE EXPOSURE SCENARIOS AND THEIR ASSOCIATED MONITORING FREQUENCIES

Action level	8-hr TWA	STEL	Required monitoring activity
– *	–	–	No 8-hr TWA or STEL monitoring required.
+ *	–	–	No STEL monitoring required. Monitor 8-hr TWA annually.
+	+	–	No STEL monitoring required. Periodic monitoring 8-hr TWA, in accordance with (d)(3)(ii).**
+	+	+	Periodic monitoring 8-hr TWA, in accordance with (d)(3)(ii)**. Periodic monitoring STEL, in accordance with (d)(3)(iii).
+	–	+	Periodic monitoring STEL, in accordance with (d)(3)(iii). Monitor 8-hr TWA, annually.

* Exposure Scenario, Limit Exceeded: + = Yes, – = No.

** The employer may decrease the frequency of exposure monitoring to annually when at least 2 consecutive measurements taken at least 7 days apart show exposures to be below the 8 hr TWA, but at or above the action level.

4. Monitoring techniques: appendix D describes the validated method of sampling and analysis which has been tested by OSHA for use with BD. The employer has the obligation of selecting a monitoring method which meets the accuracy and precision requirements of the standard under his or her unique field conditions. The standard requires that the method of monitoring must be accurate, to a 95 percent confidence level, to plus or minus 25 percent for concentrations of BD at or above 1 ppm, and to plus or minus 35 percent for concentrations below 1 ppm.

V. Personal Protective Equipment

A. Employees should be provided with and required to use impervious clothing, gloves, face shields (eight-inch minimum), and other appropriate protective clothing necessary to prevent the skin from becoming frozen from contact with liquid BD.

B. Any clothing which becomes wet with liquid BD should be removed immediately and not re-worn until the butadiene has evaporated.

C. Employees should be provided with and required to use splash proof safety goggles where liquid BD may contact the eyes.

VI. Housekeeping and Hygiene Facilities

For purposes of complying with 29 CFR 1910.141, the following items should be emphasized:

A. The workplace should be kept clean, orderly, and in a sanitary condition.

B. Adequate washing facilities with hot and cold water are to be provided and maintained in a sanitary condition.

VII. Additional Precautions

A. Store BD in tightly closed containers in a cool, well-ventilated area and take all necessary precautions to avoid any explosion hazard.

B. Non-sparking tools must be used to open and close metal containers. These containers must be effectively grounded.

C. Do not incinerate BD cartridges, tanks or other containers.

D. Employers must advise employees of all areas and operations where exposure to BD might occur.

APPENDIX C TO § 1910.1051—MEDICAL SCREENING AND SURVEILLANCE FOR 1,3-BUTADIENE (NON-MANDATORY)

I. Basis for Medical Screening and Surveillance Requirements

A. Route of Entry Inhalation

B. Toxicology

Inhalation of BD has been linked to an increased risk of cancer, damage to the reproductive organs, and fetotoxicity. Butadiene can be converted via oxidation to epoxybutene and diepoxybutane, two genotoxic metabolites that may play a role in the expression of BD's toxic effects.

BD has been tested for carcinogenicity in mice and rats. Both species responded to BD exposure by developing cancer at multiple primary organ sites. Early deaths in mice were caused by malignant lymphomas, primarily lymphocytic type, originating in the thymus.

Mice exposed to BD have developed ovarian or testicular atrophy. Sperm head morphology tests also revealed abnormal sperm in mice exposed to BD; lethal mutations were found in a dominant lethal test. In light of these results in animals, the possibility that BD may adversely affect the reproductive systems of male and female workers must be considered.

Additionally, anemia has been observed in animals exposed to butadiene. In some cases, this anemia appeared to be a primary response to exposure; in other cases, it may have been secondary to a neoplastic response.

C. Epidemiology

Epidemiologic evidence demonstrates that BD exposure poses an increased risk of leukemia. Mild alterations of hematologic parameters have also been observed in synthetic rubber workers exposed to BD.

II. Potential Adverse Health Effects

A. Acute

Skin contact with liquid BD causes characteristic burns or frostbite. BD is gaseous form can irritate the eyes, nasal passages, throat, and lungs. Blurred vision, coughing, and drowsiness may also occur. Effects are mild at 2,000 ppm and pronounced at 8,000 ppm for exposures occurring over the full workshift.

At very high concentrations in air, BD is an anesthetic, causing narcosis, respiratory paralysis, unconsciousness, and death. Such concentrations are unlikely, however, except in an extreme emergency because BD poses an explosion hazard at these levels.

B. Chronic

The principal adverse health effects of concern are BD-induced lymphoma, leukemia and potential reproductive toxicity. Anemia and other changes in the peripheral blood cells may be indicators of excessive exposure to BD.

C. Reproductive

Workers may be concerned about the possibility that their BD exposure may be affecting their ability to procreate a healthy child. For workers with high exposures to BD, especially those who have experienced difficulties in conceiving, miscarriages, or stillbirths, appropriate medical and laboratory evaluation of fertility may be necessary to determine if BD is having any adverse effect on the reproductive system or on the health of the fetus.

III. Medical Screening Components At-A-Glance

A. Health Questionnaire

The most important goal of the health questionnaire is to elicit information from the worker regarding potential signs or symptoms generally related to leukemia or other blood abnormalities. Therefore, physicians or other licensed health care professionals should be aware of the presenting symptoms and signs of lymphohematopoietic disorders and cancers, as well as the procedures necessary to confirm or exclude such diagnoses. Additionally, the health questionnaire will assist with the identification of workers at greatest risk of developing leukemia or adverse reproductive effects from their exposures to BD.

Workers with a history of reproductive difficulties or a personal or family history of immune deficiency syndromes, blood dyscrasias, lymphoma, or leukemia, and those who are or have been exposed to medicinal drugs or chemicals known to affect the hematopoietic or lymphatic systems may be at higher risk from their exposure to BD. After the initial administration, the health questionnaire must be updated annually.

B. Complete Blood Count (CBC)

The medical screening and surveillance program requires an annual CBC, with differential and platelet count, to be provided for each employee with BD exposure. This test is to be performed on a blood sample obtained by phlebotomy of the venous system or, if technically feasible, from a fingerstick sample of capillary blood. The sample is to be analyzed by an accredited laboratory.

Abnormalities in a CBC may be due to a number of different etiologies. The concern for workers exposed to BD includes, but is not limited to, timely identification of lymphohematopoietic cancers, such as leukemia and non-Hodgkin's lymphoma. Abnormalities of portions of the CBC are identified by comparing an individual's results to those of an established range of normal values for males and females. A substantial change in any individual employee's CBC may also be viewed as "abnormal" for that individual even if all measurements fall within the population-based range of normal values. It is suggested that a flowsheet for laboratory values be included in each employee's medical record so that comparisons and trends in annual CBCs can be easily made.

A determination of the clinical significance of an abnormal CBC shall be the responsibility of the examining physician, other licensed health care professional, or medical specialist to whom the employee is referred. Ideally, an abnormal CBC should be compared to previous CBC measurements for the same employee, when available. Clinical common sense may dictate that a CBC value that is very slightly outside the normal range does not warrant medical concern. A CBC abnormality may also be the result of a temporary physical stressor, such as a transient viral illness, blood donation, or menorrhagia, or laboratory error. In these cases, the CBC should be repeated in a timely fashion, i.e., within 6 weeks, to verify that return to the normal range has occurred. A clinically significant abnormal CBC should result in removal of the employee from further exposure to BD. Transfer of the employee to other work duties in a BD-free environment would be the preferred recommendation.

C. Physical Examination

The medical screening and surveillance program requires an initial physical examination for workers exposed to BD; this examination is repeated once every three years. The initial physical examination should assess each worker's baseline general health and rule out clinical signs of medical conditions that may be caused by or aggravated by occupational BD exposure. The physical examination should be directed at identification of signs of lymphohematopoietic disorders, including lymph node enlargement, splenomegaly, and hepatomegaly.

Repeated physical examinations should update objective clinical findings that could be indicative of interim development of a lymphohematopoietic disorder, such as lymphoma, leukemia, or other blood abnormality. Physical examinations may also be provided on an as needed basis in order to follow up on a positive answer on the health questionnaire, or in response to an abnormal CBC. Physical examination of workers who will no longer be working in jobs with BD exposure are intended to rule out lymphohematopoietic disorders.

The need for physical examinations for workers concerned about adverse reproductive effects from their exposure to BD should be identified by the physician or other licensed health care professional and provided accordingly. For these workers, such consultations and examinations may relate to developmental toxicity and reproductive capacity.

Physical examination of workers acutely exposed to significant levels of BD should be especially directed at the respiratory system, eyes, sinuses, skin, nervous system, and any region associated with particular complaints. If the worker has received a severe acute exposure, hospitalization may be required to assure proper medical management. Since this type of exposure may place workers at greater risk of blood abnormalities, a CBC must be obtained within 48 hours and repeated at one, two, and three months.

APPENDIX D TO § 1910.1051—SAMPLING AND ANALYTICAL METHOD FOR 1,3-BUTADIENE (NON-MANDATORY)

OSHA Method No.: 56.
Matrix: Air.
Target concentration: 1 ppm (2.21 mg/m³)

Procedure: Air samples are collected by drawing known volumes of air through sampling tubes containing charcoal adsorbent which has been coated with 4-tert-butylcatechol. The samples are desorbed with carbon disulfide and then analyzed by gas chromatography using a flame ionization detector.

Recommended sampling rate and air volume: 0.05 L/min and 3 L.

Detection limit of the overall procedure: 90 ppb (200 ug/m³) (based on 3 L air volume).

Reliable quantitation limit: 155 ppb (343 ug/m³) (based on 3 L air volume).

Standard error of estimate at the target concentration: 6.5%.

Special requirements: The sampling tubes must be coated with 4-tert-butylcatechol. Collected samples should be stored in a freezer.

Status of method: A sampling and analytical method has been subjected to the established evaluation procedures of the Organic Methods Evaluation Branch, OSHA Analytical Laboratory, Salt Lake City, Utah 84165.

1. Background

This work was undertaken to develop a sampling and analytical procedure for BD at 1 ppm. The current method recommended by OSHA for collecting BD uses activated coconut shell charcoal as the sampling medium (Ref. 5.2). This method was found to be inadequate for use at low BD levels because of sample instability.

The stability of samples has been significantly improved through the use of a specially cleaned charcoal which is coated with 4-tert-butylcatechol (TBC). TBC is a polymerization inhibitor for BD (Ref. 5.3).

1.1.1 Toxic effects

Symptoms of human exposure to BD include irritation of the eyes, nose and throat. It can also cause coughing, drowsiness and fatigue. Dermatitis and frostbite can result from skin exposure to liquid BD. (Ref. 5.1)

NIOSH recommends that BD be handled in the workplace as a potential occupational carcinogen. This recommendation is based on two inhalation studies that resulted in cancers at multiple sites in rats and in mice. BD has also demonstrated mutagenic activity in the presence of a liver microsomal activating system. It has also been reported to have adverse reproductive effects. (Ref. 5.1)

1.1.2. Potential workplace exposure

About 90% of the annual production of BD is used to manufacture styrene-butadiene rubber and Polybutadiene rubber. Other uses include: Polychloroprene rubber, acrylonitrile butadiene-stryene resins, nylon intermediates, styrene-butadiene latexes, butadiene polymers, thermoplastic elastomers, nitrile resins, methyl methacrylate-buta-

diene styrene resins and chemical intermediates. (Ref. 5.1)

1.1.3. Physical properties (Ref. 5.1)

CAS No.: 106–99–0
Molecular weight: 54.1
Appearance: Colorless gas
Boiling point: −4.41 °C (760 mm Hg)
Freezing point: −108.9 °C
Vapor pressure: 2 atm @ 15.3 °C; 5 atm @ 47 °C
Explosive limits: 2 to 11.5% (by volume in air)
Odor threshold: 0.45 ppm
Structural formula: $H_2 C{:}CHCH{:}CH_2$
Synonyms: BD; biethylene; bivinyl; butadiene; divinyl; buta-1,3-diene; alpha-gamma-butadiene; erythrene; NCI-C50602; pyrrolylene; vinylethylene.

1.2. Limit defining parameters

The analyte air concentrations listed throughout this method are based on an air volume of 3 L and a desorption volume of 1 mL. Air concentrations listed in ppm are referenced to 25 °C and 760 mm Hg.

1.2.1. Detection limit of the analytical procedure

The detection limit of the analytical procedure was 304 pg per injection. This was the amount of BD which gave a response relative to the interferences present in a standard.

1.2.2. Detection limit of the overall procedure

The detection limit of the overall procedure was 0.60 µg per sample (90 ppb or 200 µg/m³). This amount was determined graphically. It was the amount of analyte which, when spiked on the sampling device, would allow recovery approximately equal to the detection limit of the analytical procedure.

1.2.3. Reliable quantitation limit

The reliable quantitation limit was 1.03 µg per sample (155 ppb or 343 µg/m³). This was the smallest amount of analyte which could be quantitated within the limits of a recovery of at least 75% and a precision (±1.96 SD) of ±25% or better.

1.2.4. Sensitivity [1]

The sensitivity of the analytical procedure over a concentration range representing 0.6 to 2 times the target concentration, based on the recommended air volume, was 387 area

---

[1] The reliable quantitation limit and detection limits reported in the method are based upon optimization of the instrument for the smallest possible amount of analyte. When the target concentration of an analyte is exceptionally higher than these limits, they may not be attainable at the routine operation parameters.

units per µg/mL. This value was determined from the slope of the calibration curve. The sensitivity may vary with the particular instrument used in the analysis.

1.2.5. Recovery

The recovery of BD from samples used in storage tests remained above 77% when the samples were stored at ambient temperature and above 94% when the samples were stored at refrigerated temperature. These values were determined from regression lines which were calculated from the storage data. The recovery of the analyte from the collection device must be at least 75% following storage.

1.2.6. Precision (analytical method only)

The pooled coefficient of variation obtained from replicate determinations of analytical standards over the range of 0.6 to 2 times the target concentration was 0.011.

1.2.7. Precision (overall procedure)

The precision at the 95% confidence level for the refrigerated temperature storage test was ±12.7%. This value includes an additional ±5% for sampling error. The overall procedure must provide results at the target concentrations that are ±25% at the 95% confidence level.

1.2.8. Reproducibility

Samples collected from a controlled test atmosphere and a draft copy of this procedure were given to a chemist unassociated with this evaluation. The average recovery was 97.2% and the standard deviation was 6.2%.

2. Sampling procedure

2.1. Apparatus

2.1.1. Samples are collected by use of a personal sampling pump that can be calibrated to within ±5% of the recommended 0.05 L/min sampling rate with the sampling tube in line.

2.1.2. Samples are collected with laboratory prepared sampling tubes. The sampling tube is constructed of silane-treated glass and is about 5-cm long. The ID is 4 mm and the OD is 6 mm. One end of the tube is tapered so that a glass wool end plug will hold the contents of the tube in place during sampling. The opening in the tapered end of the sampling tube is at least one-half the ID of the tube (2 mm). The other end of the sampling tube is open to its full 4-mm ID to facilitate packing of the tube. Both ends of the tube are fire-polished for safety. The tube is packed with 2 sections of pretreated charcoal which has been coated with TBC. The tube is packed with a 50-mg backup section, located nearest the tapered end, and with a 100-mg sampling section of charcoal. The two sec-

tions of coated adsorbent are separated and retained with small plugs of silanized glass wool. Following packing, the sampling tubes are sealed with two 7/32 inch OD plastic end caps. Instructions for the pretreatment and coating of the charcoal are presented in Section 4.1 of this method.

2.2. Reagents

None required.

2.3. Technique

2.3.1. Properly label the sampling tube before sampling and then remove the plastic end caps.

2.3.2. Attach the sampling tube to the pump using a section of flexible plastic tubing such that the larger front section of the sampling tube is exposed directly to the atmosphere. Do not place any tubing ahead of the sampling tube. The sampling tube should be attached in the worker's breathing zone in a vertical manner such that it does not impede work performance.

2.3.3. After sampling for the appropriate time, remove the sampling tube from the pump and then seal the tube with plastic end caps. Wrap the tube lengthwise.

2.3.4. Include at least one blank for each sampling set. The blank should be handled in the same manner as the samples with the exception that air is not drawn through it.

2.3.5. List any potential interferences on the sample data sheet.

2.3.6. The samples require no special shipping precautions under normal conditions. The samples should be refrigerated if they are to be exposed to higher than normal ambient temperatures. If the samples are to be stored before they are shipped to the laboratory, they should be kept in a freezer. The samples should be placed in a freezer upon receipt at the laboratory.

2.4. Breakthrough

(Breakthrough was defined as the relative amount of analyte found on the backup section of the tube in relation to the total amount of analyte collected on the sampling tube. Five-percent breakthrough occurred after sampling a test atmosphere containing 2.0 ppm BD for 90 min at 0.05 L/min. At the end of this time 4.5 L of air had been sampled and 20.1 µg of the analyte was collected. The relative humidity of the sampled air was 80% at 23 °C.)

Breakthrough studies have shown that the recommended sampling procedure can be used at air concentrations higher than the target concentration. The sampling time, however, should be reduced to 45 min if both the expected BD level and the relative humidity of the sampled air are high.

2.5. Desorption efficiency

The average desorption efficiency for BD from TBC coated charcoal over the range from 0.6 to 2 times the target concentration was 96.4%. The efficiency was essentially constant over the range studied.

2.6. Recommended air volume and sampling rate

2.6.1. The recommended air volume is 3L.
2.6.2. The recommended sampling rate is 0.05 L/min for 1 hour.

2.7. Interferences

There are no known interferences to the sampling method.

2.8. Safety precautions

2.8.1. Attach the sampling equipment to the worker in such a manner that it will not interfere with work performance or safety.
2.8.2. Follow all safety practices that apply to the work area being sampled.

3. Analytical procedure

3.1. Apparatus

3.1.1. A gas chromatograph (GC), equipped with a flame ionization detector (FID).[2]
3.1.2. A GC column capable of resolving the analytes from any interference.[3]
3.1.3. Vials, glass 2-mL with Teflon-lined caps.
3.1.4. Disposable Pasteur-type pipets, volumetric flasks, pipets and syringes for preparing samples and standards, making dilutions and performing injections.

3.2. Reagents

3.2.1. Carbon disulfide.[4]
The benzene contaminant that was present in the carbon disulfide was used as an internal standard (ISTD) in this evaluation.
3.2.2. Nitrogen, hydrogen and air, GC grade.
3.2.3. BD of known high purity.[5]

3.3. Standard preparation

3.3.1. Prepare standards by diluting known volumes of BD gas with carbon disulfide. This can be accomplished by injecting

---

[2] A Hewlett-Packard Model 5840A GC was used for this evaluation. Injections were performed using a Hewlett-Packard Model 7671A automatic sampler.
[3] A 20-ft × ⅛-inch OD stainless steel GC column containing 20% FFAP on 80/100 mesh Chromabsorb W-AW-DMCS was used for this evaluation.
[4] Fisher Scientific Company A.C.S. Reagent Grade solvent was used in this evaluation.
[5] Matheson Gas Products, CP Grade 1,3-butadiene was used in this study.

the appropriate volume of BD into the headspace above the 1-mL of carbon disulfide contained in sealed 2-mL vial. Shake the vial after the needle is removed from the septum.[6]
3.3.2. The mass of BD gas used to prepare standards can be determined by use of the following equations:

$$MV = (760/BP)(273 + t)/(273)(22.41)$$

Where:
MV = ambient molar volume
BP = ambient barometric pressure
T = ambient temperature
μg/μL = 54.09/MV
μg/standard = (μg/μL)(μL) BD used to prepare the standard

3.4. Sample preparation

3.4.1. Transfer the 100-mg section of the sampling tube to a 2-mL vial. Place the 50-mg section in a separate vial. If the glass wool plugs contain a significant amount of charcoal, place them with the appropriate sampling tube section.
3.4.2. Add 1-mL of carbon disulfide to each vial.
3.4.3. Seal the vials with Teflon-lined caps and then allow them to desorb for one hour. Shake the vials by hand vigorously several times during the desorption period.
3.4.4. If it is not possible to analyze the samples within 4 hours, separate the carbon disulfide from the charcoal, using a disposable Pasteur-type pipet, following the one hour. This separation will improve the stability of desorbed samples.
3.4.5. Save the used sampling tubes to be cleaned and repacked with fresh adsorbent.

3.5. Analysis

3.5.1. GC Conditions
Column temperature: 95 °C
Injector temperature: 180 °C
Detector temperature: 275 °C
Carrier gas flow rate: 30 mL/min
Injection volume: 0.80 μL
GC column: 20-ft × ⅛-in OD stainless steel GC column containing 20% FFAP on 80/100 Chromabsorb W-AW-DMCS.
3.5.2. Chromatogram. See Section 4.2.
3.5.3. Use a suitable method, such as electronic or peak heights, to measure detector response.
3.5.4. Prepare a calibration curve using several standard solutions of different concentrations. Prepare the calibration curve daily. Program the integrator to report results in μg/mL.
3.5.5. Bracket sample concentrations with standards.

---

[6] A standard containing 7.71 μg/mL (at ambient temperature and pressure) was prepared by diluting 4 μL of the gas with 1-mL of carbon disulfide.

3.6. Interferences (analytical)

3.6.1. Any compound with the same general retention time as the analyte and which also gives a detector response is a potential interference. Possible interferences should be reported by the industrial hygienist to the laboratory with submitted samples.

3.6.2. GC parameters (temperature, column, etc.) may be changed to circumvent interferences.

3.6.3. A useful means of structure designation is GC/MS. It is recommended that this procedure be used to confirm samples whenever possible.

3.7. Calculations

3.7.1. Results are obtained by use of calibration curves. Calibration curves are prepared by plotting detector response against concentration for each standard. The best line through the data points is determined by curve fitting.

3.7.2. The concentration, in ug/mL, for a particular sample is determined by comparing its detector response to the calibration curve. If any analyte is found on the backup section, this amount is added to the amount found on the front section. Blank corrections should be performed before adding the results together.

3.7.3. The BD air concentration can be expressed using the following equation:

$mg/m^3 = (A)(B)/(C)(D)$

Where:

A = µg/mL from Section 3.7.2
B = volume
C = L of air sampled
D = efficiency

3.7.4. The following equation can be used to convert results in mg/m³ to ppm:

$ppm = (mg/m^3)(24.46)/54.09$

Where:

mg/m³ = result from Section 3.7.3.
24.46 = molar volume of an ideal gas at 760 mm Hg and 25 °C.

3.8. Safety precautions (analytical)

3.8.1. Avoid skin contact and inhalation of all chemicals.

3.8.2. Restrict the use of all chemicals to a fume hood whenever possible.

3.8.3. Wear safety glasses and a lab coat in all laboratory areas.

4. Additional Information

4.1. A procedure to prepare specially cleaned charcoal coated with TBC

4.1.1. Apparatus

4.1.1.1. Magnetic stirrer and stir bar.

4.1.1.2. Tube furnace capable of maintaining a temperature of 700 °C and equipped with a quartz tube that can hold 30 g of charcoal.[8]

4.1.1.3. A means to purge nitrogen gas through the charcoal inside the quartz tube.

4.1.1.4. Water bath capable of maintaining a temperature of 60 °C.

4.1.1.5. Miscellaneous laboratory equipment: One-liter vacuum flask, 1-L Erlenmeyer flask, 350-Ml Buchner funnel with a coarse fitted disc, 4-oz brown bottle, rubber stopper, Teflon tape etc.

4.1.2. Reagents

4.1.2.1. Phosphoric acid, 10% by weight, in water.[9]

4.1.2.2. 4-tert-Butylcatechol (TBC).[10]

4.1.2.3. Specially cleaned coconut shell charcoal, 20/40 mesh.[11]

4.1.2.4. Nitrogen gas, GC grade.

4.1.3. Procedure

Weigh 30g of charcoal into a 500-mL Erlenmeyer flask. Add about 250 mL of 10% phosphoric acid to the flask and then swirl the mixture. Stir the mixture for 1 hour using a magnetic stirrer. Filter the mixture using a fitted Buchner funnel. Wash the charcoal several times with 250-mL portions of deionized water to remove all traces of the acid. Transfer the washed charcoal to the tube furnace quartz tube. Place the quartz tube in the furnace and then connect the nitrogen gas purge to the tube. Fire the charcoal to 700 °C. Maintain that temperature for at least 1 hour. After the charcoal has cooled to room temperature, transfer it to a tared beaker. Determine the weight of the charcoal and then add an amount of TBC which is 10% of the charcoal, by weight.

CAUTION-TBC is toxic and should only be handled in a fume hood while wearing gloves.

Carefully mix the contents of the beaker and then transfer the mixture to a 4-oz bottle. Stopper the bottle with a clean rubber stopper which has been wrapped with Teflon tape. Clamp the bottle in a water bath so that the water level is above the charcoal level. Gently heat the bath to 60 °C and then maintain that temperature for 1 hour. Cool the charcoal to room temperature and then transfer the coated charcoal to a suitable container.

The coated charcoal is now ready to be packed into sampling tubes. The sampling tubes should be stored in a sealed container

[8] A Lindberg Type 55035 Tube furnace was used in this evaluation.
[9] Baker Analyzed" Reagent grade was diluted with water for use in this evaluation.
[10] The Aldrich Chemical Company 99% grade was used in this evaluation.
[11] Specially cleaned charcoal was obtained from Supelco, Inc. for use in this evaluation. The cleaning process used by Supelco is proprietary.

to prevent contamination. Sampling tubes should be stored in the dark at room temperature. The sampling tubes should be segregated by coated adsorbent lot number.

4.2 Chromatograms

The chromatograms were obtained using the recommended analytical method. The chart speed was set at 1 cm/min for the first three min and then at 0.2 cm/min for the time remaining in the analysis.

The peak which elutes just before BD is a reaction product between an impurity on the charcoal and TBC. This peak is always present, but it is easily resolved from the analyte. The peak which elutes immediately before benzene is an oxidation product of TBC.

5. References

5.1. "Current Intelligence Bulletin 41, 1,3-Butadiene", U.S. Dept. of Health and Human Services, Public Health Service, Center for Disease Control, NIOSH.

5.2. "NIOSH Manual of Analytical Methods", 2nd ed; U.S. Dept. of Health Education and Welfare, National Institute for Occupational Safety and Health: Cincinnati, OH. 1977, Vol. 2, Method No. S91 DHEW (NIOSH) Publ. (US), No. 77–157–B.

5.3. Hawley, G.C., Ed. "The Condensed Chemical Dictionary", 8th ed.; Van Nostrand Rienhold Company: New York, 1971; 139.5.4. *Chem. Eng. News* (June 10, 1985), (63), 22–66.

APPENDIX E TO §1910.1051 [RESERVED]

505

APPENDIX F TO § 1910.1051—MEDICAL QUESTIONNAIRES (NON-MANDATORY)

1,3 -Butadiene (BD) Initial Health Questionnaire

DIRECTIONS:

You have been asked to answer the questions on this form because you work with BD (butadiene). These questions are about your work, medical history, and health concerns. Please do your best to answer all of the questions. If you need help, please tell the doctor or health care professional who reviews this form.

This form is a confidential medical record. Only information directly related to your health and safety on the job may be given to your employer. Personal health information will not be given to anyone without your consent.

Date:_____

Name:_____ _____ ____   SSN____/____/_____
        Last   First   MI

Job Title:_____

Company's Name:_____

Supervisor's Name:_____ Supervisor's Phone No.:( )____-_____

Work History

1.   Please list all jobs you have had in the past, starting with the job you have now and moving back in time to your first job. (For more space, write on the back of this page.)

	Main Job Duty	Years	Company Name City, State	Chemicals
1				
2				
3				
4				
5				
6				
7				
8				

2. Please describe what you do during a typical work day. Be sure to tell about your work with BD.

_____

_____

3. Please check any of these chemicals that you work with now or have worked with in the past:

benzene	____	carbon tetrachloride ("carbon tet")	___
glues	____	arsine	____
toluene	____	carbon disulfide	____
inks, dyes	____	lead	____
other solvents, grease cutters	____	cement	____
insecticides (like DDT, lindane, etc.)	____	petroleum products	____
paints, varnishes, thinners, strippers	____	nitrites	____
dusts	____		

4. Please check the protective clothing or equipment you use at the job you have now:

    gloves   ____
    coveralls   ____
    respirator   ____
    dust mask   ____
    safety glasses, goggles   ____

Please circle your answer of yes or no.

5. Does your protective clothing or equipment fit you properly? yes no

6. Have you ever made changes in your protective clothing or equipment to make it fit better? yes no

7. Have you been exposed to BD when you were not wearing protective clothing or equipment? yes no

8. Where do you eat, drink and/or smoke when you are at work? (Please check all that apply.)
    Cafeteria/restaurant/snack bar   ____
    Break room/employee lounge   ____
    Smoking lounge   ____
    At my work station   ____

Please circle your answer.

9. Have you been exposed to radiation (like x-rays or nuclear material) at the job you have now or at past jobs? yes no

10. Do you have any hobbies that expose you to dusts or chemicals (including paints, glues, etc.)? yes no

11. Do you have any second or side jobs? yes no

    If yes, what are your duties there?_____

    _____

    _____

12. Where you in the military? yes   no

     If yes, what did you do in the military?_____ .

     _____

     _____

Family Health History

1. In the FAMILY MEMBER column, across from the disease name, write which family member, if any, had the disease.

DISEASE	FAMILY MEMBER
Cancer	
Lymphoma	
Sickle Cell Disease or Trait	
Immune Disease	
Leukemia	
Anemia	

2. Please fill in the following information about family health:

Relative	Alive?	Age at death?	Cause of death?
Father			
Mother			
Brother/Sister			
Brother/Sister			
Brother/Sister			

Personal Health History

Birth Date____/____/____   Age_____   Sex____   Height____   Weight_____

Please circle your answer.

1. Do you smoke any tobacco products? yes   no

2. Have you ever had any kind of surgery or operation? yes no

     If yes, what type of surgery:_____

     _____

     _____

3. Have you ever been in the hospital for any other reasons? yes no

    If yes, please describe the reason:_____

    _____

    _____

4. Do you have any on-going or current medical problems or conditions? yes no

    If yes, please describe:_____

    _____

    _____

5. Do you now have or have you ever had any of the following? Please check all that apply to you.

unexplained fever	___	bruising easily	___	still birth	___
anemia ("low blood")	___	lupus	___	eye redness	___
HIV/AIDS	___	weight loss	___	lumps you can feel	___
weakness	___	kidney problems	___	child with birth defect	___
sickle cell	___	enlarged lymph nodes	___	autoimmune disease	___
miscarriage	___	liver disease	___	overly tired	___
skin rash	___	cancer	___	lung problems	___
bloody stools	___	infertility	___	rheumatoid arthritis	___
leukemia/lymphoma	___	drinking problems	___	mononucleosis ("mono")	___
neck mass/swelling	___	thyroid problems	___	nagging cough	___
wheezing	___	night sweats	___		
yellowing of skin	___	chest pain	___		

Please circle your answer.

6. Do you have any symptoms or health problems that you think may be related to your work with BD? yes no

    If yes, please describe:_____

    _____

7. Have any of your co-workers had similar symptoms or problems?
    yes   no   don't know

    If yes, please describe:_____

    _____

8. Do you notice any irritation of your eyes, nose, throat, lungs, or skin when working with BD? yes no

9. Do you notice any blurred vision, coughing, drowsiness, nausea or headache when working with BD? yes no

10. Do you take any medications (including birth control or over-the-counter)? yes no

    If yes, please list:_____

    _____

11.   Are you allergic to any medication, food, or chemicals? yes   no

    If yes, please list:_____

    _____

12.   Do you have any health conditions not covered by this questionnaire that you think are affected by your work with BD? yes   no

    If yes, please explain:_____

    _____

13.   Did you understand all the questions? yes   no

_____

    Signature

1,3 -Butadiene (BD) Update Health Questionnaire

DIRECTIONS:

You have been asked to answer the questions on this form because you work with BD (butadiene). These questions ask about changes in your work, medical history, and health concerns since the last time you were evaluated. Please do your best to answer all of the questions. If you need help, please tell the doctor or health care professional who reviews this form.

This form is a confidential medical record. Only information directly related to your health and safety on the job may be given to your employer. Personal health information will not be given to anyone without your consent.

Date:_____

Name:_____ _____ ___   SSN____/___/____
            Last   First   MI

Job title:_____

Company's Name:_____

Supervisor's Name:_____   Supervisor's Phone No.( )____-_____

Present Work History

1. Please describe any NEW duties that you have at your job:_____
    _____
    _____
    _____

2   Please list any additional job titles you have:

    _____   _____
    _____   _____
    _____   _____

Please circle your answer.

3. Are you exposed to any other chemicals in your work since the last time you were evaluated for exposure to BD? yes no

    If yes, please list what they are:_____
    _____

4. Does your personal protective equipment and clothing fit you properly? yes   no

5. Have you made changes in this equipment or clothing to make it fit better? yes   no

6. Have you been exposed to BD when you were not wearing protective equipment or clothing?
    yes   no

7. Are you exposed to any NEW chemicals at home or while working on hobbies?
    yes no

    If yes, please list what they are:_____

    _____

8. Since your last BD health evaluation, have you started working any new second or side jobs?
    yes no

    If yes, what are your duties there?_____

    _____

    _____

Personal Health History

1. What is your current weight?_____ pounds

2. Have you been diagnosed with any new medical conditions or illness since your last evaluation?
    yes no

    If yes, please tell what they are:_____

    _____

3. Since your last evaluation, have you been in the hospital for any illnesses, injuries, or surgery?
    yes no

    If yes, please describe: _____

    _____

    _____

4. Do you have any of the following? Please place a check for all that apply to you.

unexplained fever	____	bruising easily	____	still birth	____
anemia ("low blood")	____	lupus	____	eye redness	____
HIV/AIDS	____	weight loss	____	lumps you can feel	____
weakness	____	kidney problems	____	child with birth defect	____
sickle cell	____	enlarged lymph nodes	____	autoimmune disease	____
miscarriage	____	liver disease	____	overly tired	____
skin rash	____	cancer	____	lung problems	____
bloody rash	____	infertility	____	rheumatoid arthritis	____
leukemia/lymphoma	____	drinking problems	____	mononucleosis "mono"	____
neck mass/swelling	____	thyroid problems	____	nagging cough	____
wheezing	____	night sweats	____	yellowing of skin	____

chest pain　　　____

Please circle your answer.

5.　　Do you have any symptoms or health problems that you think may be related to your work　with BD?　yes　no

If yes, please describe:_____

_____

6.　　Have any of your co-workers had similar symptoms or problems?
yes　no　don't know

If yes, please describe:_____

_____

7.　　Do you notice any irritation of your eyes, nose, throat, lungs, or skin when working with BD?
yes　no

8.　　Do you notice any blurred vision, coughing, drowsiness, nausea, or headache when working with BD? yes　no

9.　　Have you been taking any NEW medications (including birth control or over-the-counter)? yes no

If yes, please list:

_____　　_____　　_____

_____　　_____　　_____

10.　　Have you developed any NEW allergies to medications, foods, or chemicals?
yes　no

If yes, please list:

_____　　_____　　_____

_____　　_____　　_____

11.　　Do you have any health conditions not covered by this questionnaire that you think are affected by your work with BD? yes　no

If yes, please explain:_____

_____

12.　　Did you understand all the questions? yes　no

_____
Signature

[61 FR 56831, Nov. 4, 1996, as amended at 63 FR 1294, Jan. 8, 1998; 67 FR 67965, Nov. 7, 2002; 70 FR 1143, Jan. 5, 2005; 71 FR 16672, 16674, Apr. 3, 2006; 73 FR 75587, Dec. 12, 2008; 76 FR 33609, June 8, 2011; 77 FR 17785, Mar. 26, 2012; 78 FR 9313, Feb. 8, 2013]

EFFECTIVE DATE NOTE: At 84 FR 21527, May 14, 2019, § 1910.1051 was amended by revising appendix F, effective July 15, 2019. For the convenience of the user, the revised text is set forth as follows:

§ 1910.1051   1,3-Butadiene.

*   *   *   *   *

APPENDIX F TO § 1910.1051—MEDICAL QUESTIONNAIRES (NON-MANDATORY)

1,3-Butadiene (BD) Initial Health Questionnaire

DIRECTIONS:

You have been asked to answer the questions on this form because you work with

BD (butadiene). These questions are about your work, medical history, and health

concerns. Please do your best to answer all of the questions. If you need help, please tell

the doctor or health care professional who reviews this form.

This form is a confidential medical record. Only information directly related to your

health and safety on the job may be given to your employer. Personal health information

will not be given to anyone without your consent.

Date: _____

Name: _____ _____ _____

           Last   First   MI

Job Title: _____

Company's Name: _____

Supervisor's Name: _____   Supervisor's Phone No.: ( ) ____-_____

Work History

1. Please list all jobs you have had in the past, starting with the job you have now and m oving back in time to your first job. (For more space, write on the back of this page.)

Main Job Duty	Years	Company Name City, State	Chemicals
1.			
2.			
3.			
4.			
5.			
6.			
7.			
8.			

2. Please describe what you do during a typical work day. Be sure to tell about you work with BD

_____

_____

3.   Please check any of these chemicals that you work with now or have worked with

in the past:

benzene   _____

glues   _____

toluene   _____

inks, dyes   _____

other solvents, grease cutters   _____

insecticides (like DDT, lindane, etc.)   _____

paints, varnishes, thinners, strippers   _____

dusts   _____

carbon tetrachloride ("carbon tet")   _____

arsine   ____

carbon disulfide   ____

lead   ____ ·

cement   ____

petroleum products   ____

nitrites   ____

4. Please check the protective clothing or equipment you use at the job you have now:

gloves   ____

coveralls   ____

respirator   ____

dust mask   ____

safety glasses, goggles   ____

Please circle your answer of yes or no.

5. Does your protective clothing or equipment fit you properly?

    yes   no

6. Have you ever made changes in your protective clothing or equipment to make it fit better?

    yes   no

7. Have you been exposed to BD when you were not wearing protective clothing or equipment?

    yes   no

8. Where do you eat, drink and/or smoke when you are at work?

   (Please check all that apply.)

   Cafeteria/restaurant/snack bar   _____
   Break room/employee lounge   _____
   Smoking lounge   _____
   At my work station   _____

Please circle your answer.

9. Have you been exposed to radiation (like x-rays or nuclear material) at the job you have now or at past jobs?

   yes   no

10. Do you have any hobbies that expose you to dusts or chemicals (including paints, glues, etc.)?

   yes   no

11. Do you have any second or side jobs?

   yes   no

   If yes, what are your duties there? _____

   _____

   _____

   _____

12. Were you in the military?

yes   no

If yes, what did you do in the military? _____

_____

_____

_____

Family Health History

1. In the FAMILY MEMBER column, across from the disease name, write which family member, if any, had the disease.

Disease	Family Member
Cancer	
Lymphoma	
Sickle Cell Disease or Trait	
Immune Disease	
Leukemia	
Anemia	

2. Please fill in the following information about family health:

RELATIVE	ALIVE?	AGE AT DEATH?	CAUSE OF DEATH?
Father			
Mother			
Brother/Sister			
Brother/Sister			
Brother/Sister			

PERSONAL HEALTH HISTORY

Birth Date ____/____/____ Age _____ Sex ___ Height _____ Weight _____

Please circle your answer.

1. Do you smoke any tobacco products?

   yes   no

2. Have you ever had any kind of surgery or operation?

   yes   no

   If yes, what type of surgery: _____

   _____

   _____

3. Have you ever been in the hospital for any other reasons?

   yes   no

   If yes, please describe the reason: _____

   _____

   _____

4. Do you have any on-going or current medical problems or conditions?

   yes   no

   If yes, please describe: _____

   _____

5. Do you now have or have you ever had any of the following?
   Please check all that apply to you.

unexplained fever _____

anemia ("low blood") _____

HIV/AIDS _____

weakness _____

sickle cell _____

miscarriage _____

skin rash _____

bloody stools _____

leukemia/lymphoma _____

neck mass/swelling _____

wheezing _____

yellowing of skin _____

bruising easily _____

lupus _____

weight loss _____

kidney problems _____

enlarged lymph nodes _____

liver disease _____

cancer _____

infertility _____

drinking problems _____

thyroid problems _____

night sweats _____

chest pain _____

still birth _____

eye redness   ____

lumps you can feel   ____

child with birth defect   ____

autoimmune disease   ____

overly tired   ____

lung problems   ____

rheumatoid arthritis   ____

mononucleosis("mono")   ____

nagging cough   ____

Please circle your answer.

6. Do you have any symptoms or health problems that you think may be related to your work with BD?

    yes   no

If yes, please describe: _____

_____

7. Have any of your co-workers had similar symptoms or problems?

    yes   no   don't know

If yes, please describe: _____

_____

8. Do you notice any irritation of your eyes, nose, throat, lungs or skin when working with BD?

    yes   no

9. Do you notice any blurred vision, coughing, drowsiness, nausea, or headache when working with BD?

    yes   no

10. Do you take any medications (including birth control or over-the-counter)?

    yes   no

    If yes, please list: _____

    _____

11. Are you allergic to any medication, food, or chemicals?

    yes   no

    If yes, please list: _____

    _____

12. Do you have any health conditions not covered by this questionnaire that you think are affected by your work with BD?

    yes   no

If yes, please explain: _____

_____

13. Did you understand all the questions?

    yes   no

_____

    Signature

1,3-Butadiene (BD) Update Health Questionnaire

DIRECTIONS:

You have been asked to answer the questions on this form because you work with BD (butadiene). These questions ask about changes in your work, medical history, and health concerns since the last time you were evaluated. Please do your best to answer all of the questions. If you need help, please tell the doctor or health care professional who reviews this form.

This form is a confidential medical record. Only information directly related to your health and safety on the job may be given to your employer. Personal health information will not be given to anyone without your consent.

Date: _____

Name:_____

       Last   First   MI

Job Title: _____

Company's Name: _____

Supervisor's Name: _____ Supervisor's Phone No.: ( ) _____-_____

Present Work History

1. Please describe any NEW duties that you have at your job:_____

_____

_____

_____

_____

_____

2. Please list any additional job titles you have:

_____   _____

_____   _____

_____   _____

Please circle your answer.

3. Are you exposed to any other chemicals in your work since the last time you were evaluated for exposure to BD?

     yes   no

If yes, please list what they are: _____

_____

4. Does your personal protective equipment and clothing fit you properly?

     yes   no

5. Have you made changes in this equipment or clothing to make it fit better?

     yes   no

6. Have you been exposed to BD when you were not wearing protective equipment or clothing?

    yes   no

7. Are you exposed to any NEW chemicals at home or while working on hobbies?

    yes   no

    If yes, please list what they are: _____

    _____

8. Since your last BD health evaluation, have you started working any new second or side jobs?

    yes   no

    If yes, what are your duties there? _____

    _____

    _____

Personal Health History

1. What is your current weight?   _____ pounds

2. Have you been diagnosed with any new medical conditions or illness since your last evaluation?

    yes   no

If yes, please tell what they are: _____

_____

3. Since your last evaluation, have you been in the hospital for any illnesses, injuries, or surgery?

      yes   no

If yes, please describe: _____

_____

4. Do you have any of the following? Please place a check for all that apply to you.

unexplained fever	____	liver disease	____
anemia ("low blood")	____	cancer	____
HIV/AIDS	____	infertility	____
weakness	____	drinking problems	____
sickle cell	____	thyroid problems	____
miscarriage	____	night sweats	____
skin rash	____	still birth	____
bloody rash	____	eye redness	____
leukemia/lymphoma	____	lumps you can feel	____
neck mass/swelling	____	child with birth defect	____
wheezing	____	autoimmune disease	____
chest pain	____	overly tired	____
bruising easily	____	lung problems	____
lupus	____	rheumatoid arthritis	____
weight loss	____	mononucleosis "mono"	____
kidney problems	____	nagging cough	____
enlarged lymph nodes	____	yellowing of skin	____

Please circle your answer.

5. Do you have any symptoms or health problems that you think may be related to your work with BD?

    yes   no

If yes, please describe: _____

_____

6. Have any of your co-workers had similar symptoms or problems?

    yes   no   don't know

If yes, please describe: _____

_____

7. Do you notice any irritation of your eyes, nose, throat, lungs, or skin when working with BD?

    yes   no

8. Do you notice any blurred vision, coughing, drowsiness, nausea, or headache when working with BD?

    yes   no

9. Have you been taking any NEW medications (including birth control or over-the-counter)?

       yes   no

If yes, please list:

_____   _____   _____

_____   _____   _____

10. Have you developed any NEW allergies to medications, foods, or chemicals?

       yes   no

If yes, please list:

_____   _____   _____

_____   _____   _____

11. Do you have any health conditions not covered by this questionnaire that you think are affected by your work with BD?

       yes   no

If yes, please explain: _____

_____

12. Did you understand all the questions?

yes   no

___

Signature

§ 1910.1052 Methylene chloride.

This occupational health standard establishes requirements for employers to control occupational exposure to methylene chloride (MC). Employees exposed to MC are at increased risk of developing cancer, adverse effects on the heart, central nervous system and liver, and skin or eye irritation. Exposure may occur through inhalation, by absorption through the skin, or through contact with the skin. MC is a solvent which is used in many different types of work activities, such as paint stripping, polyurethane foam manufacturing, and cleaning and degreasing. Under the requirements of paragraph (d) of this section, each covered employer must make an initial determination of each employee's exposure to MC. If the employer determines that employees are exposed below the action level, the only other provisions of this section that apply are that a record must be made of the determination, the employees must receive information and training under paragraph (l) of this section and, where appropriate, employees must be protected from contact with liquid MC under paragraph (h) of this section. The provisions of the MC standard are as follows:

(a) *Scope and application.* This section applies to all occupational exposures to methylene chloride (MC), Chemical Abstracts Service Registry Number 75–09–2, in general industry, construction and shipyard employment.

(b) *Definitions.* For the purposes of this section, the following definitions shall apply:

Action level means a concentration of airborne MC of 12.5 parts per million (ppm) calculated as an eight (8)-hour time-weighted average (TWA).

Assistant Secretary means the Assistant Secretary of Labor for Occupational Safety and Health, U.S. Department of Labor, or designee.

Authorized person means any person specifically authorized by the employer and required by work duties to be present in regulated areas, or any person entering such an area as a designated representative of employees for the purpose of exercising the right to observe monitoring and measuring procedures under paragraph (d) of this section, or any other person authorized by the OSH Act or regulations issued under the Act.

Director means the Director of the National Institute for Occupational Safety and Health, U.S. Department of Health and Human Services, or designee.

Emergency means any occurrence, such as, but not limited to, equipment failure, rupture of containers, or failure of control equipment, which results, or is likely to result in an uncontrolled release of MC. If an incidental release of MC can be controlled by employees such as maintenance personnel at the time of release and in accordance with the leak/spill provisions required by paragraph (f) of this section, it is not considered an emergency as defined by this standard.

Employee exposure means exposure to airborne MC which occurs or would occur if the employee were not using respiratory protection.

531

Methylene chloride (MC) means an organic compound with chemical formula, $CH_2 Cl_2$. Its Chemical Abstracts Service Registry Number is 75-09-2. Its molecular weight is 84.9 g/mole.

Physician or other licensed health care professional is an individual whose legally permitted scope of practice (*i.e.*, license, registration, or certification) allows him or her to independently provide or be delegated the responsibility to provide some or all of the health care services required by paragraph (j) of this section.

Regulated area means an area, demarcated by the employer, where an employee's exposure to airborne concentrations of MC exceeds or can reasonably be expected to exceed either the 8-hour TWA PEL or the STEL.

Symptom means central nervous system effects such as headaches, disorientation, dizziness, fatigue, and decreased attention span; skin effects such as chapping, erythema, cracked skin, or skin burns; and cardiac effects such as chest pain or shortness of breath.

This section means this methylene chloride standard.

(c) *Permissible exposure limits (PELs)*—(1) *Eight-hour time-weighted average (TWA) PEL.* The employer shall ensure that no employee is exposed to an airborne concentration of MC in excess of twenty-five parts of MC per million parts of air (25 ppm) as an 8-hour TWA.

(2) *Short-term exposure limit (STEL).* The employer shall ensure that no employee is exposed to an airborne concentration of MC in excess of one hundred and twenty-five parts of MC per million parts of air (125 ppm) as determined over a sampling period of fifteen minutes.

(d) *Exposure monitoring*—(1) *Characterization of employee exposure.* (i) Where MC is present in the workplace, the employer shall determine each employee's exposure by either:

(A) Taking a personal breathing zone air sample of each employee's exposure; or

(B) Taking personal breathing zone air samples that are representative of each employee's exposure.

(ii) *Representative samples.* The employer may consider personal breathing zone air samples to be representative of employee exposures when they are taken as follows:

(A) *8-hour TWA PEL.* The employer has taken one or more personal breathing zone air samples for at least one employee in each job classification in a work area during every work shift, and the employee sampled is expected to have the highest MC exposure.

(B) *Short-term exposure limits.* The employer has taken one or more personal breathing zone air samples which indicate the highest likely 15-minute exposures during such operations for at least one employee in each job classification in the work area during every work shift, and the employee sampled is expected to have the highest MC exposure.

(C) *Exception.* Personal breathing zone air samples taken during one work shift may be used to represent employee exposures on other work shifts where the employer can document that the tasks performed and conditions in the workplace are similar across shifts.

(iii) *Accuracy of monitoring.* The employer shall ensure that the methods used to perform exposure monitoring produce results that are accurate to a confidence level of 95 percent, and are:

(A) Within plus or minus 25 percent for airborne concentrations of MC above the 8-hour TWA PEL or the STEL; or

(B) Within plus or minus 35 percent for airborne concentrations of MC at or above the action level but at or below the 8-hour TWA PEL.

(2) *Initial determination.* Each employer whose employees are exposed to MC shall perform initial exposure monitoring to determine each affected employee's exposure, except under the following conditions:

(i) Where objective data demonstrate that MC cannot be released in the workplace in airborne concentrations at or above the action level or above the STEL. The objective data shall represent the highest MC exposures likely to occur under reasonably foreseeable conditions of processing, use, or handling. The employer shall document the objective data exemption as specified in paragraph (m) of this section;

(ii) Where the employer has performed exposure monitoring within 12 months prior to April 10, 1997 and that exposure monitoring meets all other requirements of this section, and was conducted under conditions substantially equivalent to existing conditions; or

(iii) Where employees are exposed to MC on fewer than 30 days per year (e.g., on a construction site), and the employer has measurements by direct-reading instruments which give immediate results (such as a detector tube) and which provide sufficient informa-

tion regarding employee exposures to determine what control measures are necessary to reduce exposures to acceptable levels.

(3) *Periodic monitoring.* Where the initial determination shows employee exposures at or above the action level or above the STEL, the employer shall establish an exposure monitoring program for periodic monitoring of employee exposure to MC in accordance with Table 1:

TABLE 1—INITIAL DETERMINATION EXPOSURE SCENARIOS AND THEIR ASSOCIATED MONITORING
FREQUENCIES

Exposure scenario	Required monitoring activity
Below the action level and at or below the STEL.	No 8-hour TWA or STEL monitoring required.
Below the action level and above the STEL	No 8-hour TWA monitoring required; monitor STEL exposures every three months.
At or above the action level, at or below the TWA, and at or below the STEL.	Monitor 8-hour TWA exposures every six months.
At or above the action level, at or below the TWA, and above the STEL.	Monitor 8-hour TWA exposures every six months and monitor STEL exposures every three months.
Above the TWA and at or below the STEL	Monitor 8-hour TWA exposures every three months. In addition, without regard to the last sentence of the note to paragraph (d)(3), the following employers must monitor STEL exposures every three months until either the date by which they must achieve the 8-hour TWA PEL under paragraph (n) of this section or the date by which they in fact achieve the 8-hour TWA PEL, whichever comes first: employers engaged in polyurethane foam manufacturing; foam fabrication; furniture refinishing; general aviation aircraft stripping; product formulation; use of MC-based adhesives for boat building and repair, recreational vehicle manufacture, van conversion, or upholstery; and use of MC in construction work for restoration and preservation of buildings, painting and paint removal, cabinet making, or floor refinishing and resurfacing.
Above the TWA and above the STEL	Monitor 8-hour TWA exposures and STEL exposures every three months.

NOTE TO PARAGRAPH (d)(3): The employer may decrease the frequency of 8-hour TWA exposure monitoring to every six months when at least two consecutive measurements taken at least seven days apart show exposures to be at or below the 8-hour TWA PEL. The employer may discontinue the periodic 8-hour TWA monitoring for employees where at least two consecutive measurements taken at least seven days apart are below the action level. The employer may discontinue the periodic STEL monitoring for employees where at least two consecutive measurements taken at least 7 days apart are at or below the STEL.

(4) *Additional monitoring.* (i) The employer shall perform exposure monitoring when a change in workplace conditions indicates that employee exposure may have increased. Examples of situations that may require additional monitoring include changes in production, process, control equipment, or work practices, or a leak, rupture, or other breakdown.

(ii) Where exposure monitoring is performed due to a spill, leak, rupture or equipment breakdown, the employer shall clean-up the MC and perform the appropriate repairs before monitoring.

(5) *Employee notification of monitoring results.* (i) The employer shall, within 15 working days after the receipt of the results of any monitoring performed under this section, notify each affected employee of these results in writing, either individually or by posting of results in an appropriate location that is accessible to affected employees.

(ii) Whenever monitoring results indicate that employee exposure is above the 8-hour TWA PEL or the STEL, the employer shall describe in the written notification the corrective action being taken to reduce employee exposure to or below the 8-hour TWA PEL or STEL and the schedule for completion of this action.

533

(6) *Observation of monitoring*—(i) *Employee observation.* The employer shall provide affected employees or their designated representatives an opportunity to observe any monitoring of employee exposure to MC conducted in accordance with this section.

(ii) *Observation procedures.* When observation of the monitoring of employee exposure to MC requires entry into an area where the use of protective clothing or equipment is required, the employer shall provide, at no cost to the observer(s), and the observer(s) shall be required to use such clothing and equipment and shall comply with all other applicable safety and health procedures.

(e) *Regulated areas.* (1) The employer shall establish a regulated area wherever an employee's exposure to airborne concentrations of MC exceeds or can reasonably be expected to exceed either the 8-hour TWA PEL or the STEL.

(2) The employer shall limit access to regulated areas to authorized persons.

(3) The employer shall supply a respirator, selected in accordance with paragraph (h)(3) of this section, to each person who enters a regulated area and shall require each affected employee to use that respirator whenever MC exposures are likely to exceed the 8-hour TWA PEL or STEL.

NOTE TO PARAGRAPH (e)(3): An employer who has implemented all feasible engineering, work practice and administrative controls (as required in paragraph (f) of this section), and who has established a regulated area (as required by paragraph (e)(1) of this section) where MC exposure can be reliably predicted to exceed the 8-hour TWA PEL or the STEL only on certain days (for example, because of work or process schedule) would need to have affected employees use respirators in that regulated area only on those days.

(4) The employer shall ensure that, within a regulated area, employees do not engage in non-work activities which may increase dermal or oral MC exposure.

(5) The employer shall ensure that while employees are wearing respirators, they do not engage in activities (such as taking medication or chewing gum or tobacco) which interfere with respirator seal or performance.

(6) The employer shall demarcate regulated areas from the rest of the workplace in any manner that adequately establishes and alerts employees to the boundaries of the area and minimizes the number of authorized employees exposed to MC within the regulated area.

(7) An employer at a multi-employer worksite who establishes a regulated area shall communicate the access restrictions and locations of these areas to all other employers with work operations at that worksite.

(f) *Methods of compliance*—(1) *Engineering and work practice controls.* The employer shall institute and maintain the effectiveness of engineering controls and work practices to reduce employee exposure to or below the PELs except to the extent that the employer can demonstrate that such controls are not feasible. Wherever the feasible engineering controls and work practices which can be instituted are not sufficient to reduce employee exposure to or below the 8-TWA PEL or STEL, the employer shall use them to reduce employee exposure to the lowest levels achievable by these controls and shall supplement them by the use of respiratory protection that complies with the requirements of paragraph (g) of this section.

(2) *Prohibition of rotation.* The employer shall not implement a schedule of employee rotation as a means of compliance with the PELs.

(3) *Leak and spill detection.* (i) The employer shall implement procedures to detect leaks of MC in the workplace. In work areas where spills may occur, the employer shall make provisions to contain any spills and to safely dispose of any MC-contaminated waste materials.

(ii) The employer shall ensure that all incidental leaks are repaired and that incidental spills are cleaned promptly by employees who use the appropriate personal protective equipment and are trained in proper methods of cleanup.

NOTE TO PARAGRAPH (f)(3)(ii): See appendix A of this section for examples of procedures that satisfy this requirement. Employers covered by this standard may also be subject to the hazardous waste and emergency response provisions contained in 29 CFR 1910.120 (q).

(g) *Respiratory protection*—(1) *General.* For employees who use respirators required by this section, the employer must provide each employee an appropriate respirator that complies with the requirements of this paragraph. Respirators must be used during:

(i) Periods when an employee's exposure to MC exceeds the 8-hour TWA PEL, or STEL (for example, when an employee is using MC in a regulated area).

(ii) Periods necessary to install or implement feasible engineering and work-practice controls.

(iii) A few work operations, such as some maintenance operations and repair activities, for which the employer demonstrates that engineering and work-practice controls are infeasible.

(iv) Work operations for which feasible engineering and work-practice controls are not sufficient to reduce employee exposures to or below the PELs.

(v) Emergencies.

(2) *Respirator program.* (i) The employer must implement a respiratory protection program in accordance with §1910.13(b) through (m) (except (d)(1)(iii)), which covers each employee required by this section to use a respirator.

(ii) Employers who provide employees with gas masks with organic-vapor canisters for the purpose of emergency escape must replace the canisters after any emergency use and before the gas masks are returned to service.

(3) *Respirator selection.* Employers must:

(i) Select, and provide to employees, the appropriate atmosphere-supplying respirator specified in paragraph (d)(3)(i)(A) of 29 CFR 1910.134; however, employers must not select or use half masks of any type because MC may cause eye irritation or damage.

(ii) For emergency escape, provide employees with one of the following respirator options: A self-contained breathing apparatus operated in the continuous-flow or pressure-demand mode; or a gas mask with an organic vapor canister.

(4) *Medical evaluation.* Before having an employee use a supplied-air respirator in the negative-pressure mode, or a gas mask with an organic-vapor canister for emergency escape, the employer must:

(i) Have a physician or other licensed health-care professional (PLHCP) evaluate the employee's ability to use such respiratory protection.

(ii) Ensure that the PLHCP provides their findings in a written opinion to the employee and the employer.

(h) *Protective Work Clothing and Equipment.* (1) Where needed to prevent MC-induced skin or eye irritation, the employer shall provide clean protective clothing and equipment which is resistant to MC, at no cost to the employee, and shall ensure that each affected employee uses it. Eye and face protection shall meet the requirements of 29 CFR 1910.133 or 29 CFR 1915.153, as applicable.

(2) The employer shall clean, launder, repair and replace all protective clothing and equipment required by this paragraph as needed to maintain their effectiveness.

(3) The employer shall be responsible for the safe disposal of such clothing and equipment.

NOTE TO PARAGRAPH (h)(4): See appendix A for examples of disposal procedures that will satisfy this requirement.

(i) *Hygiene facilities.* (1) If it is reasonably foreseeable that employees' skin may contact solutions containing 0.1 percent or greater MC (for example, through splashes, spills or improper work practices), the employer shall provide conveniently located washing facilities capable of removing the MC, and shall ensure that affected employees use these facilities as needed.

(2) If it is reasonably foreseeable that an employee's eyes may contact solutions containing 0.1 percent or greater MC (for example through splashes, spills or improper work practices), the employer shall provide appropriate eyewash facilities within the immediate work area for emergency use, and shall ensure that affected employees use those facilities when necessary.

(j) *Medical surveillance*—(1) *Affected employees.* The employer shall make medical surveillance available for employees who are or may be exposed to MC as follows:

(i) At or above the action level on 30 or more days per year, or above the 8-

535

hour TWA PEL or the STEL on 10 or more days per year;

(ii) Above the 8–TWA PEL or STEL for any time period where an employee has been identified by a physician or other licensed health care professional as being at risk from cardiac disease or from some other serious MC-related health condition and such employee requests inclusion in the medical surveillance program;

(iii) During an emergency.

(2) *Costs.* The employer shall provide all required medical surveillance at no cost to affected employees, without loss of pay and at a reasonable time and place.

(3) *Medical personnel.* The employer shall ensure that all medical surveillance procedures are performed by a physician or other licensed health care professional, as defined in paragraph (b) of this section.

(4) *Frequency of medical surveillance.* The employer shall make medical surveillance available to each affected employee as follows:

(i) *Initial surveillance.* The employer shall provide initial medical surveillance under the schedule provided by paragraph (n)(2)(iii) of this section, or before the time of initial assignment of the employee, whichever is later. The employer need not provide the initial surveillance if medical records show that an affected employee has been provided with medical surveillance that complies with this section within 12 months before April 10, 1997.

(ii) *Periodic medical surveillance.* The employer shall update the medical and work history for each affected employee annually. The employer shall provide periodic physical examinations, including appropriate laboratory surveillance, as follows:

(A) For employees 45 years of age or older, within 12 months of the initial surveillance or any subsequent medical surveillance; and

(B) For employees younger than 45 years of age, within 36 months of the initial surveillance or any subsequent medical surveillance.

(iii) *Termination of employment or reassignment.* When an employee leaves the employer's workplace, or is reassigned to an area where exposure to MC is consistently at or below the action

level and STEL, medical surveillance shall be made available if six months or more have elapsed since the last medical surveillance.

(iv) *Additional surveillance.* The employer shall provide additional medical surveillance at frequencies other than those listed above when recommended in the written medical opinion. (For example, the physician or other licensed health care professional may determine an examination is warranted in less than 36 months for employees younger than 45 years of age based upon evaluation of the results of the annual medical and work history.)

(5) *Content of medical surveillance*—(i) *Medical and work history.* The comprehensive medical and work history shall emphasize neurological symptoms, skin conditions, history of hematologic or liver disease, signs or symptoms suggestive of heart disease (angina, coronary artery disease), risk factors for cardiac disease, MC exposures, and work practices and personal protective equipment used during such exposures.

NOTE TO PARAGRAPH (j)(5)(i): See appendix B of this section for an example of a medical and work history format that would satisfy this requirement.

(ii) *Physical examination.* Where physical examinations are provided as required above, the physician or other licensed health care professional shall accord particular attention to the lungs, cardiovascular system (including blood pressure and pulse), liver, nervous system, and skin. The physician or other licensed health care professional shall determine the extent and nature of the physical examination based on the health status of the employee and analysis of the medical and work history.

(iii) *Laboratory surveillance.* The physician or other licensed health care professional shall determine the extent of any required laboratory surveillance based on the employee's observed health status and the medical and work history.

NOTE TO PARAGRAPH (j)(5)(iii): See appendix B of this section for information regarding medical tests. Laboratory surveillance may include before- and after-shift carboxyhemoglobin determinations, resting

ECG, hematocrit, liver function tests and cholesterol levels.

(iv) *Other information or reports.* The medical surveillance shall also include any other information or reports the physician or other licensed health care professional determines are necessary to assess the employee's health in relation to MC exposure.

(6) *Content of emergency medical surveillance.* The employer shall ensure that medical surveillance made available when an employee has been exposed to MC in emergency situations includes, at a minimum:

(i) Appropriate emergency treatment and decontamination of the exposed employee;

(ii) Comprehensive physical examination with special emphasis on the nervous system, cardiovascular system, lungs, liver and skin, including blood pressure and pulse;

(iii) Updated medical and work history, as appropriate for the medical condition of the employee; and

(iv) Laboratory surveillance, as indicated by the employee's health status.

NOTE TO PARAGRAPH (j)(6)(iv): See appendix B for examples of tests which may be appropriate.

(7) *Additional examinations and referrals.* Where the physician or other licensed health care professional determines it is necessary, the scope of the medical examination shall be expanded and the appropriate additional medical surveillance, such as referrals for consultation or examination, shall be provided.

(8) *Information provided to the physician or other licensed health care professional.* The employer shall provide the following information to a physician or other licensed health care professional who is involved in the diagnosis of MC-induced health effects:

(i) A copy of this section including its applicable appendices;

(ii) A description of the affected employee's past, current and anticipated future duties as they relate to the employee's MC exposure;

(iii) The employee's former or current exposure levels or, for employees not yet occupationally exposed to MC, the employee's anticipated exposure levels and the frequency and exposure levels anticipated to be associated with emergencies;

(iv) A description of any personal protective equipment, such as respirators, used or to be used; and

(v) Information from previous employment-related medical surveillance of the affected employee which is not otherwise available to the physician or other licensed health care professional.

(9) *Written medical opinions.* (i) For each physical examination required by this section, the employer shall ensure that the physician or other licensed health care professional provides to the employer and to the affected employee a written opinion regarding the results of that examination within 15 days of completion of the evaluation of medical and laboratory findings, but not more than 30 days after the examination. The written medical opinion shall be limited to the following information:

(A) The physician or other licensed health care professional's opinion concerning whether exposure to MC may contribute to or aggravate the employee's existing cardiac, hepatic, neurological (including stroke) or dermal disease or whether the employee has any other medical condition(s) that would place the employee's health at increased risk of material impairment from exposure to MC.

(B) Any recommended limitations upon the employee's exposure to MC, including removal from MC exposure, or upon the employee's use of respirators, protective clothing, or other protective equipment.

(C) A statement that the employee has been informed by the physician or other licensed health care professional that MC is a potential occupational carcinogen, of risk factors for heart disease, and the potential for exacerbation of underlying heart disease by exposure to MC through its metabolism to carbon monoxide; and

(D) A statement that the employee has been informed by the physician or other licensed health care professional of the results of the medical examination and any medical conditions resulting from MC exposure which require further explanation or treatment.

(ii) The employer shall instruct the physician or other licensed health care

537

professional not to reveal to the employer, orally or in the written opinion, any specific records, findings, and diagnoses that have no bearing on occupational exposure to MC.

NOTE TO PARAGRAPH (j)(9)(ii): The written medical opinion may also include information and opinions generated to comply with other OSHA health standards.

(10) *Medical presumption.* For purposes of this paragraph (j) of this section, the physician or other licensed health care professional shall presume, unless medical evidence indicates to the contrary, that a medical condition is unlikely to require medical removal from MC exposure if the employee is not exposed to MC above the 8-hour TWA PEL. If the physician or other licensed health care professional recommends removal for an employee exposed below the 8-hour TWA PEL, the physician or other licensed health care professional shall cite specific medical evidence, sufficient to rebut the presumption that exposure below the 8-hour TWA PEL is unlikely to require removal, to support the recommendation. If such evidence is cited by the physician or other licensed health care professional, the employer must remove the employee. If such evidence is not cited by the physician or other licensed health care professional, the employer is not required to remove the employee.

(11) *Medical Removal Protection (MRP).* (i) Temporary medical removal and return of an employee.

(A) Except as provided in paragraph (j)(10) of this section, when a medical determination recommends removal because the employee's exposure to MC may contribute to or aggravate the employee's existing cardiac, hepatic, neurological (including stroke), or skin disease, the employer must provide medical removal protection benefits to the employee and either:

(1) Transfer the employee to comparable work where methylene chloride exposure is below the action level; or

(2) Remove the employee from MC exposure.

(B) If comparable work is not available and the employer is able to demonstrate that removal and the costs of extending MRP benefits to an additional employee, considering feasibility in relation to the size of the employer's business and the other requirements of this standard, make further reliance on MRP an inappropriate remedy, the employer may retain the additional employee in the existing job until transfer or removal becomes appropriate, provided:

(1) The employer ensures that the employee receives additional medical surveillance, including a physical examination at least every 60 days until transfer or removal occurs; and

(2) The employer or PLHCP informs the employee of the risk to the employee's health from continued MC exposure.

(C) The employer shall maintain in effect any job-related protective measures or limitations, other than removal, for as long as a medical determination recommends them to be necessary.

(ii) End of MRP benefits and return of the employee to former job status.

(A) The employer may cease providing MRP benefits at the earliest of the following:

(1) Six months;

(2) Return of the employee to the employee's former job status following receipt of a medical determination concluding that the employee's exposure to MC no longer will aggravate any cardiac, hepatic, neurological (including stroke), or dermal disease;

(3) Receipt of a medical determination concluding that the employee can never return to MC exposure.

(B) For the purposes of this paragraph (j), the requirement that an employer return an employee to the employee's former job status is not intended to expand upon or restrict any rights an employee has or would have had, absent temporary medical removal, to a specific job classification or position under the terms of a collective bargaining agreement.

(12) *Medical removal protection benefits.* (i) For purposes of this paragraph (j), the term medical removal protection benefits means that, for each removal, an employer must maintain for up to six months the earnings, seniority, and other employment rights and benefits of the employee as though the employee had not been removed from MC exposure or transferred to a comparable job.

(ii) During the period of time that an employee is removed from exposure to MC, the employer may condition the provision of medical removal protection benefits upon the employee's participation in follow-up medical surveillance made available pursuant to this section.

(iii) If a removed employee files a workers' compensation claim for a MC-related disability, the employer shall continue the MRP benefits required by this paragraph until either the claim is resolved or the 6-month period for payment f MRP benefits has passed, whichever occurs first. To the extent the employee is entitled to indemnity payments for earnings lost during the period of removal, the employer's obligation to provide medical removal protection benefits to the employee shall be reduced by the amount of such indemnity payments.

(iv) The employer's obligation to provide medical removal protection benefits to a removed employee shall be reduced to the extent that the employee receives compensation for earnings lost during the period of removal from either a publicly or an employer-funded compensation program, or receives income from employment with another employer made possible by virtue of the employee's removal.

(13) *Voluntary removal or restriction of an employee.* Where an employer, although not required by this section to do so, removes an employee from exposure to MC or otherwise places any limitation on an employee due to the effects of MC exposure on the employee's medical condition, the employer shall provide medical removal protection benefits to the employee equal to those required by paragraph (j)(12) of this section.

(14) *Multiple health care professional review mechanism.* (i) If the employer selects the initial physician or licensed health care professional (PLHCP) to conduct any medical examination or consultation provided to an employee under this paragraph (j)(11), the employer shall notify the employee of the right to seek a second medical opinion each time the employer provides the employee with a copy of the written opinion of that PLHCP.

(ii) If the employee does not agree with the opinion of the employer-selected PLHCP, notifies the employer of that fact, and takes steps to make an appointment with a second PLHCP within 15 days of receiving a copy of the written opinion of the initial PLHCP, the employer shall pay for the PLHCP chosen by the employee to perform at least the following:

(A) Review any findings, determinations or recommendations of the initial PLHCP; and

(B) Conduct such examinations, consultations, and laboratory tests as the PLHCP deems necessary to facilitate this review.

(iii) If the findings, determinations or recommendations of the second PLHCP differ from those of the initial PLHCP, then the employer and the employee shall instruct the two health care professionals to resolve the disagreement.

(iv) If the two health care professionals are unable to resolve their disagreement within 15 days, then those two health care professionals shall jointly designate a PLHCP who is a specialist in the field at issue. The employer shall pay for the specialist to perform at least the following:

(A) Review the findings, determinations, and recommendations of the first two PLHCPs; and

(B) Conduct such examinations, consultations, laboratory tests and discussions with the prior PLHCPs as the specialist deems necessary to resolve the disagreements of the prior health care professionals.

(v) The written opinion of the specialist shall be the definitive medical determination. The employer shall act consistent with the definitive medical determination, unless the employer and employee agree that the written opinion of one of the other two PLHCPs shall be the definitive medical determination.

(vi) The employer and the employee or authorized employee representative may agree upon the use of any expeditious alternate health care professional determination mechanism in lieu of the multiple health care professional review mechanism provided by this paragraph so long as the alternate

539

mechanism otherwise satisfies the requirements contained in this paragraph.

(k) *Hazard communication*—(1) *Hazard communication—general.* (i) Chemical manufacturers, importers, distributors and employers shall comply with all requirements of the Hazard Communication Standard (HCS) (§ 1910.1200) for MC.

(ii) In classifying the hazards of MC at least the following hazards are to be addressed: Cancer, cardiac effects (including elevation of carboxyhemoglobin), central nervous system effects, liver effects, and skin and eye irritation.

(iii) Employers shall include MC in the hazard communication program established to comply with the HCS (§ 1910.1200). Employers shall ensure that each employee has access to labels on containers of MC and to safety data sheets, and is trained in accordance with the requirements of HCS and paragraph (1) of this section.

(2) [Reserved]

(1) *Employee information and training.* (1) The employer shall provide information and training for each affected employee prior to or at the time of initial assignment to a job involving potential exposure to MC.

(2) The employer shall ensure that information and training is presented in a manner that is understandable to the employees.

(3) In addition to the information required under the Hazard Communication Standard at 29 CFR 1910.1200, 29 CFR 1915.1200, or 29 CFR 1926.59, as appropiate:

(i) The employer shall inform each affected employee of the requirements of this section and information available in its appendices, as well as how to access or obtain a copy of it in the workplace;

(ii) Wherever an employee's exposure to airborne concentrations of MC exceeds or can reasonably be expected to exceed the action level, the employer shall inform each affected employee of the quantity, location, manner of use, release, and storage of MC and the specific operations in the workplace that could result in exposure to MC, particularly noting where exposures may be above the 8-hour TWA PEL or STEL;

(4) The employer shall train each affected employee as required under the Hazard Communication standard at 29 CFR 1910.1200, 29 CFR 1915.1200, or 29 CFR 1926.59, as appropiate.

(5) The employer shall re-train each affected employee as necessary to ensure that each employee exposed above the action level or the STEL maintains the requisite understanding of the principles of safe use and handling of MC in the workplace.

(6) Whenever there are workplace changes, such as modifications of tasks or procedures or the institution of new tasks or procedures, which increase employee exposure, and where those exposures exceed or can reasonably be expected to exceed the action level, the employer shall update the training as necessary to ensure that each affected employee has the requisite proficiency.

(7) An employer whose employees are exposed to MC at a multi-employer worksite shall notify the other employers with work operations at that site in accordance with the requirements of the Hazard Communication Standard, 29 CFR 1910.1200, 29 CFR 1915.1200, or 29 CFR 1926.59, as appropiate.

(8) The employer shall provide to the Assistant Secretary or the Director, upon request, all available materials relating to employee information and training.

(m) *Recordkeeping*—(1) *Objective data.* (i) Where an employer seeks to demonstrate that initial monitoring is unnecessary through reasonable reliance on objective data showing that any materials in the workplace containing MC will not release MC at levels which exceed the action level or the STEL under foreseeable conditions of exposure, the employer shall establish and maintain an accurate record of the objective data relied upon in support of the exemption.

(ii) This record shall include at least the following information:

(A) The MC-containing material in question;

(B) The source of the objective data;

(C) The testing protocol, results of testing, and/or analysis of the material for the release of MC;

(D) A description of the operation exempted under paragraph (d)(2)(i) of this section and how the data support the exemption; and

(E) Other data relevant to the operations, materials, processing, or employee exposures covered by the exemption.

(iii) The employer shall maintain this record for the duration of the employer's reliance upon such objective data.

(2) *Exposure measurements.* (i) The employer shall establish and keep an accurate record of all measurements taken to monitor employee exposure to MC as prescribed in paragraph (d) of this section.

(ii) Where the employer has 20 or more employees, this record shall include at least the following information:

(A) The date of measurement for each sample taken;

(B) The operation involving exposure to MC which is being monitored;

(C) Sampling and analytical methods used and evidence of their accuracy;

(D) Number, duration, and results of samples taken;

(E) Type of personal protective equipment, such as respiratory protective devices, worn, if any; and

(F) Name, social security number, job classification and exposure of all of the employees represented by monitoring, indicating which employees were actually monitored.

(iii) Where the employer has fewer than 20 employees, the record shall include at least the following information:

(A) The date of measurement for each sample taken;

(B) Number, duration, and results of samples taken; and

(C) Name, social security number, job classification and exposure of all of the employees represented by monitoring, indicating which employees were actually monitored.

(iv) The employer shall maintain this record for at least thirty (30) years, in accordance with 29 CFR 1910.1020.

(3) *Medical surveillance.* (i) The employer shall establish and maintain an accurate record for each employee subject to medical surveillance under paragraph (j) of this section.

(ii) The record shall include at least the following information:

(A) The name, social security number and description of the duties of the employee;

(B) Written medical opinions; and

(C) Any employee medical conditions related to exposure to MC.

(iii) The employer shall ensure that this record is maintained for the duration of employment plus thirty (30) years, in accordance with 29 CFR 1910.1020.

(4) *Availability.* (i) The employer, upon written request, shall make all records required to be maintained by this section available to the Assistant Secretary and the Director for examination and copying in accordance with 29 CFR 1910.1020.

NOTE TO PARAGRAPH (m)(4)(i): All records required to be maintained by this section may be kept in the most administratively convenient form (for example, electronic or computer records would satisfy this requirement).

(ii) The employer, upon request, shall make any employee exposure and objective data records required by this section available for examination and copying by affected employees, former employees, and designated representatives in accordance with 29 CFR 1910.1020.

(iii) The employer, upon request, shall make employee medical records required to be kept by this section available for examination and copying by the subject employee and by anyone having the specific written consent of the subject employee in accordance with 29 CFR 1910.1020.

(5) *Transfer of records.* The employer shall comply with the requirements concerning transfer of records set forth in 29 CFR 1910.1020(h).

(n) [Reserved]

(o) *Appendices.* The information contained in the appendices does not, by itself, create any additional obligations not otherwise imposed or detract from any existing obligation.

NOTE TO PARAGRAPH (o): The requirement of 29 CFR 1910.1052(g)(1) to use respiratory protection whenever an employee's exposure to methylene chloride exceeds or can reasonably be expected to exceed the 8-hour TWA PEL is hereby stayed until August 31, 1998 for employers engaged in polyurethane foam

541

manufacturing; foam fabrication; furniture refinishing; general aviation aircraft stripping; formulation of products containing methylene chloride; boat building and repair; recreational vehicle manufacture; van conversion; upholstery; and use of methylene chloride in construction work for restoration and preservation of buildings, painting and paint removal, cabinet making and/or floor refinishing and resurfacing.

The requirement of 29 CFR 1910.1052(f)(1) to implement engineering controls to achieve the 8-hour TWA PEL and STEL is hereby stayed until December 10, 1998 for employers with more than 100 employees engaged in polyurethane foam manufacturing and for employers with more than 20 employees engaged in foam fabrication; furniture refinishing; general aviation aircraft stripping; formulation of products containing methylene chloride; boat building and repair; recreational vehicle manufacture; van conversion; upholstery; and use of methylene chloride in construction work for restoration and preservation of buildings, painting and paint removal, cabinet making and/or floor refinishing and resurfacing.

APPENDIX A TO SECTION 1910.1052—SUBSTANCE SAFETY DATA SHEET AND TECHNICAL GUIDELINES FOR METHYLENE CHLORIDE

I. SUBSTANCE IDENTIFICATION

A. Substance: Methylene chloride (CH_2Cl_2).

B. Synonyms: MC, Dichloromethane (DCM); Methylene dichloride; Methylene bichloride; Methane dichloride; CAS: 75–09–2; NCI-C50102.

C. Physical data:

1. Molecular weight: 84.9.

2. Boiling point (760 mm Hg): 39.8 °C (104 °F).

3. Specific gravity (water = 1): 1.3.

4. Vapor density (air = 1 at boiling point): 2.9.

5. Vapor pressure at 20 °C (68 °F): 350 mm Hg.

6. Solubility in water, g/100 g water at 20 °C (68 °F) = 1.32.

7. Appearance and odor: colorless liquid with a chloroform-like odor.

D. Uses:

MC is used as a solvent, especially where high volatility is required. It is a good solvent for oils, fats, waxes, resins, bitumen, rubber and cellulose acetate and is a useful paint stripper and degreaser. It is used in paint removers, in propellant mixtures for aerosol containers, as a solvent for plastics, as a degreasing agent, as an extracting agent in the pharmaceutical industry and as a blowing agent in polyurethane foams. Its solvent property is sometimes increased by mixing with methanol, petroleum naphtha or tetrachloroethylene.

E. Appearance and odor:

MC is a clear colorless liquid with a chloroform-like odor. It is slightly soluble in water and completely miscible with most organic solvents.

F. Permissible exposure:

Exposure may not exceed 25 parts MC per million parts of air (25 ppm) as an eight-hour time-weighted average (8-hour TWA PEL) or 125 parts of MC per million parts of air (125 ppm) averaged over a 15-minute period (STEL).

II. HEALTH HAZARD DATA

A. MC can affect the body if it is inhaled or if the liquid comes in contact with the eyes or skin. It can also affect the body if it is swallowed.

B. Effects of overexposure:

1. Short-term Exposure:

MC is an anesthetic. Inhaling the vapor may cause mental confusion, light-headedness, nausea, vomiting, and headache. Continued exposure may cause increased light-headedness, staggering, unconsciousness, and even death. High vapor concentrations may also cause irritation of the eyes and respiratory tract. Exposure to MC may make the symptoms of angina (chest pains) worse. Skin exposure to liquid MC may cause irritation. If liquid MC remains on the skin, it may cause skin burns. Splashes of the liquid into the eyes may cause irritation.

2. Long-term (chronic) exposure:

The best evidence that MC causes cancer is from laboratory studies in which rats, mice and hamsters inhaled MC 6 hours per day, 5 days per week for 2 years. MC exposure produced lung and liver tumors in mice and mammary tumors in rats. No carcinogenic effects of MC were found in hamsters.

There are also some human epidemiological studies which show an association between occupational exposure to MC and increases in biliary (bile duct) cancer and a type of brain cancer. Other epidemiological studies have not observed a relationship between MC exposure and cancer. OSHA interprets these results to mean that there is suggestive (but not absolute) evidence that MC is a human carcinogen.

C. Reporting signs and symptoms:

You should inform your employer if you develop any signs or symptoms and suspect that they are caused by exposure to MC.

D. Warning Properties:

1. Odor Threshold:

Different authors have reported varying odor thresholds for MC. Kirk-Othmer and Sax both reported 25 to 50 ppm; Summer and May both reported 150 ppm; Spector reports 320 ppm. Patty, however, states that since one can become adapted to the odor, MC should not be considered to have adequate warning properties.

2. Eye Irritation Level:

Kirk-Othmer reports that "MC vapor is seriously damaging to the eyes." Sax agrees with Kirk-Othmer's statement. The ACGIH Documentation of TLVs states that irritation of the eyes has been observed in workers exposed to concentrations up to 5000 ppm.

3. Evaluation of Warning Properties:

Since a wide range of MC odor thresholds are reported (25–320 ppm), and human adaptation to the odor occurs, MC is considered to be a material with poor warning properties.

III. EMERGENCY FIRST AID PROCEDURES

In the event of emergency, institute first aid procedures and send for first aid or medical assistance.

A. Eye and Skin Exposures:

If there is a potential for liquid MC to come in contact with eye or skin, face shields and skin protective equipment must be provided and used. If liquid MC comes in contact with the eye, get medical attention. Contact lenses should not be worn when working with this chemical.

B. Breathing:

If a person breathes in large amounts of MC, move the exposed person to fresh air at once. If breathing has stopped, perform cardiopulmorary resuscitation. Keep the affected person warm and at rest. Get medical attention as soon as possible.

C. Rescue:

Move the affected person from the hazardous exposure immediately. If the exposed person has been overcome, notify someone else and put into effect the established emergency rescue procedures. Understand the facility's emergency rescue procedures and know the locations of rescue equipment before the need arises. Do not become a casualty yourself.

IV. RESPIRATORS, PROTECTIVE CLOTHING, AND EYE PROTECTION

A. Respirators:

Good industrial hygiene practices recommend that engineering controls be used to reduce environmental concentrations to the permissible exposure level. However, there are some exceptions where respirators may be used to control exposure. Respirators may be used when engineering and work practice controls are not feasible, when such controls are in the process of being installed, or when these controls fail and need to be supplemented. Respirators may also be used for operations which require entry into tanks or closed vessels, and in emergency situations.

If the use of respirators is necessary, the only respirators permitted are those that have been approved by the Mine Safety and Health Administration (MSHA) or the National Institute for Occupational Safety and Health (NIOSH). Supplied-air respirators are *required* because air-purifying respirators do not provide adequate respiratory protection against MC.

In addition to respirator selection, a complete written respiratory protection program should be instituted which includes regular training, maintenance, inspection, cleaning, and evaluation. If you can smell MC while wearing a respirator, proceed immediately to fresh air. If you experience difficulty in breathing while wearing a respirator, tell your employer.

B. Protective Clothing:

Employees must be provided with and required to use impervious clothing, gloves, face shields (eight-inch minimum), and other appropriate protective clothing necessary to prevent repeated or prolonged skin contact with liquid MC or contact with vessels containing liquid MC. Any clothing which becomes wet with liquid MC should be removed immediately and not reworn until the employer has ensured that the protective clothing is fit for reuse. Contaminated protective clothing should be placed in a regulated area designated by the employer for removal of MC before the clothing is laundered or disposed of. Clothing and equipment should remain in the regulated area until all of the MC contamination has evaporated; clothing and equipment should then be laundered or disposed of as appropriate.

C. Eye Protection:

Employees should be provided with and required to use splash-proof safety goggles where liquid MC may contact the eyes.

V. HOUSEKEEPING AND HYGIENE FACILITIES

For purposes of complying with 29 CFR 1910.141, the following items should be emphasized:

A. The workplace should be kept clean, orderly, and in a sanitary condition. The employer should institute a leak and spill detection program for operations involving liquid MC in order to detect sources of fugitive MC emissions.

B. Emergency drench showers and eyewash facilities are recommended. These should be maintained in a sanitary condition. Suitable cleansing agents should also be provided to assure the effective removal of MC from the skin.

C. Because of the hazardous nature of MC, contaminated protective clothing should be placed in a regulated area designated by the employer for removal of MC before the clothing is laundered or disposed of.

VI. PRECAUTIONS FOR SAFE USE, HANDLING, AND STORAGE

A. Fire and Explosion Hazards:

MC has no flash point in a conventional closed tester, but it forms flammable vapor-air mixtures at approximately 100 °C (212 °F), or higher. It has a lower explosion limit of 12%, and an upper explosion limit of 19% in air. It has an autoignition temperature of 556.1 °C (1033 °F), and a boiling point of 39.8

543

°C (104 °F). It is heavier than water with a specific gravity of 1.3. It is slightly soluble in water.

B. Reactivity Hazards:

Conditions contributing to the instability of MC are heat and moisture. Contact with strong oxidizers, caustics, and chemically active metals such as aluminum or magnesium powder, sodium and potassium may cause fires and explosions.

Special precautions: Liquid MC will attack some forms of plastics, rubber, and coatings.

C. Toxicity:

Liquid MC is painful and irritating if splashed in the eyes or if confined on the skin by gloves, clothing, or shoes. Vapors in high concentrations may cause narcosis and death. Prolonged exposure to vapors may cause cancer or exacerbate cardiac disease.

D. Storage:

Protect against physical damage. Because of its corrosive properties, and its high vapor pressure, MC should be stored in plain, galvanized or lead lined, mild steel containers in a cool, dry, well ventilated area away from direct sunlight, heat source and acute fire hazards.

E. Piping Material:

All piping and valves at the loading or unloading station should be of material that is resistant to MC and should be carefully inspected prior to connection to the transport vehicle and periodically during the operation.

F. Usual Shipping Containers:

Glass bottles, 5- and 55-gallon steel drums, tank cars, and tank trucks.

NOTE: This section addresses MC exposure in marine terminal and longshore employment only where leaking or broken packages allow MC exposure that is not addressed through compliance with 29 CFR parts 1917 and 1918, respectively.

G. Electrical Equipment:

Electrical installations in Class I hazardous locations as defined in Article 500 of the National Electrical Code, should be installed according to Article 501 of the code; and electrical equipment should be suitable for use in atmospheres containing MC vapors. See Flammable and Combustible Liquids Code (NFPA No. 325M), Chemical Safety Data Sheet SD–86 (Manufacturing Chemists' Association, Inc.).

H. Fire Fighting:

When involved in fire, MC emits highly toxic and irritating fumes such as phosgene, hydrogen chloride and carbon monoxide. Wear breathing apparatus and use water spray to keep fire-exposed containers cool. Water spray may be used to flush spills away from exposures. Extinguishing media are dry chemical, carbon dioxide, foam. For purposes of compliance with 29 CFR 1910.307, locations classified as hazardous due to the presence of MC shall be Class I.

I. Spills and Leaks:

Persons not wearing protective equipment and clothing should be restricted from areas of spills or leaks until cleanup has been completed. If MC has spilled or leaked, the following steps should be taken:

1. Remove all ignition sources.

2. Ventilate area of spill or leak.

3. Collect for reclamation or absorb in vermiculite, dry sand, earth, or a similar material.

J. Methods of Waste Disposal:

Small spills should be absorbed onto sand and taken to a safe area for atmospheric evaporation. Incineration is the preferred method for disposal of large quantities by mixing with a combustible solvent and spraying into an incinerator equipped with acid scrubbers to remove hydrogen chloride gases formed. Complete combustion will convert carbon monoxide to carbon dioxide. Care should be taken for the presence of phosgene.

K. You should not keep food, beverage, or smoking materials, or eat or smoke in regulated areas where MC concentrations are above the permissible exposure limits.

L. Portable heating units should not be used in confined areas where MC is used.

M. Ask your supervisor where MC is used in your work area and for any additional plant safety and health rules.

VII. MEDICAL REQUIREMENTS

Your employer is required to offer you the opportunity to participate in a medical surveillance program if you are exposed to MC at concentrations at or above the action level (12.5 ppm 8-hour TWA) for more than 30 days a year or at concentrations exceeding the PELs (25 ppm 8-hour TWA or 125 ppm 15-minute STEL) for more than 10 days a year. If you are exposed to MC at concentrations over either of the PELs, your employer will also be required to have a physician or other licensed health care professional ensure that you are able to wear the respirator that you are assigned. Your employer must provide all medical examinations relating to your MC exposure at a reasonable time and place and at no cost to you.

VIII. MONITORING AND MEASUREMENT PROCEDURES

A. Exposure above the Permissible Exposure Limit:

1. Eight-hour exposure evaluation: Measurements taken for the purpose of determining employee exposure under this section are best taken with consecutive samples covering the full shift. Air samples must be taken in the employee's breathing zone.

2. Monitoring techniques: The sampling and analysis under this section may be performed by collection of the MC vapor on two charcoal adsorption tubes in series or other

composition adsorption tubes, with subsequent chemical analysis. Sampling and analysis may also be performed by instruments such as real-time continuous monitoring systems, portable direct reading instruments, or passive dosimeters as long as measurements taken using these methods accurately evaluate the concentration of MC in employees'' breathing zones.

OSHA method 80 is an example of a validated method of sampling and analysis of MC. Copies of this method are available from OSHA or can be downloaded from the Internet at *http://www.osha.gov*. The employer has the obligation of selecting a monitoring method which meets the accuracy and precision requirements of the standard under his or her unique field conditions. The standard requires that the method of monitoring must be accurate, to a 95 percent confidence level, to plus or minus 25 percent for concentrations of MC at or above 25 ppm, and to plus or minus 35 percent for concentrations at or below 25 ppm. In addition to OSHA method 80, there are numerous other methods available for monitoring for MC in the workplace.

B. Since many of the duties relating to employee exposure are dependent on the results of measurement procedures, employers must assure that the evaluation of employee exposure is performed by a technically qualified person.

IX. OBSERVATION OF MONITORING

Your employer is required to perform measurements that are representative of your exposure to MC and you or your designated representative are entitled to observe the monitoring procedure. You are entitled to observe the steps taken in the measurement procedure, and to record the results obtained. When the monitoring procedure is taking place in an area where respirators or personal protective clothing and equipment are required to be worn, you or your representative must also be provided with, and must wear, protective clothing and equipment.

X. ACCESS TO INFORMATION

A. Your employer is required to inform you of the information contained in this Appendix. In addition, your employer must instruct you in the proper work practices for using MC, emergency procedures, and the correct use of protective equipment.

B. Your employer is required to determine whether you are being exposed to MC. You or your representative has the right to observe employee measurements and to record the results obtained. Your employer is required to inform you of your exposure. If your employer determines that you are being over exposed, he or she is required to inform you of the actions which are being taken to re-

duce your exposure to within permissible exposure limits.

C. Your employer is required to keep records of your exposures and medical examinations. These records must be kept by the employer for at least thirty (30) years.

D. Your employer is required to release your exposure and medical records to you or your representative upon your request.

E. Your employer is required to provide labels and safety data sheets (SDSs) for all materials, mixtures or solutions composed of greater than 0.1 percent MC. These materials, mixtures or solutions would be classified and labeled in accordance with § 1910.1200.

DANGER CONTAINS METHYLENE CHLORIDE
POTENTIAL CANCER HAZARD

May worsen heart disease because methylene chloride is converted to carbon monoxide in the body.

May cause dizziness, headache, irritation of the throat and lungs, loss of consciousness and death at high concentrations (for example, if used in a poorly ventilated room).

Avoid Skin Contact. Contact with liquid causes skin and eye irritation.

XI. COMMON OPERATIONS AND CONTROLS

The following list includes some common operations in which exposure to MC may occur and control methods which may be effective in each case:

Operations	Controls
Use as solvent in paint and varnish removers; manufacture of aerosols; cold cleaning and ultrasonic cleaning; and as a solvent in furniture stripping.	General dilution ventilation; local exhaust ventilation; personal protective equipment; substitution.
Use as solvent in vapor degreasing.	Process enclosure; local exhaust ventilation; chilling coils; substitution.
Use as a secondary refrigerant in air conditioning and scientific testing.	General dilution ventilation; local exhaust ventilation; personal protective equipment.

APPENDIX B TO SECTION 1910.1052—MEDICAL SURVEILLANCE FOR METHYLENE CHLORIDE

I. PRIMARY ROUTE OF ENTRY

Inhalation.

II. TOXICOLOGY

Methylene Chloride (MC) is primarily an inhalation hazard. The principal acute hazardous effects are the depressant action on the central nervous system, possible cardiac toxicity and possible liver toxicity. The range of CNS effects are from decreased eye/hand coordination and decreased performance in vigilance tasks to narcosis and even death of individuals exposed at very high doses. Cardiac toxicity is due to the metabolism of MC to carbon monoxide, and the effects of carbon monoxide on heart tissue. Carbon monoxide displaces oxygen in the blood, decreases the oxygen available to heart tissue, increasing the risk of damage to the heart, which may result in heart attacks in susceptible individuals. Susceptible individuals include persons with heart disease and those with risk factors for heart disease.

·Elevated liver enzymes and irritation to the respiratory passages and eyes have also been reported for both humans and experimental animals exposed to MC vapors.

MC is metabolized to carbon monoxide and carbon dioxide via two separate pathways. Through the first pathway, MC is metabolized to carbon monoxide as an end-product via the P-450 mixed function oxidase pathway located in the microsomal fraction of the cell. This biotransformation of MC to carbon monoxide occurs through the process of microsomal oxidative dechlorination which takes place primarily in the liver. The amount of conversion to carbon monoxide is significant as measured by the concentration of carboxyhemoglobin, up to 12% measured in the blood following occupational exposure of up to 610 ppm. Through the second pathway, MC is metabolized to carbon dioxide as an end product (with formaldehyde and formic acid as metabolic intermediates) via the glutathione dependent enzyme found in the cytosolic fraction of the liver cell. Metabolites along this pathway are believed to be associated with the carcinogenic activity of MC.

MC has been tested for carcinogenicity in several laboratory rodents. These rodent studies indicate that there is clear evidence that MC is carcinogenic to male and female mice and female rats. Based on epidemiologic studies, OSHA has concluded that there is suggestive evidence of increased cancer risk in MC-related worker populations. The epidemiological evidence is consistent with the finding of excess cancer in the experimental animal studies. NIOSH regards MC as a potential occupational carcinogen and the International Agency for Research Cancer (IARC) classifies MC as an animal carcinogen. OSHA considers MC as a suspected human carcinogen.

III. MEDICAL SIGNS AND SYMPTOMS OF ACUTE EXPOSURE

Skin exposure to liquid MC may cause irritation or skin burns. Liquid MC can also be irritating to the eyes. MC is also absorbed through the skin and may contribute to the MC exposure by inhalation.

At high concentrations in air, MC may cause nausea, vomiting, light-headedness, numbness of the extremities, changes in blood enzyme levels, and breathing problems, leading to bronchitis and pulmonary edema, unconsciousness and even death.

At lower concentrations in air, MC may cause irritation to the skin, eye, and respiratory tract and occasionally headache and nausea. Perhaps the greatest problem from exposure to low concentrations of MC is the CNS effects on coordination and alertness that may cause unsafe operations of machinery and equipment, leading to self-injury or accidents.

Low levels and short duration exposures do not seem to produce permanent disability, but chronic exposures to MC have been demonstrated to produce liver toxicity in animals, and therefore, the evidence is suggestive for liver toxicity in humans after chronic exposure.

Chronic exposure to MC may also cause cancer.

IV. SURVEILLANCE AND PREVENTIVE CONSIDERATIONS

As discussed above, MC is classified as a suspect or potential human carcinogen. It is a central nervous system (CNS) depressant and a skin, eye and respiratory tract irritant. At extremely high concentrations, MC has caused liver damage in animals.

MC principally affects the CNS, where it acts as a narcotic. The observation of the symptoms characteristic of CNS depression, along with a physical examination, provides the best detection of early neurological disorders. Since exposure to MC also increases the carboxyhemoglobin level in the blood, ambient carbon monoxide levels would have an additive effect on that carboxyhemoglobin level. Based on such information, a periodic post-shift carboxyhemoglobin test as an index of the presence of carbon monoxide in the blood is recommended, but not required, for medical surveillance.

Based on the animal evidence and three epidemiologic studies previously mentioned, OSHA concludes that MC is a suspect human carcinogen. The medical surveillance program is designed to observe exposed workers on a regular basis. While the medical surveillance program cannot detect MC-induced cancer at a preneoplastic stage, OSHA anticipates that, as in the past, early detection and treatments of cancers leading to enhanced survival rates will continue to evolve.

A. Medical and Occupational History:

The medical and occupational work history plays an important role in the initial evaluation of workers exposed to MC. It is therefore extremely important for the examining physician or other licensed health care professional to evaluate the MC-exposed worker carefully and completely and to focus the examination on MC's potentially associated health hazards. The medical evaluation must include an annual detailed work and medical history with special emphasis on cardiac history and neurological symptoms.

An important goal of the medical history is to elicit information from the worker regarding potential signs or symptoms associated with increased levels of carboxyhemoglobin due to the presence of carbon monoxide in the blood. Physicians or other licensed health care professionals should ensure that the smoking history of all MC exposed employees is known. Exposure to MC may cause a significant increase in carboxyhemoglobin level in all exposed persons. However, smokers as well as workers with anemia or heart disease and those concurrently exposed to carbon monoxide are at especially high risk of toxic effects because of an already reduced oxygen carrying capacity of the blood.

A comprehensive or interim medical and work history should also include occurrence of headache, dizziness, fatigue, chest pain, shortness of breath, pain in the limbs, and irritation of the skin and eyes.

In addition, it is important for the physician or other licensed health care professional to become familiar with the operating conditions in which exposure to MC is likely to occur. The physician or other licensed health care professional also must become familiar with the signs and symptoms that may indicate that a worker is receiving otherwise unrecognized and exceptionally high exposure levels of MC.

An example of a medical and work history that would satisfy the requirement for a comprehensive or interim work history is represented by the following:

The following is a list of recommended questions and issues for the self-administered questionnaire for methylene chloride exposure.

QUESTIONNAIRE FOR METHYLENE CHLORIDE EXPOSURE

I. Demographic Information

1. Name
2. Social Security Number
3. Date
4. Date of Birth
5. Age
6. Present occupation
7. Sex
8. Race

II. Occupational History

1. Have you ever worked with methylene chloride, dichloromethane, methylene dichloride, or $CH_2 Cl_2$ (all are different names for the same chemical)? Please list which on the occupational history form if you have not already.

2. If you have worked in any of the following industries and have not listed them on the occupational history form, please do so.
Furniture stripping
Polyurethane foam manufacturing
Chemical manufacturing or formulation
Pharmaceutical manufacturing
Any industry in which you used solvents to clean and degrease equipment or parts
Construction, especially painting and refinishing
Aerosol manufacturing
Any industry in which you used aerosol adhesives

3. If you have not listed hobbies or household projects on the occupational history form, especially furniture refinishing, spray painting, or paint stripping, please do so.

III. Medical History

A. General

1. Do you consider yourself to be in good health? If no, state reason(s).
2. Do you or have you ever had:
a. Persistent thirst
b. Frequent urination (three times or more at night)
c. Dermatitis or irritated skin
d. Non-healing wounds
3. What prescription or non-prescription medications do you take, and for what reasons?
4. Are you allergic to any medications, and what type of reaction do you have?

B. Respiratory

1. Do you have or have you ever had any chest illnesses or diseases? Explain.
2. Do you have or have you ever had any of the following:
a. Asthma
b. Wheezing
c. Shortness of breath
3. Have you ever had an abnormal chest X-ray? If so, when, where, and what were the findings?
4. Have you ever had difficulty using a respirator or breathing apparatus? Explain.
5. Do any chest or lung diseases run in your family? Explain.
6. Have you ever smoked cigarettes, cigars, or a pipe? Age started?
7. Do you now smoke?
8. If you have stopped smoking completely, how old were you when you stopped?
9. On the average of the entire time you smoked, how many packs of cigarettes, cigars, or bowls of tobacco did you smoke per day?

C. Cardiovascular

1. Have you ever been diagnosed with any of the following: Which of the following apply to you now or did apply to you at some

547

time in the past, even if the problem is controlled by medication? Please explain any yes answers (*i.e.*, when problem was diagnosed, length of time on medication).

a. High cholesterol or triglyceride level
b. Hypertension (high blood pressure)
c. Diabetes
d. Family history of heart attack, stroke, or blocked arteries

2. Have you ever had chest pain? If so, answer the next five questions.

a. What was the quality of the pain (*i.e.*, crushing, stabbing, squeezing)?
b. Did the pain go anywhere (*i.e.*, into jaw, left arm)?
c. What brought the pain out?
d. How long did it last?
e. What made the pain go away?

3. Have you ever had heart disease, a heart attack, stroke, aneurysm, or blocked arteries anywhere in you body? Explain (when, treatment).

4. Have you ever had bypass surgery for blocked arteries in your heart or anywhere else? Explain.

5. Have you ever had any other procedures done to open up a blocked artery (balloon angioplasty, carotid endarterectomy, clot-dissolving drug)?

6. Do you have or have you ever had (explain each):

a. Heart murmur
b. Irregular heartbeat
c. Shortness of breath while lying flat
d. Congestive heart failure
e. Ankle swelling
f. Recurrent pain anywhere below the waist while walking

7. Have you ever had an electrocardiogram (EKG)? When?

8. Have you ever had an abnormal EKG? If so, when, where, and what were the findings?

9. Do any heart diseases, high blood pressure, diabetes, high cholesterol, or high triglycerides run in your family? Explain.

D. Hepatobiliary and Pancreas

1. Do you now or have you ever drunk alcoholic beverages? Age started: _____ Age stopped: _____.

2. Average numbers per week:

a. Beers: _____, ounces in usual container:
b. Glasses of wine: _____, ounces per glass:
c. Drinks: _____, ounces in usual container:

3. Do you have or have you ever had (explain each):

a. Hepatitis (infectious, autoimmune, drug-induced, or chemical)
b. Jaundice
c. Elevated liver enzymes or elevated bilirubin
d. Liver disease or cancer

E. Central Nervous System

1. Do you or have you ever had (explain each):

a. Headache
b. Dizziness
c. Fainting
d. Loss of consciousness
e. Garbled speech
f. Lack of balance
g. Mental/psychiatric illness
h. Forgetfulness

F. Hematologic

1. Do you have, or have you ever had (explain each):

a. Anemia
b. Sickle cell disease or trait
c. Glucose-6-phosphate dehydrogenase deficiency
d. Bleeding tendency disorder

2. If not already mentioned previously, have you ever had a reaction to sulfa drugs or to drugs used to prevent or treat malaria? What was the drug? Describe the reaction.

B. Physical Examination

The complete physical examination, when coupled with the medical and occupational history, assists the physician or other licensed health care professional in detecting pre-existing conditions that might place the employee at increased risk, and establishes a baseline for future health monitoring. These examinations should include:

1. Clinical impressions of the nervous system, cardiovascular function and pulmonary function, with additional tests conducted where indicated or determined by the examining physician or other licensed health care professional to be necessary.

2. An evaluation of the advisability of the worker using a respirator, because the use of certain respirators places an additional burden on the cardiopulmonary system. It is necessary for the attending physician or other licensed health care professional to evaluate the cardiopulmonary function of these workers, in order to inform the employer in a written medical opinion of the worker's ability or fitness to work in an area requiring the use of certain types of respiratory protective equipment. The presence of facial hair or scars that might interfere with the worker's ability to wear certain types of respirators should also be noted during the examination and in the written medical opinion.

Because of the importance of lung function to workers required to wear certain types of respirators to protect themselves from MC exposure, these workers must receive an assessment of pulmonary function before they begin to wear a negative pressure respirator and at least annually thereafter. The recommended pulmonary function tests include measurement of the employee's forced vital capacity (FVC), forced expiratory volume at one second (FEV1), as well as calculation of the ratios of FEV1 to FVC, and the ratios of measured FVC and measured FEV1 to expected respective values corrected for variation due to age, sex, race, and height. Pulmonary function evaluation must be conducted by a physician or other licensed health care professional experienced in pulmonary function tests.

The following is a summary of the elements of a physical exam which would fulfill the requirements under the MC standard:

PHYSICAL EXAM

I. Skin and appendages

1. Irritated or broken skin
2. Jaundice
3. Clubbing cyanosis, edema
4. Capillary refill time
5. Pallor

II. Head

1. Facial deformities
2. Scars
3. Hair growth

III. Eyes

1. Scleral icterus
2. Corneal arcus
3. Pupillary size and response
4. Fundoscopic exam

IV. Chest

1. Standard exam

V. Heart

1. Standard exam
2. Jugular vein distension
3. Peripheral pulses

VI. Abdomen

1. Liver span

VII. Nervous System

1. Complete standard neurologic exam

VIII. Laboratory

1. Hemoglobin and hematocrit
2. Alanine aminotransferase (ALT, SGPT)
3. Post-shift carboxyhemoglobin

IX. Studies

1. Pulmonary function testing
2. Electrocardiogram

An evaluation of the oxygen carrying capacity of the blood of employees (for example by measured red blood cell volume) is considered useful, especially for workers acutely exposed to MC.

It is also recommended, but not required, that end of shift carboxyhemoglobin levels be determined periodically, and any level

above 3% for non-smokers and above 10% for smokers should prompt an investigation of the worker and his workplace. This test is recommended because MC is metabolized to CO, which combines strongly with hemoglobin, resulting in a reduced capacity of the blood to transport oxygen in the body. This is of particular concern for cigarette smokers because they already have a diminished hemoglobin capacity due to the presence of CO in cigarette smoke.

C. Additional Examinations and Referrals

1. Examination by a Specialist

When a worker examination reveals unexplained symptoms or signs (*i.e.*, in the physical examination or in the laboratory tests), follow-up medical examinations are necessary to assure that MC exposure is not adversely affecting the worker's health. When the examining physician or other licensed health care professional finds it necessary, additional tests should be included to determine the nature of the medical problem and the underlying cause. Where relevant, the worker should be sent to a specialist for further testing and treatment as deemed necessary.

The final rule requires additional investigations to be covered and it also permits physicians or other licensed health care professionals to add appropriate or necessary tests to improve the diagnosis of disease should such tests become available in the future.

2. Emergencies

The examination of workers exposed to MC in an emergency should be directed at the organ systems most likely to be affected. If the worker has received a severe acute exposure, hospitalization may be required to assure proper medical intervention. It is not possible to precisely define "severe," but the physician or other licensed health care professional's judgement should not merely rest on hospitalization. If the worker has suffered significant conjunctival, oral, or nasal irritation, respiratory distress, or discomfort, the physician or other licensed health care professional should instigate appropriate follow-up procedures. These include attention to the eyes, lungs and the neurological system. The frequency of follow-up examinations should be determined by the attending physician or other licensed health care professional. This testing permits the early identification essential to proper medical management of such workers.

D. Employer Obligations

The employer is required to provide the responsible physician or other licensed health care professional and any specialists involved in a diagnosis with the following information: a copy of the MC standard including relevant appendices, a description of the

549

affected employee's duties as they relate to his or her exposure to MC; an estimate of the employee's exposure including duration (e.g., 15hr/wk, three 8-hour shifts/wk, full time); a description of any personal protective equipment used by the employee, including respirators; and the results of any previous medical determinations for the affected employee related to MC exposure to the extent that this information is within the employer's control.

E. Physicians' or Other Licensed Health Care Professionals' Obligations

The standard requires the employer to ensure that the physician or other licensed health care professional provides a written statement to the employee and the employer. This statement should contain the physician's or licensed health care professional's opinion as to whether the employee has any medical condition placing him or her at increased risk of impaired health from exposure to MC or use of respirators, as appropriate. The physician or other licensed health care professional should also state his or her opinion regarding any restrictions that should be placed on the employee's exposure to MC or upon the use of protective clothing or equipment such as respirators. If the employee wears a respirator as a result

of his or her exposure to MC, the physician or other licensed health care professional's opinion should also contain a statement regarding the suitability of the employee to wear the type of respirator assigned. Furthermore, the employee should be informed by the physician or other licensed health care professional about the cancer risk of MC and about risk factors for heart disease, and the potential for exacerbation of underlying heart disease by exposure to MC through its metabolism to carbon monoxide. Finally, the physician or other licensed health care professional should inform the employer that the employee has been told the results of the medical examination and of any medical conditions which require further explanation or treatment. This written opinion must not contain any information on specific findings or diagnosis unrelated to employee's occupational exposures.

The purpose in requiring the examining physician or other licensed health care professional to supply the employer with a written opinion is to provide the employer with a medical basis to assist the employer in placing employees initially, in assuring that their health is not being impaired by exposure to MC, and to assess the employee's ability to use any required protective equipment.

APPENDIX C TO SECTION 1910.1052—QUESTIONS AND ANSWERS—METHYLENE CHLORIDE CONTROL IN FURNITURE STRIPPING

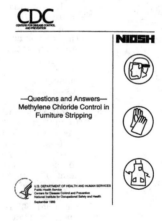

Q's & A's

DISCLAIMER

Mention of any company or product does not constitute endorsement by the Centers for Disease Control and Prevention, National Institute for Occupational Safety and Health.

This document is in the public domain and may be freely copied or reprinted.

Copies of this and other NIOSH documents are available from

Publications Dissemination, DSDTT

National Institute for Occupational Safety and Health

4676 Columbia Parkway

Cincinnati, OH 45226

FAX (513) 533-8573

For information about other occupational safety and health problems, call
1-800-35-NIOSH

DHHS (NIOSH) Publication No. 93-133

Introduction

This Pamphlet answers commonly asked questions about the hazards from exposure to methylene chloride. It also describes approaches to controlling methylene chloride exposure during the most common furniture stripping processes. Although these approaches were developed and field tested by NIOSH, each setting requires custom installation because of the different air flow interferences at each site.

What is the Stripping Solution Base?

The most common active ingredient in paint removers is a chemical called methylene chloride. Methylene chloride is present in the paint remover to penetrate, blister, and finally lift the old finish. Other chemicals in paint removers work to accelerate the stripping process, to retard evaporation, and to act as thickening agents. These other ingredients may include: methanol, toluene, acetone, or paraffin.[1]

Is Methylene Chloride Bad for Me?

Exposure to methylene chloride may cause short-term health effects or long-term health effects.

Short-Term (acute) Health Effects

Exposure to high levels of paint removers over short periods of time can cause irritation to the skin, eyes, mucous membranes, and respiratory tract. Other symptoms of high

Figure 1 — Slot Hood

exposure are dizziness headache, and lack of coordination. The occurrence of any of these symptoms indicates that you are being exposed to high levels of the methylene chloride. At the onset of any of these symptoms, you should leave the work area, get some fresh air, and determine why the levels were high.

A portion of inhaled methylene chloride is converted by the body to carbon monoxide, which can lower the blood's ability to carry oxygen. When the solvent is used properly, however, the levels of carbon monoxide should not be hazardous. Individuals with cardiovascular or pulmonary health problems should check with their physician before using the paint stripper. Individuals experiencing severe symptoms such as shortness of breath or chest pains should obtain proper medical care immediately.[2]

Long-term (Chronic) Health Effects

Methylene chloride has been shown to cause cancer in certain laboratory animal tests. The available human studies do not provide the necessary information to determine whether methylene chloride causes cancer in humans. However, as a result of the animal studies, methylene chloride is

Q's & A's

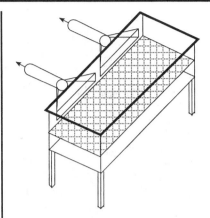

Figure 2 — Downdraft Hood

considered a potential occupational carcinogen. There is also considerable indirect evidence to suggest that workers exposed to methylene chloride may be at increased risk of developing ischemic heart disease. Therefore, it is prudent to minimize exposures to solvent vapors.[3]

What Do Federal Agencies Say About Methylene Chloride?

In 1991, the Occupational Safety and Health Administration published a Notice of Proposed Rulemaking for methylene chloride. The proposed standard would establish an eight-hour time-weighted average exposure limit of 25 parts per million (ppm), as well

as a short-term exposure limit of 125 ppm determined from a 15 minute sampling period. That is a sharp reduction from the current limit of 500 ppm. The proposed standard would also set a 12.5 ppm action level (a level that would trigger periodic exposure monitoring and medical surveillance provisions.[4]

The National Institute for Occupational Safety and Health recommends that methylene chloride be regarded as a "potential occupational carcinogen." NIOSH further recommends that occupational exposure to methylene chloride be controlled to the lowest feasible limit. This recommendation was based on the observation of cancers and tumors in both rats and mice exposed to methylene chloride in air.[5]

How Can I Be Exposed to Methylene Chloride while Stripping Furniture?

Methylene chloride can be inhaled when vapors are in the air. Inhalation of the methylene chloride vapors is generally the most important source of exposure. Methylene chloride evaporates quicker than most chemicals. The odor threshold of methylene chloride is 300 ppm.[6] Therefore, once you smell methylene chloride, you are being over-exposed. Pouring, moving, or stirring the chemical will increase the rate of evaporation.

Methylene chloride can be absorbed through the skin either by directly touching the chemical or through your gloves. Methylene chloride can be swallowed if it gets on your hands, clothes, or beard, or if food or drinks become contaminated.

How Can Breathing Exposures be Reduced?

Install a Local Exhaust Ventilation System

Local exhaust ventilation can be used to control exposures. Local exhaust ventilation systems capture contaminated air from the source before it spreads into the workers' breathing zone.[7] If engineering controls are not effective, only a self-contained breathing apparatus equipped with a full facepiece and operated in a positive-pressure mode or a supplied-air respirator affords the necessary level of protection. Air-purifying respirators such as organic vapor cartridges can only be used for escape situations.[8]

A local exhaust system consists of the following: a hood, a fan, ductwork, and a replacement air system.[9,10,11] Two processes are commonly used in furniture stripping: flow-over and dip tanks. For flow-over systems there are two common local exhaust controls for methylene chloride — a slot hood and a downdraft hood. A slot hood of different design is most often used for dip tanks. (See Figures 1, 2, and 3)

The hood is made of sheet metal and connected to the tank. All designs require a centrifugal fan to exhaust the fumes, ductwork connecting the hood and the fan, and a replacement air system to bring conditioned air into the building to replace the air exhausted.

In constructing or designing a slot or downdraft hood, use the following data:

Q's & A's

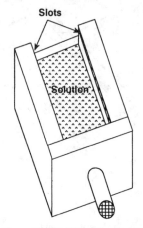

Slots

Solution

Figure 3 — Slot Hood for Dip Tank

Slot hood (Figure 1)

• At least 2200 cfm per 8' X 4' tank
• 1 - 2 inch slots
• Slot velocity - 1000 fpm
• 3 - 5 slots
• Plenum at least 1 foot deep

Downdraft hood (Figure 2)

• At least 1600 cfm per 8' X 4' tank
• Plenum at least 9" deep

Slot hood for Dip Tank (Figure 3)

• At least 2900 cfm per 8' X 4' tank
• 3/4" slot that runs the length of the front and back of the tank
• Slot velocity — 3200 fpm
• Plenum on the sides of the tank should be 6" deep by 36" long
• 12" duct leads from the center of the front plenum to the fan

Safe work practices

Workers can lower exposures by decreasing their access to the methyl-ene chloride.[12]

1) Turn on dip tank control system several minutes before entering the stripping area.

2) Avoid unnecessary transferring or moving of stripping solution.

3) Keep face out of the air stream between the solution-covered furniture and the exhaust system.

4) Keep face out of vapor zone above the stripping solution and dip tank.

5) Retrieve dropped items with a long handled tool.

6) Keep the solution-recycling system off when not in use. Cover reservoir for recycling system.

7) Cover dip tank when not in use.

8) Provide adequate ventilation for rinse area.

Q's & A's

How Can Skin Exposures be Reduced?

Skin exposures can be reduced by wearing gloves whenever you are in contact with the stripping solution.[13]

1) Two gloves should be worn. The inner glove should be made from polyethylene/ethylene vinyl alcohol (e.g. Silver Shield®, or 4H®). This material, however, does not provide good physical resistance against tears, so an outer glove made from nitrile or neoprene should be worn.

2) Shoulder-length gloves will be more protective.

3) Change gloves before the break-through time occurs. Rotate several pairs of gloves throughout the day. Let the gloves dry in a warm well ventilated area at least over night before reuse.

4) Keep gloves clean by rinsing often. Keep gloves in good condition. Inspect the gloves before use for pin-holes, cracks, thin spots, and stiffer than normal or sticky surfaces.

5) Wear a face shield or goggles to protect face and eyes.

What Other Problems Occur?

Stripping Solution Temperature

Most manufacturers of stripping solution recommend controlling the solution to a temperature of 70°F. This temperature is required for the wax in the solution to form a vapor barrier on top of the solution to keep the solution from evaporating too quickly. If the temperature is too high, the wax will not form the vapor barrier. If it is too cold, the wax will solidify and separate from the solvent causing increased evaporation. Use a belt heater to heat the solution to the correct temperature. Call your solution manufacturer for the correct temperature for your solution.[14]

Make-Up Air

Air will enter a building in an amount to equal the amount of air exhausted whether or not provision is made for this replacement. If a local exhaust system is added a make-up or replacement air system must be added to replace the air removed. Without a replacement air system, air will enter the building through cracks causing uncontrollable eddy currents. If the building perimeter is tightly sealed, it will prevent the air from entering and severely decrease the amount exhausted from the ventilation system. This will cause the building to be under negative pressure and decrease the performance of the exhaust system.[15]

Dilution Ventilation

With general or dilution ventilation, uncontaminated air is moved through the workroom by means of fans or open windows, which dilutes the pollutants in the air. Dilution ventilation does not provide effective protection to other workers and does not confine the methylene chloride vapors to one area.[16]

Phosgene Poisoning from Use of Kerosene Heaters

Do not use kerosene heaters or other open flame heaters while stripping furniture. Use of kerosene heaters in connection with methylene chloride can create lethal or dangerous concentrations of phosgene. Methylene chloride vapor is mixed with the air used for the combustion of kerosene in kerosene stoves. The vapor thus passes through the flames, coming into close contact with carbon monoxide at high temperatures. Any chlorine formed by decomposition may, under these conditions, react with carbon monoxide and form phosgene.[17]

REFERENCES

[1] Halogenated Solvents Industry Alliance and Consumer Product Safety Commission [1990]. Stripping Paint from Wood (Pamphlet for consumers on how to strip furniture and precautions to take). Washington DC: Consumer Product Safety Commission.

[2] *Ibid.*

[3] NIOSH [1992]. NIOSH Testimony on Occupational Safety and Health Administration's proposed rule on occupational exposure to methylene chloride, September 21, 1992, OSHA Docket No. H-71. NIOSH policy statements. Cincinnati, OH: U.S. Department of Health and Human Services, Public Health Service, Centers for Disease Control, National Institute for Occupational Safety and Health.

[4] 56 Fed. Reg. 57036 [1991]. Occupational Safety and Health Administration: Proposed rule on occupational exposure to methylene chloride.

[5] NIOSH [1992].

[6] Kirk, R.E. and P.F. Othmer, Eds. [1978]. Encyclopedia of Chemical Technology, 3rd Ed., Vol. 5:690. New York: John Wiley & Sons, Inc.

[7] ACGIH [1988]. Industrial Ventilation: A Manual of Recommended Practice. 20th Ed. Cincinnati, OH: American Conference of Governmental Industrial Hygienists.

[8] NIOSH [1992].

[9] Fairfield, C.L. and A.A. Beasley [1991]. In-depth Survey Report at the Association for Retarded Citizens, Meadowlands, PA. The Control of Methylene Chloride During Furniture Stripping. Cincinnati, OH: U.S. Department of Health and Human Services, Public Health Service, Centers for Disease Control, National Institute for Occupational Safety and Health.

[10] Fairfield, C.L. [1991]. In-depth Survey Report at the J.M. Murray Center, Cortland, NY. The Control of Methylene Chloride During Furniture Stripping. Cincinnati, OH: U.S. Department of Health and Human Services, Public Health Service, Centers for Disease Control, National Institute for Occupational Safety and Health.

[11] Hall, R.M., K.F. Martinez, and P.A. Jensen [1992]. In-depth Survey Report at Tri-County Furniture Stripping and Refinishing, Cincinnati, OH. The Control of Methylene Chloride During Furniture Stripping. Cincinnati, OH: U.S. Department of Health and Human Services, Public Health Service, Centers for Disease Control, National Institute for Occupational Safety and Health.

[12] Fairfield, C.L. and A.A. Beasley [1991]. In-depth Survey Report at the Association for Retarded Citizens, Meadowlands, PA. The Control of Methylene Chloride During Furniture Stripping. Cincinnati, OH: U.S. Department of Health and Human Services, Public Health Service, Centers for Disease Control, National Institute for Occupational Safety and Health.

[13] Roder, M. [1991]. Memorandum of March 11,1991 from Michael Roder of the Division of Safety Research to Cheryl L. Fairfield of the Division of Physical Sciences and Engineering, National Institute for Occupational Safety and Health, Centers for Disease Control, Public Health Service, U.S. Department of Health and Human Services.

[14] Kwick Kleen Industrial Solvents, Inc. [1981]. Operations Manual, Kwick Kleen Industrial Solvents, Inc., Vincennes, IN.

[15] ACGIH [1988].

[16] *Ibid.*

[17] Gerritsen, W.B. and C.H. Buschmann [1960]. Phosgene Poisoning Caused by the Use of Chemical Paint Removers containing Methylene Chloride in Ill-Ventilated Rooms Heated by Kerosene Stoves. British Journal of Industrial Medicine *17* :187.

Q's & A's

Where Should I go for More Information?

The NIOSH 800- number is a toll-free technical information service that provides convenient public access to NIOSH and its information resources. Callers may request information about any aspect of occupational safety and health.

1-800-35-NIOSH
(1-800-356-4674)

[62 FR 1601, Jan. 10, 1997, as amended at 62 FR 42667, Aug. 8, 1997; 62 FR 54383, Oct. 20, 1997; 62 FR 66277, Dec. 18, 1997; 63 FR 1295, Jan. 8, 1998; 63 FR 20099, Apr. 23, 1998; 63 FR 50729, Sept. 22, 1998; 71 FR 16674, Apr. 3, 2006; 71 FR 50190, Aug. 24, 2006; 73 FR 75587, Dec. 12, 2008; 77 FR 17785, Mar. 26, 2012; 78 FR 9313, Feb. 8, 2013]

EFFECTIVE DATE NOTE: At 84 FR 21544, May 14, 2019, § 1910.1052 was amended by revising appendix B, section IV, effective July 15, 2019. For the convenience of the user, the revised text is set forth as follows:

§ 1910.1052 Methylene chloride.

* * * * *

APPENDIX B TO § 1910.1052—MEDICAL SURVEILLANCE FOR METHYLENE CHLORIDE

* * * * *

IV. SURVEILLANCE AND PREVENTIVE CONSIDERATIONS

As discussed in sections II and III of this appendix, MC is classified as a suspect or potential human carcinogen. It is a central nervous system (CNS) depressant and a skin, eye and respiratory tract irritant. At extremely high concentrations, MC has caused liver damage in animals. MC principally affects the CNS, where it acts as a narcotic. The observation of the symptoms characteristic of CNS depression, along with a physical examination, provides the best detection of early neurological disorders. Since exposure to MC also increases the carboxyhemoglobin level in the blood, ambient carbon monoxide levels would have an additive effect on that carboxyhemoglobin level. Based on such information, a periodic post-shift carboxyhemoglobin test as an index of the presence of carbon monoxide in the blood is recommended, but not required, for medical surveillance.

Based on the animal evidence and three epidemiologic studies previously mentioned, OSHA concludes that MC is a suspect human carcinogen. The medical surveillance program is designed to observe exposed workers on a regular basis. While the medical surveillance program cannot detect MC-induced cancer at a preneoplastic stage, OSHA anticipates that, as in the past, early detection and treatments of cancers leading to enhanced survival rates will continue to evolve.

A. Medical and Occupational History

The medical and occupational work history plays an important role in the initial evaluation of workers exposed to MC. It is therefore extremely important for the examining physician or other licensed health care professional to evaluate the MC-exposed worker carefully and completely and to focus the examination on MC's potentially associated health hazards. The medical evaluation must include an annual detailed work and medical history with special emphasis on cardiac history and neurological symptoms.

An important goal of the medical history is to elicit information from the worker regarding potential signs or symptoms associated with increased levels of carboxyhemoglobin due to the presence of carbon monoxide in the blood. Physicians or other licensed health care professionals should ensure that the smoking history of all MC exposed employees is known. Exposure to MC may cause a significant increase in carboxyhemoglobin level in all exposed persons. However, smokers as well as workers with anemia or heart disease and those concurrently exposed to carbon monoxide are at especially high risk of toxic effects because of an already reduced oxygen carrying capacity of the blood.

A comprehensive or interim medical and work history should also include occurrence of headache, dizziness, fatigue, chest pain, shortness of breath, pain in the limbs, and irritation of the skin and eyes.

In addition, it is important for the physician or other licensed health care professional to become familiar with the operating conditions in which exposure to MC is likely to occur. The physician or other licensed health care professional also must become familiar with the signs and symptoms that may indicate that a worker is receiving otherwise unrecognized and exceptionally high exposure levels of MC.

An example of a medical and work history that would satisfy the requirement for a comprehensive or interim work history is represented by the following:

The following is a list of recommended questions and issues for the self-administered questionnaire for methylene chloride exposure.

QUESTIONNAIRE FOR METHYLENE CHLORIDE EXPOSURE

I. Demographic Information

1. Name
2. Date
3. Date of Birth
4. Age
5. Present occupation
6. Sex
7. Race (Check all that apply)

a. White ___	d. Hispanic or Latino ___
b. Black or African American ___	e. American Indian or Alaska Native ___
c. Asian ___	f. Native Hawaiian or Other Pacific Islander ___

II. Occupational History

1. Have you ever worked with methylene chloride, dichloromethane, methylene dichloride, or CH_2Cl_2 (all are different names for the same chemical)? Please list which on the occupational history form if you have not already.

2. If you have worked in any of the following industries and have not listed them on the occupational history form, please do so.

Furniture stripping
Polyurethane foam manufacturing
Chemical manufacturing or formulation
Pharmaceutical manufacturing
Any industry in which you used solvents to clean and degrease equipment or parts
Construction, especially painting and refinishing
Aerosol manufacturing
Any industry in which you used aerosol adhesives

3. If you have not listed hobbies or household projects on the occupational history form, especially furniture refinishing, spray painting, or paint stripping, please do so.

III. Medical History

A. General

1. Do you consider yourself to be in good health? If no, state reason(s).

2. Do you or have you ever had:

   a. Persistent thirst
   b. Frequent urination (three times or more at night)
   c. Dermatitis or irritated skin
   d. Non-healing wounds

3. What prescription or non-prescription medications do you take, and for what reasons?

4. Are you allergic to any medications, and what type of reaction do you have?

B. Respiratory

1. Do you have or have you ever had any chest illnesses or diseases? Explain.

2. Do you have or have you ever had any of the following:

   a. Asthma
   b. Wheezing
   c. Shortness of breath

3. Have you ever had an abnormal chest X-ray? If so, when, where, and what were the findings?

4. Have you ever had difficulty using a respirator or breathing apparatus? Explain.

5. Do any chest or lung diseases run in your family? Explain.

6. Have you ever smoked cigarettes, cigars, or a pipe? Age started:

7. Do you now smoke?

8. If you have stopped smoking completely, how old were you when you stopped?

9. On the average of the entire time you smoked, how many packs of cigarettes, cigars, or bowls of tobacco did you smoke per day?

C. Cardiovascular

1. Have you ever been diagnosed with any of the following: Which of the following apply to you now or did apply to you at some time in the past, even if the problem is controlled by medication? Please explain any yes answers (i.e., when problem was diagnosed, length of time on medication).

   a. High cholesterol or triglyceride level

   b. Hypertension (high blood pressure)

   c. Diabetes

   d. Family history of heart attack, stroke, or blocked arteries

2. Have you ever had chest pain? If so, answer the next five questions.

   a. What was the quality of the pain (i.e., crushing, stabbing, squeezing)?

   b. Did the pain go anywhere (i.e., into jaw, left arm)?

   c. What brought the pain out?

   d. How long did it last?

   e. What made the pain go away?

3. Have you ever had heart disease, a heart attack, stroke, aneurysm, or blocked arteries anywhere in your body? Explain (when, treatment).

4. Have you ever had bypass surgery for blocked arteries in your heart or anywhere else? Explain.

5. Have you ever had any other procedures done to open up a blocked artery (balloon angioplasty, carotid endarterectomy, clot-dissolving drug)?

6. Do you have or have you ever had (explain each):

    a. Heart murmur
    b. Irregular heartbeat
    c. Shortness of breath while lying flat
    d. Congestive heart failure
    e. Ankle swelling
    f. Recurrent pain anywhere below the waist while walking

7. Have you ever had an electrocardiogram (EKG)? When?

8. Have you ever had an abnormal EKG? If so, when, where, and what were the findings?

9. Do any heart diseases, high blood pressure, diabetes, high cholesterol, or high triglycerides run in your family? Explain.

D. Hepatobiliary and Pancreas

1. Do you now or have you ever drunk alcoholic beverages?
Age started: _____ Age stopped: _____.

2. Average numbers per week:

    a. Beers: _____, ounces in usual container:
    b. Glasses of wine: _____, ounces per glass:
    c. Drinks: _____, ounces in usual container:

3. Do you have or have you ever had (explain each):

    a. Hepatitis (infectious, autoimmune, drug-induced, or chemical)
    b. Jaundice
    c. Elevated liver enzymes or elevated bilirubin
    d. Liver disease or cancer

E. Central Nervous System

1. Do you or have you ever had (explain each):

    a. Headache
    b. Dizziness
    c. Fainting
    d. Loss of consciousness
    e. Garbled speech
    f. Lack of balance
    g. Mental/psychiatric illness
    h. Forgetfulness

F. Hematologic

1. Do you have, or have you ever had (explain each):

    a. Anemia
    b. Sickle cell disease or trait
    c. Glucose-6-phosphate dehydrogenase deficiency
    d. Bleeding tendency disorder

2. If not already mentioned previously, have you ever had a reaction to sulfa drugs or to drugs used to prevent or treat malaria? What was the drug? Describe the reaction.

B. Physical Examination

The complete physical examination, when coupled with the medical and occupational history, assists the physician or other licensed health care professional in detecting pre-existing conditions that might place the employee at increased risk, and establishes a baseline for future health monitoring. These examinations should include:

1. Clinical impressions of the nervous system, cardiovascular function and pulmonary function, with additional tests conducted where indicated or determined by the examining physician or other licensed health care professional to be necessary.

2. An evaluation of the advisability of the worker using a respirator, because the use of certain respirators places an additional burden on the cardiopulmonary system. It is necessary for the attending physician or other licensed health care professional to evaluate the cardiopulmonary function of these workers, in order to inform the employer in a written medical opinion of the worker's ability or fitness to work in an area requiring the use of certain types of respiratory protective equipment. The presence of facial hair or scars that might interfere with the worker's ability to wear certain types of respirators should also be noted during the examination and in the written medical opinion.

Because of the importance of lung function to workers required to wear certain types of respirators to protect themselves from MC exposure, these workers must receive an assessment of pulmonary function before they begin to wear a negative pressure respirator and at least annually thereafter. The recommended pulmonary function tests include measurement of the employee's forced vital capacity (FVC), forced expiratory volume at one second (FEV_1), as well as calculation of the ratios of FEV_1 to FVC, and the ratios of measured FVC and measured FEV_1 to expected respective values corrected for variation due to age, sex, race, and height. Pulmonary function evaluation must be conducted by a physician or other licensed health care professional experienced in pulmonary function tests.

The following is a summary of the elements of a physical exam which would fulfill the requirements under the MC standard:

PHYSICAL EXAM

I. Skin and appendages

1. Irritated or broken skin
2. Jaundice
3. Clubbing cyanosis, edema
4. Capillary refill time
5. Pallor

II. Head

1. Facial deformities
2. Scars
3. Hair growth

III. Eyes

1. Scleral icterus
2. Corneal arcus
3. Pupillary size and response
4. Fundoscopic exam

IV. Chest

1. Standard exam

V. Heart

1. Standard exam
2. Jugular vein distension
3. Peripheral pulses

VI. Abdomen

1. Liver span

VII.   Nervous System

1. Complete standard neurologic exam

VIII.   Laboratory

1. Hemoglobin and hematocrit
2. Alanine aminotransferase (ALT, SGPT)
3. Post-shift carboxyhemoglobin

IX. Studies

1. Pulmonary function testing
2. Electrocardiogram

An evaluation of the oxygen carrying capacity of the blood of employees (for example by measured red blood cell volume) is considered useful, especially for workers acutely exposed to MC.

It is also recommended, but not required, that end of shift carboxyhemoglobin levels be determined periodically, and any level above 3% for non-smokers and above 10% for smokers should prompt an investigation of the worker and his workplace. This test is recommended because MC is metabolized to CO, which combines strongly with hemoglobin, resulting in a reduced capacity of the blood to transport oxygen in the body. This is of particular concern for cigarette smokers because they already have a diminished hemoglobin capacity due to the presence of CO in cigarette smoke.

C. Additional Examinations and Referrals

1. Examination by a Specialist

When a worker examination reveals unexplained symptoms or signs (i.e. in the physical examination or in the laboratory tests), follow-up medical examinations are necessary to assure that MC exposure is not adversely affecting the worker's health. When the examining physician or other licensed health care professional finds it necessary, additional tests should be included to determine the nature of the medical problem and the underlying cause. Where relevant, the worker should be sent to a specialist for further testing and treatment as deemed necessary.

The final rule requires additional investigations to be covered and it also permits physicians or other licensed health care professionals to add appropriate or necessary tests to improve the diagnosis of disease should such tests become available in the future.

2. Emergencies

The examination of workers exposed to MC in an emergency should be directed at the organ systems most likely to be affected. If the worker has received a severe acute exposure, hospitalization may be required to assure proper medical intervention. It is not possible to precisely define "severe," but the physician or other licensed health care professional's judgment should not merely rest on hospitalization. If the worker has suffered significant conjunctival, oral, or nasal irritation, respiratory distress, or discomfort, the physician or other licensed health care professional should instigate appropriate follow-up procedures. These include attention to the eyes, lungs and the neurological system. The frequency of follow-up examinations should be determined by the attending physician or other licensed health care professional. This testing permits the early identification essential to proper medical management of such workers.

D. Employer Obligations

The employer is required to provide the responsible physician or other licensed health care professional and any specialists involved in a diagnosis with the following information: a copy of the MC standard including relevant appendices, a description of the affected employee's duties as they relate to his or her exposure to MC; an estimate of the employee's exposure including duration (e.g., 15hr/wk, three 8-hour shifts/wk, full time); a description of any personal protective equipment used by the employee, including respirators; and the results of any previous medical determinations for the affected employee related to MC exposure to the extent that this information is within the employer's control.

E. Physicians' or Other Licensed Health Care Professionals' Obligations

The standard in this section requires the employer to ensure that the physician or other licensed health care professional provides a written statement to the employee and the employer. This statement should contain the physician's or licensed health care professional's opinion as to whether the employee has any medical condition placing him or her at increased risk of impaired health from exposure to MC or use of respirators, as appropriate. The physician or other licensed health care professional should also state his or her opinion regarding any restrictions that should be placed on the employee's exposure to MC or upon the use of protective clothing or equipment such as respirators. If the employee wears a respirator as a result of his or her exposure to MC, the physician or other licensed health care professional's opinion should also contain a statement regarding the suitability of the employee to wear the type of respirator assigned. Furthermore, the employee should be informed by the physician or other licensed health care professional about the cancer risk of MC and about risk factors for heart disease, and the potential for exacerbation of underlying heart disease by exposure to MC through its metabolism to carbon monoxide. Finally, the physician or other licensed health care professional should inform the employer that the employee has been told the results of the medical examination and of any medical conditions which require further explanation or treatment. This written opinion must not contain any information on specific findings or diagnosis unrelated to employee's occupational exposures.

The purpose in requiring the examining physician or other licensed health care professional to supply the employer with a written opinion is to provide the employer with a medical basis to assist the employer in placing employees initially, in assuring that their health is not being impaired by exposure to MC, and to assess the employee's ability to use any required protective equipment.

*   *   *   *   *

§ 1910.1053 Respirable crystalline silica.

(a) *Scope and application.* (1) This section applies to all occupational exposures to respirable crystalline silica, except:

(i) Construction work as defined in 29 CFR 1910.12(b) (occupational exposures to respirable crystalline silica in construction work are covered under 29 CFR 1926.1153);

(ii) Agricultural operations covered under 29 CFR part 1928; and

(iii) Exposures that result from the processing of sorptive clays.

(2) This section does not apply where the employer has objective data demonstrating that employee exposure to respirable crystalline silica will remain below 25 micrograms per cubic meter of air (25 μg/m³) as an 8-hour time-weighted average (TWA) under any foreseeable conditions.

(3) This section does not apply if the employer complies with 29 CFR 1926.1153 and:

(i) The task performed is indistinguishable from a construction task listed on Table 1 in paragraph (c) of 29 CFR 1926.1153; and

(ii) The task will not be performed regularly in the same environment and conditions.

(b) *Definitions.* For the purposes of this section the following definitions apply:

Action level means a concentration of airborne respirable crystalline silica of 25 μg/m³, calculated as an 8-hour TWA.

Assistant Secretary means the Assistant Secretary of Labor for Occupational Safety and Health, U.S. Department of Labor, or designee.

Director means the Director of the National Institute for Occupational Safety and Health (NIOSH), U.S. Department of Health and Human Services, or designee.

Employee exposure means the exposure to airborne respirable crystalline silica that would occur if the employee were not using a respirator.

High-efficiency particulate air [HEPA] filter means a filter that is at least 99.97 percent efficient in removing mono-dispersed particles of 0.3 micrometers in diameter.

Objective data means information, such as air monitoring data from industry-wide surveys or calculations based on the composition of a substance, demonstrating employee exposure to respirable crystalline silica associated with a particular product or material or a specific process, task, or activity. The data must reflect workplace conditions closely resembling or with a higher exposure potential than the processes, types of material, control methods, work practices, and environmental conditions in the employer's current operations.

Physician or other licensed health care professional [PLHCP] means an individual whose legally permitted scope of practice (*i.e.*, license, registration, or certification) allows him or her to independently provide or be delegated the responsibility to provide some or all of the particular health care services required by paragraph (i) of this section.

Regulated area means an area, demarcated by the employer, where an employee's exposure to airborne concentrations of respirable crystalline silica exceeds, or can reasonably be expected to exceed, the PEL.

Respirable crystalline silica means quartz, cristobalite, and/or tridymite contained in airborne particles that are determined to be respirable by a sampling device designed to meet the characteristics for respirable-particle-size-selective samplers specified in the International Organization for Standardization (ISO) 7708:1995: Air Quality—Particle Size Fraction Definitions for Health-Related Sampling.

Specialist means an American Board Certified Specialist in Pulmonary Disease or an American Board Certified Specialist in Occupational Medicine.

This section means this respirable crystalline silica standard, 29 CFR 1910.1053.

(c) *Permissible exposure limit (PEL).* The employer shall ensure that no employee is exposed to an airborne concentration of respirable crystalline silica in excess of 50 μg/m³, calculated as an 8-hour TWA.

(d) *Exposure assessment*—(1) *General.* The employer shall assess the exposure of each employee who is or may reasonably be expected to be exposed to respirable crystalline silica at or above the action level in accordance with either the performance option in paragraph (d)(2) or the scheduled monitoring option in paragraph (d)(3) of this section.

(2) *Performance option.* The employer shall assess the 8-hour TWA exposure for each employee on the basis of any combination of air monitoring data or objective data sufficient to accurately characterize employee exposures to respirable crystalline silica.

(3) *Scheduled monitoring option.* (i) The employer shall perform initial monitoring to assess the 8-hour TWA exposure for each employee on the basis of one or more personal breathing zone air samples that reflect the exposures of employees on each shift, for each job classification, in each work area. Where several employees perform the same tasks on the same shift and in the same work area, the employer may sample a representative fraction of these employees in order to meet this requirement. In representative sampling, the employer shall sample the employee(s) who are expected to have the highest exposure to respirable crystalline silica.

(ii) If initial monitoring indicates that employee exposures are below the action level, the employer may discontinue monitoring for those employees whose exposures are represented by such monitoring.

(iii) Where the most recent exposure monitoring indicates that employee exposures are at or above the action level but at or below the PEL, the employer shall repeat such monitoring within six months of the most recent monitoring.

(iv) Where the most recent exposure monitoring indicates that employee exposures are above the PEL, the employer shall repeat such monitoring within three months of the most recent monitoring.

(v) Where the most recent (non-initial) exposure monitoring indicates that employee exposures are below the action level, the employer shall repeat such monitoring within six months of the most recent monitoring until two consecutive measurements, taken 7 or more days apart, are below the action level, at which time the employer may discontinue monitoring for those employees whose exposures are represented by such monitoring, except as otherwise provided in paragraph (d)(4) of this section.

(4) *Reassessment of exposures.* The employer shall reassess exposures whenever a change in the production, process, control equipment, personnel, or work practices may reasonably be expected to result in new or additional exposures at or above the action level, or when the employer has any reason to believe that new or additional exposures at or above the action level have occurred.

(5) *Methods of sample analysis.* The employer shall ensure that all samples taken to satisfy the monitoring requirements of paragraph (d) of this section are evaluated by a laboratory that analyzes air samples for respirable crystalline silica in accordance with

the procedures in Appendix A to this section.

(6) *Employee notification of assessment results.* (i) Within 15 working days after completing an exposure assessment in accordance with paragraph (d) of this section, the employer shall individually notify each affected employee in writing of the results of that assessment or post the results in an appropriate location accessible to all affected employees.

(ii) Whenever an exposure assessment indicates that employee exposure is above the PEL, the employer shall describe in the written notification the corrective action being taken to reduce employee exposure to or below the PEL.

(7) *Observation of monitoring.* (i) Where air monitoring is performed to comply with the requirements of this section, the employer shall provide affected employees or their designated representatives an opportunity to observe any monitoring of employee exposure to respirable crystalline silica.

(ii) When observation of monitoring requires entry into an area where the use of protective clothing or equipment is required for any workplace hazard, the employer shall provide the observer with protective clothing and equipment at no cost and shall ensure that the observer uses such clothing and equipment.

(e) *Regulated areas—*(1) *Establishment.* The employer shall establish a regulated area wherever an employee's exposure to airborne concentrations of respirable crystalline silica is, or can reasonably be expected to be, in excess of the PEL.

(2) *Demarcation.* (i) The employer shall demarcate regulated areas from the rest of the workplace in a manner that minimizes the number of employees exposed to respirable crystalline silica within the regulated area.

(ii) The employer shall post signs at all entrances to regulated areas that bear the legend specified in paragraph (j)(2) of this section.

(3) *Access.* The employer shall limit access to regulated areas to:

(A) Persons authorized by the employer and required by work duties to be present in the regulated area;

(B) Any person entering such an area as a designated representative of employees for the purpose of exercising the right to observe monitoring procedures under paragraph (d) of this section; and

(C) Any person authorized by the Occupational Safety and Health Act or regulations issued under it to be in a regulated area.

(4) *Provision of respirators.* The employer shall provide each employee and the employee's designated representative entering a regulated area with an appropriate respirator in accordance with paragraph (g) of this section and shall require each employee and the employee's designated representative to use the respirator while in a regulated area.

(f) *Methods of compliance—*(1) *Engineering and work practice controls.* The employer shall use engineering and work practice controls to reduce and maintain employee exposure to respirable crystalline silica to or below the PEL, unless the employer can demonstrate that such controls are not feasible. Wherever such feasible engineering and work practice controls are not sufficient to reduce employee exposure to or below the PEL, the employer shall nonetheless use them to reduce employee exposure to the lowest feasible level and shall supplement them with the use of respiratory protection that complies with the requirements of paragraph (g) of this section.

(2) *Written exposure control plan.* (i) The employer shall establish and implement a written exposure control plan that contains at least the following elements:

(A) A description of the tasks in the workplace that involve exposure to respirable crystalline silica;

(B) A description of the engineering controls, work practices, and respiratory protection used to limit employee exposure to respirable crystalline silica for each task; and

(C) A description of the housekeeping measures used to limit employee exposure to respirable crystalline silica.

(ii) The employer shall review and evaluate the effectiveness of the written exposure control plan at least annually and update it as necessary.

(iii) The employer shall make the written exposure control plan readily available for examination and copying, upon request, to each employee covered by this section, their designated representatives, the Assistant Secretary and the Director.

(3) *Abrasive blasting.* In addition to the requirements of paragraph (f)(1) of this section, the employer shall comply with other OSHA standards, when applicable, such as 29 CFR 1910.94 (Ventilation), 29 CFR 1915.34 (Mechanical paint removers), and 29 CFR 1915 Subpart I (Personal Protective Equipment), where abrasive blasting is conducted using crystalline silica-containing blasting agents, or where abrasive blasting is conducted on substrates that contain crystalline silica.

(g) *Respiratory protection—*(1) *General.* Where respiratory protection is required by this section, the employer must provide each employee an appropriate respirator that complies with the requirements of this paragraph and 29 CFR 1910.134. Respiratory protection is required:

(i) Where exposures exceed the PEL during periods necessary to install or implement feasible engineering and work practice controls;

(ii) Where exposures exceed the PEL during tasks, such as certain maintenance and repair tasks, for which engineering and work practice controls are not feasible;

(iii) During tasks for which an employer has implemented all feasible engineering and work practice controls and such controls are not sufficient to reduce exposures to or below the PEL; and

(iv) During periods when the employee is in a regulated area.

(2) *Respiratory protection program.* Where respirator use is required by this section, the employer shall institute a respiratory protection program in accordance with 29 CFR 1910.134.

(h) *Housekeeping.* (1) The employer shall not allow dry sweeping or dry brushing where such activity could contribute to employee exposure to respirable crystalline silica unless wet sweeping, HEPA-filtered vacuuming or other methods that minimize the likelihood of exposure are not feasible.

(2) The employer shall not allow compressed air to be used to clean clothing or surfaces where such activity could contribute to employee exposure to respirable crystalline silica unless:

(i) The compressed air is used in conjunction with a ventilation system that effectively captures the dust cloud created by the compressed air; or

(ii) No alternative method is feasible.

(i) *Medical surveillance—*(1) *General.* (i) The employer shall make medical surveillance available at no cost to the employee, and at a reasonable time and place, for each employee who will be occupationally exposed to respirable crystalline silica at or above the action level for 30 or more days per year.

(ii) The employer shall ensure that all medical examinations and procedures required by this section are performed by a PLHCP as defined in paragraph (b) of this section.

(2) *Initial examination.* The employer shall make available an initial (baseline) medical examination within 30 days after initial assignment, unless the employee has received a medical examination that meets the requirements of this section within the last three years. The examination shall consist of:

(i) A medical and work history, with emphasis on: Past, present, and anticipated exposure to respirable crystalline silica, dust, and other agents affecting the respiratory system; any history of respiratory system dysfunction, including signs and symptoms of respiratory disease (e.g., shortness of breath, cough, wheezing); history of tuberculosis; and smoking status and history;

(ii) A physical examination with special emphasis on the respiratory system;

(iii) A chest X-ray (a single posteroanterior radiographic projection or radiograph of the chest at full inspiration recorded on either film (no less than 14 x 17 inches and no more than 16 x 17 inches) or digital radiography systems), interpreted and classified according to the International Labour Office (ILO) International Classification of Radiographs of Pneumoconioses by a NIOSH-certified B Reader;

(iv) A pulmonary function test to include forced vital capacity (FVC) and forced expiratory volume in one second (FEV_1) and FEV_1/FVC ratio, administered by a spirometry technician with a current certificate from a NIOSH-approved spirometry course;

(v) Testing for latent tuberculosis infection; and

(vi) Any other tests deemed appropriate by the PLHCP.

(3) *Periodic examinations.* The employer shall make available medical examinations that include the procedures described in paragraph (i)(2) of this section (except paragraph (i)(2)(v)) at least every three years, or more frequently if recommended by the PLHCP.

(4) *Information provided to the PLHCP.* The employer shall ensure that the examining PLHCP has a copy of this standard, and shall provide the PLHCP with the following information:

(i) A description of the employee's former, current, and anticipated duties as they relate to the employee's occupational exposure to respirable crystalline silica;

(ii) The employee's former, current, and anticipated levels of occupational exposure to respirable crystalline silica;

(iii) A description of any personal protective equipment used or to be used by the employee, including when and for how long the employee has used or will use that equipment; and

(iv) Information from records of employment-related medical examinations previously provided to the employee and currently within the control of the employer.

(5) *PLHCP's written medical report for the employee.* The employer shall ensure that the PLHCP explains to the employee the results of the medical examination and provides each employee with a written medical report within 30 days of each medical examination performed. The written report shall contain:

(i) A statement indicating the results of the medical examination, including any medical condition(s) that would place the employee at increased risk of material impairment to health from exposure to respirable crystalline silica

and any medical conditions that require further evaluation or treatment;

(ii) Any recommended limitations on the employee's use of respirators;

(iii) Any recommended limitations on the employee's exposure to respirable crystalline silica; and

(iv) A statement that the employee should be examined by a specialist (pursuant to paragraph (i)(7) of this section) if the chest X-ray provided in accordance with this section is classified as 1/0 or higher by the B Reader, or if referral to a specialist is otherwise deemed appropriate by the PLHCP.

(6) *PLHCP's written medical opinion for the employer.* (i) The employer shall obtain a written medical opinion from the PLHCP within 30 days of the medical examination. The written opinion shall contain only the following:

(A) The date of the examination;

(B) A statement that the examination has met the requirements of this section; and

(C) Any recommended limitations on the employee's use of respirators.

(ii) If the employee provides written authorization, the written opinion shall also contain either or both of the following:

(A) Any recommended limitations on the employee's exposure to respirable crystalline silica;

(B) A statement that the employee should be examined by a specialist (pursuant to paragraph (i)(7) of this section) if the chest X-ray provided in accordance with this section is classified as 1/0 or higher by the B Reader, or if referral to a specialist is otherwise deemed appropriate by the PLHCP.

(iii) The employer shall ensure that each employee receives a copy of the written medical opinion described in paragraph (i)(6)(i) and (ii) of this section within 30 days of each medical examination performed.

(7) *Additional examinations.* (i) If the PLHCP's written medical opinion indicates that an employee should be examined by a specialist, the employer shall make available a medical examination by a specialist within 30 days after receiving the PLHCP's written opinion.

(ii) The employer shall ensure that the examining specialist is provided with all of the information that the employer is obligated to provide to the PLHCP in accordance with paragraph (i)(4) of this section.

(iii) The employer shall ensure that the specialist explains to the employee the results of the medical examination and provides each employee with a written medical report within 30 days of the examination. The written report shall meet the requirements of paragraph (i)(5) (except paragraph (i)(5)(iv)) of this section.

(iv) The employer shall obtain a written opinion from the specialist within 30 days of the medical examination. The written opinion shall meet the requirements of paragraph (i)(6) (except paragraph (i)(6)(i)(B) and (i)(6)(ii)(B)) of this section.

(j) *Communication of respirable crystalline silica hazards to employees*—(1) *Hazard communication.* The employer shall include respirable crystalline silica in the program established to comply with the hazard communication standard (HCS) (29 CFR 1910.1200). The employer shall ensure that each employee has access to labels on containers of crystalline silica and safety data sheets, and is trained in accordance with the provisions of HCS and paragraph (j)(3) of this section. The employer shall ensure that at least the following hazards are addressed: Cancer, lung effects, immune system effects, and kidney effects.

(2) *Signs.* The employer shall post signs at all entrances to regulated areas that bear the following legend:

DANGER
RESPIRABLE CRYSTALLINE SILICA
MAY CAUSE CANCER
CAUSES DAMAGE TO LUNGS
WEAR RESPIRATORY PROTECTION IN THIS AREA
AUTHORIZED PERSONNEL ONLY

(3) *Employee information and training.* (i) The employer shall ensure that each employee covered by this section can demonstrate knowledge and understanding of at least the following:

(A) The health hazards associated with exposure to respirable crystalline silica;

(B) Specific tasks in the workplace that could result in exposure to respirable crystalline silica;

(C) Specific measures the employer has implemented to protect employees

from exposure to respirable crystalline silica, including engineering controls, work practices, and respirators to be used;

(D) The contents of this section; and

(E) The purpose and a description of the medical surveillance program required by paragraph (i) of this section.

(ii) The employer shall make a copy of this section readily available without cost to each employee covered by this section.

(k) *Recordkeeping*—(1) *Air monitoring data.* (i) The employer shall make and maintain an accurate record of all exposure measurements taken to assess employee exposure to respirable crystalline silica, as prescribed in paragraph (d) of this section.

(ii) This record shall include at least the following information:

(A) The date of measurement for each sample taken;

(B) The task monitored;

(C) Sampling and analytical methods used;

(D) Number, duration, and results of samples taken;

(E) Identity of the laboratory that performed the analysis;

(F) Type of personal protective equipment, such as respirators, worn by the employees monitored; and

(G) Name, social security number, and job classification of all employees represented by the monitoring, indicating which employees were actually monitored.

(iii) The employer shall ensure that exposure records are maintained and made available in accordance with 29 CFR 1910.1020.

(2) *Objective data.* (i) The employer shall make and maintain an accurate record of all objective data relied upon to comply with the requirements of this section.

(ii) This record shall include at least the following information:

(A) The crystalline silica-containing material in question;

(B) The source of the objective data;

(C) The testing protocol and results of testing;

(D) A description of the process, task, or activity on which the objective data were based; and

(E) Other data relevant to the process, task, activity, material, or exposures on which the objective data were based.

(iii) The employer shall ensure that objective data are maintained and made available in accordance with 29 CFR 1910.1020.

(3) *Medical surveillance.* (i) The employer shall make and maintain an accurate record for each employee covered by medical surveillance under paragraph (i) of this section.

(ii) The record shall include the following information about the employee:

(A) Name and social security number;

(B) A copy of the PLHCPs' and specialists' written medical opinions; and

(C) A copy of the information provided to the PLHCPs and specialists.

(iii) The employer shall ensure that medical records are maintained and made available in accordance with 29 CFR 1910.1020.

(l) *Dates.* (1) This section is effective June 23, 2016.

(2) Except as provided for in paragraphs (l)(3) and (4) of this section, all obligations of this section commence June 23, 2018.

(3) For hydraulic fracturing operations in the oil and gas industry:

(i) All obligations of this section, except obligations for medical surveillance in paragraph (i)(1)(i) and engineering controls in paragraph (f)(1) of this section, commence June 23, 2018;

(ii) Obligations for engineering controls in paragraph (f)(1) of this section commence June 23, 2021; and

(iii) Obligations for medical surveillance in paragraph (i)(1)(i) commence in accordance with paragraph (l)(4) of this section.

(4) The medical surveillance obligations in paragraph (i)(1)(i) commence on June 23, 2018, for employees who will be occupationally exposed to respirable crystalline silica above the PEL for 30 or more days per year. Those obligations commence June 23, 2020, for employees who will be occupationally exposed to respirable crystalline silica at or above the action level for 30 or more days per year.

APPENDIX A TO § 1910.1053—METHODS OF SAMPLE ANALYSIS

This appendix specifies the procedures for analyzing air samples for respirable crystalline silica, as well as the quality control procedures that employers must ensure that laboratories use when performing an analysis required under 29 CFR 1910.1053 (d)(5). Employers must ensure that such a laboratory:

1. Evaluates all samples using the procedures specified in one of the following analytical methods: OSHA ID–142; NMAM 7500; NMAM 7602; NMAM 7603; MSHA P–2; or MSHA P–7;

2. Is accredited to ANS/ISO/IEC Standard 17025:2005 with respect to crystalline silica analyses by a body that is compliant with ISO/IEC Standard 17011:2004 for implementation of quality assessment programs;

3. Uses the most current National Institute of Standards and Technology (NIST) or NIST traceable standards for instrument calibration or instrument calibration verification;

4. Implements an internal quality control (QC) program that evaluates analytical uncertainty and provides employers with estimates of sampling and analytical error;

5. Characterizes the sample material by identifying polymorphs of respirable crystalline silica present, identifies the presence of any interfering compounds that might affect the analysis, and makes any corrections necessary in order to obtain accurate sample analysis; and

6. Analyzes quantitatively for crystalline silica only after confirming that the sample matrix is free of uncorrectable analytical interferences, corrects for analytical interferences, and uses a method that meets the following performance specifications:

6.1 Each day that samples are analyzed, performs instrument calibration checks with standards that bracket the sample concentrations;

6.2 Uses five or more calibration standard levels to prepare calibration curves and ensures that standards are distributed through the calibration range in a manner that accurately reflects the underlying calibration curve; and

6.3 Optimizes methods and instruments to obtain a quantitative limit of detection that represents a value no higher than 25 percent of the PEL based on sample air volume.

APPENDIX B TO § 1910.1053—MEDICAL SURVEILLANCE GUIDELINES

INTRODUCTION

The purpose of this Appendix is to provide medical information and recommendations to aid physicians and other licensed health care professionals (PLHCPs) regarding compliance with the medical surveillance provisions of the respirable crystalline silica standard (29 CFR 1910.1053). Appendix B is for informational and guidance purposes only and none of the statements in Appendix B should be construed as imposing a mandatory requirement on employers that is not otherwise imposed by the standard.

Medical screening and surveillance allow for early identification of exposure-related health effects in individual employee and groups of employees, so that actions can be taken to both avoid further exposure and prevent or address adverse health outcomes. Silica-related diseases can be fatal, encompass a variety of target organs, and may have public health consequences when considering the increased risk of a latent tuberculosis (TB) infection becoming active. Thus, medical surveillance of silica-exposed employees requires that PLHCPs have a thorough knowledge of silica-related health effects.

This Appendix is divided into seven sections. Section 1 reviews silica-related diseases, medical responses, and public health responses. Section 2 outlines the components of the medical surveillance program for employees exposed to silica. Section 3 describes the roles and responsibilities of the PLHCP implementing the program and of other medical specialists and public health professionals. Section 4 provides a discussion of considerations, including confidentiality. Section 5 provides a list of additional resources and Section 6 lists references. Section 7 provides sample forms for the written medical report for the employee, the written medical opinion for the employer and the written authorization.

1. RECOGNITION OF SILICA-RELATED DISEASES

1.1. Overview. The term "silica" refers specifically to the compound silicon dioxide (SiO_2). Silica is a major component of sand, rock, and mineral ores. Exposure to fine (respirable size) particles of crystalline forms of silica is associated with adverse health effects, such as silicosis, lung cancer, chronic obstructive pulmonary disease (COPD), and activation of latent TB infections. Exposure to respirable crystalline silica can occur in industry settings such as foundries, abrasive blasting operations, paint manufacturing, glass and concrete product manufacturing, brick making, china and pottery manufacturing, manufacturing of plumbing fixtures, and many construction activities including highway repair, masonry, concrete work, rock drilling, and tuck-pointing. New uses of silica continue to emerge. These include countertop manufacturing, finishing, and installation (Kramer *et al.* 2012; OSHA 2015) and hydraulic fracturing in the oil and gas industry (OSHA 2012).

Silicosis is an irreversible, often disabling, and sometimes fatal fibrotic lung disease. Progression of silicosis can occur despite removal from further exposure. Diagnosis of silicosis requires a history of exposure to silica and radiologic findings characteristic of silica exposure. Three different presentations of silicosis (chronic, accelerated, and acute) have been defined. Accelerated and acute silicosis are much less common than chronic silicosis. However, it is critical to recognize all cases of accelerated and acute silicosis because these are life-threatening illnesses and because they are caused by substantial overexposures to respirable crystalline silica. Although any case of silicosis indicates a breakdown in prevention, a case of acute or accelerated silicosis implies current high exposure and a very marked breakdown in prevention.

In addition to silicosis, employees exposed to respirable crystalline silica, especially those with accelerated or acute silicosis, are at increased risks of contracting active TB and other infections (ATS 1997; Rees and Murray 2007). Exposure to respirable crystalline silica also increases an employee's risk of developing lung cancer, and the higher the cumulative exposure, the higher the risk (Steenland *et al.* 2001; Steenland and Ward 2014). Symptoms for these diseases and other respirable crystalline silica-related diseases are discussed below.

1.2. Chronic Silicosis. Chronic silicosis is the most common presentation of silicosis and usually occurs after at least 10 years of exposure to respirable crystalline silica. The clinical presentation of chronic silicosis is:

1.2.1. Symptoms—shortness of breath and cough, although employees may not notice any symptoms early in the disease. Constitutional symptoms, such as fever, loss of appetite and fatigue, may indicate other diseases associated with silica exposure, such as TB infection or lung cancer. Employees with these symptoms should immediately receive further evaluation and treatment.

1.2.2. Physical Examination—may be normal or disclose dry rales or rhonchi on lung auscultation.

1.2.3. Spirometry—may be normal or may show only a mild restrictive or obstructive pattern.

1.2.4. Chest X-ray—classic findings are small, rounded opacities in the upper lung fields bilaterally. However, small irregular opacities and opacities in other lung areas can also occur. Rarely, "eggshell calcifications" in the hilar and mediastinal lymph nodes are seen.

1.2.5. Clinical Course—chronic silicosis in most cases is a slowly progressive disease. Under the respirable crystalline silica standard, the PLHCP is to recommend that employees with a 1/0 category X-ray be referred to an American Board Certified Specialist in Pulmonary Disease or Occupational Medicine. The PLHCP and/or Specialist should counsel employees regarding work practices and personal habits that could affect employees' respiratory health.

1.3. Accelerated Silicosis. Accelerated silicosis generally occurs within 5–10 years of exposure and results from high levels of exposure to respirable crystalline silica. The clinical presentation of accelerated silicosis is:

1.3.1. Symptoms—shortness of breath, cough, and sometimes sputum production. Employees with exposure to respirable crystalline silica, and especially those with accelerated silicosis, are at high risk for activation of TB infections, atypical mycobacterial infections, and fungal superinfections. Constitutional symptoms, such as fever, weight loss, hemoptysis (coughing up blood), and fatigue may herald one of these infections or the onset of lung cancer.

1.3.2. Physical Examination—rales, rhonchi, or other abnormal lung findings in relation to illnesses present. Clubbing of the digits, signs of heart failure, and cor pulmonale may be present in severe lung disease.

1.3.3. Spirometry—restrictive or mixed restrictive/obstructive pattern.

1.3.4. Chest X-ray—small rounded and/or irregular opacities bilaterally. Large opacities and lung abscesses may indicate infections, lung cancer, or progression to complicated silicosis, also termed progressive massive fibrosis.

1.3.5. Clinical Course—accelerated silicosis has a rapid, severe course. Under the respirable crystalline silica standard, the PLHCP can recommend referral to a Board Certified Specialist in either Pulmonary Disease or Occupational Medicine, as deemed appropriate, and referral to a Specialist is recommended whenever the diagnosis of accelerated silicosis is being considered.

1.4. Acute Silicosis. Acute silicosis is a rare disease caused by inhalation of extremely high levels of respirable crystalline silica particles. The pathology is similar to alveolar proteinosis with lipoproteinaceous material accumulating in the alveoli. Acute silicosis develops rapidly, often, within a few months to less than 2 years of exposure, and is almost always fatal. The clinical presentation of acute silicosis is as follows:

1.4.1. Symptoms—sudden, progressive, and severe shortness of breath. Constitutional symptoms are frequently present and include fever, weight loss, fatigue, productive cough, hemoptysis (coughing up blood), and pleuritic chest pain.

1.4.2. Physical Examination—dyspnea at rest, cyanosis, decreased breath sounds, inspiratory rales, clubbing of the digits, and fever.

1.4.3. Spirometry—restrictive or mixed restrictive/obstructive pattern.

1.4.4. Chest X-ray—diffuse haziness of the lungs bilaterally early in the disease. As the disease progresses, the "ground glass" appearance of interstitial fibrosis will appear.

1.4.5. Clinical Course—employees with acute silicosis are at especially high risk of TB activation, nontuberculous mycobacterial infections, and fungal superinfections. Acute silicosis is immediately life-threatening. The employee should be urgently referred to a Board Certified Specialist in Pulmonary Disease or Occupational Medicine for evaluation and treatment. Although any case of silicosis indicates a breakdown in prevention, a case of acute or accelerated silicosis implies a profoundly high level of silica exposure and may mean that other employees are currently exposed to dangerous levels of silica.

1.5. COPD. COPD, including chronic bronchitis and emphysema, has been documented in silica-exposed employees, including those who do not develop silicosis. Periodic spirometry tests are performed to evaluate each employee for progressive changes consistent with the development of COPD. In addition to evaluating spirometry results of individual employees over time, PLHCPs may want to be aware of general trends in spirometry results for groups of employees from the same workplace to identify possible problems that might exist at that workplace. (*See* Section 2 of this Appendix on Medical Surveillance for further discussion.) Heart disease may develop secondary to lung diseases such as COPD. A recent study by Liu *et al.* 2014 noted a significant exposure-response trend between cumulative silica exposure and heart disease deaths, primarily due to pulmonary heart disease, such as cor pulmonale.

1.6. Renal and Immune System. Silica exposure has been associated with several types of kidney disease, including glomerulonephritis, nephrotic syndrome, and end stage renal disease requiring dialysis. Silica exposure has also been associated with other autoimmune conditions, including progressive systemic sclerosis, systemic lupus erythematosus, and rheumatoid arthritis. Studies note an association between employees with silicosis and serologic markers for autoimmune diseases, including antinuclear antibodies, rheumatoid factor, and immune complexes (Jalloul and Banks 2007; Shtraichman *et al.* 2015).

1.7. TB and Other Infections. Silica-exposed employees with latent TB are 3 to 30 times more likely to develop active pulmonary TB infection (ATS 1997; Rees and Murray 2007). Although respirable crystalline silica exposure does not cause TB infection, individuals with latent TB infection are at increased risk for activation of disease if they have higher levels of respirable crystalline silica exposure, greater profusion of radiographic abnormalities, or a diagnosis of silicosis. Demographic characteristics, such as immigration from some countries, are associated with increased rates of latent TB infection. PLHCPs can review the latest Centers for

Disease Control and Prevention (CDC) information on TB incidence rates and high risk populations online (*See* Section 5 of this Appendix). Additionally, silica-exposed employees are at increased risk for contracting nontuberculous mycobacterial infections, including *Mycobacterium avium-intracellulare* and *Mycobacterium kansaii*.

1.8. Lung Cancer. The National Toxicology Program has listed respirable crystalline silica as a known human carcinogen since 2000 (NTP 2014). The International Agency for Research on Cancer (2012) has also classified silica as Group 1 (carcinogenic to humans). Several studies have indicated that the risk of lung cancer from exposure to respirable crystalline silica and smoking is greater than additive (Brown 2009; Liu *et al.* 2013). Employees should be counseled on smoking cessation.

2. MEDICAL SURVEILLANCE

PLHCPs who manage silica medical surveillance programs should have a thorough understanding of the many silica-related diseases and health effects outlined in Section 1 of this Appendix. At each clinical encounter, the PLHCP should consider silica-related health outcomes, with particular vigilance for acute and accelerated silicosis. In this Section, the required components of medical surveillance under the respirable crystalline silica standard are reviewed, along with additional guidance and recommendations for PLHCPs performing medical surveillance examinations for silica-exposed employees.

2.1. History

2.1.1. The respirable crystalline silica standard requires the following: A medical and work history, with emphasis on: Past, present, and anticipated exposure to respirable crystalline silica, dust, and other agents affecting the respiratory system; any history of respiratory system dysfunction, including signs and symptoms of respiratory disease (e.g., shortness of breath, cough, wheezing); history of TB; and smoking status and history.

2.1.2. Further, the employer must provide the PLHCP with the following information:

2.1.2.1. A description of the employee's former, current, and anticipated duties as they relate to the employee's occupational exposure to respirable crystalline silica;

2.1.2.2. The employee's former, current, and anticipated levels of occupational exposure to respirable crystalline silica;

2.1.2.3. A description of any personal protective equipment used or to be used by the employee, including when and for how long the employee has used or will use that equipment; and

2.1.2.4. Information from records of employment-related medical examinations pre-viously provided to the employee and currently within the control of the employer.

2.1.3. Additional guidance and recommendations: A history is particularly important both in the initial evaluation and in periodic examinations. Information on past and current medical conditions (particularly a history of kidney disease, cardiac disease, connective tissue disease, and other immune diseases), medications, hospitalizations and surgeries may uncover health risks, such as immune suppression, that could put an employee at increased health risk from exposure to silica. This information is important when counseling the employee on risks and safe work practices related to silica exposure.

2.2. Physical Examination

2.2.1. The respirable crystalline silica standard requires the following: A physical examination, with special emphasis on the respiratory system. The physical examination must be performed at the initial examination and every three years thereafter.

2.2.2. Additional guidance and recommendations: Elements of the physical examination that can assist the PHLCP include: An examination of the cardiac system, an extremity examination (for clubbing, cyanosis, edema, or joint abnormalities), and an examination of other pertinent organ systems identified during the history.

2.3. TB Testing

2.3.1. The respirable crystalline silica standard requires the following: Baseline testing for TB on initial examination.

2.3.2. Additional guidance and recommendations:

2.3.2.1. Current CDC guidelines (*See* Section 5 of this Appendix) should be followed for the application and interpretation of Tuberculin skin tests (TST). The interpretation and documentation of TST reactions should be performed within 48 to 72 hours of administration by trained PLHCPs.

2.3.2.2. PLHCPs may use alternative TB tests, such as interferon-γ release assays (IGRAs), if sensitivity and specificity are comparable to TST (Mazurek *et al.* 2010; Slater *et al.* 2013). PLHCPs can consult current CDC guidelines for acceptable tests for latent TB infection.

2.3.2.3. The silica standard allows the PLHCP to order additional tests or test at a greater frequency than required by the standard, if deemed appropriate. Therefore, PLHCPs might perform periodic (e.g., annual) TB testing as appropriate, based on employees' risk factors. For example, according to the American Thoracic Society (ATS), the diagnosis of silicosis or exposure to silica for 25 years or more are indications for annual TB testing (ATS 1997). PLHCPs should consult the current CDC guidance on risk factors for TB (*See* Section 5 of this Appendix).

2.3.2.4. Employees with positive TB tests and those with indeterminate test results should be referred to the appropriate agency or specialist, depending on the test results and clinical picture. Agencies, such as local public health departments, or specialists, such as a pulmonary or infectious disease specialist, may be the appropriate referral. Active TB is a nationally notifiable disease. PLHCPs should be aware of the reporting requirements for their region. All States have TB Control Offices that can be contacted for further information. (*See* Section 5 of this Appendix for links to CDC's TB resources and State TB Control Offices.)

2.3.2.5. The following public health principles are key to TB control in the U.S. (ATS–CDC–IDSA 2005):

(*1*) Prompt detection and reporting of persons who have contracted active TB;

(*2*) Prevention of TB spread to close contacts of active TB cases;

(*3*) Prevention of active TB in people with latent TB through targeted testing and treatment; and

(*4*) Identification of settings at high risk for TB transmission so that appropriate infection-control measures can be implemented.

2.4. Pulmonary Function Testing

2.4.1. The respirable crystalline silica standard requires the following: Pulmonary function testing must be performed on the initial examination and every three years thereafter. The required pulmonary function test is spirometry and must include forced vital capacity (FVC), forced expiratory volume in one second (FEV_1), and FEV_1/FVC ratio. Testing must be administered by a spirometry technician with a current certificate from a National Institute for Occupational Health and Safety (NIOSH)-approved spirometry course.

2.4.2. Additional guidance and recommendations: Spirometry provides information about individual respiratory status and can be used to track an employee's respiratory status over time or as a surveillance tool to follow individual and group respiratory function. For quality results, the ATS and the American College of Occupational and Environmental Medicine (ACOEM) recommend use of the third National Health and Nutrition Examination Survey (NHANES III) values, and ATS publishes recommendations for spirometry equipment (Miller *et al.* 2005; Townsend 2011; Redlich *et al.* 2014). OSHA's publication, *Spirometry Testing in Occupational Health Programs: Best Practices for Healthcare Professionals*, provides helpful guidance (See Section 5 of this Appendix). Abnormal spirometry results may warrant further clinical evaluation and possible recommenda-

tions for limitations on the employee's exposure to respirable crystalline silica.

2.5. Chest X-ray

2.5.1. The respirable crystalline silica standard requires the following: A single posteroanterior (PA) radiographic projection or radiograph of the chest at full inspiration recorded on either film (no less than 14 x 17 inches and no more than 16 x 17 inches) or digital radiography systems. A chest X-ray must be performed on the initial examination and every three years thereafter. The chest X-ray must be interpreted and classified according to the International Labour Office (ILO) International Classification of Radiographs of Pneumoconioses by a NIOSH-certified B Reader.

Chest radiography is necessary to diagnose silicosis, monitor the progression of silicosis, and identify associated conditions such as TB. If the B reading indicates small opacities in a profusion of 1/0 or higher, the employee is to receive a recommendation for referral to a Board Certified Specialist in Pulmonary Disease or Occupational Medicine.

2.5.2. Additional guidance and recommendations: Medical imaging has largely transitioned from conventional film-based radiography to digital radiography systems. The ILO Guidelines for the Classification of Pneumoconioses has historically provided film-based chest radiography as a referent standard for comparison to individual exams. However, in 2011, the ILO revised the guidelines to include a digital set of referent standards that were derived from the prior film-based standards. To assist in assuring that digitally-acquired radiographs are at least as safe and effective as film radiographs, NIOSH has prepared guidelines, based upon accepted contemporary professional recommendations (*See* Section 5 of this Appendix). Current research from Laney *et al.* 2011 and Halldin *et al.* 2014 validate the use of the ILO digital referent images. Both studies conclude that the results of pneumoconiosis classification using digital references are comparable to film-based ILO classifications. Current ILO guidance on radiography for pneumoconioses and B-reading should be reviewed by the PLHCP periodically, as needed, on the ILO or NIOSH Web sites (*See* Section 5 of this Appendix).

2.6. Other Testing. Under the respirable crystalline silica standards, the PLHCP has the option of ordering additional testing he or she deems appropriate. Additional tests can be ordered on a case-by-case basis depending on individual signs or symptoms and clinical judgment. For example, if an employee reports a history of abnormal kidney function tests, the PLHCP may want to order a baseline renal function tests (e.g., serum creatinine and urinalysis). As indicated above, the PLHCP may order annual TB testing for silica-exposed employees who are at high risk of developing active TB infections. Additional tests that PLHCPs may order based on findings of medical examinations include, but is not limited to, chest computerized tomography (CT) scan for lung cancer or COPD, testing for immunologic diseases, and cardiac testing for pulmonary-related heart disease, such as cor pulmonale.

3. ROLES AND RESPONSIBILITIES

3.1. PLHCP. The PLHCP designation refers to "an individual whose legally permitted scope of practice (*i.e.*, license, registration, or certification) allows him or her to independently provide or be delegated the responsibility to provide some or all of the particular health care services required" by the respirable crystalline silica standard. The legally permitted scope of practice for the PLHCP is determined by each State. PLHCPs who perform clinical services for a silica medical surveillance program should have a thorough knowledge of respirable crystalline silica-related diseases and symptoms. Suspected cases of silicosis, advanced COPD, or other respiratory conditions causing impairment should be promptly referred to a Board Certified Specialist in Pulmonary Disease or Occupational Medicine.

Once the medical surveillance examination is completed, the employer must ensure that the PLHCP explains to the employee the results of the medical examination and provides the employee with a written medical report within 30 days of the examination. The written medical report must contain a statement indicating the results of the medical examination, including any medical condition(s) that would place the employee at increased risk of material impairment to health from exposure to respirable crystalline silica and any medical conditions that require further evaluation or treatment. In addition, the PLHCP's written medical report must include any recommended limitations on the employee's use of respirators, any recommended limitations on the employee's exposure to respirable crystalline silica, and a statement that the employee should be examined by a Board Certified Specialist in Pulmonary Disease or Occupational medicine if the chest X-ray is classified as 1/0 or higher by the B Reader, or if referral to a Specialist is otherwise deemed appropriate by the PLHCP.

The PLHCP should discuss all findings and test results and any recommendations regarding the employee's health, worksite safety and health practices, and medical referrals for further evaluation, if indicated. In addition, it is suggested that the PLHCP offer to provide the employee with a complete copy of their examination and test results, as some employees may want this information for their own records or to provide to their personal physician or a future PLHCP. Employees are entitled to access their medical records.

Under the respirable crystalline silica standard, the employer must ensure that the PLHCP provides the employer with a written medical opinion within 30 days of the employee examination, and that the employee also gets a copy of the written medical opinion for the employer within 30 days. The PLHCP may choose to directly provide the employee a copy of the written medical opinion. This can be particularly helpful to employees, such as construction employees, who may change employers frequently. The written medical opinion can be used by the employee as proof of up-to-date medical surveillance. The following lists the elements of the written medical report for the employee and written medical opinion for the employer. (Sample forms for the written medical report for the employee, the written medical opinion for the employer, and the written authorization are provided in Section 7 of this Appendix.)

3.1.1. The written medical report for the employee must include the following information:

3.1.1.1. A statement indicating the results of the medical examination, including any medical condition(s) that would place the employee at increased risk of material impairment to health from exposure to respirable crystalline silica and any medical conditions that require further evaluation or treatment;

3.1.1.2. Any recommended limitations upon the employee's use of a respirator;

3.1.1.3. Any recommended limitations on the employee's exposure to respirable crystalline silica; and

3.1.1.4. A statement that the employee should be examined by a Board Certified Specialist in Pulmonary Disease or Occupational Medicine, where the standard requires or where the PLHCP has determined such a referral is necessary. The standard requires referral to a Board Certified Specialist in Pulmonary Disease or Occupational Medicine for a chest X-ray B reading indicating small opacities in a profusion of 1/0 or higher, or if the PHLCP determines that referral to a Specialist is necessary for other silica-related findings.

3.1.2. The PLHCP's written medical opinion for the employer must include only the following information:

3.1.2.1. The date of the examination;

3.1.2.2. A statement that the examination has met the requirements of this section; and

3.1.2.3. Any recommended limitations on the employee's use of respirators.

3.1.2.4. If the employee provides the PLHCP with written authorization, the written opinion for the employer shall also contain either or both of the following:

(1) Any recommended limitations on the employee's exposure to respirable crystalline silica; and

(2) A statement that the employee should be examined by a Board Certified Specialist in Pulmonary Disease or Occupational Medicine if the chest X-ray provided in accordance with this section is classified as 1/0 or higher by the B Reader, or if referral to a Specialist is otherwise deemed appropriate.

3.1.2.5. In addition to the above referral for abnormal chest X-ray, the PLHCP may refer an employee to a Board Certified Specialist in Pulmonary Disease or Occupational Medicine for other findings of concern during the medical surveillance examination if these findings are potentially related to silica exposure.

3.1.2.6. Although the respirable crystalline silica standard requires the employer to ensure that the PLHCP explains the results of the medical examination to the employee, the standard does not mandate how this should be done. The written medical opinion for the employer could contain a statement that the PLHCP has explained the results of the medical examination to the employee.

3.2. Medical Specialists. The silica standard requires that all employees with chest X-ray B readings of 1/0 or higher be referred to a Board Certified Specialist in Pulmonary Disease or Occupational Medicine. If the employee has given written authorization for the employer to be informed, then the employer shall make available a medical examination by a Specialist within 30 days after receiving the PLHCP's written medical opinion.

3.2.1. The employer must provide the following information to the Board Certified Specialist in Pulmonary Disease or Occupational Medicine:

3.2.1.1. A description of the employee's former, current, and anticipated duties as they relate to the employee's occupational exposure to respirable crystalline silica;

3.2.1.2. The employee's former, current, and anticipated levels of occupational exposure to respirable crystalline silica;

3.2.1.3. A description of any personal protective equipment used or to be used by the employee, including when and for how long the employee has used or will use that equipment; and

3.2.1.4. Information from records of employment-related medical examinations previously provided to the employee and currently within the control of the employer.

3.2.2. The PLHCP should make certain that, with written authorization from the employee, the Board Certified Specialist in Pulmonary Disease or Occupational Medicine has any other pertinent medical and occupational information necessary for the specialist's evaluation of the employee's condition.

3.2.3. Once the Board Certified Specialist in Pulmonary Disease or Occupational Medicine has evaluated the employee, the employer must ensure that the Specialist explains to the employee the results of the medical examination and provides the employee with a written medical report within 30 days of the examination. The employer must also ensure that the Specialist provides the employer with a written medical opinion within 30 days of the employee examination. (Sample forms for the written medical report for the employee, the written medical opinion for the employer and the written authorization are provided in Section 7 of this Appendix.)

3.2.4. The Specialist's written medical report for the employee must include the following information:

3.2.4.1. A statement indicating the results of the medical examination, including any medical condition(s) that would place the employee at increased risk of material impairment to health from exposure to respirable crystalline silica and any medical conditions that require further evaluation or treatment;

3.2.4.2. Any recommended limitations upon the employee's use of a respirator; and

3.2.4.3. Any recommended limitations on the employee's exposure to respirable crystalline silica.

3.2.5. The Specialist's written medical opinion for the employer must include the following information:

3.2.5.1. The date of the examination; and

3.2.5.2. Any recommended limitations on the employee's use of respirators.

3.2.5.3. If the employee provides the Board Certified Specialist in Pulmonary Disease or Occupational Medicine with written authorization, the written medical opinion for the employer shall also contain any recommended limitations on the employee's exposure to respirable crystalline silica.

3.2.5.4. Although the respirable crystalline silica standard requires the employer to ensure that the Board Certified Specialist in Pulmonary Disease or Occupational Medicine explains the results of the medical examination to the employee, the standard does not mandate how this should be done. The written medical opinion for the employer could contain a statement that the Specialist has explained the results of the medical examination to the employee.

3.2.6. After evaluating the employee, the Board Certified Specialist in Pulmonary Disease or Occupational Medicine should provide feedback to the PLHCP as appropriate, depending on the reason for the referral. OSHA believes that because the PLHCP has the primary relationship with the employer and employee, the Specialist may want to communicate his or her findings to the PLHCP and have the PLHCP simply update the original medical report for the employee and medical opinion for the employer. This is permitted under the standard, so long as all requirements and time deadlines are met.

3.3. Public Health Professionals. PLHCPs might refer employees or consult with public health professionals as a result of silica medical surveillance. For instance, if individual cases of active TB are identified, public health professionals from state or local health departments may assist in diagnosis and treatment of individual cases and may evaluate other potentially affected persons, including coworkers. Because silica-exposed employees are at increased risk of progression from latent to active TB, treatment of latent infection is recommended. The diagnosis of active TB, acute or accelerated silicosis, or other silica-related diseases and infections should serve as sentinel events suggesting high levels of exposure to silica and may require consultation with the appropriate public health agencies to investigate potentially similarly exposed coworkers to assess for disease clusters. These agencies include local or state health departments or OSHA. In addition, NIOSH can provide assistance upon request through their Health Hazard Evaluation program. (*See* Section 5 of this Appendix)

4. CONFIDENTIALITY AND OTHER CONSIDERATIONS

The information that is provided from the PLHCP to the employee and employer under the medical surveillance section of OSHA's respirable crystalline silica standard differs from that of medical surveillance requirements in previous OSHA standards. The standard requires two separate written communications, a written medical report for the employee and a written medical opinion for the employer. The confidentiality requirements for the written medical opinion are more stringent than in past standards. For example, the information the PLHCP can (and must) include in his or her written medical opinion for the employer is limited to: The date of the examination, a statement that the examination has met the requirements of this section, and any recommended limitations on the employee's use of respirators. If the employee provides written authorization for the disclosure of any limitations on the employee's exposure to respirable crystalline silica, then the PLHCP can (and must) include that information in the written medical opinion for the employer as well. Likewise, with the employee's written authorization, the PLHCP can (and must) disclose the PLHCP's referral recommendation (if any) as part of the written medical opinion for the employer. However, the opinion to the employer must not include information regarding recommended limitations on the employee's exposure to respirable crystalline silica or any referral

recommendations without the employee's written authorization.

The standard also places limitations on the information that the Board Certified Specialist in Pulmonary Disease or Occupational Medicine can provide to the employer without the employee's written authorization. The Specialist's written medical opinion for the employer, like the PLHCP's opinion, is limited to (and must contain): The date of the examination and any recommended limitations on the employee's use of respirators. If the employee provides written authorization, the written medical opinion can (and must) also contain any limitations on the employee's exposure to respirable crystalline silica.

The PLHCP should discuss the implication of signing or not signing the authorization with the employee (in a manner and language that he or she understands) so that the employee can make an informed decision regarding the written authorization and its consequences. The discussion should include the risk of ongoing silica exposure, personal risk factors, risk of disease progression, and possible health and economic consequences. For instance, written authorization is required for a PLHCP to advise an employer that an employee should be referred to a Board Certified Specialist in Pulmonary Disease or Occupational Medicine for evaluation of an abnormal chest X-ray (B-reading 1/0 or greater). If an employee does not sign an authorization, then the employer will not know and cannot facilitate the referral to a Specialist and is not required to pay for the Specialist's examination. In the rare case where an employee is diagnosed with acute or accelerated silicosis, co-workers are likely to be at significant risk of developing those diseases as a result of inadequate controls in the workplace. In this case, the PLHCP and/or Specialist should explain this concern to the affected employee and make a determined effort to obtain written authorization from the employee so that the PLHCP and/or Specialist can contact the employer.

Finally, without written authorization from the employee, the PLHCP and/or Board Certified Specialist in Pulmonary Disease or Occupational Medicine cannot provide feedback to an employer regarding control of workplace silica exposure, at least in relation to an individual employee. However, the regulation does not prohibit a PLHCP and/or Specialist from providing an employer with general recommendations regarding exposure controls and prevention programs in relation to silica exposure and silica-related illnesses, based on the information that the PLHCP receives from the employer such as employees' duties and exposure levels. Recommendations may include increased frequency of medical surveillance examinations, additional medical surveillance components, engineering and work practice controls, exposure monitoring and personal protective equipment. For instance, more frequent medical surveillance examinations may be a recommendation to employers for employees who do abrasive blasting with silica because of the high exposures associated with that operation.

ACOEM's Code of Ethics and discussion is a good resource to guide PLHCPs regarding the issues discussed in this section (*See* Section 5 of this Appendix).

5. RESOURCES

5.1. American College of Occupational and Environmental Medicine (ACOEM):

ACOEM Code of Ethics. Accessed at: *http://www.acoem.org/codeofconduct.aspx*

Raymond, L.W. and Wintermeyer, S. (2006) ACOEM evidenced-based statement on medical surveillance of silica-exposed workers: Medical surveillance of workers exposed to crystalline silica. *J Occup Environ Med*, 48, 95–101.

5.2. Center for Disease Control and Prevention (CDC)

Tuberculosis Web page: *http://www.cdc.gov/tb/default.htm*

State TB Control Offices Web page: *http://www.cdc.gov/tb/links/tboffices.htm*

Tuberculosis Laws and Policies Web page: *http://www.cdc.gov/tb/programs/laws/default.htm*

CDC. (2013). Latent Tuberculosis Infection: A Guide for Primary Health Care Providers. Accessed at: *http://www.cdc.gov/tb/publications/ltbi/pdf/targetedltbi.pdf*

5.3. International Labour Organization

International Labour Office (ILO). (2011) Guidelines for the use of the ILO International Classification of Radiographs of Pneumoconioses, Revised edition 2011. Occupational Safety and Health Series No. 22: *http://www.ilo.org/safework/info/publications/WCMS_168260/lang-en/index.htm*

5.4. National Institute of Occupational Safety and Health (NIOSH)

NIOSH B Reader Program Web page. (Information on interpretation of X-rays for silicosis and a list of certified B-readers). Accessed at: *http://www.cdc.gov/niosh/topics/chestradiography/breader-info.html*

NIOSH Guideline (2011). Application of Digital Radiography for the Detection and Classification of Pneumoconiosis. NIOSH publication number 2011-198. Accessed at: *http://www.cdc.gov/niosh/docs/2011-198/*.

NIOSH Hazard Review (2002), Health Effects of Occupational Exposure to Respirable Crystalline Silica. NIOSH publication

number 2002-129: Accessed at *http://www.cdc.gov/niosh/docs/2002-129/*

NIOSH Health Hazard Evaluations Programs. (Information on the NIOSH Health Hazard Evaluation (HHE) program, how to request an HHE and how to look up an HHE report). Accessed at: *http://www.cdc.gov/niosh/hhe/*

5.5. National Industrial Sand Association:

Occupational Health Program for Exposure to Crystalline Silica in the Industrial Sand Industry. National Industrial Sand Association, 2nd ed. 2010. Can be ordered at: *http://www.sand.org/silica-occupational-health-program*

5.6. Occupational Safety and Health Administration (OSHA)

Contacting OSHA: *http://www.osha.gov/html/Feed_Back.html*

OSHA's Clinicians Web page. (OSHA resources, regulations and links to help clinicians navigate OSHA's Web site and aid clinicians in caring for workers.) Accessed at: *http://www.osha.gov/dts/oom/clinicians/index.html*

OSHA's Safety and Health Topics Web page on Silica. Accessed at: *http://www.osha.gov/dsg/topics/silicacrystalline/index.html*

OSHA (2013). Spirometry Testing in Occupational Health Programs: Best Practices for Healthcare Professionals. (OSHA 3637–03 2013). Accessed at: *http://www.osha.gov/Publications/OSHA3637.pdf*

OSHA/NIOSH (2011). Spirometry: OSHA/NIOSH Spirometry InfoSheet (OSHA 3415–1–11). (Provides guidance to employers). Accessed at *http://www.osha.gov/Publications/osha3415.pdf*

OSHA/NIOSH (2011) Spirometry: OSHA/NIOSH Spirometry Worker Info. (OSHA 3418–3–11). Accessed at *http://www.osha.gov/Publications/osha3418.pdf*

5.7. Other

Steenland, K. and Ward E. (2014). Silica: A lung carcinogen. *CA Cancer J Clin*, 64, 63–69. (This article reviews not only silica and lung cancer but also all the known silica-related health effects. Further, the authors provide guidance to clinicians on medical surveillance of silica-exposed workers and worker counselling on safety practices to minimize silica exposure.)

6. REFERENCES

American Thoracic Society (ATS). Medical Section of the American Lung Association (1997). Adverse effects of crystalline silica exposure. *Am J Respir Crit Care Med*, 155, 761–765.

American Thoracic Society (ATS), Centers for Disease Control (CDC), Infectious Diseases Society of America (IDSA) (2005). Controlling Tuberculosis in the United States. *Morbidity and Mortality Weekly*

Report *(MMWR)*, 54(RR12), 1–81. Accessed at: *http://www.cdc.gov/mmwr/preview/mmwrhtml/rr5412a1.htm.*

Brown, T. (2009). Silica exposure, smoking, silicosis and lung cancer—complex interactions. *Occupational Medicine*, 59, 89–95.

Halldin, C.N., Petsonk, E.L., and Laney, A.S. (2014). Validation of the International Labour Office digitized standard images for recognition and classification of radiographs of pneumoconiosis. *Acad Radiol*, 21, 305–311.

International Agency for Research on Cancer. (2012). Monographs on the evaluation of carcinogenic risks to humans: Arsenic, Metals, Fibers, and Dusts Silica Dust, Crystalline, in the Form of Quartz or Cristobalite. A Review of Human Carcinogens. Volume 100 C. Geneva, Switzerland: World Health Organization.

Jalloul, A.S. and Banks D.E. (2007). Chapter 23. The health effects of silica exposure. In: Rom, W.N. and Markowitz, S.B. (Eds). Environmental and Occupational Medicine, 4th edition. Lippincott, Williams and Wilkins, Philadelphia, 365–387.

Kramer, M.R., Blanc, P.D., Fireman, E., Amital, A., Guber, A., Rahman, N.A., and Shitrit, D. (2012). Artifical stone silicosis: Disease resurgence among artificial stone workers. *Chest*, 142, 419–424.

Laney, A.S., Petsonk, E.L., and Attfield, M.D. (2011). Intramodality and intermodality comparisons of storage phosphor computed radiography and conventional film-screen radiography in the recognition of small pneumonconiotic opacities. *Chest*, 140, 1574–1580.

Liu, Y., Steenland, K., Rong, Y., Hnizdo, E., Huang, X., Zhang, H., Shi, T., Sun, Y., Wu, T., and Chen, W. (2013). Exposure-response analysis and risk assessment for lung cancer in relationship to silica exposure: A 44-year cohort study of 34,018 workers. *Am J Epi*, 178, 1424–1433.

Liu, Y., Rong, Y., Steenland, K., Christiani, D.C., Huang, X., Wu, T., and Chen, W. (2014). Long-term exposure to crystalline silica and risk of heart disease mortality. *Epidemiology*, 25, 689–696.

Mazurek, G.H., Jereb, J., Vernon, A., LoBue, P., Goldberg, S., Castro, K. (2010). Updated guidelines for using interferon gamma release assays to detect Mycobacterium tuberculosis infection—United States. *Morbidity and Mortality Weekly Report (MMWR)*, 59(RR05), 1–25.

Miller, M.R., Hankinson, J., Brusasco, V., Burgos, F., Casaburi, R., Coates, A., Crapo, R., Enright, P., van der Grinten, C.P., Gustafsson, P., Jensen, R., Johnson, D.C., MacIntyre, N., McKay, R., Navajas, D., Pedersen, O.F., Pellegrino, R., Viegi, G., and Wanger, J. (2005). American Thoracic Society/European Respiratory Society (ATS/ERS) Task Force:

Standardisation of Spirometry. *Eur Respir J*, 26, 319–338.

National Toxicology Program (NTP) (2014). Report on Carcinogens, Thirteenth Edition. Silica, Crystalline (respirable Size). Research Triangle Park, NC: U.S. Department of Health and Human Services, Public Health Service. *http://ntp.niehs.nih.gov/ntp/roc/content/profiles/silica.pdf.*

Occupational Safety and Health Administration/National Institute for Occupational Safety and Health (OSHA/NIOSH) (2012). Hazard Alert. Worker exposure to silica during hydraulic fracturing.

Occupational Safety and Health Administration/National Institute for Occupational Safety and Health (OSHA/NIOSH) (2015). Hazard alert. Worker exposure to silica during countertop manufacturing, finishing, and installation. (OSHA-HA-3768-2015).

Redlich, C.A., Tarlo, S.M., Hankinson, J.L., Townsend, M.C, Eschenbacher, W.L., Von Essen, S.G., Sigsgaard, T., Weissman, D.N. (2014). Official American Thoracic Society technical standards: Spirometry in the occupational setting. *Am J Respir Crit Care Med*; 189, 984–994.

Rees, D. and Murray, J. (2007). Silica, silicosis and tuberculosis. *Int J Tuberc Lung Dis*, 11(5), 474–484.

Shtraichman, O., Blanc, P.D., Ollech, J.E., Fridel, L., Fuks, L., Fireman, E., and Kramer, M.R. (2015). Outbreak of autoimmune disease in silicosis linked to artificial stone. *Occup Med*, 65, 444–450.

Slater, M.L., Welland, G., Pai, M., Parsonnet, J., and Banaei, N. (2013). Challenges with QuantiFERON-TB gold assay for large-scale, routine screening of U.S. healthcare workers. *Am J Respir Crit Care Med*, 188, 1005–1010.

Steenland, K., Mannetje, A., Boffetta, P., Stayner, L., Attfield, M., Chen, J., Dosemeci, M., DeKlerk, N., Hnizdo, E., Koskela, R., and Checkoway, H. (2001). International Agency for Research on Cancer. Pooled exposure-response analyses and risk assessment for lung cancer in 10 cohorts of silica-exposed workers: An IARC multicentre study. *Cancer Causes Control*, 12(9):773–84.

Steenland, K. and Ward E. (2014). Silica: A lung carcinogen. *CA Cancer J Clin*, 64, 63–69.

Townsend, M.C. ACOEM Guidance Statement. (2011). Spirometry in the occupational health setting—2011 Update. *J Occup Environ Med*, 53, 569–584.

7. SAMPLE FORMS

Three sample forms are provided. The first is a sample written medical report for the employee. The second is a sample written medical opinion for the employer. And the third is a sample written authorization form

that employees sign to clarify what information the employee is authorizing to be released to the employer.

WRITTEN MEDICAL REPORT FOR EMPLOYEE

EMPLOYEE NAME: _____   DATE OF EXAMINATION: _____

TYPE OF EXAMINATION:
[ ] Initial examination   [ ] Periodic examination   [ ] Specialist examination
[ ] Other: _____

RESULTS OF MEDICAL EXAMINATION:
Physical Examination –   [ ] Normal   [ ] Abnormal (see below)   [ ] Not performed
Chest X-Ray –   [ ] Normal   [ ] Abnormal (see below)   [ ] Not performed
Breathing Test (Spirometry) –   [ ] Normal   [ ] Abnormal (see below)   [ ] Not performed
Test for Tuberculosis –   [ ] Normal   [ ] Abnormal (see below)   [ ] Not performed
Other:_____   [ ] Normal   [ ] Abnormal (see below)   [ ] Not performed

Results reported as abnormal: _____
_____

[ ] Your health may be at increased risk from exposure to respirable crystalline silica due to the following:
_____

RECOMMENDATIONS:
[ ] No limitations on respirator use
[ ] Recommended limitations on use of respirator: _____
[ ] Recommended limitations on exposure to respirable crystalline silica: _____
_____

Dates for recommended limitations, if applicable: _____ to _____
                                                        MM/DD/YYYY   MM/DD/YYYY

[ ] I recommend that you be examined by a Board Certified Specialist in Pulmonary Disease or Occupational Medicine

[ ] Other recommendations*:
_____

Your next periodic examination for silica exposure should be in: [ ] 3 years   [ ] Other: _____
                                                                                              MM/DD/YYYY
Examining Provider: _____   Date: _____
                              (signature)
Provider Name: _____
Office Address: _____   Office Phone: _____

*These findings may not be related to respirable crystalline silica exposure or may not be work-related, and therefore
may not be covered by the employer. These findings may necessitate follow-up and treatment by your personal
physician.

Respirable Crystalline Silica standard (§ 1910.1053 or 1926.1153)

WRITTEN MEDICAL OPINION FOR EMPLOYER

EMPLOYER: _____

EMPLOYEE NAME: _____   DATE OF EXAMINATION: _____

TYPE OF EXAMINATION:
[ ] Initial examination   [ ] Periodic examination   [ ] Specialist examination
[ ] Other: _____

USE OF RESPIRATOR:
[ ] No limitations on respirator use
[ ] Recommended limitations on use of respirator:_____

Dates for recommended limitations, if applicable: _____ to _____
                                                               MM/DD/YYYY   MM/DD/YYYY

The employee has provided written authorization for disclosure of the following to the employer (if applicable):

[ ] This employee should be examined by an American Board Certified Specialist in Pulmonary Disease or Occupational Medicine
[ ] Recommended limitations on exposure to respirable crystalline silica:_____
_____

Dates for exposure limitations noted above: _____ to _____
                                                         MM/DD/YYYY   MM/DD/YYYY

NEXT PERIODIC EVALUATION: [ ] 3 years   [ ] Other: _____
                                                                       MM/DD/YYYY

Examining Provider: _____   Date: _____
                          (signature)
Provider Name: _____   Provider's specialty:_____

Office Address: _____   Office Phone: _____

[ ] I attest that the results have been explained to the employee.

The following is required to be checked by the Physician or other Licensed Health Care Professional (PLHCP):
[ ] I attest that this medical examination has met the requirements of the medical surveillance section of the OSHA Respirable Crystalline Silica standard (§ 1910.1053(h) or 1926.1153(h)).

AUTHORIZATION FOR CRYSTALLINE SILICA OPINION TO EMPLOYER

This medical examination for exposure to crystalline silica could reveal a medical condition that results in recommendations for (1) limitations on respirator use, (2) limitations on exposure to crystalline silica, or (3) examination by a specialist in pulmonary disease or occupational medicine. Recommended limitations on respirator use will be included in the written opinion to the employer. If you want your employer to know about limitations on crystalline silica exposure or recommendations for a specialist examination, you will need to give authorization for the written opinion to the employer to include one or both of those recommendations.

I hereby authorize the opinion to the employer to contain the following information, if relevant (please check all that apply):

☐ Recommendations for limitations on crystalline silica exposure

☐ Recommendation for a specialist examination

OR

☐ I do not authorize the opinion to the employer to contain anything other than recommended limitations on respirator use.

Please read and initial:

____ I understand that if I do not authorize my employer to receive the recommendation for specialist examination, the employer will not be responsible for arranging and covering costs of a specialist examination.

_____
Name (printed)

_____   _____
Signature   Date

[81 FR 16862, Mar. 25, 2016]

§ 1910.1096 Ionizing radiation.

(a) *Definitions applicable to this section*—(1) *Radiation* includes alpha rays, beta rays, gamma rays, X-rays, neutrons, high-speed electrons, high-speed protons, and other atomic particles; but such term does not include sound or radio waves, or visible light, or infrared or ultraviolet light.

(2) *Radioactive material* means any material which emits, by spontaneous nuclear disintegration, corpuscular or electromagnetic emanations.

(3) *Restricted area* means any area access to which is controlled by the employer for purposes of protection of individuals from exposure to radiation or radioactive materials.

(4) *Unrestricted area* means any area access to which is not controlled by the employer for purposes of protection of individuals from exposure to radiation or radioactive materials.

(5) *Dose* means the quantity of ionizing radiation absorbed, per unit of mass, by the body or by any portion of the body. When the provisions in this section specify a dose during a period of time, the dose is the total quantity of radiation absorbed, per unit of mass, by the body or by any portion of the body during such period of time. Several different units of dose are in current use. Definitions of units used in this section are set forth in paragraphs (a) (6) and (7) of this section.

(6) *Rad* means a measure of the dose of any ionizing radiation to body tissues in terms of the energy absorbed per unit of mass of the tissue. One rad is the dose corresponding to the absorption of 100 ergs per gram of tissue (1 millirad (mrad) = 0.001 rad).

(7) *Rem* means a measure of the dose of any ionizing radiation to body tissue in terms of its estimated biological effect relative to a dose of 1 roentgen (r) of X-rays (1 millirem (mrem) = 0.001 rem). The relation of the rem to other dose units depends upon the biological effect under consideration and upon the conditions for irradiation. Each of the following is considered to be equivalent to a dose of 1 rem:

(i) A dose of 1 roentgen due to X- or gamma radiation;

(ii) A dose of 1 rad due to X-, gamma, or beta radiation;

(iii) A dose of 0.1 rad due to neutrons or high energy protons;

(iv) A dose of 0.05 rad due to particles heavier than protons and with sufficient energy to reach the lens of the eye;

(v) If it is more convenient to measure the neutron flux, or equivalent, than to determine the neutron dose in rads, as provided in paragraph (a)(7)(iii) of this section, 1 rem of neutron radiation may, for purposes of the provisions in this section be assumed to be equivalent to 14 million neutrons per

square centimeter incident upon the body; or, if there is sufficient information to estimate with reasonable accuracy the approximate distribution in energy of the neutrons, the incident number of neutrons per square centimeter equivalent to 1 rem may be estimated from Table G–17:

TABLE G–17—NEUTRON FLUX DOSE EQUIVALENTS

Neutron energy (million electron volts (Mev))	Number of neutrons per square centimeter equivalent to a dose of 1 rem (neutrons/cm²)	Average flux to deliver 100 millirem in 40 hours (neutrons/cm² per sec.)
Thermal	970 × 10⁶	670
0.0001	720 × 10⁶	500
0.005	820 × 10⁶	570
0.02	400 × 10⁶	280
0.1	120 × 10⁶	80
0.5	43 × 10⁶	30
1.0	26 × 10⁶	18
2.5	29 × 10⁶	20
5.0	26 × 10⁶	18
7.5	24 × 10⁶	17
10	24 × 10⁶	17
10 to 30	14 × 10⁶	10

(8) For determining exposures to X- or gamma rays up to 3 Mev., the dose limits specified in this section may be assumed to be equivalent to the "air dose". For the purpose of this section *air dose* means that the dose is measured by a properly calibrated appropriate instrument in air at or near the body surface in the region of the highest dosage rate.

(b) *Exposure of individuals to radiation in restricted areas.* (1) Except as provided in paragraph (b)(2) of this section, no employer shall possess, use, or transfer sources of ionizing radiation in such a manner as to cause any individual in a restricted area to receive in any period of one calendar quarter from sources in the employer's possession or control a dose in excess of the limits specified in Table G–18:

TABLE G–18

	Rems per calendar quarter
Whole body: Head and trunk; active blood-forming organs; lens of eyes; or gonads	1¼
Hands and forearms; feet and ankles	18¾
Skin of whole body	7½

(2) An employer may permit an individual in a restricted area to receive doses to the whole body greater than those permitted under subparagraph (1) of this paragraph, so long as:

(i) During any calendar quarter the dose to the whole body shall not exceed 3 rems; and

(ii) The dose to the whole body, when added to the accumulated occupational dose to the whole body, shall not exceed 5 (N–18) rems, where "N" equals the individual's age in years at his last birthday; and

(iii) The employer maintains adequate past and current exposure records which show that the addition of such a dose will not cause the individual to exceed the amount authorized in this subparagraph. As used in this subparagraph *Dose to the whole body* shall be deemed to include any dose to the whole body, gonad, active bloodforming organs, head and trunk, or lens of the eye.

(3) No employer shall permit any employee who is under 18 years of age to receive in any period of one calendar quarter a dose in excess of 10 percent of the limits specified in Table G–18.

(4) *Calendar quarter* means any 3-month period determined as follows:

(i) The first period of any year may begin on any date in January: *Provided,* That the second, third, and fourth periods accordingly begin on the same date in April, July, and October, respectively, and that the fourth period extends into January of the succeeding year, if necessary to complete a 3-month quarter. During the first year of use of this method of determination, the first period for that year shall also include any additional days in January preceding the starting date for the first period; or

(ii) The first period in a calendar year of 13 complete, consecutive calendar weeks; the second period in a calendar year of 13 complete, consecutive weeks; the third period in a calendar year of 13 complete, consecutive calendar weeks; the fourth period in a calendar year of 13 complete, consecutive calendar weeks. If at the end of a calendar year there are any days not falling within a complete calendar week of that year, such days shall be included within the last complete calendar week of that year. If at the beginning of any calendar year there are days not falling within a complete calendar week of that year, such days shall be included within the last complete calendar week of the previous year; or

(iii) The four periods in a calendar year may consist of the first 14 complete, consecutive calendar weeks; the next 12 complete, consecutive calendar weeks, the next 14 complete, consecutive calendar weeks, and the last 12 complete, consecutive calendar weeks. If at the end of a calendar year there are any days not falling within a complete calendar week of that year, such days shall be included (for purposes of this section) within the last complete calendar week of the year. If at the beginning of any calendar year there are days not falling within a complete calendar week of that year, such days shall be included (for purposes of this section) within the last complete week of the previous year.

(c) *Exposure to airborne radioactive material.* (1) No employer shall possess, use or transport radioactive material in such a manner as to cause any employee, within a restricted area, to be exposed to airborne radioactive material in an average concentration in excess of the limits specified in Table 1 of appendix B to 10 CFR part 20. The limits given in Table 1 are for exposure to the concentrations specified for 40 hours in any workweek of 7 consecutive days. In any such period where the number of hours of exposure is less than 40, the limits specified in the table may be increased proportionately. In any such period where the number of hours of exposure is greater than 40, the limits specified in the table shall be decreased proportionately.

(2) No employer shall possess, use, or transfer radioactive material in such a manner as to cause any individual within a restricted area, who is under 18 years of age, to be exposed to airborne radioactive material in an average concentration in excess of the limits specified in Table II of appendix B to 10 CFR part 20. For purposes of this paragraph, concentrations may be averaged over periods not greater than 1 week.

(3) *Exposed* as used in this paragraph means that the individual is present in an airborne concentration. No allowance shall be made for the use of protective clothing or equipment, or particle size.

(d) *Precautionary procedures and personal monitoring.* (1) Every employer shall make such surveys as may be necessary for him to comply with the provisions in this section. *Survey* means an evaluation of the radiation hazards incident to the production, use, release, disposal, or presence of radioactive materials or other sources of radiation under a specific set of conditions. When appropriate, such evaluation includes a physical survey of the location of materials and equipment, and measurements of levels of radiation or concentrations of radioactive material present.

(2) Every employer shall supply appropriate personnel monitoring equipment, such as film badges, pocket chambers, pocket dosimeters, or film rings, and shall require the use of such equipment by:

(i) Each employee who enters a restricted area under such circumstances that he receives, or is likely to receive, a dose in any calendar quarter in excess of 25 percent of the applicable value specified in paragraph (b)(1) of this section; and

(ii) Each employee under 18 years of age who enters a restricted area under such circumstances that he receives, or is likely to receive, a dose in any calendar quarter in excess of 5 percent of the applicable value specified in paragraph (b)(1) of this section; and

(iii) Each employee who enters a high radiation area.

(3) As used in this section:

(i) *Personnel monitoring equipment* means devices designed to be worn or carried by an individual for the purpose of measuring the dose received (e.g., film badges, pocket chambers, pocket dosimeters, film rings, etc.);

(ii) *Radiation area* means any area, accessible to personnel, in which there exists radiation at such levels that a major portion of the body could receive in any 1 hour a dose in excess of 5 millirem, or in any 5 consecutive days a dose in excess of 100 millirem; and

(iii) *High radiation area* means any area, accessible to personnel, in which there exists radiation at such levels that a major portion of the body could receive in any one hour a dose in excess of 100 millirem.

(e) *Caution signs, labels, and signals—* (1) *General.* (i) Symbols prescribed by this paragraph shall use the conventional radiation caution colors (magenta or purple on yellow background). The symbol prescribed by this paragraph is the conventional three-bladed design:

RADIATION SYMBOL

1. Cross-hatched area is to be magenta or purple.
2. Background is to be yellow.

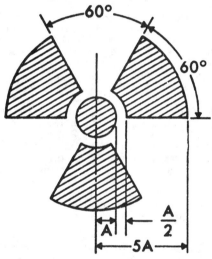

FIGURE G–10

(ii) [Reserved]

(2) *Radiation area.* Each radiation area shall be conspicuously posted with a sign or signs bearing the radiation caution symbol described in subparagraph (1) of this paragraph and the words:

CAUTION
RADIATION AREA

(3) *High radiation area.* (i) Each high radiation area shall be conspicuously posted with a sign or signs bearing the radiation caution symbol and the words:

589

CAUTION
HIGH RADIATION AREA

(ii) Each high radiation area shall be equipped with a control device which shall either cause the level of radiation to be reduced below that at which an individual might receive a dose of 100 millirems in 1 hour upon entry into the area or shall energize a conspicuous visible or audible alarm signal in such a manner that the individual entering and the employer or a supervisor of the activity are made aware of the entry. In the case of a high radiation area established for a period of 30 days or less, such control device is not required.

(4) *Airborne radioactivity area.* (i) As used in the provisions of this section, *airborne radioactivity area* means:

(*a*) Any room, enclosure, or operating area in which airborne radioactive materials, composed wholly or partly of radioactive material, exist in concentrations in excess of the amounts specified in column 1 of Table 1 of appendix B to 10 CFR part 20 or

(*b*) Any room, enclosure, or operating area in which airborne radioactive materials exist in concentrations which, averaged over the number of hours in any week during which individuals are in the area, exceed 25 percent of the amounts specified in column 1 of Table 1 of appendix B to 10 CFR part 20.

(ii) Each airborne radioactivity area shall be conspicuously posted with a sign or signs bearing the radiation caution symbol described in paragraph (e)(1) of this section and the words:

CAUTION
AIRBORNE RADIOACTIVITY AREA

(5) *Additional requirements.* (i) Each area or room in which radioactive material is used or stored and which contains any radioactive material (other than natural uranium or thorium) in any amount exceeding 10 times the quantity of such material specified in appendix C to 10 CFR part 20 shall be conspicuously posted with a sign or signs bearing the radiation caution symbol described in paragraph (e)(1) of this section and the words:

CAUTION
RADIOACTIVE MATERIALS

(ii) Each area or room in which natural uranium or thorium is used or stored in an amount exceeding 100 times the quantity of such material specified in 10 CFR part 20 shall be conspicuously posted with a sign or signs bearing the radiation caution symbol described in paragraph (e)(1) of this section and the words:

CAUTION
RADIOACTIVE MATERIALS

(6) *Containers.* (i) Each container in which is transported, stored, or used a quantity of any radioactive material (other than natural uranium or thorium) greater than the quantity of such material specified in appendix C to 10 CFR part 20 shall bear a durable, clearly visible label bearing the radiation caution symbol described in paragraph (e)(1) of this section and the words:

CAUTION
RADIOACTIVE MATERIALS

(ii) Each container in which natural uranium or thorium is transported, stored, or used in a quantity greater than 10 times the quantity specified in appendix C to 10 CFR part 20 shall bear a durable, clearly visible label bearing the radiation caution symbol described in paragraph (e)(1) of this section and the words:

CAUTION
RADIOACTIVE MATERIALS

(iii) Notwithstanding the provisions of paragraphs (e)(6) (i) and (ii) of this section a label shall not be required:

(*a*) If the concentration of the material in the container does not exceed that specified in column 2 of Table 1 of appendix B to 10 CFR part 20, or

(*b*) For laboratory containers, such as beakers, flasks, and test tubes, used transiently in laboratory procedures, when the user is present.

(iv) Where containers are used for storage, the labels required in this subparagraph shall state also the quantities and kinds of radioactive materials in the containers and the date of measurement of the quantities.

(f) *Immediate evacuation warning signal*—(1) *Signal characteristics.* (i) The signal shall be a midfrequency complex sound wave amplitude modulated at a subsonic frequency. The complex sound wave in free space shall have a fundamental frequency (f_1) between 450 and

500 hertz (Hz) modulated at a subsonic rate between 4 and 5 hertz.

(ii) The signal generator shall not be less than 75 decibels at every location where an individual may be present whose immediate, rapid, and complete evacuation is essential.

(iii) A sufficient number of signal units shall be installed such that the requirements of paragraph (f)(1)(ii) of this section are met at every location where an individual may be present whose immediate, rapid, and complete evacuation is essential.

(iv) The signal shall be unique in the plant or facility in which it is installed.

(v) The minimum duration of the signal shall be sufficient to insure that all affected persons hear the signal.

(vi) The signal-generating system shall respond automatically to an initiating event without requiring any human action to sound the signal.

(2) *Design objectives.* (i) The signal-generating system shall be designed to incorporate components which enable the system to produce the desired signal each time it is activated within one-half second of activation.

(ii) The signal-generating system shall be provided with an automatically activated secondary power supply which is adequate to simultaneously power all emergency equipment to which it is connected, if operation during power failure is necessary, except in those systems using batteries as the primary source of power.

(iii) All components of the signal-generating system shall be located to provide maximum practicable protection against damage in case of fire, explosion, corrosive atmosphere, or other environmental extremes consistent with adequate system performance.

(iv) The signal-generating system shall be designed with the minimum number of components necessary to make it function as intended, and should utilize components which do not require frequent servicing such as lubrication or cleaning.

(v) Where several activating devices feed activating information to a central signal generator, failure of any activating device shall not render the signal-generator system inoperable to ac-

tivating information from the remaining devices.

(vi) The signal-generating system shall be designed to enhance the probability that alarm occurs only when immediate evacuation is warranted. The number of false alarms shall not be so great that the signal will come to be disregarded and shall be low enough to minimize personal injuries or excessive property damage that might result from such evacuation.

(3) *Testing.* (i) Initial tests, inspections, and checks of the signal-generating system shall be made to verify that the fabrication and installation were made in accordance with design plans and specifications and to develop a thorough knowledge of the performance of the system and all components under normal and hostile conditions.

(ii) Once the system has been placed in service, periodic tests, inspections, and checks shall be made to minimize the possibility of malfunction.

(iii) Following significant alterations or revisions to the system, tests and checks similar to the initial installation tests shall be made.

(iv) Tests shall be designed to minimize hazards while conducting the tests.

(v) Prior to normal operation the signal-generating system shall be checked physically and functionally to assure reliability and to demonstrate accuracy and performance. Specific tests shall include:

(*a*) All power sources.

(*b*) Calibration and calibration stability.

(*c*) Trip levels and stability.

(*d*) Continuity of function with loss and return of required services such as AC or DC power, air pressure, etc.

(*e*) All indicators.

(*f*) Trouble indicator circuits and signals, where used.

(*g*) Air pressure (if used)

(*h*) Determine that sound level of the signal is within the limit of paragraph (f)(1)(ii) of this section at all points that require immediate evacuation.

(vi) In addition to the initial startup and operating tests, periodic scheduled performance tests and status checks must be made to insure that the system is at all times operating within design limits and capable of the required

591

response. Specific periodic tests or checks or both shall include:

(a) Adequacy of signal activation device.

(b) All power sources.

(c) Function of all alarm circuits and trouble indicator circuits including trip levels.

(d) Air pressure (if used).

(e) Function of entire system including operation without power where required.

(f) Complete operational tests including sounding of the signal and determination that sound levels are adequate.

(vii) Periodic tests shall be scheduled on the basis of need, experience, difficulty, and disruption of operations. The entire system should be operationally tested at least quarterly.

(viii) All employees whose work may necessitate their presence in an area covered by the signal shall be made familiar with the actual sound of the signal—preferably as it sounds at their work location. Before placing the system into operation, all employees normally working in the area shall be made acquainted with the signal by actual demonstration at their work locations.

(g) *Exceptions from posting requirements.* Notwithstanding the provisions of paragraph (e) of this section:

(1) A room or area is not required to be posted with a caution sign because of the presence of a sealed source, provided the radiation level 12 inches from the surface of the source container or housing does not exceed 5 millirem per hour.

(2) Rooms or other areas in onsite medical facilities are not required to be posted with caution signs because of the presence of patients containing radioactive material, provided that there are personnel in attendance who shall take the precautions necessary to prevent the exposure of any individual to radiation or radioactive material in excess of the limits established in the provisions of this section.

(3) Caution signs are not required to be posted at areas or rooms containing radioactive materials for periods of less than 8 hours: *Provided,* That

(i) The materials are constantly attended during such periods by an individual who shall take the precautions necessary to prevent the exposure of any individual to radiation or radioactive materials in excess of the limits established in the provisions of this section; and

(ii) Such area or room is subject to the employer's control.

(h) *Exemptions for radioactive materials packaged for shipment.* Radioactive materials packaged and labeled in accordance with regulations of the Department of Transportation published in 49 CFR Chapter I, are exempt from the labeling and posting requirements of this subpart during shipment, provided that the inside containers are labeled in accordance with the provisions of paragraph (e) of this section.

(i) *Instruction of personnel, posting.* (1) Employers regulated by the Nuclear Regulatory Commission shall be governed by 10 CFR part 20 standards. Employers in a State named in paragraph (p)(3) of this section shall be governed by the requirements of the laws and regulations of that State. All other employers shall be regulated by the following:

(2) All individuals working in or frequenting any portion of a radiation area shall be informed of the occurrence of radioactive materials or of radiation in such portions of the radiation area; shall be instructed in the safety problems associated with exposure to such materials or radiation and in precautions or devices to minimize exposure; shall be instructed in the applicable provisions of this section for the protection of employees from exposure to radiation or radioactive materials; and shall be advised of reports of radiation exposure which employees may request pursuant to the regulations in this section.

(3) Each employer to whom this section applies shall post a current copy of its provisions and a copy of the operating procedures applicable to the work conspicuously in such locations as to insure that employees working in or frequenting radiation areas will observe these documents on the way to and from their place of employment, or shall keep such documents available for examination of employees upon request.

(j) *Storage of radioactive materials.* Radioactive materials stored in a non-radiation area shall be secured against unauthorized removal from the place of storage.

(k) *Waste disposal.* No employer shall dispose of radioactive material except by transfer to an authorized recipient, or in a manner approved by the Nuclear Regulatory Commission or a State named in paragraph (p)(3) of this section.

(l) *Notification of incidents*—(1) *Immediate notification.* Each employer shall immediately notify the Assistant Secretary of Labor or his duly authorized representative, for employees not protected by the Nuclear Regulatory Commission by means of 10 CFR part 20; paragraph (p)(2) of this section, or the requirements of the laws and regulations of States named in paragraph (p)(3) of this section, by telephone or telegraph of any incident involving radiation which may have caused or threatens to cause:

(i) Exposure of the whole body of any individual to 25 rems or more of radiation; exposure of the skin of the whole body of any individual to 150 rems or more of radiation; or exposure of the feet, ankles, hands, or forearms of any individual to 375 rems or more of radiation; or

(ii) The release of radioactive material in concentrations which, if averaged over a period of 24 hours, would exceed 5,000 times the limit specified for such materials in Table II of appendix B to 10 CFR part 20.

(2) *Twenty-four hour notification.* Each employer shall within 24 hours following its occurrence notify the Assistant Secretary of Labor or his duly authorized representative for employees not protected by the Nuclear Regulatory Commission by means of 10 CFR part 20; paragraph (p)(2) of this section, or the requirements of the laws and applicable regulations of States named in paragraph (p)(3) of this section, by telephone or telegraph of any incident involving radiation which may have caused or threatens to cause:

(i) Exposure of the whole body of any individual to 5 rems or more of radiation; exposure of the skin of the whole body of any individual to 30 rems or more of radiation; or exposure of the feet, ankles, hands, or forearms to 75 rems or more of radiation; or

(ii) [Reserved]

(m) *Reports of overexposure and excessive levels and concentrations.* (1) In addition to any notification required by paragraph (1) of this section each employer shall make a report in writing within 30 days to the Assistant Secretary of Labor or his duly authorized representative, for employees not protected by the Nuclear Regulatory Commission by means of 10 CFR part 20; or under paragraph (p)(2) of this section, or the requirements of the laws and regulations of States named in paragraph (p)(3) of this section, of each exposure of an individual to radiation or concentrations of radioactive material in excess of any applicable limit in this section. Each report required under this paragraph shall describe the extent of exposure of persons to radiation or to radioactive material; levels of radiation and concentration of radioactive material involved, the cause of the exposure, levels of concentrations; and corrective steps taken or planned to assure against a recurrence.

(2) In any case where an employer is required pursuant to the provisions of this paragraph to report to the U.S. Department of Labor any exposure of an individual to radiation or to concentrations of radioactive material, the employer shall also notify such individual of the nature and extent of exposure. Such notice shall be in writing and shall contain the following statement: "You should preserve this report for future reference."

(n) *Records.* (1) Every employer shall maintain records of the radiation exposure of all employees for whom personnel monitoring is required under paragraph (d) of this section and advise each of his employees of his individual exposure on at least an annual basis.

(2) Every employer shall maintain records in the same units used in tables in paragraph (b) of this section and appendix B to 10 CFR part 20.

(o) *Disclosure to former employee of individual employee's record.* (1) At the request of a former employee an employer shall furnish to the employee a report of the employee's exposure to radiation as shown in records maintained by the employer pursuant to paragraph (n)(1) of this section. Such report shall be furnished within 30 days from the time the request is made, and shall cover each calendar quarter of the individual's employment involving exposure to radiation or such lesser period as may be requested by the employee. The report shall also include the results of any calculations and analysis of radioactive material deposited in the body of the employee. The report shall be in writing and contain the following statement: "You should preserve this report for future reference."

(2) [Reserved]

(p) *Nuclear Regulatory Commission licensees—NRC contractors operating NRC plants and facilities—NRC Agreement State licensees or registrants.* (1) Any employer who possesses or uses source material, byproduct material, or special nuclear material, as defined in the Atomic Energy Act of 1954, as amended, under a license issued by the Nuclear Regulatory Commission and in accordance with the requirements of 10 CFR part 20 shall be deemed to be in compliance with the requirements of this section with respect to such possession and use.

(2) NRC contractors operating NRC plants and facilities: Any employer who possesses or uses source material, byproduct material, special nuclear material, or other radiation sources under a contract with the Nuclear Regulatory Commission for the operation of NRC plants and facilities and in accordance with the standards, procedures, and other requirements for radiation protection established by the Commission for such contract pursuant to the Atomic Energy Act of 1954 as amended (42 U.S.C. 2011 *et seq.*), shall be deemed to be in compliance with the requirements of this section with respect to such possession and use.

(3) NRC-agreement State licensees or registrants:

(i) *Atomic Energy Act sources.* Any employer who possesses or uses source material, byproduct material, or special nuclear material, as defined in the Atomic Energy Act of 1954, as amended (42 U.S.C. 2011 *et seq.*), and has either registered such sources with, or is operating under a license issued by, a State which has an agreement in effect with the Nuclear Regulatory Commission pursuant to section 274(b) (42 U.S.C. 2021(b)) of the Atomic Energy Act of 1954, as amended, and in accordance with the requirements of that State's laws and regulations shall be deemed to be in compliance with the radiation requirements of this section, insofar as his possession and use of such material is concerned, unless the Secretary of Labor, after conference with the Nuclear Regulatory Commission, shall determine that the State's program for control of these radiation sources is incompatible with the requirements of this section. Such agreements currently are in effect only in the States of Alabama, Arkansas, California, Kansas, Kentucky, Florida, Mississippi, New Hampshire, New York, North Carolina, Texas, Tennessee, Oregon, Idaho, Arizona, Colorado, Louisiana, Nebraska, Washington, Maryland, North Dakota, South Carolina, and Georgia.

(ii) *Other sources.* Any employer who possesses or uses radiation sources other than source material, byproduct material, or special nuclear material, as defined in the Atomic Energy Act of 1954, as amended (42 U.S.C. 2011 *et seq.*), and has either registered such sources with, or is operating under a license issued by a State which has an agreement in effect with the Nuclear Regulatory Commission pursuant to section 274(b) (42 U.S.C. 2021(b)) of the Atomic Energy Act of 1954, as amended, and in accordance with the requirements of that State's laws and regulations shall be deemed to be in compliance with the radiation requirements of this section, insofar as his possession and use of such material is concerned, provided the State's program for control of these radiation sources is the subject of a currently effective determination by the Assistant Secretary of Labor that such program is compatible with the requirements of this section. Such determinations currently are in effect only in the States of Alabama, Arkansas, California, Kansas, Kentucky, Florida, Mississippi, New Hampshire,

New York, North Carolina, Texas, Tennessee, Oregon, Idaho, Arizona, Colorado, Louisiana, Nebraska, Washington, Maryland, North Dakota, South Carolina, and Georgia.

[39 FR 23502, June 27, 1974, as amended at 43 FR 49746, Oct. 24, 1978; 43 FR 51759, Nov. 7, 1978; 49 FR 18295, Apr. 30, 1984; 58 FR 35309, June 30, 1993. Redesignated at 61 FR 31430, June 20, 1996]

§ 1910.1200 Hazard communication.

(a) *Purpose.* (1) The purpose of this section is to ensure that the hazards of all chemicals produced or imported are classified, and that information concerning the classified hazards is transmitted to employers and employees. The requirements of this section are intended to be consistent with the provisions of the United Nations Globally Harmonized System of Classification and Labelling of Chemicals (GHS), Revision 3. The transmittal of information is to be accomplished by means of comprehensive hazard communication programs, which are to include container labeling and other forms of warning, safety data sheets and employee training.

(2) This occupational safety and health standard is intended to address comprehensively the issue of classifying the potential hazards of chemicals, and communicating information concerning hazards and appropriate protective measures to employees, and to preempt any legislative or regulatory enactments of a state, or political subdivision of a state, pertaining to this subject. Classifying the potential hazards of chemicals and communicating information concerning hazards and appropriate protective measures to employees, may include, for example, but is not limited to, provisions for: developing and maintaining a written hazard communication program for the workplace, including lists of hazardous chemicals present; labeling of containers of chemicals in the workplace, as well as of containers of chemicals being shipped to other workplaces; preparation and distribution of safety data sheets to employees and downstream employers; and development and implementation of employee training programs regarding hazards of chemicals

and protective measures. Under section 18 of the Act, no state or political subdivision of a state may adopt or enforce any requirement relating to the issue addressed by this Federal standard, except pursuant to a Federally-approved state plan.

(b) *Scope and application.* (1) This section requires chemical manufacturers or importers to classify the hazards of chemicals which they produce or import, and all employers to provide information to their employees about hazardous chemicals to which they are exposed, by means of a hazard communication program, labels and other forms of warning, safety data sheets, and information and training. In addition, this section requires distributors to transmit the required information to employers. (Employers who do not produce or import chemicals need only focus on those parts of this rule that deal with establishing a workplace program and communicating information to their workers.)

(2) This section applies to any chemical which is known to be present in the workplace in such a manner that employees may be exposed under normal conditions of use or in a foreseeable emergency.

(3) This section applies to laboratories only as follows:

(i) Employers shall ensure that labels on incoming containers of hazardous chemicals are not removed or defaced;

(ii) Employers shall maintain any safety data sheets that are received with incoming shipments of hazardous chemicals, and ensure that they are readily accessible during each workshift to laboratory employees when they are in their work areas;

(iii) Employers shall ensure that laboratory employees are provided information and training in accordance with paragraph (h) of this section, except for the location and availability of the written hazard communication program under paragraph (h)(2)(iii) of this section; and,

(iv) Laboratory employers that ship hazardous chemicals are considered to be either a chemical manufacturer or a distributor under this rule, and thus must ensure that any containers of hazardous chemicals leaving the laboratory are labeled in accordance with paragraph (f) of this section, and that a safety data sheet is provided to distributors and other employers in accordance with paragraphs (g)(6) and (g)(7) of this section.

(4) In work operations where employees only handle chemicals in sealed containers which are not opened under normal conditions of use (such as are found in marine cargo handling, warehousing, or retail sales), this section applies to these operations only as follows:

(i) Employers shall ensure that labels on incoming containers of hazardous chemicals are not removed or defaced;

(ii) Employers shall maintain copies of any safety data sheets that are received with incoming shipments of the sealed containers of hazardous chemicals, shall obtain a safety data sheet as soon as possible for sealed containers of hazardous chemicals received without a safety data sheet if an employee requests the safety data sheet, and shall ensure that the safety data sheets are readily accessible during each work shift to employees when they are in their work area(s); and,

(iii) Employers shall ensure that employees are provided with information and training in accordance with paragraph (h) of this section (except for the location and availability of the written hazard communication program under paragraph (h)(2)(iii) of this section), to the extent necessary to protect them in the event of a spill or leak of a hazardous chemical from a sealed container.

(5) This section does not require labeling of the following chemicals:

(i) Any pesticide as such term is defined in the Federal Insecticide, Fungicide, and Rodenticide Act (7 U.S.C. 136 et seq.), when subject to the labeling requirements of that Act and labeling regulations issued under that Act by the Environmental Protection Agency;

(ii) Any chemical substance or mixture as such terms are defined in the Toxic Substances Control Act (15 U.S.C. 2601 et seq.), when subject to the labeling requirements of that Act and labeling regulations issued under that Act by the Environmental Protection Agency.

(iii) Any food, food additive, color additive, drug, cosmetic, or medical or veterinary device or product, including materials intended for use as ingredients in such products (e.g., flavors and fragrances), as such terms are defined in the Federal Food, Drug, and Cosmetic Act (21 U.S.C. 301 et seq.) or the Virus-Serum-Toxin Act of 1913 (21 U.S.C. 151 et seq.), and regulations issued under those Acts, when they are subject to the labeling requirements under those Acts by either the Food and Drug Administration or the Department of Agriculture;

(iv) Any distilled spirits (beverage alcohols), wine, or malt beverage intended for nonindustrial use, as such terms are defined in the Federal Alcohol Administration Act (27 U.S.C. 201 et seq.) and regulations issued under that Act, when subject to the labeling requirements of that Act and labeling regulations issued under that Act by the Bureau of Alcohol, Tobacco, Firearms and Explosives;

(v) Any consumer product or hazardous substance as those terms are defined in the Consumer Product Safety Act (15 U.S.C. 2051 et seq.) and Federal Hazardous Substances Act (15 U.S.C. 1261 et seq.) respectively, when subject to a consumer product safety standard or labeling requirement of those Acts, or regulations issued under those Acts by the Consumer Product Safety Commission; and,

(vi) Agricultural or vegetable seed treated with pesticides and labeled in accordance with the Federal Seed Act (7 U.S.C. 1551 et seq.) and the labeling regulations issued under that Act by the Department of Agriculture.

(6) This section does not apply to: (i) Any hazardous waste as such term is defined by the Solid Waste Disposal Act, as amended by the Resource Conservation and Recovery Act of 1976, as amended (42 U.S.C. 6901 et seq.), when subject to regulations issued under that Act by the Environmental Protection Agency;

(ii) Any hazardous substance as such term is defined by the Comprehensive Environmental Response, Compensation and Liability Act (CERCLA) (42 U.S.C. 9601 et seq.) when the hazardous substance is the focus of remedial or removal action being conducted under CERCLA in accordance with Environmental Protection Agency regulations.

(iii) Tobacco or tobacco products;

(iv) Wood or wood products, including lumber which will not be processed, where the chemical manufacturer or importer can establish that the only hazard they pose to employees is the potential for flammability or combustibility (wood or wood products which have been treated with a hazardous chemical covered by this standard, and wood which may be subsequently sawed or cut, generating dust, are not exempted);

(v) Articles (as that term is defined in paragraph (c) of this section);

(vi) Food or alcoholic beverages which are sold, used, or prepared in a retail establishment (such as a grocery store, restaurant, or drinking place), and foods intended for personal consumption by employees while in the workplace;

(vii) Any drug, as that term is defined in the Federal Food, Drug, and Cosmetic Act (21 U.S.C. 301 *et seq.*), when it is in solid, final form for direct administration to the patient (e.g., tablets or pills); drugs which are packaged by the chemical manufacturer for sale to consumers in a retail establishment (e.g., over-the-counter drugs); and drugs intended for personal consumption by employees while in the workplace (e.g., first aid supplies);

(viii) Cosmetics which are packaged for sale to consumers in a retail establishment, and cosmetics intended for personal consumption by employees while in the workplace;

(ix) Any consumer product or hazardous substance, as those terms are defined in the Consumer Product Safety Act (15 U.S.C. 2051 *et seq.*) and Federal Hazardous Substances Act (15 U.S.C. 1261 *et seq.*) respectively, where the employer can show that it is used in the workplace for the purpose intended by the chemical manufacturer or importer of the product, and the use results in a duration and frequency of exposure which is not greater than the range of exposures that could reasonably be experienced by consumers when used for the purpose intended;

(x) Nuisance particulates where the chemical manufacturer or importer can establish that they do not pose any physical or health hazard covered under this section;

(xi) Ionizing and nonionizing radiation; and,

(xii) Biological hazards.

(c) *Definitions. Article* means a manufactured item other than a fluid or particle: (i) which is formed to a specific shape or design during manufacture; (ii) which has end use function(s) dependent in whole or in part upon its shape or design during end use; and (iii) which under normal conditions of use does not release more than very small quantities, e.g., minute or trace amounts of a hazardous chemical (as determined under paragraph (d) of this section), and does not pose a physical hazard or health risk to employees.

Assistant Secretary means the Assistant Secretary of Labor for Occupational Safety and Health, U.S. Department of Labor, or designee.

Chemical means any substance, or mixture of substances.

Chemical manufacturer means an employer with a workplace where chemical(s) are produced for use or distribution.

Chemical name means the scientific designation of a chemical in accordance with the nomenclature system developed by the International Union of Pure and Applied Chemistry (IUPAC) or the Chemical Abstracts Service (CAS) rules of nomenclature, or a name that will clearly identify the chemical for the purpose of conducting a hazard classification.

Classification means to identify the relevant data regarding the hazards of a chemical; review those data to ascertain the hazards associated with the chemical; and decide whether the chemical will be classified as hazardous according to the definition of hazardous chemical in this section. In addition, classification for health and physical hazards includes the determination of the degree of hazard, where appropriate, by comparing the data with the criteria for health and physical hazards.

Commercial account means an arrangement whereby a retail distributor sells hazardous chemicals to an employer, generally in large quantities over time and/or at costs that are below the regular retail price.

Common name means any designation or identification such as code name, code number, trade name, brand name or generic name used to identify a chemical other than by its chemical name.

Container means any bag, barrel, bottle, box, can, cylinder, drum, reaction vessel, storage tank, or the like that contains a hazardous chemical. For purposes of this section, pipes or piping systems, and engines, fuel tanks, or other operating systems in a vehicle, are not considered to be containers.

Designated representative means any individual or organization to whom an employee gives written authorization to exercise such employee's rights under this section. A recognized or certified collective bargaining agent shall be treated automatically as a designated representative without regard to written employee authorization.

Director means the Director, National Institute for Occupational Safety and Health, U.S. Department of Health and Human Services, or designee.

Distributor means a business, other than a chemical manufacturer or importer, which supplies hazardous chemicals to other distributors or to employers.

Employee means a worker who may be exposed to hazardous chemicals under normal operating conditions or in foreseeable emergencies. Workers such as office workers or bank tellers who encounter hazardous chemicals only in non-routine, isolated instances are not covered.

Employer means a person engaged in a business where chemicals are either used, distributed, or are produced for use or distribution, including a contractor or subcontractor.

Exposure or *exposed* means that an employee is subjected in the course of employment to a chemical that is a physical or health hazard, and includes potential (e.g., accidental or possible) exposure. "Subjected" in terms of health hazards includes any route of entry (e.g., inhalation, ingestion, skin contact or absorption.)

Foreseeable emergency means any potential occurrence such as, but not limited to, equipment failure, rupture of containers, or failure of control equipment which could result in an uncontrolled release of a hazardous chemical into the workplace.

Hazard category means the division of criteria within each hazard class, e.g., oral acute toxicity and flammable liquids include four hazard categories. These categories compare hazard severity within a hazard class and should not be taken as a comparison of hazard categories more generally.

Hazard class means the nature of the physical or health hazards, e.g., flammable solid, carcinogen, oral acute toxicity.

Hazard not otherwise classified (HNOC) means an adverse physical or health effect identified through evaluation of scientific evidence during the classification process that does not meet the specified criteria for the physical and health hazard classes addressed in this section. This does not extend coverage to adverse physical and health effects for which there is a hazard class addressed in this section, but the effect either falls below the cut-off value/concentration limit of the hazard class or is under a GHS hazard category that has not been adopted by OSHA (e.g., acute toxicity Category 5).

Hazard statement means a statement assigned to a hazard class and category that describes the nature of the hazard(s) of a chemical, including, where appropriate, the degree of hazard.

Hazardous chemical means any chemical which is classified as a physical hazard or a health hazard, a simple asphyxiant, combustible dust, pyrophoric gas, or hazard not otherwise classified.

Health hazard means a chemical which is classified as posing one of the following hazardous effects: acute toxicity (any route of exposure); skin corrosion or irritation; serious eye damage or eye irritation; respiratory or skin sensitization; germ cell mutagenicity; carcinogenicity; reproductive toxicity; specific target organ toxicity (single or repeated exposure); or aspiration hazard. The criteria for determining whether a chemical is classified as a health hazard are detailed in Appendix A to § 1910.1200—Health Hazard Criteria.

Immediate use means that the hazardous chemical will be under the control of and used only by the person who transfers it from a labeled container and only within the work shift in which it is transferred.

Importer means the first business with employees within the Customs Territory of the United States which receives hazardous chemicals produced in other countries for the purpose of supplying them to distributors or employers within the United States.

Label means an appropriate group of written, printed or graphic information elements concerning a hazardous chemical that is affixed to, printed on, or attached to the immediate container of a hazardous chemical, or to the outside packaging.

Label elements means the specified pictogram, hazard statement, signal word and precautionary statement for each hazard class and category.

Mixture means a combination or a solution composed of two or more substances in which they do not react.

Physical hazard means a chemical that is classified as posing one of the following hazardous effects: explosive; flammable (gases, aerosols, liquids, or solids); oxidizer (liquid, solid or gas); self-reactive; pyrophoric (liquid or solid); self-heating; organic peroxide; corrosive to metal; gas under pressure; or in contact with water emits flammable gas. *See* Appendix B to §1910.1200—Physical Hazard Criteria.

Pictogram means a composition that may include a symbol plus other graphic elements, such as a border, background pattern, or color, that is intended to convey specific information about the hazards of a chemical. Eight pictograms are designated under this standard for application to a hazard category.

Precautionary statement means a phrase that describes recommended measures that should be taken to minimize or prevent adverse effects resulting from exposure to a hazardous chemical, or improper storage or handling.

Produce means to manufacture, process, formulate, blend, extract, generate, emit, or repackage.

Product identifier means the name or number used for a hazardous chemical on a label or in the SDS. It provides a unique means by which the user can identify the chemical. The product identifier used shall permit cross-references to be made among the list of hazardous chemicals required in the written hazard communication program, the label and the SDS.

Pyrophoric gas means a chemical in a gaseous state that will ignite spontaneously in air at a temperature of 130 degrees F (54.4 degrees C) or below.

Responsible party means someone who can provide additional information on the hazardous chemical and appropriate emergency procedures, if necessary.

Safety data sheet (SDS) means written or printed material concerning a hazardous chemical that is prepared in accordance with paragraph (g) of this section.

Signal word means a word used to indicate the relative level of severity of hazard and alert the reader to a potential hazard on the label. The signal words used in this section are "danger" and "warning." "Danger" is used for the more severe hazards, while "warning" is used for the less severe.

Simple asphyxiant means a substance or mixture that displaces oxygen in the ambient atmosphere, and can thus cause oxygen deprivation in those who are exposed, leading to unconsciousness and death.

Specific chemical identity means the chemical name, Chemical Abstracts Service (CAS) Registry Number, or any other information that reveals the precise chemical designation of the substance.

Substance means chemical elements and their compounds in the natural state or obtained by any production process, including any additive necessary to preserve the stability of the product and any impurities deriving from the process used, but excluding any solvent which may be separated without affecting the stability of the substance or changing its composition.

Trade secret means any confidential formula, pattern, process, device, information or compilation of information that is used in an employer's business, and that gives the employer an opportunity to obtain an advantage over competitors who do not know or use it. Appendix E to §1910.1200—Definition of Trade Secret, sets out the criteria to be used in evaluating trade secrets.

Use means to package, handle, react, emit, extract, generate as a byproduct, or transfer.

Work area means a room or defined space in a workplace where hazardous chemicals are produced or used, and where employees are present.

Workplace means an establishment, job site, or project, at one geographical location containing one or more work areas.

(d) *Hazard classification.* (1) Chemical manufacturers and importers shall evaluate chemicals produced in their workplaces or imported by them to classify the chemicals in accordance with this section. For each chemical, the chemical manufacturer or importer shall determine the hazard classes, and, where appropriate, the category of each class that apply to the chemical being classified. Employers are not required to classify chemicals unless they choose not to rely on the classification performed by the chemical manufacturer or importer for the chemical to satisfy this requirement.

(2) Chemical manufacturers, importers or employers classifying chemicals shall identify and consider the full range of available scientific literature and other evidence concerning the potential hazards. There is no requirement to test the chemical to determine how to classify its hazards. Appendix A to § 1910.1200 shall be consulted for classification of health hazards, and Appendix B to § 1910.1200 shall be consulted for the classification of physical hazards.

(3) *Mixtures.* (i) Chemical manufacturers, importers, or employers evaluating chemicals shall follow the procedures described in Appendices A and B to § 1910.1200 to classify the hazards of the chemicals, including determinations regarding when mixtures of the classified chemicals are covered by this section.

(ii) When classifying mixtures they produce or import, chemical manufacturers and importers of mixtures may rely on the information provided on the current safety data sheets of the individual ingredients, except where the chemical manufacturer or importer knows, or in the exercise of reasonable diligence should know, that the safety data sheet misstates or omits information required by this section.

(e) *Written hazard communication program.* (1) Employers shall develop, im-

plement, and maintain at each workplace, a written hazard communication program which at least describes how the criteria specified in paragraphs (f), (g), and (h) of this section for labels and other forms of warning, safety data sheets, and employee information and training will be met, and which also includes the following:

(i) A list of the hazardous chemicals known to be present using a product identifier that is referenced on the appropriate safety data sheet (the list may be compiled for the workplace as a whole or for individual work areas); and,

(ii) The methods the employer will use to inform employees of the hazards of non-routine tasks (for example, the cleaning of reactor vessels), and the hazards associated with chemicals contained in unlabeled pipes in their work areas.

(2) *Multi-employer workplaces.* Employers who produce, use, or store hazardous chemicals at a workplace in such a way that the employees of other employer(s) may be exposed (for example, employees of a construction contractor working on-site) shall additionally ensure that the hazard communication programs developed and implemented under this paragraph (e) include the following:

(i) The methods the employer will use to provide the other employer(s) on-site access to safety data sheets for each hazardous chemical the other employer(s)' employees may be exposed to while working;

(ii) The methods the employer will use to inform the other employer(s) of any precautionary measures that need to be taken to protect employees during the workplace's normal operating conditions and in foreseeable emergencies; and,

(iii) The methods the employer will use to inform the other employer(s) of the labeling system used in the workplace.

(3) The employer may rely on an existing hazard communication program to comply with these requirements, provided that it meets the criteria established in this paragraph (e).

(4) The employer shall make the written hazard communication program available, upon request, to employees, their designated representatives, the Assistant Secretary and the Director, in accordance with the requirements of 29 CFR 1910.20 (e).

(5) Where employees must travel between workplaces during a workshift, *i.e.*, their work is carried out at more than one geographical location, the written hazard communication program may be kept at the primary workplace facility.

(f) *Labels and other forms of warning*— (1) *Labels on shipped containers.* The chemical manufacturer, importer, or distributor shall ensure that each container of hazardous chemicals leaving the workplace is labeled, tagged, or marked. Hazards not otherwise classified do not have to be addressed on the container. Where the chemical manufacturer or importer is required to label, tag or mark the following information shall be provided:

(i) Product identifier;

(ii) Signal word;

(iii) Hazard statement(s);

(iv) Pictogram(s);

(v) Precautionary statement(s); and,

(vi) Name, address, and telephone number of the chemical manufacturer, importer, or other responsible party.

(2) The chemical manufacturer, importer, or distributor shall ensure that the information provided under paragraphs (f)(1)(i) through (v) of this section is in accordance with Appendix C to §1910.1200, for each hazard class and associated hazard category for the hazardous chemical, prominently displayed, and in English (other languages may also be included if appropriate).

(3) The chemical manufacturer, importer, or distributor shall ensure that the information provided under paragraphs (f)(1)(ii) through (iv) of this section is located together on the label, tag, or mark.

(4) *Solid materials.* (i) For solid metal (such as a steel beam or a metal casting), solid wood, or plastic items that are not exempted as articles due to their downstream use, or shipments of whole grain, the required label may be transmitted to the customer at the time of the initial shipment, and need not be included with subsequent ship-

ments to the same employer unless the information on the label changes;

(ii) The label may be transmitted with the initial shipment itself, or with the safety data sheet that is to be provided prior to or at the time of the first shipment; and,

(iii) This exception to requiring labels on every container of hazardous chemicals is only for the solid material itself, and does not apply to hazardous chemicals used in conjunction with, or known to be present with, the material and to which employees handling the items in transit may be exposed (for example, cutting fluids or pesticides in grains).

(5) Chemical manufacturers, importers, or distributors shall ensure that each container of hazardous chemicals leaving the workplace is labeled, tagged, or marked in accordance with this section in a manner which does not conflict with the requirements of the Hazardous Materials Transportation Act (49 U.S.C. 1801 *et seq.*) and regulations issued under that Act by the Department of Transportation.

(6) *Workplace labeling.* Except as provided in paragraphs (f)(7) and (f)(8) of this section, the employer shall ensure that each container of hazardous chemicals in the workplace is labeled, tagged or marked with either:

(i) The information specified under paragraphs (f)(1)(i) through (v) of this section for labels on shipped containers; or,

(ii) Product identifier and words, pictures, symbols, or combination thereof, which provide at least general information regarding the hazards of the chemicals, and which, in conjunction with the other information immediately available to employees under the hazard communication program, will provide employees with the specific information regarding the physical and health hazards of the hazardous chemical.

(7) The employer may use signs, placards, process sheets, batch tickets, operating procedures, or other such written materials in lieu of affixing labels to individual stationary process containers, as long as the alternative method identifies the containers to which it is applicable and conveys the information required by paragraph

(f)(6) of this section to be on a label. The employer shall ensure the written materials are readily accessible to the employees in their work area throughout each work shift.

(8) The employer is not required to label portable containers into which hazardous chemicals are transferred from labeled containers, and which are intended only for the immediate use of the employee who performs the transfer. For purposes of this section, drugs which are dispensed by a pharmacy to a health care provider for direct administration to a patient are exempted from labeling.

(9) The employer shall not remove or deface existing labels on incoming containers of hazardous chemicals, unless the container is immediately marked with the required information.

(10) The employer shall ensure that workplace labels or other forms of warning are legible, in English, and prominently displayed on the container, or readily available in the work area throughout each work shift. Employers having employees who speak other languages may add the information in their language to the material presented, as long as the information is presented in English as well.

(11) Chemical manufacturers, importers, distributors, or employers who become newly aware of any significant information regarding the hazards of a chemical shall revise the labels for the chemical within six months of becoming aware of the new information, and shall ensure that labels on containers of hazardous chemicals shipped after that time contain the new information. If the chemical is not currently produced or imported, the chemical manufacturer, importer, distributor, or employer shall add the information to the label before the chemical is shipped or introduced into the workplace again.

(g) *Safety data sheets.* (1) Chemical manufacturers and importers shall obtain or develop a safety data sheet for each hazardous chemical they produce or import. Employers shall have a safety data sheet in the workplace for each hazardous chemical which they use.

(2) The chemical manufacturer or importer preparing the safety data sheet shall ensure that it is in English (although the employer may maintain copies in other languages as well), and includes at least the following section numbers and headings, and associated information under each heading, in the order listed (*See* Appendix D to § 1910.1200—Safety Data Sheets, for the specific content of each section of the safety data sheet):

(i) Section 1, Identification;

(ii) Section 2, Hazard(s) identification;

(iii) Section 3, Composition/information on ingredients;

(iv) Section 4, First-aid measures;

(v) Section 5, Fire-fighting measures;

(vi) Section 6, Accidental release measures;

(vii) Section 7, Handling and storage;

(viii) Section 8, Exposure controls/personal protection;

(ix) Section 9, Physical and chemical properties;

(x) Section 10, Stability and reactivity;

(xi) Section 11, Toxicological information;

(xii) Section 12, Ecological information;

(xiii) Section 13, Disposal considerations;

(xiv) Section 14, Transport information;

(xv) Section 15, Regulatory information; and

(xvi) Section 16, Other information, including date of preparation or last revision.

NOTE 1 TO PARAGRAPH (g)(2): To be consistent with the GHS, an SDS must also include the headings in paragraphs (g)(2)(xii) through (g)(2)(xv) in order.

NOTE 2 TO PARAGRAPH (g)(2): OSHA will not be enforcing information requirements in sections 12 through 15, as these areas are not under its jurisdiction.

(3) If no relevant information is found for any sub-heading within a section on the safety data sheet, the chemical manufacturer, importer or employer preparing the safety data sheet shall mark it to indicate that no applicable information was found.

(4) Where complex mixtures have similar hazards and contents (*i.e.,* the chemical ingredients are essentially the same, but the specific composition varies from mixture to mixture), the chemical manufacturer, importer or employer may prepare one safety data

sheet to apply to all of these similar mixtures.

(5) The chemical manufacturer, importer or employer preparing the safety data sheet shall ensure that the information provided accurately reflects the scientific evidence used in making the hazard classification. If the chemical manufacturer, importer or employer preparing the safety data sheet becomes newly aware of any significant information regarding the hazards of a chemical, or ways to protect against the hazards, this new information shall be added to the safety data sheet within three months. If the chemical is not currently being produced or imported, the chemical manufacturer or importer shall add the information to the safety data sheet before the chemical is introduced into the workplace again.

(6)(i) Chemical manufacturers or importers shall ensure that distributors and employers are provided an appropriate safety data sheet with their initial shipment, and with the first shipment after a safety data sheet is updated;

(ii) The chemical manufacturer or importer shall either provide safety data sheets with the shipped containers or send them to the distributor or employer prior to or at the time of the shipment;

(iii) If the safety data sheet is not provided with a shipment that has been labeled as a hazardous chemical, the distributor or employer shall obtain one from the chemical manufacturer or importer as soon as possible; and,

(iv) The chemical manufacturer or importer shall also provide distributors or employers with a safety data sheet upon request.

(7)(i) Distributors shall ensure that material data sheets, and updated information, are provided to other distributors and employers with their initial shipment and with the first shipment after a safety data sheet is updated;

(ii) The distributor shall either provide safety data sheets with the shipped containers, or send them to the other distributor or employer prior to or at the time of the shipment;

(iii) Retail distributors selling hazardous chemicals to employers having a commercial account shall provide a safety data sheet to such employers upon request, and shall post a sign or otherwise inform them that a material safety data sheet is available;

(iv) Wholesale distributors selling hazardous chemicals to employers over-the-counter may also provide safety data sheets upon the request of the employer at the time of the over-the-counter purchase, and shall post a sign or otherwise inform such employers that a material safety data sheet is available;

(v) If an employer without a commercial account purchases a hazardous chemical from a retail distributor not required to have safety data sheets on file (*i.e.*, the retail distributor does not have commercial accounts and does not use the materials), the retail distributor shall provide the employer, upon request, with the name, address, and telephone number of the chemical manufacturer, importer, or distributor from which a safety data sheet can be obtained;

(vi) Wholesale distributors shall also provide safety data sheets to employers or other distributors upon request; and,

(vii) Chemical manufacturers, importers, and distributors need not provide safety data sheets to retail distributors that have informed them that the retail distributor does not sell the product to commercial accounts or open the sealed container to use it in their own workplaces.

(8) The employer shall maintain in the workplace copies of the required safety data sheets for each hazardous chemical, and shall ensure that they are readily accessible during each work shift to employees when they are in their work area(s). (Electronic access and other alternatives to maintaining paper copies of the safety data sheets are permitted as long as no barriers to immediate employee access in each workplace are created by such options.)

(9) Where employees must travel between workplaces during a workshift, *i.e.*, their work is carried out at more than one geographical location, the safety data sheets may be kept at the primary workplace facility. In this situation, the employer shall ensure that employees can immediately obtain the required information in an emergency.

(10) Safety data sheets may be kept in any form, including operating procedures, and may be designed to cover groups of hazardous chemicals in a work area where it may be more appropriate to address the hazards of a process rather than individual hazardous chemicals. However, the employer shall ensure that in all cases the required information is provided for each hazardous chemical, and is readily accessible during each work shift to employees when they are in their work area(s).

(11) Safety data sheets shall also be made readily available, upon request, to designated representatives, the Assistant Secretary, and the Director, in accordance with the requirements of § 1910.1020(e).

(h) *Employee information and training.* (1) Employers shall provide employees with effective information and training on hazardous chemicals in their work area at the time of their initial assignment, and whenever a new chemical hazard the employees have not previously been trained about is introduced into their work area. Information and training may be designed to cover categories of hazards (e.g., flammability, carcinogenicity) or specific chemicals. Chemical-specific information must always be available through labels and safety data sheets.

(2) *Information.* Employees shall be informed of:

(i) The requirements of this section;

(ii) Any operations in their work area where hazardous chemicals are present; and,

(iii) The location and availability of the written hazard communication program, including the required list(s) of hazardous chemicals, and safety data sheets required by this section.

(3) *Training.* Employee training shall include at least:

(i) Methods and observations that may be used to detect the presence or release of a hazardous chemical in the work area (such as monitoring conducted by the employer, continuous monitoring devices, visual appearance or odor of hazardous chemicals when being released, etc.);

(ii) The physical, health, simple asphyxiation, combustible dust, and pyrophoric gas hazards, as well as haz-

ards not otherwise classified, of the chemicals in the work area;

(iii) The measures employees can take to protect themselves from these hazards, including specific procedures the employer has implemented to protect employees from exposure to hazardous chemicals, such as appropriate work practices, emergency procedures, and personal protective equipment to be used; and,

(iv) The details of the hazard communication program developed by the employer, including an explanation of the labels received on shipped containers and the workplace labeling system used by their employer; the safety data sheet, including the order of information and how employees can obtain and use the appropriate hazard information.

(i) *Trade secrets.* (1) The chemical manufacturer, importer, or employer may withhold the specific chemical identity, including the chemical name, other specific identification of a hazardous chemical, or the exact percentage (concentration) of the substance in a mixture, from the safety data sheet, provided that:

(i) The claim that the information withheld is a trade secret can be supported;

(ii) Information contained in the safety data sheet concerning the properties and effects of the hazardous chemical is disclosed;

(iii) The safety data sheet indicates that the specific chemical identity and/or percentage of composition is being withheld as a trade secret; and,

(iv) The specific chemical identity and percentage is made available to health professionals, employees, and designated representatives in accordance with the applicable provisions of this paragraph (i).

(2) Where a treating physician or nurse determines that a medical emergency exists and the specific chemical identity and/or specific percentage of composition of a hazardous chemical is necessary for emergency or first-aid treatment, the chemical manufacturer, importer, or employer shall immediately disclose the specific chemical identity or percentage composition of a trade secret chemical to that treating physician or nurse, regardless of the

existence of a written statement of need or a confidentiality agreement. The chemical manufacturer, importer, or employer may require a written statement of need and confidentiality agreement, in accordance with the provisions of paragraphs (i)(3) and (4) of this section, as soon as circumstances permit.

(3) In non-emergency situations, a chemical manufacturer, importer, or employer shall, upon request, disclose a specific chemical identity or percentage composition, otherwise permitted to be withheld under paragraph (i)(1) of this section, to a health professional (*i.e.*, physician, industrial hygienist, toxicologist, epidemiologist, or occupational health nurse) providing medical or other occupational health services to exposed employee(s), and to employees or designated representatives, if:

(i) The request is in writing;

(ii) The request describes with reasonable detail one or more of the following occupational health needs for the information:

(A) To assess the hazards of the chemicals to which employees will be exposed;

(B) To conduct or assess sampling of the workplace atmosphere to determine employee exposure levels;

(C) To conduct pre-assignment or periodic medical surveillance of exposed employees;

(D) To provide medical treatment to exposed employees;

(E) To select or assess appropriate personal protective equipment for exposed employees;

(F) To design or assess engineering controls or other protective measures for exposed employees; and,

(G) To conduct studies to determine the health effects of exposure.

(iii) The request explains in detail why the disclosure of the specific chemical identity or percentage composition is essential and that, in lieu thereof, the disclosure of the following information to the health professional, employee, or designated representative, would not satisfy the purposes described in paragraph (i)(3)(ii) of this section:

(A) The properties and effects of the chemical;

(B) Measures for controlling workers' exposure to the chemical;

(C) Methods of monitoring and analyzing worker exposure to the chemical; and,

(D) Methods of diagnosing and treating harmful exposures to the chemical;

(iv) The request includes a description of the procedures to be used to maintain the confidentiality of the disclosed information; and,

(v) The health professional, and the employer or contractor of the services of the health professional (*i.e.*, downstream employer, labor organization, or individual employee), employee, or designated representative, agree in a written confidentiality agreement that the health professional, employee, or designated representative, will not use the trade secret information for any purpose other than the health need(s) asserted and agree not to release the information under any circumstances other than to OSHA, as provided in paragraph (i)(6) of this section, except as authorized by the terms of the agreement or by the chemical manufacturer, importer, or employer.

(4) The confidentiality agreement authorized by paragraph (i)(3)(iv) of this section:

(i) May restrict the use of the information to the health purposes indicated in the written statement of need;

(ii) May provide for appropriate legal remedies in the event of a breach of the agreement, including stipulation of a reasonable pre-estimate of likely damages; and,

(iii) May not include requirements for the posting of a penalty bond.

(5) Nothing in this standard is meant to preclude the parties from pursuing non-contractual remedies to the extent permitted by law.

(6) If the health professional, employee, or designated representative receiving the trade secret information decides that there is a need to disclose it to OSHA, the chemical manufacturer, importer, or employer who provided the information shall be informed by the health professional, employee, or designated representative prior to, or at the same time as, such disclosure.

(7) If the chemical manufacturer, importer, or employer denies a written request for disclosure of a specific chemical identity or percentage composition, the denial must:

(i) Be provided to the health professional, employee, or designated representative, within thirty days of the request;

(ii) Be in writing;

(iii) Include evidence to support the claim that the specific chemical identity or percent of composition is a trade secret;

(iv) State the specific reasons why the request is being denied; and,

(v) Explain in detail how alternative information may satisfy the specific medical or occupational health need without revealing the trade secret.

(8) The health professional, employee, or designated representative whose request for information is denied under paragraph (i)(3) of this section may refer the request and the written denial of the request to OSHA for consideration.

(9) When a health professional, employee, or designated representative refers the denial to OSHA under paragraph (i)(8) of this section, OSHA shall consider the evidence to determine if:

(i) The chemical manufacturer, importer, or employer has supported the claim that the specific chemical identity or percentage composition is a trade secret;

(ii) The health professional, employee, or designated representative has supported the claim that there is a medical or occupational health need for the information; and,

(iii) The health professional, employee or designated representative has demonstrated adequate means to protect the confidentiality.

(10)(i) If OSHA determines that the specific chemical identity or percentage composition requested under paragraph (i)(3) of this section is not a "bona fide" trade secret, or that it is a trade secret, but the requesting health professional, employee, or designated representative has a legitimate medical or occupational health need for the information, has executed a written confidentiality agreement, and has shown adequate means to protect the confidentiality of the information, the chemical manufacturer, importer, or employer will be subject to citation by OSHA.

(ii) If a chemical manufacturer, importer, or employer demonstrates to OSHA that the execution of a confidentiality agreement would not provide sufficient protection against the potential harm from the unauthorized disclosure of a trade secret, the Assistant Secretary may issue such orders or impose such additional limitations or conditions upon the disclosure of the requested chemical information as may be appropriate to assure that the occupational health services are provided without an undue risk of harm to the chemical manufacturer, importer, or employer.

(11) If a citation for a failure to release trade secret information is contested by the chemical manufacturer, importer, or employer, the matter will be adjudicated before the Occupational Safety and Health Review Commission in accordance with the Act's enforcement scheme and the applicable Commission rules of procedure. In accordance with the Commission rules, when a chemical manufacturer, importer, or employer continues to withhold the information during the contest, the Administrative Law Judge may review the citation and supporting documentation "in camera" or issue appropriate orders to protect the confidentiality of such matters.

(12) Notwithstanding the existence of a trade secret claim, a chemical manufacturer, importer, or employer shall, upon request, disclose to the Assistant Secretary any information which this section requires the chemical manufacturer, importer, or employer to make available. Where there is a trade secret claim, such claim shall be made no later than at the time the information is provided to the Assistant Secretary so that suitable determinations of trade secret status can be made and the necessary protections can be implemented.

(13) Nothing in this paragraph shall be construed as requiring the disclosure under any circumstances of process information which is a trade secret.

(j) *Effective dates.* (1) Employers shall train employees regarding the new label elements and safety data sheets format by December 1, 2013.

(2) Chemical manufacturers, importers, distributors, and employers shall be in compliance with all modified provisions of this section no later than June 1, 2015, except:

(i) After December 1, 2015, the distributor shall not ship containers labeled by the chemical manufacturer or importer unless the label has been modified to comply with paragraph (f)(1) of this section.

(ii) All employers shall, as necessary, update any alternative workplace labeling used under paragraph (f)(6) of this section, update the hazard communication program required by paragraph (h)(1), and provide any additional employee training in accordance with paragraph (h)(3) for newly identified physical or health hazards no later than June 1, 2016.

(3) Chemical manufacturers, importers, distributors, and employers may comply with either §1910.1200 revised as of October 1, 2011, or the current version of this standard, or both during the transition period.

APPENDIX A TO §1910.1200—HEALTH HAZARD CRITERIA (MANDATORY)

A.0 GENERAL CLASSIFICATION CONSIDERATIONS

A.0.1 CLASSIFICATION

A.0.1.1 The term "hazard classification" is used to indicate that only the intrinsic hazardous properties of chemicals are considered. Hazard classification incorporates three steps:

(a) Identification of relevant data regarding the hazards of a chemical;

(b) Subsequent review of those data to ascertain the hazards associated with the chemical;

(c) Determination of whether the chemical will be classified as hazardous and the degree of hazard.

A.0.1.2 For many hazard classes, the criteria are semi-quantitative or qualitative and expert judgment is required to interpret the data for classification purposes.

A.0.2 AVAILABLE DATA, TEST METHODS AND TEST DATA QUALITY

A.0.2.1 There is no requirement for testing chemicals.

A.0.2.2 The criteria for determining health hazards are test method neutral, i.e., they do not specify particular test methods, as long as the methods are scientifically validated.

A.0.2.3 The term "scientifically validated" refers to the process by which the reliability and the relevance of a procedure are established for a particular purpose. Any test that determines hazardous properties, which is conducted according to recognized scientific principles, can be used for purposes of a hazard determination for health hazards. Test conditions need to be standardized so that the results are reproducible with a given substance, and the standardized test yields "valid" data for defining the hazard class of concern.

A.0.2.4 Existing test data are acceptable for classifying chemicals, although expert judgment also may be needed for classification purposes.

A.0.2.5 The effect of a chemical on biological systems is influenced, by the physicochemical properties of the substance and/or ingredients of the mixture and the way in which ingredient substances are biologically available. A chemical need not be classified when it can be shown by conclusive experimental data from scientifically validated test methods that the chemical is not biologically available.

A.0.2.6 For classification purposes, epidemiological data and experience on the effects of chemicals on humans (e.g., occupational data, data from accident databases) shall be taken into account in the evaluation of human health hazards of a chemical.

A.0.3 CLASSIFICATION BASED ON WEIGHT OF EVIDENCE

A.0.3.1 For some hazard classes, classification results directly when the data satisfy the criteria. For others, classification of a chemical shall be determined on the basis of the total weight of evidence using expert judgment. This means that all available information bearing on the classification of hazard shall be considered together, including the results of valid *in vitro* tests, relevant animal data, and human experience such as epidemiological and clinical studies and well-documented case reports and observations.

A.0.3.2 The quality and consistency of the data shall be considered. Information on chemicals related to the material being classified shall be considered as appropriate, as well as site of action and mechanism or mode of action study results. Both positive and negative results shall be considered together in a single weight-of-evidence determination.

A.0.3.3 Positive effects which are consistent with the criteria for classification, whether seen in humans or animals, shall

607

normally justify classification. Where evidence is available from both humans and animals and there is a conflict between the findings, the quality and reliability of the evidence from both sources shall be evaluated in order to resolve the question of classification. Reliable, good quality human data shall generally have precedence over other data. However, even well-designed and conducted epidemiological studies may lack a sufficient number of subjects to detect relatively rare but still significant effects, or to assess potentially confounding factors. Therefore, positive results from well-conducted animal studies are not necessarily negated by the lack of positive human experience but require an assessment of the robustness, quality and statistical power of both the human and animal data.

A.0.3.4 Route of exposure, mechanistic information, and metabolism studies are pertinent to determining the relevance of an effect in humans. When such information raises doubt about relevance in humans, a lower classification may be warranted. When there is scientific evidence demonstrating that the mechanism or mode of action is not relevant to humans, the chemical should not be classified.

A.0.3.5 Both positive and negative results are considered together in the weight of evidence determination. However, a single positive study performed according to good scientific principles and with statistically and biologically significant positive results may justify classification.

A.0.4 CONSIDERATIONS FOR THE CLASSIFICATION OF MIXTURES

A.0.4.1 For most hazard classes, the recommended process of classification of mixtures is based on the following sequence:

(a) Where test data are available for the complete mixture, the classification of the mixture will always be based on those data;

(b) Where test data are not available for the mixture itself, the bridging principles designated in each health hazard chapter of this appendix shall be considered for classification of the mixture;

(c) If test data are not available for the mixture itself, and the available information is not sufficient to allow application of the above-mentioned bridging principles, then the method(s) described in each chapter for estimating the hazards based on the information known will be applied to classify the mixture (e.g., application of cut-off values/concentration limits).

A.0.4.2 An exception to the above order or precedence is made for Carcinogenicity, Germ Cell Mutagenicity, and Reproductive Toxicity. For these three hazard classes, mixtures shall be classified based upon information on the ingredient substances, unless on a case-by-case basis, justification can be provided for classifying based upon the mixture as a whole. See chapters A.5, A.6, and A.7 for further information on case-by-case bases.

A.0.4.3 Use of cut-off values/concentration limits.

A.0.4.3.1 When classifying an untested mixture based on the hazards of its ingredients, cut-off values/concentration limits for the classified ingredients of the mixture are used for several hazard classes. While the adopted cut-off values/concentration limits adequately identify the hazard for most mixtures, there may be some that contain hazardous ingredients at lower concentrations than the specified cut-off values/concentration limits that still pose an identifiable hazard. There may also be cases where the cut-off value/concentration limit is considerably lower than the established non-hazardous level for an ingredient.

A.0.4.3.2 If the classifier has information that the hazard of an ingredient will be evident (i.e., it presents a health risk) below the specified cut-off value/concentration limit, the mixture containing that ingredient shall be classified accordingly.

A.0.4.3.3 In exceptional cases, conclusive data may demonstrate that the hazard of an ingredient will not be evident (i.e., it does not present a health risk) when present at a level above the specified cut-off value/concentration limit(s). In these cases the mixture may be classified according to those data. The data must exclude the possibility that the ingredient will behave in the mixture in a manner that would increase the hazard over that of the pure substance. Furthermore, the mixture must not contain ingredients that would affect that determination.

A.0.4.4 Synergistic or antagonistic effects.

When performing an assessment in accordance with these requirements, the evaluator must take into account all available information about the potential occurrence of synergistic effects among the ingredients of the mixture. Lowering classification of a mixture to a less hazardous category on the basis of antagonistic effects may be done only if the determination is supported by sufficient data.

A.0.5 BRIDGING PRINCIPLES FOR THE CLASSIFICATION OF MIXTURES WHERE TEST DATA ARE NOT AVAILABLE FOR THE COMPLETE MIXTURE

A.0.5.1 Where the mixture itself has not been tested to determine its toxicity, but there are sufficient data on both the individual ingredients and similar tested mixtures to adequately characterize the hazards of the mixture, these data shall be used in accordance with the following bridging principles, subject to any specific provisions for mixtures for each hazard class. These principles ensure that the classification process uses the available data to the greatest extent possible in characterizing the hazards of the mixture.

A.0.5.1.1 Dilution.

For mixtures classified in accordance with A.1 through A.10 of this Appendix, if a tested mixture is diluted with a diluent that has an equivalent or lower toxicity classification than the least toxic original ingredient, and which is not expected to affect the toxicity of other ingredients, then:

(a) The new diluted mixture shall be classified as equivalent to the original tested mixture; or

(b) For classification of acute toxicity in accordance with A.1 of this Appendix, paragraph A.1.3.6 (the additivity formula) shall be applied.

A.0.5.1.2 Batching.

For mixtures classified in accordance with A.1 through A.10 of this Appendix, the toxicity of a tested production batch of a mixture can be assumed to be substantially equivalent to that of another untested production batch of the same mixture, when produced by or under the control of the same *chemical manufacturer,* unless there is reason to believe there is significant variation such that the toxicity of the untested batch has changed. If the latter occurs, a new classification is necessary.

A.0.5.1.3 Concentration of mixtures.

For mixtures classified in accordance with A.1, A.2, A.3, A.8, A.9, or A.10 of this Appendix, if a tested mixture is classified in Category 1, and the concentration of the ingredients of the tested mixture that are in Category 1 is increased, the resulting untested mixture shall be classified in Category 1.

A.0.5.1.4 Interpolation within one toxicity category.

For mixtures classified in accordance with A.1, A.2, A.3, A.8, A.9, or A.10 of this Appendix, for three mixtures (A, B and C) with identical ingredients, where mixtures A and B have been tested and are in the same toxicity category, and where untested mixture C has the same toxicologically active ingredients as mixtures A and B but has concentrations of toxicologically active ingredients intermediate to the concentrations in mixtures A and B, then mixture C is assumed to be in the same toxicity category as A and B.

A.0.5.1.5 Substantially similar mixtures.

For mixtures classified in accordance with A.1 through A.10 of this Appendix, given the following set of conditions:

(a) Where there are two mixtures:

(i) A + B;

(ii) C + B;

(b) The concentration of ingredient B is essentially the same in both mixtures;

(c) The concentration of ingredient A in mixture (i) equals that of ingredient C in mixture (ii);

(d) And data on toxicity for A and C are available and substantially equivalent; i.e., they are in the same hazard category and are not expected to affect the toxicity of B; then

If mixture (i) or (ii) is already classified based on test data, the other mixture can be assigned the same hazard category.

A.0.5.1.6 Aerosols.

For mixtures classified in accordance with A.1, A.2, A.3, A.4, A.8, or A.9 of this Appendix, an aerosol form of a mixture shall be classified in the same hazard category as the tested, non-aerosolized form of the mixture, provided the added propellant does not affect the toxicity of the mixture when spraying.

A.1 ACUTE TOXICITY

A.1.1 DEFINITION

Acute toxicity refers to those adverse effects occurring following oral or dermal administration of a single dose of a substance, or multiple doses given within 24 hours, or an inhalation exposure of 4 hours.

A.1.2 CLASSIFICATION CRITERIA FOR SUBSTANCES

A.1.2.1 Substances can be allocated to one of four toxicity categories based on acute toxicity by the oral, dermal or inhalation route according to the numeric cut-off criteria as shown in Table A.1.1. Acute toxicity values are expressed as (approximate) LD50 (oral, dermal) or LC50 (inhalation) values or as acute toxicity estimates (ATE). See the footnotes following Table A.1.1 for further explanation on the application of these values.

TABLE A.1.1—ACUTE TOXICITY HAZARD CATEGORIES AND ACUTE TOXICITY ESTIMATE (ATE) VALUES DEFINING THE RESPECTIVE CATEGORIES

Exposure route	Category 1	Category 2	Category 3	Category 4
Oral (mg/kg bodyweight) *see: Note (a)* *Note (b)*	≤5	>5 and ≤50	>50 and ≤300	>300 and ≤2000.
Dermal (mg/kg bodyweight) *see: Note (a)* *Note (b)*	≤50	>50 and ≤200	>200 and ≤1000	>1000 and ≤2000.
Inhalation—Gases (ppmV) *see: Note (a)* *Note (b)* *Note (c)*	≤100	>100 and ≤500	>500 and ≤2500	>2500 and ≤20000.

TABLE A.1.1—ACUTE TOXICITY HAZARD CATEGORIES AND ACUTE TOXICITY ESTIMATE (ATE) VALUES DEFINING THE RESPECTIVE CATEGORIES—Continued

Exposure route	Category 1	Category 2	Category 3	Category 4
Inhalation—Vapors (mg/l) see: Note (a) .... Note (b) Note (c) Note (d)	≤0.5	>0.5 and ≤2.0	>2.0 and ≤10.0	>10.0 and ≤20.0.
Inhalation—Dusts and Mists (mg/l) see: Note (a) .... Note (b) Note (c)	≤0.05	>0.05 and ≤0.5	>0.5 and ≤1.0	>1.0 and ≤5.0.

Note: *Gas concentrations are expressed in parts per million per volume (ppmV).*
Notes to Table A.1.1:
(a) The acute toxicity estimate (ATE) for the classification of a substance is derived using the LD_{50}/LC_{50} where available;
(b) The acute toxicity estimate (ATE) for the classification of a substance or ingredient in a mixture is derived using:
(i) the LD_{50}/LC_{50} where available. Otherwise,
(ii) the appropriate conversion value from Table 1.2 that relates to the results of a range test, or
(iii) the appropriate conversion value from Table 1.2 that relates to a classification category;
(c) Inhalation cut-off values in the table are based on 4 hour testing exposures. Conversion of existing inhalation toxicity data which has been generated according to 1 hour exposure is achieved by dividing by a factor of 2 for gases and vapors and 4 for dusts and mists;
(d) For some substances the test atmosphere will be a vapor which consists of a combination of liquid and gaseous phases. For other substances the test atmosphere may consist of a vapor which is nearly all the gaseous phase. In these latter cases, classification is based on ppmV as follows: Category 1 (100 ppmV), Category 2 (500 ppmV), Category 3 (2500 ppmV), Category 4 (20000 ppmV).
The terms "dust", "mist" and "vapor" are defined as follows:
(i) Dust: solid particles of a substance or mixture suspended in a gas (usually air);
(ii) Mist: liquid droplets of a substance or mixture suspended in a gas (usually air);
(iii) Vapor: the gaseous form of a substance or mixture released from its liquid or solid state.

A.1.2.3 The preferred test species for evaluation of acute toxicity by the oral and inhalation routes is the rat, while the rat or rabbit are preferred for evaluation of acute dermal toxicity. Test data already generated for the classification of chemicals under existing systems should be accepted when reclassifying these chemicals under the harmonized system. When experimental data for acute toxicity are available in several animal species, scientific judgment should be used in selecting the most appropriate LD_{50}

value from among scientifically validated tests.

A.1.3 CLASSIFICATION CRITERIA FOR MIXTURES

A.1.3.1 The approach to classification of mixtures for acute toxicity is tiered, and is dependent upon the amount of information available for the mixture itself and for its ingredients. The flow chart of Figure A.1.1 indicates the process that must be followed:

Figure A.1.1: Tiered approach to classification of mixtures for acute toxicity

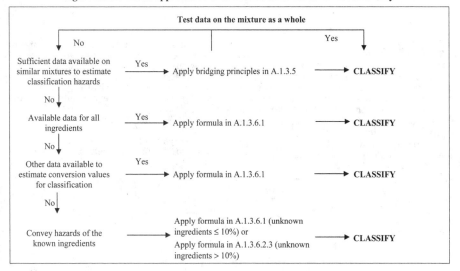

A.1.3.2 Classification of mixtures for acute toxicity may be carried out for each route of exposure, but is only required for one route of exposure as long as this route is followed (estimated or tested) for all ingredients and there is no relevant evidence to suggest acute toxicity by multiple routes. When there is relevant evidence of acute toxicity by multiple routes of exposure, classification is to be conducted for all appropriate routes of exposure. All available information shall be considered. The pictogram and signal word used shall reflect the most severe hazard category; and all relevant hazard statements shall be used.

A.1.3.3 For purposes of classifying the hazards of mixtures in the tiered approach:

(a) The "relevant ingredients" of a mixture are those which are present in concentrations ≥1% (weight/weight for solids, liquids, dusts, mists and vapors and volume/volume for gases). If there is reason to suspect that an ingredient present at a concentration <1% will affect classification of the mixture for acute toxicity, that ingredient shall also be considered relevant. Consideration of ingredients present at a concentration <1% is particularly important when classifying untested mixtures which contain ingredients that are classified in Category 1 and Category 2;

(b) Where a classified mixture is used as an ingredient of another mixture, the actual or derived acute toxicity estimate (ATE) for that mixture is used when calculating the classification of the new mixture using the formulas in A.1.3.6.1 and A.1.3.6.2.4.

(c) If the converted acute toxicity point estimates for all ingredients of a mixture are

within the same category, then the mixture should be classified in that category.

(d) When only range data (or acute toxicity hazard category information) are available for ingredients in a mixture, they may be converted to point estimates in accordance with Table A.1.2 when calculating the classification of the new mixture using the formulas in A.1.3.6.1 and A.1.3.6.2.4.

A.1.3.4 CLASSIFICATION OF MIXTURES WHERE ACUTE TOXICITY TEST DATA ARE AVAILABLE FOR THE COMPLETE MIXTURE

Where the mixture itself has been tested to determine its acute toxicity, it is classified according to the same criteria as those used for substances, presented in Table A.1.1. If test data for the mixture are not available, the procedures presented below must be followed.

A.1.3.5 CLASSIFICATION OF MIXTURES WHERE ACUTE TOXICITY TEST DATA ARE NOT AVAILABLE FOR THE COMPLETE MIXTURE: BRIDGING PRINCIPLES

A.1.3.5.1 Where the mixture itself has not been tested to determine its acute toxicity, but there are sufficient data on both the individual ingredients and similar tested mixtures to adequately characterize the hazards of the mixture, these data will be used in accordance with the following bridging principles as found in paragraph A.0.5 of this Appendix: Dilution, Batching, Concentration of mixtures, Interpolation within one toxicity category, Substantially similar mixtures, and Aerosols.

611

A.1.3.6 CLASSIFICATION OF MIXTURES BASED ON INGREDIENTS OF THE MIXTURE (ADDITIVITY FORMULA)

A.1.3.6.1 Data available for all ingredients.

The acute toxicity estimate (ATE) of ingredients is considered as follows:

(a) Include ingredients with a known acute toxicity, which fall into any of the acute toxicity categories, or have an oral or dermal LD_{50} greater than 2000 but less than or equal to 5000 mg/kg body weight (or the equivalent dose for inhalation);

(b) Ignore ingredients that are presumed not acutely toxic (e.g., water, sugar);

(c) Ignore ingredients if the data available are from a limit dose test (at the upper threshold for Category 4 for the appropriate route of exposure as provided in Table A.1.1) and do not show acute toxicity.

Ingredients that fall within the scope of this paragraph are considered to be ingredients with a known acute toxicity estimate (ATE). See note (b) to Table A.1.1 and paragraph A.1.3.3 for appropriate application of available data to the equation below, and paragraph A.1.3.6.2.4.

The ATE of the mixture is determined by calculation from the ATE values for all relevant ingredients according to the following formula below for oral, dermal or inhalation toxicity:

$$\frac{100}{ATEmix} = \sum_{n} \frac{Ci}{ATE_i}$$

Where:

Ci = concentration of ingredient i

n ingredients and i is running from 1 to n

ATEi = acute toxicity estimate of ingredient i.

A.1.3.6.2 Data are not available for one or more ingredients of the mixture.

A.1.3.6.2.1 Where an ATE is not available for an individual ingredient of the mixture, but available information provides a derived conversion value, the formula in A.1.3.6.1 may be applied. This information may include evaluation of:

(a) Extrapolation between oral, dermal and inhalation acute toxicity estimates. Such an evaluation requires appropriate pharmacodynamic and pharmacokinetic data;

(b) Evidence from human exposure that indicates toxic effects but does not provide lethal dose data;

(c) Evidence from any other toxicity tests/assays available on the substance that indicates toxic acute effects but does not necessarily provide lethal dose data; or

(d) Data from closely analogous substances using structure/activity relationships.

A.1.3.6.2.2 This approach requires substantial supplemental technical information, and a highly trained and experienced expert, to reliably estimate acute toxicity. If sufficient information is not available to reliably estimate acute toxicity, proceed to the provisions of A.1.3.6.2.3.

A.1.3.6.2.3 In the event that an ingredient with unknown acute toxicity is used in a mixture at a concentration ≥1%, and the mixture has not been classified based on testing of the mixture as a whole, the mixture cannot be attributed a definitive acute toxicity estimate. In this situation the mixture is classified based on the known ingredients only. (Note: A statement that × percent of the mixture consists of ingredient(s) of unknown toxicity is required on the label and safety data sheet in such cases; see Appendix C to this section, Allocation of Label Elements and Appendix D to this section, Safety Data Sheets.)

Where an ingredient with unknown acute toxicity is used in a mixture at a concentration ≥1%, and the mixture is not classified based on testing of the mixture as a whole, a statement that X% of the mixture consists of ingredient(s) of unknown acute toxicity is required on the label and safety data sheet in such cases; see Appendix C to this section, Allocation of Label Elements and Appendix D to this section, Safety Data Sheets.)

A.1.3.6.2.4 If the total concentration of the relevant ingredient(s) with unknown acute toxicity is ≤10% then the formula presented in A.1.3.6.1 must be used. If the total concentration of the relevant ingredient(s) with unknown acute toxicity is >10%, the formula presented in A.1.3.6.1 is corrected to adjust for the percentage of the unknown ingredient(s) as follows:

$$\frac{100 - (\Sigma C_{unknown} \text{ if } > 10\%)}{ATE_{mix}} = \sum_{n} \frac{Ci}{ATE_i}$$

TABLE A.1.2—CONVERSION FROM EXPERIMENTALLY OBTAINED ACUTE TOXICITY RANGE VALUES (OR ACUTE TOXICITY HAZARD CATEGORIES) TO ACUTE TOXICITY POINT ESTIMATES FOR USE IN THE FORMULAS FOR THE CLASSIFICATION OF MIXTURES

Exposure routes	Classification category or experimentally obtained acute toxicity range estimate	Converted acute toxicity point estimate
Oral (mg/kg bodyweight)	0 <Category 1 ≤5	0.5
	5 <Category 2 ≤50	5
	50 <Category 3 ≤300	100
	300 <Category 4 ≤2000	500
Dermal (mg/kg bodyweight)	0 <Category 1 ≤50	5
	50 <Category 2 ≤200	50
	200 <Category 3 ≤1000	300
	1000 <Category 4 ≤2000	1100
Gases (ppmV)	0 <Category 1 ≤100	10
	100 <Category 2 ≤500	100
	500 <Category 3 ≤2500	700
	2500 <Category 4 ≤20000	4500
Vapors (mg/l)	0 <Category 1 ≤0.5	0.05
	0.5 <Category 2 ≤2.0	0.5
	2.0 <Category 3 ≤10.0	3
	10.0 <Category 4 ≤20.0	11
Dust/mist (mg/l)	0 <Category 1 ≤0.05	0.005
	0.05 <Category 2 ≤0.5	0.05
	0.5 <Category 3 ≤1.0	0.5
	1.0 <Category 4 ≤5.0	1.5

Note: Gas concentrations are expressed in parts per million per volume (ppmV).

A.2 SKIN CORROSION/IRRITATION

A.2.1 DEFINITIONS AND GENERAL CONSIDERATIONS

A.2.1.1 *Skin corrosion* is the production of irreversible damage to the skin; namely, visible necrosis through the epidermis and into the dermis, following the application of a test substance for up to 4 hours. Corrosive reactions are typified by ulcers, bleeding, bloody scabs, and, by the end of observation at 14 days, by discoloration due to blanching of the skin, complete areas of alopecia, and scars. Histopathology should be considered to evaluate questionable lesions.

Skin irritation is the production of reversible damage to the skin following the application of a test substance for up to 4 hours.

A.2.1.2 Skin corrosion/irritation shall be classified using a tiered approach as detailed in figure A.2.1. Emphasis shall be placed upon existing human data (See A.0.2.6), followed by other sources of information. Classification results directly when the data satisfy the criteria in this section. In case the criteria cannot be directly applied, classification of a substance or a mixture is made on the basis of the total weight of evidence (See A.0.3.1). This means that all available information bearing on the determination of skin corrosion/irritation is considered together, including the results of appropriate scientifically validated in-vitro tests, relevant animal data, and human data such as epidemiological and clinical studies and well-documented case reports and observations.

A.2.2 CLASSIFICATION CRITERIA FOR SUBSTANCES USING ANIMAL TEST DATA

A.2.2.1 CORROSION

A.2.2.1.1 A corrosive substance is a chemical that produces destruction of skin tissue, namely, visible necrosis through the epidermis and into the dermis, in at least 1 of 3 tested animals after exposure up to a 4-hour duration. Corrosive reactions are typified by ulcers, bleeding, bloody scabs and, by the end of observation at 14 days, by discoloration due to blanching of the skin, complete areas of alopecia and scars. Histopathology should be considered to discern questionable lesions.

A.2.2.1.2 Three sub-categories of Category 1 are provided in Table A.2.1, all of which shall be regulated as Category 1.

TABLE A.2.1—SKIN CORROSION CATEGORY AND SUB-CATEGORIES

Category 1: corrosive	Corrosive sub-categories	Corrosive in ≥1 of 3 animals	
		Exposure	Observation
	1A	≤3 min	≤1 h.
	1B	>3 min ≤1 h	≤14 days.
	1C	>1 h ≤4 h	≤14 days.

A.2.2.2 IRRITATION

A.2.2.2.1 A single irritant category (Category 2) is presented in the Table A.2.2. The major criterion for the irritant category is that at least 2 tested animals have a mean score of ≥2.3 ≤4.0.

TABLE A.2.2—SKIN IRRITATION CATEGORY

	Criteria
Irritant (Category 2)	(1) Mean value of ≥2.3 ≤4.0 for erythema/eschar or for edema in at least 2 of 3 tested animals from gradings at 24, 48 and 72 hours after patch removal or, if reactions are delayed, from grades on 3 consecutive days after the onset of skin reactions; or
	(2) Inflammation that persists to the end of the observation period normally 14 days in at least 2 animals, particularly taking into account alopecia (limited area), hyperkeratosis, hyperplasia, and scaling; or
	(3) In some cases where there is pronounced variability of response among animals, with very definite positive effects related to chemical exposure in a single animal but less than the criteria above.

A.2.2.2.2 Animal irritant responses within a test can be quite variable, as they are with corrosion. A separate irritant criterion accommodates cases when there is a significant irritant response but less than the mean score criterion for a positive test. For example, a substance might be designated as an irritant if at least 1 of 3 tested animals shows a very elevated mean score throughout the study, including lesions persisting at the end of an observation period of normally 14 days. Other responses could also fulfil this criterion. However, it should be ascertained that the responses are the result of chemical exposure. Addition of this criterion increases the sensitivity of the classification system.

A.2.2.2.3 Reversibility of skin lesions is another consideration in evaluating irritant responses. When inflammation persists to the end of the observation period in 2 or more test animals, taking into consideration alopecia (limited area), hyperkeratosis, hyperplasia and scaling, then a chemical should be considered to be an irritant.

A.2.3 CLASSIFICATION CRITERIA FOR SUBSTANCES USING OTHER DATA ELEMENTS

A.2.3.1 Existing human and animal data including information from single or repeated exposure should be the first line of analysis, as they give information directly relevant to effects on the skin. If a substance is highly toxic by the dermal route, a skin corrosion/irritation study may not be practicable since the amount of test substance to be applied would considerably exceed the toxic dose and, consequently, would result in the death of the animals. When observations are made of skin corrosion/irritation in acute toxicity studies and are observed up through the limit dose, these data may be used for classification provided that the dilutions used and species tested are equivalent. In vitro alternatives that have been scientifically validated shall be used to make classification decisions. Solid substances (powders) may become corrosive or irritant when moistened or in contact with moist skin or mucous membranes. Likewise, pH extremes like ≤2 and ≥11.5 may indicate skin effects, especially when associated with significant buffering capacity. Generally, such substances are expected to produce significant effects on the skin. In the absence of any other information, a substance is considered corrosive (Skin Category 1) if it has a pH ≤2 or a pH ≥11.5. However, if consideration of alkali/acid reserve suggests the substance or mixture may not be corrosive despite the low or high pH value, then further evaluation may be necessary. In some cases enough information may be available from structurally related compounds to make classification decisions.

A.2.3.2 A tiered approach to the evaluation of initial information shall be used (Figure A.2.1) recognizing that all elements may not be relevant in certain cases.

A.2.3.3 The tiered approach explains how to organize information on a substance and to make a weight-of-evidence decision about hazard assessment and hazard classification.

A.2.3.4 All the above information that is available on a substance shall be evaluated. Although information might be gained from the evaluation of single parameters within a tier, there is merit in considering the totality of existing information and making an overall weight of evidence determination. This is especially true when there is information available on some but not all param-

eters. Emphasis shall be placed upon existing human experience and data, followed by animal experience and testing data, followed by other sources of information, but case-by-case determinations are necessary.

Figure A.2.1: Tiered evaluation of skin corrosion and irritation potential

Step	Parameter	Finding	Conclusion
1a	Existing human or animal data[1] ↓ Not corrosive or no data ↓	→ Skin corrosive	→ Category 1[2]
1b	Existing human or animal data[1] ↓ Not an irritant or no data ↓	→ Skin irritant	→ Category 2[2]
1c	Existing human or animal data[1] ↓ No/Insufficient data ↓	→ Not a skin corrosive or skin irritant	→ Not classified
2:	Other, existing skin data in animals[3] ↓ No/Insufficient data ↓	→ Skin corrosive Skin irritant	→ Category 1[2] Category 2[2]
3:	Existing skin corrosive _ex vivo / in vitro_ data[4] ↓ Not corrosive or no data ↓	→ Positive: Skin corrosive	→ Category 1[2]
	Existing skin irritation _ex vivo / in vitro_ data[4] ↓ No/Insufficient data ↓	Positive: Skin irritant Negative: Not a skin irritant[5]	Category 2[2] Not classified
4:	pH-Based assessment (with consideration of buffering capacity of the chemical, or no buffering capacity data)[5] ↓ Not a pH extreme, No pH data or extreme pH with low/no buffering capacity ↓	→ pH ≤ 2 or ≥ 11.5	→ Category 1[2]
5:	Validated Structure/Activity Relationship (SAR) models ↓ No/Insufficient data ↓	Skin corrosive Skin irritant	Category 1[2] Category 2[2]
6:	Consideration of the total Weight of Evidence[6] ↓ No concern based on consideration of the sum of available data ↓	Skin corrosive Skin irritant	Category 1[2] Category 2[2]
7:	**Not Classified**	→	Not classified

Notes to Figure A.2.1:

[1] _Evidence of existing human or animal data may be derived from single or repeated exposure(s) in occupational, consumer, transportation, or emergency response scenarios; from ethically-conducted human clinical studies; or from purposely-generated data from animal studies conducted according to scientifically validated test methods (at present, there is no internationally accepted test method for human skin irritation testing)._

[2] _Classify in the appropriate harmonized category, as shown in Tables A.2.1 and A.2.2._

<u>3</u> Pre-existing animal data (e.g. from an acute dermal toxicity test or a sensitisation test) should be carefully reviewed to determine if sufficient skin corrosion/irritation evidence is available through other, similar information. For example, classification/categorization may be done on the basis of whether a chemical has or has not produced any skin irritation in an acute dermal toxicity test in animals at the limit dose, or produces very toxic effects in an acute dermal toxicity test in animals. In the latter case, the chemical would be classified as being very hazardous by the dermal route for acute toxicity, and it would be moot whether the chemical is also irritating or corrosive on the skin. It should be kept in mind in evaluating acute dermal toxicity information that the reporting of dermal lesions may be incomplete, testing and observations may be made on a species other than the rabbit, and species may differ in sensitivity in their responses.

<u>4</u> Evidence from studies using scientifically validated protocols with isolated human/animal tissues or other, non-tissue-based, though scientifically validated, protocols should be assessed. Examples of scientifically validated test methods for skin corrosion include OECD TG 430 (Transcutaneous Electrical Resistance Test (TER)), 431 (Human Skin Model Test), and 435 (Membrane Barrier Test Method). OECD TG 439 (Reconstructed Human Epidermis Test Method) is a scientifically validated in vitro test method for skin irritation.

<u>5</u> Measurement of pH alone may be adequate, but assessment of acid or alkali reserve (buffering capacity) would be preferable. Presently, there is no scientifically validated and internationally accepted method for assessing this parameter.

<u>6</u> All information that is available on a chemical should be considered and an overall determination made on the total weight of evidence. This is especially true when there is conflict in information available on some parameters. Professional judgment should be exercised in making such a determination.

A.2.4 CLASSIFICATION CRITERIA FOR MIXTURES

A.2.4.1 CLASSIFICATION OF MIXTURES WHEN DATA ARE AVAILABLE FOR THE COMPLETE MIXTURE

A.2.4.1.1 The mixture shall be classified using the criteria for substances (See A.2.3).

A.2.4.2 CLASSIFICATION OF MIXTURES WHEN DATA ARE NOT AVAILABLE FOR THE COMPLETE MIXTURE: BRIDGING PRINCIPLES

A.2.4.2.1 Where the mixture itself has not been tested to determine its skin corrosion/irritation, but there are sufficient data on both the individual ingredients and similar tested mixtures to adequately characterize the hazards of the mixture, these data will be used in accordance with the following bridging principles, as found in paragraph A.0.5 of this Appendix: Dilution, Batching, Concentration of mixtures, Interpolation within one toxicity category, Substantially similar mixtures, and Aerosols.

A.2.4.3 CLASSIFICATION OF MIXTURES WHEN DATA ARE AVAILABLE FOR ALL INGREDIENTS OR ONLY FOR SOME INGREDIENTS OF THE MIXTURE

A.2.4.3.1 For purposes of classifying the skin corrosion/irritation hazards of mixtures in the tiered approach:

The "relevant ingredients" of a mixture are those which are present in concentrations ≥1% (weight/weight for solids, liquids, dusts, mists and vapors and volume/volume for gases.) If the classifier has reason to suspect that an ingredient present at a concentration <1% will affect classification of the mixture for skin corrosion/irritation, that ingredient shall also be considered relevant.

A.2.4.3.2 In general, the approach to classification of mixtures as irritant or corrosive to skin when data are available on the ingredients, but not on the mixture as a whole, is based on the theory of additivity, such that each corrosive or irritant ingredient contributes to the overall irritant or corrosive properties of the mixture in proportion to its potency and concentration. A weighting factor of 10 is used for corrosive ingredients when they are present at a concentration below the concentration limit for classification with Category 1, but are at a concentration that will contribute to the classification of the mixture as an irritant. The mixture is classified as corrosive or irritant when the sum of the concentrations of such ingredients exceeds a cut-off value/concentration limit.

A.2.4.3.3 Table A.2.3 below provides the cut-off value/concentration limits to be used to determine if the mixture is considered to be an irritant or a corrosive to the skin.

A.2.4.3.4 Particular care shall be taken when classifying certain types of chemicals such as acids and bases, inorganic salts, aldehydes, phenols, and surfactants. The approach explained in A.2.4.3.1 and A.2.4.3.2 might not work given that many of such substances are corrosive or irritant at concentrations <1%. For mixtures containing strong acids or bases the pH should be used as classification criteria since pH will be a better indicator of corrosion than the concentration limits of Table A.2.3. A mixture containing corrosive or irritant ingredients that cannot be classified based on the additivity approach shown in Table A.2.3, due to chemical characteristics that make this approach unworkable, should be classified as Skin Category 1 if it contains ≥1% of a corrosive ingredient and as Skin Category 2 when it contains ≥3% of an irritant ingredient. Classification of mixtures with ingredients for which the approach in Table A.2.3 does not apply is summarized in Table A.2.4 below.

A.2.4.3.5 On occasion, reliable data may show that the skin corrosion/irritation of an

ingredient will not be evident when present at a level above the generic concentration cut-off values mentioned in Tables A.2.3 and A.2.4. In these cases the mixture could be classified according to those data (See *Use of cut-off values/concentration limits,* paragraph A.0.4.3 of this Appendix).

A.2.4.3.6 If there are data showing that (an) ingredient(s) may be corrosive or irritant at a concentration of <1% (corrosive) or <3% (irritant), the mixture shall be classified accordingly (See *Use of cut-off values/concentration limits,* paragraph A.0.4.3 of this Appendix).

TABLE A.2.3—CONCENTRATION OF INGREDIENTS OF A MIXTURE CLASSIFIED AS SKIN CATEGORY 1 OR 2 THAT WOULD TRIGGER CLASSIFICATION OF THE MIXTURE AS HAZARDOUS TO SKIN

[Category 1 or 2]

Sum of ingredients classified as:	Concentration triggering classification of a mixture as:	
	Skin corrosive	Skin irritant
	Category 1	Category 2
Skin Category 1	≥5%	≥1% but <5%.
Skin Category 2		≥10%.
(10 × Skin Category 1) + Skin Category 2		≥10%.

TABLE A.2.4—CONCENTRATION OF INGREDIENTS OF A MIXTURE FOR WHICH THE ADDITIVITY APPROACH DOES NOT APPLY, THAT WOULD TRIGGER CLASSIFICATION OF THE MIXTURE AS HAZARDOUS TO SKIN

Ingredient:	Concentration:	Mixture classified as: Skin
Acid with pH ≤2	≥1%	Category 1.
Base with pH ≥11.5	≥1%	Category 1.
Other corrosive (Category 1) ingredients for which additivity does not apply	≥1%	Category 1.
Other irritant (Category 2) ingredients for which additivity does not apply, including acids and bases.	≥3%	Category 2.

A.3 SERIOUS EYE DAMAGE/EYE IRRITATION

A.3.1 DEFINITIONS AND GENERAL CONSIDERATIONS

A.3.1.1 *Serious eye damage* is the production of tissue damage in the eye, or serious physical decay of vision, following application of a test substance to the anterior surface of the eye, which is not fully reversible within 21 days of application.

Eye irritation is the production of changes in the eye following the application of test substance to the anterior surface of the eye, which are fully reversible within 21 days of application.

A.3.1.2 Serious eye damage/eye irritation shall be classified using a tiered approach as detailed in Figure A.3.1. Emphasis shall be placed upon existing human data (See A.0.2.6), followed by animal data, followed by other sources of information. Classification results directly when the data satisfy the

criteria in this section. In case the criteria cannot be directly applied, classification of a substance or a mixture is made on the basis of the total weight of evidence (See A.0.3.1). This means that all available information bearing on the determination of serious eye damage/eye irritation is considered together, including the results of appropriate scientifically validated *in vitro* tests, relevant animal data, and human data such as epidemiological and clinical studies and well-documented case reports and observations.

A.3.2 CLASSIFICATION CRITERIA FOR SUBSTANCES USING ANIMAL TEST DATA

A.3.2.1 Irreversible effects on the eye/serious damage to eyes (Category 1).

A single hazard category is provided in Table A.3.1, for substances that have the potential to seriously damage the eyes. Category 1, irreversible effects on the eye, includes the criteria listed below. These observations include animals with grade 4 cornea lesions and other severe reactions (e.g. destruction of cornea) observed at any time during the test, as well as persistent corneal opacity, discoloration of the cornea by a dye substance, adhesion, pannus, and interference with the function of the iris or other effects that impair sight. In this context, persistent lesions are considered those which are not fully reversible within an observation period of normally 21 days. Category 1 also contains substances fulfilling the criteria of corneal opacity ≥3 and/or iritis >1.5 detected in a Draize eye test with rabbits, because severe lesions like these usually do not reverse within a 21-day observation period.

TABLE A.3.1—IRREVERSIBLE EYE EFFECTS

A substance is classified as Serious Eye Damage Category 1 (irreversible effects on the eye) when it produces:
  (a) at least in one tested animal, effects on the cornea, iris or conjunctiva that are not expected to reverse or have not fully reversed within an observation period of normally 21 days; and/or
  (b) at least in 2 of 3 tested animals, a positive response of:
    (i) corneal opacity ≥3; and/or
    (ii) iritis >1.5;
    calculated as the mean scores following grading at 24, 48 and 72 hours after instillation of the substance.

A.3.2.2 Reversible effects on the eye (Category 2).

A single category is provided in Table A.3.2 for substances that have the potential to induce reversible eye irritation.

TABLE A.3.2—REVERSIBLE EYE EFFECTS

A substance is classified as Eye irritant Category 2A (irritating to eyes) when it produces in at least in 2 of 3 tested animals a positive response of:
    (i) corneal opacity ≥1; and/or
    (ii) iritis ≥1; and/or
    (iii) conjunctival redness ≥2; and/or
    (iv) conjunctival edema (chemosis) ≥2
    calculated as the mean scores following grading at 24, 48 and 72 hours after instillation of the substance, and which fully reverses within an observation period of normally 21 days.
An eye irritant is considered mildly irritating to eyes (Category 2B) when the effects listed above are fully reversible within 7 days of observation.

A.3.2.3 For those chemicals where there is pronounced variability among animal responses, this information may be taken into account in determining the classification.

A.3.3 CLASSIFICATION CRITERIA FOR SUBSTANCES USING OTHER DATA ELEMENTS

A.3.3.1 Existing human and animal data should be the first line of analysis, as they give information directly relevant to effects on the eye. Possible skin corrosion shall be evaluated prior to consideration of serious eye damage/eye irritation in order to avoid testing for local effects on eyes with skin corrosive substances. *In vitro* alternatives that have been scientifically validated and accepted shall be used to make classification decisions. Likewise, pH extremes like ≤2 and ≥11.5, may indicate serious eye damage, especially when associated with significant buffering capacity. Generally, such substances are expected to produce significant effects on the eyes. In the absence of any other information, a mixture/substance is considered to cause serious eye damage (Eye Category 1) if it has a pH ≤2 or ≥11.5. However, if consideration of acid/alkaline reserve suggests the substance may not have the potential to cause serious eye damage despite the low or high pH value, then further evaluation may be necessary. In some cases enough information may be available from structurally related compounds to make classification decisions.

A.3.3.2 A tiered approach to the evaluation of initial information shall be used where applicable, recognizing that all elements may not be relevant in certain cases (Figure A.3.1).

A.3.3.3 The tiered approach explains how to organize existing information on a substance and to make a weight-of-evidence decision, where appropriate, about hazard assessment and hazard classification.

A.3.3.4 All the above information that is available on a substance shall be evaluated.

Although information might be gained from the evaluation of single parameters within a tier, consideration should be given to the totality of existing information and making an overall weight-of-evidence determination. This is especially true when there is conflict in information available on some parameters.

Figure A.3.1 Evaluation strategy for serious eye damage and eye irritation
(See also Figure A.2.1)

Step	Parameter	Finding	Conclusion
1a:	Existing human or animal data, eye[1]	Serious Eye Damage	Category 1[2]
		Eye Irritant	Category 2[2]
	No/insufficient data or unknown		
1b:	Existing human or animal data, skin corrosion	Skin corrosive	Category 1[2]
	No/insufficient data or unknown		
1c:	Existing human or animal data, eye[1]	Existing data that show that substance does not cause serious eye damage or eye irritation	Not Classified
	No/insufficient data		
2:	Other, existing skin/eye data in animals[3]	Yes; existing data that show that substance may cause serious eye damage or eye irritation	Category 1 or Category 2[2]
	No/insufficient data		
3:	Existing *ex vivo / in vitro* data[4]	Positive: serious eye damage	Category 1[2]
		Positive: eye irritant	Category 2[2]
	No/insufficient data / negative response		
4:	pH-Based assessment (with consideration of buffering capacity of the chemical, or no buffering capacity data)[5]	pH ≤ 2 or ≥11.5	Category 1[2]
	Not a pH extreme, no pH data, or extreme pH with low/no buffering capacity		
5:	Validated structure/activity relationship (SAR) models	Severe damage to eyes	Category 1[2]
		Eye irritant	Category 2[2]
		Skin Corrosive	Category 1[2]
	No/insufficient data		
6:	Consideration of the total weight of evidence[6]	Serious eye damage	Category 1[2]
		Eye irritant	Category 2[2]
	No concern based on consideration of the sum of available data		
7:	**Not Classified**		

Notes to Figure A.3.1:

[1] *Evidence of existing human or animal data may be derived from single or repeated exposure(s) in occupational, consumer, transportation, or emergency response scenarios; from ethically-conducted human clinical studies; or from purposely-generated data from animal studies conducted according to scientifically validated test methods. At present, there are no internationally accepted test methods for human skin or eye irritation testing.*

[2] *Classify in the appropriate harmonized category, as shown in Tables A.3.1 and A.3.2.*

[3] *Pre-existing animal data should be carefully reviewed to determine if sufficient skin or eye corrosion/irritation evidence is available through other, similar information.*

[4] *Evidence from studies using scientifically validated protocols with isolated human/animal tissues or other, non-tissue-based, though scientifically validated, protocols should be assessed. Examples of, scientifically validated test methods for identifying eye corrosives and severe irritants (i.e., Serious Eye Damage) include OECD TG 437 (Bovine Corneal Opacity and Permeability (BCOP)) and TG 438 (Isolated Chicken Eye). Positive test results from a scientifically validated in vitro test for skin corrosion would likely also lead to a conclusion to classify as causing Serious Eye Damage.*

[5] *Measurement of pH alone may be adequate, but assessment of acid or alkali reserve (buffering capacity) would be preferable.*

[6] *All information that is available on a chemical should be considered and an overall determination made on the total weight of evidence. This is especially true when there is conflict in information available on some parameters. The weight of evidence including information on skin irritation could lead to classification of eye irritation. It is recognized that not all skin irritants are eye irritants as well. Professional judgment should be exercised in making such a determination.*

A.3.4 CLASSIFICATION CRITERIA FOR MIXTURES

A.3.4.1 CLASSIFICATION OF MIXTURES WHEN DATA ARE AVAILABLE FOR THE COMPLETE MIXTURE

A.3.4.1.1 The mixture will be classified using the criteria for substances.

A.3.4.1.2 Unlike other hazard classes, there are alternative tests available for skin corrosivity of certain types of chemicals that can give an accurate result for classification purposes, as well as being simple and relatively inexpensive to perform. When considering testing of the mixture, chemical manufacturers are encouraged to use a tiered weight of evidence strategy as included in the criteria for classification of substances for skin corrosion and serious eye damage and eye irritation to help ensure an accurate classification, as well as avoid unnecessary animal testing. In the absence of any other information, a mixture is considered to cause serious eye damage (Eye Category 1) if it has a pH ≤2 or ≥11.5. However, if consideration of acid/alkaline reserve suggests the substance or mixture may not have the potential to cause serious eye damage despite the low or high pH value, then further evaluation may be necessary.

A.3.4.2 CLASSIFICATION OF MIXTURES WHEN DATA ARE NOT AVAILABLE FOR THE COMPLETE MIXTURE: BRIDGING PRINCIPLES

A.3.4.2.1 Where the mixture itself has not been tested to determine its skin corrosivity or potential to cause serious eye damage or eye irritation, but there are sufficient data on both the individual ingredients and similar tested mixtures to adequately characterize the hazards of the mixture, these data will be used in accordance with the following bridging principles, as found in paragraph A.0.5 of this Appendix: Dilution, Batching, Concentration of mixtures, Interpolation within one toxicity category, Substantially similar mixtures, and Aerosols.

A.3.4.3 CLASSIFICATION OF MIXTURES WHEN DATA ARE AVAILABLE FOR ALL INGREDIENTS OR ONLY FOR SOME INGREDIENTS OF THE MIXTURE

A.3.4.3.1 For purposes of classifying the eye corrosion/irritation hazards of mixtures in the tiered approach:
The "relevant ingredients" of a mixture are those which are present in concentrations ≥1% (weight/weight for solids, liquids, dusts, mists and vapors and volume/volume for gases.) If the classifier has reason to suspect that an ingredient present at a concentration <1% will affect classification of the mixture for eye corrosion/irritation, that ingredient shall also be considered relevant.

A.3.4.3.2 In general, the approach to classification of mixtures as seriously damaging to the eye or eye irritant when data are available on the ingredients, but not on the mixture as a whole, is based on the theory of additivity, such that each corrosive or irritant ingredient contributes to the overall irritant or corrosive properties of the mixture in proportion to its potency and concentration. A weighting factor of 10 is used for corrosive ingredients when they are present at a concentration below the concentration limit for classification with Category 1, but are at a concentration that will contribute to the classification of the mixture as an irritant. The mixture is classified as seriously damaging to the eye or eye irritant when the sum of the concentrations of such ingredients exceeds a threshold cut-off value/concentration limit.

A.3.4.3.3 Table A.3.3 provides the cut-off value/concentration limits to be used to determine if the mixture should be classified as seriously damaging to the eye or an eye irritant.

A.3.4.3.4 Particular care must be taken when classifying certain types of chemicals such as acids and bases, inorganic salts, aldehydes, phenols, and surfactants. The approach explained in A.3.4.3.1 and A.3.4.3.2 might not work given that many of such substances are corrosive or irritant at concentrations <1%. For mixtures containing strong acids or bases, the pH should be used as classification criteria (See A.3.4.1) since pH will be a better indicator of serious eye damage than the concentration limits of Table A.3.3. A mixture containing corrosive or irritant ingredients that cannot be classified based on the additivity approach applied in Table A.3.3 due to chemical characteristics that make this approach unworkable, should be classified as Eye Category 1 if it contains ≥1% of a corrosive ingredient and as Eye Category 2 when it contains ≥3% of an irritant ingredient. Classification of mixtures with ingredients for which the approach in Table A.3.3 does not apply is summarized in Table A.3.4.

A.3.4.3.5 On occasion, reliable data may show that the reversible/irreversible eye effects of an ingredient will not be evident when present at a level above the generic cut-off values/concentration limits mentioned in Tables A.3.3 and A.3.4. In these cases the mixture could be classified according to those data (See also A.0.4.3 *Use of cut-off values/concentration limits*). On occasion, when it is expected that the skin corrosion/irritation or the reversible/irreversible eye effects of an ingredient will not be evident when present at a level above the generic concentration/cut-off levels mentioned in Tables A.3.3 and A.3.4, testing of the mixture may be considered. In those cases, the tiered weight of evidence strategy should be applied as referred to in section A.3.3, Figure A.3.1 and explained in detail in this chapter.

A.3.4.3.6 If there are data showing that (an) ingredient(s) may be corrosive or irritant at a concentration of <1% (corrosive) or <3% (irritant), the mixture should be classified accordingly (See also paragraph A.0.4.3, *Use of cut-off values/concentration limits*).

TABLE A.3.3—CONCENTRATION OF INGREDIENTS OF A MIXTURE CLASSIFIED AS SKIN CATEGORY 1 AND/OR EYE CATEGORY 1 OR 2 THAT WOULD TRIGGER CLASSIFICATION OF THE MIXTURES AS HAZARDOUS TO THE EYE

Sum of ingredients classified as:	Concentration triggering classification of a mixture as:	
	Irreversible eye effects	Reversible eye effects
	Category 1	Category 2
Eye or Skin Category 1	≥3%	≥1% but <3%.
Eye Category 2		≥10%.
(10 × Eye Category 1) + Eye Category 2		≥10%.
Skin Category 1 + Eye Category 1	≥3%	≥1% but <3%.
10 × (Skin Category 1 + Eye Category 1) + Eye Category 2.		≥10%.

Note: *A mixture may be classified as Eye Category 2B in cases when all relevant ingredients are classified as Eye Category 2B.*

TABLE A.3.4—CONCENTRATION OF INGREDIENTS OF A MIXTURE FOR WHICH THE ADDITIVITY APPROACH DOES NOT APPLY, THAT WOULD TRIGGER CLASSIFICATION OF THE MIXTURE AS HAZARDOUS TO THE EYE

Ingredient	Concentration	Mixture classified as: Eye
Acid with pH ≤2	≥1%	Category 1.
Base with pH ≥11.5	≥1%	Category 1.
Other corrosive (Category 1) ingredients for which additivity does not apply	≥1%	Category 1.
Other irritant (Category 2) ingredients for which additivity does not apply, including acids and bases.	≥3%	Category 2.

A.4 RESPIRATORY OR SKIN SENSITIZATION

A.4.1 DEFINITIONS AND GENERAL CONSIDERATIONS

A.4.1.1 *Respiratory sensitizer* means a chemical that will lead to hypersensitivity of the airways following inhalation of the chemical.

Skin sensitizer means a chemical that will lead to an allergic response following skin contact.

A.4.1.2 For the purpose of this chapter, sensitization includes two phases: the first phase is induction of specialized immunological memory in an individual by exposure to an allergen. The second phase is elicitation, i.e., production of a cell-mediated or antibody-mediated allergic response by exposure of a sensitized individual to an allergen.

A.4.1.3 For respiratory sensitization, the pattern of induction followed by elicitation phases is shared in common with skin sensitization. For skin sensitization, an induction phase is required in which the immune system learns to react; clinical symptoms can then arise when subsequent exposure is sufficient to elicit a visible skin reaction (elicitation phase). As a consequence, predictive tests usually follow this pattern in which there is an induction phase, the response to which is measured by a standardized elicitation phase, typically involving a patch test. The local lymph node assay is the exception, directly measuring the induction response. Evidence of skin sensitization in humans normally is assessed by a diagnostic patch test.

A.4.1.4 Usually, for both skin and respiratory sensitization, lower levels are necessary for elicitation than are required for induction.

A.4.1.5 The hazard class "respiratory or skin sensitization" is differentiated into:

(a) Respiratory sensitization; and

(b) Skin sensitization.

A.4.2 CLASSIFICATION CRITERIA FOR SUBSTANCES

A.4.2.1 RESPIRATORY SENSITIZERS

A.4.2.1.1 Hazard Categories.

A.4.2.1.1.1 Effects seen in either humans or animals will normally justify classification in a weight of evidence approach for respiratory sensitizers. Substances may be allocated to one of the two sub-categories 1A or 1B using a weight of evidence approach in accordance with the criteria given in Table A.4.1 and on the basis of reliable and good quality evidence from human cases or epidemiological studies and/or observations from appropriate studies in experimental animals.

A.4.2.1.1.2 Where data are not sufficient for sub-categorization, respiratory sensitizers shall be classified in Category 1.

TABLE A.4.1—HAZARD CATEGORY AND SUB-CATEGORIES FOR RESPIRATORY SENSITIZERS

Category 1	Respiratory sensitizer
	A substance is classified as a respiratory sensitizer. (a) if there is evidence in humans that the substance can lead to specific respiratory hypersensitivity and/or (b) if there are positive results from an appropriate animal test.[1]
Sub-category 1A	Substances showing a high frequency of occurrence in humans; or a probability of occurrence of a high sensitization rate in humans based on animal or other tests.[1] Severity of reaction may also be considered.
Sub-category 1B	Substances showing a low to moderate frequency of occurrence in humans; or a probability of occurrence of a low to moderate sensitization rate in humans based on animal or other tests.[1] Severity of reaction may also be considered.

[1] At this writing, recognized and validated animal models for the testing of respiratory hypersensitivity are not available. Under certain circumstances, data from animal studies may provide valuable information in a weight of evidence assessment.

A.4.2.1.2 Human evidence.

A.4.2.1.2.1 Evidence that a substance can lead to specific respiratory hypersensitivity will normally be based on human experience. In this context, hypersensitivity is normally seen as asthma, but other hypersensitivity reactions such as rhinitis/conjunctivitis and alveolitis are also considered. The condition will have the clinical character of an allergic reaction. However, immunological mechanisms do not have to be demonstrated.

A.4.2.1.2.2 When considering the human evidence, it is necessary that in addition to the evidence from the cases, the following be taken into account:
(a) The size of the population exposed;
(b) The extent of exposure.

A.4.2.1.2.3 The evidence referred to above could be:
(a) Clinical history and data from appropriate lung function tests related to exposure to the substance, confirmed by other supportive evidence which may include:
(i) *In vivo* immunological test (e.g., skin prick test);
(ii) *In vitro* immunological test (e.g., serological analysis);
(iii) Studies that may indicate other specific hypersensitivity reactions where immunological mechanisms of action have not been proven, e.g., repeated low-level irritation, pharmacologically mediated effects;
(iv) A chemical structure related to substances known to cause respiratory hypersensitivity;
(b) Data from positive bronchial challenge tests with the substance conducted according to accepted guidelines for the determination of a specific hypersensitivity reaction.

A.4.2.1.2.4 Clinical history should include both medical and occupational history to determine a relationship between exposure to a specific substance and development of respiratory hypersensitivity. Relevant information includes aggravating factors both in the home and workplace, the onset and progress of the disease, family history and medical history of the patient in question. The medical history should also include a note of other allergic or airway disorders from childhood and smoking history.

A.4.2.1.2.5 The results of positive bronchial challenge tests are considered to provide sufficient evidence for classification on their own. It is, however, recognized that in practice many of the examinations listed above will already have been carried out.

A.4.2.1.3 Animal studies.

A.4.2.1.3.1 Data from appropriate animal studies[2] which may be indicative of the potential of a substance to cause sensitization by inhalation in humans[3] may include:
(a) Measurements of Immunoglobulin E (IgE) and other specific immunological parameters, for example in mice
(b) Specific pulmonary responses in guinea pigs.

A.4.2.2　SKIN SENSITIZERS

A.4.2.2.1 Hazard categories.

A.4.2.2.1.1 Effects seen in either humans or animals will normally justify classification in a weight of evidence approach for skin sensitizers. Substances may be allocated to one of the two sub-categories 1A or

---

[2] At this writing, recognized and validated animal models for the testing of respiratory hypersensitivity are not available. Under certain circumstances, data from animal studies may provide valuable information in a weight of evidence assessment.

[3] The mechanisms by which substances induce symptoms of asthma are not yet fully known. For preventive measures, these substances are considered respiratory sensitizers. However, if on the basis of the evidence, it can be demonstrated that these substances induce symptoms of asthma by irritation only in people with bronchial hyperactivity, they should not be considered as respiratory sensitizers.

1B using a weight of evidence approach in accordance with the criteria given in Table A.4.2 and on the basis of reliable and good quality evidence from human cases or epidemiological studies and/or observations from appropriate studies in experimental animals according to the guidance values provided in A.4.2.2.2.1 and A.4.2.2.3.2 for sub-category 1A and in A.4.2.2.2.2 and A.4.2.2.3.3 for sub-category 1B.

A.4.2.2.1.2 Where data are not sufficient for sub-categorization, skin sensitizers shall be classified in Category 1.

TABLE A.4.2—HAZARD CATEGORY AND SUB-CATEGORIES FOR SKIN SENSITIZERS

Category 1	Skin sensitizer
	A substance is classified as a skin sensitizer. (a) if there is evidence in humans that the substance can lead to sensitization by skin contact in a substantial number of persons, or (b) if there are positive results from an appropriate animal test.
Sub-category 1A	Substances showing a high frequency of occurrence in humans and/or a high potency in animals can be presumed to have the potential to produce significant sensitization in humans. Severity of reaction may also be considered.
Sub-category 1B	Substances showing a low to moderate frequency of occurrence in humans and/or a low to moderate potency in animals can be presumed to have the potential to produce sensitization in humans. Severity of reaction may also be considered.

A.4.2.2.2 Human evidence.

A.4.2.2.2.1 Human evidence for sub-category 1A may include:

(a) Positive responses at ≤500 µg/cm² (Human Repeat Insult Patch Test (HRIPT), Human Maximization Test (HMT)—induction threshold);

(b) Diagnostic patch test data where there is a relatively high and substantial incidence of reactions in a defined population in relation to relatively low exposure;

(c) Other epidemiological evidence where there is a relatively high and substantial incidence of allergic contact dermatitis in relation to relatively low exposure.

A.4.2.2.2.2 Human evidence for sub-category 1B may include:

(a) Positive responses at >500 µg/cm² (HRIPT, HMT—induction threshold);

(b) Diagnostic patch test data where there is a relatively low but substantial incidence of reactions in a defined population in relation to relatively high exposure;

(c) Other epidemiological evidence where there is a relatively low but substantial incidence of allergic contact dermatitis in relation to relatively high exposure.

A.4.2.2.3 Animal studies

A.4.2.2.3.1 For Category 1, when an adjuvant type test method for skin sensitization is used, a response of at least 30% of the animals is considered as positive. For a non-adjuvant Guinea pig test method a response of at least 15% of the animals is considered positive. For Category 1, a stimulation index of three or more is considered a positive response in the local lymph node assay.[4]

A.4.2.2.3.2 Animal test results for sub-category 1A can include data with values indicated in Table A.4.3 below:

TABLE A.4.3—ANIMAL TEST RESULTS FOR SUB-CATEGORY 1A

Assay	Criteria
Local lymph node assay	EC3 value ≤2%.
Guinea pig maximization test	≥30% responding at ≤0.1% intradermal induction dose *or* ≥60% responding at >0.1% to ≤1% intradermal induction dose.
Buehler assay	≥15% responding at ≤0.2% topical induction dose *or* ≥60% responding at >0.2% to ≤20% topical induction dose.

Note: *EC3 refers to the estimated concentration of test chemical required to induce a stimulation index of 3 in the local lymph node assay.*

A.4.2.2.3.3 Animal test results for sub-category 1B can include data with values indicated in Table A.4.4 below:

---

[4] *Test methods for skin sensitization are described in OECD Guideline 406 (the Guinea Pig Maximization test and the Buehler guinea pig test) and Guideline 429 (Local Lymph Node Assay). Other methods may be used provided that they are scientifically validated. The Mouse Ear Swelling Test (MEST), appears to be a reliable screening test to detect moderate to strong sensitizers, and can be used, in accordance with professional judgment, as a first stage in the assessment of skin sensitization potential.*

TABLE A.4.4—ANIMAL TEST RESULTS FOR SUB-CATEGORY 1B

Assay	Criteria
Local lymph node assay	EC3 value >2%.
Guinea pig maximization test	≥30% to <60% responding at >0.1% to ≤1% intradermal induction dose or
	≥30% responding at >1% intradermal induction dose.
Buehler assay	≥15% to <60% responding at >0.2% to ≤20% topical induction dose or
	≥15% responding at >20% topical induction dose.

Note: *EC3 refers to the estimated concentration of test chemical required to induce a stimulation index of 3 in the local lymph node assay.*

A.4.2.2.4 Specific considerations.

A.4.2.2.4.1 For classification of a substance, evidence shall include one or more of the following using a weight of evidence approach:

(a) Positive data from patch testing, normally obtained in more than one dermatology clinic;

(b) Epidemiological studies showing allergic contact dermatitis caused by the substance. Situations in which a high proportion of those exposed exhibit characteristic symptoms are to be looked at with special concern, even if the number of cases is small;

(c) Positive data from appropriate animal studies;

(d) Positive data from experimental studies in man (See paragraph A.0.2.6 of this Appendix);

(e) Well documented episodes of allergic contact dermatitis, normally obtained in more than one dermatology clinic;

(f) Severity of reaction.

A.4.2.2.4.2 Evidence from animal studies is usually much more reliable than evidence from human exposure. However, in cases where evidence is available from both sources, and there is conflict between the results, the quality and reliability of the evidence from both sources must be assessed in order to resolve the question of classification on a case-by-case basis. Normally, human data are not generated in controlled experiments with volunteers for the purpose of hazard classification but rather as part of risk assessment to confirm lack of effects seen in animal tests. Consequently, positive human data on skin sensitization are usually derived from case-control or other, less defined studies. Evaluation of human data must, therefore, be carried out with caution as the frequency of cases reflect, in addition to the inherent properties of the substances, factors such as the exposure situation, bioavailability, individual predisposition and preventive measures taken. Negative human data should not normally be used to negate positive results from animal studies. For both animal and human data, consideration should be given to the impact of vehicle.

A.4.2.2.4.3 If none of the above-mentioned conditions are met, the substance need not be classified as a skin sensitizer. However, a combination of two or more indicators of skin sensitization, as listed below, may alter the decision. This shall be considered on a case-by-case basis.

(a) Isolated episodes of allergic contact dermatitis;

(b) Epidemiological studies of limited power, e.g., where chance, bias or confounders have not been ruled out fully with reasonable confidence;

(c) Data from animal tests, performed according to existing guidelines, which do not meet the criteria for a positive result described in A.4.2.2.3, but which are sufficiently close to the limit to be considered significant;

(d) Positive data from non-standard methods;

(e) Positive results from close structural analogues.

A.4.2.2.4.4 Immunological contact urticaria.

A.4.2.2.4.4.1 Substances meeting the criteria for classification as respiratory sensitizers may, in addition, cause immunological contact urticaria. Consideration shall be given to classifying these substances as skin sensitizers.

A.4.2.2.4.4.2 Substances which cause immunological contact urticaria without meeting the criteria for respiratory sensitizers shall be considered for classification as skin sensitizers.

A.4.2.2.4.4.3 There is no recognized animal model available to identify substances which cause immunological contact urticaria. Therefore, classification will normally be based on human evidence, similar to that for skin sensitization.

A.4.3 CLASSIFICATION CRITERIA FOR MIXTURES

A.4.3.1 CLASSIFICATION OF MIXTURES WHEN DATA ARE AVAILABLE FOR THE COMPLETE MIXTURE

When reliable and good quality evidence, as described in the criteria for substances, from human experience or appropriate studies in experimental animals, is available for the mixture, then the mixture shall be classified by weight of evidence evaluation of these data. Care must be exercised in evaluating data on mixtures that the dose used does not render the results inconclusive.

A.4.3.2 CLASSIFICATION OF MIXTURES WHEN DATA ARE NOT AVAILABLE FOR THE COMPLETE MIXTURE: BRIDGING PRINCIPLES

A.4.3.2.1 Where the mixture itself has not been tested to determine its sensitizing properties, but there are sufficient data on both the individual ingredients and similar tested mixtures to adequately characterize the hazards of the mixture, these data will be used in accordance with the following agreed bridging principles as found in paragraph A.0.5 of this Appendix: Dilution, Batching, Concentration of mixtures, Interpolation, Substantially similar mixtures, and Aerosols.

A.4.3.3 CLASSIFICATION OF MIXTURES WHEN DATA ARE AVAILABLE FOR ALL INGREDIENTS OR ONLY FOR SOME INGREDIENTS OF THE MIXTURE

The mixture shall be classified as a respiratory or skin sensitizer when at least one ingredient has been classified as a respiratory or skin sensitizer and is present at or above the appropriate cut-off value/concentration limit for the specific endpoint as shown in Table A.4.5.

TABLE A.4.5—CUT-OFF VALUES/CONCENTRATION LIMITS OF INGREDIENTS OF A MIXTURE CLASSIFIED AS EITHER RESPIRATORY SENSITIZERS OR SKIN SENSITIZERS THAT WOULD TRIGGER CLASSIFICATION OF THE MIXTURE

	Cut-off values/concentration limits triggering classification of a mixture as:		
Ingredient classified as:	Respiratory Sensitizer Category 1		Skin Sensitizer Category 1
	Solid/liquid	Gas	All physical states
Respiratory Sensitizer, Category 1	≥0.1%	≥0.1%	
Respiratory Sensitizer, Sub-category 1A	≥0.1%	≥0.1%	
Respiratory Sensitizer, Sub-category 1B	≥1.0%	≥0.2%	
Skin Sensitizer, Category 1	....	....	≥0.1%
Skin Sensitizer, Sub-category 1A	....	....	≥0.1%
Skin Sensitizer, Sub-category 1B	....	....	≥1.0%

A.5 GERM CELL MUTAGENICITY

A.5.1 DEFINITIONS AND GENERAL CONSIDERATIONS

A.5.1.1 A *mutation* is defined as a permanent change in the amount or structure of the genetic material in a cell. The term *mutation* applies both to heritable genetic changes that may be manifested at the phenotypic level and to the underlying DNA modifications when known (including, for example, specific base pair changes and chromosomal translocations). The term *mutagenic* and *mutagen* will be used for agents giving rise to an increased occurrence of mutations in populations of cells and/or organisms.

A.5.1.2 The more general terms *genotoxic* and *genotoxicity* apply to agents or processes which alter the structure, information content, or segregation of DNA, including those which cause DNA damage by interfering with normal replication processes, or which in a non-physiological manner (temporarily) alter its replication. Genotoxicity test results are usually taken as indicators for mutagenic effects.

A.5.1.3 This hazard class is primarily concerned with chemicals that may cause mutations in the germ cells of humans that can be transmitted to the progeny. However, mutagenicity/genotoxicity tests *in vitro* and in mammalian somatic cells *in vivo* are also considered in classifying substances and mixtures within this hazard class.

A.5.2 CLASSIFICATION CRITERIA FOR SUBSTANCES

A.5.2.1 The classification system provides for two different categories of germ cell mutagens to accommodate the weight of evidence available. The two-category system is described in the Figure A.5.1.

FIGURE A.5.1—HAZARD CATEGORIES FOR GERM CELL MUTAGENS

CATEGORY 1: Substances known to induce heritable mutations or to be regarded as if they induce heritable mutations in the germ cells of humans.

Category 1A: Substances known to induce heritable mutations in germ cells of humans.
   Positive evidence from human epidemiological studies.

Category 1B: Substances which should be regarded as if they induce heritable mutations in the germ cells of humans.

FIGURE A.5.1—HAZARD CATEGORIES FOR GERM CELL MUTAGENS—Continued

(a) Positive result(s) from *in vivo* heritable germ cell mutagenicity tests in mammals; or

(b) Positive result(s) from *in vivo* somatic cell mutagenicity tests in mammals, in combination with some evidence that the substance has potential to cause mutations to germ cells. This supporting evidence may, for example, be derived from mutagenicity/genotoxicity tests in germ cells *in vivo*, or by demonstrating the ability of the substance or its metabolite(s) to interact with the genetic material of germ cells; or

(c) Positive results from tests showing mutagenic effects in the germ cells of humans, without demonstration of transmission to progeny; for example, an increase in the frequency of aneuploidy in sperm cells of exposed people.

CATEGORY 2: Substances which cause concern for humans owing to the possibility that they may induce heritable mutations in the germ cells of humans.

Positive evidence obtained from experiments in mammals and/or in some cases from *in vitro* experiments, obtained from:

(a) Somatic cell mutagenicity tests *in vivo*, in mammals; or

(b) Other *in vivo* somatic cell genotoxicity tests which are supported by positive results from *in vitro* mutagenicity assays.

Note: *Substances which are positive in in vitro mammalian mutagenicity assays, and which also show chemical structure activity relationship to known germ cell mutagens, should be considered for classification as Category 2 mutagens.*

A.5.2.2 Specific considerations for classification of substances as germ cell mutagens:

A.5.2.2.1 To arrive at a classification, test results are considered from experiments determining mutagenic and/or genotoxic effects in germ and/or somatic cells of exposed animals. Mutagenic and/or genotoxic effects determined in *in vitro* tests shall also be considered.

A.5.2.2.2 The system is hazard based, classifying chemicals on the basis of their intrinsic ability to induce mutations in germ cells. The scheme is, therefore, not meant for the (quantitative) risk assessment of chemical substances.

A.5.2.2.3 Classification for heritable effects in human germ cells is made on the basis of scientifically validated tests. Evaluation of the test results shall be done using expert judgment and all the available evidence shall be weighed for classification.

A.5.2.2.4 The classification of substances shall be based on the total weight of evidence available, using expert judgment. In those instances where a single well-conducted test is used for classification, it shall

provide clear and unambiguously positive results. The relevance of the route of exposure used in the study of the substance compared to the route of human exposure should also be taken into account.

A.5.3 CLASSIFICATION CRITERIA FOR MIXTURES [5]

A.5.3.1 CLASSIFICATION OF MIXTURES WHEN DATA ARE AVAILABLE FOR ALL INGREDIENTS OR ONLY FOR SOME INGREDIENTS OF THE MIXTURE

A.5.3.1.1 Classification of mixtures shall be based on the available test data for the individual ingredients of the mixture using cut-off values/concentration limits for the ingredients classified as germ cell mutagens.

A.5.3.1.2 The mixture will be classified as a mutagen when at least one ingredient has been classified as a Category 1A, Category 1B or Category 2 mutagen and is present at or above the appropriate cut-off value/concentration limit as shown in Table A.5.1 below for Category 1 and 2 respectively.

_____

[5] *It should be noted that the classification criteria for health hazards usually include a tiered scheme in which test data available on the complete mixture are considered as the first tier in the evaluation, followed by the applicable bridging principles, and lastly, cut-off values/concentration limits or additivity. However, this approach is not used for Germ Cell Mutagenicity. These criteria for Germ Cell Mutagenicity con-*

sider the cut-off values/concentration limits as the primary tier and allow the classification to be modified only on a case-by-case evaluation based on available test data for the mixture as a whole.

TABLE A.5.1—CUT-OFF VALUES/CONCENTRATION LIMITS OF INGREDIENTS OF A MIXTURE CLASSIFIED AS GERM CELL MUTAGENS THAT WOULD TRIGGER CLASSIFICATION OF THE MIXTURE

Ingredient classified as:	Cut-off/concentration limits triggering classification of a mixture as:	
	Category 1 mutagen	Category 2 mutagen
Category 1A/B mutagen	≥0.1%	
Category 2 mutagen	....	≥1.0%

Note: *The cut-off values/concentration limits in the table above apply to solids and liquids (w/w units) as well as gases (v/v units).*

A.5.3.2 CLASSIFICATION OF MIXTURES WHEN DATA ARE AVAILABLE FOR THE MIXTURE ITSELF

The classification may be modified on a case-by-case basis based on the available test data for the mixture as a whole. In such cases, the test results for the mixture as a whole must be shown to be conclusive taking into account dose and other factors such as duration, observations and analysis (e.g. statistical analysis, test sensitivity) of germ cell mutagenicity test systems.

A.5.3.3 CLASSIFICATION OF MIXTURES WHEN DATA ARE NOT AVAILABLE FOR THE COMPLETE MIXTURE: BRIDGING PRINCIPLES

A.5.3.3.1 Where the mixture itself has not been tested to determine its germ cell mutagenicity hazard, but there are sufficient data on both the individual ingredients and similar tested mixtures to adequately characterize the hazards of the mixture, these data will be used in accordance with the following bridging principles as found in paragraph A.0.5 of this Appendix: Dilution, Batching, and Substantially similar mixtures.

A.5.4 EXAMPLES OF SCIENTIFICALLY VALIDATED TEST METHODS

A.5.4.1 Examples of *in vivo* heritable germ cell mutagenicity tests are:
(a) Rodent dominant lethal mutation test (OECD 478)
(b) Mouse heritable translocation assay (OECD 485)
(c) Mouse specific locus test
A.5.4.2 Examples of *in vivo* somatic cell mutagenicity tests are:
(a) Mammalian bone marrow chromosome aberration test (OECD 475)
(b) Mouse spot test (OECD 484)
(c) Mammalian erythrocyte micronucleus test (OECD 474)
A.5.4.3 Examples of mutagenicity/genotoxicity tests in germ cells are:
(a) Mutagenicity tests:
(i) Mammalian spermatogonial chromosome aberration test (OECD 483) ·
(ii) Spermatid micronucleus assay
(b) Genotoxicity tests:
(i) Sister chromatid exchange analysis in spermatogonia

(ii) Unscheduled DNA synthesis test (UDS) in testicular cells
A.5.4.4 Examples of genotoxicity tests in somatic cells are:
(a) Liver Unscheduled DNA Synthesis (UDS) *in vivo* (OECD 486)
(b) Mammalian bone marrow Sister Chromatid Exchanges (SCE)
A.5.4.5 Examples of *in vitro* mutagenicity tests are:
(a) *In vitro* mammalian chromosome aberration test (OECD 473)
(b) *In vitro* mammalian cell gene mutation test (OECD 476)
(c) Bacterial reverse mutation tests (OECD 471)
A.5.4.6 As new, scientifically validated tests arise, these may also be used in the total weight of evidence to be considered.

A.6 CARCINOGENICITY

A.6.1 DEFINITIONS

Carcinogen means a substance or a mixture of substances which induce cancer or increase its incidence. Substances and mixtures which have induced benign and malignant tumors in well-performed experimental studies on animals are considered also to be presumed or suspected human carcinogens unless there is strong evidence that the mechanism of tumor formation is not relevant for humans.

Classification of a substance or mixture as posing a carcinogenic hazard is based on its inherent properties and does not provide information on the level of the human cancer risk which the use of the substance or mixture may represent.

A.6.2 CLASSIFICATION CRITERIA FOR SUBSTANCES[6]

A.6.2.1 For the purpose of classification for carcinogenicity, substances are allocated to

_____
[6] *See Non-mandatory Appendix F Part A for further guidance regarding hazard classification for carcinogenicity. This appendix is consistent with the GHS adn is provided as guidance excerpted from the International Agency for Research on Cancer (IARC) "Monographs on the* Continued

627

one of two categories based on strength of evidence and additional weight of evidence considerations. In certain instances, route-specific classification may be warranted.

FIGURE A.6.1—HAZARD CATEGORIES FOR CARCINOGENS

CATEGORY 1: Known or presumed human carcinogens.
The classification of a substance as a Category 1 carcinogen is done on the basis of epidemiological and/or animal data. This classification is further distinguished on the basis of whether the evidence for classification is largely from human data (Category 1A) or from animal data (Category 1B):
Category 1A: Known to have carcinogenic potential for humans. Classification in this category is largely based on human evidence.
Category 1B: Presumed to have carcinogenic potential for humans. Classification in this category is largely based on animal evidence.
The classification of a substance in Category 1A and 1B is based on strength of evidence together with weight of evidence considerations (See paragraph A.6.2.5). Such evidence may be derived from:
 —human studies that establish a causal relationship between human exposure to a substance and the development of cancer (known human carcinogen); or
 —animal experiments for which there is sufficient evidence to demonstrate animal carcinogenicity (presumed human carcinogen).
In addition, on a case by case basis, scientific judgment may warrant a decision of presumed human carcinogenicity derived from studies showing limited evidence of carcinogenicity in humans together with limited evidence of carcinogenicity in experimental animals.
CATEGORY 2: Suspected human carcinogens.
The classification of a substance in Category 2 is done on the basis of evidence obtained from human and/or animal studies, but which is not sufficiently convincing to place the substance in Category 1A or B. This classification is based on strength of evidence together with weight of evidence considerations (See paragraph A.6.2.5). Such evidence may be from either limited evidence of carcinogenicity in human studies or from limited evidence of carcinogenicity in animal studies.
Other considerations: Where the weight of evidence for the carcinogenicity of a substance does not meet the above criteria, any positive study conducted in accordance with established scientific principles, and which reports statistically significant findings regarding the carcinogenic potential of the substance, must be noted on the safety data sheet.

A.6.2.2 Classification as a carcinogen is made on the basis of evidence from reliable and acceptable methods, and is intended to be used for substances which have an intrinsic property to produce such toxic effects. The evaluations are to be based on all existing data, peer-reviewed published studies and additional data accepted by regulatory agencies.

A.6.2.3 *Carcinogen classification* is a one-step, criterion-based process that involves two interrelated determinations: evaluations of strength of evidence and consideration of all other relevant information to place substances with human cancer potential into hazard categories.

A.6.2.4 *Strength of evidence* involves the enumeration of tumors in human and animal studies and determination of their level of statistical significance. Sufficient human evidence demonstrates causality between human exposure and the development of cancer, whereas sufficient evidence in animals shows a causal relationship between the agent and an increased incidence of tumors. Limited evidence in humans is demonstrated by a positive association between exposure and cancer, but a causal relationship cannot be stated. Limited evidence in animals is provided when data suggest a carcinogenic effect, but are less than sufficient. (Guidance on consideration of important factors in the classification of carcinogenicity and a more detailed description of the terms "limited" and "sufficient" have been developed by the International Agency for Research on Cancer (IARC) and are provided in non-mandatory Appendix F).

Evaluation of Carcinogenic Risks to Humans" (2006).

A.6.2.5 *Weight of evidence:* Beyond the determination of the strength of evidence for carcinogenicity, a number of other factors should be considered that influence the overall likelihood that an agent may pose a carcinogenic hazard in humans. The full list of factors that influence this determination is very lengthy, but some of the important ones are considered here.

A.6.2.5.1 These factors can be viewed as either increasing or decreasing the level of concern for human carcinogenicity. The relative emphasis accorded to each factor depends upon the amount and coherence of evidence bearing on each. Generally there is a requirement for more complete information to decrease than to increase the level of concern. Additional considerations should be used in evaluating the tumor findings and the other factors in a case-by-case manner.

A.6.2.5.2 Some important factors which may be taken into consideration, when assessing the overall level of concern are:

(a) Tumor type and background incidence;

(b) Multisite responses;

(c) Progression of lesions to malignancy;

(d) Reduced tumor latency;

Additional factors which may increase or decrease the level of concern include:

(e) Whether responses are in single or both sexes;

(f) Whether responses are in a single species or several species;

(g) Structural similarity or not to a substance(s) for which there is good evidence of carcinogenicity;

(h) Routes of exposure;

(i) Comparison of absorption, distribution, metabolism and excretion between test animals and humans;

(j) The possibility of a confounding effect of excessive toxicity at test doses; and,

(k) Mode of action and its relevance for humans, such as mutagenicity, cytotoxicity with growth stimulation, mitogenesis, immunosuppression.

Mutagenicity: It is recognized that genetic events are central in the overall process of cancer development. Therefore evidence of mutagenic activity *in vivo* may indicate that a substance has a potential for carcinogenic effects.

A.6.2.5.3 A substance that has not been tested for carcinogenicity may in certain instances be classified in Category 1A, Category 1B, or Category 2 based on tumor data from a structural analogue together with substantial support from consideration of other important factors such as formation of common significant metabolites, e.g., for benzidine congener dyes.

A.6.2.5.4 The classification should also take into consideration whether or not the substance is absorbed by a given route(s); or whether there are only local tumors at the site of administration for the tested route(s), and adequate testing by other major route(s) show lack of carcinogenicity.

A.6.2.5.5 It is important that whatever is known of the physico-chemical, toxicokinetic and toxicodynamic properties of the substances, as well as any available relevant information on chemical analogues, i.e., structure activity relationship, is taken into consideration when undertaking classification.

A.6.3 CLASSIFICATION CRITERIA FOR MIXTURES [7]

A.6.3.1 The mixture shall be classified as a carcinogen when at least one ingredient has been classified as a Category 1 or Category 2 carcinogen and is present at or above the appropriate cut-off value/concentration limit as shown in Table A.6.1.

TABLE A.6.1—CUT-OFF VALUES/CONCENTRATION LIMITS OF INGREDIENTS OF A MIXTURE CLASSIFIED AS CARCINOGEN THAT WOULD TRIGGER CLASSIFICATION OF THE MIXTURE

Ingredient classified as:	Category 1 carcinogen	Category 2 carcinogen
Category 1 carcinogen	≥0.1%	
Category 2 carcinogen		≥0.1% (note 1).

Note: *If a Category 2 carcinogen ingredient is present in the mixture at a concentration between 0.1% and 1%, information is required on the SDS for a product. However, a label warning is optional. If a Category 2 carcinogen ingredient is present in the mixture at a concentration of ≥1%, both an SDS and a label is required and the information must be included on each.*

---

[7] *It should be noted that the classification criteria for health hazards usually include a tiered scheme in which test data available on the complete mixture are considered as the first tier in the evaluation, followed by the applicable bridging principles, and lastly, cut-off values/concentration limit or additivity. However, this approach is not used for Carcinogenicity. These criteria for Carcinogenicity consider the cut-off values/concentration limits as the primary tier and allow the classification to be modified only on a case-by-case evaluation based on available test data for the mixture as a whole.*

A.6.3.2 CLASSIFICATION OF MIXTURES WHEN DATA ARE AVAILABLE FOR THE COMPLETE MIXTURE

A mixture may be classified based on the available test data for the mixture as a whole. In such cases, the test results for the mixture as a whole must be shown to be conclusive taking into account dose and other factors such as duration, observations and analysis (e.g., statistical analysis, test sensitivity) of carcinogenicity test systems.

A.6.3.3 CLASSIFICATION OF MIXTURES WHEN DATA ARE NOT AVAILABLE FOR THE COMPLETE MIXTURE: BRIDGING PRINCIPLES

Where the mixture itself has not been tested to determine its carcinogenic hazard, but there are sufficient data on both the individual ingredients and similar tested mixtures to adequately characterize the hazards of the mixture, these data will be used in accordance with the following bridging principles as found in paragraph A.0.5 of this Appendix: Dilution; Batching; and Substantially similar mixtures.

A.6.4 CLASSIFICATION OF CARCINOGENICITY [8]

A.6.4.1 Chemical manufacturers, importers and employers evaluating chemicals may treat the following sources as establishing that a substance is a carcinogen or potential carcinogen for hazard communication purposes in lieu of applying the criteria described herein:

A.6.4.1.1 National Toxicology Program (NTP), "Report on Carcinogens" (latest edition);

A.6.4.1.2 International Agency for Research on Cancer (IARC) "Monographs on the Evaluation of Carcinogenic Risks to Humans" (latest editions)

A.6.4.2 Where OSHA has included cancer as a health hazard to be considered by classifiers for a chemical covered by 29 CFR part 1910, Subpart Z, Toxic and Hazardous Substances, chemical manufacturers, importers, and employers shall classify the chemical as a carcinogen.

A.7 REPRODUCTIVE TOXICITY

A.7.1 DEFINITIONS AND GENERAL CONSIDERATIONS

A.7.1.1 *Reproductive toxicity* includes *adverse effects on sexual function and fertility* in adult males and females, as well as *adverse effects on development of the offspring*. Some reproductive toxic effects cannot be clearly assigned to either impairment of sexual function and fertility or to developmental toxicity. Nonetheless, chemicals with these effects shall be classified as reproductive toxicants.

For classification purposes, the known induction of genetically based inheritable effects in the offspring is addressed in *Germ cell mutagenicity* (See A.5).

A.7.1.2 *Adverse effects on sexual function and fertility* means any effect of chemicals that interferes with reproductive ability or sexual capacity. This includes, but is not limited to, alterations to the female and male reproductive system, adverse effects on onset of puberty, gamete production and transport, reproductive cycle normality, sexual behaviour, fertility, parturition, pregnancy outcomes, premature reproductive senescence, or modifications in other functions that are dependent on the integrity of the reproductive systems.

A.7.1.3 *Adverse effects on development of the offspring* means any effect of chemicals which interferes with normal development of the conceptus either before or after birth, which is induced during pregnancy or results from parental exposure. These effects can be manifested at any point in the life span of the organism. The major manifestations of developmental toxicity include death of the developing organism, structural abnormality, altered growth and functional deficiency.

A.7.1.4 Adverse effects on or via lactation are also included in reproductive toxicity, but for classification purposes, such effects are treated separately (See A.7.2.1).

A.7.2 CLASSIFICATION CRITERIA FOR SUBSTANCES

A.7.2.1 For the purpose of classification for reproductive toxicity, substances shall be classified in one of two categories in accordance with Figure A.7.1(a). Effects on sexual function and fertility, and on development, shall be considered. In addition, effects on or via lactation shall be classified in a separate hazard category in accordance with Figure A.7.1(b).

FIGURE A.7.1(a)—HAZARD CATEGORIES FOR REPRODUCTIVE TOXICANTS

CATEGORY 1: Known or presumed human reproductive toxicant.

---

[8] *See Non-mandatory Appendix F for further guidance regarding hazard classification for carcinogenicity and how to relate carcinogenicity classification information from IARC and NTP to GHS.*

FIGURE A.7.1(a)—HAZARD CATEGORIES FOR REPRODUCTIVE TOXICANTS—Continued

Substance shall be classified in Category 1 for reproductive toxicity when they are known to have produced an adverse effect on sexual function and fertility or on development in humans or when there is evidence from animal studies, possibly supplemented with other information, to provide a strong presumption that the substance has the capacity to interfere with reproduction in humans. The classification of a substance is further distinguished on the basis of whether the evidence for classification is primarily from human data (Category 1A) or from animal data (Category 1B).

Category 1A: Known human reproductive toxicant.
The classification of a substance in this category is largely based on evidence from humans.

Category 1B: Presumed human reproductive toxicant.
The classification of a substance in this category is largely based on evidence from experimental animals. Data from animal studies shall provide sufficient evidence of an adverse effect on sexual function and fertility or on development in the absence of other toxic effects, or if occurring together with other toxic effects the adverse effect on reproduction is considered not to be a secondary non-specific consequence of other toxic effects. However, when there is mechanistic information that raises doubt about the relevance of the effect for humans, classification in Category 2 may be more appropriate.

CATEGORY 2: Suspected human reproductive toxicant.
Substances shall be classified in Category 2 for reproductive toxicity when there is some evidence from humans or experimental animals, possibly supplemented with other information, of an adverse effect on sexual function and fertility, or on development, in the absence of other toxic effects, or if occurring together with other toxic effects the adverse effect on reproduction is considered not to be a secondary non-specific consequence of the other toxic effects, and where the evidence is not sufficiently convincing to place the substance in Category 1. For instance, deficiencies in the study may make the quality of evidence less convincing, and in view of this, Category 2 would be the more appropriate classification.

FIGURE A.7.1(b)—HAZARD CATEGORY FOR EFFECTS ON OR VIA LACTATION

EFFECTS ON OR VIA LACTATION
Effects on or via lactation shall be classified in a separate single category. Chemicals that are absorbed by women and have been shown to interfere with lactation or that may be present (including metabolites) in breast milk in amounts sufficient to cause concern for the health of a breastfed child, shall be classified to indicate this property hazardous to breastfed babies. This classification shall be assigned on the basis of:

(a) absorption, metabolism, distribution and excretion studies that indicate the likelihood the substance would be present in potentially toxic levels in breast milk; and/or

(b) results of one or two generation studies in animals which provide clear evidence of adverse effect in the offspring due to transfer in the milk or adverse effect on the quality of the milk; and/or

(c) human evidence indicating a hazard to babies during the lactation period.

A.7.2.2 BASIS OF CLASSIFICATION

A.7.2.2.1 Classification is made on the basis of the criteria, outlined above, an assessment of the total weight of evidence, and the use of expert judgment. Classification as a reproductive toxicant is intended to be used for substances which have an intrinsic, specific property to produce an adverse effect on reproduction and substances should not be so classified if such an effect is produced solely as a non-specific secondary consequence of other toxic effects.

A.7.2.2.2 In the evaluation of toxic effects on the developing offspring, it is important to consider the possible influence of maternal toxicity.

A.7.2.2.3 For human evidence to provide the primary basis for a Category 1A classification there must be reliable evidence of an adverse effect on reproduction in humans. Evidence used for classification shall be from well conducted epidemiological studies, if available, which include the use of appropriate controls, balanced assessment, and due consideration of bias or confounding factors. Less rigorous data from studies in humans may be sufficient for a Category 1A classification if supplemented with adequate data from studies in experimental animals, but classification in Category 1B may also be considered.

A.7.2.3 WEIGHT OF EVIDENCE

A.7.2.3.1 Classification as a reproductive toxicant is made on the basis of an assessment of the total weight of evidence using expert judgment. This means that all available information that bears on the determination of reproductive toxicity is considered together. Included is information such as epidemiological studies and case reports in humans and specific reproduction studies along with sub-chronic, chronic and special study results in animals that provide relevant information regarding toxicity to reproductive and related endocrine organs. Evaluation of substances chemically related to the material under study may also be included, particularly when information on the material is scarce. The weight given to the available evidence will be influenced by factors such as the quality of the studies, consistency of results, nature and severity of effects, level of statistical significance for intergroup differences, number of endpoints affected, relevance of route of administration to humans and freedom from bias. Both positive and negative results are considered together in a weight of evidence determination. However, a single, positive study performed according to good scientific principles and with statistically or biologically significant positive results may justify classification (See also A.7.2.2.3).

A.7.2.3.2 Toxicokinetic studies in animals and humans, site of action and mechanism or mode of action study results may provide relevant information, which could reduce or increase concerns about the hazard to human health. If it is conclusively demonstrated that the clearly identified mechanism or mode of action has no relevance for humans or when the toxicokinetic differences are so marked that it is certain that the hazardous property will not be expressed in humans then a chemical which produces an adverse effect on reproduction in experimental animals should not be classified.

A.7.2.3.3 In some reproductive toxicity studies in experimental animals the only effects recorded may be considered of low or minimal toxicological significance and clas-

sification may not necessarily be the outcome. These effects include, for example, small changes in semen parameters or in the incidence of spontaneous defects in the fetus, small changes in the proportions of common fetal variants such as are observed in skeletal examinations, or in fetal weights, or small differences in postnatal developmental assessments.

A.7.2.3.4 Data from animal studies shall provide sufficient evidence of specific reproductive toxicity in the absence of other systemic toxic effects. However, if developmental toxicity occurs together with other toxic effects in the dam (mother), the potential influence of the generalized adverse effects should be assessed to the extent possible. The preferred approach is to consider adverse effects in the embryo/fetus first, and then evaluate maternal toxicity, along with any other factors which are likely to have influenced these effects, as part of the weight of evidence. In general, developmental effects that are observed at maternally toxic doses should not be automatically discounted. Discounting developmental effects that are observed at maternally toxic doses can only be done on a case-by-case basis when a causal relationship is established or refuted.

A.7.2.3.5 If appropriate information is available it is important to try to determine whether developmental toxicity is due to a specific maternally mediated mechanism or to a non-specific secondary mechanism, like maternal stress and the disruption of homeostasis. Generally, the presence of maternal toxicity should not be used to negate findings of embryo/fetal effects, unless it can be clearly demonstrated that the effects are secondary non-specific effects. This is especially the case when the effects in the offspring are significant, e.g., irreversible effects such as structural malformations. In some situations it is reasonable to assume that reproductive toxicity is due to a secondary consequence of maternal toxicity and discount the effects, for example if the chemical is so toxic that dams fail to thrive and there is severe inanition; they are incapable of nursing pups; or they are prostrate or dying.

A.7.2.4 MATERNAL TOXICITY

A.7.2.4.1 Development of the offspring throughout gestation and during the early postnatal stages can be influenced by toxic effects in the mother either through non-specific mechanisms related to stress and the disruption of maternal homeostasis, or by specific maternally-mediated mechanisms. So, in the interpretation of the developmental outcome to decide classification for developmental effects it is important to consider the possible influence of maternal toxicity. This is a complex issue because of uncertainties surrounding the relationship between maternal toxicity and developmental outcome. Expert judgment and a weight of evidence approach, using all available studies, shall be used to determine the degree of influence to be attributed to maternal toxicity when interpreting the criteria for classification for developmental effects. The adverse effects in the embryo/fetus shall be first considered, and then maternal toxicity, along with any other factors which are likely to have influenced these effects, as weight of evidence, to help reach a conclusion about classification.

A.7.2.4.2 Based on pragmatic observation, it is believed that maternal toxicity may, depending on severity, influence development via non-specific secondary mechanisms, producing effects such as depressed fetal weight, retarded ossification, and possibly resorptions and certain malformations in some strains of certain species. However, the limited numbers of studies which have investigated the relationship between developmental effects and general maternal toxicity have failed to demonstrate a consistent, reproducible relationship across species. Developmental effects which occur even in the presence of maternal toxicity are considered to be evidence of developmental toxicity, unless it can be unequivocally demonstrated on a case by case basis that the developmental effects are secondary to maternal toxicity. Moreover, classification shall be considered where there is a significant toxic effect in the offspring, e.g., irreversible effects such as structural malformations, embryo/fetal lethality, or significant postnatal functional deficiencies.

A.7.2.4.3 Classification shall not automatically be discounted for chemicals that produce developmental toxicity only in association with maternal toxicity, even if a specific maternally-mediated mechanism has been demonstrated. In such a case, classification in Category 2 may be considered more appropriate than Category 1. However, when a chemical is so toxic that maternal death or severe inanition results, or the dams (mothers) are prostrate and incapable of nursing the pups, it is reasonable to assume that developmental toxicity is produced solely as a secondary consequence of maternal toxicity and discount the developmental effects. Classification is not necessarily the outcome in the case of minor developmental changes, e.g., a small reduction in fetal/pup body weight or retardation of ossification when seen in association with maternal toxicity.

A.7.2.4.4 Some of the endpoints used to assess maternal toxicity are provided below. Data on these endpoints, if available, shall be evaluated in light of their statistical or biological significance and dose-response relationship.

(a) Maternal mortality: An increased incidence of mortality among the treated dams over the controls shall be considered evidence of maternal toxicity if the increase occurs in a dose-related manner and can be attributed to the systemic toxicity of the test material. Maternal mortality greater than 10% is considered excessive and the data for that dose level shall not normally be considered to need further evaluation.

(b) Mating index (Number of animals with seminal plugs or sperm/Number of mated × 100)

(c) Fertility index (Number of animals with implants/Number of matings × 100)

(d) Gestation length (If allowed to deliver)

(e) Body weight and body weight change: Consideration of the maternal body weight change and/or adjusted (corrected) maternal body weight shall be included in the evaluation of maternal toxicity whenever such data are available. The calculation of an adjusted (corrected) mean maternal body weight change, which is the difference between the initial and terminal body weight minus the gravid uterine weight (or alternatively, the sum of the weights of the fetuses), may indicate whether the effect is maternal or intrauterine. In rabbits, the body weight gain may not be a useful indicator of maternal toxicity because of normal fluctuations in body weight during pregnancy.

(f) Food and water consumption (if relevant): The observation of a significant decrease in the average food or water consumption in treated dams (mothers) compared to the control group may be useful in evaluating maternal toxicity, particularly when the test material is administered in the diet or drinking water. Changes in food or water consumption must be evaluated in conjunction with maternal body weights when determining if the effects noted are reflective of maternal toxicity or more simply, unpalatability of the test material in feed or water.

(g) Clinical evaluations (including clinical signs, markers, and hematology and clinical chemistry studies): The observation of increased incidence of significant clinical signs of toxicity in treated dams (mothers) relative to the control group is useful in evaluating maternal toxicity. If this is to be used as the basis for the assessment of maternal toxicity, the types, incidence, degree and duration of clinical signs shall be reported in the study. Clinical signs of maternal intoxication include, but are not limited to: coma, prostration, hyperactivity, loss of righting reflex, ataxia, or labored breathing.

(h) Post-mortem data: Increased incidence and/or severity of post-mortem findings may be indicative of maternal toxicity. This can include gross or microscopic pathological findings or organ weight data, including absolute organ weight, organ-to-body weight ratio, or organ-to-brain weight ratio. When supported by findings of adverse histopathological effects in the affected organ(s), the observation of a significant change in the average weight of suspected target organ(s) of treated dams (mothers), compared to those in the control group, may be considered evidence of maternal toxicity.

A.7.2.5 ANIMAL AND EXPERIMENTAL DATA

A.7.2.5.1 A number of scientifically validated test methods are available, including methods for developmental toxicity testing (e.g., OECD Test Guideline 414, ICH Guideline S5A, 1993), methods for peri- and postnatal toxicity testing (e.g., ICH S5B, 1995), and methods for one or two-generation toxicity testing (e.g., OECD Test Guidelines 415, 416)

A.7.2.5.2 Results obtained from screening tests (e.g., OECD Guidelines 421—Reproduction/Developmental Toxicity Screening Test, and 422—Combined Repeated Dose Toxicity Study with Reproduction/Development Toxicity Screening Test) can also be used to justify classification, although the quality of this evidence is less reliable than that obtained through full studies.

A.7.2.5.3 Adverse effects or changes, seen in short- or long-term repeated dose toxicity studies, which are judged likely to impair reproductive function and which occur in the absence of significant generalized toxicity, may be used as a basis for classification, e.g., histopathological changes in the gonads.

A.7.2.5.4 Evidence from *in vitro* assays, or non-mammalian tests, and from analogous substances using structure-activity relationship (SAR), can contribute to the procedure for classification. In all cases of this nature, expert judgment must be used to assess the adequacy of the data. Inadequate data shall not be used as a primary support for classification.

A.7.2.5.5 It is preferable that animal studies are conducted using appropriate routes of administration which relate to the potential route of human exposure. However, in practice, reproductive toxicity studies are commonly conducted using the oral route, and such studies will normally be suitable for evaluating the hazardous properties of the substance with respect to reproductive toxicity. However, if it can be conclusively demonstrated that the clearly identified mechanism or mode of action has no relevance for humans or when the toxicokinetic differences are so marked that it is certain that the hazardous property will not be expressed in humans then a substance which produces an adverse effect on reproduction in experimental animals should not be classified.

A.7.2.5.6 Studies involving routes of administration such as intravenous or intraperitoneal injection, which may result in exposure of the reproductive organs to unrealistically high levels of the test substance, or elicit local damage to the reproductive organs, e.g., by irritation, must be interpreted with extreme caution and on their own are not normally the basis for classification.

A.7.2.5.7 There is general agreement about the concept of a limit dose, above which the production of an adverse effect may be considered to be outside the criteria which lead to classification. Some test guidelines specify a limit dose, other test guidelines qualify the limit dose with a statement that higher doses may be necessary if anticipated human exposure is sufficiently high that an adequate margin of exposure would not be achieved. Also, due to species differences in toxicokinetics, establishing a specific limit dose may not be adequate for situations where humans are more sensitive than the animal model.

A.7.2.5.8 In principle, adverse effects on reproduction seen only at very high dose levels in animal studies (for example doses that induce prostration, severe inappetence, excessive mortality) do not normally lead to classification, unless other information is available, for example, toxicokinetics information indicating that humans may be more susceptible than animals, to suggest that classification is appropriate.

A.7.2.5.9 However, specification of the actual "limit dose" will depend upon the test method that has been employed to provide the test results.

A.7.3 CLASSIFICATION CRITERIA FOR MIXTURES [9]

A.7.3.1 CLASSIFICATION OF MIXTURES WHEN DATA ARE AVAILABLE FOR ALL INGREDIENTS OR ONLY FOR SOME INGREDIENTS OF THE MIXTURE

A.7.3.1.1 The mixture shall be classified as a reproductive toxicant when at least one ingredient has been classified as a Category 1 or Category 2 reproductive toxicant and is present at or above the appropriate cut-off value/concentration limit specified in Table A.7.1 for Category 1 and 2, respectively.

---

[9] *It should be noted that the classification criteria for health hazards usually include a tiered scheme in which test data available on the complete mixture are considered as the first tier in the evaluation, followed by the applicable bridging principles, and lastly, cut-off values/concentration limits or additivity. However, this approach is not used for Reproductive Toxicity. These criteria for Reproductive Toxicity consider the cut-off values/concentration limits as the primary tier and allow the classification to be modified only on a case-by-case evaluation based on available test data for the mixture as a whole.*

A.7.3.1.2 The mixture shall be classified for effects on or via lactation when at least one ingredient has been classified for effects on or via lactation and is present at or above the appropriate cut-off value/concentration limit specified in Table A.7.1 for the additional category for effects on or via lactation.

TABLE A.7.1—Cut-Off Values/Concentration Limits of Ingredients of a Mixture Classified as Reproductive Toxicants or for Effects on or via Lactation That Trigger Classification of the Mixture

Ingredients classified as:	Cut-off values/concentration limits triggering classification of a mixture as:		
	Category 1 reproductive toxicant	Category 2 reproductive toxicant	Additional category for effects on or via lactation
Category 1 reproductive toxicant	≥0.1%	....	
Category 2 reproductive toxicant	....	≥0.1%	
Additional category for effects on or via lactation	....	....	≥0.1%

A.7.3.2 CLASSIFICATION OF MIXTURES WHEN DATA ARE AVAILABLE FOR THE COMPLETE MIXTURE

Available test data for the mixture as a whole may be used for classification on a case-by-case basis. In such cases, the test results for the mixture as a whole must be shown to be conclusive taking into account dose and other factors such as duration, observations and analysis (e.g., statistical analysis, test sensitivity) of reproduction test systems.

A.7.3.3 CLASSIFICATION OF MIXTURES WHEN DATA ARE NOT AVAILABLE FOR THE COMPLETE MIXTURE: BRIDGING PRINCIPLES

A.7.3.3.1 Where the mixture itself has not been tested to determine its reproductive toxicity, but there are sufficient data on both the individual ingredients and similar tested mixtures to adequately characterize the hazards of the mixture, these data shall be used in accordance with the following bridging principles as found in paragraph A.0.5 of this Appendix: Dilution, Batching, and Substantially similar mixtures.

A.8 SPECIFIC TARGET ORGAN TOXICITY SINGLE EXPOSURE

A.8.1 DEFINITIONS AND GENERAL CONSIDERATIONS

A.8.1.1 *Specific target organ toxicity—single exposure, (STOT-SE)* means specific, non-lethal target organ toxicity arising from a single exposure to a chemical. All significant health effects that can impair function, both reversible and irreversible, immediate and/or delayed and not specifically addressed in A.1 to A.7 and A.10 of this Appendix are included. Specific target organ toxicity following repeated exposure is classified in accordance with *SPECIFIC TARGET ORGAN TOXICITY— REPEATED EXPOSURE* (A.9 of this Appendix) and is therefore not included here.

A.8.1.2 Classification identifies the chemical as being a specific target organ toxicant and, as such, it presents a potential for adverse health effects in people who are exposed to it.

A.8.1.3 The adverse health effects produced by a single exposure include consistent and identifiable toxic effects in humans; or, in experimental animals, toxicologically significant changes which have affected the function or morphology of a tissue/organ, or have produced serious changes to the biochemistry or hematology of the organism, and these changes are relevant for human health. Human data is the primary source of evidence for this hazard class.

A.8.1.4 Assessment shall take into consideration not only significant changes in a single organ or biological system but also generalized changes of a less severe nature involving several organs.

A.8.1.5 Specific target organ toxicity can occur by any route that is relevant for humans, i.e., principally oral, dermal or inhalation.

A.8.1.6 The classification criteria for specific organ systemic toxicity single exposure are organized as criteria for substances Categories 1 and 2 (See A.8.2.1), criteria for substances Category 3 (See A.8.2.2) and criteria for mixtures (See A.8.3). See also Figure A.8.1.

A.8.2 CLASSIFICATION CRITERIA FOR SUBSTANCES

A.8.2.1 SUBSTANCES OF CATEGORY 1 AND CATEGORY 2

A.8.2.1.1 Substances shall be classified for immediate or delayed effects separately, by the use of expert judgment on the basis of the weight of all evidence available, including the use of recommended guidance values (See A.8.2.1.9). Substances shall then be classified in Category 1 or 2, depending upon the nature and severity of the effect(s) observed, in accordance with Figure A.8.1.

FIGURE A.8.1—HAZARD CATEGORIES FOR SPECIFIC TARGET ORGAN TOXICITY FOLLOWING SINGLE
EXPOSURE

CATEGORY 1: Substances that have produced significant toxicity in humans, or that, on the basis of evidence from studies in experimental animals can be presumed to have the potential to produce significant toxicity in humans following single exposure
Substances are classified in Category 1 for STOT–SE on the basis of:
(a) reliable and good quality evidence from human cases or epidemiological studies; or
(b) observations from appropriate studies in experimental animals in which significant and/or severe toxic effects of relevance to human health were produced at generally low exposure concentrations. Guidance dose/concentration values are provided below (See A.8.2.1.9) to be used as part of weight-of-evidence evaluation.
CATEGORY 2: Substances that, on the basis of evidence from studies in experimental animals, can be presumed to have the potential to be harmful to human health following single exposure
Substances are classified in Category 2 for STOT–SE on the basis of observations from appropriate studies in experimental animals in which significant toxic effects, of relevance to human health, were produced at generally moderate exposure concentrations. Guidance dose/concentration values are provided below (See A.8.2.1.9) in order to help in classification.
In exceptional cases, human evidence can also be used to place a substance in Category 2 (See A.8.2.1.6).
CATEGORY 3: Transient target organ effects
There are target organ effects for which a substance does not meet the criteria to be classified in Categories 1 or 2 indicated above. These are effects which adversely alter human function for a short duration after exposure and from which humans may recover in a reasonable period without leaving significant alteration of structure or function. This category only includes narcotic effects and respiratory tract irritation. Substances are classified specifically for these effects as discussed in A.8.2.2.
Note: The primary target organ/system shall be identified where possible, and where this is not possible, the substance shall be identified as a general toxicant. The data shall be evaluated and, where possible, shall not include secondary effects (e.g., a hepatotoxicant can produce secondary effects in the nervous or gastro-intestinal systems).

A.8.2.1.2 The relevant route(s) of exposure by which the classified substance produces damage shall be identified.

A.8.2.1.3 Classification is determined by expert judgment, on the basis of the weight of all evidence available including the guidance presented below.

A.8.2.1.4 Weight of evidence of all available data, including human incidents, epidemiology, and studies conducted in experimental animals is used to substantiate specific target organ toxic effects that merit classification.

A.8.2.1.5 The information required to evaluate specific target organ toxicity comes either from single exposure in humans (e.g., exposure at home, in the workplace or environmentally), or from studies conducted in experimental animals. The standard animal studies in rats or mice that provide this information are acute toxicity studies which can include clinical observations and detailed macroscopic and microscopic examination to enable the toxic effects on target tissues/organs to be identified. Results of acute toxicity studies conducted in other

species may also provide relevant information.

A.8.2.1.6 In exceptional cases, based on expert judgment, it may be appropriate to place certain substances with human evidence of target organ toxicity in Category 2: (a) when the weight of human evidence is not sufficiently convincing to warrant Category 1 classification, and/or (b) based on the nature and severity of effects. Dose/concentration levels in humans shall not be considered in the classification and any available evidence from animal studies shall be consistent with the Category 2 classification. In other words, if there are also animal data available on the substance that warrant Category 1 classification, the chemical shall be classified as Category 1.

A.8.2.1.7 Effects considered to support classification for Category 1 and 2

A.8.2.1.7.1 Classification is supported by evidence associating single exposure to the substance with a consistent and identifiable toxic effect.

A.8.2.1.7.2 Evidence from human experience/incidents is usually restricted to reports of adverse health consequences, often with uncertainty about exposure conditions, and may not provide the scientific detail that can be obtained from well-conducted studies in experimental animals.

A.8.2.1.7.3 Evidence from appropriate studies in experimental animals can furnish much more detail, in the form of clinical observations, and macroscopic and microscopic pathological examination and this can often reveal hazards that may not be life-threatening but could indicate functional impairment. Consequently all available evidence, and evidence relevance to human health, must be taken into consideration in the classification process. Relevant toxic effects in humans and/or animals include, but are not limited to:

(a) Morbidity resulting from single exposure;

(b) Significant functional changes, more than transient in nature, in the respiratory system, central or peripheral nervous systems, other organs or other organ systems, including signs of central nervous system depression and effects on special senses (e.g., sight, hearing and sense of smell);

(c) Any consistent and significant adverse change in clinical biochemistry, hematology, or urinalysis parameters;

(d) Significant organ damage that may be noted at necropsy and/or subsequently seen or confirmed at microscopic examination;

(e) Multi-focal or diffuse necrosis, fibrosis or granuloma formation in vital organs with regenerative capacity;

(f) Morphological changes that are potentially reversible but provide clear evidence of marked organ dysfunction; and,

(g) Evidence of appreciable cell death (including cell degeneration and reduced cell number) in vital organs incapable of regeneration.

A.8.2.1.8 Effects considered not to support classification for Category 1 and 2

Effects may be seen in humans and/or animals that do not justify classification. Such effects include, but are not limited to:

(a) Clinical observations or small changes in bodyweight gain, food consumption or water intake that may have some toxicological importance but that do not, by themselves, indicate "significant" toxicity;

(b) Small changes in clinical biochemistry, hematology or urinalysis parameters and/or transient effects, when such changes or effects are of doubtful or of minimal toxicological importance;

(c) Changes in organ weights with no evidence of organ dysfunction;

(d) Adaptive responses that are not considered toxicologically relevant; and,

(e) Substance-induced species-specific mechanisms of toxicity, i.e., demonstrated with reasonable certainty to be not relevant for human health, shall not justify classification.

A.8.2.1.9 Guidance values to assist with classification based on the results obtained from studies conducted in experimental animals for Category 1 and 2

A.8.2.1.9.1 In order to help reach a decision about whether a substance shall be classified or not, and to what degree it shall be classified (Category 1 vs. Category 2), dose/concentration "guidance values" are provided for consideration of the dose/concentration which has been shown to produce significant health effects. The principal argument for proposing such guidance values is that all chemicals are potentially toxic and there has to be a reasonable dose/concentration above which a degree of toxic effect is acknowledged.

A.8.2.1.9.2 Thus, in animal studies, when significant toxic effects are observed that indicate classification, consideration of the dose/concentration at which these effects were seen, in relation to the suggested guidance values, provides useful information to help assess the need to classify (since the toxic effects are a consequence of the hazardous property(ies) and also the dose/concentration).

A.8.2.1.9.3 The guidance value (C) ranges for single-dose exposure which has produced a significant non-lethal toxic effect are those applicable to acute toxicity testing, as indicated in Table A.8.1.

TABLE A.8.1—GUIDANCE VALUE RANGES FOR SINGLE-DOSE EXPOSURES

Route of exposure	Units	Guidance value ranges for:		
		Category 1	Category 2	Category 3
Oral (rat)	mg/kg body weight	C ≤300	2000 ≥C >300	Guidance values do not apply.
Dermal (rat or rabbit) ...	mg/kg body weight	C ≤1,000	2000 ≥C >1,000.	
Inhalation (rat) gas	ppmV/4h	C ≤2,500	20,000 ≥C >2,500.	
Inhalation (rat) vapor ...	mg/1/4h	C ≤10	20 ≥C >10.	
Inhalation (rat) dust/ mist/fume.	mg/l/4h	C ≤1.0	5.0 ≥C >1.0.	

A.8.2.1.9.4 The guidance values and ranges mentioned in Table A.8.1 are intended only for guidance purposes, i.e., to be used as part of the weight of evidence approach, and to assist with decisions about classification. They are not intended as strict demarcation values. Guidance values are not provided for Category 3 since this classification is primarily based on human data; animal data may be included in the weight of evidence evaluation.

A.8.2.1.9.5 Thus, it is feasible that a specific profile of toxicity occurs at a dose/concentration below the guidance value, e.g., <2000 mg/kg body weight by the oral route, however the nature of the effect may result in the decision not to classify. Conversely, a specific profile of toxicity may be seen in animal studies occurring at above a guidance value, e.g., ≥2000 mg/kg body weight by the oral route, and in addition there is supplementary information from other sources, e.g., other single dose studies, or human case experience, which supports a conclusion that, in view of the weight of evidence, classification is the prudent action to take.

A.8.2.1.10 Other considerations

A.8.2.1.10.1 When a substance is characterized only by use of animal data the classification process includes reference to dose/ concentration guidance values as one of the elements that contribute to the weight of evidence approach.

A.8.2.1.10.2 When , well-substantiated human data are available showing a specific target organ toxic effect that can be reliably attributed to single exposure to a substance, the substance shall be classified. Positive human data, regardless of probable dose, predominates over animal data. Thus, if a substance is unclassified because specific target organ toxicity observed was considered not relevant or significant to humans, if subsequent human incident data become available showing a specific target organ toxic effect, the substance shall be classified.

A.8.2.1.10.3 A substance that has not been tested for specific target organ toxicity shall, where appropriate, be classified on the basis of data from a scientifically validated structure activity relationship and expert judgment-based extrapolation from a structural analogue that has previously been classified together with substantial support from consideration of other important factors such as formation of common significant metabolites.

A.8.2.2 SUBSTANCES OF CATEGORY 3

A.8.2.2.1 Criteria for respiratory tract irritation

The criteria for classifying substances as Category 3 for respiratory tract irritation are:

(a) Respiratory irritant effects (characterized by localized redness, edema, pruritis and/or pain) that impair function with symptoms such as cough, pain, choking, and breathing difficulties are included. It is recognized that this evaluation is based primarily on human data;

(b) Subjective human observations supported by objective measurements of clear respiratory tract irritation (RTI) (e.g., electrophysiological responses, biomarkers of inflammation in nasal or bronchoalveolar lavage fluids);

(c) The symptoms observed in humans shall also be typical of those that would be produced in the exposed population rather than being an isolated idiosyncratic reaction or response triggered only in individuals with hypersensitive airways. Ambiguous reports simply of "irritation" should be excluded as this term is commonly used to describe a wide range of sensations including those such as smell, unpleasant taste, a tickling sensation, and dryness, which are outside the scope of classification for respiratory tract irritation;

(d) There are currently no scientifically validated animal tests that deal specifically with RTI; however, useful information may be obtained from the single and repeated inhalation toxicity tests. For example, animal studies may provide useful information in terms of clinical signs of toxicity (dyspnoea, rhinitis etc) and histopathology (e.g., hyperemia, edema, minimal inflammation, thickened mucous layer) which are reversible and may be reflective of the characteristic clinical symptoms described above. Such animal studies can be used as part of weight of evidence evaluation; and,

(e) This special classification will occur only when more severe organ effects including the respiratory system are not observed as those effects would require a higher classification.

A.8.2.2.2 Criteria for narcotic effects

The criteria for classifying substances in Category 3 for narcotic effects are:

(a) Central nervous system depression including narcotic effects in humans such as drowsiness, narcosis, reduced alertness, loss of reflexes, lack of coordination, and vertigo are included. These effects can also be manifested as severe headache or nausea, and can lead to reduced judgment, dizziness, irritability, fatigue, impaired memory function, deficits in perception and coordination, reaction time, or sleepiness; and,

(b) Narcotic effects observed in animal studies may include lethargy, lack of coordination righting reflex, narcosis, and ataxia. If these effects are not transient in nature, then they shall be considered for classification as Category 1 or 2.

A.8.3 CLASSIFICATION CRITERIA FOR MIXTURES

A.8.3.1 Mixtures are classified using the same criteria as for substances, or alternatively as described below. As with substances, mixtures may be classified for specific target organ toxicity following single exposure, repeated exposure, or both.

A.8.3.2 CLASSIFICATION OF MIXTURES WHEN DATA ARE AVAILABLE FOR THE COMPLETE MIXTURE

When reliable and good quality evidence from human experience or appropriate studies in experimental animals, as described in the criteria for substances, is available for the mixture, then the mixture shall be classified by weight of evidence evaluation of this data. Care shall be exercised in evaluating data on mixtures, that the dose, duration, observation or analysis, do not render the results inconclusive.

A.8.3.3 CLASSIFICATION OF MIXTURES WHEN DATA ARE NOT AVAILABLE FOR THE COMPLETE MIXTURE: BRIDGING PRINCIPLES

A.8.3.3.1 Where the mixture itself has not been tested to determine its specific target organ toxicity, but there are sufficient data on both the individual ingredients and similar tested mixtures to adequately characterize the hazards of the mixture, these data shall be used in accordance with the following bridging principles as found in paragraph A.0.5 of this Appendix: Dilution, Batching, Concentration of mixtures, Interpolation within one toxicity category, Substantially similar mixtures, or Aerosols.

A.8.3.4 CLASSIFICATION OF MIXTURES WHEN DATA ARE AVAILABLE FOR ALL INGREDIENTS OR ONLY FOR SOME INGREDIENTS OF THE MIXTURE

A.8.3.4.1 Where there is no reliable evidence or test data for the specific mixture itself, and the bridging principles cannot be used to enable classification, then classification of the mixture is based on the classification of the ingredient substances. In this case, the mixture shall be classified as a specific target organ toxicant (specific organ specified), following single exposure, repeated exposure, or both when at least one ingredient has been classified as a Category 1 or Category 2 specific target organ toxicant and is present at or above the appropriate cut-off value/concentration limit specified in Table A.8.2 for Categories 1 and 2, respectively.

TABLE A.8.2—CUT-OFF VALUES/CONCENTRATION LIMITS OF INGREDIENTS OF A MIXTURE CLASSIFIED AS A SPECIFIC TARGET ORGAN TOXICANT THAT WOULD TRIGGER CLASSIFICATION OF THE MIXTURE AS CATEGORY 1 OR 2

Ingredient classified as:	Cut-off values/concentration limits triggering classification of a mixture as:	
	Category 1	Category 2
Category 1 Target organ toxicant	≥1.0%	
Category 2 Target organ toxicant		≥1.0%

A.8.3.4.2 These cut-off values and consequent classifications shall be applied equally and appropriately to both single- and repeated-dose target organ toxicants.

A.8.3.4.3 Mixtures shall be classified for either or both single and repeated dose toxicity independently.

A.8.3.4.4 Care shall be exercised when toxicants affecting more than one organ system are combined that the potentiation or synergistic interactions are considered, because certain substances can cause target organ toxicity at <1% concentration when other ingredients in the mixture are known to potentiate its toxic effect.

A.8.3.4.5 Care shall be exercised when extrapolating the toxicity of a mixture that contains Category 3 ingredient(s). A cut-off value/concentration limit of 20%, considered as an additive of all Category 3 ingredients for each hazard endpoint, is appropriate; however, this cut-off value/concentration limit may be higher or lower depending on the Category 3 ingredient(s) involved and the fact that some effects such as respiratory tract irritation may not occur below a certain concentration while other effects such as narcotic effects may occur below this 20% value. Expert judgment shall be exercised. Respiratory tract irritation and narcotic effects are to be evaluated separately in accordance with the criteria given in A.8.2.2. When conducting classifications for these hazards, the contribution of each ingredient should be considered additive, unless there is evidence that the effects are not additive.

A.9 SPECIFIC TARGET ORGAN TOXICITY REPEATED OR PROLONGED EXPOSURE

A.9.1 DEFINITIONS AND GENERAL CONSIDERATIONS

A.9.1.1 *Specific target organ toxicity—repeated exposure (STOT–RE)* means specific target organ toxicity arising from repeated exposure to a substance or mixture. All significant health effects that can impair function, both reversible and irreversible, immediate and/or delayed and not specifically addressed in A.1 to A.7 and A.10 of this Appendix are included. Specific target organ toxicity following a single-event exposure is classified in accordance with *SPECIFIC TARGET ORGAN TOXICITY—SINGLE EXPOSURE* (A.8 of this Appendix) and is therefore not included here.

A.9.1.2 Classification identifies the substance or mixture as being a specific target organ toxicant and, as such, it may present a potential for adverse health effects in people who are exposed to it.

A.9.1.3 These adverse health effects produced by repeated exposure include consistent and identifiable toxic effects in humans, or, in experimental animals, toxicologically significant changes which have affected the function or morphology of a tissue/organ, or have produced serious changes to the biochemistry or hematology of the organism and these changes are rel-

evant for human health. Human data will be the primary source of evidence for this hazard class.

A.9.1.4 Assessment shall take into consideration not only significant changes in a single organ or biological system but also generalized changes of a less severe nature involving several organs.

A.9.1.5 Specific target organ toxicity can occur by any route that is relevant for humans, e.g., principally oral, dermal or inhalation.

A.9.2 CLASSIFICATION CRITERIA FOR SUBSTANCES

A.9.2.1 Substances shall be classified as STOT–RE by expert judgment on the basis of the weight of all evidence available, including the use of recommended guidance values which take into account the duration of exposure and the dose/concentration which produced the effect(s), (See A.9.2.9). Substances shall be placed in one of two categories, depending upon the nature and severity of the effect(s) observed, in accordance with Figure A.9.1.

FIGURE A.9.1—HAZARD CATEGORIES FOR SPECIFIC TARGET ORGAN TOXICITY FOLLOWING REPEATED EXPOSURE

CATEGORY 1: Substances that have produced significant toxicity in humans, or that, on the basis of evidence from studies in experimental animals can be presumed to have the potential to produce significant toxicity in humans following repeated or prolonged exposure

Substances are classified in Category 1 for specific target organ toxicity (repeated exposure) on the basis of:

(a) reliable and good quality evidence from human cases or epidemiological studies; or,

(b) observations from appropriate studies in experimental animals in which significant and/or severe toxic effects, of relevance to human health, were produced at generally low exposure concentrations. Guidance dose/concentration values are provided below (See A.9.2.9) to be used as part of weight-of-evidence evaluation.

CATEGORY 2: Substances that, on the basis of evidence from studies in experimental animals can be presumed to have the potential to be harmful to human health following repeated or prolonged exposure

Substances are classified in Category 2 for specific target organ toxicity (repeated exposure) on the basis of observations from appropriate studies in experimental animals in which significant toxic effects, of relevance to human health, were produced at generally moderate exposure concentrations. Guidance dose/concentration values are provided below (See A.9.2.9) in order to help in classification.

In exceptional cases human evidence can also be used to place a substance in Category 2 (See A.9.2.6).

Note: The primary target organ/system shall be identified where possible, or the substance shall be identified as a general toxicant. The data shall be carefully evaluated and, where possible, shall not include secondary effects (e.g., a hepatotoxicant can produce secondary effects in the nervous or gastro-intestinal systems).

A.9.2.2 The relevant route of exposure by which the classified substance produces damage shall be identified.

A.9.2.3 Classification is determined by expert judgment, on the basis of the weight of all evidence available including the guidance presented below.

A.9.2.4 Weight of evidence of all data, including human incidents, epidemiology, and studies conducted in experimental animals, is used to substantiate specific target organ toxic effects that merit classification.

A.9.2.5 The information required to evaluate specific target organ toxicity comes either from repeated exposure in humans, e.g., exposure at home, in the workplace or environmentally, or from studies conducted in experimental animals. The standard animal studies in rats or mice that provide this information are 28 day, 90 day or lifetime studies (up to 2 years) that include hematological, clinico-chemical and detailed macroscopic and microscopic examination to enable the toxic effects on target tissues/organs to be identified. Data from repeat dose studies performed in other species may also be used. Other long-term exposure studies, e.g., for carcinogenicity, neurotoxicity or reproductive toxicity, may also provide evidence of specific target organ toxicity that could be used in the assessment of classification.

A.9.2.6 In exceptional cases, based on expert judgment, it may be appropriate to place certain substances with human evidence of specific target organ toxicity in Category 2: (a) when the weight of human evidence is not sufficiently convincing to warrant Category 1 classification, and/or (b) based on the nature and severity of effects. Dose/concentration levels in humans shall not be considered in the classification and any available evidence from animal studies shall be consistent with the Category 2 classification. In other words, if there are also animal data available on the substance that warrant Category 1 classification, the substance shall be classified as Category 1.

A.9.2.7 EFFECTS CONSIDERED TO SUPPORT CLASSIFICATION

A.9.2.7.1 Classification is supported by reliable evidence associating repeated exposure to the substance with a consistent and identifiable toxic effect.

A.9.2.7.2 Evidence from human experience/incidents is usually restricted to reports of adverse health consequences, often with uncertainty about exposure conditions, and may not provide the scientific detail that can be obtained from well-conducted studies in experimental animals.

A.9.2.7.3 Evidence from appropriate studies in experimental animals can furnish much more detail, in the form of clinical observations, hematology, clinical chemistry, macroscopic and microscopic pathological examination and this can often reveal hazards that may not be life-threatening but could indicate functional impairment. Consequently all available evidence, and relevance to human health, must be taken into consideration in the classification process.

Relevant toxic effects in humans and/or animals include, but are not limited to:

(a) Morbidity or death resulting from repeated or long-term exposure. Morbidity or death may result from repeated exposure, even to relatively low doses/concentrations, due to bioaccumulation of the substance or its metabolites, or due to the overwhelming of the de-toxification process by repeated exposure;

(b) Significant functional changes in the central or peripheral nervous systems or other organ systems, including signs of central nervous system depression and effects on special senses (e.g., sight, hearing and sense of smell);

(c) Any consistent and significant adverse change in clinical biochemistry, hematology, or urinalysis parameters;

(d) Significant organ damage that may be noted at necropsy and/or subsequently seen or confirmed at microscopic examination;

(e) Multi-focal or diffuse necrosis, fibrosis or granuloma formation in vital organs with regenerative capacity;

(f) Morphological changes that are potentially reversible but provide clear evidence of marked organ dysfunction (e.g., severe fatty change in the liver); and,

(g) Evidence of appreciable cell death (including cell degeneration and reduced cell number) in vital organs incapable of regeneration.

A.9.2.8 EFFECTS CONSIDERED NOT TO SUPPORT CLASSIFICATION

Effects may be seen in humans and/or animals that do not justify classification. Such effects include, but are not limited to:

(a) Clinical observations or small changes in bodyweight gain, food consumption or water intake that may have some toxicological importance but that do not, by themselves, indicate "significant" toxicity;

(b) Small changes in clinical biochemistry, hematology or urinalysis parameters and/or transient effects, when such changes or effects are of doubtful or of minimal toxicological importance;

(c) Changes in organ weights with no evidence of organ dysfunction;

(d) Adaptive responses that are not considered toxicologically relevant;

(e) Substance-induced species-specific mechanisms of toxicity, i.e., demonstrated with reasonable certainty to be not relevant for human health, shall not justify classification.

A.9.2.9 GUIDANCE VALUES TO ASSIST WITH CLASSIFICATION BASED ON THE RESULTS OBTAINED FROM STUDIES CONDUCTED IN EXPERIMENTAL ANIMALS

A.9.2.9.1 In studies conducted in experimental animals, reliance on observation of effects alone, without reference to the duration of experimental exposure and dose/concentration, omits a fundamental concept of toxicology, i.e., all substances are potentially toxic, and what determines the toxicity is a function of the dose/concentration and the duration of exposure. In most studies conducted in experimental animals the test guidelines use an upper limit dose value.

A.9.2.9.2 In order to help reach a decision about whether a substance shall be classified or not, and to what degree it shall be classified (Category 1 vs. Category 2), dose/concentration "guidance values" are provided in Table A.9.1 for consideration of the dose/concentration which has been shown to produce significant health effects. The principal argument for proposing such guidance values is that all chemicals are potentially toxic and there has to be a reasonable dose/concentration above which a degree of toxic effect is acknowledged. Also, repeated-dose studies conducted in experimental animals are designed to produce toxicity at the highest dose used in order to optimize the test objective and so most studies will reveal some toxic effect at least at this highest dose. What is therefore to be decided is not only what effects have been produced, but also at what dose/concentration they were produced and how relevant is that for humans.

A.9.2.9.3 Thus, in animal studies, when significant toxic effects are observed that indicate classification, consideration of the du-ration of experimental exposure and the dose/concentration at which these effects were seen, in relation to the suggested guidance values, provides useful information to help assess the need to classify (since the toxic effects are a consequence of the hazardous property(ies) and also the duration of exposure and the dose/concentration).

A.9.2.9.4 The decision to classify at all can be influenced by reference to the dose/concentration guidance values at or below which a significant toxic effect has been observed.

A.9.2.9.5 The guidance values refer to effects seen in a standard 90-day toxicity study conducted in rats. They can be used as a basis to extrapolate equivalent guidance values for toxicity studies of greater or lesser duration, using dose/exposure time extrapolation similar to Haber's rule for inhalation, which states essentially that the effective dose is directly proportional to the exposure concentration and the duration of exposure. The assessment should be done on a case-by-case basis; for example, for a 28-day study the guidance values below would be increased by a factor of three.

A.9.2.9.6 Thus for Category 1 classification, significant toxic effects observed in a 90-day repeated-dose study conducted in experimental animals and seen to occur at or below the (suggested) guidance values (C) as indicated in Table A.9.1 would justify classification:

TABLE A.9.1—GUIDANCE VALUES TO ASSIST IN CATEGORY 1 CLASSIFICATION

[Applicable to a 90-day study]

Route of exposure	Units	Guidance values (dose/concentration)
Oral (rat)	mg/kg body weight/day	C ≤10.
Dermal (rat or rabbit)	mg/kg body weight/day	C ≤20.
Inhalation (rat) gas	ppmV/6h/day	C ≤50.
Inhalation (rat) vapor	mg/liter/6h/day	C ≤0.2.
Inhalation (rat) dust/mist/fume	mg/liter/6h/day	C ≤0.02.

A.9.2.9.7 For Category 2 classification, significant toxic effects observed in a 90-day repeated-dose study conducted in experimental animals and seen to occur within the (suggested) guidance value ranges as indicated in Table A.9.2 would justify classification:

TABLE A.9.2—GUIDANCE VALUES TO ASSIST IN CATEGORY 2 CLASSIFICATION

[Applicable to a 90-day study]

Route of exposure	Units	Guidance values (dose/concentration)
Oral (rat)	mg/kg body weight/day	10 <C ≤100.
Dermal (rat or rabbit)	mg/kg body weight/day	20 <C ≤200.
Inhalation (rat) gas	ppmV/6h/day	50 <C ≤250.
Inhalation (rat) vapor	mg/liter/6h/day	0.2 <C ≤1.0.
Inhalation (rat) dust/mist/fume	mg/liter/6h/day	0.02 <C ≤0.2.

A.9.2.9.8 The guidance values and ranges mentioned in A.2.9.9.6 and A.2.9.9.7 are intended only for guidance purposes, i.e., to be used as part of the weight of evidence approach, and to assist with decisions about classification. They are not intended as strict demarcation values.

A.9.2.9.9 Thus, it is possible that a specific profile of toxicity occurs in repeat-dose animal studies at a dose/concentration below the guidance value, e.g., <100 mg/kg body weight/day by the oral route, however the nature of the effect, e.g., nephrotoxicity seen only in male rats of a particular strain known to be susceptible to this effect, may result in the decision not to classify. Conversely, a specific profile of toxicity may be seen in animal studies occurring at above a guidance value, e.g., ≥100 mg/kg body weight/day by the oral route, and in addition there is supplementary information from other sources, e.g., other long-term administration studies, or human case experience, which supports a conclusion that, in view of the weight of evidence, classification is prudent.

A.9.2.10 OTHER CONSIDERATIONS

A.9.2.10.1 When a substance is characterized only by use of animal data the classification process includes reference to dose/concentration guidance values as one of the elements that contribute to the weight of evidence approach.

A.9.2.10.2 When well-substantiated human data are available showing a specific target organ toxic effect that can be reliably attributed to repeated or prolonged exposure to a substance, the substance shall be classified. Positive human data, regardless of probable dose, predominates over animal data. Thus, if a substance is unclassified because no specific target organ toxicity was seen at or below the dose/concentration guidance value for animal testing, if subsequent human incident data become available showing a specific target organ toxic effect, the substance shall be classified.

A.9.2.10.3 A substance that has not been tested for specific target organ toxicity may in certain instances, where appropriate, be classified on the basis of data from a scientifically validated structure activity relationship and expert judgment-based extrapolation from a structural analogue that has previously been classified together with substantial support from consideration of other important factors such as formation of common significant metabolites.

A.9.3 CLASSIFICATION CRITERIA FOR MIXTURES

A.9.3.1 Mixtures are classified using the same criteria as for substances, or alternatively as described below. As with substances, mixtures may be classified for specific target organ toxicity following single exposure, repeated exposure, or both.

A.9.3.2 CLASSIFICATION OF MIXTURES WHEN DATA ARE AVAILABLE FOR THE COMPLETE MIXTURE

When reliable and good quality evidence from human experience or appropriate studies in experimental animals, as described in the criteria for substances, is available for the mixture, then the mixture shall be classified by weight of evidence evaluation of these data. Care shall be exercised in evaluating data on mixtures, that the dose, duration, observation or analysis, do not render the results inconclusive.

A.9.3.3 CLASSIFICATION OF MIXTURES WHEN DATA ARE NOT AVAILABLE FOR THE COMPLETE MIXTURE: BRIDGING PRINCIPLES

A.9.3.3.1 Where the mixture itself has not been tested to determine its specific target organ toxicity, but there are sufficient data on both the individual ingredients and similar tested mixtures to adequately characterize the hazards of the mixture, these data shall be used in accordance with the following bridging principles as found in paragraph A.0.5 of this Appendix: Dilution; Batching; Concentration of mixtures; Interpolation within one toxicity category; Substantially similar mixtures; and Aerosols.

A.9.3.4 CLASSIFICATION OF MIXTURES WHEN DATA ARE AVAILABLE FOR ALL INGREDIENTS OR ONLY FOR SOME INGREDIENTS OF THE MIXTURE

A.9.3.4.1 Where there is no reliable evidence or test data for the specific mixture itself, and the bridging principles cannot be used to enable classification, then classification of the mixture is based on the classification of the ingredient substances. In this case, the mixture shall be classified as a specific target organ toxicant (specific organ specified), following single exposure, repeated exposure, or both when at least one ingredient has been classified as a Category 1 or Category 2 specific target organ toxicant and is present at or above the appropriate cut-off value/concentration limit specified in Table A.9.3 for Category 1 and 2 respectively.

TABLE A.9.3—CUT-OFF VALUE/CONCENTRATION LIMITS OF INGREDIENTS OF A MIXTURE CLASSIFIED AS A SPECIFIC TARGET ORGAN TOXICANT THAT WOULD TRIGGER CLASSIFICATION OF THE MIXTURE AS CATEGORY 1 OR 2

Ingredient classified as:	Cut-off values/concentration limits triggering classification of a mixture as:	
	Category 1	Category 2
Category 1 Target organ toxicant	≥1.0%	
Category 2 Target organ toxicant	....	≥1.0%

A.9.3.4.2 These cut-off values and consequent classifications shall be applied equally and appropriately to both single- and repeated-dose target organ toxicants.

A.9.3.4.3 Mixtures shall be classified for either or both single- and repeated-dose toxicity independently.

A.9.3.4.4 Care shall be exercised when toxicants affecting more than one organ system are combined that the potentiation or synergistic interactions are considered, because certain substances can cause specific target organ toxicity at <1% concentration when other ingredients in the mixture are known to potentiate its toxic effect.

A.10   ASPIRATION HAZARD

A.10.1   DEFINITIONS AND GENERAL AND SPECIFIC CONSIDERATIONS

A.10.1.1   *Aspiration* means the entry of a liquid or solid chemical directly through the oral or nasal cavity, or indirectly from vomiting, into the trachea and lower respiratory system.

A.10.1.2   Aspiration toxicity includes severe acute effects such as chemical pneumonia, varying degrees of pulmonary injury or death following aspiration.

A.10.1.3   Aspiration is initiated at the moment of inspiration, in the time required to take one breath, as the causative material lodges at the crossroad of the upper respiratory and digestive tracts in the laryngopharyngeal region.

A.10.1.4   Aspiration of a substance or mixture can occur as it is vomited following ingestion. This may have consequences for labeling, particularly where, due to acute toxicity, a recommendation may be considered to induce vomiting after ingestion. However, if the substance/mixture also presents an aspiration toxicity hazard, the recommendation to induce vomiting may need to be modified.

A.10.1.5   SPECIFIC CONSIDERATIONS

A.10.1.5.1   The classification criteria refer to kinematic viscosity. The following provides the conversion between dynamic and kinematic viscosity:

$$\frac{\text{Dynamic viscosity (mPa·s)}}{\text{Density (g/cm}^3)} = \text{Kinematic viscosity (mm}^2/\text{s)}$$

A.10.1.5.2   Although the definition of aspiration in A.10.1.1 includes the entry of solids into the respiratory system, classification according to (b) in table A.10.1 for Category 1 is intended to apply to liquid substances and mixtures only.

A.10.1.5.3   Classification of aerosol/mist products.

Aerosol and mist products are usually dispensed in containers such as self-pressurized containers, trigger and pump sprayers. Classification for these products shall be considered if their use may form a pool of product in the mouth, which then may be aspirated. If the mist or aerosol from a pressurized container is fine, a pool may not be formed. On the other hand, if a pressurized container dispenses product in a stream, a pool may be formed that may then be aspirated. Usually, the mist produced by trigger and pump sprayers is coarse and therefore, a pool may be formed that then may be aspirated. When the pump mechanism may be removed and contents are available to be swallowed then the classification of the products should be considered.

A.10.2   CLASSIFICATION CRITERIA FOR SUBSTANCES

TABLE A.10.1—CRITERIA FOR ASPIRATION TOXICITY

Category	Criteria
Category 1: Chemicals known to cause human aspiration toxicity hazards or to be regarded as if they cause human aspiration toxicity hazard.	A substance shall be classified in Category 1: (a) If reliable and good quality human evidence indicates that it causes aspiration toxicity (See note); or (b) If it is a hydrocarbon and has a kinematic viscosity ≤20.5 mm²/s, measured at 40 °C.

Note: Examples of substances included in Category 1 are certain hydrocarbons, turpentine and pine oil.

A.10.3 CLASSIFICATION CRITERIA FOR MIXTURES

A.10.3.1 CLASSIFICATION WHEN DATA ARE AVAILABLE FOR THE COMPLETE MIXTURE

A mixture shall be classified in Category 1 based on reliable and good quality human evidence.

A.10.3.2 CLASSIFICATION OF MIXTURES WHEN DATA ARE NOT AVAILABLE FOR THE COMPLETE MIXTURE: BRIDGING PRINCIPLES

A.10.3.2.1 Where the mixture itself has not been tested to determine its aspiration toxicity, but there are sufficient data on both the individual ingredients and similar tested mixtures to adequately characterize the hazard of the mixture, these data shall be used in accordance with the following bridging principles as found in paragraph A.0.5 of this Appendix: Dilution; Batching; Concentration of mixtures; Interpolation within one toxicity category; and Substantially similar mixtures. For application of the dilution bridging principle, the concentration of aspiration toxicants shall be not less than 10%.

A.10.3.3 CLASSIFICATION OF MIXTURES WHEN DATA ARE AVAILABLE FOR ALL INGREDIENTS OR ONLY FOR SOME INGREDIENTS OF THE MIXTURE

A.10.3.3.1 A mixture which contains ≥10% of an ingredient or ingredients classified in Category 1, and has a kinematic viscosity ≤20.5 mm²/s, measured at 40 °C, shall be classified in Category 1.

A.10.3.3.2 In the case of a mixture which separates into two or more distinct layers, one of which contains ≥10% of an ingredient or ingredients classified in Category 1 and has a kinematic viscosity ≤20.5 mm²/s, measured at 40 °C, then the entire mixture shall be classified in Category 1.

APPENDIX B TO §1910.1200—PHYSICAL CRITERIA (MANDATORY)

B.1 EXPLOSIVES

B.1.1 DEFINITIONS AND GENERAL CONSIDERATIONS

B.1.1.1 An *explosive chemical* is a solid or liquid chemical which is in itself capable by chemical reaction of producing gas at such a temperature and pressure and at such a speed as to cause damage to the surroundings. Pyrotechnic chemicals are included even when they do not evolve gases.

A *pyrotechnic chemical* is a chemical designed to produce an effect by heat, light, sound, gas or smoke or a combination of these as the result of non-detonative self-sustaining exothermic chemical reactions.

An *explosive item* is an item containing one or more explosive chemicals.

A *pyrotechnic item* is an item containing one or more pyrotechnic chemicals.

An *unstable explosive* is an explosive which is thermally unstable and/or too sensitive for normal handling, transport, or use.

An *intentional explosive* is a chemical or item which is manufactured with a view to produce a practical explosive or pyrotechnic effect.

B.1.1.2 The class of explosives comprises:

(a) Explosive chemicals;

(b) Explosive items, except devices containing explosive chemicals in such quantity or of such a character that their inadvertent or accidental ignition or initiation shall not cause any effect external to the device either by projection, fire, smoke, heat or loud noise; and

(c) Chemicals and items not included under (a) and (b) above which are manufactured with the view to producing a practical explosive or pyrotechnic effect.

B.1.2 CLASSIFICATION CRITERIA

Chemicals and items of this class shall be classified as unstable explosives or shall be assigned to one of the following six divisions depending on the type of hazard they present:

(a) Division 1.1—Chemicals and items which have a mass explosion hazard (a mass explosion is one which affects almost the entire quantity present virtually instantaneously);

(b) Division 1.2—Chemicals and items which have a projection hazard but not a mass explosion hazard;

(c) Division 1.3—Chemicals and items which have a fire hazard and either a minor blast hazard or a minor projection hazard or both, but not a mass explosion hazard:

(i) Combustion of which gives rise to considerable radiant heat; or

(ii) Which burn one after another, producing minor blast or projection effects or both;

(d) Division 1.4—Chemicals and items which present no significant hazard: chemicals and items which present only a small hazard in the event of ignition or initiation. The effects are largely confined to the package and no projection of fragments of appreciable size or range is to be expected. An external fire shall not cause virtually instantaneous explosion of almost the entire contents of the package;

(e) Division 1.5—Very insensitive chemicals which have a mass explosion hazard: chemicals which have a mass explosion hazard but are so insensitive that there is very little probability of initiation or of transition from burning to detonation under normal conditions;

(f) Division 1.6—Extremely insensitive items which do not have a mass explosion hazard: items which contain only extremely insensitive detonating chemicals and which demonstrate a negligible probability of accidental initiation or propagation.

B.1.3 ADDITIONAL CLASSIFICATION CONSIDERATIONS

B.1.3.1 Explosives shall be classified as unstable explosives or shall be assigned to one of the six divisions identified in B.1.2 in accordance with the three step procedure in Part I of the UN ST/SG/AC.10 (incorporated by reference; See § 1910.6). The first step is to ascertain whether the substance or mixture has explosive effects (Test Series 1). The second step is the acceptance procedure (Test Series 2 to 4) and the third step is the assignment to a hazard division (Test Series 5 to 7). The assessment whether a candidate for "ammonium nitrate emulsion or suspension or gel, intermediate for blasting explosives (ANE)" is insensitive enough for inclusion as an oxidizing liquid (See B.13) or an oxidizing solid (See B.14) is determined by Test Series 8 tests.

NOTE: Classification of solid chemicals shall be based on tests performed on the chemical as presented. If, for example, for the purposes of supply or transport, the same chemical is to be presented in a physical form different from that which was tested and which is considered likely to materially alter its performance in a classification test, classification must be based on testing of the chemical in the new form.

B.1.3.2 Explosive properties are associated with the presence of certain chemical groups in a molecule which can react to produce very rapid increases in temperature or pressure. The screening procedure in B.1.3.1 is aimed at identifying the presence of such reactive groups and the potential for rapid energy release. If the screening procedure identifies the chemical as a potential explosive, the acceptance procedure (See section 10.3 of the UN ST/SG/AC.10 (incorporated by reference; See § 1910.6)) is necessary for classification.

NOTE: Neither a Series 1 type (a) propagation of detonation test nor a Series 2 type (a) test of sensitivity to detonative shock is necessary if the exothermic decomposition energy of organic materials is less than 800 J/g.

B.1.3.3 If a mixture contains any known explosives, the acceptance procedure is necessary for classification.

B.1.3.4 A chemical is not classified as explosive if:

(a) There are no chemical groups associated with explosive properties present in the molecule. Examples of groups which may indicate explosive properties are given in Table A6.1 in Appendix 6 of the UN ST/SG/AC.10 (incorporated by reference; See § 1910.6); or

(b) The substance contains chemical groups associated with explosive properties which include oxygen and the calculated oxygen balance is less than -200.

The oxygen balance is calculated for the chemical reaction:

$$C_XH_YO_Z + [x + (y/4) - (z/2)] O_2 \rightarrow x. CO_2 + (y/2) H_2O$$

using the formula:

oxygen balance = $-1600 [2x + (y/2) -z]$/molecular weight;

or

(c) The organic substance or a homogenous mixture of organic substances contains chemical groups associated with explosive properties but the exothermic decomposition energy is less than 500 J/g and the onset of exothermic decomposition is below 500 °C (932 °F). The exothermic decomposition energy may be determined using a suitable calorimetric technique; or

(d) For mixtures of inorganic oxidizing substances with organic material(s), the concentration of the inorganic oxidizing substance is:

(i) Less than 15%, by mass, if the oxidizing substance is assigned to Category 1 or 2;

(ii) Less than 30%, by mass, if the oxidizing substance is assigned to Category 3.

B.2 FLAMMABLE GASES

B.2.1 DEFINITION

Flammable gas means a gas having a flammable range with air at 20 °C (68 °F) and a standard pressure of 101.3 kPa (14.7 psi).

B.2.2 CLASSIFICATION CRITERIA

A flammable gas shall be classified in one of the two categories for this class in accordance with Table B.2.1:

TABLE B.2.1—CRITERIA FOR FLAMMABLE GASES

Category	Criteria
1	Gases, which at 20 °C (68 °F) and a standard pressure of 101.3 kPa (14.7 psi): (a) are ignitable when in a mixture of 13% or less by volume in air; or (b) have a flammable range with air of at least 12 percentage points regardless of the lower flammable limit.
2	Gases, other than those of Category 1, which, at 20 °C (68 °F) and a standard pressure of 101.3 kPa (14.7 psi), have a flammable range while mixed in air.

NOTE: Aerosols should not be classified as flammable gases. See B.3.

B.2.3 ADDITIONAL CLASSIFICATION CONSIDERATIONS

Flammability shall be determined by tests or by calculation in accordance with ISO 10156 (incorporated by reference; See §1910.6). Where insufficient data are available to use this method, equivalent validated methods may be used.

B.3 FLAMMABLE AEROSOLS

B.3.1 DEFINITION

Aerosol means any non-refillable receptacle containing a gas compressed, liquefied or dissolved under pressure, and fitted with a release device allowing the contents to be ejected as particles in suspension in a gas, or as a foam, paste, powder, liquid or gas.

B.3.2 CLASSIFICATION CRITERIA

B.3.2.1 Aerosols shall be considered for classification as flammable if they contain any component which is classified as flammable in accordance with this Appendix, i.e.:

Flammable liquids (See B.6);
Flammable gases (See B.2);
Flammable solids (See B.7).

NOTE 1: Flammable components do not include pyrophoric, self-heating or water-reactive chemicals.

NOTE 2: Flammable aerosols do not fall additionally within the scope of flammable gases, flammable liquids, or flammable solids.

B.3.2.2 A flammable aerosol shall be classified in one of the two categories for this class in accordance with Table B.3.1.

TABLE B.3.1—CRITERIA FOR FLAMMABLE AEROSOLS

Category	Criteria

1	Contains ≥85% flammable components and the chemical heat of combustion is ≥30 kJ/g; or
	(a) For spray aerosols, in the ignition distance test, ignition occurs at a distance ≥75 cm (29.5 in), or
	(b) For foam aerosols, in the aerosol foam flammability test
	   (i) The flame height is ≥20 cm (7.87 in) and the flame duration ≥2 s; or
	   (ii) The flame height is ≥4 cm (1.57 in) and the flame duration ≥7 s

2	Contains >1% flammable components, or the heat of combustion is ≥20 kJ/g; and
	(a) for spray aerosols, in the ignition distance test, ignition occurs at a distance ≥15 cm (5.9 in), or in the enclosed space ignition test, the
	   (i) Time equivalent is ≤300 s/m³; or
	   (ii) Deflagration density is ≤300 g/m³
	(b) For foam aerosols, in the aerosol foam flammability test, the flame height is ≥4 cm and the flame duration is ≥2 s
	and it does not meet the criteria for Category 1

NOTE: Aerosols not submitted to the flammability classification procedures in this Appendix shall be classified as extremely flammable (Category 1).

B.3.3 ADDITIONAL CLASSIFICATION CONSIDERATIONS

B.3.3.1 To classify a flammable aerosol, data on its flammable components, on its chemical heat of combustion and, if applicable, the results of the aerosol foam flammability test (for foam aerosols) and of the igni-tion distance test and enclosed space test (for spray aerosols) are necessary.

B.3.3.2 The chemical heat of combustion (ΔHc), in kilojoules per gram (kJ/g), is the product of the theoretical heat of combustion ($\Delta Hcomb$), and a combustion efficiency, usually less than 1.0 (a typical combustion efficiency is 0.95 or 95%).

For a composite aerosol formulation, the chemical heat of combustion is the summation of the weighted heats of combustion for the individual components, as follows:

$$\Delta Hc \ (product) \quad = \sum_{i}^{n} \ [\ wi\% \times \Delta Hc(i)]$$

Where:

ΔHc = chemical heat of combustion (kJ/g);
wi% = mass fraction of component i in the product;
$\Delta Hc(i)$ = specific heat of combustion (kJ/g) of component i in the product;

The chemical heats of combustion shall be found in literature, calculated or determined by tests (See ASTM D240–02, ISO 13943, Sections 86.1 to 86.3, and NFPA 30B (incorporated by reference; See § 1910.6)).

B.3.3.3 The Ignition Distance Test, Enclosed Space Ignition Test and Aerosol Foam Flammability Test shall be performed in accordance with sub-sections 31.4, 31.5 and 31.6 of the of the UN ST/SG/AC.10 (incorporated by reference; See § 1910.6).

B.4 OXIDIZING GASES

B.4.1 DEFINITION

Oxidizing gas means any gas which may, generally by providing oxygen, cause or contribute to the combustion of other material more than air does.

NOTE: "Gases which cause or contribute to the combustion of other material more than air does" means pure gases or gas mixtures with an oxidizing power greater than 23.5% (as determined by a method specified in ISO 10156 or 10156–2 (incorporated by reference, See § 1910.6) or an equivalent testing method.)

B.4.2 CLASSIFICATION CRITERIA

An oxidizing gas shall be classified in a single category for this class in accordance with Table B.4.1:

TABLE B.4.1—CRITERIA FOR OXIDIZING GASES

Category	Criteria
1	Any gas which may, generally by providing oxygen, cause or contribute to the combustion of other material more than air does.

B.4.3 ADDITIONAL CLASSIFICATION CONSIDERATIONS

Classification shall be in accordance with tests or calculation methods as described in ISO 10156 (incorporated by reference; See § 1910.6) and ISO 10156–2 (incorporated by reference; See § 1910.6).

B.5 GASES UNDER PRESSURE

B.5.1 DEFINITION

Gases under pressure are gases which are contained in a receptacle at a pressure of 200 kPa (29 psi) (gauge) or more, or which are liquefied or liquefied and refrigerated.

They comprise compressed gases, liquefied gases, dissolved gases and refrigerated liquefied gases.

B.5.2 CLASSIFICATION CRITERIA

Gases under pressure shall be classified in one of four groups in accordance with Table B.5.1:

TABLE B.5.1—CRITERIA FOR GASES UNDER PRESSURE

Group	Criteria
Compressed gas	A gas which when under pressure is entirely gaseous at $-50\ °C$ ($-8\ °F$), including all gases with a critical temperature[1] $\leq -50\ °C$ ($-58\ °F$).
Liquefied gas	A gas which when under pressure is partially liquid at temperatures above $-50\ °C$ ($-58\ °F$). A distinction is made between: (a) High pressure liquefied gas: A gas with a critical temperature[1] between $-50\ °C$ ($-58\ °F$) and $+65\ °C$ ($149\ °F$); and (b) Low pressure liquefied gas: A gas with a critical temperature[1] above $+65\ °C$ ($149\ °F$).
Refrigerated liquefied gas	A gas which is made partially liquid because of its low temperature.
Dissolved gas	A gas which when under pressure is dissolved in a liquid phase solvent.

[1] *The critical temperature is the temperature above which a pure gas cannot be liquefied, regardless of the degree of compression.*

B.6 FLAMMABLE LIQUIDS

B.6.1 DEFINITION

Flammable liquid means a liquid having a flash point of not more than 93 °C (199.4 °F).

Flash point means the minimum temperature at which a liquid gives off vapor in sufficient concentration to form an ignitable mixture with air near the surface of the liquid, as determined by a method identified in Section B.6.3.

B.6.2 CLASSIFICATION CRITERIA

A flammable liquid shall be classified in one of four categories in accordance with Table B.6.1:

TABLE B.6.1—CRITERIA FOR FLAMMABLE LIQUIDS

Category	Criteria
1	Flash point <23 °C (73.4 °F) and initial boiling point ≤35 °C (95 °F).
2	Flash point <23 °C (73.4 °F) and initial boiling point >35 °C (95 °F).
3	Flash point ≥23 °C (73.4 °F) and ≤60 °C (140 °F).
4	Flash point >60 °C (140 °F) and ≤93 °C (199.4 °F).

B.6.3 ADDITIONAL CLASSIFICATION CONSIDERATIONS

The flash point shall be determined in accordance with ASTM D56–05, ASTM D3278, ASTM D3828, ASTM D93–08 (incorporated by reference; See §1910.6), or any other method specified in GHS Revision 3, Chapter 2.6. The initial boiling point shall be determined in accordance with ASTM D86–07a or ASTM D1078 (incorporated by reference; See §1910.6).

B.7 FLAMMABLE SOLIDS

B.7.1 DEFINITIONS

Flammable solid means a solid which is a readily combustible solid, or which may cause or contribute to fire through friction.

Readily combustible solids are powdered, granular, or pasty chemicals which are dangerous if they can be easily ignited by brief contact with an ignition source, such as a burning match, and if the flame spreads rapidly.

B.7.2 CLASSIFICATION CRITERIA

B.7.2.1 Powdered, granular or pasty chemicals shall be classified as flammable solids when the time of burning of one or more of the test runs, performed in accordance with the test method described in the UN ST/SG/AC.10 (incorporated by reference; See §1910.6), Part III, sub-section 33.2.1, is less than 45 s or the rate of burning is more than 2.2 mm/s (0.0866 in/s).

B.7.2.2 Powders of metals or metal alloys shall be classified as flammable solids when they can be ignited and the reaction spreads over the whole length of the sample in 10 min or less.

B.7.2.3 Solids which may cause fire through friction shall be classified in this class by analogy with existing entries (e.g., matches) until definitive criteria are established.

B.7.2.4 A flammable solid shall be classified in one of the two categories for this class using Method N.1 as described in Part III, sub-section 33.2.1 of the UN ST/SG/AC.10 (incorporated by reference; See §1910.6), in accordance with Table B.7.1:

TABLE B.7.1—CRITERIA FOR FLAMMABLE SOLIDS

Category	Criteria
1	Burning rate test: Chemicals other than metal powders: (a) Wetted zone does not stop fire; and (b) Burning time <45 s or burning rate >2.2 mm/s. Metal powders: Burning time ≤5 min.
2	Burning rate test: Chemicals other than metal powders: (a) Wetted zone stops the fire for at least 4 min; and (b) Burning time <45 s or burning rate >2.2 mm/s. Metal powders: Burning time >5 min and ≤10 min.

NOTE: Classification of solid chemicals shall be based on tests performed on the chemical as presented. If, for example, for the purposes of supply or transport, the same chemical is to be presented in a physical form different from that which was tested and which is considered likely to materially alter its performance in a classification test, classification must be based on testing of the chemical in the new form.

B.8 SELF-REACTIVE CHEMICALS

B.8.1 DEFINITIONS

Self-reactive chemicals are thermally unstable liquid or solid chemicals liable to undergo a strongly exothermic decomposition even without participation of oxygen (air). This definition excludes chemicals classified under this section as explosives, organic peroxides, oxidizing liquids or oxidizing solids. A self-reactive chemical is regarded as possessing explosive properties when in laboratory testing the formulation is liable to detonate, to deflagrate rapidly or to show a violent effect when heated under confinement.

B.8.2 CLASSIFICATION CRITERIA

B.8.2.1 A self-reactive chemical shall be considered for classification in this class unless:

(a) It is classified as an explosive according to B.1 of this appendix;

(b) It is classified as an oxidizing liquid or an oxidizing solid according to B.13 or B.14 of this appendix, except that a mixture of oxidizing substances which contains 5% or more of combustible organic substances shall be classified as a self-reactive chemical according to the procedure defined in B.8.2.2;

(c) It is classified as an organic peroxide according to B.15 of this appendix;

(d) Its heat of decomposition is less than 300 J/g; or

(e) Its self-accelerating decomposition temperature (SADT) is greater than 75 °C (167 °F) for a 50 kg (110 lb) package.

B.8.2.2 Mixtures of oxidizing substances, meeting the criteria for classification as oxidizing liquids or oxidizing solids, which contain 5% or more of combustible organic substances and which do not meet the criteria mentioned in B.8.2.1 (a), (c), (d) or (e), shall be subjected to the self-reactive chemicals classification procedure in B.8.2.3. Such a mixture showing the properties of a self-reactive chemical type B to F shall be classified as a self-reactive chemical.

B.8.2.3 Self-reactive chemicals shall be classified in one of the seven categories of "types A to G" for this class, according to the following principles:

(a) Any self-reactive chemical which can detonate or deflagrate rapidly, as packaged, will be defined as self-reactive chemical TYPE A;

(b) Any self-reactive chemical possessing explosive properties and which, as packaged, neither detonates nor deflagrates rapidly, but is liable to undergo a thermal explosion in that package will be defined as self-reactive chemical TYPE B;

(c) Any self-reactive chemical possessing explosive properties when the chemical as packaged cannot detonate or deflagrate rapidly or undergo a thermal explosion will be defined as self-reactive chemical TYPE C;

(d) Any self-reactive chemical which in laboratory testing meets the criteria in (d)(i), (ii), or (iii) will be defined as self-reactive chemical TYPE D:

(i) Detonates partially, does not deflagrate rapidly and shows no violent effect when heated under confinement; or

(ii) Does not detonate at all, deflagrates slowly and shows no violent effect when heated under confinement; or

(iii) Does not detonate or deflagrate at all and shows a medium effect when heated under confinement;

(e) Any self-reactive chemical which, in laboratory testing, neither detonates nor deflagrates at all and shows low or no effect when heated under confinement will be defined as self-reactive chemical TYPE E;

(f) Any self-reactive chemical which, in laboratory testing, neither detonates in the cavitated state nor deflagrates at all and shows only a low or no effect when heated under confinement as well as low or no explosive power will be defined as self-reactive chemical TYPE F;

(g) Any self-reactive chemical which, in laboratory testing, neither detonates in the cavitated state nor deflagrates at all and shows no effect when heated under confinement nor any explosive power, provided that it is thermally stable (self-accelerating decomposition temperature is 60 °C (140 °F) to 75 °C (167 °F) for a 50 kg (110 lb) package), and, for liquid mixtures, a diluent having a boiling point greater than or equal to 150 °C (302 °F) is used for desensitization will be defined as self-reactive chemical TYPE G. If the mixture is not thermally stable or a diluent having a boiling point less than 150 °C (302 °F) is used for desensitization, the mixture shall be defined as self-reactive chemical TYPE F.

B.8.3 ADDITIONAL CLASSIFICATION CONSIDERATIONS

B.8.3.1 For purposes of classification, the properties of self-reactive chemicals shall be determined in accordance with test series A to H as described in Part II of the UN ST/SG/AC.10 (incorporated by reference; See § 1910.6).

B.8.3.2 Self-accelerating decomposition temperature (SADT) shall be determined in accordance with the UN ST/SG/AC.10, Part II, section 28 (incorporated by reference; See § 1910.6).

B.8.3.3 The classification procedures for self-reactive substances and mixtures need not be applied if:

(a) There are no chemical groups present in the molecule associated with explosive or self-reactive properties; examples of such groups are given in Tables A6.1 and A6.2 in the Appendix 6 of the UN ST/SG/AC.10 (incorporated by reference; See § 1910.6); or

(b) For a single organic substance or a homogeneous mixture of organic substances, the estimated SADT is greater than 75 °C (167 °F) or the exothermic decomposition energy is less than 300 J/g. The onset temperature and decomposition energy may be estimated using a suitable calorimetric technique (See 20.3.3.3 in Part II of the UN ST/SG/AC.10 (incorporated by reference; See § 1910.6)).

B.9 PYROPHORIC LIQUIDS

B.9.1 DEFINITION

Pyrophoric liquid means a liquid which, even in small quantities, is liable to ignite within five minutes after coming into contact with air.

B.9.2 CLASSIFICATION CRITERIA

A pyrophoric liquid shall be classified in a single category for this class using test N.3 in Part III, sub-section 33.3.1.5 of the UN ST/SG/AC.10 (incorporated by reference; See § 1910.6), in accordance with Table B.9.1:

TABLE B.9.1—CRITERIA FOR PYROPHORIC LIQUIDS

Category	Criteria
1	The liquid ignites within 5 min when added to an inert carrier and exposed to air, or it ignites or chars a filter paper on contact with air within 5 min.

B.9.3 ADDITIONAL CLASSIFICATION CONSIDERATIONS

The classification procedure for pyrophoric liquids need not be applied when experience in production or handling shows that the chemical does not ignite spontaneously on coming into contact with air at normal temperatures (*i.e.*, the substance is known to be stable at room temperature for prolonged periods of time (days)).

B.10 PYROPHORIC SOLIDS

B.10.1 DEFINITION

Pyrophoric solid means a solid which, even in small quantities, is liable to ignite within five minutes after coming into contact with air.

B.10.2 CLASSIFICATION CRITERIA

A pyrophoric solid shall be classified in a single category for this class using test N.2 in Part III, sub-section 33.3.1.4 of the UN ST/SG/AC.10 (incorporated by reference; See § 1910.6), in accordance with Table B.10.1:

TABLE B.10.1—CRITERIA FOR PYROPHORIC SOLIDS

Category	Criteria
1	The solid ignites within 5 min of coming into contact with air.

NOTE: Classification of solid chemicals shall be based on tests performed on the chemical as presented. If, for example, for the purposes of supply or transport, the same chemical is to be presented in a physical form different from that which was tested and which is considered likely to materially alter its performance in a classification test, classification must be based on testing of the chemical in the new form.

B.10.3 ADDITIONAL CLASSIFICATION CONSIDERATIONS

The classification procedure for pyrophoric solids need not be applied when experience in production or handling shows that the chemical does not ignite spontaneously on coming into contact with air at normal temperatures (*i.e.*, the chemical is known to be stable at room temperature for prolonged periods of time (days)).

B.11 SELF-HEATING CHEMICALS

B.11.1 DEFINITION

A *self-heating chemical* is a solid or liquid chemical, other than a pyrophoric liquid or solid, which, by reaction with air and without energy supply, is liable to self-heat; this chemical differs from a pyrophoric liquid or solid in that it will ignite only when in large amounts (kilograms) and after long periods of time (hours or days).

NOTE: Self-heating of a substance or mixture is a process where the gradual reaction of that substance or mixture with oxygen (in air) generates heat. If the rate of heat production exceeds the rate of heat loss, then the temperature of the substance or mixture will rise which, after an induction time, may lead to self-ignition and combustion.

B.11.2 CLASSIFICATION CRITERIA

B.11.2.1 A self-heating chemical shall be classified in one of the two categories for this class if, in tests performed in accordance with test method N.4 in Part III, sub-section 33.3.1.6 of the UN ST/SG/AC.10 (incorporated by reference; See § 1910.6), the result meets the criteria shown in Table B.11.1.

TABLE B.11.1—CRITERIA FOR SELF-HEATING CHEMICALS

Category	Criteria
1	A positive result is obtained in a test using a 25 mm sample cube at 140 °C (284 °F).
2	A negative result is obtained in a test using a 25 mm cube sample at 140 °C (284 °F), a positive result is obtained in a test using a 100 mm sample cube at 140 °C (284 °F), and:
	(a) The unit volume of the chemical is more than 3 m³; or
	(b) A positive result is obtained in a test using a 100 mm cube sample at 120 °C (248 °F) and the unit volume of the chemical is more than 450 liters; or
	(c) A positive result is obtained in a test using a 100 mm cube sample at 100 °C (212 °F).

B.11.2.2 Chemicals with a temperature of spontaneous combustion higher than 50 °C (122 °F) for a volume of 27 m³ shall not be classified as self-heating chemicals.

B.11.2.3 Chemicals with a spontaneous ignition temperature higher than 50 °C (122 °F) for a volume of 450 liters shall not be classified in Category 1 of this class.

B.11.3 ADDITIONAL CLASSIFICATION CONSIDERATIONS

B.11.3.1 The classification procedure for self-heating chemicals need not be applied if the results of a screening test can be adequately correlated with the classification test and an appropriate safety margin is applied.

B.11.3.2 Examples of screening tests are:

(a) The Grewer Oven test (VDI guideline 2263, part 1, 1990, Test methods for the Determination of the Safety Characteristics of Dusts) with an onset temperature 80°K above the reference temperature for a volume of 1 l;

(b) The Bulk Powder Screening Test (Gibson, N. Harper, D. J. Rogers, R. Evaluation of the fire and explosion risks in drying powders, Plant Operations Progress, 4 (3), 181-189, 1985) with an onset temperature 60°K above the reference temperature for a volume of 1 l.

B.12 CHEMICALS WHICH, IN CONTACT WITH WATER, EMIT FLAMMABLE GASES

B.12.1 DEFINITION

Chemicals which, in contact with water, emit flammable gases are solid or liquid chemicals which, by interaction with water, are liable to become spontaneously flammable or to give off flammable gases in dangerous quantities.

B.12.2 CLASSIFICATION CRITERIA

B.12.2.1 A chemical which, in contact with water, emits flammable gases shall be classified in one of the three categories for this class, using test N.5 in Part III, sub-section 33.4.1.4 of the UN ST/SG/AC.10 (incorporated by reference; See § 1910.6), in accordance with Table B.12.1:

TABLE B.12.1—CRITERIA FOR CHEMICALS WHICH, IN CONTACT WITH WATER, EMIT FLAMMABLE GASES

Category	Criteria
1	Any chemical which reacts vigorously with water at ambient temperatures and demonstrates generally a tendency for the gas produced to ignite spontaneously, or which reacts readily with water at ambient temperatures such that the rate of evolution of flammable gas is equal to or greater than 10 liters per kilogram of chemical over any one minute.
2	Any chemical which reacts readily with water at ambient temperatures such that the maximum rate of evolution of flammable gas is equal to or greater than 20 liters per kilogram of chemical per hour, and which does not meet the criteria for Category 1.
3	Any chemical which reacts slowly with water at ambient temperatures such that the maximum rate of evolution of flammable gas is equal to or greater than 1 liter per kilogram of chemical per hour, and which does not meet the criteria for Categories 1 and 2.

NOTE: Classification of solid chemicals shall be based on tests performed on the chemical as presented. If, for example, the same chemical is to be presented in a physical form different from that which was tested and which is considered likely to materially alter its performance in a classification test, classification must be based on testing of the chemical in the new form.

B.12.2.2 A chemical is classified as a chemical which, in contact with water emits flammable gases if spontaneous ignition takes place in any step of the test procedure.

B.12.3 ADDITIONAL CLASSIFICATION CONSIDERATIONS

The classification procedure for this class need not be applied if:

(a) The chemical structure of the chemical does not contain metals or metalloids;

(b) Experience in production or handling shows that the chemical does not react with water, (e.g., the chemical is manufactured with water or washed with water); or

(c) The chemical is known to be soluble in water to form a stable mixture.

B.13 OXIDIZING LIQUIDS

B.13.1 DEFINITION

Oxidizing liquid means a liquid which, while in itself not necessarily combustible, may, generally by yielding oxygen, cause, or contribute to, the combustion of other material.

B.13.2 CLASSIFICATION CRITERIA

An oxidizing liquid shall be classified in one of the three categories for this class using test O.2 in Part III, sub-section 34.4.2 of the UN ST/SG/AC.10 (incorporated by reference; See § 1910.6), in accordance with Table B.13.1:

TABLE B.13.1—CRITERIA FOR OXIDIZING LIQUIDS

Category	Criteria
1	Any chemical which, in the 1:1 mixture, by mass, of chemical and cellulose tested, spontaneously ignites; or the mean pressure rise time of a 1:1 mixture, by mass, of chemical and cellulose is less than that of a 1:1 mixture, by mass, of 50% perchloric acid and cellulose;
2	Any chemical which, in the 1:1 mixture, by mass, of chemical and cellulose tested, exhibits a mean pressure rise time less than or equal to the mean pressure rise time of a 1:1 mixture, by mass, of 40% aqueous sodium chlorate solution and cellulose; and the criteria for Category 1 are not met;
3	Any chemical which, in the 1:1 mixture, by mass, of chemical and cellulose tested, exhibits a mean pressure rise time less than or equal to the mean pressure rise time of a 1:1 mixture, by mass, of 65% aqueous nitric acid and cellulose; and the criteria for Categories 1 and 2 are not met.

B.13.3 ADDITIONAL CLASSIFICATION CONSIDERATIONS

B.13.3.1 For organic chemicals, the classification procedure for this class shall not be applied if:

(a) The chemical does not contain oxygen, fluorine or chlorine; or

(b) The chemical contains oxygen, fluorine or chlorine and these elements are chemically bonded only to carbon or hydrogen.

B.13.3.2 For inorganic chemicals, the classification procedure for this class shall not be applied if the chemical does not contain oxygen or halogen atoms.

B.13.3.3 In the event of divergence between test results and known experience in the handling and use of chemicals which shows them to be oxidizing, judgments based on known experience shall take precedence over test results.

B.13.3.4 In cases where chemicals generate a pressure rise (too high or too low), caused by chemical reactions not characterizing the

oxidizing properties of the chemical, the test described in Part III, sub-section 34.4.2 of the UN ST/SG/AC.10 (incorporated by reference; See § 1910.6) shall be repeated with an inert substance (e.g., diatomite (kieselguhr)) in place of the cellulose in order to clarify the nature of the reaction.

B.14 OXIDIZING SOLIDS

B.14.1 DEFINITION

Oxidizing solid means a solid which, while in itself is not necessarily combustible, may, generally by yielding oxygen, cause, or contribute to, the combustion of other material.

B.14.2 CLASSIFICATION CRITERIA

An oxidizing solid shall be classified in one of the three categories for this class using test O.1 in Part III, sub-section 34.4.1 of the UN ST/SG/AC.10 (incorporated by reference; See § 1910.6), in accordance with Table B.14.1:

TABLE B.14.1—CRITERIA FOR OXIDIZING SOLIDS

Category	Criteria
1	Any chemical which, in the 4:1 or 1:1 sample-to-cellulose ratio (by mass) tested, exhibits a mean burning time less than the mean burning time of a 3:2 mixture, by mass, of potassium bromate and cellulose.
2	Any chemical which, in the 4:1 or 1:1 sample-to-cellulose ratio (by mass) tested, exhibits a mean burning time equal to or less than the mean burning time of a 2:3 mixture (by mass) of potassium bromate and cellulose and the criteria for Category 1 are not met.
3	Any chemical which, in the 4:1 or 1:1 sample-to-cellulose ratio (by mass) tested, exhibits a mean burning time equal to or less than the mean burning time of a 3:7 mixture (by mass) of potassium bromate and cellulose and the criteria for Categories 1 and 2 are not met.

NOTE 1: Some oxidizing solids may present explosion hazards under certain conditions (e.g., when stored in large quantities). For example, some types of ammonium nitrate may give rise to an explosion hazard under extreme conditions and the "Resistance to detonation test" (IMO: Code of Safe Practice for Solid Bulk Cargoes, 2005, Annex 3, Test 5) may be used to assess this hazard. When information indicates that an oxidizing solid may present an explosion hazard, it shall be indicated on the Safety Data Sheet.

NOTE 2: Classification of solid chemicals shall be based on tests performed on the chemical as presented. If, for example, for the purposes of supply or transport, the same chemical is to be presented in a physical form different from that which was tested and which is considered likely to materially alter its performance in a classification test, classification must be based on testing of the chemical in the new form.

B.14.3 ADDITIONAL CLASSIFICATION CONSIDERATIONS

B.14.3.1 For organic chemicals, the classification procedure for this class shall not be applied if:

(a) The chemical does not contain oxygen, fluorine or chlorine; or

(b) The chemical contains oxygen, fluorine or chlorine and these elements are chemically bonded only to carbon or hydrogen.

B.14.3.2 For inorganic chemicals, the classification procedure for this class shall not be applied if the chemical does not contain oxygen or halogen atoms.

B.14.3.3 In the event of divergence between test results and known experience in the handling and use of chemicals which shows them to be oxidizing, judgements based on known experience shall take precedence over test results.

B.15 ORGANIC PEROXIDES

B.15.1 DEFINITION

B.15.1.1 *Organic peroxide* means a liquid or solid organic chemical which contains the bivalent $-0-0-$ structure and as such is considered a derivative of hydrogen peroxide, where one or both of the hydrogen atoms have been replaced by organic radicals. The term organic peroxide includes organic peroxide mixtures containing at least one organic peroxide. Organic peroxides are thermally unstable chemicals, which may undergo exothermic self-accelerating decomposition. In addition, they may have one or more of the following properties:

(a) Be liable to explosive decomposition;

(b) Burn rapidly;

(c) Be sensitive to impact or friction;

(d) React dangerously with other substances.

B.15.1.2 An organic peroxide is regarded as possessing explosive properties when in laboratory testing the formulation is liable to detonate, to deflagrate rapidly or to show a violent effect when heated under confinement.

B.15.2 CLASSIFICATION CRITERIA

B.15.2.1 Any organic peroxide shall be considered for classification in this class, unless it contains:

(a) Not more than 1.0% available oxygen from the organic peroxides when containing not more than 1.0% hydrogen peroxide; or

(b) Not more than 0.5% available oxygen from the organic peroxides when containing more than 1.0% but not more than 7.0% hydrogen peroxide.

NOTE: The available oxygen content (%) of an organic peroxide mixture is given by the formula:

$$16 \times \sum_{i}^{n} \left(\frac{n_i \times c_i}{m_i} \right)$$

Where:

n_i = number of peroxygen groups per molecule of organic peroxide i;

c_i = concentration (mass %) of organic peroxide i;

m_i = molecular mass of organic peroxide i.

B.15.2.2 Organic peroxides shall be classified in one of the seven categories of "Types A to G" for this class, according to the following principles:

(a) Any organic peroxide which, as packaged, can detonate or deflagrate rapidly shall be defined as organic peroxide TYPE A;

(b) Any organic peroxide possessing explosive properties and which, as packaged, neither detonates nor deflagrates rapidly, but is liable to undergo a thermal explosion in that package shall be defined as organic peroxide TYPE B;

(c) Any organic peroxide possessing explosive properties when the chemical as packaged cannot detonate or deflagrate rapidly or undergo a thermal explosion shall be defined as organic peroxide TYPE C;

(d) Any organic peroxide which in laboratory testing meets the criteria in (d)(i), (ii),

or (iii) shall be defined as organic peroxide TYPE D:
(i) Detonates partially, does not deflagrate rapidly and shows no violent effect when heated under confinement; or
(ii) Does not detonate at all, deflagrates slowly and shows no violent effect when heated under confinement; or
(iii) Does not detonate or deflagrate at all and shows a medium effect when heated under confinement;
(e) Any organic peroxide which, in laboratory testing, neither detonates nor deflagrates at all and shows low or no effect when heated under confinement shall be defined as organic peroxide TYPE E;
(f) Any organic peroxide which, in laboratory testing, neither detonates in the cavitated state nor deflagrates at all and shows only a low or no effect when heated under confinement as well as low or no explosive power shall be defined as organic peroxide TYPE F;
(g) Any organic peroxide which, in laboratory testing, neither detonates in the cavitated state nor deflagrates at all and shows no effect when heated under confinement nor any explosive power, provided that it is thermally stable (self-accelerating decomposition temperature is 60 °C (140 °F) or higher for a 50 kg (110 lb) package), and, for liquid mixtures, a diluent having a boiling point of not less than 150 °C (302 °F) is used for desensitization, shall be defined as organic peroxide TYPE G. If the organic peroxide is not thermally stable or a diluent having a boiling point less than 150 °C (302 °F) is used for desensitization, it shall be defined as organic peroxide TYPE F.

B.15.3 ADDITIONAL CLASSIFICATION CONSIDERATIONS

B.15.3.1 For purposes of classification, the properties of organic peroxides shall be determined in accordance with test series A to H as described in Part II of the UN ST/SG/AC.10 (incorporated by reference; See §1910.6).

B.15.3.2 Self-accelerating decomposition temperature (SADT) shall be determined in accordance with the UN ST/SG/AC.10 (incorporated by reference; See §1910.6), Part II, section 28.

B.15.3.3 Mixtures of organic peroxides may be classified as the same type of organic peroxide as that of the most dangerous ingredient. However, as two stable ingredients can form a thermally less stable mixture, the SADT of the mixture shall be determined.

B.16 CORROSIVE TO METALS

B.16.1 DEFINITION

A *chemical which is corrosive to metals* means a chemical which by chemical action will materially damage, or even destroy, metals.

B.16.2 CLASSIFICATION CRITERIA

A chemical which is corrosive to metals shall be classified in a single category for this class, using the test in Part III, sub-section 37.4 of the UN ST/SG/AC.10 (incorporated by reference; See §1910.6), in accordance with Table B.16.1:

TABLE B.16.1—CRITERIA FOR CHEMICALS CORROSIVE TO METAL

Category	Criteria
1	Corrosion rate on either steel or aluminium surfaces exceeding 6.25 mm per year at a test temperature of 55 °C (131 °F) when tested on both materials.

NOTE: Where an initial test on either steel or aluminium indicates the chemical being tested is corrosive, the follow-up test on the other metal is not necessary.

B.16.3 ADDITIONAL CLASSIFICATION CONSIDERATIONS

The specimen to be used for the test shall be made of the following materials:
(a) For the purposes of testing steel, steel types S235JR + CR (1.0037 resp.St 37–2), S275J2G3 + CR (1.0144 resp.St 44–3), ISO 3574, Unified Numbering System (UNS) G 10200, or SAE 1020;
(b) For the purposes of testing aluminium: Non-clad types 7075–T6 or AZ5GU–T6.

APPENDIX C TO §1910.1200—ALLOCATION OF LABEL ELEMENTS (MANDATORY)

C.1 The label for each hazardous chemical shall include the product identifier used on the safety data sheet.

C.1.1 The labels on shipped containers shall also include the name, address, and telephone number of the chemical manufacturer, importer, or responsible party.

C.2 The label for each hazardous chemical that is classified shall include the signal word, hazard statement(s), pictogram(s), and precautionary statement(s) specified in C.4 for each hazard class and associated hazard category, except as provided for in C.2.1 through C.2.4.

C.2.1 PRECEDENCE OF HAZARD INFORMATION

C.2.1.1 If the signal word "Danger" is included, the signal word "Warning" shall not appear;

C.2.1.2 If the skull and crossbones pictogram is included, the exclamation mark pictogram shall not appear where it is used for acute toxicity;

C.2.1.3 If the corrosive pictogram is included, the exclamation mark pictogram shall not appear where it is used for skin or eye irritation;

C.2.1.4 If the health hazard pictogram is included for respiratory sensitization, the exclamation mark pictogram shall not appear where it is used for skin sensitization or for skin or eye irritation.

C.2.2 HAZARD STATEMENT TEXT

C.2.2.1 The text of all applicable hazard statements shall appear on the label, except as otherwise specified. The information in italics shall be included as part of the hazard statement as provided. For example: "causes damage to organs (*state all organs affected*) through prolonged or repeated exposure (*state route of exposure if no other routes of exposure cause the hazard*)". Hazard statements may be combined where appropriate to reduce the information on the label and improve readability, as long as all of the hazards are conveyed as required.

C.2.2.2 If the chemical manufacturer, importer, or responsible party can demonstrate that all or part of the hazard statement is inappropriate to a specific substance or mixture, the corresponding statement may be omitted from the label.

C.2.3 PICTOGRAMS

C.2.3.1 Pictograms shall be in the shape of a square set at a point and shall include a black hazard symbol on a white background with a red frame sufficiently wide to be clearly visible. A square red frame set at a point without a hazard symbol is not a pictogram and is not permitted on the label.

C.2.3.2 One of eight standard hazard symbols shall be used in each pictogram. The eight hazard symbols are depicted in Figure C.1. A pictogram using the exclamation mark symbol is presented in Figure C.2, for the purpose of illustration.

Figure C.1 – Hazard Symbols and Classes

Flame	Flame Over Circle	Exclamation Mark	Exploding Bomb
Flammables Self Reactives Pyrophorics Self-heating Emits Flammable Gas Organic Peroxides	Oxidizers	Irritant Dermal Sensitizer Acute Toxicity (harmful) Narcotic Effects Respiratory Tract Irritation	Explosives Self Reactives Organic Peroxides
Corrosion	Gas Cylinder	Health Hazard	Skull and Crossbones
Corrosives	Gases Under Pressure	Carcinogen Respiratory Sensitizer Reproductive Toxicity Target Organ Toxicity Mutagenicity Aspiration Toxicity	Acute Toxicity (severe)

Figure C.2 – Exclamation Mark Pictogram

C.2.3.3   Where a pictogram required by the Department of Transportation under Title 49 of the Code of Federal Regulations appears on a shipped container, the pictogram specified in C.4 for the same hazard shall not appear.

C.2.4 PRECAUTIONARY STATEMENT TEXT

C.2.4.1 There are four types of precautionary statements presented, "prevention," "response," "storage," and "disposal." The core part of the precautionary statement is presented in bold print. This is the text, except as otherwise specified, that shall appear on the label. Where additional information is required, it is indicated in plain text.

C.2.4.2 When a backslash or diagonal mark (/) appears in the precautionary statement text, it indicates that a choice has to be made between the separated phrases. In such cases, the chemical manufacturer, importer, or responsible party can choose the most appropriate phrase(s). For example, "Wear protective gloves/protective clothing/eye protection/face protection" could read "wear eye protection".

C.2.4.3 When three full stops (* * *) appear in the precautionary statement text, they indicate that all applicable conditions are not listed. For example, in "Use explosion-proof electrical/ventilating/lighting/* * */equipment", the use of "* * *" indicates that other equipment may need to be specified. In such cases, the chemical manufacturer, importer, or responsible party can choose the other conditions to be specified.

C.2.4.4 When text in *italics* is used in a precautionary statement, this indicates specific conditions applying to the use or allocation of the precautionary statement. For example, "Use explosion-proof electrical/ventilating/lighting/* * */equipment" is only required for flammable solids "*if dust clouds can occur*". Text in italics is intended to be an explanatory, conditional note and is not intended to appear on the label.

C.2.4.5 Where square brackets ([ ]) appear around text in a precautionary statement, this indicates that the text in square brackets is not appropriate in every case and should be used only in certain circumstances. In these cases, conditions for use explaining when the text should be used are provided. For example, one precautionary statement states: "[In case of inadequate ventilation] wear respiratory protection." This statement is given with the condition for use "– text in square brackets may be used if additional information is provided with the chemical at the point of use that explains what type of ventilation would be adequate for safe use". This means that, if additional information is provided with the chemical explaining what type of ventilation would be adequate for safe use, the text in square brackets should be used and the statement would read: "In case of inadequate ventilation wear respiratory protection." However, if the chemical is supplied without such ventilation information, the text in square brackets should not be used, and the precautionary statement should read: "Wear respiratory protection."

C.2.4.6 Precautionary statements may be combined or consolidated to save label space and improve readability. For example, "Keep away from heat, sparks and open flame," "Store in a well-ventilated place" and "Keep cool" can be combined to read "Keep away from heat, sparks and open flame and store in a cool, well-ventilated place."

C.2.4.7 In most cases, the precautionary statements are independent (e.g., the phrases for explosive hazards do not modify those related to certain health hazards, and products that are classified for both hazard classes shall bear appropriate precautionary statements for both). Where a chemical is classified for a number of hazards, and the precautionary statements are similar, the most stringent shall be included on the label (this will be applicable mainly to preventive measures). An order of precedence may be imposed by the chemical manufacturer, importer or responsible party in situations where phrases concern "Response." Rapid action may be crucial. For example, if a chemical is carcinogenic and acutely toxic, rapid action may be crucial, and first aid measures for acute toxicity will take precedence over those for long-term effects. In addition, medical attention to delayed health effects may be required in cases of incidental exposure, even if not associated with immediate symptoms of intoxication.

C.2.4.8 If the chemical manufacturer, importer, or responsible party can demonstrate that a precautionary statement is inappropriate to a specific substance or mixture, the precautionary statement may be omitted from the label.

C.3 SUPPLEMENTARY HAZARD INFORMATION

C.3.1 To ensure that non-standardized information does not lead to unnecessarily wide variation or undermine the required information, supplementary information on the label is limited to when it provides further detail and does not contradict or cast doubt on the validity of the standardized hazard information.

C.3.2 Where the chemical manufacturer, importer, or distributor chooses to add supplementary information on the label, placement of supplemental information shall not impede identification of information required by this section.

C.3.3 Where an ingredient with unknown acute toxicity is used in a mixture at a concentration ≥1%, and the mixture is not classified based on testing of the mixture as a whole, a statement that X% of the mixture consists of ingredient(s) of unknown acute toxicity is required on the label.

C.4 REQUIREMENTS FOR SIGNAL WORDS, HAZARD STATEMENTS, PICTOGRAMS, AND PRECAUTIONARY STATEMENTS

C.4.1 ACUTE TOXICITY – ORAL
(Classified in Accordance with Appendix A.1)

Pictogram
Skull and crossbones

Hazard category	Signal word	Hazard statement
1	Danger	Fatal if swallowed
2	Danger	Fatal if swallowed

Precautionary statements

Prevention	Response	Storage	Disposal
Wash ...thoroughly after handling. ... Chemical manufacturer, importer, or distributor to specify parts of the body to be washed after handling. **Do not eat, drink or smoke when using this product.**	**If swallowed: Immediately call a poison center/doctor/...** ... Chemical manufacturer, importer, or distributor to specify the appropriate source of emergency medical advice. **Specific treatment (see ... on this label)** ... Reference to supplemental first aid instruction. - *if immediate administration of antidote is required.* **Rinse mouth.**	Store locked up.	Dispose of contents/container to... ... in accordance with local/regional/national/international regulations (to be specified).

660

C.4.1 ACUTE TOXICITY – ORAL (CONTINUED)
(Classified in Accordance with Appendix A.1)

Hazard category	Signal word	Hazard statement	Pictogram
3	Danger	Toxic if swallowed	Skull and crossbones 

Precautionary statements

Prevention	Response	Storage	Disposal
Wash ... thoroughly after handling. ... Chemical manufacturer, importer, or distributor to specify parts of the body to be washed after handling. **Do not eat, drink or smoke when using this product.**	**If swallowed: Immediately call a poison center/doctor/...** ... Chemical manufacturer, importer, or distributor to specify the appropriate source of emergency medical advice. **Specific treatment (see ... on this label)** ... Reference to supplemental first aid instruction. - *if immediate administration of antidote is required.* **Rinse mouth.**	**Store locked up.**	**Dispose of contents/container to...** ... in accordance with local/regional/national/international regulations (to be specified).

C.4.1 ACUTE TOXICITY – ORAL (CONTINUED)
(Classified in Accordance with Appendix A.1)

Hazard category	Signal word	Hazard statement	Pictogram
4	Warning	Harmful if swallowed	Exclamation mark

Precautionary statements

Prevention	Response	Storage	Disposal
Wash ... thoroughly after handling. ... Chemical manufacturer, importer, or distributor to specify parts of the body to be washed after handling.	**If swallowed: Call a poison center/doctor/.../ if you feel unwell.** ... Chemical manufacturer, importer, or distributor to specify the appropriate source of emergency medical advice.		**Dispose of contents/container to...** ... in accordance with local/regional/national/international regulations (to be specified).
Do not eat, drink or smoke when using this product.	**Rinse mouth.**		

C.4.2 ACUTE TOXICITY - DERMAL
(Classified in Accordance with Appendix A.1)

Hazard category	Signal word	Hazard statement
1	Danger	Fatal in contact with skin
2	Danger	Fatal in contact with skin

Pictogram
Skull and crossbones

Precautionary statements

Prevention	Response	Storage	Disposal
Do not get in eyes, on skin, or on clothing.	**If on skin: Wash with plenty of water/...** ... Chemical manufacturer, importer, or distributor may specify a cleansing agent if appropriate, or may recommend an alternative agent in exceptional cases if water is clearly inappropriate.	**Store locked up.**	**Dispose of contents/container to...** ... in accordance with local/regional/national/international regulations (to be specified).
Wash ... thoroughly after handling. ... Chemical manufacturer, importer, or distributor to specify parts of the body to be washed after handling.			
Do not eat, drink or smoke when using this product.	**Immediately call a poison center/doctor/...** ... Chemical manufacturer, importer, or distributor to specify the appropriate source of emergency medical advice.		
Wear protective gloves/protective clothing. Chemical manufacturer, importer, or distributor to specify type of equipment.	**Specific treatment (see ... on this label)** ... Reference to supplemental first aid instruction. - *if immediate measures such as specific cleansing agent is advised.*		
	Take off immediately all contaminated clothing and wash it before reuse.		

C.4.2 ACUTE TOXICITY – DERMAL (CONTINUED)
(Classified in Accordance with Appendix A.1)

Hazard category	Signal word	Hazard statement		Pictogram
3	Danger	Toxic in contact with skin		Skull and crossbones

Precautionary statements

Prevention	Response	Storage	Disposal
Wear protective gloves/protective clothing. Chemical manufacturer, importer, or distributor to specify type of equipment.	**If on skin: Wash with plenty of water/...** ... Chemical manufacturer, importer, or distributor may specify a cleansing agent if appropriate, or may recommend an alternative agent in exceptional cases if water is clearly inappropriate. **Call a poison center/doctor/.../if you feel unwell.** ... Chemical manufacturer, importer, or distributor to specify the appropriate source of emergency medical advice. **Specific treatment (see ... on this label)** ... Reference to supplemental first aid instruction. - *if measures such as specific cleansing agent is advised.* **Take off immediately all contaminated clothing and wash it before reuse.**	Store locked up.	**Dispose of contents/container to...** ... in accordance with local/regional/national/international regulations (to be specified).

C.4.2 ACUTE TOXICITY – DERMAL (CONTINUED)
(Classified in Accordance with Appendix A.1)

Hazard category	Signal word	Hazard statement	Pictogram
4	Warning	Harmful in contact with skin	Exclamation mark

Precautionary statements

Prevention	Response	Storage	Disposal
Wear protective gloves/protective clothing Chemical manufacturer, importer, or distributor to specify type of equipment.	**If on skin: Wash with plenty of water/...** ... Chemical manufacturer, importer, or distributor may specify a cleansing agent if appropriate, or may recommend an alternative agent in exceptional cases if water is clearly inappropriate. **Call a poison center/doctor/.../if you feel unwell.** ... Chemical manufacturer, importer, or distributor to specify the appropriate source of emergency medical advice. **Specific treatment (see ... on this label)** ... Reference to supplemental first aid instruction. - *if measures such as specific cleansing agent is advised.* **Take off contaminated clothing and wash it before reuse.**		**Dispose of contents/container to...** ... in accordance with local/regional/national/international regulations (to be specified).

665

C.4.3 ACUTE TOXICITY - INHALATION
(Classified in Accordance with Appendix A.1)

Hazard category	Signal word	Hazard statement
1	Danger	Fatal if inhaled
2	Danger	Fatal if inhaled

Pictogram

Skull and crossbones

Precautionary statements

Prevention	Response	Storage	Disposal
Do not breathe dust/fume/gas/mist/ vapors/spray. Chemical manufacturer, importer, or distributor to specify applicable conditions.	**If inhaled: Remove person to fresh air and keep comfortable for breathing.**	**Store in a well- ventilated place. Keep container tightly closed.**	**Dispose of contents/container to...** ... in accordance with local/regional/national/international regulations (to be specified).
Use only outdoors or in a well- ventilated area.	**Immediately call a poison center/doctor/...** ... Chemical manufacturer, importer, or distributor to specify the appropriate source of emergency medical advice.	- *if product is volatile as to generate hazardous atmosphere.*	
[In case of inadequate ventilation] wear respiratory protection. Chemical manufacturer, importer, or distributor to specify equipment. - *Text in square brackets may be used if additional information is provided with the chemical at the point of use that explains what type of ventilation would be adequate for safe use.*	**Specific treatment is urgent (see ... on this label)** ... Reference to supplemental first aid instruction. - *if immediate administration of antidote is required.*	**Store locked up.**	

C.4.3 ACUTE TOXICITY – INHALATION (CONTINUED)
(Classified in Accordance with Appendix A.1)

Hazard category	Signal word	Hazard statement	Pictogram
3	Danger	Toxic if inhaled	Skull and crossbones 

Precautionary statements

Prevention	Response	Storage	Disposal
Avoid breathing dust/fume/gas/mist/vapors/spray. Chemical manufacturer, importer, or distributor to specify applicable conditions. **Use only outdoors or in a well-ventilated area.**	**If inhaled: Remove person to fresh air and keep comfortable for breathing.** **Call a poison center/doctor/...** ... Chemical manufacturer, importer, or distributor to specify the appropriate source of emergency medical advice. **Specific treatment (see ... on this label)** ... Reference to supplemental first aid instruction. - *if immediate specific measures are required.*	**Store in a well-ventilated place. Keep container tightly closed.** - *if product is volatile so as to generate hazardous atmosphere.* **Store locked up.**	**Dispose of content/container to...** ... in accordance with local/regional/national/international regulations (to be specified).

667

C.4.3 ACUTE TOXICITY – INHALATION (CONTINUED)
(Classified in Accordance with Appendix A.1)

Pictogram
Exclamation mark

Hazard category	Signal word	Hazard statement
4	Warning	Harmful if inhaled

Precautionary statements

Prevention	Response	Storage	Disposal
Avoid breathing dust/fume/gas/mist/ vapors/spray. Chemical manufacturer, importer, or distributor to specify applicable conditions.	**If inhaled: Remove person to fresh air and keep comfortable for breathing.** **Call a poison center/doctor/.../if you feel unwell.** ... Chemical manufacturer, importer, or distributor to specify the appropriate source of emergency medical advice.		
Use only outdoors or in a well-ventilated area.			

C.4.4 SKIN CORROSION/IRRITATION
(Classified in Accordance with Appendix A.2)

Hazard category	Signal word	Hazard statement		Pictogram
1A to 1C	Danger	Causes severe skin burns and eye damage		Corrosion

Precautionary statements

Prevention	Response	Storage	Disposal
Do not breathe dusts or mists. - *if inhalable particles of dusts or mists may occur during use.*	**If swallowed: Rinse mouth. Do NOT induce vomiting.**	Store locked up.	**Dispose of contents/container to...** ... in accordance with local/regional/national/internatio nal regulations (to be specified).
Wash ...thoroughly after handling. ...Chemical manufacturer, importer, or distributor to specify parts of the body to be washed after handling.	**If on skin (or hair): Take off immediately all contaminated clothing. Rinse skin with water/shower.** **Wash contaminated clothing before reuse.** **If inhaled: Remove person to fresh air and keep comfortable for breathing.**		
Wear protective gloves/protective clothing/eye protection/face protection. Chemical manufacturer, importer, or distributor to specify type of equipment.	**Immediately call a poison center/doctor/...** ... Chemical manufacturer, importer, or distributor to specify the appropriate source of emergency medical advice. **Specific treatment (see ... on this label)** ... Reference to supplemental first aid instruction. - *Manufacturer, importer, or distributor may specify a cleansing agent if appropriate.* **If in eyes: Rinse cautiously with water for several minutes. Remove contact lenses, if present and easy to do. Continue rinsing.**		

C.4.4 SKIN CORROSION/IRRITATION (CONTINUED)
(Classified in Accordance with Appendix A.2)

Hazard category	Signal word	Hazard statement
2	Warning	Causes skin irritation

Pictogram
Exclamation mark

Precautionary statements

Prevention	Response	Storage	Disposal
Wash ... thoroughly after handling. ... Chemical manufacturer, importer, or distributor to specify parts of the body to be washed after handling. **Wear protective gloves.** Chemical manufacturer, importer, or distributor to specify type of equipment.	**If on skin: Wash with plenty of water/...** ... Chemical manufacturer, importer, or distributor may specify a cleansing agent if appropriate, or may recommend an alternative agent in exceptional cases if water is clearly inappropriate. **Specific treatment (see ... on this label)** ... Reference to supplemental first aid instruction. - *Manufacturer, importer, or distributor may specify a cleansing agent if appropriate.* **If skin irritation occurs: Get medical advice/attention.** **Take off contaminated clothing and wash it before reuse.**		

C.4.5 EYE DAMAGE/IRRITATION
(Classified in Accordance with Appendix A.3)

Hazard category	Signal word	Hazard statement	Pictogram
1	Danger	Causes serious eye damage	Corrosion

Precautionary statements

Prevention	Response	Storage	Disposal
Wear eye protection/face protection. Chemical manufacturer, importer, or distributor to specify type of equipment.	**If in eyes: Rinse cautiously with water for several minutes. Remove contact lenses, if present and easy to do. Continue rinsing.** **Immediately call a poison center/doctor/...** ... Chemical manufacturer, importer, or distributor to specify the appropriate source of emergency medical advice.		

C.4.5 EYE DAMAGE/IRRITATION (CONTINUED)
(Classified in Accordance with Appendix A.3)

Hazard category	Signal word	Hazard statement
2A	Warning	Causes serious eye irritation

Pictogram
Exclamation mark

Precautionary statements

Prevention	Response	Storage	Disposal
Wash ... thoroughly after handling. ... Chemical manufacturer, importer, or distributor to specify parts of the body to be washed after handling. **Wear eye protection/face protection.** Chemical manufacturer, importer, or distributor to specify type of equipment.	**If in eyes: Rinse cautiously with water for several minutes. Remove contact lenses, if present and easy to do. Continue rinsing.** **If eye irritation persists: Get medical advice/attention.**		

C.4.5 EYE DAMAGE/IRRITATION (CONTINUED)
(Classified in Accordance with Appendix A.3)

Hazard category	Signal word	Hazard statement		Pictogram
2B	Warning	Causes eye irritation		*No Pictogram*

Precautionary statements

Prevention	Response	Storage	Disposal
Wash .... thoroughly after handling. ..., Chemical manufacturer, importer, or distributor to specify parts of the body to be washed after handling.	**If in eyes: Rinse cautiously with water for several minutes. Remove contact lenses, if present and easy to do. Continue rinsing.** **If eye irritation persists: Get medical advice/attention.**		

C.4.6 SENSITIZATION - RESPIRATORY
(Classified in Accordance with Appendix A.4)

Pictogram
Health hazard

Hazard category	**Signal word**
1 (including both sub-categories 1A and 1B)	Danger

Hazard statement

May cause allergy or asthma symptoms or breathing difficulties if inhaled

Precautionary statements

Prevention	Response	Storage	Disposal
Avoid breathing dust/fume/gas/mist/vapors/spray. Chemical manufacturer, importer, or distributor to specify applicable conditions. **[In case of inadequate ventilation] wear respiratory protection.** Chemical manufacturer, importer, or distributor to specify equipment - *Text in square brackets may be used if additional information is provided with the chemical at the point of use that explains what type of ventilation would be adequate for safe use.*	**If inhaled: If breathing is difficult, remove person to fresh air and keep comfortable for breathing.** **If experiencing respiratory symptoms: Call a poison center/doctor/...** ... Chemical manufacturer, importer, or distributor to specify the appropriate source of emergency medical advice.		**Dispose of contents/container to...** ... in accordance with local/regional/national/international regulations (to be specified).

C.4.7 SENSITIZATION - SKIN
(Classified in Accordance with Appendix A.4)

Hazard category	Signal word	Hazard statement	Pictogram
1 (including both sub-categories 1A and 1B)	Warning	May cause an allergic skin reaction	Exclamation mark 

Precautionary statements

Prevention	Response	Storage	Disposal
Avoid breathing dust/fume/gas/mist/ vapors/spray. Chemical manufacturer, importer, or distributor to specify applicable conditions.	**If on skin: Wash with plenty of water/...** ... Chemical manufacturer, importer, or distributor may specify a cleansing agent if appropriate, or may recommend an alternative agent in exceptional cases if water is clearly inappropriate.		**Dispose of contents/container to...** ... in accordance with local/regional/national/international regulations (to be specified).
Contaminated work clothing must not be allowed out of the workplace.	**If skin irritation or rash occurs: Get medical advice/attention.**		
Wear protective gloves. Chemical manufacturer, importer, or distributor to specify type of equipment.	**Specific treatment (see ... on this label)** ... Reference to supplemental first aid instruction. - *Manufacturer, importer, or distributor may specify a cleansing agent if appropriate.*		
	Wash contaminated clothing before reuse.		

C.4.8 GERM CELL MUTAGENICITY
(Classified in Accordance with Appendix A.5)

Hazard category	Signal word	Hazard statement
1A and 1B	Danger	May cause genetic defects <...>
2	Warning	Suspected of causing genetic defects <...>
		(state route of exposure if no other routes of exposure cause the hazard)

Precautionary statements

Prevention	Response	Storage	Disposal
Obtain special instructions before use.	If exposed or concerned: Get medical advice/attention.	Store locked up.	Dispose of contents/container to... ... in accordance with local/regional/national/international regulations (to be specified).
Do not handle until all safety precautions have been read and understood.			
Wear protective gloves/protective clothing/eye protection/face protection. Chemical manufacturer, importer, or distributor to specify type of equipment, as required.			

C.4.9 CARCINOGENICITY
(Classified in Accordance with Appendix A.6)

Pictogram
Health hazard

Hazard category	Signal word
1A and 1B	Danger
2	Warning

Hazard statement

May cause cancer <...>

Suspected of causing cancer <...>

(state route of exposure if no other routes of exposure cause the hazard)

Precautionary statements

Prevention	Response	Storage	Disposal
Obtain special instructions before use.	**If exposed or concerned: Get medical advice/attention.**	**Store locked up.**	**Dispose of contents/container to...** ... in accordance with local/regional/national/international regulations (to be specified).
Do not handle until all safety precautions have been read and understood.			
Wear protective gloves/protective clothing/eye protection/face protection. Chemical manufacturer, importer, or distributor to specify type of equipment, as required.			

Note: If a Category 2 carcinogen ingredient is present in the mixture at a concentration between 0.1% and 1%, information is required on the SDS for a product; however, a label warning is optional. If a Category 2 carcinogen ingredient is present in the mixture at a concentration of ≥ 1%, both an SDS and a label is required and the information must be included on each.

C.4.10 TOXIC TO REPRODUCTION
(Classified in Accordance with Appendix A.7)

Pictogram
Health hazard

Hazard category	Signal word
1A and 1B	Danger
2	Warning

Hazard statement

May damage fertility or the unborn child <...> <<...>>

Suspected of damaging fertility or the unborn child <...> <<...>>

(state specific effect if known)

(state route of exposure if no other routes of exposure cause the hazard)

Precautionary statements

Prevention	Response	Storage	Disposal
Obtain special instructions before use.	**If exposed or concerned: Get medical advice/attention.**	**Store locked up.**	**Dispose of contents/container to...** ... in accordance with local/regional/national/international regulations (to be specified).
Do not handle until all safety precautions have been read and understood.			
Wear protective gloves/protective clothing/eye protection/face protection. Chemical manufacturer, importer, or distributor to specify type of equipment, as required.			

C.4.10 TOXIC TO REPRODUCTION (CONTINUED)
(Classified in Accordance with Appendix A.7)
(EFFECTS ON OR VIA LACTATION)

Hazard category	**Signal word**	**Hazard statement**
No designated number	_No signal word_	May cause harm to breast-fed children
(See Table A.7.1 in Appendix A.7)		

Pictogram
No Pictogram

Precautionary statements

Prevention	Response	Storage	Disposal
Obtain special instructions before use.	**If exposed or concerned: Get medical advice/attention.**		
Do not breathe dusts or mists. - _if inhalable particles of dusts or mists may occur during use._			
Avoid contact during pregnancy/while nursing.			
Wash ... thoroughly after handling. ...Chemical manufacturer, importer, or distributor to specify parts of the body to be washed after handling.			
Do not eat, drink or smoke when using this product.			

C.4.11 SPECIFIC TARGET ORGAN TOXICITY (Single Exposure)
(Classified in Accordance with Appendix A.8)

Hazard category	Signal word	Hazard statement	Pictogram
1	Danger	Causes damage to organs <...> <<...>> <...> *(or state all organs affected if known)* <<...>> *(state route of exposure if no other routes of exposure cause the hazard)*	Health hazard

Precautionary statements

Prevention	Response	Storage	Disposal
Do not breathe dust/fume/gas/mist/ vapors/spray. Chemical manufacturer, importer, or distributor to specify applicable conditions. **Wash ...thoroughly after handling.** ... Chemical manufacturer, importer, or distributor to specify parts of the body to be washed after handling. **Do not eat, drink or smoke when using this product.**	**If exposed: Call a poison center/doctor/...** ... Chemical manufacturer, importer, or distributor to specify the appropriate source of emergency medical advice. **Specific treatment (see ... on this label)** ... Reference to supplemental first aid instruction. - *if immediate measures are required.*	**Store locked up.**	**Dispose of contents/container to...** ... in accordance with local/regional/national/international regulations (to be specified).

C.4.11 SPECIFIC TARGET ORGAN TOXICITY (Single Exposure) (CONTINUED)
(Classified in Accordance with Appendix A.8)

Hazard category	Signal word	Hazard statement	Pictogram
2	Warning	May cause damage to organs <...> <<...>> <..> *(or state all organs affected, if known)* <<...>> *(state route of exposure if no other routes of exposure cause the hazard)*	Health hazard

Precautionary statements

Prevention	Response	Storage	Disposal
Do not breathe dust/fume/gas/mist/ vapors/spray. Chemical manufacturer, importer, or distributor to specify applicable conditions.	**If exposed or concerned: Call a poison center/doctor/...** ... Chemical manufacturer, importer, or distributor to specify the appropriate source of emergency medical advice.	**Store locked up.**	**Dispose of contents/container to...** ... in accordance with local/regional/national/international regulations (to be specified).
Wash ... thoroughly after handling. ... Chemical manufacturer, importer, or distributor to specify parts of the body to be washed after handling.			
Do not eat, drink or smoke when using this product.			

C.4.11 SPECIFIC TARGET ORGAN TOXICITY (Single Exposure) (CONTINUED)
(Classified in Accordance with Appendix A.8)

Hazard category	Signal word	Hazard statement	Pictogram
3	Warning	May cause respiratory irritation; or May cause drowsiness or dizziness	Exclamation mark

Precautionary statements

Prevention	Response	Storage	Disposal
Avoid breathing dust/fume/gas/mist/ vapors/spray. Chemical manufacturer, importer, or distributor to specify applicable conditions. **Use only outdoors or in a well-ventilated area.**	**If inhaled: Remove person to fresh air and keep comfortable for breathing.** **Call a poison center/doctor/.../if you feel unwell.** ... Chemical manufacturer, importer, or distributor to specify the appropriate source of emergency medical advice.	**Store in a well-ventilated place. Keep container tightly closed.** - *if product is volatile so as to generate hazardous atmosphere.* **Store locked up.**	**Dispose of contents/container to...** ... in accordance with local/regional/national/international regulations (to be specified).

682

C.4.12 SPECIFIC TARGET ORGAN TOXICITY (Repeated Exposure)
(Classified in Accordance with Appendix A.9)

Hazard category	Signal word	Hazard statement	Pictogram
1	Danger	**Causes damage to organs** <...> **through prolonged or repeated exposure** <<...>> <...> *(state all organs affected, if known)* <<...>> *(state route of exposure if no other routes of exposure cause the hazard)*	Health hazard

Precautionary statements

Prevention	Response	Storage	Disposal
Do not breathe dust/fume/gas/mist/vapors/spray. Chemical manufacturer, importer, or distributor to specify applicable conditions. **Wash ... thoroughly after handling.** ...Chemical manufacturer, importer, or distributor to specify parts of the body to be washed after handling. **Do not eat, drink or smoke when using this product.**	**Get medical advice/attention if you feel unwell.**		**Dispose of contents/container to...** ...in accordance with local/regional/national/international regulations (to be specified).

C.4.12 SPECIFIC TARGET ORGAN TOXICITY (Repeated Exposure) (CONTINUED)
(Classified in Accordance with Appendix A.9)

Hazard category	Signal word	Hazard statement	Pictogram
2	Warning	May cause damage to organs <...> through prolonged or repeated exposure <<...>> <...> *[state all organs affected, if known]* <<...>> *[state route of exposure if no other routes of exposure cause the hazard]*	Health hazard

Precautionary statements

Prevention	Response	Storage	Disposal
Do not breathe dust/fume/gas/mist/vapors/spray. Chemical manufacturer, importer, or distributor to specify applicable conditions.	**Get medical advice/attention if you feel unwell.**		**Dispose of contents/container to...** ... in accordance with local/regional/national/international regulations (to be specified).

C.4.13 ASPIRATION HAZARD
(Classified in Accordance with Appendix A.10)

Hazard category	Signal word	Hazard statement		Pictogram
1	Danger	May be fatal if swallowed and enters airways		Health hazard

Precautionary statements

Prevention	Response	Storage	Disposal
	If swallowed: Immediately call a poison center/doctor/... ... Chemical manufacturer, importer, or distributor to specify the appropriate source of emergency medical advice. Do NOT induce vomiting.	Store locked up.	Dispose of contents/container to... ... in accordance with local/regional/national/international regulations (to be specified).

C.4.14 EXPLOSIVES
(Classified in Accordance with Appendix B.1)

Hazard category	Signal word	Hazard statement
Unstable explosive	Danger	Unstable explosive

Pictogram
Exploding bomb

Precautionary statements

Prevention	Response	Storage	Disposal
Obtain special instructions before use.	**Explosion risk in case of fire.**	**Store ...** ...in accordance with local/regional/ national/international regulations (to be specified).	**Dispose of contents/container to ...** ...in accordance with local/regional/ national/international regulations (to be specified).
Do not handle until all safety precautions have been read and understood.	**Do NOT fight fire when fire reaches explosives.**		
Wear personal protective equipment/face protection. Chemical manufacturer, importer, or distributor to specify type of equipment, as required.	**Evacuate area.**		

686

C.4.14 EXPLOSIVES (CONTINUED)
(Classified in Accordance with Appendix B.1)

Pictogram
Exploding bomb

Hazard category	Signal word	Hazard statement
Division 1.1	Danger	Explosive; mass explosion hazard
Division 1.2	Danger	Explosive; severe projection hazard
Division 1.3	Danger	Explosive; fire, blast or projection hazard

Precautionary statements

Prevention	Response	Storage	Disposal
Keep away from heat/sparks/open flames/hot surfaces. - No smoking. Chemical manufacturer, importer, or distributor to specify applicable ignition source(s).	**In case of fire:** evacuate area.	Store ... ...in accordance with local/regional/national/ international regulations (to be specified).	**Dispose of contents/container to ...** ... in accordance with local/ regional/national/ international regulations (to be specified).
Keep wetted with... ... Chemical manufacturer, importer, or distributor to specify appropriate material.	**Explosion risk in case of fire.**		
- *if drying out increases explosion hazard, except as needed for manufacturing or operating processes (e.g., nitrocellulose).*	**Do NOT fight fire when fire reaches explosives.**		
Ground/bond container and receiving equipment.			
- *if the explosive is electrostatically sensitive.*			
Do not subject to grinding/shock/.../friction. ...Chemical manufacturer, importer, or distributor to specify applicable rough handling.			
Wear face protection. Chemical manufacturer, importer, or distributor to specify type of equipment.			

Note: Unpackaged explosives or explosives repacked in packagings other than the original or similar packaging shall have the label elements assigned to Division 1.1 unless the hazard is shown to correspond to one of the hazard categories in Appendix B.1, in which case the corresponding symbol, signal word and/or the hazard statement shall be assigned.

C.4.14 EXPLOSIVES (CONTINUED)
(Classified in Accordance with Appendix B.1)

Hazard category	**Signal word**	**Hazard statement**	**Pictogram**
Division 1.4	Warning	Fire or projection hazard	 Exploding bomb[1]

Precautionary statements[1]			
Prevention	**Response**	**Storage**	**Disposal**
Keep away from heat/sparks/open flames/hot surfaces. - No smoking. Chemical manufacturer, importer, or distributor to specify applicable ignition source(s).	**In case of fire: Evacuate area.**	**Store ...** ...in accordance with local/regional/ national/internation al regulations (to be specified).	**Dispose of contents/container to...** ... in accordance with local/regional/national/i nternational regulations (to be specified).
Ground/bond container and receiving equipment. - *if the explosive is electrostatically sensitive.*	**Explosion risk in case of fire.** - *except if explosives are 1.4S ammunition and components thereof.*		
Do not subject to grinding/shock/.../friction. Chemical manufacturer, importer, or distributor to specify applicable rough handling.	**Do NOT fight fire when fire reaches explosives.**		
Wear face protection. Chemical manufacturer, importer, or distributor to specify type of equipment.	**Fight fire with normal precautions from a reasonable distance** - *if explosives are 1.4S ammunition and components thereof.*		

Note: Unpackaged explosives or explosives repacked in packagings other than the original or similar packaging shall have the label elements assigned to Division 1.1 unless the hazard is shown to correspond to one of the hazard categories in Appendix B.1, in which case the corresponding symbol, signal word and/or the hazard statement shall be assigned.[1]

---

[1] *Except no pictogram is required for explosives that are 1.4S small arms ammunition and components thereof. Labels for 1.4S small arms ammunition and components shall include appropriate precautionary statements.*

C.4.14 EXPLOSIVES (CONTINUED)
(Classified in Accordance with Appendix B.1)

Hazard category	Signal word	Hazard statement	Pictogram
Division 1.5	Danger	May mass explode in fire	*No pictogram*

Precautionary statements

Prevention	Response	Storage	Disposal
Keep away from heat/sparks/open flames/hot surfaces. - No smoking. Chemical manufacturer, importer, or distributor to specify applicable ignition source(s).	**In case of fire: Evacuate area.**	Store ... ...in accordance with local/regional/ national/international regulations (to be specified).	**Dispose of contents/container to ...** ... in accordance with local/regional/ national/international regulations (to be specified).
Keep wetted with... ... Chemical manufacturer, importer, or distributor to specify appropriate material. - *if drying out increases explosion hazard, except as needed for manufacturing or operating processes (e.g., nitrocellulose).*	**Explosion risk in case of fire.** **Do NOT fight fire when fire reaches explosives.**		
Ground/bond container and receiving equipment - *if the explosive is electrostatically sensitive.*			
Do not subject to grinding/shock/.../friction. ...Chemical manufacturer, importer, or distributor to specify applicable rough handling.			
Wear face protection. Chemical manufacturer, importer, or distributor to specify type of equipment.			

Note: Unpackaged explosives or explosives repacked in packagings other than the original or similar packaging shall have the label elements assigned to Division 1.1 unless the hazard is shown to correspond to one of the hazard categories in Appendix B.1, in which case the corresponding symbol, signal word and/or the hazard statement shall be assigned.

689

C.4.14 EXPLOSIVES (CONTINUED)
(Classified in Accordance with Appendix B.1)

			Pictogram
			No pictogram

Hazard category
Division 1.6

Signal word
No signal word

Hazard statement
No hazard statement

Precautionary statements

Prevention	Response	Storage	Disposal
None assigned.	None assigned	None assigned	None assigned

Note: Unpackaged explosives or explosives repacked in packagings other than the original or similar packaging shall have the label elements assigned to Division 1.1 unless the hazard is shown to correspond to one of the hazard categories in Appendix B.1, in which case the corresponding symbol, signal word and/or the hazard statement shall be assigned.

C.4.15 FLAMMABLE GASES
(Classified in Accordance with Appendix B.2)

Hazard category	Signal word	Hazard statement	Pictogram
1	Danger	Extremely flammable gas	Flame

Precautionary statements

Prevention	Response	Storage	Disposal
Keep away from heat/sparks/open flames/hot surfaces. –No smoking. Chemical manufacturer, importer, or distributor to specify applicable ignition source(s).	**Leaking gas fire: Do not extinguish, unless leak can be stopped safely.** **Eliminate all ignition sources if safe to do so.**	Store in well-ventilated place.	

C.4.15 FLAMMABLE GASES (CONTINUED)
(Classified in Accordance with Appendix B.2)

Hazard category	Signal word	Hazard statement
2	Warning	Flammable gas

Pictogram
No Pictogram

Precautionary statements

Prevention	Response	Storage	Disposal
Keep away from heat/sparks/open flames/hot surfaces. –No smoking. Chemical manufacturer, importer, or distributor to specify applicable ignition sources(s).	**Leaking gas fire: Do not extinguish, unless leak can be stopped safely.** **Eliminate all ignition sources if safe to do so.**	**Store in well-ventilated place.**	

C.4.16 FLAMMABLE AEROSOLS
(Classified in Accordance with Appendix B.3)

Pictogram
Flame

Hazard category	Signal word
1	Danger
2	Warning

Hazard statement
Extremely flammable aerosol
Flammable aerosol

Precautionary statements

Prevention	Response	Storage	Disposal
Keep away from heat/sparks/open flames/hot surfaces. –No smoking. Chemical manufacturer, importer, or distributor to specify applicable ignition sources(s).		**Protect from sunlight. Do not expose to temperatures exceeding 50 °C/122 °F.**	
Do not spray on an open flame or other ignition source.			
Pressurized container: Do not pierce or burn, even after use.			

693

C.4.17 OXIDIZING GASES
(Classified in Accordance with Appendix B.4)

		Pictogram
		Flame over circle

Hazard category	Signal word	Hazard statement
1	Danger	May cause or intensify fire; oxidizer

Precautionary statements

Prevention	Response	Storage	Disposal
Keep/Store away from clothing/.../combustible materials. ...Chemical manufacturer, importer, or distributor to specify other incompatible materials. **Keep reduction valves/valves and fittings free from oil and grease.**	**In case of fire: Stop leak if safe to do so.**	**Store in well-ventilated place.**	

C.4.18 GASES UNDER PRESSURE
(Classified in Accordance with Appendix B.5)

Hazard category	Signal word	Hazard statement
Compressed gas	Warning	Contains gas under pressure; may explode if heated
Liquefied gas	Warning	Contains gas under pressure; may explode if heated
Dissolved gas	Warning	Contains gas under pressure; may explode if heated

Pictogram
Gas cylinder

Precautionary statements

Prevention	Response	Storage	Disposal
		Protect from sunlight. Store in a well-ventilated place.	

C.4.18 GASES UNDER PRESSURE (CONTINUED)
(Classified in Accordance with Appendix B.5)

		Pictogram Gas cylinder

Hazard category   **Signal word**   **Hazard statement**

Refrigerated liquefied gas   Warning   Contains refrigerated gas; may cause cryogenic burns or injury

Precautionary statements

Prevention	Response	Storage	Disposal
Wear cold insulating gloves/face shield/eye protection.	Thaw frosted parts with lukewarm water. Do not rub affected area. Get immediate medical advice/attention	Store in well-ventilated place.	

C.4.19 FLAMMABLE LIQUIDS
(Classified in Accordance with Appendix B.6)

			Pictogram
			Flame

Hazard category	Signal word	Hazard statement
1	Danger	Extremely flammable liquid and vapor
2	Danger	Highly flammable liquid and vapor
3	Warning	Flammable liquid and vapor

Precautionary statements

Prevention	Response	Storage	Disposal
Keep away from heat/sparks/open flames/hot surfaces.– No smoking. Chemical manufacturer, importer, or distributor to specify applicable ignition source(s). **Keep container tightly closed.** **Ground/Bond container and receiving equipment** - *if electrostatically sensitive material is for reloading.* - *if product is volatile so as to generate hazardous atmosphere.* **Use explosion-proof electrical/ventilating/ lighting/.../equipment.** ... Chemical manufacturer, importer, or distributor to specify other equipment. **Use only non-sparking tools.** **Take precautionary measures against static discharge.** **Wear protective gloves/eye protection/face protection** Chemical manufacturer, importer, or distributor to specify type of equipment.	**If on skin (or hair): Take off immediately all contaminated clothing. Rinse skin with water/shower.** **In case of fire: Use ... to extinguish.** ... Chemical manufacturer, importer, or distributor to specify appropriate media. - *if water increases risk*	Store in a well-ventilated place. Keep cool.	Dispose of contents/container to... ... in accordance with local/regional/national/ international regulations (to be specified).

C.4.19 FLAMMABLE LIQUIDS (CONTINUED)
(Classified in Accordance with Appendix B.6)

Hazard category	Signal word	Hazard statement
4	Warning	Combustible liquid

Pictogram
No Pictogram

Precautionary statements

Prevention	Response	Storage	Disposal
Keep away from flames and hot surfaces. – No smoking. **Wear protective gloves/eye protection/face protection** Chemical manufacturer, importer, or distributor to specify type of equipment.	**In case of fire: Use ... to extinguish.** ... Chemical manufacturer, importer, or distributor to specify appropriate media. - *if water increases risk.*	**Store in a well-ventilated place. Keep cool.**	**Dispose of contents/container to...** in accordance with local/regional/national/international regulations (to be specified).

C.4.20 FLAMMABLE SOLIDS
(Classified in Accordance with Appendix B.7)

Hazard category	Signal word	Hazard statement	Pictogram
1	Danger	Flammable solid	Flame
2	Warning	Flammable solid	

Precautionary statements			
Prevention	**Response**	**Storage**	**Disposal**
Keep away from heat/sparks/open flames/hot surfaces. - No smoking. Chemical manufacturer, importer, or distributor to specify applicable ignition source(s). **Ground/Bond container and receiving equipment.** - *if electrostatically sensitive material is for reloading.* **Use explosion-proof electrical/ventilating/ lighting/... /equipment.** ... Chemical manufacturer, importer, or distributor to specify other equipment. - *if dust clouds can occur.* **Wear protective gloves/eye protection/face protection** Chemical manufacturer, importer, or distributor to specify type of equipment.	**In case of fire: Use ... to extinguish** ... Chemical manufacturer, importer, or distributor to specify appropriate media. - *if water increases risk.*		

C.4.21 SELF-REACTIVE SUBSTANCES AND MIXTURES
(Classified in Accordance with Appendix B.8)

		Pictogram
		Exploding bomb

Hazard category	**Signal word**	**Hazard statement**
Type A	Danger	Heating may cause an explosion

Precautionary statements

Prevention	Response	Storage	Disposal
Keep away from heat/sparks/open flames/hot surfaces. - No smoking. Chemical manufacturer, importer, or distributor to specify applicable ignition source(s).	**In case of fire: Use ... to extinguish** ... Chemical manufacturer, importer, or distributor to specify appropriate media. - *if water increases risk.*	**Store in a well-ventilated place. Keep cool.**	**Dispose of contents/container to...** ... in accordance with local/regional/national/international regulations (to be specified).
Keep/Store away from clothing/.../combustible materials. ... Chemical manufacturer, importer, or distributor to specify other incompatible materials.	**In case of fire: Evacuate area. Fight fire remotely due to the risk of explosion.**	**Store at temperatures not exceeding** ...°C/...°F. ... Chemical manufacturer, importer, or distributor to specify temperature.	
Keep only in original container.		**Store away from other materials.**	
Wear protective gloves/eye protection/face protection. Chemical manufacturer, importer, or distributor to specify type of equipment.			

C.4.21 SELF-REACTIVE SUBSTANCES AND MIXTURES (CONTINUED)
(Classified in Accordance with Appendix B.8)

Hazard category	Signal word	Hazard statement	Pictograms
Type B	Danger	Heating may cause a fire or explosion	Exploding bomb and flame 

Precautionary statements

Prevention	Response	Storage	Disposal
Keep away from heat/sparks/open flames/hot surfaces. - No smoking. Chemical manufacturer, importer, or distributor to specify applicable ignition source(s).	**In case of fire: Use ... to extinguish.** ... Chemical manufacturer, importer, or distributor to specify appropriate media. - *if water increases risk.*	**Store in a well-ventilated place. Keep cool.**	Dispose of contents/container to... ...in accordance with local/regional/national/international regulations (to be specified).
Keep/Store away from clothing/...combustible materials. ... Chemical manufacturer, importer, or distributor to specify other incompatible materials.	**In case of fire: Evacuate area. Fight fire remotely due to the risk of explosion.**	**Store at temperatures not exceeding** ...°C/...°F. ... Chemical manufacturer, importer, or distributor to specify temperature.	
Keep only in original container.		**Store away from other materials.**	
Wear protective gloves/eye protection/face protection. Chemical manufacturer, importer, or distributor to specify type of equipment.			

701

C.4.21 SELF-REACTIVE SUBSTANCES AND MIXTURES(CONTINUED)
(Classified in Accordance with Appendix B.8)

Pictogram
Flame

Hazard category	Signal word	Hazard statement
Type C	Danger	Heating may cause a fire
Type D	Danger	Heating may cause a fire
Type E	Warning	Heating may cause a fire
Type F	Warning	Heating may cause a fire

Precautionary statements

Prevention	Response	Storage	Disposal
Keep away from heat/sparks/open flames/hot surfaces. - No smoking. Chemical manufacturer, importer, or distributor to specify applicable ignition source(s).	**In case of fire: Use ... to extinguish** ... Chemical manufacturer, importer, or distributor to specify appropriate media. - *if water increases risk.*	**Store in a well-ventilated place. Keep cool.**	**Dispose of contents/container to...** ...in accordance with local/regional/national/international regulations (to be specified).
Keep/Store away from clothing/.../combustible materials. ...Chemical manufacturer, importer, or distributor to specify other incompatible materials.		**Store at temperatures not exceeding ...°C/...°F.** ...Chemical manufacturer, importer, or distributor to specify temperature.	
Keep only in original container.		**Store away from other materials.**	
Wear protective gloves/eye protection/face protection. Chemical manufacturer, importer, or distributor to specify type of equipment.			

C.4.22 PYROPHORIC LIQUIDS
(Classified in Accordance with Appendix B.9)

Hazard category	Signal word	Hazard statement	Pictogram
1	Danger	**Hazard statement** Catches fire spontaneously if exposed to air	Flame

Precautionary statements

Prevention	Response	Storage	Disposal
Keep away from heat/sparks/open flames. - No smoking. - *Chemical manufacturer, importer, or distributor to specify applicable ignition sources(s).* **Do not allow contact with air.** **Wear protective gloves/eye protection/face protection.** *Chemical manufacturer, importer, or distributor to specify type of equipment.*	**If on skin: Immerse in cool water/wrap with wet bandages** **In case of fire: Use ... to extinguish** *... Chemical manufacturer, importer, or distributor to specify appropriate media.* - *if water increases risk.*	**Store contents under** *... Chemical manufacturer, importer, or distributor to specify appropriate liquid or inert gas.*	

C.4.23 PYROPHORIC SOLIDS
(Classified in Accordance with Appendix B.10)

Hazard category	Signal word	Hazard statement	Pictogram
1	Danger	Catches fire spontaneously if exposed to air	Flame

Precautionary statements

Prevention	Response	Storage	Disposal
Keep away from heat/sparks/open flames/hot surfaces. - No smoking. Chemical manufacturer, importer, or distributor to specify applicable ignition source(s). **Do not allow contact with air.** **Wear protective gloves/eye protection/face protection** Chemical manufacturer, importer, or distributor to specify type of equipment.	**Brush off loose particles from skin. Immerse in cool water/wrap/wrap in wet bandages.** **In case of fire: Use ... to extinguish** ... Chemical manufacturer, importer, or distributor to specify appropriate media. - *if water increases risk.*	**Store contents under** ... Chemical manufacturer, importer, or distributor to specify appropriate liquid or inert gas.	

C.4.24 SELF-HEATING SUBSTANCES AND MIXTURES
(Classified in Accordance with Appendix B.11)

Hazard category	Signal word
1	Danger
2	Warning

Hazard statement

Self-heating; may catch fire

Self-heating in large quantities; may catch fire

Pictogram
Flame

Precautionary statements

Prevention	Response	Storage	Disposal
Keep cool. Protect from sunlight. **Wear protective gloves/eye protection/face protection.** Chemical manufacturer, importer, or distributor to specify type of equipment.		**Maintain air gap between stacks/pallets.** **Store bulk masses greater than ... kg/...lbs at temperatures not exceeding ...°C/...°F.** ... Chemical manufacturer, importer, or distributor to specify mass and temperature. **Store away from other materials.**	

705

C.4.25 SUBSTANCES AND MIXTURES WHICH, IN CONTACT WITH WATER, EMIT FLAMMABLE GASES
(Classified in Accordance with Appendix B.12)

Hazard category	Signal word	Hazard statement
1	Danger	In contact with water releases flammable gases, which may ignite spontaneously
2	Danger	In contact with water releases flammable gas

Pictogram
Flame

Precautionary statements

Prevention	Response	Storage	Disposal
Do not allow contact with water. **Handle under inert gas. Protect from moisture.** **Wear protective gloves/eye protection/face protection.** Chemical manufacturer, importer, or distributor to specify type of equipment.	**Brush off loose particles from skin and immerse in cool water/wrap in wet bandages.** **In case of fire: Use ... to extinguish** ... Chemical manufacturer, importer, or distributor to specify appropriate media. - *if water increases risk.*	**Store in a dry place. Store in a closed container.**	**Dispose of contents/container to...** ...in accordance with local/regional/national/ international regulations (to be specified).

C.4.25 SUBSTANCES AND MIXTURES WHICH, IN CONTACT WITH WATER, EMIT FLAMMABLE GASES
(CONTINUED)

(Classified in Accordance with Appendix B.12)

			Pictogram
			Flame

Hazard category	Signal word	Hazard statement	
3	Warning	In contact with water releases flammable gas	

Precautionary statements			
Prevention	**Response**	**Storage**	**Disposal**
Handle under inert gas. Protect from moisture. **Wear protective gloves/eye protection/face protection.** Chemical manufacturer, importer, or distributor to specify type of equipment.	**In case of fire: Use ... to extinguish.** ... Chemical manufacturer, importer, or distributor to specify appropriate media. - *if water increases risk.*	**Store in a dry place.** **Store in a closed container.**	**Dispose of contents/container to...** ... in accordance with local/regional/national/international regulations (to be specified).

C.4.26 OXIDIZING LIQUIDS
(Classified in Accordance with Appendix B.13)

Hazard category	Signal word	Hazard statement	Pictogram
1	Danger	May cause fire or explosion; strong oxidizer	Flame over circle

Precautionary statements			
Prevention	Response	Storage	Disposal
Keep away from heat.	If on clothing: Rinse immediately contaminated clothing and skin with plenty of water before removing clothes.		Dispose of contents/container to... ...in accordance with local/regional/ national/international regulations (to be specified).
Keep/Store away from clothing and other combustible materials.	In case of major fire and large quantities: Evacuate area. Fight fire remotely due to the risk of explosion.		
Take any precaution to avoid mixing with combustibles/... ... Chemical manufacturer, importer, or distributor to specify other incompatible materials.	In case of fire: Use ... to extinguish. ... Chemical manufacturer, importer, or distributor to specify appropriate media. - *if water increases risk.*		
Wear protective gloves /eye protection/face protection. Chemical manufacturer, importer, or distributor to specify type of equipment.			
Wear fire/flame resistant/retardant clothing.			

C.4.26 OXIDIZING LIQUIDS (CONTINUED)
(Classified in Accordance with Appendix B.13)

Hazard category	Signal word	Hazard statement
2	Danger	May intensify fire; oxidizer
3	Warning	May intensify fire; oxidizer

Pictogram
Flame over circle

Precautionary statements

Prevention	Response	Storage	Disposal
Keep away from heat. **Keep/Store away from clothing/.../combustible materials.** ...Chemical manufacturer, importer, or distributor to specify other incompatible materials. **Take any precaution to avoid mixing with combustibles/...** ...Chemical manufacturer, importer, or distributor to specify other incompatible materials. **Wear protective gloves/eye protection/face protection.** Chemical manufacturer, importer, or distributor to specify type of equipment.	**In case of fire: Use ... to extinguish.** ... Chemical manufacturer, importer, or distributor to specify appropriate media. - *if water increases risk.*		**Dispose of contents/container to...** ...in accordance with local/regional/ national/international regulations (to be specified).

709

C.4.27 OXIDIZING SOLIDS
(Classified in Accordance with Appendix B.14)

Hazard category	Signal word	Hazard statement	Pictogram
1	Danger	May cause fire or explosion; strong oxidizer	Flame over circle

Precautionary statements

Prevention	Response	Storage	Disposal
Keep away from heat.	**If on clothing: Rinse immediately contaminated clothing and skin with plenty of water before removing clothes.**		**Dispose of contents/container to...** ...in accordance with local/regional/ national/international regulations (to be specified).
Keep away from clothing and other combustible materials.			
Take any precaution to avoid mixing with combustibles/... ...Chemical manufacturer, importer, or distributor to specify other incompatible materials.	**In case of major fire and large quantities: Evacuate area. Fight fire remotely due to the risk of explosion.**		
	In case of fire: Use ... to extinguish. ... Chemical manufacturer, importer, or distributor to specify appropriate media.		
Wear protective gloves/eye protection/face protection. Chemical manufacturer, importer, or distributor to specify type of equipment.	- *if water increases risk.*		
Wear fire/flame resistant/retardant clothing.			

C.4.27 OXIDIZING SOLIDS (CONTINUED)
(Classified in Accordance with Appendix B.14)

Hazard category	Signal word	Hazard statement
2	Danger	May intensify fire; oxidizer
3	Warning	May intensify fire; oxidizer

Pictogram
Flame over circle

Precautionary statements

Prevention	Response	Storage	Disposal
Keep away from heat. **Keep/Store away from clothing/.../ combustible materials.** … Chemical manufacturer, importer, or distributor to specify incompatible materials. **Take any precaution to avoid mixing with combustibles/...** …Chemical manufacturer, importer, or distributor to specify other incompatible materials. **Wear protective gloves/eye protection/face protection.** Chemical manufacturer, importer, or distributor to specify type of equipment.	**In case of fire: Use ... to extinguish.** … Chemical manufacturer, importer, or distributor to specify appropriate media. - *if water increases risk.*		**Dispose of contents/container to...** … in accordance with local/regional/national/international regulations (to be specified).

711

C.4.28 ORGANIC PEROXIDES
(Classified in Accordance with Appendix B.15)

		Pictogram
		Exploding bomb

Hazard category	Signal word
Type A	Danger

Hazard statement

Heating may cause an explosion

Precautionary statements

Prevention	Response	Storage	Disposal
Keep away from heat/sparks/open flames/hot surfaces.- No smoking. Chemical manufacturer, importer, or distributor to specify applicable ignition source(s).		**Store at temperatures not exceeding ...°C/...°F. Keep cool.** ...Chemical manufacturer, importer, or distributor to specify temperature.	**Dispose of contents/container to...** ... in accordance with local/regional/national/international regulations (to be specified).
Keep/Store away from clothing/.../combustible materials. ... Chemical manufacturer, importer, or distributor to specify incompatible materials.		**Protect from sunlight.** **Store away from other materials.**	
Keep only in original container.			
Wear protective gloves/eye protection/face protection. Chemical manufacturer, importer, or distributor to specify type of equipment.			

712

C.4.28 ORGANIC PEROXIDES (CONTINUED)
(Classified in Accordance with Appendix B.15)

Hazard category	Signal word	Hazard statement
Type B	Danger	Heating may cause a fire or explosion

	Pictograms
	Exploding bomb and flame

Precautionary statements

Prevention	Response	Storage	Disposal
Keep away from heat/sparks/open flames/hot surfaces. - No smoking. Chemical manufacturer, importer, or distributor to specify applicable ignition source(s).		**Store at temperatures not exceeding ...°C/...°F. Keep cool.** Chemical manufacturer, importer, or distributor to specify temperature.	**Dispose of contents/container to...** ... in accordance with local/regional/national/international regulations (to be specified).
Keep /Store away from clothing/.../combustible materials. ... Chemical manufacturer, importer, or distributor to specify incompatible materials.		**Protect from sunlight.** **Store away from other materials.**	
Keep only in original container.			
Wear protective gloves/eye protection/face protection. Chemical manufacturer, importer, or distributor to specify type of equipment.			

713

C.4.28 ORGANIC PEROXIDES (CONTINUED)
(Classified in Accordance with Appendix B.15)

Hazard category	Signal word	Hazard statement
Type C	Danger	Heating may cause a fire
Type D	Danger	Heating may cause a fire
Type E	Warning	Heating may cause a fire
Type F	Warning	Heating may cause a fire

Pictogram
Flame

Precautionary statements

Prevention	Response	Storage	Disposal
Keep away from heat/sparks/open flames/hot surfaces. - No smoking. Chemical manufacturer, importer, or distributor to specify applicable ignition source(s).		**Store at temperatures not exceeding ...°C/...°F. Keep cool.** ... Chemical manufacturer, importer, or distributor to specify temperature.	**Dispose of contents/container to...** ... in accordance with local/regional/national/international regulations (to be specified).
Keep/Store away from clothing/.../ combustible materials ... Chemical manufacturer, importer, or distributor to specify incompatible materials.		**Protect from sunlight.**	
Keep only in original container.		**Store away from other materials.**	
Wear protective gloves/eye protection/face protection. Chemical manufacturer, importer, or distributor to specify type of equipment.			

C.4.29 CORROSIVE TO METALS
(Classified in Accordance with Appendix B.16)

Hazard category	Signal word	Hazard statement
1	Warning	May be corrosive to metals

Pictogram
Corrosion

Precautionary statements

Prevention	Response	Storage	Disposal
Keep only in original container.	**Absorb spillage to prevent material damage.**	**Store in corrosive resistant/... container with a resistant inner liner.** ... Chemical manufacturer, importer, or distributor to specify other compatible materials.	

C.4.30 Label elements for OSHA defined hazards

Hazard	Signal word	Hazard statement	Pictogram
Pyrophoric Gas	Danger	Catches fire spontaneously if exposed to air	Flame
Simple Asphyxiant	Warning	May displace oxygen and cause rapid suffocation	*No Pictogram*
Combustible Dust[2]	Warning	May form combustible dust concentrations in air	*No Pictogram*

[2] *The chemical manufacturer or importer shall label chemicals that are shipped in dust form, and present a combustible dust hazard in that form when used downstream, under paragraph (f)(1); 2) the chemical manufacturer or importer shipping chemicals that are in a form that is not yet a dust must provide a label to customers under paragraph (f)(4) if, under normal conditions of use, the chemicals are processed in a downstream workplace in such a way that they present a combustible dust hazard; and 3) the employer shall follow the workplace labeling requirements under paragraph (f)(6) where combustible dust hazards are present.*

APPENDIX D TO § 1910.1200—SAFETY DATA
SHEETS (MANDATORY)

A safety data sheet (SDS) shall include the information specified in Table D.1 under the section number and heading indicated for sections 1–11 and 16. If no relevant information is found for any given subheading within a section, the SDS shall clearly indicate that no applicable information is available. Sections 12–15 may be included in the SDS, but are not mandatory.

TABLE D.1—MINIMUM INFORMATION FOR AN SDS

Heading	Subheading
1. Identification	(a) Product identifier used on the label; (b) Other means of identification; (c) Recommended use of the chemical and restrictions on use; (d) Name, address, and telephone number of the chemical manufacturer, importer, or other responsible party; (e) Emergency phone number.
2. Hazard(s) identification	(a) Classification of the chemical in accordance with paragraph (d) of § 1910.1200; (b) Signal word, hazard statement(s), symbol(s) and precautionary statement(s) in accordance with paragraph (f) of § 1910.1200. (Hazard symbols may be provided as graphical reproductions in black and white or the name of the symbol, e.g., flame, skull and crossbones); (c) Describe any hazards not otherwise classified that have been identified during the classification process; (d) Where an ingredient with unknown acute toxicity is used in a mixture at a concentration ≥1% and the mixture is not classified based on testing of the mixture as a whole, a statement that X% of the mixture consists of ingredient(s) of unknown acute toxicity is required.
3. Composition/information on ingredients	Except as provided for in paragraph (i) of § 1910.1200 on trade secrets: For Substances (a) Chemical name; (b) Common name and synonyms; (c) CAS number and other unique identifiers; (d) Impurities and stabilizing additives which are themselves classified and which contribute to the classification of the substance. For Mixtures In addition to the information required for substances: (a) The chemical name and concentration (exact percentage) or concentration ranges of all ingredients which are classified as health hazards in accordance with paragraph (d) of § 1910.1200 and (1) Are present above their cut-off/concentration limits; or (2) Present a health risk below the cut-off/concentration limits. (b) The concentration (exact percentage) shall be specified unless a trade secret claim is made in accordance with paragraph (i) of § 1910.1200, when there is batch-to-batch variability in the production of a mixture, or for a group of substantially similar mixtures (*See* A.0.5.1.2) with similar chemical composition. In these cases, concentration ranges may be used. For All Chemicals Where a Trade Secret is Claimed Where a trade secret is claimed in accordance with paragraph (i) of § 1910.1200, a statement that the specific chemical identity and/or exact percentage (concentration) of composition has been withheld as a trade secret is required.
4. First-aid measures	(a) Description of necessary measures, subdivided according to the different routes of exposure, i.e., inhalation, skin and eye contact, and ingestion; (b) Most important symptoms/effects, acute and delayed; (c) Indication of immediate medical attention and special treatment needed, if necessary.
5. Fire-fighting measures	(a) Suitable (and unsuitable) extinguishing media. (b) Specific hazards arising from the chemical (e.g., nature of any hazardous combustion products). (c) Special protective equipment and precautions for fire-fighters.
6. Accidental release measures	(a) Personal precautions, protective equipment, and emergency procedures. (b) Methods and materials for containment and cleaning up.
7. Handling and storage	(a) Precautions for safe handling. (b) Conditions for safe storage, including any incompatibilities.
8. Exposure controls/personal protection ...	(a) OSHA permissible exposure limit (PEL), American Conference of Governmental Industrial Hygienists (ACGIH) Threshold Limit Value (TLV), and any other exposure limit used or recommended by the chemical manufacturer, importer, or employer preparing the safety data sheet, where available. (b) Appropriate engineering controls. (c) Individual protection measures, such as personal protective equipment.
9. Physical and chemical properties	(a) Appearance (physical state, color, etc.); (b) Odor; (c) Odor threshold; (d) pH; (e) Melting point/freezing point; (f) Initial boiling point and boiling range; (g) Flash point; (h) Evaporation rate; (i) Flammability (solid, gas);

717

TABLE D.1—MINIMUM INFORMATION FOR AN SDS—Continued

Heading	Subheading
	(j) Upper/lower flammability or explosive limits;
	(k) Vapor pressure;
	(l) Vapor density;
	(m) Relative density;
	(n) Solubility(ies);
	(o) Partition coefficient: n-octanol/water;
	(p) Auto-ignition temperature;
	(q) Decomposition temperature;
	(r) Viscosity.
10. Stability and reactivity	(a) Reactivity;
	(b) Chemical stability;
	(c) Possibility of hazardous reactions;
	(d) Conditions to avoid (e.g., static discharge, shock, or vibration);
	(e) Incompatible materials;
	(f) Hazardous decomposition products.
11. Toxicological information	Description of the various toxicological (health) effects and the available data used to identify those effects, including:
	(a) Information on the likely routes of exposure (inhalation, ingestion, skin and eye contact);
	(b) Symptoms related to the physical, chemical and toxicological characteristics;
	(c) Delayed and immediate effects and also chronic effects from short- and long-term exposure;
	(d) Numerical measures of toxicity (such as acute toxicity estimates).
	(e) Whether the hazardous chemical is listed in the National Toxicology Program (NTP) Report on Carcinogens (latest edition) or has been found to be a potential carcinogen in the International Agency for Research on Cancer (IARC) Monographs (latest edition), or by OSHA.
12. Ecological information (Non-mandatory)	(a) Ecotoxicity (aquatic and terrestrial, where available);
	(b) Persistence and degradability;
	(c) Bioaccumulative potential;
	(d) Mobility in soil;
	(e) Other adverse effects (such as hazardous to the ozone layer).
13. Disposal considerations (Non-mandatory).	Description of waste residues and information on their safe handling and methods of disposal, including the disposal of any contaminated packaging.
14. Transport information (Non-mandatory)	(a) UN number;
	(b) UN proper shipping name;
	(c) Transport hazard class(es);
	(d) Packing group, if applicable;
	(e) Environmental hazards (e.g., Marine pollutant (Yes/No));
	(f) Transport in bulk (according to Annex II of MARPOL 73/78 and the IBC Code);
	(g) Special precautions which a user needs to be aware of, or needs to comply with, in connection with transport or conveyance either within or outside their premises.
15. Regulatory information (Non-mandatory).	Safety, health and environmental regulations specific for the product in question.
16. Other information, including date of preparation or last revision.	The date of preparation of the SDS or the last change to it.

APPENDIX E TO § 1910.1200—DEFINITION OF "TRADE SECRET" (MANDATORY)

The following is a reprint of the *Restatement of Torts* section 757, comment *b* (1939):

b. Definition of trade secret. A trade secret may consist of any formula, pattern, device or compilation of information which is used in one's business, and which gives him an opportunity to obtain an advantage over competitors who do not know or use it. It may be a formula for a chemical compound, a process of manufacturing, treating or preserving materials, a pattern for a machine or other device, or a list of customers. It differs from other secret information in a business (see s759 of the *Restatement of Torts* which is not included in this Appendix) in that it is not simply information as to single or ephemeral events in the conduct of the business, as, for example, the amount or other terms of a secret bid for a contract or the salary of certain employees, or the security investments made or contemplated, or the date fixed for the announcement of a new policy or for bringing out a new model or the like. A trade secret is a process or device for continuous use in the operations of the business. Generally it relates to the production of goods, as, for example, a machine or formula for the production of an article. It may, however, relate to the sale of goods or to other operations in the business, such as a code for determining discounts, rebates or other concessions in a price list or catalogue, or a list of specialized customers, or a method of bookkeeping or other office management.

Secrecy. The subject matter of a trade secret must be secret. Matters of public knowledge or of general knowledge in an industry cannot be appropriated by one as his secret. Matters which are completely disclosed by the goods which one markets cannot be his secret. Substantially, a trade secret is known only in the particular business in which it is used. It is not requisite that only the proprietor of the business know it. He may, without losing his protection, communicate it to employees involved in its use. He may likewise communicate it to others pledged to secrecy. Others may also know of it independently, as, for example, when they have discovered the process or formula by independent invention and are keeping it secret. Nevertheless, a substantial element of secrecy must exist, so that, except by the use of improper means, there would be difficulty in acquiring the information. An exact definition of a trade secret is not possible. Some factors to be considered in determining whether given information is one's trade secret are: (1) The extent to which the information is known outside of his business; (2) the extent to which it is known by employees and others involved in his business; (3) the extent of measures taken by him to guard the secrecy of the information; (4) the value of the information to him and his competitors; (5) the amount of effort or money expended by him in developing the information; (6) the ease or difficulty with which the information could be properly acquired or duplicated by others.

Novelty and prior art. A trade secret may be a device or process which is patentable; but it need not be that. It may be a device or process which is clearly anticipated in the prior art or one which is merely a mechanical improvement that a good mechanic can make. Novelty and invention are not requisite for a trade secret as they are for patentability. These requirements are essential to patentability because a patent protects against unlicensed use of the patented device or process even by one who discovers it properly through independent research. The patent monopoly is a reward to the inventor. But such is not the case with a trade secret. Its protection is not based on a policy of rewarding or otherwise encouraging the development of secret processes or devices. The protection is merely against breach of faith and reprehensible means of learning another's secret. For this limited protection it is not appropriate to require also the kind of novelty and invention which is a requisite of patentability. The nature of the secret is, however, an important factor in determining the kind of relief that is appropriate against one who is subject to liability under the rule stated in this Section. Thus, if the secret consists of a device or process which is a novel invention, one who acquires the secret wrongfully is ordinarily enjoined from fur-

ther use of it and is required to account for the profits derived from his past use. If, on the other hand, the secret consists of mechanical improvements that a good mechanic can make without resort to the secret, the wrongdoer's liability may be limited to damages, and an injunction against future use of the improvements made with the aid of the secret may be inappropriate.

APPENDIX F TO § 1910.1200—GUIDANCE FOR HAZARD CLASSIFICATIONS RE: CARCINOGENICITY (NON-MANDATORY)

The mandatory criteria for classification of a chemical for carcinogenicity under HCS (§ 1910.1200) are found in Appendix A.6 to this section. This non-mandatory Appendix provides additional guidance on hazard classification for carcinogenicity. Part A of Appendix F includes background guidance provided by GHS based on the Preamble of the International Agency for Research on Cancer (IARC) "Monographs on the Evaluation of Carcinogenic Risks to Humans" (2006). Part B provides IARC classification information. Part C provides background guidance from the National Toxicology Program (NTP) "Report on Carcinogens" (RoC), and Part D is a table that compares GHS carcinogen hazard categories to carcinogen classifications under IARC and NTP, allowing classifiers to be able to use information from IARC and NTP RoC carcinogen classifications to complete their classifications under the GHS, and thus the HCS.

PART A: BACKGROUND GUIDANCE [1]

As noted in Footnote 6 of Appendix A.6. to this section, the GHS includes as guidance for classifiers information taken from the Preamble of the International Agency for Research on Cancer (IARC) "Monographs on the Evaluation of Carcinogenic Risks to Humans" (2006), providing guidance on the evaluation of the strength and evidence of carcinogenic risks to humans. This guidance also discusses some additional considerations in classification and an approach to analysis, rather than hard-and-fast rules. Part A is consistent with Appendix A.6, and should help in evaluating information to determine carcinogenicity.

Carcinogenicity in humans:

The evidence relevant to carcinogenicity from studies in humans is classified into one of the following categories:

---

[1] *The text of Appendix F, Part A, on the IARC Monographs, is paraphrased from the 2006 Preamble to the "Monographs on the Evaluation of Carcinogenic Risks to Humans"; the Classifier is referred to the full IARC Preamble for the complete text. The text is not part of the agreed GHS text on the harmonized system developed by the OECD Task Force-HCL.*

(a) Sufficient evidence of carcinogenicity: A causal relationship has been established between exposure to the agent and human cancer. That is, a positive relationship has been observed between the exposure and cancer in studies in which chance, bias and confounding could be ruled out with reasonable confidence.

(b) Limited evidence of carcinogenicity: A positive association has been observed between exposure to the agent and cancer for which a causal interpretation is considered by the Working Group to be credible, but chance, bias or confounding could not be ruled out with reasonable confidence.

In some instances, the above categories may be used to classify the degree of evidence related to carcinogenicity in specific organs or tissues.

Carcinogenicity in experimental animals:

The evidence relevant to carcinogenicity in experimental animals is classified into one of the following categories:

(a) Sufficient evidence of carcinogenicity: A causal relationship has been established between the agent and an increased incidence of malignant neoplasms or of an appropriate combination of benign and malignant neoplasms in two or more species of animals or two or more independent studies in one species carried out at different times or in different laboratories or under different protocols. An increased incidence of tumors in both sexes of a single species in a well-conducted study, ideally conducted under Good Laboratory Practices, can also provide sufficient evidence.

Exceptionally, a single study in one species and sex might be considered to provide sufficient evidence of carcinogenicity when malignant neoplasms occur to an unusual degree with regard to incidence, site, type of tumor or age at onset, or when there are strong findings of tumors at multiple sites.

(b) Limited evidence of carcinogenicity: The data suggest a carcinogenic effect but are limited for making a definitive evaluation because, e.g. the evidence of carcinogenicity is restricted to a single experiment; there are unresolved questions regarding the adequacy of the design, conduct or interpretation of the studies; the agent increases the incidence only of benign neoplasms or lesions of uncertain neoplastic potential; or the evidence of carcinogenicity is restricted to studies that demonstrate only promoting activity in a narrow range of tissues or organs.

Guidance on How To Consider Important Factors in Classification of Carcinogenicity (See Reference Section)

The weight of evidence analysis called for in GHS and the HCS (§ 1910.1200) is an integrative approach that considers important factors in determining carcinogenic potential along with the strength of evidence analysis. The IPCS *"Conceptual Framework for Evaluating a Mode of Action for Chemical Carcinogenesis"* (2001), International Life Sciences Institute (ILSI) *"Framework for Human Relevance Analysis of Information on Carcinogenic Modes of Action"* (Meek, *et al.*, 2003; Cohen *et al.*, 2003, 2004), and Preamble to the IARC Monographs (2006; Section B.6. (Scientific Review and Evaluation; Evaluation and Rationale)) provide a basis for systematic assessments that may be performed in a consistent fashion. The IPCS also convened a panel in 2004 to further develop and clarify the human relevance framework. However, the above documents are not intended to dictate answers, nor provide lists of criteria to be checked off.

Mode of Action

Various documents on carcinogen assessment all note that mode of action in and of itself, or consideration of comparative metabolism, should be evaluated on a case-by-case basis and are part of an analytic evaluative approach. One must look closely at any mode of action in animal experiments, taking into consideration comparative toxicokinetics/toxicodynamics between the animal test species and humans to determine the relevance of the results to humans. This may lead to the possibility of discounting very specific effects of certain types of substances. Life stage-dependent effects on cellular differentiation may also lead to qualitative differences between animals and humans. Only if a mode of action of tumor development is conclusively determined not to be operative in humans may the carcinogenic evidence for that tumor be discounted. However, a weight of evidence evaluation for a substance calls for any other tumorigenic activity to be evaluated, as well.

Responses in Multiple Animal Experiments

Positive responses in several species add to the weight of evidence that a substance is a carcinogen. Taking into account all of the factors listed in A.6.2.5.2 and more, such chemicals with positive outcomes in two or more species would be provisionally considered to be classified in GHS Category 1B until human relevance of animal results are assessed in their entirety. It should be noted, however, that positive results for one species in at least two independent studies, or a single positive study showing unusually strong evidence of malignancy may also lead to Category 1B.

Responses Are in One Sex or Both Sexes

Any case of gender-specific tumors should be evaluated in light of the total tumorigenic response to the substance observed at other sites (multi-site responses or incidence above background) in determining the carcinogenic potential of the substance.

If tumors are seen only in one sex of an animal species, the mode of action should be carefully evaluated to see if the response is consistent with the postulated mode of action. Effects seen only in one sex in a test species may be less convincing than effects seen in both sexes, unless there is a clear patho-physiological difference consistent with the mode of action to explain the single sex response.

Confounding Effects of Excessive Toxicity or Localized Effects

Tumors occurring only at excessive doses associated with severe toxicity generally have doubtful potential for carcinogenicity in humans. In addition, tumors occurring only at sites of contact and/or only at excessive doses need to be carefully evaluated for human relevance for carcinogenic hazard. For example, forestomach tumors, following administration by gavage of an irritating or corrosive, non-mutagenic chemical, may be of questionable relevance. However, such determinations must be evaluated carefully in justifying the carcinogenic potential for humans; any occurrence of other tumors at distant sites must also be considered.

Tumor Type, Reduced Tumor Latency

Unusual tumor types or tumors occurring with reduced latency may add to the weight of evidence for the carcinogenic potential of a substance, even if the tumors are not statistically significant.

Toxicokinetic behavior is normally assumed to be similar in animals and humans, at least from a qualitative perspective. On the other hand, certain tumor types in animals may be associated with toxicokinetics or toxicodynamics that are unique to the animal species tested and may not be predictive of carcinogenicity in humans. Very few such examples have been agreed internationally. However, one example is the lack of human relevance of kidney tumors in male rats associated with compounds causing α2u-globulin nephropathy (IARC, Scientific Publication N° 147[2]). Even when a particular tumor type may be discounted, expert judgment must be used in assessing the total tumor profile in any animal experiment.

PART B: INTERNATIONAL AGENCY FOR RESEARCH ON CANCER (IARC)[3]

IARC Carcinogen Classification Categories:

---

[2] *While most international agencies do not consider kidney tumors coincident with α2u-globulin nephropathy to be a predictor of risk in humans, this view is not universally held. (See: Doi et al., 2007).*

[3] *Preamble of the International Agency for Research on Cancer (IARC) "Monographs on the*

Group 1: The agent is *carcinogenic to humans*

This category is used when there is *sufficient evidence of carcinogenicity* in humans. Exceptionally, an agent may be placed in this category when evidence of carcinogenicity in humans is less than *sufficient* but there is *sufficient evidence of carcinogenicity* in experimental animals and strong evidence in exposed humans that the agent acts through a relevant mechanism of carcinogenicity.

Group 2:

This category includes agents for which, at one extreme, the degree of evidence of carcinogenicity in humans is almost *sufficient*, as well as those for which, at the other extreme, there are no human data but for which there is evidence of carcinogenicity in experimental animals. Agents are assigned to either Group 2A (*probably carcinogenic to humans*) or Group 2B (*possibly carcinogenic to humans*) on the basis of epidemiological and experimental evidence of carcinogenicity and mechanistic and other relevant data. The terms *probably carcinogenic* and *possibly carcinogenic* have no quantitative significance and are used simply as descriptors of different levels of evidence of human carcinogenicity, with *probably carcinogenic* signifying a higher level of evidence than *possibly carcinogenic*.

Group 2A: The agent is *probably carcinogenic to human.*

This category is used when there is *limited evidence of carcinogenicity* in humans and *sufficient evidence of carcinogenicity* in experimental animals. In some cases, an agent may be classified in this category when there is *inadequate evidence of carcinogenicity* in humans and *sufficient evidence of carcinogenicity* in experimental animals and strong evidence that the carcinogenesis is mediated by a mechanism that also operates in humans. Exceptionally, an agent may be classified in this category solely on the basis of *limited evidence of carcinogenicity* in humans. An agent may be assigned to this category if it clearly belongs, based on mechanistic considerations, to a class of agents for which one or more members have been classified in Group 1 or Group 2A.

Group 2B: The agent is *possibly carcinogenic to humans.*

This category is used for agents for which there is *limited evidence of carcinogenicity* in humans and less than *sufficient evidence of carcinogenicity* in experimental animals. It may also be used when there is *inadequate evidence of carcinogenicity* in humans but there is *sufficient evidence of carcinogenicity* in experimental animals. In some instances,

---

Evaluation of Carcinogenic Risks to Humans" (2006).

an agent for which there is *inadequate evidence of carcinogenicity* in humans and less than *sufficient evidence of carcinogenicity* in experimental animals together with supporting evidence from mechanistic and other relevant data may be placed in this group. An agent may be classified in this category solely on the basis of strong evidence from mechanistic and other relevant data.

PART C: NATIONAL TOXICOLOGY PROGRAM (NTP), "REPORT ON CARCINOGENS", BACKGROUND GUIDANCE

NTP Listing Criteria[4]:

The criteria for listing an agent, substance, mixture, or exposure circumstance in the Report on Carcinogens (RoC) are as follows:

Known To Be A Human Carcinogen: There is sufficient evidence of carcinogenicity from studies in humans[5] that indicates a causal relationship between exposure to the agent, substance, or mixture, and human cancer.

Reasonably Anticipated To Be A Human Carcinogen: There is limited evidence of carcinogenicity from studies in humans that indicates that a causal interpretation is credible, but that alternative explanations, such as chance, bias, or confounding factors, could not adequately be excluded,

or

there is sufficient evidence of carcinogenicity from studies in experimental animals that indicates there is an increased incidence of malignant and/or a combination of malignant and benign tumors in multiple species or at multiple tissue sites, or by multiple routes of exposure, or to an unusual degree with regard to incidence, site, or type of tumor, or age at onset,

or

there is less than sufficient evidence of carcinogenicity in humans or laboratory animals; however, the agent, substance, or mixture belongs to a well-defined, structurally-related class of substances whose members are listed in a previous Report on Carcinogens as either known to be a human carcinogen or reasonably anticipated to be a human carcinogen, or there is convincing relevant information that the agent acts through mechanisms indicating it would likely cause cancer in humans.

Conclusions regarding carcinogenicity in humans or experimental animals are based on scientific judgment, with consideration given to all relevant information. Relevant information includes, but is not limited to, dose response, route of exposure, chemical structure, metabolism, pharmacokinetics, sensitive sub-populations, genetic effects, or other data relating to mechanism of action or factors that may be unique to a given substance. For example, there may be substances for which there is evidence of carcinogenicity in laboratory animals, but there are compelling data indicating that the agent acts through mechanisms that do not operate in humans and would therefore not reasonably be anticipated to cause cancer in humans.

PART D: TABLE RELATING APPROXIMATE EQUIVALENCES AMONG IARC, NTP RoC, AND GHS CARCINOGENICITY CLASSIFICATIONS

The following table may be used to perform hazard classifications for carcinogenicity under the HCS (§ 1910.1200). It relates the approximated GHS hazard categories for carcinogenicity to the classifications provided by IARC and NTP, as described in Parts B and C of this Appendix.

APPROXIMATE EQUIVALENCES AMONG CARCINOGEN CLASSIFICATION SCHEMES

IARC	GHS	NTP RoC
Group 1	Category 1A	Known.
Group 2A	Category 1B	Reasonably Anticipated (See Note 1).
Group 2B	Category 2	Reasonably Anticipated (See Note 1).

Note 1:

1. *Limited evidence of carcinogenicity from studies in humans (corresponding to IARC 2A/ GHS 1B);*

2. *Sufficient evidence of carcinogenicity from studies in experimental animals (again, essentially corresponding to IARC 2A/GHS 1B);*

3. *Less than sufficient evidence of carcinogenicity in humans or laboratory animals; however:*

a. *The agent, substance, or mixture belongs to a well-defined, structurally-related class of substances whose members are listed in a previous RoC as either "Known" or "Reasonably Anticipated" to be a human carcinogen, or*

---

[4] *See: http://ntp.niehs.nih.gov/go/15209.*
[5] *This evidence can include traditional cancer epidemiology studies, data from clinical studies, and/or data derived from the study of tissues or*

cells from humans exposed to the substance in question that can be useful for evaluating whether a relevant cancer mechanism is operating in people.

b. *There is convincing relevant information that the agent acts through mechanisms indicating it would likely cause cancer in humans.*

*REFERENCES

Cohen, S.M., J. Klaunig, M.E. Meek, R.N. Hill, T. Pastoor, L. Lehman-McKeeman, J. Bucher, D.G. Longfellow, J. Seed, V. Dellarco, P. Fenner-Crisp, and D. Patton. 2004. Evaluating the human relevance of chemically induced animal tumors. *Toxicol. Sci.* 78(2):181–186.

Cohen, S.M., M.E. Meek, J.E. Klaunig, D.E. Patton, P.A. Fenner-Crisp. 2003. The human relevance of information on carcinogenic modes of action: Overview. *Crit. Rev. Toxicol.* 33(6):581–9.

Meek, M.E., J.R. Bucher, S.M. Cohen, V. Dellarco, R.N. Hill, L. Lehman-McKeeman, D.G. Longfellow, T. Pastoor, J. Seed, D.E. Patton. 2003. A framework for human relevance analysis of information on carcinogenic modes of action. *Crit. Rev. Toxicol.* 33(6):591–653.

Sonich-Mullin, C., R. Fielder, J. Wiltse, K. Baetcke, J. Dempsey, P. Fenner-Crisp, D. Grant, M. Hartley, A. Knapp, D. Kroese, I. Mangelsdorf, E. Meek, J.M. Rice, and M. Younes. 2001. The conceptual framework for evaluating a mode of action for chemical carcinogenesis. *Reg. Toxicol. Pharm.* 34:146–152.

International Programme on Chemical Safety Harmonization Group. 2004. Report of the First Meeting of the Cancer Working Group. World Health Organization. Report IPCS/HSC–CWG–1/04. Geneva.

International Agency for Research on Cancer. IARC Monographs on the Evaluation of Carcinogenic Risks to Human. Preambles to Volumes. World Health Organization. Lyon, France.

Cohen, S.M., P.A. Fenner-Crisp, and D.E. Patton. 2003. Special Issue: Cancer Modes of Action and Human Relevance. Critical Reviews in Toxicology, R.O. McClellan, ed., Volume 33/Issue 6. CRC Press.

Capen, C.C., E. Dybing, and J.D. Wilbourn. 1999. Species differences in thyroid, kidney and urinary bladder carcinogenesis. International Agency for Research on Cancer, Scientific Publication N° 147.

Doi, A.M., G. Hill, J. Seely, J.R. Hailey, G. Kissling, and J.R. Buchera. 2007. α2u-Globulin nephropathy and renal tumors in National Toxicology Program studies. *Toxicol. Pathol.* 35:533–540.

[59 FR 6170, Feb. 9, 1994, as amended at 59 FR 17479, Apr. 13, 1994; 59 FR 65948, Dec. 22, 1994; 61 FR 9245, Mar. 7, 1996; 77 FR 17785, Mar. 26, 2012; 78 FR 9313, Feb. 8, 2013]

§ 1910.1201 Retention of DOT markings, placards and labels.

(a) Any employer who receives a package of hazardous material which is required to be marked, labeled or placarded in accordance with the U. S. Department of Transportation's Hazardous Materials Regulations (49 CFR Parts 171 through 180) shall retain those markings, labels and placards on the package until the packaging is sufficiently cleaned of residue and purged of vapors to remove any potential hazards.

(b) Any employer who receives a freight container, rail freight car, motor vehicle, or transport vehicle that is required to be marked or placarded in accordance with the Hazardous Materials Regulations shall retain those markings and placards on the freight container, rail freight car, motor vehicle or transport vehicle until the hazardous materials which require the marking or placarding are sufficiently removed to prevent any potential hazards.

(c) Markings, placards and labels shall be maintained in a manner that ensures that they are readily visible.

(d) For non-bulk packages which will not be reshipped, the provisions of this section are met if a label or other acceptable marking is affixed in accordance with the Hazard Communication Standard (29 CFR 1910.1200).

(e) For the purposes of this section, the term "hazardous material" and any other terms not defined in this section have the same definition as in the Hazardous Materials Regulations (49 CFR Parts 171 through 180).

[59 FR 36700, July 19, 1994]

§ 1910.1450 Occupational exposure to hazardous chemicals in laboratories.

(a) *Scope and application.* (1) This section shall apply to all employers engaged in the laboratory use of hazardous chemicals as defined below.

(2) Where this section applies, it shall supersede, for laboratories, the requirements of all other OSHA health standards in 29 CFR part 1910, subpart Z, except as follows:

(i) For any OSHA health standard, only the requirement to limit employee exposure to the specific permissible exposure limit shall apply for laboratories, unless that particular standard states otherwise or unless the conditions of paragraph (a)(2)(iii) of this section apply.

(ii) Prohibition of eye and skin contact where specified by any OSHA health standard shall be observed.

(iii) Where the action level (or in the absence of an action level, the permissible exposure limit) is routinely exceeded for an OSHA regulated substance with exposure monitoring and medical surveillance requirements, paragraphs (d) and (g)(1)(ii) of this section shall apply.

(3) This section shall not apply to:

(i) Uses of hazardous chemicals which do not meet the definition of laboratory use, and in such cases, the employer shall comply with the relevant standard in 29 CFR part 1910, subpart Z, even if such use occurs in a laboratory.

(ii) Laboratory uses of hazardous chemicals which provide no potential for employee exposure. Examples of such conditions might include:

(A) Procedures using chemically-impregnated test media such as Dip-and-Read tests where a reagent strip is dipped into the specimen to be tested and the results are interpreted by comparing the color reaction to a color chart supplied by the manufacturer of the test strip; and

(B) Commercially prepared kits such as those used in performing pregnancy tests in which all of the reagents needed to conduct the test are contained in the kit.

(b) *Definitions—*

Action level means a concentration designated in 29 CFR part 1910 for a specific substance, calculated as an eight (8)-hour time-weighted average, which initiates certain required activities such as exposure monitoring and medical surveillance.

Assistant Secretary means the Assistant Secretary of Labor for Occupational Safety and Health, U.S. Department of Labor, or designee.

Carcinogen (see *select carcinogen*).

Chemical Hygiene Officer means an employee who is designated by the employer, and who is qualified by training or experience, to provide technical guidance in the development and implementation of the provisions of the Chemical Hygiene Plan. This definition is not intended to place limitations on the position description or job classification that the designated indvidual shall hold within the employer's organizational structure.

Chemical Hygiene Plan means a written program developed and implemented by the employer which sets forth procedures, equipment, personal protective equipment and work practices that (i) are capable of protecting employees from the health hazards presented by hazardous chemicals used in that particular workplace and (ii) meets the requirements of paragraph (e) of this section.

Designated area means an area which may be used for work with "select carcinogens," reproductive toxins or substances which have a high degree of acute toxicity. A designated area may be the entire laboratory, an area of a laboratory or a device such as a laboratory hood.

Emergency means any occurrence such as, but not limited to, equipment failure, rupture of containers or failure of control equipment which results in an uncontrolled release of a hazardous chemical into the workplace.

Employee means an individual employed in a laboratory workplace who may be exposed to hazardous chemicals in the course of his or her assignments.

Hazardous chemical means any chemical which is classified as health hazard or simple asphyxiant in accordance with the Hazard Communication Standard (§ 1910.1200).

Health hazard means a chemical that is classified as posing one of the following hazardous effects: Acute toxicity (any route of exposure); skin corrosion or irritation; serious eye damage or eye irritation; respiratory or skin sensitization; germ cell mutagenicity; carcinogenity; reproductive toxicity; specific target organ toxicity (single or repeated exposure); aspiration hazard. The criteria for determining whether a chemical is classified as a health hazard are detailed in appendix A of the Hazard Communication Standard (§ 1910.1200) and § 1910.1200(c) (definition of "simple asphyxiant").

Laboratory means a facility where the "laboratory use of hazardous chemicals" occurs. It is a workplace where relatively small quantities of hazardous chemicals are used on a non-production basis.

Laboratory scale means work with substances in which the containers used for reactions, transfers, and other handling of substances are designed to be easily and safely manipulated by one person. "Laboratory scale" excludes those workplaces whose function is to produce commercial quantities of materials.

Laboratory-type hood means a device located in a laboratory, enclosure on five sides with a moveable sash or fixed partial enclosed on the remaining side; constructed and maintained to draw air from the laboratory and to prevent or minimize the escape of air contaminants into the laboratory; and allows chemical manipulations to be conducted in the enclosure without insertion of any portion of the employee's body other than hands and arms. Walk-in hoods with adjustable sashes meet the above definition provided that the sashes are adjusted during use so that the airflow and the exhaust of air contaminants are not compromised and employees do not work inside the enclosure during the release of airborne hazardous chemicals.

Laboratory use of hazardous chemicals means handling or use of such chemicals in which all of the following conditions are met:

(i) Chemical manipulations are carried out on a "laboratory scale;"

(ii) Multiple chemical procedures or chemicals are used;

(iii) The procedures involved are not part of a production process, nor in any way simulate a production process; and

(iv) "Protective laboratory practices and equipment" are available and in common use to minimize the potential for employee exposure to hazardous chemicals.

Medical consultation means a consultation which takes place between an employee and a licensed physician for the purpose of determining what medical examinations or procedures, if any, are appropriate in cases where a significant exposure to a hazardous chemical may have taken place.

Mutagen means chemicals that cause permanent changes in the amount or structure of the genetic material in a cell. Chemicals classified as mutagens in accordance with the Hazard Communication Standard (§1910.1200) shall be considered mutagens for purposes of this section.

Physical hazard means a chemical that is classified as posing one of the following hazardous effects: Explosive; flammable (gases, aerosols, liquids, or solids); oxidizer (liquid, solid, or gas); self reactive; pyrophoric (gas, liquid or solid); self-heating; organic peroxide; corrosive to metal; gas under pressure; in contact with water emits flammable gas; or combustible dust. The criteria for determining whether a chemical is classified as a physical hazard are in appendix B of the Hazard Communication Standard (§1910.1200) and §1910.1200(c) (definitions of "combustible dust" and "pyrophoric gas").

Protective laboratory practices and equipment means those laboratory procedures, practices and equipment accepted by laboratory health and safety experts as effective, or that the employer can show to be effective, in minimizing the potential for employee exposure to hazardous chemicals.

Reproductive toxins mean chemicals that affect the reproductive capabilities including adverse effects on sexual function and fertility in adult males and females, as well as adverse effects on the development of the offspring. Chemicals classified as reproductive toxins in accordance with the Hazard Communication Standard (§1910.1200) shall be considered reproductive toxins for purposes of this section.

Select carcinogen means any substance which meets one of the following criteria:

(i) It is regulated by OSHA as a carcinogen; or

(ii) It is listed under the category, "known to be carcinogens," in the Annual Report on Carcinogens published by the National Toxicology Program (NTP) (latest edition); or

(iii) It is listed under Group 1 ("carcinogenic to humans") by the International Agency for Research on Cancer Monographs (IARC) (latest editions); or

(iv) It is listed in either Group 2A or 2B by IARC or under the category, "reasonably anticipated to be carcinogens" by NTP, and causes statistically significant tumor incidence in experimental animals in accordance with any of the following criteria:

(A) After inhalation exposure of 6–7 hours per day, 5 days per week, for a significant portion of a lifetime to dosages of less than 10 mg/m^3;

(B) After repeated skin application of less than 300 (mg/kg of body weight) per week; or

(C) After oral dosages of less than 50 mg/kg of body weight per day.

(c) *Permissible exposure limits.* For laboratory uses of OSHA regulated substances, the employer shall assure that laboratory employees' exposures to such substances do not exceed the permissible exposure limits specified in 29 CFR part 1910, subpart Z.

(d) *Employee exposure determination*— (1) *Initial monitoring.* The employer shall measure the employee's exposure to any substance regulated by a standard which requires monitoring if there is reason to believe that exposure levels for that substance routinely exceed the action level (or in the absence of an action level, the PEL).

(2) *Periodic monitoring.* If the initial monitoring prescribed by paragraph (d)(1) of this section discloses employee exposure over the action level (or in the absence of an action level, the PEL), the employer shall immediately comply with the exposure monitoring provisions of the relevant standard.

(3) *Termination of monitoring.* Monitoring may be terminated in accordance with the relevant standard.

(4) *Employee notification of monitoring results.* The employer shall, within 15 working days after the receipt of any monitoring results, notify the employee of these results in writing either individually or by posting results in an appropriate location that is accessible to employees.

(e) *Chemical hygiene plan—General.* (Appendix A of this section is non-mandatory but provides guidance to assist employers in the development of the Chemical Hygiene Plan.)

(1) Where hazardous chemicals as defined by this standard are used in the workplace, the employer shall develop and carry out the provisions of a written Chemical Hygiene Plan which is:

(i) Capable of protecting employees from health hazards associated with hazardous chemicals in that laboratory and

(ii) Capable of keeping exposures below the limits specified in paragraph (c) of this section.

(2) The Chemical Hygiene Plan shall be readily available to employees, employee representatives and, upon request, to the Assistant Secretary.

(3) The Chemical Hygiene Plan shall include each of the following elements and shall indicate specific measures that the employer will take to ensure laboratory employee protection:

(i) Standard operating procedures relevant to safety and health considerations to be followed when laboratory work involves the use of hazardous chemicals;

(ii) Criteria that the employer will use to determine and implement control measures to reduce employee exposure to hazardous chemicals including engineering controls, the use of personal protective equipment and hygiene practices; particular attention shall be given to the selection of control measures for chemicals that are known to be extremely hazardous;

(iii) A requirement that fume hoods and other protective equipment are functioning properly and specific measures that shall be taken to ensure proper and adequate performance of such equipment;

(iv) Provisions for employee information and training as prescribed in paragraph (f) of this section;

(v) The circumstances under which a particular laboratory operation, procedure or activity shall require prior approval from the employer or the employer's designee before implementation;

(vi) Provisions for medical consultation and medical examinations in accordance with paragraph (g) of this section;

(vii) Designation of personnel responsible for implementation of the Chemical Hygiene Plan including the assignment of a Chemical Hygiene Officer and, if appropriate, establishment of a Chemical Hygiene Committee; and

(viii) Provisions for additional employee protection for work with particularly hazardous substances. These include "select carcinogens," reproductive toxins and substances which have a high degree of acute toxicity. Specific consideration shall be given to the following provisions which shall be included where appropriate:

(A) Establishment of a designated area;

(B) Use of containment devices such as fume hoods or glove boxes;

(C) Procedures for safe removal of contaminated waste; and

(D) Decontamination procedures.

(4) The employer shall review and evaluate the effectiveness of the Chemical Hygiene Plan at least annually and update it as necessary.

(f) *Employee information and training.* (1) The employer shall provide employees with information and training to ensure that they are apprised of the hazards of chemicals present in their work area.

(2) Such information shall be provided at the time of an employee's initial assignment to a work area where hazardous chemicals are present and prior to assignments involving new exposure situations. The frequency of refresher information and training shall be determined by the employer.

(3) *Information.* Employees shall be informed of:

(i) The contents of this standard and its appendices which shall be made available to employees;

(ii) The location and availability of the employer's Chemical Hygiene Plan;

(iii) The permissible exposure limits for OSHA regulated substances or recommended exposure limits for other hazardous chemicals where there is no applicable OSHA standard;

(iv) Signs and symptoms associated with exposures to hazardous chemicals used in the laboratory; and

(v) The location and availability of known reference material on the hazards, safe handling, storage and disposal of hazardous chemicals found in the laboratory including, but not limited to, safety data sheets received from the chemical supplier.

(4) *Training.* (i) Employee training shall include:

(A) Methods and observations that may be used to detect the presence or release of a hazardous chemical (such as monitoring conducted by the employer, continuous monitoring devices, visual appearance or odor of hazardous chemicals when being released, etc.);

(B) The physical and health hazards of chemicals in the work area; and

(C) The measures employees can take to protect themselves from these hazards, including specific procedures the employer has implemented to protect employees from exposure to hazardous chemicals, such as appropriate work practices, emergency procedures, and personal protective equipment to be used.

(ii) The employee shall be trained on the applicable details of the employer's written Chemical Hygiene Plan.

(g) *Medical consultation and medical examinations.* (1) The employer shall provide all employees who work with hazardous chemicals an opportunity to receive medical attention, including any follow-up examinations which the examining physician determines to be necessary, under the following circumstances:

(i) Whenever an employee develops signs or symptoms associated with a hazardous chemical to which the employee may have been exposed in the laboratory, the employee shall be provided an opportunity to receive an appropriate medical examination.

(ii) Where exposure monitoring reveals an exposure level routinely above the action level (or in the absence of an action level, the PEL) for an OSHA regulated substance for which there are exposure monitoring and medical surveillance requirements, medical surveillance shall be established for the affected employee as prescribed by the particular standard.

(iii) Whenever an event takes place in the work area such as a spill, leak, explosion or other occurrence resulting in the likelihood of a hazardous exposure, the affected employee shall be provided an opportunity for a medical consultation. Such consultation shall be for the purpose of determining the need for a medical examination.

(2) All medical examinations and consultations shall be performed by or

under the direct supervision of a licensed physician and shall be provided without cost to the employee, without loss of pay and at a reasonable time and place.

(3) *Information provided to the physician.* The employer shall provide the following information to the physician:

(i) The identity of the hazardous chemical(s) to which the employee may have been exposed;

(ii) A description of the conditions under which the exposure occurred including quantitative exposure data, if available; and

(iii) A description of the signs and symptoms of exposure that the employee is experiencing, if any.

(4) *Physician's written opinion.* (i) For examination or consultation required under this standard, the employer shall obtain a written opinion from the examining physician which shall include the following:

(A) Any recommendation for further medical follow-up;

(B) The results of the medical examination and any associated tests;

(C) Any medical condition which may be revealed in the course of the examination which may place the employee at increased risk as a result of exposure to a hazardous chemical found in the workplace; and

(D) A statement that the employee has been informed by the physician of the results of the consultation or medical examination and any medical condition that may require further examination or treatment.

(ii) The written opinion shall not reveal specific findings of diagnoses unrelated to occupational exposure.

(h) *Hazard identification.* (1) With respect to labels and safety data sheets:

(i) Employers shall ensure that labels on incoming containers of hazardous chemicals are not removed or defaced.

(ii) Employers shall maintain any safety data sheets that are received with incoming shipments of hazardous chemicals, and ensure that they are readily accessible to laboratory employees.

(2) The following provisions shall apply to chemical substances developed in the laboratory:

(i) If the composition of the chemical substance which is produced exclu-sively for the laboratory's use is known, the employer shall determine if it is a hazardous chemical as defined in paragraph (b) of this section. If the chemical is determined to be hazardous, the employer shall provide appropriate training as required under paragraph (f) of this section.

(ii) If the chemical produced is a by-product whose composition is not known, the employer shall assume that the substance is hazardous and shall implement paragraph (e) of this section.

(iii) If the chemical substance is produced for another user outside of the laboratory, the employer shall comply with the Hazard Communication Standard (29 CFR 1910.1200) including the requirements for preparation of safety data sheets and labeling.

(i) *Use of respirators.* Where the use of respirators is necessary to maintain exposure below permissible exposure limits, the employer shall provide, at no cost to the employee, the proper respiratory equipment. Respirators shall be selected and used in accordance with the requirements of 29 CFR 1910.134.

(j) *Recordkeeping.* (1) The employer shall establish and maintain for each employee an accurate record of any measurements taken to monitor employee exposures and any medical consultation and examinations including tests or written opinions required by this standard.

(2) The employer shall assure that such records are kept, transferred, and made available in accordance with 29 CFR 1910.20.

(k) [Reserved]

(l) *Appendices.* The information contained in the appendices is not intended, by itself, to create any additional obligations not otherwise imposed or to detract from any existing obligation.

APPENDIX A TO § 1910.1450—NATIONAL RE-
SEARCH COUNCIL RECOMMENDATIONS CON-
CERNING CHEMICAL HYGIENE IN LABORA-
TORIES (NON-MANDATORY)

To assist employers in developing an appropriate laboratory Chemical Hygiene Plan (CHP), the following non-mandatory recommendations were based on the National Research Council's (NRC) 2011 edition of

"Prudent Practices in the Laboratory: Handling and Management of Chemical Hazards." This reference, henceforth referred to as "Prudent Practices," is available from the National Academies Press, 500 Fifth Street NW., Washington DC 20001 (*www.nap.edu*). "Prudent Practices" is cited because of its wide distribution and acceptance and because of its preparation by recognized authorities in the laboratory community through the sponsorship of the NRC. However, these recommendations do not modify any requirements of the OSHA Laboratory standard. This appendix presents pertinent recommendations from "Prudent Practices," organized into a form convenient for quick reference during operation of a laboratory and during development and application of a CHP. For a detailed explanation and justification for each recommendation, consult "Prudent Practices."

"Prudent Practices" deals with both general laboratory safety and many types of chemical hazards, while the Laboratory standard is concerned primarily with chemical health hazards as a result of chemical exposures. The recommendations from "Prudent Practices" have been paraphrased, combined, or otherwise reorganized in order to adapt them for this purpose. However, their sense has not been changed.

Section F contains information from the U.S. Chemical Safety Board's (CSB) Fiscal Year 2011 Annual Performance and Accountability report and Section F contains recommendations extracted from the CSB's 2011 case study, "Texas Tech University Laboratory Explosion," available from: *http://www.csb.gov/*.

CULTURE OF SAFETY

With the promulgation of the Occupational Safety and Health Administration (OSHA) Laboratory standard (29 CFR 1910.1450), a culture of safety consciousness, accountability, organization, and education has developed in industrial, governmental, and academic laboratories. Safety and training programs have been implemented to promote the safe handling of chemicals from ordering to disposal, and to train laboratory personnel in safe practices. Laboratory personnel must realize that the welfare and safety of each individual depends on clearly defined attitudes of teamwork and personal responsibility. Learning to participate in this culture of habitual risk assessment, experiment planning, and consideration of worst-case possibilities—for oneself and one's fellow workers—is as much part of a scientific education as learning the theoretical background of experiments or the step-by-step protocols for doing them in a professional manner. A crucial component of chemical education for all personnel is to nurture basic attitudes and habits of prudent

behavior so that safety is a valued and inseparable part of all laboratory activities throughout their career.

Over the years, special techniques have been developed for handling chemicals safely. Local, state, and federal regulations hold institutions that sponsor chemical laboratories accountable for providing safe working environments. Beyond regulation, employers and scientists also hold themselves personally responsible for their own safety, the safety of their colleagues and the safety of the general public. A sound safety organization that is respected by all requires the participation and support of laboratory administrators, workers, and students. A successful health and safety program requires a daily commitment from everyone in the organization. To be most effective, safety and health must be balanced with, and incorporated into, laboratory processes. A strong safety and health culture is the result of positive workplace attitudes—from the chief executive officer to the newest hire; involvement and buy-in of all members of the workforce; mutual, meaningful, and measurable safety and health improvement goals; and policies and procedures that serve as reference tools, rather than obscure rules.

In order to perform their work in a prudent manner, laboratory personnel must consider the health, physical, and environmental hazards of the chemicals they plan to use in an experiment. However, the ability to accurately identify and assess laboratory hazards must be taught and encouraged through training and ongoing organizational support. This training must be at the core of every good health and safety program. For management to lead, personnel to assess worksite hazards, and hazards to be eliminated or controlled, everyone involved must be trained.

A. General Principles

1. Minimize All Chemical Exposures and Risks

Because few laboratory chemicals are without hazards, general precautions for handling all laboratory chemicals should be adopted. In addition to these general guidelines, specific guidelines for chemicals that are used frequently or are particularly hazardous should be adopted.

Laboratory personnel should conduct their work under conditions that minimize the risks from both known and unknown hazardous substances. Before beginning any laboratory work, the hazards and risks associated with an experiment or activity should be determined and the necessary safety precautions implemented. Every laboratory should develop facility-specific policies and procedures for the highest-risk materials and procedures used in their laboratory. To identify these, consideration should be given to past accidents, process conditions, chemicals used in large volumes, and particularly hazardous chemicals.

Perform Risk Assessments for Hazardous Chemicals and Procedures Prior to Laboratory Work:

(a) Identify chemicals to be used, amounts required, and circumstances of use in the experiment. Consider any special employee or laboratory conditions that could create or increase a hazard. Consult sources of safety and health information and experienced scientists to ensure that those conducting the risk assessment have sufficient expertise.

(b) Evaluate the hazards posed by the chemicals and the experimental conditions. The evaluation should cover toxic, physical, reactive, flammable, explosive, radiation, and biological hazards, as well as any other potential hazards posed by the chemicals.

(c) For a variety of physical and chemical reasons, reaction scale-ups pose special risks, which merit additional prior review and precautions.

(d) Select appropriate controls to minimize risk, including use of engineering controls, administrative controls, and personal protective equipment (PPE) to protect workers from hazards. The controls must ensure that OSHA's Permissible Exposure Limits (PELs) are not exceeded. Prepare for contingencies and be aware of the institutional procedures in the event of emergencies and accidents.

One sample approach to risk assessment is to answer these five questions:

(a) What are the hazards?

(b) What is the worst thing that could happen?

(c) What can be done to prevent this from happening?

(d) What can be done to protect from these hazards?

(e) What should be done if something goes wrong?

2. Avoid Underestimation of Risk

Even for substances of no known significant hazard, exposure should be minimized; when working with substances that present special hazards, special precautions should be taken. Reference should be made to the safety data sheet (SDS) that is provided for each chemical. Unless otherwise known, one should assume that any mixture will be more toxic than its most toxic component and that all substances of unknown toxicity are toxic.

Determine the physical and health hazards associated with chemicals before working with them. This determination may involve consulting literature references, laboratory chemical safety summaries (LCSSs), SDSs, or other reference materials. Consider how the chemicals will be processed and determine whether the changing states or forms will change the nature of the hazard. Review your plan, operating limits, chemical evalua-

tions and detailed risk assessment with other chemists, especially those with experience with similar materials and protocols.

Before working with chemicals, know your facility's policies and procedures for how to handle an accidental spill or fire. Emergency telephone numbers should be posted in a prominent area. Know the location of all safety equipment and the nearest fire alarm and telephone.

3. Adhere to the Hierarchy of Controls

The hierarchy of controls prioritizes intervention strategies based on the premise that the best way to control a hazard is to systematically remove it from the workplace, rather than relying on employees to reduce their exposure. The types of measures that may be used to protect employees (listed from most effective to least effective) are: engineering controls, administrative controls, work practices, and PPE. Engineering controls, such as chemical hoods, physically separate the employee from the hazard. Administrative controls, such as employee scheduling, are established by management to help minimize the employees' exposure time to hazardous chemicals. Work practice controls are tasks that are performed in a designated way to minimize or eliminate hazards. Personal protective equipment and apparel are additional protection provided under special circumstances and when exposure is unavoidable.

Face and eye protection is necessary to prevent ingestion and skin absorption of hazardous chemicals. At a minimum, safety glasses, with side shields, should be used for all laboratory work. Chemical splash goggles are more appropriate than regular safety glasses to protect against hazards such as projectiles, as well as when working with glassware under reduced or elevated pressures (e.g., sealed tube reactions), when handling potentially explosive compounds (particularly during distillations), and when using glassware in high-temperature operations. Do not allow laboratory chemicals to come in contact with skin. Select gloves carefully to ensure that they are impervious to the chemicals being used and are of correct thickness to allow reasonable dexterity while also ensuring adequate barrier protection.

Lab coats and gloves should be worn when working with hazardous materials in a laboratory. Wear closed-toe shoes and long pants or other clothing that covers the legs when in a laboratory where hazardous chemicals are used. Additional protective clothing should be used when there is significant potential for skin-contact exposure to chemicals. The protective characteristics of this clothing must be matched to the hazard. Never wear gloves or laboratory coats outside the laboratory or into areas where food is stored and consumed.

4. Provide Laboratory Ventilation

The best way to prevent exposure to airborne substances is to prevent their escape into the working atmosphere by the use of hoods and other ventilation devices. To determine the best choice for laboratory ventilation using engineering controls for personal protection, employers are referred to Table 9.3 of the 2011 edition of "Prudent Practices." Laboratory chemical hoods are the most important components used to protect laboratory personnel from exposure to hazardous chemicals.

(a) Toxic or corrosive chemicals that require vented storage should be stored in vented cabinets instead of in a chemical hood.

(b) Chemical waste should not be disposed of by evaporation in a chemical hood.

(c) Keep chemical hood areas clean and free of debris at all times.

(d) Solid objects and materials, such as paper, should be prevented from entering the exhaust ducts as they can reduce the air flow.

(e) Chemical hoods should be maintained, monitored and routinely tested for proper performance.

A laboratory ventilation system should include the following characteristics and practices:

(a) Heating and cooling should be adequate for the comfort of workers and operation of equipment. Before modification of any building HVAC, the impact on laboratory or hood ventilation should be considered, as well as how laboratory ventilation changes may affect the building HVAC.

(b) A negative pressure differential should exist between the amount of air exhausted from the laboratory and the amount supplied to the laboratory to prevent uncontrolled chemical vapors from leaving the laboratory.

(c) Local exhaust ventilation devices should be appropriate to the materials and operations in the laboratory.

(d) The air in chemical laboratories should be continuously replaced so that concentrations of odoriferous or toxic substances do not increase during the workday.

(e) Laboratory air should not be recirculated but exhausted directly outdoors.

(f) Air pressure should be negative with respect to the rest of the building. Local capture equipment and systems should be designed only by an experienced engineer or industrial hygienist.

(g) Ventilation systems should be inspected and maintained on a regular basis. There should be no areas where air remains static or areas that have unusually high airflow velocities.

Before work begins, laboratory workers should be provided with proper training that includes how to use the ventilation equipment, how to ensure that it is functioning properly, the consequences of improper use, what to do in the event of a system failure or power outage, special considerations, and the importance of signage and postings.

5. Institute a Chemical Hygiene Program

A comprehensive chemical hygiene program is required. It should be designed to minimize exposures, injuries, illnesses and incidents. There should be a regular, continuing effort that includes program oversight, safe facilities, chemical hygiene planning, training, emergency preparedness and chemical security. The chemical hygiene program must be reviewed annually and updated as necessary whenever new processes, chemicals, or equipment is implemented. Its recommendations should be followed in all laboratories.

6. Observe the PELs and TLVs

OSHA's Permissible Exposure Limits (PELs) must not be exceeded. The American Conference of Governmental Industrial Hygienists' Threshold Limit Values (TLVs) should also not be exceeded.

B. Responsibilities

Persons responsible for chemical hygiene include, but are not limited to, the following:

1. Chemical Hygiene Officer

(a) Establishes, maintains, and revises the chemical hygiene plan (CHP).

(b) Creates and revises safety rules and regulations.

(c) Monitors procurement, use, storage, and disposal of chemicals.

(d) Conducts regular inspections of the laboratories, preparations rooms, and chemical storage rooms, and submits detailed laboratory inspection reports to administration.

(e) Maintains inspection, personnel training, and inventory records.

(f) Assists laboratory supervisors in developing and maintaining adequate facilities.

(g) Seeks ways to improve the chemical hygiene program.

2. Department Chairperson or Director

(a) Assumes responsibility for personnel engaged in the laboratory use of hazardous chemicals.

(b) Provides the chemical hygiene officer (CHO) with the support necessary to implement and maintain the CHP.

(c) After receipt of laboratory inspection report from the CHO, meets with laboratory supervisors to discuss cited violations and to ensure timely actions to protect trained laboratory personnel and facilities and to ensure that the department remains in compliance with all applicable federal, state, university, local and departmental codes and regulations.

(d) Provides budgetary arrangements to ensure the health and safety of the departmental personnel, visitors, and students.

3. Departmental Safety Committee reviews accident reports and makes appropriate recommendations to the department chairperson regarding proposed changes in the laboratory procedures.

4. Laboratory Supervisor or Principal Investigator has overall responsibility for chemical hygiene in the laboratory, including responsibility to:

(a) Ensure that laboratory personnel comply with the departmental CHP and do not operate equipment or handle hazardous chemicals without proper training and authorization.

(b) Always wear personal protective equipment (PPE) that is compatible to the degree of hazard of the chemical.

(c) Follow all pertinent safety rules when working in the laboratory to set an example.

(d) Review laboratory procedures for potential safety problems before assigning to other laboratory personnel.

(e) Ensure that visitors follow the laboratory rules and assumes responsibility for laboratory visitors.

(f) Ensure that PPE is available and properly used by each laboratory employee and visitor.

(g) Maintain and implement safe laboratory practices.

(h) Provide regular, formal chemical hygiene and housekeeping inspections, including routine inspections of emergency equipment;

(i) Monitor the facilities and the chemical fume hoods to ensure that they are maintained and function properly. Contact the appropriate person, as designated by the department chairperson, to report problems with the facilities or the chemical fume hoods.

5. Laboratory Personnel

(a) Read, understand, and follow all safety rules and regulations that apply to the work area;

(b) Plan and conduct each operation in accordance with the institutional chemical hygiene procedures;

(c) Promote good housekeeping practices in the laboratory or work area.

(d) Notify the supervisor of any hazardous conditions or unsafe work practices in the work area.

(e) Use PPE as appropriate for each procedure that involves hazardous chemicals.

C. The Laboratory Facility

General Laboratory Design Considerations

Wet chemical spaces and those with a higher degree of hazard should be separated from other spaces by a wall or protective barrier wherever possible. If the areas cannot be separated, then workers in lower hazard spaces may require additional protection from the hazards in connected spaces.

1. Laboratory Layout and Furnishing

(a) Work surfaces should be chemically resistant, smooth, and easy to clean.

(b) Hand washing sinks for hazardous materials may require elbow, foot, or electronic controls for safe operation.

(c) Wet laboratory areas should have chemically resistant, impermeable, slip-resistant flooring.

(d) Walls should be finished with a material that is easy to clean and maintain.

(e) Doors should have view panels to prevent accidents and should open in the direction of egress.

(f) Operable windows should not be present in laboratories, particularly if there are chemical hoods or other local ventilation systems present.

2. Safety Equipment and Utilities

(a) An adequate number and placement of safety showers, eyewash units, and fire extinguishers should be provided for the laboratory.

(b) Use of water sprinkler systems is resisted by some laboratories because of the presence of electrical equipment or water-reactive materials, but it is still generally safer to have sprinkler systems installed. A fire large enough to trigger the sprinkler system would have the potential to cause far more destruction than the local water damage.

D. Chemical Hygiene Plan (CHP)

The OSHA Laboratory standard defines a CHP as "a written program developed and implemented by the employer which sets forth procedures, equipment, personal protective equipment and work practices that are capable of protecting employees from the health hazards presented by hazardous chemicals used in that particular workplace." (29 CFR 1910.1450(b)). The Laboratory Standard requires a CHP: "Where hazardous chemicals as defined by this standard are used in the workplace, the employer shall develop and carry out the provisions of a written Chemical Hygiene Plan." (29 CFR 1910.1450(e)(1)). The CHP is the foundation of the laboratory safety program and must be reviewed and updated, as needed, and at least on an annual basis to reflect changes in policies and personnel. A CHP should be facility specific and can assist in promoting a culture of safety to protect workers from exposure to hazardous materials.

1. The Laboratory's CHP must be readily available to workers and capable of protecting workers from health hazards and minimizing exposure. Include the following topics in the CHP:

(a) Individual chemical hygiene responsibilities;
(b) Standard operating procedures;
(c) Personal protective equipment, engineering controls and apparel;
(d) Laboratory equipment;
(e) Safety equipment;
(f) Chemical management;
(g) Housekeeping;
(h) Emergency procedures for accidents and spills;
(i) Chemical waste;
(j) Training;
(k) Safety rules and regulations;
(l) Laboratory design and ventilation;
(m) Exposure monitoring;
(n) Compressed gas safety;
(o) Medical consultation and examination.
It should be noted that the nature of laboratory work may necessitate addressing biological safety, radiation safety and security issues.

2. Chemical Procurement, Distribution, and Storage

Prudent chemical management includes the following processes:
Chemical Procurement:
(a) Information on proper handling, storage, and disposal should be known to those who will be involved before a substance is received.
(b) Only containers with adequate identifying labels should be accepted.
(c) Ideally, a central location should be used for receiving all chemical shipments.
(d) Shipments with breakage or leakage should be refused or opened in a chemical hood.
(e) Only the minimum amount of the chemical needed to perform the planned work should be ordered.
(f) Purchases of high risk chemicals should be reviewed and approved by the CHO.
(g) Proper protective equipment and handling and storage procedures should be in place before receiving a shipment.
Chemical Storage:
(a) Chemicals should be separated and stored according to hazard category and compatibility.
(b) SDS and label information should be followed for storage requirements.
(c) Maintain existing labels on incoming containers of chemicals and other materials.
(d) Labels on containers used for storing hazardous chemicals must include the chemical identification and appropriate hazard warnings.
(e) The contents of all other chemical containers and transfer vessels, including, but not limited to, beakers, flasks, reaction vessels, and process equipment, should be properly identified.
(f) Chemical shipments should be dated upon receipt and stock rotated.

(g) Peroxide formers should be dated upon receipt, again dated upon opening, and stored away from heat and light with tight-fitting, nonmetal lids.
(h) Open shelves used for chemical storage should be secured to the wall and contain ¾-inch lips. Secondary containment devices should be used as necessary.
(i) Consult the SDS and keep incompatibles separate during transport, storage, use, and disposal.
(j) Oxidizers, reducing agents, and fuels should be stored separately to prevent contact in the event of an accident.
(k) Chemicals should not be stored in the chemical hood, on the floor, in areas of egress, on the benchtop, or in areas near heat or in direct sunlight.
(l) Laboratory-grade, flammable-rated refrigerators and freezers should be used to store sealed chemical containers of flammable liquids that require cool storage. Do not store food or beverages in the laboratory refrigerator.
(m) Highly hazardous chemicals should be stored in a well-ventilated and secure area designated for that purpose.
(n) Flammable chemicals should be stored in a spark-free environment and in approved flammable-liquid containers and storage cabinets. Grounding and bonding should be used to prevent static charge buildups when dispensing solvents.
(o) Chemical storage and handling rooms should be controlled-access areas. They should have proper ventilation, appropriate signage, diked floors, and fire suppression systems.
Chemical Handling:
(a) As described above, a risk assessment should be conducted prior to beginning work with any hazardous chemical for the first time.
(b) All SDS and label information should be read before using a chemical for the first time.
(c) Trained laboratory workers should ensure that proper engineering controls (ventilation) and PPE are in place.
Chemical Inventory:
(a) Prudent management of chemicals in any laboratory is greatly facilitated by keeping an accurate inventory of the chemicals stored.
(b) Unneeded items should be discarded or returned to the storeroom.
Transporting Chemicals:
(a) Secondary containment devices should be used when transporting chemicals.
(b) When transporting chemicals outside of the laboratory or between stockrooms and laboratories, the transport container should be break-resistant.
(c) High-traffic areas should be avoided.
Transferring Chemicals:
(a) Use adequate ventilation (such as a fume hood) when transferring even a small

amount of a particularly hazardous substance (PHS).

(b) While drum storage is not appropriate for laboratories, chemical stockrooms may purchase drum quantities of solvents used in high volumes. Ground and bond the drum and receiving vessel when transferring flammable liquids from a drum to prevent static charge buildup.

(c) If chemicals from commercial sources are repackaged into transfer vessels, the new containers should be labeled with all essential information on the original container.

Shipping Chemicals: Outgoing chemical shipments must meet all applicable Department of Transportation (DOT) regulations and should be authorized and handled by the institutional shipper.

3. Waste Management

A waste management plan should be in place before work begins on any laboratory activity. The plan should utilize the following hierarchy of practices:

(a) Reduce waste sources. The best approach to minimize waste generation is by reducing the scale of operations, reducing its formation during operations, and, if possible, substituting less hazardous chemicals for a particular operation.

(b) Reuse surplus materials. Only the amount of material necessary for an experiment should be purchased, and, if possible, materials should be reused.

(c) Recycle waste. If waste cannot be prevented or minimized, the organization should consider recycling chemicals that can be safely recovered or used as fuel.

(d) Dispose of waste properly. Sink disposal may not be appropriate. Proper waste disposal methods include incineration, treatment, and land disposal. The organization's environmental health and safety (EHS) office should be consulted in determining which methods are appropriate for different types of waste.

Collection and Storage of Waste:

(a) Chemical waste should be accumulated at or near the point of generation, under the control of laboratory workers.

(b) Each waste type should be stored in a compatible container pending transfer or disposal. Waste containers should be clearly labeled and kept sealed when not in use.

(c) Incompatible waste types should be kept separate to ensure that heat generation, gas evolution, or another reaction does not occur.

(d) Waste containers should be segregated by how they will be managed. Waste containers should be stored in a designated location that does not interfere with normal laboratory operations. Ventilated storage and secondary containment may be appropriate for certain waste types.

(e) Waste containers should be clearly labeled and kept sealed when not in use. La-

bels should include the accumulation start date and hazard warnings as appropriate.

(f) Non-explosive electrical systems, grounding and bonding between floors and containers, and non-sparking conductive floors and containers should be used in the central waste accumulation area to minimize fire and explosion hazards. Fire suppression systems, specialized ventilation systems, and dikes should be installed in the central waste accumulation area. Waste management workers should be trained in proper waste handling procedures as well as contingency planning and emergency response. Trained laboratory workers most familiar with the waste should be actively involved in waste management decisions to ensure that the waste is managed safely and efficiently. Engineering controls should be implemented as necessary, and personal protective equipment should be worn by workers involved in waste management.

4. Inspection Program

Maintenance and regular inspection of laboratory equipment are essential parts of the laboratory safety program. Management should participate in the design of a laboratory inspection program to ensure that the facility is safe and healthy, workers are adequately trained, and proper procedures are being followed.

Types of inspections: The program should include an appropriate combination of routine inspections, self-audits, program audits, peer inspections, EHS inspections, and inspections by external entities.

Elements of an inspection:

(a) Inspectors should bring a checklist to ensure that all issues are covered and a camera to document issues that require correction.

(b) Conversations with workers should occur during the inspection, as they can provide valuable information and allow inspectors an opportunity to show workers how to fix problems.

(c) Issues resolved during the inspection should be noted.

(d) An inspection report containing all findings and recommendations should be prepared for management and other appropriate workers.

(e) Management should follow-up on the inspection to ensure that all corrections are implemented.

5. Medical Consultation and Examination

The employer must provide all employees who work with hazardous chemicals an opportunity to receive medical attention, including any follow-up examinations that the examining physician determines to be necessary, whenever an employee develops signs or symptoms associated with a hazardous chemical to which the employee may have been exposed in the laboratory. If an employee encounters a spill, leak, explosion or other occurrence resulting in the likelihood of a hazardous exposure, the affected employee must be provided an opportunity for a medical consultation by a licensed physician. All medical examinations and consultations must be performed by or under the direct supervision of a licensed physician and must be provided without cost to the employee, without loss of pay and at a reasonable time and place. The identity of the hazardous chemical, a description of the incident, and any signs and symptoms that the employee may experience must be relayed to the physician.

6. Records

All accident, fatality, illness, injury, and medical records and exposure monitoring records must be retained by the institution in accordance with the requirements of state and federal regulations (see 29 CFR part 1904 and § 1910.1450(j)). Any exposure monitoring results must be provided to affected laboratory staff within 15 working days after receipt of the results (29 CFR 1910.1450(d)(4)).

7. Signs

Prominent signs of the following types should be posted:

(a) Emergency telephone numbers of emergency personnel/facilities, supervisors, and laboratory workers;

(b) Location signs for safety showers, eyewash stations, other safety and first aid equipment, and exits; and

(c) Warnings at areas or equipment where special or unusual hazards exist.

8. Spills and Accidents

Before beginning an experiment, know your facility's policies and procedures for how to handle an accidental release of a hazardous substance, a spill or a fire. Emergency response planning and training are especially important when working with highly toxic compounds. Emergency telephone numbers should be posted in a prominent area. Know the location of all safety equipment and the nearest fire alarm and telephone. Know who to notify in the event of an emergency. Be prepared to provide basic emergency treatment. Keep your co-workers informed of your activities so they can respond appropriately. Safety equipment, including spill control kits, safety shields, fire safety equipment, PPE, safety showers and eyewash units, and emergency equipment should be available in well-marked highly visible locations in all chemical laboratories. The laboratory supervisor or CHO is responsible for ensuring that all personnel are aware of the locations of fire extinguishers and are trained in their use. After an extinguisher has been used, designated personnel

must promptly recharge or replace it (29 CFR 1910.157(c)(4)). The laboratory supervisor or CHO is also responsible for ensuring proper training and providing supplementary equipment as needed.

Special care must be used when handling solutions of chemicals in syringes with needles. Do not recap needles, especially when they have been in contact with chemicals. Remove the needle and discard it immediately after use in the appropriate sharps containers. Blunt-tip needles are available from a number of commercial sources and should be used unless a sharp needle is required to puncture rubber septa or for subcutaneous injection.

For unattended operations, laboratory lights should be left on, and signs should be posted to identify the nature of the experiment and the hazardous substances in use. Arrangements should be made, if possible, for other workers to periodically inspect the operation. Information should be clearly posted indicating who to contact in the event of an emergency. Depending on the nature of the hazard, special rules, precautions, and alert systems may be necessary.

9. Training and Information

Personnel training at all levels within the organization, is essential. Responsibility and accountability throughout the organization are key elements in a strong safety and health program. The employer is required to provide employees with information and training to ensure that they are apprised of the hazards of chemicals present in their work area (29 CFR 1910.1450(f)). This information must be provided at the time of an employee's initial assignment to a work area where hazardous chemicals are present and prior to assignments involving new exposure situations. The frequency of refresher information and training should be determined by the employer. At a minimum, laboratory personnel should be trained on their facility's specific CHP, methods and observations that may be used to detect the presence or release of a hazardous chemical (such as monitoring conducted by the employer, continuous monitoring devices, visual appearance or odor of hazardous chemicals when being released), the physical and health hazards of chemicals in the work area and means to protect themselves from these hazards. Trained laboratory personnel must know shut-off procedures in case of an emergency. All SDSs must be made available to the employees.

E. General Procedures for Working With Chemicals

The risk of laboratory injuries can be reduced through adequate training, improved engineering, good housekeeping, safe work practice and personal behavior.

1. General Rules for Laboratory Work With Chemicals

(a) Assigned work schedules should be followed unless a deviation is authorized by the laboratory supervisor.

(b) Unauthorized experiments should not be performed.

(c) Plan safety procedures before beginning any operation.

(d) Follow standard operating procedures at all times.

(e) Always read the SDS and label before using a chemical.

(f) Wear appropriate PPE at all times.

(g) To protect your skin from splashes, spills and drips, always wear long pants and closed-toe shoes.

(h) Use appropriate ventilation when working with hazardous chemicals.

(i) Pipetting should never be done by mouth.

(j) Hands should be washed with soap and water immediately after working with any laboratory chemicals, even if gloves have been worn.

(k) Eating, drinking, smoking, gum chewing, applying cosmetics, and taking medicine in laboratories where hazardous chemicals are used or stored should be strictly prohibited.

(l) Food, beverages, cups, and other drinking and eating utensils should not be stored in areas where hazardous chemicals are handled or stored.

(m) Laboratory refrigerators, ice chests, cold rooms, and ovens should not be used for food storage or preparation.

(n) Contact the laboratory supervisor, Principal Investigator, CHO or EHS office with all safety questions or concerns.

(o) Know the location and proper use of safety equipment.

(p) Maintain situational awareness.

(q) Make others aware of special hazards associated with your work.

(r) Notify supervisors of chemical sensitivities or allergies.

(s) Report all injuries, accidents, incidents, and near misses.

(t) Unauthorized persons should not be allowed in the laboratory.

(u) Report unsafe conditions to the laboratory supervisor or CHO.

(v) Properly dispose of chemical wastes.

Working Alone in the Laboratory

Working alone in a laboratory is dangerous and should be strictly avoided. There have been many tragic accidents that illustrate this danger. Accidents are unexpected by definition, which is why coworkers should always be present. Workers should coordinate schedules to avoid working alone.

Housekeeping

Housekeeping can help reduce or eliminate a number of laboratory hazards. Proper housekeeping includes appropriate labeling and storage of chemicals, safe and regular cleaning of the facility, and proper arrangement of laboratory equipment.

2. Nanoparticles and Nanomaterials

Nanoparticles and nanomaterials have different reactivities and interactions with biological systems than bulk materials, and understanding and exploiting these differences is an active area of research. However, these differences also mean that the risks and hazards associated with exposure to engineered nanomaterials are not well known. Because this is an area of ongoing research, consult trusted sources for the most up to date information available. Note that the higher reactivity of many nanoscale materials suggests that they should be treated as potential sources of ignition, accelerants, and fuel that could result in fire or explosion. Easily dispersed dry nanomaterials may pose the greatest health hazard because of the risk of inhalation. Operations involving these nanomaterials deserve more attention and more stringent controls than those where the nanomaterials are embedded in solid or suspended in liquid matrixes.

Consideration should be given to all possible routes of exposure to nanomaterials including inhalation, ingestion, injection, and dermal contact (including eye and mucous membranes). Avoid handling nanomaterials in the open air in a free-particle state. Whenever possible, handle and store dispersible nanomaterials, whether suspended in liquids or in a dry particle form, in closed (tightly-sealed) containers. Unless cutting or grinding occurs, nanomaterials that are not in a free form (encapsulated in a solid or a nanocomposite) typically will not require engineering controls. If a synthesis is being performed to create nanomaterials, it is not enough to only consider the final material in the risk assessment, but consider the hazardous properties of the precursor materials as well.

To minimize laboratory personnel exposure, conduct any work that could generate engineered nanoparticles in an enclosure that operates at a negative pressure differential compared to the laboratory personnel breathing zone. Limited data exist regarding the efficacy of PPE and ventilation systems against exposure to nanoparticles. However, until further information is available, it is prudent to follow standard chemical hygiene practices. Conduct a hazard evaluation to determine PPE appropriate for the level of hazard according to the requirements set forth in OSHA's Personal Protective Equipment standard (29 CFR 1910.132).

3. Highly Toxic and Explosive/Reactive Chemicals/Materials

The use of highly toxic and explosive/reactive chemicals and materials has been an area of growing concern. The frequency of academic laboratory incidents in the U.S. is an area of significant concern for the Chemical Safety Board (CSB). The CSB issued a case study on an explosion at Texas Tech University in Lubbock, Texas, which severely injured a graduate student handling a high-energy metal compound. Since 2001, the CSB has gathered preliminary information on 120 different university laboratory incidents that resulted in 87 evacuations, 96 injuries, and three deaths.

It is recommended that each facility keep a detailed inventory of highly toxic chemicals and explosive/reactive materials. There should be a record of the date of receipt, amount, location, and responsible individual for all acquisitions, syntheses, and disposal of these chemicals. A physical inventory should be performed annually to verify active inventory records. There should be a procedure in place to report security breaches, inventory discrepancies, losses, diversions, or suspected thefts.

Procedures for disposal of highly toxic materials should be established before any experiments begin, possibly even before the chemicals are ordered. The procedures should address methods for decontamination of any laboratory equipment that comes into contact with highly toxic chemicals. All waste should be accumulated in clearly labeled impervious containers that are stored in unbreakable secondary containment.

Highly reactive and explosive materials that may be used in the laboratory require appropriate procedures and training. An explosion can occur when a material undergoes a rapid reaction that results in a violent release of energy. Such reactions can happen spontaneously and can produce pressures, gases, and fumes that are hazardous. Some reagents pose a risk on contact with the atmosphere. It is prudent laboratory practice to use a safer alternative whenever possible. If at all possible, substitutes for highly acute, chronic, explosive, or reactive chemicals should be considered prior to beginning work and used whenever possible.

4. Compressed Gas

Compressed gases expose laboratory personnel to both chemical and physical hazards. It is essential that these are monitored for leaks and have the proper labeling. By monitoring compressed gas inventories and disposing of or returning gases for which there is no immediate need, the laboratory can substantially reduce these risks. Leaking gas cylinders can cause serious hazards that may require an immediate evacuation of the area and activation of the emergency response system. Only appropriately trained hazmat responders may respond to stop a leaking gas cylinder under this situation.

F. Safety Recommendations—Physical Hazards

Physical hazards in the laboratory include combustible liquids, compressed gases, reactives, explosives and flammable chemicals, as well as high pressure/energy procedures, sharp objects and moving equipment. Injuries can result from bodily contact with rotating or moving objects, including mechanical equipment, parts, and devices. Personnel should not wear loose-fitting clothing, jewelry, or unrestrained long hair around machinery with moving parts.

The Chemical Safety Board has identified the following key lessons for laboratories that address both physical and other hazards:

(1) Ensure that research-specific hazards are evaluated and then controlled by developing specific written protocols and training.

(2) Expand existing laboratory safety plans to ensure that all safety hazards, including physical hazards of chemicals, are addressed.

(3) Ensure that the organization's EHS office reports directly to an identified individual/office with organizational authority to implement safety improvements.

(4) Develop a verification program that ensures that the safety provisions of the CHP are communicated, followed, and enforced at all levels within the organization.

(5) Document and communicate all laboratory near-misses and previous incidents to track safety, provide opportunities for education and improvement to drive safety changes at the university.

(6) Manage the hazards unique to laboratory chemical research in the academic environment. Utilize available practice guidance that identifies and describes methodologies to assess and control hazards.

(7) Written safety protocols and training are necessary to manage laboratory risk.

G. Emergency Planning

In addition to laboratory safety issues, laboratory personnel should be familiar with established facility policies and procedures regarding emergency situations. Topics may include, but are not limited to:

(1) Evacuation procedures—when it is appropriate and alternate routes;

(2) Emergency shutdown procedures—equipment shutdown and materials that should be stored safely;

(3) Communications during an emergency—what to expect, how to report, where to call or look for information;

(4) How and when to use a fire extinguisher;

(5) Security issues—preventing tailgating and unauthorized access;

(6) Protocol for absences due to travel restrictions or illness;

(7) Safe practices for power outage;

(8) Shelter in place—when it is appropriate;

(9) Handling suspicious mail or phone calls;

(10) Laboratory-specific protocols relating to emergency planning and response;

(11) Handling violent behavior in the workplace; and

(12) First-aid and CPR training, including automated external defibrillator training if available.

It is prudent that laboratory personnel are also trained in how to respond to short-term, long-term and large-scale emergencies. Laboratory security can play a role in reducing the likelihood of some emergencies and assisting in preparation and response for others. Every institution, department, and individual laboratory should consider having an emergency preparedness plan. The level of detail of the plan will vary depending on the function of the group and institutional planning efforts already in place.

Emergency planning is a dynamic process. As personnel, operations, and events change, plans will need to be updated and modified. To determine the type and level of emergency planning needed, laboratory personnel need to perform a vulnerability assessment. Periodic drills to assist in training and evaluation of the emergency plan are recommended as part of the training program.

H. Emergency Procedures

(1) Fire alarm policy. Most organizations use fire alarms whenever a building needs to be evacuated—for any reason. When a fire alarm sounds in the facility, evacuate immediately after extinguishing all equipment flames. Check on and assist others who may require help evacuating.

(2) Emergency safety equipment. The following safety elements should be met:

a. A written emergency action plan has been provided to workers;

b. Fire extinguishers, eyewash units, and safety showers are available and tested on a regular basis; and

c. Fire blankets, first-aid equipment, fire alarms, and telephones are available and accessible.

(3) Chemical spills. Workers should contact the CHO or EHS office for instructions before cleaning up a chemical spill. All SDS and label instructions should be followed, and appropriate PPE should be worn during spill cleanup.

(4) Accident procedures. In the event of an accident, immediately notify appropriate personnel and local emergency responders. Provide an SDS of any chemical involved to the attending physician. Complete an accident report and submit it to the appropriate office or individual within 24 hours.

(5) Employee safety training program. New workers should attend safety training before they begin any activities. Additional training should be provided when they advance in their duties or are required to perform a task for the first time. Training documents should be recorded and maintained. Training should include hands-on instruction of how to use safety equipment appropriately.

(6) Conduct drills. Practice building evacuations, including the use of alternate routes. Practice shelter-in-place, including plans for extended stays. Walk the fastest route from your work area to the nearest fire alarm, emergency eye wash and emergency shower. Learn how each is activated. In the excitement of an actual emergency, people rely on what they learned from drills, practice and training.

(7) Contingency plans. All laboratories should have long-term contingency plans in place (e.g., for pandemics). Scheduling, workload, utilities and alternate work sites may need to be considered.

I. Laboratory Security

Laboratory security has evolved in the past decade, reducing the likelihood of some emergencies and assisting in preparation and response for others. Most security measures are based on the laboratory's vulnerability. Risks to laboratory security include, but are not limited to:

(1) Theft or diversion of chemicals, biologicals, and radioactive or proprietary materials, mission-critical or high-value equipment;

(2) Threats from activist groups;

(3) Intentional release of, or exposure to, hazardous materials;

(4) Sabotage or vandalism of chemicals or high-value equipment;

(5) Loss or release of sensitive information; and

(6) Rogue work or unauthorized laboratory experimentation. Security systems in the laboratory are used to detect and respond to a security breach, or a potential security breach, as well as to delay criminal activity by imposing multiple layered barriers of increasing stringency. A good laboratory security system will increase overall safety for laboratory personnel and the public, improve emergency preparedness by assisting with preplanning, and lower the organization's liability by incorporating more rigorous planning, staffing, training, and command systems and implementing emergency communications protocols, drills, background checks, card access systems, video surveillance, and other measures. The security plan should clearly delineate response to security issues, including the coordination of institution and laboratory personnel with both internal and external responders.

APPENDIX B TO § 1910.1450—REFERENCES (NON-MANDATORY)

The following references are provided to assist the employer in the development of a Chemical Hygiene Plan. The materials listed below are offered as non-mandatory guidance. References listed here do not imply specific endorsement of a book, opinion, technique, policy or a specific solution for a safety or health problem. Other references not listed here may better meet the needs of a specific laboratory. (a) Materials for the development of the Chemical Hygiene Plan:

1. American Chemical Society, Safety in Academic Chemistry Laboratories, 4th edition, 1985.

2. Fawcett, H.H. and W. S. Wood, Safety and Accident Prevention in Chemical Operations, 2nd edition, Wiley-Interscience, New York, 1982.

3. Flury, Patricia A., Environmental Health and Safety in the Hospital Laboratory, Charles C. Thomas Publisher, Springfield IL, 1978.

4. Green, Michael E. and Turk, Amos, Safety in Working with Chemicals, Macmillan Publishing Co., NY, 1978.

5. Kaufman, James A., Laboratory Safety Guidelines, Dow Chemical Co., Box 1713, Midland, MI 48640, 1977.

6. National Institutes of Health, NIH Guidelines for the Laboratory use of Chemical Carcinogens, NIH Pub. No. 81-2385, GPO, Washington, DC 20402, 1981.

7. National Research Council, Prudent Practices for Disposal of Chemicals from Laboratories, National Academy Press, Washington, DC, 1983.

8. National Research Council, Prudent Practices for Handling Hazardous Chemicals in Laboratories, National Academy Press, Washington, DC, 1981.

9. Renfrew, Malcolm, Ed., Safety in the Chemical Laboratory, Vol. IV, *J. Chem. Ed.*, American Chemical Society, Easlon, PA, 1981.

10. Steere, Norman V., Ed., Safety in the Chemical Laboratory, *J. Chem. Ed.* American Chemical Society, Easlon, PA, 18042, Vol. I, 1967, Vol. II, 1971, Vol. III 1974.

11. Steere, Norman V., Handbook of Laboratory Safety, the Chemical Rubber Company Cleveland, OH, 1971.

12. Young, Jay A., Ed., Improving Safety in the Chemical Laboratory, John Wiley & Sons, Inc. New York, 1987.

(b) Hazardous Substances Information:

1. American Conference of Governmental Industrial Hygienists, Threshold Limit Values for Chemical Substances and Physical Agents in the Workroom Environment with Intended Changes, 6500 Glenway Avenue, Bldg. D–7 Cincinnati, OH 45211–4438 (latest edition).

2. Annual Report on Carcinogens, National Toxicology Program U.S. Department of Health and Human Services, Public Health Service, U.S. Government Printing Office, Washington, DC, (latest edition).

3. Best Company, Best Safety Directory, Vols. I and II, Oldwick, N.J., 1981.

4. Bretherick, L., Handbook of Reactive Chemical Hazards, 2nd edition, Butterworths, London, 1979.

5. Bretherick, L., Hazards in the Chemical Laboratory, 3rd edition, Royal Society of Chemistry, London, 1986.

6. Code of Federal Regulations, 29 CFR part 1910 subpart Z. U.S. Govt. Printing Office, Washington, DC 20402 (latest edition).

7. IARC Monographs on the Evaluation of the Carcinogenic Risk of Chemicals to Man, World Health Organization Publications Center, 49 Sheridan Avenue, Albany, New York 12210 (latest editions).

8. NIOSH/OSHA Pocket Guide to Chemical Hazards. NIOSH Pub. No. 85–114, U.S. Government Printing Office, Washington, DC, 1985 (or latest edition).

9. Occupational Health Guidelines, NIOSH/OSHA NIOSH Pub. No. 81–123 U.S. Government Printing Office, Washington, DC, 1981.

10. Patty, F.A., Industrial Hygiene and Toxicology, John Wiley & Sons, Inc., New York, NY (Five Volumes).

11. Registry of Toxic Effects of Chemical Substances, U.S. Department of Health and Human Services, Public Health Service, Centers for Disease Control, National Institute for Occupational Safety and Health, Revised Annually, for sale from Superintendent of Documents U.S. Govt. Printing Office, Washington, DC 20402.

12. The Merck Index: An Encyclopedia of Chemicals and Drugs. Merck and Company Inc. Rahway, N.J., 1976 (or latest edition).

13. Sax, N.I. Dangerous Properties of Industrial Materials, 5th edition, Van Nostrand Reinhold, NY., 1979.

14. Sittig, Marshall, Handbook of Toxic and Hazardous Chemicals, Noyes Publications, Park Ridge, NJ, 1981.

(c) Information on Ventilation:

1. American Conference of Governmental Industrial Hygienists Industrial Ventilation (latest edition), 6500 Glenway Avenue, Bldg. D–7, Cincinnati, Ohio 45211–4438.

2. American National Standards Institute, Inc. American National Standards Fundamentals Governing the Design and Operation of Local Exhaust Systems ANSI Z 9.2–1979 American National Standards Institute, N.Y. 1979.

3. Imad, A.P. and Watson, C.L. Ventilation Index: An Easy Way to Decide about Hazardous Liquids, Professional Safety pp 15–18, April 1980.

4. National Fire Protection Association, Fire Protection for Laboratories Using Chemicals NFPA–45, 1982.

Safety Standard for Laboratories in Health Related Institutions, NFPA, 56c, 1980.

Fire Protection Guide on Hazardous Materials, 7th edition, 1978.

National Fire Protection Association, Batterymarch Park, Quincy, MA 02269.

5. Scientific Apparatus Makers Association (SAMA), Standard for Laboratory Fume Hoods, SAMA LF7–1980, 1101 16th Street, NW., Washington, DC 20036.

(d) Information on Availability of Referenced Material:

1. American National Standards Institute (ANSI), 1430 Broadway, New York, NY 10018.

2. American Society for Testing and Materials (ASTM), 1916 Race Street, Philadelphia, PA 19103.

[55 FR 3327, Jan. 31, 1990; 55 FR 7967, Mar. 6, 1990; 55 FR 12111, Mar. 30, 1990; 57 FR 29204, July 1, 1992; 61 FR 5508, Feb. 13, 1996; 71 FR 16674, Apr. 3, 2006; 76 FR 33609, June 8, 2011; 77 FR 17887, Mar. 26, 2012; 78 FR 4325, Jan. 22, 2013]

§§ 1910.1451–1910.1499   [Reserved]

FINDING AIDS

A list of CFR titles, subtitles, chapters, subchapters and parts and an alphabetical list of agencies publishing in the CFR are included in the CFR Index and Finding Aids volume to the Code of Federal Regulations which is published separately and revised annually.

Table of CFR Titles and Chapters
(Revised as of July 1, 2019)

Title 1—General Provisions

Title 2—Grants and Agreements

Title 2—Grants and Agreements—Continued

Title 3—The President

Title 4—Accounts

Title 5—Administrative Personnel

Title 5—Administrative Personnel—Continued

Title 6—Domestic Security

Title 7—Agriculture

748

Title 15—Commerce and Foreign Trade—Continued

Title 16—Commercial Practices

Title 17—Commodity and Securities Exchanges

Title 18—Conservation of Power and Water Resources

Title 19—Customs Duties

Title 20—Employees' Benefits

751

752

753

Title 29—Labor—Continued

Title 30—Mineral Resources

Title 31—Money and Finance: Treasury

Title 31—Money and Finance: Treasury—Continued

Title 32—National Defense

Title 33—Navigation and Navigable Waters

Title 34—Education

Title 34—Education—Continued

Title 35 [Reserved]

Title 36—Parks, Forests, and Public Property

Title 37—Patents, Trademarks, and Copyrights

Title 38—Pensions, Bonuses, and Veterans' Relief

Title 39—Postal Service

Title 40—Protection of Environment

Title 41—Public Contracts and Property Management

Title 41—Public Contracts and Property Management—Continued

Chap.

302   Relocation Allowances (Parts 302–1—302–99)

303   Payment of Expenses Connected with the Death of Certain Employees (Part 303–1—303–99)

304   Payment of Travel Expenses from a Non-Federal Source (Parts 304–1—304–99)

Title 42—Public Health

I   Public Health Service, Department of Health and Human Services (Parts 1—199)

II—III   [Reserved]

IV   Centers for Medicare & Medicaid Services, Department of Health and Human Services (Parts 400—699)

V   Office of Inspector General-Health Care, Department of Health and Human Services (Parts 1000—1099)

Title 43—Public Lands: Interior

SUBTITLE A—OFFICE OF THE SECRETARY OF THE INTERIOR (PARTS 1—199)

SUBTITLE B—REGULATIONS RELATING TO PUBLIC LANDS

I   Bureau of Reclamation, Department of the Interior (Parts 400—999)

II   Bureau of Land Management, Department of the Interior (Parts 1000—9999)

III   Utah Reclamation Mitigation and Conservation Commission (Parts 10000—10099)

Title 44—Emergency Management and Assistance

I   Federal Emergency Management Agency, Department of Homeland Security (Parts 0—399)

IV   Department of Commerce and Department of Transportation (Parts 400—499)

Title 45—Public Welfare

SUBTITLE A—DEPARTMENT OF HEALTH AND HUMAN SERVICES (PARTS 1—199)

SUBTITLE B—REGULATIONS RELATING TO PUBLIC WELFARE

II   Office of Family Assistance (Assistance Programs), Administration for Children and Families, Department of Health and Human Services (Parts 200—299)

III   Office of Child Support Enforcement (Child Support Enforcement Program), Administration for Children and Families, Department of Health and Human Services (Parts 300—399)

IV   Office of Refugee Resettlement, Administration for Children and Families, Department of Health and Human Services (Parts 400—499)

Title 45—Public Welfare—Continued

Title 46—Shipping

Title 47—Telecommunication

Title 48—Federal Acquisition Regulations System

Title 49—Transportation

Title 50—Wildlife and Fisheries

Alphabetical List of Agencies Appearing in the CFR

(Revised as of July 1, 2019)

Agency	CFR Title, Subtitle or Chapter
Administrative Conference of the United States	1, III
Advisory Council on Historic Preservation	36, VIII
Advocacy and Outreach, Office of	7, XXV
Afghanistan Reconstruction, Special Inspector General for	5, LXXXIII
African Development Foundation	22, XV
Federal Acquisition Regulation	48, 57
Agency for International Development	2, VII; 22, II
Federal Acquisition Regulation	48, 7
Agricultural Marketing Service	7, I, IX, X, XI
Agricultural Research Service	7, V
Agriculture, Department of	2, IV; 5, LXXIII
Advocacy and Outreach, Office of	7, XXV
Agricultural Marketing Service	7, I, IX, X, XI
Agricultural Research Service	7, V
Animal and Plant Health Inspection Service	7, III; 9, I
Chief Financial Officer, Office of	7, XXX
Commodity Credit Corporation	7, XIV
Economic Research Service	7, XXXVII
Energy Policy and New Uses, Office of	2, IX; 7, XXIX
Environmental Quality, Office of	7, XXXI
Farm Service Agency	7, VII, XVIII
Federal Acquisition Regulation	48, 4
Federal Crop Insurance Corporation	7, IV
Food and Nutrition Service	7, II
Food Safety and Inspection Service	9, III
Foreign Agricultural Service	7, XV
Forest Service	36, II
Grain Inspection, Packers and Stockyards Administration	7, VIII; 9, II
Information Resources Management, Office of	7, XXVII
Inspector General, Office of	7, XXVI
National Agricultural Library	7, XLI
National Agricultural Statistics Service	7, XXXVI
National Institute of Food and Agriculture	7, XXXIV
Natural Resources Conservation Service	7, VI
Operations, Office of	7, XXVIII
Procurement and Property Management, Office of	7, XXXII
Rural Business-Cooperative Service	7, XVIII, XLII
Rural Development Administration	7, XLII
Rural Housing Service	7, XVIII, XXXV
Rural Telephone Bank	7, XVI
Rural Utilities Service	7, XVII, XVIII, XLII
Secretary of Agriculture, Office of	7, Subtitle A
Transportation, Office of	7, XXXIII
World Agricultural Outlook Board	7, XXXVIII
Air Force, Department of	32, VII
Federal Acquisition Regulation Supplement	48, 53
Air Transportation Stabilization Board	14, VI
Alcohol and Tobacco Tax and Trade Bureau	27, I
Alcohol, Tobacco, Firearms, and Explosives, Bureau of	27, II
AMTRAK	49, VII
American Battle Monuments Commission	36, IV
American Indians, Office of the Special Trustee	25, VII
Animal and Plant Health Inspection Service	7, III; 9, I

764

765

Table of OMB Control Numbers

The OMB control numbers for part 1910 of title 29 were consolidated into §1910.8 at 61 FR 5508, Feb. 13, 1996. Section 1910.8 is reprinted below for the convenience of the user.

§1910.8 OMB control numbers under the Paperwork Reduction Act.

The following sections or paragraphs each contain a collection of information requirement which has been approved by the Office of Management and Budget under the control number listed.

29 CFR citation	OMB control No.
1910.7	1218–0147
1910.23	1218–0199
1910.27	1218–0199
1910.28	1218–0199
1910.66	1218–0121
1910.67(b)	1218–0230
1910.68	1218–0226
1910.95	1218–0048
1910.111	1218–0208
1910.119	1218–0200
1910.120	1218–0202
1910.132	1218–0205
1910.134	1218–0099
1910.137	1218–0190
1910.142	1218–0096
1910.145	1218–0132
1910.146	1218–0203
1910.147	1218–0150
1910.156	1218–0075
1910.157(e)(3)	1218–0210
1910.157(f)(16)	1218–0218
1910.177(d)(3)(iv)	1218–0219
1910.179(j)(2)(iii) and (iv)	1218–0224
1910.179(m)(1) and (m)(2)	1218–0224
1910.180(d)(6)	1218–0221
1910.180(g)(1) and (g)(2)(ii)	1218–0221
1910.181(g)(1) and (g)(3)	1218–0222
1910.184(e)(4), (f)(4) and (i)(8)(ii)	1218–0223
1910.217(e)(1)(i) and (ii)	1218–0229
1910.217(g)	1218–0070
1910.217(h)	1218–0143
1910.218(a)(2)(i) and (ii)	1218–0228
1910.252(a)(2)(xiii)(c)	1218–0207
1910.255(e)	1218–0207
1910.266	1218–0198
1910.268	1218–0225
1910.269	1218–0190
1910.272	1218–0206
1910.302	1218–0256
1910.303	1218–0256
1910.304	1218–0256
1910.305	1218–0256
1910.306	1218–0256

29 CFR citation	OMB control No.
1910.307	1218–0256
1910.308	1218–0256
1910.420	1218–0069
1910.421	1218–0069
1910.423	1218–0069
1910.430	1218–0069
1910.440	1218–0069
1910.1001	1218–0133
1910.1003	1218–0085
1910.1004	1218–0084
1910.1006	1218–0086
1910.1007	1218–0083
1910.1008	1218–0087
1910.1009	1218–0089
1910.1010	1218–0082
1910.1011	1218–0090
1910.1012	1218–0080
1910.1013	1218–0079
1910.1014	1218–0088
1910.1015	1218–0044
1910.1016	1218–0081
1910.1017	1218–0010
1910.1018	1218–0104
1910.1020	1218–0065
1910.1024	1218–0267
1910.1025	1218–0092
1910.1026	1218–0252
1910.1027	1218–0185
1910.1028	1218–0129
1910.1029	1218–0128
1910.1030	1218–0180
1910.1043	1218–0061
1910.1044	1218–0101
1910.1045	1218–0126
1910.1047	1218–0108
1910.1048	1218–0145
1910.1050	1218–0184
1910.1051	1218–0170
1910.1052	1218–0179
1910.1053	1218–0266
1910.1096	1218–0103
1910.1200	1218–0072
1910.1450	1218–0131

[61 FR 5508, Feb. 13, 1996, as amended at 62 FR 29668, June 2, 1997; 62 FR 42666, Aug. 8, 1997; 62 FR 43581, Aug. 14, 1997; 62 FR 65203, Dec. 11, 1997; 63 FR 13340, Mar. 19, 1998; 63 FR 17093, Apr. 8, 1998; 71 FR 38086, July 5, 2006; 72 FR 40075, July 23, 2007; 81 FR 48710, July 26, 2016; 82 FR 31253, July 6, 2017; 83 FR 9702, Mar. 7, 2018]

List of CFR Sections Affected

All changes in this volume of the Code of Federal Regulations (CFR) that were made by documents published in the FEDERAL REGISTER since January 1, 2014 are enumerated in the following list. Entries indicate the nature of the changes effected. Page numbers refer to FEDERAL REGISTER pages. The user should consult the entries for chapters, parts and subparts as well as sections for revisions.

For changes to this volume of the CFR prior to this listing, consult the annual edition of the monthly List of CFR Sections Affected (LSA). The LSA is available at *www.govinfo.gov*. For changes to this volume of the CFR prior to 2001, see the "List of CFR Sections Affected, 1949–1963, 1964–1972, 1973–1985, and 1986–2000" published in 11 separate volumes. The "List of CFR Sections Affected 1986–2000" is available at *www.govinfo.gov*.

2019

29 CFR—Continued

84 FR
Page

○